Organizational Behavior
Ninth Edition

Organizational Behavior

Ninth Edition

Robert Kreitner

Angelo Kinicki

Both of Arizona State University

McGraw-Hill Irwin

McGraw-Hill
Irwin

ORGANIZATIONAL BEHAVIOR

Published by McGraw-Hill/Irwin, a business unit of The McGraw-Hill Companies, Inc., 1221 Avenue of the Americas, New York, NY, 10020. Copyright © 2010, 2008, 2007, 2004, 2001, 1998, 1994, 1992, 1989 by The McGraw-Hill Companies, Inc. All rights reserved. No part of this publication may be reproduced or distributed in any form or by any means, or stored in a database or retrieval system, without the prior written consent of The McGraw-Hill Companies, Inc., including, but not limited to, in any network or other electronic storage or transmission, or broadcast for distance learning.

Some ancillaries, including electronic and print components, may not be available to customers outside the United States.

This book is printed on acid-free paper.

1 2 3 4 5 6 7 8 9 0 DOW/DOW 0 9

ISBN   978-0-07-018261-5
MHID   0-07-018261-2

About the Authors

Robert Kreitner, PhD (pictured left) is a professor emeritus of management at Arizona State University and a member of ASU's W P Carey School of Business Faculty Hall of Fame. Prior to joining ASU in 1975, Bob taught at Western Illinois University. He also taught organizational behavior at Thunderbird. Bob has addressed a diverse array of audiences worldwide on management topics. He has authored articles for journals such as *Organizational Dynamics, Business Horizons, Educational and Psychological Measurement, Journal of Organizational Behavior Management,* and *Journal of Business Ethics.* He also is the coauthor (with Fred Luthans) of the award-winning book *Organizational Behavior Modification and Beyond: An Operant and Social Learning Approach;* the author of *Management,* 11th edition, a best-selling introductory management text; and coauthor (with Carlene Cassidy) of *Supervision: Setting People Up for Success,* 1st edition. His textbooks collectively have been through 29 editions.

Among his consulting and executive development clients have been American Express, SABRE Computer Services, Honeywell, Motorola, Amdahl, the Hopi Indian Tribe, State Farm Insurance, Goodyear Aerospace, Doubletree Hotels, Bank One–Arizona, Nazarene School of Large Church Management, US Steel, and Allied-Signal. In 1981–82 he served as chairman of the Academy of Management's Management Education and Development Division. Bob was born in Buffalo, New York. After a four-year enlistment in the US Coast Guard, including service on the icebreaker EASTWIND in Antarctica, Bob attended the University of Nebraska–Omaha on a football scholarship. Bob also holds an MBA from the University of Nebraska–Omaha and a PhD from the University of Nebraska–Lincoln. While working on his PhD in business at Nebraska, he spent six months teaching management courses for the University in Micronesia. In 1996, Bob taught two courses in Albania's first-ever MBA program. He taught a summer leadership program in Switzerland from 1995 to 1998. Bob and his wife Margaret, a retired Intel Corp. manager, live in Phoenix with their two cats Yahoo and Sweetie Pie. They enjoy world travel, lots of hiking, and fishing in Alaska.

Angelo Kinicki is a professor of management at the W P Carey School of Business at Arizona State University. He was awarded the Weatherup/Overby Chair in Leadership in 2005. He has held his current position since receiving his doctorate in organizational behavior from Kent State University in 1982.

Angelo is recognized for both his teaching and research. As a teacher, Angelo has been the recipient of several awards, including the Outstanding Teaching Award–MBA and Master's Program (2007–08), the John W Teets Outstanding Graduate Teacher Award (2004–05), Graduate Teaching Excellence Award (1998–99), Continuing Education Excellence Award (1991–92), and Undergraduate Teaching Excellence Award (1987–88). He also was selected into *Who's Who of American Colleges and Universities* and *Beta Gamma Sigma.* He has published more than 80 articles in a variety of leading academic and professional journals and has coauthored six college textbooks (21 including revisions). His textbooks have been used by hundreds of universities around the world and have been translated into multiple languages. Angelo's experience as a researcher resulted in his selection to serve on the editorial review boards for the *Academy of Management Journal,* the *Journal of Management,* and the *Journal of Vocational Behavior.* He also received the All-Time Best Reviewer Award from the *Academy of Management Journal* for the period of 1996 to 1999. Angelo's current research interests include the study of leadership, organizational culture, and coping with organizational change and involuntary job loss.

Angelo is an active international consultant who works with management groups to create organizational change aimed at increasing organizational effectiveness and profitability. He enjoys delivering a variety of executive development programs on many topics related to organizational behavior. He has worked with many *Fortune* 500 firms as well as numerous entrepreneurial organizations in diverse industries. His work on leadership development led to the creation of a 360-degree leadership feedback instrument called the Performance Management Leadership Survey (PMLS) that has been used by companies throughout the United States and Europe.

One of Angelo's strengths is his ability to teach students at all levels within a university. He uses an interactive environment to enhance undergraduates' understanding about management and organizational behavior. He focuses MBAs on applying management concepts to solve complex problems; PhD students learn the art and science of conducting scholarly research.

Angelo and his wife, Joyce, have enjoyed living in the beautiful Arizona desert for 25 years but are natives of Cleveland, Ohio. They enjoy traveling, golfing, and spoiling Nala, their golden retriever.

Brief Contents

Contents

Organizational Behavior
Ninth Edition

Part 1

The World of Organizational Behavior

Chapter I

Organizational Behavior: The Quest for People-Centered Organizations and Ethical Conduct

LEARNING OBJECTIVES

When you finish studying the material in this chapter, you should be able to:

LO.1 Define the term *organizational behavior,* and contrast McGregor's Theory X and Theory Y assumptions about employees.

LO.2 Identify the four principles of total quality management (TQM).

LO.3 Define the term *e-business,* and specify at least three OB-related issues raised by e-leadership.

LO.4 Contrast human and social capital, and explain why we need to build both.

LO.5 Define the term *management,* and identify at least five of the eleven managerial skills in Wilson's profile of effective managers.

LO.6 Characterize 21st-century managers.

LO.7 Describe Carroll's global corporate social responsibility pyramid, and discuss the problem of moral erosion.

LO.8 Identify four of the seven general ethical principles, and explain how to improve an organization's ethical climate.

LO.9 Describe the sources of organizational behavior research evidence.

Student Resources for Studying Chapter 1

The Web site for your text includes resources that will help you master the concepts in this chapter. As you read, you'll want to visit the site for these helpful tools:

- Your online Study Guide includes learning objectives, a chapter summary, a glossary of key terms, and discussion questions.

- Take a practice quiz and test your knowledge!

- Scroll through a PowerPoint presentation with key concepts for this chapter.

Your instructor might also direct you to the Web site for these exercises:

- Self-assessments that correspond with the chapter content and a Group Exercise.

- You'll also find Video Cases and Internet Exercises for this chapter online.

www.mhhe.com/kreitner

Michelle Peluso, President and Chief Executive Officer, Travelocity

A few months before I was born, my father founded an environmental-engineering firm. I literally grew up watching him build it. Even as a little kid, I was struck by Dad's obsessive interest in and care for the people who worked for him.

Nights when our family's dinner-table conversation didn't include discussion of his employees were rare. "Sally's gotten accepted into an MBA program," he'd say excitedly, "and we're going to figure out how she can do that part-time." Or "John's wife just had a baby girl! We're going over this weekend to see her." Before company picnics we were thoroughly briefed: Bill had just won a new client; Mary was about to make an important presentation. His concern was authentic and unwavering, and it extended to all aspects of his employees' lives. When two of his top employees were killed in a plane crash coming back from a business trip, Dad spent time with their grieving families.

Now, my father's attitude and behavior were just part of his personality, not some maneuver to produce results—but they produced them all the same. He grew that start-up into a thriving 300-person business and then sold it to a larger company but continued to run it successfully. Two years ago, when he left to begin a new venture, more than half of his former employees sent him their résumés. So although my father never gave me management advice directly, his example provided a profound lesson: If you treat your employees as unique individuals, they'll be loyal to you and they'll perform—and your business will perform, too.

The longer I'm in my own career, the more I attempt to put that lesson into practice. At a 5,000-person global organization, I simply can't know everyone personally. But I can apply my dad's techniques in a scaled-up way that lets me know as many people as possible, that encourages managers to do the same, and that makes our employees generally feel that this is a place where someone's looking out for them. I often visit our different offices; I hold brown-bag lunches every week; I regularly e-mail the whole staff about what's going well and what needs to improve; I hold quarterly talent management sessions with my direct reports; and I constantly walk the halls. When anyone at Travelocity e-mails me, I respond within 24 hours. I read every single word of our annual employee survey results and of my managers' 360-degree performance feedback—and I rate those managers in large part on how well they know and lead their own people.

Focusing on individuals instead of "the team" isn't easy. It takes a lot of time and genuine caring, and requires a long-term view—which can be tough when you've got a big business to run. Ultimately, however, it's worth

Michelle Peluso, President and CEO of Travelocity, learned from her entrepreneurial father to focus on the individual employee.

the effort, for your employees and for the organization. A few years ago one of our senior managers was leading a huge project that had high visibility with our investor community when she began having pregnancy complications. I fully supported her in taking several months off, for her own health and for her kids. It was a daunting time, but the team worked through it, and that manager is still working here—as our COO (chief operating officer).

I describe my leadership style in all humility. I don't have all the answers on how to lead people, and I learn from colleagues every day. But I share Dad's entrepreneurial belief: People aren't your "greatest asset"—they're your only asset.[1]

FOR DISCUSSION

What practical management lessons have you just learned from Michelle Peluso?

Travelocity's Michelle Peluso does more than just talk about the importance of her company's people; she trusts, empowers, and listens to them. She has helped create what Stanford University's Jeffrey Pfeffer calls a "people-centered" organization. Research evidence from companies in both the United States and Germany shows the following seven *people-centered practices* to be strongly associated with much higher profits and significantly lower employee turnover:

1. Job security (to eliminate fear of layoffs).
2. Careful hiring (emphasizing a good fit with the company culture).
3. Power to the people (via decentralization and self-managed teams).
4. Generous pay for performance.
5. Lots of training.
6. Less emphasis on status (to build a "we" feeling).
7. Trust building (through the sharing of critical information).[2]

Importantly, these factors are a *package* deal, meaning they need to be installed in a coordinated and systematic manner—not in bits and pieces.

According to Pfeffer, only 12% of today's organizations have the systematic approaches and persistence to qualify as true people-centered organizations, thus giving them a competitive advantage.[3] To us, an 88% shortfall in the quest for people-centered organizations represents a tragic waste of human and economic potential. There are profound ethical implications as well, especially during the recent deep recession with millions of layoffs[4] (see the Ethical Dilemma at the end of this chapter). As the head of a model people-centered company, Gary Kelly, CEO of Southwest Airlines, put it this way:

> We've never had a layoff. We've never had a pay cut. And we're going to strive mightily, especially this year [2009], to avoid them once again. I worry about that every day. And I don't worry about much, but I worry about that.[5]

At people-centered organizations such as Southwest Airlines, layoffs are a very last resort, not a knee-jerk first response to bad news. Both practical experience and research tell us that layoffs hurt everyone, including the "survivors" who keep their jobs. A recent study of 318 companies led to this conclusion: "Three-fourths of 4,172 workers who have kept their jobs say their productivity has dropped since their organizations let people go."[6] Of course, layoffs are sometimes unavoidable. But imaginative people-centered organizations can make layoffs a last resort with tactics such as across-the-board pay cuts and/or reduced hours and voluntary unpaid leaves of absence. Additionally, consider these unique people-centered tactics:

> Vermont's Rhino Foods, which makes the cookie dough for Ben & Jerry's ice cream, recently sent 15 factory workers to nearby lip balm manufacturer Autumn Harp for a

week to help it handle a holiday rush. The employees were paid by Rhino, which then invoiced its neighbor for the hours worked. President Ted Castle is looking to adopt a similar approach with salaried managers, too. "It's a lot easier to just do the layoff," says Castle. "But in the long term, it's not easier for the business." . . .

Matt Cooper, vice-president of Larkspur (Calif.) recruiting firm Accolo, asked employees to take five days of unpaid leave this quarter but won't dock paychecks until March. If big deals come through, he'll lift the pay cut.[7]

Each of us needs to accept the challenge to do a better job of creating and maintaining people-centered organizations, whatever our role(s) in society—employer/entrepreneur, employee, manager, stockholder, student, teacher, voter, elected official, social/political activist. Toward that end, the mission of this book is to help increase the number of people-centered and ethically managed organizations around the world to improve the general quality of life.[8]

The purpose of this first chapter is to define organizational behavior (OB); examine its contemporary relevance; explore its historical, managerial, and ethical contexts; and introduce a topical roadmap for the balance of this book.

Welcome to the World of OB

to the point

Why is it important to study organizational behavior, regardless of one's organizational level or specialty?

Organizational behavior deals with how people act and react in organizations of all kinds. Think of the many organizations that touch your life on a regular basis; organizations that employ, educate, connect, inform, feed, heal, protect, and entertain you. Cradle to grave, we interface with organizations at every turn. According to Chester I Barnard's classic definition, an **organization** is "a system of consciously coordinated activities or forces of two or more persons."[9] Organizations are a social invention helping us to achieve things collectively that we could not achieve alone. For better or for worse, they extend our reach. Consider the inspiring example of the World Health Organization (WHO):

Organization

System of consciously coordinated activities of two or more people.

In 1967, 10 to 15 million people around the globe were struck annually by smallpox. That year, the World Health Organization set up its smallpox-eradication unit. In 13 years it was able to declare the world free of the disease. In 1988, 350,000 people were afflicted by polio when the WHO set up a similar eradication unit. Since then it has spent $3 billion and received the help of 20 million volunteers from around the world. The result: in 2003 there were only 784 reported cases of polio.[10]

On the other hand, organizations such as *Al Qaeda* kill and terrorize, and others such as General Motors squander our resources. Organizations are the chessboard upon which the game of life is played. To know more about *organizational behavior*—life within organizations—is to know more about the nature, possibilities, and rules of that game.

LO.1 Organizational Behavior: An Interdisciplinary Field

Organizational behavior

Interdisciplinary field dedicated to better understanding and managing people at work.

Organizational behavior, commonly referred to as OB, is an interdisciplinary field dedicated to better understanding and managing people at work. By definition, organizational behavior is both research and application oriented. Three basic levels of analysis in OB are individual, group, and organizational. OB draws upon a diverse array of disciplines, including psychology, management, sociology, organization theory, social psychology, statistics, anthropology, general systems theory, economics, information technology, political science, vocational counseling, human stress management, psychometrics, ergonomics, decision theory, and ethics. This rich heritage has spawned many competing perspectives and theories about human work behavior. By 2003, one researcher had identified 73 distinct theories about behavior within the field of OB.[11]

Some FAQs about Studying OB

Through the years we (and our colleagues) have fielded some frequently asked questions (FAQs) from our students about our field. Here are the most common ones, along with our answers.

Why Study OB?   If you thoughtfully study this book, you will learn more about yourself, how to interact effectively with others, and how to thrive (not just survive) in organizations. Lots of insights about your own personality, emotions, values, job satisfaction, perceptions, needs, and goals are available in Part Two. Relative to your interpersonal effectiveness, you will learn about being a team player, building trust, managing conflict, negotiating, communicating, and influencing and leading others. We conclude virtually every major topic with practical how-to-do-it instructions. The idea is to build your skills in areas such as self-management, making ethical decisions, avoiding groupthink, listening, coping with organizational politics, handling change, and managing stress. Respected OB scholar Edward E Lawler III created the "virtuous career spiral" in Figure 1–1 to illustrate how OB-related skills point you toward career success. "It shows that increased skills and performance can lead to better jobs and higher rewards."[12]

Figure 1–1   *OB-Related Skills Are the Ticket to Ride the Virtuous Career Spiral*

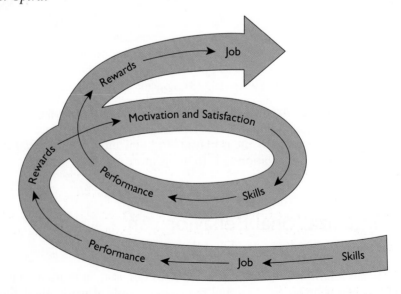

SOURCE: Edward E Lawler III, *Treat People Right! How Organizations and Individuals Can Propel Each Other into a Virtuous Spiral of Success,* Jossey-Bass, 2003, p. 21. Reprinted with permission of John Wiley & Sons, Inc.

**If I'm an Accounting (or Other Technical Major), Why Should
I Study OB?**   Many students in technical fields such as accounting, finance, computer science, and engineering consider OB to be a "soft" discipline with little or no relevance. You may indeed start out in a narrow specialty, but eventually your hard-won success will catch up with you and you will be tapped for some sort of supervisory or leadership position. Your so-called soft people skills will make or break your career at that point.[13] Also, in today's team-oriented and globalized workplace, your teamwork, cross-cultural, communication, conflict handling, and negotiation skills and your powers of persuasion will be needed early and often. Jack Welch, the legendary CEO of General Electric, and Suzy Welch, the former editor of *Harvard Business Review,* offered this answer to a business school professor's question about how best to prepare students for today's global business environment:

> We'd make the case that the nitty-gritty of managing people should rank higher in the educational hierarchy. In the past two years we've visited 35 B-schools around the world and have been repeatedly surprised by how little classroom attention is paid to hiring, motivating, team-building, and firing. Instead, B-schools seem far more invested in teaching brainiac concepts—disruptive technologies, complexity modeling, and the like. Those may be useful, particularly if you join a consulting firm, but real managers need to know how to get the most out of people....
>
> We hope you have the clout to make sure people management is front and center at your university. If you do, you'll launch your students' careers with a real head start.[14]

Can I Get a Job in OB?   Organizational behavior is an academic designation. With the exception of teaching/research positions, OB is not an everyday job category such as accounting, marketing, information technology, or finance. Students of OB typically do not get jobs in organizational behavior, per se. This reality in no way demeans OB or lessens its importance in effective organizational management. OB is a *horizontal* discipline cutting across virtually every job category, business function, and professional specialty. Anyone who plans to make a living in a large or small, public or private, organization needs to study organizational behavior.

A Historical Perspective of OB

A historical perspective of the study of people at work helps in studying organizational behavior. According to a management history expert, this is important because

> Historical perspective is the study of a subject in light of its earliest phases and subsequent evolution. Historical perspective differs from history in that the object of historical perspective is to sharpen one's vision of the present, not the past.[15]

In other words, we can better understand where the field of OB is today and where it appears to be headed by appreciating where it has been and how it is being redirected.[16] Let us examine four significant landmarks in the understanding and management of people in the workplace.

1. The human relations movement.
2. The quality movement.
3. The e-business revolution.
4. The age of human and social capital.

to the point

What lessons from McGregor and Deming can help managers build human and social capital?

The Human Relations Movement

A unique combination of factors during the 1930s fostered the human relations movement. First, following legalization of union–management collective bargaining in the United States in 1935, management began looking for new ways of handling employees. Second, behavioral scientists conducting on-the-job research started calling for more attention to the "human" factor. Managers who had lost the battle to keep unions out of their factories heeded the call for better human relations and improved working conditions. One such study, conducted at Western Electric's Chicago-area Hawthorne plant, was a prime stimulus for the human relations movement. Ironically, many of the Hawthorne findings have turned out to be more myth than fact.

These relay assembly test room employees in the classic Hawthorne Western Electric studies turned in record performance. Why? No one knows for certain, and debate continues to this day. Supportive supervision was long believed to be the key factor. Whatever the reason, Hawthorne gave the budding human relations movement needed research credibility.

The Hawthorne Legacy   Interviews conducted decades later with three subjects of the Hawthorne studies and reanalysis of the original data with modern statistical techniques do not support initial conclusions about the positive effect of supportive supervision. Specifically, money, fear of unemployment during the Great Depression, managerial discipline, and high-quality raw materials—not supportive supervision—turned out to be responsible for high output in the relay assembly test room experiments.[17] Nonetheless, the human relations movement gathered momentum through the 1950s, as academics and managers alike made stirring claims about the powerful effect that individual needs, supportive supervision, and group dynamics apparently had on job performance.

The Writings of Mayo and Follett   Essential to the human relations movement were the writings of Elton Mayo and Mary Parker Follett. Australian-born Mayo, who headed the Harvard researchers at Hawthorne, advised managers to attend to employees' emotional needs in his 1933 classic *The Human Problems of an Industrial Civilization.* Follett was a true pioneer, not only as a woman management consultant in the male-dominated industrial world of the 1920s, but also as a writer who saw employees as complex combinations of attitudes, beliefs, and needs. Mary Parker Follett was way ahead of her time in telling managers to motivate job performance instead of merely demanding it, a "pull" rather than "push" strategy. She also built a logical bridge between political democracy and a cooperative spirit in the workplace.[18]

Theory Y

McGregor's modern and positive assumptions about employees being responsible and creative.

McGregor's Theory Y   In 1960, Douglas McGregor wrote a book entitled *The Human Side of Enterprise,* which has become an important philosophical base for the modern view of people at work.[19] Drawing upon his experience as a management consultant, McGregor formulated two sharply contrasting sets of assumptions about human nature (see Table 1–1). His Theory X assumptions were pessimistic and negative and, according to McGregor's interpretation, typical of how managers traditionally perceived employees. To help managers break with this negative tradition, McGregor formulated his **Theory Y,** a modern and positive set of assumptions about people. McGregor believed managers could accomplish more through others by viewing them as self-energized, committed, responsible, and creative beings.[20]

Table 1–1   *McGregor's Theory X and Theory Y*

OUTDATED (THEORY X) ASSUMPTIONS ABOUT PEOPLE AT WORK	MODERN (THEORY Y) ASSUMPTIONS ABOUT PEOPLE AT WORK
1. Most people dislike work; they avoid it when they can.	1. Work is a natural activity, like play or rest.
2. Most people must be coerced and threatened with punishment before they will work. People require close direction when they are working.	2. People are capable of self-direction and self-control if they are committed to objectives.
3. Most people actually prefer to be directed. They tend to avoid responsibility and exhibit little ambition. They are interested only in security.	3. People generally become committed to organizational objectives if they are rewarded for doing so.
	4. The typical employee can learn to accept and seek responsibility.
	5. The typical member of the general population has imagination, ingenuity, and creativity.

SOURCE: From D McGregor, *The Human Side of Enterprise*, McGraw-Hill, 1960, Ch 4. Copyright © 2008 The McGraw-Hill Companies. Reprinted with permission.

According to this overview from *HR Magazine,* McGregor's Theory Y is still a distant vision in the American workplace:

> With strikingly similar statistics, several highly respected research and consulting organizations have found that there's a huge population of workers—roughly half of all Americans in the workforce—who show up, do what's expected of them, but don't go that extra mile, don't turn on the creative juices, don't get inspired to create great products or services.
>
> Perhaps the most significant finding: These are people, for the most part, who want to go above and beyond, to be an integral part of the company's success. Something—often a disconnect with an immediate supervisor or a feeling that the organization doesn't care about them—is getting in the way. There is a huge, untapped potential that many executives, managers and employees do not recognize and, therefore, have not addressed. And it's sapping organizations' potential.
>
> "We're running as an economy at 30% efficiency" because so many workers are not contributing as much as they could, says Curt Coffman [from the Gallup Organization].[21]

New Assumptions about Human Nature   Unfortunately, unsophisticated behavioral research methods caused the human relationists to embrace some naive and misleading conclusions.[22] For example, human relationists believed in the axiom, "A satisfied employee is a hardworking employee." Subsequent research, as discussed later in this book, shows the satisfaction–performance linkage to be more complex than originally thought.

Despite its shortcomings, the human relations movement opened the door to more progressive thinking about human nature. Rather than continuing to view employees as passive economic beings, managers began to see them as active social beings and took steps to create more humane work environments.

The Quality Movement

In 1980, NBC aired a television documentary titled "If Japan Can . . . Why Can't We?" It was a wake-up call for North American companies to dramatically improve product quality or continue losing market share to Japanese electronics and automobile companies. A full-fledged movement ensued during the 1980s and 1990s. Much was written, said, and done about improving the quality of both goods and services.[23] Thanks to the concept of *total quality management* (TQM) and Six Sigma programs, the quality of the goods and services we purchase today is significantly better than in years past. Six Sigma was developed in 1986 at Motorola by engineer Bill Smith to achieve an astounding 99.9997% quality target by eliminating defects and cutting waste. It was licensed to companies such as General Electric that became avid users. An estimated 35% of U.S. companies have adopted Six Sigma.

> Six Sigma, broadly speaking, expresses a way of thinking about business problems that encourages precision and predictability. The mantra of Six Sigma "black belts" is DMAIC, for "define, measure, analyze, improve, control." The "sigma" refers to the Greek letter, which in statistics is used to measure how far something deviates from perfection. The "six" comes from the goal to be no more than six standard deviations away from that perfect measure.[24]

The underlying principles of TQM and Six Sigma are more important than ever given customers' steadily rising expectations:

> Establish a reputation for great value, top quality, or pulling late-night miracles in time for crucial client meetings, and soon enough, the goalposts move. "Greatness" lasts only as long as someone fails to imagine something better. Inevitably, the exceptional becomes the expected.
>
> Call it the performance paradox: If you deliver, you only qualify to deliver more. Great companies and their employees have always endured this treadmill of expectations. But these days, the brewing forces of technology, productivity, and transparency have accelerated the cycle to breakneck speed.[25]

The quality movement has profound practical implications for managing people today.

Total quality management

An organizational culture dedicated to training, continuous improvement, and customer satisfaction.

What Is TQM?   Experts on the subject offered this definition of **total quality management:**

> TQM means that the organization's culture is defined by and supports the constant attainment of customer satisfaction through an integrated system of tools, techniques, and training. This involves the continuous improvement of organizational processes, resulting in high-quality products and services.[26]

Quality consultant Richard J Schonberger sums up TQM as "continuous, customer-centered, employee-driven improvement."[27] TQM is necessarily employee driven because product/service quality cannot be continuously improved without the active learning and participation of *every* employee. Thus, in successful quality improvement programs, TQM principles are embedded in the organization's culture. In fact, according to the results of a field experiment, bank customers had higher satisfaction after interacting with bank employees who had been trained to provide excellent service.[28]

The Deming Legacy   Quality is in the corporate DNA today thanks in large part to the pioneering work of W Edwards Deming.[29] Ironically, the mathematician credited with Japan's post–World War II quality revolution rarely talked in terms of quality. He instead preferred to discuss "good management" during the hard-hitting seminars he delivered right up until his death at age 93 in 1993.[30] Although Deming's passion was the statistical measurement and reduction of variations in industrial processes, he had much to say about how employees should be treated. Regarding the human side of quality improvement, Deming called for the following:

- Formal training in statistical process control techniques and teamwork.
- Helpful leadership, rather than order giving and punishment.
- Elimination of fear so employees will feel free to ask questions.
- Emphasis on continuous process improvements rather than on numerical quotas.
- Teamwork.
- Elimination of barriers to good workmanship.[31]

One of Deming's most enduring lessons for managers is his 85–15 rule.[32] Specifically, when things go wrong, there is roughly an 85% chance the *system* (including management, machinery, and rules) is at fault. Only about 15% of the time is the individual employee at fault. Unfortunately, as Deming observed, the typical manager spends most of his or her time wrongly blaming and punishing individuals for system failures. Statistical analysis is required to uncover system failures.

LO.2 **Principles of TQM**   Despite variations in the language and scope of TQM programs, it is possible to identify four common TQM principles:

1. Do it right the first time to eliminate costly rework and product recalls.
2. Listen to and learn from customers and employees.
3. Make continuous improvement an everyday matter.
4. Build teamwork, trust, and mutual respect.[33]

Deming's influence is clearly evident in this list. Once again, as with the human relations movement, we see *people* as the key factor in organizational success.

In summary, TQM advocates have made a valuable contribution to the field of OB by providing a *practical* context for managing people. The case for TQM is strong because, as discovered in two comprehensive studies, *it works*.[34] When people are managed according to TQM principles, more of them are likely to get the employment opportunities and high-quality goods and services they demand. As you will see many times in later chapters, this book is anchored to Deming's philosophy and TQM principles.

LO.3 # The Internet and E-Business Revolution

In the early 1990s, when Internet applications were undergoing a growth spurt, advocates said it would change everything. Then came the tech crash of 2001 and the Internet promise was ridiculed as pure hype. But after some adolescent growing pains, *the Internet has in fact changed everything*. The raw numbers are impressive: 190 million Americans on the Internet; over 1 billion Internet users worldwide; 3,000 Google

E-business

Running the entire business via the Internet.

searches every second in the United States.[35] What was once *e-commerce* (buying and selling goods and services over the Internet) has evolved into **e-business,** using the Internet to facilitate *every* aspect of running a business.[36] Said one industry observer: "Strip away the highfalutin talk, and at bottom, the Internet is a tool that dramatically lowers the cost of communication. That means it can radically alter any industry or activity that depends heavily on the flow of information."[37]

Relative to OB, we need to focus on how the Internet has changed the behavior of those who have grown up with the Internet and take activities such as Googling, Facebooking, YouTubing, and tweeting on Twitter for granted. Don Tapscott, author of the intriguing new book *Grown Up Digital: How the Net Generation Is Changing the World*, says the 81 million Americans born between January 1977 and December 1997 have a unique worldview shaped by the Internet:

> These are the eight norms of the Net Generation. They value freedom—freedom to be who they are, freedom of choice. They want to customize everything, even their jobs. They learn to be skeptical, to scrutinize what they see and read in the media, including the Internet. They value integrity—being honest, considerate, transparent, and abiding by their commitment. They're great collaborators, with friends online and at work. They thrive on speed. They love to innovate.
>
> …[I]f you understand these norms, you can change your company, school or university, government, or family for the twenty-first century.[38]

(Tapscott's ideas about the Net Generation are expanded upon in Chapter 14.) In short, organizations and organizational life will never be the same because of e-mail, e-learning, e-management, e-leadership (see Table 1–2), virtual teams, and virtual organizations.[39]

Table 1–2   *The Brave New World of E-Leadership*

Because it involves electronically mediated interactions, in combination with the traditional face-to-face variety, experts say e-leadership raises these major issues for modern management:

1. Leaders and followers have more access to information and each other, and this is changing the nature and content of their interactions.

2. Leadership is migrating to lower and lower organizational levels and out through the boundaries of the organization to both customers and suppliers.

3. Leadership creates and exists in networks that go across traditional organizational and community boundaries.

4. Followers know more at earlier points in the decision-making process, and this is potentially affecting the credibility and influence of leaders.

5. Unethical leaders with limited resources can now impact negatively a much broader audience of potential followers.

6. The amount of time and contact that even the most senior leaders can have with their followers has increased, although the contact is not in the traditional face-to-face mode.

Making wise hiring and job assignment decisions, nurturing productive relationships, and building trust are more important than ever in the age of e-leadership.

SOURCE: Six implications excerpted from *Organizational Dynamics*, vol. 4, B J Avolio and S S Kahai, "Adding the 'E' to E-Leadership: How It May Impact Your Leadership," p 333. Copyright © 2003 with permission from Elsevier Science.

LO.4 The Need to Build Human and Social Capital

Knowledge workers, those who add value by using their brains rather than the sweat off their backs, are more important than ever in today's global economy. What you know and who you know increasingly are the keys to both personal and organizational success[40] (see Figure 1–2). In the United States, the following "perfect storm" of current and emerging trends heightens the importance and urgency of building human capital:

• Spread of advanced technology to developing countries with rapidly growing middle classes (e.g., China, India, Russia, and Brazil).

• Offshoring of increasingly sophisticated jobs (e.g., product design, architecture, medical diagnosis).

• Comparatively poor math and science skills among America's youth.

• Massive brain drain caused by retiring post–World War II baby-boom generation.[41]

Figure 1–2   *The Strategic Importance and Dimensions of Human and Social Capital*

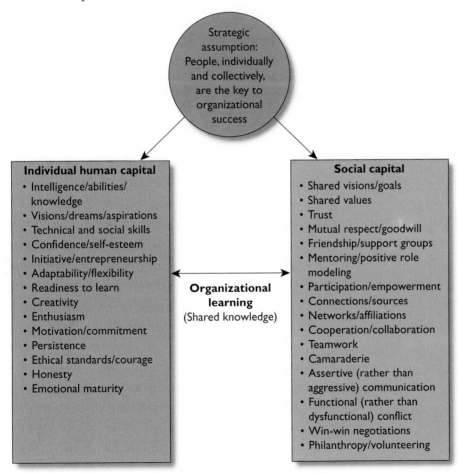

What Is Human Capital? (Hint: Think BIG)

A team of human resource management authors offered this perspective:

> We're living in a time when a new economic paradigm—characterized by speed, innovation, short cycle times, quality, and customer satisfaction—is highlighting the importance of intangible assets, such as brand recognition, knowledge, innovation, and particularly human capital.[42]

Human capital

The productive potential of one's knowledge and actions.

Human capital is the productive potential of an individual's knowledge and actions. *Potential* is the operative word in this intentionally broad definition. When you are hungry, money in your pocket is good because it has the potential to buy a meal. Likewise, a present or future employee with the right combination of knowledge, skills, and motivation to excel represents human capital with the potential to give the organization a competitive advantage. For example, Intel is a high-tech computer chip manufacturer whose future depends on innovative engineering. It takes years of math and science studies to make world-class engineers. Not wanting to leave the future supply of engineers to chance, Intel annually spends $100 million funding education initiatives at all levels worldwide.[43] The company encourages youngsters to study math and science and sponsors rigorous science competitions with scholarships up to $100,000 for the winners.[44] Will all of the students end up working for Intel? No. That's not the point. The point is much bigger—namely, to build the *world's* human capital.

What Is Social Capital?

Our focus now shifts from the individual to social units (e.g., friends, family, company, group or club, nation). Think *relationships*.

Social capital

The productive potential of strong, trusting, and cooperative relationships.

Social capital is productive potential resulting from strong relationships, goodwill, trust, and cooperative effort.[45] Again, the word *potential* is key (see the Real World/Real People feature on page 15). According to experts on the subject: "It's true: the social capital that used to be a given in organizations is now rare and endangered. But the social capital we can build will allow us to capitalize on the volatile, virtual possibilities of today's business environment."[46] Relationships do matter. In a general survey, 77% of the women and 63% of the men rated "Good relationship with boss" extremely important. Other factors—including good equipment, resources, easy commute, and flexible hours—received lower ratings.[47] Moreover, research indicates the favorable impacts positive social interactions can have on cardiovascular health and the immune system.[48]

Building Human and Social Capital

Various dimensions of human and social capital are listed in Figure 1–2. They are a preview of what lies ahead in this book, including our discussion of organizational learning in Chapter 17. Formal organizational learning and *knowledge management* programs, as discussed in Chapter 12, need social capital to leverage individual human capital for the greater good. It is a straightforward formula for success. Growth depends on the timely sharing of valuable knowledge. After all, what good are bright employees who do not network, teach, and inspire?

Debt-Burdened Students Help Themselves by Building Human and Social Capital

Tufts University junior Dean Ladin expected to owe as much as $40,000 in student loans upon graduation and assumed he'd need to postpone for years his dream of working in youth services.

But with the nation's economy struggling, he's planning to apply for a low-paying teaching job in a high-need setting. By doing so, he will become eligible for a program . . . to help Tufts graduates pay down their debts if they go to work in public service. . . .

Eager to encourage public service and give debt-burdened graduates more options, several colleges and universities are trying new initiatives. . . .

Undergraduates at 15 colleges are . . . receiving stipends to discuss their federal internships and recruit classmates. Meanwhile, the year-old Public Service Loan Forgiveness Program eventually will discharge outstanding balances on federal student loans for anyone who . . . works full-time for 10 years in government non-profit groups.

Is this "carrot" approach to building human and social capital a good (or bad) idea?

SOURCE: Excerpted from G J MacDonald, "Tuition Paid with Service," *USA Today*, November 18, 2008, p 6D.

In a win-win approach to building human and social capital, some colleges are helping graduates pay down their student loans in return for teaching in high-need areas. Interested?

LO.5 The Managerial Context: Getting Things Done with and through Others

Like the organizations they run, managers touch our lives in many ways. Schools, hospitals, government agencies, and large and small businesses all require systematic management. Formally defined, **management** is the process of working with and through others to achieve organizational objectives, efficiently and ethically, in the face of constant change. For students of OB, the central feature of this definition is "working with and through others."[49] Managers play a constantly evolving role. Today's successful managers are no longer the I've-got-everything-under-control order givers of yesteryear. Rather, they need to creatively envision and actively sell bold new directions in an ethical and people-friendly manner. Effective managers are team players empowered by the willing and active support of others who are driven by conflicting self-interests.[50] Each of us has a huge stake in how well managers carry out their evolving role. A recent review of 30 years of business literature led to this conclusion about what good management involves: "Find a clear purpose. Be aware that past experience and a mass of information can interfere with wise decisions. Maintain a bias toward action. Be open to change. Seek feedback."[51] A good managerial role model is Todd Bradley, who guided Hewlett-Packard's personal computer division to No. 1:

> Three years ago, when Bradley was brought in, investors wanted HP to jettison the PC business. IBM had just sold its unit to Lenovo, and it looked like Dell would dominate

Management
Process of working with and through others to achieve organizational objectives, efficiently and ethically, amid constant change.

the industry with its low-cost, no frills, direct-sales model. With remarkable speed, however, HP has knocked Dell on its heels and shown it's not just Apple that can innovate in the computer business.[52]

Quality of management can make a big difference for employees and customers, alike.

Let us take a closer look at the skills managers need to perform and the future direction of management.

What Do Managers Do? A Skills Profile

Observational studies by Henry Mintzberg and others have found the typical manager's day to be a fragmented collection of brief episodes.[53] Interruptions are commonplace, while large blocks of time for planning and reflective thinking are not. In one particular study, four top-level managers spent 63% of their time on activities lasting less than nine minutes each. Only 5% of the managers' time was devoted to activities lasting more than an hour.[54] But what specific skills do effective managers perform during their hectic and fragmented workdays?

Many attempts have been made over the years to paint a realistic picture of what managers do. Diverse and confusing lists of managerial functions and roles have been suggested. Fortunately, a stream of research over the past 20 years by Clark Wilson and others has given us a practical and statistically validated profile of managerial *skills*[55] (see Table 1–3). Wilson's managerial skills profile focuses on 11 observable categories of managerial behavior. This is very much in tune with today's emphasis on managerial competency. Wilson's unique skills-assessment technique goes beyond the usual self-report approach with its natural bias. In addition to surveying a given manager about his or her 11 skills, the Wilson approach also asks those who report directly to the manager to answer questions about their boss's skills. According to Wilson and his colleagues, the result is an assessment of skill *mastery*, not simply skill

Table 1–3   *Skills Exhibited by an Effective Manager*

1. **Clarifies goals and objectives** for everyone involved.
2. **Encourages participation,** upward communication, and suggestions.
3. **Plans and organizes** for an orderly work flow.
4. Has **technical and administrative expertise** to answer organization-related questions.
5. **Facilitates work** through team building, training, coaching, and support.
6. **Provides feedback** honestly and constructively.
7. **Keeps things moving** by relying on schedules, deadlines, and helpful reminders.
8. **Controls details** without being overbearing.
9. Applies reasonable **pressure for goal accomplishment.**
10. **Empowers and delegates** key duties to others while maintaining goal clarity and commitment.
11. **Recognizes good performance** with rewards and positive reinforcement.

SOURCES: Adapted from material in F Shipper, "A Study of the Psychometric Properties of the Managerial Skill Scales of the Survey of Management Practices," *Educational and Psychological Measurement,* June 1995, pp 468–79; and C L Wilson, *How and Why Effective Managers Balance Their Skills: Technical, Teambuilding, Drive* (Columbia, MD: Rockatech Multimedia Publishing, 2003).

awareness.[56] The logic behind Wilson's approach is both simple and compelling. Who better to assess a manager's skills than the people who experience those behaviors on a day-to-day basis—those who report directly to the manager?

The Wilson managerial skills research yields four useful lessons:

1. Dealing effectively with *people* is what management is all about. The 11 skills in Table 1–3 constitute a goal creation/commitment/feedback/reward/accomplishment cycle with human interaction at every turn.

2. Managers with high skills mastery tend to have better subunit performance and employee morale than managers with low skills mastery.[57]

3. *Effective* female and male managers *do not* have significantly different skill profiles,[58] contrary to claims in the popular business press in recent years.[59]

4. At all career stages, *derailed* managers (those who failed to achieve their potential) tended to be the ones who *overestimated* their skill mastery (rated themselves higher than their employees did).[60] This prompted the following conclusion from the researcher: "when selecting individuals for promotion to managerial positions, those who are arrogant, aloof, insensitive, and defensive should be avoided."[61]

go to the Web for the Self-Exercise: How Strong Is Your Motivation to Manage?

LO.6 21st-Century Managers

Today's workplace is indeed undergoing immense and permanent changes.[62] Organizations have been "reengineered" for greater speed, efficiency, and flexibility. Teams are pushing aside the individual as the primary building block of organizations.[63] Command-and-control management is giving way to participative management and empowerment. Ego-centered leaders are being replaced by customer-centered leaders. Employees increasingly are being viewed as internal customers. A 2008 summit of 35 executives and management scholars prompted a call for a *reinvention* of management. Lead researcher Gary Hamel framed the challenge this way:

© 2002 Ted Goff

"So what's the problem with morale now?"

Copyright © 2002 Ted Goff. Reprinted with permission.

> [Historically,] the problems were efficiency and scale, and the solution was bureaucracy, with its hierarchical structure, cascading goals, precise role definitions, and elaborate rules and procedures.

> Managers today face a new set of problems, products of a volatile and unforgiving environment. Some of the most critical: How in an age of rapid change do you create organizations that are as adaptable and resilient as they are focused and efficient? How in a world where the winds of creative destruction blow at gale force can a company innovate quickly and boldly enough to stay relevant and profitable? How in a creative economy where entrepreneurial genius is the secret to success do you inspire employees to bring the gifts of initiative, imagination, and passion to work every day? How ... do you encourage executives to fulfill their responsibilities to all stakeholders?[64]

All this creates a mandate for more flexible, innovative, and responsive organizations and a new kind of manager in the 21st century (see Table 1–4).

Table 1–4   *Evolution of the 21st-Century Manager*

	PAST MANAGERS	FUTURE MANAGERS
Primary role	Order giver, privileged elite, manipulator, controller	Facilitator, team member, teacher, advocate, sponsor, coach
Learning and knowledge	Periodic learning, narrow specialist	Continuous life-long learning, generalist with multiple specialties
Compensation criteria	Time, effort, rank	Skills, results
Cultural orientation	Monocultural, monolingual	Multicultural, multilingual
Primary source of influence	Formal authority	Knowledge (technical and interpersonal)
View of people	Potential problem	Primary resource; human capital
Primary communication pattern	Vertical	Multidirectional
Decision-making style	Limited input for individual decisions	Broad-based input for joint decisions
Ethical considerations	Afterthought	Forethought
Nature of interpersonal relationships	Competitive (win–lose)	Cooperative (win–win)
Handling of power and key information	Hoard and restrict access	Share and broaden access for greater transparency
Approach to change	Resist	Facilitate

The Contingency Approach to Management

Scholars have wrestled for many years with the problem of how best to apply the diverse and growing collection of management tools and techniques. Their answer is the contingency approach. The **contingency approach** calls for using management techniques in a situationally appropriate manner, instead of trying to rely on "one best way" or "one size fits all."

The contingency approach encourages managers to view organizational behavior within a situational context. According to this modern perspective, evolving situations, not hard-and-fast rules, determine when and where various management techniques are appropriate. Harvard's Clayton Christensen put it this way: "Many of the widely accepted principles of good management are only situationally appropriate."[65] For example, as discussed in Chapter 16, contingency researchers have determined that there is no single best style of leadership. Organizational behavior specialists embrace the contingency approach because it helps them realistically interrelate individuals, groups, and evolving circumstances inside and outside the organization.[66] Moreover, the contingency approach sends a clear message to managers in today's global economy: Carefully read the situation and then be flexible enough to adapt (see the Real World/Real People feature on page 19).

Contingency approach

Using management tools and techniques in a situationally appropriate manner; avoiding the one-best-way mentality.

Businesses Help Develop Nonprofit Sector Leaders

Nothing about the executive dining room at American Express, on the 50th floor at the company's downtown Manhattan headquarters, suggests not-for-profit. But on a recent afternoon, 24 employees of nonprofits sank into oversized dinner chairs, listening to AmEx Chief Executive Kenneth I. Chenault. "You can learn a great deal about leadership if you take it as seriously as other disciplines," Chenault said. "Most people don't."

The visitors, handpicked by their bosses, made up the first class of a weeklong "Nonprofit Leadership Academy." AmEx, like most big companies, has long supported nonprofits with donations. Its new program is part of a growing effort to address one of the nonprofit world's acute problems—the lack of well-trained managers.

Others are doing it, too.... [In 2008], IBM announced a collaboration with Bridgespan Group, a consultancy for nonprofits, to help employees facing retirement transition into nonprofit work. Bank of America has a training program for nonprofit executives, and the Gap Foundation has one in the works. The goal, says Chenault, is to have everyone "leverage our existing tools to make a major impact in the nonprofit world."

What leadership and management challenges are unique to nonprofit organizations such as universities, hospitals, and charities?

SOURCE: Alison Damast, "Narrowing the Nonprofit Talent Gap," *BusinessWeek*, August 11, 2008, p 58.

American Express CEO Kenneth I Chenault.

The Ethics Challenge

to the point

How can an understanding of Carroll's social responsibility pyramid and the seven moral principles lead to more ethical conduct in the workplace?

Thanks to highly publicized criminal acts of now-jailed executives from the likes of Enron, Tyco, and WorldCom,[67] corporate officers in the United States became subject to high accountability standards and harsh penalties under the Sarbanes-Oxley Act of 2002.[68] Sadly, instead of improving, business ethics continued to hit new lows, as symbolized by $50 billion Ponzi schemer Bernard Madoff's trip to prison in 2009.[69] The general public and elected officials (who have their own criminal hall of shame) continue to call for greater attention to ethical conduct.[70]

Clearly, *everyone* needs to join in the effort to stem this tide of unethical conduct. There are a variety of individual and organizational factors that contribute to unethical behavior. OB is an excellent vantage point for better understanding and improving workplace ethics. If OB can provide insights about managing human work behavior, then it can teach us something about avoiding *misbehavior*.

Ethics involves the study of moral issues and choices. It is concerned with right versus wrong, good versus bad, and the many shades of gray in supposedly black-and-white issues. Moral implications spring from virtually every decision, both on and off the job. Managers are challenged to have more imagination and the courage to do the right thing to make the world a better place.

To enhance our understanding of ethics within an OB context, we will discuss (1) a corporate social responsibility model, (2) the general erosion of morality, (3) seven moral principles for managers, (4) how to improve an organization's ethical climate, and (5) a personal call to action.

Ethics

Study of moral issues and choices.

Pennies Add Up at JCPenney

In Appleton, Wis., the after-school center at Horizons School has several kids who couldn't be there if not for the JCPenney Afterschool Fund—one of the more than 600 after-school programs the department store helps fund. . . . [In 2008], Penney's provided 20,000 grants to cover or defray costs for kids to attend after-school programs.

The retailer contributed more than $70 million since 1999 to programs run by YMCAs, Boys and Girls Clubs, 4-H Clubs and United Way-funded agencies. In addition, Penney sometimes raises money for the after-school fund by asking customers whether they'd be willing to round their purchases up to the next dollar. On Dec. 5–14 [2008], Penney raised a record $1.5 million in the fourth such "Round Up."

Companies like JCPenney have provided millions of dollars for children's after-school programs to fulfill their corporate social responsibility.

How would you respond to someone who called this simply a public relations campaign?

SOURCE: Excerpted from J O'Donnell, "20,000 Grants Help Kids," *USA Today*, December 24, 2008, p 2B.

LO.7 A Model of Global Corporate Social Responsibility and Ethics

Corporate social responsibility

Corporations are expected to go above and beyond following the law and making a profit.

Corporate social responsibility (CSR) is defined as "the notion that corporations have an obligation to constituent groups in society other than stockholders and beyond that prescribed by law or union contract."[71] CSR challenges businesses to go above and beyond just making a profit to serve the interests and needs of "stakeholders," including past and present employees, customers, suppliers, and countries and communities where facilities are located[72] (see the Real World/Real People feature above). A good deal of controversy surrounds the drive for greater CSR because classical economic theory says businesses are responsible for producing goods and services to make profits, not solving the world's social, political, and environmental ills.[73] What is your opinion?

University of Georgia business ethics scholar Archie B Carroll views CSR in broad terms. So broad, in fact, that he created a model of CSR/business ethics with the global economy and multinational corporations in mind (see Figure 1–3). This model is very timely because it effectively triangulates three major trends: (1) economic globalization, (2) expanding CSR expectations, and (3) the call for improved business ethics. Carroll's global CSR pyramid, from the bottom up, advises organizations in the global economy to

- *Make a profit* consistent with expectations for international businesses.

- *Obey the law* of host countries as well as international law.

- *Be ethical in its practices,* taking host-country and global standards into consideration.

- *Be a good corporate citizen,* especially as defined by the host country's expectations.[74]

Figure 1–3   *Carroll's Global Corporate Social Responsibility Pyramid*

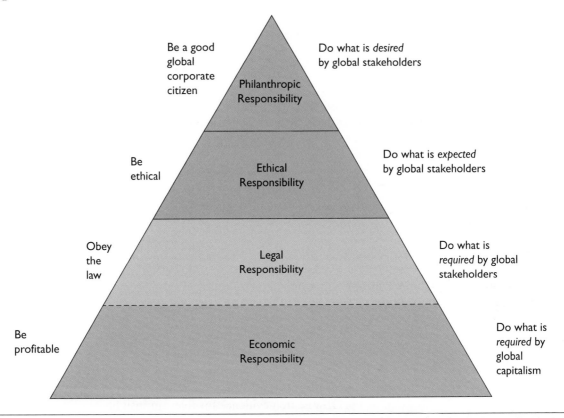

Be a good global corporate citizen

Philanthropic Responsibility

Do what is *desired* by global stakeholders

Be ethical

Ethical Responsibility

Do what is *expected* by global stakeholders

Obey the law

Legal Responsibility

Do what is *required* by global stakeholders

Be profitable

Economic Responsibility

Do what is *required* by global capitalism

SOURCE: From *Academy of Management Executive: The Thinking Manager's Source* by A B Carroll. Copyright © 2004 by The Aademy of Management. Reproduced by permission of The Academy of Management via Copyright Clearance Center.

In keeping with the pyramid idea, Carroll emphasizes that each level needs to be solid if the structure is to stand. A pick-and-choose approach to CSR is inappropriate. The top level of the pyramid, according to Carroll, reflects "global society's expectations that business will engage in social activities that are not mandated by law nor generally expected of business in an ethical sense."[75] The spirit of Carroll's global corporate social responsibility pyramid is evident in Nike's ongoing quest to shake its sweatshop image:

Progress has been slow in coming to Nike's global supply chain, which employs nearly 800,000 workers in 52 countries. Still, Nike . . . has made strides since it embraced corporate responsibility. What started as a massive PR shield has evolved into a broader mandate for the way it makes and sells products. Nike has been particularly inventive at weaving environmental awareness

By transforming its business practices to embrace global corporate social responsibility standards, Nike has improved its image. Does corporate reputation influence your buying decisions?

into its design process, rating each sneaker according to a sustainability index. On labor, the company admits that its initial efforts—setting a code of conduct and monitoring compliance—haven't ended abuses across the hundreds of factories that produce its goods. But the lessons from the 1990s—to own up to problems, then find companywide solutions—are helping the world's biggest shoemaker … with labor issues. "I'm proud of what we've accomplished, but we're still not where we need to be," says Nike's current CEO, Mark Parker.[76]

Our OB in Action Case Study on Patagonia at the end of this chapter is a good CSR example. With this global CSR perspective in mind, we now narrow the focus to individual moral behavior.

An Erosion of Morality?

David Callahan, in his book *The Cheating Culture: Why More Americans Are Doing Wrong to Get Ahead*, paints this disturbing picture of modern society:

> … the character of Americans has changed. Those values associated with the market hold sway in their most caricatured form: individualism and self-reliance have morphed into selfishness and self-absorption; competitiveness has become social Darwinism; desire for the good life has turned into materialism; aspiration has become envy. There is a growing gap between the life that many Americans want and the life they can afford—a problem that bedevils even those who would seem to have everything. Other values in our culture have been sidelined; belief in community, social responsibility, compassion for the less able or less fortunate.[77]

Does this portrayal of a "cheating culture" have merit and, if so, to what extent? Let us examine the OB research evidence for relevant insights.

Taking Local Norms and Conduct into Consideration   National culture, as discussed in Chapter 4, affects how people think and act about everything, including ethical issues. This reality was supported in a multination study (including the United States, Great Britain, France, Germany, Spain, Switzerland, India, China, and Australia) of management ethics. Managers from each country were asked to judge the ethicality of 12 questionable behaviors, including such things as giving and accepting gifts, passing blame, sharing confidential information, and concealing errors. Results revealed significant differences across the 10 nations in the study. That is, managers in some countries approved of practices that were frowned upon in other countries.[78] Consequently, care needs to be taken when extrapolating Callahan's characterization of American morality to other cultures. Each culture requires its own ethical analysis, taking local norms into consideration.

Ethical Lapses in the Workplace   A nationwide survey of 581 human resource professionals revealed that 62% of the respondents occasionally observed unethical behavior at their companies.[79] Unethical behavior occurs at all organizational levels, although recent research indicates that senior executives tend to have significantly more positive perceptions of ethics in their organizations than do lower-level employees.[80] Perhaps that is because lower-level employees regularly witness common ethical lapses such as lying about being sick, fudging a report, bullying and sexual harassment, personal use of company equipment, and stealing

company property or funds. Executives are not immune to being victims of unethical conduct, however. For example, a survey of job applicants for executive positions indicated that 64% had been misinformed about the financial condition of potential employers, and 58% of these individuals were negatively affected by this misinformation.[81] It is very likely that some of those affected individuals moved their families and left their friends only to discover the promise of a great job in a financially stable organization was a lie. Job applicants, for their part, also have ethical lapses. An analysis of 2.6 million background checks by ADP Screening and Selection Services, revealed that "44% of applicants lied about their work histories, 41% lied about their education, and 23% falsified credentials or licenses."[82]

Experts estimate that US companies lost about $994 billion to fraud in 2008, much of it at the hands of insiders.[83] A slumping economy worsens the situation:

> Corporate grifters seem to be getting nervier. Recently, a Maryland man swiped 32 laptops from his nonprofit health-care employer and put them on eBay. A chief financial officer changed the color of the type on some spreadsheet data from black to white so as to render the fake numbers invisible while juicing the totals—and his bonus. One regional vice-president for sales billed his corporate card $4,000 for Victoria's Secret lingerie—and not for his wife, either.
>
> That these schemers are getting caught is a testament to the strides made by the corporate fraud police. Sleuthing technologies are light-years beyond where they were in the last recession, of 2001. And with most companies looking to cut costs, managers are eager to crack down on insider malfeasance, which on average equals 7% of revenues, says the Association of Certified Fraud Examiners.[84]

On a global scale, the World Bank says, "bribery has become a $1 trillion industry."[85]

Intense Pressure for Results Starts Early

Lower-level managers generally want to "look good" for their bosses. In support of this conclusion, many studies have found a tendency among middle- and lower-level managers to act unethically in the face of perceived pressure for results. Further, this tendency is particularly pronounced when individuals are significantly rewarded for accomplishing their goals.[86] By fostering a pressure-cooker atmosphere for results, managers can unwittingly set the stage for unethical shortcuts by employees who seek to please and be loyal to the company.

Unfortunately, the seeds of this problem are planted early in life. A survey of 787 youngsters ages 13 to 18 found "that 44% of teens feel they're under strong pressure to succeed in school, no matter the cost. Of those, 81% believe the pressure will be the same or worse in the workplace."[87] Sixty-nine percent of the students admitted to lying in the past year (with 27% confessing they even lied on the survey!).[88] Anonymous surveys by the Josephson Institute of almost 30,000 students from private and public high schools across the United States found 60% admittedly had cheated on a test in 2006 and 64% in 2008. Thirty-six percent reportedly had plagiarized via the Internet in 2008, up from 33% in 2006. According to the 2008 survey: "Students attending non-religious independent schools reported the lowest cheating rate (47 percent) while 63 percent of students from religious schools cheated."[89]

In summary, Callahan's earlier characterization of America's cheating culture is an appropriate wake-up call. The challenge to improve is immense because unethical behavior is pervasive.

L0.8 General Moral Principles

Management consultant and writer Kent Hodgson has helpfully taken managers a step closer to ethical decisions by identifying seven general moral principles (see Table 1–5). Hodgson calls them "the magnificent seven" to emphasize their timeless and worldwide relevance. Notions of both justice and care are clearly evident in the magnificent seven, which are detailed and, hence, more practical. Importantly, according to Hodgson, there are no absolute ethical answers for decision makers. The goal for managers should be to rely on moral principles so their decisions are *principled, appropriate,* and *defensible.*[90]

Table 1–5   *The Magnificent Seven: General Moral Principles for Managers*

1. *Dignity of human life:* The lives of people are to be respected. Human beings, by the fact of their existence, have value and dignity. We may not act in ways that directly intend to harm or kill an innocent person. Human beings have a right to live; we have an obligation to respect that right to life. Human life is to be preserved and treated as sacred.

2. *Autonomy:* All persons are intrinsically valuable and have the right to self-determination. We should act in ways that demonstrate each person's worth, dignity, and right to free choice. We have a right to act in ways that assert our own worth and legitimate needs. We should not use others as mere "things" or only as means to an end. Each person has an equal right to basic human liberty, compatible with a similar liberty for others.

3. *Honesty:* The truth should be told to those who have a right to know it. Honesty is also known as integrity, truth telling, and honor. One should speak and act so as to reflect the reality of the situation. Speaking and acting should mirror the way things really are. There are times when others have the right to hear the truth from us; there are times when they do not.

4. *Loyalty:* Promises, contracts, and commitments should be honored. Loyalty includes fidelity, promise keeping, keeping the public trust, good citizenship, excellence in quality of work, reliability, commitment, and honoring just laws, rules, and policies.

5. *Fairness:* People should be treated justly. One has the right to be treated fairly, impartially, and equitably. One has the obligation to treat others fairly and justly. All have the right to the necessities of life—especially those in deep need and the helpless. Justice includes equal, impartial, unbiased treatment. Fairness tolerates diversity and accepts differences in people and their ideas.

6. *Humaneness:* There are two parts: (1) Our actions ought to accomplish good, and (2) we should avoid doing evil. We should do good to others and to ourselves. We should have concern for the well-being of others; usually, we show this concern in the form of compassion, giving, kindness, serving, and caring.

7. *The common good:* Actions should accomplish the "greatest good for the greatest number" of people. One should act and speak in ways that benefit the welfare of the largest number of people, while trying to protect the rights of individuals.

SOURCE: From Kent Hodgson, *A Rock and a Hard Place: How to Make Ethical Business Decisions When the Choices Are Tough,* © 1992. Reprinted with permission of the author.

How to Improve the Organization's Ethical Climate

Improving workplace ethics is not just a nice thing to do; it also can have a positive impact on the bottom line. Studies in the United States and the United Kingdom demonstrated that corporate commitment to ethics can be profitable. Evidence suggested that profitability is enhanced by a reputation for honesty and corporate citizenship.[91] Ethics also can impact the quality of people who apply to work in an organization. An online survey of 1,020 individuals indicated that 83% rated a company's record of business ethics as "very important" when deciding to accept a job offer. Only 2% rated it as "unimportant."[92]

A team of management researchers recommended the following actions for improving on-the-job ethics.[93]

- *Behave ethically yourself.* Managers are potent role models whose habits and actual behavior send clear signals about the importance of ethical conduct. Ethical behavior is a top-to-bottom proposition and executives are challenged "to simultaneously maximize the so-called triple bottom line, or 'People, Planet, Profit.'"[94]

- *Screen potential employees.* Surprisingly, employers are generally lax when it comes to checking references, credentials, transcripts, and other information on applicant résumés. More diligent action in this area can screen out those given to fraud and misrepresentation. Integrity testing is fairly valid but is no panacea.[95]

- *Develop a meaningful code of ethics.* Codes of ethics can have a positive impact if they satisfy these four criteria:

  1. They are *distributed* to every employee.
  2. They are firmly *supported* by top management.
  3. They refer to *specific* practices and ethical dilemmas likely to be encountered by target employees (e.g., salespersons paying kickbacks, purchasing agents receiving payoffs, laboratory scientists doctoring data, or accountants "cooking the books").
  4. They are evenly *enforced* with rewards for compliance and strict penalties for noncompliance.

- *Provide ethics training.* Employees can be trained to identify and deal with ethical issues during orientation and through seminar, video, and Internet training sessions.[96]

- *Reinforce ethical behavior.* Behavior that is reinforced tends to be repeated, whereas behavior that is not reinforced tends to disappear. Ethical conduct too often is ignored or even punished while unethical behavior is rewarded.

- *Create positions, units, and other structural mechanisms to deal with ethics.* Ethics needs to be an everyday affair, not a one-time announcement of a new ethical code that gets filed away and forgotten. A growing number of large companies in the United States have chief ethics officers who report directly to the CEO, thus making ethical conduct and accountability priority issues.

- *Create a climate in which whistle-blowing becomes unnecessary.* **Whistle-blowing** occurs when an employee reports a perceived unethical and/or illegal activity to a third party such as government agencies, news media,

Whistle-blowing

Reporting unethical/illegal acts to outside third parties.

or public-interest groups. Enron's Sherron Watkins was a highly publicized whistle-blower.[97] Organizations can reduce the need for whistle-blowing by encouraging free and open expression of dissenting viewpoints and giving employees a voice through fair grievance procedures and/or anonymous ethics hot lines.[98]

A Personal Call to Action

In the final analysis, ethics comes down to individual perception and motivation. Organizational climate, role models, structure, training, and rewards all can point employees in the right direction. But individuals first must be **morally attentive,** meaning they faithfully consider the ethical implications of their actions and circumstances.[99] Second, they must *want* to do the right thing and have the courage to act. Bill George, the respected former CEO of Medtronic, the maker of life-saving devices such as heart pacemakers, gave us this call to action: "Each of us needs to determine . . . where our ethical boundaries are and, if asked to violate (them), refuse. . . . If this means refusing a direct order, we must be prepared to resign."[100] Rising to this challenge requires strong personal *values* (more about values in Chapter 6) and the *courage* to adhere to them during adversity.

Morally attentive
Faithfully considering the ethical implications of one's actions.

Learning about OB: Research and a Road Map

to the point
Which of the five research methodologies is likely to provide the best insights about OB?

OB is a broad and growing field. We have a lot of ground to cover. To make the trip as instructive and efficient as possible, we use a theory→research→practice strategy. For virtually all major topics in this book, we begin by presenting the underlying theoretical framework (often with graphical models showing how key variables are related) and defining key terms. Next, we tap the latest research findings for valuable insights. Finally, we round out the discussion with illustrative practical examples and, when applicable, how-to-do-it advice.

LO.9 Five Sources of OB Research Insights

OB gains its credibility as an academic discipline by being research driven. Scientific rigor pushes aside speculation, prejudice, and untested assumptions about workplace behavior. We systematically cite "hard" evidence from five different categories. Worthwhile evidence was obtained by drawing upon the following *priority* of research methodologies:

Meta-analysis
Pools the results of many studies through statistical procedure.

- *Meta-analyses.* A **meta-analysis** is a statistical pooling technique that permits behavioral scientists to draw general conclusions about certain variables from many different studies.[101] It typically encompasses a vast number of subjects, often reaching the thousands. Meta-analyses are instructive because they focus on general patterns of research evidence, not fragmented bits and pieces or isolated studies.[102]

Field study
Examination of variables in real-life settings.

- *Field studies.* In OB, a **field study** probes individual or group processes in an organizational setting. Because field studies involve real-life situations, their results often have immediate and practical relevance for managers.

- *Laboratory studies.* In a **laboratory study,** variables are manipulated and measured in contrived situations. College students are commonly used as subjects. The highly controlled nature of laboratory studies enhances research precision. But generalizing the results to organizational management requires caution.

- *Sample surveys.* In a **sample survey,** samples of people from specified populations respond to questionnaires. The researchers then draw conclusions about the relevant population. Generalizability of the results depends on the quality of the sampling and questioning techniques.

- *Case studies,* A **case study** is an in-depth analysis of a single individual, group, or organization, Because of their limited scope, case studies yield realistic but not very generalizable results.

Laboratory study

Manipulation and measurement of variables in contrived situations.

Sample survey

Questionnaire responses from a sample of people.

Case study

In-depth study of a single person, group, or organization.

go to the Web for the Group Exercise: Timeless Advice

A Topical Model for Understanding and Managing OB

Figure 1–4 is a topical road map for our journey through this book. Our destination is organizational effectiveness through continuous improvement. Four different criteria for determining whether or not an organization is effective are discussed in Chapter 17. The study of OB can be a wandering and pointless trip if we overlook the need to translate OB lessons into an effective and efficient organized endeavor.

At the far left side of our topical road map are managers and team leaders, those who are responsible for accomplishing organizational results with and through others. The three circles at the center of our road map correspond to Parts Two, Three, and Four of this text. Logically, the flow of topical coverage in this book (following introductory Part One) goes from individuals, to group processes, to organizational processes. Around the core of our topical road map in Figure 1–4 is the organization. Accordingly, we end our journey with organization-related material in Part Four. Organizational structure and design are covered there in Chapter 17 to establish and develop the *organizational* context of organizational behavior. Rounding out our organizational context is a discussion of organizational change in Chapter 18. Chapters 3 and 4 provide a *cultural* context for OB.

The dotted line represents a permeable boundary between the organization and its environment. Energy and influence flow both ways across this permeable boundary. Truly, no organization is an island in today's highly interactive and interdependent world. Relative to the *external* environment, international cultures are explored in Chapter 4. Organization–environment contingencies are examined in Chapter 17.

Chapter 2 examines the OB implications of significant demographic and social trends. These discussions provide a realistic context for studying and managing people at work.

Bon voyage! Enjoy your trip through the challenging, interesting, and often surprising world of OB.

Figure 1–4   *A Topical Model for What Lies Ahead*

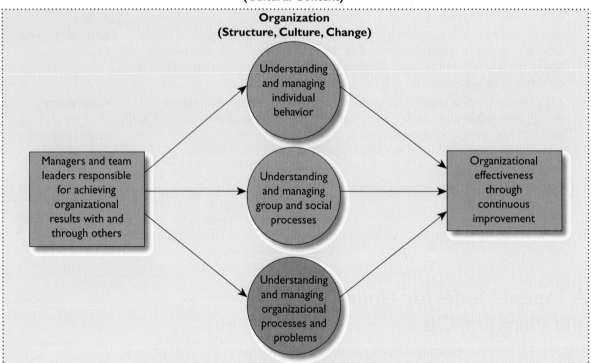

**External Environment
(Cultural Context)**

**Organization
(Structure, Culture, Change)**

Understanding and managing individual behavior

Managers and team leaders responsible for achieving organizational results with and through others

Understanding and managing group and social processes

Organizational effectiveness through continuous improvement

Understanding and managing organizational processes and problems

Summary of Key Concepts

1. *Define the term* organizational behavior, *and contrast McGregor's Theory X and Theory Y assumptions about employees.* Organizational behavior (OB) is an interdisciplinary field dedicated to better understanding and managing people at work. It is both research and application oriented. Theory X employees, according to traditional thinking, dislike work, require close supervision, and are primarily interested in security. According to the modern Theory Y view, employees are capable of self-direction, of seeking responsibility, and of being creative.

2. *Identify the four principles of total quality management (TQM).* (*a*) Do it right the first time to eliminate costly rework. (*b*) Listen to and learn from customers and employees. (*c*) Make continuous improvement an everyday matter. (*d*) Build teamwork, trust, and mutual respect.

3. *Define the term* e-business, *and specify at least three OB-related issues raised by e-leadership.* E-business involves using the Internet to more effectively and efficiently manage every aspect of a business. Six OB-related issues raised by the advent of e-leadership are (*a*) greater access to information for everyone, (*b*) leadership is migrating to lower levels and outside the organization, (*c*) development of nontraditional leadership networks, (*d*) followers have more information earlier in the decision-making process, (*e*) greater influence for unethical leaders with limited resources, and (*f*) more contact between senior leaders and their followers.

4. *Contrast human and social capital, and explain why we need to build both.* The first involves *individual* characteristics; the second involves *social* relationships. Human capital is the productive potential of an individual's knowledge and actions. Dimensions include

such things as intelligence, visions, skills, self-esteem, creativity, motivation, ethics, and emotional maturity. Social capital is productive potential resulting from strong relationships, goodwill, trust, and cooperative effort. Dimensions include such things as shared visions and goals, trust, mutual respect, friendships, empowerment, teamwork, win-win negotiations, and volunteering. Social capital is necessary to tap individual human capital for the good of the organization through knowledge sharing and networking.

5. *Define the term* management, *and identify at least five of the eleven managerial skills in Wilson's profile of effective managers.* Management is the process of working with and through others to achieve organizational objectives in an efficient and ethical manner. According to the Wilson skills profile, an effective manager (*a*) clarifies goals and objectives, (*b*) encourages participation, (*c*) plans and organizes, (*d*) has technical and administrative expertise, (*e*) facilitates work through team building and coaching, (*f*) provides feedback, (*g*) keeps things moving, (*h*) controls details, (*i*) applies reasonable pressure for goals accomplishment, (*j*) empowers and delegates, and (*k*) recognizes and rewards good performance.

6. *Characterize 21st-century managers.* They will be team players who will get things done cooperatively by relying on joint decision making, their knowledge instead of formal authority, and their multicultural skills. They will engage in life-long learning and be compensated on the basis of their skills and results. They will facilitate rather than resist change, share rather than hoard power and key information, and be multidirectional communicators. Ethics will be a forethought instead of an afterthought. They will be generalists with multiple specialties.

7. *Describe Carroll's global corporate social responsibility pyramid, and discuss the problem of moral erosion.* From bottom to top, the four levels of corporate responsibility in Carroll's pyramid are: *economic* (make a profit); *legal* (obey the law); *ethical* (be ethical in its practices); and *philanthropic* (be a good corporate citizen). Progress needs to be made on all levels. Callahan's claim that America has developed a "cheating culture" is supported by unethical conduct at all organizational levels. An unintended but serious consequence of excessive pressure for results, beginning in school and carrying over to the workplace, is expedient unethical behavior. Moral erosion is evident in high school and workplace surveys about misconduct.

8. *Identify four of the seven general ethical principles, and explain how to improve an organization's ethical climate.* The "magnificent seven" moral principles are (*a*) dignity of human life, (*b*) autonomy, (*c*) honesty, (*d*) loyalty, (*e*) fairness, (*f*) humaneness (by doing good and avoiding evil), and (*g*) the common good (accomplishing the greatest good for the greatest number of people). An organization's ethical climate can be improved by managers being good role models, carefully screening job applicants, creating and firmly enforcing a code of ethics mentioning specific practices, providing ethics training, rewarding ethical behavior, creating ethics-related positions and structures, and reducing the need for whistle-blowing (reporting unethical conduct to outside third parties) through open and honest debate.

9. *Describe the sources of organizational behavior research evidence.* Five sources of OB research evidence are meta-analyses (statistically pooled evidence from several studies), field studies (evidence from real-life situations), laboratory studies (evidence from contrived situations), sample surveys (questionnaire data), and case studies (observation of a single person, group, or organization).

Key Terms

OB in Action Case Study

A Passion for the Planet[103]

BusinessWeek Southern Californian Scott Robinson had quite a résumé when he returned from studying in France last Christmas. The 26-year-old had an undergraduate degree from Bucknell University, two MBAs, and internships at two of Europe's most respected corporations, Nestlé and Unilever Group. Yet, when it came time to take the next career step, he chose a job as a stock handler in a surf shop in Cardiff-by-the-Sea, California. Actually, he begged for the job. What gives? Simple, he says: "I wanted to work for a company that's driven by values."

The company is Patagonia Inc., a Ventura, California, seller of outdoor clothing and equipment that has a reputation as an enlightened employer and champion of the environment. On his return from France, Robinson read *Let My People Go Surfing,* a memoir and manifesto of sustainable business practices by Patagonia founder and chairman Yvon Chouinard. The company's goal is as simple as it is challenging: to produce the highest-quality products while doing the least possible harm to the environment.

That mission is a daily inspiration for Patagonia's 1,275 employees, from Chouinard to the flip-flop-wearing guy who answers the phone in the headquarters lobby. Most corporate mission statements are empty platitudes. This one guides every decision. And it's the centerpiece of a set of management practices that have helped Patagonia grow at a healthy rate and retain what is arguably the best reputation in its industry even while it faces increasing competition from much larger companies.

Patagonia's philosophy is the handiwork of Chouinard, a gruff yet funny outdoorsman who, despite his 67 years and arthritic hands, hasn't slowed down much. He helped pioneer modern rock-climbing techniques in his youth and now prowls the globe in search of outdoor adventures and product ideas. That is, when he's not shaking up his 33-year-old company, helping to preserve the environment, or advocating radical changes in the way Americans do business. "Most people want to do good things, but don't. At Patagonia, it's an essential part of your life," says Chouinard.

At a time when companies must adapt to an ever-quickening competitive pace, a highly motivated workforce can provide a crucial edge. Until now, there have been two primary approaches to keeping employees at the top of their game. At the high-stress workplace, bosses rule by fear, kicking ass, and taking names. At feel-good places, managers try to motivate employees with kind words and generous benefits. Neither approach is optimal. In a recent Gallup poll, only one-third of Americans considered themselves passionate about their jobs.

A few companies have found a better way. "There are companies that stress continuous improvement and being way better than the competition but also make people feel comfortable," says Stanford University professor Jeffrey Pfeffer. These companies range from publicly traded giants such as FedEx and Southwest Airlines to a small fry like Patagonia. They are meritocracies with ambitious goals that trust their employees to do the right thing—and give them the tools and time they need to do it.

Patagonia, with 39 stores in seven countries, works hard at achieving that delicate balance. It offers an on-site day-care center at its headquarters and full medical benefits to all employees, including part-timers. When the surf's up, Chouinard himself urges people to hit the beach. At the same time, the company demands hard work, creativity, collaboration, and results. Management isn't shy about axing employees who aren't up to snuff. . . .

Patagonia enjoys an unrivaled reputation among outdoor aficionados, and its green philosophy is gaining broader appeal as more Americans embrace sustainable consumption. Chouinard's goal for Patagonia's own sustainability: "I look at this company as an experiment to see if we can run it so it's here 100 years from now and always makes the best-quality stuff," he says. That means keeping growth relatively slow but steady, at about 5% per year. Revenues were up a healthy 7% last year, to $260 million. Operating margins typically come in at the high end of the 12% to 15% industry average, according to people who have seen the numbers, and that's after it donates 1% of revenues to environmental groups. Patagonia, which declined to comment on its financials, is owned by a Chouinard family trust. . . .

Few Patagonians are in it just for the money. The company recently raised salaries to adjust for the cost of living, and everybody gets an annual bonus based on profits, but, overall, Patagonia pays at, or just slightly above, the market rate. However, the most significant rewards aren't monetary. One popular perk is a program that allows employees to take off up to two months at full pay and work for environmental groups. Lisa Myers, who works on the company's giving programs, tracked wolves in Yellowstone National Park during her sabbatical. The company also pays 50% of her college expenses as she pursues a wildlife biology degree. "It's easy to go to work when you get paid to do what you love to do," she says.

Patagonia's culture makes it a magnet for talented people. The company receives an average of 900 résumés for every job opening, so it can afford to be picky. . . .

Can others capture some of Patagonia's magic? Most companies—especially ones with demanding public shareholders—simply can't let employees take a surfing break. They can, however, foster creativity and provide a sense of purpose. Perhaps the most valuable and easily applied lesson from Patagonia's experience is this: To think outside the box, sometimes you need to get out of the cubicle.

Questions for Discussion

1. What role, if any, does McGregor's Theory Y play at Patagonia? Explain.
2. How does Patagonia build human and social capital?
3. How does this case bring the profile of the 21st-century manager (Table 1–4) to life? Explain.
4. Which of the seven moral principles in Table 1–5 apear to be in force at Patagonia? Explain.
5. What appeals to you (or does not appeal to you) about working at Patagonia? Explain.

Ethical Dilemma

Caught in the Layoff Wringer

"I'm the purchasing manager for an engineering company, and I've been told to lay off one employee. All my staffers are hard-working, and I don't feel morally right about laying off one of them. My boss says every department needs to participate in the cut. What should I do?"[104]

What Advice Would You Offer This Troubled Manager?

1. It's not about *you*, it's about doing your job as a manager. Show some courage; pick someone. (What general criteria should be applied to determine who gets laid off? What is your ethical reasoning for this approach?)
2. Suggest to upper management that there are many good alternatives to layoffs, such as voluntary leave without pay, reduced hours across the board, and lending workers to local companies that are temporarily short-handed. (What is your preferred approach and how would you present your case to management? What is your ethical argument?)
3. Tell management that it is arbitrary to cut one person from every work unit because some units may have all winners while other units may have a number of marginal people. (State your business case and ethical argument for this line of thinking.)
4. Go to the wall to defend your group and tell management you'll quit rather than "sacrifice" a perfectly good employee. (What is your ethical reasoning here?)
5. Invent other interpretations or options. Discuss.

Web Resources

For study material and exercises that apply to this chapter, visit our Web site, **www.mhhe.com/kreitner**

Chapter 2

Managing Diversity: Releasing Every Employee's Potential

LEARNING OBJECTIVES

When you finish studying the material in this chapter, you should be able to:

LO.1 Define diversity and review the four layers of diversity.

LO.2 Explain the difference between affirmative action and managing diversity.

LO.3 Explain why Alice Eagly and Linda Carli believe that a woman's career is best viewed as traveling through a labyrinth.

LO.4 Review the demographic trends pertaining to racial groups, educational mismatches, and an aging workforce.

LO.5 Highlight the managerial implications of increasing diversity in the workforce.

LO.6 Describe the positive and negative effects of diversity by using social categorization theory and information/decision-making theory.

LO.7 Identify the barriers and challenges to managing diversity.

LO.8 Discuss the organizational practices used to effectively manage diversity as identified by R Roosevelt Thomas Jr.

Student Resources for Studying Chapter 2

The Web site for your text includes resources that will help you master the concepts in this chapter. As you read, you'll want to visit the site for these helpful tools:

- Your online Study Guide includes learning objectives, a chapter summary, a glossary of key terms, and discussion questions.
- Take a practice quiz and test your knowledge!
- Scroll through a PowerPoint presentation with key concepts for this chapter.

Your instructor might also direct you to the Web site for these exercises:

- Self-assessments that correspond with the chapter content and a Group Exercise.
- You'll also find Video Cases and Internet Exercises for this chapter online.

www.mhhe.com/kreitner

In a recent class at Abraham Clark High School in Roselle, New Jersey, business teacher Barbara Govahn distributed glossy classroom materials that invited students to think about what they want to be when they grow up. Eighteen career paths were profiled, including a writer, a magician, a town mayor—and five employees from accounting giant Deloitte LLP.

"Consider a career you may never have imagined," the book suggests. "Working as a professional auditor."

The curriculum, provided free to the public school by a nonprofit arm of Deloitte, aims to persuade students to join the company's ranks. One 18-year-old senior in Ms. Govahn's class, Hipolito Rivera, says the company-sponsored lesson drove home how professionals in all fields need accountants. "They make it sound pretty good," he says.

Deloitte and other corporations are reaching out to classrooms—drafting curricula while also conveying the benefits of working for the sponsor companies. Hoping to create a pipeline of workers far into the future, these corporations furnish free lesson plans and may also underwrite classroom materials, computers, or training seminars for teachers.

The programs represent a new dimension of the business world's influence in public schools. Companies such as McDonald's Corp. and Yum Brands Inc.'s Pizza Hut have long attempted to use school promotions to turn students into customers. The latest initiatives would turn them into employees.

Companies that employ engineers, fearful of a coming labor shortage, are at the movement's forefront. Lockheed Martin Corp. began funding engineering courses two years ago at schools near its aircraft testing and development site in Palmdale, California, saying it hopes to replenish its local workforce. Starting in 2004, British engine-maker Rolls-Royce PLC has helped fund high-school courses in topics such as engine propulsion. Intel Corp. supports curricula in school districts where engineering concepts are taught as early as the elementary level.

Schools are increasingly accepting curriculum and funds from corporations concerned about labor shortages in the accounting and engineering fields.

Schools, for their part, have embraced corporate support as state education funding has remained flat for a decade and declining housing values now threaten to eat into property-tax revenues. Teachers, meanwhile, often welcome the lesson plans, classroom equipment, and the corporate-sponsored professional development sessions. . . .

Lockheed is bracing for a worker shortage. The company estimates that about half of its science- and engineering-based workforce will be retiring in the next decade or so. Meanwhile, interest in engineering as a career is declining among US students. In a 2007 survey of more than 270,000 college freshmen conducted by the Higher Education Research Institute at UCLA, 7.5% said they intended to major in engineering—the lowest level since the 1970s. National-security restrictions preclude the Bethesda, Maryland, company and other major defense contractors from outsourcing many jobs overseas.

"We're already within the window of criticality to get tomorrow's engineers in the classroom today," says Jim Knotts, director of corporate citizenship for Lockheed. "We want to address a national need to develop the next generation of engineers—but with some affinity toward Lockheed Martin."[1]

The chapter opening vignette highlights two key reasons why it is important for managers to effectively manage diversity. Effectively managing diversity is not only a good thing to do in order to attract and retain the most talented employees, but it makes good business sense. Unfortunately, however, some organizations are missing the mark when it comes to managing diversity, and the result can be costly lawsuits. Consider the following examples:

- Lockheed Martin Corp. settled a discrimination lawsuit for $2.5 million with Charles Daniels, an aviation electrician. Daniels claimed that he "was subjected to racial harassment by co-workers on a daily basis and to threats of retaliation—including threats of lynching and other death threats—once he complained to supervisors."[2] Lockheed officials dismissed the incidents saying, "boys will be boys," and continued to assign Mr. Daniels to the same team that was harassing him; he was ultimately laid off.[3]

- An 18-year-old male salesclerk for a baby products retailer in New Jersey alleged that he was subjected to a sexually hostile environment—he was called "fag," "faggot," and "happy pants," and he was forcefully stripped of his trousers by co-workers. The retailer settled for $205,000.[4]

- Janet Orlando, a former employee at Alarm One, a home security firm in Fresno, California, was awarded $1.7 million by a jury "after she was spanked in front of her colleagues in what her employer called a camaraderie-building exercise. Sales teams were encouraged to compete, and the losers were made fun of, forced to eat baby food, required to wear diapers and spanked with a rival company's yard signs, according to court documents."[5]

It is important to note that these things occurred in these companies despite the existence of laws that prohibit such behaviors. As you will learn in this chapter, managing diversity entails much more than following laws and creating policies and procedures proscribing equal treatment of employees.

Managing diversity is a sensitive, potentially volatile, and sometimes uncomfortable issue. Yet managers are required to deal with it in the name of organizational survival. Accordingly, the purpose of this chapter is to help you get a better understanding of this important context for organizational behavior. We begin by defining diversity. Next, we build the business case for diversity and then discuss the barriers and challenges associated with managing diversity. The chapter concludes by describing the organizational practices used to manage diversity effectively.

LO.1 Defining Diversity

to the point
Why is it important for managers to focus on managing diversity?

Diversity represents the multitude of individual differences and similarities that exist among people. It is not an issue of age, race, or gender. It is not an issue of being heterosexual, gay, or lesbian or of being Catholic, Jewish, Protestant, Muslim, or Buddhist. Diversity also does not pit white males against all other groups of people. Diversity pertains to the host of individual differences that make all of us unique and different from others.

This section begins our journey into managing diversity by first reviewing the key dimensions of diversity. Because many people associate diversity with affirmative action, this section compares affirmative action with managing diversity. They are not the same.

Diversity
The host of individual differences that make people different from and similar to each other.

Layers of Diversity

Like seashells on a beach, people come in a variety of shapes, sizes, and colors. This variety represents the essence of diversity. Lee Gardenswartz and Anita Rowe, a team of diversity experts, identified four layers of diversity to help distinguish the important ways in which people differ (see Figure 2–1). Taken together, these layers define your personal identity and influence how each of us sees the world.

Figure 2–1 shows that personality is at the center of the diversity wheel. Personality is at the center because it represents a stable set of characteristics that is responsible for a person's identity. The dimensions of personality are discussed later in Chapter 5. The next layer of diversity consists of a set of internal dimensions that are referred to as surface-level dimensions of diversity. These dimensions, for the most part, are not within our control, but they strongly influence our attitudes and expectations and assumptions about others, which, in turn, influence our behavior. Take the encounter experienced by an African-American woman in middle management while vacationing at a resort:

> While I was sitting by the pool, "a large 50-ish white male approached me and demanded that I get him extra towels. I said, 'Excuse me?' He then said, 'Oh, you don't work here,' with no shred of embarrassment or apology in his voice."[6]

Stereotypes regarding one or more of the surface-level dimensions of diversity most likely influenced this man's behavior toward the woman.

Figure 2–1 reveals that the next layer of diversity is composed of external influences, which are referred to as secondary dimensions of diversity. They represent individual differences that we have a greater ability to influence or control. Examples include where you grew up and live today, your religious affiliation, whether you are married and have children, and your work experiences. These dimensions also exert a significant influence on our perceptions, behavior, and attitudes.

Consider religion as an illustration. Organizations are paying more attention to religious discrimination in light of the fact that the frequency of religious discrimination claims has doubled in the last 15 years. Employment laws require organizations to "reasonably accommodate employees' sincerely held religious practices unless doing so would impose an undue hardship on the employer. A reasonable religious accommodation is any adjustment to the work environment that will allow the employee to practice his religion. Examples of reasonable accommodation include: flexible scheduling, voluntary substitutions or swaps, job reassignments and lateral transfers, and modification of grooming requirements."[7]

Figure 2–1   *The Four Layers of Diversity*

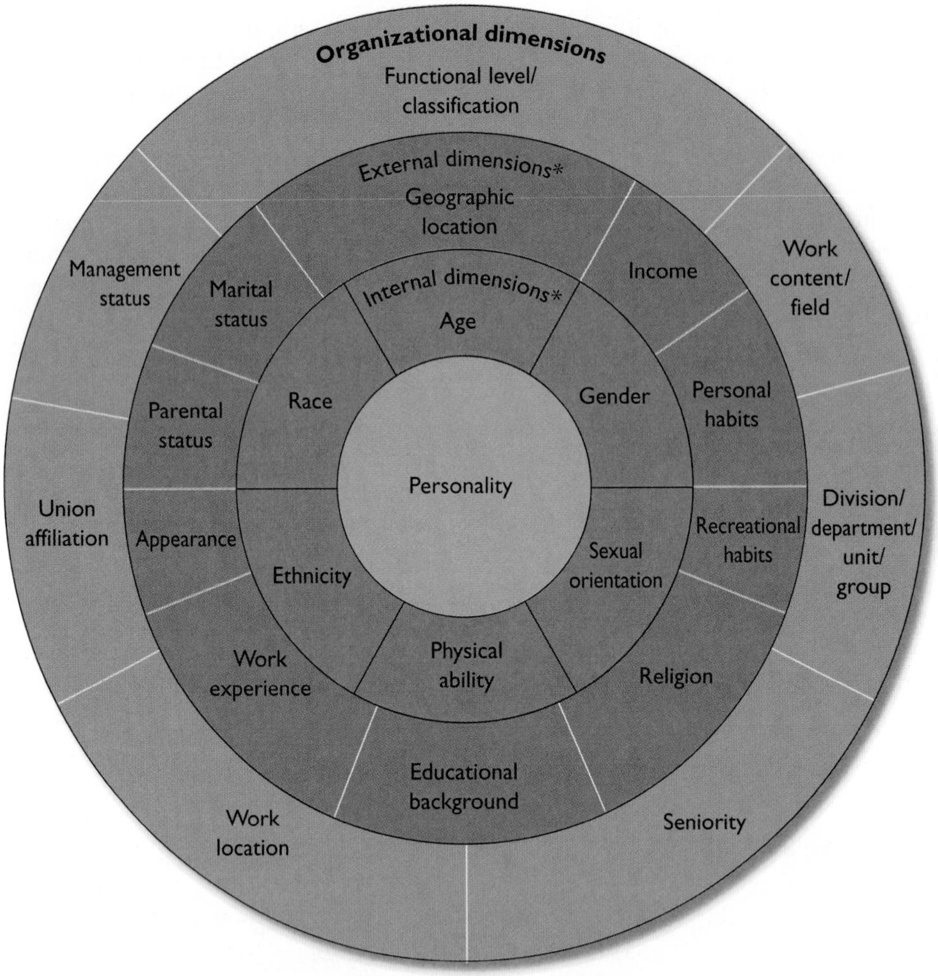

Organizational dimensions
Functional level/classification

External dimensions*
Geographic location

Internal dimensions*
Age

Management status   Marital status   Income   Work content/field

Parental status   Race   Gender   Personal habits

Union affiliation   Appearance   Personality   Sexual orientation   Recreational habits   Division/department/unit/group

Ethnicity   Physical ability   Religion

Work experience   Educational background   Seniority

Work location

*Internal dimensions and external dimensions are adapted from Marilyn Loden and Judy B Rosener, *Workforce America!* (Homewood, IL: Business One Irwin, 1991).

SOURCE: L Gardenswartz and A Rowe, *Diverse Teams at Work: Capitalizing on the Power of Diversity* (New York: McGraw-Hill, 1994), p. 33. © 1994.

The final layer of diversity includes organizational dimensions such as seniority, job title and function, and work location.

go to the Web for the Self-Exercise: How Does Your Diversity Profile Affect Your Relationships with Other People?

LO.2 Affirmative Action and Managing Diversity

Effectively managing diversity requires organizations to adopt a new way of thinking about differences among people. Rather than pitting one group against another, managing diversity entails recognition of the unique contribution every employee can make. For example, Aetna Inc., EMC Corporation, IBM, PepsiCo, and Nordstrom's focus on hiring and promoting diverse employees as part of a strategy to create and market products appealing to a broader and more diverse customer base.[8] This section highlights the differences between affirmative action and managing diversity.

Affirmative Action

Affirmative action is an outgrowth of equal employment opportunity (EEO) legislation. The goal of this legislation is to outlaw discrimination and to encourage organizations to proactively prevent discrimination. **Discrimination** occurs when employment decisions about an individual are due to reasons not associated with performance or are not related to the job. Table 2–1 provides a review of major federal laws pertaining to equal employment opportunity. As you can see from this table, many forms of discrimination are outlawed. For example, organizations cannot discriminate on the basis of race, color, religion, national origin, sex, age, physical and mental disabilities, and pregnancy. Many of these federal laws are enforced by the Equal Employment Opportunity Commission (EEOC), and individuals may sue for back pay and punitive damages when they feel that they have been discriminated against.[9]

> **Discrimination**
> Occurs when employment decisions are based on factors that are not job related.

In contrast to the proactive perspective of EEO legislation, **affirmative action** is an artificial intervention aimed at giving management a chance to correct an imbalance, an injustice, a mistake, or outright discrimination that occurred in the past. Affirmative action does not legitimize quotas. Quotas are illegal. They can only be imposed by judges who conclude that a company has engaged in discriminatory practices. It also is important to note that under no circumstances does affirmative action require companies to hire unqualified people.

> **Affirmative action**
> Focuses on achieving equality of opportunity in an organization.

Although affirmative action created tremendous opportunities for women and minorities, it does not foster the type of thinking that is needed to effectively manage diversity. For example, a recent meta-analysis summarizing 35 years of research involving 29,000 people uncovered the following results: (1) affirmative action plans are perceived more negatively by white males than women and minorities because it is perceived to work against their own self-interests; (2) affirmative action plans are viewed more positively by people who are liberals and Democrats than conservatives and Republicans; and (3) affirmative action plans are not supported by people who possess racist or sexist attitudes.[10]

Affirmative action programs also were found to negatively affect the women and minorities expected to benefit from them. Research demonstrated that women and minorities, supposedly hired on the basis of affirmative action, felt negatively stigmatized as unqualified or incompetent. They also experienced lower job satisfaction and more stress than employees supposedly selected on the basis of merit.[11] Another study, however, showed that these negative consequences were reduced for women when a merit criterion was included in hiring decisions. In other words, women hired under affirmative action programs felt better about themselves and exhibited higher performance when they believed they were hired because of their competence rather than their gender.[12]

Managing Diversity

Managing diversity entails enabling people to perform up to their maximum potential. It focuses on changing an organization's culture and infrastructure such that people provide the highest productivity possible. ATA Engineering Inc., rated by *The Wall Street Journal* as one of the top 15 small workplaces in 2008, is a good example of a company that effectively manages

> **Managing diversity**
> Creating organizational changes that enable all people to perform up to their maximum potential.

Table 2–1   *Some Important U.S. Federal Laws and Regulations Protecting Employees*

YEAR LABOR RELATIONS	LAW OR REGULATION	PROVISIONS
1974	Privacy Act	Gives employees legal right to examine letters of reference concerning them
1986	Immigration Reform & Control Act	Requires employers to verify the eligibility for employment of all their new hires (including US citizens)
1988	Polygraph Protection Act	Limits employer's ability to use lie detectors
1988	Worker Adjustment & Retraining Notification Act	Requires organizations with 100 or more employees to give 60 days' notice for mass layoffs or plant closings
2003	Sarbanes-Oxley Act	Prohibits employers from demoting or firing employees who raise accusations of fraud to a federal agency
COMPENSATION AND BENEFITS		
1974	Employee Retirement Income Security Act (ERISA)	Sets rules for managing pension plans; provides federal insurance to cover bankrupt plans
1993	Family & Medical Leave Act	Requires employers to provide 12 weeks of unpaid leave for medical and family reasons, including for childbirth, adoption, or family emergency
1996	Health Insurance Portability & Accountability Act (HIPAA)	Allows employees to switch health insurance plans when changing jobs and receive new coverage regardless of preexisting health conditions; prohibits group plans from dropping ill employees
HEALTH AND SAFETY		
1970	Occupational Safety & Health Act (OSHA)	Establishes minimum health and safety standards in organizations
1985	Consolidated Omnibus Budget Reconciliation Act (COBRA)	Requires an extension of health insurance benefits after termination
EQUAL EMPLOYMENT OPPORTUNITY		
1963	Equal Pay Act	Requires men and women be paid equally for performing equal work
1964, amended 1972	Civil Rights Act, Title VII	Prohibits discrimination on basis of race, color, religion, national origin, or sex
1967, amended 1978 and 1986	Age Discrimination in Employment Act (ADEA)	Prohibits discrimination of employees over 40 years old; restricts mandatory retirement
1978	Pregnancy Discrimination Act	Broadens discrimination to cover pregnancy, childbirth, and related medical conditions; protects job security during maternity leave

1990, amended 2009	Americans with Disablities Act (ADA)	Prohibits discrimination against essentially qualified employees with physical or mental disabilities or chronic illness; requires "reasonable accommodation" be provided so they can perform duties
1991	Civil Rights Act	Amends and clarifies Title VII, ADA, and other laws; permits suits against employers for punitive damages in cases of intentional discrimination

SOURCE: From A Kinicki and B Williams, *Management: A Practical Introduction,* 3/e, McGraw-Hill, 2008, p 293. Copyright © 2008 The McGraw-Hill Companies. Reprinted with permission.

diversity (see the Real World/Real People feature on page 40). Ann Morrison, a diversity expert, conducted a study of 16 organizations that successfully managed diversity. Her results uncovered three key strategies for success: education, enforcement, and exposure. She describes them as follows:

> The education component of the strategy has two thrusts: one is to prepare nontraditional managers for increasingly responsible posts, and the other is to help traditional managers overcome their prejudice in thinking about and interacting with people who are of a different sex or ethnicity. The second component of the strategy, enforcement, puts teeth in diversity goals and encourages behavior change. The third component, exposure to people with different backgrounds and characteristics, adds a more personal approach to diversity by helping managers get to know and respect others who are different.[13]

In summary, both consultants and academics believe that organizations should strive to manage diversity rather than simply using affirmative action. This conclusion was supported by a recent study of 62 R&D teams from a multinational pharmaceutical company. Results revealed that the effects of age, nationality, and educational diversity on team performance were more positive when team leaders displayed transformational leadership.[14] Transformational leadership, which is thoroughly discussed in Chapter 16, involves behaviors in which leaders foster trust, commitment, and loyalty from followers. More is said about managing diversity later in this chapter.

Building the Business Case for Managing Diversity

The rationale for managing diversity goes well beyond legal, social, and moral reasons. Quite simply, the primary reason for managing diversity is the ability to grow and maintain a business in an increasingly competitive marketplace. Many companies understand and endorse this proposition. For example, IBM, PepsiCo, Deloitte, Zappos, and Nordstrom's decided to focus on hiring and promoting diverse employees in order to help create and market products to a broader and more diverse customer base.[15] Research indirectly supports the logic of this strategy. For example, a recent study of 207 companies in 11 industries demonstrated that financial performance was higher when the organization's top management

to the point
Which of the managerial implications of diversity are consistent with recommendations for reconciling the effects of diverse work environments?

ATA Engineering Inc. Effectively Manages Diversity

Managers often talk about the merits of "teamwork" and a "flat" culture. But few can claim to implement those practices as well as ATA Engineering Inc.

When ATA spun off from another engineering firm in 2000, the new leaders—managers from the former firm—wanted to preserve the collegial and collaborative spirit they had as a part of a bigger company. So, they sought out practices that emphasized equality and teamwork in compensation and decision making.

In 2004, the 28 employees from the former firm agreed to make the company 100% employee-owned by starting an employee stock-ownership plan. What's more, every ATA engineer, manager, and executive is paid on the same engineering pay scale—there's not a separate scale for managers. So there aren't big differences in pay between managers and the people they supervise.

Bonuses also have an egalitarian flavor: All workers receive an equal percentage of their salary as an annual bonus. The setup works that way for a couple of reasons. ATA leaders believe that every employee should reap the rewards of the whole team. Managers also feel it's too hard to accurately assess how much one employee deserves a bonus over another; singling people out could result in unfairness and resentment. . . .

The company also believes in group decision making. At least eight to 10 ATA employees are involved in interviewing every job candidate. If one employee objects to the hire, the candidate may not be offered a job unless the employee changes his or her mind.

Sometimes even the biggest company decisions are made by workers. When the lease was up on the company's building, for instance, ATA formed a committee of employees to address the issue. The group decided to stay put, after determining the current location was convenient to the majority of employees.

Would you like to work at ATA Engineering? Explain why.

SOURCE: Excerpted from K K Spors, "Top Small Workplaces 2008," *The Wall Street Journal,* October 13, 2008, p R4. Copyright © 2008 by Dow Jones & Company, Inc. Reproduced with permission of Dow Jones & Company, Inc. via Copyright Clearance Center.

Organizations like ATA make every important decision as a group. What are the pros and cons of group decision making?

---

team (TMT) was diverse and collocated in the same location. The positive effects of diversity were not obtained when the TMT was geographically dispersed.[16] Sony, L'Oreal, Ford Motor Company, Microsoft, and Retirement Living TV, on the other hand, are trying to increase their revenue streams by targeting sales and promotion activities toward an older group of potential customers. In a similar vein, the firearms industry is targeting women as a source of new revenue by creating weapons (e.g., pink guns, shorter gun stocks and barrels, and lighter crossbows) and camouflage more suited for women.[17]

Organizations cannot use diversity as a strategic advantage if employees fail to contribute their full talents, abilities, motivation, and commitment. It is thus essential for an organization to create an environment or culture that allows all employees to reach their full potential. Managing diversity is a critical component of creating such an organization.

This section explores the business need to manage diversity by first reviewing the demographic trends that are creating an increasingly diverse workforce. We then summarize the managerial implications of demographic diversity and review evidence pertaining to the positive and negative effects associated with diverse work environments.

Increasing Diversity in the Workforce

Workforce demographics, which are statistical profiles of the characteristics and composition of the adult working population, are an invaluable human-resource planning aid. They enable managers to anticipate and adjust for surpluses or shortages of appropriately skilled individuals. Consider the implications associated with an aging population that will be retiring in record numbers over the next decade, a US birthrate that is too low to provide enough workers to meet future demands, a workforce in 2050 that is composed of 55% minority employees, over 21 million illegal immigrants working in the United States, and 1 in 7 US adults who lack the literacy skills to read anything beyond a child's picture book.[18] Experts predict that these demographic trends will create a serious shortage of skilled workers in the future and that immigration will affect the ethnic composition of the population.

> **Workforce demographics**
> Statistical profiles of adult workers.

Moreover, general population demographics give managers a preview of the values and motives of current and future employees. Demographic changes in the US workforce during the last two or three decades have immense implications for organizational behavior. This section explores the managerial implications of four demographic-based characteristics of the workforce: (1) women navigate a labyrinth after breaking the glass ceiling, (2) racial groups are encountering a glass ceiling and perceived discrimination, (3) there is a mismatch between workers' educational attainment and occupational requirements, and (4) generational differences in an aging workforce.

LO.3 Women Navigate a Labyrinth After Breaking the Glass Ceiling

The Wall Street Journal journalists—Carol Hymowitz and Timothy Schellhardt—coined the term **glass ceiling** in 1986. The term *glass ceiling* was used to represent an absolute barrier or solid roadblock that prevented women from advancing to higher-level positions. This ceiling resulted in women finding themselves stuck in lower-level jobs, ones that do not have profit-and-loss responsibility, and those with less visibility, power, and influence. There are a variety of statistics that support the prior existence of a glass ceiling. For example, women earned 78 cents on the dollar relative to men's earnings in 2008, and women received fewer stock options than male executives, even after controlling for level of education, performance, and job function. A study of 13,503 female managers and 17,493 male managers further demonstrated that women at higher levels in the managerial hierarchy received fewer promotions than males at comparable positions.[19] These differences are a function of several potential causes:[20]

> **Glass ceiling**
> Invisible barrier blocking women and minorities from top management positions.

- Women face discrimination.
- Women spend more time handling domestic and child-care issues then men.
- Women encounter more obstacles to their leadership and authority than men (e.g., negative stereotypes).
- Women have less social capital and lower breadth of personal networks than men.

Indra Nooyi, CEO of Pepsi, is a good example of someone who has successfully moved through a career labyrinth. She was rated as one of America's Best Leaders in 2008 by U.S. News and World Report.

- Organizations have increased demands for longer hours, travel, and relocation and these demands conflict with the domestic roles held by many married women.

Carol Hymowitz, the same journalist who initially introduced the metaphor of a glass ceiling, wrote an article in *The Wall Street Journal* in 2004 that concluded women had broken through the glass ceiling. This led renowned researcher Alice Eagly and her colleague Linda Carli to conduct a thorough investigation into the organizational life of women. They summarized their findings in a 2007 book titled *Through the Labyrinth.*[21] These authors agreed with Hymowitz after analyzing many types of longitudinal data. For example, they noted that there are many more female CEOs in 2008 (12 and 24 female CEOs within *Fortune* 500 and *Fortune* 1000 firms, respectively) and more women in managerial and administrative positions (e.g., a 24% increase from 1972 to 2006) than there were in the 1980s and 1990s. Statistics further showed that women made great strides in terms of (1) educational attainment (women earned the majority of bachelor's, master's, and PhD degrees in 2007); (2) holding seats on boards of directors of *Fortune* 500 firms (a 10% increase between 1995 and 2007); (3) obtaining leadership positions in educational institutions (64 percent of administrators in 2007 were women and 23 percent were college and/or university presidents); and (4) receiving federal court appointments (in 2007, 23% and 24% of federal district court judges and federal circuit court judges, respectively, were women).[22]

You can interpret the above statistics in one of two ways. On the one hand, you might believe that women are underpaid and underrepresented in leadership positions and that they are victims of discriminatory organizational practices. Alternatively, you can agree with Alice Eagly and Linda Carli's conclusion that "women have made substantial progress but still have quite far to go to achieve equal representation as leaders. . . . These statistics demonstrate considerable social change and show that women's careers have become far more successful than they were in the past. Men still have more authority and higher wages, but women have been catching up. Because some women have moved into the most elite leadership roles, absolute barriers are a thing of the past."[23] These authors believe that women are not victims. Rather, they propose that a woman's career follow a pattern more characteristic of traveling through a labyrinth.

A labyrinth is represented by a maze and is defined as "an intricate structure of interconnecting passages through which it is difficult to find one's way."[24] Eagly and Carli used the labyrinth metaphor because they believe that a woman's path to success is not direct or simple, but rather contains twists, turns, and obstructions, particularly for married women with children. Managers and organizations thus are advised to develop policies, procedures, and programs aimed at helping women to navigate their way through the maze of career success (see the Real World/Real People box featuring Best Buy on page 43). More will be said about this later in this section.

LO.4 **Racial Groups Are Encountering a Glass Ceiling and Perceived Discrimination** Historically, the United States has been a black-and-white country. The percentage change in US population between 2000

Best Buy Uses a Women's Leadership Forum to Build Employee and Customer Loyalty

Best Buy's Women's Leadership Forum (WOLF) engages female and male employees, from line-level to executives, empowering them to reinvent the company for the retailer's female customers and employees through their ideas and experiences.

WOLF focuses on a simple objective: "If we want to be a great place for women to shop, we have to be a great place for women to work." As such, WOLF is grounded in three pillars:

- Commitment—to the business, customers, and to each other.
- Networking—employees build a strong, diverse circle of individuals they trust to help them both professionally and personally.
- Give back—employees give their time and energy to help and support women and girls in need in their local communities, building valuable leadership skills.

How does WOLF develop a woman's skills?

SOURCE: Excerpted from "Best Practices & Outstanding Initiatives," *Training,* February 2008, p 118.

Julie Gilbert, founder of Best Buy's Women's Leadership Forum.

---

and 2050 by race reveals that this pattern no longer exists (see Figure 2–2). Figure 2–2 shows that Asians and Hispanics are expected to have the largest growth in population between 2000 and 2050. The Asian population will triple to 33 million by 2050, and the Hispanics will increase their ranks by 118% to 102.6 million. Hispanics will account for 25% of the population in 2050. All told, the so-called minority groups will constitute approximately 55% of the workforce in 2050 according to the Census Bureau.[25]

Unfortunately, three additional trends suggest that current-day minority groups are experiencing their own glass ceiling. First, minorities in general are advancing less in the managerial and professional ranks than whites. For example, whites, blacks, Asians, and Hispanics or Latinos held 36.1%, 27.1%, 48.1%, and 17.8% of all managerial and professional jobs in the United States in 2007.[26] Second, the number of race-based charges of discrimination that were deemed to show reasonable cause by the US Equal Employment Opportunity Commission increased from 294 in 1995 to 998 in 2007. Companies paid a total of $67.7 million to resolve these claims outside of litigation in 2007.[27] Third, minorities also tend

The gun industry has created pink guns as a way to get women to purchase their products. The industry hopes to increase sales by offering more attractive guns to women. Are you swayed?

Figure 2–2   *Percentage Change in US Population by Race*

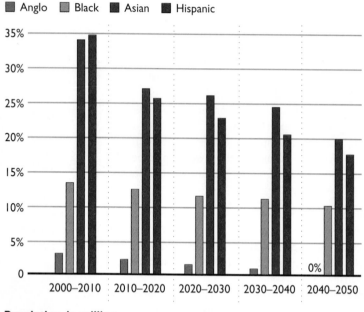

Population, in millions

	2000–2010	2010–2020	2020–2030	2030–2040	2040–2050
Anglo	201.1 mil	205.9 mil	209.2 mil	210.3 mil	210.3 mil
Black	40.5	45.4	50.4	55.9	61.4
Asian	14.2	18.0	22.6	28.0	33.4
Hispanic	47.8	59.8	73.1	87.6	102.6

Source: US Census Bureau   Associated Press

SOURCE: G C Armas, "Almost Half of US Likely to Be Minorities by 2050," *Arizona Republic*, March 18, 2004, p A5. US Census Bureau, Tbl. 1a., "Projected Population of the US by Race and Hispanic Origin: 2000–2050 (www.census.gov/ipc/www/usinterimproj/), March 2004. Used by permission of the Associated Press.

to earn less personal income than whites. Median weekly earnings in 2007 were $569, $503, and $716 for African Americans, Hispanics, and whites, respectively. Interestingly, Asians had the highest median income—$830 per week.[28] Finally, a number of studies showed that minorities experienced more perceived discrimination, racism-related stress, and less psychological support than whites.[29]

go to the Web for the Self-Exercise: What Are the Strategies for Breaking the Glass Ceiling?

Mismatch between Educational Attainment and Occupational Requirements
Approximately 28% of the labor force has a college degree, and college graduates earn substantially more than workers with less education.[30] At the same time, however, three trends suggest a mismatch between educational attainment and the knowledge and skills needed by employers. First, recent studies show that college graduates, while technically and functionally competent, are lacking in terms of teamwork skills, critical thinking, and analytic reasoning. Second, there is a shortage of college graduates in technical

fields related to science, math, and engineering. Third, organizations are finding that high school graduates working in entry-level positions do not possess the basic skills needed to perform effectively.[31] This latter trend is partly due to a national high-school dropout rate estimated at over 9% and the existence of about 32 million adults in the United States that are functionally illiterate. Literacy is defined as "an individual's ability to read, write, and speak English, compute and solve problems at levels of proficiency necessary to function on the job and in society, to achieve one's goals, and develop one's knowledge and potential."[32] Illiteracy costs corporate America around $60 billion a year in lost productivity.[33] These statistics are worrisome to both government officials and business leaders.

The key issue confronting organizations in the United States, and any country that wants to compete in a global economy, is whether or not the population has the skills and abilities needed to drive economic growth. Unfortunately, results from a study commissioned by the National Center on Education and the Economy suggests that the United States is losing ground on this issue. Findings were summarized in a book titled *Tough Choice or Tough Times: The Report of the New Commission on the Skills of the American Workforce.* The authors arrived at the following conclusions based on their analysis.

> Whereas for most of the 20th century the United States could take pride in having the best-educated workforce in the world, that is no longer true. Over the past 30 years, one country after another has surpassed us in the proportion of their entering workforce with the equivalent of a high school diploma, and many more are on the verge of doing so. Thirty years ago, the United States could lay claim to having 30 percent of the world's population of college students. Today that proportion has fallen to 14 percent and is continuing to fall.
>
> While our international counterparts are increasingly getting more education, their young people are getting a better education as well. American students and young adults place anywhere from the middle to the bottom of the back in all three continuing comparative studies of achievement in mathematics, science, and general literacy in the advanced industrial nations.
>
> While our relative position in the world's education league tables has continued its long slow decline, the structure of the global economy has continued to evolve. Every day, more and more of the work that people do ends up in a digitized form. From X-rays used for medical diagnostic purposes, to songs, movies, architectural drawings, technical papers, and novels, that work is saved on a hard disk and transmitted instantly over the Internet to someone near or far who makes use of it in an endless variety of ways. Because this is so, employers everywhere have access to a worldwide workforce composed of people who do not have to move to participate in work teams that are truly global. Because this is so, a swiftly rising number of American workers at every skill level are in direct competition with workers in every corner of the globe.[34]

These conclusions underscore the fact that the mismatch between educational attainment and occupational requirements have both short- and long-term implications for organizations and countries alike. American companies are more likely to outsource technical work to countries like India and China, to hire more immigrants to fill entry-level positions, to spend more money on employee training, and to use phased retirement programs that encourage skilled employees to work beyond retirement age.[35]

Generational Differences in an Aging Workforce   America's population and workforce are getting older. By 2011, half of the US workforce will be over 50 years of age, and 80% will be over 50 by 2018.[36] Life expectancy is increasing as well. The number of people living into their 80s is increasing rapidly, and this group disproportionately suffers from chronic illness. The United States is not the only country with an aging population. Germany, China, Japan, Russia, Brazil, Italy, and other countries in both eastern and western Europe, for example, are expected to encounter significant economic, social, and political problems due to an aging population.

An aging population in the United States underscores a potential skill gap in the future. As those employees in the baby-boom generation retire—the 78 million people born between 1946 and 1964—the US workforce will lose the skills, knowledge, experience, and relationships possessed by the more than a quarter of all Americans. This situation will likely create skill shortages in fast-growing technical fields.

In addition to the challenges associated with an aging workforce, it is important for managers to effectively deal with generational differences in values, attitudes, and behaviors that exist in the workforce. For example, companies such as IBM, Lockheed Martin, Ernst & Young LLP, and Aetna have addressed this issue by providing training workshops on generational diversity.[37] Table 2–2 presents a summary of generational differences that exist across commonly labeled groups of people: Millennials, also known as Gen Ys; Gen Xers; Baby Boomers; and Traditionalists. Before examining these proposed differences, it is important to note that these labels and distinctions are generalizations and are used for sake of discussion. There are always exceptions to the characterizations shown in Table 2–2 and all conclusions should be interpreted with caution.[38] Table 2–2 reveals that Millennials account for the largest block of employees in the workforce, followed by Baby Boomers. This is important because many Millennials are being managed by Boomers who possess a very different set of personal traits. Traits, which are discussed in Chapter 5, represent stable physical and mental characteristics that form an individual's identity. Conflicting traits are likely to create friction between people. For example, the workaholic and competitive nature of Boomers is likely to conflict with the entitled and work-life balance perspective of Millennials. As discussed in the next section, managers and employees alike will need to be sensitive to the generational differences highlighted in Table 2–2 in the pursuit of effectively managing diversity.

We would like to close our discussion about age by highlighting results from a recent meta-analysis of 118 studies involving over 52,000 people. The researchers wanted to investigate the relationship between age and 10 dimensions of performance: core task performance, creativity, performance in training workshops, helping behavior at work, safety performance, counterproductive work behaviors, aggression at work, substance abuse, tardiness, and absenteeism. Results demonstrated that older workers displayed more helping and safety-oriented behavior. Older workers also exhibited less workplace aggression, substance abuse, tardiness, and absenteeism. Age was predominantly unrelated to core task performance, creativity, and performance in training workshops.[39] The researchers concluded that "these observations suggest either that older workers are as motivated as younger workers to contribute to their organizations or that they are more consciously engaged in discretionary behaviors to compensate for any losses in technical core performance."[40]

Table 2–2   *Workforce Generational Differences*

	MILLENNIALS (GEN YS)	GEN XERS	BABY BOOMERS	TRADITIONALISTS
Time Span Estimated	1980–2001	1965–1979	1946–1964	1925–1945
Current US Residents	92 Million	62 Million	78.3 Million	38.6 Million
Key Historical Events	Columbine High School shootings, September 11 terrorist attacks, Enron and other corporate scandals, wars in Afghanistan and Iraq, Hurricane Katrina	AIDS epidemic, space shuttle *Challenger* catastrophe, fall of the Berlin Wall, Oklahoma City bombing, Bill Clinton–Monica Lewinsky scandal	Vietnam War, assassinations of John and Robert Kennedy and Martin Luther King Jr., first man on the moon, Kent State killings, Watergate	Great Depression, Pearl Harbor, World War II, Korean War, Cold War era, Cuban missile crisis
Traits	Entitled, optimistic, civic minded, close parental involvement, values work-life balance, impatient, multitasking, team-oriented	self-reliant, adaptable, cynical, distrust of authority, resourceful, entrepreneurial, technology savvy	Workaholic, idealistic, competitive, loyal, materialistic, seeks personal fulfillment, values titles and the corner office	Patriotic, dependable, conformist, respects authority, rigid, socially and financially conservative, solid work ethic

SOURCE: R Alsop, *The Trophy Kids Grow Up* (San Francisco: Jossey-Bass, 2008), p 5. [permission needed.]

L0.5 Managerial Implications of Demographic Diversity

Regardless of gender, race, education, or age, all organizations need employees who possess the skills and abilities required to successfully complete their jobs. Hiring, retaining, and developing a diverse workforce not only gives an organization access to a deeper pool of talent, it also may introduce perspectives that help the organization identify and meet the needs of a diverse customer base. For example, a Citizens Union Bank branch in Louisville, Kentucky, designed and staffed the branch with the goal of attracting more Latin American customers. The interior contains "bright, colorful walls of yellows and blues, large-scale photos of Latin American countries, comfortable couches, sit-down desks, a children's play area, a television tuned to Hispanic programming and even a vending area stocked with popular Latin American-brand soft drinks and snacks. Along with its interior design, this branch has a different name: 'Nuestro Banco,' Spanish for 'Our Bank.'"[41] Branch deposits are setting records, and the CEO is planning to use this same model in other locations. The point to remember is that companies need to adopt policies and procedures that meet the needs of all employees. As such, programs such as day care, elder care, flexible work schedules, and benefits such as paternal leaves, less-rigid relocation policies, concierge services, and mentoring programs are likely to become more popular.[42] In addition to this general conclusion, this section summarizes some unique managerial implications associated with effectively managing diversity in regards to demographic trends related to gender, race, education, and age.

Managing Gender-Based Diversity   Special effort is needed to help women navigate through the labyrinth of career success. Organizations can do this by providing women the developmental assignments that prepare them for promotional opportunities.[43] Laura Desmond, CEO of Starcom Media Vest/The Americas, suggests that women need to help themselves advance to senior-level positions. She believes that "getting to the top requires setting goals and persevering—along with a willingness to seek stretch assignments that challenge and yield broader experiences." Andrea Jung, chair and CEO of Avon Products, further recommends that women should find a company or industry that they love because "the hard work and sacrifices required are only possible if you are fully engaged in your company and enjoy what you do."[44]

Women also can help their own cause by following seven recommendations proposed by Alice Eagly and Linda Carli, authors of *Through the Labyrinth*.[45] First, focus on being exceptionally competent and seek mentors for different purposes. Second, build social capital. Social capital, as you may recall from Chapter 1, represents the totality of one's professional and personal relationships. Learning to play the game of golf may represent one viable strategy in this pursuit. For example, Susan Reed, editor in chief of *Golf for Women,* concluded that "[w]omen are just now learning what men have known for years: that golf may be one of the best relationship-building tools there is—both for business and for pleasure. Women resist going out for the afternoon because they're generally too responsible, shortsightedly so. Like men, they need to realize that leaving the work on the desk (which will be there anyway) and going out to play golf with a valuable business prospect is a good decision."[46] Third, seek work-life balance by delegating housework or hiring domestic help. Fourth, improve your negotiating skills. Fifth, take credit for your accomplishments; men do. Sixth, work toward creating a partnership with your spouse that leads to a mutually supportive relationship. Finally, develop an interpersonal style that balances the need to be assertive and communal.

Managing Racially Based Diversity   Given the projected increase in the number of Hispanics entering the workforce over the next 25 years, managers should consider progressive methods to recruit, retain, and integrate this segment of the population into their organizations. For example, Miami Children's Hospital and Shaw Industries Inc. in Dalton, Georgia, attempted to improve employee productivity, satisfaction, and motivation by developing customized training programs to improve the commmunication skills of their Spanish-speaking employees (see the Real World/Real People feature on page 49).[47] Research further reveals that the retention and career progression of minorities can be significantly enhanced through effective mentoring.

Miami Children's Hospital and Shaw Industries Inc. Focus on Improving Employees' English Proficiency

Miami Children's Hospital

- Language class meets twice a week.
- Language training is tied to the work environment (i.e., participants taught how to speak to customers).
- English-speaking managers participate in a customized "Spanish as a Second Language" program.

Shaw Industries Inc.

- Program participants are selected from the facilities, shifts, and departments where language barriers are most pronounced; classes contain an equal number of English and native Spanish speakers.
- Participants complete 30 hours of computer-based instruction prior to attending class. The computerized instruction contains pictures and associated words of objects found in the company's facilities.
- Participants take a four-day immersion class in the language they want to learn. Teams of Spanish-speaking and English groups join on the last day to work on activities and games in which they speak their native and new language 50 percent of the time, respectively.
- Post-class training assignments require participants to speak with five targeted individuals in the new language.

Why is it important that employees can adequately speak English in the US? Explain.

SOURCE: Excerpted and adapted from S Boehle, "Voices of Opportunity," *Training*, January 2009, p 39.

David Thomas, a researcher from Harvard University, conducted a three-year study of mentoring practices at three US corporations: a manufacturer, an electronics company, and a high-tech firm. His results revealed that successful people of color who advanced the furthest had a strong network of mentors and sponsors who nurtured their professional development. Findings also demonstrated that people of color should be mentored differently than their white counterparts. He recommended that organizations

> should provide a range of career paths, all uncorrelated with race, that lead to the executive suite. . . . Achieving this system, however, would require integrating the principles of opportunity, development, and diversity into the fabric of the organization's management practices and human resource systems. And an important element in the process would be to identify potential mentors, train them, and ensure that they are paired with promising professionals of color.[48]

Managing Education-Based Diversity Mismatches between the amount of education needed to perform current jobs and the amount of education possessed by members of the workforce are growing. This trend creates two potential problems for organizations. First, there will be a shortage of qualified people in technical fields. To combat this issue, both Lockheed Martin and Agilent Technologies offer some type of paid apprenticeship or internship to attract high-school students interested in the sciences. Other companies such as State Street, Fidelity, and Cisco are attempting to overcome skill gaps by encouraging employees to participate in skills-based volunteering projects. The goal of these projects is to increase targeted skills through volunteer activities.[49] Second, underemployment among college graduates threatens to erode job satisfaction and work motivation. As well-educated workers begin to look for jobs commensurate with their qualifications and expectations, absenteeism and turnover likely will increase. This problem underscores the need for job redesign (see the discussion in Chapter 8). In addition, organizations will need to consider interventions, such as realistic job previews and positive reinforcement programs (discussed in Chapter 9), to reduce absenteeism and turnover. On-the-job remedial skills and literacy training will be necessary to help the growing number of dropouts and illiterates cope with job demands.

Managing Age-Related Diversity

Organizations can take advantage of an aging workforce by capitalizing on the human and social capital possessed by older employees. For example, John Deere, Boeing, Borders, CVS Caremark, and Baystate Health are targeting "productive" Baby Boomers for retention, recruitment, and mentoring. These companies believe that boomers can help overcome skill gaps in today's workforce.[50] In order to make this strategy work, however, the *Wall Street Journal* suggests that organizations will need to encourage baby boomers to remain in the workforce in lieu of retiring.[51] The following seven initiatives can help to keep older workers engaged and committed to working.[52]

1. Provide challenging work assignments that make a difference to the firm.
2. Give the employee considerable autonomy and latitude in completing a task.
3. Provide equal access to training and learning opportunities when it comes to new technology.
4. Provide frequent recognition for skills, experience, and wisdom gained over the years.
5. Provide mentoring opportunities whereby older workers can pass on accumulated knowledge to younger employees.
6. Ensure that older workers receive sensitive, high-quality supervision.
7. Design a work environment that is both stimulating and fun.

Generational differences outlined in Table 2–2 can affect employee motivation and productivity, thereby necessitating a managerial response. For example, recent in-depth interviews with 50 workers over the age of 50 revealed that older workers felt blocked from important communication networks by younger employees and that their experience and skills were not valued. One respondent commented that "when older colleagues spoke during company meetings, younger colleagues would yawn, avoid eye contact with the speaker, doodle, or send text or instant messages under the table.[53] In contrast, some Gen Y employees believe that Baby Boomers want to be rewarded for the amount of time they spend at work rather than productivity. Best Buy's headquarters has attempted to reconcile this concern by creating an evaluation system that judges people only on task completion and performance. People are encouraged to work only as many hours as needed to get the job done.[54] Further, Gen X employees also report feeling "stuck in the middle." A Gen Xer named Michael noted, "I have an executive management team who are 8 to 12 years older than I am, with no plans for retirement in the near future. This leaves me stuck."

Age-related diversity can cause unnecessary friction in the workplace. How can managers help facilitate helpful interactions across all generations?

I have been searching for business opportunities due to my distrust of Corporate America's motives."[55] Companies clearly need to find ways to motivate and retain Gen X employees who may be stuck in organizational hierarchies.

The shortage of skilled employees in the future underscores the need for organizations to recruit Millennials. Not only do Gen Ys represent the largest block of employees in the workforce (see Table 2–2), but they possess traits and skills needed in an increasingly technologically advanced economy. Organizations are responding to this issue by trying to create work environments that meet the needs of this segment of the workforce. For example, Growth Works Capital, Ernst & Young, Philip Morris USA, IBM, and Bearing Point implemented new rewards programs and job design interventions aimed at attracting and retaining Gen Y employees. Unilever similarly created a "consumerization architect" position that focuses on helping employees use popular technology after learning that Gen Y employees were dissatisfied with the company's use of information technology.[56]

LO.6 The Positive and Negative Effects of Diverse Work Environments

Earlier in this chapter we stated that effectively managing diversity is not only a good thing to do in order to attract and retain the most talented employees, but it makes good business sense. Although one can easily find testimonials from managers and organizations supporting this conclusion, we need to examine the validity of this claim by considering the evidence provided by OB research. As you will learn shortly, this research reveals that there are both positive and negative effects of diversity on important work outcomes. Organizational behavior researchers have explained these conflicting results by integrating two competing explanations of how diversity impacts employee attitudes, behavior, and performance. These explanations are based on what is called *social categorization theory* and *information/decision-making* theory. This section focuses on helping you understand how to garner the positive benefits of diversity by presenting a process model of diversity that integrates these two explanations.

Social Categorization Theory   A team of OB researchers describe the **social categorization theory** of diversity as follows:

> The social categorization perspective holds that similarities and differences are used as a basis for categorizing self and others into groups, with ensuing categorizations distinguishing between one's own in-group and one or more out-groups. People tend to like and trust in-group members more than out-group members and thus generally tend to favor in-groups over out-groups.... [W]ork group members are more positively inclined toward their group and the people within it if fellow group members are similar rather than dissimilar to the self.[57]

This perspective further implies that similarity leads to liking and attraction, thereby fostering a host of positive outcomes. If this were the case, one would expect that the more homogeneous a work group, the higher the member commitment and group cohesion, and the lower the amount of interpersonal conflicts. There is a large body of research supporting propositions derived from the social categorization model.[58]

For example, past research revealed that people who were different from their work units in racial or ethnic background were less psychologically committed

Social categorization theory
Similarity leads to liking and attraction.

to their organizations and less satisfied with their careers.[59] Additional studies showed that demographic diversity was associated with less cooperation among team members and more negative impressions toward people who were demographically different.[60] Finally, recent studies demonstrated that demographic diversity was associated with higher employee turnover and employee deviance (i.e., exhibiting behavior that violates norms and threatens the well-being of the organization) and lower profits.[61] All told then, the social categorization model supports the idea that homogeneity is better than heterogeneity in terms of affecting work-related attitudes, behavior, and performance.

Information/Decision-Making Theory   The second theoretical point of view, referred to as **information/decision-making theory,** arrives at opposite predictions, proposing that diverse groups should outperform homogenous groups. The logic of this theory was described as follows:

> The idea is that diverse groups are more likely to possess a broader range of task-relevant knowledge, skills, and abilities that are distinct and nonredundant and to have different opinions and perspectives on the task at hand. This not only gives diverse groups a larger pool of resources, but may also have other beneficial effects.[62]

This perspective highlights three positive effects of diverse work groups.[63] First, diverse groups are expected to do a better job in earlier phases of problem solving because they are more likely to use their diverse backgrounds to generate a more comprehensive view of a problem. For example, gender and ethnic diversity can help work teams to better understand the needs and perspectives of a multicultural customer base. Second, the existence of diverse perspectives can help groups to brainstorm or uncover more novel alternatives during problem-solving activities. Finally, diversity can enhance the number of contacts a group or work unit has at its disposal. This broad network enables groups to gain access to new information and expertise, which results in more support for decisions than homogenous groups. Research supports this theory of diversity.

Team performance was positively related to a team's diversity in gender, ethnicity, age, and education.[64] Heterogeneous groups also were found to produce better-quality decisions and demonstrated higher productivity than homogenous groups.[65] Preliminary research also supports the idea that workforce diversity promotes creativity and innovation. This occurs through the sharing of diverse ideas and perspectives. Rosabeth Moss-Kanter, a management expert, was one of the first to investigate this relationship. Her results indicated that innovative companies deliberately used heterogeneous teams to solve problems, and they employed more women and minorities than less innovative companies. She also noted that innovative companies did a better job of eliminating racism, sexism, and classism.[66] A summary of 40 years of diversity research supported Moss-Kanter's conclusion that diversity can promote creativity and improve a team's decision making.[67]

Reconciling the Effects of Diverse Work Environments   Our previous discussion about social categorization theory and information/decision-making theory revealed that there are both positive and negative effects associated with diversity. The model in Figure 2–3 summarizes the process underlying these effects. Consistent with social categorization theory, there is a negative relationship between the amount of diversity in a work group and the quality of interpersonal

Information/ decision-making theory

Diversity leads to better task-relevant processes and decision making.

Figure 2–3   *A Process Model of Diversity*

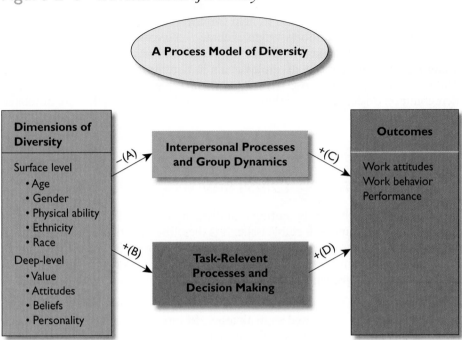

processes and group dynamics within a work group (path A in Figure 2–3). This negative relationship ultimately results in negative outcomes because of the positive relationship between the quality of interpersonal processes and group dynamics and outcomes (path C). For example, gender and racial diversity in a work group foster more interpersonal conflict, which in turn results in lower job satisfaction, higher turnover, and lower productivity. Recent research shows that this type of negative pattern is more pronounced when groups have salient demographic fault-lines.[68] A **demographic faultline** is defined as "hypothetical dividing lines that may split a group into subgroups based on one or more attributes."[69] Faultlines form when work group members possess varying demographic characteristics (e.g., gender, age, ethnicity), and negative interpersonal processes occur when people align themselves based on salient faultlines or demographic characteristics.[70]

In contrast, research regarding the information/decision-making theory tells us that the amount of diversity in a work group is positively associated with task-relevant processes and decision making (path B), which in turn fosters positive outcomes (path D). Gender and racial diversity in this case lead to positive outcomes because they lead to improved task-related processes and decision making. Two recent studies demonstrated that the positive effects of diversity were stronger when work groups were open-minded, more readily discussed and shared information, and displayed more integrative behavior.[71]

Given that work-group diversity is associated with positive and negative outcomes, we need to consider what management can do to reduce the potential negative effects of diversity. First, organizations can target training to improve the inherent negative relationship between a work group's diversity and its interpersonal processes and group dynamics (path A in Figure 2–3). For example, training can be used to help employees develop interpersonal skills that foster integrative

Demographic faultline

A hypothetical dividing line that splits groups into demographically based subgroups.

and collaborative behavior. This training might focus on conflict management, interpersonal influence, giving feedback, communication, and valuing differences. Second, managers can seek ways to help employees ease the tensions of working in diverse groups. Such efforts might include the creation of support groups.[72] Finally, steps could be taken to reduce the negative effects of unconscious stereotyping and increase the use of group goals in heterogenous groups. Rewarding groups to accomplish group goals might encourage group members to focus on their common objectives rather than on demographic faultlines that are unrelated to performance.

to the point

What are the most common barriers to implementing successful diversity programs?

LO.7 Barriers and Challenges to Managing Diversity

We introduced this chapter by noting that diversity is a sensitive, potentially volatile, and sometimes uncomfortable issue. It is therefore not surprising that organizations encounter significant barriers when trying to move forward with managing diversity. The following is a list of the most common barriers to implementing successful diversity programs:[73]

1. *Inaccurate stereotypes and prejudice.* This barrier manifests itself in the belief that differences are viewed as weaknesses. In turn, this promotes the view that diversity hiring will mean sacrificing competence and quality.

2. *Ethnocentrism.* The ethnocentrism barrier represents the feeling that one's cultural rules and norms are superior or more appropriate than the rules and norms of another culture. This barrier is thoroughly discussed in Chapter 4.

3. *Poor career planning.* This barrier is associated with the lack of opportunities for diverse employees to get the type of work assignments that qualify them for senior management positions.

4. *A negative diversity climate.* Climate is generally viewed as employee perceptions about an organization's formal and informal policies, practices, and procedures.[74] **Diversity climate** is a subcomponent of an organization's overall climate and is defined as the employees' aggregate "perceptions about the organization's diversity-related formal structure characteristics and informal values."[75] Diversity climate is positive when employees view the organization as being fair to all types of employees; the concept of organizational fairness is discussed in Chapter 8. Recent research revealed that a positive diversity climate enhanced the positive effects of diversity while a negative diversity climate reduced the positive aspects of employee diversity.[76]

Diversity climate

Employees' aggregate perceptions about an organization's policies, practices, and procedures pertaining to diversity

5. *An unsupportive and hostile working environment for diverse employees.* Sexual, racial, and age harassment are common examples of hostile work environments. Whether perpetrated against women, men, or older individuals, hostile environments are demeaning, unethical, and appropriately called "work environment pollution." Moreover, the EEOC holds employers legally accountable for behavior that creates a hostile work environment. An expert on the subject explains:

> An employer violates Title VII of the Civil Rights [Act] of 1964 [see Table 2–1] if it engages in unlawful discrimination by maintaining a hostile work environment. To prove a hostile work environment claim involving co-workers, an employee must show that she was subject to unwelcome harassment based on a

protected characteristic [e.g., race, color, religion, national origin, sex, age] and that the harassment was severe or pervasive enough to create a hostile or abusive working environment. In addition, the employee must show that the employer knew or should have known about the environment and failed to act promptly to prevent or end the harassment.[77]

Sexual harassment, which we discuss in Chapter 11 under the context of men and women working together in groups, is the most frequent type of hostile environment charge filed with the EEOC.

6. *Lack of political savvy on the part of diverse employees.* Diverse employees may not get promoted because they do not know how to "play the game" of getting along and getting ahead in an organization. Research reveals that women and people of color are excluded from organizational networks.[78]

7. *Difficulty in balancing career and family issues.* Women still assume the majority of the responsibilities associated with raising children. This makes it harder for women to work evenings and weekends or to frequently travel once they have children. Even without children in the picture, household chores take more of a woman's time than a man's time.

8. *Fears of reverse discrimination.* Some employees believe that managing diversity is a smoke screen for reverse discrimination. This belief leads to very strong resistance because people feel that one person's gain is another's loss.

9. *Diversity is not seen as an organizational priority.* This leads to subtle resistance that shows up in the form of complaints and negative attitudes. Employees may complain about the time, energy, and resources devoted to diversity that could have been spent doing "real work."

10. *The need to revamp the organization's performance appraisal and reward system.* Performance appraisals and reward systems must reinforce the need to effectively manage diversity. This means that success will be based on a new set of criteria. For example, General Electric evaluates the extent to which its managers are inclusive of employees with different backgrounds. These evaluations are used in salary and promotion decisions.[79]

11. *Resistance to change.* Effectively managing diversity entails significant organizational and personal change. As discussed in Chapter 18, people resist change for many different reasons.

In summary, managing diversity is a critical component of organizational success.

go to the Web for the Group Exercise: Managing Diversity-Related Interactions

LO.8 Organizational Practices Used to Effectively Manage Diversity

to the point

Why is fostering mutual adaptation the best action option for managing diversity?

So what are organizations doing to effectively manage diversity? Answering this question requires that we provide a framework for categorizing organizational initiatives. Researchers and practitioners have developed relevant frameworks. One was developed by R Roosevelt Thomas Jr, a diversity expert. He identified eight generic action options that can be used to address any type of diversity issue. This section reviews Thomas's framework in order to provide you with a broad understanding about how organizations are effectively managing diversity.

R Roosevelt Thomas Jr's Generic Action Options

Thomas identified eight basic responses for handling any diversity issue. After describing each action option, we discuss relationships among them.[80]

Option 1: Include/Exclude

This choice is an outgrowth of affirmative action programs. Its primary goal is to either increase or decrease the number of diverse people at all levels of the organizations. Shoney's restaurant represents a good example of a company that attempted to include diverse employees after settling a discrimination lawsuit. The company subsequently hired African Americans into positions of dining-room supervisors and vice presidents, added more franchises owned by African Americans, and purchased more goods and services from minority-owned companies.[81]

Option 2: Deny

People using this option deny that differences exist. Denial may manifest itself in proclamations that all decisions are color, gender, and age blind and that success is solely determined by merit and performance. Consider State Farm Insurance, for example. "Although it was traditional for male agents and their regional managers to hire male relatives, State Farm Insurance avoided change and denied any alleged effects in a nine-year gender-bias suit that the company lost."[82]

Option 3: Assimilate

The basic premise behind this alternative is that all diverse people will learn to fit in or become like the dominant group. It only takes time and reinforcement for people to see the light. Organizations initially assimilate employees through their recruitment practices and the use of company orientation programs. New hires generally are put through orientation programs that aim to provide employees with the organization's preferred values and a set of standard operating procedures. Employees then are encouraged to refer to the policies and procedures manual when they are confused about what to do in a specific situation. These practices create homogeneity among employees.

Option 4: Suppress

Differences are squelched or discouraged when using this approach. This can be done by telling or reinforcing others to quit whining and complaining about issues. The old "you've got to pay your dues" line is another frequently used way to promote the status quo.

Option 5: Isolate

This option maintains the current way of doing things by setting the diverse person off to the side. In this way the individual is unable to influence organizational change. Managers can isolate people by putting them on special projects. Entire work groups or departments are isolated by creating functionally independent entities, frequently referred to as "silos." Shoney Inc.'s employees commented to a *Wall Street Journal* reporter about isolation practices formerly used by the company:

> White managers told of how Mr. Danner [previous chairman of the company] told them to fire blacks if they became too numerous in restaurants in white neighborhoods;

if they refused, they would lose their jobs, too. Some also said that when Mr. Danner was expected to visit their restaurant, they scheduled black employees off that day or, in one case, hid them in the bathroom. Others said blacks' applications were coded and discarded.[83]

Option 6: Tolerate

Toleration entails acknowledging differences but not valuing or accepting them. It represents a live-and-let-live approach that superficially allows organizations to give lip service to the issue of managing diversity. Toleration is different from isolation in that it allows for the inclusion of diverse people. However, differences are not really valued or accepted when an organization uses this option.

Option 7: Build Relationships

This approach is based on the premise that good relationships can overcome differences. It addresses diversity by fostering quality relationships—characterized by acceptance and understanding—among diverse groups. Rockwell Collins, Inc., a producer of aviation electronics in Cedar Rapids, Iowa, is a good example of a company attempting to use this diversity option. Rockwell is motivated to pursue this option because it has a shortage of qualified employees in a state that is about 6% nonwhite. To attract minority candidates the company "is building closer relationships with schools that have strong engineering programs as well as sizable minority populations. It also is working more closely with minority-focused professional societies."[84] The city of Cedar Rapids is also getting involved in the effort by trying to offer more cultural activities and ethnic-food stores that cater to a more diverse population base.

Option 8: Foster Mutual Adaptation

In this option, people are willing to adapt or change their views for the sake of creating positive relationships with others. This implies that employees and management alike must be willing to accept differences and, most important, agree that everyone and everything is open for change. Sodexho Inc., the largest provider of integrated food and facilities management services in the United States, Canada, and Mexico, is a good example of a company trying to implement this option (see Real World/Real People box featuring Sodexho USA on page 58).

Conclusions about Action Options

Although the action options can be used alone or in combination, some are clearly better than others. Exclusion, denial, assimilation, suppression, isolation, and toleration are among the least preferred options. Inclusion, building relationships, and mutual adaptation are the preferred strategies. That said, Thomas reminds us that mutual adaptation is the only approach that unquestionably endorses the philosophy behind managing diversity. In closing this discussion, it is important to note that choosing how to best manage diversity is a dynamic process that is determined by the context at hand. For instance, some organizations are not ready for mutual adaptation. The best one might hope for in this case is the inclusion of diverse people.

Raytheon is a good example of a company that is trying to eliminate the barriers to managing diversity. With a large number of employees needed in the near future, the chief diversity officer has claimed that they won't be turning their backs on anyone.

Sodexho USA Fosters Mutual Adaptation

At Sohexho USA, Chief Diversity Officer Rohini Anand partners with Sodexho University to create training that encourages diversity at the company. "Our learning strategy is phased, starting with a foundational training event that explains the business case for diversity and how it fits with the company strategy," Anand says. "It then moves to a mandatory one-day event for compliance and the spirit of diversity or an inclusive strategy. After that, skill-based learning labs teach about gender, cross-cultural differences, sexual orientation, and micro-iniquities. They look to include diversity content in all of the training department's offerings, and have train-the-trainer programs to build an internal capacity for inclusion in the organization....

Sodexho has a diversity scorecard for managers, which includes the manager's success in recruitment, retention, promotion, and development of all employees. A substantial portion of managers' bonuses is determined by their success in these areas.

What do you like best about Sodexho's approach toward diversity? Discuss.

SOURCE: H Dolezalek, "The Path to Inclusion," *Training*, May 2008, p 54.

Summary of Key Concepts

1. *Define diversity and review the four layers of diversity.* Diversity represents the individual differences that make people different from and similar to each other. Diversity pertains to everybody. It is not simply an issue of age, race, gender, or sexual orientation. The layers of diversity define an individual's personal identity and constitute a perceptual filter that influences how we interpret the world. Personality is at the center of the diversity wheel. The second layer of diversity consists of a set of internal dimensions that are referred to as surface-level dimensions of diversity. The third layer is composed of external influences and is called secondary dimensions of diversity. The final layer of diversity includes organizational dimensions.

2. *Explain the difference between affirmative action and managing diversity.* Affirmative action is an outgrowth of equal employment opportunity legislation and is an artificial intervention aimed at giving management a chance to correct past discrimination. Managing diversity entails creating a host of organizational changes that enable all people to perform up to their maximum potential.

3. *Explain why Alice Eagly and Linda Carli believe that a woman's career is best viewed as traveling through a labyrinth.* Eagly and Carli believe that women were barred from achieving high-level managerial positions in the past, but that women now have busted through these barriers. They cite statistics showing that women have made progress in terms of obtaining CEO positions, managerial and administrative positions, and educational attainment; holding seats on boards of directors; obtaining leadership positions in educational institutions; and receiving federal court appointments. Eagly and Carli propose that women have made these strides by successfully navigating a labyrinth of twists, turns, and obstacles.

4. *Review the demographic trends pertaining to racial groups, educational mismatches, and an aging workforce.*

With respect to racial groups, Asians and Hispanics are expected to have the largest growth in the population between 2000 and 2050, and minority groups will constitute 49.9% of the population in 2050. Minority groups also are experiencing a glass ceiling. There is a mismatch between workers' educational attainment and occupational requirements. The workforce is aging.

5. *Highlight the managerial implications of increasing diversity in the workforce.* There are seven broad managerial implications: (*a*) To attract the best workers, companies need to adopt policies and programs that meet the needs of all employees; (*b*) managers should consider progressive methods to recruit, retain, and integrate Hispanic workers into their organizations; (*c*) mentoring programs are needed to help minorities advance within the organizational hierarchy; (*d*) there will be a shortage of qualified people in technical fields; (*e*) on-the-job remedial skills and literacy training will be needed to help the growing number of dropouts and illiterates cope with job demands; (*f*) organizations will need to provide tangible support education if the United States is to remain globally competitive; and (*g*) there are three broad recommendations for managing an aging workforce.

6. *Describe the positive and negative effects of diversity by using social categorization theory and information/decision-making theory.* Social categorization theory implies that similarity leads to liking and attraction, thereby fostering a host of positive outcomes. This theory supports the idea that homogeneity is better than heterogeneity because diversity causes negative interpersonal processes and group dynamics. The information/decision-making theory is based on the notion that diverse groups should outperform homogenous groups because diversity is positively associated with task-relevant processes and decision making.

7. *Identify the barriers and challenges to managing diversity.* There are 10 barriers to successfully implementing diversity initiatives: (*a*) inaccurate stereotypes and prejudice, (*b*) ethnocentrism, (*c*) poor career planning, (*d*) an unsupportive and hostile working environment for diverse employees, (*e*) lack of political savvy on the part of diverse employees, (*f*) difficulty in balancing career and family issues, (*g*) fears of reverse discrimination, (*h*) diversity is not seen as an organizational priority, (*i*) the need to revamp the organization's performance appraisal and reward system, and (*j*) resistance to change.

8. *Discuss the organizational practices used to effectively manage diversity as identified by R Roosevelt Thomas Jr.* There are many different practices organizations can use to manage diversity. R Roosevelt Thomas Jr identified eight basic responses for handling any diversity issue: include/exclude, deny, assimilate, suppress, isolate, tolerate, build relationships, and foster mutual adaptation. Exclusion, denial, assimilation, suppression, isolation, and toleration are among the least preferred options. Inclusion, building relationships, and mutual adaptation are the preferred strategies.

Key Terms

Diversity, 35
Discrimination, 37
Affirmative action, 37
Managing diversity, 37
Workforce demographics, 41

Glass ceiling, 41
Social categorization theory, 51
Information/decision-making theory, 52
Demographic faultline, 53
Diversity climate, 54

OB in Action Case Study

LeasePlan Effectively Manages Diversity[85]

Shortly after joining LeasePlan USA as its head of sales and marketing in 2003, Mike Pitcher met with representatives of the vehicle-leasing company's top customers. To his surprise, most were women.

Women also outnumbered men among LeasePlan's 450 employees. Yet the vast majority of top managers at the company, a subsidiary of Netherlands-based LeasePlan Corp., were men.

Soon after, LeasePlan began an effort to transform its corporate culture—rooted in the old-boy network of fleet managers—and promote more women. Executives hired a consultant to offer women career counseling, revised the company's pay plan to stress performance over longevity, and displaced some longtime managers. Today, three of the eight top executives are women, up from one in seven two years ago.

Women employees say LeasePlan is a more supportive and collaborative employer. Mr. Pitcher, now the company's chief executive, calls the initiative a strategic investment rather than the "the politically correct thing to do."

"LeasePlan doesn't build anything," he says. "Our sustainable competitive advantage is our people."...

Such efforts require sustained commitment at the top, says Sheila Wellington, clinical professor of management at New York University's Stern School of Business. Executives "need to make it very clear that this isn't the flavor of the month," says Ms. Wellington, a former president of Catalyst, a research firm for focusing on women's workplace issues.

Ms. Wellington says executives must hold middle managers accountable for supporting and promoting female subordinates, particularly at smaller companies...

LeasePlan executives launched their initiative in 2006. They hired Pathbuilders, Inc., an Atlanta human-resources consultancy that focuses on women, to craft a program that includes a skills assessment, career guidance, and tips on communicating and building a "brand." The program, which taps about 30 women each year, also features networking events and a panel discussion with female executives from other firms.

The broader effort to transform the corporate culture distinguishes LeasePlan from other companies trying to promote women, says Maria Goldsholl, chief operating officer of Mom Corps, a staffing company specializing in flexible employment for women...

The program also appears to be boosting job satisfaction and engagement among LeasePlan's women employees. In a 2006 survey, 35% of women agreed the "management supports my efforts to manage my career." The following year, 47% of all female employees and 71% of program participants agreed. The percentage of women who said they think positions at LeasePlan are awarded fairly increased to 30% from 22%.

Gerri Patton, director of client activation, says the program helped her become more confident and outspoken. The 23-year LeasePlan veteran encourages her female subordinates to apply. "I wish I would have done that program 10 or 15 years ago," she says. "There's no telling where I would be . . . The sky would have been the limit."

SOURCE: Excerpted from C Tuna, "Initiative Moves Women Up Corporate Ladder," *The Wall Street Journal*, October 20, 2008, p B4. Copyright © 2008 by Dow Jones & Company, Inc. Reproduced with permission of Dow Jones & Company, Inc. via Copyright Clearance Center.

Questions for Discussion

1. What is the business case that is driving LeasePlan's interest in managing diversity? Discuss.

2. Compare and contrast the extent to which LeasePlan is using principles from affirmative action and managing diversity. Explain your rationale.

3. To what extent are LeasePlan's efforts consistent with recommendations derived from Alice Eagly and Linda Carli? Discuss.

4. Which of R Roosevelt Thomas Jr's eight generic diversity options is LeasePlan using to manage diversity? Explain.

5. While LeasePlan's diversity initiative is clearly working, what recommendations would you make for improving their program? Explain.

Ethical Dilemma

Should Wal-Mart Pull the Plug on Ningbo Beifa Group?[85]

TANG YINGHONG WAS CAUGHT IN AN IMPOSSIBLE squeeze. For years, his employer, Ningbo Beifa Group, had prospered as a top supplier of pens, mechanical pencils, and highlighters to Wal-Mart Stores and other major retailers. But late last year, Tang learned that auditors from Wal-Mart, Beifa's biggest customer, were about to inspect labor conditions at the factory in the Chinese coastal city of Ningbo where he worked as an administrator. Wal-Mart had already on three occasions caught Beifa paying its 3,000 workers less than China's minimum wage and violating overtime rules, Tang says. Under the U.S. chain's labor rules, a fourth offense would end the relationship.

Help arrived suddenly in the form of an unexpected phone call from a man calling himself Lai Mingwei. The caller said he was with Shanghai Corporate Responsibility Management & Consulting Co., and for a $5,000 fee, he'd take care of Tang's Wal-Mart problem. "He promised us he could definitely get us a pass for the audit," Tang says.

Lai provided advice on how to create fake but authentic-looking records and suggested that Beifa hustle any workers with grievances out of the factory on the day of the audit, Tang recounts. The consultant also coached Beifa managers on what questions they could expect from Wal-Mart's inspectors, says Tang. After following much of Lai's advice, the Beifa factory in Ningbo passed the audit earlier this year, Tang says, even though the company didn't change any of its practices.

For more than a decade, major American retailers and name brands have answered accusations that they exploit "sweatshop" labor with elaborate codes of conduct and on-site monitoring. But in China many factories have just gotten better at concealing abuses.

Internal industry documents reviewed by *Business Week* reveal that numerous Chinese factories keep double sets of books to fool auditors and distribute scripts for employees to recite if they are questioned. And a new breed of Chinese consultant has sprung up to assist companies like Beifa in evading audits. "Tutoring and helping factories deal with audits has become an industry in China," says Tang, 34, who recently left Beifa of his own volition to start a Web site for workers.

A lawyer for Beifa, Zhou Jie, confirms that the company employed the Shanghai consulting firm but denies any dishonesty related to wages, hours, or outside monitoring. Past audits had "disclosed some problems, and we took necessary measures correspondingly," he explains in a letter responding to questions. The lawyer adds that Beifa has "become the target of accusations" by former employees "whose unreasonable demands have not been satisfied." Reached by cell phone, a man identifying himself as Lai says that the Shanghai consulting firm helps suppliers pass audits, but he declines to comment on his work for Beifa.

Business Week has informed executives at Wal-Mart about these allegations. What would you do if you were an executive at Wal-Mart?

1. Ningbo Beifa Group passed the most recent audit, so I would let these results stand for now.

2. What is done is done. However, I would investigate the allegations and then improve the future auditing procedures based on the results.

3. Investigate the allegations and discontinue working with Beifa if they are true.

4. Invent other options. Discuss.

Web Resources

For study material and exercises that apply to this chapter, visit our Web site, **www.mhhe.com/kreitner**

Chapter 3

Organizational Culture, Socialization, and Mentoring

When you finish studying the material in this chapter, you should be able to:

LO.1 Define organizational culture and discuss its three layers.

LO.2 Discuss the difference between espoused and enacted values.

LO.3 Describe the four functions of organizational culture.

LO.4 Discuss the four types of organizational culture associated with the competing values framework.

LO.5 Summarize the seven conclusions derived from research about the outcomes associated with organizational culture.

LO.6 Review the three caveats about culture change.

LO.7 Summarize the methods used by organizations to change organizational culture.

LO.8 Describe the three phases in Feldman's model of organizational socialization.

LO.9 Discuss the various socialization tactics used to socialize employees.

LO.10 Explain the four developmental networks associated with mentoring.

Southwest Airline's Culture permeates every aspect of our company. It is our essence, our DNA, our past, our present, and our future. It is so important, in fact, that I wish I had more space to discuss it.

We often say that other airlines can copy our business plan from top to bottom but Southwest stands apart from the clones because of our People. But I would still wager that if another company somehow managed to hire all our fantastic Employees, that company wouldn't match up to Southwest.

Why? The new employer wouldn't possess the Southwest Culture, the secret sauce, if you will, of our organization. That Culture motivates and sustains us. For many of us, being part of Southwest is not just a vocation, but a mission. I don't dictate the Culture; neither do our other Officers. Rather, it stems from the collective personality of our Employees. It took us more than 30 years just to establish some definitions of our Culture upon which we could all agree. Those definitions are laid out in what we call "Living the Southwest Way." That creed consists of three values: A Warrior Spirit that recognizes courage, hard work, and desire to be the best; a Servant's Heart that follows the Golden Rule and treats others with respect; and a Fun-LUVing Attitude that includes FUN, of course, but also passion and celebration.

In January, we observed the 18th anniversary of the founding of our Corporate Culture Committee, a group dedicated to preserving our Culture for the present and the future. This Committee stresses that the Southwest Culture resides in each Employee, no matter the Employee's title. But the Culture Committee also recognizes how fragile Culture can be. I've talked with some of our Employees who have come to us from other airlines and firms that, long ago, maintained a strong culture. These Employees often said that they witnessed how a little benign neglect was able to destroy that culture almost overnight.

Their experiences confirm what I have always believed: Lip service can be a great danger. It's easy to write columns like this bragging about our Culture; the hard work is living up to it every day. Thus, the Committee Members act as examples for all of our

Southwest employees make up the personality of the organization.

other Employees to see. They show that Culture comes from the heart, not from the memo. As you might imagine, they have a difficult job, but we are fortunate to have the dedication of these Culture Warriors who battle indifference and complacency on a daily basis. With their help, our Culture continues to fly high.[1]

FOR DISCUSSION

How would you describe the organizational culture at Southwest Airlines?

The opening vignette highlights three key conclusions about organizational culture. First, an organization's culture can impact employee motivation, satisfaction, and turnover. Southwest is able to maintain low employee turnover and high job satisfaction by creating a positive, employee-focused culture. The same can be said about the top five companies to work for in America in 2008 according to *Fortune*—NetApp, Edward Jones, Boston Consulting Group, Google, and Wegmans Food Markets.[2] Second, organizational culture can be a source of competitive advantage. Southwest Airlines, for example, relies on its employees and customer-focused culture to produce sustained profits and high productivity. Dov Seidman, CEO of LRN, a company that helps organizations to create ethical cultures, also believes in the power of organizational culture. According to Seidman, "We are witnessing a trend in business where values-based behaviors and cultures are being shaped as a source of competitive advantage."[3] Finally, managers can influence organizational culture. Southwest uses its culture committee as a vehicle to shape and reinforce the values desired by senior management.

This chapter will help you better understand how managers can use organizational culture as a competitive advantage. After defining and discussing the context of organizational culture, we examine (1) the dynamics of organizational culture, (2) the process of culture change, (3) the organization socialization process, and (4) the embedding of organizational culture through mentoring.

LO.1 Organizational Culture: Definition and Context

to the point
How does organizational culture influence organizational outcomes?

Organizational culture
Shared values and beliefs that underlie a company's identity.

Organizational culture is "the set of shared, taken-for-granted implicit assumptions that a group holds and that determines how it perceives, thinks about, and reacts to its various environments."[4] This definition highlights three important characteristics of organizational culture. First, organizational culture is passed on to new employees through the process of socialization, a topic discussed later in this chapter. Second, organizational culture influences our behavior at work. Finally, organizational culture operates at different levels.

Figure 3–1 provides a conceptual framework for reviewing the widespread impact organizational culture has on organizational behavior. It also shows the linkage between this chapter—culture, socialization, and mentoring—and other key topics in this book. Figure 3–1 reveals organizational culture is shaped by four key components: the founder's values, the industry and business environment, the national culture, and the senior leaders' vision and behavior: The impact of national culture on organizational behavior is discussed in detail in Chapter 4. In turn, organizational culture influences the type of organizational structure adopted by a company and a host of practices, policies, and

Figure 3–1   *A Conceptual Framework for Understanding Organizational Culture*

Antecedents	Organizational culture	Organizational structure and practices	Group and social processes	Collective attitudes and behavior	Organizational outcomes
• Founder's values • Industry and business environment • National culture (Ch. 4) • Senior leaders' vision and behavior (Ch. 16)	• Observable artifacts ↓ ↑ • Espoused values ↓ ↑ • Basic assumptions	• Reward systems (Ch. 9) • Organizational design (Ch. 17)	• Socialization • Mentoring • Decision making (Ch. 12) • Group dynamics (Ch. 10) • Communication (Ch. 14) • Influence and empowerment (Ch. 15) • Leadership (Ch. 16)	• Work attitudes (Ch. 6) • Job satisfaction (Ch. 6) • Motivation (Ch. 8)	• Effectiveness (Ch. 17) • Stress (Ch. 18)

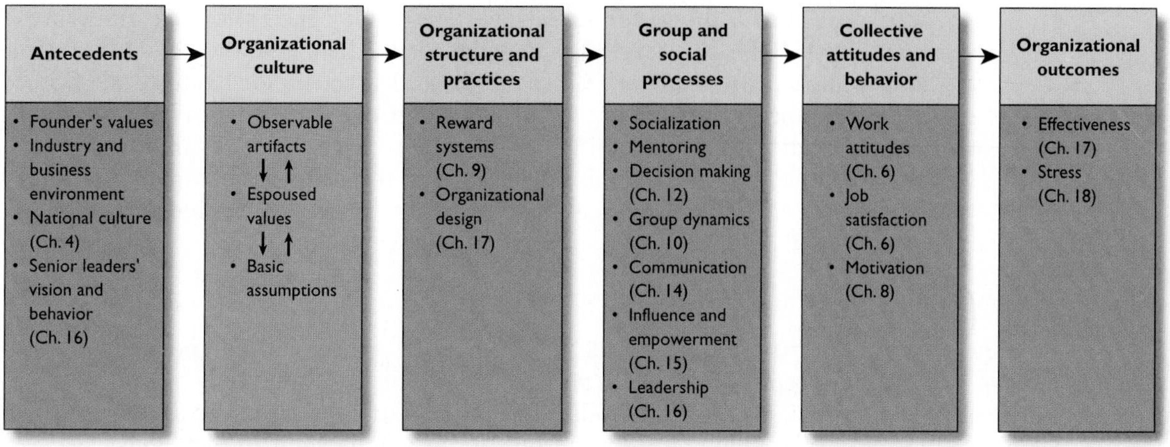

SOURCE: From C Ostroff, A Kinicki, and M Tamkins,"Organizational Culture and Climate," *Handbook of Psychology,* vol. 12, edited by Walter C Borman, Daniel R Ilgen, Richard J Klimoski, and Irving B Weiner, pp 565–93, Copyright © 2003. Reprinted with permission of John Wiley & Sons, Inc.

procedures implemented in pursuit of organizational goals. These organizational characteristics then affect a variety of group and social processes. This sequence ultimately affects employees' attitudes and behavior and a variety of organizational outcomes. All told, Figure 3–1 reveals that organizational culture is a contextual variable influencing individual, group, and organizational behavior.

Dynamics of Organizational Culture

To gain a better understanding of how organizational culture is formed and used by employees, this section begins by discussing the layers of organizational culture. We then review the four functions of organizational culture, types of organizational culture, and outcomes associated with organizational culture.

Layers of Organizational Culture

Figure 3–1 shows the three fundamental layers of organizational culture: observable artifacts, espoused values, and basic assumptions. Each level varies in terms of outward visibility and resistance to change, and each level influences another level.

Observable Artifacts   At the more visible level, culture represents observable artifacts. Artifacts consist of the physical manifestation of an organization's culture. Organizational examples include acronyms, manner of dress, awards, myths and stories told about the organization, published lists of values, observable rituals and ceremonies, special parking spaces, decorations, and so on. For example, the Ritz-Carlton hotel uses storytelling to reinforce a culture that is focused on exceeding customers' expectations. The company shares "wow stories"

to the point
What are the key conclusions regarding layers of culture, functions of culture, types of culture, and outcomes associated with organizational culture?

at meetings each week that relay guests' tales of staff members going above and beyond the call of duty. Each "wow" winner, such as a laundry attendant who dove into a dumpster to retrieve one young guest's stuffed gingerbread man, gets $100.[5] This level also includes visible behaviors exhibited by people and groups. Jeffrey Immelt, CEO of General Electric, for instance, reinforced a performance-based culture by declining an earned bonus of $12 million in 2008. He felt it was inappropriate to take the bonus because earnings were below expectations and he wants his compensation to reflect the company's financial performance.[6] Artifacts are easier to change than the less visible aspects of organizational culture.

Values

Enduring belief in a mode of conduct or end-state.

Espoused values

The stated values and norms that are preferred by an organization.

Sustainability

Meeting humanity's needs without harming future generations.

LO.2 Espoused Values   Values possess five key components. "**Values** (1) are concepts or beliefs, (2) pertain to desirable end-states or behaviors, (3) transcend situations, (4) guide selection or evaluation of behavior and events, and (5) are ordered by relative importance."[7] It is important to distinguish between values that are espoused versus those that are enacted.

Espoused values represent the explicitly stated values and norms that are preferred by an organization. They are generally established by the founder of a new or small company and by the top management team in a larger organization.[8] Consider, for example, the espoused values of Williams-Sonoma, Inc. (see the Real World/Real People feature on page 67). This specialty retailer of home furnishings was founded in 1956 and has experienced substantial growth since its inception.

On a positive note, Williams-Sonoma and many more companies are espousing the value of sustainability. **Sustainability** represents "a company's ability to make a profit without sacrificing the resources of its people, the community, and the planet."[9] Sustainability also is referred to as "being green," and Pulitzer Prize winner Thomas Friedman believes that "outgreening" other nations can renew America and defeat al-Qaeda.[10] Others believe that outgreening can produce competitive advantage for organizations. For example, insurer Safeco and Microsoft have significantly cut costs and increased productivity by implementing employer-subsidized transportation that reinforces the idea that people be encouraged not to drive to work.[11] Unilever is a great example of a company committed to sustainability.

> The world is Unilever's laboratory. In Brazil, the company operates a free community laundry in a São Paulo slum, provides financing to help tomato growers convert to eco-friendly "drip" irrigation, and recycles 17 tons of waste annually at a toothpaste factory. Unilever funds a floating hospital that offers free medical care in Bangladesh, a nation with just 20 doctors for every 10,000 people. In Ghana, it teaches palm oil producers to reuse plant waste while providing potable water to deprived communities. In India, Unilever staff help thousands of women in remote villages start micro-enterprises. And responding to green activists, the company discloses how much carbon dioxide and hazardous waste its factories spew out around the world.[12]

Because espoused values represent aspirations that are explicitly communicated to employees, managers hope that those values will directly influence employee behavior. Unfortunately, aspirations do not automatically produce the desired behaviors because people do not always "walk the talk."

Williams-Sonoma's Espoused Values Focus on Employees, Customers, Shareholders, and Ethical Behavior

People First

We believe the potential of our company has no limit and is driven by our associates and their imagination. We are committed to an environment that attracts, motivates and recognizes high performance.

Customers

We are here to please our customers—without them nothing else matters.

Quality

We must take pride in everything we do. From our people, to our products and in our relationships with business partners and our community, quality is our signature.

Shareholders

We must provide a superior return to our shareholders. It's everyone's job.

Ethical Sourcing

Williams-Sonoma, Inc., and all of its brands are committed to maintaining the highest level of integrity and honesty throughout all aspects of our business, and strive to ensure that our business associates, including agents, vendors and suppliers, share our commitment to socially responsible employment conditions.

Environmental Paper Procurement Policy

Williams-Sonoma, Inc., is committed to environmental stewardship, and more specifically, to sound paper procurement practices that ensure the sustainability of forests and other natural resources.

Recycling

The launch of Williams-Sonoma Inc.'s Recycle 100 brings our company-wide *Greening Our Home* initiative to our customers' homes. 50% of American households recycle their paper products. Our customers recyle 60%, but, in sharing their environmental concern, we're making 100% recycling the goal for this innovative new program.

To what extent are these values consistent with your own values? Would you like to work at Williams-Sonoma?

SOURCE: Excerpted from "Corporate Values," www.williams-sonomainc.com/careers/corporate-values.html, accessed February 19, 2009.

Enacted values, on the other hand, represent the values and norms that actually are exhibited or converted into employee behavior. They represent the values that employees ascribe to an organization based on their observations of what occurs on a daily basis. Starbucks and Hoar Construction LLC, rated as the 19th Best Medium Company to Work For in America, are excellent examples of the difference between espoused and enacted values.

Enacted values

The values and norms that are exhibited by employees.

Starbucks, once the undisputed leader in premium-priced caffeine fixes, long has cultivated a corporate reputation for social responsibility, environmental awareness, and sensitivity to workers' rights. Now that carefully crafted image is under assault because of a messy legal dispute with a group called the Starbucks Workers Union (SWU), which started recruiting employees in 2004 and now claims 300 members. On December 23, 2008, a National Labor Relations Board judge found that Starbucks had illegally fired three New York City baristas as it tried to squelch the union-organizing effort.[13] In contrast, a male assistant project manager at Hoar Construction, which espouses that it values employees, was told to take at least one week off and maybe two after the birth of his child. The employee originally asked for two days off.[14]

Starbucks espoused that it valued employees and then behaved in an untrusting manner by trying to squash union organizing efforts. Oppositely, Hoar Construction's espoused and enacted values were identical.

It is important for managers to reduce gaps between espoused and enacted values because they can significantly influence employee attitudes and organizational performance. For example, a survey administered by the Ethics Resource Center showed that employees were more likely to behave ethically when management behaved in a way that set a good ethical example and kept its promises and commitments.[15] Another study of 7,500 employees from four continents revealed that employees did not trust senior management because they did not "walk-the-talk." This discrepancy creates problems because employees' satisfaction, performance, and turnover are affected when they feel that their values do not match the organization's enacted values.[16] Managers can use a "cultural fit assessment" survey to determine the match between espoused and enacted values. Results can then be used to improve the work environment and to align the organization's espoused and enacted values.[17]

Basic Assumptions
Basic underlying assumptions are unobservable and represent the core of organizational culture. They constitute organizational values that have become so taken for granted over time that they become assumptions that guide organizational behavior. They thus are highly resistant to change. When basic assumptions are widely held among employees, people will find behavior based on an inconsistent value inconceivable. Southwest Airlines, for example, is noted for operating according to basic assumptions that value employees' welfare and providing high-quality service. Employees at Southwest Airlines would be shocked to see management act in ways that did not value employees' and customers' needs.

Practical Application of Research on Values
Organizations subscribe to a constellation of values rather than to only one and can be profiled according to their values. This enables managers to determine whether or not the organization's values are consistent and supportive of its corporate goals and initiatives. Organizations are less likely to accomplish their corporate goals when employees perceive an inconsistency between espoused values (e.g., honesty) and the behaviors needed to accomplish the goals (e.g., shredding financial documents). Similarly, organizational change is unlikely to succeed if it is based on a set of values highly inconsistent with employees' individual values. This underscores the need for organizations to use creative methods during the hiring process to ensure a match between applicant-organizational values. Consider the selection process used by ReThink Rewards, a Toronto-based company, when hiring salespeople.

> The process includes group interviews, each with 10 candidates and two employees—a sales representative and a human resource representative. The interviewers then select 10 finalist candidates and ask each to review one of the company's case studies and give a 20-minute PowerPoint presentation to two other employees. The presentations are followed by 10-minute question-and-answer sessions. Finalists are interviewed by the hiring manager and HR representative, who use "Topgrading" methods—an approach that involves an extensive interview with each candidate about his or her experiences in high school, college and the workplace. . . . During the Topgrading interview, the candidate is asked 15 questions about each job he or she has held in the past 10 years, including opportunities, challenges, mistakes and accomplishments.[18]

LO.3 Four Functions of Organizational Culture

As illustrated in Figure 3–2, an organization's culture fulfills four functions. To help bring these four functions to life, let us consider how each of them has taken shape at Southwest Airlines. Southwest is a particularly instructive example because it has grown to become the largest carrier in the United States based on scheduled departures since its inception in 1971 and has achieved 37 consecutive years of profitability. *Fortune* has ranked Southwest in the top five of the Best Companies to Work For in America from 1997 to 2000; Southwest has chosen not to participate in this ranking process since 2000. Southwest also was ranked as the twelfth most admired company in the United States by *Fortune* in 2008, partly due to its strong and distinctive culture.[19]

1. *Give members an organizational identity.* Southwest Airlines is known as a fun place to work that values employee satisfaction and customer loyalty over corporate profits. Gary Kelly, Southwest's CEO, highlighted this theme by noting that "our people are our single greatest strength and our most enduring longterm competitive advantage."[20]

   The company also has a catastrophe fund based on voluntary contributions for distribution to employees who are experiencing serious personal difficulties. Southwest's people-focused identity is reinforced by the fact that it is an employer of choice. For example, Southwest received 329,000 résumés and hired 4,200

Figure 3–2   *Four Functions of Organizational Culture*

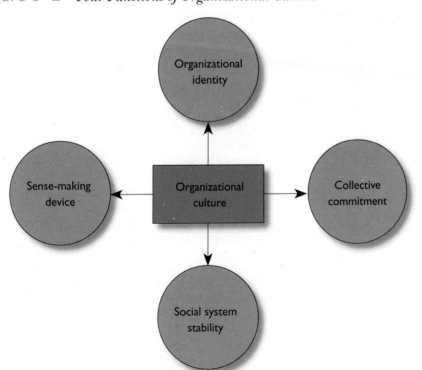

SOURCE: Adapted from discussion in L Smircich, "Concepts of Culture and Organizational Analysis," *Administrative Science Quarterly,* September 1983, pp 339–58. Reprinted with permission.

new employees in 2007. The company also was rated as providing outstanding opportunities for women and Hispanics by *Professional Women* magazine and *Hispanic* magazine, respectively, and *Business Ethics* ranked Southwest among the 100 Best Corporate Citizens seven years in a row.

2. *Facilitate collective commitment.* The mission of Southwest Airlines "is dedication to the highest quality of Customer Service delivered with a sense of warmth, friendliness, individual pride, and Company Spirit."[21] Southwest's more than 35,000 employees are committed to this mission. The Department of Transportation's Air Travel Consumer Report reported Southwest was ranked number one in fewest customer complaints since 1987.

3. *Promote social system stability.* Social system stability reflects the extent to which the work environment is perceived as positive and reinforcing, and the extent to which conflict and change are effectively managed. Southwest is noted for its philosophy of having fun, having parties, and celebrating. For example, each city in which the firm operates is given a budget for parties. Southwest also uses a variety of performance-based awards and service awards to reinforce employees. The company's positive and enriching environment is supported by the lowest turnover rates in the airline industry and the employment of 1,165 married couples.

The smile on this Southwest Airlines employee demonstrates the four functions of culture. Southwest employees have high job satisfaction and low employee turnover in part attributable to its philosophy of having fun and celebrating. Would you like to work at Southwest?

4. *Shape behavior by helping members make sense of their surroundings.* This function of culture helps employees understand why the organization does what it does and how it intends to accomplish its long-term goals. Keeping in mind that Southwest's leadership originally viewed ground transportation as their main competitor in 1971, employees come to understand why the airline's primary vision is to be the best primarily short-haul, low-fare, high-frequency, point-to-point carrier in the United States. Employees understand they must achieve exceptional performance, such as turning a plane in 20 minutes, because they must keep costs down in order to compete against Greyhound and the use of automobiles. In turn, the company reinforces the importance of outstanding customer service and high performance expectations by using performance-based awards and profit sharing. Employees own about 8% of the company stock.

LO.4 Types of Organizational Culture

Organizational behavior researchers have proposed three different frameworks to capture the various types of organizational culture: the Organizational Culture Inventory, the Competing Values Framework, and the Organizational Culture Profile.[22] This section discusses the Competing Values Framework because it is the most widely used approach for classifying organizational culture. It also was named as one of the 40 most important frameworks in the study of organizations and has been shown to be a valid approach for classifying organizational culture.[23]

Figure 3–3   *Competing Values Framework*

Flexibility and discretion

	Clan	Adhocracy	
	Thrust: Collaborate	**Thrust:** Create	
	Means: Cohesion, participation, communication, empowerment	**Means:** Adaptability, creativity, agility	
Internal focus and integration	**Ends:** Morale, people development, commitment	**Ends:** Innovation, Growth, cutting-edge output	**External focus and differentiation**
	Hierarchy	Market	
	Thrust: Control	**Thrust:** Compete	
	Means: Capable processes, consistency, process control, measurement	**Means:** Customer focus, productivity, enhancing competitiveness	
	Ends: Efficiency, timeliness, smooth functioning	**Ends:** Market share, profitability, goal achievement	

Stability and control

SOURCE: Adapted from K S Cameron, R E Quinn, J Degraff, and A V Thakor, *Competing Values Leadership* (Northampton, MA: Edward Elgar, 2006), p 32.

The **competing values framework** (CVF) provides a practical way for managers to understand, measure, and change organizational culture. It was originally developed by a team of researchers who were trying to classify different ways to assess organizational effectiveness. This research showed that measures of organizational effectiveness vary along two fundamental dimensions or axes. One axis pertains to whether an organization focuses its attention and efforts on internal dynamics and employees or outward toward its external environment and its customers and shareholders. The second is concerned with an organization's preference for flexibility and discretion or control and stability. Combining these two axes creates four types of organizational culture that are based on different core values and different sets of criteria for accessing organizational effectiveness. The CVF is shown in Figure 3–3.[24]

Figure 3–3 shows the strategic thrust associated with each cultural type along with the means used to accomplish this thrust and the resulting ends or goals pursued by each cultural type. Before beginning our exploration of the CVF, it is important to note that organizations can possess characteristics associated with each culture type. That said, however, organizations tend to have one type of culture that is more dominant than the others. Let us begin our discussion of culture types by starting in the upper-left-hand quadrant of the CVF.

Clan Culture   A **clan culture** has an internal focus and values flexibility rather than stability and control. It resembles a family-type organization in which effectiveness is achieved by encouraging collaboration between employees. This type of culture is very "employee-focused" and strives to instill cohesion through consensus and job satisfaction and commitment through employee involvement.

Competing values framework

A framework for categorizing organizational culture.

Clan culture

A culture that has an internal focus and values flexibility rather than stability and control.

Clan organizations devote considerable resources to hiring and developing their employees, and they view customers as partners.

A company with a strong clan culture is Decagon Devices Inc. in Pullman, Washington. The company may be small, but senior management tries to maintain a family atmosphere at work. The company's CEO, Tamsin Jolley, noted that "the way that we like to see it is that as we add employees we're just adding members to the family." This feeling starts with a profit-sharing program that distributes 20% of pretax profits to employees on a quarterly basis. "Then there are day-to-day activities that bring workers closer together. Each Wednesday, some employees take turns bringing home-cooked meals to work for their colleagues. Then, all the workers eat lunch together. The weekly meal is an opportunity for managers to share news about the company, introduce new employees, and teach workers how to read the company's financial statements. The company also encourages employees to socialize at work. The office has a ping-pong table and slot-car track, and there's a long tradition of employees playing soccer on their breaks."[25] Decagon Devices also provides generous employee health benefits and hosts annual catered family picnics and holiday parties.

Southwest Airlines; NetApp, rated as the number 1 Best Company to Work For in America in 2008 by *Fortune;* Nucor; and Zappos represent other good examples of successful companies with clan cultures.[26] Zappos, for example, encourages managers to spend between 10% and 20% of their spare time with employees during off-work hours.[27]

Zappos's clan culture can be seen in these employees. It is no wonder the company was rated as the 23rd best company to work for by *Fortune.* Would you like to work for Zappos?

Adhocracy Culture

Adhocracy culture

A culture that has an external focus and values flexibility.

An **adhocracy culture** has an external focus and values flexibility. This type of culture fosters the creation of innovative products and services by being adaptable, creative, and fast to respond to changes in the marketplace. Adhocracy cultures do not rely on the type of centralized power and authority relationships that are part of market and hierarchical cultures. They also encourage employees to take risks, think outside the box, and experiment with new ways of getting things done. This type of culture is well suited for start-up companies, those in industries undergoing constant change, and those in mature industries that are in need of innovation to enhance growth. Consider how Jeff Immelt, CEO of General Electric, is trying to instill characteristics of an adhocracy in order to fuel revenue growth.

The company, which is well-known for sharing best practices across its many units, has recently begun formally discussing failures, too. Last September the company set up a two-hour conference call for managers of eight "imagination breakthroughs" that didn't live up to expectations and were being shelved, or "retired," in GE's parlance. ("Imagination Breakthroughs"—IBs—are new businesses or products that have potential sales of $100 million within three to five years.)

Such discussions can be nerve-racking, especially in companies where failure has traditionally been met with tough consequences. . . ."I had some offline conversations with some of the IB leaders reassuring them that this was not a call where they were going to get their pink slips," says Patia McGrath, a GE marketing director who helped put together the call. "The notion of taking big swings, and that it's O.K. to miss the swing, is something that's quite new with Jeff."[28]

W. L. Gore, Intel, and Google are other companies that possess cultural characteristics consistent with an adhocracy.

Market Culture   A **market culture** has a strong external focus and values stability and control. Organizations with this culture are driven by competition and a strong desire to deliver results and accomplish goals. Because this type of culture is focused on the external environment, customers and profits take precedence over employee development and satisfaction. The major goal of managers is to drive toward productivity, profits, and customer satisfaction. Employees are expected to react fast, work hard, and deliver quality work on time. Organizations with this culture tend to reward people who deliver results. Byung Mo Ahn, president of Kia Motors, is a good example of a leader who desires to promote a market culture. He fired two senior executives from Kia Motors America in February 2008 because they were not meeting their expected sales goals. Employees from North America note that Mr. Ahn has created a very aggressive and competitive work environment. Some describe the environment as militaristic. Intel is another example of a company with a market culture. The company eliminated more than 10,000 jobs between 2006 and 2007 in a restructuring to reduce costs and improve efficiency and profitability.[29] Jack and Suzy Welch believe that more organizations will try to cultivate a market culture in response to the economic problems facing the world in 2009. Their rationale is that a market culture can help organizations to focus on productivity and results, thereby reducing costs, increasing profitability, and improving customer satisfaction.[30]

Home Depot is an example of a company focused on competition and results due to the actions of former CEO Robert Nardelli. What other companies do you think fit into a market culture?

Market culture
A culture that has a strong external focus and values stability and control.

Hierarchy Culture   Control is the driving force within a hierarchy culture. The **hierarchy culture** has an internal focus, which produces a more formalized and structured work environment, and values stability and control over flexibility. This orientation leads to the development of reliable internal processes, extensive measurement, and the implementation of a variety of control mechanisms. For example, companies with a hierachy culture are more likely to use the type of total quality management (TQM) programs discussed in Chapter 1. Effectiveness in a company with this type of culture is likely to be assessed with measures of efficiency, timeliness, and reliability of producing and delivering products and services. Home Depot is a good example of a company that tried to use a hierarchy culture to cut costs and increase profitability. Although this culture did help to lower costs, it also led to employee job dissatisfaction and reduced customer satisfaction (see the Real World/Real People feature on page 74). In contrast, Exelon, the No. 1 US nuclear power generator, has successfully used its hierarchy culture to boost efficiency, safety, and profit.[31]

Hierarchy culture
A culture that has an internal focus and values stability and control over flexibility.

Cultural Types Represent Competing Values   It is important to note that certain cultural types reflect opposing core values. These contradicting cultures are found along the two diagonals in Figure 3–3. For example, the clan culture—upper-left quadrant—is represented by values that emphasize an internal focus and flexibility, whereas the market culture—bottom-right quadrant—has an external focus and concern for stability and control. You can see the same conflict between an adhocracy culture that values flexibility and an external focus and a

Home Depot's Former CEO, Robert Nardelli, Fostered a Hierarchy Culture

Store managers were suddenly measured on a bewildering array of metrics, such as the average hourly labor rate, none related to customer service. By centralizing, Home Depot saved money—but robbed managers of the power they'd had to make decisions based on neighborhood quirks . . . or the regional popularity of small iridescent tiles. "There were beach chairs in Kansas City when it was snowing outside," says a regional manager during a visit to Southlake, Texas. "The focus was on the metrics below the sales line, but not sales itself." Stores became dirty; employees, surly or scarce. The result: a company that looked better on paper but felt much unhappier in person. And in the retail business, where the customer experience is what matters most, that unhappiness eventually showed up at the cash register.

Why did a hierarchy culture create problems at Home Depot?

SOURCE: Excerpted from J Reingold, "Home Depot's Total Rehab," *Fortune*, September 29, 2009, p 162.

---

hierarchy culture that endorses stability and control along with an internal focus. Why are these contradictions important?

They are important because an organization's success may depend on its ability to possess core values that are associated with competing cultural types. While this is difficult to pull off, it can be done. Consider Toyota, for example. The company is known for its Toyota Production System (TPS) that allows it to produce high-quality, low-cost vehicles while also developing new products quickly. A research study aimed at identifying the sources of TPS's success revealed an organizational culture that accommodates the following contradictions: (1) the company moves slowly, yet makes big innovations such as the Prius; (2) the company's operations are efficient, but decision making is slow due to extensive participation among employees; (3) the company is very hierarchical, yet it encourages employees to challenge and criticize management; and (4) the company pushes employees to communicate in a simple and short fashion, but fosters extensive social networks among employees.[32] The Ritz-Carlton, a high-end luxury hotel, has similarly found a way to overcome competing values associated with clan and market cultures. The company spends 10% of its payroll on employee training and empowers its employees to determine the best way to provide customer service. At the same time, the company is fiercely focused on providing world-class customer service.[33]

go to the Web for the Group Exercise: Assessing the Organizational Culture at Your School

LO.5 Outcomes Associated with Organizational Culture

Both managers and academic researchers believe that organizational culture can be a driver of employee attitudes, performance, and organizational effectiveness. To test this possibility, various measures of organizational culture have been correlated with a variety of individual and organizational outcomes. So what have we learned? A team of researchers recently conducted a meta-analysis to answer this

Table 3–1   *Correlates of Organizational Culture*

ORGANIZATIONAL OUTCOMES	TYPE OF ORGANIZATIONAL CULTURE							
	CLAN		ADHOCRACY		MARKET		HIERARCHY	
	DIRECTION	STRENGTH	DIRECTION	STRENGTH	DIRECTION	STRENGTH	DIRECTION	STRENGTH
Job satisfaction	+	S	+	M	+	M	*	*
Organizational commitment	+	S	+	M	+	M	*	*
Quality of products and services	+	M	+	M	+	M	*	*
Growth in revenue	+	W	+	W	+	M	*	*
Innovation	+	M	+	M	+	S	–	NS
Profit	+	NS	+	W	+	W	–	NS
Customer satisfaction	+	W	*	*	+	M	*	*
Market performance (e.g., market share)	+	W	+	M	+	M	–	NS
Overall subjective performance	+	M	+	M	+	M	–	M

NOTE: For the direction of the relationship, "+" indicates a positive relationship and "–" a negative relationship. For the strength of relationships, "S" indicates a strong relationship, "M" a moderate relationship, "W" a weak relationship, and "NS" a non significant relationship. An asterisk means that there was no data available.

SOURCE: See Chad Hartnell, Yi Ou, and Angelo Kinicki. Under review at the Academy of Management Journal, March 2009. Assessing the Organizational Culture-Organizational Effectiveness Link: A Meta-Analytic Review.

question. Their results were based on 93 studies involving 16,803 companies and 59,467 employees. Table 3–1 summarizes results from this study.[34]

Table 3–1 shows the direction and strength of relationships between nine different organizational outcomes and the four types of culture represented by the CVF. Keep in mind while reading this table that a positive relationship indicates that the two variables move in the same direction. For example, the positive relationship between job satisfaction and clan culture means that employees' job satisfaction goes up as a culture becomes more clannish. The reverse is true for a negative relationship such as the one between innovation and a hierarchy culture. In this case, innovation goes down as a culture becomes more hierarchical.

Table 3–1 reveals that the nine types of organizational outcomes had significant and positive relationships with clan, adhocracy, and market cultures. The majority of these relationships were of moderate strength, indicating that they are important to today's managers. Closer examination of Table 3–1 leads to the following seven conclusions:

1. Organizational culture is clearly related to measures of organizational effectiveness. This reinforces the conclusion that an organization's culture can be a source of competitive advantage.

2. Employees are more satisfied and committed to organizations with clan cultures. These results suggest that employees prefer to work in organizations that value

flexibility over stability and control and those that are more concerned with satisfying employees' needs than customer or shareholder desires.

3. An organization's financial performance (i.e., growth in revenue and profit) is not very strongly related to organizational culture. Managers should not expect to increase financial performance by trying to change their organization's culture.

4. Companies with market cultures tend to have more positive organizational outcomes. Managers are encouraged to consider how they might make their cultures more market oriented.

5. Innovation and quality can be increased by building characteristics associated with clan, adhocracy, and market cultures into the organization.

6. Customer satisfaction is most strongly related to market cultures. This finding implies that it is important for organizations to have an external focus on its customers.

7. Hierarchy cultures are not associated with positive outcomes. Managers are encouraged to monitor the extent to which employees feel under wraps, unempowered, and controlled by management or organizational systems. This conclusion underscores the importance of employee empowerment, which is discussed in Chapter 15.

Researchers also have investigated the importance of organizational culture within the context of a merger. These studies indicated that mergers frequently failed due to incompatible cultures. Due to the increasing number of corporate mergers around the world, and the conclusion that 7 out of 10 mergers and acquisitions failed to meet their financial promise, managers within merged companies would be well advised to consider the role of organizational culture in creating a new organization.[35]

In summary, research underscores the significance of organizational culture. It also reinforces the need to learn more about the process of cultivating and changing an organization's culture. An organization's culture is not determined by fate. It is formed and shaped by the combination and integration of everyone who works in the organization. A change-resistant culture, for instance, can undermine the effectiveness of any type of organizational change. Although it is not an easy task to change an organization's culture, the next section provides a preliminary overview of how to create cultural change.

Vision
Long-term goal describing "what" an organization wants to become.

to the point
What are the specific methods or techniques managers can use to change an organization's culture?

L0.6 The Process of Culture Change

Before describing the specific ways in which managers can change organizational culture, let us review three caveats about culture change. First, it is possible to change an organization's culture, and the process essentially begins with targeting one of the three layers of organizational culture previously discussed—observable artifacts, espoused values, and basic assumptions—for change. Ultimately, culture change involves changing people's minds and their behavior.[36] Second, it is important to consider the extent to which the current culture is aligned with the organization's vision and strategic plan before attempting to change any aspect of organizational culture. A **vision** represents a long-term goal that describes "what" an organization wants to become. For example, Walt Disney's original vision for Disneyland included the following components:

Disneyland will be something of a fair, an exhibition, a playground, a community center, a museum of living facts, and a showplace of beauty and magic. It will be filled with the accomplishments, the joys and hopes of the world we live in. And it will remind and show us how to make those wonders part of our lives.[37]

A **strategic plan** outlines an organization's long-term goals and the actions necessary to achieve these goals. Mark Fields, executive vice president, Ford Motor Company, and president, The Americas, firmly believes that culture, vision, and strategic plans should be aligned. According to Fields, "Culture eats strategy for breakfast. You can have the best plan in the world, and if the culture isn't going to let it happen, it's going to die on the vine."[38]

Finally, it is important to use a structured approach when implementing culture change. Chapter 18 can help you in this regard as it presents several models that provide specific steps to follow when implementing any type of organizational change. Let us now consider the specific methods or techniques that managers can use to change an organization's culture.

Strategic plan
A long-term plan outlining actions needed to achieve desired results.

LO.7 Edgar Schein, a well-known OB scholar, notes that changing organizational culture involves a teaching process. That is, organizational members teach each other about the organization's preferred values, beliefs, norms, expectations, and behaviors. This is accomplished by using one or more of the following mechanisms:[39]

1. *Formal statements of organizational philosophy, mission, vision, values, and materials used for recruiting, selection, and socialization.* Sam Walton, the founder of Wal-Mart, established three basic beliefs or values that represent the core of the organization's culture. They are (1) respect for the individual, (2) service to our customer, and (3) striving for excellence. Further, Nucor Corp. attempts to emphasize the value it places on its people by including the name of all employees, more than 18,000, in its annual report. This practice also reinforces the clan type of culture the company wants to encourage.[40] Would you like to work at Nucor?

2. *The design of physical space, work environments, and buildings.* Intel originally had all its staff work in uniform cubicles, consistent with the value it places on equality. (Top managers don't have reserved parking spaces either.) However, the cubicle arrangement conflicted with another Intel value—innovation—so the company is experimenting with open-seating arrangements combined with small conference rooms. Not only are open-seating arrangements thought to encourage collaboration, they can reduce noise because employees can see when their activities are annoying to other workers. Intel hopes that this environment will better support creative thinking.[41]

3. *Slogans, language, acronyms, and sayings.* For example, Robert Mittelstaedt, dean of the W.P. Carey School of Business at Arizona State University, promotes his vision of having one of the best business schools in the world through the slogan "Top-of-mind business school." Employees are encouraged to engage in activities that promote the quality and reputation of the school's academic programs.

4. *Deliberate role modeling, training programs, teaching, and coaching by managers and supervisors.* Fluor Corporation, one of the leading design, engineering, and contracting firms in the world, desires an ethical culture that fights corruption within the construction industry. The company, which derives more than

half of its $17 billion in revenues overseas, puts all its employees through online anticorruption training sessions and teaches specialized workers, such as field operators, in person. Executives promote an open-door policy and a hotline for reporting crimes—as well as tough penalties for violators, who receive zero tolerance for infractions.[42]

5. *Explicit rewards, status symbols (e.g., titles), and promotion criteria.* At Triage Consulting Group, employees at the same level of their career earn the same pay, but employees are eligible for merit bonuses, reinforcing the culture of achievement. The merit bonuses are partly based on coworkers' votes for who contributed most to the company's success, and the employees who received the most votes are recognized each year at the company's "State of Triage" meeting.[43]

6. *Stories, legends, or myths about key people and events.* Time is a highly valued resource at The Associates, a financial services firm. To reinforce the importance of not wasting time, many stories circulate about senior managers missing planes or being locked out of meetings because they were late.[44] Managers can develop and tell motivating stories by noticing relevant actions and tying them to values. Good stories also can come from listening to customers. It is important when telling stories that you are factual and authentic because someone may check out the story.[45]

7. *The organizational activities, processes, or outcomes that leaders pay attention to, measure, and control.* When Ron Sargent took over as chief executive of Staples, he wanted to increase the focus on customer service. He started by investigating what values the office supply retailer's employees already held, and they told him they cared about helping others. Sargent used that value as the basis for developing their skill in serving customers. Staples began teaching employees more about the products they sell and now offers bonuses for team performance. Sargent also pays frequent visits to stores so he can talk directly to employees about what customers like and dislike.[46]

8. *Leader reactions to critical incidents and organizational crises.* Consider the cultural messages sent by Jerry Lukens, a supervisor at Lincoln Industries: Lincoln is the leading supplier of products that need high-performance metal finishing. Jerry received a phone call at 2:00 a.m. from Pella Corp., one of Lincoln's customers. Pella, which is a window and door manufacturer, did not have enough patio door hinges to complete a job. Lukens loaded up his car in Lincoln, Nebraska, and headed toward Pella, Iowa, which was 230 miles away. He reached Pella's loading dock by 6:00 a.m. and was able to deliver the hinges needed to complete the job.[47] It is no wonder that Lincoln Industries is known for providing outstanding customer service.

9. *The workflow and organizational structure.* Hierarchical structures are more likely to embed an orientation toward control and authority than a flatter organization. Results shown in Table 3–1 further showed that hierarchical cultures tended to be associated with lower overall subjective performance. This partly explains why leaders from many organizations are increasingly reducing the number of organizational layers in an attempt to empower employees (see Chapter 17) and increase employee involvement. Toyota represents a case in point. Akio Toyoda, the company's new president, has decided to change the organizational culture and structure in an attempt to manage Toyota's first annual operating loss in 70 years (see the Real World/Real People feature on page 79).[48]

Toyota Plans to Restructure in Order to Change Its Culture

Mr. Toyoda is expected to try to implement changes quickly, including a transformation of Toyota's corporate culture. According to individuals familiar with the situation, Mr. Toyoda believes Toyota, long known for its cautious management, has become even more conservative and bureaucratic in recent years and needs a new structure to speed up decision making.

These people said Mr. Toyoda may try, among other things, to streamline Toyota's management ranks, which he believes have become bloated. He may also try to shake up the company's current top management, they said, possibly bringing in talent from outside the

company. That could include bringing in former Toyota executives who left to manage Toyota affiliates in recent years. . . .

One of Mr. Toyoda's biggest challenges will be to persuade some reluctant Toyota employees to follow his lead.

Which of the mechanisms for changing culture are being used by Mr. Toyoda?

SOURCE: Excerpted from N Shirouzu, "Toyota, Needing Change, Taps a Scion to Lead," *The Wall Street Journal,* January 12, 2009, p B2.

---

10. *Organizational systems and procedures.* Companies are increasingly using electronic networks to enhance collaboration among employees in order to achieve innovation, quality, and efficiency. For example, Serena Software Inc., a California-based company with 800 employees located in 29 offices across 14 countries, encouraged its employees to sign up for Facebook for free, and to use the network as a vehicle for getting to know each other. In contrast to using a public site for networking, Dow Chemical launched its own internal social network in order to create relationships between current, past, and temporary employees.[49]

11. *Organizational goals and the associated criteria used for recruitment, selection, development, promotion, layoffs, and retirement of people.* Aflac, for example, has spent considerable time establishing performance expectations for its employees in pursuit of a market-based culture that focuses on customer service.

> Aflac has embarked on a process to quantify service expectations for all positions, and Sharon Douglas, vice president and chief people officer, has been integrally involved in this process. . . . The process involved focus groups and quantitative studies involving customers, staff and managers. . . . Douglas stresses that expectations should be specific and explicitly stated, not assumed. For example, at Aflac there is an expectation that when employees field a phone call that is not directly related to their area of expertise, they will not transfer the call. "We expect them to take in all of the information and then go back to find the proper response," Douglas says.[50]

Organizational socialization

Process by which employees learn an organization's values, norms, and required behaviors.

The Organizational Socialization Process

Organizational socialization is defined as "the process by which a person learns the values, norms, and required behaviors which permit him to participate as a member of the organization."[51] As previously discussed, organizational socialization is a key mechanism used by organizations to embed their organizational cultures. In short, organizational socialization turns outsiders into fully functioning insiders

to the point

How can the practical lessons of socialization research be integrated within the three phases of socialization?

by promoting and reinforcing the organization's core values and beliefs. This section introduces a three-phase model of organizational socialization and examines the practical application of socialization research.

LO.8 A Three-Phase Model of Organizational Socialization

© 2003 Ted Goff

"We're in awe of your ability to fit in here, Ms. Stoughton."

Ted Goff. Reprinted by permission.

One's first year in a complex organization can be confusing. There is a constant swirl of new faces, strange jargon, conflicting expectations, and apparently unrelated events. Some organizations treat new members in a rather haphazard, sink-or-swim manner. More typically, though, the socialization process is characterized by a sequence of identifiable steps.

Organizational behavior researcher Daniel Feldman has proposed a three-phase model of organizational socialization that promotes deeper understanding of this important process. As illustrated in Figure 3–4, the three phases are (1) anticipatory socialization, (2) encounter, and (3) change and acquisition. Each phase has its associated perceptual and social processes. Feldman's model also specifies behavioral and affective outcomes that can be used to judge how well an individual has been socialized. The entire three-phase sequence may take from a few weeks to a year to complete, depending on individual differences and the complexity of the situation.

Anticipatory socialization phase

Occurs before an individual joins an organization, and involves the information people learn about different careers, occupations, professions, and organizations.

Phase 1: Anticipatory Socialization   The **anticipatory socialization phase** occurs before an individual actually joins an organization. It is represented by the information people have learned about different careers, occupations, professions, and organizations. For example, anticipatory socialization partially explains the different perceptions you might have about working for the US government versus a high-technology company like Intel or Microsoft. Anticipatory socialization information comes from many sources. An organization's current employees are a powerful source of anticipatory socialization. The recruiting or wooing of parents is another anticipatory socialization technique used by a variety of companies. Ogilvy Public Relations, Office Depot Inc., Enterprise Rent-A-Car, Capital One, and Northwestern Mutual Life Insurance all include parents in the recruiting process. These firms find that parental involvement is particularly helpful when trying to recruit Millennials; remember our discussion in Chapter 2.[52]

Unrealistic expectations about the nature of the work, pay, and promotions are often formulated during phase 1. Because employees with unrealistic expectations are more likely to quit their jobs in the future, organizations may want to use realistic job previews.[53] A **realistic job preview** (RJP) involves giving recruits a realistic idea of what lies ahead by presenting both positive and negative aspects of the job. Whirlpool, for example, uses its career Web site to post candid comments from employees about what it is like to work at the company.[54] RJPs may be electronic, verbal, in booklet form, audiovisual, or hands-on. Research supports the practical benefits of using RJPs. A meta-analysis of 40 studies revealed that RJPs were related to higher performance and to lower attrition from the recruitment process.

Realistic job preview

Presents both positive and negative aspects of a job.

Figure 3–4   *A Model of Organizational Socialization*

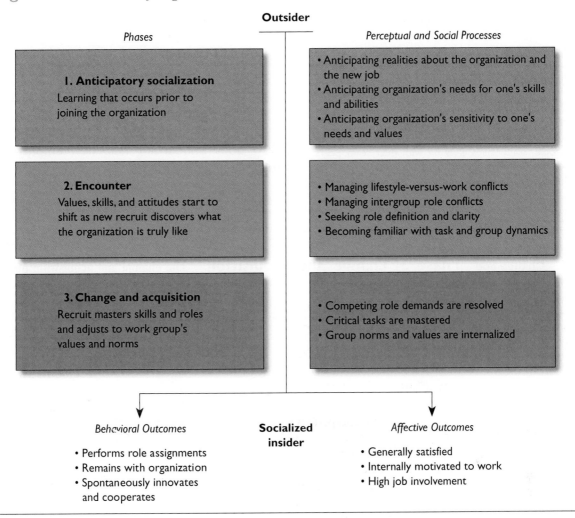

SOURCE: Adapted from material in D C Feldman, "The Multiple Socialization of Organization Members," *Academy of Management Review*, April 1981, pp 309–18. Copyright © 1981 by The Academy of Management. Reproduced by permission of The Academy of Management via Copyright Clearance Center.

Results also demonstrated that RJPs lowered job applicants' initial expectations and led to lower turnover among those applicants who were hired.[55]

Phase 2: Encounter   This second phase begins when the employment contract has been signed. During the **encounter phase** employees come to learn what the organization is really like. It is a time for reconciling unmet expectations and making sense of a new work environment. Many companies use a combination of orientation and training programs to socialize employees during the encounter phase. Onboarding is one such technique. **Onboarding** programs help employees to integrate, assimilate, and transition to new jobs by making them familiar with corporate policies, procedures, culture, and politics and by clarifying work role expectations and responsibilities.[56] The Real World/Real People box on page 82 illustrates how Herbalife International is successfully using onboarding to retain and enhance the productivity of newly hired executives.

Encounter phase

Employees learn what the organization is really like and reconcile unmet expectations.

Onboarding

Programs aimed at helping employees integrate, assimilate, and transition to new jobs.

Herbalife International Effectively Uses Onboarding with Executives

Eighteen months ago, Michele Crocker, vice president of worldwide distributor optimization for Herbalife International, established an executive onboarding program called "The First 100 Days Hit the Ground Running Work Plan." . . . The program takes a structured approach focused on three vital areas.

"The first one is ensuring that they establish solid people relationships early on with their team, peers, key internal and external customers, and any global business partners," says Crocker. "We also put a lot of emphasis up front on understanding the philosophy, the culture, and how we operate as a company. The other

area we look at is operational: how the functions work and the executive's role in Herbalife's success." . . .

Every 30 to 45 days during the program, Herbalife also conducts a progress check with the new executive and some of his or her teammates.

How does onboarding help new employees adjust to a new job?

SOURCE: Excerpted from S Fall, "The Executive Entrance," *Training*, August 2008, p 47.

Change and acquisition phase

Requires employees to master tasks and roles and to adjust to work group values and norms.

Phase 3: Change and Acquisition   The **change and acquisition phase** requires employees to master important tasks and roles and to adjust to their work group's values and norms. To achieve that adjustment, employees should be clear about their roles, feel confident they can do what is expected of them, and have the acceptance of their coworkers. Additionally, organizations such as Schlumberger, a large multinational oil company, use incentives and social gatherings to reinforce the new behaviors expected of employees.

> The company is gradually changing its old Soviet culture of blame. Luc Ollivier, a 50-year-old Frenchman, was installed as the boss of regional operations Siberian Geophysical. He's trying to reward performance and, more critical, systematically eliminate mistakes rather than simply punish the people who make them. Ollivier says the company's veteran drillers have immense experience, "but they don't like to teach the young people." So he is working to forge better ties through daylong get-togethers that conclude with a beer bash. Ollivier says the pace of work is up by more than 30% in the past two years, and Siberian Geophysical's drilling revenues reached about $250 million last year [2007], about double their level in 2006.[57]

Table 3–2 presents a list of socialization processes or tactics used by organizations to help employees through this adjustment process. Returning to Table 3–2, can you identify the socialization tactics used by Schlumberger?

go to the Web for the Self-Exercise: Have You Been Adequately Socialized?

Practical Application of Socialization Research

Past research suggests six practical guidelines for managing organizational socialization.

I. A recent survey showed that effective onboarding programs resulted in increased retention, productivity, and rates of task completion for new hires.[58] This reinforces the conclusion that managers should avoid a haphazard, sink-or-swim

LO.9 Table 3–2   *Socialization Tactics*

TACTIC	DESCRIPTION
Collective vs. individual	Collective socialization consists of grouping newcomers and exposing them to a common set of experiences rather than treating each newcomer individually and exposing him or her to more or less unique experiences.
Formal vs. informal	Formal socialization is the practice of segregating a newcomer from regular organization members during a defined socialization period versus not clearly distinguishing a newcomer from more experienced members. Army recruits must attend boot camp before they are allowed to work alongside established soldiers.
Sequential vs. random	Sequential socialization refers to a fixed progression of steps that culminate in the new role, compared to an ambiguous or dynamic progression. The socialization of doctors involves a lock-step sequence from medical school, to internship, to residency before they are allowed to practice on their own.
Fixed vs. variable	Fixed socialization provides a timetable for the assumption of the role, whereas a variable process does not. American university students typically spend one year apiece as freshmen, sophomores, juniors, and seniors.
Serial vs. disjunctive	A serial process is one in which the newcomer is socialized by an experienced member, whereas a disjunctive process does not use a role model.
Investiture vs. divestiture	Investiture refers to the affirmation of a newcomer's incoming global and specific role identities and attributes. Divestiture is the denial and stripping away of the newcomer's existing sense of self and the reconstruction of self in the organization's image. During police training, cadets are required to wear uniforms and maintain an immaculate appearance; they are addressed as "officer" and told they are no longer ordinary citizens but representatives of the police force.

SOURCE: Descriptions were taken from B E Ashforth, *Role Transitions in Organizational Life: An Identity-Based Perspective* (Mahwah, NJ: Lawrence Erlbaum Associates, 2001), pp 149–83.

approach to organizational socialization because formalized socialization tactics positively affect new hires. Formalized or institutionalized socialization tactics were found to positively help employees in both domestic and international operations.[59]

2. Organizations like the United States Military Academy at West Point use socialization tactics to reinforce a culture that promotes ethical behavior. Managers are encouraged to consider how they might best set expectations regarding ethical behavior during all three phases of the socialization process.[60]

3. The type of orientation program used to socialize employees affects their expectations and behavior. A recent study of 72 new Asian international graduate students revealed that they had more accurate expectations, felt less stress, reported better adjustment, and had higher retention rates when the orientation program focused on coping with new entry stress.[61] Managers need to help new

hires integrate within the organizational culture and overcome the stress associated with working in a new environment. Consider the approach used by John Chambers, CEO of Cisco Systems: "He meets with groups of new hires to welcome them soon after they start, and at monthly breakfast meetings workers are encouraged to ask him tough questions.[62]

4. Support for stage models is mixed. Although there are different stages of socialization, they are not identical in order, length, or content for all people or jobs.[63] Managers are advised to use a contingency approach toward organizational socialization. In other words, different techniques are appropriate for different people at different times.

5. The organization can benefit by training new employees to use proactive socialization behaviors. A study of 154 entry-level professionals showed that effectively using proactive socialization behaviors influenced the newcomers' general anxiety and stress during the first month of employment and their motivation and anxiety six months later.[64]

6. Managers should pay attention to the socialization of diverse employees. Research demonstrated that diverse employees, particularly those with disabilities, experienced different socialization activities than other newcomers. In turn, these different experiences affected their long-term success and job satisfaction.[65]

Mentoring
Process of forming and maintaining developmental relationships between a mentor and a junior person.

to the point
What are the four developmental networks and how can you use them to advance your career?

Embedding Organizational Culture through Mentoring

The modern word *mentor* derives from Mentor, the name of a wise and trusted counselor in Greek mythology. Terms typically used in connection with mentoring are *teacher, coach, sponsor,* and *peer*. **Mentoring** is defined as the process of forming and maintaining intensive and lasting developmental relationships between a variety of developers (i.e., people who provide career and psychosocial support) and a junior person (the protégé, if male; or protégée, if female).[66] Mentoring can serve to embed an organization's culture when developers and the protégé/protégée work in the same organization for two reasons. First, mentoring contributes to creating a sense of oneness by promoting the acceptance of the organization's core values throughout the organization. Second, the socialization aspect of mentoring also promotes a sense of membership.

Not only is mentoring important as a tactic for embedding organizational culture, but research suggests it can significantly influence the protégé/protégée's

In today's high-technology work environments, helping or coaching others on the use of computer programs is a key function of mentoring. This type of mentoring is important in embedding an organization's culture because it contributes to a sense of oneness and it enhances employees' feelings of competence. Have you ever been mentored?

future career. For example, a meta-analysis revealed that mentored employees had higher compensation and more promotions than nonmentored employees. Mentored employees also were found to have higher organizational knowledge, job performance, and salary over time.[67] This section focuses on how people can use mentoring to their advantage. We discuss the functions of mentoring, the developmental networks underlying mentoring, and the personal and organizational implications of mentoring.

Functions of Mentoring

Kathy Kram, a Boston University researcher, conducted in-depth interviews with both members of 18 pairs of senior and junior managers. As a by-product of this study, Kram identified two general functions—career and psychosocial—of the mentoring process. Five *career functions* that enhanced career development were sponsorship, exposure-and-visibility, coaching, protection, and challenging assignments. Four *psychosocial functions* were role modeling, acceptance-and-confirmation, counseling, and friendship. The psychosocial functions clarified the participants' identities and enhanced their feelings of competence.[68]

LO.10 Developmental Networks Underlying Mentoring

Historically, it was thought that mentoring was primarily provided by one person who was called a mentor. Today, however, the changing nature of technology, organizational structures, and marketplace dynamics requires that people seek career information and support from many sources. Mentoring is currently viewed as a process in which protégés and protégées seek developmental guidance from a network of people, who are referred to as *developers*. McKinsey & Company tells its associates, "Build your own McKinsey." This slogan means the consulting firm expects its people to identify partners, colleagues, and subordinates who have related goals and interests so that they can help one another develop their expertise. Each McKinsey associate is thus responsible for his or her own career development—and for mentoring others. As McKinsey's approach recognizes, the diversity and strength of a person's network of relationships is instrumental in obtaining the type of career assistance needed to manage his or her career.[69] Figure 3–5 presents a developmental network typology based on integrating the diversity and strength of developmental relationships.[70]

The **diversity of developmental relationships** reflects the variety of people within the network an individual uses for developmental assistance. There are two subcomponents associated with network diversity: (1) the number of different people the person is networked with and (2) the various social systems from which the networked relationships stem (e.g., employer, school, family, community, professional associations, and religious affiliations). As shown in Figure 3–5, developmental relationship diversity ranges from low (few people or social systems) to high (multiple people or social systems).

Developmental relationship strength reflects the quality of relationships among the individual and those involved in his or her developmental network. For

Diversity of developmental relationships

The variety of people in a network used for developmental assistance.

Developmental relationship strength

The quality of relationships among people in a network.

Figure 3–5   *Developmental Networks Associated with Mentoring*

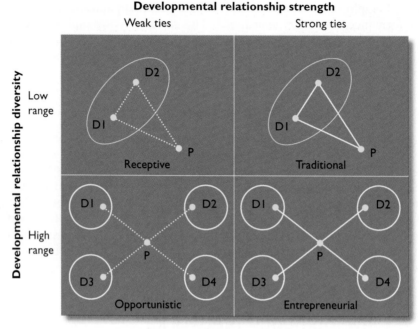

Key: D, developer; P, protégé

SOURCE: From M Higgins and K Kram, "Reconceptualizing Mentoring at Work: A Developmental Network Perspective," *Academy of Management Review*, April 2001, p 270. Copyright © 2001 by The Academy of Management. Reproduced by permission of The Academy of Management via Copyright Clearance Center.

example, strong ties are reflective of relationships based on frequent interactions, reciprocity, and positive affect. Weak ties, in contrast, are based more on superficial relationships. Together, the diversity and strength of developmental relationships result in four types of developmental networks (see Figure 3–5): receptive, traditional, entrepreneurial, and opportunistic.

A *receptive* developmental network is composed of a few weak ties from one social system such as an employer or a professional association. The single oval around D1 and D2 in Figure 3–5 is indicative of two developers who come from one social system. In contrast, a *traditional* network contains a few strong ties between an employee and developers that all come from one social system. An entrepreneurial network, which is the strongest type of developmental network, is made up of strong ties among several developers (D1–D4) who come from four different social systems. Finally, an opportunistic network is associated with having weak ties with multiple developers from different social systems.

Personal and Organizational Implications

There are five key personal implications to consider. First, it is important to foster a broad developmental network because the number and quality of your contacts will influence your career success. This is particularly true in today's economy.[71]

Second, job and career satisfaction are likely to be influenced by the consistency between an individual's career goals and the type of developmental network at his or her disposal. For example, people with an entrepreneurial developmental network are more likely to experience change in their careers and to benefit from personal learning than people with receptive, traditional, and opportunistic networks. If this sounds attractive to you, you should try to increase the diversity and strength of your developmental relationships. In contrast, lower levels of job satisfaction are expected when employees have receptive developmental networks and they desire to experience career advancement in multiple organizations. Receptive developmental networks, however, can be satisfying to someone who does not desire to be promoted up the career ladder.[72] Third, a developer's willingness to provide career and psychosocial assistance is a function of the protégé/protégée's ability and potential and the quality of the interpersonal relationship.[73] This implies that you must take ownership for enhancing your skills, abilities, and developmental networks if you desire to experience career advancement throughout your life.

Fourth, it is important to become proficient at using social networking tools such as Twitter, LinkedIn.com, and Facebook. These tools not only enable you to increase the breadth of your social network, but they also can increase your productivity. A recent study demonstrated that people with the broadest digital networks were 7% more productive than employees without such networks.[74] Fifth, develop a mentoring plan. Experts suggest that this plan should include the following components:[75]

- Identify and prioritize your mentoring goals. These goals should be based on a determination of what you want to learn.

- Identify people who are skilled or experienced in areas you want to improve. Don't overlook your peers as they are a good source of functional, technical, and organizational knowledge.[76]

- Determine how best to build a relationship with these "targeted" individuals.

- Determine how you can provide value to your mentor. Because mentoring is a two-way street, others are more likely to help you if they see some value in assisting you in the pursuit of your career goals.

- Determine when it is time to move on. Mentors are not forever. If you believe that your mentor is ineffective, or worse yet, causing more harm than benefit, find a new mentor. Finally, although mentoring can help your career, and some mediocre people advance because of a strong mentor, don't be fooled into thinking that "who you know" is a replacement for talent, knowledge, and motivation. We strongly encourage you to use your own passion, motivation, talents, and networking skills to accomplish your personal and professional goals.

Research also supports the organizational benefits of mentoring. For example, mentoring enhances the effectiveness of organizational communication. Specifically, mentoring increases the amount of vertical communication both up and down an organization, and it provides a mechanism for modifying or reinforcing organizational culture. Benefits such as these are leading more and more companies to set up formal mentoring programs. A recent survey found that 6 out of 10 companies already have programs for coaching or mentoring, and of the remaining companies, 8 out of 10 are planning such a program.[77]

Summary of Key Concepts

1. *Define organizational culture and discuss its three layers.* Organizational culture represents the shared assumptions that a group holds. It influences employees' perceptions and behavior at work. The three layers of organizational culture include observable artifacts, espoused values, and basic assumptions. Artifacts are the physical manifestations of an organization's culture. Espoused values represent the explicitly stated values and norms that are preferred by an organization. Basic underlying assumptions are unobservable and represent the core of organizational culture.

2. *Discuss the difference between espoused and enacted values.* Espoused values represent the explicitly stated values and norms that are preferred by an organization. Enacted values, in contrast, reflect the values and norms that actually are exhibited or converted into employee behavior. Employees become cynical when management espouses one set of values and norms and then behaves in an inconsistent fashion.

3. *Describe the four functions of organizational culture.* Four functions of organizational culture are organizational identity, collective commitment, social system stability, and sense-making device.

4. *Discuss the four types of organizational culture associated with the competing values framework.* The competing values framework identifies four different types of organizational culture. A clan culture has an internal focus and values flexibility rather than stability and control. An adhocracy culture has an external focus and values flexibility. A market culture has a strong external focus and values stability and control. A hierarchy culture has an internal focus and values stability and control over flexibility.

5. *Summarize the seven conclusions derived from research about the outcomes associated with organizational culture.* Organizational culture is related to measures of organizational effectiveness. Employees are more satisfied and committed to organizations with clan cultures. An organization's financial performance is not very strongly related to organizational culture. Companies with market cultures tend to have more positive organizational outcomes. Innovation and quality can be increased by building characteristics associated with clan, adhocracy, and market cultures into the organization. Customer satisfaction is most strongly related to market cultures. Hierarchy cultures are not associated with positive outcomes.

6. *Review the three caveats about culture change.* First, it is possible to change an organization's culture, and the process essentially begins with targeting one of the three layers of culture for change. Second, it is important to consider the extent to which the current culture is aligned with the organization's vision and strategic plans before attempting to change any aspect of organizational culture. Finally, it is important to use a structured approach when implementing culture change.

7. *Summarize the methods used by organizations to change organizational culture.* Changing culture amounts to teaching employees about the organization's preferred values, beliefs, expectations, and behaviors. This is accomplished by using one or more of the following 11 mechanisms: (*a*) formal statements of organizational philosophy, mission, vision, values, and materials used for recruiting, selection, and socialization; (*b*) the design of physical space, work environments, and buildings; (*c*) slogans, language, acronyms, and sayings; (*d*) deliberate role modeling, training programs, teaching, and coaching by managers and supervisors; (*e*) explicit rewards, status symbols, and promotion criteria; (*f*) stories, legends, and myths about key people and events; (*g*) the organizational activities, processes, or outcomes that leaders pay attention to, measure, and control; (*h*) leader reactions to critical incidents and organizational crises; (*i*) the workflow and organizational structure; (*j*) organizational systems and procedures; and (*k*) organizational goals and associated criteria used for recruitment, selection, development, promotion, layoffs, and retirement of people.

8. *Describe the three phases in Feldman's model of organizational socialization.* The three phases of Feldman's model are anticipatory socialization, encounter, and change and acquisition. Anticipatory socialization begins before an individual actually joins the organization. The encounter phase begins when the employment contract has been signed. Phase 3 involves the period in which employees master important tasks and resolve any role conflicts.

9. *Discuss the various socialization tactics used to socialize employees.* There are six key socialization tactics. They are collective versus individual, formal versus informal, sequential versus random, fixed versus variable, serial versus disjunctive, and investiture versus divestiture (see Table 3–2). Each tactic provides organizations with two opposing options for socializing employees.

10. *Explain the four developmental networks associated with mentoring.* The four developmental networks are based on integrating the diversity and strength of an individual's developmental relationships. The

four resulting developmental networks are receptive, traditional, entrepreneurial, and opportunistic. A receptive network is composed of a few weak ties from one social system. Having a few strong ties with developers from one social system is referred to as a traditional network. An entrepreneurial network is made up of strong ties among several developers; and an opportunistic network is associated with having weak ties from different social systems.

Key Terms

OB in Action Case Study

Cisco Systems Uses Its Culture for Competitive Advantage[78]

Manny Rivelo, a senior vice president at Cisco Systems, belongs to more internal company teams than he can count on both hands. "I'm on a litany of them—three councils, maybe six boards, and five working groups," he says.

They're part of an organizational web dreamed up by CEO John Chambers—a structure so complex that it takes 15 minutes and a whiteboard to fully explain. Chambers, however, uses just three words to describe the benefits of the San Jose networking giant's management system: "speed, skill, and flexibility."

It seems paradoxical that a multilayered organizational model would actually speed things up. But Chambers, whose company landed on the World's Most Admired Companies list partly for its management prowess, says his system of boards and councils has indeed made Cisco (CSCO, *Fortune* 500) more agile—and that it will help the company grow in the recession.

Chambers' idea originated at the tail end of the 2001 downturn, after Cisco wrote off $2.2 billion in losses. He realized that the company's hierarchical structure precluded it from moving quickly into new markets, so he began to group executives into cross-functional teams.

Chambers figured that putting together managers in sales and leaders in engineering, say, would break down traditional silos and lead to faster decision making.

Not all Cisco executives felt the same way. "It took seven years, and the first three years were bumpy," says Rivelo. Chambers has said that as many as 20% of Cisco's executives couldn't handle working with unfamiliar colleagues; some were irked by the new compensation structure, which is tied to teamwork.

Rivelo is part of a nine-person council that the company created to replace its chief development officer, who departed in December 2007. Some 70% of Rivelo's compensation is based on the council's ability to meet revenue targets and collaborate.

As Cisco has entered new lines of business (the router company now makes thousands of products, including high-end teleconferencing systems and cable boxes), its teams and councils have multiplied. Today there are at least 10 boards and more than 30 councils, says Rivelo, who admits that he doesn't know the exact number.

The total is hard to pin down because it's constantly evolving. Padmasree Warrior, Cisco's new chief technology officer, belongs to the enterprise council—teams at that level target $10 billion-plus market opportunities. She recently saw a chance to deliver services over the Internet and formed a smaller working group to research the idea. Four months later that group evolved into a board, which is a subset of a council.

Although the system has been in place for years, its success is difficult to quantify. Cisco says the team approach helped it figure out in only eight days that it should acquire Web-conferencing company WebEx, for example. But Yankee Group analyst Zeus Kerravala says he's still waiting for productivity metric. "Nothing will show success more than proof," he says.

Technology chief Warrior says that she was skeptical when she first came to Cisco in March from Motorola (MOT, *Fortune* 500). But she became a believer when she and others from different divisions forged a partnership with an outside company in a single council meeting. What would have required multiple meetings at other firms "took the four of us on a phone call," she says.

Such quick decision making could help Cisco execute some key acquisitions in the current slowdown. For many big companies, belt-tightening usually means putting off big decisions until conditions improve.

Cisco, with $26 billion in cash, has the coffers—and apparently the management structure—to immediately start shopping.

Questions for Discussion

1. What are the observable artifacts, espoused values, and basic assumptions associated with Cisco's culture? Explain.
2. Use the competing values framework to diagnose Cisco's culture. To what extent does it possess characteristics associated with clan, adhocracy, market, and hierarchy cultures? Discuss.
3. Begin by looking up Cisco's mission or vision statement on the company's Web site. Now answer the following question: To what extent is the culture type you identified in question 2 consistent with the accomplishment of this mission or vision? Explain.
4. What techniques for changing organizational culture has Cisco used to form its culture? Discuss.
5. Would you like to work at Cisco? Explain your rationale.

Ethical Dilemma

Credit-Card Issuers Have Cultures That Focus on Growth by Targeting Financially Strapped People[79]

The troubles sound familiar. Borrowers falling behind on their payments. Defaults rising. Huge swaths of loans souring. Investors getting burned. But forget the now-familiar tales of mortgages gone bad. The next horror for beaten-down financial firms is the $950 billion worth of outstanding credit-card debt—much of it toxic. . . . The consumer debt bomb is already beginning to spray shrapnel throughout the financial markets, further weakening the U.S. economy. "The next meltdown will be in credit cards," says Gregory Larkin, senior analyst at research firm Innovest Strategic Value Advisors. . . .

But some banks and credit-card companies may be exacerbating their problems. To boost profits and get ahead of coming regulation, they're hiking interest rates. But that's making it harder for consumers to keep up. . . . Sure the credit-card market is just a fraction of the $11.9 trillion mortgage market. But sometimes the losses can be more painful. That's because most credit-card debt is unsecured, meaning consumers don't have to make down payments when opening up their accounts. If they stop making monthly payments and the account goes bad, there are no underlying assets for

credit-card companies to recoup. With mortgages, in contrast, some banks are protected both by down payments and by the ability to recover at least some of the money by selling the property. . . .

The industry's practices during the lending boom are coming back to haunt many credit-card lenders now. Cate Colombo, a former call center staffer at MBNA, the big issuer bought by Bank of America in 2005, says her job was to develop a rapport with credit-card customers and advise them to use more of their available credit. Colleagues would often gather around her chair when she was on the phone with a customer and chant: "Sell, sell." "It was like *Boiler Room*," says Colombo, referring to the 2000 movie about unscrupulous stock brokers. "I knew that they would probably be in debt for the rest of their lives." Unless, of course, they default.

Assume that you are member of Congress. What would you do in light of the facts in this case?

1. Create legislation that does not allow credit-card issuers to raise interest rates for those who cannot pay their bills.

2. Create legislation that makes it a crime for people like Cate Columbo to entice people to spend money on a credit card when they can't afford it.
3. I would not create any legislation. Credit-card issuers and people like Cate Columbo are not to blame for our financial problems. People must be responsible for their own behavior.
4. Invent other options.

Web Resources

Additional tools and resources are available to help you master the content of this chapter on the Web site at www.mhhe.com/kreitner

Chapter 4

International OB: Managing across Cultures

LEARNING OBJECTIVES

When you finish studying the material in this chapter, you should be able to:

LO.1 Define the term *culture,* and explain how societal culture and organizational culture combine to influence on-the-job behavior.

LO.2 Define *ethnocentrism,* and explain how to develop cultural intelligence.

LO.3 Distinguish between high-context and low-context cultures and identify and describe the nine cultural dimensions from Project GLOBE.

LO.4 Distinguish between individualistic and collectivist cultures, and explain the difference between monochronic and polychronic cultures.

LO.5 Specify the practical lesson from the Hofstede cross-cultural study.

LO.6 Explain what Project GLOBE researchers discovered about leadership.

LO.7 Explain why U.S. managers have a comparatively high failure rate on foreign assignments.

LO.8 Summarize the research findings about North American women on foreign assignments.

LO.9 Identify four stages of the foreign assignment cycle and the OB trouble spot associated with each stage.

Student Resources for Studying Chapter 4

The Web site for your text includes resources that will help you master the concepts in this chapter. As you read, you'll want to visit the site for these helpful tools:

- Your online Study Guide includes learning objectives, a chapter summary, a glossary of key terms, and discussion questions.
- Take a practice quiz and test your knowledge!
- Scroll through a PowerPoint presentation with key concepts for this chapter.

Your instructor might also direct you to the Web site for these exercises:

- Self-assessments that correspond with the chapter content and a Group Exercise.
- You'll also find Video Cases and Internet Exercises for this chapter online.

www.mhhe.com/kreitner

In the business world, to "table something" means that it will be discussed later, right? Not always. In some European cultures, to table something means that it will be put on the table and discussed now.

This particular contradiction often leads to a stalemate during team meetings as one group tries to move to the next agenda item while another group tries to discuss the "tabled" item. These types of misunderstandings have become common in multicultural teams. In fact, communication is the No. 1 issue facing multicultural teams.

With the U.S. population becoming increasingly diverse, odds are high that employees are or soon will be working on multicultural teams. Yet many corporate leaders mistakenly assume that efficient operation of multicultural teams based in the United States will not be an issue because they are not working globally. Hence, teamwork training typically doesn't cover issues relating to operation of multicultural teams, even as the United States continues to evolve into one of the world's most multicultural societies.

Multicultural teams may have members in other countries or may consist only of Americans with different ethnic, racial, and national origins. They can all be U.S. residents or U.S. citizens and still hail from different parts of the world. For example, one

defense company has a U.S.-based team of 20 with origins in 14 countries, all doing classified work.

And, in fact, a multicultural team of members from different parts of the United States still faces issues of communication, working styles, and leadership similar to those faced by multinational teams. Members from New York may function very differently from members from the Midwest or the South, with marked distinctions in matters such as business etiquette and attire.

Sharon Powell, learning and development manager for Parker Hannifin Corp., a provider of motion and control technologies in Cleveland, says, "We need to

think about culture in a different way. It is not just the country you come from but also from what part of the country you come from. What is your value system? What is your communication style? What is important to you?"[1]

FOR DISCUSSION

How comfortable and effective are you in dealing with people from other cultural backgrounds?

We hear a lot about globalization and the global economy these days. Signs and symptoms of economic globalization making headlines in recent years have been the controversial North American Free Trade Agreement, riots at World Trade Organization meetings, complaints about the offshoring of jobs, trade imbalances, foreign sweatshops, and intellectual property abuses.[2] These are legitimate concerns, but some have been exaggerated out of proportion as circumstances evolve. For instance, take the offshoring of jobs—replacing domestic employees with lower-paid workers in foreign countries. According to a recent research report, "About half of offshore service work arrangements fail, and often it's because executives don't take into account the 'invisible costs' of communication and cultural friction."[3] Rising wages in India, China, and elsewhere also are making offshoring less attractive.[4] Still, a global economic earthquake is underway:

> For more than half a century, Americans could take for granted that the world economy would orbit around them. No longer. . . .
>
> "The change is from globalization going one way to globalization going every way. It's as much about what developing countries are doing as developed countries," said Mark Foster, a London-based Accenture consultant.
>
> Assuming continued economic growth in the developing world, the ranks of the global middle class are expected to triple by 2030 to 1.2 billion, according to the World Bank. Today, a bit more than half of that free-spending group resides in developing countries. By 2030, almost all of it, 92%, will call the developing world home.
>
> For multinational corporations, that means paying ever more attention to what's happening outside the United States and especially in Asia, Latin America, parts of the Middle East and Africa.[5]

Global managers, who can move comfortably from one culture to another while conducting business, have an advantage in the new global economy. Consider, for example, the story of Google's Ken Tokusei.

> The job of overseeing Google's mobile lab in Japan falls to Tokusei. Born and raised in Tokyo, he moved to Boston in the mid-1980s while still in high school because he felt he "had no future in Japan." After undergraduate studies at Cornell, Tokusei got a master's in computer science from Stanford, then worked at several Silicon Valley tech startups. Five years ago, he landed a job with Google. The 39-year-old speaks at a machine-gun pace, switching effortlessly between Japanese and English, and shuttles between Google headquarters in Mountain View, Calif., and Asia about 20 times a year.[6]

Indeed, according to one study, US multinational companies headed by CEOs with international assignments on their résumés tended to outperform the competition.[7] Even managers and employees who stay in their native country, as discussed in the opening vignette, will find it hard to escape today's global economy and cross-cultural interactions. This is particularly true in countries such as the United States and Canada, culturally diverse nations populated by both indigenous people and generations of immigrants.[8] (In fact, you will learn some interesting things about Navajo culture later in this chapter.) Employees who do stay home will be thrust into international relationships by working for foreign-owned companies or by dealing with foreign suppliers, customers, and co-workers. Perhaps they will be offered an unexpected foreign assignment. *Management Review* offered this helpful perspective:

> It's easy to think that people who have lived abroad or who are multilingual have global brains, while those who still live in their hometowns are parochial. But both notions are fallacies. Managers who have never left their home states can have global brains if they are interested in the greater world around them, make an effort to learn about other people's perspectives, and integrate those perspectives into their own way of thinking.[9]

The global economy is a rich mix of opportunities, problems, and cultures, and now is the time to prepare to thrive in it. Accordingly, the purpose of this chapter is to help you take a step in that direction by exploring the impacts of culture in today's increasingly internationalized organizations. This chapter draws upon the area of cultural anthropology. We begin with a model that shows how societal culture and organizational culture (covered in Chapter 3) combine to influence work behavior. Next, we discuss how to develop *cultural intelligence*. Key dimensions of societal culture are presented with the goal of enhancing cross-cultural awareness. Practical lessons from cross-cultural management research are then reviewed. The chapter concludes by exploring the challenge of accepting a foreign assignment and avoiding *culture shock*.

Courtesy of Vahan Shirvanian
www.cartoonstock.com

LO.1 Culture and Organizational Behavior

to the point
What does culture involve and how are societal and organizational culture related?

How would you, as a manager, interpret the following situations?

> An Asian executive for a multinational company, transferred from Taiwan to the Midwest, appears aloof and autocratic to his peers.

> A West Coast bank embarks on a "friendly teller" campaign, but its Filipino female tellers won't cooperate.

> A white manager criticizes a black male employee's work. Instead of getting an explanation, the manager is met with silence and a firm stare.[10]

If you attribute the behavior in these situations to personalities, three descriptions come to mind: arrogant, unfriendly, and hostile. These are reasonable conclusions. Unfortunately, they are probably wrong, being based more on prejudice and stereotypes than on actual fact. However, if you attribute the behavioral outcomes to *cultural* differences, you stand a better chance of making the following more valid interpretations: "As it turns out, Asian culture encourages a more distant managing style, Filipinos associate overly friendly behavior in women with prostitution, and blacks as a group act more deliberately, studying visual cues, than most white men."[11] One cannot afford to overlook relevant cultural contexts when trying to understand and manage organizational behavior.

Societal Culture Is Complex and Multilayered

Culture

Beliefs and values about how a community of people should and do act.

In Chapter 3, we discussed *organizational* culture. Here, the focus is more broadly on *societal* culture. "**Culture** is a set of beliefs and values about what is desirable and undesirable in a community of people, and a set of formal or informal practices to support the values."[12] So culture has both prescriptive (what people should do) and descriptive (what they actually do) elements. Culture is passed from one generation to the next by family, friends, teachers, and relevant others. Most cultural lessons are learned by observing and imitating role models as they go about their daily affairs or as observed in the media.[13]

Culture is difficult to grasp because it is multilayered. International management experts Fons Trompenaars (from the Netherlands) and Charles Hampden-Turner (from Britain) offered this instructive analogy in their landmark book, *Riding the Waves of Culture:*

> Culture comes in layers, like an onion. To understand it you have to unpeel it layer by layer.
>
> On the outer layer are the products of culture, like the soaring skyscrapers of Manhattan, pillars of private power, with congested public streets between them. These are expressions of deeper values and norms in a society that are not directly visible (values such as upward mobility, "the more-the-better," status, material success). The layers of values and norms are deeper within the "onion," and are more difficult to identify.[14]

The best way to "peel the cultural onion" is to be proactive and get to know people from different cultures. IBM's CEO, Samuel Palmisano, recently put it this way: "I enjoy spending time in many countries, especially in the developing world. There is tremendous optimism and excitement about their future. You can't learn about these diverse cultures and immense opportunities by staying in your corporate headquarters."[15] The same goes for students in classrooms.

Culture Is a Subtle but Pervasive Force

Culture generally remains below the threshold of conscious awareness because it involves *taken-for-granted assumptions* about how one should perceive, think, act, and feel. Pioneering cultural anthropologist Edward T Hall put it this way:

> Since much of culture operates outside our awareness, frequently we don't even know what we know. We pick . . . [expectations and assumptions] up in the cradle. We unconsciously learn what to notice and what not to notice, how to divide time and space, how to walk and talk and use our bodies, how to behave as men or women, how to relate to other people, how to handle responsibility, whether experience is seen as whole or fragmented. This applies to all people. The Chinese or the Japanese or the Arabs are as unaware of their assumptions as we are of our own. We each assume that they're part of human nature. What we think of as "mind" is really internalized culture.[16]

In sum, it has been said: "you are your culture, and your culture is you." As part of the growing sophistication of marketing practices in the global economy, companies are hiring anthropologists to decipher the cultural roots of customer needs and preferences (see the Real World/Real People feature on page 97).

Should Anthropologists Go to War?

The military for years has enlisted anthropologists, depending on their expertise, to write up analyses of distant places and cultures.

But debate is growing among those scientists over whether it is appropriate for them to be involved in actually working alongside soldiers in combat or to contribute to the growing field of counterterrorism research....

In Iraq and Afghanistan, field anthropologists study culture, kinship, and networks in societies, "particularly key" factors in the insurgencies, according to the Army's counterinsurgency manual. For example, in these countries it is considered reasonable to put family ties above the needs of society, and nepotism is seen as positive, not negative. That's something young soldiers raised in the USA, with our veneration of the rugged individualist, may not immediately understand.

Is this right or wrong? A necessary tool in the defense of the nation and the world? Or a misuse of science to advance warfare?

Where do you come down on this issue? What is your ethical argument?

SOURCE: Excerpted from D Vergano and E Weise, "Should Anthropologists Work Alongside Soldiers?" *USA Today*, December 9, 2008, p 5D.

A Model of Societal and Organizational Cultures

As illustrated in Figure 4–1, culture influences organizational behavior in two ways. Employees bring their societal culture to work with them in the form of customs and language. Organizational culture, a by-product of societal culture, in turn affects the individual's values, ethics, attitudes, assumptions, and expectations. Societal culture is shaped by the various environmental factors listed in the left-hand side of Figure 4–1.

Once inside the organization's sphere of influence, the individual is further affected by the *organization's* culture. Mixing of societal and organizational cultures can produce interesting dynamics in multinational companies. For example, with French and American employees working side by side at General Electric's medical imaging production facility in Waukesha, Wisconsin, unit head Claude Benchimol has witnessed some culture shock:

The French are surprised the American parking lots empty out as early as 5 PM; the Americans are surprised the French don't start work at 8 AM. Benchimol feels the French are more talkative and candid. Americans have more of a sense of hierarchy and are less likely to criticize. But they may be growing closer to the French. Says Benchimol: "It's taken a year to get across the idea that we are all entitled to say what we don't like to become more productive and work better."[17]

Figure 4–1   *Cultural Influences on Organizational Behavior*

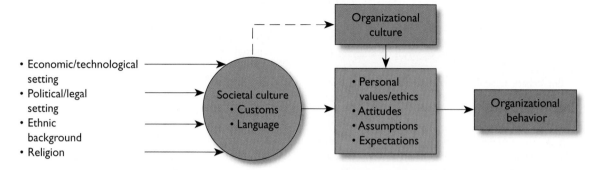

Same company, same company culture, yet GE's French and American coworkers have different attitudes about time, hierarchy, and communication. They are the products of different societal cultures.

When managing people at work, the individual's societal culture, the organizational culture, and any interaction between the two need to be taken into consideration. For example, American workers' cultural orientation toward quality improvement differs significantly from the Japanese cultural pattern.

> Unlike Japanese workers, Americans aren't interested in making small step-by-step improvements to increase quality. They want to achieve the breakthrough, the impossible dream. The way to motivate them: Ask for the big leap, rather than for tiny steps.[18]

to the point

Can cultural intelligence reduce ethnocentrism?

Developing Cultural Intelligence

What is your readiness to interact effectively with people from other cultures? To help answer that question, imagine a continuum with *ethnocentrism* on the low-readiness end and *cultural intelligence* on the high-readiness end. Let's explore these two extremes, with the goal of decreasing ethnocentrism and increasing cultural intelligence.

L0.2 Ethnocentrism: A Cross-Cultural Roadblock

Ethnocentrism

Belief that one's native country, culture, language, and behavior are superior.

Ethnocentrism, the belief that one's native country, culture, language, and modes of behavior are superior to all others, has its roots in the dawn of civilization. First identified as a behavioral science concept in 1906, involving the tendency of groups to reject outsiders,[19] the term *ethnocentrism* generally has a more encompassing (national or societal) meaning today. Worldwide evidence of ethnocentrism is plentiful. As a case in point, listen to Hiwa Assad, a former Kurdish guerilla fighter who lives in the city of Kirkuk in the Kurdish region of northern Iraq. "People in Kirkuk have two faces. . . . They sit with you and talk as if they're angels. They say, 'I have no enemies and don't hate other religions and nationalities.' But the minute they are alone with their own sect, they are the first ones to insult and hate."[20] Militant ethnocentrism led to deadly "ethnic cleansing" in Bosnia and Kosovo and genocide in the African nations of Rwanda, Burundi, and the Darfur region of Sudan.

Less dramatic, but still troublesome, is ethnocentrism within managerial and organizational contexts. Experts on the subject framed the problem this way:

> [Ethnocentric managers have] a preference for putting home-country people in key positions everywhere in the world and rewarding them more handsomely for work, along with a tendency to feel that this group is more intelligent, more capable, or more reliable. . . . Ethnocentrism is often not attributable to prejudice as much as to inexperience or lack of knowledge about foreign persons and situations. This is not too surprising, since most executives know far more about employees in their home environments. As one executive put it, "At least I understand why our own managers make mistakes. With our foreigners, I never know. The foreign managers may be better. But if I can't trust a person, should I hire him or her just to prove we're multinational?"[21]

Research suggests ethnocentrism is bad for business. A survey of 918 companies with home offices in the United States (272 companies), Japan (309), and Europe (337) found ethnocentric staffing and human resource policies to be associated with increased personnel problems. Those problems included recruiting difficulties, high turnover rates, and lawsuits over personnel policies. Among the three regional samples, Japanese companies had the most ethnocentric human resource practices and the most international human resource problems.[22]

Current and future managers, and people in general, can effectively deal with ethnocentrism through education, greater cross-cultural awareness, international experience, and a conscious effort to value cultural diversity. Fareed Zakaria, a *Newsweek* and CNN correspondent born in India, recently offered this wake-up call about the risks of ethnocentrism:

CNN correspondent Fareed Zakaria.

> Americans speak few languages, know little about foreign cultures, and remain unconvinced that they need to rectify this. Americans rarely benchmark to global standards because they are sure that their way must be the best and most advanced. The result is that they are increasingly suspicious of the emerging global era. There is a growing gap between America's worldly business elite and cosmopolitan class, on the one hand, and the majority of the American people, on the other. Without real efforts to bridge it, this divide could destroy America's competitive edge and its political future.[23]

Here are a couple of positive signs: 2008 saw record numbers of foreign students (623,805) studying in the United States and US students (241,791) studying abroad.[24]

Cultural Paradoxes Require Cultural Intelligence

An important qualification needs to be offered at this juncture. All of the cultural differences in this chapter and elsewhere need to be viewed as *tendencies* and *patterns* rather than as absolutes.[25] As soon as one falls into the trap of assuming *all* Italians are this, and *all* Koreans will do that, and so on, potentially instructive generalizations become mindless stereotypes. Two professors with extensive foreign work experience offer this advice: "As teachers, researchers, and managers in cross-cultural contexts, we need to recognize that our original characterizations of other cultures are best guesses that we need to modify as we gain more experience."[26] Consequently, they contend, we will be better prepared to deal with inevitable *cultural paradoxes.* By paradox, they mean there are always exceptions to the rule; individuals who do not fit the expected cultural pattern. A good example is the head of Canon. "By Japanese CEO standards, Canon Inc.'s Fujio Mitarai is something of an anomaly. For starters, he's fast and decisive—a far cry from the consensus builders who typically run Japan Inc."[27] One also encounters lots of cultural paradoxes in large and culturally diverse nations such as the United States and Brazil. This is where the need for cultural intelligence arises.

Cultural intelligence

The ability to interpret ambiguous cross-cultural situations accurately.

   Cultural intelligence, the ability to accurately interpret ambiguous cross-cultural situations, is an important skill in today's diverse workplaces. Two OB scholars explain:

> A person with high cultural intelligence can somehow tease out of a person's or group's behavior those features that would be true of all people and all groups, those peculiar to this person or this group, and those that are neither universal nor idiosyncratic. The vast realm that lies between those poles is culture.[28]

Those interested in developing their cultural intelligence need to first polish their *emotional* intelligence, discussed in detail in Chapter 5, and then practice in unfamiliar cross-cultural situations.[29] Of course, as in all human interaction, there is no adequate substitute for really getting to know, listen to, and care about others. Imagine the opportunities for students to build cultural intelligence at the IE Business School in Madrid, Spain, ranked number 2 in *BusinessWeek*'s 2008 list of the best international MBA programs:

High-context cultures

Primary meaning derived from nonverbal situational cues.

> … last year's class of 287 included 55 nationalities. With the highest student satisfaction rating of all of *BusinessWeek*'s ranked schools, U.S. and international, IE's student body is among the most diverse in the world. Rodrigo Sanchez Hidalgo, who graduated from the program in December, worked with classmates from 15 countries, including Kazakhstan and El Salvador. To help attract an even more international mix of students, IE recently opened marketing and admissions offices in Singapore, Dubai, Berlin, and Lisbon. The goal: producing graduates adept at navigating a multicultural business environment. "This is not a melting pot where participants share a common culture," says Santiago Iñiguez de Ozoño, dean of the business school.[30]

to the point

How can knowing about high-context cultures and the GLOBE dimensions improve managerial effectiveness?

LO.3 Understanding Cultural Differences

This section explores basic ways of describing and comparing cultures. As a foundation, we contrast high-context and low-context cultures and introduce nine cultural dimensions identified in the GLOBE project. Then our attention turns to examining cross-cultural differences in terms of individualism, time, space, and religion.

High-Context and Low-Context Cultures

This is a broadly applicable and very useful cultural distinction[31] (see Figure 4–2). People from **high-context cultures**—including China, Korea, Japan, Vietnam, Mexico, and Arab cultures—rely heavily on situational cues for meaning when

Figure 4–2 *Contrasting High-Context and Low-Context Cultures*

High-Context
- Establish social trust first
- Value personal relations and goodwill
- Agreement by general trust
- Negotiations slow and ritualistic

Low-Context
- Get down to business first
- Value expertise and performance
- Agreement by specific, legalistic contract
- Negotiations as efficient as possible

SOURCE: Reprinted from *Business Horizons*, vol. 36, No. 3, M Munter, "Cross-Cultural Communication for Managers," p 72, © 1993, with permission from Elsevier.

perceiving and communicating with others. Nonverbal cues such as one's official position, status, or family connections convey messages more powerfully than do spoken words. Take, for example, Arif M Naqvi, a native of Pakistan doing business in Dubai, United Arab Emirates:

> Naqvi is an insider, doing business with some of the most influential people in the region, including Khalid bin Sultan, the son of Saudi Crown Prince Sultan. His contacts and experience are crucial when it comes to making deals happen; relationships are often more important than money in the Middle East. . . .
>
> It takes finesse to close a deal, as it did for Naqvi with Aramex International, a courier company. Fadi Ghandour, founder and CEO of Aramex, recalls a series of . . . [long, drawn-out] lunches and dinners over several months with Naqvi.[32]

go to the Web for the Group Exercise: Looking into a Cultural Mirror

Reading the Fine Print in Low-Context Cultures

In **low-context cultures,** written and spoken words carry the burden of shared meanings. Low-context cultures include those found in Germany, Switzerland, Scandinavia, North America, and Great Britain. True to form, Germany has precise written rules for even the smallest details of daily life.[33] In *high*-context cultures, agreements tend to be made on the basis of someone's word or a handshake, after a prolonged get-acquainted and trust-building period. Low-context Americans and Canadians, at least those with cultural roots in Northern Europe, see the handshake as a signal to get a signature on a detailed, lawyer-approved, ironclad contract.

Low-context cultures

Primary meaning derived from written and spoken words.

Avoiding Cultural Collisions   Misunderstanding and miscommunication often are problems in international business dealings when the parties are from high- versus low-context cultures. A Mexican business professor made this instructive observation:

> Over the years, I have noticed that across cultures there are different opinions on what is expected from a business report. US managers, for instance, take a pragmatic, get-to-the-point approach, and expect reports to be concise and action-oriented. They don't have time to read long explanations: "Just the facts, ma'am."
>
> Latin American managers will usually provide long explanations that go beyond the simple facts. . . .
>
> I have a friend who is the Latin America representative for a United States firm and has been asked by his boss to provide regular reports on sales activities. His reports are long, including detailed explanations on the context in which the events he is reporting on occur and the possible interpretations that they might have. His boss regularly answers these reports with very brief messages, telling him to "cut the crap and get to the point!"[34]

Awkward situations such as this can be avoided when those on both sides of the context divide make good-faith attempts to understand and accommodate their counterparts. Here are some practical tips:

- People on both sides of the context barrier must be trained to make adjustments.
- A new employee should be greeted by a group consisting of his or her boss, several colleagues who have similar duties, and an individual located near the newcomer.
- Background information is essential when explaining anything. Include the history and personalities involved.
- Do not assume the newcomer is self-reliant. Give explicit instructions not only about objectives, but also about the process involved.
- High-context workers from abroad need to learn to ask questions outside their department and function.
- Foreign workers must make an effort to become more self-reliant.[35]

Nine Cultural Dimensions from the GLOBE Project

Project GLOBE (Global Leadership and Organizational Behavior Effectiveness) is the brainchild of University of Pennsylvania professor Robert J House.[36] It is a massive and ongoing attempt to "develop an empirically based theory to describe, understand, and predict the impact of specific cultural variables on leadership and organizational processes and the effectiveness of these processes."[37] GLOBE has evolved into a network of more than 150 scholars from 62 societies since the project was launched in Calgary, Canada, in 1994. Most of the researchers are native to the particular cultures they study, thus greatly enhancing the credibility of the project. During the first two phases of the GLOBE project, a list of nine basic cultural dimensions was developed and statistically validated. Translated questionnaires based on the nine dimensions were administered to thousands of managers in the banking, food, and telecommunications industries around the world to build a database. Results are being published on a regular basis. Much work and many years are needed if the project's goal, as stated above, is to be achieved. In the meantime, we have been given a comprehensive, valid, and up-to-date tool for better understanding cross-cultural similarities and differences.

The nine cultural dimensions from the GLOBE project are

- *Power distance.* How much unequal distribution of power should there be in organizations and society?
- *Uncertainty avoidance.* How much should people rely on social norms and rules to avoid uncertainty and limit unpredictability?
- *Institutional collectivism.* How much should leaders encourage and reward loyalty to the social unit, as opposed to the pursuit of individual goals?
- *In-group collectivism.* How much pride and loyalty should individuals have for their family or organization?
- *Gender egalitarianism.* How much effort should be put into minimizing gender discrimination and role inequalities?
- *Assertiveness.* How confrontational and dominant should individuals be in social relationships?
- *Future orientation.* How much should people delay gratification by planning and saving for the future?
- *Performance orientation.* How much should individuals be rewarded for improvement and excellence?
- *Humane orientation.* How much should society encourage and reward people for being kind, fair, friendly, and generous?[38]

What about Your Culture?   Take a short break from your reading and go to the Web to complete the Self-Exercise. It will help you better comprehend the nine GLOBE cultural dimensions. Can you trace your cultural profile to family history and country of origin of your ancestors? For example, one of your author's German roots are evident in his cultural profile. What are the personal implications of any cultural "gaps" that surfaced?

go to the Web for the Self-Exercise: What Is Your Cultural Profile?

Country Profiles and Practical Implications   How do different countries score on the GLOBE cultural dimensions? Data from 18,000 managers yielded the profiles in Table 4–1. A quick overview shows a great deal of cultural diversity around the world. But thanks to the nine GLOBE dimensions, we have a more precise understanding of *how* cultures vary. Closer study reveals telling cultural *patterns,* or cultural fingerprints for nations. The US managerial sample, for instance, scored high on assertiveness and performance orientation. Accordingly, Americans are widely perceived as pushy and hardworking. Switzerland's high scores on uncertainty avoidance and future orientation help explain its centuries of political neutrality and world-renowned banking industry. Singapore is known as a great place to do business because it is clean and safe and its people are well educated and hardworking. This is no surprise, considering Singapore's high scores on social collectivism, future orientation, and performance orientation.[39]

Table 4–1   *Countries Ranking Highest and Lowest on the GLOBE Cultural Dimensions*

DIMENSION	HIGHEST	LOWEST
Power distance	Morocco, Argentina, Thailand, Spain, Russia	Denmark, Netherlands, South Africa—black sample, Israel, Costa Rica
Uncertainty avoidance	Switzerland, Sweden, Germany—former West, Denmark, Austria	Russia, Hungary, Bolivia, Greece, Venezuela
Institutional collectivism	Sweden, South Korea, Japan, Singapore, Denmark	Greece, Hungary, Germany—former East, Argentina, Italy
In-group collectivism	Iran, India, Morocco, China, Egypt	Denmark, Sweden, New Zealand, Netherlands, Finland
Gender egalitarianism	Hungary, Poland, Slovenia, Denmark, Sweden	South Korea, Egypt, Morocco, India, China
Assertiveness	Germany—former East, Austria, Greece, US, Spain	Sweden, New Zealand, Switzerland, Japan, Kuwait
Future orientation	Singapore, Switzerland, Netherlands, Canada—English-speaking, Denmark	Russia, Argentina, Poland, Italy, Kuwait
Performance orientation	Singapore, Hong Kong, New Zealand, Taiwan, US	Russia, Argentina, Greece, Venezuela, Italy
Humane orientation	Philippines, Ireland, Malaysia, Egypt, Indonesia	Germany—former West, Spain, France, Singapore, Brazil

SOURCE: Adapted from M Javidan, R J House, and P W Dorfman, "A Nontechnical Summary of GLOBE Findings," in *Culture, Leadership, and Organizations: The GLOBE Study of 62 Societies*, ed R J House, P J Hanges, M Javidan, P W Dorfman, and V Gupta (Thousand Oaks, CA: Sage, 2004), pp 29–48.

In contrast, Russia's low scores on future orientation and performance orientation could foreshadow a slower-than-hoped-for transition from a centrally planned economy to free enterprise capitalism.

As explained by business and science author Malcolm Gladwell, cultural tendencies can become a life-and-death matter in hazardous occupations. Despite having modern aircraft and well-trained pilots, Korean Air experienced too many crashes during the 1990s.

> What they were struggling with was a cultural legacy, that Korean culture is hierarchical. You are obliged to be deferential toward your elders and superiors in a way that would be unimaginable in the United States. But Boeing and Airbus design modern, complex airplanes to be flown by two equals. That works beautifully in low-power-distance cultures [like the United States, where hierarchies aren't as relevant]. But in cultures that have high power distance, it's very difficult. I use the case study of a very famous plane crash in Guam of Korean Air. They're flying along, and they run into a little bit of trouble, the weather's bad. The pilot makes an error, and the co-pilot doesn't correct him. But once Korean Air figured out that their problem was cultural, they fixed it.[40]

These illustrations bring us to an important practical lesson: *Knowing the cultural tendencies of your coworkers, foreign business partners, and competitors can give you a strategic competitive advantage (and even save lives in hazardous occupations).*

LO.4 Individualism versus Collectivism

Have you ever been torn between what you personally wanted and what the group, organization, or society expected of you? If so, you have firsthand experience with a fundamental and important cultural distinction: individualism versus collectivism. This source of cultural variation—represented by two of the nine GLOBE dimensions—deserves a closer look. As might be expected with an extensively researched topic, individualism–collectivism has many interpretations.[41] Let us examine the basic concept for greater cultural awareness.

Individualistic cultures, characterized as "I" and "me" cultures, give priority to individual freedom and choice. Accordingly, they emphasize *personal* responsibility for one's affairs. This is no small matter in an aging society:

> A strong feeling of "social solidarity," as [Johns Hopkins University professor Gerald F] Anderson sees it, makes Europeans inclined to be generous to older people, more willing to support them. "Their attitude is, we're older and we'll need some help," he says. "The US attitude is, we're all rugged individualists and we're going to take care of ourselves, not others."[42]

This cultural distinction was borne out in a recent survey of the quality of life among senior citizens in 16 industrialized nations. The Netherlands was number one and the United States ranked number 13.[43]

Collectivist cultures, oppositely called "we" and "us" cultures, rank shared goals higher than individual desires and goals. People in collectivist cultures are expected to subordinate their own wishes and goals to those of the relevant social unit. A worldwide survey of 30,000 managers by Trompenaars and Hampden-Turner, who prefer the term *communitarianism* to *collectivism,* found the highest degree of individualism in Israel, Romania, Nigeria, Canada, and the United States. Countries ranking lowest in individualism—thus qualifying as collectivist cultures—were Egypt, Nepal, Mexico, India, and Japan. Brazil, China, and France also ended up toward the collectivist end of the scale.[44]

A Business Success Factor   Of course, one can expect to encounter both individualists and collectivists in culturally diverse countries such as the United States. For example, imagine the frustration of Dave Murphy, a Boston-based mutual fund salesperson, when he tried to get Navajo Indians in Arizona interested in saving money for their retirement. After several fruitless meetings with groups of Navajo employees, he was given this cultural insight by a local official: "If you come to this environment, you have to understand that money is different. It's there to be spent. If you have some, you help your family."[45] (This suggests Navajos generally would score high on in-group collectivism and low on future orientation on the GLOBE scale.) To traditional Navajos, enculturated as collectivists, saving money is an unworthy act of selfishness. Subsequently, the sales pitch was tailored to emphasize the *family* benefits of individual retirement savings plans.

Allegiance to Whom?   The Navajo example brings up an important point about collectivist cultures. Specifically, which unit of society predominates? For the Navajos, family is the key reference group. But, as Trompenaars and Hampden-Turner observe, important differences exist among collectivist (or communitarian) cultures:

> For each single society, it is necessary to determine the group with which individuals have the closest identification. They could be keen to identify with their trade union,

Individualistic culture
Primary emphasis on personal freedom and choice.

Collectivist culture
Personal goals less important than community goals and interests.

their family, their corporation, their religion, their profession, their nation, or the state apparatus. The French tend to identify with *la France, la famille, le cadre;* the Japanese with the corporation; the former eastern bloc with the Communist Party; and Ireland with the Roman Catholic Church. Communitarian goals may be good or bad for industry depending on the community concerned, its attitude and relevance to business development.[46]

This observation validates GLOBE's distinction between institutional and in-group collectivism.

Cultural Perceptions of Time

In North American and Northern European cultures, time seems to be a simple matter. It is linear, relentlessly marching forward, never backward, in standardized chunks. Time-crunched Americans believe in Ben Franklin's advice that "time is money." It is spent, saved, or wasted.[47] A prime example is William P Lauder, CEO of Esteé Lauder Companies, the cosmetics giant. Lauder declared in a recent interview: "When I see people waste time, I call them on it immediately. Time is their greatest resource, and when it's gone, it's lost forever."[48] Lauder's opposite is actor Johnny Depp. According to a *Newsweek* reporter, "He seems like a man who has never rushed to, or from, anywhere in his life. He is chronically late for interviews—sometimes four or five hours, sometimes days—but this time around a gentlemanly 50 minutes."[49] Kentucky-born Depp certainly doesn't fit the stereotypical American who shows up 10 minutes early for appointments. When working across cultures, time becomes a very complex matter. Imagine a New Yorker's chagrin when left in a waiting room for 45 minutes, only to find a Latin American government official dealing with three other people at once. The North American resents the lack of prompt and undivided attention. The Latin American official resents the North American's impatience and apparent self-centeredness. This vicious cycle of resentment can be explained by the distinction between **monochronic time** and **polychronic time:**

Monochronic time

Belief that time is limited, precisely segmented, and schedule driven.

> The former is revealed in the ordered, precise, schedule-driven use of public time that typifies and even caricatures efficient Northern Europeans and North Americans. The latter is seen in the multiple and cyclical activities and concurrent involvement with different people in Mediterranean, Latin American, and especially Arab cultures.[50]

Polychronic time

Belief that time is flexible, multidimensional, and based on relationships and situations.

Low-context cultures, such as in the United States, tend to run on monochronic time, while higher-context cultures, such as in Central America's Costa Rica, tend to run on polychronic time. People in polychronic cultures view time as flexible, fluid, and multidimensional. During the Islamic holy month of Ramadan in Middle Eastern nations, for example, the faithful fast during daylight hours, and the general pace of things markedly slows. However, economic globalization has spawned monochronic global business practices that create exceptions to the rule.

> Travel guides about Spain warn tourists that because of the siesta—the tradition of a long break for lunch and a nap—shops and businesses may be closed for a good part of the afternoon. But at least in Spain's major cities, the siesta gradually is giving way to the influences of globalization and work/life balance.
>
> Employers in Spain have been re-thinking their practice of permitting long afternoon breaks that extend the Spanish workday far into the evening. The siesta can interrupt

Spanish companies' dealings with other European businesses for a large portion of the workday. Moreover, it is becoming impractical for employees in the larger cities to travel home for lunch, and the length of the workday is becoming an issue for many employees.[51]

Managers need to adjust their mental clocks when doing business across cultures.

Interpersonal Space

Anthropologist Edward T Hall noticed a connection between culture and preferred interpersonal distance. People from high-context cultures were observed standing close when talking to someone. Low-context cultures appeared to dictate a greater amount of interpersonal space. Hall applied the term **proxemics** to the study of cultural expectations about interpersonal space.[52] He specified four interpersonal distance zones. Some call them space bubbles. They are *intimate* distance, *personal* distance, *social* distance, and *public* distance. Ranges for the four interpersonal distance zones are illustrated in Figure 4–3, along with selected cultural differences.

North American business conversations normally are conducted at about a three- to four-foot range, within the personal zone in Figure 4–3. A range of approximately one foot is common in Latin American and Asian cultures, uncomfortably close for Northern Europeans and North Americans. Some Arab traditionalists like to get even closer. Mismatches in culturally dictated interpersonal space zones can prove very distracting for the unprepared. Hall explains,

> Arabs tend to get very close and breathe on you. It's part of the high sensory involvement of a high-context culture. . . .
>
> The American on the receiving end can't identify all the sources of his discomfort but feels that the Arab is pushy. The Arab comes close, the American backs up. The Arab follows, because he can only interact at certain distances. Once the American learns that Arabs handle space differently and that breathing on people is a form of communication, the situation can sometimes be redefined so the American relaxes.[53]

Proxemics

Hall's term for the study of cultural expectations about interpersonal space.

Figure 4–3 *Interpersonal Distance Zones for Business Conversations Vary from Culture to Culture*

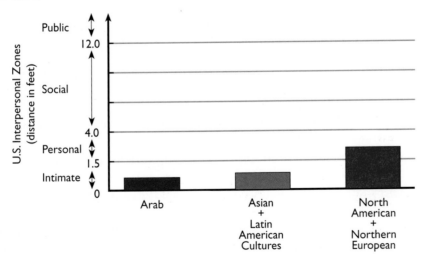

Arizona Hospital Blends Modern Medicine with Navajo Traditions

When a Navajo woman delivers a baby at Banner Page Hospital in northern Arizona, she invites her entire family—often more than 10 people—into the birthing room. She may give birth squatting, as is custom among Native Americans. A medicine man will offer ancient prayers and herbs for the mother to ease childbirth. After the baby is delivered, nurses will save the placenta so the family can take it home and bury it in a sacred place.

In this desert town flanked by canyons and Lake Powell, traditional Navajo healing is merging with modern medicine. The hospital's Native American Cultural Committee, formed in 2002, is working toward an inclusive medical community by tackling the cultural sensitivities of the Navajo people, many of whom are wary of modern medicine.

[According to the head of the hospital's Native American Cultural Committee,] "You have to consider the entire person, family and culture."

As a hospital administrator, what business and ethical arguments would you offer to defend this accommodation to Navajo traditions?

SOURCE: Excerpted from A Haupt, "Hospital Honors its Navajo Ties," *USA Today*, August 18, 2008, p 10B.

Asian and Middle-Eastern hosts grow weary of having to seemingly chase their low-context guests around at social gatherings to maintain what they feel is proper conversational range. Backing up all evening to keep conversational partners at a proper distance is an awkward experience as well. Awareness of cultural differences, along with skillful accommodation, are essential to productive intercultural business dealings.

Religion

Religious beliefs and practices can have a profound effect on cross-cultural relations (see the Real World/Real People feature above). A comprehensive treatment of different religions is beyond the scope of our current discussion.[54] However, we can examine the relationship between religious affiliation and work-related values. A study of 484 international students at a Midwestern US university uncovered wide variability. The following list gives the most important work-related value for each of five religious affiliations:

Catholic—Consideration ("Concern that employees be taken seriously, be kept informed, and that their judgments be used.")

Protestant—Employer effectiveness ("Desire to work for a company that is efficient, successful, and a technological leader.")

Buddhist—Social responsibility ("Concern that the employer be a responsible part of society.")

Muslim—Continuity ("Desire for stable environment, job longevity, reduction of uncertainty.")

No religious preference—Professional challenge ("Concern with having a job that provides learning opportunities and opportunities to use skills well.")[55]

Thus, there was virtually *no agreement* across religions about the primary work value. This led the researchers to conclude: "Employers might be wise to consider the impact that religious differences (and more broadly, cultural factors) appear to have on the values of employee groups."[56] Of course, in the United States and other selected countries, equal employment opportunity laws forbid managers from basing employment-related decisions on an applicant's religious preference.

Practical Insights from Cross-Cultural Management Research

to the point

Is American-style leadership effective worldwide?

Nancy Adler, an international OB specialist at Canada's McGill University, has offered the following definition: "**Cross-cultural management** explains the behavior of people in organizations around the world and shows people how to work in organizations with employee and client populations from many different cultures."[57] Historically, cross-cultural management research has focused almost exclusively on cultural differences. One researcher, troubled by inappropriate cross-cultural comparisons, recently called this approach "comparing chopsticks with forks."[58] But GLOBE researchers Mansour Javidan and Robert J House recommend studying *similarities* as well as differences. They believe tracking cultural similarities will help us judge how applicable specific management practices are in foreign cultures. "For example, leadership theories developed in the US are probably more easily generalizable to UK managers (another member of the Anglo cluster) than to managers in an Arab country."[59] In this section we will examine two different streams of cross-cultural management research. Both offer useful lessons for today's managers.

Cross-cultural management

Understanding and teaching behavioral patterns in different cultures.

LO.5 The Hofstede Study: How Well Do US Management Theories Apply in Other Countries?

The short answer to this important question: *not very well*. This answer derives from a landmark study conducted 30 years ago by Dutch researcher Geert Hofstede. His unique cross-cultural comparison of 116,000 IBM employees from 53 countries worldwide focused on four cultural dimensions:

- *Power distance.* How much inequality does someone expect in social situations?
- *Individualism–collectivism.* How loosely or closely is the person socially bonded?
- *Masculinity–femininity.* Does the person embrace stereotypically competitive, performance-oriented masculine traits or nurturing, relationship-oriented feminine traits?
- *Uncertainty avoidance.* How strongly does the person desire highly structured situations?

Welcome to the Gateway Language Village, a total-immersion English-language school in Zhuhai, China. Students from China and elsewhere are forbidden to converse in anything but English when they set foot on campus. GLV was founded by Ping Hong, who grew up in China and holds a master's degree from Purdue University in the United States. He and his Colombian wife have a boy and a girl who speak Chinese, Spanish, and English. They will be well-equipped to succeed in the global economy.

The US sample ranked relatively low on power distance, very high on individualism, moderately high on masculinity, and low on uncertainty avoidance.[60]

The high degree of variation among cultures led Hofstede to two major conclusions: (1) Management theories and practices need to be adapted to local cultures. This is particularly true for made-in-America management theories (e.g., Maslow's need hierarchy) and Japanese team management practices. *There is no one best way to manage across cultures.*[61] (2) Cultural arrogance is a luxury individuals, companies, and nations can no longer afford in a global economy.

LO.6 Leadership Lessons from the GLOBE Project

In phase 2, the GLOBE researchers set out to discover which, if any, attributes of leadership were universally liked or disliked. They surveyed 17,000 middle managers working for 951 organizations across 62 countries. Their results, summarized in Table 4–2, have important implications for trainers and present and future global managers.[62] Visionary and inspirational *charismatic leaders* who are good team builders generally do the best. On the other hand, *self-centered leaders* seen as loners or face-savers generally receive a poor reception worldwide. (See Chapter 16 for a comprehensive treatment of leadership.) Local and foreign managers who heed these results are still advised to use a contingency approach to leadership after using their cultural intelligence to read the local people and culture. David Whitwam, the longtime CEO of appliance maker Whirlpool, frames the challenge this way:

> Leading a company today is different from the 1980s and '90s, especially in a global company. It requires a new set of competencies. Bureaucratic structures don't work anymore. You have to take the command-and-control types out of the system. You need to allow and encourage broad-based involvement in the company. Especially in consumer kinds of companies, we need a diverse workforce with diverse leadership. You need strong regional leadership that lives in the culture. We have a North American running the North American business, and a Latin American running the Latin American business.[63]

Table 4–2   *Leadership Attributes Universally Liked and Disliked across 62 Nations*

UNIVERSALLY POSITIVE LEADER ATTRIBUTES	UNIVERSALLY NEGATIVE LEADER ATTRIBUTES
Trustworthy	Loner
Just	Asocial
Honest	Noncooperative
Foresight	Irritable
Plans ahead	Nonexplicit
Encouraging	Egocentric
Positive	Ruthless
Dynamic	Dictatorial
Motive arouser	
Confidence builder	
Motivational	
Dependable	
Intelligent	
Decisive	
Effective bargainer	
Win–win problem solver	
Administrative skilled	
Communicative	
Informed	
Coordinator	
Team builder	
Excellence oriented	

SOURCE: Excerpted and adapted from P W Dorfman, P J Hanges, and F C Brodbeck, "Leadership and Cultural Variation: The Identification of Culturally Endorsed Leadership Profiles," in *Culture, Leadership, and Organizations: The GLOBE Study of 62 Societies*, ed R J House, P J Hanges, M Javidan, P W Dorfman, and V Gupta (Thousand Oaks, CA: Sage, 2004), Tables 21.2 and 21.3, pp 677–78.

go to the Web for the Self-Exercise: How Do Your Work Goals Compare Internationally?

Preparing Employees for Successful Foreign Assignments

to the point
What does it take to succeed on a foreign assignment?

As the reach of global companies continues to grow, many opportunities for living and working in foreign countries will arise. Imagine, for example, the opportunities for foreign duty and cross-cultural experiences at Siemens, the German electronics giant. "While Siemens' corporate headquarters is near Munich, nearly 80% of the firm's business is international. Worldwide the company has 470,000 employees, including 75,000 in the United States and 25,000 in China."[64] Siemens and other global players need a vibrant and growing cadre of employees who are willing and able to do business across cultures.[65] Jack and Suzy Welch, in their *BusinessWeek* column, recently offered this view of the next ten years: "There's gold in them-thar hills for any experienced manager who's got the ambition, interest, and global mind-set to work abroad for several years."[66] Thus, the purpose of this final section is to help you prepare yourself and others to work successfully in foreign countries, because a foreign assignment can be a real résumé builder these days.

LO.7 Why Do US Expatriates Fail on Foreign Assignments?

Expatriate

Anyone living or working in a foreign country.

As we use the term here, **expatriate** refers to anyone living or working outside their home country. Hence, they are said to be *expatriated* when transferred to another country and *repatriated* when transferred back home. Reliable statistics of how many Americans, both civilian and military, are presently working outside the country are not available, although it is certainly in the millions. We do know that only 27% of US citizens hold a valid passport (compared to 40% in Canada, 64% in the United Kingdom, and 90% in Germany).[67] This rough indicator of low global engagement helps explain why Americans are commonly characterized as cross-culturally inept and prone to failure on international assignments. Research supports this view. A pair of international management experts offered this assessment:

> Over the past decade, we have studied the management of expatriates at about 750 US, European, and Japanese companies. We asked both the expatriates themselves and the executives who sent them abroad to evaluate their experiences. In addition, we looked at what happened after expatriates returned home. . . .
>
> Overall, the results of our research were alarming. We found that between 10% and 20% of all US managers sent abroad returned early because of job dissatisfaction or difficulties in adjusting to a foreign country. Of those who stayed for the duration, nearly one-third did not perform up to the expectations of their superiors. And perhaps most problematic, one-fourth of those who completed an assignment left their company, often to join a competitor, within one year after repatriation. That's a turnover rate double that of managers who did not go abroad.[68]

A more recent study of why expatriate employees returned home early found the situation to be slowly improving. Still, *personal and family adjustment problems* (36.6%) and *homesickness* (31%) were found to be major stumbling blocks for American managers working in foreign countries.[69] A survey asking 72 human resource managers at multinational corporations to identify the most important success factor in a foreign assignment provided this insight: "Nearly 35% said cultural adaptability: patience, flexibility, and tolerance for others' beliefs."[70]

US multinational companies clearly need to do a better job of preparing employees and their families for foreign assignments, particularly in light of the high costs involved:

> The tab for sending an executive who earns $160,000 in the US, plus a spouse and two children, to India for two years is about $900,000, says Jacqui Hauser, vice president of consulting services for Cendant Mobility, a relocation-services firm in Danbury, Conn.

This includes housing and cost-of-living allowances, foreign- and hardship-pay premiums, tax-assistance, education and car allowances and paid transportation home each year for the entire family.[71]

L0.8 A Bright Spot: North American Women on Foreign Assignments

Historically, a woman from the United States or Canada on a foreign assignment was a rarity. Things are changing, albeit slowly. A review of research evidence and anecdotal accounts uncovered these insights:

- The proportion of corporate women from North America on foreign assignments grew from about 3% in the early 1980s to between 11% and 15% in recent years.

- Self-disqualification and management's assumption that women would not be welcome in foreign cultures—not foreign prejudice, itself—are the primary barriers for potential female expatriates.

- Expatriate North American women are viewed first and foremost by their hosts as being foreigners, and only secondarily as being female.

- North American women have a very high success rate on foreign assignments.[72]

Considering the rapidly growing demand for global managers today,[73] self-disqualification by women and management's prejudicial policies are counterproductive. For their part, women and others who desire a foreign assignment need to be proactive by becoming culturally intelligent and announcing their desire for a foreign assignment. The CEO of tobacco giant Reynolds American is a good case in point: "Susan Ivey says her big break came in 1990, when she was asked to take an overseas assignment and given 48 hours to decide. She went for it. The experience, Ivey says, was 'broadening in every way.'"[74] When Irene Rosenfeld, CEO of Kraft Foods, was asked about her best decision, she said: "My move to Canada in 1996 was a terrific growth opportunity. All my direct reports were very experienced men who had never worked for a woman before. The team was not wild about Americans either. . . . I really learned the difference between managing and leading."[75]

L0.9 Avoiding OB Trouble Spots in Foreign Assignments

Finding the right person (often along with a supportive and adventurous family) for a foreign position is a complex, time-consuming, and costly process.[76] For our purposes, it is sufficient to narrow the focus to common OB trouble spots in the foreign assignment cycle. As illustrated in Figure 4–4, the first and last stages of the cycle occur at home. The middle two stages occur in the foreign or host country. Each stage hides an OB-related trouble spot that needs to be anticipated and neutralized. Otherwise, the bill for another failed foreign assignment will grow.

Avoiding Unrealistic Expectations with Cross-Cultural Training

Realistic job previews (RJPs) have proven effective at bringing people's unrealistic expectations about a pending job assignment down to earth by providing a

Figure 4–4 *The Foreign Assignment Cycle (with OB Trouble Spots)*

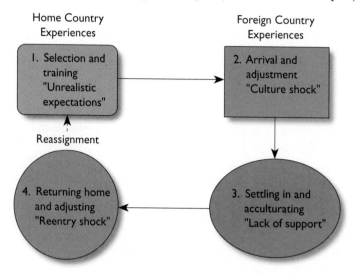

realistic balance of good and bad news. People with realistic expectations tend to quit less often and be more satisfied than those with unrealistic expectations. RJPs are a must for future expatriates. In addition, cross-cultural training is required. (For training tips in different cultures, see the Real World/Real People feature on page 115.)

Cross-cultural training

Structured experiences to help people adjust to a new culture/country.

Cross-cultural training is any type of structured experience designed to help departing employees adjust to a foreign culture. The trend is toward more such training in the United States. But there is a great deal of room for improvement, as indicated by the results of a *Training* magazine survey. Only 12% rated cross-cultural/diversity training as "very important" for preparing employees for international assignments.[77] Experts believe that cross-cultural training, although costly, is less expensive than failed foreign assignments. Programs vary widely in type and also in rigor. Of course, the greater the difficulty, the greater the time and expense:

- *Easiest.* Predeparture training is limited to informational materials, including books, lectures, films, videos, and Internet searches.
- *Moderately difficult.* Experiential training is conducted through case studies, role playing, simulations, and introductory language instruction.
- *Most difficult.* Departing employees are given some combination of the preceding methods plus comprehensive language instruction and field experience in the target culture. As an example of the latter, PepsiCo Inc. transfers "about 25 young foreign managers a year to the US for one-year assignments in bottling plants."[78]

Which approach is the best? Research to date does not offer a final answer. One study involving US employees in South Korea led the researcher to recommend a *combination* of informational and experiential predeparture training.[79] As a general rule of thumb, the more rigorous the cross-cultural training, the better.

Training Needs to Fit the Local Culture

Brazil

- Building personal relationships is key in Brazilian culture, so talk about yourself.
- Time is much more event oriented in Brazil. In terms of personal space, program participants who approach you during class activities may stand much closer to you than you are used to. Power is accepted and respected. Those who have high status positions are not questioned, even when the individual has doubts about a stance taken.... What may seem like fighting or arguing to a trainer [during group discussions] is normal communication behavior in Brazil.*

China

- Trainees expect the trainer to lead the class as the expert, and lecture is the preferred delivery method.
- Harmony and order are valued in China. Your trainees do not want to stand out. Make sure not to highlight the performance of any one individual. This praise could cause the individual and class to feel uncomfortable.
- Although China is a group-oriented culture, try to minimize your use of small group discussions. There is a belief that learning is more powerful when the knowledge comes from the trainer as opposed to the trainees.
- Because relationships are critical in this culture, [right at the start] tell your trainees about yourself and your organization.**

France

- Although English is the predominant business language in France, a trainer's credibility is dependent on his/her mastery of the French language, and training delivery in French is preferred. The same applies for all support material (books, evaluation forms, multimedia, etc.). Videos should be in French or contain French subtitles.
- Participants seek the intellectual stimulation of debate and exchange. Provide ample time for discussions, and be flexible with your program.
- Expect to be continuously challenged. The relatively direct communication style of French audiences can be perceived as confrontational. However, please note that the challenge is a positive sign, as it reveals the participants' passionate interest in the subject.***

What cultural dimensions discussed in this chapter are evident in these training tips? Explain.

SOURCES: *Excerpted from N Orkin, "Focus on Brazil," *Training*, May 2008, p 20. **Excerpted from N Orkin, "Focus on China," *Training*, July–August 2008, p 18. ***Excerpted from K Blanchard-Cattarossi and S Redrupp, "Focus on France," *Training*, January 2009, p 18.

Ideally, trainees should walk away with the nine cross-cultural competencies in Table 4–3.

Our personal experience with teaching OB to foreign students both in the United States and around the world reminds us there really is no substitute for an intimate knowledge of the local culture, language, customs, and etiquette. A good example is Jeremy Shepherd, owner of Pearl Paradise, a Santa Monica, California, online jewelry business. "[He] speaks the Chinese Mandarin dialect, buys directly from pearl farmers in China and cuts out the middleman. That lets him sell high-quality pearls at lower prices to everyone from college students to investment bankers."[80] Who

Table 4–3   *Key Cross-Cultural Competencies*

CROSS-CULTURAL COMPETENCY CLUSTER	KNOWLEDGE OR SKILL REQUIRED
Building relationships	Ability to gain access to and maintain relationships with members of host culture
Valuing people of different cultures	Empathy for difference; sensitivity to diversity
Listening and observation	Knows cultural history and reasons for certain cultural actions and customs
Coping with ambiguity	Recognizes and interprets implicit behavior, especially nonverbal cues
Translating complex information	Knowledge of local language, symbols or other forms of verbal language, and written language
Taking action and initiative	Understands intended and potentially unintended consequences of actions
Managing others	Ability to manage details of a job including maintaining cohesion in a group
Adaptability and flexibility	Views change from multiple perspectives
Managing stress	Understands own and other's mood, emotions, and personality

SOURCE: Excerpted from Y Yamazaki and D C Kayes, "An Experiential Approach to Cross-Cultural Learning: A Review and Integration of Competencies for Successful Expatriate Adaptation," *Academy of Management Learning and Education,* December 2004, Table 2, p 372.

will likely have the language advantage as the global economy evolves, given these recent figures? According to the US Department of Education, 24,000 American children are studying Chinese, while 200 million Chinese are studying English.[81] Meanwhile, nearly 81% of all Americans speak only English.[82]

Avoiding Culture Shock

Culture shock
Anxiety and doubt caused by an overload of new expectations and cues.

Have you ever been in a totally unfamiliar situation and felt disoriented and perhaps a bit frightened? If so, you already know something about culture shock. According to anthropologists, **culture shock** involves anxiety and doubt caused by an overload of unfamiliar expectations and social cues.[83] College freshmen often experience a variation of culture shock. An expatriate manager, or family member, may be thrown off balance by an avalanche of strange sights, sounds, and behaviors. Among them may be unreadable road signs, strange-tasting food, inability to use your left hand for social activities (in Islamic countries, the left hand is the toilet hand), or failure to get a laugh with your surefire joke. For the expatriate manager trying to concentrate on the fine details of a business negotiation, culture shock is more than an embarrassing inconvenience. It is a disaster! Like the confused college freshman who quits and goes home, culture-shocked employees often panic and go home early.

The best defense against culture shock is comprehensive cross-cultural training, including intensive language study. Once again, the best way to pick up subtle—yet important—social cues is via the local language.

Support during the Foreign Assignment

Especially during the first six months, when everything is so new to the expatriate, a support system needs to be in place.[84] *Host-country sponsors,* assigned to individual managers or families, are recommended because they serve as "cultural seeing-eye dogs." In a foreign country, where even the smallest errand can turn into an utterly exhausting production, sponsors can get things done quickly because they know the cultural and geographical territory. Honda's Ohio employees, for example, enjoyed the help of family sponsors when training in Japan:

> Honda smoothed the way with Japanese wives who once lived in the US. They handled emergencies such as when Diana Jett's daughter Ashley needed stitches in her chin. When task force senior manager Kim Smalley's daughter, desperate to fit in at elementary school, had to have a precisely shaped bag for her harmonica, a Japanese volunteer stayed up late to make it.[85]

Avoiding Reentry Shock   Strange as it may seem, many otherwise successful expatriate managers encounter their first major difficulty only after their foreign assignment is over. Why? Returning to one's native culture is taken for granted because it seems so routine and ordinary. But having adjusted to another country's way of doing things for an extended period of time can put one's own culture and surroundings in a strange new light. Three areas for potential reentry shock are work, social activities, and general environment (e.g., politics, climate, transportation, food). Ira Caplan's return to New York City exemplifies reentry shock:

> During the past 12 years, living mostly in Japan, he and his wife had spent their vacations cruising the Nile or trekking in Nepal. They hadn't seen much of the US. They are getting an eyeful now. . . .
>
> Prices astonish him. The obsession with crime unnerves him. What unsettles Mr Caplan more, though, is how much of himself he has left behind.
>
> In a syndrome of return no less stressful than that of departure, he feels displaced, disregarded, and diminished. . . .
>
> In an Italian restaurant, crowded at lunchtime, the waiter sets a bowl of linguine in front of him. Mr Caplan stares at it. "In Asia, we have smaller portions and smaller people," he says.
>
> Asia is on his mind. He has spent years cultivating an expertise in a region of huge importance. So what? This is New York.[86]

Work-related adjustments were found to be a major problem for samples of repatriated Finnish, Japanese, and American employees.[87] Upon being repatriated, a 12-year veteran of one US company said: "Our organizational culture was turned upside down. We now have a different strategic focus, different 'tools' to get the job done, and different buzzwords to make it happen. I had to learn a whole new corporate 'language.'"[88] Reentry shock can be reduced through employee career counseling and home-country sponsors. Simply being aware of the problem of reentry shock is a big step toward effectively dealing with it.[89]

Overall, the key to a successful foreign assignment is making it a well-integrated link in a career chain rather than treating it as an isolated adventure.

Summary of Key Concepts

1. *Define the term* culture, *and explain how societal culture and organizational culture combine to influence on-the-job behavior.* Culture is a set of beliefs and values about what is desirable and undesirable in a community of people, and a set of formal or informal practices to support the values. Culture has both prescriptive and

descriptive elements and involves taken-for-granted assumptions about how to think, act, and feel. Culture overrides national boundaries. Key aspects of societal culture, such as customs and language, are brought to work by the individual. Working together, societal and organizational culture influence the person's values, ethics, attitudes, and expectations.

2. *Define* ethnocentrism, *and explain how to develop cultural intelligence.* Ethnocentrism is the belief that one's native culture, language, and ways of doing things are superior to all others. Cultural intelligence, the ability to interpret ambiguous cross-cultural situations, is an extension of emotional intelligence (discussed in Chapter 5). It can be developed through comprehensive experience with foreign people and cultures.

3. *Distinguish between high-context and low-context cultures and identify and describe the nine cultural dimensions from Project GLOBE.* People from low-context cultures infer relatively less from situational cues and extract more meaning from spoken and written words. In high-context cultures such as China and Japan, managers prefer slow negotiations and trust-building meetings, which tend to frustrate low-context Northern Europeans and North Americans who prefer to get right down to business. The nine GLOBE cultural dimensions are: (1) Power distance—How equally should power be distributed? (2) Uncertainty avoidance—How much should social norms and rules reduce uncertainty and unpredictability? (3) Institutional collectivism—How much should loyalty to the social unit override individual interests? (4) In-group collectivism—How strong should one's loyalty be to family or organization? (5) Gender egalitarianism—How much should gender discrimination and role inequalities be minimized? (6) Assertiveness—How confrontational and dominant should one be in social relationships? (7) Future orientation—How much should one delay gratification by planning and saving for the future? (8) Performance orientation—How much should individuals be rewarded for improvement and excellence? (9) Humane orientation—How much should individuals be rewarded for being kind, fair, friendly, and generous?

4. *Distinguish between individualistic and collectivist cultures, and explain the difference between monochronic and polychronic cultures.* People in individualistic cultures think primarily in terms of "I" and "me" and place a high value on freedom and personal choice. Collectivist cultures teach people to be "we" and "us" oriented and to subordinate personal wishes and goals to the interests of the relevant social unit (such as family, group, organization, or society). People in monochronic cultures are schedule driven and prefer to do one thing at a time. To them, time is like money; it is spent wisely or wasted. In polychronic cultures, there is a tendency to do many things at once and to perceive time as flexible and multidimensional. Polychronic people view monochronic people as being too preoccupied with time.

5. *Specify the practical lesson from the Hofstede cross-cultural study.* There is no one best way to manage across cultures. Management theories and practices need to be adapted to the local culture.

6. *Explain what Project GLOBE researchers discovered about leadership.* Across 62 cultures, they identified leader attributes that are universally liked and universally disliked. The universally liked leader attributes—including trustworthy, dynamic, motive arouser, decisive, and intelligent—are associated with the charismatic/transformational leadership style that is widely applicable. Universally disliked leader attributes—such as noncooperative, irritable, egocentric, and dictatorial—should be avoided in all cultures.

7. *Explain why US managers have a comparatively high failure rate on foreign assignments.* American expatriates are troubled by personal and family adjustment problems and homesickness. A great deal of money is wasted when expatriates come home early. More extensive cross-cultural training is needed.

8. *Summarize the research findings about North American women on foreign assignments.* The number of North American women on foreign assignments is still small, but growing. Self-disqualification and prejudicial home-country supervisors and staffing policies are largely to blame. Foreigners tend to view North American women primarily as foreigners and secondarily as women. North American women have a high success rate on foreign assignments. Foreign language skills, a strong and formally announced desire, foreign experience, networking, family and supervisory support, and visibility with upper management can increase the chances of getting a desired foreign assignment for both women and men.

9. *Identify four stages of the foreign assignment cycle and the OB trouble spot associated with each stage.* Stages of the foreign assignment cycle (with OB trouble spots) are (1) selection and training (unrealistic expectations); (2) arrival and adjustment (culture shock); (3) settling in and acculturating (lack of support); and (4) returning home and adjusting (reentry shock).

Key Terms

Culture, 96
Ethnocentrism, 98
Cultural intelligence, 100

High-context cultures, 100
Low-context cultures, 101
Individualistic culture, 105

OB in Action Case Study

It's All About Face-to-Face[90]

BusinessWeek Some road warriors fly commercial. Others take the corporate jet. Some pack their own bags. Others keep complete wardrobes in major cities. Some work through the entire plane ride. Others sleep. But if there is one thing these globetrotters agree on, it's that there is no substitute for face time—with the Abu Dhabi moneyman who holds the key to the future; with the underling who is AWOL on e-mail; with the spouse and kids, who have been a little sullen and exasperated of late.

Schmoozing, humoring, hammering the table—all must be done in person. "I don't want to sound like a whirling dervish," says Paul Calello, Credit Suisse's (CS) investment banking chief. "But in a global world you have to get in front of your employees, spend time with your clients, and show commitment when it comes to joint ventures, mergers, and alliances. The key is thoughtful travel—traveling when necessary."

Yes, many predicted the end of face time. But, paradoxically, the great work diaspora unleashed by technology is making physical connection all the more important. As companies open more outposts in more emerging markets, the need to gather intensifies. That's why executives increasingly feel the inhuman pull of having to be in two, three, four places at one time. The road warrior's art is all about finessing the strategic calculation of where to be when; of what bets to make with one's time. How do road warriors do this? By knowing cultures, organizations, and who has the power. Their jobs may be global, but their understanding must be local. It's not just companies' operations that have gotten bigger. So have these jobs.

Not so long ago it seemed as though technology might make business travel, if not obsolete, then a whole lot rarer. We're not talking about teleporting— just simple things like smartphones, corporate wikis, and videoconferencing. Coca-Cola's president and CEO-designate, Muhtar Kent, has been flying around the globe for Coke since the late 1970s. "I thought 10 or 15 years ago when the concept of videoconferencing first came out that it's really going to take the place of travel," he recalls. Of course that didn't happen, and he now spends about 150 days a year in the corporate jet.

Outreach Pays

Kent considers travel key to meeting new people who might one day prove useful. Several years ago, he was eager to open a bottling plant in Albania but frustrated that Coke couldn't get the approvals it needed from the rudderless young government. A friend urged Kent to visit a doctor who was well-versed in local politics. He found the man's patients sitting on tangerine boxes because there were no chairs in the waiting room. "I'm interested in investing in your country," Kent recalls saying during the chat. Three years later, the doctor was Albania's first elected president, and 24 months after that Coke opened its first bottling plant in the country. The doctor-turned-president, Sali Berisha, cut the ribbon.

Kent has never forgotten the lesson. More recently, Coke was hoping to win the rights to the Vitaminwater brand from Glacéau, the U.S. beverage maker known for its so-called enhanced waters. Kent knew one of the company's minority owners was Ratan Tata of Tata Group. He'd never met Tata. So during a business trip to India, Kent requested a dinner with him—no agenda, just to get to know each other, he said. Oh, and by the way, was it O.K. to bring along a Glacéau executive? It was. "And 72 days later, we closed the deal."

Meeting the right people is all very well, but road warriors who haven't done their homework on the local potentate can run into big problems. Few understand this better than Bill Roedy, the chief of MTV Networks International. His job requires getting often risqué programming into as many countries as he can without offending local sensibilities. A history enthusiast, Roedy is pretty good at figuring out the local scene. Yet he found himself with a rare case of butterflies in mid-September as his flight from London was set to touch down in the Saudi Arabian city of Jiddah. Roedy was in town to persuade the mayor of Mecca to give his blessing to MTV Arabia, the network's biggest global launch, which had the potential to reach 200 million Arabs across the region. "Presidents and sheiks don't normally watch MTV, so we have to help them overcome stereotypical views they have," says Roedy. "Nobody was more important than the mayor of Mecca, the religious center of Islam. We had to get it right."

Despite a hectic schedule that included trips to Budapest (to launch MTV Hungary), Prague (to attend a sales meeting), and New York (to discuss . . . budgets), Roedy carved out as much time in Saudi Arabia as he could. While there he attended recording sessions with the Arab rappers Jeddah Legends, where he learned that their lyrics tended to be about family and religion—themes that he would draw on during his meeting with the mayor of Mecca.

Finally the day arrived, and Roedy found himself providing assurances to a barrage of questions: Will there be opportunities to educate young people? (Yes.) Will there be a regular call to prayer? (Yes.) And, of course, there will be no skin, right, Mr. Roedy? (Correct.) To help seal the deal, Roedy attended an elaborate dinner in tents by the Red Sea. Ten days later, back at his London base, Roedy learned MTV Arabia could launch as scheduled in November. "Those meetings were crucial," he says.

Mark Sullivan, CEO of WhittmanHart Consulting, which advises clients about information management, flies up to 300,000 miles a year and knows well the strain constant travel can put on a family. "My profession is riddled with failed marriages, broken families, and people who get swept up with the lifestyle," he says.

Sullivan remains a road warrior for one reason: face time with his employees. About a year ago the firm's popular founder died. Sullivan, then president, knew voice messages, e-mail blasts, and memos wouldn't do. So he and two board members hopped on a plane and in two weeks traveled to nine offices around the U.S. to console bereft employees. "They needed a chance to swing away at you, to air concerns," says Sullivan. "If it's urgent, you've got to be physically there."

Questions for Discussion

1. If someone was under the impression that modern information and communication technology would significantly reduce the need for foreign business travel, how would you explain the real-life situation to them, based on what you just read?

2. Is face-to-face communication more important in high-context or low-context cultures? Explain.

3. Which of the cross-cultural competencies listed in Table 4–3 are evident in this case study? Explain.

4. Based on what you just read, are you more or less interested in getting a foreign assignment someday? Explain.

Ethical Dilemma

3M Tries to Make a Difference in Russia[91]

Russian managers aren't inclined . . . to reward people for improved performance. They spurn making investments for the future in favor of realizing immediate gains. They avoid establishing consistent business practices that can reduce uncertainty. Add in the country's high political risk and level of corruption, and it's no wonder that many multinationals have all but given up on Russia. . . .

The Russian business environment can be corrupt and dangerous; bribes and protection money are facts of life. But unlike many international companies, which try to distance themselves from such practices by simply banning them, 3M Russia actively promotes not only ethical behavior but also the personal security of its employees. . . .

3M Russia also strives to differentiate itself from competitors by being an ethical leader. For example, it holds training courses in business ethics for its customers.

Should 3M Export Its American Ethical Standards to Russia?

1. If 3M doesn't like the way things are done in Russia, it shouldn't do business there. Explain your rationale.

2. 3M should do business in Russia but not meddle in Russian culture. "When in Russia, do things the Russian way." Explain your rationale.

3. 3M has a basic moral responsibility to improve the ethical climate in foreign countries where it does business. Explain your rationale.

4. 3M should find a practical middle ground between the American and Russian ways of doing business. How should that happen?

5. Invent other options. Discuss.

Web Resources

For study material and exercises that apply to this chapter, visit our Web site,
www.mhhe.com/kreitner

Part 2

Individual Behavior in Organizations

Chapter 5

Key Individual Differences and the Road to Success

Student Resources for Studying Chapter 5

The Web site for your text includes resources that will help you master the concepts in this chapter. As you read, you'll want to visit the site for these helpful tools:

- Your online Study Guide includes learning objectives, a chapter summary, a glossary of key terms, and discussion questions.
- Take a practice quiz and test your knowledge!
- Scroll through a PowerPoint presentation with key concepts for this chapter.

Your instructor might also direct you to the Web site for these exercises:

- Self-assessments that correspond with the chapter content and a Group Exercise.
- You'll also find Video Cases and Internet Exercises for this chapter online.

www.mhhe.com/kreitner

Paradoxically, adult stem cells may be both the cause of cancer and a cure for it.

That theory, barely discussed even five years ago, has captivated the country's leading researchers, including Alfredo Quiñones-Hinojosa, M.D., a 40-year-old one-time farm worker from Mexico who now heads the Brain Tumor Center at the Johns Hopkins Bayview Medical Center in Baltimore.

Quiñones is a researcher with a difference. Dressed in his green scrubs and fresh from the second of what will be three brain surgeries that day, Quiñones puts in punishing 16-hour shifts, working not just in the operating room but in a brain cancer research lab as well. "The surgery can be perfect, a beautiful work of art," he says. "But I still know that no matter what I do, these patients will eventually succumb to this disease. So how can I not look for a cure when I see my patients and their families and the suffering this cancer causes?"

It's that work and passion that last year led *Popular Science* to name Quiñones to its annual Brilliant Ten list of "the most creative, the most groundbreaking, the most brilliant young scientists in the country."

Quiñones is convinced that adult stem cells act as triggers for brain cancer. (Unlike the use of embryonic stem cells, which requires the creation and destruction of an embryo, the use of adult stem cells found in children and adults is not politically controversial.) . . .

Quiñones' pursuit of a cure for brain cancer is marked by the same grit and determination that have shaped every facet of his life. This is a doctor, after all, whose life here began one cold, dark January night when, as a frightened 19-year-old, he climbed a chain-link fence along the border between Mexico and the United States. The first time he clambered over the fence he was caught and sent back across the border. Just hours later he was back. This time he made it over and escaped into the night.

An undocumented immigrant, Quiñones spoke no English and had no job skills. He labored as a farm worker in California, "One day a friend said to me, 'You will always be a migrant worker,' and something snapped, I just couldn't accept that," he says.

Quiñones, who lived in a dilapidated trailer, took English lessons and enrolled at a community college while juggling jobs as a painter and welder. He won a scholarship to the University of California, Berkeley. From there, he went on to medical school at Harvard University. He became a citizen.

Now, his office walls at Hopkins are covered in awards.

"This is a man who won't take no for an answer," says Henry Brem, M.D., chair of neurosurgery at Hopkins. "He's an inspired scientist, and an extraordinarily hard-working one."[1]

FOR DISCUSSION

What does this amazing success story tell us about what it takes to get ahead in this world?

As the world's population continues to grow (more than 6.7 billion at the time of this writing),[2] many of us seek a unique identity that sets us apart from the crowd. This makes understanding and managing people and trying to please them increasingly difficult. For instance, consider Cold Stone Creamery's ice cream stores, where customer-selected mix-ins and toppings make more than 11.5 million variations possible![3] What's your favorite? Likewise, how do you express yourself in the workplace? Are you a go-getter, like Dr. Quiñones featured in the opening vignette, or a slacker? Are you a loner or highly social? Do you see yourself as master of your own fate, or a victim of circumstances? Are you emotional or calm and cool? Is your job satisfaction through the roof or stuck in the basement? Thanks to a vast array of individual differences such as these, modern organizations have a rich and interesting human texture. On the other hand, individual differences make the manager's job endlessly challenging. In fact, according to research, "variability among workers is substantial at all levels but increases dramatically with job complexity. In life insurance sales, for example, variability in performance is around six times as great as in routine clerical jobs."[4]

Growing workforce diversity compels managers to view individual differences in a fresh new way. Rather than stifling diversity, as in the past, today's managers need to better understand and accommodate employee diversity and individual differences.[5]

Both this chapter and the next explore the key individual differences portrayed in Figure 5–1. The figure is intended to be an instructional road map showing the bridges between self-concept and self-expression. This chapter focuses on self-concept, personality, abilities, and emotions. Personal values, attitudes, and job satisfaction are covered in Chapter 6. Taken as an integrated whole, all these factors provide a foundation for better understanding each organizational contributor (including yourself) as a unique and special individual. This chapter ends with a practical capstone section about achieving success, however you choose to define that form of self-expression.

Self-Concept

to the point

What can managers do to build their employees' self-esteem and self-efficacy?

When you look in the mirror, you recognize who it is. You see your*self*.[6] This is a remarkable talent in the animal kingdom, according to scientists. Only humans, apes, dolphins, and elephants can recognize themselves in a mirror.[7] But what exactly do you know about that person in the mirror? People ages 16 to 70 were asked what they would do differently if they could live life over again; 48% chose the response category "Get in touch with self."[8] Toward that end, this section helps you get in better touch with yourself on the way to better understanding and

Figure 5–1   *An Instructional Road Map for the Study of Individual Differences in Chapters 5 and 6*

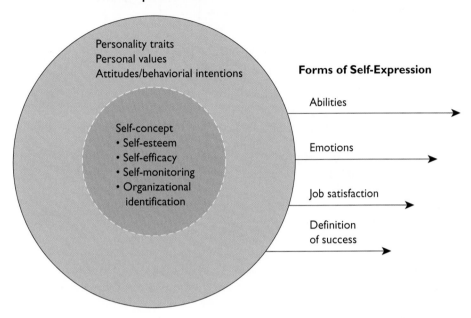

managing yourself and others in the workplace. Former General Electric CEO Jack Welch tells us: "You've got to be comfortable with yourself to make a good boss."[9]

Sociologist Viktor Gecas defines **self-concept** as "the concept the individual has of himself as a physical, social, and spiritual or moral being."[10] In other words, because you have a self-concept, you recognize yourself as a distinct human being. A self-concept would be impossible without the capacity to think about complex things and processes. This brings us to the role of cognitions. **Cognitions** represent "any knowledge, opinion, or belief about the environment, about oneself, or about one's behavior."[11] Among many different types of cognitions, those involving anticipation, introspection, planning, goal setting, evaluating, and setting personal standards are particularly relevant to OB.

Our attention now turns to three topics invariably mentioned when behavioral scientists discuss self-concept. They are self-esteem, self-efficacy, and self-monitoring. We also consider the ethical implications of organizational identification, a social aspect of self. A practical social learning model of self-management can be found in Learning Module A (Learning Module A is located on our Web site at www.mhhe .com/kreitner). Each of these areas deserves a closer look by those who want to better understand and effectively manage themselves and others.

Self-concept
Person's self-perception as a physical, social, spiritual being.

Cognitions
A person's knowledge, opinions, or beliefs.

LO.1 Self-Esteem

Self-esteem is a belief about one's own self-worth based on an overall self-evaluation.[12] Self-esteem is measured by having survey respondents indicate their agreement or disagreement with both positive and negative statements. A positive statement on one general self-esteem survey is: "I feel I am a person of worth, the

Self-esteem
One's overall self-evaluation.

"Well, whenever I lose my sense of identity, I Google myself"

From *Harvard Business Review*, November 2008, page 100, by Chris Wildt.

equal of other people."[13] Among the negative items is: "I feel I do not have much to be proud of."[14] Those who agree with the positive statements and disagree with the negative statements have high self-esteem. They see themselves as worthwhile, capable, and acceptable. People with low self-esteem view themselves in negative terms, do not feel good about themselves, and experience self-doubts. Recent research shows they tend to have health problems and low-quality social relationships, as well as being vulnerable to depression.[15]

Employment and Self-Esteem

What researchers call organization-based self-esteem makes paid employment a prime determinant of overall self-esteem in modern life.[16] Consequently, unemployment can have a devastating impact on one's self-esteem. Consider these instructive remarks from Arthur J Fiacco, a 56-year-old executive who was laid off without any warning during an economic downturn:

> I had never felt so lonely and helpless. I had been working since I was 16 years old. . . .
> A job isn't just about working. A job helps define who we are. It is what we talk with our neighbors about. It is the place we go. It is how we are introduced. It is one of the first things people ask about when we meet them. And most important, we measure ourselves from our very first job onward. Without a job, I felt I had lost my identity.[17]

Fiacco eventually turned things around by building a successful consulting business. He says now, "I am making a contribution and feel good. . . . I have learned to listen to what others are trying to tell me."[18]

Self-Esteem across Cultures

What are the cross-cultural implications for self-esteem, a concept that has been called uniquely Western? In a survey of 13,118 students from 31 countries worldwide, a moderate positive correlation was found between self-esteem and life satisfaction. But the relationship was stronger in individualistic cultures (e.g., United States, Canada, New Zealand, Netherlands) than in collectivist cultures (e.g., Korea, Kenya, Japan). The researchers concluded that individualistic cultures socialize people to focus more on themselves, while people in collectivist cultures "are socialized to fit into the community and to do their duty. Thus, how a collectivist feels about him- or herself is less relevant to . . . life satisfaction."[19] Global managers need to remember to deemphasize self-esteem when doing business in collectivist ("we") cultures, as opposed to emphasizing it in individualistic ("me") cultures.

Can General Self-Esteem Be Improved?   The short answer is yes (see Table 5–1). More detailed answers come from research. In one study, youth-league baseball coaches who were trained in supportive teaching techniques had a positive effect on the self-esteem of young boys. A control group of untrained coaches had no such positive effect.[20] Another study led to this conclusion: "Low self-esteem can be raised more by having the person think of desirable characteristics possessed rather than of undesirable characteristics from which he or she is free."[21] This approach can help neutralize the self-defeating negative thoughts among those with low self-esteem. Meanwhile, a lively debate continues among educational policy makers over the relative importance of boosting students' self-esteem versus making sure they master the basics of reading, writing, and math.[22] When researchers recently reviewed data from 1975 through 2006, they found that the self-esteem movement had carried the day. But at what cost? Results showed

Table 5–1   *Branden's Six Pillars of Self-Esteem*

What nurtures and sustains self-esteem in grown-ups is not how others deal with us but how we ourselves operate in the face of life's challenges—the choices we make and the actions we take.

This leads us to the six pillars of self-esteem.

1. *Live consciously.* Be actively and fully engaged in what you do and with whom you interact.

2. *Be self-accepting.* Don't be overly judgmental or critical of your thoughts and actions.

3. *Take personal responsibility.* Take full responsibility for your decisions and actions in life's journey.

4. *Be self-assertive.* Be authentic and willing to defend your beliefs when interacting with others, rather than bending to their will to be accepted or liked.

5. *Live purposefully.* Have clear near-term and long-term goals and realistic plans for achieving them to create a sense of control over your life.

6. *Have personal integrity.* Be true to your word and your values.

Between self-esteem and the practices that support it, there is reciprocal causation. This means that the behaviors that generate good self-esteem are also expressions of good self-esteem.

SOURCE: From Nathaniel Branden, *Self-Esteem at Work: How Confident People Make Powerful Companies,* 1998, pp 33–36. Reprinted with permission of John Wiley & Sons, Inc.

Military Veterans Bring High Self-Efficacy to MBA Programs

Ryan McDermott, a second-year student at Darden [the University of Virginia's School of Business], led a combat mission down the most dangerous road in Baghdad, fought four battles, and wrote a plan for training and deploying 3,600 soldiers, all by the age of 26. Summer Jones, a former Naval officer, by 26 had launched Tomahawk missiles off a ship in the Persian Gulf, commanded 200 sailors, and delivered the news of Sept. 11 Pentagon casualties to their families. When her Georgetown University evening MBA classmates wonder how the 32-year-old maintains a full-time job, raises two children, supports her husband in law school, and earns her MBA at the same time, she tells them: "When you've been in a wartime environment, you step back and say, 'This is easy.'" As if to prove it, she gave birth to her second son just after the first week of the MBA program without missing a day of class.

What is the ethical argument for hiring military veterans?

SOURCE: J Porter, "From the Battlefield to B-School," *BusinessWeek,* March 24, 2008, p 80.

Summer Jones and her growing family.

that while self-esteem among high school seniors had risen over the years, self-perceptions of *competence* had not. This left the researchers worried that "over-praised" kids who were confident about becoming "very good" spouses, parents, and employees could be primed for a big letdown in real life.[23] What are your thoughts on this?

LO.2 Self-Efficacy

Self-confidence that leads to results is important in today's demanding workplaces. In fact, when 2,500 managers and executives in the United States were polled by *BusinessWeek,* 72% of the women and 66% of the men said *self-confidence* was the most important quality for succeeding in business.[24] Self-confidence that can be backed up with real results involves more than high self-esteem; it also requires self-efficacy.[25] **Self-efficacy** is a person's belief about his or her chances of successfully accomplishing a specific task. According to one OB writer, "Self-efficacy arises from the gradual acquisition of complex cognitive, social, linguistic, and/or physical skills through experience."[26] Role models can inspire us to build self-efficacy (see Real World/Real People feature about military veterans above).

Self-efficacy

Belief in one's ability to do a task.

The relationship between self-efficacy and performance is a cyclical one. Efficacy → performance cycles can spiral upward toward success or downward toward failure.[27] Researchers have documented strong linkages between high self-efficacy expectations and success in widely varied physical and mental tasks, anxiety reduction, addiction control, pain tolerance, illness recovery, avoidance of seasickness in naval cadets, physical exercise, and stress avoidance.[28] Oppositely, those with low self-efficacy expectations tend to have low success rates. Although self-efficacy sounds like some sort of mental magic, it operates in a very straight-forward manner, as a model will show.

What Are the Mechanisms of Self-Efficacy? A basic model of self-efficacy is displayed in Figure 5–2. It draws upon the work of Stanford psychologist Albert Bandura. Let us explore this model with a simple illustrative task. Imagine you have been told to prepare and deliver a 10-minute talk to an OB class of 50 students on the workings of the self-efficacy model in Figure 5–2.

Figure 5–2   *A Model of How Self-Efficacy Beliefs Can Pave the Way for Success or Failure*

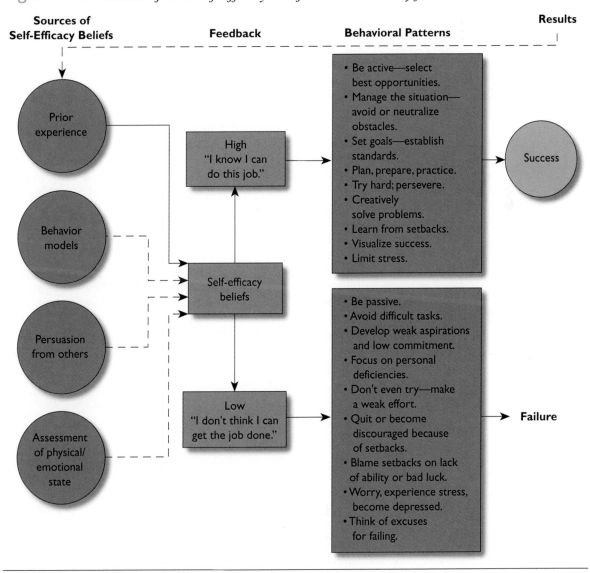

SOURCES: Adapted from discussion in A Bandura, "Regulation of Cognitive Processes through Perceived Self-Efficacy," *Developmental Psychology,* September 1989, pp 729–35; and R Wood and A Bandura, "Social Cognitive Theory of Organizational Management," *Academy of Management Review,* July 1989, pp 361–84.

Your self-efficacy calculation would involve cognitive appraisal of the interaction between your perceived capability and situational opportunities and obstacles.

As you begin to prepare for your presentation, the four sources of self-efficacy beliefs would come into play. Because prior experience is the most potent source, according to Bandura, it is listed first and connected to self-efficacy beliefs with a solid line. Past success in public speaking would boost your self-efficacy. But bad experiences with delivering speeches would foster low self-efficacy. Regarding behavior models as a source of self-efficacy beliefs, you would be influenced by the success or failure of your classmates in delivering similar talks. Their successes would tend to bolster you (or perhaps their failure would if you were very competitive and had high self-esteem). Likewise, any supportive persuasion from your classmates that you will do a good job would enhance your self-efficacy. Physical and emotional factors also might affect your self-confidence. A sudden case of laryngitis or a bout of stage fright could cause your self-efficacy expectations to plunge. Your cognitive evaluation of the situation then would yield a self-efficacy belief—ranging from high to low expectations for success. Importantly, self-efficacy beliefs are not merely boastful statements based on bravado; they are deep convictions supported by experience.

Moving to the *behavioral patterns* portion of Figure 5–2, we see how self-efficacy beliefs are acted out. In short, if you have high self-efficacy about giving your 10-minute speech, you will work harder, more creatively, and longer when preparing for your talk than will your low-self-efficacy classmates. The results would then take shape accordingly. People program themselves for success or failure by enacting their self-efficacy expectations. Positive or negative results subsequently become feedback for one's base of personal experience. Along those lines, a national panel of scholars convened to discover why American students don't do better in math concluded: "Effort counts. Students who believe that working hard will make them smarter in math actually do achieve better."[29]

Self-Efficacy Implications for Managers   On-the-job research evidence encourages managers to nurture self-efficacy, both in themselves and in others. In fact, a meta-analysis encompassing 21,616 subjects found a significant positive correlation between self-efficacy and job performance.[30] Self-efficacy can be boosted in the workplace through careful hiring, challenging assignments, training and coaching, goal setting, supportive leadership and mentoring, and rewards for improvement. Boeing's CEO, James McNerney, offered this perspective:

> [S]uccess and achievement can feed on themselves. It feels good to keep succeeding. It feels great to see the people you work with grow and achieve. Maybe the ignition happens when you're younger, and then it feeds on itself. The next question is how you give it to people who weren't fortunate enough to have it given to them when they were young. It gets back to leadership attributes—expect a lot, inspire people, ask them to take the values that are important to them at home or at church and bring them to work.[31]

L0.3 Self-Monitoring

Consider these contrasting scenarios:

1. You are rushing to an important meeting when a coworker pulls you aside and starts to discuss a personal problem. You want to break off the conversation, so you glance up at the clock. He keeps talking. You say, "I'm late for a big meeting." He continues. You turn and start to walk away. The person keeps talking as

if he never received any of your verbal and nonverbal signals that the conversation was over.

2. Same situation. Only this time, when you glance at the clock, the person immediately says, "I know, you've got to go. Sorry. We'll talk later."

In the first all-too-familiar scenario, you are talking to a "low self-monitor." The second scenario involves a "high self-monitor." But more is involved here than an irritating situation. A significant and measurable individual difference in self-expression behavior, called self-monitoring, is highlighted. **Self-monitoring** is the extent to which a person observes his or her own self-expressive behavior and adapts it to the demands of the situation. Experts on the subject offer this explanation:

> Individuals high in self-monitoring are thought to regulate their expressive self-presentation for the sake of desired public appearances, and thus be highly responsive to social and interpersonal cues of situationally appropriate performances. Individuals low in self-monitoring are thought to lack either the ability or the motivation to so regulate their expressive self-presentations. Their expressive behaviors, instead, are thought to functionally reflect their own enduring and momentary inner states, including their attitudes, traits, and feelings.[32]

Self-monitoring
Observing one's own behavior and adapting it to the situation.

In organizational life, both high and low monitors are subject to criticism. High self-monitors are sometimes called *chameleons,* who readily adapt their self-presentation to their surroundings. Low self-monitors, on the other hand, often are criticized for being on their own planet and insensitive to others.

A Matter of Degree   Self-monitoring is not an either-or proposition. It is a matter of degree; a matter of being relatively high or low in terms of related patterns of self-expression. As a quick comprehension check, does the following scenario involve a relatively high or low self-monitoring individual?

go to the Web for the Self-Exercise: What Are Your Self-Monitoring Tendencies?

> We have an employee who turns every interaction—work-related or not—into a conversation about her. She's otherwise good at her job, but folks are beginning to avoid meetings with her or task forces on which she serves. "She sucks the air out of the room," a co-worker complained.[33]

If you said a low self-monitor, you understand the concept. What are your self-monitoring tendencies?

Research Findings and Practical Recommendations   A meta-analysis encompassing 23,191 subjects in 136 samples found self-monitoring to be relevant and useful when dealing with job performance and emerging leaders.[34] According to field research, there is a positive relationship between high self-monitoring and career success. Among 139 MBA graduates who were tracked for five years, high self-monitors enjoyed more internal and external promotions than did their low self-monitoring classmates.[35] Another study of 147 managers and professionals found that high self-monitors had a better record of acquiring a mentor (someone to act as a personal career coach and professional sponsor).[36]

These results mesh well with an earlier study that found managerial success (in terms of speed of promotions) tied to political savvy (knowing how to socialize, network, and engage in organizational politics).[37]

The foregoing evidence and practical experience lead us to make these practical recommendations:

For high, moderate, and low self-monitors: Become more consciously aware of your self-image and how it affects others.

For high self-monitors: Don't overdo it by evolving from a successful chameleon into someone who is widely perceived as insincere, dishonest, phoney, and untrustworthy. You cannot be everything to everyone.

For low self-monitors: You can bend without breaking, so try to be a bit more accommodating while being true to your basic beliefs. Don't wear out your welcome when communicating. Practice reading and adjusting to nonverbal cues in various public situations. If your conversation partner is bored or distracted, stop—because he or she is not really listening.

Organizational Identification: A *Social* Aspect of Self-Concept with Ethical Implications

Organizational identification

Organizational values or beliefs become part of one's self-identity.

The dividing line between self and others is not a neat and precise one. A certain amount of blurring occurs, for example, when an employee comes to define him- or herself with a *specific* organization—a psychological process called *organizational identification.* According to an expert on this evolving OB topic, "**organizational identification** occurs when one comes to integrate beliefs about one's organization into one's identity."[38] Organizational identification goes to the heart of organizational culture and socialization (recall our discussion in Chapter 3).

Managers put a good deal of emphasis today on organizational mission, philosophy, and values with the express intent of integrating the company into each employee's self-identity. Hopefully, as the logic goes, employees who identify closely with the organization will be more loyal, more committed, and harder working. For example, consider this snapshot of American Express:

Credit card behemoth breeds loyalty: Nearly a quarter of employees have been with the company more than 15 years. "It is my honor to serve my brand, my creed, my company," says one.[39]

As an extreme case in point, organizational identification among employees at Harley-Davidson's motorcycle factories is so strong that many sport tattoos with the company's logo.[40] Working at Harley is not just a job, it's a lifestyle. (Somehow, your authors have a hard time imagining an employee with a General Motors or Burger King tattoo!)

A company tattoo may be a bit extreme, but the ethical implications of identifying too closely with one's employer are profound. Phyllis Anzalone, a former Enron employee, is a good case in point. She admitted that Enron *was* her self-identity and she ended up with emotional scars:

What did working at Enron do for Anzalone? For one thing, it made her a lot of money, so much that the company's failure cost her about $1 million. More important, it made her. It took her from being a reasonably successful facilities management salesperson from rural Louisiana and propelled her into the ranks of sales superstars. It changed her view of herself; it confirmed what she thought she could achieve. "Enron had a profound effect on my life," she says. As devastating as it was, I'm glad I did it. It was like being on steroids every day."

And what does Anzalone think of the executives who ran Enron—and then ran it into the ground? "They are scum," she says, "They are crooks, and they are traitors. They betrayed many people's trust, including mine."[41]

Anzalone distanced herself from Enron's most unsavory characters during her years with the company. But some of her colleagues, with equally strong organizational identification, evidently turned their backs on their personal ethical standards and values when working on clearly illegal deals. When employees suspend their critical thinking and lose their objectivity, unhealthy groupthink can occur and needed constructive conflict does *not* occur. (Groupthink is covered in Chapter 10 and functional conflict is discussed in Chapter 13.) Whistle-blowing, as defined in Chapter 1, is unlikely to occur when organizational identification is excessive. Company loyalty and dedication are one thing; blind obedience to unethical leaders is quite another.[42]

Personality: Concepts and Controversy

Individuals have their own way of thinking and acting, their own unique style or *personality*. **Personality** is defined as the combination of stable physical and mental characteristics that give the individual his or her identity.[43] These characteristics or traits—including how one looks, thinks, acts, and feels—are the product of interacting genetic and environmental influences.[44] In this section, we introduce the Big Five personality dimensions, explore the proactive personality, and issue some cautions about workplace personality testing.

LO.4 The Big Five Personality Dimensions

Decades of research produced cumbersome lists of personality traits. In fact, one recent study identified 1,710 English-language adjectives used to describe aspects of personality.[45] Fortunately, this confusing situation has been statistically distilled to the Big Five.[46] They are extraversion, agreeableness, conscientiousness, emotional stability, and openness to experience (see Table 5–2 for descriptions).

to the point
How would someone with a proactive personality likely score on the Big Five dimensions?

Personality
Stable physical and mental characteristics responsible for a person's identity.

Table 5–2   *The Big Five Personality Dimensions*

PERSONALITY DIMENSION	CHARACTERISTICS OF A PERSON SCORING POSITIVELY ON THE DIMENSION
1. Extraversion	Outgoing, talkative, sociable, assertive
2. Agreeableness	Trusting, good-natured, cooperative, softhearted
3. Conscientiousness	Dependable, responsible, achievement oriented, persistent
4. Emotional stability	Relaxed, secure, unworried
5. Openness to experience	Intellectual, imaginative, curious, broad-minded

SOURCE: Adapted from M R Barrick and M K Mount, "Autonomy as a Moderator of the Relationships between the Big Five Personality Dimensions and Job Performance," *Journal of Applied Psychology*, February 1993, pp 111–18.

Standardized personality tests determine how positively or negatively a person scores on each of the Big Five. For example, someone scoring negatively on extraversion would be an introverted person prone to shy and withdrawn behavior. Someone scoring negatively on emotional security would be nervous, tense, angry, and worried. Appropriately, the negative end of the emotional stability scale is labeled neuroticism.

A person's scores on the Big Five reveal a personality profile as unique as his or her fingerprints. One's personality profile is relatively durable, too. Extraversion and conscientiousness were found to be the most stable of the Big Five, according to data on 799 people covering the 40 years between their elementary-school days and midlife.[47] So don't be surprised when many of your high-school classmates seem pretty much the same at your 20th reunion, except for some extra pounds and thinning hair, of course.

But one important question lingers: Are personality models ethnocentric and unique to the culture in which they were developed? At least as far as the Big Five model goes, cross-cultural research evidence points in the direction of no. Specifically, the Big Five personality structure held up very well in one study of women and men from Russia, Canada, Hong Kong, Poland, Germany, and Finland and a second study (85% male) of South Korean managers and stockbrokers.[48] A recent comprehensive analysis of Big Five studies led the researchers to this conclusion: "To date, there is no compelling evidence that culture affects personality structure."[49] However, a recent study of Dutch personality traits, using an updated assessment tool, added three more personality traits to the Big Five— *virtue*, *competence*, and *hedonism*.[50]

Those interested in OB want to know the connection between the Big Five and job performance. Ideally, Big Five personality dimensions that correlate positively and strongly with job performance would be helpful in the selection, training, and appraisal of employees. A meta-analysis of 117 studies involving 23,994 subjects from many professions offers guidance.[51] Among the Big Five, *conscientiousness* had the strongest positive correlation with job performance and training performance. According to the researchers, "those individuals who exhibit traits associated with a strong sense of purpose, obligation, and persistence generally perform better than those who do not."[52] Not surprisingly, entrepreneurs score high on conscientiousness.[53] Another recent finding: Extraversion (an outgoing personality) correlated positively with promotions, salary level, and career satisfaction. And, as one might expect, neuroticism (low emotional stability) was associated with low career satisfaction.[54]

go to the Web for the Self-Exercise: How Do You Score on the Big Five Personality Factors?

Proactive personality

Action-oriented person who shows initiative and perseveres to change things.

LO.5 The Proactive Personality

As suggested by the previous discussion, someone who scores high on the Big Five dimension of conscientiousness is probably a good worker. Thomas S Bateman and J Michael Crant took this important linkage an additional step by formulating the concept of the proactive personality. They define and characterize the **proactive personality** in these terms: "someone who is relatively unconstrained by situational

Climbing Life's Mountains Requires the Right People with Proactive Personalities

Jim Collins, author of the best-seller *Good to Great* and expert rock climber:

> The right people don't need to be managed. The moment you feel the need to tightly manage someone, you've made a hiring mistake.
>
> The right people don't think they have a job: They have responsibilities. . . .
>
> The right people do what they say they will do, which means being really careful about what they say they will do. It's key in difficult times. In difficult environments our results are our responsibility. People who take credit in good times and blame external forces in bad times do not deserve to lead. . . .
>
> As a rock climber, the one thing you learn is that those who panic, die on the mountain. You don't just sit on the mountain. You either go up or go down, but don't just sit and wait to get clobbered. If you go down and survive, you can come back another day.

What ethical themes and responsibilities are evident here?

SOURCE: As quoted in J Reingold, "Jim Collins: How Great Companies Turn Crisis into Opportunity," *Fortune*, February 2, 2009, p 52.

forces and who effects environmental change. Proactive people identify opportunities and act on them, show initiative, take action, and persevere until meaningful change occurs."[55] They have what researchers have long called an **internal locus of control,** the belief that one controls the events and consequences affecting one's life.[56] For example, an "internal" tends to attribute positive outcomes, such as getting a passing grade on an exam, to her or his own abilities. Accordingly, an "internal" tends to blame negative events, such as failing an exam, on personal shortcomings—not studying hard enough, perhaps. Oppositely, people with an **external locus of control** tend to attribute key outcomes in their lives to environmental causes, such as luck or fate. In a review of relevant studies, Crant found the proactive personality to be positively associated with individual, team, and organizational success.[57]

Internal locus of control

Attributing outcomes to one's own actions.

External locus of control

Attributing outcomes to circumstances beyond one's control.

go to the Web for the Self-Exercise: Where Is Your Locus of Control?

Successful entrepreneurs exemplify the proactive personality.[58] People with proactive personalities truly are valuable *human capital,* as defined in Chapter 1. Those wanting to get ahead would do well to cultivate the initiative, drive, courage, and perseverance of someone with a proactive personality—and managers would do well to hire them. Matt Glotzbach, product management director for Google Enterprise, is a good case in point:

> My first morning at Google, I put my name and address on one form online, and it went everywhere it needed to go electronically. That's how this place works.

I went to a staff meeting that afternoon and got assigned to figure out how Google could launch Enterprise [applications for corporations] in Europe. I was told to come back with the answer at the end of the week. It was like, "Hey, New Guy, you don't know anything about our business yet, and you don't have any international experience, but here are some people who can help you. Go figure it out." We launched in Europe a few months later.[59]

Issue: What about Personality Testing in the Workplace?

Personality testing as a tool for making decisions about hiring, training, and promotion is commonplace. "According to the Association of Test Publishers, overall employment testing, including personality tests, has been growing at a rate of 10% to 15% in each of the past three years."[60]

Unfortunately, there is the major issue of *sloppy administration*. Annie Murphy Paul, author of the new book *The Cult of Personality*,[61] explains:

> You hear a lot from psychologists who are supportive of personality testing, and sometimes from testing companies, that there are ideal ways to use these tests. An example would be to bring in a psychologist to do a study of the job itself and design or tailor a test specifically for that position, and then have it administered by a psychologist, and have the results remain confidential. I think the way these tests are actually used is that they're usually bought off the shelf, they're given indiscriminately, often by people who aren't trained or qualified, and then the results aren't kept confidential or private at all. For all the talk about standards on how [these tests] should be used, the way they're used in the real world is more hit-or-miss.[62]

Faking, cheating, and illegal discrimination also are potential problems with on-the-job personality testing. A recent computer simulation revealed the potential for faking conscientiousness, a key Big Five factor.[63] Regarding the problem of cheating, the case of Anton Smith is a cautionary tale: Prior to taking a 130-item personality test when applying for a job at an athletic footwear store in North Carolina, Smith got an edge when a friend found a pirated answer key on the Internet. Smith, who got the job but later left when the store went out of business, had this to say about the test: "It isn't useful. People are hip to it."[64] The problem of illegal discrimination was summed up by Dallas employment attorney Allan King when he told a group of human resource professionals in 2008 that, because society is so diverse, "every test has an adverse impact against somebody."[65] A recent meta-analysis of personality testing across five racial groups in the United States came to essentially the same conclusion.[66]

Ability

Stable characteristic responsible for a person's maximum physical or mental performance.

The practical tips in Table 5–3 can help managers avoid abuses and costly discrimination lawsuits when using personality and psychological testing for employment-related decisions. Job-related skills testing and behavioral interviewing are workable alternatives to personality testing.

We now shift our focus to abilities and intelligence.

to the point

What are the major abilities and eight multiple intelligences?

Abilities (Intelligence) and Performance

Individual differences in abilities and accompanying skills are a central concern for managers because nothing can be accomplished without appropriately skilled personnel. An **ability** represents a broad and stable characteristic responsible for a person's maximum—as opposed to typical—performance on mental and physical

Table 5–3   *Advice and Words of Caution about Personality Testing in the Workplace*

Researchers, test developers, and organizations that administer personality assessments offer the following suggestions for getting started or for evaluating whether tests already in use are appropriate for forecasting job performance:

- Determine what you hope to accomplish. If you are looking to find the best fit of job and applicant, analyze the aspects of the position that are most critical for it.

- Look for outside help to determine if a test exists or can be developed to screen applicants for the traits that best fit the position. Industrial psychologists, professional organizations, and a number of Internet sites provide resources.

- Insist that any test recommended by a consultant or vendor be validated scientifically for the specific purpose that you have defined. Vendors should be able to cite some independent, credible research supporting a test's correlation with job performance.

- Ask the test provider to document the legal basis for any assessment: Is it fair? Is it job-related? Is it biased against any racial or ethnic group? Does it violate an applicant's right to privacy under state or federal laws? Vendors should provide a lawyer's statement that a test does not adversely affect any protected class, and employers may want to get their own lawyer's opinion, as well.

- Make sure that every staff member who will be administering tests or analyzing results is educated about how to do so properly and keeps results confidential. Use the scores on personality tests in tandem with other factors that you believe are essential to the job—such as skills and experience—to create a comprehensive evaluation of the merits of each candidate, and apply those criteria identically to each applicant.

SOURCE: From S Bates, "Personality Counts," *HR Magazine*, February 2002, p 34. Copyright 2008 by Society for Human Resource Management (SHRM). Reproduced with permission of Society for Human Resource Management via Copyright Clearance Center.

tasks. A **skill,** on the other hand, is the specific capacity to physically manipulate objects. Consider this difference as you imagine yourself being the only passenger on a small commuter airplane in which the pilot has just passed out. As the plane nose-dives, your effort and abilities will not be enough to save yourself and the pilot if you do not possess flying skills. As shown in Figure 5–3 successful performance (be it landing an airplane or performing any other job) depends on the right combination of effort, ability, and skill.

Skill
Specific capacity to manipulate objects.

Abilities and skills are being developed in some unique ways today, thanks to modern technology. For example, a biomedical professor at Arizona State University and a Phoenix surgeon "conducted studies in which trainee surgeons played a Nintendo Wii video game called Marble Mania, which requires players to develop dexterity in their hand movements to succeed at the game. . . . The Wii game players showed 48 percent more improvement in their surgical techniques than the non-players."[67] So video game–obsessed youngsters can now tell their worried parents and teachers, "I'm just refining my surgical techique."

Among the many desirable skills and competencies in organizational life are written and spoken communication, initiative, decisiveness, tolerance, problem solving, adaptability, and resilience. Importantly, our cautions about on-the-job personality testing extend to ability, intelligence, and skill testing and certification.[68]

Before moving on, we need to say something about a modern-day threat to abilities, skills, and general competence. That threat, according to public health officials, is *sleep deprivation.*

Figure 5–3   *Performance Depends on the Right Combination of Effort, Ability, and Skill*

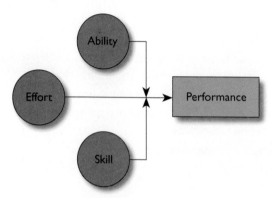

Abilities and the Need for Sleep

In a recent survey of 1,506 adults in the United States, only 49% reported getting a "good night's sleep" every night or almost every night.[69] If you are routinely short-changing your basic sleep needs, you are likely to be a less effective decision maker and problem solver, more stressed (see Chapter 18), and more prone to health problems than you should be.[70] Habitually sleep-deprived people need to be aware of this stunning fact: "Staying awake 24 hours impairs cognitive psychomotor performance to the same degree as having a 0.1 percent blood alcohol level."[71] That exceeds the 0.08 percent blood alcohol limit for drivers in the United States. In fact, experts estimate "that sleep-deprived drivers cause more than 100,000 automobile crashes a year and more than 1,500 deaths."[72] According to sleep researcher Sara Mednick:

> Without sleep you don't learn. My research shows that people deteriorate during the day. It's difficult to sustain productivity. Naps can add back to the sleep you're deprived of at night. And a nap enhances productivity even if you have enough nocturnal sleep....

> A 20-minute nap in the afternoon, between 1 PM and 3 PM, right after lunch, would be ideal. You don't want to get into deep sleep, because you need to be alert. This nap will allow you to be as productive right after the nap as you were before. That's what a lot of businesspeople need for on-your-feet thinking.[73]

Employers have taken note and are making changes:

> Many workplaces, including shoe retailer Zappos.com and New York City–based Workman Publishing, have designated

sleep areas. Metal distributor Yarde Metals goes a step further. Its Southington, Conn., headquarters features the "Z Lounge," a darkened room equipped with a reclining chair that vibrates to music as a TV screen plays video of a babbling brook, crackling fireplace, beach scene or fish tank. "If some people just need a nap for 15 minutes and they can finish out their day with a clear mind, there's benefit to the company to do that," says Yarde marketing director Susan Kozikowski.[74]

The balance of this section explores intelligence, specific cognitive abilities, and the controversial idea of multiple intelligences.

Intelligence and Cognitive Abilities

Although experts do not agree on a specific definition, **intelligence** represents an individual's capacity for constructive thinking, reasoning, and problem solving.[75] Historically, intelligence was believed to be an innate capacity, passed genetically from one generation to the next. Research since has shown, however, that intelligence (like personality) also is a function of environmental influences.[76] Organic factors have more recently been added to the formula as a result of mounting evidence of the connection between alcohol and drug abuse and poor eating habits among pregnant women and intellectual development problems in their children.[77]

Intelligence
Capacity for constructive thinking, reasoning, problem solving.

Researchers have produced some interesting findings about intelligence in recent years. A steady and significant rise in average intelligence among those in developed countries has been observed over the last 70 years. Why? Experts at an American Psychological Association conference concluded, "Some combination of better schooling, improved socioeconomic status, healthier nutrition, and a more technologically complex society might account for the gains in IQ scores."[78] So if you think you're smarter than your parents and your teachers, despite being criticized for not knowing a lot a facts they think are important, you're probably right!

Two Types of Abilities   Human intelligence has been studied predominantly through the empirical approach. By examining the relationships between measures of mental abilities and behavior, researchers have statistically isolated major components of intelligence. Using this empirical procedure, pioneering psychologist Charles Spearman proposed in 1927 that all cognitive performance is determined by two types of abilities. The first can be characterized as a general mental ability needed for *all* cognitive tasks. The second is unique to the task at hand.[79] For example, an individual's ability to complete crossword puzzles is a function of his or her broad mental abilities as well as the specific ability to perceive patterns in partially completed words.

Seven Major Mental Abilities   Through the years, much research has been devoted to developing and expanding Spearman's ideas on the relationship between cognitive abilities and intelligence. One research psychologist listed 120 distinct mental abilities. Table 5–4 contains definitions of the seven most frequently cited mental abilities. Of the seven abilities, personnel selection researchers have found verbal ability, numerical ability, spatial ability, and inductive reasoning to be valid predictors of job performance for both minority and majority applicants.[80]

Table 5–4 *Mental Abilities Underlying Performance*

ABILITY	DESCRIPTION
1. Verbal comprehension	The ability to understand what words mean and to readily comprehend what is read.
2. Word fluency	The ability to produce isolated words that fulfill specific symbolic or structural requirements (such as all words that begin with the letter *b* and have two vowels).
3. Numerical	The ability to make quick and accurate arithmetic computations such as adding and subtracting.
4. Spatial	Being able to perceive spatial patterns and to visualize how geometric shapes would look if transformed in shape or position.
5. Memory	Having good rote memory for paired words, symbols, lists of numbers, or other associated items.
6. Perceptual speed	The ability to perceive figures, identify similarities and differences, and carry out tasks involving visual perception.
7. Inductive reasoning	The ability to reason from specifics to general conclusions.

SOURCE: From M D Dunnette, "Aptitudes, Abilities, and Skills," in *Handbook of Industrial and Organizational Psychology*, ed M D Dunnette, Rand McNally, 1976, pp 478–83. Reprinted with permission.

LO.6 Do We Have Multiple Intelligences?

Howard Gardner, a professor at Harvard's Graduate School of Education, offered a new paradigm for human intelligence in his 1983 book *Frames of Mind: The Theory of Multiple Intelligences*.[81] He has subsequently identified eight different intelligences that vastly broaden the long-standing concept of intelligence. Gardner's concept of multiple intelligences (MI) includes not only cognitive abilities but social and physical abilities and skills as well:

- *Linguistic intelligence:* potential to learn and use spoken and written languages.
- *Logical-mathematical intelligence:* potential for deductive reasoning, problem analysis, and mathematical calculation.
- *Musical intelligence:* potential to appreciate, compose, and perform music.
- *Bodily-kinesthetic intelligence:* potential to use mind and body to coordinate physical movement.
- *Spatial intelligence:* potential to recognize and use patterns.
- *Interpersonal intelligence:* potential to understand, connect with, and effectively work with others.
- *Intrapersonal intelligence:* potential to understand and regulate oneself.
- *Naturalist intelligence:* potential to live in harmony with one's environment.[82]

Many educators and parents have embraced MI because it helps explain how a child could score poorly on a standard IQ test yet be obviously gifted in one or more ways (e.g., music, sports, relationship building). Moreover, they believe the concept of MI underscores the need to help each child develop in his or her own unique way and at his or her own pace. They say standard IQ tests deal only with the first two intelligences on Gardner's list. Meanwhile, most academic psychologists and intelligence specialists continue to criticize Gardner's model as too subjective and poorly integrated. They prefer the traditional model of intelligence as a unified variable measured by a single test. We keep an open mind about MI, as evidenced by our coverage of cultural intelligence and emotional intelligence in this textbook.

"Enough with the Beethoven, Mom! How about some Jay-Z?" Some parents strive to develop their baby's multiple intelligences by exposing them to unconventional stimuli. Research tells us the vote is still out on whether or not they are wasting their time. Hmmm. Come to think of it, Tiger Woods' Dad had him playing golf at a very young age.

Emotions in the Workplace

to the point
What is the meaning of emotional intelligence, emotional contagion, and emotional labor?

In the ideal world of management theory, employees pursue organizational goals in a logical and rational manner. Emotional behavior seldom is factored into the equation. Yet day-to-day organizational life shows us how prevalent and powerful emotions can be.[83] Anger and jealousy, both potent emotions, often push aside logic and rationality in the workplace. Managers use fear and other emotions to both motivate and intimidate. Sadness and anxiety creep in, too. For example, consider this 2008 meeting at Microsoft:

> Steve Ballmer was sobbing. He repeatedly tried to speak and couldn't get the words out. Minutes passed as he tried to regain his composure. But the audience of 130 of Microsoft's senior leaders waited patiently, many of them crying too. They knew that the CEO was choked up because this executive retreat, held in late March at a resort north of Seattle, was the last ever for company co-founder Bill Gates, as well as for Jeff Raikes, one of the company's longest-tenured executives. "I've spent more time with these two human beings than with anyone else in my life," Ballmer finally said. "Bill and Jeff have been my North Star and kept me going. Now I'm going to count on all of you to be there for me."[84]

Less dramatic, but still emotion laden, is John Chambers's tightrope act as CEO of Cisco Systems:

> Any company that thinks it's utterly unbeatable is already beaten. So when I begin to think we're getting a little bit too confident, you'll see me emphasizing the paranoia side. And then when I feel that there's a little bit too much fear and apprehension, I'll just jump back to the other side. My job is to keep those scales perfectly balanced.[85]

These admired corporate leaders would not have achieved what they have without the ability to be logical and rational decision makers *and* be emotionally charged.

In this section, our examination of individual differences turns to defining emotions, reviewing a typology of 10 positive and negative emotions, exploring emotional intelligence and maturity, and focusing on the interesting topics of emotional contagion and emotional labor.

LO.7 Positive and Negative Emotions

Emotions

Complex human reactions to personal achievements and setbacks that may be felt and displayed.

Richard S Lazarus, a leading authority on the subject, defines **emotions** as "complex, patterned, organismic reactions to how we think we are doing in our lifelong efforts to survive and flourish and to achieve what we wish for ourselves."[86] The word *organismic* is appropriate because emotions involve the *whole* person—biological, psychological, and social. Importantly, psychologists draw a distinction between *felt* and *displayed* emotions.[87] For example, a person might feel angry (felt emotion) at a rude coworker but not make a nasty remark in return (displayed emotion). As discussed in Chapter 18, emotions play roles in both causing and adapting to stress and its associated biological and psychological problems. The destructive effect of emotional behavior on social relationships is all too obvious in daily life.

Lazarus's definition of emotions centers on a person's goals. Accordingly, his distinction between positive and negative emotions is goal oriented. Some emotions are triggered by frustration and failure when pursuing one's goals. Lazarus calls these *negative* emotions. They are said to be goal incongruent. For example, which of the six negative emotions in Figure 5–4 are you likely to experience if you fail the final exam in a required course? Failing the exam would be incongruent with your goal of graduating on time. On the other hand, which of the four *positive* emotions

Figure 5–4   *Positive and Negative Emotions*

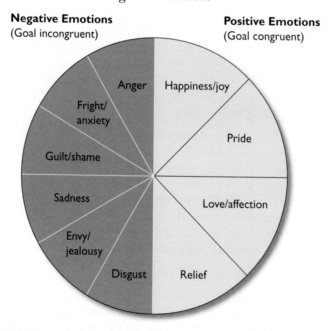

SOURCE: Adapted from discussion in R S Lazarus, *Emotion and Adaptation* (New York: Oxford University Press, 1991), Chs. 6, 7.

in Figure 5–4 would you probably experience if you graduated on time and with honors? The emotions you would experience in this situation are positive because they are congruent (or consistent) with an important lifetime goal. The individual's goals, it is important to note, may or may not be socially acceptable. Thus, a positive emotion, such as love/affection, may be undesirable if associated with sexual harassment. Oppositely, slight pangs of guilt, anxiety, and envy can motivate extra effort. On balance, the constructive or destructive nature of a particular emotion must be judged in terms of both its intensity and the person's relevant goal.

For a dramatic real-life example of the interplay between negative and positive emotions, consider the situation Kenneth I Chenault faced just 10 months after becoming CEO of American Express. The September 11, 2001, terrorist attacks claimed the lives of 11 employees, and the firm's headquarters building, across the street from ground zero in Lower Manhattan, had to be abandoned for what turned out to be eight months of repairs.

> Chenault gathered 5,000 American Express employees at the Paramount Theater in New York on September 20 for a highly emotional "town hall meeting." During the session, Chenault demonstrated the poise, compassion, and decisiveness that vaulted him to the top. He told employees that he had been filled with such despair, sadness, and anger that he had seen a counselor. Twice, he rushed to spontaneously embrace grief-stricken employees. Chenault said he would donate $1 million of the company's profits to the families of the AmEx victims. "I represent the best company and the best people in the world," he concluded." In fact, you are my strength, and I love you."[88]

Thus, Chenault masterfully used positive emotions to cope with profound negative emotions.

LO.8 Developing Emotional Intelligence

People cope with powerful emotions in lots of different ways. Take Taryn Rose, for example. She followed in her physician father's footsteps by attending medical school. However, near the end of her residency, she was bitten by the entrepreneurial bug and set her sights on developing and selling stylish shoes that would not ruin women's feet. But she did not want to disappoint her family. "I feared regret more than I feared failure,"[89] she recalled for *Fast Company* magazine, so she followed her dream. Now that she is the CEO of her own $20-million-a-year company, her family understands. For Taryn Rose, it took a good idea and determination to conquer her fears. Another way to deal effectively with fear and other emotions is to become more emotionally mature by developing emotional intelligence.

In 1995, Daniel Goleman, a psychologist turned journalist, created a stir in education and management circles with the publication of his book *Emotional Intelligence*. Hence, an obscure topic among psychologists became mainstream. Building upon Howard Gardner's concept of interpersonal

Talk about baptism by fire. Just 10 months after being named CEO of American Express, Kenneth I Chenault addressed 5,000 of his coworkers in an emotional meeting to begin the healing process following the September 11, 2001, terrorist attacks. The tragedy claimed the lives of 11 AmEx employees and closed the firm's New York headquarters for eight months of repairs. Chenault, seen here presiding over AmEx's May 13, 2002, headquarters homecoming celebration, reportedly handled the post-9/11 meeting with great skill and compassion.

intelligence, Goleman criticizes the traditional model of intelligence (IQ) for being too narrow, thus failing to consider interpersonal competence. Goleman's broader agenda includes "abilities such as being able to motivate oneself and persist in the face of frustrations; to control impulse and delay gratification; to regulate one's moods and keep distress from swamping the ability to think; to empathize and to hope."[90] Thus, **emotional intelligence** is the ability to manage oneself and one's relationships in mature and constructive ways. Referred to by some as EI and others as EQ, emotional intelligence is said to have four key components: self-awareness, self-management, social awareness, and relationship management. The first two constitute *personal competence;* the second two feed into *social competence* (see Table 5–5).

Emotional intelligence

Ability to manage oneself and interact with others in mature and constructive ways.

Table 5–5   *Developing Personal and Social Competence through Emotional Intelligence*

Personal Competence: These capabilities determine how we manage ourselves.
Self-Awareness
- *Emotional self-awareness:* Reading one's own emotions and recognizing their impact; using "gut sense" to guide decisions.
- *Accurate self-assessment:* Knowing one's strengths and limits.
- *Self-confidence:* A sound sense of one's self-worth and capabilities.

Self-Management
- *Emotional self-control:* Keeping disruptive emotions and impulses under control.
- *Transparency:* Displaying honesty and integrity; trustworthiness.
- *Adaptability:* Flexibility in adapting to changing situations or overcoming obstacles.
- *Achievement:* The drive to improve performance to meet inner standards of excellence.
- *Initiative:* Readiness to act and seize opportunities.
- *Optimism:* Seeing the upside in events.

Social Competence: These capabilities determine how we manage relationships.
Social Awareness
- *Empathy:* Sensing others' emotions, understanding their perspective, and taking active interest in their concerns.
- *Organizational awareness:* Reading the currents, decision networks, and politics at the organizational level.
- *Service:* Recognizing and meeting follower, client, or customer needs.

Relationship Management
- *Inspirational leadership:* Guiding and motivating with a compelling vision.
- *Influence:* Wielding a range of tactics for persuasion.
- *Developing others:* Bolstering others' abilities through feedback and guidance.
- *Change catalyst:* Initiating, managing, and leading in a new direction.
- *Conflict management:* Resolving disagreements.
- *Building bonds:* Cultivating and maintaining a web of relationships.
- *Teamwork and collaboration:* Cooperation and team building.

SOURCE: Reprinted by permission of Harvard Business School Publishing. Exhibit from *Primal Leadership: Realizing the Power of Emotional Intelligence,* by D Goleman, R Boyatzis, and A McKee, 2002, p 398. Copyright 2002 by the Harvard Business School Publishing Corporation; all rights reserved.

As an integrated package, the proactive personality discussed earlier and the characteristics listed in Table 5–5 constitute a challenging self-development agenda for each of us.

Practical Research Insights about Emotional Contagion and Emotional Labor

Two streams of OB research on emotions are beginning to yield interesting and instructive insights:

- *Emotional contagion.* Have you ever had someone's bad mood sour your mood? That person could have been a parent, supervisor, coworker, friend, or someone serving you in a store or restaurant. Appropriately, researchers call this emotional contagion. We, quite literally, can catch another person's bad mood or displayed negative emotions. This effect was documented in a study of 131 bank tellers (92% female) and 220 exit interviews with their customers. Tellers who expressed positive emotions tended to have more satisfied customers. Two field studies with nurses and accountants as subjects found a strong linkage between the work group's collective mood and the individual's mood.[91] Both foul moods and good moods turned out to be contagious.

- *Emotional labor.* Generations of managers have known about the power of emotional contagion in the marketplace. "Smile, look happy for the customers," employees are told over and over. But what if the employee is having a rotten day? What if they have to mask their true feelings and emotions? What if they have to fake it? Researchers have begun studying the dynamics of what they call emotional labor. A pair of authors, one from Australia the other from the United States, summarized the research lessons to date:

> Emotional labor can be particularly detrimental to the employee performing the labor and can take its toll both psychologically and physically. Employees . . . may bottle up feelings of frustration, resentment, and anger, which are not appropriate to express. These feelings result, in part, from the constant requirement to monitor one's negative emotions and express positive ones. If not given a healthy expressive outlet, this emotional repression can lead to a syndrome of emotional exhaustion and burnout.[92]

Interestingly, a pair of laboratory studies with US college students as subjects found no gender difference in *felt* emotions. But the women were more emotionally *expressive* than the men.[93] Managers clearly need to be attuned to (and responsive to) the emotional states and needs of their people. This requires emotional intelligence.

Paving Your Road to Success with Lessons from OB

to the point

What do psychological capital and deliberate practice involve and how can we make our own luck?

Let's put your new knowledge about yourself and others to practical use by exploring the road to success. Of course, we cannot define *success* for you—it depends upon your own history, expectations, goals and dreams, and opportunities. We can share a couple of helpful perspectives, however. The first comes from legendary Omaha investor Warren Buffett: "They say success is getting what you want and happiness is wanting what you get."[94] The second comes from College

go to the Web for the Group Exercise: Anger Control Role Play

Football Hall of Fame coach Lou Holtz: "Make sure you always have four things in your life: Something to do, someone to love, something to hope for and something to believe in."[95] With these inspirational words in mind, we explore four key paving stones for your road to success: psychological capital, deliberate practice, luck, and humility (see the Real World/Real People feature about failure not being an option).

Psychological Capital

In Chapter 1, we introduced the concepts of human and social capital. To those we now add psychological capital (PsyCap). PsyCap is derived from the positive psychology movement that emphasizes what is *right* with people rather than what is wrong or dysfunctional. This approach focuses on human strengths and potential as a way to possibly *prevent* mental and behavioral problems and improve the general quality of life. University of Nebraska OB scholar Fred Luthans and his colleagues offer this definition of **psychological capital:**

Psychological capital

Striving for success by developing one's self-efficacy, optimism, hope, and resiliency.

> [PsyCap is] an individual's positive psychological state of development and is characterized by (1) having confidence (*self-efficacy*) to take on and put in the necessary effort to succeed at challenging tasks; (2) making a positive attribution (*optimism*) about succeeding now and in the future; (3) persevering toward goals, and when necessary, redirecting paths to goals (*hope*) in order to succeed; and (4) when beset by problems and adversity, sustaining and bouncing back and even beyond (*resiliency*) to attain success.[96]

Importantly, you can build your own PsyCap by applying lessons from this textbook relating to self-efficacy, positive attributions (Chapter 7), and goal setting (Chapter 9). **Resiliency** can be developed through deliberate practice, discussed below, and being inspired by role models such as jazz/folk singer Melody Gardot:

> When a car crashes your bike and leaves you bed-ridden for a year, people don't expect to hear that you feel blessed. But despite months of rehab and ongoing chronic pain and sensitivity to light, that accident changed my life in beautiful ways.
>
> The doctor recommended music therapy. Research suggests the melodies can help rebuild neural pathways, so I strummed a few notes on a little guitar. The songs led to recordings and to live performances. Now I'm about to tour on a new album, *Worrisome Heart*.[97]

Deliberate Practice

Is there something you want to become really, *really* good at—world-class good? Maybe a sport, a musical instrument, speaking in pubic, writing a blog, playing a video game, designing products, coding software, singing and dancing, or woodworking. Then take this good advice from an old New York City joke: *Tourist*: "How do I get to Carnegie Hall?" *New Yorker*: "Practice, practice, practice." Okay, so how much practice? Try the "10,000-hour rule." After studying relevant research evidence, Malcolm Gladwell came to this conclusion in his recent book *Outliers: The Story of Success*: ". . . the closer psychologists look at the careers of the gifted, the smaller the role innate talent seems to play and the bigger the role preparation seems to play. . . . [T]he people at the very top don't work just harder or even much harder than everyone else. They work much, *much* harder. . . . Ten thousand hours is the magic number of greatness."[98] Generally, that works out to about ten years of "deliberate" practice.

Fortune magazine's Geoff Colvin, in his interesting new book *Talent Is Overrated: What* Really *Separates World-Class Performers from Everybody Else*, identifies the key elements of **deliberate practice:**

> It is activity designed specifically to improve performance, often with a teacher's help; it can be repeated a lot; feedback on results is continuously available; it's highly demanding mentally, whether the activity is purely intellectual, such as chess or business-related activities, or heavily physical, such as sports; and it isn't much fun.[99]

Tiger Woods, who has relentlessly polished every aspect of his golf game since he was a toddler—first under his father's tutelage and later with the best coaches—shows where deliberate practice can take you. This situation, in addition to his titles and trophies, illustrates Tiger's uncanny "feel" for the game of golf:

> A few years ago, Nike was developing a driver and had Woods test the prototype. He hit three and said he liked the light one.
>
> The clubs weighed the same, Woods was told. No they don't, he replied.
>
> Nike's research crew put the drivers on a scale and discovered Woods was right. The club he liked weighed 2 grams less than the others.[100]

Resiliency

The ability to handle pressure and quickly bounce back from personal and career setbacks.

Deliberate practice

A demanding, repetitive, and assisted program to improve one's performance.

Luck

If you want to know about luck, then talk to lucky and unlucky people to see how they differ. That simple premise is behind more than a decade of innovative research by Richard Wiseman, a psychology professor in the UK. It turns out that luck involves much more than simply random chance or coincidence. Lucky people, through how they think and behave, make their own good fortune. Here are Wiseman's four guidelines for improving your luck:

1. *Be active and involved.* Be open to new experiences and networking with others to encounter more lucky chance opportunities.
2. *Listen to your hunches about luck.* Learn when to listen to your intuitive gut feelings. Meditation and mind-clearing activities can help.
3. *Expect to be lucky no matter how bad the situation.* Remain optimistic and work to make your expectations a self-fulfilling prophecy.
4. *Turn your bad luck into good fortune.* Take control of bad situations by remaining calm, positive, and focused on a better future.[101]

Now we know why singer Melody Gardot, in the example above, feels blessed. She made her own luck by turning bad luck into good fortune.

Humility

Humility

Considering the contributions of others and good fortune when gauging one's success.

Before you declare yourself Grade A executive material, here is one more thing to toss into your tool kit: a touch of humility. **Humility** is "a realistic assessment of one's own contribution and the recognition of the contribution of others, along with luck and good fortune that made one's own success possible."[102] Humility has been called the silent virtue. How many truly humble people brag about being humble? Two OB experts offered this instructive perspective:

> Humble individuals have a down-to-earth perspective of themselves and of the events and relationships in their lives. Humility involves a capability to evaluate success, failure, work, and life without exaggeration. Furthermore, humility enables leaders to distinguish the delicate line between such characteristics as healthy self-confidence, self-esteem, and self-assessment, and those of over-confidence, narcissism, and stubbornness. Humility is the mid-point between the two negative extremes of arrogance and lack of self-esteem. This depiction allows one to see that a person can be humble and competitive or humble and ambitious at the same time, which contradicts common—but mistaken—views about humility.[103]

Someone has to be great. Why not you? Go for it!

Summary of Key Concepts

1. *Define self-esteem, and explain how it can be improved with Branden's six pillars of self-esteem.* Self-esteem is how people perceive themselves as physical, social, and spiritual beings. Branden's six pillars of self-esteem are live consciously, be self-accepting, take personal responsibility, be self-assertive, live purposefully, and have personal integrity.

2. *Define self-efficacy, and explain its sources.* Self-efficacy involves one's belief about his or her ability to

accomplish specific tasks. Those extremely low in self-efficacy suffer from learned helplessness. Four sources of self-efficacy beliefs are prior experience, behavior models, persuasion from others, and assessment of one's physical and emotional states. High self-efficacy beliefs foster constructive and goal-oriented action, whereas low self-efficacy fosters passive, failure-prone activities and emotions.

3. *Contrast high and low self-monitoring individuals, and discuss the ethical implications of organizational identification.* A high self-monitor strives to make a good public impression by closely monitoring his or her behavior and adapting it to the situation. Very high self-monitoring can create a "chameleon" who is seen as insincere and dishonest. Low self-monitors do the opposite by acting out their momentary feelings, regardless of their surroundings. Very low self-monitoring can lead to a one-way communicator who seems to ignore verbal and nonverbal cues from others. People who supplant their own identity with that of their organization run the risk of blind obedience and groupthink because of a failure to engage in critical thinking and not being objective about what they are asked to do.

4. *Identify and describe the Big Five personality dimensions, and specify which one is correlated most strongly with job performance.* The Big Five personality dimensions are extraversion (social and talkative), agreeableness (trusting and cooperative), conscientiousness (responsible and persistent), emotional stability (relaxed and unworried), and openness to experience (intellectual and curious). Conscientiousness is the best predictor of job performance.

5. *Describe the proactive personality and an internal locus of control.* Someone with a proactive personality shows initiative, takes action, and perseveres to bring about change. People with an internal locus of control, such as entrepreneurs, believe they are masters of their own fate.

6. *Identify at least five of Gardner's eight multiple intelligences.* Harvard's Howard Gardner broadens the traditional cognitive abilities model of intelligence to include social and physical abilities. His eight multiple

intelligences include linguistic, logical-mathematical, musical, bodily-kinesthetic, spatial, interpersonal, intrapersonal, and naturalist.

7. *Distinguish between positive and negative emotions, and explain how they can be judged.* Positive emotions—happiness/joy, pride, love/affection, and relief—are personal reactions to circumstances congruent with one's goals. Negative emotions—anger, fright/anxiety, guilt/shame, sadness, envy/jealousy, and disgust—are personal reactions to circumstances incongruent with one's goals. Both types of emotions need to be judged in terms of intensity and the appropriateness of the person's relevant goal.

8. *Identify the four key components of emotional intelligence, and discuss the practical significance of emotional contagion and emotional labor.* Goleman's model says the four components are self-awareness, self-management, social awareness, and relationship management. People can, in fact, catch another person's good or bad moods and expressed emotions, much as they would catch a contagious disease. Managers and others in the workplace need to avoid spreading counterproductive emotions. People in service jobs who are asked to suppress their own negative emotions and display positive emotions, regardless of their true feelings at the time, pay a physical and mental price for their emotional labor. Managers who are not mindful of emotional labor may experience lower productivity, reduced job satisfaction, and possibly aggression and even violence.

9. *Explain how psychological capital, deliberate practice, luck, and humility can pave your road to success.* Psychological capital (PsyCap) can be built through self-efficacy, optimism (positive attributions), hope (goal setting), and resiliency. Deliberate practice involves following the 10,000-hour rule with a demanding, repetitive, and assisted program of improvement. Lucky people stay involved to maximize their chance opportunities, follow their lucky hunches, expect to be lucky no matter the circumstances, and turn bad luck into good fortune. Humble people factor the contributions of others and good fortune into their perceived success.

Key Terms

The Best Advice I Ever Got

Stephen A. Schwarzman, Chairman and Chief Executive Officer, the Blackstone Group

I grew up in a small town outside Philadelphia and went to the local high school, where I ran track all four years. Our team practiced outdoors, and in the winter, in the bitter cold, the experience was pretty miserable. The school was set on a hill, and as we ran around the parking lot the wind would come whipping around the building and hit us. We had to watch our steps carefully so as not to slip and fall on the ice. While we were doing our laps, the coach—a 50-year-old named Jack Armstrong—would stand against one wall protected from the wind, bundled up in a huge coat and wool hat and gloves, clapping and smiling cheerfully. Every time the pack shuffled past, he'd shout, "Remember—you've got to make your deposits before you can make a withdrawal!"

Now, this was a public school with no special facilities, and the team was made up of average athletes with differing levels of intelligence and motivation. But we never lost one single meet. And because of that success, and maybe because of the way in which the advice itself was delivered—I remember it when people yell at me—Coach Armstrong's words resonated. I've thought of them a million times throughout my career in finance, and they've guided this firm, too.

Coach Armstrong came to mind in one of my first weeks on Wall Street, 35 years ago. I'd stayed up all night building a massive spreadsheet to be ready for a morning meeting. These were the days before Excel, and it was a huge feat for someone as bad at statistical stuff as I was to do this all by hand; I was pretty proud of myself. The partner on the deal, however, took one look at my work, spotted a tiny error, and went ballistic. As I sat there while he yelled at me, I realized I was getting the MBA version of Coach Armstrong's words. Making an effort and meeting the deadline simply weren't enough. To put it in Coach Armstrong's terms, it wasn't sufficient to make some deposits; I had to be certain that the deposits would cover any withdrawal 100% before we made a decision or did a deal. If I hadn't done all the up-front work and made completely sure that my analysis was correct, I shouldn't have put anything forth. Inaccurate analysis produces faulty insights and bad decisions—which lead to losing a tremendous amount of money.

Today, whenever I'm under pressure to make a decision on a transaction but I don't know what the right one is, I try desperately to postpone it. I'll insist on more information—on doing extra laps around the intellectual parking lot—before committing. . . .

Every year I speak to our new associates and give them this advice, although in my own words. This isn't like school, I tell them, where you want to get your hand in the air and give an answer quickly. The only grade here is 100. Deadlines are important, but at Blackstone you can always get help in meeting them. As a firm, we can always figure out how to do another lap around the parking lot. Because what's true when running track is true when doing deals: The person who's the most ready for game day will be the one who wins.[104]

Questions for Discussion

1. How would you describe Stephen Schwarzman's personality?

2. Relative to the concepts you have just read about, what traits and characteristics would describe the "ideal" Blackstone job candidate? Explain your rationale for selecting each characteristic.

3. Ranked 1 = most important to 8 = least important, which of Gardner's eight multiple intelligences are most critical to being successful at a major investment company like Blackstone? Explain your ranking.

4. Using Table 5–5 as a guide, how important are the various emotional intelligence competencies for making good investment decisions? Explain.

5. Do you have what it takes to work for someone like Stephen Schwarzman? Explain in terms of the concepts in this chapter.

Ethical Dilemma

Is It Time for Performance-Enhancing Drugs in the Workplace?

BusinessWeek Facing an important job interview, the college graduate searches her closet for the perfect outfit, then rifles through her medicine cabinet for just the right cognitive-enhancement pill. Adderall, perhaps, to help her concentrate. Or Provigil, for alertness . . . or maybe a beta blocker to combat jitters?

Doctors in the U.S. who track drug trends say scenarios like this could play out in a thousand variations as college students who grew up using prescription drugs as study aids enter the workforce. Many high-powered professionals are already popping such pills in secret. Within a few years they could be joined by millions of older adults, including baby boomers who decide there's nothing wrong with using "smart drugs" to ward off senior moments. The drug industry will benefit mightily if public opinion swings this way.

Many healthy people have trepidations about tinkering with the brain using addictive or otherwise risky pharmaceuticals. But those reservations are eroding for several reasons. A whole generation has come of age using attention-deficit drugs such as Adderall and Ritalin, a category valued at nearly $4.7 billion in 2007. A lot of teenagers have used them casually as study aids, often buying them on the Internet. And now, overworked professionals are seeing the appeal. "From assembly-line workers to surgeons, many different kinds of employee may benefit from enhancement and want access to it," wrote Martha J. Farah, director of the Center for Cognitive Neuroscience at the University of Pennsylvania, in a recent commentary in the science journal *Nature*. In the controversial essay, she and her co-authors, including Stanford Law School Professor Henry T. Greely, declared it's time for people to overcome their squeamishness: "Mentally competent adults should be able to engage in cognitive enhancement using drugs."[105]

Do Cognitive Enhancement Drugs Belong in the Workplace?

1. If they provide a competitive edge and are used by consenting adults, then it's an acceptable business practice. Explain.
2. This is a dangerous game. Companies should have clear policies forbidding the use of these drugs (along with alcohol and illegal drugs) in the workplace. Explain.
3. This is a personal matter that could boost performance, so companies would be wise to passively accept it. Explain.
4. Invent other options. Discuss.

Web Resources

For study material and exercises that apply to this chapter, visit our Web site, www.mhhe.com/kreitner

Chapter 6

Values, Attitudes, Job Satisfaction, and Counterproductive Work Behaviors

When you finish studying the material in this chapter, you should be able to:

LO.1 Explain Schwartz's value theory, and describe three types of value conflict.

LO.2 Describe the values model of work/family conflict, and specify at least three practical lessons from work/family conflict research.

LO.3 Identify the three components of attitudes and discuss cognitive dissonance.

LO.4 Explain how attitudes affect behavior in terms of Ajzen's theory of planned behavior.

LO.5 Describe the model of organizational commitment.

LO.6 Define the work attitudes of job involvement/employee engagement and job satisfaction.

LO.7 Identify and briefly describe five alternative causes of job satisfaction.

LO.8 Identify eight important correlates/consequences of job satisfaction, and summarize how each one relates to job satisfaction.

LO.9 Identify the causes of counterproductive work behaviors and the measures used to prevent them.

Asked what job they would take if they could have any, people unleash their imaginations and dream of exotic places, powerful positions, or work that involves alcohol and a paycheck at the same time.

Or so you'd think.

None of that appeals to Lori Miller who, as a lead word processor, has to do things that don't seem so dreamy, including proofreading, spell-checking, and formatting. But she loves it.

"I like and respect nearly all my coworkers, and most of them feel the same way about me," she says. "Just a few things would make it a little better," she says, including a shorter commute and the return of some great people who used to work there. And one more thing: She'd appreciate if everyone would put their dishes in the dishwasher.

One person's idea of a dream job is as simple as a place where coworkers would put their dishes in the dishwasher. What is your idea of a dream job?

It's not a lot to ask for and it turns out a surprising number of people dreaming up their dream job don't ask for much. One could attribute it to lack of imagination, setting the bar low, or "anchoring," the term referring to the place people start and never move far from. One could chalk it up to rationalizing your plight.

But maybe people simply like what they do and aren't, as some management would have you believe, asking for too much—just the elimination of a small but disproportionately powerful amount of office inanity.

That may be one reason why two-thirds of Americans would take the same job again "without hesitation" and why 90% of Americans are at least somewhat satisfied with their jobs, according to a Gallup Poll. . . .

So, money doesn't interest Elizabeth Gray as much as a level playing field. "I like what I do," says the city project manager who once witnessed former colleagues award a contractor, paid for work he never completed, with the title of "Contractor of the Year." Thus: "My dream job would be one free of politics," she says. "All advancement would be based on merit. The people who really did the work would be the ones who received the credit."

Frank Gastner has a similar ideal: "VP in charge of destroying inane policies." Over the years, he's had to hassle with the simplest of design flaws that would cost virtually nothing to fix were it not for the bureaucracies that entrenched them. So, the retired manufacturer's representative says he would address product and process problems with the attitude, "It's not right; let's fix it now without a committee meeting."

A dream job does not have to be extravagant to be the ideal job for you.

Monique Huston actually has her dream job—and many tell her it's theirs, too. She's general manager of a pub in Omaha, the Dundee Dell, which boasts 650 single-malt scotches on its menu. She visits bars, country clubs, people's homes, and Scotland for whiskey tastings. "I stumbled on my passion in life," she says.

Still, some nights she doesn't feel like drinking—or smiling. "Your face hurts," she complains. And when you have your dream job you wonder what in the world you'll do next.[1]

The chapter-opening vignette highlights that one person's dream job can be someone else's misery. For example, Lori Miller loves proofreading whereas we don't enjoy this task. The bigger point to remember, however, is that individual differences influence our values, attitudes, job satisfaction, and tendency to exhibit counterproductive workplace behaviors. It thus is important for managers to consider individual differences, which were discussed in Chapter 5, when trying to satisfy and motivate employees.

The overall goal of this chapter is to continue our investigation of individual differences from Chapter 5 so that you can get a better idea of how managers and organizations can use knowledge of individual differences to attract, motivate, and retain quality employees. We explore and discuss the impact of personal values and attitudes on important outcomes such as job satisfaction, performance, turnover, and counterproductive work behaviors.

> **to the point**
> Why is it important for managers to understand an employee's values?

Personal Values

When discussing organizational culture in Chapter 3, we defined *values* as desired ways of behaving or desired end-states. Our focus in Chapter 3 was on collective or shared values; here the focus shifts to *personal* values. Personal values essentially represent the things that have meaning to us in our lives. Values are important to your understanding of organizational behavior because they influence our behavior across different settings.

Shalom Schwartz has developed a comprehensive and well-accepted theory of personal values.[2] Let us learn more about personal values by exploring Schwartz's theory, discussing value conflicts, and examining the timely value-related topic of work versus family life conflicts.

LO.1 Schwartz's Value Theory

Schwartz believes that values are motivational in that they "represent broad goals that apply across contexts and time."[3] For example, valuing achievement will likely result in your working hard to earn a promotion at work just at it will drive you to compete against friends in a weekly golf game. Values also are relatively stable and can influence behavior outside of our awareness.

Schwartz proposed that there are 10 broad values that guide behavior. He also identified the motivational mechanisms that underlie each value (see Table 6–1). It is these motivational mechanisms that give values their ability to influence our behavior. For example, Table 6–1 shows that the desire for social power, authority, and wealth drive someone who values power. In contrast, the value of conformity is driven by motives related to politeness, obedience, self-discipline, and honoring one's parents and elders. Not only have these 10 values been found to predict behavior as outlined in the theory, but they also generalize across cultures.[4] A recent study showed that the 10 basic values were relevant to understanding behavior across 20 countries.[5]

Table 6–1   *Definition of Values and Motives in Schwartz's Theory*

VALUE	DEFINITION AND UNDERLYING MOTIVES
Power	Social status and prestige, control or dominance over people and resources (social power, authority, wealth)
Achievement	Personal success through demonstrating competence according to social standards (successful, capable, ambitious, influential)
Hedonism	Pleasure and sensuous gratification for oneself (pleasure, enjoying life)
Stimulation	Excitement, novelty, and challenge in life (daring, a varied life, an exciting life)
Self-direction	Independent thought and action choosing, creating, exploring (creativity, freedom, independent, curious, choosing own goals)
Universalism	Understanding, appreciation, tolerance and protection of the welfare of all people and of nature (broadminded, wisdom, social justice, equality, a world at peace, a world of beauty, unity with nature, protecting the environment)
Benevolence	Preservation and enhancement of the welfare of people with whom one is in frequent personal contact (helpful, honest, forgiving, loyal, responsible)
Tradition	Respect, commitment, and acceptance of the customs and ideas that traditional culture or religion provides the self (humble, accepting my portion in life, devout, respect for tradition, moderate)
Conformity	Restraint of actions, inclinations, and impulses likely to upset or harm others and violate social expectations or norms (politeness, obedient, self-discipline, honoring parents and elders)
Security	Safety, harmony, and stability of society, of relationships, and of self (family security, national security, social order, clean, reciprocation of favors)

SOURCE: From Anat Bardi and Shalom H Schwartz, "Values and Behavior: Strength and Structure of Relations," *Personality & Social Psychology Bulletin*, October 2003, p 1208. Copyright © 2003 by Sage Publications.

Figure 6–1 shows the proposed relationships among the 10 values. The circular pattern reveals which values are most strongly related and which ones are in conflict. In general, adjacent values like self-direction and universalism are positively related, whereas values that are further apart (e.g., self-direction and power) are less strongly related. Taking this one step further, Schwartz proposes that values that are in opposing directions from the center conflict with each other. Examples are power and universalism or stimulation and conformity/tradition. For instance, the drive to live a stimulating life by engaging in activities like skydiving or mountain climbing would conflict with the desire to live a moderate or traditional life. Research provides partial support for these predictions.[6]

Value Conflicts

There are three types of value conflict that are related to an individual's attitudes, job satisfaction, turnover, performance, and counterproductive behavior. They are *intra*personal value conflict, *inter*personal value conflict, and individual–organization value conflict. These sources of conflict are, respectively, from inside the person, between people, and between the person and the organization.

Figure 6–1   *Relationship among Schwartz's Values*

SOURCE: Anat Bardi and Shalom H Schwartz, "Values and Behavior: Strength and Structure of Relations," *Personality and Social Psychology Bulletin,* October 2003, p 1208. Copyright © 2003 by Sage Publications.

Intrapersonal Value Conflict   Our discussion of Schwartz's theory of values revealed that people are likely to experience inner conflict and stress when personal values conflict with each other. For employees who want balance in their lives, a stressful conflict can arise when one values, for example, "achievement" and "tradition." Paul Wenske, a former investigative reporter for the *Kansas City Star,* is experiencing intrapersonal value conflict after being forced to take a buyout from his employer. He was an award-winning journalist for 30 years that strongly identified with his work role. He told *The Wall Street Journal* that "Suddenly you're not the same person you used to be. You look in the mirror. Who are you?" Therapists suggest that this type of value conflict can be reduced by "taking pride in characteristics that can't be stripped away—virtue, integrity, honesty, generosity. They also recommend investing more time and pride in relationships with family, friends, and community."[7] In general, people are happier and less stressed when their personal values are aligned.

Interpersonal Value Conflict   This type of value conflict often is at the core of personality conflicts, and such conflicts can negatively affect one's career. Consider the case of Jeffrey Johnson. He was fired by the owner of the *Los Angeles Times*—the Tribune Co.—when his values collided with those possessed by senior management. Senior management wanted Johnson to improve the paper's financial results by cutting costs. Johnson then was asked to eliminate employees from the payroll. The conflict for Mr. Johnson was that he did not believe that the newspaper's problems would be solved by employee layoffs. He wanted to improve the newspaper's financial status by exploring creative ways to generate revenue as opposed to cutting costs.[8] This example highlights how important it is to carefully evaluate the pros and cons of handling interpersonal value conflicts with our superiors.

Individual–Organization Value Conflict   As we saw in Chapter 3, companies actively seek to embed certain values into their corporate cultures. Conflict can occur when values espoused and enacted by the organization collide with employees' personal values. OB researchers refer to this type of conflict as value congruence or person–culture fit.[9] **Value congruence or person–culture fit** reflects the similarity between an individual's personal values and the cultural value system of an organization. This is an important type of conflict to consider when accepting future jobs because positive outcomes such as satisfaction, commitment, performance, career success, reduced stress, and lower turnover intentions are realized when an individual's personal values are similar or aligned with organizational values.[10]

Value congruence or person–culture fit

The similarity between personal values and organizational values.

go to the Web for the Self-Exercise: Personal Values Clarification

L0.2 Work versus Family Life Conflict

A complex web of demographic and economic factors makes the balancing act between job and life very challenging for most of us. This is particularly true during a recession.[11] The Real World/Real People feature on page 158 illustrates what happened to Karyn Couvillion as she tried to balance the increased demands of doing more work with less resources. Unfortunately, this type of imbalance is not expected to disappear in the near future.

In this section, we seek to better understand work versus family life conflict by introducing a values-based model and discussing practical research insights.

A Values-Based Model of Work/Family Conflict   Pamela L Perrewé and Wayne A Hochwarter proposed a model of work/family conflict (see Figure 6–2). On the left, we see one's general life values feeding into one's family-related values and work-related values. Family values involve enduring beliefs about the importance of family and who should play key family roles (e.g., child rearing, housekeeping, and income earning). Work values center on the relative importance of work and career goals in one's life. *Value similarity* relates to the degree of consensus among family members about family values. When a housewife launches a business venture despite her husband's desire to be the sole breadwinner, lack of family value similarity causes work/family conflict. *Value congruence,* on the other hand, involves the amount of value agreement between employee and employer. If, for example, refusing to go on a business trip to stay home for a child's birthday is viewed as disloyalty to the company, lack of value congruence can trigger work/family conflict.

In turn, "work-family conflict can take two distinct forms: work interference with family and family interference with work."[12] For example, suppose two managers in the same department have daughters playing on the same soccer team. One manager misses the big soccer game to attend a last-minute department meeting; the other manager skips the meeting to attend the game. Both may experience work/family conflict, but for different reasons.[13]

The last two boxes in the model—value attainment and job and life satisfaction—are a package deal. Satisfaction tends to be higher for those who live according to

Karyn Couvillion Quit Her Job in Response to Work/Family Conflict

Does this sound familiar? 350 e-mails a day in my inbox. Blackberry, cell phone, and laptop constantly in tow. Check my Outlook calendar and see that I'm double—or triple—booked in meetings every hour, plus a 7 a.m. global conference call. Being told by management that we cannot hire additional head count because of a hiring freeze, despite the hefty increase in responsibilities for my team. That was me a year ago. The red tape, politics, ridiculous expectations, and meager resources made it nearly impossible to do my job as an advertising and brand manager for a large tech company. On top of it, I had just returned from maternity leave after having my first child. And my father was very sick with leukemia, but I could not take the out-of-state trip to visit him due to a company policy that burned vacation and sick time as part of maternity leave.

So I quit. So did my husband, who worked in a top advertising agency. In fact, we both quit on the same day: Sept. 11, 2007. We decided that life was too short and we had had enough. . . . I wanted to spend some time with my ill father. . . . When my father died on Dec. 2, 2007, I was there by his side.

Using the Schwartz theory of values, which conflicting values led Karyn to quit?

SOURCE: Excerpted from M Conlin, "How to Get a Life and Do Your Job," *BusinessWeek*, August 25, 2008, pp 37–38.

Karyn's work/family conflict led her to quit her job. How would you respond in a similar situation?

Figure 6–2   *A Values Model of Work/Family Conflict*

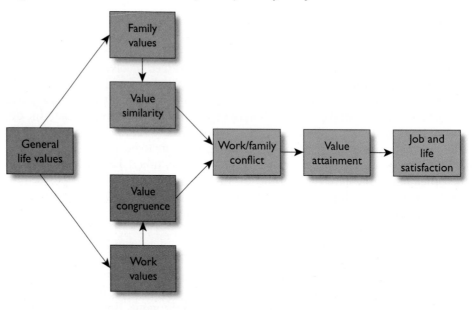

SOURCE: From Pamela L Perrewé and Wayne A Hochwarter, "Can We Really Have It All? The Attainment of Work and Family Values," *Current Directions in Psychological Science*, February 2001, p 30. Reprinted with permission of Wiley-Blackwell.

their values and lower for those who do not. Overall, this model reflects much common sense. How does *your* life track through the model? Sadly, it is a painful trip for many these days.

go to the Web for the Self-Exercise: Are Your Values and Commitments Aligned?

Practical Research Insights about Work/Family Conflict   This is a new but very active area of OB research. Let us consider five practical conclusions derived from this research.

- *Work/family balance begins at home.* As discussed in Chapter 2, women shoulder the majority of the standard household chores and child-rearing responsibilities. Fortunately, recent research shows that men are beginning to share more of the work associated with running a home.[14] These results suggest that both men and women need help with domestic responsibilities if there is any chance of achieving work/family balance. You are encouraged to hire domestic help if you need and can afford it.

- *An employer's family-supportive philosophy is more important than specific programs.* Many employers offer family-friendly programs today, including child and elder day care assistance, parental leave, telecommuting, and flexible work schedules. However, if employees are afraid or reluctant to take advantage of those programs because the organization's culture values hard work and long hours above all else, families will inevitably suffer. To be truly family-friendly, the organization needs to provide programs and back them up with a family-supportive philosophy and culture.[15] Satyam Computer Services Limited is a good example. The company implemented a Family Learning program aimed at helping its employees' families to "bond with each other and the organization." The program "aims to guide children through a smooth transition to adulthood, while teaching them skills intended to improve their quality of life. Their parents learn about the dynamics of adult relationships; self-guided improvement; and life management skills."[16]

Great companies recognize that the ability to take care of family concerns is an important part of an employee's job satisfaction. How can a company's policies reflect a family-supportive philosophy?

- *Informal flexibility in work hours and in allowing people to work at home is essential to promoting work/family balance.* Quite simply, flexibility allows people to cope more effectively with competing demands across their personal and work lives. Dell Inc., for example, is allowing some work teams to eliminate "firm office hours and handing employees control over when and how they achieve goals." Bristol-Myers Squibb similarly tried to enhance worker flexibility by enabling people to choose one of six different work schedules.[17] In support of these practices, a recent survey of 560 organizations revealed that flexible schedules resulted in increased employee morale and retention.[18]

- *Supportive bosses and spouses can help.* A recent field survey of 792 information technology employees from 10 companies revealed that work/family conflict was lower when employees had good relationships with their direct supervisor. Similarly, a study of 168 couples demonstrated that work/family conflict was reduced when spouses helped each other to balance their individual work/family demands.[19]

- *Take a proactive approach to managing work/family conflict.* Two recent meta-analyses of more than 60 different studies and 43,000 people demonstrated that an individual's personal life spills over to his or her work life and vice versa. This means that employees' job satisfaction, organizational commitment, and intentions to quit are significantly related to the amount of work/family conflict that exists in their lives.[20] We thus encourage you to identify and manage the sources of work/family conflict. The importance of this recommendation is underscored by recent results from a study of 9,627 managers from 33 countries. Findings indicated that managers were rated as more promotable when they were perceived as having higher work-life balance.[21]

Organizational Response to Work/Family Issues   Organizations have implemented a variety of family-friendly programs and services aimed at helping employees to balance the interplay between their work and personal lives. Although these programs are positively received by employees, experts now believe that such efforts are partially misguided because they focus on balancing work/family issues rather than integrating them. Balance is needed for opposites, and work and family are not opposites. Rather, our work and personal lives should be a well-integrated whole.

go to the Web for the Self-Exercise: How Family-Supportive Is Your Employer?

to the point

Why is it important for managers to understand an employee's attitudes and how do attitudes influence employee behavior?

LO.3   Attitudes

Hardly a day goes by without the popular media reporting the results of another attitude survey. The idea is to take the pulse of public opinion. What do we think about President Obama, terrorism, the war on drugs, gun control, or taxes? In the workplace, meanwhile, managers conduct attitude surveys to monitor such things as job and pay satisfaction. All this attention to attitudes is based on the realization that our attitudes influence our behavior. For example, research demonstrated that seniors with a positive attitude about aging had better memory, had better hearing, and lived longer than those with negative attitudes.[22] In a work setting, two recent meta-analyses revealed that job attitudes were positively related to performance and negatively associated with indicators of withdrawal—lateness, absenteeism, and turnover.[23] In this section, we discuss the components of attitudes and examine the connection between attitudes and behavior.

Attitude

Learned predisposition toward a given object.

The Nature of Attitudes

An **attitude** is defined as "a learned predisposition to respond in a consistently favorable or unfavorable manner with respect to a given object."[24] Consider your attitude toward chocolate ice cream. You are more likely to purchase a chocolate ice cream cone if you have a positive attitude toward chocolate ice cream. In contrast, you are more likely to purchase some other flavor, say vanilla caramel swirl, if you have a positive attitude toward vanilla and a neutral or negative attitude toward chocolate ice cream. Let us consider a work example. If you have a positive attitude about your job (i.e., you like what you are doing), you would be more willing to extend yourself at work by working longer and harder. These examples illustrate that attitudes propel us to act in a specific way in a specific context. That is, attitudes affect behavior at a different level than do values. While values represent global beliefs that influence behavior across *all* situations, attitudes relate only to behavior directed toward *specific* objects, persons, or situations. Values and attitudes generally, but not always, are in harmony. A manager who strongly values helpful behavior may have a negative attitude toward helping an unethical coworker. The difference between attitudes and values is clarified by considering the three components of attitudes: affective, cognitive, and behavioral.[25] It is important to note that your overall attitude toward someone or something is a function of the combined influence of all three components.

Affective Component

The **affective component** of an attitude contains the feelings or emotions one has about a given object or situation. For example, how do you *feel* about people who talk on cell phones in restaurants? If you feel annoyed or angry with such people, you are expressing negative affect or feelings toward people who talk on cell phones in restaurants. In contrast, the affective component of your attitude is neutral if you are indifferent about people talking on cell phones in restaurants.

Affective component
The feelings or emotions one has about an object or situation.

Cognitive Component

What do you *think* about people who talk on cell phones in restaurants? Do you believe this behavior is inconsiderate, productive, completely acceptable, or rude? Your answer represents the cognitive component of your attitude toward people talking on cell phones in restaurants. The **cognitive component** of an attitude reflects the beliefs or ideas one has about an object or situation.

Cognitive component
The beliefs or ideas one has about an object or situation.

Behavioral Component

The **behavioral component** refers to how one intends or expects to act toward someone or something. For example, how would you intend to respond to someone talking on a cell phone during dinner at a restaurant if this individual were sitting in close proximity to you and your guest? Attitude theory suggests that your ultimate behavior in this situation is a function of all three attitudinal components. You are unlikely to say anything to someone using a cell phone in a restaurant if you are not irritated by this behavior (affective), if you believe cell phone use helps people to manage their lives (cognitive), and you have no intention of confronting this individual (behavioral).[26]

Behavioral component
How one intends to act or behave toward someone or something.

What Happens When Attitudes and Reality Collide? Cognitive Dissonance

What happens when a strongly held attitude is contradicted by reality? Suppose you are extremely concerned about getting AIDS, which you believe is transferred from contact with body fluids, including blood. Then you find yourself in a life-threatening accident in a foreign country and need surgery and blood transfusions—including transfusions of blood (possibly AIDS-infected) from a blood bank with unknown quality control. Would you reject the blood to remain consistent with your beliefs about getting AIDS? According to social psychologist Leon Festinger, this situation would create cognitive dissonance.

Cognitive dissonance

Psychological discomfort experienced when attitudes and behavior are inconsistent.

Cognitive dissonance represents the psychological discomfort a person experiences when his or her attitudes or beliefs are incompatible with his or her behavior.[27] Festinger proposed that people are motivated to maintain consistency between their attitudes and beliefs and their behavior. He therefore theorized that people will seek to reduce the "dissonance," or psychological tension, through one of three main methods:

1. *Change your attitude or behavior, or both.* This is the simplest solution when confronted with cognitive dissonance. Returning to our example about needing a blood transfusion, this would amount to either (1) telling yourself that you can't get AIDS through blood and take the transfusion or (2) simply refusing to take the transfusion.

2. *Belittle the importance of the inconsistent behavior.* This happens all the time. In our example, you could belittle the belief that you can get AIDS from the foreign blood bank. (The doctor said she regularly uses blood from that blood bank.)

3. *Find consonant elements that outweigh dissonant ones.* This approach entails rationalizing away the dissonance. You can tell yourself that you are taking the transfusion because you have no other options. After all, you could die if you don't get the required surgery.

How Stable Are Attitudes?

In one landmark study, researchers found the *job* attitudes of 5,000 middle-aged male employees to be very stable over a five-year period. Positive job attitudes remained positive; negative ones remained negative. Even those who changed jobs or occupations tended to maintain their prior job attitudes.[28] More recent research suggests the foregoing study may have overstated the stability of attitudes because it was restricted to a middle-aged sample. This time, researchers asked: What happens to attitudes over the entire span of adulthood? *General* attitudes were found to be more susceptible to change during early and late adulthood than during middle adulthood. Three factors accounted for middle-age attitude stability: (1) greater personal certainty, (2) perceived abundance of knowledge, and (3) a need for strong attitudes. Thus, the conventional notion that general attitudes become less likely to change as the person ages was rejected. Elderly people, along with young adults, can and do change their general attitudes because they are more open and less self-assured.[29]

Because our cultural backgrounds and experiences vary, our attitudes and behavior vary. Attitudes are translated into behavior via behavioral intentions. Let us examine an established model of this important process.

L0.4 Attitudes Affect Behavior via Intentions

Building on Leon Festinger's work on cognitive dissonance, Icek Ajzen and Martin Fishbein further delved into understanding the reason for discrepancies between individuals' attitudes and behavior. Ajzen ultimately developed and refined a model focusing on intentions as the key link between attitudes and planned behavior. His theory of planned behavior in Figure 6–3 shows three separate but interacting determinants of one's intention (a person's readiness to perform a given behavior) to exhibit a specific behavior.

Figure 6–3   *Ajzen's Theory of Planned Behavior*

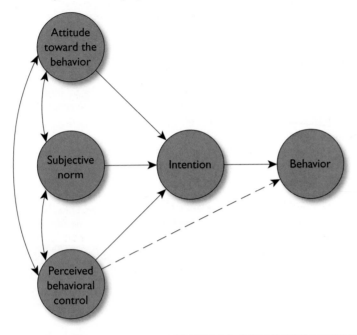

SOURCE: From I Ajzen, "The Theory of Planned Behavior," *Organizational Behavior and Human Decision Processes*, Figure 1, p 182. Copyright © 1991, with permission from Elsevier Science.

Importantly, this model only predicts behavior under an individual's control, not behavior due to circumstances beyond one's control. For example, this model can predict the likelihood that Boeing Co.'s machinists would strike against the company in late 2008. But it would be a poor model for predicting whether or not a specific machinist would arrive at the picket line at a designated time and date because uncontrolled circumstances such as traffic delays or an accident could intervene.[30]

Determinants of Intention   Ajzen has explained the nature and roles of the three determinants of intention as follows:

> The first is the *attitude toward the behavior* and refers to the degree to which a person has a favorable or unfavorable evaluation or appraisal of the behavior in question. The second predictor is a social factor termed *subjective norm*; it refers to the perceived social pressure to perform or not to perform the behavior. The third antecedent of intention is the degree of *perceived behavior control*, which . . . refers to the perceived ease or difficulty of performing the behavior and it is assumed to reflect past experience as well as anticipated impediments and obstacles.[31]

To bring these three determinants of intention to life, let us return to the example of the machinist strike against Boeing (see the Real World/Real People feature on page 164). The machinists have a positive attitude about striking because they believe the company is going to outsource their jobs. There also is a strong subjective norm to strike that is being promoted by the union. Regarding perceived behavior control, the machinists are completely in charge of acting on their intentions to strike.

Attitudes and Beliefs at the Core of Machinists' Strike at Boeing

At the heart of the union machinists' strike against Boeing Co. is a high-stakes showdown over something the aerospace giant once touted as a manufacturing innovation: Its efforts to outsource key roles in producing its new 787 Dreamliner jet. . . .

Boeing says it needs flexibility in its manufacturing to avoid the problems that have befallen other big industrial companies, while the union is fighting to keep as many jobs as possible. . . .

Resentment over outsourcing has been festering since the mid-1990s, when Boeing began a sweeping campaign to modernize its factories. The company has relied increasingly on contractors around the world to build larger and larger sections of its airplanes. By adopting many of the methods pioneered in the automobile industry, Boeing has been able to reduce the time it takes to build some of its jets by more than 50%. . . .

"We want the company to be extremely successful, but it seems like every time we make a big leap forward in efficiency, Boeing finds a way to send more jobs to outside contractors," said John Jorgensen, who has worked on Boeing's assembly lines for 43 years.

Their fear is that Boeing will eventually seek to allow contractors to go one step further and install their components directly on the airplane. Boeing officials insist that they have no plans to do this, but at the same time, they have refused to give the union blanket assurances in writing.

According to people familiar with the situation, Boeing had hoped that IAM President Tom Buffenbarger would help break the impasse with local union officials over the job security issue. . . . Instead, Mr. Buffenbarger agreed that job security was one of the union's priorities. "It's time for Boeing to listen to us on this," Mr. Buffenbarger said in a telephone interview from Florida.

What beliefs are driving the machinists' desire to strike?

SOURCE: Excerpted from J L Lunsford, "Outsourcing at Crux of Boeing Strike," *The Wall Street Journal,* September 8, 2008. Copyright © 2008 by Dow Jones & Company, Inc. via Copyright Clearance Center.

This machinist is on strike at Boeing due to the threat of outsourcing.

Intentions and Behavior Research Lessons and Implications

According to the model of planned behavior, someone's intention to engage in a given behavior is a strong predictor of that behavior. For example, the quickest and possibly most accurate way of determining whether an individual will quit his or her job is to have an objective third party ask if he or she intends to quit. A meta-analysis of 34 studies of employee turnover involving more than 83,000 employees validated this direct approach. The researchers found stated behavioral intentions to be a better predictor of employee turnover than job satisfaction, satisfaction with the work itself, or organizational commitment.[32] Another study took these findings one step further by considering whether or not job applicants' intention to quit a job before they were hired would predict voluntary turnover six months after being hired. Results demonstrated that intentions to quit significantly predicted turnover.[33]

Research has demonstrated that Ajzen's model accurately predicted intentions to buy consumer products, to search for a new job, to have children, to vote for specific political candidates, and to share information with others at work. Attitudes and behaviors regarding affirmative action programs, weight loss intentions and behavior, using Internet services to facilitate the shipping of products, nurses' willingness to work with older patients, and reenlisting in the National Guard also have been predicted successfully by the model.[34] From a practical standpoint, the theory of planned behavior has important managerial implications. Managers are encouraged to use prescriptions derived from the model to implement interventions aimed at changing employees' behavior.

According to this model, changing behavior starts with the recognition that behavior is modified through intentions, which in turn are influenced by three different determinants (see Figure 6–3). Managers can thus influence behavioral change by doing or saying things that affect the three determinants of employees' intentions to exhibit a specific behavior: attitude toward the behavior, subjective norms, and perceived behavioral control.[35] Let us return to the example of striking machinists at Boeing to explain how this can be done. Boeing management might attempt to change employees' attitude toward striking by making statements and commitments to reinforce the belief that machinists will not lose jobs due to outsourcing. This also might reduce the subjective norm to strike. Further, management can try to gain the support of union President Tom Buffenbarger by allowing the union to have input on outsourcing decisions. This support is needed to reduce the subjective norm regarding the strike.

It is important to remember that employee beliefs can be influenced through the information management provides on a day-by-day basis, the organization's culture, the content of training programs, the behavior of key employees, and the rewards that are targeted to reinforce certain beliefs. Consider how H C Jackson, founder of Jackson's Hardware in San Rafael, California, used these ideas to change employees' beliefs about taking over ownership of the company.

> As part of creating an ownership culture, Jackson's spends ample time teaching employees about the benefits of ownership....The company has a committee whose role is to educate employees about stock ownership and how their work is directly related to the success of the business—and thus their own financial well-being. Jackson's also puts out an annual ownership plan newsletter and selects an "Employee Owner for the Month" who receives a gas card and $600 toward a weekend getaway and dinner or store purchase.[36]

On a personal level, you also can use this model to influence your own behavior. If you want to increase the amount of time you spend studying, for example, you might begin by trying to influence your attitude toward studying. You could tell yourself that more studying leads to better grades, which in turn can help you find a rewarding job after graduation. You also can reward yourself for reaching a target score on the next exam. Subjective norms to study can be influenced by arranging to study with other students who are doing well in the class or by talking with your parents about what is going on in the class. Finally, it is important to remember that the amount of time you have for studying might be somewhat outside of your control. Our advice: control what you can and plan for contingencies.

Key Work Attitudes

to the point
What is the meaning of organizational commitment, job involvement, and employee engagement?

Work attitudes such as organizational commitment, job involvement/employee engagement, and job satisfaction have a dual interest to managers. On the one hand, they represent important outcomes that managers may want to enhance. On the other, they are symptomatic of other potential problems. For example, low job satisfaction may be a symptom of an employee's intention to quit. It thus is important for managers to understand the causes and consequences of key work attitudes.

What is your attitude toward work? Is work something meaningful that defines and fulfills you, or is it just a way to pay the bills? Interestingly, attitudes toward work have changed significantly throughout recorded history. For the early Greeks, for instance, work was something done by enslaved people. Today, in contrast, work is viewed by many as a source of satisfaction and enjoyment, and there is growing sentiment that work should be fun. While everyone does not agree about having fun at work, organizations such as Southwest Airlines have turned it into a strategic competitive advantage. Key employee selection factors at Southwest Airlines are a keen sense of humor and a general positive attitude. Consider how CEO Bob Pike's positive attitude toward work would set the tone for his employees at Creative Training Techniques International, Inc.:

> It is not a choice between fun and work, it is a choice for fun and work. I find it depressing that so many people spend 8 hours a day at work and 16 hours trying to forget that they did! It's time for us to replace the common definition of work: if it is not dull and boring then it can't be work! Work should be about passion, it should have a sense of purpose, it should be about involvement and participation. High-performing teams who do challenging work also know how to have fun. They have an attitude that says they enjoy what they do and that they belong to a diverse group of committed individuals who know the mission, values, and vision of the team. And they look forward to making a contribution.
>
> Understand that there will always be both fun-loving and fun-killing people. Fun-killers don't actually object to the fun; they feel that the fun isn't relevant to the work and therefore not important.[37]

How would you like to work for Bob Pike?

People have a multitude of attitudes about things that happen to them at work, but OB researchers have focused on a limited number of them. This section specifically examines two work attitudes—organizational commitment and job involvement/employee engagement—that have important practical implications. Job satisfaction, the most frequently studied work attitude, is thoroughly discussed in the next section of this chapter.

L0.5 Organizational Commitment

Before discussing a model of organizational commitment, it is important to consider the meaning of the term *commitment*. What does it mean to commit? Common sense suggests that commitment is an agreement to do something for yourself, another individual, group, or organization.[38] Formally, OB researchers define commitment as "a force that binds an individual to a course of action of relevance to one or more targets."[39] This definition highlights that commitment is associated with behavior and that commitment can be aimed at multiple targets or entities. For example, an individual can be committed to his or her job, family, girl- or boyfriend, faith, friends, career, organization, or a variety of professional associations. Let us now consider the application of commitment to a work organization.

Organizational commitment reflects the extent to which an individual identifies with an organization and is committed to its goals. It is an important work attitude because committed individuals are expected to display a willingness to work harder to achieve organizational goals and a greater desire to stay employed at an organization. Figure 6–4 presents a model of organizational commitment that identifies its causes and consequences.

Organizational commitment

Extent to which an individual identifies with an organization and its goals.

Figure 6–4   *A Model of Organizational Commitment*

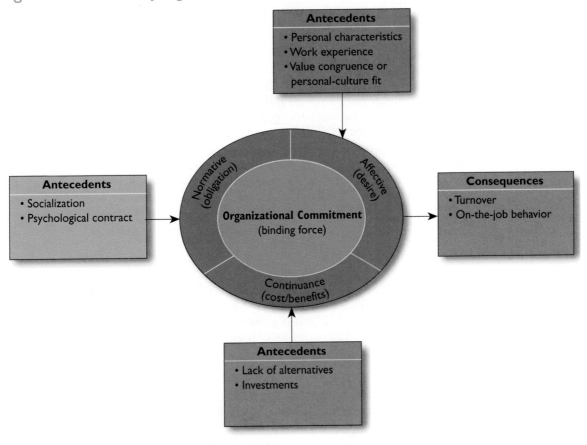

SOURCE: Adapted from J P Meyer and L Herscovitch, "Commitment in the Workplace: Toward a General Model," *Human Resource Management Review*, Autumn 2001, p 317.

A Model of Organizational Commitment

Figure 6–4 shows that organizational commitment is composed of three separate but related components: affective commitment, normative commitment, and continuance commitment. John Meyer and Natalie Allen, a pair of commitment experts, define these components as follows:

> *Affective commitment* refers to the employee's emotional attachment to, identification with, and involvement in the organization. Employees with a strong affective commitment continue employment with an organization because they *want* to do so. *Continuance commitment* refers to an awareness of the costs associated with leaving the organization. Employees whose primary link to the organization is based on continuance commitment remain because they *need* to do so. Finally, *normative commitment* reflects a feeling of obligation to continue employment. Employees with a high level of normative commitment feel that they *ought* to remain with the organization.[40]

Figure 6–4 also reveals that these three components combine to produce a binding force that influences the consequences of employee turnover and on-the-job behavior such as performance, absenteeism, and organizational citizenship, which is discussed later in this chapter.

Each component of commitment is influenced by a separate set of antecedents (see Figure 6–4). In the current context, an antecedent is something that causes the component of commitment to occur. For example, affective commitment is related to a variety of personal characteristics such as personality and locus of control (recall our discussion in Chapter 5), past work experience, and value congruence, which was discussed earlier in this chapter.[41] Because continuance commitment reflects a ratio of the costs and benefits associated with leaving an organization, antecedents are anything that affects the costs and benefits of leaving. Examples are a lack of job/career alternatives and the amount of real and psychological investments a person has in a particular organization or community. Continuance commitment would be high if an individual has no job alternatives, is actively involved in his or her church, has many friends in the community, owns shares of the company stock, and needs medical benefits for a family of five. Nancy Kramer, CEO of Resource Interactive, implemented a creative approach toward enhancing employees' continuance commitment.

> She launched the Resource Employee Equity Fund, or Reef. Here's how it works: The company buys stock in each of its 20 or so publicly held company clients. On employees' first anniversary, they each get one share of the Reef, which includes one share of each client's stock and 1/100th of a share of Warren Buffett's Berkshire Hathaway Inc. Class A shares. Each Reef share is worth abou $1,900 right now, she says.[42]

Psychological contract

An individual's perception about the terms and conditions of a reciprocal exchange with another party.

Finally, normative commitment is influenced by the socialization process discussed in Chapter 3 and what is termed the psychological contract. **Psychological contracts** represent an individual's perception about the terms and conditions of a reciprocal exchange between him- or herself and another party.[43] In a work environment, the psychological contract represents an employee's beliefs about what he or she is entitled to receive in return for what he or she provides to the organization. Research shows that an employer breach of the psychological contract is associated with lower organizational commitment, job satisfaction, and performance, and greater intentions to quit.[44]

Research and Practical Applications

Organizational commitment matters. A meta-analysis of 183 studies and almost 26,000 individuals uncovered a significant and strong positive relationship between organizational commitment and job satisfaction.[45] This finding encourages managers to increase job satisfaction in order to elicit higher levels of commitment. In turn, another meta-analysis involving 26,344 individuals revealed organizational commitment was significantly correlated with job performance.[46] This is an important finding because it implies managers can increase productivity by enhancing employees' organizational commitment.

Finally, a third meta-analysis summarizing results across 67 studies and 27,500 people uncovered a significant, negative relationship between organizational commitment and turnover.[47] This finding underscores the importance of paying attention to employees' organizational commitment because high commitment helps reduce the costs of employee turnover. In summary, managers are encouraged to focus on improving employees' organizational commitment.

Interestingly, companies use a variety of methods to increase employees' organizational commitment. Burns & McDonnell and TDIndustries use an employee stock ownership plan while Mayo Clinic and Mattel employ a host of progressive benefits.[48] All told, people are more likely to be committed to their organizations when they believe that the organization truly cares about their welfare and well-being.[49] Managers also can increase the components of employee commitment through the following activities:

- Affective commitment is enhanced by hiring people whose personal values are consistent with the organization's values. A positive, satisfying work environment also should increase employees' desire to stay. Harley-Davidson is following this advice. "Employee surveys show 90% strongly identify with the company's riding culture. Some employees get to work at biker rallies at Harley's expense."[50]

- Continuance commitment is enhanced by offering employees a variety of progressive benefits and human resource programs. At Mattell, for instance, perks include "13 paid holidays, two paid days to volunteer in schools, two onsite child-care centers, five paid days of parental leave . . . half-days on Fridays all year long, and onsite toy stores that offer discounts."[51]

- Normative commitment can be increased by making sure that management does not breach its psychological contracts and by trying to enhance the level of trust throughout the organization. We provide specific recommendation for building and maintaining trust in Chapter 11.

go to the Web for the Group Exercise: The Paper Airplane Contest

L0.6 Job Involvement and Employee Engagement

Job involvement is defined as "the degree to which one is cognitively preoccupied with, engaged in, and concerned with one's present job."[52] This work attitude manifests itself through the extent to which people are immersed in their job tasks. Take Vinton Studios' animators/directors Sean Burns and Doug Aberle for example. (Vinton Studios trademarked an animation process known as Claymation.® The process has been used in television commercials involving the California Raisins and M&Ms and the television series *The PJs.*) Sean says, "This is a great place to work. We work on truly interesting and cutting-edge stuff. Plus I get to work on things that interest me. Each project is a new situation every time. We suggest interesting twists, new ideas." Doug is involved in his work. "At the end of the day, you've never been so tired—or had so much fun! There's a lot of variety in working on a TV show. There's something different every day."[53] This suggests it is important for managers to understand the causes and consequences of job involvement because of its association with motivation and satisfaction. Let us now consider results from a meta-analytic study involving thousands of people, to learn more about job involvement.[54]

Job involvement
Extent to which an individual is immersed in his or her present job.

Job involvement was positively associated with job satisfaction, organizational commitment, and intrinsic motivation, and negatively related to intentions to quit. There are three key managerial implications associated with these results. First, managerial attempts to improve either of the two work attitudes discussed in this section are likely to positively affect the other work attitude. Second, managers can increase employees' job involvement by providing work environments that fuel intrinsic motivation. Specific recommendations for doing this are discussed in the section on

Although this little Claymation character seems a bit skeptical, the artists at Vinton Studios exhibit high job involvement. They love working on creative projects that hold their interest and turn hard work into fun. Task variety also is a big plus. An added bonus: their uncooperative subjects can be tossed back into the clay bucket.

intrinsic motivation in Chapter 9. Third, improving job involvement can reduce employee turnover.

Past results pertaining to the relationship between job involvement and performance are controversial. While the earlier meta-analysis failed to uncover a significant relationship between job involvement and performance, poor measures of job involvement used in past studies may have biased the results. A more recent study corrected this problem and found a positive relationship between job involvement and performance.[55] Managers thus are encouraged to increase employees' job involvement as a viable strategy for improving job performance.

Research on job involvement has evolved into the study of an individual difference variable called **employee engagement.** Employee engagement is defined as an individual's involvement, satisfaction, and enthusiasm for work.[56] Managers and organizations are interested in this personal characteristic because engaged employees are expected to put more effort into their jobs and to be more committed and loyal to their employers. While there is little academic research to substantiate this claim, consulting firms such as Gallup and Hewitt Associates LLC have collected proprietary data supporting the practical value of employee engagement.[57] For example, Gallup researchers conducted a meta-analysis involving 198,514 individuals from 7,930 business units and found that employee engagement was significantly associated with organizational-level customer satisfaction/loyalty, profitability, productivity, turnover, and safety outcomes.[58] Gallup estimates that organizations can achieve 12% higher customer satisfaction/loyalty, 18% more productivity, and 12% greater profitability when their employees are highly engaged.[59]

While academic research still is needed to validate measures of employee engagement, we believe that organizations can find value in measuring, tracking, and responding to surveys of employee engagement.[60] The Ritz-Carlton, for instance, was able to significantly lower employee turnover (18% versus an industry average of 158%) and increase both customer satisfaction and customer spending by following this recommendation.[61]

Employee engagement

Individual's involvement, satisfaction, and enthusiasm for work.

Job satisfaction

An affective or emotional response to one's job.

Job Satisfaction

to the point

What are the causes, correlates, and consequences of job satisfaction?

Job satisfaction essentially reflects the extent to which an individual likes his or her job. Formally defined, **job satisfaction** is an affective or emotional response toward various facets of one's job. This definition implies job satisfaction is not a unitary concept. Rather, a person can be relatively satisfied with one aspect of his or her job and dissatisfied with one or more other aspects. For example, a recent survey of job satisfaction across generational groups uncovered the following trends: Traditionalists, Baby Boomers, Gen Xers, and Gen Ys were most satisfied with their employers and least satisfied with compensation; Baby Boomers had lower satisfaction with employers, the jobs they perform, and compensation than Traditionalists, Gen Xers, and Gen Ys; and Traditionalists had higher job satisfaction than the other groups across all aspects of satisfaction.[62]

Researchers at Cornell University developed the Job Descriptive Index (JDI) to assess one's satisfaction with the following job dimensions: work, pay, promotions, coworkers, and supervision.[63] Researchers at the University of Minnesota concluded there are 20 different dimensions underlying job satisfaction. Although researchers do not have consensus about the exact number of dimensions that constitute job satisfaction, they do agree that it has five predominant causes. We believe that knowledge about the causes of job satisfaction can assist managers in using a multifaceted approach toward increasing this key work attitude. Let us now examine the causes of job satisfaction.

LO.7 The Causes of Job Satisfaction

Five predominant models of job satisfaction focus on different causes. They are need fulfillment, discrepancy, value attainment, equity, and dispositional/genetic components. A brief review of these models provides insight into the variety of methods that can be used to increase employees' job satisfaction.[64]

Need Fulfillment   These models propose that satisfaction is determined by the extent to which the characteristics of a job allow an individual to fulfill his or her needs. For example, a survey by the Society for Human Resource Management asked employees to choose the aspects of their job that were very important to their job satisfaction. Their top four choices were compensation, benefits, job security, and work/life balance—all directly related to employees' ability to meet a variety of basic needs.[65] We suspect that the need for job security will become more important for employees during our current recession. Although need fulfillment models generated a great degree of controversy, it is generally accepted that need fulfillment is correlated with job satisfaction.[66]

Discrepancies   These models propose that satisfaction is a result of met expectations. **Met expectations** represent the difference between what an individual expects to receive from a job, such as good pay and promotional opportunities, and what he or she actually receives. When expectations are greater than what is received, a person will be dissatisfied. In contrast, this model predicts that an individual will be satisfied when he or she attains outcomes above and beyond expectations. A meta-analysis of 31 studies that included 17,241 people demonstrated that met expectations were significantly related to job satisfaction.[67] Many companies use employee attitude or opinion surveys to assess employees' expectations and concerns, even during bad economic conditions (see the Real World/Real People feature about assessing employees' job satisfaction on page 172).

Met expectations

The extent to which one receives what he or she expects from a job.

Value Attainment   The idea underlying **value attainment** is that satisfaction results from the perception that a job allows for fulfillment of an individual's important work values.[68] For example, New Belgium Brewing Co., brewers of Fat Tire, attracts employees who value bicycling and environmental sustainability. The company gives each employee a cruiser bike after working for the company for one year and it established on-site recycling centers. Almost 50% of employees working at the corporate headquarters in Fort Collins, Colorado, commute by

Value attainment

The extent to which a job allows fulfillment of one's work values.

Organizations Assess Employees' Job Satisfaction Even during Bad Times

Your company has been seeing declining sales for several quarters; you've already made salary cuts and are considering additional cuts and possibly layoffs. You wonder what employees might be thinking right now, but are a little afraid to ask. Is this the right time to conduct a survey?

While some HR professionals suggest that introducing an employee survey during difficult times is not a good idea, others disagree. Marc Effron, vice president of talent management for beauty products manufacturer Avon products in New York, says Avon started its engagement survey about three years ago, immediately after a major turnaround effort. "It was probably one of the most difficult times in our company's history," he says. Yet Effron suspects that the survey sent a positive message, serving as "a good demonstration that we care about employee opinions."

Think about "the positive impact that an employee survey can have," says Ilene Gochman, HR consultancy Watson Wyatt's organization effectiveness practice leader. An adverse environment is "precisely the time you want to know what's on the minds of employees, because those that are staying are the ones you want to engage."

Joseph Cabral, senior vice president and chief human resources officer for the North Shore–LIJ Health System in Long Island, New York, says North Shore has been surveying its 38,000 employees annually for the past three years, but it recently went to a quarterly survey to provide more real-time and actionable results and to allow comparisons across worksites and departments.

"During these uncertain times, employees are a little more on edge, but if we're effective in our communication and we're clear and we're honest and we're doing all the right things, it really helps the employees feel comfortable and it builds trust," he says.

What are the pros and cons of conducting an employee survey during a bad economy?

SOURCE: Excerpted from L Grensing-Pophal, "To Ask or Not to Ask," *HR Magazine*, February 2009, pp 53–55.

---

bike during the summer.[69] In general, research consistently supports the prediction that value fulfillment is positively related to job satisfaction. Managers can thus enhance employee satisfaction by structuring the work environment and its associated rewards and recognition to reinforce employees' values.

Equity　In this model, satisfaction is a function of how "fairly" an individual is treated at work. Satisfaction results from one's perception that work outcomes, relative to inputs, compare favorably with a significant other's outcomes/inputs. A meta-analysis involving 190 studies and 64,757 people supported this model. Employees' perceptions of being treated fairly at work were highly related to overall job satisfaction.[70] Managers thus are encouraged to monitor employees' fairness perceptions and to interact with employees in such a way that they feel equitably treated. Chapter 8 explores this promising model in more detail.

Dispositional/Genetic Components　Have you ever noticed that some of your coworkers or friends appear to be satisfied across a variety of job circumstances, whereas others always seem dissatisfied? This model of satisfaction attempts to explain this pattern.[71] Specifically, the dispositional/genetic model is based on the belief that job satisfaction is partly a function of both personal traits and genetic factors. As such, this model implies that stable individual differences are just as important in explaining job satisfaction as are characteristics of the work environment. Although only a few studies have tested these propositions, results support a positive, significant relationship between personal traits and job satisfaction over time periods ranging from 2 to 50 years.[72] Genetic factors also were found to significantly predict life satisfaction, well-being, and general job satisfaction.[73] Overall, researchers estimate that 30% of an individual's job satisfaction is associated with dispositional and genetic components.[74] Pete and Laura Wakeman, founders of Great Harvest Bread Company, have used this model of job satisfaction while running their company for more than 25 years.

These employees appear to be enjoying their jobs. Research suggests that they are more likely to enjoy their job based on genetic factors and personal traits.

> Our hiring ads say clearly that we need people with "strong personal loves as important as their work." This is not a little thing. You can't have a great life unless you have a buffer of like-minded people all around you. If you want to be nice, you can't surround yourself with crabby people and expect it to work. You might stay nice for a while, just because—but it isn't sustainable over years. If you want a happy company, you can do it only by hiring naturally happy people. You'll never build a happy company by "making people happy"—you can't really "make" people any way that they aren't already. Laura and I want to be in love with life, and our business has been a good thing for us in that journey.[75]

Although Pete and Laura's hiring approach is consistent with the dispositional and genetic model of job satisfaction, it is important to note that hiring "like-minded" people can potentially lead to discriminatory decisions. Managers are advised not to discriminate on the basis of race, gender, religion, color, national origin, and age.

go to the Web for the Self-Exercise: How Satisfied Are You with Your Present Job?

LO.8 Major Correlates and Consequences of Job Satisfaction

This topic has significant managerial implications because thousands of studies have examined the relationship between job satisfaction and other organizational variables. Because it is impossible to examine them all, we will consider a subset of the more important variables from the standpoint of managerial relevance.

Table 6–2 summarizes the pattern of results. The relationship between job satisfaction and these other variables is either positive or negative. The strength of the relationship ranges from weak (very little relationship) to strong. Strong relationships imply that managers can significantly influence the variable of interest by increasing job satisfaction. Let us now consider eight key correlates of job satisfaction.

Motivation   A recent meta-analysis of nine studies and 1,739 workers revealed a significant positive relationship between motivation and job satisfaction. Because satisfaction with supervision also was significantly correlated with motivation, managers are advised to consider how their behavior affects employee satisfaction.[76] Managers can potentially enhance employees' motivation through various attempts to increase job satisfaction.

Table 6–2   *Correlates of Job Satisfaction*

VARIABLES RELATED WITH SATISFACTION	DIRECTION OF RELATIONSHIP	STRENGTH OF RELATIONSHIP
Motivation	Positive	Moderate
Job involvement	Positive	Moderate
Organizational commitment	Positive	Moderate
Organizational citizenship behavior	Positive	Moderate
Absenteeism	Negative	Weak
Tardiness	Negative	Weak
Withdrawal cognitions	Negative	Strong
Turnover	Negative	Moderate
Heart disease	Negative	Moderate
Perceived stress	Negative	Strong
Pro-union voting	Negative	Moderate
Job performance	Positive	Moderate
Life satisfaction	Positive	Moderate
Mental health	Positive	Moderate

Job Involvement   Job involvement represents the extent to which an individual is personally involved with his or her work role. A meta-analysis involving 27,925 individuals from 87 different studies demonstrated that job involvement was moderately related with job satisfaction.[77] Managers are thus encouraged to foster satisfying work environments in order to fuel employees' job involvement.

Organizational citizenship behaviors (OCBs)

Employee behaviors that exceed work-role requirements.

Organizational Citizenship Behavior   Organizational citizenship behaviors (OCBs) consist of employee behaviors that are beyond the call of duty. Examples include "such gestures as constructive statements about the department, expression of personal interest in the work of others, suggestions for improvement, training new people, respect for the spirit as well as the letter of housekeeping rules, care for organizational property, and punctuality and attendance well beyond standard or enforceable levels."[78] Managers certainly would like employees to exhibit these behaviors. A meta-analysis covering 7,031 people and 21 separate studies revealed a significant and moderately positive correlation between organizational citizenship behaviors and job satisfaction.[79] Moreover, a more extensive meta-analysis involving 51,235 individuals and 168 studies indicated that OCBs were significantly related to both individual-level consequences (e.g., performance appraisal ratings, intentions to quit, absenteeism, and turnover) and organizational-level outcomes (e.g., productivity, efficiency, lower costs, customer satisfaction, and unit-level turnover).[80] These results are important for two reasons. First, exhibiting OCBs is likely to create positive impressions about you among your colleagues and manager. In turn, these impressions affect your ability to work with others, your manager's evaluation of your performance, and ultimately your promotability. Second, the aggregate amount of employees' OCBs affects important organizational outcomes. It thus is important for managers to

Phenomenex Inc. Uses Fun to Reduce Absenteeism

Fasha Mahjoor, founder and chief executive of Phenomenex Inc., wanted to build a workplace that was more than just a place to clock out every evening. He wanted to create an environment where employees could have lots of fun together and feel appreciated.

"Our company is not one where you just come to work," says Mr. Mahjoor. It's one where (employees) love coming to work."

Team sports are a central part of the culture. The company hosts an annual soccer game and PhenOlympics, where employees compete in 10 athletic contests. The company also organizes recreational trips, such as an annual skiing and whitewater rafting trip, for employees and their families. The trips are often free or highly subsidized by Phenomenex.

. . . "About every six weeks we have a little event," says Donna Valenzuela, a 32-year-old customer-service representative who has worked at Phenomenex's Torrance, Calif., offices since 2005.

Ms. Valenzuela sits on an employee committee that helps come up with trips and company events. That might be a family picnic in the summer, for instance, or a trip to a Los Angeles Dodgers game.

She says all the activity helps break the monotony: "Here, it's not just work, work, work."

Would you like to work at Phenomenex?

SOURCE: Excerpted from "Top Small Workplaces 2008," *The Wall Street Journal*, October 13, 2008, p R9.

---

foster an environment that promotes OCBs.[81] Managers are encouraged to make and implement employee-related decisions in an equitable fashion in order to foster OCBs.[82] More is said about this in Chapter 8.

Absenteeism   Absenteeism is not always what it appears to be, and it can be costly. For example, a survey of 700 managers indicated that 20% of them called in sick because they simply did not feel like going to work that day. The top three reasons given for the bogus excuse of being sick were doing personal errands, catching up on sleep, and relaxing.[83] While it is difficult to provide a precise estimate of the cost of absenteeism, a recent survey by Mercer Consulting estimated that unplanned absenteeism costs as much as 9% of a company's total payroll.[84] Because of these costs, managers are constantly on the lookout for ways to reduce it. Phenomenex Inc.'s attempt involves creating a fun environment that motivates employees to want to come to work (see the Real World/Real People feature above). One recommendation has been to increase job satisfaction. If this is a valid recommendation, there should be a strong negative relationship (or negative correlation) between satisfaction and absenteeism. In other words, as satisfaction increases, absenteeism should decrease. A researcher tracked this prediction by synthesizing three separate meta-analyses containing a total of 74 studies. Results revealed a weak negative relationship between satisfaction and absenteeism.[85] It is unlikely, therefore, that managers will realize any significant decrease in absenteeism by increasing job satisfaction.

Withdrawal Cognitions   Although some people quit their jobs impulsively or in a fit of anger, most go through a process of thinking about whether or not they should quit. **Withdrawal cognitions** encapsulate this thought process by representing an individual's overall thoughts and feelings about quitting. What causes an individual to think about quitting his or her job? Job satisfaction is believed to be one of the most significant contributors. For example, a study of managers, salespersons, and auto mechanics from a national automotive retail

Withdrawal cognitions

Overall thoughts and feelings about quitting a job.

store chain demonstrated that job dissatisfaction caused employees to begin the process of thinking about quitting. In turn, withdrawal cognitions had a greater impact on employee turnover than job satisfaction in this sample.[86] Results from this study imply that managers can indirectly help to reduce employee turnover by enhancing employee job satisfaction.

Turnover   In spite of the economic problems facing the world in 2008, a survey of 600 organizations indicated that 81% of them viewed employee retention as a critical business priority. This was an increase from 41% in 2007.[87] This result is consistent with another survey of 1,200 U.S. employees. Forty percent of the respondents reported that they were open to looking for another job while 13% were actively searching.[88] Turnover is important to companies because it disrupts organizational continuity and is very costly. Costs of turnover fall into two categories: separation costs and replacement costs.

> Separation costs may include severance pay, costs associated with an exit interview, outplacement fees, and possible litigation costs, particularly for involuntary separation. Replacement costs are the well-known costs of a hire, including sourcing expenses, HR processing costs for screening and assessing candidates, the time spent by hiring managers interviewing candidates, travel and relocation expenses, signing bonuses, if applicable, and orientation and training costs.[89]

Experts estimate that the cost of turnover for an hourly employee is roughly 30% of annual salary, whereas the cost can range up to 150% of yearly salary for professional employees.[90]

Although there are various things a manager can do to reduce employee turnover, many of them revolve around attempts to improve employees' job satisfaction. This trend is supported by results from a meta-analysis of 67 studies covering 24,556 people. Job satisfaction obtained a moderate negative relationship with employee turnover.[91] Given the strength of this relationship, managers are advised to try to reduce employee turnover by increasing employee job satisfaction.

Perceived Stress   Stress can have very negative effects on organizational behavior and an individual's health. Stress is positively related to absenteeism, turnover, coronary heart disease, and viral infections. Based on a meta-analysis of 32 studies covering 11,063 individuals, Table 6–2 reveals that perceived stress has a strong, negative relationship with job satisfaction.[92] It is hoped that managers would attempt to reduce the negative effects of stress by improving job satisfaction.

Job Performance   One of the biggest controversies within OB research centers on the relationship between job satisfaction and job performance. Although researchers have identified eight different ways in which these variables are related, the dominant beliefs are either that satisfaction causes performance or performance causes satisfaction.[93] A team of researchers recently attempted to resolve this controversy through a meta-analysis of data from 312 samples involving 54,417 individuals.[94] There were two key findings from this study. First, job satisfaction and performance are moderately related. This is an important finding because it supports the belief that employee job satisfaction is a key work attitude managers should consider when attempting to increase employees' job performance. Second, the relationship between job satisfaction and performance is much more complex than originally thought. It is not as simple as satisfaction causing performance or performance causing satisfaction. Rather, researchers now believe both variables indirectly influence each other through a host of individual differences and work-environment characteristics.[95] There is one additional consideration to keep in mind regarding the relationship between job satisfaction and job performance.

Researchers believe the relationship between satisfaction and performance is understated due to incomplete measures of individual-level performance. For example, if performance ratings used in past research did not reflect the actual interactions and interdependencies at work, inaccurate measures of performance served to lower the reported correlations between satisfaction and performance. Examining the relationship between *aggregate* measures of job satisfaction and organizational performance is one solution to correct this problem. In support of these ideas, a team of researchers conducted a recent meta-analysis of 7,939 business units in 36 companies. Results uncovered significant positive relationships between business-unit-level employee satisfaction and business-unit outcomes of customer satisfaction, productivity, profit, employee turnover, and accidents.[96] It thus appears managers can positively affect a variety of important organizational outcomes, including performance, by increasing employee job satisfaction.

> **Counterproductive work behaviors (CWBs)**
>
> Types of behavior that harm employees and the organization as a whole.

LO.9 Counterproductive Work Behaviors

> **to the point**
>
> What are the causes of counterproductive work behaviors and how can managers prevent them?

In our discussion of job satisfaction, we noted that an absence of satisfaction may be associated with some types of undesirable behavior, such as absenteeism and employee turnover. These costly behaviors, along with some that are even more disturbing, are part of a category of behavior known as **counterproductive work behaviors (CWBs),** types of behavior that harm employees and the organization as a whole. CWBs "include but are not limited to theft, white collar crime, absenteeism, tardiness, drug and alcohol abuse, disciplinary problems, accidents, sabotage, sexual harassment, and violence."[97] Consider the following three examples:

> Recently, a Maryland man swiped 32 laptops from his nonprofit healthcare employer and put them on eBay. A chief financial officer changed the color of the type on some spreadsheet data from black to white so as to render the fake numbers invisible while juicing the totals—and his bonus. One regional vice-president for sales billed his corporate card $4,000 for Victoria's Secret lingerie—and not for his wife, either.[98]

Experts expect incidents like this to increase during the current recession.

Occurrences of counterproductive work behavior like this generally increase during a recession.

Mistreatment of Others

Some forms of CWBs involve mistreatment of coworkers, subordinates, or even customers. For example, employees engage in harassment, bullying, or blatant unfairness. Unfortunately, in a recent survey of U.S. employees, 45% said they have had a boss who was abusive.[99] Abuse by supervisors is especially toxic because employees report that when they feel they have been intimidated, humiliated, or undermined by an abusive supervisor, they are more likely to retaliate with counterproductive behavior aimed at the supervisor or their coworkers.[100] This type of response is especially likely when the organization does not provide channels through which employees can complain and find a resolution to the problem of mistreatment.[101]

Violence at Work

Terrifying images of the shootings at Virginia Tech and Northern Illinois University have brought home the urgency of protecting people in organizations from sudden acts of violence committed by insiders or outsiders. Often, coworkers are first to notice that an employee explodes in anger or seems depressed or troubled. Psychiatrist and consultant Roger Brunswick says, "Violence rarely begins with someone walking in and shooting others. Violence usually builds slowly and starts with bullying, intimidation and threats."[102] A first line of defense should be for the organization to set up and publicize how employees can report troubling behavior to their supervisor or human resource department. Pitney Bowes set up a hotline that employees can call anonymously to report any concerns, and it has trained managers in identifying signs that something is wrong with an employee.[103]

Causes and Prevention of CWBs

Employers obviously want to prevent CWBs, so they need to know the causes of such behavior. A study that followed the work behaviors of more than 900 young adults for 23 years found that a diagnosis of conduct disorder in adolescence was associated with CWBs, but criminal convictions before entering the workforce were not associated with CWBs.[104] Personality traits and job conditions also could make CWBs more likely. For example, young adults who scored higher on compulsion to adhere to norms, control their impulses, and avoid hostility tended not to use CWBs. They also were less likely to engage in CWBs if they had satisfying jobs that offered autonomy—and more likely to engage in CWBs if they had more resource power (such as more people to supervise). Intelligence may play a role, too. A study of applicants for law enforcement jobs found that higher scores for cognitive ability were associated with fewer reports of CWBs such as violence and destruction of property after candidates were hired.[105]

These findings suggest the following implications for management:

- Organizations can limit CWBs by hiring individuals who are less prone to engage in this type of behavior. Cognitive ability is associated with many measures of success, so it is a logical quality to screen for in hiring decisions. Personality tests also may be relevant.

- Organizations should ensure they are motivating desired behaviors and not CWBs, for example, by designing jobs that promote satisfaction and by preventing abusive supervision. A study of 265 restaurants found that CWBs were greater in restaurants where employees reported abuse by supervisors and where managers had more employees to supervise.[106] CWBs in these restaurants were associated with lower profits and lower levels of customer satisfaction, so adequate staffing and management development could not only make employees' lives more pleasant but also improve the bottom line.

- If an employee does engage in CWBs, the organization should respond quickly and appropriately, defining the specific behaviors that are unacceptable and the requirements for acceptable behavior. Chapter 9 describes guidelines for giving effective feedback.

Summary of Key Concepts

1. *Explain Schwartz's value theory, and describe three types of value conflict.* Schwartz proposed that 10 core values guide our behavior across contexts and time (see Table 6–1). Each value possesses motivational mechanisms that drive behavior. Figure 6–1 further shows the relationships among the ten values. Some are consistent and positively related, whereas others are inconsistent and conflict with each other. Three types of value conflict are intrapersonal, interpersonal, and individual–organization.

2. *Describe the values model of work/family conflict, and specify at least three practical lessons from work/family conflict research.* General life values determine one's values about family and work. Work/family conflict can occur when there is a lack of value similarity with family members. Likewise, work/family conflict can occur when one's own work values are not congruent with the company's values. When someone does not attain his or her values because of work/family conflicts, job or life satisfaction, or both, can suffer. Six practical lessons from work/family conflict research are (1) work/family balance begins at home, (2) an employer's family-supportive philosophy is more important than specific programs, (3) informal flexibility in work hours and in allowing people to work at home is essential to promoting work/family balance, (4) mentors can help, (5) individuals should take a proactive approach to managing work/family conflict, and (6) self-employment has its rewards, but it is associated with higher work/family conflict and lower family satisfaction.

3. *Identify the three components of attitudes and discuss cognitive dissonance.* The three components of attitudes are affective, cognitive, and behavioral. The affective component represents the feelings or emotions one has about a given object or situation. The cognitive component reflects the beliefs or ideas one has about an object or situation. The behavioral component refers to how one intends or expects to act toward someone or something. Cognitive dissonance represents the psychological discomfort an individual experiences when his or her attitudes or beliefs are incompatible with his or her behavior. There are three main methods for reducing cognitive dissonance: change an attitude or behavior, belittle the importance of the inconsistent behavior, and find consonant elements that outweigh dissonant ones.

4. *Explain how attitudes affect behavior in terms of Ajzen's theory of planned behavior.* Intentions are the key link between attitudes and behavior in Ajzen's model. Three determinants of the strength of an intention are one's attitude toward the behavior, subjective norm (social expectations and role models), and the perceived degree of one's control over the behavior. Intentions, in turn, are powerful determinants of behavior.

5. *Describe the model of organizational commitment.* Organizational commitment reflects how strongly a person identifies with an organization and is committed to its goals. Organizational commitment is composed of three related components: affective commitment, continuance commitment, and normative commitment. In turn, each of these components is influenced by a separate set of antecedents: An antecedent is something that causes the component of commitment to occur.

6. *Define the work attitudes of job involvement/employee engagement and job satisfaction.* Job involvement is the extent to which a person is preoccupied with, immersed in, and concerned with his/her job. Employee engagement is similar to job involvement and represents an individual's satisfaction, involvement, and enthusiasm for his/her work. Job satisfaction reflects how much people like or dislike their jobs.

7. *Identify and briefly describe five alternative causes of job satisfaction.* They are need fulfillment (the degree to which one's own needs are met), discrepancies (satisfaction depends on the extent to which one's expectations are met), value attainment (satisfaction depends on the degree to which one's work values are fulfilled), equity (perceived fairness of input/outcomes determines one's level of satisfaction), and dispositional/genetic (job satisfaction is dictated by one's personal traits and genetic makeup).

8. *Identify eight important correlates/consequences of job satisfaction, and summarize how each one relates to job satisfaction.* Eight major correlates/consequences of job satisfaction are motivation (moderate positive relationship), job involvement (moderate positive), organizational citizenship behavior (moderate positive), absenteeism (weak negative), withdrawal cognitions (strong negative), turnover (moderate negative), perceived stress (strong negative), and job performance (moderate positive).

9. *Identify the causes of counterproductive work behaviors and the measures used to prevent them.* Counterproductive work behaviors (CWBs) may result from personal characteristics coupled with a lack of autonomy and job satisfaction. CWBs are more likely in situations where supervisors are abusive and responsible for many employees. Organizations can limit CWBs by hiring individuals with appropriate cognitive skills and personality traits. They can design jobs to promote satisfaction. They can develop managers to supervise effectively without abuse and should deliver immediate feedback and discipline if anyone engages in CWBs.

OB in Action Case Study

Companies Are Trying to Improve Employee Attitudes during the Recession[107]

BusinessWeek CEOs may have cut back sharply on management consulting in the last downturn, but that's not stopping Bain & Co.'s worldwide managing director, Steve Ellis, from doing the same thing Bain did during the dot-com bust: hiring. He's adding consultants in hot-growth areas such as emerging markets and corporate turnarounds, and he's more aggressively targeting former consultants who went to financial-services firms and are now "stranded." Plus, despite expectations that 2009 will be a challenging year for consulting, he's pushing full speed ahead in recruiting from an MBA class that suddenly has far fewer options. "This is a huge opportunity to grab very talented people," says Ellis.

For many managers, recessions prompt a near-autonomic reflex: Hunker down, reduce head count, and cut every cost you can. While a certain dose of those bitter pills is unavoidable, smart leaders see downturns as having plenty of upside, too. Talent is cheaper. Companies can gain market share as others cut back. And savvy investments give bold players a head start when the economy picks up.

Nowhere is that more true than in the care and feeding of employees. Even amid a hiring freeze or a workforce reduction, there are ways to engage top workers. As the housing market crumbled, Home Depot cut jobs in its corporate offices. It also closed 15 locations. Still, Chairman and Chief Executive Frank Blake wanted to boost morale and set realistic goals. In addition to extending restricted stock grants to assistant store managers, he lowered sales and profit targets that hourly employees have to meet to receive bonuses. As a result, says Marvin Ellison, Home Depot's new executive vice-president for U.S. stores, the highest percentage ever of in-store employees got bonuses in the first half of this year. "We still challenged people to hit some pretty tough numbers," Ellison says.

Keeping people focused amid mounting layoffs often requires a more emotional approach. Talking about the company's nonfinancial goals can help prevent productivity from grinding to a halt as anxious employees await their fate. And once cuts are made, managers need to take time to discuss them and why they happened. Ignoring the matter, says Christopher Rice, president and CEO of leadership consulting firm BlessingWhite, creates an atmosphere that's "like the most awkward Thanksgiving dinner. And it doesn't go away."

Amid pressure to downsize, it's easy to forget that talent retention is a critical concern during a recession. Michael Kesner, a principal at Deloitte Consulting's human capital practice, notes that "companies who took advantage of employees in past downturns were rewarded with people bailing when things turned around." To avoid that, some of Kesner's clients are adding more weight to factors employees can control—such as customer satisfaction scores or production levels—when deciding on bonuses. Others are creating discretionary bonus pools to reward poachable stars. And with some 63% of companies reporting that all or most of the stock options they've granted in the past five years are underwater, according to a Deloitte survey of 151 companies, a few are considering the controversial step of repricing or exchanging them. Compensation research firm Equilar reports that 23 companies have done so since the beginning of the year, including R.H. Donnelley and software maker VMware.

Plain, Unvarnished Communication

There are other ways to make employees feel valued. Consider Best Buy, which has watched its stock plummet 40% over the past month and announced it will hire fewer seasonal employees amid a dismal holiday shopping outlook. One way the company has also tried to keep employees engaged is by setting up online surveys to solicit ideas for cutting costs. Some 900 ideas have emerged since the surveys were sent out three weeks ago. A couple of them: save shipping costs by consolidating distribution of in-store signs and use a computerized phone system to schedule service calls. As John Pershing, Best Buy's executive vice-president for human capital, says: "When you know you can make a difference and you're part of a solution, it can change your mind completely."

Indeed the best strategy for managing talent, in good times and bad, remains plain, unvarnished communication. "People are looking for reassurances, for transparency, and they're not looking for surprises," says Edward E. Lawler III, director of the Center for Effective Organizations at the University of Southern California. A CEO town hall meeting is fine, but it's no substitute for reassurances from managers further down the line. Says Jon R. Katzenbach, a senior partner and founder at consultant Katzenbach Partners: "If you're scared and your worried about your job, hearing the CEO telling you things are good isn't nearly as effective as (hearing it from) the person you have respect for because you've worked with them all along."

That said, symbolic gestures from CEOs can help employees feel that everyone is sharing the pain. JetBlue Airways CEO David Barger has cut back across the board over the past year—delaying aircraft orders, trimming head count through voluntary unpaid leaves, even shedding the free pillows from his planes. In July he cut his own salary, from $500,000 to $375,000 for the year. "There's an awful lot of pain that's taking place across the industry," says Barger. "It was just the right thing to do."

Questions for Discussion

1. Which of Schwartz's 10 values are driving the behavior of managers at Bain & Co., Home Depot, and Best Buy? Provide examples to support your conclusions.
2. How would you describe Steve Ellis's affective, cognitive, and behavioral components of his attitude toward managing in a recession? Be specific.
3. How are Home Depot and Best Buy trying to increase employee involvement?
4. Use Ajzen's theory of planned behavior (Figure 6–3) to analyze how managers can increase employee performance during a recession. Be sure to explain what managers can do to affect each aspect of the theory.
5. Based on what you learned in this chapter, what advice would you give to managers trying increase employees' organizational commitment and job satisfaction in a recession? Be specific.

Ethical Dilemma

How Would You Handle Employees Who Fake Illnesses to Take Sick Leave?[108]

Dirk Cuypers, the top official at Belgium's health ministry, is sick of sick leave.

Belgians, like many Europeans, are entitled to extensive or even unlimited sick leave—and they tend to stretch the definition of the word. One study showed government employees in droves were calling in sick to pack before vacations and to sleep off holiday hangovers. Some government departments were averaging 35 days of paid sick leave per employee each year, more than twice the national rate and seven times the U.S. average.

Dr. Cuypers and the minister for civil service set up a network of doctor-inspectors around the nation to smoke out malingerers. . . . Once, says Dr. Quoidbach, he discovered that a man taking time off was really working a black-market job, given away by the paint on his hands. Another man answered his door with an undone belt as a woman hurried out the door. Others, faking backs, go to the door too fast.

What Would You Do If You Were Dirk Cuypers?

1. Prosecute the cheaters. They are causing Belgian companies to be inefficient, thereby increasing costs.
2. Push for national legislation aimed at reducing the amount of sick days that people are allowed to take.
3. There is nothing you can do because people just find other ways to cheat.
4. Continue the doctor-inspectors, and do not pay people found to be lying about being sick.
5. Invent other options.

Web Resources

For study material and exercises that apply to this chapter, visit our Web site, www.mhhe.com/kreitner

Chapter 7

Social Perception and Attributions

When you finish studying the material in this chapter, you should be able to:

LO.1 Describe perception in terms of the information-processing model.

LO.2 Identify and briefly explain seven managerial implications of social perception.

LO.3 Discuss stereotypes and the process of stereotype formation.

LO.4 Summarize the managerial challenges and recommendations of sex-role, age, racial and ethnic, and disability stereotypes.

LO.5 Describe and contrast the Pygmalion effect, the Galatea effect, and the Golem effect.

LO.6 Discuss how the self-fulfilling prophecy is created and how it can be used to improve individual and group productivity.

LO.7 Explain, according to Kelley's model, how external and internal causal attributions are formulated.

LO.8 Contrast the fundamental attribution bias and the self-serving bias.

Smart dressing involves sending subliminal messages, particularly when a serious job is at stake. This is something that even high-ranking business leaders can underestimate.

In commerce, unlike in Hollywood, fashion plays a largely uncredited role. Business schools train graduates to shine their shoes for an interview. But once established, apart from avoiding the obvious gaffe—a coffee stained shirt or a visible rhinestone bra strap—many executives spend little time contemplating what they wear to a job interview. At their peril....

"People don't understand the messages that their clothes send," says Ms. Waldt, a recruiter with CTPartners. Women sometimes don't realize how often a tight shirt or a low neckline comes across as seductive. People who meet them are likely to assume the sexual innuendo is intentional. It's harder for men to goof, but they do—for instance, by being sloppy with untucked or wrinkled shirts or wearing beeping sports watches to staid business events. Sagging socks, dangling earrings and obvious designer logos all send messages that register with the people on the other side of the table....

Ms. Waldt recalls a candidate sent to an interview with a retailer that had a casual culture. Unfortunately for him, he dressed up. "The clothes that he was wearing were so polar-opposite of what the company did that they thought he just didn't get them at all," says Ms. Waldt. "They never bothered to interview him. He sat in a holding pen all day and flew home."

Possibly, that job candidate wouldn't have wanted to work at a company that dismissed him so summarily. Yet boards of directors routinely size up executive-level candidates by inspecting the clues in their clothes.

Hal Reiter, an executive recruiter and chairman and chief executive of Herbert Mines Associates, recalls meeting with a CEO candidate for a mainstream retailer.

The man, chief financial officer of a major big-box retailer, showed up in a navy-blue necktie with a gold circular symbol surrounded by what looked like leaves and red blotches. Upon closer inspection, Mr. Reiter discovered that the red was blood dripping from a crown of thorns. The tie isn't the main reason he didn't get the job, but the distractingly graphic religious imagery didn't help....

Female politicians know what a tightrope fashion can be: Smart clothes might not win votes, but the wrong style can lose them votes. The wardrobes of female political candidates are so closely scrutinized that the media has reported who shops for House Speaker Nancy Pelosi (her husband Paul) and that former

What message is this man's clothing sending in contrast to the other interview candidates?

French presidential candidate Ségolène Royal buys at Zara....

David Goldhill, president and chief executive of the Game Show Network, has been overhauling the television network's senior management lately. He highlighted the subliminal nature of the interviewing process when I asked if his decisions have been influenced by what a job candidate or subordinate wore, for better or for worse. "Probably," he responded, "but I'm not aware of it."[1]

FOR DISCUSSION

Are you surprised by interviewing gaffes discussed in this vignette? Explain.

How important is the perception process? As highlighted in the chapter-opening vignette, perception can determine whether or not you get a job offer following an employment interview. Our perceptions and feelings are influenced by information we receive from newspapers, magazines, television, radio, family, and friends. You see, we all use information stored in our memories to interpret the world around us, and our interpretations, in turn, influence how we respond and interact with others. As human beings, we constantly strive to make sense of our surroundings. The resulting knowledge influences our behavior and helps us navigate our way through life. Think of the perceptual process that occurs when meeting someone for the first time. Your attention is drawn to the individual's physical appearance, mannerisms, actions, and reactions to what you say and do. You ultimately arrive at conclusions based on your perceptions of this social interaction. The brown-haired, green-eyed individual turns out to be friendly and fond of outdoor activities. You further conclude that you like this person and then ask him or her to go to a concert, calling the person by the name you stored in memory.

The reciprocal process of perception, interpretation, and behavioral response also applies at work. Bernie Madoff, for example, used the perception process to help orchestrate a $50-billion Ponzi scheme against unsuspecting investors. Madoff, who was described as "entrepreneurial, rich, and charming," used the success of his company in the 1980s and 1990s to create an image of a can't-lose investment strategist. His offices "oozed success" and the trading room looked "very profitable—and totally legitimate." He was active in social circles and charitable organizations. All told, these perceptions helped Madoff to recruit wealthy investors and money managers and to maintain the perception that he was running one of the most exclusive and successful investment firms in the world. Unfortunately, it was a lie that continued to exist partly because of the perception process.[2]

The perception process influences much more than the impressions people make about each other. For example, companies use knowledge about perceptions when designing and marketing their products, and political candidates use it to get elected.[3] The Transportation Security Administration also uses research about perception to design training programs aimed at helping airport security screeners to detect threatening objects more accurately.[4] An error in the perception process in this context can lead to catastrophic consequences! The point we are trying to make is that the perception process influences a host of managerial activities, organizational processes, and quality-of-life issues. We have written this chapter with this conclusion in mind. You will gain a thorough understanding of how perception works and how you can use it to enhance your future personal and professional success.

Let us now begin our exploration of the perceptual process and its associated outcomes. In this chapter we focus on (1) an information-processing model of perception, (2) stereotypes, (3) the self-fulfilling prophecy, and (4) how causal attributions are used to interpret behavior.

LO.1 An Information-Processing Model of Perception

to the point
How can the information-processing model of perception explain poor hiring decisions, inaccurate performance appraisals, perceptions of leaders, and poor physical and psychological well-being?

Perception is a cognitive process that enables us to interpret and understand our surroundings. Recognition of objects is one of this process's major functions. For example, both people and animals recognize familiar objects in their environments. You would recognize a picture of your best friend; dogs and cats can recognize their food dishes or a favorite toy. Reading involves recognition of visual patterns representing letters in the alphabet. People must recognize objects to meaningfully interact with their environment. But since OB's principal focus is on people, the following discussion emphasizes *social* perception rather than object perception.

The study of how people perceive one another has been labeled *social cognition* and *social information processing.* In contrast to the perception of objects,

> [s]ocial cognition is the study of how people make sense of other people and themselves. It focuses on how ordinary people think about people and how they think they think about people....
>
> Research on social cognition also goes beyond naive psychology. The study of social cognition entails a fine-grained analysis of how people think about themselves and others, and it leans heavily on the theory and methods of cognitive psychology.[5]

Let us now examine the fundamental processes underlying perception.

Perception

Process of interpreting one's environment.

Four-Stage Sequence and a Working Example

Perception involves a four-stage information-processing sequence (hence, the label "information processing"). Figure 7–1 illustrates a basic information-processing model of perception. Three of the stages in this model—selective attention/comprehension, encoding and simplification, and storage and retention—describe how specific information and environmental stimuli are observed and stored in memory. The fourth and final stage, retrieval and response, involves turning mental representations into real-world judgments and decisions.

Keep the following everyday example in mind as we look at the four stages of perception. Suppose you were thinking of taking a course in, say, personal finance. Three professors teach the same course, using different types of instruction and testing procedures. Through personal experience, you have come to prefer good

Figure 7–1   *Perception: An Information-Processing Model*

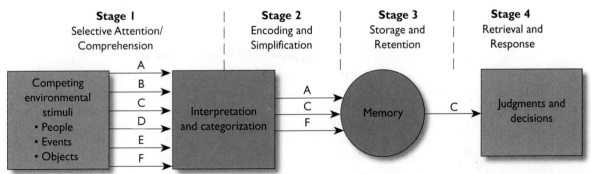

professors who rely on the case method of instruction and essay tests. According to the information-processing model of perception, you would likely arrive at a decision regarding which professor to take as follows:

Stage 1: Selective Attention/Comprehension

People are constantly bombarded by physical and social stimuli in the environment. Since they do not have the mental capacity to fully comprehend all this information, they selectively perceive subsets of environmental stimuli. This is where attention plays a role. **Attention** is the process of becoming consciously aware of something or someone. Attention can be focused on information either from the environment or from memory. Regarding the latter situation, if you sometimes find yourself thinking about totally unrelated events or people while reading a textbook, your memory is the focus of your attention. Research has shown that people tend to pay attention to salient stimuli.

Attention
Being consciously aware of something or someone.

Salient Stimuli   Something is salient when it stands out from its context. For example, a 250-pound man would certainly be salient in a women's aerobics class but not at a meeting of the National Football League Players' Association. One's needs and goals often dictate which stimuli are salient. For a driver whose gas gauge is on empty, an Exxon or Mobil sign is more salient than a McDonald's or Burger King sign. The reverse would be true for a hungry driver with a full gas tank. Paco Underhill, founder and CEO of Envirosell, an organization that helps companies understand consumer behavior, uses the concept of salience to help stores sell more products (see the Real World/Real People feature on page 187). Moreover, research shows that people have a tendency to pay more attention to negative than positive information. This leads to a negativity bias.[6] This bias helps explain the gawking factor that slows traffic to a crawl following a car accident.

Back to Our Example   You begin your search for the "right" personal finance professor by asking friends who have taken classes from the three professors. You also may interview the various professors who teach the class to gather still more relevant information. Returning to Figure 7–1, all the information you obtain represents competing environmental stimuli labeled A through F. Because you are concerned about the method of instruction (e.g., line A in Figure 7–1), testing procedures (e.g., line C), and past grade distributions (e.g., line F), information in those areas is particularly salient to you. Figure 7–1 shows that these three salient pieces of information thus are perceived, and you then progress to the second stage of information processing. Meanwhile, competing stimuli represented by lines B, D, and E in Figure 7–1 fail to get your attention and are discarded from further consideration.

Stage 2: Encoding and Simplification

Observed information is not stored in memory in its original form. Encoding is required; raw information is interpreted or translated into mental representations. To accomplish this, perceivers assign pieces of information to **cognitive categories**. "By *category* we mean a number of objects that are considered equivalent. Categories are generally designated by names, e.g., *dog, animal*."[7] People, events, and objects are interpreted and evaluated by comparing their characteristics with information contained in schemata (or schema in singular form).

Cognitive categories
Mental depositories for storing information.

In-Store Displays Help Generate Sales

For a while, he has been telling merchants that there are no new customers, which is his way of saying that stores must get better at persuading existing customers to purchase more. He has also noticed that people more often make a decision about what to buy when they are out shopping, not before. This gives stores an opportunity: If they can compellingly present information about merchandise—following Underhill's rules, of course—they might exert greater influence on consumers. "It's all about in-store marketing," he says. "It's making things occur to the shopper." . . .

Then there is the matter of choice: Underhill says some shoppers can't deal with it, and if the item isn't a necessity, they'll just walk away. "Merchants have to take some control over the consumer's eye," he says.

"Put up a sign that says 'Our Best Seller' or 'Our Best Student Computer.'" . . .

When Underhill talks to his clients about signs, he is concerned with what he calls the dropout rate, or the percentage of people who don't read through an important piece of information. When there's a problem, it's because the sign isn't in a place where people feel comfortable shopping, or it's facing the wrong way, or the text is not big, simple, or helpful enough.

To what extent is Mr. Paco being manipulative?

SOURCE: S Berfield, "Getting the Most Out of Every Shopper," *BusinessWeek*, February 9, 2009, p 45.

Schemata   A **schema** represents a person's mental picture or summary of a particular event or type of stimulus. A schema for an event, like going out to dinner in a restaurant, is called a **script.** Your memory for going out to dinner probably is quite similar to the restaurant script shown in Table 7–1.

Cognitive-category labels are needed to make schemata meaningful. For example, you have a category label for "going to dinner" and another titled "sports car." Each schema contains information. Let us consider what you have stored in memory about sports cars. Does your schema contain a smaller vehicle with two doors? Is it red? If you answered yes, you would tend to classify all small, two-door, fire-engine-red vehicles as sports cars because this type of car possesses characteristics that are consistent with your "sports car schema."

Schema
Mental picture of an event or object.

Script
A mental picture of an event.

Is this consistent with your "sports car schema"? If it is, you'll likely classify all small, two-door, red vehicles as sports cars. Can you think of another example of a common schema in today's culture?

Encoding Outcomes   We use the encoding process to interpret and evaluate our environment. Interestingly, this process can result in differing interpretations and evaluations of the same person or event. Varying interpretations of what we observe occur due to four key reasons.

First, people possess different information in the schemata used for interpretation. For instance, a recent meta-analysis of 62 studies revealed women and men had different opinions about what type of behaviors constituted sexual harassment. Women defined a broader range of behaviors as harassing.[8] Second, our moods and emotions influence our focus of attention and evaluations of others.[9] Third, people tend to apply recently used cognitive

Table 7–1   *Restaurant Schema*

Schema: **Restaurant.**
Characters: **Customers, hostess, waiter, chef, cashier.**
Scene 1: **Entering.**
  Customer goes into restaurant.
  Customer finds a place to sit.
    He may find it himself.
    He may be seated by a hostess.
      He asks the hostess for a table.
      She gives him permission to go to the table.
Scene 2: **Ordering.**
  Customer receives a menu.
  Customer reads it.
  Customer decides what to order.
  Waiter takes the order.
    Waiter sees the customer.
    Waiter goes to the customer.
    Customer orders what he wants.
  Chef cooks the meal.
Scene 3: **Eating.**
  After some time the waiter brings the meal from the chef.
  Customer eats the meal.
Scene 4: **Exiting.**
  Customer asks the waiter for the check.
  Waiter gives the check to the customer.
  Customer leaves a tip.
    The size of the tip depends on the goodness of the service.
  Customer pays the cashier.
  Customer leaves the restaurant.

SOURCE: From D Rumelhart, *Introduction to Human Information Processing* (New York: John Wiley & Sons, Inc., 1977). Reprinted with permission of John Wiley & Sons, Inc.

categories during encoding. For example, you are more likely to interpret a neutral behavior exhibited by a professor as positive if you were recently thinking about positive categories and events.[10] Fourth, individual differences influence encoding. Pessimistic or depressed individuals, for instance, tend to interpret their surroundings more negatively than optimistic and happy people. The point is that we should not be surprised when people interpret and evaluate the same situation or event differently. Researchers are currently trying to identify the host of factors that influence the encoding process.

Back to Our Example   Having collected relevant information about the three personal finance professors and their approaches, you compare this information with other details contained in schemata. This leads you to form an impression and evaluation of what it would be like to take a course from each professor.

In turn, the relevant information contained on paths A, C, and F in Figure 7–1 are passed along to the third stage of information processing.

go to the Web for the Self-Exercise: Does a Schema Improve the Comprehension of Written Material?

Stage 3: Storage and Retention

This phase involves storage of information in long-term memory. Long-term memory is like an apartment complex consisting of separate units connected to one another. Although different people live in each apartment, they sometimes interact. In addition, large apartment complexes have different wings (such as A, B, and C). Long-term memory similarly consists of separate but related categories. Like the individual apartments inhabited by unique residents, the connected categories contain different types of information. Information also passes among these categories. Finally, long-term memory is made up of three compartments (or wings) containing categories of information about events, semantic materials, and people.[11]

Event Memory   This compartment is composed of categories containing information about both specific and general events. These memories describe appropriate sequences of events in well-known situations, such as going to a restaurant (refer back to Table 7–1), going on a job interview, going to a food store, or going to a movie.

Semantic Memory   Semantic memory refers to general knowledge about the world. In so doing, it functions as a mental dictionary of concepts. Each concept contains a definition (e.g., a good leader) and associated traits (outgoing), emotional states (happy), physical characteristics (tall), and behaviors (works hard). Just as there are schemata for general events, concepts in semantic memory are stored as schemata. Given our previous discussion of managing diversity in Chapter 2 and International OB in Chapter 4, it should come as no surprise that there are cultural differences in the type of information stored in semantic memory.

Person Memory   Categories within this compartment contain information about a single individual (your supervisor) or groups of people (managers). The manner in which Yukihiro Yamazaki, chief Lexus GS technician for dynamic evaluation, does his job provides a good example of using all three compartments of long-term memory. Yamazaki's role is to evaluate the performance of a new car (see the Real World/Real People feature on page 190). His evaluation is based on comparing characteristics he observes about a new car against information stored in memory.

Back to Our Example   As the time draws near for you to decide which personal finance professor to take, your schemata of them are stored in the three categories of long-term memory. These schemata are available for immediate comparison or retrieval.

Yukihiro Yamazaki Uses Information in Long-Term Memory to Evaluate a Vehicle's Performance

Yamazaki notes that he uses four senses to evaluate a car.

- **Sight:** I observe everything—the overall tone of the car, its shape and color, whether everything matches. I look for anything that may look unusual.
- **Sound:** I listen for any kind of out-of-place noise, such as a ticking, that might indicate the presence of a mechanical or assembly problem.
- **Smell:** I study the scent of the leather seats, air from the air conditioning, the exhaust gas—and try to detect any anomalies.

- **Touch:** I feel the interior and exterior of the car—the contour of the sheet metal, the action of the button and switches. When I'm driving, I use my entire body to feel the road and other vibrations.

What is your opinion of Mr. Yamazaki's approach?

SOURCE: Excerpted from A Taylor III, "Test Driver," *Fortune*, October 30, 2006, p 106.

Stage 4: Retrieval and Response

People retrieve information from memory when they make judgments and decisions. Our ultimate judgments and decisions are either based on the process of drawing on, interpreting, and integrating categorical information stored in long-term memory or on retrieving a summary judgment that was already made.

Concluding our example, it is registration day and you have to choose which professor to take for personal finance. After retrieving from memory your schemata-based impressions of the three professors, you select a good one who uses the case method and gives essay tests (line C in Figure 7–1). In contrast, you may choose your preferred professor by simply recalling the decision you made two weeks ago.

LO.2 Managerial Implications

Social cognition is the window through which we all observe, interpret, and prepare our responses to people and events. A wide variety of managerial activities, organizational processes, and quality-of-life issues are thus affected by perception. Consider, for example, the following seven implications.

Hiring   Interviewers make hiring decisions based on their impression of how an applicant fits the perceived requirements of a job. Unfortunately, many of these decisions are made on the basis of implicit cognition. **Implicit cognition** represents any thoughts or beliefs that are automatically activated from memory without our conscious awareness. The existence of implicit cognition leads people to make biased decisions without an understanding that it is occurring.[12] This tendency has been used as an explanation of alleged discriminatory behavior at Wal-Mart, FedEx, Johnson & Johnson, and Cargill. Experts recommend two solutions for reducing this problem.[13] First, managers can be trained to understand and reduce this type of hidden bias. For example, one study demonstrated that training improved interviewers' ability to obtain high-quality, job-related information and to stay focused on the interview task. Trained interviewers provide more balanced judgments about applicants than nontrained interviewers.[14] Second, bias can be

Implicit cognition
Any thought or belief that is automatically activated without conscious awareness.

reduced by using structured as opposed to unstructured interviews, and by relying on evaluations from multiple interviewers rather than just one or two people.

Performance Appraisal   Faulty schemata about what constitutes good versus poor performance can lead to inaccurate performance appraisals, which erode work motivation, commitment, and loyalty. For example, a study of 166 production employees indicated that they had greater trust in management when they perceived that the performance appraisal process provided accurate evaluations of their performance.[15] Therefore, it is important for managers to accurately identify the behavioral characteristics and results indicative of good performance at the beginning of a performance review cycle. These characteristics then can serve as the standards for evaluating employee performance. The importance of using objective rather than subjective measures of employee performance was highlighted in a meta-analysis involving 50 studies and 8,341 individuals. Results revealed that objective and subjective measures of employee performance were only moderately related. The researchers concluded that objective and subjective measures of performance are not interchangeable.[16] Managers are thus advised to use more objectively based measures of performance as much as possible because subjective indicators are prone to bias and inaccuracy. In those cases where the job does not possess objective measures of performance, however, managers should still use subjective evaluations. Furthermore, because memory for specific instances of employee performance deteriorates over time, managers need a mechanism for accurately recalling employee behavior.[17] Research reveals that individuals can be trained to be more accurate raters of performance.[18]

Leadership   Research demonstrated that employees' evaluations of leader effectiveness were influenced strongly by their schemata of good and poor leaders. A leader will have a difficult time influencing employees when he or she exhibits behaviors contained in employees' schemata of poor leaders. A team of researchers investigated the behaviors contained in our schemata of good and poor leaders. Good leaders were perceived as exhibiting the following behaviors: (1) assigning specific tasks to group members, (2) telling others that they had done well, (3) setting specific goals for the group, (4) letting other group members make decisions, (5) trying to get the group to work as a team, and (6) maintaining definite standards of performance.[19]

Communication and Interpersonal Influence   Managers need to remember that social perception is a screening process that can distort communication, both coming and going. Because people interpret oral and written communications by using schemata developed through past experiences, your ability to influence others is affected by information contained in others' schemata regarding age, gender, ethnicity, appearance, speech, mannerisms, personality, and other personal characteristics. It is important to keep this in mind when trying to influence others or when trying to sell your ideas. Experts suggest that you can increase your ability to influence others by following these four basic guidelines: (1) convey a positive attitude, (2) dress professionally, (3) don't check your cell phone when interacting with others, and (4) determine how others perceive you by asking for feedback.[20]

Counterproductive Work Behaviors   Past research showed that employees exhibited a variety of counterproductive work behaviors (recall our discussion in Chapter 6) when they perceived that they were treated unfairly.[21] It is very important for managers to treat employees fairly, remembering that perceptions of fairness are in the eye of the beholder. Chapter 8 discusses how this can be done in greater detail.

Physical and Psychological Well-Being

The negativity bias can lead to both physical and psychological problems. Specifically, research shows that perceptions of fear, harm, and anxiety are associated with the onset of illnesses, absenteeism, and intentions to quit.[22] We should all attempt to avoid the tendency of giving negative thoughts too much attention. Try to let negative thoughts roll off yourself just like water off a duck.

Designing Web Pages

Researchers have recently begun to explore what catches viewers' attention on Web pages by using sophisticated eye-tracking equipment. This research can help organizations to spend their money wisely when designing Web pages. Kara Pernice Coyne, director of a research project studying Web page design, praised the Web pages of JetBlue Airways and Sears while noting problems with the one used by Agree Systems.[23] One expert provided the following recommendations for designing an effective Web page.

- Individuals read Web pages in an F pattern. They're more inclined to read longer sentences at the top of a page and less as they scroll down. That makes the first two words of a sentence very important.

- Surfers connect well with images of people looking directly at them. It helps if the person in the photo is attractive, but not too good looking.

- Images in the middle of a page can present an obstacle course.

- People respond to pictures that provide useful information, not just decoration.[24]

to the point

How can managers use knowledge of stereotypes and stereotype formation to more effectively reduce problems associated with sex-role, age, racial, and disability stereotypes?

LO.3 Stereotypes: Perceptions about Groups of People

While it is often true that beauty is in the eye of the beholder, perception does result in some predictable outcomes. Managers aware of the perception process and its outcomes enjoy a competitive edge. The Walt Disney Company, for instance, takes full advantage of perceptual tendencies to influence customers' reactions to waiting in long lines at its theme parks:

> In Orlando, at Disney-MGM Studios, visitors waiting to get into a Muppet attraction watch tapes of Kermit the Frog on TV monitors. At the Magic Kingdom, visitors to the Extra Terrestrial Alien Encounter attraction are entertained by a talking robot before the show. At some rides, the company uses simple toys, like blocks, to help parents keep small children busy and happy during the wait.[25]

This example illustrates how the focus of one's attention influences the perception of standing in long lines.

Likewise, managers can use knowledge of perceptual outcomes to help them interact more effectively with employees. For example, Table 7–2 describes five common perceptual errors. Since these perceptual errors often distort the evaluation

Table 7–2   *Commonly Found Perceptual Errors*

PERCEPTUAL ERROR	DESCRIPTION	EXAMPLE	RECOMMENDED SOLUTION
Halo	A rater forms an overall impression about an object and then uses that impression to bias ratings about the object.	Rating a professor high on the teaching dimensions of ability to motivate students, knowledge, and communication because we like him or her.	Remember that an employee's behavior tends to vary across different dimensions of performance. Keep a file or diary to record examples of positive and negative employee performance throughout the year.
Leniency	A personal characteristic that leads an individual to consistently evaluate other people or objects in an extremely positive fashion.	Rating a professor high on all dimensions of performance regardless of his or her actual performance. The rater that hates to say negative things about others.	It does not help employees when they are given positive feedback that is inaccurate. Try to be fair and realistic when evaluating others.
Central tendency	The tendency to avoid all extreme judgments and rate people and objects as average or neutral.	Rating a professor average on all dimensions of performance regardless of his or her actual performance.	It is normal to provide feedback that contains both positive and negative information. The use of a performance diary can help to remember examples of employee performance.
Recency effects	The tendency to remember recent information. If the recent information is negative, the person or object is evaluated negatively.	Although a professor has given good lectures for 12 to 15 weeks, he or she is evaluated negatively because lectures over the last 3 weeks were done poorly.	It is critical to accumulate examples of performance that span the entire rating period. Keep a file or diary to record examples of performance throughout the year.
Contrast effects	The tendency to evaluate people or objects by comparing them with characteristics of recently observed people or objects.	Rating a good professor as average because you compared his or her performance with three of the best professors you have ever had in college. You are currently taking courses from the three excellent professors.	It is important to evaluate employees against a standard rather than your memory of the best or worst person in a particular job.

of job applicants and of employee performance, managers need to guard against them. This section examines one of the most important and potentially harmful perceptual outcomes associated with person perception: stereotypes. After exploring the process of stereotype formation and maintenance, we discuss sex-role stereotypes, age stereotypes, race stereotypes, disability stereotypes, and the managerial challenge to avoid stereotypical biases.

Stereotype Formation and Maintenance

Stereotype

Beliefs about the characteristics of a group.

"A **stereotype** is an individual's set of beliefs about the characteristics or attributes of a group."[26] Stereotypes are not always negative. For example, the belief that engineers are good at math is certainly part of a stereotype. Stereotypes may or may not be accurate. Engineers may in fact be better at math than the general population. In general, stereotypic characteristics are used to differentiate a particular group of people from other groups.[27]

It is important to remember that stereotypes are a fundamental component of the perception process and we use them to help process the large amount of information that bombards us daily. As such, it is not immoral or bad to possess stereotypes. That said, however, inappropriate use of stereotypes can lead to poor decisions; can create barriers for women, older individuals, people of color, and people with disabilities; and can undermine loyalty and job satisfaction.

Stereotyping is a four-step process. It begins by categorizing people into groups according to various criteria, such as gender, age, race, and occupation. Next, we infer that all people within a particular category possess the same traits or characteristics (e.g., all women are nurturing, older people have more job-related accidents, all African Americans are good athletes, all professors are absentminded). Then, we form expectations of others and interpret their behavior according to our stereotypes. Finally, stereotypes are maintained by (1) overestimating the frequency of stereotypic behaviors exhibited by others, (2) incorrectly explaining expected and unexpected behaviors, and (3) differentiating minority individuals from oneself.[28] It is hard to stop people from using stereotypes because these four steps are self-reinforcing. The good news, however, is that researchers have identified a few ways to break the chain of stereotyping.

Research shows that the use of stereotypes is influenced by the amount and type of information available to an individual and his or her motivation to accurately process information.[29] People are less apt to use stereotypes to judge others when they encounter salient information that is highly inconsistent with a stereotype. For instance, you are unlikely to assign stereotypic "professor" traits to a new professor you have this semester if he or she rides a Harley-Davidson, wears leather pants to class, and has a pierced nose. People also are less likely to rely on stereotypes when they are motivated to avoid using them. That is, accurate information processing requires mental effort. Stereotyping is generally viewed as a less effortful strategy of information processing. Let us now take a look at different types of stereotypes and consider additional methods for reducing their biasing effects.

Sex-role stereotype

Beliefs about appropriate roles for men and women.

L0.4 Sex-Role Stereotypes

A **sex-role stereotype** is the belief that differing traits and abilities make men and women particularly well suited to different roles. A survey of 61,647 people—50% female and 50% male—sheds light on the sex-role stereotypes held by adults within the United States. Results revealed that women were labeled as moody, gossipy, emotional, and catty. A similar set of negative stereotypes was not uncovered when it came to perceptions about men. When asked who would be more likely to lead effectively, males were preferred by a 2 to 1 margin by both men and women.[30] Researchers suggest that this pattern of results is related to gender-based expectations or stereotypes that people use without any conscious awareness.[31] The key question, however, is whether or not these stereotypes influence the hiring, evaluation, and promotion of people at work.

A meta-analysis of 19 studies comprising 1,842 individuals found no significant relationships between applicant gender and hiring recommendations.[32] A second meta-analysis of 24 experimental studies revealed that men and women received similar performance ratings for the same level of task performance. Stated differently, there was no pro-male bias. These experimental results were further supported in a field study of female and male professors.[33] Unfortunately, results pertaining to promotion decisions are not as promising. A field study of 682 employees in a multinational *Fortune* 500 company demonstrated that gender was significantly related to promotion potential ratings. Men received more favorable evaluations than women in spite of controlling for age, education, organizational tenure, salary grade, and type of job.[34] Another study of 448 upper-level managers showed that gender bias influenced the performance ratings and promotional opportunities for women, particularly when women worked in nontraditional jobs. The researchers conducting this study concluded that sex-role stereotypes partially explained these findings.[35]

Age Stereotypes

Age stereotypes reinforce age discrimination because of their negative orientation. For example, long-standing age stereotypes depict older workers as less satisfied, not as involved with their work, less motivated, not as committed, less productive than their younger coworkers, and more apt to be absent from work. Older employees are also perceived as being more accident prone. As with sex-role stereotypes, these age stereotypes are based more on fiction than fact.

OB researcher Susan Rhodes sought to determine whether age stereotypes were supported by data from 185 different studies. She discovered that as age increases so do employees' job satisfaction, job involvement, internal work motivation, and organizational commitment. Moreover, older workers were not more accident prone.[36] With respect to performance, a meta-analysis involving over 52,000 people showed that age was unrelated to task performance, creativity, and performance in training workshops.[37] Some OB researchers, however, believe that this finding does not reflect the true relationship between age and performance. They propose that the relationship between age and performance changes as people grow older. This idea was tested on data obtained from 24,219 individuals. In support of this hypothesis, results revealed that age was positively related to performance for younger employees (25 to 30 years of age) and then plateaued: Older employees were not less productive. Age and experience also predicted performance better for more complex jobs than other jobs, and job experience had a stronger relationship with performance than age.[38] Another study examined memory, reasoning, spatial relations, and dual tasking for 1,000 doctors, ages 25 to 92, and 600 other adults. The researchers concluded "that a large proportion of older individuals scored as well or better on aptitude tests as those in the prime of life. We call these intellectually vigorous individuals 'optimal agers.'"[39]

What about turnover and absenteeism? A meta-analysis containing 45 samples and a total of 21,656 individuals revealed that age and turnover were negatively related.[40] That is, older employees quit less often than did younger employees. Similarly, another meta-analysis of 34 studies encompassing 7,772 workers indicated that age was inversely related to both voluntary (a day at the beach) and involuntary (sick day) absenteeism.[41] Contrary to stereotypes, older workers are ready and able to meet their job requirements. Moreover, results from the two meta-analyses suggest managers should focus more attention on the turnover and absenteeism among younger workers than among older workers.

Racial and Ethnic Stereotypes

There are many different racial and ethnic stereotypes that exist. For instance, African Americans have been viewed as athletic, aggressive, and angry; Asians, as quiet, introverted, smarter, and more quantitatively oriented; Hispanics, as family oriented and religious; and Arabs, as angry. Racial and ethnic stereotypes are particularly problematic because they are automatically triggered and lead to what researchers call *micro aggressions*. **Micro aggressions** represent "biased thoughts, attitudes, and feelings" that exist at an unconsious level.[42] Unfortunately, they can affect our behavior and negatively affect people of color. Consider the following scenario:

Micro aggressions
Biased thoughts, attitudes, and feelings that exist at an unconscious level.

> Two colleagues—one Asian-American, the other African-American—board a small plane. A flight attendant tells them they can sit anywhere, so they choose seats near the front of the plane and across the aisle from each other so they can talk. At the last minute, three white men enter the plane and take the seats in front of them. Just before takeoff, the flight attendant, who is white, asks the two colleagues if they would mind moving to the back of the plane to better balance the plane's load. Both react with anger, sharing the same sense that they are being singled out to symbolically "sit at the back of the bus." When they express these feelings to the attendant, she indignantly denies the charge, saying she was merely trying to ensure the flight's safety and give the two some privacy.[43]

What do you think, was the flight attendant exhibiting a micro aggression or were the colleagues being too sensitive?

Negative racial and ethnic stereotypes are still apparent in many aspects of life and in many organizations.[44] Consider the experience of Eldrick (Tiger) Woods. Tiger was raised in two different cultures. His mother was from Thailand and his father was African American. Since becoming a professional golfer in 1996, Tiger has won 87 tournaments and has more career victories than any other active player on the PGA Tour. He also has the lowest career scoring average and greatest amount of career earnings than any other golfer in the history of the game. He also is the only golfer in history to hold the title for all four major tournaments at the same time.[45] Unfortunately, Tiger has experienced a host of racial stereotypes and biases (see the Real World/Real People feature on page 197). Let us now consider the following evidence regarding racial and ethnic stereotypes in organizations.

A meta-analysis of interview decisions from 31 studies with total samples of 4,169 African Americans and 6,307 whites revealed that whites received higher interviewer evaluations. Another study of 2,805 interviews uncovered a same-race bias for Hispanics and African Americans but not for whites. That is, Hispanics and

Tiger Woods Experiences Racial Bias

"I became aware of my racial identity on my first day of school, on my first day of kindergarten. A group of sixth graders tied me to a tree, spray-painted the word 'nigger' on me, and threw rocks at me. That was my first day at school. And the teacher really didn't do much of anything. I used to live across the street from school and kind of down the way a little bit. The teacher said, 'Okay, just go home.' So I had to outrun all these kids going home, which I was able to do. It was certainly an eye-opening experience, you know, being five years old. We were the only minority family in all of Cypress, California.

"When my parents moved in, before I was born, they used to have these oranges come through the window all the time. And it could have not been racially initiated or it could have been. We don't know. But it was very interesting, though people don't necessarily know it, that I grew up in the 1980s and still had incidents. I had a racial incident even in the 1990s at my home course where I grew up, the Navy golf course. And right before the 1994 US Amateur, I was 18 years old, I was out practicing, just hitting pitch shots and some guy just yelled over the fence and used the N word numerous times at me. That's in 1994."

Despite his international acclaim and reputation, Tiger Woods battled racial stereotypes into the mid-90s. What can be done to stop the spread of racism and racial stereotypes?

SOURCE: C Barkley, *Who's Afraid of a Large Black Man?* (New York: Penguin Press, 2005), p 7.

African-American interviewers evaluated applicants of their own race more favorably than applicants of other races. White interviewers did not exhibit any such bias.[46] Performance ratings were found to be unbiased in two studies that used large samples of 21,547 and 39,537 rater–ratee pairs of African-American and white employees, respectively, from throughout the United States. These findings revealed that African-American and white managers did not differentially evaluate their employees based on race.[47] Given the increasing number of people of color that will enter the workforce over the next 10 years (recall our discussion in Chapter 2), employers should focus on nurturing and developing women and people of color as well as increasing managers' sensitivities to invalid racial stereotypes and what is called *stereotype threat*. **Stereotype threat** "refers to the 'predicament' in which members of a social group (e.g., African-Americans, women) 'must deal with the possibility of being judged or treated stereotypically, or of doing something that would confirm the stereotype.'"[48] Research has documented that stereotype threat was associated with lower performance on evaluative tasks for women and nonwhites. For example, African Americans and women performed worse on academic tests when something primed them to think about race or gender. The drop in performance was higher when people experienced a race/ethnicity-based stereotype.[49] These results suggest that it is important for teachers and managers to avoid activating any race/ethnicity or gender stereotypes (e.g., asking people about their race or gender) when people are taking evaluative tests such as an academic test, an employment test, or a graduate school admissions test.

Stereotype threat
The predicament in which members of a social group (e.g., African Americans, women) must deal with the possibility of being judged or treated stereotypically, or of doing something that would confirm the stereotype.

Disability Stereotypes

People with disabilities not only face negative stereotypes that affect their employability, but they also can be stigmatized by the general population.[50] These trends create a host of problems for people with disabilities. For example, people with disabilities are more likely to be unemployed—the unemployment rate in January 2009 was 13.2% for people with disabilities and 8.3% for those without disabilities—and to make less money than those without disabilities.[51] People with disabilities also were found to be two-and-a half times as likely to live in poverty as people without disabilities.[52] The problem is even more pronounced for people with serious mental illness. The Americans with Disabilities Act (ADA) was created in 1990 in response to these statistics. As mentioned in Chapter 2, this act prohibits discrimination against qualified employees with physical or mental disabilities or chronic illness and requires "reasonable accommodation" of employees with disabilities.[53]

go to the Web for the Self-Exercise: How Do Diversity Assumptions Influence Team Member Interactions?

Managerial Challenges and Recommendations

The key managerial challenge is to reduce the extent to which stereotypes influence decision making and interpersonal processes throughout the organization.[54] We recommend that an organization first needs to inform its workforce about the problem of stereotyping through employee education and training. Training also can be used to equip managers with the skills needed to handle situations associated with managing employees with disabilities. The next step entails engaging in a broad effort to reduce stereotypes throughout the organization. Social scientists believe that "quality" interpersonal contact among mixed groups is the best way to reduce stereotypes because it provides people with more accurate data about the characteristics of other groups of people. As such, organizations should create opportunities for diverse employees to meet and work together in cooperative groups of equal status.

Another recommendation is for managers to identify valid individual differences (discussed in Chapter 5) that differentiate between successful and unsuccessful performers. As previously discussed, for instance, research reveals experience is a better predictor of performance than age. Research also shows that managers can be trained to use these valid criteria when hiring applicants and evaluating employee performance.[55]

Removing promotional barriers for men and women, people of color, and persons with disabilities is another viable solution to alleviating the stereotyping problem. Walgreens represents a good example of how companies can assist people with disabilities to obtain meaningful work (see the Real World/Real People box on page 199). This can be accomplished by minimizing the differences in job experience across groups of people. Similar experience, coupled with the accurate evaluation of performance, helps managers to make decisions that are less influenced by stereotypes.

Walgreens Effectively Accommodates People with Disabilities

In November, Walgreens—one of the nation's largest drugstore retailers—will open a state-of-the-art distribution center in Windsor, Conn. It will be the company's second facility designed specifically to employ people with disabilities and is patterned after the 5,571-store group's Anderson, S.C., center that opened last summer.

Managers at both facilities share a goal of having people with disabilities fill at least one-third of the available jobs.

Many observers laud the retailer's plans as a source of meaningful jobs with equal opportunities for advancement and job mobility. And the outcomes so far suggest that the company's latest prescription for diversification works well, contends Deb Russell, Walgreen's manager of outreach and employee services, based at headquarters in Deerfield, Ill. Company leaders intend to launch similar initiatives at future distribution centers—and use the experience to provide managers in other divisions with information and guidance they expect will result in even more hiring of people with disabilities.

"We know of no other facility of its kind where such a significant portion of the workforce has disabilities," Russell says of the $175 million South Carolina location. Currently, 40 percent of the distribution center's 400 employees have disclosed physical or cognitive disabilities. Yet the facility's efficiency rose by 20 percent since opening, after technology and process changes originally intended to accommodate workers with disabilities improved everyone's jobs. At full capacity, the center will employ 800. Workers will include those challenged by cognitive disabilities and autism.

Why don't more companies take a proactive approach toward hiring people with disabilities?

SOURCE: From S Wells, "Counting on Workers with Disabilities," *HR Magazine,* April 2008, pp 45–46. Copyright 2008 by Society for Human Resource Management (SHRM). Reproduced with permission of Society for Human Resource Management via Copyright Clearance Center.

In conclusion, it is important to obtain top management's commitment and support to eliminate the organizational practices that support or reinforce stereotyping and discriminatory decisions. Research clearly demonstrates that top management support is essential to successful implementation of the types of organizational changes being recommended.

Self-fulfilling prophecy

Someone's high expectations for another person result in high performance.

L0.5 Self-Fulfilling Prophecy: The Pygmalion Effect

Historical roots of the self-fulfilling prophecy are found in Greek mythology. According to mythology, Pygmalion was a sculptor who hated women yet fell in love with an ivory statue he carved of a beautiful woman. He became so infatuated with the statue that he prayed to the goddess Aphrodite to bring her to life. The goddess heard his prayer, granted his wish, and Pygmalion's statue came to life. The essence of the **self-fulfilling prophecy,** or Pygmalion effect, is that someone's high expectations for another person result in high performance for that person. A related self-fulfilling prophecy effect is referred to as the Galatea effect. The **Galatea effect** occurs when an individual's high self-expectations for him- or herself lead to high performance. The key process underlying both the Pygmalion and Galatea effects is the idea that people's expectations or beliefs determine their behavior and performance, thus serving to make their expectations come true. In other words, we strive to validate our perceptions of reality, no matter how faulty they may be. Thus, the self-fulfilling prophecy is an important perceptual outcome we need to better understand.

to the point
What is the self-fulfilling prophecy and how can managers use it to bolster individual and organizational productivity?

Galatea effect

An individual's high self-expectations lead to high performance.

Oprah Winfrey is a great example of the Galatea effect. Born in Kosciusko, Mississippi, where she lived on a farm and was raised by her grandmother, she has evolved into one of the 100 Most Influential People of the 20th Century by *Time* magazine.

Research and an Explanatory Model

The self-fulfilling prophecy was first demonstrated in an academic environment. After giving a bogus test of academic potential to students from grades 1 to 6, researchers informed teachers that certain students had high potential for achievement. In reality, students were randomly assigned to the "high potential" and "control" (normal potential) groups. Results showed that children designated as having high potential obtained significantly greater increases in both IQ scores and reading ability than did the control students.[56] The teachers of the supposedly high potential group got better results because their high expectations caused them to give harder assignments, more feedback, and more recognition of achievement. Students in the normal potential group did not excel because their teachers did not expect outstanding results.

Research similarly has shown that by raising instructors' and managers' expectations for individuals performing a wide variety of tasks, higher levels of achievement/productivity can be obtained. Results from a meta-analysis of 17 studies involving 2,874 people working in a variety of industries and occupations demonstrated the Pygmalion effect was quite strong.[57] This finding implies that higher levels of achievement and productivity can be obtained by raising managers' performance expectations of their employees. Further, the performance-enhancing Pygmalion effect was stronger in the military, with men, and for people possessing low performance expectations. Extending these results, a recent study confirmed that female leaders can produce the Pygmalion effect on male subordinates.[58] This is an important finding in light of the increasing number of women in managerial roles (recall our discussion in Chapter 2).

Figure 7–2 presents a model that integrates the self-fulfilling prophecy, the Galatea effect, and self-efficacy, which was discussed in Chapter 5. The model shows that the self-fulfilling process begins with a manager's expectations for his or her direct reports. In turn, these expectations influence the type of leadership used by a leader (linkage 1). Positive expectations beget positive and supportive leadership, which subsequently leads employees to develop higher self-expectations (linkage 2). The positive Galatea effect created by these higher expectations then motivates employees to exert more effort (linkage 3), ultimately increasing performance (linkage 4) and supervisory expectations (linkage 5). Successful performance also improves an employee's self-efficacy, which

Figure 7–2   *A Model of the Self-Fulfilling Prophecy*

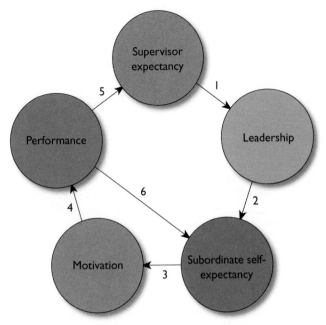

SOURCE: From D Eden, "Self-Fulfilling Prophecy as a Management Tool: Harnessing Pygmalion," *Academy of Management Review,* January 1984, p 67. Copyright © 1984 by The Academy of Management. Reproduced by permission of The Academy of Management via Copyright Clearance Center.

then fuels additional self-expectations of success (linkage 6). Research provides support for this model.[59] Researchers coined the term *Golem effect* to represent the negative side of the performance enhancing process depicted in Figure 7–2. The **Golem effect** is a loss in performance resulting from low leader expectations.[60] Let us consider how it works.

Golem effect

Loss in performance due to low leader expectations.

Say that an employee makes a mistake such as losing notes during a meeting or exhibits poor performance on a task—turning in a report a day late. A manager then begins to wonder if this person has what it takes to be successful in the organization. This doubt leads the manager to watch this person more carefully. The employee, of course, notices this doubt and begins to sense a loss of trust. The suspect employee then responds in one of two ways. He or she may doubt his or her own judgment and competence. This in turn leads the individual to become more risk averse and to decrease the amount of ideas and suggestions for the manager's critical review. The manager notices this behavior and interprets it as an example of less initiative. Oppositely, the employee may take on more and more responsibility so that he or she can demonstrate his or her competence and worth. This is likely to cause the employee to screw up on something, which in turn reinforces the manager's suspicions. You can see that this process results in a destructive relationship that is fueled by negative expectations. The point to remember is that the self-fulfilling prophecy works in both directions. The next section discusses ideas for enhancing the Pygmalion effect and reducing the Golem effect.

LO.6 Putting the Self-Fulfilling Prophecy to Work

Largely due to the Pygmalion effect, managerial expectations powerfully influence employee behavior and performance. Consequently, managers need to harness the Pygmalion effect by building a hierarchical framework that reinforces positive performance expectations throughout the organization.

Employees' self-expectations are the foundation of this framework. In turn, positive self-expectations improve interpersonal expectations by encouraging people to work toward common goals. This cooperation enhances group-level productivity and promotes positive performance expectations within the work group. At Google, for example, employees routinely work long hours, especially when work groups are trying to meet deadlines for the launch of new products. Because Google is known for creating innovative products in a timely fashion, positive group-level expectations help create and reinforce an organizational culture of high expectancy for success. This process then excites people about working for the organization, thereby reducing turnover.[61]

Because positive self-expectations are the foundation for creating an organizationwide Pygmalion effect, let us consider how managers can create positive performance expectations. This task may be accomplished by using various combinations of the following:

1. Recognize that everyone has the potential to increase his or her performance.
2. Set high performance goals.
3. Positively reinforce employees for a job well done.
4. Provide frequent feedback that conveys your belief in employees' ability to complete their tasks.
5. Give employees the opportunity to experience increasingly challenging tasks and projects.
6. Communicate by using facial expressions, voice intonations, body language, and encouraging comments that reflect high expectations.
7. Provide employees with the input, information, and resources they need to achieve their goals.
8. Introduce new employees as if they have outstanding potential.
9. Become aware of your personal prejudices and nonverbal messages that may discourage others.
10. Help employees master key skills and tasks.[62]

Causal attributions
Suspected or inferred causes of behavior.

to the point
How does Kelley's model of attribution, the fundamental attribution bias, and the self-serving bias explain how managers tend to manage both good- and poor-performing employees?

Causal Attributions

Attribution theory is based on the premise that people attempt to infer causes for observed behavior. Rightly or wrongly, we constantly formulate cause-and-effect explanations for our own and others' behavior. Attributional statements such as the following are common: "Joe drinks too much because he has no willpower; but I need a couple of drinks after work because I'm under a lot of pressure." Formally defined, **causal attributions** are suspected or inferred causes of behavior. Even though our causal attributions tend to be self-serving and are often invalid, it is important to understand how people formulate attributions because they profoundly affect organizational behavior. For example, a supervisor who attributes an employee's poor performance to a lack of effort might reprimand that individual. However, training might be deemed necessary if the supervisor attributes the poor performance to a lack of ability.

Generally speaking, people formulate causal attributions by considering the events preceding an observed behavior. This section explores Harold Kelley's model of attribution, two important attributional tendencies, and related managerial implications.

L0.7 Kelley's Model of Attribution

Current models of attribution, such as Kelley's, are based on the pioneering work of the late Fritz Heider. Heider, the founder of attribution theory, proposed that behavior can be attributed either to **internal factors** within a person (such as ability and effort) or to **external factors** within the environment (such as task difficulty, help from others, and good/bad luck). This line of thought parallels the idea of an internal versus external locus of control, as discussed in Chapter 5. Building on Heider's work, Kelley attempted to pinpoint major antecedents of internal and external attributions. Kelley hypothesized that people make causal attributions after gathering information about three dimensions of behavior: consensus, distinctiveness, and consistency.[63] These dimensions vary independently, thus forming various combinations and leading to differing attributions.

Figure 7–3 presents performance charts showing low versus high consensus, distinctiveness, and consistency. These charts are now used to help develop a working knowledge of all three dimensions in Kelley's model.

Internal factors

Personal characteristics that cause behavior.

External factors

Environmental characteristics that cause behavior.

- *Consensus* involves a comparison of an individual's behavior with that of his or her peers. There is high consensus when one acts like the rest of the group and low consensus when one acts differently. As shown in Figure 7–3, high consensus is indicated when persons A, B, C, D, and E obtain similar levels of individual performance. In contrast, person C's performance is low in consensus because it significantly varies from the performance of persons A, B, D, and E.

- *Distinctiveness* is determined by comparing a person's behavior on one task with his or her behavior on other tasks. High distinctiveness means the individual has performed the task in question in a significantly different manner than he or she has performed other tasks. Low distinctiveness means stable performance or quality from one task to another. Figure 7–3 reveals that

Figure 7–3   *Performance Charts Showing Low and High Consensus, Distinctiveness, and Consistency Information*

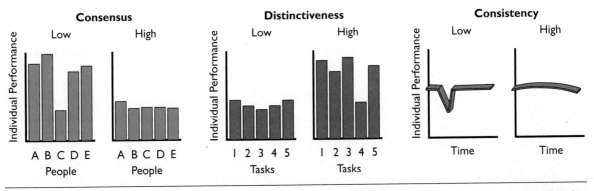

the employee's performance on task 4 is highly distinctive because it significantly varies from his or her performance on tasks 1, 2, 3, and 5.

- *Consistency* is determined by judging if the individual's performance on a given task is consistent over time. High consistency implies that a person performs a certain task the same, time after time. Unstable performance of a given task over time would mean low consistency. The downward spike in performance depicted in the consistency graph of Figure 7–3 represents low consistency. In this case, the employee's performance on a given task varied over time.

It is important to remember that consensus relates to other *people,* distinctiveness relates to other *tasks,* and consistency relates to *time.* The question now is: How does information about these three dimensions of behavior lead to internal or external attributions?

Kelley hypothesized that people attribute behavior to *external* causes (environmental factors) when they perceive high consensus, high distinctiveness, and low consistency. *Internal* attributions (personal factors) tend to be made when observed behavior is characterized by low consensus, low distinctiveness, and high consistency. So, for example, when all employees are performing poorly (high consensus), when the poor performance occurs on only one of several tasks (high distinctiveness), and the poor performance occurs during only one time period (low consistency), a supervisor will probably attribute an employee's poor performance to an external source such as peer pressure or an overly difficult task. In contrast, performance will be attributed to an employee's personal characteristics (an internal attribution) when only the individual in question is performing poorly (low consensus), when the inferior performance is found across several tasks (low distinctiveness), and when the low performance has persisted over time (high consistency). Many studies have supported this predicted pattern of attributions in a work setting.[64] The attribution process also has been extended by marketing researchers to examine consumers' attributions about customer service, product characteristics, and advertising and by OB researchers to study leadership.[65]

go to the Web for the Group Exercise: Using Attribution Theory to Resolve Performance Problems

LO.8 Attributional Tendencies

Researchers have uncovered two attributional tendencies that distort one's interpretation of observed behavior—*fundamental attribution bias* and *self-serving bias.*

Fundamental attribution bias

Ignoring environmental factors that affect behavior.

Fundamental Attribution Bias   The **fundamental attribution bias** reflects one's tendency to attribute another person's behavior to his or her personal characteristics, as opposed to situational factors. This bias causes perceivers to ignore important environmental forces that often significantly affect behavior. For example, a study of 1,420 employees of a large utility company demonstrated that supervisors tended to make more internal attributions about worker accidents than did the workers. Interestingly, research also shows that people from Westernized cultures tend to exhibit the fundamental attribution bias more than individuals from East

Asia.[66] A recent study of shareholders similarly showed that shareholders attributed the price of stocks more to CEO behavior and less to market fluctuations.[67]

Self-Serving Bias   The **self-serving bias** represents one's tendency to take more personal responsibility for success than for failure. The self-serving bias suggests employees will attribute their success to internal factors (high ability or hard work) and their failures to uncontrollable external factors (tough job, bad luck, unproductive coworkers, or an unsympathetic boss). This tendency seems to have been in play at companies where employees filed high-profile discrimination lawsuits. In one case, an employee of a major accounting firm was, as the court judge wrote, "generally viewed as a highly competent project leader who worked long hours, pushed vigorously to meet deadlines, and demanded much from the multidisciplinary staffs." She was denied a partnership. The employee blamed the firm for discriminating against her because she was a woman; the firm blamed her for being "sometimes overly aggressive, unduly harsh, difficult to work with, and impatient with staff." And in another case, a woman who was not promoted to dean blamed the university for discriminating against her, while the university, like the accounting firm, said this employee was hard to get along with. In both cases, the courts could not take either point of view for granted but had to look for objective performance measures and evidence of how the organization treated its male employees.[68]

Alex Rodriguez, who currently plays third base for the New York Yankees, speaking at a conference on steroid use. He signed the richest contract in baseball history in 2007 for $275 million over 10 years. In 2009, he admitted to taking banned substances in the past. How does taking banned substances affect the self-serving bias of an accomplished athlete like Alex?

Much research has investigated the self-serving bias.[69] Two studies, for instance, examined whether or not senior executives fell prey to the self-serving bias when communicating with stockholders in their annual letter to shareholders. Results revealed executives in the United States and Singapore took credit for themselves when their companies did well and blamed negative outcomes on the environment.[70] Overall, however, research on the self-serving bias has produced inconsistent results. Two general patterns of attributions have been observed in past research. The first reveals that individuals make internal attributions for success as predicted by a self-serving bias. In contrast, people make both internal and external attributions for failure.[71] This means people do not automatically blame failure on external factors as originally expected from a self-serving bias. A team of researchers concluded, "When highly self-focused people feel that failure can be rapidly remedied, they will attribute failure to self; when the likelihood of improvement seems low, however, failure will be attributed externally."[72]

Managerial Application and Implications

Attribution models can be used to explain how managers handle poorly performing employees. One study revealed that managers gave employees more immediate, frequent, and negative feedback when they attributed their performance to low effort. This reaction was even more pronounced when the manager's success was dependent on an employee's performance. A second study indicated that managers tended to transfer employees whose poor performance was attributed to a lack of ability. These same managers also decided to take no immediate action when poor performance was attributed to external factors beyond an individual's control.[73]

The preceding discussion has several important implications for managers. First, men and women have different attributions regarding the causes of being promoted. Results from a recent survey of 140,000 people from 80 countries revealed that men and women had different attributions about what it takes to be promoted to a senior-level position. Men concluded that promotions were based on hard work whereas women reported that promotions were based more on luck and connections. As discussed in Chapter 2, these results, which were consistent across countries, suggest that a woman's promotional track resembles more of a labyrinth than a straight upward path. Managers thus are encouraged to help women develop social capital and to promote people on the basis of job-related criteria that are accurately measured.[74]

Second, managers tend to disproportionately attribute behavior to *internal* causes.[75] This can result in inaccurate evaluations of performance, leading to reduced employee motivation. No one likes to be blamed because of factors they perceive to be beyond their control. Further, because managers' responses to employee performance vary according to their attributions, attributional biases may lead to inappropriate managerial actions, including promotions, transfers, layoffs, and so forth. This can dampen motivation and performance. Attributional training sessions for managers are in order. Basic attributional processes can be explained, and managers can be taught to detect and avoid attributional biases. Finally, an employee's attributions for his or her own performance have dramatic effects on subsequent motivation, performance, and personal attitudes such as self-esteem. For instance, people tend to give up, develop lower expectations for future success, and experience decreased self-esteem when they attribute failure to a lack of ability. Fortunately, attributional retraining can improve both motivation and performance. Research shows that employees can be taught to attribute their failures to a lack of effort rather than to a lack of ability.[76] This attributional realignment paves the way for improved motivation and performance. It also is important to remember the implications of the self-serving bias. If managers want employees to accept personal responsibility for failure and correspondingly modify their effort and behavior, it is essential for employees to believe that they can improve upon their performance in the future. Otherwise, employees are likely to attribute failure to external causes and they will not change their behavior.

Summary of Key Concepts

1. *Describe perception in terms of the information-processing model.* Perception is a mental and cognitive process that enables us to interpret and understand our surroundings. Social perception, also known as social cognition and social information processing, is a four-stage process. The four stages are selective attention/comprehension, encoding and simplification, storage and retention, and retrieval and response. During social cognition, salient stimuli are matched with schemata, assigned to cognitive categories, and stored in long-term memory for events, semantic materials, or people.

2. *Identify and briefly explain seven managerial implications of social perception.* Social perception affects hiring decisions, performance appraisals, leadership

perceptions, communication and interpersonal influence, counterproductive work behaviors, physical and psychological well-being, and the design of Web pages. Inaccurate schemata or racist and sexist schemata may be used to evaluate job applicants. Similarly, faulty schemata about what constitutes good versus poor performance can lead to inaccurate performance appraisals. Invalid schemata need to be identified and replaced with appropriate schemata through coaching and training. Further, managers are advised to use objective rather than subjective measures of performance. With respect to leadership, a leader will have a difficult time influencing employees when he or she exhibits behaviors contained in employees' schemata of poor leaders. Because people interpret oral and written communications by using schemata developed through past experiences, an individual's ability to influence others is affected by information contained in others' schemata regarding age, gender, ethnicity, appearance, speech, mannerisms, personality, and other personal characteristics. It is very important to treat employees fairly, as perceptions of unfairness are associated with counterproductive work behaviors. Try to let negative thoughts roll off yourself like water off a duck to avoid the physical and psychological effects of negative thoughts.

3. *Discuss stereotypes and the process of stereotype formation.* Stereotypes represent grossly oversimplified beliefs or expectations about groups of people. Stereotyping is a four-step process that begins by categorizing people into groups according to various criteria. Next, we infer that all people within a particular group possess the same traits or characteristics. Then, we form expectations of others and interpret their behavior according to our stereotypes. Finally, stereotypes are maintained by (*a*) overestimating the frequency of stereotypic behaviors exhibited by others, (*b*) incorrectly explaining expected and unexpected behaviors, and (*c*) differentiating minority individuals from oneself. The use of stereotypes is influenced by the amount and type of information available to an individual and his or her motivation to accurately process information.

4. *Summarize the managerial challenges and recommendations of sex-role, age, racial and ethnic, and disability stereotypes.* The key managerial challenge is to reduce the extent to which stereotypes influence decision making and interpersonal processes throughout the organization. Training can be used to educate employees about the problem of stereotyping and to equip managers with the skills needed to handle situations associated with managing employees with disabilities. Because mixed-group contact reduces stereotyping, organizations should create opportunities for diverse employees to meet and work together in cooperative groups of equal status. Hiring decisions should be based on valid individual differences, and managers can be trained to use valid criteria when evaluating employee performance. Minimizing differences in job opportunities and experiences across groups of people can help alleviate promotional barriers. It is critical to obtain top management's commitment and support to eliminate stereotyping and discriminatory decisions.

5. *Describe and contrast the Pygmalion effect, the Galatea effect, and the Golem effect.* The Pygmalion effect, also known as the self-fulfilling prophecy, describes how someone's high expectations for another person result in high performance for that person. The Galatea effect occurs when an individual's high self-expectations lead to high self-performance. The Golem effect is a loss of performance resulting from low leader expectations.

6. *Discuss how the self-fulfilling prophecy is created and how it can be used to improve individual and group productivity.* According to the self-fulfilling prophecy, high managerial expectations foster high employee self-expectations. These expectations in turn lead to greater effort and better performance and yet higher expectations.

7. *Explain, according to Kelley's model, how external and internal causal attributions are formulated.* Attribution theory attempts to describe how people infer causes for observed behavior. According to Kelley's model of causal attribution, external attributions tend to be made when consensus and distinctiveness are high and consistency is low. Internal (personal responsibility) attributions tend to be made when consensus and distinctiveness are low and consistency is high.

8. *Contrast the fundamental attribution bias and the self-serving bias.* Fundamental attribution bias involves emphasizing personal factors more than situational factors while formulating causal attributions for the behavior of others. Self-serving bias involves personalizing the causes of one's successes and externalizing the causes of one's failures.

Key Terms

Perception, 185
Attention, 186
Cognitive categories, 186
Schema, 187
Script, 187

Implicit cognition, 190
Stereotype, 194
Sex-role stereotype, 194
Micro aggressions, 196
Stereotype threat, 197

OB in Action Case Study

Job Offers Are Won and Lost Based on Interviewers' Perceptions of Responses to the Question "What Are Your Weaknesses"[77]

Worldwide Panel LLC, a small market-research firm, is getting flooded with resumes for four vacancies in sales and information technology.

However, officials expect to reject numerous applicants after asking them: "What is your greatest weakness?" Candidates often respond "with something that is not a weakness," says Christopher Morrow, senior vice president of the Calabasas, Calif., concern. "It is a deal breaker."

The weakness question represents the most common and most stressful one posed during interviews. Yet in today's weak job market, the wrong answer weakens your chances of winning employment.

Some people offer replies that they mistakenly assume that the bosses love, such as "I am a perfectionist." That response "will be used against you" because you appear incapable of delegating, warns Joshua Ehrlich, dean of a master's program in executive coaching sponsored by BeamPines Inc., a New York coaching firm, and Middlesex University in London.

A careful game plan could help you with the shortcoming query in a way that highlights your fit for a desired position. Job seekers who field the question well demonstrate that they can "take initiative and improve themselves," Mr. Morrow says. . . .

It's equally important that you consider an employer's corporate culture. While being interviewed by a start-up, "you could say, 'My weakness is I get bored by routine,'" says Ben Dattner, a New York industrial psychologist.

Last month, an aspiring executive director of a nonprofit group in suburban San Francisco nearly jeopardized his selection because his reply to a variation of the weakness question ignored one of its core values, according to Ms. Klaus, a board member there. Near the end of his interview, she wondered whether he might have problems with any aspects of the job. "No, I am confident I could do it all," the prospect declared. His flip comment dismayed Ms. Klaus, because she felt he lacked awareness of his weakness. She says his response raises doubts among board members that "he would be able to take critical feedback," an attribute the organization values highly.

Because the man was well qualified, the board gave him a second interview—and demanded a fuller explanation of his weak spots. He said he had been "unprepared for that question and nervous about coming out with a big fatal flaw," then described his tendency to make decisions too fast during workplace crises. Board members' doubts disappeared, and they picked him for the nonprofit's top job.

Ideally, your reply also should exclude the word "weakness" and cover your corrective steps. Dubbing your greatest fault a "window of opportunity" signals your improvement efforts should benefit the workplace, says Oscar Adler, a retired Maidenform Brands sales executive and author of the book, *Sell Yourself in Any Interview.* For instance, he suggests, a salesman might note that he sold more after strengthening his facility with numbers.

When an interviewer pops this nerve-wracking query, your body language counts as well. The wrong nonverbal cues undercut your credibility. Certain candidates hunch over, glance furtively around the room or wring their sweaty palms. "They sort of look like they're being asked a question they can't handle," says Mr. Adler.

Maintaining eye contact, regular breathing, and a broad smile impress employers that "you're prepared for the weakness question," says psychotherapist Pat Pearson, author of *Stop Self-Sabotage!*

For the same reason, you seem thoughtful if you pause before responding. But don't wait too long. "If you're going to take a minute," Mr. Morrow cautions, "I've just identified your weakness."

Questions for Discussion

1. Which of the perceptual errors listed in Table 7–2 are affecting recruiters' perceptions in this case? Discuss.

2. What negative stereotypes are fueling recruiters' perceptions?

3. To what extent do the Pygmalion effect, the Galatea effect, and the Golem effect play a role in this case? Explain.

4. What lessons about perception did you learn from this case? Explain.

5. How would you answer the "weakness" question? Explain how it might be perceived by recruiters.

Ethical Dilemma

Should Brain Scans Be Used to Craft Advertising?[78]

IT MIGHT SOON BE time to redefine MRI machines as "market research imaging" devices. At Harvard's McLean Hospital not long ago, six male whiskey drinkers, ages 25 to 34, lined up to have their brains scanned for Arnold Worldwide. The Boston-based ad shop was using functional magnetic resonance imaging (fMRI) to gauge the emotional power of various images, including college kids drinking cocktails on spring break, twentysomethings with flasks around a campfire, and older guys at a swanky bar. The scans "help give us empirical evidence of the emotion of decision making," says Baysie Wightman, head of Arnold's new, science-focused Human Nature Dept. The results will help shape the 2007 ad campaign for client Brown-Forman, which owns Jack Daniels.

The idea of peeking into the brain for consumer insights isn't new. More than a dozen universities have been using fMRI to study how people respond to products (prompting Ralph Nader's Commercial Alert group to assert that "it's wrong to use a medical technology for marketing, not healing"). But now a few agencies like Arnold—whose clients also include McDonald's and Fidelity—and Digitas, another Boston-based shop, are offering fMRI research. "Neuromarketing" consultants, like Los Angeles-based FKF Applied Research, are springing up, too, to link companies with hospitals seeking to lease time on their pricey MRI machines.

Should We Allow Companies to Use Brain Scans to Test Advertising Campaigns?

1. Absolutely not! Ralph Nader is right; it's wrong to use medical equipment for marketing.
2. Why not? People participate voluntarily in these studies and they get paid for the experience.
3. Ad campaigns are expensive, and it is good business sense to test their effectiveness with brain scans.
4. Using medical equipment in this way is a good way to share the costs of an expensive MRI. In the end, reducing the costs of medical equipment is good for society at large.
5. Invent other options.

Web Resources

For study material and exercises that apply to this chapter, visit our Web site, www.mhhe.com/kreitner

Chapter 8

Foundations of Motivation

LEARNING OBJECTIVES

When you finish studying the material in this chapter, you should be able to:

LO.1 Contrast Maslow's, Alderfer's, and McClelland's need theories.

LO.2 Explain the practical significance of Herzberg's distinction between motivators and hygiene factors.

LO.3 Discuss the role of perceived inequity in employee motivation.

LO.4 Explain the differences among distributive, procedural, and interactional justice.

LO.5 Describe the practical lessons derived from equity theory.

LO.6 Explain Vroom's expectancy theory, and review its practical implications.

LO.7 Explain how goal setting motivates an individual, and review the four practical lessons from goal-setting research.

LO.8 Review the mechanistic, motivational, biological, and perceptual-motor approaches to job design.

LO.9 Specify issues that should be addressed before implementing a motivational program.

Student Resources for Studying Chapter 8

You might suppose that the stars are in near-perfect alignment for major reform of CEO pay. The mammoth pay and disastrous performance of Countrywide Financial's Angelo Mozilo, Citigroup's Chuck Prince, and Merrill Lynch's Stan O'Neal should be enough to make the public furious. Each CEO departed with $100-million-plus compensation after misadventures with subprime mortgages. Now add the economic slowdown to the mix; ordinary Americans are worried about making ends meet while failed pooh-bahs rake it in....

The answer is that whatever remedies reformers enact, corporate boards can always find a way to pay the boss whatever they like. Over the past 25 years CEO pay has risen regardless of the economic or political climate. It rises faster than corporate profits, economic growth, or average workforce compensation. A recent study by the compensation consulting firm DolmatConnell & Partners found that CEO pay in the companies of the Dow Jones industrials increased at a blowout 15.1% annual rate over the past decade.

A more sensible alternative to the current compensation system would require CEOs to own a lot of company stock. If the stock is given to the boss, his salary and bonus should be docked to reflect its value. As for bonuses, they should be based on improving a company's cash earnings relative to its cost of capital, not to more easily manipulated measures like earnings per share. They should not be capped, but they should be banked—unavailable to the CEO for some period of years—to prevent short-term gaming.

To see why that is unlikely to happen, check out this spring's crop of corporate proxy statements, which are still being filed. You'll note that this year many companies are reporting the specific performance targets on which CEO pay is based—saying not just that pay is based partly on free cash flow, for example, but reporting the amount that must be achieved. Companies are doing that because the SEC is making them. But by wangling pay formulas in a dozen ways, they can still pay CEOs as crazily as they like. Look, for example, at one of America's legendary pay abusers, Occidental Petroleum. Its latest proxy is full of impressive-looking targets and formulas, but the bottom line is that the company has consistently paid CEO Ray Irani huge sums ($110 million for 2007) during his 17 years at the top, regardless of performance, which has mostly been terrible.[1]

Angelo Mozilo, former CEO of Countrywide Financial left the company with a hefty bonus package.

FOR DISCUSSION

Do you think that CEOs' pay should be tied to corporate performance? Explain.

As you will learn later in this chapter, expectancy theory is based on the principle that an individual's pay should be tied to his or her performance. The fundamental concept underlying this theory is that employee motivation is higher when people are rewarded with rewards they value. Contrary to this theory, the chapter-opening vignette illustrates that many CEOs receive excessive salaries even when they fail to lead their organizations toward profitability and growth. This practice is likely to result in lower employee motivation for the average worker.

Many managers and executives understand that effective employee motivation is one of management's most important duties. Jeff Immelt, General Electric's CEO, understands this premise. He noted in a GE annual report that "[d]eveloping and motivating people is the most important part of my job. I spend one-third of my time on people."[2] Similarly, Best Buy CEO Brad Anderson concluded that his company's key competitive differentiator was "how we inspire our employees. Without that capability, you won't last."[3] As you will read in this chapter, an employee's motivation is a function of several components, including an individual's needs, the extent to which a work environment is positive and supportive, perceptions of being treated fairly, creating a strong relationship between performance and the receipt of valued rewards, the use of accurate measures of performance, and the setting of specific goals.

The term *motivation* derives from the Latin word *movere*, meaning "to move." In the present context, **motivation** represents "those psychological processes that cause the arousal, direction, and persistence of voluntary actions that are goal directed."[4] Researchers have proposed two general categories of motivation theories to explain the psychological processes underlying employee motivation: content theories and process theories. **Content theories of motivation** focus on identifying internal factors such as instincts, needs, satisfaction, and job characteristics that energize employee motivation. These theories do not explain how motivation is influenced by the dynamic interaction between an individual and the environment in which he or she works. This limitation led to the creation of process theories of motivation. **Process theories of motivation** focus on explaining the process by which internal factors and cognitions influence employee motivation.[5] Process theories are more dynamic than content theories.

Table 8–1 provides an overview of the various content and process theories discussed in this chapter. As you study these seven theories, remember that they offer different recommendations about how to motivate employees because they are based on different sets of assumptions regarding the causes of motivation. We help you to integrate and apply these varying recommendations by summarizing the managerial implications for each theory before discussing an alternative perspective.

After discussing the major content and process theories of motivation, this chapter provides an overview of job design methods used to motivate employees and concludes by focusing on practical recommendations for putting motivational theories to work.

Motivation

Psychological processes that arouse and direct goal-directed behavior.

Content theories of motivation

Identify internal factors influencing motivation.

Process theories of motivation

Identify the process by which internal factors and cognitions influence motivation.

Table 8–1   *Overview of Motivation Theories*

CONTENT THEORIES	PROCESS THEORIES
Maslow's Need Hierarchy Theory	Adam's Equity Theory
Alderfer's ERG Theory	Vroom's Expectancy Theory
McClelland's Need Theory	Goal Setting Theory
Herzberg's Motivator-Hygiene Theory	

LO.1 Content Theories of Motivation

to the point
How would you contrast the content theories of motivation proposed by Maslow, Alderfer, McClelland, and Herzberg?

Most content theories of motivation revolve around the notion that an employee's needs influence motivation. **Needs** are physiological or psychological deficiencies that arouse behavior. They can be strong or weak and are influenced by environmental factors. Thus, human needs vary over time and place. The general idea behind need theories of motivation is that unmet needs motivate people to satisfy them. Conversely, people are not motivated to pursue a satisfied need. Let us now consider four popular content theories of motivation: Maslow's need hierarchy theory, Alderfer's ERG theory, McClelland's need theory, and Herzberg's motivator–hygiene model.

Needs
Physiological or psychological deficiencies that arouse behavior.

Maslow's Need Hierarchy Theory

In 1943, psychologist Abraham Maslow published his now-famous **need hierarchy theory** of motivation. Although the theory was based on his clinical observation of a few neurotic individuals, it has subsequently been used to explain the entire spectrum of human behavior. Maslow proposed that motivation is a function of five basic needs. These needs are

Need hierarchy theory
Five basic needs—physiological, safety, love, esteem, and self-actualization—influence behavior.

1. *Physiological.* Most basic need. Entails having enough food, air, and water to survive.
2. *Safety.* Consists of the need to be safe from physical and psychological harm.
3. *Love.* The desire to be loved and to love. Contains the needs for affection and belonging.
4. *Esteem.* Need for reputation, prestige, and recognition from others. Also contains need for self-confidence and strength.
5. *Self-actualization.* Desire for self-fulfillment—to become the best one is capable of becoming.

Maslow said these five needs are arranged in the prepotent hierarchy shown in Figure 8–1. In other words, he believed human needs generally emerge in a predictable stair-step fashion. Accordingly, when one's physiological needs are relatively satisfied, one's safety needs emerge, and so on up the need hierarchy, one step at a

Figure 8–1   *Maslow's Need Hierarchy*

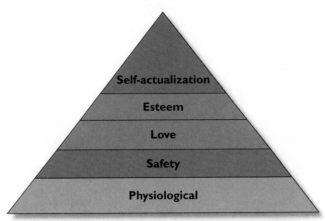

time. Once a need is satisfied, it activates the next higher need in the hierarchy. This process continues until the need for self-actualization is activated.[6]

Although research does not clearly support this theory of motivation, two key managerial implications of Maslow's theory are worth noting. First, it is important for managers to focus on satisfying employee needs related to self concepts—self-esteem and self-actualization—because their satisfaction is significantly associated with a host of important outcomes such as academic achievement, physical illness, psychological well-being (e.g., anxiety disorders, depression), criminal convictions, drug abuse, marital satisfaction, money and work problems, and performance at work.[7]

Second, a satisfied need may lose its motivational potential. Therefore, managers are advised to motivate employees by devising programs or practices aimed at satisfying emerging or unmet needs. Many companies have responded to this recommendation by offering employees targeted benefits that meet their specific needs. Consider Joie de Vivre, a hotel chain in California's Bay Area. Management uses Maslow's principles to verify that the company is building employee satisfaction and loyalty in a variety of ways. For example, Joie de Vivre managers provide recognition with formal processes to identify and comment on occasions when employees have provided exceptional service. They try to help housekeepers derive meaning from their jobs by bringing them together to talk about what the guests' experience would be like if the housekeepers weren't making their stay more comfortable.[8] Managers also can use customized surveys in order to assess the specific needs of their employees.[9] In conclusion, managers are more likely to fuel employee motivation by offering benefits and rewards that meet individual needs.

Alderfer's ERG Theory

Clayton Alderfer developed an alternative theory of human needs in the late 1960s. Alderfer's theory differs from Maslow's in three major respects. First, a smaller set of core needs is used to explain behavior. From lowest to highest level they are *existence needs* (E)—the desire for physiological and materialistic well-being; *relatedness needs* (R)—the desire to have meaningful relationships with significant others; and *growth needs* (G)—the desire to grow as a human being and to use one's abilities to their fullest potential; hence, the label **ERG theory.** Second, ERG theory does not assume needs are related to each other in a stair-step hierarchy as does Maslow. Alderfer believes that more than one need may be activated at a time. Finally, ERG theory contains a frustration-regression component. That is, frustration of higher-order needs can influence the desire for lower-order needs.[10] For example, employees may demand higher pay or better benefits (existence needs) when they are frustrated or dissatisfied with the quality of their interpersonal relationships (relatedness needs) at work.

ERG theory

Three basic needs—existence, relatedness, and growth—influence behavior.

Research on ERG theory has provided mixed support for some of the theory's key propositions. That said, however, there are two key managerial implications associated with ERG. The first revolves around the frustration-regression aspect of the theory. Managers should keep in mind that employees may be motivated to pursue lower-level needs because they are frustrated with a higher-order need. For instance, the solution for a stifling work environment may be a request for higher pay or better benefits. Second, ERG theory is consistent with the finding that individual and cultural differences influence our need states. People are motivated by different needs at different times in their lives. This implies that managers should customize their reward and recognition programs to meet employees' varying needs. Consider how Marc Albin, CEO of Albin Engineering Services, Inc., handles this recommendation.

> To identify which parts of individual employees' egos need scratching, Albin takes an unconventional approach. "My experience in managing people is, they're all different," says Albin. "Some people want to be recognized for their cheerful attitude and their ability to spread their cheerful attitude. Some want to be recognized for the quality of their work, some for the quantity of their work. Some like to be recognized individually; others want to be recognized in groups." Consequently, at the end of each employee-orientation session Albin e-mails his new hires and asks them how and in what form they prefer their strokes. "It helps me understand what they think of themselves and their abilities, and I make a mental note to pay special attention to them when they're working in that particular arena," he says. "No one has ever said, 'Just recognize me for anything I do well.'"[11]

McClelland's Need Theory

David McClelland, a well-known psychologist, has been studying the relationship between needs and behavior since the late 1940s. Although he is most recognized for his research on the need for achievement, he also investigated the needs for affiliation and power. Let us consider each of these needs.

The Need for Achievement

Need for achievement

Desire to accomplish something difficult.

The **need for achievement** is defined by the following desires:

> To accomplish something difficult. To master, manipulate, or organize physical objects, human beings, or ideas. To do this as rapidly and as independently as possible. To overcome obstacles and attain a high standard. To excel one's self. To rival and surpass others. To increase self-regard by the successful exercise of talent.[12]

Achievement-motivated people share three common characteristics: (1) they prefer working on tasks of moderate difficulty; (2) they prefer situations in which performance is due to their efforts rather than other factors, such as luck; and (3) they desire more feedback on their successes and failures than do low achievers. A review of research on the "entrepreneurial" personality showed that entrepreneurs were found to have a higher need for achievement than nonentrepreneurs.[13]

The Need for Affiliation

Need for affiliation

Desire to spend time in social relationships and activities.

People with a high **need for affiliation** prefer to spend more time maintaining social relationships, joining groups, and wanting to be loved. Individuals high in this need are not the most effective managers or leaders because they tend to avoid conflict, have a hard time making difficult decisions without worrying about being disliked, and avoid giving others negative feedback.[14]

The Need for Power

Need for power

Desire to influence, coach, teach, or encourage others to achieve.

The **need for power** reflects an individual's desire to influence, coach, teach, or encourage others to achieve. People with a high need for power like to work and are concerned with discipline and self-respect. There are positive and negative sides to this need. The negative face of power is characterized by an "if I win, you lose" mentality. In contrast, people with a positive orientation to power focus on accomplishing group goals and helping employees obtain the feeling of competence. More is said about the two faces of power in Chapter 13.

Because effective managers must positively influence others, McClelland proposes that top managers should have a high need for power coupled with a low need for affiliation.

Managerial Implications   Given that adults can be trained to increase their achievement motivation,[15] organizations should consider the benefits of providing achievement training for employees. Moreover, achievement, affiliation, and power needs can be considered during the selection process, for better placement. For example, a study revealed that individuals' need for achievement affected their preference to work in different companies. People with a high need for achievement were more attracted to companies that had a pay-for-performance environment than were those with a low achievement motivation.[16] Finally, it is important to balance the above recommendations with the downside of high achievement. McClelland noted that people with high achievement might be more prone to "cheat and cut corners and to leave people out of the loop." He also noted that some high achievers "are so fixated on finding a shortcut to the goal that they may not be too particular about the means they use to reach it."[17] Byrraju Ramalinga Raju, former founder and chairman of Satyam Computers, is a good example. Mr. Raju was known as a highly driven executive who had a grand vision for using technology to help develop rural India. He also was highly involved with several foundations in India. Unfortunately, Mr. Raju apparently took some illegal shortcuts to meet Satyam's short-term financial goals (see the Real World/Real People feature on page 217).[18]

L0.2 Herzberg's Motivator–Hygiene Theory

Frederick Herzberg's theory is based on a landmark study in which he interviewed 203 accountants and engineers.[19] These interviews sought to determine the factors responsible for job satisfaction and dissatisfaction. Herzberg found separate and distinct clusters of factors associated with job satisfaction and dissatisfaction. Job satisfaction was more frequently associated with achievement, recognition, characteristics of the work, responsibility, and advancement. These factors were all related to outcomes associated with the *content* of the task being performed.

Motivators

Job characteristics associated with job satisfaction.

Herzberg labeled these factors **motivators** because each was associated with strong effort and good performance. He hypothesized that motivators cause a person to move from a state of no satisfaction to satisfaction (see Figure 8–2). Therefore, Herzberg's theory predicts managers can motivate individuals by incorporating "motivators" into an individual's job.

Herzberg found job *dissatisfaction* to be associated primarily with factors in the work *context* or environment. Specifically, company policy and administration, technical supervision, salary, interpersonal relations with one's supervisor, and working conditions were most frequently mentioned by employees expressing job dissatisfaction. Herzberg labeled this second cluster of factors

Hygiene factors

Job characteristics associated with job dissatisfaction.

hygiene factors. He further proposed that they were not motivational. At best, according to Herzberg's interpretation, an individual will experience no job dissatisfaction when he or she has no grievances about hygiene factors (refer to Figure 8–2). Research reveals that pay is one of the most important contributors to dissatisfaction, and employees are more likely to quit when faced with poor hygiene factors.[20]

High Achievement Needs Can Lead to Negative Outcomes

Satyam was created by Ramalinga Raju and others and was, until recently, perceived to be amongst the top Indian IT vendors. Raju has allegedly admitted overstating its cash reserves by one billion US dollars. Later, allegations have been made that the company's assets were not inflated, but instead siphoned off by Ramalinga Raju. Ramalinga Raju is currently lodged in Hyderabad's Chanchalguda jail as Prisoner No. 213 on various criminal charges including fraud, forgery, cheating, embezzlement, and insider trading to name just a few. It has been estimated that more than one billion US dollars' worth of investor's wealth was illegally siphoned out of Satyam Computers into numerous private accounts by prime accused Raju and possibly a few others in what has become known as the single biggest corporate fraud in India's history.

Why would high achievement lead Mr. Raju to commit these crimes?

SOURCE: Excerpted from "Ramalinga Raju," Wikipedia, last updated February 27, 2009, http:wikipedia.org.

The key to adequately understanding Herzberg's motivator–hygiene theory is recognizing that he believes that satisfaction is not the opposite of dissatisfaction. Herzberg concludes that "the opposite of job satisfaction is not job dissatisfaction, but rather no job satisfaction; and similarly, the opposite of job dissatisfaction is not job satisfaction, but no dissatisfaction."[21] Herzberg thus asserts that the dissatisfaction–satisfaction continuum contains a zero midpoint at which dissatisfaction and satisfaction are absent. Conceivably, an organization member who has good supervision, pay, and working conditions but a tedious and unchallenging task with little chance of advancement would be at the zero midpoint. That person

Figure 8–2   *Herzberg's Motivator–Hygiene Model*

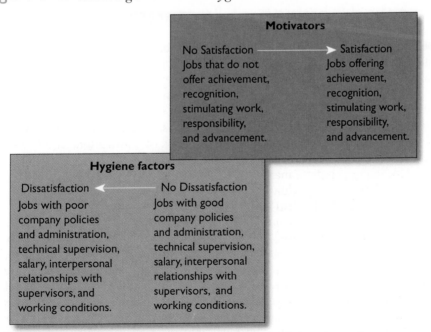

SOURCE: Adapted in part from D A Whitsett and E K Winslow, "An Analysis of Studies Critical of the Motivator–Hygiene Theory," *Personnel Psychology*, Winter 1967, pp 391–415.

would have no dissatisfaction (because of good hygiene factors) and no satisfaction (because of a lack of motivators).

Herzberg's theory has generated a great deal of research and controversy.[22] Research does not support the two-factor aspect of his theory nor the proposition that hygiene factors are unrelated to job satisfaction. Just the same, there are two key implications associated with this theory. First, managers are encouraged to pay attention to hygiene factors and motivators because they both are related to employees' job satisfaction. This is precisely what Grant Lundberg, CEO of Wehah Farms Inc., is doing to maintain employee motivation and satisfaction. Second, recognizing good performance is important, particularly in a down economy when raises are sparse. It is important to recognize behaviors and results that are linked to the organization's goals. Managers also should be careful that they don't recognize too frequently or infrequently. Recognition should be earned, not a given.[23]

> The company shows employees that they're valued in many ways, including an employee garden where they grow fruits and vegetables, an annual bonus tied to company performance, and an extensive wellness program. The company also works to make sure all employees have ample opportunities to move into management positions and provide input. The "Above and Beyond" program gives $200 cash prizes each month to employees who suggest ideas that are implemented or who do something exceptional. (One employee won for helping a choking colleague.) And, once a month, Mr. Lundberg hosts a "Meet the CEO" event where a small group of seven or eight employees chat with him to provide feedback and discuss any concerns.[24]

Equity theory
Holds that motivation is a function of fairness in social exchanges.

to the point
What is the difference between a content and a process theory of motivation?

Process Theories of Motivation

Earlier in the chapter we discussed the difference between content theories of motivation, which focus on the impact of internal factors on motivation, and process theories. Process theories go one step further in explaining motivation by identifying the process by which various internal factors influence motivation. These models also are cognitive in nature. That is, they are based on the premise that motivation is a function of employees' perceptions, thoughts, and beliefs. We now explore the three most common process theories of motivation: equity theory, expectancy theory, and goal-setting theory.

to the point
How does the concept of organizational justice expand Adam's theory of equity and what are the practical lessons derived from equity theory?

LO.3 Adams's Equity Theory of Motivation

Defined generally, **equity theory** is a model of motivation that explains how people strive for fairness and justice in social exchanges or give-and-take relationships. As a process theory of motivation, equity theory explains how an individual's motivation to behave in a certain way is fueled by feelings of inequity or a lack of justice. For example, contractor Rajendrasinh Babubhai Makwana was powerfully motivated to seek revenge against Fannie Mae after he was fired (see the Real World/Real People feature on page 219). Experts believe that this type of motivated vengeance is likely to increase as companies lay off more employees.[25] Psychologist J Stacy Adams pioneered application of the equity principle to the

Fired Contractor Seeks Revenge against Fannie Mae

Mr Makwana, a native of India in the US, on a work visa, was indicted by a federal grand jury Tuesday in Baltimore. He pleaded not guilty. . . . Mr. Makwana worked at Fannie as a contract computer engineer, specializing in the Unix operating system, and was fired on Oct. 24. That day, according to the affidavit, someone using Mr. Makwana's laptop inserted malicious code into a routine computer program on Fannie computer servers. The code was set to execute on Jan. 31, 2009, and was programmed to attack all 4,000 of the company's servers. Prosecutors allege the code would have wiped out all the data on the servers.

The code was tucked at the end of a legitimate software program scheduled to run each morning. It was discovered by chance by a Fannie technician five days later, according to the affidavit.

How can companies prevent this type of event from happening?

SOURCE: Excerpted from S Gorman, "Virus Was Set to Destroy Fannie Mae Data," *The Wall Street Journal*, February 1, 2009, p A2.

workplace. Central to understanding Adams's equity theory of motivation is an awareness of key components of the individual–organization exchange relationship. This relationship is pivotal in the formation of employees' perceptions of equity and inequity.

The Individual–Organization Exchange Relationship

Adams points out that two primary components are involved in the employee–employer exchange, *inputs* and *outcomes*. An employee's inputs, for which he or she expects a just return, include education/training, skills, creativity, seniority, age, personality traits, effort expended, and personal appearance. On the outcome side of the exchange, the organization provides such things as pay/bonuses, fringe benefits, challenging assignments, job security, promotions, status symbols, and participation in important decisions.

Negative and Positive Inequity

On the job, feelings of inequity revolve around a person's evaluation of whether he or she receives adequate rewards to compensate for his or her contributive inputs. People perform these evaluations by comparing the perceived fairness of their employment exchange to that of relevant others.[26] This comparative process, which is based on an equity norm, was found to vary across countries.[27] People tend to compare themselves to other individuals with whom they have close interpersonalties—such as friends—or to similar others—such as people performing the same job or individuals of the same gender or educational level—rather than dissimilar others. For example, do you consider the average CEO in the United States a relevant comparison person to yourself? If not, then you should not feel inequity because the average CEO earns about 344 times what the average worker is paid. In contrast, a CEO in Japan may feel inequity in light of knowing that the average salary of CEOs at Japan's 100 largest companies was $1.5 million, compared with $13.3 million for big firms in the United States.[28]

Three different equity relationships are illustrated in Figure 8–3: equity, negative inequity, and positive inequity. Assume the two people in each of the equity relationships in Figure 8–3 have equivalent backgrounds (equal education, seniority, and so forth) and perform identical tasks. Only their hourly pay rates differ. Equity exists for an individual when his or her ratio of perceived outcomes to inputs is equal to the ratio of outcomes to inputs for a relevant coworker (part A in Figure 8–3). Because equity is based on comparing *ratios* of outcomes to inputs, inequity will not necessarily be perceived just because someone else receives greater rewards. If the other person's additional outcomes are due to his or her greater inputs, a sense of equity may still exist. However, if the comparison person enjoys greater outcomes for similar inputs, **negative inequity** will be perceived (part B in Figure 8–3). On the other hand, a person will experience **positive inequity** when his or her outcome to input ratio is greater than that of a relevant coworker (part C in Figure 8–3). Interestingly, the current economy is creating a lot of positive inequity for layoff survivors like Jeff Jacobs.

Negative inequity

Comparison in which another person receives greater outcomes for similar inputs.

Positive inequity

Comparison in which another person receives lesser outcomes for similar inputs.

Last August, on the eve of a planned trip to cover the 2008 Olympic Games in China, Jeff Jacobs, sports columnist for *The Hartford Courant,* found himself with mixed feelings. Excitement about the plum assignment was tempered by nagging anxiety: In the past month, 25 percent of the news staff at Connecticut's largest daily had been laid off or offered buyouts, a result of sagging ad sales. "I'm so riddled with guilt and anxiety," Jacobs wrote in his column before making the trip. "One-fourth of the friends, colleagues,

Figure 8–3   *Negative and Positive Inequity*

A. An Equitable Situation

B. Negative Inequity

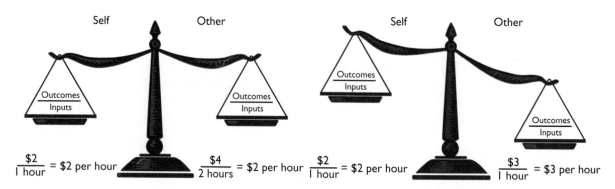

C. Positive Inequity

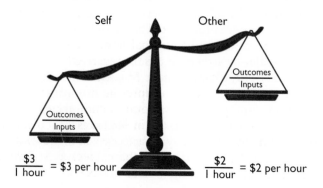

journalists I have admired are gone. One-fourth of my soul is gone. In its place is survivor's guilt. The trip of a lifetime suddenly feels like the regret of a lifetime."[29]

Dynamics of Perceived Inequity

Managers can derive practical benefits from Adams's equity theory by recognizing that (1) people have varying sensitivities to perceived equity and inequity and (2) inequity can be reduced in a variety of ways.

Thresholds of Equity and Inequity
Have you ever noticed that some people become very upset over the slightest inequity whereas others are not bothered at all? Research has shown that people respond differently to the same level of inequity due to an individual difference called *equity sensitivity*. **Equity sensitivity** reflects an individual's "different preferences for, tolerances for, and reactions to the level of equity associated with any given situation."[30] Equity sensitivity spans a continuum ranging from benevolents to sensitives to entitleds.

Benevolents are people who have a higher tolerance for negative inequity. They are altruistic in the sense that they prefer their outcome/input ratio to be lower than ratios from comparison others. In contrast, equity *sensitives* are described as individuals who adhere to a strict norm of reciprocity and are quickly motivated to resolve both negative and positive inequity. Finally, *entitleds* have no tolerance for negative inequity. They actually expect to obtain greater output/input ratios than comparison others and become upset when this is not the case.[31]

Reducing Inequity
Equity ratios can be changed by attempting to alter one's outcomes or adjusting one's inputs. For example, negative inequity might be resolved by asking for a raise or a promotion (i.e., raising outputs) or by reducing inputs (i.e., working fewer hours or exerting less effort). It also is important to note that equity can be restored by altering one's equity ratios behaviorally or cognitively, or both. A cognitive strategy entails psychologically distorting perceptions of one's own or one's comparison person's outcomes and inputs (e.g., conclude that comparison other has more experience or works harder).

LO.4 Expanding the Concept of Equity: Organizational Justice

Beginning in the late 1970s, researchers began to expand the role of equity theory in explaining employee attitudes and behavior. This led to a domain of research called *organizational justice*. Organizational justice reflects the extent to which people perceive that they are treated fairly at work. This, in turn, led to the identification of three different components of organizational justice: distributive, procedural, and interactional.[32] **Distributive justice** reflects the perceived fairness of how resources and rewards are distributed or allocated. **Procedural justice** is defined as the perceived fairness of the process and procedures used to make allocation decisions. Research shows that positive perceptions of distributive and procedural justice are enhanced by giving employees a "voice" in decisions that affect them. Voice represents the extent to which employees who are affected by a decision can present relevant information about the decision to others. Voice is analogous to asking employees for their input into the decision-making process.

Equity sensitivity
An individual's tolerance for negative and positive equity.

Distributive justice
The perceived fairness of how resources and rewards are distributed.

Procedural justice
The perceived fairness of the process and procedures used to make allocation decisions.

Interactional justice

Extent to which people feel fairly treated when procedures are implemented.

The last justice component, **interactional justice,** relates to the "quality of the interpersonal treatment people receive when procedures are implemented."[33] This form of justice does not pertain to the outcomes or procedures associated with decision making, but rather it focuses on whether or not people feel they are treated fairly when decisions are implemented. Fair interpersonal treatment necessitates that managers communicate truthfully and treat people with courtesy and respect.

Many studies of organizational justice have been conducted over the last two decades. Fortunately, four meta-analyses of more than 200 studies help summarize what has been learned from this research.[34] The following trends were uncovered: (1) job performance was positively associated with both distributive and procedural justice, but procedural justice was the best predictor of this outcome; (2) all three forms of justice were positively correlated with job satisfaction, organizational commitment, organizational citizenship behaviors, and employees' trust, and negatively with employees' withdrawal cognitions and turnover; (3) distributive and procedural injustice were negatively related to negative emotions such as anger; and all three forms of justice were negatively associated with aggressive behavior at work.[35] These results suggest a host of practical lessons for managers.

LO.5 Practical Lessons from Equity Theory

Equity theory has at least six important practical implications. First, research on equity theory emphasizes the need for managers to pay attention to employees' perceptions of what is fair and equitable. No matter how fair management thinks the organization's policies, procedures, and reward system are, each employee's *perception* of the equity of those factors is what counts. For example, a nationwide study of 3,000 US workers revealed that 39% felt underpaid and only 37% reported feeling valued by their employer.[36] Managers thus are encouraged to make hiring decisions on merit-based, job-related information, and to make more attempts at providing positive recognition about employee behavior and performance. Moreover, because justice perceptions are influenced by the extent to which managers explain their decisions, managers are encouraged to explain the rationale behind their decisions.

Fred Smith, CEO and founder of FedEx. The word "FedEx" was added to the Merriam-Webster's Collegiate Dictionary in 2006. How often do you use the word "FedEx" when you need to mail something?

Second, managers benefit by allowing employees to participate in making decisions about important work outcomes. In general, employees' perceptions of procedural justice are enhanced when they have a voice in the decision-making process.[37] Managers are encouraged to seek employee input on organizational changes that are likely to impact the workforce. For instance, managers at Shell Refining decided to ask top-performing supervisors at its Port Arthur, Texas, refinery for input on how to improve plant performance. The result of this action was higher employee morale and a 30% reduction in unplanned maintenance repairs.[38]

Third, employees should be given the opportunity to appeal decisions that affect their welfare. Being able to appeal a decision fosters perceptions of distributive and procedural justice. Fourth, managers can promote cooperation and teamwork among group members by treating them equitably. Research reveals that people are just as concerned with fairness in group settings as they are with their own personal interests.[39] Fifth, employees' perceptions of justice are strongly influenced by the leadership behavior exhibited by their managers (leadership is discussed in Chapter 16).[40] It thus is important for managers to consider the justice-related implications of their decisions, actions, and public communications. Consider the decisions made by FedEX CEO Frederick Smith.

> FedEx has undergone layoffs, but it has also cut pay, and the higher you go in the company, the greater the percentage cut. That saves jobs and helps stabilize the company. "All of our management compensation is heavily related to the performance of the company," says founder and CEO Fred Smith. "At the first-line management level it's maybe 15% or 20%. At my level it's 90%. So obviously, as the economy has gotten weaker, a lot of that expense has simply gone away." On top of those automatic adjustments, FedEx also announced in December that it was cutting the pay of salaried employees by 5% this year. Smith cut his own pay 20%.[41]

Finally, managers need to pay attention to the organization's climate for justice. For example, an organization's climate for justice was found to significantly influence employees' organizational commitment and job satisfaction.[42] Researchers also believe a climate of justice can significantly influence the type of customer service provided by employees. In turn, this level of service is likely to influence customers' perceptions of "fair service" and their subsequent loyalty and satisfaction.[43]

Managers can attempt to follow these practical implications by monitoring equity and justice perceptions through informal conversations, interviews, or attitude surveys. Researchers have developed and validated a host of surveys that can be used for this purpose.

go to the Web for the Self-Exercise: Measuring Perceived Fair Interpersonal Treatment

L0.6 Vroom's Expectancy Theory

to the point
What are the main components of expectancy theory and how can managers put this theory into practice?

Expectancy theory holds that people are motivated to behave in ways that produce desired combinations of expected outcomes. Generally, expectancy theory can be used to predict motivation and behavior in any situation in which a choice between two or more alternatives must be made. For instance, it can be used to predict whether to quit or stay at a job; whether to exert substantial or minimal effort at a task; and whether to major in management, finance, marketing, psychology, or communication.

Victor Vroom formulated a mathematical model of expectancy in his 1964 book *Work and Motivation.*[44] Vroom's theory has been summarized as follows:

> The strength of a tendency to act in a certain way depends on the strength of an expectancy that the act will be followed by a given consequence (or outcome) and on the value or attractiveness of that consequence (or outcome) to the actor.[45]

Expectancy theory
Holds that people are motivated to behave in ways that produce valued outcomes.

Motivation, according to Vroom, boils down to the decision of how much effort to exert in a specific task situation. This choice is based on a two-stage sequence of expectations (effort→performance and performance→outcome). First, motivation is affected by an individual's expectation that a certain level of effort will produce the intended performance goal. For example, if you do not believe increasing the amount of time you spend studying will significantly raise your grade on an exam, you probably will not study any harder than usual. Motivation also is influenced by the employee's perceived chances of getting various outcomes as a result of accomplishing his or her performance goal. Finally, individuals are motivated to the extent that they value the outcomes received.

Vroom used a mathematical equation to integrate the above concepts into a predictive model of motivational force or strength. For our purposes, however, it is sufficient to define and explain the three key concepts within Vroom's model—*expectancy, instrumentality,* and *valence.*

Expectancy

Expectancy
Belief that effort leads to a specific level of performance.

An **expectancy,** according to Vroom's terminology, represents an individual's belief that a particular degree of effort will be followed by a particular level of performance. In other words, it is an effort→performance expectation. Expectancies take the form of subjective probabilities. As you may recall from a course in statistics, probabilities range from 0 to 1. An expectancy of 0 indicates effort has no anticipated impact on performance.

For example, suppose you have not memorized the keys on a keyboard. No matter how much effort you exert, your perceived probability of typing 30 error-free words per minute likely would be 0. An expectancy of 1 suggests that performance is totally dependent on effort. If you decided to memorize the letters on a keyboard as well as practice a couple of hours a day for a few weeks (high effort), you should be able to type 30 words per minute without any errors. In contrast, if you do not memorize the letters on a keyboard and only practice an hour or two per week (low effort), there is a very low probability (say, a 20% chance) of being able to type 30 words per minute without any errors.

The following factors influence an employee's expectancy perceptions:

- Self-esteem.
- Self-efficacy (recall the discussion in Chapter 5).
- Previous success at the task.
- Help received from a supervisor and subordinates.
- Information necessary to complete the task.
- Good materials and equipment to work with.[46]

Instrumentality

Instrumentality
A performance→ outcome perception.

An **instrumentality** is a performance→outcome perception. It represents a person's belief that a particular outcome is contingent on accomplishing a specific level of performance. Performance is instrumental when it leads to something else. For example, passing exams is instrumental to graduating from college.

Instrumentalities range from −1.0 to 1.0. An instrumentality of 1.0 indicates attainment of a particular outcome is totally dependent on task performance. An instrumentality of 0 indicates there is no relationship between performance and outcome. For example, most companies link the number of vacation days to seniority, not job performance. Finally, an instrumentality of −1.0 reveals that high performance reduces the chance of obtaining an outcome while low performance increases the chance. For example, the more time you spend studying to get an A on an exam (high performance), the less time you will have for enjoying leisure activities. Similarly, as you lower the amount of time spent studying (low performance), you increase the amount of time that may be devoted to leisure activities.

The concept of instrumentality is illustrated by the pay practices being used at Aflac (see the Real World/Real People feature on page 226). Aflac's profit-sharing plan makes an individual's bonus instrumental on the company's overall performance.

Valence

As Vroom used the term, **valence** refers to the positive or negative value people place on outcomes. Valence mirrors our personal preferences. For example, most employees have a positive valence for receiving additional money or recognition. In contrast, job stress and being laid off would likely result in negative valence for most individuals. In Vroom's expectancy model, *outcomes* refer to different consequences that are contingent on performance, such as pay, promotions, or recognition. An outcome's valence depends on an individual's needs and can be measured for research purposes with scales ranging from a negative value to a positive value. For example, an individual's valence toward more recognition can be assessed on a scale ranging from −2 (very undesirable) to 0 (neutral) to +2 (very desirable).

Farcus   by David Waisglass
Gordon Coulthart

© 1994 Farcus Cartoons   WAISGLASS/COULTHART

"Frankly, I didn't think they'd go for this performance incentive stuff."

SOURCE: FARCUS® is reprinted with permission from LaughingStock Licensing Inc., Ottawa, Canada. All rights reserved.

Valence
The value of a reward or outcome.

Vroom's Expectancy Theory in Action

Vroom's expectancy model of motivation can be used to analyze a real-life motivation program. Consider the following performance problem described by Frederick W Smith, founder and chief executive officer of Federal Express Corporation:

[W]e were having a helluva problem keeping things running on time. The airplanes would come in and everything would get backed up. We tried every kind of control mechanism that you could think of, and none of them worked. Finally, it became obvious that the underlying problem was that it was in the interest of the employees at the cargo terminal—they were college kids, mostly—to run late, because it meant that they made more money. So what we did was give them all a minimum guarantee and say, "Look, if you get through before a certain time, just go home, and you will have beat the system." Well, it was unbelievable. I mean, in the space of about 45 days, the place was way ahead of schedule. And I don't even think it was a conscious thing on their part.[47]

How did Federal Express get its college-age cargo handlers to switch from low effort to high effort? According to Vroom's model, the student workers originally exerted low effort because they were paid on the basis of time, not output. It was in their best interest to work slowly and accumulate as many hours as possible. By offering to let the student workers *go home early if and when they completed their assigned duties,* Federal Express prompted high effort. This new arrangement created two positively

Aflac Uses the Principles of Expectancy Theory

Dan Amos, CEO of Aflac, the insurer based in Columbus, GA, says the best way to promote loyalty and teamwork is to link all staff pay to the company's performance, to varying degrees. The company is expected at its annual meeting next Monday to become the first US public company to give investors a vote on top officers' pay packages.

When he took charge 16 years ago, Mr. Amos replaced the company's traditional Christmas bonus with a profit-sharing one for all employees, from call-center personnel to top executives. In 2007, Aflac's 4,500 US employees received an average of 6.7% of their annual salaries in bonuses. "We want everyone participating in making the company better and everyone benefiting when it does," says Mr. Amos, who received $4.1 million in salary, bonus, and other compensation last year and was granted restricted stock and stock options valued at $8.4 million.

Do you like Aflac's approach to paying bonuses? Explain.

SOURCE: Excerpted from C Hymowitz, "Pay Gap Fuels Worker Woes," *The Wall Street Journal*, April 2008, p B8.

---

valued outcomes: guaranteed pay plus the opportunity to leave early. The motivation to exert high effort became greater than the motivation to exert low effort.

Judging from the impressive results, the student workers had both high effort→ performance expectancies and positive performance→outcome instrumentalities. Moreover, the guaranteed pay and early departure opportunity evidently had strongly positive valences for the student workers.

Research on Expectancy Theory and Managerial Implications

Many researchers have tested expectancy theory. In support of the theory, a meta-analysis of 77 studies indicated that expectancy theory significantly predicted performance, effort, intentions, preferences, and choice.[48] Another summary of 16 studies revealed that expectancy theory correctly predicted occupational or organizational choice 63.4% of the time; this was significantly better than chance predictions.[49] All told, there is widespread agreement that behavior and attitudes are influenced when organizations link rewards to targeted behaviors.[50] This relationship is discussed in more detail in Chapter 9.

Nonetheless, expectancy theory has been criticized for a variety of reasons. For example, the theory is difficult to test, and the measures used to assess expectancy, instrumentality, and valence have questionable validity.[51] In the final analysis, however, expectancy theory has important practical implications for individual managers and organizations as a whole (see Table 8–2).

Managers are advised to enhance effort→performance expectancies by helping employees accomplish their performance goals. Managers can do this by providing support and coaching and by increasing employees' self-efficacy. It also is important for managers to influence employees' instrumentalities and to monitor valences for various rewards.

In summary, there is no one best type of reward. Individual differences and need theories tell us that people are motivated by different rewards. Managers should therefore focus on linking employee performance to valued rewards regardless of the type of reward used to enhance motivation. For example, trucking company J A Frate Inc. uses a variety of rewards to motivate its truck drivers.

Table 8–2   *Managerial and Organizational Implications of Expectancy Theory*

IMPLICATIONS FOR MANAGERS	IMPLICATIONS FOR ORGANIZATIONS
Determine the outcomes employees value.	Reward people for desired performance; and do not keep pay decisions secret.
Identify good performance so appropriate behaviors can be rewarded.	Design challenging jobs.
Make sure employees can achieve targeted performance levels.	Tie some rewards to group accomplishments to build teamwork and encourage cooperation.
Link desired outcomes to targeted levels of performance.	Reward managers for creating, monitoring, and maintaining expectancies, instrumentalities, and outcomes that lead to high effort and goal attainment.
Make sure changes in outcomes are large enough to motivate high effort.	Monitor employee motivation through interviews or anonymous questionnaires.
Monitor the reward system for inequities.	Accommodate individual differences by building flexibility into the motivation program.

"Each month the company's Driver Recognition Committee selects 'Drivers of the Month' and usually divvies $200 in Wal-Mart gift certificates among them. The recognition is based on a point system where drivers can be docked points for issues such as damaged freight, tardiness, or sloppy log books. Each year, one driver is designated 'Driver of the Year' and wins a large prize. . . . Employees are also encouraged to suggest changes, with the top three suggestion makers each quarter winning $100, $50, and $25, respectively."[52]

go to the Web for the Self-Exercise: What Outcomes Motivate Employees?

LO.7 Motivation through Goal Setting

to the point
What is the process by which goals affect employee performance and what are the practical lessons from goal-setting research?

Regardless of the nature of their specific achievements, successful people tend to have one thing in common. Their lives are goal oriented. Consider Mike Proulx, for example. "When Mike Proulx was bagging groceries as a teenager in the 1960s, he decided he would become president of Bashas. [Bashas is a privately held grocery chain in Arizona with over 150 stores.] That's the job he has now held for three years. . . . When I was 18 I made a series of goals that included by age such and such I would be a store manager, and by a certain age, I was going to be district manager and then vice president and then president."[53] As a process model of motivation, goal-setting theory explains how the simple behavior of setting goals activates a powerful motivational process that leads to sustained, high performance. This section explores the theory and research pertaining to goal setting, and Chapter 9 continues the discussion by focusing on the practical application of goal setting.

Goals: Definition and Background

Goal

What an individual is trying to accomplish.

Edwin Locke, a leading authority on goal setting, and his colleagues define a **goal** as "what an individual is trying to accomplish; it is the object or aim of an action."[54] The motivational effect of performance goals and goal-based reward plans has been recognized for a long time. At the turn of the 20th century, Frederick Taylor attempted to scientifically establish how much work of a specified quality an individual should be assigned each day. He proposed that bonuses be based on accomplishing those output standards: Taylor's theory is discussed in the next section of this chapter. More recently, goal setting has been promoted through a widely used management technique called *management by objectives (MBO)*. The application of MBO is outlined in Chapter 9.

How Does Goal Setting Work?

Despite abundant goal-setting research and practice, goal-setting theories are surprisingly scarce. An instructive model was formulated by Locke and his associates. According to Locke's model, goal setting has four motivational mechanisms.

Goals Direct Attention   Goals direct one's attention and effort toward goal-relevant activities and away from goal-irrelevant activities. If, for example, you have a term project due in a few days, your thoughts and actions tend to revolve around completing that project. For example, both Mitsubishi and Emory University used the power of goals to direct their organizations toward the pursuit of sustainability initiatives (see the Real World/Real People feature on page 229).[55]

Goals Regulate Effort   Not only do goals make us selectively perceptive, they also motivate us to act. The instructor's deadline for turning in your term project would prompt you to complete it, as opposed to going out with friends, watching television, or studying for another course. Generally, the level of effort expended is proportionate to the difficulty of the goal.

Goals Increase Persistence   Within the context of goal setting, persistence represents the effort expended on a task over an extended period of time: It takes effort to run 100 meters; it takes persistence to run a 26-mile marathon. Persistent people tend to see obstacles as challenges to be overcome rather than as reasons to fail. A difficult goal that is important to an individual is a constant reminder to keep exerting effort in the appropriate direction. This is a fundamental reason why investors are keenly interested in the goals executives must meet in order to earn incentives such as stock grants and bonuses. In today's highly competitive marketplace, companies are linking a growing share of executives' pay to profits and share price. Executives know that investors are watching to see whether they meet the targets and won't hesitate to push for their ouster if they fail to deliver.[56] Therefore, says Ira Kay, a director of the consulting firm Watson Wyatt, "Setting sufficiently challenging performance goals and appropriate corporate performance metrics is an extremely important part of the executive pay process."[57] Similarly,

Mitsubishi and Emory University Attempt to Set Sustainability Goals

Because sustainability officers are a fairly new breed, setting and prioritizing goals can be overwhelming. Most companies have already begun some green initiatives, so the first step is to look at what has already been accomplished and what else needs attention. Mitsubishi started with a corporate social responsibility survey to look at the activities it was already doing so its CSO could determine which areas needed special attention. The idea was to take a fresh look at the impact that climate change, resource depletion, and oil and gas prices were having on the business and see these issues as business risks—not just from a compliance standpoint, but also from a strategic planning standpoint.

Emory University looked at what it could do quickly without much effort to jump-start its goal setting. School leaders also decided that before they talked about going beyond mere compliance in environmental

health and safety, they needed to make sure they were absolutely compliant with current regulations. The Emory team also listed some purely aspirational goals, such as reducing energy consumption by 25 percent and having 75 percent local or sustainable foods in their hospitals and cafeterias by 2015. Team members weren't sure how they were going to reach the energy reduction goal when they set it, but since have found ways to accomplish it.

Why would it be hard to set sustainability goals? Explain.

SOURCE: From N H Woodward, "New Breed of Human Resource Leader," *HR Magazine*, June 2008, p 56. Copyright 2008 by Society for Human Resource Management (SHRM). Reproduced with permission of Society for Human Resource Management via Copyright Clearance Center.

---

in the world of sports, after Irish golfer Padraig Harrington won the British Open, he announced that his goal was to win more major titles, saying, "You have to have goals to keep you moving forward. If your goal is to win one major, then that would be it. I am definitely focused on winning more than one."[58]

Goals Foster the Development and Application of Task Strategies and Action Plans   If you are here and your goal is out there somewhere, you face the problem of getting from here to there. For example, think about the challenge of starting a business. Do you want to earn profits, grow larger, or make the world a better place? To get there, you have to make a tremendous number of decisions and complete a myriad of tasks. Goals can help because they encourage people to develop strategies and action plans that enable them to achieve their goals. A series of studies conducted in South Africa, Zimbabwe, and Namibia found that small businesses were more likely to grow and succeed if their owners engaged in "elaborate and proactive planning."[59]

Irish golfer, Padraig Harrington, won the PGA Championship in 2008.

Practical Lessons from Goal-Setting Research

Research consistently has supported goal setting as a motivational technique. Setting performance goals increases individual, group, and organizational performance. Further, the positive effects of goal setting were found in six other countries or regions: Australia, Canada, the Caribbean, England, West Germany, and Japan. Goal setting works in different cultures. Reviews of the many goal-setting studies conducted over the past few decades have given managers five practical insights:

I. *Specific high goals lead to greater performance.* **Goal specificity** pertains to the quantifiability of a goal. For example, a goal of selling nine cars a month

Goal specificity

Quantifiability of a goal.

229

is more specific than telling a salesperson to do his or her best. Results from more than 1,000 studies entailing over 88 different tasks and 40,000 people demonstrated that performance was greater when people had specific high goals.[60]

2. *Feedback enhances the effect of specific, difficult goals.* Feedback plays a key role in all of our lives. Feedback lets people know if they are headed toward their goals or if they are off course and need to redirect their efforts. Goals plus feedback is the recommended approach.[61] Goals inform people about performance standards and expectations so that they can channel their energies accordingly. In turn, feedback provides the information needed to adjust direction, effort, and strategies for goal accomplishment.

3. *Participative goals, assigned goals, and self-set goals are equally effective.* Both managers and researchers are interested in identifying the best way to set goals. Should goals be participatively set, assigned, or set by the employee him or herself? A summary of goal-setting research indicated that no single approach was consistently more effective than others in increasing performance.[62] Managers are advised to use a contingency approach by picking a method that seems best suited for the individual and situation at hand.

Action plan

Activities or tasks to be accomplished to obtain a goal.

4. *Action planning facilitates goal accomplishment.* An **action plan** outlines the activities or tasks that need to be accomplished in order to obtain a goal. They can also include dates associated with completing each task, resources needed, and obstacles that must be overcome. Managers can use action plans as a vehicle to have performance discussions with employees, and employees can use them to monitor progress toward goal achievement. An action plan also serves as a cue to remind us of what we should be working on, which in turn was found to lead to goal-relevant behavior and success.[63] Finally, managers are encouraged to allow employees to develop their own action plans because this autonomy fuels higher goal commitment and a sense of doing meaningful work.[64]

Goal commitment

Amount of commitment to achieving a goal.

5. *Goal commitment and monetary incentives affect goal-setting outcomes.* **Goal commitment** is the extent to which an individual is personally committed to achieving a goal. In general, an individual is expected to persist in attempts to accomplish a goal when he or she is committed to it. Researchers believe that goal commitment moderates the relationship between the difficulty of a goal and performance. That is, difficult goals lead to higher performance only when employees are committed to their goals. Conversely, difficult goals are hypothesized to lead to lower performance when people are not committed to their goals. A meta-analysis of 21 studies based on 2,360 people supported these predictions.[65] It also is important to note that people are more likely to commit to high goals when they have high self-efficacy about successfully accomplishing their goals.

Like goal setting, the use of monetary incentives to motivate employees is seldom questioned. Unfortunately, research uncovered some negative consequences when goal achievement is linked to individual incentives. Empirical studies demonstrated that goal-based bonus incentives produced higher commitment to easy goals and lower commitment to difficult goals. People were reluctant to commit to high goals that were tied to monetary incentives. People with high goal commitment also offered less help to their coworkers when they received goal-based bonus incentives to accomplish difficult individual goals. Individuals also neglected aspects of the job that were not covered in the performance goals.[66]

These findings underscore some of the dangers of using goal-based incentives, particularly for employees in complex, interdependent jobs requiring cooperation. Managers need to consider the advantages, disadvantages, and dilemmas of goal-based incentives prior to implementation.

LO.8 Motivating Employees through Job Design

to the point

What are the similarities and differences between the mechanistic, motivational, biological, and perceptual-motor approaches to job design?

Job design is used when a manager suspects that the type of work an employee performs or characteristics of the work environment are causing motivational problems. **Job design,** also referred to as *job redesign,* "refers to any set of activities that involve the alteration of specific jobs or interdependent systems of jobs with the intent of improving the quality of employee job experience and their on-the-job productivity."[67] A team of researchers examined the various methods for conducting job design and integrated them into an interdisciplinary framework that contains four major approaches: mechanistic, motivational, biological, and perceptual-motor.[68] As you will learn, each approach to job design emphasizes different outcomes. This section discusses these four approaches to job design and focuses most heavily on the motivational methods.

Job design

Changing the content or process of a specific job to increase job satisfaction and performance.

The Mechanistic Approach

The mechanistic approach draws from research in industrial engineering and scientific management and is most heavily influenced by the work of Frederick Taylor. Taylor, a mechanical engineer, developed the principles of scientific management while working at both Midvale Steel Works and Bethlehem Steel in Pennsylvania. He observed very little cooperation between management and workers and found that employees were underachieving by engaging in output restriction, which Taylor called "systematic soldiering." Taylor's interest in scientific management grew from his desire to improve upon this situation.

  Scientific management is "that kind of management which conducts a business or affairs by *standards* established by facts or truths gained through *systematic* observation, experiment, or reasoning."[69] Taylor's approach focused on using research and experimentation to determine the most efficient way to perform jobs. The application of scientific management involves the following five steps: (1) develop standard methods for performing jobs by using time and motion studies, (2) carefully select employees with the appropriate abilities, (3) train workers to use the standard methods and procedures, (4) support workers and reduce interruptions, and (5) provide incentives to reinforce performance.[70] Because jobs are highly specialized and standardized when they are designed according to the principles of scientific management, this approach to job design targets efficiency, flexibility, and employee productivity.

  Designing jobs according to the principles of scientific management has both positive and negative consequences. Positively, employee efficiency and productivity are increased. On the other hand, research reveals that simplified, repetitive jobs also lead to job dissatisfaction, poor mental health, higher levels of stress, and low sense of accomplishment and personal growth.[71] These negative consequences paved the way for the motivational approach to job design.

Scientific management

Using research and experimentation to find the most efficient way to perform a job.

Motivational Approaches

The motivational approaches to job design attempt to improve employees' affective and attitudinal reactions such as job satisfaction and intrinsic motivation as well as a host of behavioral outcomes such as absenteeism, turnover, and performance. We discuss four key motivational techniques: job enlargement, job enrichment, job rotation, and a contingency approach called the job characteristics model.

Job enlargement

Putting more variety into a job.

Job Enlargement
This technique was first used in the late 1940s in response to complaints about tedious and overspecialized jobs. **Job enlargement** involves putting more variety into a worker's job by combining specialized tasks of comparable difficulty. Some call this *horizontally loading* the job. Researchers recommend using job enlargement as part of a broader approach that uses multiple motivational methods because it does not have a significant and lasting positive effect on job performance by itself.[72]

Job rotation

Moving employees from one specialized job to another.

Job Rotation
As with job enlargement, job rotation's purpose is to give employees greater variety in their work. **Job rotation** calls for moving employees from one specialized job to another. Rather than performing only one job, workers are trained and given the opportunity to perform two or more separate jobs on a rotating basis. By rotating employees from job to job, managers believe they can stimulate interest and motivation while providing employees with a broader perspective of the organization. Tata Consultancy Services (TCS), for example, uses job rotation as a way to develop its workforce and provide employees with exposure to international operations (see the Real World/Real People feature on page 233).[73] Other proposed advantages of job rotation include increased worker flexibility and easier scheduling because employees are cross-trained to perform different jobs. Organizations also use job rotation as a vehicle to place new employees into jobs of their choice. The idea is that turnover is reduced and performance increases because people self-select their jobs.[74]

Despite positive experiences from companies like TCS, it is not possible to draw firm conclusions about the value of job rotation programs because they have not been adequately researched.

Job enrichment

Building achievement, recognition, stimulating work, responsibility, and advancement into a job.

Job Enrichment
Job enrichment is the practical application of Frederick Herzberg's motivator–hygiene theory of job satisfaction that we discussed earlier in this chapter. Specifically, **job enrichment** entails modifying a job such that an employee has the opportunity to experience achievement, recognition, stimulating work, responsibility, and advancement. These characteristics are incorporated into a job through vertical loading. Rather than giving employees additional tasks of similar difficulty (horizontal loading), *vertical loading* consists of giving workers more responsibility. In other words, employees take on tasks normally performed by their supervisors.

Intrinsic motivation

Motivation caused by positive internal feelings.

The Job Characteristics Model
Two OB researchers, J Richard Hackman and Greg Oldham, played a central role in developing the job characteristics approach. These researchers tried to determine how work can be structured so that employees are internally or intrinsically motivated. **Intrinsic motivation** occurs when an individual is "turned on to one's work because of the positive internal feelings

Tata Consultancy Services Uses Job Rotation

India-based Tata Consultancy Services (TCS), a software services and consulting company, considers job rotation a key strategy for developing its workforce and delivering added value to customers. The overseas program sends employees native to India to contribute to TCS operations in countries such as China, Hungary, and South America, among others. With offices in 42 countries globally and customers spread throughout the world, the ability to send skilled workers overseas is a must. But it also helps TCS provide better service since it draws on the strength of its entire workforce, rather than simply relying on whatever talent can be found in the office located closest to the customer. "It gives us the opportunity to offer a value proposition to our customers from the point of view of quality and knowledge," says Ajoy Mukherjee, vice president, head, global human resources.

Overseas assignments at TCS usually span 18 to 24 months, with employees learning both from their work with the customer, as well as from fellow TCS employees who are based permanently at that location. When the employee returns to India, he or she usually will continue working on the same kind of projects that were worked on abroad, thereby transferring the knowledge gained overseas to the home office. "The rotation is essential in building the competency of our people," says Mukherjee. "They were able to go onsite and meet face-to-face with our customers, and see how things work in another country." In addition to enhancing technical skills, the international people skills of those on overseas assignments are boosted.

Why would this rotation program increase employee satisfaction and performance?

SOURCE: Excerpted from M Weinstein, "Foreign but Familiar," *Training*, January 2009, p 22. Used with permission of Nielsen Business Media, Inc.

---

that are generated by doing well, rather than being dependent on external factors (such as incentive pay or compliments from the boss) for the motivation to work effectively."[75] These positive feelings power a self-perpetuating cycle of motivation. As shown in Figure 8–4, internal work motivation is determined by three psychological states. In turn, these psychological states are fostered by the presence of five core job dimensions. The object of this approach is to promote high intrinsic motivation by designing jobs that possess the five core job characteristics shown in Figure 8–4. Let us examine the core job dimensions.

In general terms, **core job dimensions** are common characteristics found to a varying degree in all jobs. Three of the job characteristics shown in Figure 8–4 combine to determine experienced meaningfulness of work:

Core job dimensions
Job characteristics found to various degrees in all jobs.

- *Skill variety.* The extent to which the job requires an individual to perform a variety of tasks that require him or her to use different skills and abilities.

- *Task identity.* The extent to which the job requires an individual to perform a whole or completely identifiable piece of work. In other words, task identity is high when a person works on a product or project from beginning to end and sees a tangible result.

- *Task significance.* The extent to which the job affects the lives of other people within or outside the organization.

Experienced responsibility is elicited by the job characteristic of autonomy, defined as follows:

- *Autonomy.* The extent to which the job enables an individual to experience freedom, independence, and discretion in both scheduling and determining the procedures used in completing the job.

Figure 8–4   *The Job Characteristics Model*

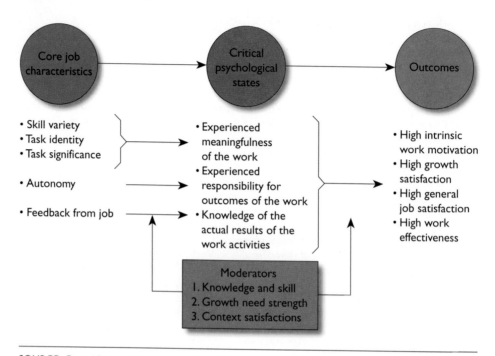

SOURCE: From J Richard Hackman and Greg R Oldham, *Work Redesign* (Prentice Hall Organizational Development Series), 1st, © 1980, p 90. Reproduced by permission of Pearson Education, Inc., Upper Saddle River, New Jersey.

Finally, knowledge of results is fostered by the job characteristic of feedback, defined as follows:

*   *Feedback.* The extent to which an individual receives direct and clear information about how effectively he or she is performing the job.[76]

Hackman and Oldham recognized that everyone does not want a job containing high amounts of the five core job characteristics. They incorporated this conclusion into their model by identifying three attributes that affect how individuals respond to job enrichment. These attributes are concerned with the individual's knowledge and skill, growth need strength (representing the desire to grow and develop as an individual), and context satisfactions (see the box labeled Moderators in Figure 8–4). Context satisfactions represent the extent to which employees are satisfied with various aspects of their job, such as satisfaction with pay, coworkers, and supervision.

There are several practical implications associated with using the job characteristics model to enhance intrinsic motivation: Steps for applying this model are shown in Table 8–3. Managers may want to use this model to increase employee job satisfaction and organizational commitment. A recent meta-analysis involving 259 studies and over 75,000 people demonstrated a moderately strong relationship between job characteristics and satisfaction.[77] Consistent with this finding, The Container Store in Coppell, Texas, and Principal Financial Group in Des Moines, Iowa, attempted to enhance employees' satisfaction by designing more autonomy into employees' jobs. Both organizations allow employees to select from a variety of work schedules that meet their needs.[78] Research supports this motivational

Table 8–3   *Steps for Applying the Job Characteristics Model*

1. Diagnose the work environment to determine if a performance problem is due to de-motivating job characteristics. Hackman and Oldham developed a self-report instrument for managers to use called the job diagnostic survey: It is shown and used in the Group Exercise, which can be found on the book's Web site. Diagnosis begins by determining whether the core job characteristics are low or high. If the job characteristics are lower than desired, a manager proceeds to step 2. If the performance problem is not due to low job characteristics, then a manager looks to apply another model of motivation or human behavior to solve the performance problem.

2. Determine whether job redesign is appropriate for a given group of employees. Job redesign is most likely to work in a participative environment in which employees have the necessary knowledge and skills to perform the enriched tasks and their job satisfaction is average to high.

3. Determine how to best redesign the job. The focus of this effort is to increase those core job characteristics that are low. Employee input is essential during this step to determine the details of a redesign initiative.

strategy, as autonomy was found to be positively associated with job performance and proactive work behaviors.[79]

The same large-scale meta-analysis mentioned above further showed that managers can enhance employees' intrinsic motivation, job involvement, and performance, while reducing absenteeism and stress by increasing the core job characteristics.[80] On the negative side, however, job redesign appears to reduce the quantity of output just as often as it has a positive effect. Caution and situational appropriateness are advised. For example, one study demonstrated that job redesign works better in less-complex organizations (small plants or companies).[81] Nonetheless, managers are likely to find noticeable increases in the quality of performance after a job redesign program. Results from 21 experimental studies revealed that job redesign resulted in a median increase of 28% in the quality of performance.[82]

go to the Web for the Group Exercise: Applying the Job Characteristics Model

Biological and Perceptual-Motor Approaches

The biological approach to job design is based on research from biomechanics, work physiology, and ergonomics and focuses on designing the work environment to reduce employees' physical strain, fatigue, and health complaints. An attempt is made to redesign jobs so that they eliminate or reduce the amount of repetitive motions from a worker's job. Ford Motor Company uses virtual reality in its biological approach to job design. In a Dearborn, Michigan, laboratory, technicians wearing sensors and virtual-reality goggles go through the motions required to assemble newly designed vehicles. Cameras and motion-capture software collect data from the sensors and create animated images of the assembly jobs. Then

Ford Motor Co. ergonomics specialist places virtual reality goggles on an employee. How does this approach lower costs and boost quality of their vehicles and their jobs?

ergonomics specialists analyze each job, looking for potentially painful, difficult, or repetitive movements that could cause discomfort and injuries. Jobs—or the vehicles themselves—are redesigned to prevent these problems before the vehicle assembly even begins. Besides making assembly-line jobs less painful, the approach has lowered costs and boosted quality.[83]

The perceptual-motor approach is derived from research that examines human factors engineering, perceptual and cognitive skills, and information processing. This approach to job design emphasizes the reliability of work outcomes by examining error rates, accidents, and workers' feedback about facilities and equipment.[84] Toyota Motor Company applies such principles in developing standard procedures and training for its manufacturing plants around the world. To prepare workers in China, the company taught 3,000 detailed assembly-line tasks by displaying videos above workstations simulating factory setups. The videos teach workers how to perform tasks as basic as holding a screw or air gun in the way that is most efficient, delivers consistent quality, and is least tiring. As the company simplifies jobs for inexperienced workers in places like China, it discovers solutions that can apply anywhere in the world. For example, instead of asking workers to go to bins to choose parts, Toyota started delivering all the needed parts to workers inside containers placed in the otherwise empty car bodies. The process is so efficient that Toyota is starting to use it in its Mississippi factory.[85]

Repetitive motion disorders (RMDs)

Muscular disorders caused by repeated motions.

The frequency of using both the biological and perceptual-motor approaches to job redesign is increasing in light of the number of workers who experience injuries related to overexertion or repetitive motion. **Repetitive motion disorders (RMDs)** are "a family of muscular conditions that result from repeated motions performed in the course of normal work or daily activities. RMDs include carpal tunnel syndrome, bursitis, tendonitis, epicondylitis, ganglion cyst, tenosynovitis, and trigger finger. RMDs are caused by too many uninterrupted repetitions of an activity or motion, unnatural or awkward motions such as twisting the arm or wrist, overexertion, incorrect posture, or muscle fatigue."[86] According to data from the Bureau of Labor Statistics, the incidence of some types of RMDs—in particular, carpal tunnel syndrome—has declined, but among the types of events that led to injury, repetitive motion resulted in the longest absences from work (a median of 19 days).[87] Injuries caused by repetitive motion are by far most likely in production jobs, especially among meat cutters, plumbers, and welders. To combat this problem, the Occupational Safety and Health Administration (OSHA) implemented guidelines regarding ergonomic standards in the workplace.

to the point

What are the issues managers should consider before implementing a motivational program?

LO.9 Putting Motivational Theories to Work

We started this chapter by noting that motivating employees is a key aspect of being an effective manager. That said, managers face two key challenges when trying to devise motivational programs. First, many managers are stretched in their job duties. They feel pulled in multiple dimensions and spend far too much time fighting fires instead of proactively focusing on employees' needs. This situation is frustrating and can lead to lower job satisfaction and motivation for managers. Although we feel sorry for people in this situation, it still is imperative for managers to find the time, and a positive attitude, to apply to the task of employee motivation. Jack and Suzy Welch commented on this issue and concluded that "no boss is doing his job properly if he's not letting each of his people know where they stand in constructive detail" and delivering "outsize rewards for outsize performance."[88] Second, managers may not know how to motivate people beyond the simple use of monetary rewards. It is important for managers to use a broader or more integrated approach when trying to motivate employees. This approach should consider the various theories and models discussed in this chapter as well as concepts covered in previous chapters. Organizations can help managers by providing them with training and coaching that focuses on how they can improve their ability to "motivate others."[89]

With the aforementioned in mind, this section raises several issues to be considered when designing an integrated approach toward employee motivation. Our intent is not to discuss all relevant considerations but rather to highlight a few important ones.

Assuming a motivational program is being considered to improve productivity, quality, or customer satisfaction, the first issue revolves around the difference between motivation and performance. Motivation and performance are not one and the same. Motivation is only one of several factors that influence performance. For example, poor performance may be more a function of outdated or inefficient materials and machinery, not having goals to direct one's attention, a monotonous job, feelings of inequity, a negative work environment characterized by political behavior and conflict, poor supervisory support and coaching, or poor work flow. Motivation cannot make up for a deficient job context. Managers, therefore, need to carefully consider the causes of poor performance and employee misbehavior.

Individual differences represent one of the first causes of low motivation that should be considered. For example, low motivation may be due to issues associated with managing diversity (recall our discussion in Chapter 2). The individual differences discussed in Chapters 5 and 6 (self-esteem, self-efficacy, personality, locus of control, intelligence, mental abilities, emotions, values, and attitudes) also are important causes of employee motivation. Managers are advised to develop employees so they have the ability and job knowledge to perform their jobs effectively. In addition, attempts should be made to nurture positive employee characteristics such as self-esteem, self-efficacy, positive emotions, and the need for achievement.

Because motivation is goal directed, the process of developing and setting goals should be consistent with our previous discussion. Moreover, the method used to evaluate performance also needs to be considered. Without a valid performance appraisal system, it is difficult, if not impossible, to accurately distinguish good and poor performers.

Finally, it is important for organizations to train their managers to properly assess people. Consistent with expectancy theory, managers should make extrinsic rewards contingent on performance. In doing so, however, it is important to consider three issues. First, managers need to ensure that performance goals are directed to achieve the "right" end results. For example, health insurers and medical groups wrestle over the relative focus on cost savings versus patient satisfaction. Consider the case of Oakland-based Kaiser Permanente:

Telephone clerks at California's largest HMO received bonuses for keeping calls with patients brief and limiting the number of doctor visits they set up. . . . The California

Nurses Association, the union representing Kaiser's registered nurses, derided the program as deceitful and harmful to patients with serious medical problems.

"Patients don't understand they're talking to a high school graduate with no nursing background," [Jim] Anderson said.

The clerks, who generally have little to no medical training, answer phone calls from customers wanting to set up doctor appointments or asking simple medical questions.

Cash bonuses were paid to those who made appointments for fewer than 35% of callers and spent less than an average of three minutes, 45 seconds on the phone with each patient. Clerks were also encouraged to transfer fewer than 50% of the calls to registered nurses for further evaluation.[90]

How do you feel about Kaiser Permanente's plan? How might it be changed to more effectively motivate employees to provide higher-quality care?

Second, the promise of increased rewards will not prompt higher effort and good performance unless those rewards are clearly tied to performance and they are large enough to gain employees' interests or attention.[91]

Third, equity theory tells us that motivation is influenced by employee perceptions about the fairness of reward allocations. Motivation is decreased when employees believe rewards are inequitably allocated. Rewards also need to be integrated appropriately into the appraisal system. If performance is measured at the individual level, individual achievements need to be rewarded. On the other hand, when performance is the result of group effort, rewards should be allocated to the group.

Feedback also should be linked with performance. Feedback provides the information and direction needed to keep employees focused on relevant tasks, activities, and goals. Managers should strive to provide specific, timely, and accurate feedback to employees.

Finally, we end this chapter by noting that an organization's culture (recall our discussion in Chapter 3) significantly influences employee motivation and behavior. A positive self-enhancing culture is more likely to engender higher motivation and commitment than a culture dominated by suspicion, faultfinding, and blame.

Summary of Key Concepts

1. *Contrast Maslow's, Alderfer's, and McClelland's need theories.* Maslow proposed that motivation is a function of five basic needs arranged in a prepotent hierarchy. The concept of a stair-step hierarchy has not stood up well under research. Alderfer concluded that three core needs explain behavior—existence, relatedness, and growth. He proposed that more than one need can be activated at a time and frustration of higher-order needs can influence the desire for lower-level needs. McClelland argued that motivation and performance vary according to the strength of an individual's need for achievement. High achievers prefer tasks of moderate difficulty, situations under their control, and a desire for more performance feedback than low achievers. Top managers should have a high need for power coupled with a low need for affiliation.

2. *Explain the practical significance of Herzberg's distinction between motivators and hygiene factors.* Herzberg believes job satisfaction motivates better job performance. His hygiene factors, such as policies, supervision, and salary, erase sources of dissatisfaction. On the other hand, his motivators, such as achievement, responsibility, and recognition, foster job satisfaction. Although Herzberg's motivator–hygiene theory of job satisfaction has been criticized on methodological grounds, it offers practical advice for motivating employees.

3. *Discuss the role of perceived inequity in employee motivation.* Equity theory is a model of motivation that explains how people strive for fairness and justice in social exchanges. On the job, feelings of inequity revolve around a person's evaluation of whether he or she receives adequate rewards to compensate for his or her contributive inputs. People perform these evaluations by comparing the perceived fairness of their employment exchange with that of relevant others. Perceived inequity creates motivation to restore equity.

4. *Explain the differences among distributive, procedural, and interactional justice.* Distributive, procedural, and interactional justice are the three key components underlying organizational justice. Distributive justice reflects the perceived fairness of how resources and rewards are distributed. Procedural justice represents the perceived fairness of the process and procedures used to make allocation decisions. Interactional justice entails the perceived fairness of a decision maker's behavior in the process of decision making.

5. *Describe the practical lessons derived from equity theory.* Equity theory has at least six practical implications. First, managers should pay attention to employees' perceptions of what is fair and equitable. It is the employee's view of reality that counts when trying to motivate someone, according to equity theory. Second, employees should be given a voice in decisions that affect them. Third, employees should be given the opportunity to appeal decisions that affect their welfare. Fourth, managers can promote cooperation and teamwork among group members by treating them equitably. Fifth, treating employees inequitably can lead to litigation and costly court settlements. Sixth, perceptions of justice are influenced by the leadership behavior exhibited by managers. Finally, managers need to pay attention to the organization's climate for justice because it influences employee attitudes and behavior.

6. *Explain Vroom's expectancy theory, and review its practical implications.* Expectancy theory assumes motivation is determined by one's perceived chances of achieving valued outcomes. Vroom's expectancy model of motivation reveals how effort→performance expectancies and performance→outcome instrumentalities influence the degree of effort expended to achieve desired (positively valent) outcomes. Managers are advised to enhance effort→performance expectancies by helping employees accomplish their performance goals.

With respect to instrumentalities and valences, managers should attempt to link employee performance and valued rewards.

7. *Explain how goal setting motivates an individual, and review the four practical lessons from goal-setting research.* Four motivational mechanisms of goal setting are as follows: (1) Goals direct one's attention, (2) goals regulate effort, (3) goals increase one's persistence, and (4) goals encourage development of goal-attainment strategies and action plans. Research identifies four practical lessons about goal setting. First, specific high goals lead to greater performance. Second, feedback enhances the effect of specific, difficult goals. Third, participative goals, assigned goals, and self-set goals are equally effective. Fourth, goal commitment and monetary incentives affect goal-setting outcomes.

8. *Review the mechanistic, motivational, biological, and perceptual-motor approaches to job design.* The mechanistic approach is based on industrial engineering and scientific management and focuses on increasing efficiency, flexibility, and employee productivity. Motivational approaches aim to improve employees' affective and attitudinal reactions and behavioral outcomes. Job enlargement, job enrichment, job rotation, and a contingency approach called the job characteristics model are motivational approaches to job design. The biological approach focuses on designing the work environment to reduce employees' physical strain, fatigue, and health complaints. The perceptual-motor approach emphasizes the reliability of work outcomes.

9. *Specify issues that should be addressed before implementing a motivational program.* Managers need to consider the variety of causes of poor performance. Motivation is only one of several factors that influence performance. Managers should not ignore the many individual differences that affect motivation. The goal-setting process should be consistent with the four practical lessons derived from goal-setting research. The method used to evaluate performance as well as the link between performance and rewards must be examined. Performance must be accurately evaluated, and rewards should be equitably distributed. Rewards should also be directly tied to performance. Finally, managers should recognize that employee motivation and behavior are influenced by organizational culture.

Key Terms

Motivation, 212
Content theories of motivation, 212
Process theories of motivation, 212
Needs, 213

Need hierarchy theory, 213
ERG theory, 214
Need for achievement, 215
Need for affiliation, 215

239

OB in Action Case Study

The Pay-for-Performance Program among Denver Teachers Hits a Roadblock[92]

The Denver Public Schools' pay-for-performance plan to motivate teachers was hailed as a model for the rest of the country when it took effect three years ago. It now stands on the verge of collapse after months of contract negotiations have stalemated.

Some teachers have staged sick-outs; others plan to welcome families back to school this week by handing out fliers denouncing the district's contract offer. There is even talk of a strike.

National education experts are dismayed. If merit pay can't work in Denver, "future initiatives are destined to fail," said Matthew Springer, director of the National Center on Performance Incentives at Vanderbilt University in Tennessee.

The breakdown stems from a philosophical disagreement between the school district and the union.

The district is offering large increases in incentive pay, but the biggest rewards will go to early—and to midcareer teachers—and to those willing to take risks by working in impoverished schools or taking jobs few others want, such as teaching middle-school math. Yearly bonuses for such work would nearly triple, to about $3,000.

The union is all for boosting bonuses but also wants an across-the-board pay increase. Most crucially, union leadership objects to proposed changes that would hold down salaries of veteran teachers to free more money for novices . . . . Nationwide, most teachers are paid based on two factors: education and experience. Denver's plan sets a base salary, but most raises depend on a teacher's accomplishments, and teachers aren't automatically rewarded for making it through another year. All new teachers must enroll in the incentive plan; it is optional for veterans.

One way to earn a salary bump is to guide students to high scores on Colorado's standardized tests, which is also used to measure progress under the federal No Child Left Behind Act.

Teachers are also rewarded for getting good evaluations and for continuing their own educations. And they get bonuses for meeting student-achievement goals that have nothing to do with test scores.

Greg Ahrnsbrak, a gym teacher at a public high school here, earned a $356 increase last year by achieving his goal of boosting student fitness with a weight-training program.

Many such bonuses are tacked on to a teacher's base salary. And they are cumulative. So when a teacher earning $38,000 notches $3,000 in bonuses, the base salary rises to $41,000 the following year. If the teacher earns another $3,000 in incentives, the salary jumps again, to $44,000. . . .

Superintendent Michael Bennet wants to raise incentives for all teachers, but under his proposal only those with less than 13 years' experience would continue to get bonuses incorporated into their salaries. Veteran teachers would get annual bonus checks, but their base salaries wouldn't grow, except for cost-of-living adjustments. Mr. Bennet also aims to expand team incentives, such as facultywide bonuses for schools that show academic growth.

"It's a significant step forward," Mr. Bennet said.

Kim Ursetta, president of the teachers union, calls the modifications unacceptable, but she still says pay-for-performance deserves a shot.

Questions for Discussion

1. What is the source of conflict between the school system and the union?
2. To what extent does Denver's pay plan build on recommendations from equity and expectancy theory? Explain.
3. What role does organizational culture play in this case?
4. Using the various motivation theories discussed in this chapter, how would you revise the pay plan so that it would be acceptable to both the school system and union? Provide specific recommendations.

Should Retrocessions Be Allowed in the United States?[93]

A retrocession is a kickback that "asset managers may be skimming off investments. While little known in the US, the practice has been an open secret in European private banking for decades—and it recently surfaced as a perk that Zurich-based Credit Suisse may have received from Bernie Madoff's feeder funds.

"How does this work? Essentially, bankers get rebates from fund managers they park money with—and pocket the commissions instead of passing the savings on to clients. Retrocessions typically match 25% of a fund's management fee, says British hedge fund manager Fabien Pictet. So on a $2 billion investment, a management fee of 2%, or $40 million, would yield a $10 million kickback."

What Is Your Opinion about Retrocessions?

1. A retrocession is like getting a sales commission and thus should be allowed.
2. This is another way that bankers are taking advantage of investors. Commissions should be passed to investors and not kept by bankers. This practice should be against the law.
3. Bankers should be required to disclose this issue to potential investors and then let individuals decide for themselves. A person may be okay with this practice because they have a long-term relationship with the banker.
4. Invent other options.

For study material and exercises that apply to this chapter, visit our Web site, **www.mhhe.com/kreitner**

Chapter 9

Improving Job Performance with Goals, Feedback, Rewards, and Positive Reinforcement

It's the rare employer that can offer up the perfect blend of training, advancement opportunity, camaraderie, and perks. But Ultimate [Software], No. 1 on this year's list of the Best Medium Companies to Work for in America, comes as close as any. Founded in 1990 with four employees, Ultimate launched its first product in 1993, a DOS-based human resource, benefits, and payroll package. Scott Scherr, Ultimate's founder and chief executive officer, took the company public five years later.

Today, most of Ultimate's 810 employees work out of two sunny lakeside buildings on the edge of the Everglades [in Weston, Florida]. Last year, the company posted revenue of more than $151 million—a 33 percent increase over the previous year's earnings, even during these tough economic times. Company officials maintain that their business model—based on month-to-month payments rather than pricey long-term licenses—makes it easier to hold onto cash-strapped clients.

Employees credit Scherr for setting a tone that fosters loyalty and trust and makes the company a great place to work. Scherr sees the relationship with employees more pragmatically.

"If you take care of your employees, then they take care of you," says Scherr, a Bronx native who cut his teeth working for ADP, now one of Ultimate's competitors.

Ultimate employees rave about such uncommon benefits as fully paid health premiums for themselves, family members, and domestic partners; a 30 percent company match on 401(k) contributions; stock options; and annual tuition reimbursement of up to $5,280.

The education benefit—the maximum eligible for tax benefits—enables employees such as Jose Chinea, systems engineer, to return to school to hone their skills and, in turn, become more valuable.

"Ultimate understands the importance of helping to grow their employees and helping educate them," says Chinea, who received a master's degree in management and information systems in January and hopes to parlay that into a promotion.

Sales Analyst Lisa Jameson, who works out of her home in Dallas, still tears up when she recalls how Ultimate took her suggestion that the company offer paid adoption leave just before she adopted her oldest

Generous employee rewards have helped Florida-based Ultimate Software prosper during tough economic times.

son, Conner, in 2004. "I just thought I would ask," she says, adding that the congratulatory note she received from Scherr following the adoption was icing on the cake. Jameson used the benefit—six weeks of paid leave, on par with maternity leave—again in 2007 when she adopted son Tyler.

Several workers devastated in 2005 by back-to-back hurricanes also say the company came through for them, providing financial assistance and emotional support.

When sales representative Kathy Collins tried to return an advance she had requested after her home was destroyed by Hurricane Katrina, company officials waved her off. "That's the type of family I have at Ultimate Software," she says.[1]

FOR DISCUSSION

What appeals most to you about working at Ultimate Software? Why?

LO.1 This final chapter of Part Two serves as a practical capstone for what we have learned so far in Parts One and Two. Our focus here is on improving individual job performance. We need to put to work what we have learned about cultural and individual differences, perception, and motivation. Some companies, such as Ultimate Software in the opening vignette, do a good job in this regard. A rewarding and employee-friendly culture, with lots of personal touches, creates loyal and motivated employees. Unfortunately, research shows that most managers fall far short when it comes to carefully nurturing job performance. A consulting firm's ongoing study of more than 500 managers since 1993 led to this conclusion:

> Only one out of 100 managers provides every direct report with these five basics every day:
>
> - Performance requirements and standard operating procedures related to tasks and responsibilities.
> - Defined parameters, measurable goals and concrete deadlines for all work assignments for which the direct report will be held accountable.
> - Accurate monitoring, evaluation, and documentation of work performance.
> - Specific feedback on work performance with guidance for improvement.
> - Fairly distributed rewards and detriments [penalties].[2]

The researchers call this situation "under-management." The consequences of under-management are not good. According to the Society for Human Resource Management, "a new survey finds that only one in seven employees worldwide is fully engaged with their work. There is a vast, largely untapped reserve of employee performance potential."[3] A comprehensive approach to tapping this vast potential is performance management. **Performance management** is an organizationwide system whereby managers integrate the activities of goal setting, monitoring and evaluating, providing feedback and coaching, and rewarding employees on a continuous basis.[4] This contrasts with the haphazard tradition of annual performance appraisals,[5] a largely unsatisfying experience for everyone involved.[6] (See Learning Module B, on the book's Web site, for more on performance appraisal.) OB can shed valuable light on key aspects of performance management—namely, goal setting, feedback and coaching, and rewards and positive reinforcement.

As indicated in Figure 9–1, job performance needs a life-support system. Like an astronaut drifting in space without the protection and support of a space suit, job performance will not thrive without a support system. First, people with the

Performance management

Continuous cycle of improving job performance with goal setting, feedback and coaching, and rewards and positive reinforcement.

Figure 9–1   *Improving Individual Job Performance: A Continuous Process*

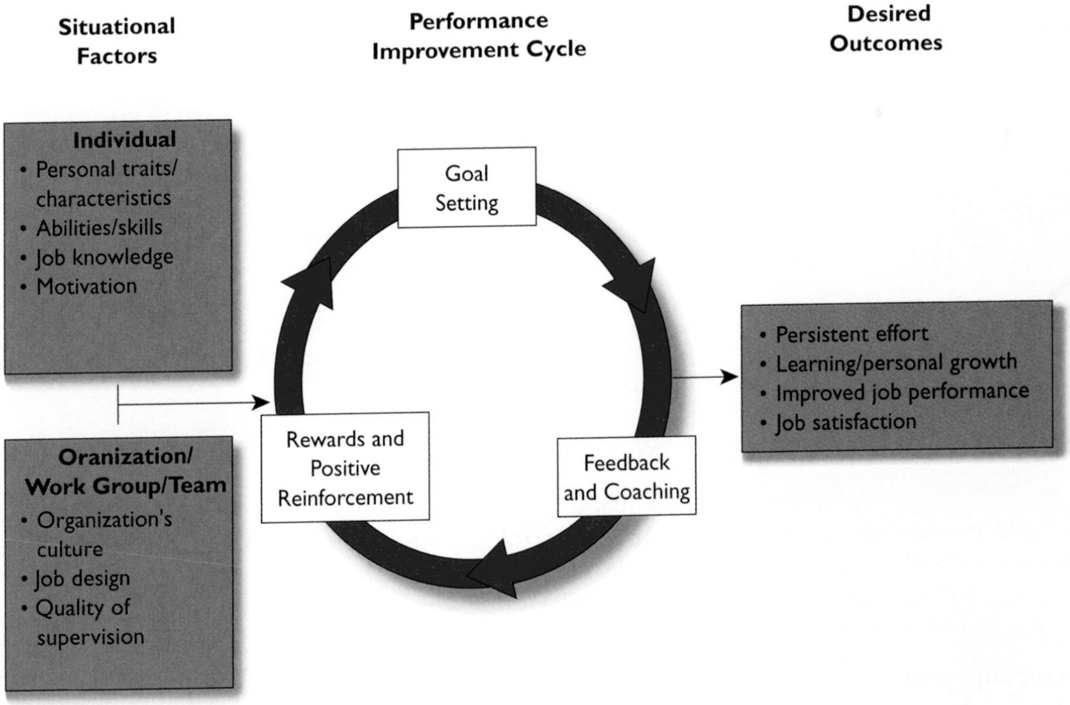

| Situational Factors | Performance Improvement Cycle | Desired Outcomes |

Individual
- Personal traits/ characteristics
- Abilities/skills
- Job knowledge
- Motivation

Oranization/ Work Group/Team
- Organization's culture
- Job design
- Quality of supervision

Goal Setting

Rewards and Positive Reinforcement

Feedback and Coaching

- Persistent effort
- Learning/personal growth
- Improved job performance
- Job satisfaction

requisite abilities, skills, and job knowledge need to be hired. Joe Kraus, co-founder and CEO of Jotspot, a Web page hosting service, offers this blunt advice:

Never compromise on hiring. Every time I've compromised, I've come to regret it. You have to be tough, even if that means not hiring people who could turn out to be great, because of the damage one person who isn't great can do.

Nothing demotivates people like the equal treatment of unequals. When you hire a bozo and treat him the same as a rock star, it deflates the rock star.[7]

Next, training is required to correct any job knowledge shortfalls.[8] The organization's structure, culture, and job design and supervisory practices also can facilitate or hinder job performance. At the heart of the model in Figure 9–1 are the key aspects of the performance improvement cycle that we explore in depth in this chapter. Importantly, it is a dynamic and continuous cycle requiring management's strategic oversight, followed up with day-to-day attention.

Line of sight

Employees know the organization's strategic goals and how they need to contribute.

Goal Setting

Goal setting in the workplace could use an extreme makeover. According to a Franklin Covey survey of workers in the United States, 56% don't "clearly understand their organization's most important goals" and an astounding 81% "don't have clearly defined goals."[9] These figures could be cut in half and still represent a very unproductive situation. The missing element here is what goal-setting experts call line of sight. Employees with a clear **line of sight** understand the organization's

to the point
What are the keys to an effective goal-setting process?

strategic goals and know what actions they need to take, both individually and as team members.[10] A good case in point is Bloomberg LP, the 9,400-employee financial information services company founded by New York City Mayor Michael Bloomberg:

> The company has a highly unusual compensation system that ties employee pay directly to the sale of terminals—or more precisely, to net installations, or "net installs." The concept behind this system is that *everyone* at the company should be driving toward only one goal: selling more Bloombergs. To underscore that point, large electronic signs hanging from the ceilings in the Bloomberg offices report progress on both sales and installations. Bells ring to mark a sale—multiple times if the news justifies it.[11]

To help you fully comprehend the power of goal setting, this section distinguishes between two types of goals, discusses management by objectives, and explains how to manage the goal-setting process.

Two Types of Goals

Goal-setting researchers have drawn an instructive distinction between performance outcome goals and learning goals. A **performance outcome goal** targets a specific end-result. A **learning goal,** in contrast, strives to improve creativity and develop skills (see the Real World/Real People feature on page 247). Managers typically overemphasize the former and ignore the latter as they try to "motivate" greater effort and achieve final results. But for employees who lack the necessary skills, performance outcome goals are more frustrating than motivating. When skills are lacking, a developmental process is needed wherein learning goals precede performance outcome goals. Goal researchers Gerard Seijts and Gary Latham explain with a golfing analogy:

> A performance outcome goal often distracts attention from the discovery of task-relevant strategies. For example, focusing on a golf score of 95 by novices may prevent them from focusing on the mastery of the swing and weight transfer and using the proper clubs necessary for attaining that score. . . .
>
> In short, the novice golfer must learn how to play the game before becoming concerned with attaining a challenging performance outcome (e.g., score equals 95).[12]

Management by Objectives

The motivational impact of performance goals and goal-based reward plans has been known for a long time. More than a century ago, Frederick Taylor attempted to scientifically establish how much work of a specified quality an individual should be assigned each day. He proposed that bonuses be based on accomplishing specific output quotas. Since the 1950s, goal setting has been promoted through a widely used management technique called management by objectives (MBO). **Management by objectives** is a management system that incorporates participation into decision making, goal setting, and objective feedback.[13] The central idea of MBO, getting individual employees to "own" a piece of a collective effort, is evident in this recent bit of advice from Google executive Paul Russell:

> Help your people map out their goals. Ask them to apply those aspirations to what they do every day. You'll build their sense of affiliation with the company and make them feel they belong. And they'll believe that they don't have to leave to accomplish their ambitions.[14]

Performance outcome goal

Targets a specific end-result.

Learning goal

Encourages learning, creativity, and skill development.

Management by objectives

Management system incorporating participation into decision making, goal setting, and feedback.

Starwood's New CEO Frits van Paasschen Runs on Goals

[Chairman of the board Bruce] Duncan says that van Paasschen, (pronounced "van passion") 47, stood out because of his "intellectual firepower," success-shaping global strategies for consumer products at Disney, Nike and Coors, his likable personality and the aggressive way he promised to tackle the job. Because he lacked hotel experience, he vowed to immerse himself in the industry. Since joining, he's visited 132 hotels in 20 countries and 45 cities. [He is fluent in English, Dutch, German, Italian, and Spanish.]

Van Paasschen's passion for running didn't hurt, either.

"That shows someone who has a plan and gets it done," Duncan says. "It shows he'll do whatever it takes."

Van Paasschen credits running with much of his management style. Business, he says, is about conquering personal fears, setting high goals for yourself and breaking barriers, which in many ways meshes with Starwood's culture.

What role have goals played in your life? Explain.

SOURCE: B De Lollis, "Starwood's CEO Takes an Idea and Runs with It," *USA Today*, June 23, 2008, pp 1B–2B.

Getting in shape for marathons helps Starwood's CEO Frits van Paasschen set tough goals to keep pace in the competitive hotel business.

A meta-analysis of MBO programs showed productivity gains in 68 of 70 different organizations. Specifically, results uncovered an average gain in productivity of 56% when top-management commitment was high. The average gain was only 6% when commitment was low. A second meta-analysis of 18 studies further demonstrated that employees' job satisfaction was significantly related to top management's commitment to an MBO implementation.[15] These impressive results are tempered by reports of ethical problems stemming from *extreme* pressure for results. Such was the case at IndyMac Bancorp, a mortgage lender seized by the government during the financial meltdown of 2008. According to one investigator: "There was a culture of top-down pressure to push through as many loans as possible—and to ignore the problems."[16] Ethically sound MBO programs marry learning goals and performance outcome goals anchored to high ethical standards.

Managing the Goal-Setting Process

There are three general steps to follow when implementing a goal-setting program.[17] Serious deficiencies in one step cannot make up for strength in the other two. The three steps need to be implemented in a systematic fashion.

Step 1: Set Goals A number of sources can be used as input during this goal-setting stage. Time and motion studies are one source. Goals also may be based on the average past performance of job holders. Third, the employee and his or her manager may set the goal participatively, through give-and-take negotiation.

Fourth, goals can be set by conducting external or internal benchmarking. Benchmarking is used when an organization wants to compare its performance or internal work processes to those of other organizations (external benchmarking) or to other internal units, branches, departments, or divisions within the organization (internal benchmarking). For example, a company might set a goal to surpass the customer service levels or profit of a benchmarked competitor. Finally, the overall strategy of a company (e.g., become the lowest-cost producer) may affect the goals set by employees at various levels in the organization.

In accordance with available research evidence, goals should be "SMART." SMART is an acronym that stands for specific, measurable, attainable, results oriented, and time bound. Table 9–1 contains a set of guidelines for writing SMART goals. There are two additional recommendations to consider when setting goals. First, for complex tasks, managers should train employees in problem-solving techniques and encourage them to develop a performance action plan. Action plans specify the strategies or tactics to be used in order to accomplish a goal.

Second, because of individual differences (recall our discussion in Chapter 5), it may be necessary to establish different goals for employees performing the same

Table 9–1   *Guidelines for Writing SMART Goals*

Specific	Goals should be stated in precise rather than vague terms. For example, a goal that provides for 20 hours of technical training for each employee is more specific than stating that a manager should send as many people as possible to training classes. Goals should be quantified when possible.
Measurable	A measurement device is needed to assess the extent to which a goal is accomplished. Goals thus need to be measurable. It also is critical to consider the quality aspect of the goal when establishing measurement criteria. For example, if the goal is to complete a managerial study of methods to increase productivity, one must consider how to measure the quality of this effort. Goals should not be set without considering the interplay between quantity and quality of output.
Attainable	Goals should be realistic, challenging, and attainable. Impossible goals reduce motivation because people do not like to fail. Remember, people have different levels of ability and skill.
Results oriented	Corporate goals should focus on desired end-results that support the organization's vision. In turn, an individual's goals should directly support the accomplishment of corporate goals. Activities support the achievement of goals and are outlined in action plans. To focus goals on desired end-results, goals should start with the word *to*, followed by verbs such as *complete, acquire, produce, increase*, and *decrease*. Verbs such as *develop, conduct, implement*, or *monitor* imply activities and should not be used in a goal statement.
Time bound	Goals specify target dates for completion.

SOURCE: From A J Kinicki, *Performance Management Systems* (Superstition Mt., AZ: Kinicki & Associates, Inc., 2009), pp 2–9. Reprinted with permission; all rights reserved.

job. For example, a study of 103 undergraduate business students revealed that individuals high in conscientiousness had higher motivation, had greater goal commitment, and obtained higher grades than students low in conscientiousness.[18]

An individual's goal orientation is another important individual difference to consider when setting goals. Three types of goal orientations are a learning goal orientation, a performance-prove goal orientation, and a performance-avoid goal orientation. A team of researchers described the differences and implications for goal setting in the following way:

> People with a high learning goal orientation view skills as malleable. They make efforts not only to achieve current tasks but also to develop the ability to accomplish future tasks. People with a high performance-prove goal orientation tend to focus on performance and try to demonstrate their ability by looking better than others. People with a high performance-avoid goal orientation also focus on performance, but this focus is grounded in trying to avoid negative outcomes.[19]

Although some studies showed that people set higher goals, exerted more effort, had higher self-efficacy, and achieved higher performance when they possessed a learning goal orientation as opposed to either a performance-prove or performance-avoid goal orientation, other research demonstrated a more complex series of relationships.[20] The best we can conclude is that an individual's goal orientation influences the actions that he or she takes in the pursuit of accomplishing goals in specific situations. Thus, managers are encouraged to consider individual differences when setting goals.

Step 2: Promote Goal Commitment
Obtaining goal commitment is important because employees are more motivated to pursue goals they view as reasonable, obtainable, and fair. Goal commitment may be increased by using an appropriate mix of the following techniques:

1. Provide an explanation for why the organization is implementing a goal-setting program.
2. Present the corporate goals, and explain how and why an individual's personal goals support them. Jeroen van der Veer, CEO of Royal Dutch Shell, advises: "The task of leaders is to simplify."[21] He says it should take no more than two minutes to communicate the direction of the organization.
3. Have employees establish their own goals and action plans. Encourage them to set challenging, stretch goals. Goals should be difficult, but not impossible.[22]
4. Train managers in how to conduct participative goal-setting sessions, and train employees in how to develop effective action plans.
5. Be supportive, and do not use goals to threaten employees.
6. Set goals that are under the employees' control, and provide them with the necessary resources.
7. Provide monetary incentives or other rewards for accomplishing goals.[23]

Step 3: Provide Support and Feedback
Step 3 calls for providing employees with the necessary support elements or resources to get the job done. This includes ensuring that each employee has the necessary abilities and information to reach his or her goals. As a pair of goal-setting experts succinctly stated, "Motivation without knowledge is useless."[24] Training often is required to

help employees achieve difficult goals. Moreover, managers should pay attention to employees' perceptions of effort→performance expectancies, self-efficacy, and valence of rewards. Finally, as we discuss next, employees should be provided with timely, specific feedback (knowledge of results) on how they are doing.

Feedback

to the point

Why is feedback important and how should it be given?

Employees' hearty appetite for feedback too often goes unfulfilled. For example, according to one survey, "43% of employees feel they don't get enough guidance to improve their performance."[25] Achievement-oriented students also want feedback. Following a difficult exam, for instance, students want to know two things: how they did and how their peers did. By letting students know how their work measures up to grading and competitive standards, an instructor's feedback permits the students to adjust their study habits so they can reach their goals. Likewise, managers in well-run organizations follow up goal setting with a feedback program to provide a rational basis for adjustment and improvement. For instance, consider the following remarks by Fred Smith, the founder and CEO of FedEx, the overnight delivery pioneer with over $35 billion in annual revenues and nearly 239,000 employees.[26] Smith's experience as a US Marine company commander during the Vietnam War helped shape his leadership style.

Fred Smith, CEO of FedEx, believes strong leadership involves providing specific and steady feedback to all employees.

> My leadership philosophy is a synthesis of the principles taught by the marines and every organization for the past 200 years.
>
> When people walk in the door, they want to know: What do you expect out of me? What's in this deal for me? What do I have to do to get ahead? Where do I go in this organization to get justice if I'm not treated appropriately? They want to know how they're doing. They want some feedback. And they want to know that what they are doing is important.
>
> If you take the basic principles of leadership and answer those questions over and over again, you can be successful dealing with people.[27]

Feedback

Objective information about performance.

As the term is used here, **feedback** is objective information about individual or collective performance. Subjective assessments such as "You're doing a poor job," "You're lazy," or "We really appreciate your hard work" do not qualify as objective feedback. But hard data such as units sold, days absent, dollars saved, projects completed, customers satisfied, and quality rejects are all candidates for objective feedback programs. Christopher D Lee, author of the book *Performance Conversations: An Alternative to Appraisals,* clarifies the concept of feedback by contrasting it with performance appraisals:

> Feedback is the exchange of information about the status and quality of work products. It provides a road map to success. It is used to motivate, support, direct, correct and regulate work efforts and outcomes. Feedback ensures that the manager and employees are in sync and agree on the standards and expectations of the work to be performed.

Traditional appraisals, on the other hand, discourage two-way communication and treat employee involvement as a bad thing. Employees are discouraged from participating in a performance review, and when they do, their responses are often considered "rebuttals."

To reverse this, successful performance management must contain a healthy degree of feedback and employee involvement.[28]

LO.2 Two Functions of Feedback

Experts say feedback serves two functions for those who receive it: one is *instructional* and the other *motivational*. Feedback instructs when it clarifies roles or teaches new behavior. For example, an assistant accountant might be advised to handle a certain entry as a capital item rather than as an expense item. On the other hand, feedback motivates when it serves as a reward or promises a reward.[29] Having the boss tell you that a grueling project you worked on earlier has just been completed can be a rewarding piece of news. As documented by researchers, the motivational function of feedback can be significantly enhanced by pairing *specific,* challenging goals with *specific* feedback about results.[30] With these two functions of feedback in mind, we now explore the vital role of feedback recipients, some practical lessons from feedback research, 360-degree feedback, and how to give feedback for coaching purposes.

Are the Feedback Recipients Ready, Willing, and Able?

Conventional wisdom says the more feedback organizational members get, the better. An underlying assumption is that feedback works automatically. Managers simply need to be motivated to give it. According to a meta-analysis of 23,663 feedback incidents, however, feedback is far from automatically effective. While feedback did, in fact, have a generally positive impact on performance, performance actually *declined* in more than 38% of the feedback incidents.[31] Feedback also can be warped by nontask factors, such as race. A laboratory study at Stanford University focused on cross-race feedback on the content (subjective feedback) and writing mechanics (objective feedback) of written essays. White students gave African-American students *less* critical *subjective* feedback than they did to white students. This positive racial bias disappeared with objective feedback.[32] These results are a bright caution light for those interested in improving job performance with feedback. Subjective feedback is easily contaminated by situational factors. Moreover, if objective feedback is to work as intended, managers need to understand the interaction between feedback recipients and their environment.[33]

The Recipient's Characteristics   Personality characteristics such as self-esteem and self-efficacy can help or hinder one's readiness for feedback. Those having low self-esteem and low self-efficacy generally do not actively seek feedback that, unfortunately, would tend to confirm those problems. Needs and goals also influence one's openness to feedback. In a laboratory study, Japanese psychology students who scored high on need for achievement responded more favorably to feedback than did their classmates who had low need for achievement.[34] This particular relationship likely exists in Western cultures as well. For example, 331 employees in the marketing department of a large public utility in the United States were found to seek feedback on important issues or when faced with uncertain situations. Long-tenured employees from this sample also were less likely to seek feedback than employees with little time on the job.[35] High self-monitors, those chameleonlike people we discussed in Chapter 5, are also more open to feedback because it helps them adapt their behavior to the situation. Recall from Chapter 5 that high self-monitoring employees were found to be better at initiating relationships with mentors (who typically provide feedback).[36] Low self-monitoring people, in contrast, are tuned into their own internal feelings more than they are to external cues. For example, someone observed that talking to media kingpin Ted Turner, a very low self-monitor, was like having a conversation with a radio!

Researchers have started to focus more directly on the recipient's actual desire for feedback, as opposed to indirectly on personality characteristics, needs, and goals. Everyday experience tells us that not everyone really wants the performance feedback they supposedly seek. Restaurant servers who ask, "How was everything?" while presenting the bill, typically are not interested in a detailed reply. (See the Real World/Real People feature on page 253.)

The Recipient's Perception of Feedback

The *sign* of feedback, a term used in feedback research, refers to whether it is positive or negative. Generally, people tend to perceive and recall positive feedback more accurately than they do negative feedback.[37] But feedback with a negative sign (e.g., being told your performance is below average) can have a positive motivational impact. In fact, in one study, those who were told they were below average on a creativity test subsequently outperformed those who were led to believe their results were above average. The subjects apparently took the negative feedback as a challenge and set and pursued higher goals. Those receiving positive feedback apparently were less motivated to do better.[38] Nonetheless, feedback with a negative sign or threatening content needs to be administered carefully to avoid creating insecurity and defensiveness. Self-efficacy also can be damaged by negative feedback, as discovered in a pair of experiments with business students. The researchers concluded, "To facilitate the development of strong efficacy beliefs, managers should be careful about the provision of negative feedback. Destructive criticism by managers which attributes the cause of poor performance to internal factors reduces both the beliefs of self-efficacy and the self-set goals of recipients."[39]

The Recipient's Cognitive Evaluation of Feedback

Upon receiving feedback, people cognitively evaluate factors such as its accuracy, the credibility of the source, the fairness of the system (e.g., performance appraisal system), their performance-reward expectancies, and the reasonableness of the standards. Any feedback that fails to clear one or more of these cognitive hurdles will be rejected or downplayed. Personal experience largely dictates how these factors are weighed. For instance, you would probably discount feedback from someone who exaggerates or from someone who performed poorly on the same task you have just successfully completed. In view of the "trust gap," discussed in Chapter 11, managerial credibility is an ethical matter of central importance today. According to the authors of the book *Credibility: How Leaders Gain and Lose It, Why People Demand It,* "without a solid foundation of personal credibility, leaders can have no hope of enlisting others in a common vision."[40] Managers who have proven untrustworthy and not credible have a hard time improving job performance through feedback.

Feedback from a source who apparently shows favoritism or relies on unreasonable behavior standards would be suspect.[41] Also, as predicted by expectancy

Culture Trumped Performance Ratings at ITT

Why was turnover so high? That's what ITT China President William E Taylor wanted to know when he visited the Shanghai sales office three years ago. The local manager had a simple answer for Taylor, then head of ITT's industrial products division. If the sales boss gave workers an average "3" on the 1–5 performance scale, they'd stop talking to him and in some cases, quit shortly after. "They're losing face in the organization," the manager lamented. "It would be great if we could do something about the scores."

It was comments like that, popping up around the globe, that helped ITT ultimately make the radical decision to ditch performance ratings altogether. In southern Europe, the focus on individual performance didn't sit well with the region's more "collective ethos," says James Durcan, director of ITT's talent development. And in Scandinavia, where there's more of "a sense of equality between bosses and workers," says Durcan, some workers asked, "What gives you the right to rate me a 3?"

Why is this an ethical matter, in addition to being good cross-cultural management?

SOURCE: Reprinted from J McGregor, "Case Study: To Adapt, ITT Let's Go of Unpopular Ratings," January 28, 2008, issue of *BusinessWeek* by special permission. Copyright © 2008 by The McGraw-Hill Companies, Inc.

motivation theory, feedback must foster high effort→performance expectancies and performance→reward instrumentalities if it is to motivate desired behavior.

> **go to the Web for the Self-Exercise:** How Strong Is Your Desire for Performance Feedback?

Practical Lessons from Feedback Research

After reviewing dozens of laboratory and field studies of feedback, a trio of OB researchers cited the following practical implications for managers:

- The acceptance of feedback should not be treated as a given; it is often misperceived or rejected. This is especially true in intercultural situations.
- Managers can enhance their credibility as sources of feedback by developing their expertise and creating a climate of trust.
- Negative feedback is typically misperceived or rejected.
- Although very frequent feedback may erode one's sense of personal control and initiative, feedback is too *infrequent* in most work organizations.
- Feedback needs to be tailored to the recipient.
- While average and below-average performers need extrinsic rewards for performance, high performers respond to feedback that enhances their feelings of competence and personal control.[42]

More recent research insights about feedback include the following:

- Computer-based performance feedback leads to greater improvements in performance when it is received directly from the computer system rather than via an immediate supervisor.[43]
- Recipients of feedback perceive it to be more accurate when they actively participate in the feedback session versus passively receiving feedback.[44]

Table 9–2   *Six Common Trouble Signs for Organizational Feedback Systems*

1. Feedback is used to punish, embarrass, or put down employees.
2. Those receiving the feedback see it as irrelevant to their work.
3. Feedback information is provided too late to do any good.
4. People receiving feedback believe it relates to matters beyond their control.
5. Employees complain about wasting too much time collecting and recording feedback data.
6. Feedback recipients complain about feedback being too complex or difficult to understand.

SOURCE: Adapted from C Bell and R Zemke, "On-Target Feedback," *Training*, June 1992, pp 36–44.

- Destructive criticism tends to cause conflict and reduce motivation.[45]
- "The higher one rises in an organization the less likely one is to receive quality feedback about job performance."[46]

Managers who act on these research implications and the trouble signs in Table 9–2 can build credible and effective feedback systems.

Our discussion to this point has focused on traditional downward feedback. Let us explore a newer and interesting approach to feedback in the workplace.

360-degree feedback

Comparison of anonymous feedback from one's superior, subordinates, and peers with self-perceptions.

LO.3 360-Degree Feedback

The concept of **360-degree feedback** involves letting individuals compare their own perceived performance with behaviorally specific (and usually anonymous) performance information from their manager, subordinates, and peers. Even outsiders may be involved in what is sometimes called full-circle feedback.[47]

A recent meta-analysis of twenty-four 360-degree feedback studies in which the recipients were rated two or more times prompted this helpful conclusion from the researchers:

Improvement is most likely to occur when feedback indicates that change is necessary, recipients have a positive feedback orientation, perceive a need to change their behavior, react positively to the feedback, believe change is feasible, set appropriate goals to regulate their behavior, and take actions that lead to skill and performance improvement.[48]

Top management support and an organizational climate of openness can help 360-degree feedback programs succeed. For example,

A G Lafley, chairman of Procter & Gamble, has the courage to handle 360-degree feedback and the common sense to make changes.

Procter & Gamble [chairman] A G Lafley finds out what his employees really think about him when he receives the results of his 360-degree feedback evaluation.

The human resources tool that assesses strengths and weaknesses can be brutally honest because it lets a circle of people from executives on down give him anonymous performance reviews. The results show that others at P&G think Lafley is impatient. Lafley must also test the patience of others, because he is excoriated for being chronically late to meetings.[49]

Research evidence and personal experience lead us to *favor* anonymity and *discourage* linking 360-degree feedback to pay and promotion decisions.

According to one expert, *trust* is the issue:

Trust is at the core of using 360-degree feedback to enhance productivity. Trust determines how much an individual is willing to contribute for an employer. Using 360 confidentially, for developmental purposes, builds trust; using it to trigger pay and personnel decisions puts trust at risk.[50]

Thus, 360-degree feedback definitely has a place in the development of managerial skills, especially in today's team-based organizations.

How to Give Feedback for Coaching Purposes and Organizational Effectiveness

Managers need to keep the following tips in mind when giving feedback as part of a comprehensive performance management program:

- Focus on *performance,* not personalities.
- Give *specific* feedback linked to learning goals and performance outcome goals.
- Channel feedback toward *key result areas* for the organization.
- Give feedback as *soon* as possible.
- Give feedback to coach *improvement,* not just for final results.
- Base feedback on *accurate* and *credible* information.
- Pair feedback with *clear expectations* for improvement.[51]

go to the Web for the Self-Exercise: What Kind of Feedback Are You Getting?

Organizational Reward Systems

to the point

What should managers do to improve job performance with intrinsic and extrinsic rewards?

Rewards are an ever-present and always controversial feature of organizational life. (Think of the ongoing debate over CEO compensation packages in the hundreds of millions of dollars.)[52] Some employees see their jobs as the source of a paycheck and little else. Others derive great pleasure from their jobs and association with coworkers. In fact, according to a Gallup survey, 55% of American workers said "they would continue to work even if they won a lottery jackpot to the tune of $10 million."[53] (How about you?) Even volunteers who donate their time to charitable organizations, such as the Red Cross, walk away with rewards in

Figure 9–2   *A General Model of Organizational Reward Systems*

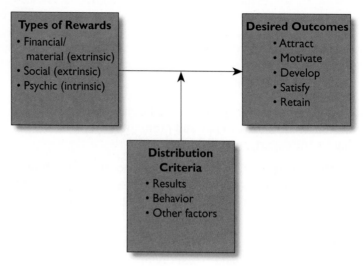

the form of social recognition and pride of having given unselfishly of their time. Hence, the subject of organizational rewards includes, but goes far beyond, monetary compensation.[54] This section examines key components of organizational reward systems to provide a conceptual background for discussing the timely topic of pay for performance.

Despite the fact that reward systems vary widely, it is possible to identify and interrelate some common components. The model in Figure 9–2 focuses on three important components: (1) types of rewards, (2) distribution criteria, and (3) desired outcomes. Let us examine these components.

L0.4 Types of Rewards

Extrinsic rewards

Financial, material, or social rewards from the environment.

Intrinsic rewards

Self-granted, psychic rewards.

Financial, material, and social rewards qualify as **extrinsic rewards** because they come from the environment. Psychic rewards, however, are **intrinsic rewards** because they are self-granted. An employee who works to obtain extrinsic rewards, such as money or praise, is said to be extrinsically motivated. One who derives pleasure from the task itself or experiences a sense of competence or self-determination is said to be intrinsically motivated. The relative importance of extrinsic and intrinsic rewards is a matter of culture and personal tastes.[55]

Reward Distribution Criteria

According to one expert on organizational reward systems, three general criteria for the distribution of rewards are as follows:

- *Performance: results.* Tangible outcomes such as individual, group, or organization performance; quantity and quality of performance.

- *Performance: actions and behaviors.* Such as teamwork, cooperation, risk taking, creativity.

- *Nonperformance considerations.* Customary or contractual, where the type of job, nature of the work, equity, tenure, level in hierarchy, and so forth are rewarded.[56]

One trend today is toward performance criteria and away from nonperformance criteria such as seniority. Another trend involves mixing reward distribution criteria: Westinghouse Electric is a recent case in point: "To ensure the rank and file get in gear, managers are now being graded not just on the dollars they generate but also on how many customers they've spoken to and how many proposals they've sent out."[57]

Desired Outcomes of the Reward System

As listed in Figure 9–2, a good reward system should attract talented people and motivate and satisfy them once they have joined the organization.

"We don't have medical or a 401(k) but there *are* treats"
SOURCE: *Harvard Business Review*, March 2008, p 82.

Further, a good reward system should foster personal growth and development and keep talented people from leaving. A prime example is Tulsa-based QuikTrip: "Employees are treated so well at this 24-hour convenience chain—wages, benefits, and training—that they stay around for the long haul. More than 200 have been here more than 20 years."[58]

The Building Blocks of Intrinsic Rewards and Motivation

As defined earlier, intrinsic rewards are self-granted. But this does not leave management out of the picture. Indeed, there is a great deal managers can do to create situations in which employees are more likely to experience intrinsic rewards and be intrinsically motivated. Kenneth Thomas's model of intrinsic motivation provides helpful direction.[59] His model combines the job characteristics model of job design (discussed in Chapter 8), the concept of empowerment (discussed in Chapter 15), and Edward Deci and Richard Ryan's cognitive evaluation theory. Deci and Ryan contend that people must satisfy their needs for autonomy and competence when completing a task for it to be intrinsically motivating.[60] Thomas uses the concept of *building blocks* to show managers how to construct the right conditions for four basic intrinsic rewards: meaningfulness, choice, competence, and progress (see Figure 9–3). Let us examine management's leadership challenges for each building block.

Actress Emma Watson (Hermione to Harry Potter movie fans) is worth $20 million, yet leads a simple life and plans on college. What would you do in her situation?

Leading for Meaningfulness   Managers lead for meaningfulness by *inspiring* their employees and *modeling* desired behaviors. Figure 9–3 reveals how managers can accomplish this by helping employees to identify their passions at work and creating an exciting organizational vision employees feel connected to. In support of this

Figure 9–3 *Thomas's Building Blocks for Intrinsic Rewards and Motivation*

Choice • Delegated authority • Trust in workers • Security (no punishment) for honest mistakes • A clear purpose • Information	**Competence** • Knowledge • Positive feedback • Skill recognition • Challenge • High, noncomparative standards
Meaningfulness • A non-cynical climate • Clearly identified passions • An exciting vision • Relevant task purposes • Whole tasks	**Progress** • A collaborative climate • Milestones • Celebrations • Access to customers • Measurement of improvement

SOURCE: Reprinted with permission of the publisher. From K Thomas, *Intrinsic Motivation at Work: Building Energy and Commitment.* Copyright © 2000 by K Thomas, Berrett-Koehler Publishers, Inc., San Francisco, CA. All rights reserved. www.bkconnection.com.

recommendation, results from Gallup poll surveys show that employees are more engaged and productive when they see the connection between their work and the organization's vision.[61] This connection creates a sense of purpose for employees. Some jobs are so vital that they inherently foster a strong sense of meaningfulness. For example, consider this unique job at America's largest nuclear power plant near Phoenix:

> By 6 a.m., Michelle Catts is making her way to the office past guards armed with automatic weapons, ultrasensitive X-ray machines, electronic gates and sensors that sniff out explosives. . . .
>
> Catts is one of four Nuclear Regulatory Commission inspectors at the plant serving as government watchdogs to make sure Arizona Public Service Co. finds problems before they affect safety. . . .
>
> "My job every day is to make sure this plant is operating safely," Catts said. "That's a pretty important job. It's a good feeling at the end of the day to know I found important things to ask about."[62]

Leading for Choice Managers lead for choice by *empowering* employees and *delegating* meaningful assignments and tasks. This is how Gail Evans, an executive vice president at Atlanta-based CNN, feels about leading for choice.

> [She] says delegating is essential. If you refuse to let your staff handle their own projects, you're jeopardizing their advancement—because they aren't learning new skills and adding successes to their resume—and you're wasting your precious hours doing someone else's work.[63]

Leading for Competence This involves *supporting* and *coaching* employees. Figure 9–3 lists key factors and actions for enhancing a sense of competence. Managers first need to make sure employees have the knowledge needed to successfully perform their jobs. Deficiencies can be handled through training and mentoring. Providing positive feedback and sincere recognition can also be coupled with the assignment of a challenging task to fuel employees' intrinsic motivation.

Leading for Progress   Managers lead for progress by *monitoring* and *rewarding* others. Douglas R Conant, CEO of Campbell Soup Company, has engineered a remarkable turnaround and is a good role model in this regard:

> The turnaround has been catalyzed by cost-cutting, smart innovations, and a concerted effort to reinvigorate the workforce....
>
>   Conant hasn't shaken up a complacent 137-year-old company by being in-your-face. He happily gives others credit and deflects praise. He's not brash.... In his time at Campbell, he has sent out more than 16,000 hand-written thank-you notes to staffers, from the chief investment officer to the receptionist at headquarters—notes often found hanging in people's offices or above their desks. "[In business] we're trained to find things that are wrong, but I try to celebrate what's right," says Conant.[64]

We now direct our attention to *extrinsic* rewards—money, opportunities, and recognition granted by others.

LO.5 Why Do Extrinsic Rewards Too Often Fail to Motivate?

Despite huge investments of time and money for monetary and nonmonetary compensation, the desired motivational impact often is not achieved. A management consultant/writer offers these eight reasons:

1. Too much emphasis on monetary rewards.
2. Rewards lack an "appreciation effect."
3. Extensive benefits become entitlements.
4. Counterproductive behavior is rewarded. (For example, "a pizza delivery company focused its rewards on the on-time performance of its drivers, only to discover that it was inadvertently rewarding reckless driving."[65])
5. Too long a delay between performance and rewards.
6. Too many one-size-fits-all rewards.
7. Use of one-shot rewards with a short-lived motivational impact.
8. Continued use of demotivating practices such as layoffs, across-the-board raises and cuts, and excessive executive compensation.[66]

These stubborn problems have fostered a search for more effective extrinsic reward practices. While a thorough discussion of modern compensation practices[67] is way beyond our present scope, we can explore a general approach to boosting the motivational impact of monetary rewards—pay for performance.

Pay for Performance

Pay for performance is the popular term for monetary incentives linking at least some portion of the paycheck directly to results or accomplishments. Many refer to it simply as *incentive pay,* while others call it *variable pay.* "Broad-based variable pay programs are offered by 80% of US companies."[68] The general idea behind pay-for-performance schemes—including but not limited to merit pay, bonuses, and profit sharing—is to give employees an incentive for working harder

Pay for performance

Monetary incentives tied to one's results or accomplishments.

These folks not only make really cool picnic baskets, they actually work *inside* one! Longaberger's headquarters building in Frazeyburg, Ohio, is a giant replica of the firm's famous maple wood baskets. Each day, 2,500 employees who are paid on a piece-rate basis weave 40,000 hand-crafted baskets. This team of Longaberger employees recently won a prestigious quality award for cutting waste and improving productivity.

or smarter. Pay for performance is something extra, compensation above and beyond basic wages and salaries. Proponents of incentive compensation say something extra is needed because hourly wages and fixed salaries do little more than motivate people to show up at work and put in the required hours.[69] The most basic form of pay for performance is the traditional piece-rate plan, whereby the employee is paid a specified amount of money for each unit of work. For example, 2,500 artisans at Longaberger's, in Frazeyburg, Ohio, are paid a fixed amount for each handcrafted wooden basket they weave. Together, they produce 40,000 of the prized maple baskets daily.[70] Sales commissions, whereby a salesperson receives a specified amount of money for each unit sold, is another long-standing example of pay for performance. Today's service economy is forcing management to creatively adapt and go beyond piece rate and sales commission plans to accommodate greater emphasis on product and service quality, interdependence, and teamwork.

Current Practices   For an indication of current practices, see Table 9–3, which is based on a survey of 156 US executives. The lack of clear patterns in Table 9–3 is indicative of the still experimental nature of incentive compensation today. Much remains to be learned from research and practice.

Research Insights   According to available expert opinion and research results, pay for performance too often falls short of its goal of improved job performance. "Experts say that roughly half the incentive plans they see don't work, victims of poor design and administration."[71] In fact, one study documented how incentive pay had a *negative* effect on the performance of 150,000 managers from 500 financially distressed companies.[72] A meta-analysis of 39 studies found only a modest positive correlation between financial incentives and performance *quantity* and no impact on performance *quality*.[73] Other researchers have found only a weak statistical link between large executive bonuses paid out in good years and subsequent improvement in corporate profitability.[74] Also, in a survey of small business owners, more than half said their commission plans failed to motivate extra effort from their salespeople.[75] Linking teachers' merit pay to student performance, a highly-touted school reform idea, has had mixed results (see the Real World/Real People feature about teacher pay on page 262).

A study of variable pay plans by Hewitt Associates, a leading human resources consulting firm, uncovered this instructive pattern:

> [M]ore than one-third (41%) of the companies with single-digit revenue growth said the cost outweighed the benefits for them. Not only have the plans failed to improve business results for a quarter of these organizations, they have actually led to adverse results for 26% of those surveyed.
>
> The situation was reversed, however, for companies experiencing double-digit revenue growth. These companies reported that their programs achieved positive outcomes and contributed to business results. "We've found that companies achieving

Table 9–3   *The Use and Effectiveness of Modern Incentive Pay Plans*

PLAN TYPE	PRESENTLY HAVE	RATED HIGHLY EFFECTIVE
Annual bonus	74%	20%
Special one-time spot awards (after the fact)	42	38
Individual incentives	39	27
Long-term incentives (executive level)	32	44
Lump-sum merit pay	28	19
Competency-based pay	22	31
Profit-sharing (apart from retirement program)	22	43
Profit-sharing (as part of retirement program)	22	46
ESOP* stock plan	21	33
Suggestion/proposal programs	17	19
Team-based pay	15	29
Long-term incentives (below executive levels)	13	43
Skill-/knowledge-based pay	12	58
Group incentives (not team-based)	11	24
Pay for quality	9	29
Gainsharing	8	38
Special key-contributor programs (before the fact)	7	55

*Employee stock ownership plan.

SOURCE: From "Incentive Pay Plans: Which Ones Work . . . and Why?" April 2001 HRfocus. This was originally published in IOMA's *HRfocus* newsletter and is republished here with the express written permission of IOMA. Copyright © 2009. Further use of, electronic distribution, or reproduction of this material requires the permission of IOMA. For more information, go to www.ioma.com.

high-revenue growth have successful programs because they provide the appropriate amount of administrative, communication and monetary support," says Paul Shafer, a business leader for Hewitt. If not implemented well, he says, variable pay "will be seen as an entitlement by employees and a substantial loss to employers."[76]

Clearly, the pay-for-performance area is still very much up in the air.

L0.6 Getting the Most out of Extrinsic Rewards and Pay for Performance

Based on what we have learned to date,[77] here is a workable plan for maximizing the motivational impact of extrinsic rewards:

- Tie praise, recognition, and noncash awards to *specific* results.
- Make pay for performance an integral part of the organization's basic strategy (e.g., pursuit of best-in-the-industry product or service quality).
- Base incentive determinations on objective performance data.
- Have all employees actively participate in the development, implementation, and revision of the performance-pay formulas.
- Encourage two-way communication so problems with the incentive plan will be detected early.

Should Teachers' Pay Be Tied to Student Performance?

At least eight states are moving away from a traditional pay model, which increases salaries based on seniority and advanced degrees. . . . In dozens of districts, test scores already have earned teachers more money. . . .

- In Chicago, teachers at a handful of schools can earn up to $8,000 in annual bonuses for improved scores, while mentor teachers and "lead teachers" can earn an extra $7,000 or $15,000, respectively.
- In Nashville, middle-school math teachers can earn up to $15,000 based on student performance.

Do such plans work? A research center launched at Vanderbilt University to study performance pay has found mostly promising, if limited, results. . . .

Teachers are sharply divided. A survey . . . found 88% support bonuses for those who agree to work in hard-to-staff schools; 35% support them for improved test scores. Many say they don't trust test scores to accurately reflect their efforts.

What is your position on this pay-for-performance issue? Explain.

SOURCE: Excerpted from G Toppo, "Teachers Take Test Scores to Bank," *USA Today*, October 22, 2008, p 1A. For more, see D Jones, "CEOs Split on Paying for Good Grades," *USA Today*, September 11, 2008, pp 1B–2B.

In some schools, teachers' pay is directly linked to their students' ability to score well on tests. Is that a good idea?

- Build pay-for-performance plans around participative structures such as suggestion systems or problem-solving teams.
- Reward teamwork and cooperation whenever possible.
- Actively sell the plan to supervisors and middle managers who may view employee participation as a threat to their traditional notion of authority.
- If annual cash bonuses are granted, pay them in a lump sum to maximize their motivational impact.
- Selectively use creative noncash rewards to create buzz and excitement.

go to the Web for the Group Exercise: Rewards, Rewards, Rewards

to the point

What role does positive reinforcement play in behavior shaping?

L0.7 Positive Reinforcement

Feedback and extrinsic reward programs too often are ineffective because they are administered in haphazard ways.[78] For example, consider these scenarios:

- A young programmer stops e-mailing creative suggestions to his boss because she never responds.

- The office politician gets a great promotion while her more skilled coworkers scratch their heads and gossip about the injustice.

In the first instance, a productive behavior faded away for lack of encouragement. In the second situation, unproductive behavior was unwittingly rewarded. Feedback and rewards need to be handled more precisely. Fortunately, the field of behavioral psychology can help. Thanks to the pioneering work of Edward L Thorndike, B F Skinner, and many others, a behavior modification technique called *positive reinforcement* helps managers achieve needed discipline and desired effect when providing feedback and granting extrinsic rewards.

Thorndike's Law of Effect

During the early 1900s, Edward L Thorndike observed in his psychology laboratory that a cat would behave randomly and wildly when placed in a small box with a secret trip lever that opened a door. However, once the cat accidentally tripped the lever and escaped, the animal would go straight to the lever when placed back in the box. Hence, Thorndike formulated his famous **law of effect,** which says *behavior with favorable consequences tends to be repeated, while behavior with unfavorable consequences tends to disappear.*[79] This was a dramatic departure from the prevailing notion a century ago that behavior was the product of inborn instincts.

Skinner's Operant Conditioning Model

Skinner refined Thorndike's conclusion that behavior is controlled by its consequences. Skinner's work became known as *behaviorism* because he dealt strictly with observable behavior.[80] As a behaviorist, Skinner believed it was pointless to explain behavior in terms of unobservable inner states such as needs, drives, attitudes, or thought processes.[81] He similarly put little stock in the idea of self-determination.

In his 1938 classic, *The Behavior of Organisms,* Skinner drew an important distinction between the two types of behavior: respondent and operant behavior.[82] He labeled unlearned reflexes, or stimulus–response (S–R) connections, **respondent behavior.** This category of behavior was said to describe a very small proportion of adult human behavior. Examples of respondent behavior would include shedding tears while peeling onions and reflexively withdrawing one's hand from a hot stove.[83] Skinner attached the label **operant behavior** to behavior that is learned when one "operates on" the environment to produce desired consequences. Some call this the response–stimulus (R–S) model. Years of controlled experiments with pigeons in "Skinner boxes" helped Skinner develop a sophisticated technology of behavior control, or operant conditioning. For example, he taught pigeons how to pace figure-eights and how to bowl by reinforcing the under-weight (and thus hungry) birds with food whenever

Law of effect

Behavior with favorable consequences is repeated; behavior with unfavorable consequences disappears.

Respondent behavior

Skinner's term for unlearned stimulus–response reflexes.

Operant behavior

Skinner's term for learned, consequence-shaped behavior.

Renowned behavioral psychologist B F Skinner and your co-author Bob Kreitner met and posed for a snapshot at an Academy of Management meeting in Boston. As a behaviorist, Skinner preferred to deal with observable behavior and its antecedents and consequences in the environment rather than with inner states such as attitudes and cognitive processes. Professor Skinner was a fascinating man who left a permanent mark on modern psychology.

Figure 9–4   *Contingent Consequences in Operant Conditioning*

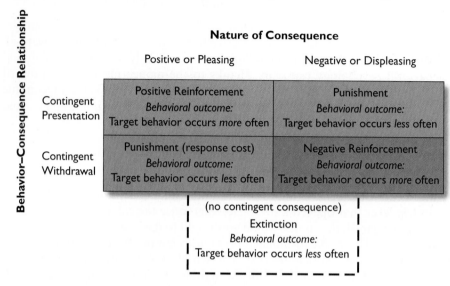

they more closely approximated target behaviors. Skinner's work spawned the field of behavior modification and has significant implications for OB because the vast majority of organizational behavior falls into the operant category.[84]

Contingent Consequences

Contingent consequences, according to Skinner's operant theory, control behavior in four ways: positive reinforcement, negative reinforcement, punishment, and extinction. The term *contingent* means there is a systematic if-then linkage between the target behavior and the consequence. Remember Mom (and Pink Floyd) saying something to this effect: "If you don't finish your dinner, you don't get dessert" (see Figure 9–4)? To avoid the all-too-common mislabeling of these consequences, let us review some formal definitions.

Positive reinforcement

Making behavior occur more often by contingently presenting something positive.

LO.8 **Positive Reinforcement Strengthens Behavior** Positive **reinforcement** is the process of strengthening a behavior by contingently presenting something pleasing. (Importantly, a behavior is strengthened when it increases in frequency and weakened when it decreases in frequency.) A design engineer who works overtime because of praise and recognition from the boss is responding to positive reinforcement.[85]

A corporate culture built on positive reinforcement can foster loyalty, hard work, and creativity. This is especially true in hard economic times, as exemplified by JM Family Enterprises in Deerfield Beach, Florida:

> Amid falling sales, many intensely loyal employees at this privately held Toyota distributor volunteered to forgo bonuses. CEO Colin Brown rejected their offers and paid out bonuses, but asked for their support in cutting costs elsewhere in the company.[86]

Negative reinforcement

Making behavior occur more often by contingently withdrawing something negative.

Negative Reinforcement Also Strengthens Behavior Negative **reinforcement** is the process of strengthening a behavior by contingently withdrawing something displeasing. For example, an army sergeant who stops yelling when a recruit jumps out of bed has negatively reinforced that particular behavior.

Similarly, the behavior of clamping our hands over our ears when watching a jumbo jet take off is negatively reinforced by relief from the noise. Negative reinforcement is often confused with punishment. But the two strategies have opposite effects on behavior. Negative reinforcement, as the word *reinforcement* indicates, strengthens a behavior because it provides relief from an unpleasant situation.

Punishment Weakens Behavior   **Punishment** is the process of weakening behavior through either the contingent presentation of something displeasing or the contingent withdrawal of something positive. A manager assigning a tardy employee to a dirty job exemplifies the first type of punishment. Docking a tardy employee's pay is an example of the second type of punishment, called *response cost punishment*. Legal fines involve response cost punishment. Salespeople who must make up any cash register shortages out of their own pockets are being managed through response cost punishment. Ethical questions can and should be raised about this type of on-the-job punishment.[87]

Extinction Also Weakens Behavior   **Extinction** is the weakening of a behavior by ignoring it or making sure it is not reinforced. Getting rid of a former boyfriend or girlfriend by refusing to answer his or her phone calls is an extinction strategy. A good analogy for extinction is to imagine what would happen to your houseplants if you stopped watering them. Like a plant without water, a behavior without occasional reinforcement eventually dies. Although very different processes, both punishment and extinction have the same weakening effect on behavior.

Schedules of Reinforcement

As just illustrated, contingent consequences are an important determinant of future behavior. The *timing* of behavioral consequences can be even more important. Based on years of tedious laboratory experiments with pigeons in highly controlled environments, Skinner and his colleagues discovered distinct patterns of responding for various schedules of reinforcement.[88]

Although some of their conclusions can be generalized to negative reinforcement, punishment, and extinction, it is best to think only of positive reinforcement when discussing schedules.

Continuous Reinforcement   Every instance of a target behavior is reinforced when a **continuous reinforcement** (CRF) schedule is in effect. For instance, when your television set is operating properly, you are reinforced with a picture every time you turn it on (a CRF schedule). But, as with any CRF schedule of reinforcement, the behavior of turning on the television will undergo rapid extinction if the set breaks.

Intermittent reinforcement   Unlike CRF schedules, **intermittent reinforcement** involves reinforcement of *some* but not all instances of a target behavior. Four subcategories of intermittent schedules are fixed and variable ratio schedules and fixed and variable interval schedules. Reinforcement in *ratio* schedules is contingent on the number of responses observed. *Interval* reinforcement is tied to the passage of time. Some common examples of the four types of intermittent reinforcement are as follows:

- *Fixed ratio*—piece-rate pay; bonuses tied to the sale of a fixed number of units.
- *Variable ratio*—slot machines that pay off after a variable number of lever pulls; lotteries that pay off after the purchase of a variable number of tickets.
- *Fixed interval*—hourly pay; annual salary paid on a regular basis.

Punishment

Making behavior occur less often by contingently presenting something negative or withdrawing something positive.

Extinction

Making behavior occur less often by ignoring or not reinforcing it.

Continuous reinforcement

Reinforcing every instance of a behavior.

Intermittent Reinforcement

Reinforcing some but not all instances of behavior.

- *Variable interval*—random supervisory praise and pats on the back for employees who have been doing a good job.

Scheduling Is Critical   The schedule of reinforcement can more powerfully influence behavior than the magnitude of reinforcement. Although this proposition grew out of experiments with pigeons, subsequent on-the-job research confirmed it. Consider, for example, a field study of 12 unionized beaver trappers employed by a lumber company to keep the large rodents from eating newly planted tree seedlings.[89]

The beaver trappers were randomly divided into two groups that alternated weekly between two different bonus plans. Under the first schedule, each trapper earned his regular $7 per hour wage plus $1 for each beaver caught. Technically, this bonus was paid on a CRF schedule. The second bonus plan involved the regular $7 per hour wage plus a one-in-four chance (as determined by rolling the dice) of receiving $4 for each beaver trapped. This second bonus plan qualified as a variable ratio (VR-4) schedule. In the long run, both incentive schemes averaged out to a $1-per-beaver bonus. Surprisingly, however, when the trappers were under the VR-4 schedule, they were 58% more productive than under the CRF schedule, despite the fact that the net amount of pay averaged out the same for the two groups during the 12-week trapping season.

Work Organizations Typically Rely on the Weakest Schedule
Generally, variable ratio and variable interval schedules of reinforcement produce the strongest behavior that is most resistant to extinction. As gamblers will attest, variable schedules hold the promise of reinforcement after the next target response. For example, the following drama at a Laughlin, Nevada, gambling casino is one more illustration of the potency of variable ratio reinforcement:

> An elderly woman with a walker had lost her grip on the slot [machine] handle and had collapsed on the floor.
>
> "Help," she cried weakly.
>
> The woman at the machine next to her interrupted her play for a few seconds to try to help her to her feet, but all around her the army of slot players continued feeding coins to the machines.
>
> A security man arrived to soothe the woman and take her away.
>
> "Thank you," she told him appreciatively.
>
> "But don't forget my winnings."[90]

Organizations without at least some variable reinforcement are less likely to prompt this type of dedication to task. A good example is Zappos, the Las Vegas–based online retailer, where "any employee can give any other employee a $50 bonus for a job well done."[91]

Unfortunately, time-based pay schemes such as hourly wages and yearly salaries that rely on the weakest schedule of reinforcement (fixed interval) are still the rule in today's workplaces. In fact, according to the US Bureau of Labor Statistics, "59 percent of U.S. workers are paid by the hour."[92]

LO.9 Behavior Shaping

Have you ever wondered how trainers at aquarium parks manage to get bottle-nosed dolphins to do flips, killer whales to carry people on their backs, and seals to juggle balls? The results are seemingly magical. Actually, a mundane learning process called *shaping* is responsible for the animals' antics.

Two-ton killer whales, for example, have a big appetite, and they find buckets of fish very reinforcing. So if the trainer wants to ride a killer whale, he or she reinforces very basic behaviors that will eventually lead to the whale being ridden. The killer whale is contingently reinforced with a few fish for coming near the trainer, then for being touched, then for putting its nose in a harness, then for being straddled, and eventually for swimming with the trainer on its back. In effect, the trainer systematically raises the behavioral requirement for reinforcement.[93] Thus, **shaping** is defined as the process of reinforcing closer and closer approximations to a target behavior.

Shaping works very well with people, too, especially in training and quality programs involving continuous improvement. Praise, recognition, and instructive and credible feedback cost managers little more than moments of their time. Yet, when used in conjunction with learning goals and a behavior-shaping program, these consequences can efficiently foster significant improvements in job performance. The key to successful behavior shaping lies in reducing a complex target behavior to easily learned steps and then faithfully (and patiently) reinforcing any improvement. For example, Continental Airlines used a cash bonus program to improve its on-time arrival record from one of the worst in the industry to one of the best. Employees originally were promised a $65 bonus each month Continental earned a top-five ranking. Now it takes a second- or third-place ranking to earn the $65 bonus and a $100 bonus awaits employees when they achieve a number one ranking.[94] (Table 9–4 lists practical tips on shaping.)

Shaping
Reinforcing closer and closer approximations to a target behavior.

Table 9–4   *Ten Practical Tips for Shaping Job Behavior*

1. *Accommodate the process of behavioral change.* Behaviors change in gradual stages, not in broad, sweeping motions.

2. *Define new behavior patterns specifically.* State what you wish to accomplish in explicit terms and in small amounts that can be easily grasped.

3. *Give individuals feedback on their performance.* A once-a-year performance appraisal is not sufficient.

4. *Reinforce behavior as quickly as possible.*

5. *Use powerful reinforcement.* To be effective, rewards must be important to the employee—not to the manager.

6. *Use a continuous reinforcement schedule.* New behaviors should be reinforced every time they occur. This reinforcement should continue until these behaviors become habitual.

7. *Use a variable reinforcement schedule for maintenance.* Even after behavior has become habitual, it still needs to be rewarded, though not necessarily every time it occurs.

8. *Reward teamwork—not competition.* Group goals and group rewards are one way to encourage cooperation in situations in which jobs and performance are interdependent.

9. *Make all rewards contingent on performance.*

10. *Never take good performance for granted.* Even superior performance, if left unrewarded, will eventually deteriorate.

SOURCE: Adapted from A T Hollingsworth and D Tanquay Hoyer, "How Supervisors Can Shape Behavior," *Personnel Journal*, May 1985, pp 86, 88.

Summary of Key Concepts

1. *Define the term* performance management, *distinguish between learning goals and performance outcome goals, and explain the three-step goal-setting process.* Performance management is a continuous cycle of improving individual job performance with goal setting, feedback and coaching, and rewards and positive reinforcement. Learning goals encourage learning, creativity, and skill development. Performance outcome goals target specified end-results. The three-step goal-setting process includes (1) set goals that are SMART—specific, measurable, attainable, results oriented, and time bound; (2) promote goal commitment with clear explanations, participation, and supportiveness; (3) provide support and feedback by providing information, needed training, and knowledge of results.

2. *Identify the two basic functions of feedback, and specify at least three practical lessons from feedback research.* Feedback, in the form of objective information about performance, both instructs and motivates. Feedback is not automatically accepted as intended, especially negative feedback. Managerial credibility can be enhanced through expertise and a climate of trust. Feedback must not be too frequent or too scarce and must be tailored to the individual. Feedback directly from computers is effective. Active participation in the feedback session helps people perceive feedback as more accurate. The quality of feedback received decreases as one moves up the organizational hierarchy.

3. *Define 360-degree feedback, and summarize how to give good feedback in a performance management program.* A focal person receives anonymous 360-degree feedback from subordinates, the manager, peers, and selected others such as customers or suppliers. Good feedback is tied to performance goals and clear expectations, linked with specific behavior or results, reserved for key result areas, given as soon as possible, provided for improvement as well as for final results, focused on performance rather than on personalities, and based on accurate and credible information.

4. *Distinguish between extrinsic and intrinsic rewards, and explain the four building blocks of intrinsic rewards and motivation.* Extrinsic rewards—including pay, material goods, and social recognition—are granted by others. Intrinsic rewards are psychic rewards, such as a sense of competence or a feeling of accomplishment, that are self-granted and experienced internally. According to Thomas's model, the four basic intrinsic rewards are meaningfulness, choice, competence, and progress. Managers can boost intrinsic motivation by letting employees work on important whole tasks (meaningfulness), delegating and trusting (choice), providing challenge and feedback (competence), and collaboratively celebrating improvement (progress).

5. *Summarize the reasons why extrinsic rewards often fail to motivate employees.* Extrinsic reward systems can fail to motivate employees for these reasons: overemphasis on money, no appreciation effect, benefits become entitlements, wrong behavior is rewarded, rewards are delayed too long, use of one-size-fits-all rewards, one-shot rewards with temporary impact, and demotivating practices such as layoffs.

6. *Discuss how managers can generally improve extrinsic reward and pay-for-performance plans.* They need to be strategically anchored, based on quantified performance data, highly participative, actively sold to supervisors and middle managers, and teamwork oriented. Annual bonuses of significant size are helpful.

7. *State Thorndike's law of effect, and explain Skinner's distinction between respondent and operant behavior.* According to Edward L Thorndike's law of effect, behavior with favorable consequences tends to be repeated, while behavior with unfavorable consequences tends to disappear. B F Skinner called unlearned stimulus–response reflexes *respondent behavior.* He applied the term *operant behavior* to all behavior learned through experience with environmental consequences.

8. *Define positive reinforcement, negative reinforcement, punishment, and extinction, and distinguish between continuous and intermittent schedules of reinforcement.* Positive and negative reinforcement are consequence management strategies that strengthen behavior, whereas punishment and extinction weaken behavior. These strategies need to be defined objectively in terms of their actual impact on behavior frequency, not subjectively on the basis of intended impact.

   Every instance of a behavior is reinforced with a continuous reinforcement (CRF) schedule. Under intermittent reinforcement schedules—fixed and variable ratio or fixed and variable interval—some, rather than all, instances of a target behavior are reinforced. Variable schedules produce the most extinction-resistant behavior.

9. *Demonstrate your knowledge of behavior shaping.* Behavior shaping occurs when closer and closer approximations of a target behavior are reinforced. In effect, the standard for reinforcement is made more difficult as the individual learns. The process begins with continuous reinforcement, which gives way to intermittent reinforcement when the target behavior becomes strong and habitual.

OB in Action Case Study

The Employee Whisperer[95]

At the suburban Philadelphia offices of Kenexa, people grin at one another all day long. Sometimes they hug. Bright posters of the company's guiding principles dot the walls: YOU'RE ALLOWED TO LAUGH YOUR WAY THROUGH A PROBLEM and MAKING FRIENDS REPLACES OUR ORGANIZATIONAL HIERARCHY. The CEO, Rudy Karsan, spouts odd koanlike talk: "The world is like a roomful of jars. Every time you open a jar, there's untold treasure in there."

Ah, but there's treasure in such psychobabble. Kenexa is the leading human-resources-services company in America. Sixty percent of the Fortune 100, including Caterpillar, General Motors, Time Warner, and Wachovia, hire Kenexa to help get inside the minds of their employees and build worker loyalty. It has what analysts say is the sector's most sophisticated data-crunching software, as well as a squad of scientists—statisticians and industrial and organizational psychologists—to help turn correlations into action plans as well as profit: Kenexa's revenue has tripled since its 2005 IPO [initial public offering of stock], to $182 million. In HR [human resources], a discipline viewed by workers at most companies as unhelpful at best and horrendous at worst, the company's secret is its Cyndi Lauper–like conviction that employees just want to have fun.

According to Kenexa, turnover among managers who feel pride in their company is 21% lower than among those who don't. Adds the Kenyan-born, Canadian-educated Karsan: "When you're in a job that you enjoy and you're good at, you're not just a better worker. You're a better spouse, a better parent, a better citizen."

But this isn't just about group hugs. Kenexa's scientists do interviews and surveys to learn what inspires employees. (Managers: Apparently, employees love sessions where you just listen to them.) Its industry-leading software runs the data through sophisticated algorithms, identifying correlations and possible causations. Then Kenexa devises strategies to improve work environments and recruit, evaluate, and keep talent. For example, after studying several service industries, Kenexa recently developed a program in which potential hires use avatars to act out scenarios—from remembering the proper arrangement of items in a hotel room to making judgment calls about inebriated drinkers at a bar—to measure how naturally engaged an applicant would be on the job.

But first, Kenexa has to get itself hired. When Aetna's HR head for business operations, Craig Hurty, first approached Aetna CEO Ronald Williams about measuring employee motivation, Williams had just one question: How does it change financial performance? Kenexa's researchers presented statistics showing that companies with higher satisfaction scores had 700% higher shareholder return. "When I sent those results to our CEO, I was up in his office that same day, and we spent half an hour going through the results," Hurty says.

Karsan notes that knowing employees are passionate is pointless if a company doesn't know how to exploit the passion. Kenexa's software helps suggest action plans drawn partly from a 4,000-client database of what has worked in the past for its highest-scoring clients. Last year, the company took on a huge and complex case at Boeing, where it drilled down to departmental groups as small as 30 people and delivered tailored plans directly to the company's 15,000 managers. "It used to be that we'd take the survey, we'd look at the results, everybody would say, 'Oh, that's nice,' and we'd put it on the shelf where it would gather dust until we did the next one," says John Messman, Boeing's employee-relations director. Today, he says, everyone from the CEO down to division managers discusses not just scores, but also strategies to goose engagement.

Karsan says Kenexa "sells its own dog food internally." Everything from recognition programs to in-house competitions to the corporate structure is constantly subject to employee feedback, and everything is meant to boost involvement and loyalty.

Kenexa draws a line straight from its employees' behavior to its success. The company now has offices in 18 countries, including a newly opened 25-acre research campus in India. "It doesn't matter where in the world you go," he explains. "Through their work, people find dignity."

Questions for Discussion

1. What makes a workplace "fun?" What are your personal on-the-job experiences with productivity-enhancing fun? Describe them.

2. Why do Kenexa's leaders have no excuses when it comes to creating a productive performance management program?

3. If you worked as a salesperson for Kenexa, what would be the key talking points in your sales pitch?

4. In terms of Thomas's four building blocks in Figure 9–3, how would you rate Kenexa's potential for generating intrinsic motivation? Explain.

5. Would you like to work at Kenexa? Why or why not?

Ethical Dilemma

Rewarding and Motivating Employees by Ignoring Their Unethical Actions[96]

Using company resources to work on personal projects, especially on company time, is a no-no for employees in most organizations. But supervisors often operate in what I call a gray zone, turning a blind eye to such officially forbidden behavior. They realize that stamping it out may do more harm than good, because many employees have a deep-seated need to engage in it.

My three-year study of an aeronautic manufacturing plant with 4,000 workers gave me insight into why gray zones persist in work settings. Employees produced personal artifacts such as kitchen utensils, toys for their kids, and window frames, using company time and materials. Managers overlooked all this, because they could count on people when official work needed to be cranked out.

Consider the similar case of a competent, productive junior editor at a newspaper who works on her novel at the office. Despite company policies prohibiting this, her boss winks at the habit. By tolerating the editor's behavior,

the supervisor holds on to a loyal, self-motivated, and engaged worker.

How Should Managers Respond to This Issue?

1. Let's be practical, this is a good commonsense motivational practice in today's workplaces. Explain your ethical reasoning.

2. This practice is okay on a case-by-case basis. Explain how managers should selectively enforce a "no personal work on company time" policy.

3. This is bad management because it serves to condone and even encourage unethical conduct. Clear ethical rules against doing personal work on company time need to be written, promulgated, and enforced. Agree or disagree? Explain.

4. Invent other options. Explain and discuss.

Web Resources

For study material and exercises that apply to this chapter, visit our Web site, www.mhhe.com/kreitner

Part 3

Group and Social Processes

Chapter 10

Group Dynamics

LEARNING OBJECTIVES

When you finish studying the material in this chapter, you should be able to:

LO.1 Identify the four sociological criteria of a group, and discuss the impact of social networking on group dynamics.

LO.2 Describe the five stages in Tuckman's theory of group development, and discuss the threat of group decay.

LO.3 Distinguish between role conflict and role ambiguity.

LO.4 Contrast roles and norms, and specify four reasons norms are enforced in organizations.

LO.5 Distinguish between task and maintenance roles in groups.

LO.6 Summarize the practical contingency management implications for group size.

LO.7 Discuss why managers need to carefully handle mixed-gender task groups.

LO.8 Describe groupthink, and identify at least four of its symptoms.

LO.9 Define social loafing, and explain how managers can prevent it.

Businesses have been teching-up customer Web sites with blogs, videos, rating tools, and other interactive features for years. But it's the rare employer that puts the same tools to work inside the company.

That's where the McLean, Va.-based bank and financial services company Capital One stands out.

Impressed by explosive growth of social networking sites such as Facebook, MySpace, and YouTube, Capital One added similar collaborative technologies to the company's own intranet, Oneplace, in 2007–08.

"We noticed that the workplace was not as collaborative as it could be," says Matt Schuyler, Capital One's chief human resources officer. "We wanted a way to encourage open and honest dialogue." . . .

Earlier generation Web sites, including most corporate intranets, allowed only select administrators to add content. Material usually has to pass muster with top brass and then be specially formatted and coded to be readable by a Web browser.

But so-called Web 2.0 technologies—the hallmark of social networking sites including Facebook—allow virtually anyone with access to the site to instantaneously contribute and make changes. By integrating similar technology into Oneplace, Capital One's [human resource] team transformed the organization's site from a static tool—mostly housing HR materials from benefits forms and training schedules to the employee handbook—to a lively forum for employees to post, share, and critique ideas. . . .

The Capital One employee directory serves as the cornerstone of Oneplace.

In line with Facebook and MySpace, the site allows staff members to post personal profiles and photos. Currently, about 2,000 employees list themselves, including descriptions of their job duties and areas of expertise. . . .

Employees can search the ever-growing site using a Google-type search engine.

As Schuyler sees it, online collaboration fits in with Capital One's management philosophy.

"We view work not as a place you go, but a thing you do," he says, noting that the company has a tradition of supporting flexible workplaces since many employees work at home or from more than one office.

In such an environment, he says, online communication, including state-of-the-art collaborative tools, become a business imperative.

Schuyler admits the idea of giving employees unfettered access to the intranet raises some eyebrows among corporate traditionalists, including the company's lawyers. But concerns about hurtful, inappropriate, or potentially inflammatory postings have so far been unwarranted—in part because each posting includes the author's name.

"Collaborative technology is self-policing," says Schuyler. "If someone writes something inappropriate, the next person has something to say about it."

Schuyler maintains that the success of the enhanced intranet is reflected in employees' growing reliance on it and by the feedback employees are encouraged to provide. A recent survey found that in the previous month, 96 percent of employees used Oneplace at least once and the typical employee visited the site 14 different days and accessed 85 pages of content. Meanwhile, the site's developers are using a model known as "agile development" that allows them to roll out features gradually and make improvements to the system based on user feedback.

For Capital One, Schuyler adds, this collaborative process is a natural extension of the culture.[1]

Organizations, by definition, are collections of people constantly interacting to achieve something greater than individuals could accomplish on their own. Research consistently reveals the importance of social skills for both individual and organizational success. For example, a recent study of 1,040 managers employed by 100 manufacturing and service organizations in the United States found 15 reasons why managers fail in the face of rapid change. The top two reasons were "ineffective communication skills/practices" and "poor work relationships/interpersonal skills."[2] Relationships *do* matter in the workplace, as acknowledged by Capital One's lively social networking intitiative.

Management, as defined in Chapter 1, involves getting things done with and through others. Experts say managers need to build *social capital* with four key social skills: social perception, impression management, persuasion and social influence, and social adaptability (see Table 10–1).[3] How polished are your social skills? Where do you need improvement? Daniel Goleman recommends an expanded form of emotional intelligence he calls *social intelligence*, "being intelligent not just *about* our relationships but also *in* them."[4]

Let us begin by defining the term *group* as a prelude to examining types of groups, functions of group members, social networking in the workplace, and the group development process. Our attention then turns to group roles and norms, the basic building blocks of group dynamics. Effects of group structure and member characteristics on group outcomes are explored next. Finally, three serious

Table 10–1   *Key Social Skills Managers Need for Building Social Capital*

SOCIAL SKILL	DESCRIPTION	TOPICAL LINKAGES IN THIS TEXT
Social perception	Ability to perceive accurately the emotions, traits, motives, and intentions of others	• Individual differences, Chapters 5 and 6 • Emotional intelligence, Chapter 5 • Social perception, Chapter 7 • Employee motivation, Chapters 8 and 9
Impression management	Tactics designed to induce liking and a favorable first impression by others	• Impression management, Chapter 15
Persuasion and social influence	Ability to change others' attitudes or behavior in desired directions	• Influence tactics and social power, Chapter 15 • Leadership, Chapter 16
Social adaptability	Ability to adapt to, or feel comfortable in, a wide range of social situations	• Cultural intelligence, Chapter 4 • Managing change, Chapter 18

SOURCE: Columns 1 and 2 excerpted from R A Baron and G D Markman, "Beyond Social Capital: How Social Skills Can Enhance Entrepreneurs' Success," *Academy of Management Executive*, February 2000, table 1, p 110.

threats to group effectiveness are discussed. (This chapter serves as a foundation for our discussion of teams and teamwork in the following chapter.)

LO.1 Groups and Social Networking

to the point

What can managers do about social networking technology blurring the line between formal and informal groups?

Groups and teams are inescapable features of modern life.[5] College students are often teamed with their peers for class projects. Parents serve on community advisory boards at their local schools. Managers find themselves on product planning committees and productivity task forces. Productive organizations simply cannot function without gathering individuals into groups and teams. But as personal experience shows, group effort can bring out both the best and the worst in people. A marketing department meeting, where several people excitedly brainstorm and refine a creative new advertising campaign, can yield results beyond the capabilities of individual contributors. Conversely, committees have become the butt of jokes (e.g., a committee is a place where they take minutes and waste hours; a camel is a horse designed by a committee) because they all too often are plagued by lack of direction and by conflict. Modern managers need a solid understanding of groups and group processes so as to both avoid their pitfalls and tap their vast potential. Moreover, the huge and growing presence of the Internet and modern communication technologies—with their own unique networks of informal and formal social relationships—is a major challenge for profit-minded business managers.

Although other definitions of groups exist, we draw from the field of sociology and define a **group** as two or more freely interacting individuals who share collective norms and goals and have a common identity.[6] Figure 10–1 illustrates how the four criteria in this definition combine to form a conceptual whole. Organizational psychologist Edgar Schein shed additional light on this concept by drawing instructive distinctions between a group, a crowd, and an organization:

Group

Two or more freely interacting people with shared norms and goals and a common identity.

> The size of a group is thus limited by the possibilities of mutual interaction and mutual awareness. Mere aggregates of people do not fit this definition because they do not interact

Figure 10–1 *Four Sociological Criteria of a Group*

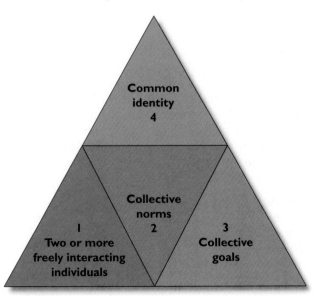

and do not perceive themselves to be a group even if they are aware of each other as, for instance, a crowd on a street corner watching some event. A total department, a union, or a whole organization would not be a group in spite of thinking of themselves as "we," because they generally do not all interact and are not all aware of each other. However, work teams, committees, subparts of departments, cliques, and various other informal associations among organizational members would fit this definition of a group.[7]

Take a moment now to think of various groups of which you are a member. Does each of your groups satisfy the four criteria in Figure 10–1?

Formal and Informal Groups

Formal group

Formed by the organization.

Informal group

Formed by friends or those with common interests.

Individuals join groups, or are assigned to groups, to accomplish various purposes. If the group is formed by a manager to help the organization accomplish its goals, then it qualifies as a **formal group.** Formal groups typically wear such labels as work group, project team, committee, corporate board, or task force. An **informal group** exists when the members' overriding purpose of getting together is friendship or common interests. Although formal and informal groups often overlap, such as a team of corporate auditors heading for the tennis courts after work, some employees are not friends with their coworkers.[8] Off-the-job informal groups can be a very important source of emotional support, especially in hard times. This recent gathering in San Francisco is a good case in point:

> One by one, they answer the question: What's your favorite holiday dish? When all eight are through, an imaginary feast fills an austere white room that buzzes with the hum of a neon light.
>
> "We should swap recipes," says Gary Sanchez, 43. "We may not have jobs, but at least we'll be well-fed."
>
> The group breaks into laughter. It's a welcome emotion.
>
> This is not a summit of would-be chefs but a session of Job Club, a weekly gathering of area unemployed whose mission is to both soothe nerves frayed by layoffs as well as help steer those assembled back to a steady paycheck.
>
> Such informal gatherings have always existed, typically sponsored by church groups and local career centers. But the economic collapse has placed renewed importance on this homespun salve, one that some attendees describe as a lifeline out of anger, fear and loneliness.[9]

Functions of Formal Groups

Researchers point out that formal groups fulfill two basic functions: *organizational* and *individual.* The various functions are listed in Table 10–2. Complex combinations of these functions can be found in formal groups at any given time.

For example, consider what Mazda's new American employees experienced when they spent a month working in Japan before the opening of the firm's Flat Rock, Michigan, plant:

> After a month of training in Mazda's factory methods, whipping their new Japanese buddies at softball and sampling local watering holes, the Americans were fired up. . . . [A maintenance manager] even faintly praised the Japanese practice of holding group calisthenics at the start of each working day: "I didn't think I'd like doing exercises every morning, but I kind of like it."[10]

While Mazda pursued the organizational functions it wanted—interdependent teamwork, creativity, coordination, problem solving, and training—the American

Table 10–2 *Formal Groups Fulfill Organizational and Individual Functions*

ORGANIZATIONAL FUNCTIONS	INDIVIDUAL FUNCTIONS
1. Accomplish complex, interdependent tasks that are beyond the capabilities of individuals.	1. Satisfy the individual's need for affiliation.
2. Generate new or creative ideas and solutions.	2. Develop, enhance, and confirm the individual's self-esteem and sense of identity.
3. Coordinate interdepartmental efforts.	3. Give individuals an opportunity to test and share their perceptions of social reality.
4. Provide a problem-solving mechanism for complex problems requiring varied information and assessments.	4. Reduce the individual's anxieties and feelings of insecurity and powerlessness.
5. Implement complex decisions.	5. Provide a problem-solving mechanism for personal and interpersonal problems.
6. Socialize and train newcomers.	

SOURCE: Adapted from E H Schein, *Organizational Psychology*, 3rd ed (Englewood Cliffs, NJ: Prentice Hall, 1980), pp 149–51.

workers benefited from the individual functions of formal groups. Among those benefits were affiliation with new friends, enhanced self-esteem, exposure to the Japanese social reality, and reduction of anxieties about working for a foreign-owned company. In short, Mazda created a workable blend of organizational and individual group functions by training its newly hired American employees in Japan.

Social Networking Is Blurring the Formal/Informal Boundaries

Social relationships are complex, alive, and dynamic. They have little regard for arbitrary boundaries. The desirability of overlapping formal and informal groups is problematic. Some managers firmly believe personal friendship fosters productive teamwork on the job while others view workplace "bull sessions" as a serious threat to productivity. Both situations are common, and it is the manager's job to strike a workable balance, based on the maturity and goals of the people involved. Additionally, there is the ethics-laden issue of managers being friends with the people they oversee.

The Social Networking Revolution   For many years, the term *networking* simply meant building a modest list of personal and professional contacts. But thanks to Internet innovations such as e-mail, blogs, MySpace, Facebook, and LinkedIn, the age of *social networking* has arrived.[11] The traditional notion of networking has gone hyper. Why settle for a static list of contacts when you can have instant and comprehensive interaction with countless thousands? But technology is running far ahead of precise definition, research, and organizational policies.

    PC Magazine offers this working definition of **social networking site (SNS):**

A Web site that provides a virtual community for people interested in a particular subject or just to "hang out" together. Members create their own online "profile" with biographical data, pictures, likes, dislikes and any other information they choose to post. They communicate with each other by voice, chat, instant message, videoconference

Social networking site (SNS)
A Web-enabled community of people who share all types of information.

and blogs, and the service typically provides a way for members to contact friends of other members.[12]

Members of a SNS may or may not know each other on a face-to-face basis and SNS use is dominated by, but not restricted to, young people. According to a recent Pew Research Center survey, 75% of online users ages 18–24 and 30% of online users ages 35–44 have at least one profile on a SNS.[13]

As SNSs continue to mushroom and new applications such as Twitter emerge,[14] organizational leaders generally have been left scratching their heads. Their unanswered questions abound: How can we profit from this? How can we embrace and/or control it? (See the Real World/Real People feature on page 279.) Is it a good or bad thing (see the Ethical Dilemma at end of this chapter)? What are the implications of this massive connectivity for productivity, privacy, harassment, confidentiality, protection of intellectual property, and information systems security? Social networking truly is the Wild West of organizational life, with mostly unanswered questions and unknown consequences.[15] The lines between formal and informal groups have been blurred almost beyond recognition. Still, managers need to establish some boundaries.

Should Managers Be Friends with Those Who Report to Them?

One long-standing group dynamics dilemma magnified by the social networking revolution involves manager-employee friendships. In their *BusinessWeek* column, Jack and Suzy Welch offered this sound advice:

> . . . you don't need to be friends with your subordinates, as long as you share the same values for the business. But if you are friends with them, lucky you. Working with people you really like for 8 or 10 hours a day adds fun to everything.
>
> That said, remember that boss-subordinate friendships live or die because of one thing: complete, unrelenting candor. Candor is imperative in any working relationship, but it's especially necessary when there's a social aspect involved. You don't want your liking someone's personality to automatically communicate that you like his or her performance. You may, but performance evaluations have to come in a distinct and separate set of conversations at work—as often as four times a year—in which you sit down with your subordinate, put the shared laughs from last weekend's barbecue in the corner, and talk about what's expected and what has been delivered.
>
> Do these candid conversations require a certain ability to compartmentalize? You bet they do. But when you recognize that fact and practice discipline, confident you're being fair to everyone, you should be able to enjoy one of work's best built-in perks: hanging out with friends.[16]

Add *compartmentalizing* to the list of essential managerial social skills in the age of social networking.

to the point

Why is it important to know the stages of group development when creating effective work groups and teams?

LO.2 The Group Development Process

Groups and teams in the workplace go through a maturation process, such as one would find in any life-cycle situation (e.g., humans, organizations, products). While there is general agreement among theorists that the group development process occurs in identifiable stages, they disagree about the exact number, sequence, length, and nature of those stages.[17] One oft-cited model is the one proposed in 1965 by educational psychologist Bruce W Tuckman. His original model involved only four stages (forming, storming, norming, and performing).

For Better or for Worse, Social Networking Is Breaking Down Walls

. . . [B]logs, it turns out, are just one of the do-it-yourself tools to emerge on the Internet. Vast social networks such as Facebook and MySpace offer people new ways to meet and exchange information. Sites like LinkedIn help millions forge important work relationships and alliances. New applications pop up every week. While only a small slice of the population wants to blog, a far larger swath of humanity is eager to make friends and contacts, to exchange pictures and music, to share activities and ideas.

These social connectors are changing the dynamics of companies around the world. Millions of us are now hanging out on the Internet with customers, befriending rivals, clicking through pictures of our boss at a barbecue, or seeing what she read at the beach. It's as if the walls around our companies are vanishing and old org charts are lying on their sides.

This can be disturbing for top management, who are losing control, at least in the traditional sense. Workers can fritter away hours on YouTube. They can use social networks to pillory a colleague or leak secrets. That's the downside, and companies that don't adapt are sure to get lots of it.

But there's an upside to the loss of control. Ambitious workers use these tools to land new deals and to assemble global teams for collaborative projects. The potential for both better and worse is huge, and it's growing. . . . .

Work and Leisure, colleague and rival; they all blend on these networks.

What is your personal experience with the positives and negatives of social networking? What ethical red flags do you see for the workplace? Explain.

SOURCE: Excerpted from S Baker and H Green, "Beyond Blogs," June 2, 2008, issue of *BusinessWeek* by special permission. Copyright © 2008 by The McGraw-Hill Companies, Inc.

For better or for worse, social networking sites like Facebook and MySpace are impacting group dynamics in the workplace.

The five-stage model in Figure 10–2 evolved when Tuckman and a doctoral student added "adjourning" in 1977.[18] A word of caution is in order. Somewhat akin to Maslow's need hierarchy theory, Tuckman's theory has been repeated and taught so often and for so long that many have come to view it as documented fact, not merely a theory. Even today, it is good to remember Tuckman's own caution that his group development model was derived more from group therapy sessions than from natural-life groups. Still, many in the OB field like Tuckman's five-stage model of group development because of its easy-to-remember labels and commonsense appeal.

Five Stages

Let us briefly examine each of the five stages in Tuckman's model. Notice in Figure 10–2 how individuals give up a measure of their independence when they join and participate in a group. Also, the various stages are not necessarily of the same

Figure 10–2   *Tuckman's Five-Stage Theory of Group Development*

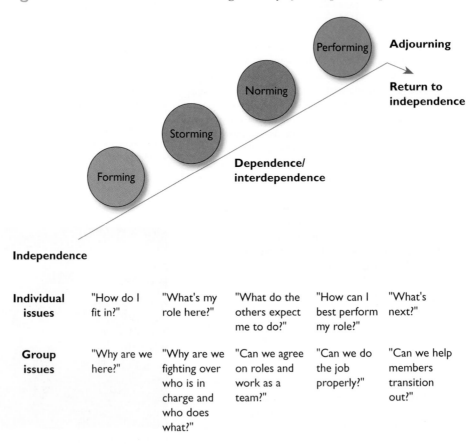

Individual issues	"How do I fit in?"	"What's my role here?"	"What do the others expect me to do?"	"How can I best perform my role?"	"What's next?"
Group issues	"Why are we here?"	"Why are we fighting over who is in charge and who does what?"	"Can we agree on roles and work as a team?"	"Can we do the job properly?"	"Can we help members transition out?"

duration or intensity. For instance, the storming stage may be practically nonexistent or painfully long, depending on the goal clarity and the commitment and maturity of the members. You can make this process come to life by relating the various stages to your own experiences with work groups, committees, athletic teams, social or religious groups, or class project teams. Some group happenings that surprised you when they occurred may now make sense or strike you as inevitable when seen as part of a natural development process.

Stage 1: Forming   During this ice-breaking stage, group members tend to be uncertain and anxious about such things as their roles, who is in charge, and the group's goals. Mutual trust is low, and there is a good deal of holding back to see who takes charge and how. If the formal leader (e.g., a supervisor) does not assert his or her authority, an emergent leader will eventually step in to fulfill the group's need for leadership and direction. Leaders typically mistake this honeymoon period as a mandate for permanent control. But later problems may force a leadership change.[19]

Stage 2: Storming   This is a time of testing. Individuals test the leader's policies and assumptions as they try to determine how they fit into the power structure. Subgroups take shape, and subtle forms of rebellion, such as procrastination, occur. Many groups stall in stage 2 because power politics erupts into open rebellion.[20]

Stage 3: Norming

Groups that make it through stage 2 generally do so because a respected member, other than the leader, challenges the group to resolve its power struggles so something can be accomplished. Questions about authority and power are resolved through unemotional, matter-of-fact group discussion. A feeling of team spirit is experienced because members believe they have found their proper roles. **Group cohesiveness,** defined as the "we feeling" that binds members of a group together, is the principal by-product of stage 3.[21] (For a good laugh, see the golfing explanation below the photo.)

Stage 4: Performing

Activity during this vital stage is focused on solving task problems. As members of a mature group, contributors get their work done without hampering others. There is a climate of open communication, strong cooperation, and lots of helping behavior. Conflicts and job boundary disputes are handled constructively and efficiently. Cohesiveness and personal commitment to group goals help the group achieve more than could any one individual acting alone. According to a pair of group development experts,

> the group structure can become flexible and adjust to fit the requirements of the situation without causing problems for the members. Influence can shift depending on who has the particular expertise or skills required for the group task or activity. Subgroups can work on special problems or subproblems without posing threats to the authority or cohesiveness of the rest of the group.[22]

Stage 5: Adjourning

The work is done; it is time to move on to other things. Having worked so hard to get along and get something done, many members feel a compelling sense of loss. The return to independence can be eased by rituals celebrating "the end" and "new beginnings." Parties, award ceremonies, graduations, or mock funerals can provide the needed punctuation at the end of a significant group project. Leaders need to emphasize valuable lessons learned in group dynamics to prepare everyone for future group and team efforts.

A *Fortune* article examined the question, Why do people love to mix golf and business? (Hint: It's all about group dynamics.):

> Ask people why they golf with business associates, and the answer is always the same: It's a great way to build relationships. They say this far more about golf than about going to dinner or attending a baseball game, and for good reason. Indeed, this may be the central fact about corporate golf, though it's rarely said: When people golf together, they see one another humiliated. At least 95% of all golfers are terrible, which means that in 18 holes everyone in the foursome will hit a tree, take three strokes in one bunker, or four-putt, with everyone else watching. Bonding is simply a matter of people jointly going through adversity, and a round of golf will furnish plenty of it. Of course it's only a game, but of course it isn't, so the bonds can be surprisingly strong. And what's that worth?

SOURCE: G Colvin, "Why Execs Love Golf," *Fortune*, April 30, 2001, p 46.

Group Development: Research and Practical Implications

A growing body of group development research provides managers with some practical insights.

Group cohesiveness

A "we feeling" binding group members together.

Extending the Tuckman Model: Group Decay   An interesting study of 10 software development teams, ranging in size from 5 to 16 members, enhanced the practical significance of Tuckman's model.[23] Unlike Tuckman's laboratory groups who worked together only briefly, the teams of software engineers worked on projects lasting *years*. Consequently, the researchers discovered more than simply a five-stage group development process. Groups were observed actually shifting into reverse once Tuckman's "performing" stage was reached, in what the researchers called *group decay*. In keeping with Tuckman's terminology, the three observed stages of group decay were labeled "de-norming," "de-storming," and "de-forming." These additional stages take shape as follows:

- *De-norming*. As the project evolves, there is a natural erosion of standards of conduct. Group members drift in different directions as their interests and expectations change.

- *De-storming*. This stage of group decay is a mirror opposite of the storming stage. Whereas disagreements and conflicts arise rather suddenly during the storming stage, an undercurrent of discontent slowly comes to the surface during the de-storming stage. Individual resistance increases and cohesiveness declines.

- *De-forming*. The work group literally falls apart as subgroups battle for control. Those pieces of the project that are not claimed by individuals or subgroups are abandoned. "Group members begin isolating themselves from each other and from their leaders. Performance declines rapidly because the whole job is no longer being done and group members little care what happens beyond their self-imposed borders."[24]

The primary management lesson from this study is that group leaders should not become complacent upon reaching the performing stage. According to the researchers: "The performing stage is a knife edge or saddle point, not a point of static equilibrium."[25] Awareness is the first line of defense. Beyond that, constructive steps need to be taken to reinforce norms, bolster cohesiveness, and reaffirm the common goal—*even when work groups seem to be doing their best.*

Feedback   Another fruitful study was carried out by a pair of Dutch social psychologists. They hypothesized that interpersonal feedback would vary systematically during the group development process. "The unit of feedback measured was a verbal message directed from one participant to another in which some aspect of behavior was addressed."[26] After collecting and categorizing 1,600 instances of feedback from four different eight-person groups, they concluded the following:

- Interpersonal feedback increases as the group develops through successive stages.

- As the group develops, positive feedback increases and negative feedback decreases.

- Interpersonal feedback becomes more specific as the group develops.

- The credibility of peer feedback increases as the group develops.[27]

These findings hold important lessons for managers. The content and delivery of interpersonal feedback among work group or committee members can be used as a gauge of whether the group is developing properly. For example, the onset of stage 2 (storming) will be signaled by a noticeable increase in *negative* feedback.

Effort can then be directed at generating specific, positive feedback among the members so the group's development will not stall. Our discussion of feedback in Chapter 9 is helpful in this regard.

Deadlines   Field and laboratory studies found uncertainty about deadlines to be a major disruptive force in both group development and intergroup relations. The practical implications of this finding were summed up by the researcher as follows:

> Uncertain or shifting deadlines are a fact of life in many organizations. Interdependent organizational units and groups may keep each other waiting, may suddenly move deadlines forward or back, or may create deadlines that are known to be earlier than is necessary in efforts to control erratic workflows. The current research suggests that the consequences of such uncertainty may involve more than stress, wasted time, overtime work, and intergroup conflicts. Synchrony in group members' expectations about deadlines may be critical to groups' abilities to accomplish successful transitions in their work.[28]

Thus, effective group management involves clarifying not only tasks and goals, but schedules and deadlines as well. When group members accurately perceive important deadlines, the pacing of work and timing of interdependent tasks tend to be more efficient.

Leadership Styles   Along a somewhat different line, experts in the area of leadership contend that different leadership styles are needed as work groups develop.

> In general, it has been documented that leadership behavior that is active, aggressive, directive, structured, and task-oriented seems to have favorable results early in the group's history. However, when those behaviors are maintained throughout the life of the group, they seem to have a negative impact on cohesiveness and quality of work. Conversely, leadership behavior that is supportive, democratic, decentralized, and participative seems to be related to poorer functioning in the early group development stages. However, when these behaviors are maintained throughout the life of the group, more productivity, satisfaction, and creativity result.[29]

The practical punch line here is that managers are advised to shift from a directive and structured leadership style to a participative and supportive style as the group develops.[30]

go to the Web for the Self-Exercise: Is This a Mature Work Group or Team?

Roles and Norms: Social Building Blocks for Group and Organizational Behavior

to the point

What are roles and norms and how do they affect workplace behavior?

Work groups transform individuals into functioning organizational members through subtle yet powerful social forces.[31] These social forces, in effect, turn "I" into "we" and "me" into "us." Group influence weaves individuals into the organization's social fabric by communicating and enforcing both role expectations and norms. We need to understand roles and norms if we are to effectively manage group and organizational behavior.

Roles

Four centuries have passed since William Shakespeare had his character Jaques speak the following memorable lines in Act II of *As You Like It:* "All the world's a stage, And all the men and women merely players; They have their exits and their entrances; And one man in his time plays many parts." This intriguing notion of all people as actors in a universal play was not lost on 20th-century sociologists who developed a complex theory of human interaction based on roles. According to an OB scholar, "**roles** are sets of behaviors that persons expect of occupants of a position."[32] Role theory attempts to explain how these social expectations influence employee behavior. This section explores role theory by analyzing a role episode and defining the terms *role overload, role conflict,* and *role ambiguity.*

Roles

Expected behaviors for a given position.

Role Episodes

A role episode, as illustrated in Figure 10–3, consists of a snapshot of the ongoing interaction between two people. In any given role episode, there is a role sender and a focal person who is expected to act out the role. Within a broader context, one may be simultaneously a role sender and a focal person. For the sake of social analysis, however, it is instructive to deal with separate role episodes.

Role episodes begin with the role sender's perception of the relevant organization's or group's behavioral requirements. Those requirements serve as a standard for formulating expectations for the focal person's behavior. The role sender then cognitively evaluates the focal person's actual behavior against those expectations. Appropriate verbal and behavioral messages are then sent to the focal person to pressure him or her into behaving as expected. A recent meta-analysis of the results from 160 different studies involving 77,954 employees confirmed that positive and negative peer pressure powerfully influence role performance.[33] This is how Westinghouse used a carrot-and-stick approach to communicate role expectations:

> The carrot is a plan, that . . . rewarded 134 managers with options to buy 764,000 shares of stock for boosting the company's financial performance.
>
> The stick is quarterly meetings that are used to rank managers by how much their operations contribute to earnings per share. The soft-spoken . . . [chairman of the board]

Figure 10–3   *A Role Episode*

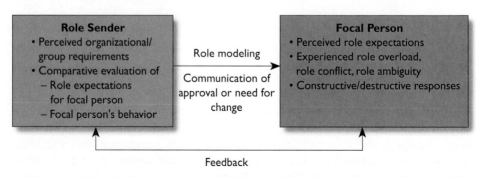

SOURCE: Adapted in part from R L Kohn, D M Wolfe, R P Quinn, and J D Snoek, *Organizational Stress: Studies in Role Conflict and Ambiguity,* 1981 ed. (Malabar, FL: Robert E Krieger Publishing, 1964), p 26.

doesn't scold. He just charts in green the results of the sectors that have met their goals and charts the laggards in red. Peer pressure does the rest. Shame "is a powerful tool," says one executive.[34]

On the receiving end of the role episode, the focal person accurately or inaccurately perceives the communicated role expectations and modeled behavior. Various combinations of role overload, role conflict, and role ambiguity are then experienced. (These three outcomes are defined and discussed in the following sections.) The focal person then responds constructively by engaging in problem solving, for example, or destructively because of undue tension, stress, and strain.

Role Overload

According to organizational psychologist Edgar Schein, **role overload** occurs when "the sum total of what role senders expect of the focal person far exceeds what he or she is able to do."[35] Students who attempt to handle a full course load and maintain a decent social life while working 30 or more hours a week know full well the consequences of role overload. As the individual tries to do more and more in less and less time, stress mounts and personal effectiveness slips.

Role overload
Others' expectations exceed one's ability.

LO.3 Role Conflict

Have you ever felt like you are being torn apart by the conflicting demands of those around you? If so, you are a victim of role conflict. **Role conflict** is experienced when "different members of the role set expect different things of the focal person."[36] Managers often face conflicting demands between work and family, as discussed in Chapter 6. Women tend to experience greater work-versus-family role conflict than men because they typically shoulder more of the household and child care duties. In a telephone survey of 1,009 adults in the United States, 81% of the women said they do most of the cooking, while 39% of the men claimed to handle the cooking. And who usually cleans up after meals? Seventy-eight percent of the women said they do, while 54% of the men took credit for that chore.[37] Employees in single-person households have their own version of role conflict between work and outside interests. (See the Real World/ Real People feature on page 286.)

Role conflict
Others have conflicting or inconsistent expectations.

Role conflict also may be experienced when internalized values, ethics, or personal standards collide with others' expectations. For instance, an otherwise ethical production supervisor may be told by a superior to "fudge a little" on the quality control reports so an important deadline will be met. The resulting role conflict forces the supervisor to choose between being loyal but unethical or ethical but disloyal. Tough ethical choices such as this mean personal turmoil, interpersonal conflict, and even resignation. Consequently, experts say business schools should do a better job of weaving ethics education into their course requirements.[38]

Role Ambiguity

Those who experience role conflict may have trouble complying with role demands, but they at least know what is expected of them. Such is not the case with **role ambiguity,** which occurs when "members of the role set fail to communicate to the focal person expectations they have or information needed to perform the role, either because they do not have the information or because they deliberately withhold it."[39] In short, people experience role ambiguity when they do not know what is expected of them. Organizational newcomers often complain about unclear job descriptions and vague promotion criteria. According to role theory, prolonged role ambiguity can foster job dissatisfaction, erode self-confidence, and hamper job performance.

Role ambiguity
Others' expectations are unknown.

As might be expected, role ambiguity varies across cultures. In a 21-nation study, people in individualistic cultures were found to have higher role ambiguity

Take Charge of the Role Conflict in Your Busy Life

In my research and coaching work over the past two decades, I have met many people who feel unfulfilled, overwhelmed, or stagnant because they are forsaking performance in one or more aspects of their lives. They aren't bringing their leadership abilities to bear in all of life's domains—work, home, community, and self (mind, body, and spirit). Of course, there will always be some tension among the different roles we play. But, contrary to the common wisdom, there's no reason to assume that it's a zero-sum game. It makes more sense to pursue excellent performance as a leader in all four domains—achieving what I call "four-way wins"—not trading off one for another but finding mutual value among them.

This is the main idea in a program called Total Leadership that I teach at the Wharton School [the University of Pennsylvania's Business School] and at companies and workshops around the world. "Total" because it's about the whole person and "Leadership" because it's about creating sustainable change to benefit not just you but the most important people around you.

Scoring four-way wins starts by taking a clear view of what you want from and can contribute to each domain of your life, now and in the future, with thoughtful consideration of the people who matter most to you and the expectations you have for one another. This is followed by systematically designing and implementing carefully crafted experiments—doing something new for a short period to see how it affects all four domains. If an experiment doesn't work out, you stop or adjust, and little is lost. If it does work out, it's a small win; over time these add up so that your overall efforts are focused increasingly on what and who matter most. Either way, you learn more about how to lead in all parts of your life.

Any useful advice here for you? Explain.

Role overload and role conflict are common today. How can you keep perspective and balance in your life?

---

than people in collectivist cultures.[40] In other words, people in collectivist or "we" cultures had a clearer idea of others' expectations. Collectivist cultures make sure everyone knows their proper place in society. People in individualistic "me" cultures, such as the United States, may enjoy more individual discretion, but comparatively less input from others has its price—namely, greater role ambiguity.

As mentioned earlier, these role outcomes typically are experienced in some combination, usually to the detriment of the individual and the organization. In fact, a study in Israel documented lower job performance when employees experienced a combination of role conflict and role ambiguity.[41]

go to the Web for the Self-Exercise: Measuring Role Conflict and Role Ambiguity

LO.4 Norms

Norms are more encompassing than roles. While roles involve behavioral expectations for specific positions, norms help organizational members determine right from wrong and good from bad. According to one respected team of management consultants: "A **norm** is an attitude, opinion, feeling, or action—shared by two or more people—that guides their behavior."[42] Although norms are typically unwritten and seldom discussed openly, they have a powerful influence on group and organizational behavior.[43] PepsiCo Inc., for instance, has evolved a norm that equates corporate competitiveness with physical fitness. According to observers,

> [l]eanness and nimbleness are qualities that pervade the company. When Pepsi's brash young managers take a few minutes away from the office, they often head straight for the company's physical fitness center or for a jog around the museum-quality sculptures outside of PepsiCo's Purchase, New York, headquarters.[44]

At PepsiCo and elsewhere, group members positively reinforce those who adhere to current norms with friendship and acceptance. On the other hand, nonconformists experience criticism and even **ostracism,** or rejection by group members. Anyone who has experienced the "silent treatment" from a group of friends knows what a potent social weapon ostracism can be.[45] Norms can be put into proper perspective by understanding how they develop and why they are enforced.

Norm
Shared attitudes, opinions, feelings, or actions that guide social behavior.

Ostracism
Rejection by other group members.

How Norms Are Developed

Experts say norms evolve in an informal manner as the group or organization determines what it takes to be effective. Generally speaking, norms develop in various combinations of the following four ways:

1. *Explicit statements by supervisors or coworkers.* For instance, a group leader might explicitly set norms about not drinking (alcohol) at lunch.

2. *Critical events in the group's history.* At times there is a critical event in the group's history that establishes an important precedent. (For example, a key recruit may have decided to work elsewhere because a group member said too many negative things about the organization. Hence, a norm against such "sour grapes" behavior might evolve.)

3. *Primacy.* The first behavior pattern that emerges in a group often sets group expectations. If the first group meeting is marked by very formal interaction between supervisors and employees, then the group often expects future meetings to be conducted in the same way.

4. *Carryover behaviors from past situations.* Such carryover of individual behaviors from past situations can increase the predictability of group members' behaviors in new settings and facilitate task accomplishment. For instance, students and professors carry fairly constant sets of expectations from class to class.[46]

We would like you to take a few moments and think about the norms that are currently in effect in your classroom. List the norms on a sheet of paper. Do these norms help or hinder your ability to learn? Norms can affect performance either positively or negatively.

Why Norms Are Enforced

Norms tend to be enforced by group members when they

- Help the group or organization survive.
- Clarify or simplify behavioral expectations.

Table 10–3   *Four Reasons Norms Are Enforced*

NORM	REASON FOR ENFORCEMENT	EXAMPLE
"Make our department look good in top management's eyes."	Group/organization survival	After vigorously defending the vital role played by the Human Resources Management Department at a divisional meeting, a staff specialist is complimented by her boss.
"Success comes to those who work hard and don't make waves."	Clarification of behavioral expectations	A senior manager takes a young associate aside and cautions him to be a bit more patient with coworkers who see things differently.
"Be a team player, not a star."	Avoidance of embarrassment	A project team member is ridiculed by her peers for dominating the discussion during a progress report to top management.
"Customer service is our top priority."	Clarification of central values/unique identity	Two sales representatives are given a surprise Friday afternoon party for having received prestigious best-in-the-industry customer service awards from an industry association.

- Help individuals avoid embarrassing situations.
- Clarify the group's or organization's central values and/or unique identity.[47]

Working examples of each of these four situations are presented in Table 10–3.

Relevant Research Insights and Managerial Implications

Although instruments used to measure role conflict and role ambiguity have questionable validity,[48] two separate meta-analyses indicated that role conflict and role ambiguity negatively affected employees. Specifically, role conflict and role ambiguity were associated with job dissatisfaction, tension and anxiety, lack of organizational commitment, intentions to quit, and, to a lesser extent, poor job performance.[49]

The meta-analyses' results hold few surprises for managers. Generally, because of the negative association reported, it makes sense for management to reduce both role conflict and role ambiguity. In this endeavor, managers can use feedback, formal rules and procedures, directive leadership, setting of specific (difficult) goals, and participation. Managers also can use the mentoring process discussed in Chapter 3 to reduce role conflict and ambiguity.

Regarding norms, a recent set of laboratory studies involving a total of 1,504 college students as subjects has important implications for workplace diversity programs. Subjects in groups where the norm was to express prejudices, condone discrimination, and laugh at hostile jokes tended to engage in these undesirable behaviors. Conversely, subjects tended to disapprove of prejudicial and discriminatory conduct when exposed to groups with more socially acceptable norms.[50] So, once again, Mom and our teachers were right when they warned us about the dangers of hanging out with "the wrong crowd." Managers who want to build strong diversity programs need to cultivate favorable role models and group norms. Poor role models and antisocial norms need to be identified and weeded out.

Group Structure and Composition

to the point

How do task and maintenance roles vary and what does research tell us about group size and mixed-gender groups?

Work groups of varying size are made up of individuals with varying ability and motivation.[51] Moreover, those individuals perform different roles, on either an assigned or voluntary basis. No wonder some work groups are more productive than others. No wonder some committees are tightly knit while others wallow in conflict. In this section, we examine three important dimensions of group structure and composition: (1) functional roles of group members, (2) group size, and (3) gender composition. Each of these dimensions alternatively can enhance or hinder group effectiveness, depending on how it is managed.

Functional Roles Performed by Group Members

As described in Table 10–4, both task and maintenance roles need to be performed if a work group is to accomplish anything.[52]

Table 10–4   *Functional Roles Performed by Group Members*

TASK ROLES	DESCRIPTION
Initiator	Suggests new goals or ideas.
Information seeker/giver	Clarifies key issues.
Opinion seeker/giver	Clarifies pertinent values.
Elaborator	Promotes greater understanding through examples or exploration of implications.
Coordinator	Pulls together ideas and suggestions.
Orienter	Keeps group headed toward its stated goal(s).
Evaluator	Tests group's accomplishments with various criteria such as logic and practicality.
Energizer	Prods group to move along or to accomplish more.
Procedural technician	Performs routine duties (e.g., handing out materials or rearranging seats).
Recorder	Performs a "group memory" function by documenting discussion and outcomes.
MAINTENANCE ROLES	**DESCRIPTION**
Encourager	Fosters group solidarity by accepting and praising various points of view.
Harmonizer	Mediates conflict through reconciliation or humor.
Compromiser	Helps resolve conflict by meeting others half way.
Gatekeeper	Encourages all group members to participate.
Standard setter	Evaluates the quality of group processes.
Commentator	Records and comments on group processes/dynamics.
Follower	Serves as a passive audience.

SOURCE: Adapted from discussion in K D Benne and P Sheats, "Functional Roles of Group Members," *Journal of Social Issues,* Spring 1948, pp 41–49.

Task roles

Task-oriented
group behavior.

Maintenance roles

Relationship-building
group behavior.

LO.5 Task versus Maintenance Roles   **Task roles** enable the work group to define, clarify, and pursue a common purpose. Meanwhile, **maintenance roles** foster supportive and constructive interpersonal relationships. In short, task roles keep the group *on track* while maintenance roles keep the group *together*. A project team member is performing a task function when he or she stands at an update meeting and says, "What is the real issue here? We don't seem to be getting anywhere." Another individual who says, "Let's hear from those who oppose this plan," is performing a maintenance function. Importantly, each of the various task and maintenance roles may be played in varying combinations and sequences by either the group's leader or any of its members.

Checklist for Managers   The task and maintenance roles listed in Table 10–4 can serve as a handy checklist for managers and group leaders who wish to ensure proper group development. Roles that are not always performed when needed, such as those of coordinator, evaluator, and gatekeeper, can be performed in a timely manner by the formal leader or assigned to other members. The task roles of initiator, orienter, and energizer are especially important because they are *goal-directed* roles. Research studies on group goal setting confirm the motivational power of challenging goals. As with individual goal setting (in Chapter 9), difficult but achievable goals are associated with better group results.[53] Also in line with individual goal-setting theory and research, group goals are more effective if group members clearly understand them and are both individually and collectively committed to achieving them. Initiators, orienters, and energizers can be very helpful in this regard.

International managers need to be sensitive to cultural differences regarding the relative importance of task and maintenance roles. In Japan, for example, cultural tradition calls for more emphasis on maintenance roles, especially the roles of harmonizer and compromiser:

> Courtesy requires that members not be conspicuous or disputatious in a meeting or classroom. If two or more members discover that their views differ—a fact that is tactfully taken to be unfortunate—they adjourn to find more information and to work toward a stance that all can accept. They do not press their personal opinions through strong arguments, neat logic, or rewards and threats. And they do not hesitate to shift their beliefs if doing so will preserve smooth interpersonal relations. (To lose is to win.)[54]

Group Size

How many group members is too many? The answer to this deceptively simple question has intrigued managers and academics for years. Folk wisdom says "two heads are better than one" but that "too many cooks spoil the broth." Recent employee survey evidence shows 3-person work groups to be the most popular (54%), followed by groups of 4 or more (27%) and 2-person groups (9%).[55] So where should a manager draw the line when staffing a committee? At 3? At 5 or 6? At 10 or more? Researchers have taken two different approaches to pinpointing optimum group size: mathematical modeling and laboratory simulations. Let us briefly review research evidence from these two approaches.

The Mathematical Modeling Approach

This approach involves building a mathematical model around certain desired outcomes of group action such as decision quality. Due to differing assumptions and statistical techniques, the results of this research are inconclusive. Statistical estimates of optimum group size have ranged from 3 to 13.[56]

How big is too big when it comes to work groups? Here we see the press monitoring the situation as President Obama, key cabinet members, and advisors discuss the Swine Flu epidemic.

The Laboratory Simulation Approach

This stream of research is based on the assumption that group behavior needs to be observed firsthand in controlled laboratory settings. A laboratory study by respected Australian researcher Philip Yetton and his colleague, Preston Bottger, provides useful insights about group size and performance.[57]

A total of 555 subjects (330 managers and 225 graduate management students, of whom 20% were female) were assigned to task teams ranging in size from 2 to 6. The teams worked on the National Aeronautics and Space Administration moon survival exercise. (This exercise involves the rank ordering of 15 pieces of equipment that would enable a spaceship crew on the moon to survive a 200-mile trip between a crash-landing site and home base.)[58] After analyzing the relationships between group size and group performance, Yetton and Bottger concluded the following:

> It would be difficult, at least with respect to decision quality, to justify groups larger than five members. . . . Of course, to meet needs other than high decision quality, organizations may employ groups significantly larger than four or five.[59]

More recent laboratory studies exploring the brainstorming productivity of various size groups (2 to 12 people), in face-to-face versus computer-mediated situations, proved fruitful. In the usual face-to-face brainstorming sessions, productivity of ideas did not increase as the size of the group increased. But brainstorming productivity increased as the size of the group increased when ideas were typed into networked computers.[60] These results suggest that computer networks are helping to deliver on the promise of productivity improvement through modern information technology.

LO.6 **Managerial Implications**   Within a contingency management framework, there is no hard-and-fast rule about group size. It depends on the manager's objective for the group. If a high-quality decision is the main objective, then a three- to five-member group would be appropriate. However, if the objective is to generate creative ideas, encourage participation, socialize new members, engage in training, or communicate policies, then groups much larger than five could be justified. But even in this developmental domain, researchers have found upward limits on group size. According to a meta-analysis, the positive effects of team-building activities diminished as group size increased.[61] Managers also need to be aware of *qualitative* changes that occur when group size increases. A meta-analysis of eight studies found the following relationships: As group size increased, group leaders tended to become more directive, and group member satisfaction tended to decline slightly.[62]

Odd-numbered groups (e.g., three, five, seven members) are recommended if the issue is to be settled by a majority vote. Voting deadlocks (e.g., 2–2, 3–3) too often hamper effectiveness of even-numbered groups.

L0.7 Effects of Men and Women Working Together in Groups

One study suggests that females entering male-dominated fields, such as law enforcement, face greater challenges than do males entering female-dominated fields, such as nursing.

As pointed out in Chapter 2, the female portion of the US labor force has grown significantly in recent decades. This demographic shift has impacted attitudes. For example, in a recent report about a longitudinal study of US executives, the researchers observed:

> Men and women are . . . responding similarly to the statement "I would feel comfortable working for a woman." Most female respondents continue to say they would, though there's been a slight drop since 1985. Of the men, 71% say they would. That figure is up significantly from 1965 (27%) and 1985 (47%).[63]

With more committees and teams requiring collaboration between women and men, some profound effects on group dynamics might be expected.[64] Let us see what researchers have found in the way of group gender composition effects and what managers can do about them.

Women Face an Uphill Battle in Mixed-Gender Task Groups

Laboratory and field studies paint a picture of inequality for women working in mixed-gender groups. Both women and men need to be aware of these often subtle but powerful group dynamics so corrective steps can be taken. Here is a prime example from a recent study of the link between handshake strength and job interview ratings. The researchers concluded:

> . . . we demonstrate that women overcome the effects of weaker handshakes, such that on average they do not receive lower interview performance ratings from interviewers, and that women may actually benefit more than do men if they present a strong and complete grip when they shake hands.[65]

Of course, the cultural context of this study (US university students as subjects) needs to be taken into consideration. Handshake etiquette varies across cultures.

In a laboratory study of six-person task groups, a clear pattern of gender inequality was found in the way group members interrupted each other. Men interrupted women significantly more often than they did other men. Women, who tended to interrupt less frequently and less successfully than men, interrupted men and women equally.[66] Another laboratory study involving Canadian college students found "both men and women exhibiting higher levels of interruption behavior in male-dominated groups."[67]

A field study of mixed-gender police and nursing teams in the Netherlands found another group dynamics disadvantage for women. These two particular professions—police work and nursing—were fruitful research areas because men dominate the former while women dominate the latter. As women move into male-dominated police forces and men gain employment opportunities in the female-dominated world of nursing, who faces the greatest resistance? The answer from this study was the women police officers. As the representation of the minority gender (either female police officers or male nurses) increased in the work groups, the following changes in attitude were observed:

> The attitude of the male majority changes from neutral to resistant, whereas the attitude of the female majority changes from favorable to neutral. In other words, men increasingly want to keep their domain for themselves, while women remain willing to share their domain with men.[68]

Again, managers are faced with the challenge of countering discriminatory tendencies in group dynamics.

The Issue of Sexual Harassment

According to an industry survey by a New York law firm specializing in workplace issues, the problem of sexual harassment refuses to go away:

> 63% of [234] respondents noted that they had handled a sexual harassment complaint at their company. That's up from 2003, when 57% said they had handled one. At least there was some good news here; that's way down from 1995, when 95% of respondents said that they'd handled one.[69]

The problem persists outside the business sector as well:

> About one out of seven female veterans of Afghanistan or Iraq who visit a Veterans Affairs center for medical care report being a victim of sexual assault or harassment during military duty.[70]

Making matters worse, a recent field study of five organizations found sexual harassment compounded by ethnic discrimination. According to the researchers, "Women experienced more sexual harassment than men, minorities experienced more ethnic harassment than whites, and minority women experienced more harassment overall than majority men, minority men, and majority women."[71] Thus, it was double jeopardy for the minority women. On-the-job harassment is persistent because it is rooted in widespread abusive behavior among teenagers (both face-to-face and electronically).[72]

Another study of social-sexual behavior among 1,232 working men ($n = 405$) and women ($n = 827$) in the Los Angeles area found *nonharassing* sexual behavior to be very common, with 80% of the total sample reporting experience with such behavior. Indeed, according to the researchers, increased social contact between women and men in work groups and organizations has led to increased sexualization (e.g., flirting and romance) in the workplace.[73]

Table 10−5   *Behavioral Categories of Sexual Harassment*

CATEGORY	DESCRIPTION	BEHAVIORAL EXAMPLES
Derogatory attitudes— impersonal	Behaviors that reflect derogatory attitudes about men or women in general	Obscene gestures not directed at target Sex-stereotyped jokes
Derogatory attitudes— personal	Behaviors that are directed at the target that reflect derogatory attitudes about the target's gender	Obscene phone calls Belittling the target's competence
Unwanted dating pressure	Persistent requests for dates after the target has refused	Repeated requests to go out after work or school
Sexual propositions	Explicit requests for sexual encounters	Proposition for an affair
Physical sexual contact	Behaviors in which the harasser makes physical sexual contact with the target	Embracing the target Kissing the target
Physical nonsexual contact	Behaviors in which the harasser makes physical nonsexual contact with the target	Congratulatory hug
Sexual coercion	Requests for sexual encounters or forced encounters that are made a condition of employment or promotion	Threatening punishment unless sexual favors are given Sexual bribery

SOURCE: From M Rotundo, D Nguyen, and P R Sackett, "A Meta-Analytic Review of Gender Differences in Perceptions of Sexual Harassment," *Journal of Applied Psychology*, October 2001, Article 914–922. Copyright © 2001 by the American Psychological Association. Reprinted with permission.

From an OB research standpoint, sexual harassment is a complex and multifaceted problem. For example, a meta-analysis of 62 studies found women perceiving a broader range of behaviors as sexual harassment (see Table 10–5), as opposed to what men perceived. Women and men tended to agree that sexual propositions and coercion qualified as sexual harassment, but there was less agreement about other aspects of a hostile work environment.[74]

Constructive Managerial Action   Male and female employees can and often do work well together in groups. A survey of 387 male US government employees sought to determine how they were affected by the growing number of female coworkers. The researchers concluded, "Under many circumstances, including intergender interaction in work groups, frequent contact leads to cooperative and supportive social relations."[75] More recently, a field study of 1,158 US Air Force officers divided into mixed-gender teams for a five-week officer development program determined that "a higher female proportion within teams contributed to better team problem solving."[76] Still, managers need to take affirmative steps to ensure that the documented sexualization of work environments does not erode into sexual harassment. Whether perpetrated against women or men, sexual harassment is demeaning, unethical, and appropriately called "work environment pollution." Moreover, the US

Equal Employment Opportunity Commission holds employers legally accountable for behavior it considers sexually harassing. An expert on the subject explains:

> What exactly is sexual harassment? The Equal Employment Opportunity Commission (EEOC) says that unwelcome sexual advances, requests for sexual favors, and other verbal or physical conduct of a sexual nature constitute sexual harassment when submission to such conduct is made a condition of employment; when submission to or rejection of sexual advances is used as a basis for employment decisions; or when such conduct creates an intimidating, hostile, or offensive work environment. These EEOC guidelines interpreting Title VII of the Civil Rights Act of 1964 further state that employers are responsible for the actions of their supervisors and agents and that employers are responsible for the actions of other employees if the employer knows or should have known about the sexual harassment.[77]

A *Training* magazine survey of 1,652 US companies with at least 100 employees found 91% conducting some sort of sexual harassment training and 68% doing so at least annually.[78] Given the disagreement between women and men about what constitutes sexual harassment, this type of education is very important.

Beyond avoiding lawsuits by establishing and enforcing antidiscrimination and sexual harassment policies, managers need to take additional steps. Workforce diversity training is a popular approach today. Gender-issue workshops are another option.

Threats to Group Effectiveness

to the point
What are the Asch effect, groupthink, and social loafing and how can they be prevented?

Even when managers carefully staff and organize task groups, group dynamics can still go haywire. Forehand knowledge of three major threats to group effectiveness—the Asch effect, groupthink, and social loafing—can help managers take necessary preventive steps. Because the first two problems relate to blind conformity, some brief background work is in order.

Very little would be accomplished in task groups and organizations without conformity to norms, role expectations, policies, and rules and regulations. After all, deadlines, commitments, and product/service quality standards need to be established and adhered to if the organization is to survive. But conformity is a two-edged sword. Excessive or blind conformity can stifle critical thinking, the first line of defense against unethical conduct. Almost daily accounts in the popular media of executive misdeeds, insider trading scandals, price fixing, illegal dumping of hazardous wastes, and other unethical practices make it imperative that future managers understand the mechanics of blind conformity.[79]

"I caught Barclay lip-synching when everyone else was saying yes."
SOURCE: *Harvard Business Review*, December 2006, p. 122.

Figure 10–4   *The Asch Experiment*

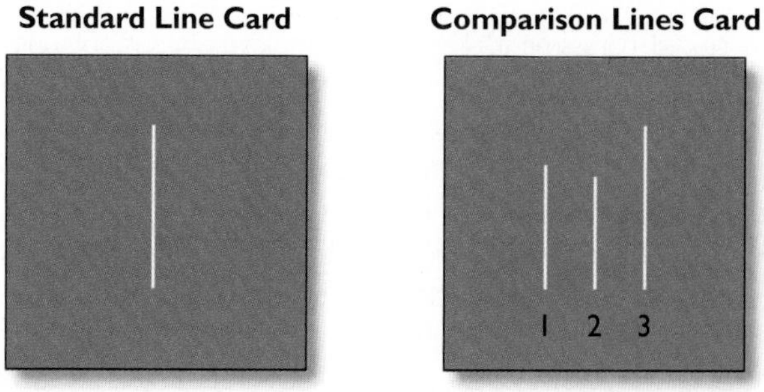

Standard Line Card   **Comparison Lines Card**

The Asch Effect

More than 55 years ago, social psychologist Solomon Asch conducted a series of laboratory experiments that revealed a negative side of group dynamics.[80] Under the guise of a "perception test," Asch had groups of seven to nine volunteer college students look at 12 pairs of cards such as the ones in Figure 10–4. The object was to identify the line that was the same length as the standard line. Each individual was told to announce his or her choice to the group. Since the differences among the comparison lines were obvious, there should have been unanimous agreement during each of the 12 rounds. But that was not the case.

A Minority of One   All but one member of each group were Asch's confederates who agreed to systematically select the wrong line during seven of the rounds (the other five rounds were control rounds for comparison purposes). The remaining individual was the naive subject who was being tricked. Group pressure was created by having the naive subject in each group be among the last to announce his or her choice. Thirty-one subjects were tested. Asch's research question was: "How often would the naive subjects conform to a majority opinion that was obviously wrong?"

Only 20% of Asch's subjects remained entirely independent; 80% yielded to the pressures of group opinion at least once! And 58% knuckled under to the "immoral majority" at least twice. Hence, the **Asch effect,** the distortion of individual judgment by a unanimous but incorrect opposition, was documented.

Asch effect

Giving in to a unanimous but wrong opposition.

A Managerial Perspective   Asch's experiment has been widely replicated with mixed results. Both high and low degrees of blind conformity have been observed with various situations and subjects. Replications in Japan and Kuwait have demonstrated that the Asch effect is not unique to the United States.[81] A 1996 meta-analysis of 133 Asch-line experiments from 17 countries found a *decline* in conformity among US subjects since the 1950s. Internationally, collectivist countries, where the group prevails over the individual, produced higher levels of conformity than individualistic countries.[82] The point is not precisely how great the Asch effect is in a given situation or culture, but rather, managers committed to ethical conduct need to be concerned that the Asch effect exists.

For Jeffrey Skilling, the now-jailed former CEO of Enron, the Asch effect was something to cultivate and nurture. Consider this organizational climate for blind obedience:

Skilling was filling headquarters with his own troops. He was not looking for "fuzzy skills," a former employee recalls. His recruits talked about a socialization process called

"Enronizing." Family time? Quality of life? Forget it. Anybody who did not embrace the elbows-out culture "didn't get it." They were "damaged goods" and "shipwrecks," likely to be fired by their bosses at blistering annual job reviews known as rank-and-yank sessions. The culture turned paranoid: former CIA and FBI agents were hired to enforce security. Using "sniffer" programs, they would pounce on anyone e-mailing a potential competitor. The "spooks," as the former agents were called, were known to barge into offices and confiscate computers.[83]

Even isolated instances of blind, unthinking conformity seriously threaten the effectiveness and integrity of work groups and organizations.[84] Functional conflict and assertiveness, discussed in Chapters 13 and 14, can help employees respond appropriately when they find themselves facing an immoral majority. Ethical codes mentioning specific practices also can provide support and guidance.

LO.8 Groupthink

Why did President Lyndon B Johnson and his group of intelligent White House advisers make some very *unintelligent* decisions that escalated the Vietnam War? Those fateful decisions were made despite obvious warning signals, including stronger than expected resistance from the North Vietnamese and withering support at home and abroad. Systematic analysis of the decision-making processes underlying the war in Vietnam and other US foreign policy fiascoes prompted Yale University's Irving Janis to coin the term *groupthink*.[85] Modern managers can all too easily become victims of groupthink, just like President Johnson's staff, if they passively ignore the danger.

Definition and Symptoms of Groupthink
Janis defines **groupthink** as "a mode of thinking that people engage in when they are deeply involved in a cohesive in-group, when members' strivings for unanimity override their motivation to realistically appraise alternative courses of action."[86] He adds, "Groupthink refers to a deterioration of mental efficiency, reality testing, and moral judgment that results from in-group pressures."[87] Unlike Asch's subjects, who were strangers to each other, members of groups victimized by groupthink are friendly, tightly knit, and cohesive.

The symptoms of groupthink listed in Figure 10–5 thrived in US corporate boardrooms of the past where cohesive directors too often caved in to strong-willed CEOs and signed off on bad decisions. But, as recently noted by *BusinessWeek*, circumstances are changing:

> A new era for directors dawned with the passage of the Sarbanes-Oxley Act of 2002. Then board members were hit with the frightening prospect of real financial liability in a smattering of lawsuits that followed the corporate crime wave. Now the heat on directors is growing more intense. Their reputations are increasingly at risk when the companies they watch over are tainted by scandal. Their judgment is being questioned by activist shareholders outraged by sky-high pay packages. And investors and regulators are subjecting their actions to higher scrutiny. Long gone are the days when a director could get away with a quick rubber-stamp of a CEO's plans. . . .
>
> The old rules of civility that discouraged directors from asking managers tough or embarrassing questions are eroding.[88]

Groupthink

Janis's term for a cohesive in-group's unwillingness to realistically view alternatives.

Figure 10–5 *Symptoms of Groupthink Lead to Defective Decision Making*

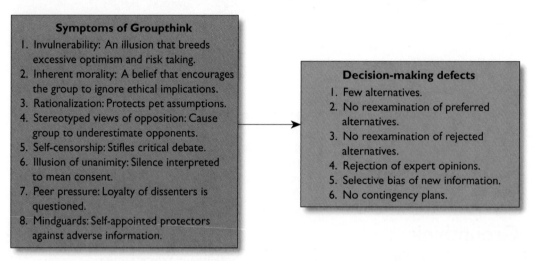

SOURCES: Symptoms from I L Janis, *Groupthink: Psychological Studies of Policy, Decisions and Fiascoes*, 2E. Copyright © 1982 by Wadsworth, a part of Cengage Learning, Inc. Reproduced by permission. www.cengage.com/permission. Defects excerpted from G Moorhead, "Groupthink: Hypothesis in Need of Testing," *Group & Organization Studies*, December 1982, p 434. Copyright © 1982 by Sage Publications. Reprinted by permission of Sage Publications.

Groupthink Research and Prevention Laboratory studies using college students as subjects validate portions of Janis's groupthink concept. Specifically, it has been found that

- Groups with a moderate amount of cohesiveness produce better decisions than low- or high-cohesive groups.
- Highly cohesive groups victimized by groupthink make the poorest decisions, despite high confidence in those decisions.[89]

Janis believes prevention is better than cure when dealing with groupthink. He recommends the following preventive measures:

1. Each member of the group should be assigned the role of critical evaluator. This role involves actively voicing objections and doubts.
2. Top-level executives should not use policy committees to rubber-stamp decisions that have already been made.
3. Different groups with different leaders should explore the same policy questions.
4. Subgroup debates and outside experts should be used to introduce fresh perspectives.
5. Someone should be given the role of devil's advocate when discussing major alternatives. This person tries to uncover every conceivable negative factor.
6. Once a consensus has been reached, everyone should be encouraged to rethink their position to check for flaws.[90]

These antigroupthink measures can help cohesive groups produce sound recommendations and decisions. A G Lafley, the widely respected chairman of

Procter & Gamble, offers his own constructive twist:

> Some of the strongest, most courageous people are on the minority side of a decision. It doesn't mean they're wrong. It means they have the courage to speak. . . . I've been trying to change from an advocacy system to what I call an inquiry system. First, I make sure we have a clear definition of the problem. We hold off on the advocacy. We get all the possible solutions and sort through the options. Then, and only then, do we want people to advocate.[91]

Avoiding groupthink is a powerful argument in favor of *diversity;* not only racial and gender diversity, but diversity in age, background, religion, education, and world views as well. (See the Real World/Real People feature on page 300.)

LO.9 Social Loafing

Is group performance less than, equal to, or greater than the sum of its parts? Can three people, for example, working together accomplish less than, the same as, or more than they would working separately? An interesting study conducted more than a half century ago by a French agricultural engineer named Ringelmann found the answer to be "less than."[92] In a rope-pulling exercise, Ringelmann reportedly found that three people pulling together could achieve only two and a half times the average individual rate. Eight pullers achieved less than four times the individual rate. This tendency for individual effort to decline as group size increases has come to be called **social loafing**.[93] Let us briefly analyze this threat to group effectiveness and synergy with an eye toward avoiding it.

Social loafing
Decrease in individual effort as group size increases.

Social Loafing Theory and Research   Among the theoretical explanations for the social loafing effect are (1) equity of effort ("Everyone else is goofing off, so why shouldn't I?"), (2) loss of personal accountability ("I'm lost in the crowd, so who cares?"), (3) motivational loss due to the sharing of rewards ("Why should I work harder than the others when everyone gets the same reward?"), and (4) coordination loss as more people perform the task ("We're getting in each other's way.").

Laboratory studies refined these theories by identifying situational factors that moderated the social loafing effect. Social loafing occurred when

- The task was perceived to be unimportant, simple, or not interesting.[94]
- Group members thought their individual output was not identifiable.[95]
- Group members expected their coworkers to loaf.[96]

But social loafing did *not* occur when group members in two laboratory studies expected to be evaluated.[97] Also, research suggests that self-reliant "individualists" are more prone to social loafing than are group-oriented "collectivists." But individualists can be made more cooperative by keeping the group small and holding each member personally accountable for results.[98]

Practical Implications   These findings demonstrate that social loafing is not an inevitable part of group effort. Management can curb this threat to group effectiveness by making sure the task is challenging and perceived as

A Call for Better Corporate Governance

When boards are operating as they should, directors are engaged in a vigorous, candid dialogue with the CEO and his lieutenants about strategy and having the right talent in place to execute key initiatives. And they're spending time in the guts of the organization, talking to "regular" employees and looking for signs that the CEO's vision is understood and shared, that company values are more than lip service proffered for the board's entertainment. They're protecting shareholders not by wielding calculators but by deploying good judgment. . . .

But that can happen only when boards have the right kind of people serving on them: Members who, in very limited time, can exercise good judgment and act with courage. Members who have a special ear, the kind that can hear a presentation and discern between overpromisers and overdeliverers, between glib salesmen and those they would bet their own money on. Members who have skin in the game, know the company, and care about it deeply.

Can more diligent corporate governance help executives avoid groupthink?

SOURCE: Excerpted from J Welch and S Welch, "Of Boards and Blame," January 26–February 2, 2009, issue of *BusinessWeek* by special permission. Copyright © 2009 by The McGraw-Hill Companies, Inc.

An active corporate board of directors can help keep companies on an effective and ethical track and be the first line of defense against groupthink. Why are corporate boards often criticized for being too passive?

Table 10–6   *How to Avoid Social Loafing in Groups and Teams: The Stepladder Technique*

The stepladder technique is intended to enhance group decision making by structuring the entry of group members into a core group. Increasing or decreasing the number of group members alters the number of steps. In a four-person group, the stepladder technique has three steps. Initially, two group members (the initial core group) work together on the problem at hand. Next, a third member joins the core group and presents his or her preliminary solutions for the same problem. The entering member's presentation is followed by a three-person discussion. Finally, the fourth group member joins the core group and pre-sents his or her preliminary solutions. This is followed by a four-person discussion, which has as its goal the rendering of a final group decision.

The stepladder technique has four requirements. First, each group member must be given the group's task and sufficient time to think about the problem before entering the core group. Second, the entering member must present his or her preliminary solutions before hearing the core group's preliminary solutions. Third, with the entry of each additional member to the core group, sufficient time to discuss the problem is necessary. Fourth, a final decision must be purposely delayed until the group has been formed in its entirety.

SOURCE: Excerpted from S G Rogelberg, J L Barnes-Farrell, and C A Lowe, "The Stepladder Technique: An Alternative Group Structure Facilitating Effective Group Decision Making," *Journal of Applied Psychology* 77 (October 1992), p 731. Copyright © 1992 by the American Psychological Association. Reprinted with permission.

---

go to the Web for the Group Exercise: A Committee Decision

important. Additionally, it is a good idea to hold group members personally accountable for identifiable portions of the group's task. One way to do this is with the *stepladder technique,* a group decision-making process proven effective by researchers (see Table 10–6). Compared with conventional groups, stepladder groups produced significantly better decisions in the same amount of time. "Furthermore, stepladder groups' decisions surpassed the quality of their best individual members' decisions 56% of the time. In contrast, conventional groups' decisions surpassed the quality of their best members' decisions only 13% of the time."[99] The stepladder technique could be a useful tool for organizations relying on any sort of teams, including self-managed and virtual teams (discussed in the next chapter).

Summary of Key Concepts

1. *Identify the four sociological criteria of a group, and discuss the impact of social networking on group dynamics.* Sociologically, a *group* is defined as two or more freely interacting individuals who share collective norms and goals and have a common identity. Social networking sites such as MySpace and Facebook have blurred the line between formal and informal groups by giving people unprecedented access to one's personal life. This has magnified the long-standing dilemma of how friendly managers should be with their direct reports. They are urged to compartmentalize their official and unofficial roles.

2. *Describe the five stages in Tuckman's theory of group development, and discuss the threat of group decay.* The five stages in Tuckman's theory are forming (the group comes together), storming (members test the limits and each other), norming (questions about authority and power are resolved as the group becomes more cohesive), performing (effective communication and cooperation help the group get things done), and adjourning (group members go their own way). According to recent research, group decay occurs when a work group achieves the "performing" stage and then shifts into reverse. Group decay occurs through de-norming (erosion of standards), de-storming (growing discontent and loss of cohesiveness), and de-forming (fragmentation and breakup of the group).

3. *Distinguish between role conflict and role ambiguity.* Organizational roles are sets of behaviors persons expect of occupants of a position. One may experience role overload (too much to do in too little time), role conflict (conflicting role expectations), or role ambiguity (unclear role expectations).

4. *Contrast roles and norms, and specify four reasons norms are enforced in organizations.* While roles are specific to the person's position, norms are shared attitudes that differentiate appropriate from inappropriate behavior in a variety of situations. Norms evolve informally and are enforced because they help the group or organization survive, clarify behavioral expectations, help people avoid embarrassing situations, and clarify the group's or organization's central values.

5. *Distinguish between task and maintenance roles in groups.* Members of formal groups need to perform both task (goal-oriented) and maintenance (relationship-oriented) roles if anything is to be accomplished.

6. *Summarize the practical contingency management implications for group size.* Laboratory simulation studies suggest decision-making groups should be limited to five or fewer members. Larger groups are appropriate when creativity, participation, and socialization are the main objectives. If majority votes are to be taken, odd-numbered groups are recommended to avoid deadlocks.

7. *Discuss why managers need to carefully handle mixed-gender task groups.* Women face special group dynamics challenges in mixed-gender task groups. Steps need to be taken to make sure increased sexualization of work environments does not erode into illegal sexual harassment.

8. *Describe groupthink, and identify at least four of its symptoms.* Groupthink plagues cohesive in-groups that shortchange moral judgment while putting too much emphasis on unanimity. Symptoms of groupthink include invulnerability, inherent morality, rationalization,

stereotyped views of opposition, self-censorship, illusion of unanimity, peer pressure, and mindguards. Critical evaluators, outside expertise, and devil's advocates are among the preventive measures recommended by Irving Janis, who coined the term *groupthink*.

9. *Define social loafing, and explain how managers can prevent it*. Social loafing involves the tendency for individual effort to decrease as group size increases. This problem can be contained if the task is challenging and important, individuals are held accountable for results, and group members expect everyone to work hard. The stepladder technique, a structured approach to group decision making, can reduce social loafing by increasing personal effort and accountability.

Key Terms

Group, 275
Formal group, 276
Informal group, 276
Social networking site (SNS), 277
Group cohesiveness, 281
Roles, 284
Role overload, 285
Role conflict, 285

Role ambiguity, 285
Norm, 287
Ostracism, 287
Task roles, 290
Maintenance roles, 290
Asch effect, 296
Groupthink, 297
Social loafing, 299

OB in Action Case Study

Unmasking Manly Men

What can managers in white-collar firms learn from roughnecks and roustabouts on an offshore oil rig? That extinguishing macho behavior is vital to achieving top performance. That's a key finding from our study of life on two oil platforms, during which we spent several weeks over the course of 19 months living, eating, and working alongside crews offshore.

Oil rigs are dirty, dangerous, and demanding workplaces that have traditionally encouraged displays of masculine strength, daring, and technical prowess. But over the past 15 years or so the platforms we studied have deliberately jettisoned their hard-driving, macho cultures in favor of an environment in which men admit when they've made mistakes and explore how anxiety, stress, or lack of experience may have caused them; appreciate one another publicly; and routinely ask for and offer help. These workers shifted their focus from proving their masculinity to larger, more compelling goals: maximizing the safety and well-being of coworkers and doing their jobs effectively.

The shift required a new attitude toward work, which was pushed from the top down. If you can't expose errors and learn from them, management's thinking went, you can't be safe or effective. Workers came to appreciate that to improve safety and performance in a potentially deadly environment, they had to be open to new information that challenged their assumptions, and they had to acknowledge when they were wrong.

Their altered stance revealed two things: First, that much of their macho behavior was not only unnecessary but actually got in the way of doing their jobs; and second, that their notions about what constituted strong leadership needed to change. They discovered that the people who used to rise to the top—the "biggest, baddest roughnecks," as one worker described them—weren't necessarily the best at improving safety and effectiveness. Rather, the ones who excelled were mission-driven guys who cared about their fellow workers, were good listeners, and were willing to learn.

Over the 15-year period these changes in work practices, norms, perceptions, and behaviors were implemented company-wide. The company's accident rate declined by 84%, while productivity (number of barrels produced), efficiency (cost per barrel), and reliability (production "up" time) increased beyond the industry's previous benchmark.

But the changes had an unintended effect as well. The men's willingness to risk a blow to their image—by, for example, exposing their incompetence or weakness when necessary in order to do their jobs well—profoundly influenced their sense of who they were and could be as men. No longer focused on affirming their masculinity, they felt able to behave in ways that conventional masculine norms would have precluded.

If men in the hypermasculine environment of oil rigs can let go of the macho ideal and improve their performance, then men in corporate America might be able to do likewise. Numerous studies have examined the costs of macho displays in contexts ranging from aeronautics to manufacturing to high tech to the law. They show that men's attempts to prove their masculinity interfere with the training of recruits, compromise decision quality, marginalize women workers, lead to civil- and human-rights violations, and alienate men from their health, feelings, and relationships with others. The price of men's striving to demonstrate their masculinity is high, and both individuals and organizations pay it.

The problem lies not in traditionally masculine attributes per se—many tasks require aggressiveness, strength, or emotional detachment—but in men's efforts to prove themselves on these dimensions, whether in the hazardous setting of an offshore oil platform or in the posh, protected surroundings of the executive suite. By creating conditions that focus people on the real requirements of the job, rather than on stereotypical images believed to equate with competence, organizations can free employees to do their best work.[100]

Questions for Discussion

1. How do the concepts of roles and norms figure into this case? Explain.
2. What are the implications for mixed-gender work groups? Is this a good way to combat sexual harassment? Explain.
3. Does this attitude shift make groupthink more or less likely? Explain.

Ethical Dilemma

My Boss Wants to "Friend" Me Online

Paul Dyer always was able to hold off his boss's invitations to party by employing that arm's-length response: "We'll have to do that sometime," he'd say.

But when his boss, in his 30s, invited Dyer, 24, to be friends on the social-networking sites MySpace and Facebook, dodging wasn't so easy.

On the one hand, accepting a person's request to be friends online grants them access to the kind of intimacy never meant for office consumption, such as recent photos of keggers. . . .

But declining a "friend" request from a colleague or a boss is a slight. So Dyer accepted the invitation, then removed any inappropriate or incriminating photos of himself. . . .

Dyer, it turns out, wasn't the one who had to be embarrassed. His boss had photos of himself attempting to imbibe two drinks at once, ostensibly, Dyer ventures, to send the message: "I'm a crazy, young party guy."[101]

If You Were Paul Dyer, What Would You Do Now?

1. Big mistake. Unwind the situation as quickly and graciously as possible, preferably in person. Explain how.
2. Don't panic. Let the online relationship whither away from lack of attention.
3. Play along for awhile in hopes the boss has a short online attention span and will flit off to pester others.
4. You've made a bad decision; now don't compound it by alienating your boss. Participate in the virtual relationship, applying your own ethical boundaries. Explain those boundaries.
5. Invent other interpretations or options. Discuss.

NOTE: In a recent survey of 1,070 employees, 30% considered their boss a friend.[102]

Web Resources

For study material and exercises that apply to this chapter, visit our Web site, **www.mhhe.com/kreitner**

Chapter 11

Developing and Leading Effective Teams

When you finish studying the material in this chapter, you should be able to:

LO.1 Explain how a work group becomes a team.

LO.2 Identify and describe four types of work teams.

LO.3 Explain the model of effective work teams, and specify the two criteria of team effectiveness.

LO.4 Identify five teamwork competencies team members need to possess.

LO.5 Discuss why teams fail.

LO.6 List at least four things managers can do to build trust.

LO.7 Distinguish two types of group cohesiveness, and summarize cohesiveness research findings.

LO.8 Define virtual teams and self-managed teams.

LO.9 Describe high-performance teams and discuss team leadership.

Student Resources for Studying Chapter 11

The Web site for your text includes resources that will help you master the concepts in this chapter. As you read, you'll want to visit the site for these helpful tools:

- Your online Study Guide includes learning objectives, a chapter summary, a glossary of key terms, and discussion questions.
- Take a practice quiz and test your knowledge!
- Scroll through a PowerPoint presentation with key concepts for this chapter.

Your instructor might also direct you to the Web site for these exercises:

- Self-assessments that correspond with the chapter content and a Group Exercise.
- You'll also find Video Cases and Internet Exercises for this chapter online.

www.mhhe.com/kreitner

BusinessWeek Like the other 149 passengers on US Airways' Flight 1549, all of whom survived a harrowing landing in New York's Hudson River, Baltimore attorney James J Hanks Jr. was amazed by the pilot's deft response to losing power in both engines. But Hanks, a partner at law firm Venable LLP, was also impressed with the velvet-rope care US Airways employees provided following the forced landing—from the dry clothes, warm meals, and free hotel room they had waiting for him onshore to their efforts to replace all of his lost possessions, down to his BlackBerry. "I felt completely comfortable in their hands," says Hanks.

For a company that's not known for its customer service—the Tempe (Ariz.) carrier has perennially finished near the bottom of customer service rankings—US Airways' handling of the near-disaster has cast a halo around its brand. It provided passengers with everything from flights for loved ones to daily calls from counselors. Crisis-management experts say the carrier's "Miracle on the Hudson" follow-up will stand as a case study in how to treat customers after a crisis. "The airmanship was spectacular, but US Airways did an outstanding job of helping the passengers with their emotional reentry as well," says airline consultant Robert W Mann Jr.

Like all carriers, US Airways has a playbook for such incidents. It stages "dry run" emergency exercises at least three times a year at each airport it serves and has a far-flung network of gate agents, reservation clerks, and other employees who double as "Care Team" members who are dispatched to emergencies at a moment's notice. When news broke of the water landing, US Airways activated a special 800 number for families to call and dispatched more than 100 employees on a Boeing 757 from headquarters. Scott Stewart, managing director for corporate finance, was armed with a bag of emergency cash for passengers and credit cards for employees to buy any medicines, toiletries, or personal items that passengers needed.

Other responders arrived with suitcases full of prepaid cell phones and sweatsuits for anyone who needed dry clothes. Staffers escorted each passenger to a new flight or a local New York hotel, where it arranged for round-the-clock buffets. They also arranged train tickets and rental cars for those who didn't want to fly. "Some people lost their driver's licenses, so we

Passengers from US Airways' Flight 1549 being rescued from the Hudson River.

reached out to high-level executives at Hertz and Amtrak to make sure they had no trouble getting a rental or a ticket," says Kerry Hester, vice-president for customer-service planning. The airline also retained locksmiths to help passengers who had lost their keys get back into their cars and homes.[1]

FOR DISCUSSION

From the time Flight 1549 was first is trouble through the customer follow-up process, what types of teamwork were required for positive outcomes?

Extensive media coverage documented how Captain Sullenberger's skilled US Airways' flight crew helped save 155 lives on January 15, 2009.[2] Less heralded was the follow-up customer service teamwork covered in the opening vignette. Well-practiced teamwork—by the flight crew, first responders, medical professionals, and airline support staff—was a key contributor to the "miracle on the Hudson." On a less dramatic but still important level is the teamwork required on a day-to-day basis to get the job done in organizations of all sizes and types. The concept of *social capital,* covered in Chapter 1, really comes to life when our attention turns to teams and teamwork in today's organizations. *BusinessWeek* columnists Jack and Suzy Welch offered this perspective:

> It is the excitement of being part of something bigger than yourself and the thrill of building something—a product, a service, or a team. It is the fun of laughing, debating, sweating it out with fellow travelers—friends and allies in the never-ending competition for customers and profits.... It just doesn't get any better.[3]

Cooperation, trust, and camaraderie energize organizations. Judging from a recent survey that asked corporate leaders to look ahead five years, we all need to polish our teamwork skills: "Teamwork/collaboration" (74%) was among the top three most important knowledge/skill areas, just behind "critical thinking/problem solving" (78%) and "information technology application" (77%).[4] Jeff Vijungco, director of recruiting at Adobe Systems, tells how he finds team players: "I actually count the number of times a candidate says 'I' in an interview. We'd much rather hear 'we'."[5]

Team

Small group with complementary skills who hold themselves mutually accountable for common purpose, goals, and approach.

Emphasis in this chapter is on tapping the full and promising potential of work groups and teams. We will (1) identify different types of work teams; (2) look at what makes teams succeed or fail; (3) examine keys to effective teamwork, such as trust; (4) explore modern applications of the team concept, including virtual teams; and (5) discuss team building and team leadership.

to the point

How can you help a work group evolve into an effective team?

LO.1 Work Teams: Types, Effectiveness, and Stumbling Blocks

Jon R Katzenbach and Douglas K Smith, management consultants at McKinsey & Company, say it is a mistake to use the terms *group* and *team* interchangeably. After studying many different kinds of teams—from athletic to corporate to military—they concluded that successful teams tend to take on a life of their own. Katzenbach and Smith define a **team** as "a small number of people with complementary skills who are committed to a common purpose, performance goals, and approach for which they hold themselves mutually accountable."[6] Relative

Table 11–1   *The Evolution of a Team*

A work group becomes a team when
1. Leadership becomes a shared activity.
2. Accountability shifts from strictly individual to both individual and collective.
3. The group develops its own purpose or mission.
4. Problem solving becomes a way of life, not a part-time activity.
5. Effectiveness is measured by the group's collective outcomes and products.

SOURCE: Condensed and adapted from J R Katzenbach and D K Smith, *The Wisdom of Teams: Creating the High-Performance Organization* (New York: HarperBusiness, 1999), p 214.

to Tuckman's theory of group development in Chapter 10—forming, storming, norming, performing, and adjourning—teams are task groups that have matured to the *performing* stage (but not slipped into decay). Because of conflicts over power and authority and unstable interpersonal relations, many work groups never qualify as a real team.[7] Katzenbach and Smith clarified the distinction this way: "The essence of a team is *common commitment*. Without it, groups perform as individuals; with it, they become a powerful unit of collective performance."[8] (See Table 11–1.) A prime example of melding a group of individuals into a team involves East Carolina University's successful football coach Skip Holtz. Coach Holtz sent a powerful signal when he first met with his new team on the Greenville, North Carolina, campus:

> The first thing he did was take the players' names off the back of the jerseys.
>
> "I came away from our first meeting with the feeling that this was a very selfish, self-centered team," Holtz says. "There weren't a lot of people talking about goals and the big picture. We needed to change the culture and the attitude and change it fast."
>
> Defensive end Zack Slate was a freshman on a 2–9 team in 2004 and remembers the meeting.
>
> "We had a lot of guys split in a lot of different ways. There was no sense of team," Slate says. "Coach Holtz started building from the ground up with discipline and precision."[9]

When Katzenbach and Smith refer to "a small number of people" in their definition, they mean between 2 and 25 team members. They found effective teams to typically have fewer than 10 members. This conclusion was echoed in a survey of 400 workplace team members in the United States and Canada: "The average North American team consists of 10 members. Eight is the most common size."[10]

LO.2 A General Typology of Work Teams

Work teams are created for various purposes and thus face different challenges. Managers can deal more effectively with those challenges when they understand how teams differ. A helpful way of sorting things out is to consider a typology of work teams developed by Eric Sundstrom and his colleagues.[11] Four general types of work teams listed in Table 11–2 are (1) advice, (2) production, (3) project, and (4) action. Each of these labels identifies a basic *purpose*. For instance, advice teams generally make recommendations for managerial decisions. Less commonly do they actually make final decisions. In contrast, production and action teams carry out management's decisions.

Table 11–2   *Four General Types of Work Teams and Their Outputs*

TYPES AND EXAMPLES	DEGREE OF TECHNICAL SPECIALIZATION	DEGREE OF COORDINATION WITH OTHER WORK UNITS	WORK CYCLES	TYPICAL OUTPUTS
Advice Committees Review panels, boards Quality circles Employee involvement groups Advisory councils	Low	Low	Work cycles can be brief or long; one cycle can be team life span.	Decisions Selections Suggestions Proposals Recommendations
Production Assembly teams Manufacturing crews Mining teams Flight attendant crews Data processing groups Maintenance crews	Low	High	Work cycles typically repeated or continuous process; cycles often briefer than team life span.	Food, chemicals Components Assemblies Retail sales Customer service Equipment repairs
Project Research groups Planning teams Architect teams Engineering teams Development teams Task forces	High	Low (for traditional units) or High (for cross-functional units)	Work cycles typically differ for each new project; one cycle can be team life span.	Plans, designs Investigations Presentations Prototypes Reports, findings
Action Sports teams Entertainment groups Expeditions Negotiating teams Surgery teams Cockpit crews Military platoons and squads Police and fire teams	High	High	Brief performance events, often repeated under new conditions, requiring extended training or preparation.	Combat missions Expeditions Contracts, lawsuits Concerts Surgical operations Competitive events Disaster assistance

SOURCE: Excerpted and adapted from E Sundstrom, K P DeMeuse, and D Futrell, "Work Teams," *American Psychologist,* February 1990, p 125. Reprinted with permission of the author.

Four key variables in Table 11–2 deal with technical specialization, coordination, work cycles, and outputs. Technical specialization is low when the team draws upon members' general experience and problem-solving ability. It is high when team members are required to apply technical skills acquired through higher education or extensive training. The degree of coordination with other work units is determined by the team's relative independence (low coordination) or interdependence (high coordination). Work cycles are the amount of time teams need to discharge their missions. The various outputs listed in Table 11–2 are intended to illustrate real-life impacts. A closer look at each type of work team is in order.[12]

Advice Teams   As their name implies, advice teams are created to broaden the information base for managerial decisions. Advice teams tend to have a low degree of technical specialization. Coordination also is low because advice teams work pretty much on their own. Ad hoc committees (e.g., the annual picnic committee) have shorter life cycles than standing committees (e.g., the grievance committee).

Production Teams   This second type of team is responsible for performing day-to-day operations. Minimal training for routine tasks accounts for the low degree of technical specialization. But coordination typically is high because work flows from one team to another. For example, railroad maintenance crews require fresh information about needed repairs from train crews, and the train crews, in turn, need to know exactly where maintenance crews are working.

Project Teams   Projects require creative problem solving, often involving the application of specialized knowledge. Since projects focus on a specific outcome (e.g., developing a new vaccine, producing a movie, or building a skyscraper), time is critical and the team may disband upon completion of the project. The trend in product development today is toward cross-functional teams that bring together specialists from production, marketing, and finance from around the world. Take Lenovo's ThinkPad X300 PC, for example:

> Like most ThinkPads, this one got its start in the U.S. The planners, project leaders, and some of the designers are in North Carolina. The more detailed design and engineering work is done by a team in Yamato, Japan. Manufacturing and purchasing take place in Shenzhen, China.[13]

A high-tech global project team such as this requires a high degree of coordination and efficient communication. Project teams also can bring realism into academic settings.

Action Teams   This last type of team is best exemplified by a baseball team. High specialization is combined with high coordination. Nine highly trained athletes play specialized defensive positions. But good defensive play is not enough because effective hitting is necessary. Moreover, coordination between the manager, base runners, base coaches, and the bull pen needs to be precise. So it is with airline cockpit crews, firefighters, hospital surgery teams, mountain-climbing expeditions, rock music groups, labor contract negotiating teams, and police SWAT teams, among others. A unique challenge for action teams is to exhibit peak performance on demand.[14]

This four-way typology of work teams is dynamic and changing, not static. Some teams evolve from one type to another. Other teams represent a combination of types. For example, consider the work of a team at General Foods: "The company

These firefighters qualify as an action team because they are capable of synchronized peak performance at a moment's notice.

launched a line of ready-to-eat desserts by setting up a team of nine people with the freedom to operate like entrepreneurs starting their own business. The team even had to oversee construction of a factory with the technology required to manufacture their product."[15] This particular team was a combination advice-project-action team. In short, the General Foods team did everything but manufacture the end product themselves (that was done by production teams).

L0.3 Effective Work Teams

The effectiveness of athletic teams is a straightforward matter of wins and losses. Things become more complicated, however, when the focus shifts to work teams in today's organizations.[16] Figure 11–1 lists two effectiveness criteria for work teams: performance and viability. Conceptually, the first one is simple: Did the team get the job done? The second criterion is more subtle and easily ignored or overlooked, to the

Team viability

Team members satisfied and willing to contribute.

longer-term detriment of the organization. **Team viability** is defined as team members' satisfaction and continued willingness to contribute. Are the team members better or worse off for having contributed to the team effort? A work team is not truly effective if it gets the job done but self-destructs in the process and burns everyone out.

Also, as indicated in Figure 11–1, work teams require a team-friendly organization if they are to be effective. Work teams need a support system. They have a much greater chance of success if they are nurtured and facilitated by the organization. The team's purpose needs to be in concert with the organization's strategy. Similarly, team participation and autonomy require an organizational culture that values those processes. A good role model is Linda Hunt, president of St. Joseph's Hospital and Medical Center in Phoenix, Arizona. She recently noted,

> We live the model of collaboration. We promote it in our centers of excellence and in our teaching programs, and we incorporate teams into quality care wherever possible.[17]

Team members also need appropriate technological tools, *reasonable* schedules, and training. Teamwork needs to be rewarded by the organizational reward system.[18] Such is not the case when pay and bonuses are tied solely to individual

Figure 11–1   *Effective Work Teams*

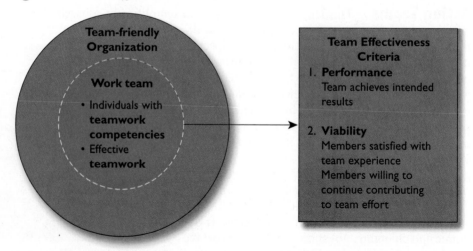

SOURCES: Adapted in part from E Sundstrom, K P DeMeuse, and D Futrell, "Work Teams," *American Psychologist,* February 1990, pp 120–33; and C A Beatty and B A Barker Scott, *Building Smart Teams: A Roadmap to High Performance* (Thousand Oaks, CA: Sage, 2004), pp 5–8.

output. For a positive example, consider what has taken place at Internet equipment maker Cisco Systems:

> [CEO John] Chambers took . . . steps to rein in Cisco's Wild West culture during 2002. Most pointedly, he made teamwork a critical part of top execs' bonus plans. He told them 30% of their bonuses for the 2003 fiscal year would depend on how well they collaborated with others. "It tends to formalize the discussion around how can I help you and how can you help me," says Sue Bostrom, head of Cisco's Internet consulting group.[19]

LO.4 **Contributors Need Teamwork Competencies** Forming workplace teams and urging employees to be good team players are good starting points on the road to effective teams. But much more is needed today.[20] Jeff Zucker, president of NBC Universal Television Group, initially faced this situation:

> My biggest challenge is getting the new team to maximize our potential and combine together into one culture. We have a bunch of people with strong personalities who are extremely good at what they do. I want them to feel they are the best, and yet have us work together as a team.[21]

In short, Zucker's leadership group had not yet melded into a true team, as defined earlier. He needed to make sure his people possessed the teamwork competencies in Table 11–3. Teamwork skills and competencies need to be role modeled and

Table 11–3 *How Strong Are Your Teamwork Competencies?*

Orients Team to Problem-Solving Situation
Assists the team in arriving at a common understanding of the situation or problem. Determines the important elements of a problem situation. Seeks out relevant data related to the situation or problem.

Organizes and Manages Team Performance
Helps team establish specific, challenging, and accepted team goals. Monitors, evaluates, and provides feedback on team performance. Identifies alternative strategies or reallocates resources to address feedback on team performance.

Promotes a Positive Team Environment
Assists in creating and reinforcing norms of tolerance, respect, and excellence. Recognizes and praises other team members' efforts. Helps and supports other team members. Models desirable team member behavior.

Facilitates and Manages Task Conflict
Encourages desirable and discourages undesirable team conflict. Recognizes the type and source of conflict confronting the team and implements an appropriate resolution strategy. Employs "win–win" negotiation strategies to resolve team conflicts.

Appropriately Promotes Perspective
Defends stated preferences, argues for a particular point of view, and withstands pressure to change position for another that is not supported by logical or knowledge-based arguments. Changes or modifies position if a defensible argument is made by another team member. Projects courtesy and friendliness to others while arguing position.

SOURCE: From G Chen, L M Donahue, and R I Klimoski, "Training Undergraduates to Work in Organizational Teams," *Academy of Management Learning and Education,* March 2004, App. A, p 40. Copyright © 2004 by The Academy of Management. Reproduced by permission of The Academy of Management via Copyright Clearance Center.

Table 11–4   *Characteristics of Effective Teamwork*

1. Clear purpose	The vision, mission, goal, or task of the team has been defined and is now accepted by everyone. There is an action plan.
2. Informality	The climate tends to be informal, comfortable, and relaxed. There are no obvious tensions or signs of boredom.
3. Participation	There is much discussion, and everyone is encouraged to participate.
4. Listening	The members use effective listening techniques such as questioning, paraphrasing, and summarizing to get out ideas.
5. Civilized disagreement	There is disagreement, but the team is comfortable with this and shows no signs of avoiding, smoothing over, or suppressing conflict.
6. Consensus decisions	For important decisions, the goal is substantial but not necessarily unanimous agreement through open discussion of everyone's ideas, avoidance of formal voting, or easy compromises.
7. Open communication	Team members feel free to express their feelings on the tasks as well as on the group's operation. There are few hidden agendas. Communication takes place outside of meetings.
8. Clear roles and work assignments	There are clear expectations about the roles played by each team member. When action is taken, clear assignments are made, accepted, and carried out. Work is fairly distributed among team members.
9. Shared leadership	While the team has a formal leader, leadership functions shift from time to time depending on the circumstances, the needs of the group, and the skills of the members. The formal leader models the appropriate behavior and helps establish positive norms.
10. External relations	The team spends time developing key outside relationships, mobilizing resources, and building credibility with important players in other parts of the organization.
11. Style diversity	The team has a broad spectrum of team-player types including members who emphasize attention to task, goal setting, focus on process, and questions about how the team is functioning.
12. Self-assessment	Periodically, the team stops to examine how well it is functioning and what may be interfering with its effectiveness.

SOURCE: From G M Parker, *Team Players and Teamwork: The New Competitive Business Strategy* (San Francisco: Jossey-Bass, 1990), table 2, p 33. Reprinted with permission of John Wiley & Sons, Inc.

taught. For example, when Jim Vesterman was an MBA student at the University of Pennsylvania's Wharton School, he recalled lifelong teamwork lessons he learned as a combat US Marine serving in Iraq:

> We were one team. Our platoon commander would often quote Kipling to describe Marines: "The strength of the pack is the wolf, and the strength of the wolf is the pack." The Marine Corps recruits wolves. But its strength comes from training them to fight as a pack . . .
>
> When I'm working with a group now, I can honestly say that I think about the team first. The "I first" approach has been drilled out of me.[22]

Notice in Table 11–3 the importance of group problem solving, mentoring, and conflict management skills.

What Does Effective Teamwork Involve?

Unfortunately, the terms *team* and *teamwork* are tossed around rather casually today. Many work groups are called teams when they are far from it. Real teamwork requires a concerted collective effort (see Table 11–4). It requires lots of tolerance, practice, and trial-and-error learning.[23] Using Table 11–4 as a guide, have you ever personally experienced *real* teamwork?

Military units know the wisdom behind the old saying that there is no letter "I" in the word *team*.

LO.5 Why Do Work Teams Fail?

Advocates of the team approach to management paint a very optimistic and bright picture. Yet there is a dark side to teams.[24] While exact statistics are not available, they can and often do fail. Anyone contemplating the use of team structures in the workplace needs a balanced perspective of advantages and limitations.

Common Management Mistakes with Teams

The main threats to team effectiveness, according to the center of Figure 11–2, are *unrealistic expectations* leading to *frustration*. Frustration, in turn, encourages people to abandon teams. Both managers and team members can be victimized by unrealistic expectations.

On the left side of Figure 11–2 is a list of common management mistakes. These mistakes generally involve doing a poor job of creating a supportive environment for teams and teamwork.

Problems for Team Members

The lower-right portion of Figure 11–2 lists common problems for team members. Contrary to critics' Theory X contention about employees lacking the motivation and creativity for real teamwork, it is common for teams to take on too much too quickly and to drive themselves too hard for fast results. Important group dynamics and team skills get lost in the rush for results. Consequently, team members' expectations need to be given a reality check by management and team members themselves. Also, teams need to be counseled against quitting when they run into an unanticipated obstacle. Failure is part of the learning process with teams, as it is elsewhere in life. Comprehensive training in interpersonal skills can prevent many common teamwork problems.

Figure 11–2   *Why Work Teams Fail*

Mistakes typically made by management

- Teams cannot overcome weak strategies and poor business practices.
- Hostile environment for teams (command-and-control culture; competitive/individual reward plans; management resistance).
- Teams adopted as a fad, a quick-fix; no long-term commitment.
- Lessons from one team not transferred to others (limited experimentation with teams).
- Vague or conflicting team assignments.
- Inadequate team skills training.
- Poor staffing of teams.
- Lack of trust.

Unrealistic expectations resulting in frustration

Problems typically experienced by team members

- Team tries to do too much too soon.
- Conflict over differences in personal work styles (and/or personality conflicts).
- Too much emphasis on results, not enough on team processes and group dynamics.
- Unanticipated obstacle causes team to give up.
- Resistance to doing things differently.
- Poor interpersonal skills (aggressive rather than assertive communication, destructive conflict, win-lose negotiation).
- Poor interpersonal chemistry (loners, dominators, self-appointed experts do not fit in).
- Lack of trust.

SOURCES: Adapted from discussion in S R Rayner, "Team Traps: What They Are, How to Avoid Them," *National Productivity Review,* Summer 1996, pp 101–15; L Holpp and R Phillips, "When Is a Team Its Own Worst Enemy?" *Training,* September 1995, pp 71–82; B Richardson, "Why Work Teams Flop—and What Can Be Done about It," *National Productivity Review,* Winter 1994/95, pp 9–13; and C O Longenecker and M Neubert, "Barriers and Gateways to Management Cooperation and Teamwork," *Business Horizons,* September–October 2000, pp 37–44.

to the point

What can be done to improve cooperation, trust, and cohesiveness in work teams?

Effective Teamwork through Cooperation, Trust, and Cohesiveness

As competitive pressures intensify, experts say organizational success increasingly will depend on teamwork rather than individual stars. Nowhere is this more true than in hospitals. Imagine yourself or a loved one being in this terrible situation:

A 67-year-old woman was admitted to the hospital for treatment of cerebral aneurysms—weakened blood vessels in the brain. Doctors examined her and sent her to her room.

The next day, she was wheeled into cardiology, of all places, where a doctor had threaded a catheter into her heart before someone noticed he had the wrong patient. The procedure was stopped; the patient recovered.[25]

Analysis of this case by researchers revealed the need for better communication and teamwork.

Whether in hospitals or the world of business, three components of teamwork receiving the greatest attention are cooperation, trust, and cohesiveness. Let us explore the contributions each can make to effective teamwork.

Cooperation

Individuals are said to be cooperating when their efforts are systematically *integrated* to achieve a collective objective.[26] The greater the integration, the greater the degree of cooperation. Ritz-Carlton, the luxury hotel chain, effectively integrates cooperation into its service quality improvement strategy:

> The whole approach ... depends upon identifying and correcting things that go wrong. To ensure that errors are reported rather than covered up, Ritz-Carlton tries hard to de-stigmatize them, shifting the focus from blame to correction. Mistakes are referred to as "Mr. BIVs," after a cartoon character whose name stands for breakdowns, inefficiencies, and variations. The point is that "a Mr. BIV occurred, and we want to surface it and get rid of it forever," explains [training director Diana] Oreck.
>
> At the start of every shift, every day, at every Ritz-Carlton property, a 15-minute staff meeting takes place. Part of it is devoted to refresher training on one of the 12 "Service Values" incorporated into the company's Gold Standards. ... Another part alerts the staff to Mr. BIVs that have arisen and the guests affected.[27]

Cooperation versus Competition   A widely held assumption among managers is that "competition brings out the best in people." From an economic standpoint, business survival depends on staying ahead of the competition. But from an interpersonal standpoint, critics contend competition has been overemphasized, primarily at the expense of cooperation.[28] UK-born Sandra Dawson, an expert on organizational change who teaches management at the University of Cambridge, recently offered these helpful insights:

> I am a very strong advocate for collaboration.... [I tell my students,] "You need no lessons in competition. You will be as competitive as anyone, because you are here and because you are determined about where you want to go. But I am not sure how you will collaborate, though that may well differentiate you in tomorrow's global business world."
>
> I found women likelier to agree initially that collaboration is important. I found men much more difficult to get to the door of collaboration. Men maybe have a tougher time looking beyond themselves and those like them. They have got to believe that there is value in the "Other," who will by definition have different interests and ways to see the world.
>
> ... [W]e teach collaboration by demonstrating its success in action [through group projects with local companies]. ... The groups have to deliver on very tight deadlines they can meet only if they take the best from each member and do not allow one member to dominate in all respects.[29]

Research Support for Cooperation   After conducting a meta-analysis of 122 studies encompassing a wide variety of subjects and settings, one team of researchers concluded that

1. Cooperation is superior to competition in promoting achievement and productivity.
2. Cooperation is superior to individualistic efforts in promoting achievement and productivity.

Farcus

by David Waisglass
Gordon Coulthart

© 1995 Farcus Cartoons

WAISGLASS/COULTHART

www.farcus.com

3. Cooperation without intergroup competition promotes higher achievement and productivity than cooperation with intergroup competition.[30]

Given the size and diversity of the research base, these findings strongly endorse cooperation in modern organizations. Cooperation can be encouraged by reward systems that reinforce teamwork, along with individual achievement.

Interestingly, cooperation can be encouraged by quite literally tearing down walls, or not building them in the first place. A study of 229 managers and professionals employed by eight small businesses proved insightful:

> The researchers looked at the effects of private offices, shared private offices, cubicles, and team-oriented open offices on productivity, and found to their initial surprise that the small team, open-office configuration (desks scattered about in a small area with no partitions) to be significantly correlated with superior performance. In addition, they found that the open-office configuration was particularly favored by the youngest employees, who believe open offices provide them greater access to colleagues and the opportunity to learn from their more seasoned senior compatriots.[31]

There is a movement among architects and urban planners to design and build structures that encourage spontaneous interaction, cooperation, and teamwork (see the Real World/Real People feature on page 317).

A study involving 84 male US Air Force trainees uncovered an encouraging link between cooperation and favorable race relations. After observing the subjects interact in three-man teams during a management game, the researchers concluded: "[Helpful] teammates, both black and white, attract greater respect and liking than do teammates who have not helped. This is particularly true when the helping occurs voluntarily."[32] These findings suggest that managers can enhance equal employment opportunity and diversity programs by encouraging *voluntary* helping behavior in interracial work teams. Accordingly, it is reasonable to conclude that voluntary helping behavior could build cooperation in mixed-gender teams and groups as well.

Another study involving 72 health care professionals in a US Veterans Affairs Medical Center found a negative correlation between cooperation and team size. In other words, cooperation diminished as the health care team became larger.[33] Managers thus need to restrict the size of work teams if they desire to facilitate cooperation.

LO.6 Trust

These have not been good times for trust. Years of wasteful government spending, massive layoffs, bloated executive bonuses, corporate scandals, and broken promises have left many people justly cynical about trusting what leaders say and do.[34] In a 2008 Harvard University public opinion survey, 80% said the United States was

Designing Buildings with Employee Collaboration in Mind

Edmunds.com, a publisher of automotive information, moved its staff of 300 to a new building in Santa
Monica, Calif., in 2005. The 90,000-sq.-ft. building,
designed by Studios Architecture, is meant to emphasize collaboration. It has only five private offices for
executives. The rest of the staff, now numbering 423,
stretch across the top and bottom floors of open-plan
space, with an airy reception area on the middle floor
doubling as an all-staff gathering spot and coffee area.
Since relocating, the company's employee turnover
rate has been halved.

From an architectural standpoint, what would your ideal workspace look like?

SOURCE: H Walters, "Efficiency Trumps Opulence," *BusinessWeek*,
December 15, 2008, p 74.

Teamwork today begins with how architects
design buildings and workspaces to foster human
interaction and cooperation rather than isolation.

in a government and business leadership crisis. Sixty-five percent said so in 2005.[35]
So it is no surprise that a recent international survey found only about 50% of US,
Canadian, and Mexican employees trusted top management. Significantly, 75% of
those surveyed in all three countries reportedly trusted their immediate supervisors.
This prompted the following observation: "The findings should matter to management because of the close link between trust and employee engagement: The more
employees trust management, the more engaged and productive they will be—and
vice versa."[36] This contention is reinforced by another survey: "In a study of 500
business professionals, conducted by MasterWorks, Annandale, Virginia, 95% said
the main factor in deciding to stay or leave their job was whether they had a trusting relationship with their manager."[37] Clearly, remedial action is needed to close
the trust gap, especially the huge one between employees and top management.

In this section, we examine the concept of trust and introduce six practical
guidelines for building trust.

go to the Web for the Self-Exercise: How Trusting Are You?

Trust

Reciprocal faith in others' intentions and behavior.

Reciprocal Faith and a Cognitive Leap   **Trust** is defined as reciprocal faith in others' intentions and behavior.[38] Experts on the subject explain the reciprocal (give-and-take) aspect of trust as follows:

> When we see others acting in ways that imply that they trust us, we become more disposed to reciprocate by trusting in them more. Conversely, we come to distrust those whose actions appear to violate our trust or to distrust us.[39]

In short, we tend to give what we get: trust begets trust; distrust begets distrust. Trust can be fragile, too. Syndicated business columnist Harvey Mackay reminds us that "[i]t takes years to build up trust, but only seconds to destroy it."[40] Appropriately, an interesting new line of management research centers on *trust repair*, both organizational and interpersonal.[41]

Propensity to trust

A personality trait involving one's general willingness to trust others.

One model of organizational trust includes a personality trait called **propensity to trust.** The developers of the model explain:

> Propensity might be thought of as the *general willingness to trust others*. Propensity will influence how much trust one has for a trustee prior to data on that particular party being available. People with different developmental experiences, personality types, and cultural backgrounds vary in their propensity to trust. . . . An example of an extreme case of this is what is commonly called blind trust. Some individuals can be observed to repeatedly trust in situations that most people would agree do not warrant trust. Conversely, others are unwilling to trust in most situations, regardless of circumstances that would support doing so.[42]

What is your propensity to trust? How did you develop that personality trait?

Trust involves "a cognitive 'leap' beyond the expectations that reason and experience alone would warrant"[43] (see Figure 11–3). For example, suppose a member of a newly formed class project team works hard, based on the assumption that her teammates also are working hard. That assumption, on which her trust is based, is a cognitive leap that goes beyond her actual experience with her teammates. When you trust someone, you have *faith* in their good intentions. The act of trusting someone, however, carries with it the inherent risk of betrayal. Progressive managers believe that the benefits of interpersonal trust far outweigh any risks of betrayed trust. For example, Michael Powell, who founded the chain of bookstores bearing his name more than 25 years ago, built his business around the principles of open-book management, empowerment, and trust. Powell's propensity to trust was sorely tested when one of his employees stole more than $60,000

Figure 11–3   *Interpersonal Trust Involves a Cognitive Leap*

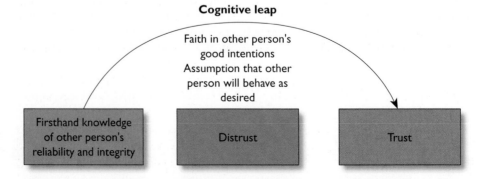

in a used-book purchasing scheme. After putting in some accounting safeguards, Powell's propensity to trust remains intact. He observed,

> The incident was a watershed for me and my staff, dispelling any naïveté we may have had about crime. We realized that not only *can* theft happen; it *will* happen. At the same time, dealing with the matter forced us to revisit our basic values and managerial philosophies. We believe that the modern demands of business call for an empowered and fully flexible staff, and we know that such a staff will often have to handle valuable commodities and money. We also believe that most people are not going to abuse our trust if they are put in a position with a reasonable amount of review and responsibility.[44]

How to Build Trust   Management professor/consultant Fernando Bartolomé offers the following six guidelines for building and maintaining trust:

1. *Communication.* Keep team members and employees informed by explaining policies and decisions and providing accurate feedback. Be candid about one's own problems and limitations. Tell the truth.
2. *Support.* Be available and approachable. Provide help, advice, coaching, and support for team members' ideas.
3. *Respect.* Delegation, in the form of real decision-making authority, is the most important expression of managerial respect. Actively listening to the ideas of others is a close second. (Empowerment, discussed in Chapter 15, is not possible without trust.)
4. *Fairness.* Be quick to give credit and recognition to those who deserve it. Make sure all performance appraisals and evaluations are objective and impartial.
5. *Predictability.* Be consistent and predictable in your daily affairs. Keep both expressed and implied promises.
6. *Competence.* Enhance your credibility by demonstrating good business sense, technical ability, and professionalism.[45]

Trust needs to be earned; it cannot be demanded. Trust is anchored to **credibility**— "developing the integrity, intent, capabilities, and results that make you *believable,* both to yourself and to others."[46] How credible and trustworthy are you? How about those in your personal and professional circles?

Credibility
Being believable through integrity, intent, capabilities, and results.

L0.7 Cohesiveness

Cohesiveness is a process whereby "a sense of 'we-ness' emerges to transcend individual differences and motives."[47] Members of a cohesive group stick together. They are reluctant to leave the group. Cohesive group members stick together for one or both of the following reasons: (1) because they enjoy each others' company or (2) because they need each other to accomplish a common goal. Accordingly, two types of group cohesiveness, identified by sociologists, are socio-emotional cohesiveness and instrumental cohesiveness.[48]

Cohesiveness
A sense of "we-ness" helps group stick together.

Socio-emotional cohesiveness
Sense of togetherness based on emotional satisfaction.

Socio-Emotional and Instrumental Cohesiveness   **Socio-emotional cohesiveness** is a sense of togetherness that develops when individuals derive emotional satisfaction from group participation. Most general discussions of group cohesiveness are limited to this type. However, from the standpoint of getting things accomplished in task groups and teams, we cannot afford to ignore instrumental cohesiveness. **Instrumental cohesiveness** is a sense of togetherness that develops when group members are mutually dependent on one another because they believe they could not achieve the group's goal by acting separately. A feeling

Instrumental cohesiveness
Sense of togetherness based on mutual dependency needed to get the job done.

of "we-ness" is *instrumental* in achieving the common goal. Team advocates generally assume both types of cohesiveness are essential to productive teamwork. But is this really true?

Lessons from Group Cohesiveness Research   What is the connection between group cohesiveness and performance? A landmark meta-analysis of 49 studies involving 8,702 subjects provided these insights:

- There is a small but statistically significant cohesiveness → performance effect.
- The cohesiveness → performance effect was stronger for smaller and real groups (as opposed to contrived groups in laboratory studies).
- The cohesiveness → performance effect becomes stronger as one moves from nonmilitary real groups to military groups to sports teams.
- Commitment to the task at hand (meaning the individual sees the performance standards as legitimate) has the most powerful impact on the cohesiveness → performance linkage.

- The *performance → cohesiveness* linkage is stronger than the cohesiveness → performance linkage. Thus, success tends to bind group or team members together rather than closely knit groups being more successful.
- Contrary to the popular view, cohesiveness is not "a 'lubricant' that minimizes friction due to the human 'grit' in the system."[49]
- All this evidence led the researchers to this practical conclusion: "Efforts to enhance group performance by fostering interpersonal attraction or 'pumping up' group pride are not likely to be effective."[50]

Sergey Brin (left) and Larry Page have a lot to smile about these days. The Moscow and Michigan natives teamed up while pursuing graduate degrees at Stanford University and founded Google in 1998. Who says teamwork doesn't pay? Can you say "billionaire?"

A second meta-analysis found no significant relationship between cohesiveness and the quality of group decisions. However, support was found for Janis's contention that *groupthink* tends to afflict cohesive in-groups with strong leadership. Groups whose members liked each other a great deal tended to make poorer quality decisions.[51]

Getting Some Positive Impact from Group Cohesiveness   Research tells us that group cohesiveness is no secret weapon in the quest for improved group or team performance. The trick is to keep task groups small, make sure performance standards and goals are clear and accepted, achieve some early successes, and follow the tips in Table 11–5. A good example is Westinghouse's highly automated military radar electronics plant in College Station, Texas. Compared with

Table 11–5   *Steps Managers Can Take to Enhance the Two Types of Group Cohesiveness*

Socio-Emotional Cohesiveness
Keep the group relatively small.
Strive for a favorable public image to increase the status and prestige of belonging.
Encourage interaction and cooperation.
Emphasize members' common characteristics and interests.
Point out environmental threats (e.g., competitors' achievements) to rally the group.
Instrumental Cohesiveness
Regularly update and clarify the group's goal(s).
Give every group member a vital "piece of the action."
Channel each group member's special talents toward the common goal(s).
Recognize and equitably reinforce every member's contributions.
Frequently remind group members they need each other to get the job done.

their counterparts at a traditional factory in Baltimore, each of the Texas plant's 500 employees produces eight times more, at half the per-unit cost:

> The key, says Westinghouse, is not the robots but the people. Employees work in teams of 8 to 12. Members devise their own solutions to problems. Teams measure daily how each person's performance compares with that of other members and how the team's performance compares with the plant's. Joseph L Johnson, 28, a robotics technician, says that is a big change from a previous hourly factory job where he cared only about "picking up my paycheck." Here, peer pressure "makes sure you get the job done."[52]

Self-selected work teams (in which people pick their own teammates) and off-the-job social events can stimulate socio-emotional cohesiveness.[53] The fostering of socio-emotional cohesiveness needs to be balanced with instrumental cohesiveness. The latter can be encouraged by making sure everyone in the group recognizes and appreciates each member's vital contribution to the group goal. While balancing the two types of cohesiveness, managers need to remember that group-think theory and research cautions against too much cohesiveness.

LO.8 Teams in Action: Virtual Teams and Self-Managed Teams

to the point
What are the keys to success for virtual and self-managed teams?

All sorts of interesting approaches to teams and teamwork can be found in the workplace today. A great deal of experimentation is taking place as organizations struggle to be more flexible and responsive (see the Real World/Real People feature on page 322). New information technologies also have spurred experimentation with team formats. This section profiles two different approaches to teams: virtual teams and self-managed teams. We have selected these particular types of teams for three reasons: (1) they have recognizable labels, (2) they have at least some research evidence, (3) they vary in degree of empowerment (refer to Figure 15–2 in Chapter 15).

As indicated in Table 11–6, the two types of teams are distinct but not totally unique. Overlaps exist. For instance, computer-networked virtual teams may or may not have volunteer members and may or may not be self-managed. Another

Xerox's "Future of Work" Project Foresees a Flexible Global Workplace

Xerox has a dedicated team of ethnographers—yes, as in social scientists who study people in their natural habitats—following workers as they go about their business. One goal is to pass their findings on to big customers, which can use the information to harness global workforces. . . .

Steve Hoover, who runs one of Xerox's research labs in Webster, N.Y., has a theory about what the next generation of work will look like. Work, he reckons, will be like making a movie. Instead of teaming up with the same people day in and day out, "hundreds of people [with very diverse work styles] will come together for a year and then break apart." . . . By gaining a better understanding of how different people collaborate, Xerox hopes to ensure that each movie has a happy ending.

What will happen to personal accountability and ethics in a more flexible and global project-oriented workplace? Explain.

SOURCE: J Mero, "Field Study: The Evolution of Work," *Fortune*, September 29, 2008, pp 224–25.

The long-standing dream of working from the beach is now a reality, thanks to modern telecommunications and wireless Internet technology. Your virtual office on Hawaii's Waikiki Beach awaits. Interested?

point of overlap involves the fifth variable in Table 11–6: relationship to organization structure. Teams are called *parallel* structures when they exist outside normal channels of authority and communication.[54] Self-managed teams, on the other hand, are *integrated* into the basic organizational structure. Virtual teams vary in this regard, although they tend to be parallel because they are made up of functional specialists (engineers, accountants, marketers, etc.) who team up on temporary projects. Keeping these basic distinctions in mind, let us explore virtual teams and self-managed teams.

Table 11–6   *Basic Distinctions between Virtual Teams and Self-Managed Teams*

	VIRTUAL TEAMS	SELF-MANAGED TEAMS
Type of team (see Table 11–2)	Advice or project (usually project)	Production, project, or action
Type of empowerment (see Figure 15–2)	Consultation, participation, or delegation	Delegation
Members	Managers and technical specialists	Production/service, technical specialists
Basis of membership	Assigned (some voluntary)	Assigned
Relationship to organization structure	Parallel or integrated	Integrated
Amount of face-to-face communication	Periodic to none	Varies, depending on use of information technology

Virtual Teams

Virtual teams are a product of modern times. They take their name from *virtual reality* computer simulations, where "it's almost like the real thing." Thanks to evolving information technologies such as the Internet, e-mail, instant messaging, videoconferencing, groupware, and fax machines, you can be a member of a work team without really being there.[55] Traditional team meetings are location specific. Team members are either physically present or absent. Virtual teams, in contrast, convene electronically with members reporting in from different locations, different organizations, and even different time zones.

Because virtual teams are relatively new, there is no consensual definition. Our working definition of a **virtual team** is a physically dispersed task group that conducts its business primarily through modern information technology. Advocates say virtual teams are very flexible and efficient because they are driven by information and skills, not by time and location. People with needed information or skills can be team members, regardless of where or when they actually do their work. Virtual teams are second nature to many who grew up with the Internet. *USA Today* recently observed:

> Online communities have become so vital that close to half of those in the USA who participate—43%—say their online friends and associates are as important as groups they participate in face to face.[56]

On the negative side, lack of face-to-face interaction can weaken trust, communication, and accountability. Working remotely may also negatively impact how management perceives work quality. In a survey of 1,465 employees, 55% said yes and 45% said no to the question: "Do you think your work quality is perceived the same when you work remotely as when you are physically in the office?"[57] Also, as covered in Chapter 1 under the discussion of e-leadership, leading and managing from a distance can be very challenging.[58]

Research Insights　　As one might expect with a new and ill-defined area, research evidence to date is a bit spotty. Here is what we have learned so far from recent studies of computer-mediated groups:

- Virtual groups formed over the Internet follow a group development process similar to that for face-to-face groups.[59] (Recall our discussion of Tuckman's model in Chapter 10.)
- Internet chat rooms create more work and yield poorer decisions than face-to-face meetings and telephone conferences.[60]
- Successful use of groupware (software that facilitates interaction among virtual group members) requires training and hands-on experience.[61]
- Inspirational leadership has a positive impact on creativity in electronic brainstorming groups.[62]
- Conflict management is particularly difficult for *asynchronous* virtual teams (those not interacting in real time) that have no opportunity for face-to-face interaction.[63]
- Having at least one member of a team working remotely "prompts the group to be more disciplined in its coordination and communication—yielding a better and more productive experience for all members. . . . But turn that isolate into a pair—by adding a coworker at the same location—and the team

Virtual team

Information technology allows group members in different locations to conduct business.

suffers."[64] The latter problem occurs because the remote pair tends to bond with each other, all too often against "headquarters."

Practical Considerations   Virtual teams may be in fashion, but they are not a cure-all. In fact, they may be a giant step backward for those not well versed in modern information technology. Managers who rely on virtual teams agree on one point: *Meaningful face-to-face contact, especially during early phases of the group development process, is absolutely essential.* Virtual group members need "faces" in their minds to go with names and electronic messages. Periodic face-to-face interaction not only fosters social bonding among virtual team members, it also facilitates conflict resolution. Additionally, virtual teams cannot succeed without some old-fashioned factors such as top-management support, hands-on training, a clear mission and specific objectives, effective leadership, and schedules and deadlines. (See the practical tips listed in Table 11–7.)

Table 11–7   *How to Create and Manage a Virtual Team*

Forming the Team
- Develop a team mission statement along with teamwork expectations and norms, project goals, and deadlines.
- Recruit team members with complementary skills and diverse backgrounds who have the ability and willingness to contribute.
- Get a high-level sponsor to champion the project.
- Post a skill, biographical sketch, contact information, and "local time" matrix to familiarize members with each other and their geographic dispersion.

Preparing the Team
- Make sure everyone has a broadband connection and is comfortable with virtual teamwork technologies (e.g., e-mail, instant messaging, conference calls, online meeting and collaboration programs such as WebEx, and videoconferencing).
- Establish hardware and software compatibility.
- Make sure everyone is comfortable with synchronous (interacting at the same time) and asynchronous (interacting at different times) teamwork.
- Get individuals to buy in on team goals, deadlines, and individual tasks.

Building Teamwork and Trust
- Make sure everyone is involved (during meetings and overall).
- Arrange periodic face-to-face work meetings, team-building exercises, and leisure activities.
- Encourage collaboration between and among team members and subtasks.
- Establish an early-warning system for conflict (e.g., gripe sessions).

Motivating and Leading the Team
- Post a scoreboard to mark team progress toward goals.
- Celebrate team accomplishments both virtually and face-to-face.
- Begin each virtual team meeting with praise and recognition for outstanding contributions.
- Keep team members' line managers informed of their accomplishments and progress.

SOURCE: From Robert Kreitner, *Management*, 11th ed (Boston: Houghton Mifflin Harcourt, 2009), p 385. Copyright © 2009 SouthWestern, a part of Cengage Learning, Inc. Reproduced by permission. www.cengage.com/permission.

Self-Managed Teams

Have you ever thought you could do a better job than your boss? Well, if the trend toward self-managed work teams continues to grow as predicted, you just may get your chance. For example, "[a]t a General Mills cereal plant in Lodi, California, teams . . . schedule, operate, and maintain machinery so effectively that the factory runs with no managers present during the night shift."[65] More typically, managers are present to serve as trainers and facilitators. Self-managed teams come in every conceivable format today, some more autonomous than others.

Self-managed teams are defined as groups of workers who are given administrative oversight for their task domains. Administrative oversight involves delegated activities such as planning, scheduling, monitoring, and staffing. These are chores normally performed by managers. In short, employees in these unique work groups act as their own supervisor. Accountability is maintained *indirectly* by outside managers and leaders. According to a study of a company with 300 self-managed teams, 66 "team advisers" relied on these four indirect influence tactics:

- *Relating.* Understanding the organization's power structure, building trust, showing concern for individual team members.
- *Scouting.* Seeking outside information, diagnosing teamwork problems, facilitating group problem solving.
- *Persuading.* Gathering outside support and resources, influencing team to be more effective and pursue organizational goals.
- *Empowering.* Delegating decision-making authority, facilitating team decision-making process, coaching.[66]

Self-managed teams are variously referred to as semiautonomous work groups, autonomous work groups, and superteams.

Managerial Resistance   Something much more complex is involved than this apparently simple label suggests. The term *self-managed* does not mean simply turning workers loose to do their own thing. Indeed, an organization embracing self-managed teams should be prepared to undergo revolutionary changes in management philosophy, structure, staffing and training practices, and reward systems. Moreover, the traditional notions of managerial authority and control are turned on their heads. Not surprisingly, many managers strongly resist giving up the reins of power to people they view as subordinates. They see self-managed teams as a threat to their job security.

Cross-Functionalism   A common feature of self-managed teams, particularly among those above the shop-floor or clerical level, is **cross-functionalism.**[67] In other words, specialists from different areas are put on the same team. For example, you can thank a cross-functional team for that little musical riff you hear every time you fire up Microsoft's Windows Vista operating system: "In the end, it took 18 months—and a team of 20 composers, sound designers, engineers, and developers."[68] Mark Stefik, a manager at the world-renowned Palo Alto Research Center in California, explains the wisdom of cross-functionalism:

> Something magical happens when you bring together a group of people from different disciplines with a common purpose. It's a middle zone, the breakthrough zone. The idea is to start a team on a problem—a hard problem, to keep people motivated. When there's an obstacle, instead of dodging it, bring in another point of view: an electrical

Self-managed teams
Groups of employees granted administrative oversight for their work.

Cross-functionalism
Team made up of technical specialists from different areas.

engineer, a user interface expert, a sociologist, whatever spin on the market is needed. Give people new eyeglasses to cross-pollinate ideas.[69]

Are Self-Managed Teams Effective? The Research Evidence

Among companies with self-managed teams, the most commonly delegated tasks are work scheduling and dealing directly with outside customers. The least common team chores are hiring and firing.[70] Most of today's self-managed teams remain bunched at the shop-floor level in factory settings. Experts predict growth of the practice in the managerial ranks and in service operations.[71]

Table 11–8   *There Are Many Ways to Empower Self-Managed Teams*

External Leader Behavior

1. Make team members responsible and accountable for the work they do.
2. Ask for and use team suggestions when making decisions.
3. Encourage team members to take control of their work.
4. Create an environment in which team members set their own team goals.
5. Stay out of the way when team members attempt to solve work-related problems.
6. Generate high team expectations.
7. Display trust and confidence in the team's abilities.

Production/Service Responsibilities

1. The team sets its own production/service goals and standards.
2. The team assigns jobs and tasks to its members.
3. Team members develop their own quality standards and measurement techniques.
4. Team members take on production/service learning and development opportunities.
5. Team members handle their own problems with internal and external customers.
6. The team works with a whole product or service, not just a part.

Human Resource Management System

1. The team gets paid, at least in part, as a team.
2. Team members are cross-trained on jobs within their team.
3. Team members are cross-trained on jobs in other teams.
4. Team members are responsible for hiring, training, punishment, and firing.
5. Team members use peer evaluations to formally evaluate each other.

Social Structure

1. The team gets support from other teams and departments when needed.
2. The team has access to and uses important and strategic information.
3. The team has access to and uses the resources of other teams.
4. The team has access to and uses resources inside and outside the organization.
5. The team frequently communicates with other teams.
6. The team makes its own rules and policies.

SOURCE: From B L Kirkman and B Rosen, "Powering Up Teams," *Organizational Dynamics,* Winter 2000, p 56. Copyright © 2000 with permission from Elsevier Science.

Much of what we know about self-managed teams comes from testimonials and case studies. Fortunately, a body of higher quality field research is slowly developing. A review of three meta-analyses covering 70 individual studies concluded that self-managed teams had

- A positive effect on productivity.
- A positive effect on specific attitudes relating to self-management (e.g., responsibility and control).
- No significant effect on general attitudes (e.g., job satisfaction and organizational commitment).
- No significant effect on absenteeism or turnover.[72]

Although encouraging, these results do not qualify as a sweeping endorsement of self-managed teams. Nonetheless, experts say the trend toward self-managed work teams will continue upward in North America because of a strong cultural bias in favor of direct participation (see Table 11–8). Managers need to be prepared for the resulting shift in organizational administration.[73]

go to the Web for the Self-Exercise: Measuring Work Group Autonomy

Team Building and Team Leadership

Helping a work group evolve into a true team requires imaginative and cost-effective team building and a special set of leadership skills. Let us explore what these requirements entail.

to the point

How can team building and team leadership create a high-performance team?

Team Building

Team building is a catch-all term for a whole host of techniques aimed at improving the internal functioning of work groups. Whether conducted by company trainers or outside consultants, team-building activities and workshops strive for greater cooperation, better communication, and less dysfunctional conflict.

Rote memorization and lectures/discussions are discouraged by team-building experts who prefer *active* versus passive learning. Greater emphasis is placed on *how* work groups get the job done than on the job itself. Experiential learning techniques such as interpersonal trust exercises, conflict-handling role-play sessions, creative activities (see the Real World/Real People feature on page 328), and competitive games are common. Outdoor activities can be a nice change of pace for office and factory dwellers. An extreme case in point: "Each year Seagate Technology spends $2 million for 200 employees to spend a week hiking, kayaking, and adventure racing in the mountains of New Zealand."[74] Company officials insist it's worth it. But ethical red flags have been raised about lavish off-site events during the recent deep recession (see the Ethical Dilemma at the end of this chapter). Less costly team-building activities, such as volunteering to build a Habitat for Humanity home, can be both effective and socially responsible. Jeffrey Katzenberg, CEO of Dreamworks Animation SKG, the studio that gave us *Shrek,* prefers celebrations for team building: "When a movie opens, when a DVD comes

Team building

Experiential learning aimed at better internal functioning of groups.

Team Building: Turning Managers into Business Maestros

What CEO doesn't wish his team could function like a well-rehearsed orchestra? To learn how managers can make such music, companies hire Slovenia-born concert violinist Miha Pogačnik. For a song (O.K., for $16,000 a day), Pogačnik, based in Hamburg, teaches executives at companies such as Oracle how musical compositions are organized and ways to apply those principles to business. Last year he spoke, and played, at Northwestern's Kellogg School of Management. Recently he had European Union environment ministers sit with members of an orchestra in Ljubljana (Slovenia's capital) as they played to experience how leaders relate to teams. Such exposure "builds up almost new organs of perception" in executives, claims Pogačnik, who will also arrange for a CEO to wield the baton.

If given the task by your manager, what specific team-building activity would you select and what would you do to make it an effective learning event?

SOURCE: Reprinted from J Ewing, "Turning Managers into Business Maestros," August 4, 2008, issue of *BusinessWeek* by special permission. Copyright © 2008 by The McGraw-Hill Companies, Inc.

Concert violinists, such as Miha Pogačnik, are the ultimate team players.

---

out, or when awards are won, all of those milestones are celebrated in a big way."[75] Free online resources, such as www.businessballs.com (named for the art of juggling balls), are an excellent way to spark your imagination about how to go about building your team in a cost-effective manner.

The Bottom Line: Without clear goals, proper leadership, careful attention to details, and transfer of learning back to the job, both on-site and off-site team-building sessions can become an expensive disappointment.[76]

LO.9 **The Goal of Team Building: High-Performance Teams** Team building allows team members to wrestle with simulated or real-life problems. Outcomes are then analyzed by the group to determine what group processes need improvement. Learning stems from recognizing and addressing faulty group dynamics. Perhaps one subgroup withheld key information from another, thereby hampering group progress. With cross-cultural teams becoming commonplace in today's global economy, team building is more important than ever.[77]

A nationwide survey of team members from many organizations, by Wilson Learning Corporation, provides a useful model or benchmark

Pat Summitt, head coach of the University of Tennessee's women's basketball team has over 1,000 wins and 8 national championships because of her ability to meld diverse and talented individuals into high-performance teams.

of what we should expect of teams. The researchers' question was simply: "What is a high-performance team?"[78] The respondents were asked to describe their peak experiences in work teams. Analysis of the survey results yielded the following eight attributes of high-performance teams:

1. *Participative leadership.* Creating an interdependency by empowering, freeing up, and serving others.
2. *Shared responsibility.* Establishing an environment in which all team members feel as responsible as the manager for the performance of the work unit.
3. *Aligned on purpose.* Having a sense of common purpose about why the team exists and the function it serves.
4. *High communication.* Creating a climate of trust and open, honest communication.
5. *Future focused.* Seeing change as an opportunity for growth.
6. *Focused on task.* Keeping meetings focused on results.
7. *Creative talents.* Applying individual talents and creativity.
8. *Rapid response.* Identifying and acting on opportunities.[79]

These eight attributes effectively combine many of today's most progressive ideas on management, among them being participation, empowerment, service ethic, individual responsibility and development, self-management, trust, active listening, and envisioning. But patience and diligence are required. According to a manager familiar with work teams, "high-performance teams may take three to five years to build."[80]

Assessing the Effectivensss of Team Building

Managers are accountable for knowing if their team-building activities are effective. The most widely used assessment framework among corporate trainers was first developed in 1959 by University of Wisconsin professor Donald L Kirkpatrick. His four-level evaluation model, from most superficial to most comprehensive, consists of the following:

- *Reaction*—How did the participants feel about the activity?
- *Learning*—Did the experience increase knowledge or improve skills?
- *Behavior*—Did participants' on-the-job behavior improve as a result of the activity?
- *Results*—Did participants subsequently achieve better measurable results?[81]

Unfortunately, managers too often settle for a quick post-activity survey of participants (e.g., Did you enjoy the activity? Was it worthwhile?). Adequate assessment requires a more comprehensive approach. Tony Hsieh, CEO of online retailer Zappos, is headed in the right direction by quizzing managers responsible for team building:

> [He] polls managers after they've taken teams to dinner or on a hike, and they invariably talk about communication, greater trust, and budding friendships. "Then we ask, 'How much more efficient do you think your team is now?'" Hsieh says. "The range is anywhere from 20% to 100%."[82]

go to the Web for the Group Exercise: Student Team Development Project

Leading Teams

Practical experience and a growing body of research have made it apparent that leading a team is not the same as leading individuals.[83] Parallel sets of skills are needed. This is somewhat akin to the difference between conducting a group exercise with a classroom full of students and discussing a problem with one student after class. Very different interaction dynamics are involved in the two situations. As a prelude to our comprehensive coverage of leadership in Chapter 16, this final section highlights the importance of being able to lead both individuals and teams. Harvard Business School professor Linda A Hill framed the challenge for new managers this way:

> . . .[T]he new manager must figure out how to harness the power of a team. Simply focusing on one-on-one relationships with members of the team can undermine that process.
>
> . . . [M]any new managers fail to recognize, rnuch less address, their team-building responsibilities. Instead, they conceive of their people-management role as building the most effective relationships they can with each individual subordinate, erroneously equating the management of their team with managing the individuals on the team.
>
> They attend primarily to individual performance and pay little or no attention to team culture and performance. They hardly ever rely on group forums for identifying and solving problems. Some spend too much time with a small number of trusted subordinates, often those who seem most supportive. New managers tend to handle issues, even those with teamwide implications, one-on-one. This leads them to make decisions based on unnecessarily limited information.[84]

These are cautionary words for aspiring, new, and experienced managers alike. Keep them in mind as you reflect back on our discussion of groupthink in Chapter 10 and our discussions in later chapters of group decision making, functional conflict, communication, influence and power, leadership, and managing change.[85]

Summary of Key Concepts

1. *Explain how a work group becomes a team.* A team is a mature group where leadership is shared, accountability is both individual and collective, the members have developed their own purpose, problem solving is a way of life, and effectiveness is measured by collective outcomes.

2. *Identify and describe four types of work teams.* Advice teams provide information for managerial decisions. Production teams perform an organization's day-to-day operations. Project teams apply specialized knowledge to solve problems needed to complete a specific project. Action teams are highly skilled and highly coordinated to provide peak performance on demand.

3. *Explain the model of effective work teams, and specify the two criteria of team effectiveness.* Work teams need three things: (*a*) a team-friendly organization to provide a support system, (*b*) individuals with teamwork competencies, and (*c*) effective teamwork. The two team effectiveness criteria are performance (getting the job done) and team viability (satisfied members who are willing to continue contributing to the team).

4. *Identify five teamwork competencies team members need to possess.* They are (*a*) orients team to problem-solving situation, (*b*) organizes and manages team performance, (*c*) promotes a positive team environment,

(*d*) facilitates and manages task conflict, and (*e*) appropriately promotes perspective.

5. *Discuss why teams fail.* Teams fail because unrealistic expectations cause frustration and failure. Common management mistakes include weak strategies, creating a hostile environment for teams, faddish use of teams, not learning from team experience, vague team assignments, poor team staffing, inadequate training, and lack of trust. Team members typically try too much too soon, experience conflict over differing work styles and personalities, ignore important group dynamics, resist change, exhibit poor interpersonal skills and chemistry, and display a lack of trust.

6. *List at least four things managers can do to build trust.* Six recommended ways to build trust are through communication, support, respect (especially delegation), fairness, predictability, and competence.

7. *Distinguish two types of group cohesiveness, and summarize cohesiveness research findings.* Cohesive groups have a shared sense of togetherness or a "we" feeling. Socio-emotional cohesiveness involves emotional satisfaction. Instrumental cohesiveness involves goal-directed togetherness. There is a small but significant relationship between cohesiveness and performance. The effect is stronger for smaller groups. Commitment to task among group members strengthens the cohesiveness-performance linkage. Success can build group cohesiveness. Cohesiveness is not a cure-all for group problems. Too much cohesiveness can lead to groupthink.

8. *Define virtual teams and self-managed teams.* Virtual teams are physically dispersed work groups that conduct their business via modern information technologies such as the Internet, e-mail, and videoconferences. Self-managed teams are work groups that perform their own administrative chores such as planning, scheduling, and staffing.

9. *Describe high-performance teams and discuss team leadership.* Eight attributes of high-performance teams are participative leadership, shared responsibility, aligned on purpose, high communication, future focused for growth, focused on task, creative talents applied, and rapid response. Leading a team is not the same as leading the individuals within it. Parallel sets of leadership skills are required. More emphasis is needed on team building, broader input, and group problem solving.

Key Terms

OB in Action Case Study

A Trans-Atlantic Team Learns the Ropes[86]

Of all the things Dave Gray worried about when he branched out overseas, tripe never entered the equation.

Gray, founder and chairman of Xplane, a consulting and design firm based in Portland, Oregon, acquired a small firm in Madrid in late 2006, hoping to establish a European outpost and break into Spanish-speaking markets worldwide. Gray was eager to establish rapport between his Spanish and American staff members, and face-to-face meetings seemed like the best way to forge a bond. But during one dinner meeting in Madrid shortly after the acquisition, a visitor from Xplane's St. Louis office refused to sample the tripe—considered a delicacy in Spain—and proceeded to make crude jokes about it.

It was a minor incident, but only one in a series of minor incidents that ultimately created tensions between the six employees in Xplane's Madrid office and the 45 in its U.S. offices. "I expected to come in and say, 'This is how we do things,'" says Gray, who relocated to Madrid to oversee the transition. But he quickly learned that the Madrid and American offices were separated by more than just an ocean.

Most companies have a standard formula for team building: Spring for an annual off-site, throw in a few happy hours and a holiday party, and hope for chemistry. That approach may suffice when employees work under the same roof or even in the same country. But in a global workplace, misunderstandings and resentments can pile up, says Anil Gupta, a professor at the University of Maryland's Robert H. Smith School of Business and co-author of *The Quest for Global Dominance: Transforming Global Presence into Global Competitive Advantage.* The result, all too often, is an us-against-them mentality that makes the already challenging task of running a global organization much more difficult. Small companies, Gupta says, need to establish guidelines early, before tensions start to rise.

At Xplane, the culture clashes were starting to hurt morale. Gray noticed, for example, that some Spanish staff members grumbled when they learned that they had been excluded from e-mails sent to everyone in the two U.S. locations. The exclusion sent a clear message to the Spanish staff: You're not one of us. "They would always forget there was a third office," says Stephen O'Flynn, an Irish citizen and a project manager in the Madrid office.

Gray knew he had to make changes. "These cultural aspects don't show up in numbers," he says. "But a good culture is the fuel that keeps things going." He told employees that too much information is better than not enough and that seemingly minor statements could be misinterpreted. Meanwhile, Xplane's CEO, Aric Wood, asked the Madrid staff members to fill out surveys about their experiences, then discussed the results with them during one-on-one sessions. . . .

Lack of communication was a major complaint. "Not only did they feel distant, but technology was a major obstacle," Wood says. To make communicating easier, Xplane switched to Web-based phone service; now, co-workers dial only four numbers to call one another instead of 13. Wood set up a wiki with pictures of employees from all three offices. O'Flynn became an unofficial ambassador to the U.S., going out of his way to call colleagues in Portland and St. Louis for input and urging his office mates to do the same. "I did a lot of brokering to get people talking," he says.

The technology has improved communication, but it's no substitute for face time, Wood says. Instead of spending money on a one-off team-building trip, Xplane started a year-round employee exchange program. Last year, the company rented apartments in Madrid and Portland and spent $20,000 flying employees back and forth for weeklong visits. About 16 employees have crossed the Atlantic. "We tried to close the gap through technology," Wood says, "but ultimately we had to buy a lot of airline tickets."

Of course, there is no one-size-fits-all solution for building an effective global team. Part of the problem is that each country has its own cultural peccadilloes. In China, for example, many employees are reluctant to disagree with their managers or assume leadership roles—a trait linked to the legacy of the Cultural Revolution of the 1960s and 1970s, when speaking out was dangerous. By contrast, companies moving into India often contend with ego clashes and power struggles, according to Gupta, who researched more than 200 companies for his book. "People in India, especially in tech companies, believe they are just as competent as those in the United States," he says. That's a problem if their American counterparts see them as second class.

Questions for Discussion

1. Using Table 11–1 as a guide, what did Xplane have to do to create a *team* when the Madrid firm was acquired? Explain.

2. Should Xplane's employees have been instructed ahead of time in both the cross-cultural competencies back in Table 4–4 and the teamwork competencies in Table 11–3? Explain how it should have been done.

3. How important is trust with this sort of international virtual team? Explain how you would have established trust more quickly.

4. Which type of cohesiveness, socio-emotional or instrumental, is more important in this type of team building? Explain.

5. What advice would you give Xplane's CEO Aric Wood about managing a virtual team, team building, and team leadership?

Ethical Dilemma

Thanks, But No Thanks![87]

BusinessWeek On Mar. 2, [2009], Wayzata (Minn.)-based TCF Financial announced it would return $361 million to the Treasury Dept. TCF's decision came weeks after politicians pilloried the bank for holding a company-bonding event at a ski resort. "From Congress' point of view, any dollar a bank spends is subject to government review," says TCF Chief Executive William Cooper. "It's another regulatory push on top of all the regulation we have [already]."

1. TCF shouldn't have taken government bailout money if it didn't really need it. Explain your ethical reasoning.

2. Cooper did the right thing to protect management's right to run the company as it sees fit. Explain your ethical reasoning.

3. Congress doesn't understand the value of first-rate team building in competitive business organizations.

How would you explain the ethics and practical value of such expenditures if you were called to testify before a congressional committee?

4. Invent other options. Discuss.

Web Resources

For study material and exercises that apply to this chapter, visit our Web site, **www.mhhe.com/kreitner**

Chapter 12

Individual and Group Decision Making

From suggestion boxes to "open door" policies, managers frequently claim they solicit input and new ideas from their employees. But few companies generate—and implement—as many ideas from their employees as Landscape Forms Inc.

The commercial-outdoor furniture manufacturer was originally formed to provide winter work opportunities to summer landscaping crews in snowy Michigan. In the early 1980s, the company adopted Frost/Scanlon principles—a set of processes developed by university researchers to improve organizational effectiveness, such as teaching employees the importance of taking part in workplace decision making. The object is to create a participatory workforce that understands and feels connected to the goals of the organization.

Today the company still practices and teaches those principles and has devised several of its own ways for employees to be actively engaged in decisions that affect their immediate work. One way: an employee-suggestion system dubbed "muda removas." A play on a Japanese term, it translates as "getting rid of waste."

In this process, developed by Landscape management, employees and their teams come up with ways to make their jobs more efficient and effective. If the whole team agrees on the employee's idea, it can be implemented—without approval from senior management.

Landscape documents how many muda removas are implemented and publishes them in its employee newsletter. So far this year, the company has implemented more than 1,400. Many are small changes,

such as slightly altering the manufacturing process in a way that makes assembly easier, but they can make a big difference in one employee's job satisfaction or efficiency....

Landscape has also encouraged the use of its muda-remova procedures to enlist employees to come up with cost-saving ideas in their immediate areas that would save the company money, at a time when it's struggling to compete with companies moving manufacturing overseas.

Mardi White, a 57-year-old customer service representative, has worked at Landscape for 21 years and says she's had "many" of her ideas implemented. Last

Landscape Forms employees celebrating the opening of their new manufacturing area that was designed with the input of all employees.

year, she realized how time-consuming it was to find furniture-assembly instructions in the computer system when talking with a customer by phone. She suggested that the company put a customer's assembly instructions and other information in one computer program, so they were easy to access. Her manager consulted with the IT department to see if it was feasible. It was.

"If you can find ways to make your job easier, the company is very open to that," Ms. White says.[1]

FOR DISCUSSION

What are the strengths of Landscape Forms's approach to decision making?

We all make decisions on a daily basis. From deciding what clothes to wear to whom we want to marry, our decisions impact our lives in many ways. Sometimes our choices are good and other times they are bad. At work, however, decision making is one of the primary responsibilities of being a manager, and the quality of one's decisions can have serious consequences. Consider the cases of former General Motors Chairman and CEO Richard Wagoner Jr. and John Thain, former CEO of Merrill Lynch. In April 2005, GM's management team met and debated whether or not to build another electric car: The company's first electric car resulted in a loss of $1 billion. Wagoner and his team decided to stay with gas guzzlers and to fight congressional proposals aimed at improving fuel economy instead of building an electric car. Four years later, Toyota's hybrids have gained market share and GM is on the verge of bankruptcy. Some believe that this decision cost Wagoner his job.[2] In contrast, John Thain's decisions caused Ken Lewis, Bank of America's former CEO, to ask Thain for his resignation in 2009: BofA bought Merrill in December 2008. While Merrill was losing over $27 billion in 2008, Thain spent $1.2 million decorating his office. "Thain also handed out lavish packages to new hires. Peter Kraus, whom Thain lured from Goldman to head strategic planning, got a guarantee of around $25 million, which he received even though he left the company after three weeks . . . Thain was even more generous to Thomas Montag, installing him as head of sales and trading with a $39.4 million package." One of Thain's last decisions was to award around $4 billion in 2008 bonuses for Merrill employees despite a fourth quarter loss of $15.84 billion. Shortly after, he left town for a skiing trip to Vail rather than deal with the financial crisis.[3] In contrast, the chapter-opening vignette illustrates how decision making contributed to Landscape Forms' success.

The overall goal of this chapter is to provide you with a thorough understanding of decision making so that you can improve the quality of your personal and group-based decisions. To help in this pursuit, this chapter focuses on (1) models of decision making, (2) decision-making biases, (3) the dynamics of decision making, (4) group decision making, and (5) creativity.

Decision making

Identifying and choosing solutions that lead to a desired end result.

to the point

What are the key differences between rational and nonrational models of decision making and how can these models be integrated?

LO.1 Models of Decision Making

Decision making entails identifying and choosing alternative solutions that lead to a desired state of affairs. For example, you may be reading this book as part of an online course that you decided to take because you are working full time. Alternatively, you may be a full-time student reading this book as part of a course being taken on campus. Identifying and sorting out alternatives like when and how to take a course is the process of decision making.

You can use two broad approaches to make decisions. You can follow a *rational model* or various *nonrational models*. Let us now consider how each of these approaches works. We begin by examining the rational model of decision making.

The Rational Model

The **rational model** proposes that managers use a rational, four-step sequence when making decisions: (1) identifying the problem, (2) generating alternative solutions, (3) selecting a solution, and (4) implementing and evaluating the solution. According to this model, managers are completely objective and possess complete information to make a decision. Despite criticism for being unrealistic, the rational model is instructive because it analytically breaks down the decision-making process and serves as a conceptual anchor for newer models.[4] Let us now consider each of these four steps.

Rational model

Logical four-step approach to decision making.

Identifying the Problem

A **problem** exists when the actual situation and the desired situation differ. For example, a problem exists when you have to pay rent at the end of the month and don't have enough money. Your problem is not that you have to pay rent. Your problem is obtaining the needed funds. Mattel's CEO, Bob Eckert, learned that his company had a problem when two of his top managers arrived in his office to tell him lead had been discovered in one of the company's toys. Around the same time, newspapers were publishing reports that magnets were becoming dislodged from other Mattel toys: If a small child swallowed them, they could cause serious damage by attaching themselves together in the child's intestines. Eckert had to decide whether his company had a publicity problem, a design problem, or a production problem—and if it were a production problem, where that problem was occurring and why.[5] In general, how do individuals or organizations know when a problem exists or will occur soon? Three methods are commonly used for identifying problems: historical cues, planning, and other people's perceptions:

Problem

Gap between an actual and a desired situation.

1. Using historical cues to identify problems assumes that the recent past is the best estimate of the future. Thus, managers rely on past experience to identify discrepancies (problems) from expected trends. For example, a sales manager may conclude that a problem exists because the first-quarter sales are less than they were a year ago. This method is prone to error because it is highly subjective.

Scenario technique

Speculative forecasting method.

2. A planning approach is more systematic and can lead to more accurate results. This method consists of using projections or scenarios to estimate what is expected to occur in the future. A time period of one or more years is generally used. The **scenario technique** is a speculative, conjectural forecast tool used to identify future states, given a certain set of environmental conditions. Once different scenarios are developed, companies devise alternative strategies to survive in the various situations. This process helps to create contingency plans far into the future.[6] Companies like Royal Dutch/Shell, Fleet Financial Group, IBM, Pfizer, and Deutsche Bank are increasingly using the scenario technique as a planning tool.

"Our task, then, is to decide how to decide how to decide."

© 2002 Ted Goff. Used by permission.

McDonald's Used Multiple Methods to Identify a Problem

McDonald's executives watching the growth of Starbucks at the beginning of this decade realized that they were missing out on the fastest-growing parts of the beverage business. Data showed that soda sales had flattened while sales of specialty coffee and smoothies were growing at a double-digit rate outside McDonald's. Customers were buying food at McDonald's, then going to convenience stores to get bottled energy drinks, sports drinks and tea, as well as sodas by Coke competitors....

McDonald's researchers contacted customers of Starbucks and other coffee purveyors and conducted three-hour interviews where they videotaped the customers talking about their coffee-buying habits. The researchers got in the cars of the customers and drove with them to their favorite coffee place, then took them to McDonald's and had them try the espresso drinks.

What methods were used to identify the cause of why McDonald's was missing out on the fastest-growing components of the beverage business?

SOURCE: Excerpted from J Adamy, "McDonald's Takes On a Weakened Starbucks," *The Wall Street Journal,* January 7, 2008, pp A1, A10.

Consumers even use coffee shops to conduct business meetings. What can McDonald's do to tap that market?

---

3. A final approach to identifying problems is to rely on the perceptions of others. A restaurant manager may realize that his or her restaurant provides poor service when a large number of customers complain about how long it takes to receive food after placing an order. In other words, customers' comments signal that a problem exists. Interestingly, companies frequently compound their problems by ignoring customer complaints or feedback.

Some companies use multiple methods to identify problems. McDonald's is a good example (see the Real World/Real People feature above).

Generating Solutions   After identifying a problem, the next logical step is generating alternative solutions. For repetitive and routine decisions such as deciding when to send customers a bill, alternatives are readily available through decision rules. For example, a company might routinely bill customers three days after shipping a product. This is not the case for novel and unstructured decisions. Because there are no cut-and-dried procedures for dealing with novel problems, managers must creatively generate alternative solutions. Unfortunately, a study of 400 strategic decisions revealed that this recommendation is easier said than done. Results showed that managers fell prey to three decision-making blunders that restricted the number of solutions they considered when trying to solve a problem. These blunders were (1) rushing to judgment, (2) selecting readily available ideas or solutions, and (3) making poor allocation of resources to study alternative solutions. Decision makers thus are encouraged to slow down when making decisions, to evaluate a broader set of alternatives, and to invest in studying a greater number of potential solutions.[7]

Selecting a Solution   Optimally, decision makers want to choose the alternative with the greatest value. Decision theorists refer to this as maximizing the expected utility of an outcome. This is no easy task. First, assigning values to alternatives is complicated and prone to error. Not only are values subjective, but they also vary according to the preferences of the decision maker. Research demonstrates that people vary in their preferences for safety or risk when making decisions. For example, a meta-analysis summarizing 150 studies revealed that males displayed more risk taking than females.[8] Further, evaluating alternatives assumes they can be judged according to some standards or criteria. This further assumes that (1) valid criteria exist, (2) each alternative can be compared against these criteria, and (3) the decision maker actually uses the criteria. As you know from making your own key life decisions, people frequently violate these assumptions. Finally, the ethics of the solution should be considered. In the earlier example of Mattel's problems, CEO Eckert said, "How you achieve success is just as important as success itself."[9] He announced a recall of 18.2 million toys, the largest recall in Mattel's history. The company also announced that its magnet toys had been redesigned to make them safer and that it had investigated the Chinese contractor that had used the paint containing lead. Would you conclude that these options maximized utility for Mattel?

Implementing and Evaluating the Solution   Once a solution is chosen, it needs to be implemented. After the solution is implemented, the evaluation phase assesses its effectiveness. If the solution is effective, it should reduce the difference between the actual and desired states that created the problem. If the gap is not closed, the implementation was not successful, and one of the following is true: Either the problem was incorrectly identified or the solution was inappropriate. Assuming the implementation was unsuccessful, management can return to the first step, problem identification. If the problem was correctly identified, management should consider implementing one of the previously identified, but untried, solutions. This process can continue until all feasible solutions have been tried or the problem has changed.

Summarizing the Rational Model   The rational model is prescriptive, outlining a logical process that managers should use when making decisions. As such, the rational model is based on the notion that managers optimize when making decisions. **Optimizing** involves solving problems by producing the best possible solution and is based on a set of highly desirable assumptions—having complete information, leaving emotions out of the decision-making process, honestly and accurately evaluating all alternatives, time and resources are abundant and accessible, and people are willing to implement and support decisions. Practical experience, of course, tells us that these assumptions are unrealistic. As noted by Herbert Simon, a decision theorist who in 1978 earned the Nobel Prize for his work on decision making, "The assumptions of perfect rationality are contrary to fact. It is not a question of approximation; they do not even remotely describe the processes that human beings use for making decisions in complex situations."[10]

Optimizing
Choosing the best possible solution.

That said, there are three benefits of trying to follow a rational process as much as realistically possible.

- The quality of decisions may be enhanced, in the sense that they follow more logically from all available knowledge and expertise.
- It makes the reasoning behind a decision transparent and available to scrutiny.
- If made public, it discourages the decider from acting on suspect considerations (such as personal advancement or avoiding bureaucratic embarrassment).[11]

Nonrational Models of Decision Making

Nonrational models

Explain how decisions actually are made.

In contrast to the rational model's focus on how decisions should be made, **nonrational models** attempt to explain how decisions actually are made. They are based on the assumption that decision making is uncertain, that decision makers do not possess complete information, and that it is difficult for managers to make optimal decisions. Two nonrational models are Herbert Simon's *normative* model and the *garbage can model*.

Simon's Normative Model

Bounded rationality

Constraints that restrict rational decision making.

Herbert Simon proposed this model to describe the process that managers actually use when making decisions. The process is guided by a decision maker's bounded rationality. **Bounded rationality** represents the notion that decision makers are "bounded" or restricted by a variety of constraints when making decisions. These constraints include any personal or environmental characteristics that reduce rational decision making. Examples are the limited capacity of the human mind, problem complexity and uncertainty, amount and timelines of information at hand, criticality of the decision, and time demands.[12]

Ultimately, these limitations result in the tendency to acquire manageable rather than optimal amounts of information. In turn, this practice makes it difficult for managers to identify all possible alternative solutions. In the long run, the constraints of bounded rationality cause decision makers to fail to evaluate all potential alternatives, thereby causing them to satisfice.

Satisficing

Choosing a solution that meets a minimum standard of acceptance.

Satisficing consists of choosing a solution that meets some minimum qualifications, one that is "good enough." Satisficing resolves problems by producing solutions that are satisfactory, as opposed to optimal. Finding a radio station to listen to in your car is a good example of satisficing. You cannot optimize because it is impossible to listen to all stations at the same time. You thus stop searching for a station when you find one playing a song you like or do not mind hearing.

A recent national survey by the Business Performance Management Forum underscores the existence of satisficing: only 26% of respondents indicated that their companies had formal, well-understood decision-making processes. Respondents noted that the most frequent causes of poor decision making included:

- Poorly defined processes and practices.
- Unclear company vision, mission, and goals.
- Unwillingness of leaders to take responsibility.
- A lack of reliable, timely information.[13]

The Garbage Can Model

As is true of Simon's normative model, this approach grew from the rational model's inability to explain how decisions are actually made. It assumes that organizational decision making is a sloppy and haphazard process. This contrasts sharply with the rational model, which proposed that decision makers follow a sequential series of steps beginning with a problem and ending with a solution. According to the **garbage can model,** decisions result from a complex interaction between four independent streams of events: problems, solutions, participants, and choice opportunities.[14] The interaction of these events creates "a collection of choices looking for problems, issues and feelings looking for decision situations in which they might be aired, solutions looking for issues to which they might be the answer, and decision makers looking for work."[15] A similar type of process occurs in your kitchen garbage basket. We randomly discard our trash and it gets mashed together based on chance interactions. Consider, for instance, going to your kitchen trash container and noticing that the used coffee grounds are stuck to a banana peel. Can you explain how this might occur? The answer is simple: because they both got thrown in around the same time. Just like the process of mixing garbage in a trash container, the garbage can model of decision making assumes that decision making does not follow an orderly series of steps. Rather, attractive solutions can get matched up with whatever handy problems exist at a given point in time or people get assigned to projects because their work load is low at that moment. This model of decision making thus attempts to explain how problems, solutions, participants, and choice opportunities interact and lead to a decision.

> **Garbage can model**
>
> Holds that decision making is sloppy and haphazard.

The garbage can model has four practical implications.[16] First, many decisions are made by oversight or by the presence of a salient opportunity. For example, the Campbell Soup Company needed to find a way to motivate supermarkets to give them more space on the shelves. They thus decided to create a new shelving system that automatically slides soup cans to the front when a shopper picks up a can. The decision was a success. Customers bought more soup, increasing the revenue for both Campbell and the supermarkets, and the supermarkets reduced their restocking costs.[17]

Second, political motives frequently guide the process by which participants make decisions. It thus is important for you to consider the political ramifications of your decisions. Organizational politics are discussed in Chapter 15. Third, the decision-making process is sensitive to load. That is, as the number of problems increases, relative to the amount of time available to solve them, problems are less likely to be solved. Finally, important problems are more likely to be solved than unimportant ones because they are more salient to organizational participants.[18]

Integrating Rational and Nonrational Models

Applying the idea that decisions are shaped by characteristics of problems and decision makers, consultants David Snowden and Mary Boone have come up with their own approach that is not as haphazard as the garbage can model but acknowledges the challenges facing today's organizations. They essentially integrate rational and nonrational models by identifying four kinds of decision environments and an effective method of decision making for each.[19]

1. A simple context is stable, and clear cause-and-effect relationships can be discerned, so the best answer can be agreed on. This context calls for the rational model, where the decision maker gathers information, categorizes it, and responds in an established way.

2. In a complicated context, there is a clear relationship between cause and effect, but some people may not see it, and more than one solution may be effective. Here, too, the rational model applies, but it requires the investigation of options, along with analysis of them.

3. In a complex context, there is one right answer, but there are so many unknowns that decision makers don't understand cause-and-effect relationships. Decision makers therefore need to start out by experimenting, testing options, and probing to see what might happen as they look for a creative solution.

4. In a chaotic context, cause-and-effect relationships are changing so fast that no pattern emerges. In this context, decision makers have to act first to establish order and then find areas where it is possible to identify patterns so that aspects of the problem can be managed.

Some situations are in the even more troubling state of disorder where those involved cannot even agree on the context. The solution then is to see aspects of the situation as a separate context and address them accordingly. For example, following the murder of seven people in a fast-food restaurant, Deputy Chief Walter Gasior had to

> take immediate action via the media to stem the tide of initial panic by keeping the community informed (chaotic); . . . help keep the department running routinely and according to established procedure (simple); . . . call in experts (complicated); and . . . continue to calm the community . . . (complex). That last situation proved the most challenging. . . . Gasior set up a forum for business owners, high school students, teachers, and parents to share concerns and hear the facts. . . . He allowed solutions to emerge from the community itself rather than trying to impose them.[20]

to the point

How would you describe the eight decision-making biases?

L0.2 Decision-Making Biases

People make a variety of systematic mistakes when making decisions. These mistakes are generally associated with a host of biases that occur when we use judgmental heuristics. **Judgmental heuristics** represent rules of thumb or shortcuts that people use to reduce information-processing demands.[21] We automatically use them without conscious awareness. The use of heuristics helps decision makers to reduce the uncertainty inherent within the decision-making process. Because these shortcuts represent knowledge gained from past experience, they can help decision makers evaluate current problems. But they also can lead to systematic errors that erode the quality of decisions. For example, Dr. Jerome Groopman estimates that these biases might account for 15% to 20% of all misdiagnoses of medical conditions (see the Real World/Real People feature on page 343).

Judgmental heuristics

Rules of thumb or shortcuts that people use to reduce information-processing demands.

There are both pros and cons to the use of heuristics. In this section we focus on discussing eight biases that affect decision making: (1) availability, (2) representativeness, (3) confirmation, (4) anchoring, (5) overconfidence, (6) hindsight, (7) framing, and (8) escalation of commitment. Knowledge about these biases can help you to avoid using them in the wrong situation.[22]

1. **Availability heuristic.** The availability heuristic represents a decision maker's tendency to base decisions on information that is readily available in memory. Information is more accessible in memory when it involves an event that recently occurred, when it is salient (e.g., a plane crash), and when it evokes strong emotions (e.g., a high-school student shooting other students). This heuristic is likely to cause people to overestimate the occurrence of unlikely events such as a plane crash or a high school shooting. This bias also is partially responsible for the recency effect discussed in Chapter 7. For example, a manager is more likely to give an employee

Decision-Making Biases Affect the Misdiagnosis of Medical Conditions

Operational mistakes account for only a small percentage of medical errors. The overwhelming majority reflect poor thinking. . . . My extensive research on misdiagnoses shows that even the most seasoned physicians are highly susceptible to anchoring error, or seizing on the first bit of clinical information that makes an impression. Similarly, all doctors recall dramatic past cases of theirs and mistakenly apply them to the case at hand, a so-called availability error. Another cognitive trap is attribution error, whereby a physician relies on a stereotype to which he attributes all of his patient's complaints. Menopause, old age, and stress are common categories that physicians glibly invoke as explanation for vague symptoms without digging more deeply for other causes.

Are you surprised that medical doctors fall prey to decision-making biases? Explain.

SOURCE: Excerpted from J Groopman, "A Doctor's Rx for CEO Decision Makers," *Harvard Business Review,* February 2008, pp 19–20.

---

a positive performance evaluation if the employee exhibited excellent performance over the last few months.

2. **Representativeness heuristic.** The representativeness heuristic is used when people estimate the probability of an event occurring. It reflects the tendency to assess the likelihood of an event occurring based on one's impressions about similar occurrences. A manager, for example, may hire a graduate from a particular university because the past three people hired from this university turned out to be good performers. In this case, the "school attended" criterion is used to facilitate complex information processing associated with employment interviews. Unfortunately, this shortcut can result in a biased decision. Similarly, an individual may believe that he or she can master a new software package in a short period of time because a different type of software was easy to learn. This estimate may or may not be accurate. For example, it may take the individual a much longer period of time to learn the new software because it involves learning a new programming language.

3. **Confirmation bias.** The confirmation bias has two components. The first is to subconsciously decide something before investigating why it is the right decision; for example, deciding to purchase a particular type of PDA (personal digital assistant). This directly leads to the second component, which is to seek information that supports purchasing this PDA while discounting information that does not.

These stock traders make investment decisions in a pressure-filled environment. What type of decision-making biases are likely to influence their decisions?

4. **Anchoring bias.** How would you answer the following two questions? Is the population of Iraq greater than 40 million? What's your best guess about the population of Iraq? Was your answer to the second question influenced by the number *40 million* suggested by the first question? If yes, you were affected by the anchoring bias. The anchoring bias occurs when decision makers are influenced by the first information received about a decision, even if it is irrelevant. This bias happens because initial information, impressions, data, feedback, or stereotypes anchor our subsequent judgments and decisions.[23]

5. **Overconfidence bias.** The overconfidence bias relates to our tendency to be over-confident about estimates or forecasts. This bias is particularly strong when you are asked moderate to extremely difficult questions rather than easy ones. Imagine the problem this bias might create for a sales manager estimating sales revenue for the next year. Research shows that overoptimism significantly influences entrepreneurs' decisions to start and sustain new ventures.[24] Imagine the challenges this bias might create for managers in difficult and dangerous situations. Recently, five US Forest Service firefighters died while fighting a fire in the mountains east of Los Angeles because their command officers were over-confident about their ability to protect a vacation home. According to an investigation, the highly motivated firefighters tackled the hazardous situation, even though they lacked an adequate escape route.[25]

6. **Hindsight bias.** Imagine yourself in the following scenario: You are taking an OB course that meets Tuesday and Thursday, and your professor gives unannounced quizzes each week. It's the Monday before a class, and you are deciding whether to study for a potential quiz or to watch Monday night football. Two of your classmates have decided to watch the game rather than study because they don't think there will be a quiz the next day. The next morning you walk into class and the professor says, "Take out a sheet of paper for the quiz." You turn to your friends and say, "I knew we were going to have a quiz; why did I listen to you?" The hindsight bias occurs when knowledge of an outcome influences our belief about the probability that we could have predicted the outcome earlier. We are affected by this bias when we look back on a decision and try to reconstruct why we decided to do something.

7. **Framing bias.** This bias relates to the manner in which a question is posed. Consider the following scenario: Imagine that the United States is preparing for the outbreak of an unusual Asian disease that is expected to kill 600 people. Two alternative programs to combat the disease have been proposed. Assume that the exact scientific estimates of the consequences of the programs are as follows:

> *Program A:* If Program A is adopted, 200 people will be saved.
>
> *Program B:* If Program B is adopted, there is a one-third probability that 600 people will be saved and a two-thirds probability that no people will be saved.

Which of the two programs would you recommend?[26] Research shows that most people chose Program A even though the two programs produce the same results. This result is due to the framing bias. The framing bias is the tendency to consider risks about gains—saving lives–differently than risks pertaining to losses—losing lives. You are encouraged to frame decision questions in alternative ways in order to avoid this bias.[27]

8. **Escalation of commitment bias.** The escalation of commitment bias refers to the tendency to stick to an ineffective course of action when it is unlikely that the bad situation can be reversed. Personal examples include investing more money into an old or broken car or waiting an extremely long time for a bus to take you somewhere when you could have walked just as easily. A business example pertains to whether or not the US government will continue to bail out GM above the already committed $13.4 billion even though the company shows limited signs of improvement.[28] Researchers recommend the following actions to reduce the escalation of commitment:

- Set minimum targets for performance, and have decision makers compare their performance against these targets.
- Regularly rotate managers in key positions throughout a project.

- Encourage decision makers to become less ego-involved with a project.
- Make decision makers aware of the costs of persistence.[29]

Dynamics of Decision Making

Decision making is part science and part art. Accordingly, this section examines two dynamics of decision making—knowledge management and decision-making styles—that affect the "science" component. It is important to understand the "science" side because knowledge management processes provide managers with the information they need to make decisions, and decision-making styles are individual differences that influence the manner in which people make decisions. We also examine the "art" side of the equation by discussing the role of intuition in decision making and a decision tree for making ethical decisions. An understanding of these dynamics can help managers make better decisions.

to the point
What are the key conclusions regarding knowledge management, decision-making styles, intuition in decision making, and ethical decision making?

L0.3 Improving Decision Making through Effective Knowledge Management

Have you ever had to make a decision with either too much or too little information? If you have, then you know the quality of a decision is only as good as the information used to make the decision. This realization has spawned a growing interest in the concept of knowledge management. **Knowledge management** (KM) is "the development of tools, processes, systems, structures, and cultures explicitly to improve the creation, sharing, and use of knowledge critical for decision making."[30] The effective use of KM helps organizations improve the quality of their decision making and correspondingly reduce costs and increase productivity.[31]

This section explores the fundamentals of KM so that you can use them to improve your decision making.

Knowledge Comes in Different Forms   There are two types of knowledge that impact the quality of decisions: tacit knowledge and explicit knowledge. **Tacit knowledge** "entails information that is difficult to express, formalize, or share. It . . . is unconsciously acquired from the experiences one has while immersed in an environment."[32] Many skills, for example, swinging a golf club or writing a speech, are difficult to describe in words because they involve tacit knowledge. Tacit knowledge is intuitive and is acquired by having considerable experience and expertise at some task or job. We more thoroughly discuss the role of intuition in decision making later in this section. In contrast, **explicit knowledge** can easily be put into words and explained to others. This type of knowledge is shared verbally or in written documents or numerical reports. In summary, tacit knowledge represents private information that is difficult to share, whereas explicit knowledge is external or public and is more easily communicated. Although both types of knowledge affect decision making, experts suggest competitive advantages are created when tacit knowledge is shared among employees.[33] King Arthur Flour Company is a good example of how employees can teach tacit knowledge to others.

Knowledge management

Implementing systems and practices that increase the sharing of knowledge and information throughout an organization.

Tacit knowledge

Information gained through experience that is difficult to express and formalize.

Explicit knowledge

Information that can be easily put into words and shared with others.

Company executives believe that teaching its employee owners about baking and baking culture will give them an enthusiasm that will spill into how they perform their jobs and deal with customers. Even employees who don't work directly with flour are encouraged to learn about baking…. Employees are offered about 15 "Brain Food" classes each year, in which workers teach their peers everything from how to bake whole-grain breads and pies to more general-interests topics such as reading company financial statements and managing personal finances. The classes are voluntary and held during work hours, but all employees are encouraged to attend. What's more, employees can attend classes the company offers for professional and home bakers when there's room available.[34]

Let us now examine how companies foster this type of information sharing.

Knowledge Sharing   Organizations increasingly rely on sophisticated KM software to share explicit knowledge. This software allows companies to amass large amounts of information that can be accessed quickly from around the world. In contrast, tacit knowledge is shared most directly by observing, participating, or working with experts or coaches. For example, organizations try to facilitate knowledge sharing at the highest levels by allowing retired CEOs to maintain offices in the corporate headquarters. Mentoring, which was discussed in Chapter 3, is another method for spreading tacit knowledge. Finally, informal networking, periodic meetings, and the design of office space can be used to facilitate KM. LyondellBasell, a worldwide manufacturer of polymer products, uses a combination of these suggestions in order to ensure that employee knowledge is preserved and passed on to future employees (see the Real World/Real People feature on page 347).

It is important to remember that the best-laid plans for increasing KM are unlikely to succeed without the proper organizational culture. Effective KM requires a knowledge-sharing culture that both encourages and reinforces the spread of tacit knowledge.[35]

L0.4 General Decision-Making Styles

Decision-making style

A combination of how individuals perceive and respond to information.

This section focuses on how an individual's decision-making style affects his or her approach to decision making. A **decision-making style** reflects the combination of how an individual perceives and comprehends stimuli and the general manner in which he or she chooses to respond to such information.[36] A team of researchers developed a model of decision-making styles that is based on the idea that styles vary along two different dimensions: value orientation and tolerance for ambiguity.[37] *Value orientation* reflects the extent to which an individual focuses on either task and technical concerns or people and social concerns when making decisions. Some people, for instance, are very task focused at work and do not pay much attention to people issues, whereas others are just the opposite. The second dimension pertains to a person's *tolerance for ambiguity.* This individual difference indicates the extent to which a person has a high need for structure or control in his or her life. Some people desire a lot of structure in their lives (a low tolerance for ambiguity) and find ambiguous situations stressful and psychologically uncomfortable. In contrast, others do not have a high need for structure and can thrive in uncertain situations (a high tolerance for ambiguity). Ambiguous situations can energize people with a high tolerance for ambiguity. When the dimensions of value orientation and tolerance for ambiguity are combined, they form

LydondellBasell Focuses on Retaining Employee Knowledge

How a company implements a knowledge-capture program depends on its structure, size, and specialty as well as its business practices, says Darlene Lamp, a technical superintendent at LyondellBasell, a worldwide polymer manufacturer based in Clinton, Iowa.

Foreseeing a spate of retirements, LyondellBasell kicked off a knowledge retention program early last year. The first step was asking key employees to take notes on what they'd learned during their tenures, items "that they knew weren't already documented," Lamp says.

Though the practice was somewhat effective, Lamp's team soon sought a more formal method to capture and disseminate vital job knowledge. Last fall, the company contracted with Knowledge Harvesting, a Birmingham, Ala.-based consulting firm whose employees capture and formally record the sometimes-amorphous information departing employees have learned on the job. LyondellBasell chose two soon-to-retire experts with vital job skills to work with Knowledge Harvesting.

One of the employees was a chemical specialist who had become an expert on a chemical catalyst process. During the course of one week, Pam Holloway, co-partner of Knowledge Harvesting, conducted structural interviews, of two to three hours each, with the employee.

"The majority of the important knowledge in an organization is in somebody's head. You really don't know what you have until you've lost it," Holloway says. "Our focus is on the difficult stuff that people do. That's not the same as documenting procedures that could be collected and made easily explicit."

As she did with the retiring chemical specialist at LyondellBasell, Holloway carefully structures interviews with departing workers to elicit employees' soft knowledge . . .

She videotapes portions of the sessions that she finds need visual aids. When she interviewed the chemical specialist, for example, he told her that when the chemical reached a particular fluidity and color, it was ready—a tidbit of information hard to pick up on the job. She videotaped the solution at the moment it achieved the desired color so future employees would have a visual reference.

The second LyondellBasell subject-matter specialist selected for the Knowledge Harvesting process rebuilt special mechanical equipment. Although the employee had previously been involved in training other workers during one-on-one sessions, trainees left those sessions with few documents to refer to, Lamp says. . . .

But after Holloway interviewed the mechanical equipment expert, she encapsulated his know-how on a searchable Web-based system accessible via the company intranet. Information gleaned from the chemical specialist also now resides on the intranet in a searchable format. For some segments, employees can click on video aids.

How does the company's approach ensure that tacit knowledge is passed on to future employees?

SOURCE: Excerpted from J Thilmany, "Passing on Know-How," *HR Magazine*, June 2008, pp 101–102. Reprinted with permission of Society for Human Resource Management.

---

four styles of decision making (see Figure 12–1): directive, analytical, conceptual, and behavioral.

Directive   People with a *directive* style have a low tolerance for ambiguity and are oriented toward task and technical concerns when making decisions. They are efficient, logical, practical, and systematic in their approach to solving problems. People with this style are action oriented and decisive and like to focus on facts. In their pursuit of speed and results, however, these individuals tend to be autocratic, exercise power and control, and focus on the short run.

Interestingly, a directive style seems well suited for an air-traffic controller. Here is what Paul Rinaldi had to say about his decision-making style to a reporter from *Fortune*.

It's not so much analytical as it is making a decision quickly and sticking with it. You have to do that knowing that some of the decisions you're going to make are going to be wrong, but you're going to make that decision be right. You can't back out. You've

Figure 12–1   *Decision-Making Styles*

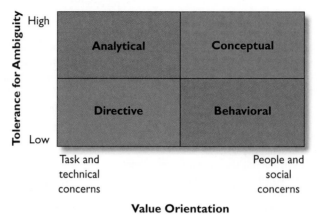

SOURCE: Based on discussion contained in A J Rowe and R O Mason, *Managing with Style: A Guide to Understanding, Assessing, and Improving Decision Making* (San Francisco: Jossey-Bass, 1987), pp 1–17.

constantly got to be taking into account the speed of the airplane, its characteristics, the climb rate, and how fast it's going to react to your instructions. You're taking all that in and processing it in a split second, hoping that it'll all work together. If it doesn't, then you go to plan B. . . . The percentage of us that make it to retirement is not real high. It takes a toll on you. We can't make mistakes.[38]

Analytical   This style has a much higher tolerance for ambiguity and is characterized by the tendency to overanalyze a situation. People with this style like to consider more information and alternatives than do directives. Analytic individuals are careful decision makers who take longer to make decisions but who also respond well to new or uncertain situations. They can often be autocratic.

Zhang Guangming is a good example of someone with an analytical style. "Zhang Guangming's car-buying synapses have been in overdrive for months. He has spent hours poring over Chinese car buff magazines, surfing Web sites to mine data on various models, and trekking out to a dozen dealerships across Beijing. Finally, Zhang settled on either a Volkswagen Bora or a Hyundai Sonata sedan. But with cutthroat competition forcing dealers to slash prices, he's not sure whether to buy now or wait."[39]

Conceptual   People with a conceptual style have a high tolerance for ambiguity and tend to focus on the people or social aspects of a work situation. They take a broad perspective to problem solving and like to consider many options and future possibilities. Conceptual types adopt a long-term perspective and rely on intuition and discussions with others to acquire information. They also are willing to take risks and are good at finding creative solutions to problems. On the downside, however, a conceptual style can foster an idealistic and indecisive approach to decision making. Howard Stringer, Sony Corporation's first foreign-born CEO, possesses characteristics of a conceptual style.

Mr. Stringer's dilemma is that he is caught between different management styles and cultures. He says he recognizes the risk of falling behind amid breakneck changes in electronics. But he says there's an equal risk of moving too aggressively. "I don't want to change Sony's culture to the point where it's unrecognizable from the founder's vision," he says. . . . Mr. Stringer, 65 years old, stuck with [an] executive team he inherited. He tried gently persuading managers to cooperate with one another and urged them to think about developing products in a new way.[40]

Behavioral   This style is the most people oriented of the four styles. People with this style work well with others and enjoy social interactions in which opinions are openly exchanged. Behavioral types are supportive, receptive to suggestions, show warmth, and prefer verbal to written information. Although they like to hold meetings, people with this style have a tendency to avoid conflict and to be too concerned about others. This can lead behavioral types to adopt a wishy-washy approach to decision making and to have a hard time saying no to others and to have difficulty making difficult decisions.

Research and Practical Implications   Research shows that very few people have only one dominant decision-making style. Rather, most managers have characteristics that fall into two or three styles. Studies also show that decision-making styles vary by age, occupations, job level, gender, and countries.[41] You can use knowledge of decision-making styles in four ways. First, knowledge of styles helps you to understand yourself. Awareness of your style assists you in identifying your strengths and weaknesses as a decision maker and facilitates the potential for self-improvement.[42] Second, you can increase your ability to influence others by being aware of styles. For example, if you are dealing with an analytical person, you should provide as much information as possible to support your ideas. This same approach is more likely to frustrate a directive type. Third, knowledge of styles gives you an awareness of how people can take the same information and yet arrive at different decisions by using a variety of decision-making strategies. Different decision-making styles represent one likely source of interpersonal conflict at work (conflict is thoroughly discussed in Chapter 13). Finally, it is important to remember that there is not a best decision-making style that applies in all situations. You are best off to use a contingency approach in which you use a style that is best suited for the situation at hand. For example, if the context requires a quick decision, then a directive style might be best. In contrast, a behavioral approach would be more appropriate when making decisions that involve employees' welfare. At this point we cannot provide more detailed recommendations because researchers have not developed a complete contingency theory that outlines when to use the different decision-making styles.

go to the Web for the Self-Exercise: What Is Your Decision Making Style?

L0.5 The Role of Intuition in Decision Making

In the recent book *How We Decide,* author Jonah Lehrer concluded that intuition is effectively used by many people when making decisions.[43] **Intuition** "is a capacity for attaining direct knowledge or understanding without the apparent intrusion of rational thought or logical inference."[44] As a process, intuition is automatic and involuntary. It is important to understand the sources of intuition and to develop your intuitive skills because intuition is as important as rational analysis in many decisions. Consider the following examples:

> Ignoring recommendations from advisers, Ray Kroc purchased the McDonald's brand from the McDonald brothers: "I'm not a gambler and I didn't have that kind of money,

Intuition

Making a choice without the use of conscious thought or logical inference.

but my funny bone instinct kept urging me on." Ignoring numerous naysayers and a lack of supporting market research, Bob Lutz, former president of Chrysler, made the Dodge Viper a reality. "It was this subconscious, visceral feeling. And it just felt right." Ignoring the fact that 24 publishing houses had rejected the book and her own publishing house was opposed, Eleanor Friede gambled on a "little nothing book," called *Jonathan Livingston Seagull*: "I felt there were truths in this simple story that would make it an international classic."[45]

Unfortunately, the use of intuition does not always lead to blockbuster decisions such as those by Ray Kroc or Eleanor Friede. To enhance your understanding about the role of intuition in decision making, this section reviews a model of intuition and discusses the pros and cons of using intuition to make decisions.

A Model of Intuition

Figure 12–2 presents a model of intuition. Starting at the far right, the model shows there are two types of intuition:[46]

1. A holistic hunch represents a judgment that is based on a subconscious integration of information stored in memory. People using this form of intuition may not be able to explain why they want to make a certain decision, except that the choice "feels right."

2. Automated experiences represent a choice that is based on a familiar situation and a partially subconscious application of previously learned information related to that situation. For example, when you have years of experience driving a car, you react to a variety of situations without conscious analysis.

Returning to Figure 12–2, you can see that there are two sources of intuition: expertise and feelings. Expertise represents an individual's combined explicit and tacit knowledge regarding an object, person, situation, or decision opportunity. This source of intuition increases with age and experience. The feelings component reflects the automatic, underlying effect one experiences in response to an object, person, situation, or decision opportunity. An intuitive response is based on the interaction between one's expertise and feelings in a given situation.

Figure 12–2   *A Model of Intuition*

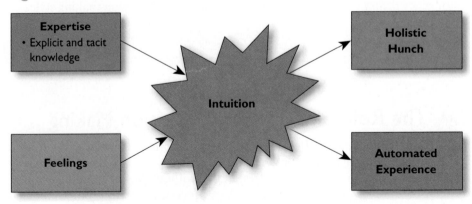

SOURCES: Based in part on E Sadler-Smith and E Shefy, "The Intuitive Executive: Understanding and Applying 'Gut Feel' in Decision-Making," *Academy of Management Executive*, November 2004, pp 76–91; and C C Miller and R D Ireland, "Intuition in Strategic Decision Making: Friend or Foe in the Fast-Paced 21st Century," *Academy of Management Executive*, February 2005, pp 19–30.

Pros and Cons of Using Intuition When Making Decisions

On the positive side, intuition can speed up the decision-making process.[47] Intuition thus can be valuable in our complex and ever-changing world. Intuition may be a practical approach when resources are limited and deadlines are tight. Intuition based on deep knowledge and active preparation informs quick and complicated decisions in an effective hospital emergency department. Recalling her work as director of an emergency department, Kathleen Gallo says, "While the arrival of a helicopter with a whole family of car-wreck victims might look like a crisis and might be a crisis for the family, it is not a crisis for the staff . . . because they are prepared."[48]

On the downside, intuition is subject to the same types of biases associated with rational decision making. It is particularly susceptible to the availability and representativeness heuristics, as well as the overconfidence and hindsight biases.[49] In addition, the decision maker may have difficulty convincing others that the intuitive decision makes sense, so a good idea may be ignored.

Where does that leave us with respect to using intuition? We believe that intuition and rationality are complementary and that managers should attempt to use both when making decisions. For example, a recent study showed that scenario planning increased the use of intuitive-based decision making.[50] Research further revealed that experts rely quite heavily on intuition when making decisions.[51] We thus encourage you to use intuition when making decisions. You can develop your intuitive awareness by using the guidelines shown in Table 12–1.

Table 12–1   *Guidelines for Developing Intuitive Awareness*

RECOMMENDATION	DESCRIPTION
1. Open up the closet	To what extent do you experience intuition; trust your feelings; count on intuitive judgments; suppress hunches; covertly rely upon gut feel?
2. Don't mix up your I's	Instinct, insight, and intuition are not synonymous; practice distinguishing between your instincts, your insights, and your intuitions.
3. Elicit good feedback	Seek feedback on your intuitive judgments; build confidence in your gut feel; create a learning environment in which you can develop better intuitive awareness.
4. Get a feel for your batting average	Benchmark your intuitions; get a sense for how reliable your hunches are; ask yourself how your intuitive judgment might be improved.
5. Use imagery	Use imagery rather than words; literally visualize potential future scenarios that take your gut feelings into account.
6. Play devil's advocate	Test out intuitive judgments; raise objections to them; generate counter-arguments; probe how robust gut feel is when challenged.
7. Capture and validate your intuitions	Create the inner state to give your intuitive mind the freedom to roam; capture your creative intuitions; log them before they are censored by rational analysis.

SOURCE: From E Sadler-Smith and E Shefy, "The Intuitive Executive: Understanding and Applying 'Gut Feel' in Decision-Making," *Academy of Management Executive*, November 2004, p 88. Copyright © 2004 by The Academy of Management. Reproduced by permission of The Academy of Management via Copyright Clearance Center.

Road Map to Ethical Decision Making: A Decision Tree

In Chapter 1 we discussed the importance of ethics and the growing concern about the lack of ethical behavior among business leaders. For example, a US Roper poll revealed that 72% of respondents perceived that corporate wrongdoing was rampant, and only 2% believed that leaders of large organizations were trustworthy.[52] While this trend partially explains the passage of laws to regulate ethical behavior in corporate America, we believe that ethical acts ultimately involve individual or group decisions. It thus is important to consider the issue of ethical decision making. Harvard Business School professor Constance Bagley suggests that a decision tree can help managers to make more ethical decisions.[53]

Decision tree

Graphical representation of the process underlying decision making.

A **decision tree** is a graphical representation of the process underlying decisions and it shows the resulting consequences of making various choices. Decision trees are used as an aid in decision making. Ethical decision making frequently involves trade-offs, and a decision tree helps managers navigate through them. The decision tree shown in Figure 12–3 can be applied to any type of decision or action that an individual manager or corporation is contemplating. Looking at the tree,

Figure 12–3   *An Ethical Decision Tree*

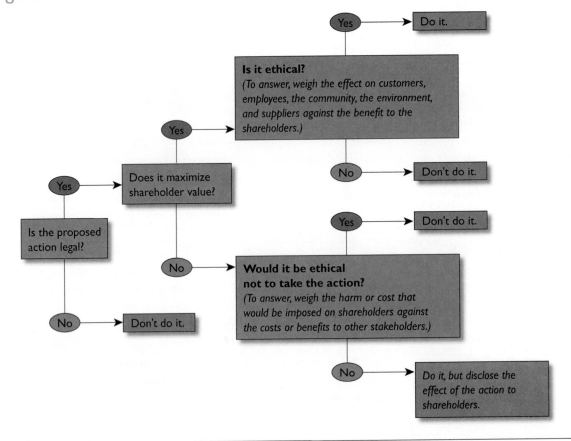

the first question to ask is whether or not the proposed action is legal. If the action is illegal, do not do it. If the action is legal, then consider the impact of the action on shareholder value. A decision maximizes shareholder value when it results in a more favorable financial position (e.g., increased profits) for an organization. Whether or not an action maximizes shareholder value, the decision tree shows that managers still need to consider the ethical implications of the decision or action. For example, if an action maximizes shareholder value, the next question to consider is whether or not the action is ethical. The answer to this question is based on considering the positive effect of the action on an organization's other key constituents (i.e., customers, employees, the community, the environment, and suppliers) against the benefit to the shareholders. According to the decision tree framework, managers should make the decision to engage in an action if the benefits to the shareholders exceed the benefits to the other key constituents. Managers should not engage in the action if the other key constituents would benefit more from the action than shareholders.

Figure 12–3 illustrates that managers use a slightly different perspective when their initial conclusion is that an action does not maximize shareholder value. In this case, the question becomes Would it be ethical not to take action? This question necessitates that a manager consider the *harm or cost* of an action to shareholders against the *costs or benefits* to other key constituents. If the costs to shareholders from a managerial decision exceed the costs or benefits to other constituents, the manager or company should not engage in the action. Conversely, the manager or company should take action when the perceived costs or benefits to the other constituents are greater than the costs to shareholders. Let us apply this decision tree to IBM's decision to raise the amount of money it required retirees to contribute to their health benefits.[54] The company made this decision in order to save money.

Is it legal for a company to decrease its contribution to retiree health care benefits while simultaneously raising retirees' contributions? The answer is yes. Does an organization maximize shareholder value by decreasing its retiree health care expenses? Again, the answer is yes. We now have to consider the overall benefits to shareholders against the overall benefits to other key constituents. The answer to this question is more complex than it appears and is contingent on an organization's corporate values. Consider the following two examples. In company one, the organization is losing money and it needs cash in order to invest in new product development. Management believes that new products will fuel the company's economic growth and ultimate survival. This company's statement of corporate values also reveals that the organization values profits and shareholder return more than employee loyalty. In this case, the company should make the decision to increase retirees' health care contributions. Company two, in contrast, is profitable and has been experiencing increased market share with its products. This company's statement of corporate values also indicates that employees are the most important constituent it has, even more than shareholders: Southwest Airlines is a good example of a company with these corporate values. In this case, the company should not make the decision to decrease its contribution to retirees' benefits.

It is important to keep in mind that the decision tree cannot provide a quick formula that managers and organizations can use to evaluate every ethical question. Ethical decision making is not always clear-cut and it is affected by cross-cultural differences. Organizations are encouraged to train employees and managers about cross-cultural issues when the work involves people with mixed cultural backgrounds.[55] That said, the decision tree does provide a framework for considering the trade-offs between managerial and corporate actions and managerial and corporate ethics. Try using this decision tree the next time you are faced with a significant ethical question or problem.

go to the *Web for the Group Exercise:* Ethical Decision Making

to the point

What are the pros and cons of group decision making and the various problem-solving techniques?

Group Decision Making

Groups such as committees, task forces, project teams, or review panels often play a key role in the decision-making process. ATA Engineering Inc., for example, is committed to group decision making.

> At least eight to 10 ATA employees are involved in interviewing every job candidate. If one employee objects to the hire, the candidate may not be offered a job unless that employee changes his or her mind. Sometimes, even the biggest company decisions are made by workers. When the lease was up on the company's building, for instance, ATA formed a committee of employees to address the issue. The group decided to stay put, after determining the current location was convenient to the majority of employees.[56]

Is ATA right in assuming that two or more heads are always better than one? Do all employees desire to have a say in the decision-making process? To what extent are managers involving employees in the decision-making process? What techniques do groups use to improve their decision making? Are face-to-face meetings more effective than computer-aided decision making? This section provides the background for answering these questions. We discuss (1) group involvement in decision making, (2) advantages and disadvantages of group-aided decision making, and (3) group problem-solving techniques.

LO.6 Group Involvement in Decision Making

Whether groups assemble in face-to-face meetings or rely on other technologically based methods to communicate, they can contribute to each stage of the decision-making process. In order to maximize the value of group-aided decision making, however, it is important to create an environment in which group members feel free to participate and express their opinions. Research sheds light on how managers can create such an environment.

A team of researchers conducted two studies to determine whether a group's innovativeness was related to *minority dissent,* defined as the extent to which group members feel comfortable disagreeing with other group members, and a group's level of participation in decision making. Results showed that the most innovative groups possessed high levels of both minority dissent and participation in decision making.[57] These findings encourage managers to seek divergent views from group members during decision making. They also support the practice of not seeking compliance from group members or punishing group members who disagree with the majority opinion.

The aforementioned study reinforces the notion that the quality of group decision making varies across groups. This in turn raises the issue of how to best assess a group's decision-making effectiveness. Although experts do not agree on the one "best" criterion, there is agreement that groups need to work through various aspects of decision making in order to be effective. Experts suggest that decision-making effectiveness in a group is dependent on successfully accomplishing the following:[58]

1. Developing a clear understanding of the problem. This requires that the group possess the information needed to make a good decision.

2. Developing decision criteria. In other words, the group needs to determine the criteria that will be used to select a solution.

3. Thoroughly and accurately assessing the positive and negative qualities of alternative solutions.

4. Encouraging minority dissent and norms of constructive conflict. Groups should embrace conflict rather than try to avoid it.

go to the Web for the Self-Exercise: Assessing Participation in Group Decision Making

Advantages and Disadvantages of Group-Aided Decision Making

Including groups in the decision-making process has both pros and cons (see Table 12–2). On the positive side, groups contain a greater pool of knowledge, provide more varied perspectives, create more comprehension of decisions, increase decision acceptance, and create a training ground for inexperienced employees. These advantages must be balanced, however, with the disadvantages listed in Table 12–2. In doing so, managers need to determine the extent to which the advantages and disadvantages apply to the decision situation. The following three guidelines may then be applied to help decide whether groups should be included in the decision-making process.

1. If additional information would increase the quality of the decision, managers should involve those people who can provide the needed information.

2. If acceptance is important, managers need to involve those individuals whose acceptance and commitment are important.

3. If people can be developed through their participation, managers may want to involve those whose development is most important.[59]

Group versus Individual Performance   Before recommending that managers involve groups in decision making, it is important to examine whether groups perform better or worse than individuals. After reviewing 61 years of relevant research, a decision-making expert concluded that "[g]roup performance was generally qualitatively and quantitatively superior to the performance of the average individual."[60] Although subsequent research of small-group decision making generally supported this conclusion, there are five important issues to consider when using groups to make decisions:

1. Groups were less efficient than individuals. It thus is important to consider time constraints when determining whether to involve groups in decision making.

Table 12–2   *Advantages and Disadvantages of Group-Aided Decision Making*

ADVANTAGES	DISADVANTAGES
1. **Greater pool of knowledge.** A group can bring much more information and experience to bear on a decision or problem than can an individual acting alone.	1. **Social pressure.** Unwillingness to "rock the boat" and pressure to conform may combine to stifle the creativity of individual contributors.
2. **Different perspectives.** Individuals with varied experience and interests help the group see decision situations and problems from different angles.	2. **Domination by a vocal few.** Sometimes the quality of group action is reduced when the group gives in to those who talk the loudest and longest.
3. **Greater comprehension.** Those who personally experience the give-and-take of group discussion about alternative courses of action tend to understand the rationale behind the final decision.	3. **Logrolling.** Political wheeling and dealing can displace sound thinking when an individual's pet project or vested interest is at stake.
4. **Increased acceptance.** Those who play an active role in group decision making and problem solving tend to view the outcome as "ours" rather than "theirs."	4. **Goal displacement.** Sometimes secondary considerations such as winning an argument, making a point, or getting back at a rival displace the primary task of making a sound decision or solving a problem.
5. **Training ground.** Less experienced participants in group action learn how to cope with group dynamics by actually being involved.	5. **Groupthink.** Sometimes cohesive in-groups let the desire for unanimity override sound judgment when generating and evaluating alternative courses of action. (Groupthink was discussed in Chapter 10.)

SOURCE: From R Kreitner, *Management*, 8E. Copyright © 2001 by SouthWestern, a part of Cengage Learning, Inc. Reproduced by permission. www.cengage.com/permission.

2. Groups were more confident about their judgments and choices than individuals. Because group confidence is not a surrogate for group decision quality, this overconfidence can fuel groupthink—groupthink was discussed in Chapter 10—and a resistance to consider alternative solutions proposed by individuals outside the group.

3. Group size affected decision outcomes. Decision quality was negatively related to group size.[61]

4. Decision-making accuracy was higher when (a) groups knew a great deal about the issues at hand and (b) group leaders possessed the ability to effectively evaluate the group members' opinions and judgments. Groups need to give more weight to relevant and accurate judgments while downplaying irrelevant or inaccurate judgments made by its members.[62]

These employees are conducting a brainstorming session. Brainstorming can be fun and is used to generate multiple ideas and solutions for solving problems.

5. The composition of a group affects its decision-making processes and ultimately performance. For example, groups of familiar people are more likely to make better decisions when members share a lot of unique information. In contrast, unacquainted group members should outperform groups of friends when most group members possess common knowledge.[63]

Additional research suggests that managers should use a contingency approach when determining whether to include others in the decision-making process. Let us now consider these contingency recommendations.

Practical Contingency Recommendations   If the decision occurs frequently, such as deciding on promotions or who qualifies for a loan, use groups because they tend to produce more consistent decisions than do individuals. Given time constraints, let the most competent individual, rather than a group, make the decision. In the face of environmental threats such as time pressure and potential serious effects of a decision, groups use less information and fewer communication channels. This increases the probability of a bad decision. This conclusion underscores a general recommendation that managers should keep in mind: Because the quality of communication strongly affects a group's productivity, on complex tasks it is essential to devise mechanisms to enhance communication effectiveness.

L0.7 Group Problem-Solving Techniques

Using groups to make decisions generally requires that they reach a consensus. According to a decision-making expert, a **consensus** "is reached when all members can say they either agree with the decision or have had their 'day in court' and were unable to convince the others of their viewpoint. In the final analysis, everyone agrees to support the outcome."[64] This definition indicates that consensus does not require unanimous agreement because group members may still disagree with the final decision but are willing to work toward its success.

Groups can experience roadblocks when trying to arrive at a consensus decision. For one, groups may not generate all relevant alternatives to a problem because an individual dominates or intimidates other group members. This can be overt or subtle. For instance, group members who possess power and authority, such as a CEO, can be intimidating, regardless of interpersonal style, simply by being present in the room. Moreover, shyness inhibits the generation of alternatives. Shy or socially anxious individuals may withhold their input for fear of embarrassment or lack of confidence. Satisficing is another hurdle to effective group decision making. As previously noted, groups satisfice due to limited time, information, or ability to handle large amounts of information. A management expert offered the following dos and don'ts for successfully achieving consensus: Groups should use active listening skills, involve as many members as possible, seek out the reasons behind arguments, and dig for the facts. At the same time, groups should not horse trade (I'll support you on this decision because you supported me on the last one), vote, or agree just to avoid "rocking the boat."[65] Voting is not encouraged because it can split the group into winners and losers.

Decision-making experts have developed three group problem-solving techniques—brainstorming, the nominal group technique, and the Delphi

Consensus

Presenting opinions and gaining agreement to support a decision.

technique—to reduce the above roadblocks. Knowledge of these techniques can help current and future managers to more effectively use group-aided decision making. Further, the advent of computer-aided decision making enables managers to use these techniques to solve complex problems with large groups of people.

Brainstorming

Brainstorming

Process to generate a quantity of ideas.

Brainstorming was developed by A F Osborn, an advertising executive, to increase creativity.[66] **Brainstorming** is used to help groups generate multiple ideas and alternatives for solving problems. This technique is effective because it helps reduce interference caused by critical and judgmental reactions to one's ideas from other group members.

When brainstorming, a group is convened, and the problem at hand is reviewed. Individual members then are asked to silently generate ideas/alternatives for solving the problem. Silent idea generation is recommended over the practice of having group members randomly shout out their ideas because it leads to a greater number of unique ideas.[67] Next, these ideas/alternatives are solicited and written on a board or flip chart. Managers or team leaders may want to collect the brainstormed ideas anonymously, as research demonstrated that more controversial ideas and more nonredundant ideas were generated by anonymous than nonanonymous brainstorming groups.[68] Finally, a second session is used to critique and evaluate the alternatives. Managers are advised to follow the seven rules for brainstorming used by IDEO, a product design company:[69]

1. *Defer judgment.* Don't criticize during the initial stage of idea generation. Phrases such as "we've never done it that way," "it won't work," "it's too expensive," and "our manager will never agree" should not be used.

2. *Build on the ideas of others.* Encourage participants to extend others' ideas by avoiding "buts" and using "ands."

3. *Encourage wild ideas.* Encourage out-of-the-box thinking. The wilder and more outrageous the ideas, the better.

4. *Go for quantity over quality.* Participants should try to generate and write down as many new ideas as possible. Focusing on quantity encourages people to think beyond their favorite ideas.

5. *Be visual.* Use different colored pens (e.g., red, purple, blue) to write on big sheets of flip chart paper, white boards, or poster board that are put on the wall.

6. *Stay focused on the topic.* A facilitator should be used for keeping the discussion on target.

7. *One conversation at a time.* The ground rules are that no one interrupts another person, no dismissing of someone's ideas, no disrespect, and no rudeness.

Brainstorming is an effective technique for generating new ideas/alternatives, and a recent study revealed that people can be trained to improve their brainstorming skills.[70] Brainstorming is not appropriate for evaluating alternatives or selecting solutions.

The Nominal Group Technique

Nominal group technique

Process to generate ideas and evaluate solutions.

The **nominal group technique** (NGT) helps groups generate ideas and evaluate and select solutions. NGT is a structured group meeting that follows this format:[71] A group is convened to discuss a particular problem or issue. After the problem is understood, individuals silently generate ideas in writing. Each individual, in round-robin fashion, then offers one idea from his or her list. Ideas are recorded on a blackboard or flip chart; they are not discussed at this stage of the process. Once all ideas are elicited, the group discusses them. Anyone may criticize or defend any item. During this step, clarification is provided as well as general agreement or disagreement with the idea. The "30-second soap box" technique, which entails giving each participant a maximum of 30 seconds to argue for or against any of the ideas under consideration, can be used to facilitate this discussion. Alternatively, groups can create an effort/benefit matrix to facilitate this discussion. This is done by identifying the amount of effort and the costs required to implement each idea and comparing these to the potential benefits associated with each idea. Finally, group members anonymously vote for their top choices. The group leader then adds the votes to determine the group's choice. Prior to making a final decision, the group may decide to discuss the top-ranked items and conduct a second round of voting.

The nominal group technique reduces the roadblocks to group decision making by (1) separating brainstorming from evaluation, (2) promoting balanced participation among group members, and (3) incorporating mathematical voting techniques in order to reach consensus. CKE Restaurants, for example, uses a combination of brainstorming and NGT in its new product development process (see the Real World/Real People feature on page 360).[72] NGT has been successfully used in many different decision-making situations and has been found to generate more ideas than a standard brainstorming session.[73]

The Delphi Technique   This problem-solving method was originally developed by the Rand Corporation for technological forecasting.[74] It now is used as a multipurpose planning tool. The **Delphi technique** is a group process that anonymously generates ideas or judgments from physically dispersed experts. Unlike NGT, experts' ideas are obtained from questionnaires or via the Internet as opposed to face-to-face group discussions.

A manager begins the Delphi process by identifying the issue(s) he or she wants to investigate. For example, a manager might want to inquire about customer demand, customers' future preferences, or the effect of locating a plant in a certain region of the country. Next, participants are identified and a questionnaire is developed. The questionnaire is sent to participants and returned to the manager. In today's computer-networked environments, this often means that the questionnaires are e-mailed to participants. The manager then summarizes the responses and sends feedback to the participants. At this stage, participants are asked to (1) review the feedback, (2) prioritize the issues being considered, and (3) return the survey within a specified time period. This cycle repeats until the manager obtains the necessary information.

The Delphi technique is useful when face-to-face discussions are impractical, when disagreements and conflict are likely to impair communication, when certain individuals might severely dominate group discussion, and when groupthink is a probable outcome of the group process.[75]

Computer-Aided Decision Making   The increased globalization of organizations coupled with the advancement of information technology has led to the development of computer-aided decision-making systems. Computerization is being used in two general ways. First, many organizations are using a variety of computer, software, and electronic devices to improve decision making. Such systems allow managers to quickly obtain larger amounts of information from employees, customers, or suppliers around the world. For example, Best Buy Co., Google, GE, Intel, and Microsoft all use internal intranets, which are discussed in Chapter 14, to obtain input from employees. Both Best Buy and Google found

Delphi technique

Process to generate ideas from physically dispersed experts.

CKE Restaurants Combines Brainstorming, NGT, and Intuition to Make Decisions about New Products

AT CKE Restaurants, which includes the Hardee's and Carl's Jr. quick-service restaurant chains, the process for new product introduction calls for rigorous testing at a certain stage. It starts with brainstorming, in which several cross-functional groups develop a variety of new product ideas. Only some of them make it past the next phase, judgmental screening, during which a group of marketing, product development, and operations people will evaluate ideas based on experience and intuition. Those that make the cut are actually developed and then tested in stores, with well-defined measures and control groups. At that point, executives decide whether to roll out a product systemwide, modify it for retesting, or kill the whole idea.

CKE has attained an enviable hit rate in new product introductions—about one in four new products is successful, versus one in 50 or 60 for consumer products.

How many different groups of people are involved in the decision-making process at CKE Restaurants?

SOURCE: Excerpted from T H Davenport, "How to Design Smart Business Experiments," *Harvard Business Review,* February 2009, p 72–73.

that these systems were helpful in estimating the demand for new products and services.[76] Wal-Mart also is well known for using computer-aided decision making to improve decision making. For example, Wal-Mart stores are using a new computerized system to schedule its 1.3 million workers. The system creates staffing levels for each store based on the number of customers in the store at any given point in time.[77] These systems also were found to improve information processing and decision making within virtual teams—recall our discussion in Chapter 11.[78]

The second general application of computer-aided decision making relates to the running of meetings. Two types of systems are used: chauffeur driven and group driven. Chauffeur-driven systems ask participants to answer predetermined questions on electronic keypads or dials. Live television audiences on shows such as *Who Wants to Be a Millionaire?* are frequently polled with this system. The computer system tabulates participants' responses in a matter of seconds.

Group-driven electronic meetings are conducted in one of two major ways. First, managers can use e-mail systems, which are discussed in Chapter 14, or the Internet to collect information or brainstorm about a decision that must be made. For example, Miami Children's Hospital uses a combination of the Internet and a conferencing software technology to make decisions about the design of its training programs. Here is what Loubna Noureddin, director of staff and community education, had to say about the organization's computer-aided decision making:

"What I truly like about it is my connection to other hospitals," Noureddin says. "I'm able to understand what other hospitals are doing about specific things. I put my question out, and people can respond, and I can answer back." She explains, for instance, that using the system, she and her colleagues have received guidance from other corporate educators, and even subject matter experts, on how to best train workers in such fields as critical care. "You get many other hospitals logging into the system, and telling us what they do," she says.[79]

Noureddin claims that the system has saved the company time and money.

The second method of computer-aided, group-driven meetings is conducted in special facilities equipped with individual workstations that are networked to each other. Instead of talking, participants type their input, ideas, comments, reactions, or evaluations on their keyboards. The input simultaneously appears on a large projector screen at the front of the room, thereby enabling all participants to see all input. This computer-driven process reduces consensus roadblocks because input is anonymous, everyone gets a chance to contribute, and no one can dominate the process. Research demonstrated that computer-aided decision making produced greater quality and quantity of ideas than either traditional brainstorming or the nominal group technique for both small and large groups of people.[80]

In conclusion, we expect the use of computer-aided decision making to increase in the future. These systems are well suited for modern organizational life and for the large number of Millennials or Gen Ys entering the workforce.[81]

Creativity

to the point
How can managers increase creativity throughout each stage of the creative process?

In light of today's need for fast-paced decisions, an organization's ability to stimulate the creativity and innovation of its employees is becoming increasingly important. Many organizations believe that creativity and innovation, which is discussed in Chapter 17, are the seeds of success.[82] Relative to our discussion in this chapter, creativity can be used in all four steps of rational decision making and any time an individual or group is trying solve a problem, make a decision, or develop something new. Creativity is particularly important during brainstorming sessions.

To gain further insight into managing the creative process, we begin by defining creativity and highlighting the individual characteristics associated with creativity. We then review the stages underlying the creative process and conclude with practical recommendations for increasing creativity in organizations.

L0.8 Definition and Individual Characteristics Associated with Creativity

Creativity
Process of developing something new or unique.

Although many definitions have been proposed, **creativity** is defined here as the process of using imagination and skill to develop a new or unique product, object, process, or thought.[83] It can be as simple as locating a new place to hang your car keys or as complex as developing a pocket-size microcomputer. Creativity can also be applied to the context of cutting costs. For example, companies such as medical device creator Olympus and energy firms Royal Dutch Shell and Chevron are looking for creative ways to cut costs.[84] This definition highlights three broad types of creativity. One can create something new (creation), one can combine or synthesize things (synthesis), or one can improve or change things (modification).

Individual creative behavior is directly affected by a variety of individual characteristics. First off, creativity requires motivation.[85] In other words, people make a decision whether or not they want to apply their knowledge and capabilities to create new ideas, things, or products. In addition to motivation, creative people typically march to the beat of a different drummer. They are highly motivated individuals who spend considerable time developing both tacit and explicit knowledge about their field of interest or occupation. But contrary to stereotypes, creative people are not necessarily geniuses or introverted nerds. In addition, they are not *adaptors.* "Adaptors are those who . . . prefer to resolve difficulties or make decisions in such a way as to have the least impact upon the assumptions, procedures, and values of the organization."[86] In contrast, creative individuals are dissatisfied with the status quo. They look for new and exciting solutions to problems. Because of this, creative organizational members can be perceived as disruptive and hard to get along with.[87] Further, research indicates that male and female managers do not differ in levels of creativity, and there are a host of personality characteristics that are associated with creativity.[88] These characteristics include, but are not limited to, those shown in Table 12–3. This discussion comes to life by considering the following example.

The Post-it Notes story represents a good illustration of how the individual characteristics shown in Table 12–3 promote creative behavior/performance. Post-it Notes are a $200 million-a-year product for 3M Corporation:

> The idea originated with Art Fry, a 3M employee who used bits of paper to mark hymns when he sat in his church choir. These markers kept falling out of the hymn books. He decided that he needed an adhesive-backed paper that would stick as long as necessary but could be removed easily. He soon found what he wanted in the 3M laboratory, and the Post-it Note was born.
>
> Fry saw the market potential of his invention, but others did not. Market-survey results were negative; major office-supply distributors were skeptical. So he began giving samples to 3M executives and their secretaries. Once they actually used the little pieces

Table 12–3   *Individual Characteristics Associated with Creativity*

Intellectual Abilities
- Ability to see problems in new ways and to escape bounds of conventional thinking.
- Ability to recognize which ideas are worth pursuing and which are not.
- Ability to persuade and influence others.

Tacit (Implied) and Explicit Knowledge (about field of interest, occupation, issue, product, service, etc.)

Styles of Thinking
- Preference for thinking in novel ways of one's own choosing.

Personality Traits
- Willingness to overcome obstacles.
- Willingness to take sensible risks.
- Willingness to tolerate ambiguity.
- Self-efficacy.
- Openness to experience and conscientiousness.

Intrinsic Task Motivation

SOURCES: Based on discussion in T Brown, "Thinking," *Harvard Business Review,* June 2008, pp 85–92; and R J Sternberg and R I Lubart, "Investing in Creativity," *American Psychologist,* July 1996, pp 677–78.

of adhesive paper, they were hooked. Having sold 3M on the project, Fry used the same approach with other executives throughout the United States.[89]

Notice how Fry had to influence others to try out his idea. Table 12–3 shows that creative people have the ability to persuade and influence others.

The Steps or Stages of Creativity

Researchers are not absolutely certain how creativity takes place. Nonetheless, we do know that creativity involves "making remote associations" between unconnected events, ideas, information stored in memory (recall our discussion in Chapter 7), or physical objects. Consider how Dr William Foege, then working for the US Centers for Disease Control and Prevention, led the effort to eradicate smallpox in Nigeria. Foege realized that his supply of vaccine was insufficient for the whole population. But he observed how people congregated to shop in markets, so he targeted his campaign to vaccinate the people in those crowded areas, even if they were merely visitors. In so doing, Foege (now a senior fellow with the Carter Center and the Bill and Melinda Gates Foundation) created a model for future vaccination campaigns that efficiently interrupt the paths by which a virus spreads.[90]

The idea of "remote associations" describes thinking such as Foege's connection of shopping behavior and a virus's spread. But it doesn't explain how Foege was able to make this creative link. Researchers, however, have identified five stages underlying the creative process: preparation, concentration, incubation, illumination, and verification. Let us consider these stages.

The preparation stage reflects the notion that creativity starts from a base of knowledge. Experts suggest that creativity involves a convergence between tacit or implied knowledge and explicit knowledge. Renowned choreographer Twyla Tharp emphasizes the significance of preparation in the creative process: "I think everyone can be creative, but you have to prepare for it with routine." Tharp's creativity-feeding habits include reading literature, keeping physically active (which stimulates the brain as well as the rest of the body), and choosing new projects that are very different from whatever she has just completed. Even an activity as simple as looking up a word in the dictionary offers an opportunity for preparation: Tharp looks at the word before and after, too, just to see if it gives her an idea.[91]

During the concentration stage, an individual focuses on the problem at hand. Research shows that creative ideas at work are often triggered by work-related problems, incongruities, or failures. This was precisely the case for Jason Jiang, 35-year-old founder of Focus Media Holding.

> Focus was born of a simple observation. In 2002, Jiang was waiting for an elevator at a Shanghai shopping mall and found himself staring at a poster featuring sultry Taiwanese actress Shu Qi pushing Red Earth cosmetics. Jiang figured he'd make buckets of money by replacing such posters with video screens. His hunch was that people would be grateful for something to watch—yes, even ads—while they waited for the ride up to their office or apartment. (In China, it's not uncommon to wait several minutes for an elevator.)[92]

Jiang's creative idea was a hit. Focus's advertising sales surpassed $489 million in 2007 and the stock has increased sixfold since 2005.

Interestingly, Japanese companies are noted for encouraging this stage as part of a quality improvement process more than American companies. For example, the average number of ideas per employee was 37.4 for Japanese workers versus 0.12 for US workers.[93]

Incubation is done unconsciously. During this stage, people engage in daily activities while their minds simultaneously mull over information and make remote associations. These associations ultimately are generated in the *illumination* stage. Finally, *verification* entails going through the entire process to verify, modify, or try out the new idea.

Let us examine the stages of creativity to determine why Japanese organizations propose and implement more ideas than do American companies. To address this issue, a creativity expert visited and extensively interviewed employees from five major Japanese companies. He observed that Japanese firms have created a management infrastructure that encourages and reinforces creativity. People were taught to identify problems (discontents) on their first day of employment. In turn, discontents were referred to as "golden eggs" to reinforce the notion that it is good to identify problems.

These organizations also promoted the stages of incubation, illumination, and verification through teamwork and incentives. For example, some companies posted the golden eggs on large wall posters in the work area; employees were then encouraged to interact with each other to execute the final three stages of the creative process. Employees eventually received monetary awards for any suggestions that passed all five phases of this process.[94] This research underscores the conclusion that creativity can be enhanced by effectively managing the creativity process and by fostering a positive and supportive work environment.

L0.9 Practical Recommendations for Increasing Creativity

While some consultants recommend hypnotism as a good way to increase employees' creativity,[95] we prefer suggestions derived from research and three executives leading creative or innovative companies: Jeffrey Katzenberg, CEO of Dreamworks Animation; Ed Catmull, cofounder of Pixar; and David Kelley, founder of Ideo. Both research and practical experience underscore the conclusion that creativity can be enhanced by effectively managing the stages of creativity and by fostering a positive and supportive work environment.[96] To that end, managers are encouraged to establish corporate values that emphasize innovation, to establish innovation goals (e.g., develop five new patents), and to allocate rewards and resources to innovative activities. At a minimum, individuals need the time and space to reflect and think about whatever issues or problems need creative solutions (see the Real World/Real People feature on page 365).

All three executives further recommend that management should create a "safe" work environment that encourages risk taking, autonomy, collaboration, and trusting relationships among employees.[97] These executives suggest that it is important to develop a "peer environment" in which people are more concerned about working for the greater good then their own personal success. This norm can be nurtured through the use of transformational leadership, which is discussed in Chapter 16.[98] The willingness to give and accept ongoing feedback in a nondefensive manner is another critical component of a culture dedicated to creativity. For example, Pixar uses daily reviews or "dailies" as a process of giving

Employees at the Blanchard Schaefer Agency Are Given the Time and Space to Be Creative

Lynaia Lutes is taking time to focus.

An account supervisor at a small Texas advertising and public relations agency, Lutes not long ago was a master of executing the details of work, without always focusing on strategy and long-term vision. Glued to her personal digital assistant, she shot off e-mails night and day, yet felt overwhelmed and sometimes did work that didn't pass muster with her bosses.

"A couple of times, I basically completed an assignment" but didn't approach it strategically, admits Lutes.

Now, taking time to think and focus deeply has become one of Lutes' performance goals. And she and the 14 other employees at the Blanchard Schaefer agency in Arlington are expected to make appointments with themselves just to contemplate, even daydream, for an hour. New on the premises, a "womb room," Spartan and unwired, allows employees to retreat to let the ideas flow without interruption.

Do you think people need quiet space to be creative?

SOURCE: Excerpted from M Jackson, "Quelling Distraction," *HRMagazine*, August 2008, p 43.

and receiving constant feedback. This will be most effective if organizations train managers in the process of providing effective feedback. Mr. Catmull and Mr. Kelly also emphasize the importance of hiring great people who possess some of the individual characteristics shown in Table 12–3. Matt Bowen, president of Aloft Group, a marketing firm in Massachusetts, suggests that this can be done by trying to determine how people think. He does this by asking job applicants to tell stories about their previous jobs.[99] Finally, these executives also suggest that management should stay connected with innovations taking place in the academic community. For example, Dreamworks invites academics to deliver lectures and Pixar encourages technical artists to publish and attend academic conferences. In summary, creativity is a process that can be managed, and it is built around the philosophy of hiring and retaining great people to work in a positive and supportive work environment.

Summary of Key Concepts

1. *Compare and contrast the rational model of decision making, Simon's normative model, and the garbage can model.* The rational decision-making model consists of identifying the problem, generating alternative solutions, evaluating and selecting a solution, and implementing and evaluating the solution. Research indicates that decision makers do not follow the series of steps outlined in the rational model.

Simon's normative model is guided by a decision maker's bounded rationality. Bounded rationality means that decision makers are bounded or restricted by a variety of constraints when making decisions.

The normative model suggests that decision making is characterized by (*a*) limited information processing, (*b*) the use of judgmental heuristics, and (*c*) satisficing.

The garbage can model is based on the assumption that decision making is sloppy and haphazard. Decisions result from an interaction between four independent streams of events: problems, solutions, participants, and choice opportunities.

2. *Discuss eight decision-making biases.* Decision-making bias occurs as the result of using judgmental heuristics. The eight biases that affect decision

making include (1) availability, (2) representativeness, (3) confirmation, (4) anchoring, (5) overconfidence, (6) hindsight, (7) framing, and (8) escalation of commitment.

3. *Discuss knowledge management and techniques used by companies to increase knowledge sharing.* Knowledge management involves the implementation of systems and practices that increase the sharing of knowledge and information throughout an organization. There are two types of knowledge that impact the quality of decisions: tacit knowledge and explicit knowledge. Organizations use computer systems to share explicit knowledge. Tacit knowledge is shared by observing, participating, or working with experts or coaches. Mentoring, informal networking, meetings, and design of office space also influence knowledge sharing.

4. *Explain the model of decision-making styles.* The model of decision-making styles is based on the idea that styles vary along two different dimensions: value orientation and tolerance for ambiguity. When these two dimensions are combined, they form four styles of decision making: directive, analytical, conceptual, and behavioral. People with a directive style have a low tolerance for ambiguity and are oriented toward task and technical concerns. Analytics have a higher tolerance for ambiguity and are characterized by a tendency to overanalyze a situation. People with a conceptual style have a high threshold for ambiguity and tend to focus on people or social aspects of a work situation. This behavioral style is the most people oriented of the four styles.

5. *Explain the model of intuition and the ethical decision tree.* Intuition consists of insight or knowledge that is obtained without the use of rational thought or logical inference. There are two types of intuition: holistic hunches and automated experiences. In turn, there are two sources of intuition: expertise, which consists of an individual's combined explicit and tacit knowledge regarding an object, person, situation, or decision opportunity; and feelings. Intuition is based on the interaction between one's expertise and feelings in a given situation.

   The ethical decision tree presents a structured approach for making ethical decisions. Managers work through the tree by answering a series of questions and the process leads to a recommended decision.

6. *Summarize the pros and cons of involving groups in the decision-making process.* There are both pros and cons to involving groups in the decision-making process. Although research shows that groups typically outperform the average individual, there are five important issues to consider when using groups to make decisions. (*a*) Groups are less efficient than individuals. (*b*) A group's overconfidence can fuel groupthink. (*c*) Decision quality is negatively related to group size. (*d*) Groups are more accurate when they know a great deal about the issues at hand and when the leader possesses the ability to effectively evaluate the group members' opinions and judgments. (*e*) The composition of a group affects its decision-making processes and performance. In the final analysis, managers are encouraged to use a contingency approach when determining whether to include others in the decision-making process.

7. *Contrast brainstorming, the nominal group technique, the Delphi technique, and computer-aided decision making.* Group problem-solving techniques facilitate better decision making within groups. Brainstorming is used to help groups generate multiple ideas and alternatives for solving problems. The nominal group technique assists groups both to generate ideas and to evaluate and select solutions. The Delphi technique is a group process that anonymously generates ideas or judgments from physically dispersed experts. The purpose of computer-aided decision making is to reduce consensus roadblocks while collecting more information in a shorter period of time.

8. *Describe the stages of the creative process.* Creativity is defined as the process of using imagination and skill to develop a new or unique product, object, process, or thought. There are five stages of the creative process: preparation, concentration, incubation, illumination, and verification.

9. *Discuss practical recommendations for increasing creativity.* Creativity can be enhanced by effectively managing the stages of creativity and by fostering a positive and supportive work environment. People need the time and space to be creative. Managers are encouraged to create a "safe" work environment that encourages risk taking, autonomy, collaboration, and trusting relationships among employees. It also is important to develop a "peer environment" in which people are more concerned about working for the greater good than their own personal success.

Key Terms

OB in Action Case Study

Ford's CEO Alan Mulally Adopts a New Approach to Decision Making[100]

BusinessWeek Almost 30 months after Alan R Mulally left Boeing to become chief executive of Ford Motor, it's still easy to peg him as an industry outsider. . . . Outsider CEOs have a decidedly varied track record. Some bring in their own people and impose a jarring management philosophy on a corporate culture, as Robert Nardelli did at Home Depot with such mixed results that the board pushed him out. Some are unsuited to running an unfamiliar business. Former S C Johnson CEO William Perez's 13 month stint at Nike comes to mind. Others tread more softly and succeed, like Eric Schmidt, the former Novell guy who runs Google. Mulally arguably falls into the latter category. Since arriving he has left most of the team he inherited in place and quieted talk that an aerospace guy couldn't run an automaker. . . .

Clay Ford Jr. says his CEO's progress in shaking up a calcified culture has thus far kept Ford independent and away from the US Treasury's loan window. Under Mulally, decision making is more transparent, once-fractious divisions are working together, and cars of better quality are moving faster from design studio to showroom. . . .

If Ford had one key insight to share, it was this: "Ford," he told Mulally, "is a place where they wait for the leader to tell them what to do." His point was that Ford staffers below the top echelon weren't sufficiently involved in decision-making. . . .

Mulally told employees Ford's existing turnaround blueprint was essentially sound. Besides dramatically reducing head count and closing factories, the "Way Forward Plan" called for Ford to modernize plants so they could handle multiple models rather than just one. A second piece of the plan was more controversial: a switch to vehicles that could be sold in several markets. This required a centralization that was anathema to the divisions around the world—fiefdoms used to developing cars themselves. This was the part of the plan that Mulally wanted to accelerate. Some executives sought meetings with Bill Ford to complain. "I didn't permit it," he says.

Mulally knew that to get his way, he would have to change Ford's culture. In the coming months, Ford employees would hear him say, over and over: "That doesn't work for me." This included Ford's penchant for cycling executives into new jobs every few years. The idea was to groom well-rounded managers. But no one was in a job long enough to make a difference or feel accountable. In the five years before Mulally arrived, executive Mark Fields ran the Mazda Motor affiliate, Ford Europe, the luxury Premier Auto Group, and the North and South American businesses. "I'm going into my fourth year in the same job," says Fields, still president of the Americas. "I've never had such consistency of purpose before."

Another thing that had to change: a culture that "loved to meet," as Bill Ford puts it. Managers commonly held "pre-meetings," where they schemed how to get their stories straight for higher-ups. It was a classic CYA maneuver and antiethical to problem solving. Mulally had seen this kind of thing before when he was running engineering at Boeing's commercial plane division. In 1997, Boeing took a $2.7 billion charge when commercial suffered a communications breakdown and failed to match production to rising demand; two assembly lines closed down for a month. When Mulally became CEO of the commercial plane division in 1999, he kicked off a new era of radical transparency that made it harder to hide problems.

He took the philosophy to Ford. As at Boeing, Mulally was determined to have a constant stream of data that would give his team a weekly snapshot of Ford's global operations and hold executives' performance up against profit targets. Constantly updated numbers—later validated by pre-earnings quarterly audits—would make it impossible for executives to hide unpleasant truths. But that wasn't the only objective. "Information should never be used as a weapon on a team," says Mulally. Rather, the numbers would help executives anticipate problems and tweak strategy accordingly.

The heart of Mulally's data operation is located in the Taurus and Continental rooms (named after the cars). They are beige and white spaces, about 10 foot by 20, down a flight of stairs from his 12th-floor office. The walls are covered with color-coded tables, bar charts, and line graphs. They represent what's going on in every corner of Ford's operation—China, Russia, South America, Ford Motor Credit, and so forth. Divisions that aren't living up to profit projections on a given week are red. Those that are hitting their numbers are green. Yellow means the results could go either way at the next meeting.

When Mulally first instituted the weekly Business Plan Review system, it was viewed not only as a pain in the neck but also like playing poker with all your cards showing. James Farley, a former Toyota hand Mulally hired as his chief global marketing executive, had his own reasons to be uncomfortable. In 22 years at Toyota, Farley had experienced uninterrupted growth. So it was a blow when his key metric, market share, turned red last September. GM was heavily discounting its pickups, making it tough for Ford to clear out its 2008 trucks before an all new F-series arrived in October. "I am my market share," Farley recalls. "So I didn't like it one bit."

But when he saw how Mulally used the data, he became a believer. The team agreed to delay the launch of the F-series truck by about six weeks, dial down fourth quarter production by 40%, and focus on clearing out the '08 trucks that had piled up when gas prices soared last summer. The team swallowed hard because delaying the new F-series, Ford's biggest moneymaker, would worsen already dismal yearend losses. But, says Farley, "we had total consensus that it was the right thing to do."

In November, Mulally decided that the dire business conditions, and Ford's new ability to react to rapidly changing circumstances, warranted daily meetings with the global team. Insiders say these led Ford to strike a new deal with the union on retiree health care before GM and Chrysler, and helped it price discounts and boost market share four months in a row. . . .

Mulally has imposed discipline on a company that veered from one strategy to the next. Brands such as Lincoln and Mercury changed their positioning every year. Today the plan, hashed over with dealers who have been given more say, is locked: Lincoln will focus on premium sedans and SUVs, while Mercury will sell premium small cars and crossovers.

Questions for Discussion

1. How would you describe Mulally's approach to decision making?

2. Is Mulally's approach more characteristic of the rational, normative, or garbage can models of decision making? Discuss your rationale.

3. What type of decision-making styles are most and least consistent with Mulally's approach to decision making? To what extent is Ford following the practical recommendations of increasing creativity? Explain.

4. What are your key takeaways from this case?

Ethical Dilemma

Should Hospitals Be Allowed to Use Credit Scores in Determining What Type of Care Patients Receive?[101]

BusinessWeek In the hospital business they call it a "wallet biopsy." A growing number of medical centers are using sophisticated software that digs into patients' finances to help determine whether they will receive free or discounted care.

The procedure, which is not understood by most patients or even many doctors, generally doesn't come into play when there is an emergency. But it has raised eyebrows for several reasons: Hospital administrators are looking at patient data—credit scores, credit-card limits, and 401(k) balances—not usually associated with treatment decisions. . . .

Debbie Maupin, 41, already has felt the procedure's sting. The Dallas resident fractured her skull, neck, and back in a car crash in April 2005. Parkland Health & Hospital System gave her free care worth more than $100,000 because her job as a mortgage adviser offered no health insurance. When she returned in June 2006 for a scheduled CAT scan, however, Parkland told her she no longer qualified as a charity case "because my credit score was too high," she says. A hospital financial counselor, she adds, refused to show her a copy of her credit report. Unable to work because of her injuries, she says she's "living off borrowed money from my father and friends . . . I have nothing in the bank." She never got the scan.

Should Hospitals or Medical Centers Be Allowed to Make Patient Care Decisions Based on Credit Scores?

1. Absolutely. Hospitals should not have to provide free care to someone who has money stashed away in the bank or 401(k) plans. This is a good way to detect if someone is lying or trying to "game" the system.

2. Absolutely not. A hospital has no business accessing private information about patients without their knowledge.

3. Yes, under three stipulations: (1) the patient gives permission, (2) the patient gets to see the report, and (3) credit scores are not used as the sole criteria to make decisions about getting care.

4. Invent other options.

Web Resources

For study material and exercises that apply to this chapter, visit our Web site, www.mhhe.com/kreitner

Chapter 13

Managing Conflict and Negotiating

LEARNING OBJECTIVES

When you finish studying the material in this chapter, you should be able to:

LO.1 Define the term *conflict,* and put the three metaphors of conflict into proper perspective for the workplace.

LO.2 Distinguish between functional and dysfunctional conflict, and discuss why people avoid conflict.

LO.3 List six antecedents of conflict, and identify the desired outcomes of conflict.

LO.4 Define *personality conflicts,* and explain how managers should handle them.

LO.5 Discuss the role of in-group thinking in intergroup conflict, and explain what management can do about intergroup conflict.

LO.6 Discuss what can be done about cross-cultural conflict.

LO.7 Explain how managers can stimulate functional conflict, and identify the five conflict-handling styles.

LO.8 Explain the nature and practical significance of conflict triangles and alternative dispute resolution for third-party conflict intervention.

LO.9 Explain the difference between distributive and integrative negotiation, and discuss the concept of added-value negotiation.

Student Resources for Studying Chapter 13

The Web site for your text includes resources that will help you master the concepts in this chapter. As you read, you'll want to visit the site for these helpful tools:

- Your online Study Guide includes learning objectives, a chapter summary, a glossary of key terms, and discussion questions.
- Take a practice quiz and test your knowledge!
- Scroll through a PowerPoint presentation with key concepts for this chapter.

Your instructor might also direct you to the Web site for these exercises:

- Self-assessments that correspond with the chapter content and a Group Exercise.
- You'll also find Video Cases and Internet Exercises for this chapter online.

www.mhhe.com/kreitner

Lowrie Beacham didn't like confronting people or making decisions that favored one staffer over another, including the time two of his people were vying to be in charge of the new fitness center.

"Instead of having one bad day and getting over it, it went on for literally years," he recalls. "You just kick the can a little farther down the road—'Let's have a meeting on this next month'—anything you can try to keep from having that confrontation."

Anytime his employees bristled at his gentle criticisms, he'd change the subject: "You're getting to work on time; that's wonderful!" he'd say, "Never mind that your clients say you're difficult to work with."

What resulted was a dysfunctional department, he admits, "with no discipline, no confidence in where they stood, lots of scheming and kvetching, back-stabbing." He gave up his management role. "I'm extremely happy not managing," he says.

The bad manager tends to conjure images of the blood-vessel-bursting screamer looking for a handle to fly off. But these types are increasingly rare. Far more common, and more insidious, are the managers who won't say a critical word to the staffers who need to hear it. In avoiding an unpleasant conversation, they allow something worse to ferment in the delay. They achieve kindness in the short term but heartlessness

in the long run, dooming the problem employee to nonimprovement. You can't fix what you can't say is broken.[1]

Conflict-avoiding managers can unwittingly create unproductive and dysfunctional workplaces.

FOR DISCUSSION

How good are you at constructive confrontation? If you need improvement, what should you do differently?

How would you handle this situation?

Your name is Annie and you are a product development manager for Amazon.com. As you were eating lunch today in your cubicle, Laura, a software project manager with an office nearby, asked if she could talk to you for a few minutes. You barely know Laura and you have heard both good and bad things about her work habits. Although your mind was more on how to meet Friday's deadline than on lunch, you waved her in.

She proceeded to pour out her woes about how she is having an impossible time partnering with Hans on a new special project. He is regarded as a top-notch software project manager, but Laura has found him to be ill-tempered and uncooperative. Laura thought you and Hans were friends because she has seen the two of you talking in the cafeteria and parking lot. You told Laura you have a good working relationship with Hans, but he's not really a friend. Still, Laura pressed on. "Would you straighten Hans out for me?" she asked. "We've got to get moving on this special project."

"Why this?" "Why now?" "Why me?!!" you thought as your eyes left Laura and drifted back to your desk.

Write down some ideas about how to handle this all-too-common conflict situation. Set it aside. We'll revisit your recommendation later in the chapter. In the meantime, we need to explore the world of conflict because, as indicated in the opening vignette, walking the tightrope between too much and too little conflict is a never-ending challenge in organizational life. After discussing a modern view of conflict and four major types of conflict, we learn how to manage conflict both as a participant and as a third party. The related topic of negotiation is examined next. We conclude with a contingency approach to conflict management and negotiation.

LO.1 Conflict: A Modern Perspective

Make no mistake about it. Conflict is an unavoidable aspect of organizational life. These major trends conspire to make *organizational* conflict inevitable:

- Constant change.
- Greater employee diversity.
- More teams (virtual and self-managed).
- Less face-to-face communication (more electronic interaction).
- A global economy with increased cross-cultural dealings.

Dean Tjosvold, at Hong Kong's Lingnan University, notes that "[c]hange begets conflict, conflict begets change"[2] and challenges us to do better with this sobering global perspective:

Learning to manage conflict is a critical investment in improving how we, our families, and our organizations adapt and take advantage of change. Managing conflicts well does not insulate us from change, nor does it mean that we will always come out on top or get all that we want. However, effective conflict management helps us keep in touch with new developments and create solutions appropriate for new threats and opportunities.

Much evidence shows we have often failed to manage our conflicts and respond to change effectively. High divorce rates, disheartening examples of sexual and physical abuse of children, the expensive failures of international joint ventures, and bloody ethnic violence have convinced many people that we do not have the abilities to cope with our complex interpersonal, organizational, and global conflicts.[3]

But respond we must. As outlined in this chapter, tools and solutions are available, if only we develop the ability and will to use them persistently. The choice is ours: Be active managers of conflict, or be managed by conflict.

A comprehensive review of the conflict literature yielded this consensus definition: "**conflict** is a process in which one party perceives that its interests are being opposed or negatively affected by another party."[4] The word *perceives* reminds us that sources of conflict and issues can be real or imagined. The resulting conflict is the same. Conflict can escalate (strengthen) or deescalate (weaken) over time. "The conflict process unfolds in a context, and whenever conflict, escalated or not, occurs the disputants or third parties can attempt to manage it in some manner."[5] Consequently, current and future managers need to understand the dynamics of conflict and know how to handle it effectively (both as disputants and as third parties). This call to action is bolstered by a survey asking employees what their manager's New Year's resolution should be. The number one response was "Deal with workplace conflicts faster."[6]

Conflict
One party perceives its interests are being opposed or set back by another party.

The Language of Conflict: Metaphors and Meaning

Conflict is a complex subject for several reasons.[7] Primary among them is the reality that conflict often carries a lot of emotional luggage. Fear of losing or fear of change quickly raises the emotional stakes in a conflict. Conflicts also vary widely in magnitude. Conflicts have both participants and observers. Some observers may be interested and active; others, disinterested and passive. Consequently, the term *conflict* can take on vastly different meanings, depending on the circumstances and one's involvement. For example, consider these three metaphors and accompanying workplace expressions:

- *Conflict as war:* "We shot down that idea."
- *Conflict as opportunity:* "What are all the possibilities for solving this problem?"
- *Conflict as journey:* "Let's search for common ground."[8]

Anyone viewing a conflict as war or a sports contest will try to win at all costs and wipe out the enemy. For example, *BusinessWeek* quoted Donald Trump as saying, "In life, you have fighters and nonfighters. You have winners and losers. I am both a fighter and a winner."[9] Alternatively, those seeing a conflict as an opportunity and a journey will tend to be more positive, open-minded, and constructive. In a hostile world, combative and destructive warlike thinking often prevails. But typical daily workplace conflicts are *not* war. So when dealing with organizational conflicts, we are challenged to rely less on the metaphor and language of war and more on the metaphors and language of *opportunity* and *journey*. For instance, Christine Day, CEO of yoga apparel retailer Lululemon Athletica, offers this advice: "You might disagree with your co-workers on how to get there, but make sure you agree on what you're trying to accomplish."[10] We need to monitor our choice of words in conflict situations carefully.

While explaining the three metaphors, conflict experts Kenneth Cloke and Joan Goldsmith made this instructive observation that we want to keep in mind for the balance of this chapter:

> Conflict gives you an opportunity to deepen your capacity for empathy and intimacy with your opponent. Your anger transforms the "Other" into a stereotyped demon or villain.

Similarly, defensiveness will prevent you from communicating openly with your opponents, or listening carefully to what they are saying. On the other hand, once you engage in dialogue with that person, you will resurrect the human side of their personality—and express your own as well.

Moreover, when you process your conflicts with integrity, they lead to growth, increased awareness, and self-improvement. Uncontrolled anger, defensiveness, and shame defeat these possibilities. Everyone feels better when they overcome their problems and reach resolution, and worse when they succumb and fail to resolve them. It is a bitter truth that victories won in anger lead to long-term defeat. Those defeated turn away, feeling betrayed and lost, and carry this feeling with them into their next conflict.

Conflict can be seen simply as a way of learning more about what is not working and discovering how to fix it. The usefulness of the solution depends on the depth of your understanding of the problem. This depends on your ability to listen to the issue as you would to a teacher, which depends on halting the cycle of escalation and searching for opportunities for improvement.[11]

In short, win–win beats win–lose in both conflict management and negotiation.

A Conflict Continuum

Ideas about managing conflict underwent an interesting evolution during the 20th century. Initially, scientific management experts such as Frederick W Taylor believed all conflict ultimately threatened management's authority and thus had to be avoided or quickly resolved. Later, human relationists recognized the inevitability of conflict and advised managers to learn to live with it. Emphasis remained on resolving conflict whenever possible, however. Beginning in the 1970s, OB specialists realized conflict had both positive and negative outcomes, depending on its nature and intensity. This perspective introduced the revolutionary idea that organizations could suffer from *too little* conflict. Figure 13–1 illustrates the relationship between conflict intensity and outcomes.

Work groups, departments, or organizations experiencing too little conflict tend to be plagued by apathy, lack of creativity, indecision, and missed deadlines. Excessive conflict, on the other hand, can erode organizational performance because

Figure 13–1 *The Relationship between Conflict Intensity and Outcomes*

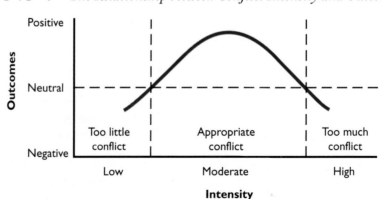

of political infighting, dissatisfaction, lack of teamwork, and turnover. Workplace aggression and violence can be manifestations of excessive conflict.[12] Appropriate types and levels of conflict energize people in constructive directions.[13]

L0.2 Functional versus Dysfunctional Conflict

The distinction between **functional conflict** and **dysfunctional conflict** pivots on whether the organization's interests are served. According to one conflict expert,

> [s]ome [types of conflict] support the goals of the organization and improve performance; these are functional, constructive forms of conflict. They benefit or support the main purposes of the organization. Additionally, there are those types of conflict that hinder organizational performance; these are dysfunctional or destructive forms. They are undesirable and the manager should seek their eradication.[14]

Functional conflict is commonly referred to in management circles as constructive or cooperative conflict. In terms of what we just discussed about the language of conflict, those engaging in functional conflict apply a win–win attitude to solve problems and find common ground (see the Real World/Real People feature about Google on page 376). Organizational psychologist Kerry Sulkowicz recently drew an important distinction between aggressiveness and assertiveness when giving this advice about functional conflict:

> The best CEOs I work with know how to exert pressure, say no, and start and win a fight when necessary. So much for teamwork? Actually, collaboration and confrontation aren't mutually exclusive. There's aggression—a basic survival mechanism—and then there's its tamer, more socially adaptive cousin, assertiveness, which can be deployed usefully, including with people working on the "same side."
>
> The need to be assertive comes up all the time. It's essential in negotiating contracts, rejecting bad work, criticizing a strategy, or firing (or defending) an employee. Yet some people will do almost anything to avoid confrontation. . . .
>
> The key, oddly enough, is to empathize with the person you're confronting. To that end, marshal useful facts rather than impressions, offer alternatives along with your objections, and limit comments to the deed, not the doer. Your opponent won't hear anything you say after an attack on his or her character. And don't be self-righteous. Or gloat if you prevail. Nobody likes a poor winner.[15]

Functional conflict
Serves organization's interests.

Dysfunctional conflict
Threatens organization's interests.

Why People Avoid Conflict

Are you uncomfortable in conflict situations? Do you go out of your way to avoid conflict? If so, you're not alone. Many of us avoid conflict for a variety of both good and bad reasons. Tim Ursiny, in his entertaining and instructive book *The Coward's Guide to Conflict,* contends that we avoid conflict because we fear various combinations of the following things: "harm," "rejection," "loss of relationship," "anger," "being seen as selfish," "saying the wrong thing," "failing," "hurting someone else," "getting what you want," and "intimacy."[16] This list is self-explanatory, except for the fear of "getting what you want." By this, Ursiny is referring to those who, for personal reasons, feel undeserving or fear the consequences of success, or both (so they tend to sabotage themselves).[17] For our present purposes, it is sufficient to become consciously aware of our fears and practice overcoming them. Reading, understanding, and acting upon the material in this chapter are steps in a positive direction.

Lots of Friendly Fighting at Google

Douglas Merrill, Chief Information Officer and V.P. of Engineering:

Organizations that exist for a long time almost always have strong cultures. But any sociologist will tell you it's rare for people to talk about the elements of their culture. Google lives out loud. We argue about strategy and whether our products are good or bad. We argue about everything. But you want conflict to thrive in a supportive way. At heart, I'm an introvert, but I've learned to enjoy the give and take of ideas here. We work hard to protect people who argue.

How comfortable would you be working in this sort of confrontational environment?

SOURCE: As quoted in C Salter, "The Faces and Voices of the World's Most Innovative Company," *Fast Company*, March 2008, p 77.

Lively but positive debate is a staple of Google's corporate culture. How do you handle disagreements at work?

L0.3 Antecedents of Conflict

Certain situations produce more conflict than others. By knowing the antecedents of conflict, managers are better able to anticipate it and take steps to resolve it if it becomes dysfunctional. Among the situations tending to produce either functional or dysfunctional conflict are

- Incompatible personalities or value systems.
- Overlapping or unclear job boundaries.
- Competition for limited resources.
- Interdepartment/intergroup competition.
- Inadequate communication.
- Interdependent tasks (e.g., one person cannot complete his or her assignment until others have completed their work).
- Organizational complexity (conflict tends to increase as the number of hierarchical layers and specialized tasks increase).
- Unreasonable or unclear policies, standards, or rules.
- Unreasonable deadlines or extreme time pressure.
- Collective decision making (the greater the number of people participating in a decision, the greater the potential for conflict).
- Decision making by consensus.
- Unmet expectations (employees who have unrealistic expectations about job assignments, pay, or promotions are more prone to conflict).
- Unresolved or suppressed conflicts.[18]

Proactive managers carefully read these early warnings and take appropriate action.

Desired Conflict Outcomes

Within organizations, conflict management is more than simply a quest for agreement. If progress is to be made and dysfunctional conflict minimized, a broader agenda is in order. Tjosvold's cooperative conflict model calls for three desired outcomes:

1. *Agreement.* But at what cost? Equitable and fair agreements are best. An agreement that leaves one party feeling exploited or defeated will tend to breed resentment and subsequent conflict.

2. *Stronger relationships.* Good agreements enable conflicting parties to build bridges of goodwill and trust for future use. Moreover, conflicting parties who trust each other are more likely to keep their end of the bargain.

3. *Learning.* Functional conflict can promote greater self-awareness and creative problem solving. Like the practice of management itself, successful conflict handling is learned primarily by doing. Knowledge of the concepts and techniques in this chapter is a necessary first step, but there is no substitute for hands-on practice. In a contentious world, there are plenty of opportunities to practice conflict management.[19]

Types of Conflict

Certain antecedents of conflict, highlighted earlier, deserve a closer look. This section probes the nature and organizational implications of three basic types of conflict: personality conflict, intergroup conflict, and cross-cultural conflict. Our discussion of each type of conflict includes some practical tips and techniques.

to the point
What are the keys to effectively handling personality, intergroup, and cross-cultural conflict?

L0.4 Personality Conflict

We visited the topic of personalities in our Chapter 2 discussion of diversity. Also, recall the Big Five personality dimensions introduced in Chapter 5. Once again, your *personality* is the package of stable traits and characteristics creating your unique identity. According to experts on the subject:

Each of us has a unique way of interacting with others. Whether we are seen as charming, irritating, fascinating, nondescript, approachable, or intimidating depends in part on our personality, or what others might describe as our style.[20]

Given the many possible combinations of personality traits, it is clear why personality conflicts are inevitable. We define a **personality conflict** as interpersonal opposition based on personal dislike, disagreement, or different styles. For example, imagine the potential for a top-level personality conflict at EMC Corp., a leading maker of data storage equipment and services. Michael C Ruettgers, executive chairman of the Massachusetts-based firm, gave up his CEO position in January 2001 after running the company for nine years.

Personality conflict

Interpersonal opposition driven by personal dislike or disagreement.

In a January [2002] interview, Ruettgers gave CEO Joseph M Tucci A's in innovation and strategic management, but F's in stock-price performance and financial management because the company lost $508 million in 2001. Ruettgers added that he was disappointed Tucci has attracted so little outside talent during his year at the helm. . . .

At the same time, some former execs say, Tucci has wanted to move faster to cut costs, make acquisitions, and introduce new software but Ruettgers and EMC have

A personality conflict with his former boss didn't keep EMC's CEO Joseph M Tucci from succeeding with a more people-friendly style of management.

slowed the pace of change. And Ruettgers, who had planned to be less active in daily affairs, has continued to attend weekly meetings to review operations. This has analysts and insiders speculating that Tucci could soon take the fall for EMC's poor performance. "In that culture, someone must fail," says a former EMC executive. "There will be a scapegoat."...

The personal and management styles of Tucci, a salesman, and Ruettgers, who started at EMC as an operations expert, couldn't be more different. Tucci likes to build one-on-one relationships, while Ruettgers is more aloof. Tucci seems to be more willing than Ruettgers to make tough decisions quickly. Bill Scannell, EMC's senior vice president for global sales, says Tucci gives him an answer immediately when he asks for advice. Ruettgers tends to chew on things awhile. And Tucci praises and thanks his troops regularly, while Ruettgers once told a former executive that saying thank-you is a sign of weakness.[21]

Any way you look at it, Tucci was in a tough spot, and conflicting personalities only made it worse. How did things turn out? By 2006, Tucci's strategy and personal style were vindicated as EMC posted impressive results from hot new products.[22] Good guys don't always finish last!

Workplace Incivility: The Seeds of Personality Conflict

Somewhat akin to physical pain, chronic personality conflicts often begin with seemingly insignificant irritations. A pair of OB researchers recently offered this cautionary overview of the problem and its consequences:

> Incivility, or employees' lack of regard for one another, is costly to organizations in subtle and pervasive ways. Although uncivil behaviors occur commonly, many organizations fail to recognize them, few understand their harmful effects, and most managers and executives are ill-equipped to deal with them. Over the past eight years, as we have learned about this phenomenon through interviews, focus groups, questionnaires, experiments, and executive forums with more than 2,400 people across the US and Canada, we have found that incivility causes its targets, witnesses, and additional stakeholders to act in ways that erode organizational values and deplete organizational resources. Because of their experiences of workplace incivility, employees decrease work effort, time on the job, productivity, and performance. Where incivility is not curtailed, job satisfaction and organizational loyalty diminish as well. Some employees leave their jobs solely because of the impact of this subtle form of deviance.[23]

Vicious cycles of incivility need to be avoided, or broken early, with an organizational culture that places a high value on respect for coworkers. This requires managers and leaders to act as caring and courteous role models. A positive spirit of cooperation, as opposed to one based on negativism and aggression, also helps. Proactive steps need to be taken because of these troubling survey results:

- "Twenty-five percent to 30% of US employees are bullied and emotionally abused sometime during their work histories."[24]

- In a 2007 survey, "38% of women said they heard sexual innuendo, wisecracks, or taunts at the office last year, up from 22%. . . . [M]en were more likely than women to hear all types of tasteless or questionable comments, with 44% saying they heard racial slurs, for instance, compared with 24% of women."[25]

- In a 2008 survey of 11,251 adults, 86% answered yes to the question, "Do you work with one or more annoying co-workers?"[26]

Some organizations have resorted to workplace etiquette training. More specifically, constructive feedback or skillful behavior shaping can keep a single irritating behavior from precipitating a full-blown personality conflict (or worse). Another promising tool for nipping workplace incivility in the bud is a **day of contemplation,** defined as "a *paid* day off where an employee showing lack of dedication to the job is granted the opportunity to rethink his commitment to working at your company."[27] This tactic, also called *decision-making leave,* is not part of the organization's formal disciplinary process, nor is it a traditional suspension without pay. A day of contemplation is a one-time-only-per-employee option.

Day of contemplation
A one-time-only day off with pay to allow a problem employee to recommit to the organization's values and mission.

Dealing with Personality Conflicts   Personality conflicts are a potential minefield for managers. Let us frame the situation. Personality traits, by definition, are stable and resistant to change. Moreover, according to the American Psychiatric Association's *Diagnostic and Statistical Manual of Mental Disorders,* there are 410 psychological disorders that can and do show up in the workplace.[28] This brings up legal issues. Employees in the United States suffering from psychological disorders such as depression and mood-altering diseases such as alcoholism are protected from discrimination by the Americans with Disabilities Act.[29] (Other nations have similar laws.) Also, sexual harassment and other forms of discrimination can grow out of apparent personality conflicts. Finally, personality conflicts can spawn workplace aggression and violence.

Traditionally, managers dealt with personality conflicts by either ignoring them or transferring one party. In view of the legal implications, just discussed, both of these options may be open invitations to discrimination lawsuits. Table 13–1

Table 13–1   *How to Deal with Personality Conflicts*

TIPS FOR EMPLOYEES HAVING A PERSONALITY CONFLICT	TIPS FOR THIRD-PARTY OBSERVERS OF A PERSONALITY CONFLICT	TIPS FOR MANAGERS WHOSE EMPLOYEES ARE HAVING A PERSONALITY CONFLICT
• Communicate directly with the other person to resolve the perceived conflict (emphasize problem solving and common objectives, not personalities). • Avoid dragging coworkers into the conflict. • If dysfunctional conflict persists, seek help from direct supervisors or human resource specialists.	• Do not take sides in someone else's personality conflict. • Suggest the parties work things out themselves in a constructive and positive way. • If dysfunctional conflict persists, refer the problem to parties' direct supervisors.	• Investigate and document conflict. • If appropriate, take corrective action (e.g., feedback or behavior shaping). • If necessary, attempt informal dispute resolution. • Refer difficult conflicts to human resource specialists or hired counselors for formal resolution attempts and other interventions.

NOTE: All employees need to be familiar with and *follow* company policies for diversity, antidiscrimination, and sexual harassment.

presents practical tips for both nonmanagers and managers who are involved in or affected by personality conflicts. Our later discussions of handling dysfunctional conflict and alternative dispute resolution techniques also apply.

go to the Web for the Self-Exercise: What Is Your Primary Conflict-Handling Style?

L0.5 Intergroup Conflict

Conflict among work groups, teams, and departments is a common threat to organizational competitiveness. For example, when Michael Volkema became CEO of Herman Miller, he found an inward-focused company with divisions fighting over budgets. He curbed intergroup conflict at the Michigan-based furniture maker by emphasizing collaboration and redirecting everyone's attention outward, to the customer.[30] Managers who understand the mechanics of intergroup conflict are better equipped to face this sort of challenge.

In-Group Thinking: The Seeds of Intergroup Conflict   As we discussed in previous chapters, *cohesiveness*—a "we feeling" binding group members together—can be a good or bad thing. A certain amount of cohesiveness can turn a group of individuals into a smooth-running team. Too much cohesiveness, however, can breed groupthink because a desire to get along pushes aside critical thinking. The study of in-groups by small group researchers has revealed a whole package of changes associated with increased group cohesiveness. Specifically,

- Members of in-groups view themselves as a collection of unique individuals, while they stereotype members of other groups as being "all alike."
- In-group members see themselves positively and as morally correct, while they view members of other groups negatively and as immoral.
- In-groups view outsiders as a threat.
- In-group members exaggerate the differences between their group and other groups. This typically involves a distorted perception of reality.[31]

Avid sports fans who simply can't imagine how someone would support the opposing team exemplify one form of in-group thinking. Also, this pattern of behavior is a form of ethnocentrism, discussed as a cross-cultural barrier in Chapter 4. Reflect for a moment on evidence of in-group behavior in your life. Does your circle of friends make fun of others because of their race, gender, nationality, religion, sexual preference, weight, or major in college?

Talk about in-group thinking. Don't get between these rabid fans and their beloved Pittsburgh Steelers.

In-group thinking is one more fact of organizational life that virtually guarantees conflict. Managers cannot eliminate in-group thinking, but they certainly should not ignore it when handling intergroup conflicts.

Research Lessons for Handling Intergroup Conflict   Sociologists have long recommended the contact hypothesis for reducing intergroup conflict. According to the *contact hypothesis,* the more the members of different groups interact, the less intergroup conflict they will experience. Those interested in improving race, international, and union–management relations typically encourage cross-group interaction. The hope is that *any* type of interaction, short of actual conflict, will reduce stereotyping and combat in-group thinking. But research evidence has been mixed. A recent meta-analysis of 515 different studies did indeed support the contact hypothesis, with greater intergroup contact associated with less prejudice.[32] On the other hand, a field study of 83 health center employees (83% female) at a Midwest US university probed the specific nature of intergroup relations and concluded that

> [t]he number of *negative* relationships was significantly related to higher perceptions of intergroup conflict. Thus, it seems that negative relationships have a salience that overwhelms any possible positive effects from friendship links across groups.[33]

Intergroup contact and friendships are still desirable, as documented in many studies,[34] but they are readily overpowered by negative intergroup interactions. Thus, *priority number one for managers faced with intergroup conflict is to identify and root out specific negative linkages among groups.* A single personality conflict, for instance, may contaminate the entire intergroup experience. The same goes for an employee who voices negative opinions or spreads negative rumors about another group. Our updated contact model in Figure 13–2 is based on this and other research insights, such as the need to foster positive attitudes toward other groups. Also, notice how conflict within the group and negative gossip from third parties are threats that need to be neutralized if intergroup conflict is to be minimized.[35]

L0.6 Cross-Cultural Conflict

Doing business with people from different cultures is commonplace in our global economy where cross-border mergers, joint ventures, and alliances are the order of the day.[36] Because of differing assumptions about how to think and act, the potential for cross-cultural conflict is both immediate and huge.[37] Success or failure, when conducting business across cultures, often hinges on avoiding and minimizing actual or perceived conflict. For example, consider this cultural mismatch:

> Mexicans place great importance on saving face, so they tend to expect any conflicts that occur during negotiations to be downplayed or kept private. The prevailing attitude in the [United States], however, is

Cross-cultural conflict is a major challenge in international dealings.

Figure 13–2   *An Updated Contact Model for Minimizing Intergroup Conflict*

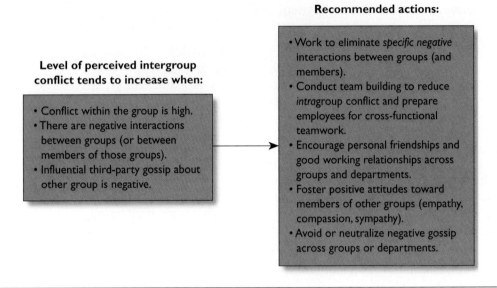

Level of perceived intergroup conflict tends to increase when:

- Conflict within the group is high.
- There are negative interactions between groups (or between members of those groups).
- Influential third-party gossip about other group is negative.

Recommended actions:

- Work to eliminate *specific negative interactions* between groups (and members).
- Conduct team building to reduce *intragroup* conflict and prepare employees for cross-functional teamwork.
- Encourage personal friendships and good working relationships across groups and departments.
- Foster positive attitudes toward members of other groups (empathy, compassion, sympathy).
- Avoid or neutralize negative gossip across groups or departments.

SOURCES: Based on research evidence in G Labianca, D J Brass, and B Gray, "Social Networks and Perceptions of Intergroup Conflict: The Role of Negative Relationships and Third Parties," *Academy of Management Journal,* February 1998, pp 55–67; C D Batson et al., "Empathy and Attitudes: Can Feeling for a Member of a Stigmatized Group Improve Feelings toward the Group?" *Journal of Personality and Social Psychology,* January 1997, pp 105–18; and S C Wright et al., "The Extended Contact Effect: Knowledge of Cross-Group Friendships and Prejudice," *Journal of Personality and Social Psychology,* July 1997, pp 73–90.

that conflict should be dealt with directly and publicly to prevent hard feelings from developing on a personal level.[38]

This is not a matter of who is right and who is wrong; rather it is a matter of accommodating cultural differences for a successful business transaction. Awareness of the GLOBE project's cross-cultural dimensions, discussed in Chapter 4, is an important first step. Stereotypes also need to be identified and neutralized. Beyond that, cross-cultural conflict can be moderated by using international consultants and building cross-cultural relationships.

International Consultants   In response to broad demand, there is a growing army of management consultants specializing in cross-cultural relations. Competency and fees vary widely, of course. But a carefully selected cross-cultural consultant can be helpful, as this illustration shows:

[W]hen electronics-maker Canon planned to set up a subsidiary in Dubai through its Netherlands division, it asked consultant Sahid Mirza of Glocom, based in Dubai, to find out how the two cultures would work together.

Mirza sent out the test questionnaires and got a sizeable response. "The findings were somewhat surprising," he recalls. "We found that, at the bedrock level, there were relatively few differences. Many of the Arab businessmen came from former British colonies and viewed business in much the same way as the Dutch."

But at the level of behavior, there was a real conflict. "The Dutch are blunt and honest in expression, and such expression is very offensive to Arab sensibilities." ... As a result of Mirza's research, Canon did start the subsidiary in Dubai, but it trained both the Dutch and the Arab executives first.[39]

Table 13–2   *Ways to Build Cross-Cultural Relationships*

BEHAVIOR	RANK
Be a good listener	1
Be sensitive to needs of others	2
Be cooperative, rather than overly competitive	2
Advocate inclusive (participative) leadership	3
Compromise rather than dominate	4
Build rapport through conversations	5
Be compassionate and understanding	6
Avoid conflict by emphasizing harmony	7
Nurture others (develop and mentor)	8

> Tie (for rank 2 items)

SOURCE: Adapted from R L Tung, "American Expatriates Abroad: From Neophytes to Cosmopolitans," *Journal of World Business*, Summer 1998, table 6, p 136. © 1998, with permission from Elsevier.

Consultants also can help untangle possible personality and intergroup conflicts from conflicts rooted in differing national cultures. *Note:* Although we have discussed these three basic types of conflict separately, they typically are encountered in complex, messy bundles.

Building Cross-Cultural Relationships to Avoid Dysfunctional Conflict
Rosalie L Tung's study of 409 expatriates from US and Canadian multinational firms is very instructive.[40] Her survey sought to pinpoint success factors for the expatriates (14% female) who were working in 51 different countries worldwide. Nine specific ways to facilitate interaction with host-country nationals, as ranked from most useful to least useful by the respondents, are listed in Table 13–2. Good listening skills topped the list, followed by sensitivity to others and cooperativeness rather than competitiveness. Interestingly, US managers are culturally characterized as just the opposite: poor listeners, blunt to the point of insensitivity, and excessively competitive. Some managers need to add self-management to the list of ways to minimize cross-cultural conflict.[41]

Managing Conflict

As we have seen, conflict has many faces and is a constant challenge for managers who are responsible for reaching organizational goals. Our attention now turns to the active management of both functional and dysfunctional conflict. We discuss how to stimulate functional conflict, how to handle dysfunctional conflict, and how third parties can deal effectively with conflict. Relevant research lessons also are examined.

to the point

How can managers stimulate functional conflict, manage dysfunctional conflict, and avoid conflict triangles?

L0.7 Stimulating Functional Conflict

Sometimes committees and decision-making groups become so bogged down in details and procedures that nothing substantive is accomplished. Carefully monitored functional conflict can help get the creative juices flowing once again.

Programmed conflict

Encourages different opinions without protecting management's personal feelings.

Managers basically have two options. They can fan the fires of naturally occurring conflict—but this approach can be unreliable and slow. Alternatively, managers can resort to programmed conflict.[42] Experts in the field define **programmed conflict** as "conflict that raises different opinions *regardless of the personal feelings of the managers.*"[43] The trick is to get contributors to either defend or criticize ideas based on relevant facts rather than on the basis of personal preference or political interests. This requires disciplined role playing. Two programmed conflict techniques with proven track records are devil's advocacy and the dialectic method. Let us explore these two ways of stimulating functional conflict.

Devil's Advocacy　　This technique gets its name from a traditional practice within the Roman Catholic Church. When someone's name came before the

Figure 13–3　　*Techniques for Stimulating Functional Conflict: Devil's Advocacy and the Dialectic Method*

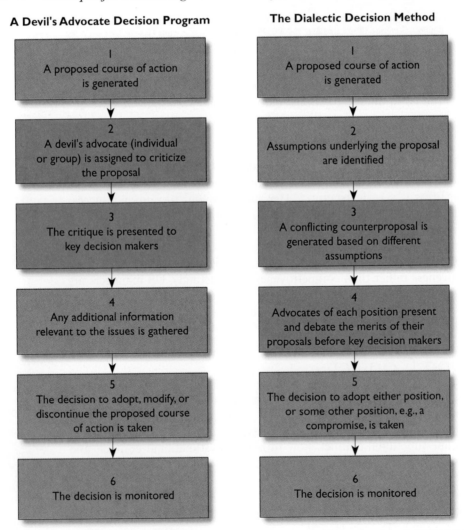

A Devil's Advocate Decision Program

1. A proposed course of action is generated
2. A devil's advocate (individual or group) is assigned to criticize the proposal
3. The critique is presented to key decision makers
4. Any additional information relevant to the issues is gathered
5. The decision to adopt, modify, or discontinue the proposed course of action is taken
6. The decision is monitored

The Dialectic Decision Method

1. A proposed course of action is generated
2. Assumptions underlying the proposal are identified
3. A conflicting counterproposal is generated based on different assumptions
4. Advocates of each position present and debate the merits of their proposals before key decision makers
5. The decision to adopt either position, or some other position, e.g., a compromise, is taken
6. The decision is monitored

SOURCE: From R A Cosier and C R Schwenk, "Agreement and Thinking Alike: Ingredients for Poor Decisions," *Academy of Management Executive*, February 1990, pp 72–73. Copyright © 1990 by The Academy of Management. Reproduced by permission of The Academy of Management via Copyright Clearance Center.

College of Cardinals for elevation to sainthood, it was absolutely essential to ensure that he or she had a spotless record. Consequently, one individual was assigned the role of *devil's advocate* to uncover and air all possible objections to the person's canonization. In accordance with this practice, **devil's advocacy** in today's organizations involves assigning someone the role of critic.[44] Recall from Chapter 10, Irving Janis recommended the devil's advocate role for preventing groupthink.

In the left half of Figure 13–3, note how devil's advocacy alters the usual decision-making process in steps 2 and 3. This approach to programmed conflict is intended to generate critical thinking and reality testing.[45] It is a good idea to rotate the job of devil's advocate so no one person or group develops a strictly negative reputation. Moreover, periodic devil's advocacy role-playing is good training for developing analytical and communication skills and emotional intelligence.

Devil's advocacy

Assigning someone the role of critic.

The Dialectic Method   Like devil's advocacy, the dialectic method is a time-honored practice. This particular approach to programmed conflict traces back to the dialectic school of philosophy in ancient Greece. Plato and his followers attempted to synthesize truths by exploring opposite positions (called *thesis* and *antithesis*). Court systems in the United States and elsewhere rely on directly opposing points of view for determining guilt or innocence. Accordingly, today's **dialectic method** calls for managers to foster a structured debate of opposing viewpoints prior to making a decision.[46] Steps 3 and 4 in the right half of Figure 13–3 set the dialectic approach apart from the normal decision-making process. For an example of the dialectic method in action, see the Real World/Real People feature on page 386.

Dialectic method

Fostering a debate of opposing viewpoints to better understand an issue.

A major drawback of the dialectic method is that "winning the debate" may overshadow the issue at hand. Also, the dialectic method requires more skill training than does devil's advocacy. Regarding the comparative effectiveness of these two approaches to stimulating functional conflict, however, a laboratory study ended in a tie. Compared with groups that strived to reach a consensus, decision-making groups using either devil's advocacy or the dialectic method yielded equally higher quality decisions.[47] But in a more recent laboratory study, groups using devil's advocacy produced more potential solutions and made better recommendations for a case problem than did groups using the dialectic method.[48]

In light of this mixed evidence, managers have some latitude in using either devil's advocacy or the dialectic method for pumping creative life back into stalled deliberations. Personal preference and the role players' experience may well be the deciding factors in choosing one approach over the other. The important thing is to actively stimulate functional conflict when necessary, such as when the risk of blind conformity or groupthink is high. Joseph M Tucci, the CEO of EMC introduced previously, fosters functional conflict by creating a supportive climate for dissent:

Good leaders always leave room for debate and different opinions. . . .

The team has to be in harmony. But before you move out, there needs to be a debate. Leadership is not a right. You have to earn it.

. . . . [E]very company needs a healthy paranoia. It's the CEO's job to keep it on the edge, to put tension in the system. You have to do the right thing for the right circumstances.[49]

How Toro Mows Down Bad Ideas

Toro, the $1.8 billion lawn-mower giant, knows how to curb the urge to merge. Anytime an M&A [merger and acquisition] pitch reaches the desk of CEO Mike Hoffman, he asks a due-diligence group to make the case to the company's board. But he also turns to the "contra team"—half a dozen vice presidents and directors—to deliver the voice of dissent. According to chairman Ken Melrose . . . a few years ago the contras killed an eight-figure acquisition of a manufacturer that had pitched itself as a turnaround success. The contras' number crunching showed that its sector was facing a slump.

The prospect's revenues have since tanked, while Toro has nearly doubled its sales. "Naysaying in corporate America isn't popular," Melrose says. "The contra team is a way to create negative views that are in the shareholders' best interest and the company's best interest."

What factors can limit the effectiveness of this technique?

SOURCE: Excerpted from P Kaihla, "Toro: The Contra Team," *Business 2.0*, April 2006, p 83.

This meshes well with the results of a pair of laboratory studies that found a positive relationship between the degree of minority dissent and team innovation, *but only when participative decision making was used.*[50]

Alternative Styles for Handling Dysfunctional Conflict

People tend to handle negative conflict in patterned ways referred to as *styles*. Several conflict styles have been categorized over the years. According to conflict specialist Afzalur Rahim's model, five different conflict-handling styles can be plotted on a 2 × 2 grid. High to low concern for *self* is found on the horizontal axis of the grid, while low to high concern for *others* forms the vertical axis (see Figure 13–4). Various combinations of these variables produce the five different conflict-handling styles: integrating, obliging, dominating, avoiding, and compromising.[51] There is no single best style; each has strengths and limitations and is subject to situational constraints.

Integrating (Problem Solving)   In this style, interested parties confront the issue and cooperatively identify the problem, generate and weigh alternative

Figure 13–4   *Five Conflict-Handling Styles*

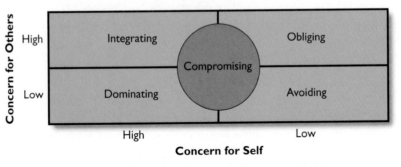

SOURCE: From M Afzalur Rahim, "A Strategy for Managing Conflict in Complex Organizations," *Human Relations*, January 1985, p 84. Copyright © 1985, The Tavistock Institute.

Let's Go Play Some Golf

Ed Henkes, national account manager at an electrical-parts maker, wanted to repair a relationship with a key customer that had been frayed by a personality clash with one of his former reps. Henkes, who works for FCI-Burndy Products in Manchester, NH, knew that buyers at the other company, Graybar Electric, shared his passion for golf. So he thought the course would be a perfect place for the two parties to reconnect. Rather than propose a competitive round that could reignite old grudges, Henkes had a better idea: a corporate golf school where everyone could work side by side on improving their games.

So in [early 2008]. . . , Henkes sprang for the equivalent of a "corporate buddies trip" to Las Vegas. After three days of on-course instruction from the VIP Golf Academy's teaching staff, everyone was on the same page again. "Our sales guys said [we] couldn't have done anything better to improve relations," Henkes recalls. "This really brought them together."

Why was this an effective conflict resolution tactic? In a belt-tightening era, how would you justify (or condemn) this golf outing to Las Vegas?

SOURCE: Reprinted from R O Crockett, "Golf School as a Tool," November 10, 2008, issue of *BusinessWeek* by special permission. Copyright © 2008 by The McGraw-Hill Companies.

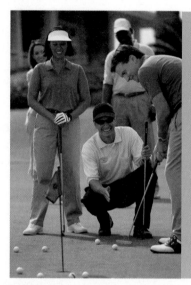

Is golf school a secret weapon in the fight against dysfunctional conflict?

---

solutions, and select a solution. Integrating is appropriate for complex issues plagued by misunderstanding. However, it is inappropriate for resolving conflicts rooted in opposing value systems. Its primary strength is its longer lasting impact because it deals with the underlying problem rather than merely with symptoms. The primary weakness of this style is that it is very time consuming.

Obliging (Smoothing)   "An obliging person neglects his or her own concern to satisfy the concern of the other party."[52] This style, often called *smoothing,* involves playing down differences while emphasizing commonalities (see the Real World/Real People feature above). Obliging may be an appropriate conflict-handling strategy when it is possible to eventually get something in return. But it is inappropriate for complex or worsening problems. Its primary strength is that it encourages cooperation.[53] Its main weakness is that it's a temporary fix that fails to confront the underlying problem.

Dominating (Forcing)   High concern for self and low concern for others encourages "I win, you lose" tactics. The other party's needs are largely ignored. This style is often called *forcing* because it relies on formal authority to force compliance. Dominating is appropriate when an unpopular solution must be implemented, the issue is minor, a deadline is near, or a crisis looms. It can be awkward in an open and participative climate. Speed is its primary strength. The primary weakness of this domineering style is that it often breeds resentment. Interestingly, the National Center for Women and Policing cites this particular conflict-handling style as a reason for hiring more women.

> Women are 12.7% of the personnel in large police departments but account for 2% of excessive-force cases that are upheld.... [T]he findings support their contention that women's negotiating and communication skills should prompt police departments to hire more women.[54]

Avoiding   This tactic may involve either passive withdrawal from the problem or active suppression of the issue. Avoidance is appropriate for trivial issues or when the costs of confrontation outweigh the benefits of resolving the conflict. It is inappropriate for difficult and worsening problems. The main strength of this style is that it buys time in unfolding or ambiguous situations. The primary weakness is that the tactic provides a temporary fix that sidesteps the underlying problem.

Compromising   This is a give-and-take approach involving moderate concern for both self and others. Compromise is appropriate when parties have opposite goals or possess equal power. But compromise is inappropriate when overuse would lead to inconclusive action (e.g., failure to meet important deadlines). The primary strength of this tactic is that it has no disgruntled losers, but it's a temporary fix that can stifle creative problem solving.

go to the Web for the Group Exercise: Bangkok Blowup—A Role-Playing Exercise

LO.8 Third-Party Interventions

In a perfect world, people would creatively avoid conflict and handle actual conflicts directly and positively. Dream on! Organizational politics being what they are, we can find ourselves as unwilling (and often unready) third parties to someone else's conflict. Thus, a working knowledge of conflict triangles and alternative dispute resolution techniques, the focus of this section, is essential to effective management today.

Conflict Triangles   Remember Annie, the Amazon.com manager at the start of this chapter? Her busy day was interrupted by her coworker Laura's tale of a conflict situation. Laura was recruiting Annie to help settle the situation. This is a classic conflict triangle. A **conflict triangle** "occurs when two people are having a problem and, instead of addressing the problem directly with each other, one of them gets a third person involved."[55] As discussed under the heading of organizational politics, in Chapter 15, employees tend to form political *coalitions* because there is power in numbers. In Annie's case, Laura was engaged in a not-so-subtle attempt to gang up against her adversary, Hans. Moreover, Laura was using Annie to vent her pent-up frustrations. This is a common and often very disruptive situation in today's organizations. The question is, What to do?

Those finding themselves in conflict triangles have a wide range of options, according to experts on the subject. Figure 13–5 shows how responses can promote either functional or dysfunctional conflict. Preferred options 1 and 2, called

Conflict triangle

Conflicting parties involve a third person rather than dealing directly with each other.

Figure 13–5   *Third-Party Intervention Options for Handling Conflict Triangles*

Detriangling
(least political; low risk of dysfunctional conflict)

More triangling
(most political; high risk of dysfunctional conflict)

1. Reroute complaints by coaching the sender to find ways to constructively bring up the matter with the receiver. Do not carry messages for the sender.
2. Facilitate a meeting with the sender and receiver to coach them to speak directly and constructively with each other.
3. Transmit verbatim messages with the sender's name included and coach the receiver on constructive ways to discuss the message with the sender.
4. Carry the message verbatim but protect the sender's name.
5. Soften the message to protect the sender.
6. Add your spin to the message to protect the sender.
7. Do nothing. The participants will triangle in someone else.
8. Do nothing and spread the gossip. You will triangle in others.

SOURCE: List of options excerpted from P Ruzich, "Triangles: Tools for Untangling Interpersonal Messes," *HR Magazine*, July 1999, p 134.

detriangling, involve the third party channeling the disputants' energy in a direct and positive manner toward each other. Importantly, the third party avoids becoming part of a political coalition in options 1 and 2. Options 3 through 8 can be a slippery slope toward further counterproductive triangling. Also, political and ethical implications multiply as the third party progresses to option 3 and beyond.

Alternative Dispute Resolution (ADR)   Disputes between employees, between employees and their employer, and between companies too often end up in lengthy and costly court battles. For example, while discussing the steady rise in wrongful termination lawsuits, *BusinessWeek* recently cited these figures: "A company can easily spend $100,000 to get a meritless lawsuit tossed out before trial. And if a case goes to a jury, the fees skyrocket to $300,000, and often much higher."[56] A more constructive, less expensive approach called *alternative dispute resolution* has enjoyed enthusiastic growth in recent years.[57] In fact, the widely imitated *People's Court*–type television shows operating outside the formal judicial system are part of this trend toward what one writer calls "do-it-yourself justice."[58] **Alternative dispute resolution** (ADR), according to a pair of Canadian labor lawyers, "uses faster, more user-friendly methods of dispute resolution, instead of traditional, adversarial approaches (such as unilateral decision making or litigation)."[59] The following ADR techniques represent a progression of steps third parties can take to resolve organizational conflicts.[60] They are ranked from easiest and least expensive to most difficult and costly. A growing number of organizations have formal ADR policies involving an established sequence of various combinations of these techniques:

Alternative dispute resolution
Avoiding costly lawsuits by resolving conflicts informally or through mediation or arbitration.

- *Facilitation.* A third party, usually a manager, informally urges disputing parties to deal directly with each other in a positive and constructive manner. This can be a form of detriangling, as discussed earlier.

- *Conciliation.* A neutral third party informally acts as a communication conduit between disputing parties. This is appropriate when conflicting parties refuse to meet face to face. The immediate goal is to establish direct communication, with the broader aim of finding common ground and a constructive solution.

- *Peer review.* A panel of trustworthy coworkers, selected for their ability to remain objective, hears both sides of a dispute in an informal and confidential meeting. Any decision by the review panel may or may not be binding, depending on the company's ADR policy. Membership on the peer review panel often is rotated among employees.

- *Ombudsman.* Someone who works for the organization, and is widely respected and trusted by his or her coworkers, hears grievances on a confidential basis, and attempts to arrange a solution. This approach, more common in Europe than North America, permits someone to get help from above without relying on the formal hierarchy chain.

- *Mediation.* "The mediator—a trained, third-party neutral—actively guides the disputing parties in exploring innovative solutions to the conflict. Although some companies have in-house mediators who have received ADR training, most also use external mediators who have no ties to the company."[61] Unlike an arbitrator, a mediator does *not* render a decision. It is up to the disputants to reach a mutually acceptable decision.

- *Arbitration.* Disputing parties agree ahead of time to accept the decision of a neutral arbitrator in a formal courtlike setting, often complete with evidence and witnesses. Participation in this form of ADR can be voluntary or mandatory, depending upon company policy or union contracts.[62] Statements are confidential. Decisions are based on legal merits. Trained arbitrators, typically from outside agencies such as the American Arbitration Association, are versed in relevant laws and case precedents.[63]

Practical Lessons from Conflict Research

Laboratory studies, relying on college students as subjects, uncovered the following insights about organizational conflict:

- People with a high need for affiliation tended to rely on a smoothing (obliging) style while avoiding a forcing (dominating) style.[64] Thus, personality traits affect how people handle conflict.

- Disagreement expressed in an arrogant and demeaning manner produced significantly more negative effects than the same sort of disagreement expressed in a reasonable manner.[65] In other words, *how* you disagree with someone is very important in conflict situations.

- Threats and punishment, by one party in a disagreement, tended to produce intensifying threats and punishment from the other party.[66] In short, aggression breeds aggression.

- As conflict increased, group satisfaction decreased. An integrative style of handling conflict led to higher group satisfaction than did an avoidance style.[67]

- A recent study of 252 MBA students (27% female) broken up into 65 self-managing teams underscored the importance of taking a *proactive* rather than reactive approach to conflict resolution. Each team pooled their talents for 40% of their grade across four core courses during one semester. According to the researchers, the more successful teams were more proactive:

"they make decisions about group resources (time, member skills, materials, etc.) in a way that integrates individual interests by identifying issues and creating solutions to potential conflicts before they arise."[68] The less successful teams tended to reactively make decisions looking backward instead of toward the future. Thus, the old saying "an ounce of prevention is worth a pound of cure" is true when it comes to dysfunctional conflict.

• Companies with mandatory or binding arbitration policies were viewed *less* favorably than companies without such policies.[69] Apparently, mandatory or binding arbitration policies are a turn-off for job applicants who dislike the idea of being forced to do something.

Field studies involving managers and real organizations have given us the following insights:

• Both intradepartmental and interdepartmental conflict decreased as goal difficulty and goal clarity increased. Thus, challenging and clear goals can defuse conflict.

• Higher levels of conflict tended to erode job satisfaction and internal work motivation.[70]

• Men and women at the same managerial level tended to handle conflict similarly. In short, there was no gender effect.[71]

• Conflict tended to move around the organization in a case study of a public school system.[72] Thus, managers need to be alerted to the fact that conflict often originates in one area or level and becomes evident somewhere else. Conflict needs to be traced back to its source if there is to be lasting improvement.

• Samples of Japanese, German, and American managers who were presented with the same conflict scenario preferred different resolution techniques. Japanese and German managers did not share the Americans' enthusiasm for integrating the interests of all parties. The Japanese tended to look upward to management for direction, whereas the Germans were more bound by rules and regulations. In cross-cultural conflict resolution, there is no one best approach. Culture-specific preferences need to be taken into consideration prior to beginning the conflict resolution process.[73]

As we transition from conflict to negotiation, take a short break from your reading and reflect on how you can better handle conflict in your daily life. Think win–win.

Negotiation
Give-and-take process between conflicting interdependent parties.

go to the Web for the Self-Exercise: The Conflict Iceberg

L0.9 Negotiation

to the point
What are the two types of negotiation and what does added-value negotiation involve?

Formally defined, **negotiation** is a give-and-take decision-making process involving interdependent parties with different preferences.[74] Common examples include labor–management negotiations over wages, hours, and working conditions and negotiations between supply chain specialists and vendors involving price, delivery schedules, and credit terms. Self-managed work teams with overlapping task boundaries also need to rely on negotiated agreements. Negotiating skills are more important today than ever[75] (see the Real World/Real People feature on page 392). In fact, in a recent survey of 3,600 professional employees in 18 countries, only 52% said yes to the question, "Have you ever asked for or negotiated a pay raise?"[76]

You Won't Get a Better Price If You Don't Ask

At Lowe's, Linda Palmer had $48 skimmed from the $248 cost of a stainless-steel GE microwave. At ABC Warehouse, Fielding Fowler had $54 shaved from the price of a Frigidaire refrigerator.

Whether through sweet talk or tough talk, all that these and a growing number of other savvy shoppers essentially did was point to the price tag and ask, "Can you do better?"

The answer these days is often yes.

It's basic bookkeeping: With the economy in dire straits, retailers have to move those refrigerators (and color TVs and sofa sets), which means that crafty consumers are getting their mattresses for something less than the sticker price—and their delivery for free.

Long the method for shopping real estate, car dealerships, flea markets and antiques stores, haggling is invading recession-era retail.

How good a negotiator are you? What holds you back if you're not?

SOURCE: Excerpted from O Barker, "Hagglers Thrive in New Economy," *USA Today*, March 16, 2009, p 1D.

Tough economic times have brought price haggling to the shopping mall. How effective are you at negotiating good deals?

Two Basic Types of Negotiation

Negotiation experts distinguish between two types of negotiation—*distributive* and *integrative.* Understanding the difference requires a change in traditional fixed-pie thinking:

"Never, EVER purr during the negotiating process, Derwood!"

Copyright Scott Arthur Masear. Reprinted with permission.

A *distributive* negotiation usually involves a single issue—a "fixed-pie"—in which one person gains at the expense of the other. For example, haggling over the price of a rug in a bazaar is a distributive negotiation. In most conflicts, however, more than one issue is at stake, and each party values the issues differently. The outcomes available are no longer a fixed-pie divided among all parties. An agreement can be found that is better for both parties than what they would have reached through distributive negotiation. This is an *integrative* negotiation.

However, parties in a negotiation often don't find these beneficial trade-offs because each *assumes* its interests *directly* conflict with those of the other party. "What is good for the other side must be bad for us" is a common and unfortunate perspective that most people have. This is the mind-set we call the *mythical* "fixed-pie."[77]

Distributive negotiation involves traditional win–lose thinking. Integrative negotiation calls for a progressive win–win strategy.[78] In a laboratory study of joint

Figure 13–6　*An Integrative Approach: Added-Value Negotiation*

	Separately	**Jointly**
Step 1: Clarify interests	• Identify tangible and intangible needs	• Discuss respective needs • Find *common ground* for negotiation
Step 2: Identify options	• Identify *elements of value* (e.g., property, money, behavior, rights, risks)	• Create a *marketplace of value* by discussing respective elements of value
Step 3: Design alternative deal packages	• Mix and match *elements of value* in various workable combinations • Think in terms of *multiple deals*	• Exchange *deal packages*
Step 4: Select a deal	• Analyze deal packages proposed by other party	• Discuss and select from feasible deal packages • Think in terms of *creative agreement*
Step 5: Perfect the deal		• Discuss unresolved issues • Develop written agreement • *Build relationships* for future negotiations

SOURCE: From K Albrecht and S Albrecht, "Added Value Negotiating," *Training,* April 1993, pp 26–29. Used with permission of Nielsen Business Media, Inc.

venture negotiations, teams trained in integrative tactics achieved better outcomes for *both* sides than did untrained teams.[79] North American negotiators generally are too short-term oriented and poor relationship builders when negotiating in Asia, Latin America, and the Middle East.[80] The added-value negotiation technique illustrated in Figure 13–6 is an integrative approach that can correct these shortcomings.

Ethical Pitfalls in Negotiation

The success of integrative negotiation, such as added-value negotiation, hinges to a large extent on the *quality* of information exchanged, as researchers have documented.[81] Telling lies, hiding key facts, and engaging in the other potentially unethical tactics listed in Table 13–3 erode trust and goodwill, both vital in win–win negotiations.[82] An awareness of these dirty tricks can keep good faith bargainers from being unfairly exploited.[83] Unethical negotiating tactics need to be factored into organizational codes of ethics.

Table 13–3   *Questionable/Unethical Tactics in Negotiation*

TACTIC	DESCRIPTION/CLARIFICATION/RANGE
Lies	Subject matter for lies can include limits, alternatives, the negotiator's intent, authority to bargain, other commitments, acceptability of the opponent's offers, time pressures, and available resources.
Puffery	Among the items that can be puffed up are the value of one's payoffs to the opponent, the negotiator's own alternatives, the costs of what one is giving up or is prepared to yield, importance of issues, and attributes of the products or services.
Deception	Acts and statements may include promises or threats, excessive initial demands, careless misstatements of facts, or asking for concessions not wanted.
Weakening the opponent	The negotiator here may cut off or eliminate some of the opponent's alternatives, blame the opponent for his own actions, use personally abrasive statements to or about the opponent, or undermine the opponent's alliances.
Strengthening one's own position	This tactic includes building one's own resources, including expertise, finances, and alliances. It also includes presentations of persuasive rationales to the opponent or third parties (e.g., the public, the media) or getting mandates for one's position.
Nondisclosure	Includes partial disclosure of facts, failure to disclose a hidden fact, failure to correct the opponents' misperceptions or ignorance, and concealment of the negotiator's own position or circumstances.
Information exploitation	Information provided by the opponent can be used to exploit his weaknesses, close off his alternatives, generate demands against him, or weaken his alliances.
Change of mind	Includes accepting offers one had claimed one would not accept, changing demands, withdrawing promised offers, and making threats one promised would not be made. Also includes the failure to behave as predicted.
Distraction	These acts or statements can be as simple as providing excessive information to the opponent, asking many questions, evading questions, or burying the issue. Or they can be more complex, such as feigning weakness in one area so that the opponent concentrates on it and ignores another.
Maximization	Includes demanding the opponent make concessions that result in the negotiator's gain and the opponent's equal or greater loss. Also entails converting a win–win situation into win–lose.

SOURCE: Reprinted from H J Reitz, J A Wall Jr, and M S Love, "Ethics in Negotiation: Oil and Water or Good Lubrication?" *Business Horizons,* May–June 1998, p 6. © 1998, with permission from Elsevier.

Practical Lessons from Negotiation Research

Laboratory and field studies have yielded these insights:

- Negotiators with fixed-pie expectations produced poor joint outcomes because they restricted and mismanaged information.[84]

- A meta-analysis of 62 studies found a *slight* tendency for women to negotiate more cooperatively than men. But when faced with a tit-for-tat bargaining strategy (equivalent countermoves), women were significantly more competitive than men.[85]

- Personality characteristics can affect negotiating success. Negotiators who scored high on the Big Five personality dimensions of extraversion and agreeableness (refer back to Table 5–2) tended to do poorly with distributive (fixed-pie; win–lose) negotiations.[86]

- Good and bad moods can have positive and negative effects, respectively, on negotiators' plans and outcomes.[87] So wait until both you and your boss are in a good mood before you ask for a raise.

- Subjects in a study trained in goal setting and problem solving enjoyed more satisfying and optimistic dialogues on a controversial subject than did those with no particular strategy.[88] Practical implication: don't negotiate without being adequately prepared.

- Studies of negotiations between Japanese, between Americans, and between Japanese and Americans found less productive joint outcomes across cultures than within cultures.[89] Less understanding of the other party makes cross-cultural negotiation more difficult than negotiations at home.

Conflict Management and Negotiation: A Contingency Approach

to the point

What are the practical lessons from the contingency approach to conflict management and negotiation?

Three realities dictate how organizational conflict should be managed. First, various types of conflict are inevitable because they are triggered by a wide variety of antecedents. Second, too little conflict may be as counterproductive as too much. Third, there is no single best way of avoiding or resolving conflict. Consequently, conflict specialists recommend a contingency approach to managing conflict. Antecedents of conflict and actual conflict need to be monitored. If signs of too little conflict such as apathy or lack of creativity appear, then functional conflict needs to be stimulated. This can be done by nurturing appropriate antecedents of conflict or programming conflict with techniques such as devil's advocacy and the dialectic method. On the other hand, when conflict becomes dysfunctional, the appropriate conflict-handling style needs to be used. Realistic training involving role playing can prepare managers to try alternative conflict-handling styles.

Third-party interventions are necessary when conflicting parties are unwilling or unable to engage in conflict resolution or integrative negotiation. Integrative or added-value negotiation is most appropriate for intergroup and interorganizational conflict. The key is to get the conflicting parties to abandon traditional fixed-pie thinking and their win–lose expectations.

Managers can keep from getting too deeply embroiled in conflict by applying four lessons from recent research: (1) establish challenging and clear goals, (2) disagree in a constructive and reasonable manner, (3) do not get caught up in conflict triangles, and (4) refuse to get caught in the aggression-breeds-aggression spiral.

Summary of Key Concepts

1. *Define the term* conflict, *and put the three metaphors of conflict into proper perspective for the workplace.* Conflict is a process in which one party perceives that its interests are being opposed or negatively affected by another party. Conflict is inevitable but not necessarily destructive. Metaphorically, conflict can be viewed as war (win at all costs), an opportunity (be creative, grow, and improve), or a journey (a search for common ground and a better way). Within organizations, we are challenged to see conflicts as win–win opportunities and journeys rather than as win–lose wars.

2. *Distinguish between functional and dysfunctional conflict, and discuss why people avoid conflict.* Functional conflict enhances organizational interests while dysfunctional conflict is counterproductive. Three desired conflict outcomes are agreement, stronger relationships, and learning. People avoid conflict because of the following fears: harm, rejection, loss of relationship, anger, being seen as selfish, saying the wrong thing, failing, hurting someone else, getting what we want, and intimacy.

3. *List six antecedents of conflict, and identify the desired outcomes of conflict.* Among the many antecedents of conflict are incompatible personalities or value systems; competition for limited resources; inadequate communication; unreasonable or unclear policies, standards, or rules; unreasonable deadlines or extreme time pressure; collective decision making; unmet expectations; and unresolved or suppressed conflicts. The three desired outcomes of conflict are agreement, stronger relationships, and learning.

4. *Define personality conflicts, and explain how managers should handle them.* Personality conflicts involve interpersonal opposition based on personal dislike or disagreement (or as an outgrowth of workplace incivility). Care needs to be taken with personality conflicts in the workplace because of the legal implications of diversity, antidiscrimination, and sexual harassment. Managers should investigate and document personality conflict, take corrective actions such as feedback or behavior modification if appropriate, or attempt informal dispute resolution. Difficult or persistent personality conflicts need to be referred to human resource specialists or counselors.

5. *Discuss the role of in-group thinking in intergroup conflict, and explain what management can do about intergroup conflict.* Members of in-groups tend to see themselves as unique individuals who are more moral than outsiders, whom they view as a threat and stereotypically as all alike. In-group thinking is associated with ethnocentric behavior. According to the updated contact model, managers first must strive to eliminate negative relationships between conflicting groups. Beyond that, they need to provide team building,

encourage personal friendships across groups, foster positive attitudes about other groups, and minimize negative gossip about groups.

6. *Discuss what can be done about cross-cultural conflict.* International consultants can prepare people from different cultures to work effectively together. Cross-cultural conflict can be minimized by having expatriates build strong cross-cultural relationships with their hosts (primarily by being good listeners, being sensitive to others, and being more cooperative than competitive).

7. *Explain how managers can stimulate functional conflict, and identify the five conflict-handling styles.* There are many antecedents of conflict—including incompatible personalities, competition for limited resources, and unrealized expectations—that need to be monitored. Functional conflict can be stimulated by permitting antecedents of conflict to persist or programming conflict during decision making with devil's advocates or the dialectic method. The five conflict-handling styles are integrating (problem solving), obliging (smoothing), dominating (forcing), avoiding, and compromising. There is no single best style.

8. *Explain the nature and practical significance of conflict triangles and alternative dispute resolution for third-party conflict intervention.* A conflict triangle occurs when one member of a conflict seeks the help of a third party rather than facing the opponent directly. Detriangling is advised, whereby the third-party redirects the disputants' energy toward each other in a positive and constructive manner. Alternative dispute resolution involves avoiding costly court battles with more informal and user-friendly techniques such as facilitation, conciliation, peer review, ombudsman, mediation, and arbitration.

9. *Explain the difference between distributive and integrative negotiation, and discuss the concept of added-value negotiation.* Distributive negotiation involves fixed-pie and win–lose thinking. Integrative negotiation is a win–win approach to better results for both parties. The five steps in added-value negotiation are as follows: step 1, clarify interests; step 2, identify options; step 3, design alternative deal packages; step 4, select a deal; and step 5, perfect the deal. Elements of value, multiple deal packages, and creative agreement are central to this approach.

Key Terms

Selina Lo Sees the Light[90]

Throughout the 1990s, Selina Lo had a reputation as one of Silicon Valley's most aggressive and successful salespeople. But anyone who was not part of what Lo deemed the solution, she treated as her personal problem. Her bag of management tools included yelling, fist pounding, and stomach-curdling sarcasm.

David Callisch, director of marketing at switchmaker Alteon WebSystems in the late '90s, was among those she shot down, rolled over, and put in their place. After two years of working for Lo, who was vice president of marketing at the time, Callisch begged her to please, please let him report to someone else. "I said, 'I can't handle working for you,'" he recalls. "'You cause me huge amounts of anxiety. I don't want to go on like this.'"

"She'd stick her head in your office and bark out a bunch of commands," Callisch says. "We used to call them 'drive-bys.' If we ever wanted to motivate someone, we'd say, 'We're going to tell Selina that you can't do this.' It would put the fear of God into them."

The Big-Cheese Challenge

In 2004, Lo became CEO of Ruckus Wireless, a Wi-Fi start-up in Sunnyvale, California. And that was when she realized she needed to change. The first inkling came as she was trying to recruit executives she had known in other jobs. She made them financial offers they couldn't refuse. They refused anyway. They also told her why. "I had heard complaints before," says Lo. "But I always shrugged that off. Hey, stress is part of this profession; it's part of the package. I didn't realize I was making people physically sick."

Lo had also grown accustomed to ripping into her bosses, who generally tolerated it because her fierceness served their companies. But shortly after taking over at Ruckus, she got into a heated argument with a major investor, and even Lo realized she had crossed a line. Dominic Orr, chairman of the board at Ruckus and Lo's boss at Alteon, was present at that investor meeting and calls it a moment of truth. "It became clear that Selina Lo might win—but Ruckus might lose," he says.

The final straw came as Lo found herself for the first time managing people she had recruited and hired. She felt an unfamiliar obligation for the lives and happiness of employees—all employees, not just the engineers and marketers she usually favored. "When I was VP of marketing, I could go nuts, and the damage would be limited," she says. "When the CEO screams, the impact is much greater. I can't build a company with nervous people."

The Softening

What Lo calls her "directness" is bred in her bones, the result of being raised by hypercompetitive parents in fast-paced Hong Kong. It also stems from being a woman in a male-dominated industry, she says. Changing required a huge effort of will. And she was no stranger to management training. "I tried to do what the books said: be hands-off and let people make their own mistakes," says Lo. "But I hated it, hated it, hated it."

Disenchanted with the classes-and-books route to better leadership, Lo resolved to reform her own way. Impatience, she recognized, was her greatest foe. Lo likes things settled, which means arguments end when she leaves the room. Winner: Selina Lo. At Ruckus, she adopted a group decision-making process that forces her to consider the opinions of others. Now, when a disagreement arises, she quickly convenes a meeting of herself, her disputant, and one or two other people affected by the decision. "If they agree with me, he gets more data points about why I am correct," says Lo. "If they agree with him, I ask myself, Am I being blind or unfair?"

She also gets a group assist in matters of emotional intelligence. In the past, Lo had always been stingy with praise, because she herself doesn't need it. "In Chinese culture, it's considered bad manners to praise your kid, so I never got that from my parents," she says. "I became very self-driven." At Ruckus, Lo has asked colleagues to help her recognize when and how to dole out the kudos. Before an all-hands meeting, for example, someone might suggest she acknowledge an individual for a job well done. "The process has been like learning to be a parent," she says. "People learn to be good parents without going to school. If you care, over time, you figure out how to do it."

Questions for Discussion

1. How did Selina Lo's interpersonal style evolve in terms of the conflict metaphors discussed in this chapter?

2. What evidence of functional and dysfunctional conflict is apparent in this case?

3. What did Selina Lo need to learn early on about emotional intelligence, as discussed in Chapter 5? How would it have impacted her management style?

4. How would you handle a boss with the win–lose style Selina Lo exhibited early in her career? Explain.

5. Using Table 13–2 as a guide, what lessons about cross-cultural conflict did Selina Lo need to learn early in her career?

6. Which conflict-handing styles are evident in this case? What was their comparative effectiveness?

Ethical Dilemma

Break It Up!

BusinessWeek At the company where I work—we make creative products for children—two of the top executives are at war with each other. They go off on rants, they use foul language, and from time to time they actually have shoving matches. Both of these men are top producers, I might add. What lies behind this behavior? And is there anything coworkers can do? We're appalled, but the boss won't step in.[91]

What Is the Right Thing to Do in This Situation? (What Are the Ethical Implications for Your Choice?)

1. These guys are simply high-spirited thoroughbreds who kick up some dust while helping us win the race. Just stay out of their way.
2. The good results these men get are more than offset by the negative impact their feud has on company productivity and morale. A coalition of employees needs to confront the boss with the facts and recommend corrective action.
3. In this obvious clash of personalities, one of these bullies must be fired. Or should the company fire both?
4. The boss is clueless, so someone needs to elevate the issue to the board of directors.
5. A brave coworker who has the respect of these feuding men needs to take them aside for a little talk about workplace civility, to break the cycle of dysfunctional conflict. This would be a win–win option, where everyone could save face and upper management wouldn't be dragged into the fray.
6. Let's take sides in this feud and fight it out until there's a clear winner and loser.
7. Invent other options. Discuss.

Web Resources

For study material and exercises that apply to this chapter, visit our Web site,
www.mhhe.com/kreitner

Part 4

Organizational Processes

Chapter 14

Communicating in the Digital Age

LEARNING OBJECTIVES

When you finish studying the material in this chapter, you should be able to:

LO.1 Describe the perceptual process model of communication.

LO.2 Describe the barriers to effective communication.

LO.3 Contrast the communication styles of assertiveness, aggressiveness, and nonassertiveness.

LO.4 Discuss the primary sources of nonverbal communication.

LO.5 Review the five dominant listening styles and 10 keys to effective listening.

LO.6 Describe the communication differences between men and women, and explain the source of these differences.

LO.7 Discuss the formal and informal communication channels.

LO.8 Explain the contingency approach to media selection.

LO.9 Describe the Internet Generation, and discuss the pros and cons of teleworking.

LO.10 Specify practical tips for more effective e-mail and cell phone etiquette.

Student Resources for Studying Chapter 14

The Web site for your text includes resources that will help you master the concepts in this chapter. As you read, you'll want to visit the site for these helpful tools:

- Your online Study Guide includes learning objectives, a chapter summary, a glossary of key terms, and discussion questions.
- Take a practice quiz and test your knowledge!
- Scroll through a PowerPoint presentation with key concepts for this chapter.

Your instructor might also direct you to the Web site for these exercises:

- Self-assessments that correspond with the chapter content and a Group Exercise.
- You'll also find Video Cases and Internet Exercises for this chapter online.

www.mhhe.com/kreitner

BusinessWeek In the world of Facebook or Twitter, people love to hear feedback about what they're up to. But sit them down for a performance review, and suddenly the experience becomes traumatic.

Now companies are taking a page from social networking sites to make the performance evaluation process more fun and useful. Accenture has developed a Facebook-style program called Performance Multiplier in which, among other things, employees post status updates, photos, and two or three weekly goals that can be viewed by fellow staffers. Even more immediate: new software from a Toronto startup called Rypple that lets people post Twitter-length questions about their performance in exchange for anonymous feedback. Companies ranging from sandwich chain Great Harvest Bread Co. to Firefox developer Mozilla have signed on as clients.

Such initiatives upend the dreaded rite of annual reviews by making performance feedback a much more real-time and ongoing process. Stanford University management professor Robert Sutton argues that performance reviews "mostly suck" because they're conceived from the top rather than designed with employees' needs in mind. "If you have regular conversations with people, and they know where they stand, then the performance evaluation is maybe unnecessary," says Sutton.

What Rypple's and Accenture's tools do is create a process in which evaluations become dynamic—and more democratic. Rypple, for example, gives employees the chance to post brief, 140-character questions, such as "What did you think of my presentation?" or "How can I run meetings better?" The queries are e-mailed to managers, peers, or anyone else the user selects. Short anonymous responses are then aggregated and sent back, providing a quick-and-dirty 360-degree review. The basic service is free. But corporate clients can pay for a premium version that includes tech support, extra security, and analysis of which topics figure highest in employee posts. Rypple's co-founders have also launched software called TouchBase that's meant to replace the standard annual review with quick monthly surveys and discussions. . . .

If having your performance goals posted for the world to see sounds a bit Orwellian, consider this: Rypple reports that some two-thirds of the questions posted on its service come from managers wanting feedback about business questions or their own performance. The biggest payoff of these social network-style tools may prove to be better performance by the boss.[1]

FOR DISCUSSION

What do you like or dislike about using information technology for more intensive performance management?

Modern information technology is connecting us and transforming our lives in unprecedented ways. The chapter-opening vignette offers a glimpse of what is occurring in the workplace. There are positives, negatives, and unintended consequences of living in a "wired world." So it is important for all of us to understand the underlying communication process and the dynamics of communicating as technology continues to evolve.

The study of communication is fundamentally important because every managerial function and activity involves some form of direct or indirect communication. Whether planning and organizing or directing and leading, managers find themselves communicating with and through others. This implies that everyone's communication skills affect both personal and organizational effectiveness.[2] For example, one study found that 70% of "preventable hospital mishaps" resulted from a lack of communication between employees, particularly during handoffs of patient care.[3] A survey of 336 organizations revealed that 66% of the respondents did not know or understand their organization's mission and business strategy, which subsequently led them to feel disengaged at work. This sort of communication breakdown leads to lower productivity and product quality, and higher labor costs and turnover.[4]

This chapter will help you to better understand how managers can both improve their communication skills and design more effective communication programs. We discuss (1) basic dimensions of the communication process, focusing on a perceptual process model and barriers to effective communication; (2) interpersonal communication; (3) organizational communication; and (4) communicating in the information technology age.

to the point

Why is knowledge of the basic communication process essential for communicating more effectively?

Communication

Interpersonal exchange of information and understanding.

Basic Dimensions of the Communication Process

Communication is defined as "the exchange of information between a sender and a receiver, and the inference (perception) of meaning between the individuals involved."[5] Managers who understand this process can analyze their own communication patterns as well as design communication programs that fit organizational needs. This section reviews a perceptual process model of communication and discusses the barriers to effective communication.

LO.1 Perceptual Process Model of Communication

Historically, the communication process was described in terms of a conduit model. This model depicts communication as a pipeline in which information and meaning are transferred from person to person. Today, communication experts criticize the conduit model for being unrealistic. The conduit model assumes communication transfers *intended meanings* from person to person. If this assumption were true, miscommunication would not exist and there would be no need to worry about being misunderstood. We could simply say or write what we want and assume the listener or reader accurately understands our intended meaning.

As we all know, communicating is not that simple or clear-cut. Communication is fraught with misunderstanding. In recognition of this, researchers have begun to examine communication as a form of social information processing (recall the discussion in Chapter 7) in which receivers interpret messages by cognitively processing information. This view led to development of a **perceptual model of communication** that depicts communication as a process in which receivers create meaning in their own minds. Let us consider the parts of this process and then integrate them with an example.

Perceptual model of communication
Process in which receivers create their own meaning.

Sender, Message, and Receiver

The sender is the person wanting to communicate information—the message—and the receiver is the person, group, or organization for whom the message is intended.

Encoding

Encoding entails translating thoughts into a code or language that can be understood by others. This forms the foundation of the message. For example, if a professor wants to inform students about an assignment, she must first think about what information she wants to communicate. Once the professor resolves this issue in her mind and encodes it into spoken or written words, she needs to select a medium for sharing the message. Word choice is very important because the English language, for one example, has upwards of one million words.[6]

Selecting a Medium

Managers have a wide variety of media at their disposal. Typical media in organizations include face-to-face conversations, telephone calls, e-mail, voice mail, videoconferencing, written memos or letters, photographs or drawings, meetings, bulletin boards, computer output, and charts or graphs. Choosing the appropriate medium depends on many factors, including the nature of the message, its intended purpose, the audience, proximity to the audience, time constraints, and personal skills and preferences.

All media have advantages and disadvantages. Face-to-face conversations, for instance, are useful for communicating about important or emotionally charged issues and those requiring immediate feedback and intensive interaction. Telephones are convenient, fast, and sometimes private, but lack nonverbal information. Although writing memos or letters is time consuming, it is a good medium when it is difficult to meet with the other person, when formality and a written record are important, and when face-to-face interaction is not necessary to enhance understanding. We have more to say later about choosing media.

Decoding and Creating Meaning

Decoding occurs when receivers receive a message. It is the process of interpreting and making sense of a message. Returning to our example of a professor communicating about an assignment, decoding would occur among students when they receive the message from the professor.

In contrast to the conduit model's assumption that senders give messages their meaning, the perceptual model says that *receivers* give messages their meaning. Intended meaning can be an elusive thing. Consider this cross-cultural experience of a *Wall Street Journal* reporter on assignment in China.

> I was riding the elevator a few weeks ago with a Chinese colleague here in the *Journal's* Asian headquarters. I smiled and said, "Hi." She responded, "You've gained weight." I might have been appalled, but at least three other Chinese co-workers also have told me I'm fat. I probably should cut back on the pork dumplings. In China, such an intimate observation from a colleague isn't necessarily an insult. It's probably just friendliness.[7]

This example highlights how decoding and creating meaning are influenced by cultural norms and values.

Figure 14–1 *Communication Process in Action*

Let's meet at Starbucks to study.	**2. Message** is transmitted through a medium (e.g., text message).	Which Starbucks? We have two classes togther; which one are you thinking about?

Noise (any interference)

I. Sender encodes message, selects medium (e.g., cell phone).	**4. Receiver** sends feedback through a medium (e.g., text message via cell phone).	**3. Receiver** decodes message and decides that feedback is needed.

Noise

Interference with the transmission and understanding of a message.

Feedback   How often do you think you have lost your cell phone connection with the other person? Something like this usually occurs: "Hello, are you there?" "Can you hear me?" The other person may say back, "Yes, I can hear you, but you're fading in and out." This is an example of feedback; the sender gets a reaction from the receiver.

Trying to communicate via cell phone while sitting in a café is likely to be affected by noise. The person's cell phone conversation can also represent noise to someone at the next table.

Noise   Noise represents anything that interferes with the transmission and understanding of a message. It can affect any part of the communication process. This broad definition of noise includes many situations such as a speech impairment or accent, poor telephone connection, illegible handwriting, bad photocopy, inaccurate statistics, lies, background sounds, poor hearing and eyesight, and physical distance between sender and receiver.

Figure 14–1 provides an example of the perceptual communication process. Notice the cyclical nature of this exchange of meaning, as the sender becomes a receiver and so on.

LO.2 Barriers to Effective Communication

There are two key components of effective communication. First, senders need to accurately communicate their intended message. Understanding is unlikely, otherwise. Second, receivers need to correspondingly perceive and interpret the message accurately. Anything that gets in the way of the accurate transmission and reception of a message is a barrier to effective communication. It is important to be aware of and avoid these barriers when communicating.

Table 14–1   *Potential Breakdowns in the Communication Process Itself*

- **Sender barrier (e.g., forgetting to send a message, fearing to send a message, or procrastinating with a difficult message).**
- **Encoding barrier (e.g., poor language skills, poor word choice, or incomprehensible delivery).**
- **Medium barrier (e.g., faulty transmission, battery failure on wireless device, busy signal, shouting in a noisy place, or computer network failure).**
- **Decoding barrier (e.g., poor language skills; mixed signals from verbal and nonverbal messages; or failure to understand humor, slang, or technical jargon).**
- **Receiver barrier (e.g., no message received, unwillingness to receive message, or strong emotional reaction to message).**
- **Feedback barrier (e.g., blank stare, lack of verbal or written response, mixed signals from verbal and nonverbal messages).**

Some barriers actually are part of the communication process itself (see Table 14–1). Communication will fail if any step in the communication process is disrupted or blocked. More broadly, there are three types of barriers likely to impact communication effectiveness: (1) personal barriers, (2) physical barriers, and (3) semantic barriers.

Personal Barriers   Have you ever communicated with someone and felt totally confused? This may have prompted you to wonder: "Is it them or is it me?" **Personal barriers** represent any individual attributes that hinder communication. Let's examine nine common personal barriers that foster miscommunication.

Personal barriers

Any individual attribute that hinders communication.

1. *Variable skills in communicating effectively.* Some people are simply better communicators than others. They may know one or more foreign languages.[8] They have the speaking and listening skills, the ability to use gestures for dramatic effect, the vocabulary to alter the message to fit the audience, the writing skills to convey concepts in simple and concise terms, and the social skills to make others feel comfortable. Others suffer for lack of these skills. Fortunately, practice and communication skills training can help.[9]

2. *Variations in how information is processed and interpreted.* Did you grow up in a rural setting, in the suburbs, or in a city? Did you attend private or public school? What were your parents' attitudes about your doing chores and playing sports? Are you from a loving home or one marred with fighting, yelling, and lack of structure?

Answers to these questions are relevant because they make up the different frames of reference and experiences people use to interpret the world around them. As you may recall from Chapter 7, people selectively attend to various stimuli based on their unique frames of reference. This means that these differences affect our interpretations of what we see and hear.

3. *Variations in interpersonal trust.* Chapter 11 discussed the manner in which trust affects interpersonal relationships. Communication is more likely to be distorted when people do not trust each other.[10] Rather than focusing on the message, a lack of trust is likely to cause people to be defensive and question the accuracy of what is being communicated.

4. *Stereotypes and prejudices.* We noted in Chapter 7 that stereotypes are oversimplified beliefs about specific groups of people. They potentially distort communication because their use causes people to misperceive and filter information.[11] It is important for all of us to be aware of our stereotypes and to recognize that they may subconsciously affect the messages we send and how we interpret messages we receive.

5. *Big egos.* Our ego—whether due to pride, inflated self-esteem, superior ability, or arrogance—can be a major communication barrier. Egos can cause political battles, turf wars, and pursuit of power, credit, and resources. Egos influence how we treat others as well as our receptiveness to being influenced by others. Have you ever had someone put you down in public? Then you know how ego-related feelings can influence communication.

6. *Poor listening skills.* How many times have you been in class when one student asks the same question that was asked minutes earlier? How about going to a party and meeting a low self-monitoring person (as described in Chapter 5) who only talks about himself and never asks questions about you? This experience certainly doesn't make one feel important or memorable. It's hard to communicate effectively when one of the parties is not listening. Listening skills are discussed later in this chapter.

7. *Natural tendency to evaluate others' messages.* What do you say to someone after watching the latest movie in a theater? "What did you think of the movie?" He or she might reply, "It was great, best movie I've seen all year." You then may say, "I agree," or alternatively, "I disagree; that movie stunk." The point is that we all have a natural tendency, according to renowned psychologist Carl Rogers, to evaluate messages from our own point of view or frame of reference, particularly when we have strong feelings about the issue.[12]

8. *Inability to listen with understanding.* Listening with understanding occurs when a receiver can "see the expressed idea and attitude from the other person's point of view, to sense how it feels to him, to achieve his frame of reference in regard to the thing he is talking about."[13] Try to listen with understanding; it will make you less defensive and can improve your accuracy in perceiving messages.

9. *Nonverbal communication.* Communication accuracy is enhanced when one's facial expression and gestures are consistent with the intent of a message. Interestingly, people may not even be aware of their nonverbal messages. More is said about this important aspect of communication a bit later.

Physical Barriers: Sound, Time, Space, and More

Have you ever been talking to someone on a cell phone while standing in a busy area with traffic noise and people talking loudly next to you? Then you know what physical barriers are. Other such barriers include time-zone differences, telephone-line static, distance from others, and crashed computers. Office design is another physical barrier, which is why more organizations are hiring experts to design facilities that promote open interactions, yet provide space for private meetings.[14]

Semantic Barriers: When Words Matter

Semantics
The study of words.

When your boss tells you, "We need to complete this project right away," what does it mean? Does "we" mean just you? You and your coworkers? Or you, your coworkers, and the boss? Does "right away" mean today, tomorrow, or next week? These are examples of semantic barriers. **Semantics** is the study of words.

Semantic barriers are more likely in today's global and multicultural workforce. Their frequency also is fueled by the growing trend to outsource customer service operations to foreign countries, particularly to India. In response to complaints from American customers, Indian outsourcers such as Wipro have instituted training programs aimed at reducing cross-cultural semantic barriers:

> In an American-culture training class at Wipro, students identify Indian stereotypes (superstitious, religious, and helpful) and American stereotypes (sports-loving, punctual, not as knowledgeable about computers as they think). The point is to identify shallow images as barriers to good communication so they can be overcome.
>
> The class reviews cultural differences—big and small. As a "high-context" culture where what is communicated is more internalized (say, in a family), Indians can seem to be beating around the bush to Americans, who are part of a low-context culture in which communications need to be more explicit. "If you like to talk and you're dealing with a low-context person," explains the instructor, Roger George, "you might want to keep it simple and get to the point."[15]

Jargon
Language or terminology that is specific to a particular profession, group, or company.

Jargon and buzzwords constitute another category of semantic barrier. **Jargon** represents language or terminology that is specific to a particular profession, group, or company. The use of jargon has increased as our society has become more technologically oriented. (For example, "The CIO wants the RFP to go out ASAP" means "The Chief Information Officer wants the Request for Proposal to go out as soon as possible.") *Buzzwords* are overused words or faddish phrases that become a form of verbal or written shorthand. (For example, an economist who says, "At the end of the day, the bottom line is that there's a lack of visibility" simply means, "I don't know what's going to happen.") Words or phrases that are ordinary to you may be mysterious to outsiders or nonspecialists. If we want to be clearly understood, it is important to choose our words and craft our messages with the receiver's situation and frame of reference in mind.[16]

"I love the way you get them to hang on your every buzzword."
SOURCE: Paul Kales, *Harvard Business Review*, December 2008, p 18.

go to the Web for the Self-Exercise: What Is Your Business Etiquette?

to the point

What is involved in assertive communication, nonverbal communication, active listening, and genderflex communication?

Communication competence

Ability to communicate effectively in specific situations.

Interpersonal Communication

The quality of interpersonal communication within an organization is very important. Researchers found that people with good communication skills helped groups to make more innovative decisions and were promoted more frequently than individuals with less developed abilities.[17] **Communication competence** is defined as the ability to communicate effectively in specific situations. Business etiquette, for example, is one component of communication competence.

While there are a host of communication abilities and skills under the umbrella of communication competence, we focus on five that you can control: assertiveness, aggressiveness, nonassertiveness, nonverbal communication, and active listening. We conclude this section by discussing gender differences in communication.

L0.3 Assertiveness, Aggressiveness, and Nonassertiveness

Table 14–2 describes the styles of assertiveness, aggressiveness, and nonassertiveness and identifies nonverbal and verbal behavior patterns associated with each one. Here's a quick quiz to see if you understand the three contrasting communication styles. Which style did Carol Bartz, the very successful former CEO of Autodesk, display upon taking the top spot at struggling Yahoo in 2009?

> Just a few minutes after being introduced at a hastily arranged conference call, the self-described straight shooter told analysts she intends to ensure Yahoo gets "some friggin' breathing room" so the company can "kick some butt."[18]

Only time will tell if Bartz's in-your-face aggressive communication style will turn things around at Yahoo, or build resentment, mistrust, and resistance. In general, you can improve your communication competence by trying to be more assertive and less aggressive or nonassertive. Let's apply this recommendation in the context of saying no to someone.

We all get asked to do things we really don't want to do. For example, you may have been asked by a lazy friend to share a homework assignment or, alternatively, to purchase a product you don't need. The communication goal in these cases is to say no in an assertive manner. Below are several tips for saying no.

- Don't feel like you have to provide a yes or no answer on the spot. You can ask for more time to think over the request.

- Be honest, and start your response with the word *no*. It's easier to be steadfast in your commitment to saying no if you start out by saying the word up front.

- Use nonverbal assertive behaviors to reinforce your words. For example, you can shake your head from side to side while saying no and you can look into the requester's eyes as you say no; but don't glare.

- Use verbal assertive behaviors. Say no with a firm, direct tone. Use "I" statements when necessary. For example, "I feel it is unfair to give you my homework so you can sleep in and skip class."[19]

Table 14–2   *Communication Styles*

COMMUNICATION STYLE	DESCRIPTION	NONVERBAL BEHAVIOR PATTERN	VERBAL BEHAVIOR PATTERN
Assertive	Pushing hard without attacking; permits others to influence outcome; expressive and self-enhancing without intruding on others	Good eye contact Comfortable but firm posture Strong, steady, and audible voice Facial expressions matched to message Appropriately serious tone Selective interruptions to ensure understanding	Direct and unambiguous language No attributions or evaluations of other's behavior Use of "I" statements and cooperative "we" statements
Aggressive	Taking advantage of others; expressive and self-enhancing at other's expense	Glaring eye contact Moving or leaning too close Threatening gestures (pointed finger; clenched fist) Loud voice Frequent interruptions	Swear words and abusive language Attributions and evaluations of other's behavior Sexist or racist terms Explicit threats or put-downs
Nonassertive	Encouraging others to take advantage of us; inhibited; self-denying	Little eye contact Downward glances Slumped posture Constantly shifting weight Wringing hands Weak or whiny voice	Qualifiers ("maybe"; "kind of") Fillers ("uh," "you know," "well") Negaters ("It's not really that important"; "I'm not sure")

SOURCE: Adapted in part from J A Waters, "Managerial Assertiveness," *Business Horizons,* September–October 1982, pp 24–29.

It is okay to say no. Remember, the more you say yes to others, the less time you have to yourself. Saying yes when you want to say no can lead to guilt, anger, resentment, and potentially failure.

go to the Web for the Group Exercise: Practicing Different Styles of Communication

LO.4 Nonverbal Communication

Nonverbal communication is "[a]ny message, sent or received independent of the written or spoken word . . . [It] includes such factors as use of time and space, distance between persons when conversing, use of color, dress, walking behavior, standing, positioning, seating arrangement, office locations and furnishing."[20]

Nonverbal communication

Messages sent outside of the written or spoken word.

ethics

Reading the Nonverbal Signs of a Possible Layoff

Marcia Finberg's relationship with her boss had been cordial during the three years she worked as vice president of marketing and business development for a Phoenix hospital. Her boss, the CEO, always made small talk and followed up with her on projects. When this rapport suddenly stopped, Ms. Finberg knew something was up. Three months later her job was eliminated. . . .

Ms. Finberg's boss went from being friendly with her to avoiding her and being curt. She knew the hospital was losing patients to a new medical center in the area and that her employer's financial situation had become precarious.

From an ethical standpoint, what should the hospital's CEO have done differently?

SOURCE: Excerpted from D Mattioli, "Layoff Sign: Boss's Cold Shoulder," *The Wall Street Journal*, October 23, 2008, p D6.

Communication experts estimate that 65% of every conversation is partially interpreted through nonverbal communication.[21] It thus is important to ensure that your nonverbal signals are consistent with your intended verbal messages. Inconsistencies create noise and promote miscommunications.[22] Because of the prevalence of nonverbal communication and its significant impact on organizational behavior (including, but not limited to, perceptions of others, hiring decisions, work attitudes, and turnover), managers need to become consciously aware of the nonverbal signals they give and receive (see the Real World/Real People feature above).

Body Movements and Gestures   Body movements, such as leaning forward or backward, and gestures, such as pointing, provide additional nonverbal information that can either enhance or detract from the communication process. Open body positions such as leaning forward communicate *immediacy,* a term used to represent openness, warmth, closeness, and availability for communication. *Defensiveness* is communicated by gestures such as folding arms, crossing hands, and crossing one's legs. Judith Hall, a communication researcher, conducted a meta-analysis of gender differences in body movements and gestures. Results revealed that women nodded their heads and moved their hands more than men. Leaning forward, large body shifts, and foot and leg movements were exhibited more frequently by men than women.[23]

Although it is fun to interpret body movements and gestures when playing charades, it is important to remember that body language is easily misinterpreted and highly dependent on context. Hand gestures are especially problematic in cross-cultural situations. For example, President Barack Obama's enthusiastic use of the thumbs-up sign at the 2009 G-20 meeting in London could have been interpreted as "great" in the US and China; the "number 1" in France; the "number 5" in Japan; and "up yours" in Australia, Italy, and many other places.[24]

President Obama's well-intentioned thumbs-up sign at the 2009 G-20 economic summit in London is an insulting gesture in some countries and cultures. Nonverbal communication is problematic in cross-cultural situations.

Touch   Touching is another powerful nonverbal cue. People tend to touch those they like. A meta-analysis of gender differences in touching indicated that women do more touching during conversations than men.[25] Of particular note, however, is the fact that men and women interpret touching differently. Sexual harassment claims might be reduced by keeping this perceptual difference in mind.

Moreover, norms for touching vary significantly around the world. Consider the example of two males walking across campus holding hands. In the Middle East, this behavior would be quite normal for males who are friends or have great respect for each other. In contrast, this behavior is not commonplace in the United States.

Facial Expressions   Facial expressions convey a wealth of information. Smiling at a business meeting in Kansas City, for instance, typically represents warmth, happiness, or friendship, whereas frowning conveys dissatisfaction or anger. But are these interpretations universal across cultures? The short answer is no. A summary of relevant research revealed that the association between facial expressions and emotions varies across cultures.[26] Smiling, for example, conveys different emotions around the world. Once again, we need to be careful when using and reading facial expressions among diverse groups of employees and when working across cultures.

Eye Contact   Eye contact is a strong nonverbal cue that serves four functions in communication. First, eye contact regulates the flow of communication by signaling the beginning and end of conversation. There is a tendency to look away from others when beginning to speak and to look at them when done. Second, gazing (as opposed to glaring) facilitates and monitors feedback because it reflects interest and attention. Third, eye contact conveys emotion. People tend to avoid eye contact when discussing bad news or providing negative feedback. Fourth, gazing relates to the type of relationship between communicators.

As is true for body movements, gestures, and facial expressions, norms for eye contact vary across cultures. Westerners are taught at an early age to look at their parents when spoken to. In contrast, Asians are taught to avoid eye contact with a parent or superior in order to show obedience and subservience.[27] Once again, managers should be sensitive to different orientations toward maintaining eye contact with diverse employees.

Practical Tips   Good nonverbal communication skills are essential for building positive interpersonal relationships. Communication experts offer the following advice to improve nonverbal skills:[28]

Positive Nonverbal Actions That Help Communication

- Maintaining appropriate eye contact.
- Occasionally using affirmative nods to indicate agreement.
- Smiling and showing interest.
- Leaning slightly toward the speaker.
- Keeping your voice low and relaxed.
- Being aware of your facial expressions.

Actions to Avoid

- Licking your lips or playing with your hair or mustache.
- Turning away from the person you are communicating with.
- Closing your eyes and displaying uninterested facial expressions such as yawning.
- Excessively moving in your chair or tapping your feet.

- Using an unpleasant tone and speaking too quickly or too slowly.
- Biting your nails, picking your teeth, and constantly adjusting your glasses.

Of course, these tips are culturally specific to conducting business in North America and need to be adjusted elsewhere.

LO.5 Active Listening

Some communication experts contend that listening is the keystone communication skill for employees involved in sales, customer service, or management. In support of this conclusion, listening effectiveness was positively associated with customer satisfaction and negatively associated with employee intentions to quit. Poor communication between employees and management also was cited as a primary cause of employee discontent and turnover.[29] Listening skills are particularly important for all of us because we spend a great deal of time listening to others.

Listening

Actively decoding and interpreting verbal messages.

Listening involves much more than hearing a message. Hearing is merely the physical component of listening. **Listening** is the process of *actively* decoding and interpreting verbal messages. Listening requires cognitive attention and information processing; hearing does not. With these distinctions in mind, we examine listening styles and offer some practical advice for becoming a more effective listener.

Listening Styles   Communication experts believe that people listen with a preferred listening style. While people may lean toward one dominant listening style, we tend to use a combination of two or three. There are five dominant listening styles: appreciative, empathetic, comprehensive, discerning, and evaluative.[30] Let us consider each style.

An *appreciative* listener listens in a relaxed manner, preferring to listen for pleasure, entertainment, or inspiration. He or she tends to tune out speakers who provide no amusement or humor in their communications. *Empathetic* listeners interpret messages by focusing on the emotions and body language being displayed by the speaker as well as the presentation media. They also tend to listen without judging. A *comprehensive* listener makes sense of a message by first organizing specific thoughts and actions and then integrates this information by focusing on relationships among ideas. These listeners prefer logical presentations without interruptions. *Discerning* listeners attempt to understand the main message and determine important points. They like to take notes and prefer logical presentations. Finally, *evaluative* listeners listen analytically and continually formulate arguments and challenges to what is being said. They tend to accept or reject messages based on personal beliefs, ask a lot of questions, and can become interruptive.

You can improve your listening skills by first becoming aware of the effectiveness of the different listening styles you use in various situations. This awareness can then help you to modify your style to fit a specific situation. For example, if you are listening to a presidential debate, you may want to focus on using a comprehensive and discerning style. In contrast, an evaluative style may be more appropriate if you are listening to a sales presentation.

Becoming a More Effective Listener   Effective listening is a learned skill that requires effort and motivation. Patricia A Woertz, CEO of Archer Daniels Midland, the $44 billion-a-year agricultural commodities giant, recently offered this homespun advice: "My mom says we have two ears and one mouth for a reason. . . . We should be listening twice as much as we speak."[31] That's right; it

Table 14–3   *The Keys to Effective Listening*

KEYS TO EFFECTIVE LISTENING	THE BAD LISTENER	THE GOOD LISTENER
1. Capitalize on thought speed	Tends to daydream	Stays with the speaker, mentally summarizes the speaker, weighs evidence, and listens between the lines
2. Listen for ideas	Listens for facts	Listens for central or overall ideas
3. Find an area of interest	Tunes out dry speakers or subjects	Listens for any useful information
4. Judge content, not delivery	Tunes out dry or monotone speakers	Assesses content by listening to entire message before making judgments
5. Hold your fire	Gets too emotional or worked up by something said by the speaker and enters into an argument	Withholds judgment until comprehension is complete
6. Work at listening	Does not expend energy on listening	Gives the speaker full attention
7. Resist distractions	Is easily distracted	Fights distractions and concentrates on the speaker
8. Hear what is said	Shuts out or denies unfavorable information	Listens to both favorable and unfavorable information
9. Challenge yourself	Resists listening to presentations of difficult subject matter	Treats complex presentations as an exercise for the mind
10. Use handouts, overheads, or other visual aids	Does not take notes or pay attention to visual aids	Takes notes as required and uses visual aids to enhance understanding of the presentation

SOURCES: Derived from N Skinner, "Communication Skills," *Selling Power,* July–August 1999, pp 32–34; and G Manning, K Curtis, and S McMillen, *Building the Human Side of Work Community* (Cincinnati: Thomson Executive Press, 1996), pp 127–54.

takes energy and desire to really listen to others. Unfortunately, it may seem like there are no rewards for listening, but there are negative consequences when we don't. Think of a time, for example, when someone did not pay attention to you by looking at his or her watch or doing some other activity such as typing on a keyboard. How did you feel? You may have felt put down, unimportant, or offended. In turn, such feelings can erode the quality of interpersonal relationships as well as fuel job dissatisfaction, lower productivity, and result in poor customer service. Listening is an important skill that can be improved by avoiding the 10 habits of bad listeners while cultivating the 10 good listening habits (see Table 14–3).

In addition, a communication expert suggests that we can all improve our listening skills by adhering to the following three fundamental recommendations:[32]

- Attend closely to what's being said, not to what you want to say next.
- Allow others to finish speaking before taking our turn.
- Repeat back what you've heard to give the speaker the opportunity to clarify the message.

go to the Web for the Self-Exercise: Assessing Your Listening Skills

LO.6 Women and Men Communicate Differently

Women and men have communicated differently since the dawn of time. These differences can create communication problems that undermine productivity and interpersonal communication. Gender-based differences in communication are partly caused by linguistic styles commonly used by women and men. Deborah Tannen, a communication expert, defines **linguistic style** as follows:

Linguistic style

A person's typical speaking pattern.

> Linguistic style refers to a person's characteristic speaking pattern. It includes such features as directness or indirectness, pacing and pausing, word choice, and the use of such elements as jokes, figures of speech, stories, questions, and apologies. In other words, linguistic style is a set of culturally learned signals by which we not only communicate what we mean but also interpret others' meaning and evaluate one another as people.[33]

Linguistic style not only helps explain communication differences between women and men, but it also influences our perceptions of others' confidence, competence, and abilities. Increased awareness of linguistic styles can thus improve communication accuracy and your communication competence. This section strives to increase your understanding of interpersonal communication between women and men by discussing alternative explanations for differences in linguistic styles, various communication differences between women and men, and recommendations for improving communication across the gender divide.

Why Do Linguistic Styles Vary between Women and Men?

Although researchers do not completely agree on the cause of communication differences between women and men, there are two competing explanations that involve the well-worn debate between *nature* and *nurture*. Some researchers believe that interpersonal differences between women and men are due to inherited biological differences between the sexes. More specifically, this perspective, which also is called the *Darwinian perspective* or *evolutionary psychology,* attributes gender differences in communication to drives, needs, and conflicts associated with reproductive strategies used by women and men. For example, proponents would say that males communicate more aggressively, interrupt others more than women, and hide their emotions because they have an inherent desire to possess features

attractive to females in order to compete with other males for purposes of mate selection. Although males may not be competing for mate selection during a business meeting, evolutionary psychologists propose that men cannot turn off their biologically based determinants of behavior.[34]

In contrast, social role theory is based on the idea that females and males learn ways of speaking as children growing up. Research shows that girls learn conversational skills and habits that focus on rapport and relationships, whereas boys learn skills and habits that focus on status and hierarchies. Accordingly, women come to view communication

Men and women possess different communication styles. Do you think that these differences can impede brainstorming sessions like the one shown here? If yes, what can be done to overcome this type of communication roadblock?

as a network of connections in which conversations are negotiations for closeness. This orientation leads women to seek and give confirmation and support more so than men. Men, on the other hand, see conversations as negotiations in which people try to achieve and maintain the upper hand. It thus is important for males to protect themselves from others' attempts to put them down or push them around. This perspective increases a male's need to maintain independence and avoid failure.[35]

Gender Differences in Communication   Research demonstrates that women and men communicate differently in a number of ways.[36] Table 14–4 illustrates 10 different communication patterns that vary between women and men. There are two important issues to keep in mind about the tendencies identified in Table 14–4. First, they are not stereotypes for all women and men. Some men are less likely to boast about their achievements, and some women are less likely to share the credit. The point is that there are always exceptions to the rule. Second, your linguistic style influences perceptions about your confidence, competence, and authority. These judgments may, in turn, affect your future job assignments and subsequent promotability. Consider, for instance, linguistic styles displayed by Greg and Mindy. Greg downplays any uncertainties he has about issues and asks very few questions. He does this even when he is unsure about an issue being

Table 14–4   *Communication Differences between Women and Men*

1. Men are less likely to ask for information or directions in a public situation that would reveal their lack of knowledge.

2. In decision making, women are more likely to downplay their certainty; men are more likely to downplay their doubts.

3. Women tend to apologize even when they have done nothing wrong. Men tend to avoid apologies as signs of weakness or concession.

4. Women tend to accept blame as a way of smoothing awkward situations. Men tend to ignore blame and place it elsewhere.

5. Women tend to temper criticism with positive buffers. Men tend to give criticism directly.

6. Women tend to insert unnecessary and unwarranted thank-you's in conversations. Men may avoid thanks altogether as a sign of weakness.

7. Women tend to ask "What do you think?" to build consensus. Men often perceive that question to be a sign of incompetence and lack of confidence.

8. Women tend to give directions in indirect ways, a technique that may be perceived as confusing, less confident, or manipulative by men.

9. Men tend to usurp [take] ideas stated by women and claim them as their own. Women tend to allow this process to take place without protest.

10. Women use softer voice volume to encourage persuasion and approval. Men use louder voice volume to attract attention and maintain control.

SOURCE: From Dayle M Smith, *Women at Work: Leadership for the Next Century*, 1st. Copyright © 2000. Reproduced by permission of Pearson Education, Inc., Upper Saddle River, New Jersey.

discussed. In contrast, Mindy is more forthright at admitting when she does not understand something, and she tends to ask a lot of questions. Some people may perceive Greg as more competent than Mindy because he displays confidence and acts as if he understands the issues being discussed.

Improving Communication between Women and Men   Author

Genderflex

Temporarily using communication behaviors typical of the other gender.

Judith Tingley suggests that women and men should learn to genderflex. **Genderflex** entails the temporary use of communication behaviors typical of the other gender in order to increase the potential for influence.[37]

In contrast, Deborah Tannen recommends that everyone needs to become aware of how linguistic styles work and how they influence our perceptions and judgments. She believes that knowledge of linguistic styles helps to ensure that people with valuable insights or ideas get heard. Consider how gender-based linguistic differences affect who gets heard at a meeting:

> Those who are comfortable speaking up in groups, who need little or no silence before raising their hands, or who speak out easily without waiting to be recognized are far more likely to get heard at meetings. Those who refrain from talking until it's clear that the previous speaker is finished, who wait to be recognized, and who are inclined to link their comments to those of others will do fine at a meeting where everyone else is following the same rules but will have a hard time getting heard in a meeting with people whose styles are more like the first pattern. Given the socialization typical of boys and girls, men are more likely to have learned the first style and women the second, making meetings more congenial for men than for women.[38]

Knowledge of these linguistic differences can assist managers in devising methods to ensure that everyone's ideas are heard and given fair credit both in and out of meetings. Furthermore, it is useful to consider the organizational strengths and limitations of your linguistic style. You may want to consider modifying a linguistic characteristic that is a detriment to perceptions of your confidence, competence, and authority. In conclusion, cross-gender communication can be improved by remembering that women and men have different ways of saying the same thing.

to the point

How should the grapevine and media selection be managed?

Organizational Communication

Examining the broader issue of organizational communication is a good way to identify factors contributing to effective and ineffective management. We structure this discussion by focusing on the "who" and "how" of communication. For example, the first step in any type of communication is deciding who is going to be the recipient of the message. In work settings, you can communicate upward to your boss, downward to direct reports, horizontally with peers, and externally with customers and suppliers. We discuss the who of organizational communication by reviewing the various formal and informal channels used to communicate. We then delve into the how of communication by reviewing a contingency model for selecting the medium. You will learn that communication effectiveness is determined by an appropriate match between the content of a message and the media used to communicate—the how.

L0.7 Formal Communication Channels: Up, Down, Horizontal, and External

Formal communication channels follow the chain of command or organizational structure. Messages communicated on formal channels are viewed as official and are transmitted via one or more of three different routes: (1) vertical—either upward or downward, (2) horizontal, and (3) external.

Vertical Communication: Communicating Up and Down the Organization

Vertical communication involves the flow of information between people at different organizational levels. As discussed later in this section, communication distortion is more likely to occur when a message passes through multiple levels of an organization.

- *Upward communication* involves sending a message to someone at a higher level in the organization. Employees commonly communicate information upward about themselves, problems with coworkers, organizational practices and policies they do not understand or dislike, and results they have or have not achieved. Organizations and managers are increasingly encouraging upward communication in the spirit of fostering organizational justice, intrinsic motivation, and empowerment (more on empowerment in the next chapter). Upward communication also is a key component of organizational efforts to increase productivity and improve customer service because frontline employees generally know what it takes to get the job done. Managers can encourage upward communication via employee attitude and opinion surveys, suggestion systems, formal grievance procedures, open-door policies, informal meetings, e-mail, and town hall meetings.[39] Asking open-ended and nonjudgmental questions also is a good way to stimulate productive upward communication. A manager faced with a performance issue is better off asking, "How can we avoid this problem in the future?" rather than asking, "What did you do wrong this time?"[40]

- *Downward communication* occurs when someone at a higher level in the organization sends information or a message to someone at a lower level (or levels). Managers generally provide five types of information through downward communication: strategies/goals, job instructions, job rationale, organizational policies and practices, and feedback about performance. Recent surveys highlight the need for improvement in this area. In a survey of 1,198 workers, the top-ranked workplace frustration was "[p]oor communication by senior management about the business."[41] Seventy percent of 1,006 employees in a second survey answered no to the question: "Have your company's leaders communicated with employees about how the current economy might affect the company?"[42]

Because town hall meetings are increasingly used in organizations to facilitate vertical communication, tips for conducting them more effectively are offered below.

- The size of the meeting depends on the logistics of your workforce and the message being delivered. If you have good news to tell a number of employees, you can split them into more intimate groups if you like. But if the news is bad, it's better to have everyone hear it at the same time.

- Consider using speakers other than your senior executives.

Formal communication channels
Follow the chain of command or organizational structure.

- Broadcast town meetings so employees in other locations can participate. Taping allows absent employees to view the meeting later.
- When making a presentation, take the educational level of your audience into account.
- Don't make presentations too technical.
- Send invitations to all employees who are eligible to attend.
- Employees should be strongly encouraged to attend meetings, but attendance should not be mandatory. If your meeting is being held after business hours, consider paying employees for their time.[43]

Horizontal Communication: Communicating within and between Work Units

Horizontal communication flows among coworkers and between different work units, and its main purpose is coordination. During this sideways communication, employees share information and best practices, coordinate work activities and schedules, solve problems, offer advice and coaching, and resolve conflicts (see the Real World/Real People feature on page 419). Horizontal communication is facilitated by project meetings, committees, team building (recall our discussion in Chapter 11), social gatherings, and matrix structures (discussed in Chapter 17.)

Horizontal communication is impeded in three ways: (1) by specialization that causes people to work alone; (2) by encouraging competition that reduces information sharing; and (3) by an organizational culture that does not promote collaboration and cooperation.

External Communication: Communicating with Others outside the Organization

External communication is a two-way flow of information between employees and a variety of stakeholders outside the organization. External stakeholders include customers, suppliers, shareholders/owners, labor unions, government officials, community residents, and so on. Many organizations create formal departments, such as public or community relations, to coordinate their external communications. To protect competitive strategies, trade secrets, and the integrity of nondisclosure agreements, employees need to be fully informed about what they should *not* communicate to outsiders in everything from casual conversations to blogs.[44]

Informal Communication Channels

Informal communication channels
Do not follow the chain of command or organizational structure.

Informal communication channels do not follow the chain of command. They skip management levels and bypass lines of authority. Let us consider two commonly used informal channels: the grapevine and management by wandering around.

Grapevine
Unofficial communication system of the informal organization.

The Grapevine   The **grapevine** represents the unofficial communication system of the informal organization and encompasses all types of communication media. For example, an employee may share a bit of office gossip via e-mail, a face-to-face conversation, a text or Twitter message, or a phone call or voice mail. Although the grapevine often is a source of inaccurate rumors, it can function positively as an early warning signal for organizational changes, a medium for facilitating organizational changes, a medium for embedding organizational culture, a mechanism for fostering group cohesiveness, and a way of getting employee and customer feedback.

REAL WORLD | real people ethics

Surgical Team Communication Is a Life-or-Death Matter

Eight hospitals reduced the number of deaths from surgeries by more than 40% by using a checklist that helps doctors and nurses avoid errors, according to a [recent] report. . . .

If all hospitals used the same checklist, they could save tens of thousands of lives and $20 billion in medical costs each year, says author Atul Gawande, a surgeon and associate professor at the Harvard School of Public Health. . . .

The study shows that an operation's success depends far more on teamwork and clear communication than the brillance of individual doctors, says co-author Alex Haynes, also of Harvard. And that's good news, he says, because it means hospitals everywhere can improve.

Researchers modeled the checklist, which takes only two minutes to go through, after ones used by the aviation industry, which has dramatically reduced the number of crashes in recent years.

What is the ethical imperative for hospital administrators?

SOURCE: Excerpted from L Szabo, "Checklist Reduces Surgery Deaths," *USA Today*, January 15, 2009, p 8D.

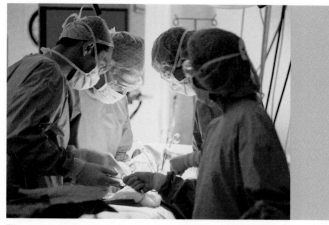

The success of a surgical procedure depends not only on medical skills, but also on the team's communication skills.

People who consistently pass along grapevine information to others are called **liaison individuals** or gossips:

> About 10% of the employees on an average grapevine will be highly active participants. They serve as liaisons with the rest of the staff members who receive information but spread it to only a few other people. Usually these liaisons are friendly, outgoing people who are in positions that allow them to cross departmental lines. For example, secretaries tend to be liaisons because they can communicate with the top executive, the janitor, and everyone in between without raising eyebrows.[45]

Effective managers monitor the pulse of work groups by regularly communicating with known liaisons.

In contrast to liaison individuals, **organizational moles** use the grapevine for a different purpose. They obtain information, often negative, in order to enhance their power and status. They do this by secretly reporting their perceptions and hearsay about the difficulties, conflicts, or failure of other employees to powerful members of management. This enables a mole to divert attention away from him- or herself and to position him- or herself as more competent than others. Management should attempt to create an open, trusting environment that discourages mole behavior because moles can destroy teamwork, create conflict, and impair productivity.

Although research activity on the grapevine has slowed in recent years, we have gained the following insights: (1) it is faster than formal channels; (2) it is about 75% accurate; (3) people rely on it when they are insecure, threatened, or faced with organizational changes; and (4) employees use the grapevine to acquire

Liaison individuals
Those who consistently pass along grapevine information to others.

Organizational moles
Those who use the grapevine to enhance their power and status.

the majority of their on-the-job information.[46] Managers tend to view the grapevine negatively. In fact, when 250 advertising executives were asked in a recent survey, "Do you think office gossip has a positive or negative effect on the workplace?" 63% said negative.[47]

The key managerial recommendation is to *monitor* and *influence* the grapevine rather than attempt to extinguish it. Effective managers accomplish this by vigorously promoting upward communication, as just discussed. Information technology enables the following proactive approach to monitoring the grapevine:

> What if managers and employees could listen in on any gripe fests and hallway brainstorms taking place at the office, all at one time? That's the concept, in digital form, behind Hewlett-Packard's WaterCooler, a new tool from its research labs that indexes what employees say on their internal and external blogs.
>
> Workers can opt in or out of the index, but many—about 11,000 at HP—choose to let their musings on everything from iPhone rumors to speculation about HP reorgs be aggregated on the site. Users can click on a "zeitgeist" link to see what's hot each week.[48]

Management by walking around

Managers walk around and informally talk to people from all areas and levels.

Management by Walking Around (MBWA)   Management by walking around (MBWA) involves managers literally walking around the organization and informally talking to people from all departments and levels.[49] It is an effective way to communicate because employees prefer to get information directly from their manager. Linda Dulye, a communications expert, concluded that employees "favor it more than e-mails, Web sites or intranet sites, or town hall meetings—even more than the grapevine. . . . The most effective channel for employees is the informal workplace 'walk-around'—having their manager come to their desk and sit and chat about work."[50] She offers the following tips for conducting MBWA:[51]

1. Dedicate a certain amount of time each week for MBWA.
2. Don't take your cell phone. It is important to stay focused on the person/people you are talking with and to avoid distractions.
3. Use active listening and don't take the approach that business is the only available topic for discussion. Employees may enjoy some amount of casual conversation.
4. The experience should be a two-way conversation. Show interest in your employees' issues and concerns.
5. Don't hesitate to take a notepad and record things requiring follow-up. Don't bring formal charts and graphs; the goal is to maintain an informal conversation.
6. Thank the individual or group for their time and feedback.

LO.8 Choosing Media: A Contingency Perspective

In this section we turn our attention to discussing the how of the communication process. Specifically, we examine how managers can determine the best method or medium to use when communicating via the various formal and informal channels of communication.

Today's managers can choose from a dizzying array of communication media (telephone, e-mail, voice mail, cell phone, standard and express mail, text messaging, video, blogs, and so forth). Tony Hsieh, CEO of online retailer Zappos, reportedly has 30,000 people both inside and outside the company receiving his

Twitter feeds.[52] Fortunately, research tells us that managers can help reduce information overload and improve communication effectiveness by more rigorously selecting communication media. If an inappropriate medium is used, managerial decisions may be based on inaccurate information, important messages may not reach the intended audience, and employees may become dissatisfied and unproductive. The recent recession severely tested management's ability to select appropriate communication media. Consider this positive example involving Johnson Financial Group, based in Racine, Wisconsin:

> Employees at the 63 locations of this financial services company were assured their jobs were safe and kept in the loop about the industry upheaval via town halls and voicemails from the CEO.[53]

Media selection is a key component of communication effectiveness. The following section explores a contingency model designed to help managers select communication media in a systematic and effective manner. Media selection in this model is based on the interaction between media richness and complexity of the problem/situation at hand.

Media Richness
Respected organizational theorists Richard Daft and Robert Lengel explain the communication concept of richness this way:

> Richness is defined as the potential information-carrying capacity of data. If the communication of an item of data, such as a wink, provides substantial new understanding, it would be considered rich. If the datum provides little understanding, it would be low in richness.[54]

Media richness involves the capacity of a given communication medium to convey information and promote understanding. Alternative media can vary from rich to lean.

Media richness
Capacity of a communication medium to convey information and promote understanding.

Media richness is based on four factors: (1) feedback (ranging from fast to very slow), (2) channel (ranging from the combined visual and audio characteristics of a video conference to the limited visual aspects of a computer report), (3) type of communication (ranging from personal to impersonal), and (4) language source (ranging from the natural body language and speech involved in a face-to-face conversation to the numbers contained in a financial statement).

A two-way face-to-face conversation is the richest form of communication. It provides immediate feedback and allows for the observation of multiple cues such as body language and tone of voice. Although relatively high in richness, telephone conversations and video conferencing are not as informative as face-to-face exchanges. At the other end of the scale, newsletters, computer reports, and general e-mail are lean media because feedback is very slow, the channels involve only limited visual information, and the information provided is generic or impersonal.

Complexity of the Managerial Problem/Situation
Managers face problems and situations that range from low to high in complexity. Low-complexity situations are routine, predictable, and managed by using objective or standard procedures. Calculating an employee's paycheck is an example of low complexity. Highly complex situations, such as a corporate reorganization, are ambiguous, unpredictable, hard to analyze, and often emotionally laden. Managers spend considerably more time analyzing these situations because they rely on more sources of information during their deliberations. There are no set solutions to complex problems or situations.

Figure 14–2   *A Contingency Model for Selecting Communication Media*

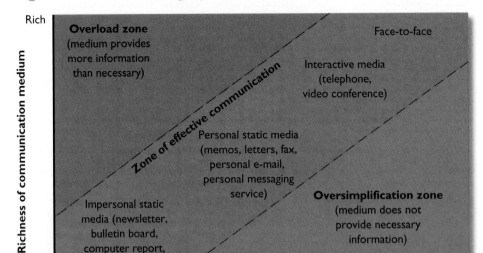

SOURCES: Adapted and updated from R Lengel and R L Daft, "The Selection of Communication Media as an Executive Skill," *Academy of Management Executive*, August 1988, p 226, and R L Daft and R H Lengel, "Information Richness: A New Approach to Managerial Behavior and Organization Design," in *Research in Organizational Behavior*, ed B M Staw and L L Cummings (Greenwich, CT: JAI Press, 1984), p 199.

Contingency Recommendations   The contingency model for selecting media is graphically shown in Figure 14–2. As indicated, there are three zones of communication effectiveness. Effective communication occurs when the richness of the medium is matched appropriately with the complexity of the problem or situation. Media low in richness—impersonal static and personal static—are better suited for simple problems; media high in richness—interactive media and face-to-face—are appropriate for complex problems or situations. Sun Microsystems, for example, followed this recommendation when communicating with employees about upcoming layoffs. The organization used a series of face-to-face sessions to deliver the bad news and provided managers with a set of slides and speaking points to help disseminate the necessary information.[55]

Conversely, ineffective communication occurs when the richness of the medium is either too high or too low for the complexity of the problem or situation. For example, a district sales manager would fall into the *overload zone* if he or she communicated monthly sales reports through richer media. Conducting face-to-face meetings or telephoning each salesperson would provide excessive information and take more time than necessary to communicate monthly sales data. The *oversimplification zone* represents another ineffective choice of communication media. In this situation, media with inadequate richness are used to communicate about complicated or emotional issues. For example, Radio Shack Corporation used e-mail to notify 400 employees at its Texas headquarters that they were being let go. Worse yet, a London-based body-piercing and jewelry store used a text message to fire an employee. This choice of medium is ineffective in this context because it does not preserve privacy and it does not allow employees to ask questions.

Further, dismissing employees in this manner can lower morale among remaining employees and damage a company's image.[56]

Research Evidence   The relationship between media richness and problem/ situation complexity has not been researched extensively. Available evidence indicates that managers used richer sources when confronted with ambiguous and complicated events, and miscommunication increased when rich media were used to transmit information that was traditionally communicated through lean media.[57] Moreover, a meta-analysis of more than 40 studies revealed that media usage was significantly different across organizational levels. Upper-level executives/managers spent more time in face-to-face meetings than did lower-level managers.[58] This finding is consistent with recommendations derived from the contingency model just discussed.

How Digital Communication Is Impacting Organizational Behavior

to the point

What distinguishes the Internet Generation and what are the keys to effective telecommuting, e-mail, and cell phone etiquette?

Imagine how a universal language would make worldwide communication much easier. While there may be no universally understood written and spoken languages, a universal *digital* language of 1s and 0s is reshaping the way we live, work, and play. Digitized words (wireless e-mail on a BlackBerry), pictures (video clips on YouTube), sounds (talking and listening to music on an iPhone), and motions (hitting and throwing on a Wii game) are conveniently packaged and readily shared communication content. In turn, the transmission of digitized content has been revolutionized by technologies such as the Internet, communication satellites, and Wi-Fi. Put it all together and we have virtually immediate access to unprecedented amounts of information and globe-spanning communication opportunities (for example, see the Real World/Real People feature on page 424).

The purpose of this concluding section is to explore how the digital communication revolution is affecting organizational behavior, both positively and negatively. Importantly, our focus here is not on the technological finepoints of digital communication innovations (e.g., cloud computing, mobile Internet, texting, blogging, and social networking on Facebook and Twitter),[59] but rather on how digital communication affects how we act and interact in work settings. For instance, researchers wanted to know if "peers rate each other differently depending on what medium they use. It turns out people are far more likely to trash their colleagues via e-mail than when filling out a paper form."[60] Also, we are interested in assessing the impact of communication technology on employee productivity. For example,

> [a] recent MIT study found that in one organization the employees with the most extensive personal digital networks were 7% more productive than their colleagues— so Wikis and Web 2.0 tools may indeed improve productivity. In the same organization, however, the employees with the most cohesive face-to-face networks were 30% more productive. Electronic tools may well be suited to information discovery, but face-to-face communication ... best supports information integration.[61]

More and faster digital communication does not necessarily mean *better* communication.

Global E-Mentoring at IBM

It may be time-tested, but there's something uninspiring about the corporate mentoring protocol, wherein a seasoned veteran gets assigned to impart wisdom to an ambitious young talent. IBM is putting a fresh spin on the practice by democratizing its mentoring program. As of January [2009], the company began empowering employees to reach across its global empire with the click of a button for advice on everything from preparing for a promotion to learning how to innovate.

The changes reflect the company's effort to become a truly global enterprise that relies on cross-border information-sharing and collaboration. "It became obvious that we had to make mentoring a tool for transferring knowledge globally," says Sheila Forte-Trammell, an IBM human resources consultant who helped launch the initiative.

Any IBM employee can now sign up to give or receive advice by filling out a profile in a Web-based employee directory called BluePages. Think of it as Match.com for mentoring. In less than two months, 3,000 people have joined.

How easy and useful would it be for you to find an e-mentor on your own at this time?

SOURCE: Reprinted from S Hamm, "Match.Com for Mentors," March 23, 30, 2009, issue of *BusinessWeek* by special permission. Copyright © 2009 by The McGraw-Hill Companies.

IBM employees can now connect via computer to "virtual mentors" anywhere in the world.

After highlighting two strategic concerns for management, we discuss eight norms of the Internet Generation, the dynamics of work-connecting technologies, and some unintended consequences of today's communication/information technologies.

Strategic Concerns: Security and Privacy

Because much of today's communication involves complex Internet-linked computer systems, careless and malicious actions can wreak havoc in terms of costly downtime and lost or stolen data. Any discussion of digital communication and information technology must necessarily address the twin concerns of security and privacy. Failure in those areas compromises the integrity and reliability of the entire electronic communication process. According to the FBI's Internet Crime Complaint Center, 275,284 complaints involving a record $265 million in losses were recorded in 2008.[62] Experts say the losses are much higher because companies report only a small fraction of Internet fraud for fear of bad publicity. The following specific cases are instructive and cautionary:

Alpharetta, Ga.-based data broker ChoicePoint Inc. . . . paid a record $10 million in civil penalties and $5 million in consumer redress in 2006 to settle Federal Trade Commission (FTC) charges that its security and record handling procedures violated consumers' privacy rights and various federal laws. And drug manufacturer Eli Lilly and Co.

Table 14–5   *Protecting against Security and Privacy Breaches on the Internet*

- **Pick strong passwords.** Use a mix of letters, symbols, and numbers, following the guidelines at www.microsoft.com/protect/yourself/password/create.mspx.
- **Use different passwords** for different Web services. And never use your Web passwords for PIN codes on credit, debit, or ATM cards.
- **Don't reveal sensitive information**—not even in "private" areas of services such as Facebook or Flickr that offer public access to most material.
- **Don't share files** on services that offer optional sharing, such as Google Docs, unless there is a real need.
- **Keep data** whose disclosure would create legal liability or embarrassment on your personal hard drives and storage devices.
- **Avoid file-sharing services** such as Lime Wire that distribute pirated files. Both the services and the downloads can open your computer to prying eyes.
- **Apply the latest security updates** to all your software, including operating systems, browsers, and antivirus programs.

SOURCE: Reprinted from S H Wildstrom, "Security Smarts," April 6, 2009, issue of *BusinessWeek* by special permission. Copyright © 2009 by The McGraw-Hill Companies, Inc.

agreed to follow a four-stage information security program for 20 years to settle an FTC complaint lodged after an employee mistakenly released nearly 700 e-mail addresses collected through the company's Prozac.com web site.[63]

For our present purposes, it is sufficient to review the Internet security and privacy protection tips in Table 14–5. *Prevention* is the key when it comes to protecting digital communication systems against hackers, identity theft, and fraud. How faithfully do you practice "safe computing"?[64]

LO.9 Here Comes the Huge Internet Generation

The largest generation in US history, more than 81 million people born between the beginning of 1977 and the end of 1997, is unique for another reason other than its size: they grew up with the Internet as a central feature of their lives. Author, consultant, and University of Toronto professor Don Tapscott, in his new book *Grown Up Digital: How the Net Generation Is Changing Your World*, calls them the Net Gen. Understanding their worldview, as shaped by the Internet and digital communication technologies, is a good preview of how workplaces are changing. Tapscott offers this overview:

> As talent, the Net Generation is already transforming the workforce. The biggest generation ever is flooding into a talent vortex being created by the expansion of the global economy, the mobility of labor, and the fastest and biggest generational retirement ever. They are bringing new approaches to collaboration, knowledge sharing, and innovation in businesses and governments around the world. There is strong evidence that the organizations that embrace these new ways of working experience better performance, growth, and success. To win the battle for talent, organizations need to rethink many aspects of how they recruit, compensate, develop, collaborate with, and supervise talent. I believe the very idea of management is changing.[65]

Table 14–6   *What Makes the Internet Generation Tick? Eight Norms*

1. **Freedom.** A desire to experience new and different things takes precedence over long-term commitments. Flexible work hours and locations, a say in how things are done, and freedom of choice are desirable.

2. **Customization.** Everything from personalized cell phone ring tones to lifestyle choices to unique Facebook layouts make life interesting and fun.

3. **Scrutiny.** With both trash and treasure on the Internet, Net Geners have learned to be skeptical, check things out, and ask probing questions. Candor and straight talk are favored. Authority figures and "facts" are not taken at face value.

4. **Integrity.** "Net Geners care about integrity—being honest, considerate, transparent, and abiding by their commitments. This is also a generation with profound tolerance." Trust in employers, people, and products is important. Some ethical elasticity (e.g., pirating music and plagiarizing) when in cyberspace is an open issue.

5. **Collaboration.** Relationships are of key importance. They know how to work and play with others and are eager to offer up opinions and suggestions. Volunteering is valued.

6. **Entertainment.** A job should not be a life sentence; it should be both challenging and fun. The Internet is a productivity tool, personal communication device, information source, and "fun tool of choice." Multitasking is a way of life to keep things moving and interesting.

7. **Speed.** "They're used to instant response, 24/7. Video games give them instant feedback; Google answers their inquiries within nanoseconds." Rapid-fire texting, instant messaging, and Tweeting are far faster and superior to e-mail and slow organizational decision making. Fast, accurate, and helpful feedback on job performance is demanded.

8. **Innovation.** An impatience for new and different user experiences is evident. "In the workplace, innovation means rejecting the traditional command-and-control hierarchy and devising work processes that encourage collaboration and creativity."

SOURCE: Quoted and adapted from discussion in D Tapscott, *Grown Up Digital: How the Net Generation Is Changing Your World* (New York: McGraw-Hill, 2009), pp 73–96.

Years of focus groups and interviews with nearly 10,000 people worldwide (with an emphasis on young people) led Tapscott and his research team to identify eight Net Gen norms (see Table 14–6). These norms reflect general patterns of experiences, attitudes, preferences, and expectations. Net Gen members expect the same instant access to comprehensive information and people, and the accompanying empowerment, in their work lives as they had growing up and going to school. Change-resistant managers who stubbornly stand in the way of Net Gen's digital lifelines will get run over.

How many of the eight Net Gen norms in Table 14–6 are evident in this recent situation?

Like just about every twentysomething, Jamie Varon, 23, had her heart set on working at Twitter. She had already applied for a position through the company's website. *And* asked a contact at Google to put in a good word for her. *And* showed up at the company's headquarters with a bag of cookies in an attempt to charm a recruiter into talking to her. But she still hadn't landed an interview. What Varon did next made her feel a little crazy. But then, it's a crazy time to be looking for a job. She created a website called twittershouldhireme.com, including her résumé, recommendations, and a blog tracking her quest. Within 24 hours the company contacted her. She had a lunch meeting set up at Twitter, and in the meantime got two job offers from tech companies that had noticed her site.[66]

The Two Faces of Telecommuting/Teleworking

Digital communication has significantly altered the traditional linkages between work, place, and time. This is especially true for knowledge workers who do not produce tangible products such as cars or provide tangible services such as haircuts. Thanks to advanced telecommunications technology and Internet tools such as Web conferencing, many variations of telecommuting are possible.[67] Rather than the person physically traveling to and from an office, **telecommuting** allows the work to travel electronically to and from the person's home. Wireless Internet access and cell phones have further evolved telecommuting into **teleworking** (connecting to the office from practically anywhere). All this has altered the traditional work and *place* connection, as employees can now perform their work in various locations rather than always physically gathering in one place. Because of computerized memory capabilities, the traditional work and *time* connection also has been altered. Employees in different locations and time zones can work simultaneously (called synchronous communication) and team members can work on the same project at different times (asynchronous communication).

Telecommuting/ Teleworking

Doing work generally performed in the office at home or in other convenient locations using advanced communication technologies.

Use and Benefits   Among US companies with at least 500 employees, 28% have some full-time telecommuters and 40% have some part-time telecommuters.[68] Behind the statistics are real people with altered lives:

> Eve Gelb's life was once a blur of hour-and-a-half commutes on the 405 Freeway in Los Angeles. What memories: The NPR fatigue. The stale minivan air….But that's all in the past. Gelb, a project manager at a giant HMO, SCAN Health Plan, has given up her Ethan Allen-style office, yanked down the family photos, and moved into her home office. Members of the professional class normally have to beg their managers—or at least delicately negotiate—to allow them to work remotely. But in Gelb's case, it was her boss's idea.
>
> SCAN is one of a growing number of companies encouraging workers to toil from home. Sure, employers have been doing this for years. But as the recession bites and companies look to save money on real estate costs, what was once a cushy perk is now deemed a business necessity. And that, along with a few choice enticements—voila!, a shiny new BlackBerry—is how companies are selling it to employees, whose emotions range from ecstasy to befuddlement.[69]

As your authors will readily attest, telecommuting from home sometimes means sharing your chair with a four-legged office mate. Or is it the other way around?

An expert recently listed the benefits of telecommuting: "(1) increases employee productivity, (2) increases the attractiveness of the employer, (3) decreases operating costs, (4) increases operationality during a crisis, and (5) contributes to green initiatives."[70] Additionally, telecommuting can bring homebound disabled people and prison inmates into the workforce.

Problems   The benefits of telecommuting/teleworking have been documented primarily through testimonial claims rather than through rigorous research. For example, IBM reported saving $100 million in capital facilities and equipment costs by letting 42% of its employees work from home. Teleworking reportedly resulted in productivity increases of 25 to 35% at FourGen Software and Continental Traffic Services, respectively.[71] Meanwhile, managerial doubts and negative research evidence have accumulated. According to *BusinessWeek,* "[w]ell into the work-from-anywhere era, managers are beginning to ask: Are the underlings working remotely . . . or remotely working?"[72] Working from home, the grocery store, or the beach takes self-discipline. There also are career implications. A survey of 1,300 executives from 71 countries found a general belief that people who telework are less likely to get promoted.[73] This is the "out of sight, out of mind" dilemma. Another problem is a sense of professional isolation among teleworkers. In a recent study, "a matched sample of 261 professional-level teleworkers and their managers revealed that professional isolation negatively impacts job performance."[74] Finally, as the following summary of another recent study points out, the "freedom" of teleworking can create major work-life imbalance:

> Utilizing both surveys and follow-up focus group interactions, this study found that while work-connecting technologies permitted a greater range of options regarding when and where work was done, this same connectivity provided constant availability to work and often drove expectations that more must be done, thereby increasing the likelihood of longer work hours and—surprisingly—leading to a diminished sense of flexibility.[75]

Building on what we emphasized in our Chapter 11 discussion of virtual teams, regular professional or recreational face-to-face interaction is vital to group development, cohesiveness, and team spirit. Your authors, who have worked on this book in their home offices for many years, also recommend that teleworkers practice using the "off" switches in their heads and on their *electronic leashes.*

LO.10 Dealing with Unintended Consequences of the Digital Age

An interesting thing happened on the way to our digital future. Convenient, speedy, and fun technologies spawned some unproductive, obnoxious, and even unsafe behaviors. For instance, language specialists lament how digital tools such as e-mail, text messaging, and Twitter have further eroded already poor writing skills. Teachers and managers are not pleased with research papers, formal documents, and official correspondence containing smiley faces and texting-style shorthand such as "OMG & U R GR8."[76] Another digital age bone of contention is what Microsoft vice president Linda Stone calls "continuous partial attention." Stone explains: "You're in a conference room, and all the people around the table are glancing—frequently and surreptitiously—at the cell phones or BlackBerrys they're holding just below the table. . . . This constant checking of handheld electronic devices has become epidemic."[77] Sound familiar? Let us explore the unintended behavioral consequences of e-mail and cell phones, two ubiquitous and vital forms of digital age communication, with the goal of more effective communication.

E-mail Overkill   People tend to have a love-hate relationship with e-mail. No wonder. "We're drowning in it. The average worker receives 200 a day, according to the research firm Basex."[78] Mobile Internet computers and handheld devices allow us to send and receive e-mail around the clock from practically anywhere—including, sometimes tragically, from behind the steering wheel. In addition to the hazards of distracted driving, unintended behavioral consequences of e-mail documented by researchers include (1) there has been a decrease in all other forms of communication among coworkers—including greetings and informal conversations; (2) emotions often are poorly communicated or miscommunicated via e-mail messages; and (3) the greater the use of e-mail, the less connected coworkers reportedly feel.[79] While endorsing formal policy statements for technology use in organizations, one expert recently observed:

> E-mail continues to be fraught with legal, ethical and productivity issues. One problem: Users think of e-mail the way they think of oral communication—as informal, not as a medium that sticks if the wrong words come out. But written e-mail, stored on hard drives, is not like oral communication: A wrong word or phrase offered inadvertently, mischievously or angrily can have legal repercussions.[80]

Along with a formally written and communicated organizational e-mail policy, embracing the tips in Table 14–7, managers can curb e-mail overkill in creative

Table 14–7   *Some Practical E-mail Tips*

- **Do not assume e-mail is confidential.** Employers are increasingly monitoring all e-mail. Assume your messages will be a matter of permanent record and can be read by anyone.
- **Be professional and courteous.** Recommendations include delete trailing messages, don't send chain letters and jokes, don't type in all caps—it's equivalent to shouting, don't respond immediately to a nasty e-mail, refrain from using colored text and background, don't expose your contact list to strangers, and be patient about receiving replies.
- **Avoid sloppiness.** Use a spell checker or reread the message before sending.
- **Don't use e-mail for volatile or complex issues.** Use a medium that is appropriate for the situation at hand.
- **Keep messages brief and clear.** Use accurate subject headings and let the reader know what you want right up front. Use bullets, as in this table, for conciseness.
- **Save people time.** Type "no reply necessary" in the subject line or at the top of your message if appropriate. Write a descriptive subject line to help the receiver prioritize messages.
- **Be careful with attachments.** Large attachments can crash other systems and use up valuable time downloading. Send only what is necessary, and get permission to send multiple attachments.

SOURCES: Adapted from C Graham, "In-Box Overload," *Arizona Republic*, March 16, 2007, p A14; M Totty, "Rethinking the Inbox," *The Wall Street Journal*, March 26, 2007, p R8; F C Leffler and L Palais, "Filter Out Perilous Company E-Mails," SHRM Legal Report, *HR Magazine*, August 2008, pp 1–3; and P Bathurst, "Watch What You Type," *Arizona Republic*, September 28, 2008, p EC1.

ways. For example, an engineering group at computer chip maker Intel instituted e-mail-free Fridays.

> E-mail isn't forbidden, but everyone is encouraged to phone or meet face-to-face. The goal is more direct, free flowing communication and better exchange of ideas, Intel principal engineer Nathan Zeldes said in a company blog post.[81]

Cell Phone Use and Abuse   Eighty-four percent of US households have a cell phone and the technology is deeply imbedded in the culture. In fact, in a nationwide Pew survey, the majority of respondents said they would give up their landline phones, television, the Internet, and e-mail before they would surrender their cell phones.[82] As with e-mail, the widespread use of cell phones, about half with built-in cameras, has generated plenty of unintended behavioral consequences. Cell phone problems range from merely annoying (loud ring tones and conversations in public places) to unethical and illegal (sending pornographic photos and photographing restricted areas or materials) to deadly.[83] Evidence of the latter was underscored on September 12, 2008, when a Los Angeles area commuter train crash killed 25 people and injured 130 others. The engineer, who also was killed, reportedly "sent and received 43 text messages and made four phone calls while on duty that day, including a text message he sent 22 seconds before the collision."[84] Not surprisingly, lawmakers across the United States are trying to outlaw hands-on cell phone use and text messaging while driving.[85] Recent brain scan research indicates the hazards of listening intently while driving, be it on a cell phone, to a passenger, or to talk radio:

> Researchers collected fMRI images of 29 undergraduates as they simulated steering a vehicle along a curving road, either undisturbed or while listening to spoken sentences that they judged as true or false. They found that the listening task reduced driving-related brain activity—the spatial processing that takes place in the parietal lobe—by almost 40 percent.[86]

Heeding this research and following the general cell phone etiquette tips in Table 14–8 can make for better and safer digital age communication.[87]

Table 14–8   *Five Commandments of Cell Phone Etiquette*

1. **Thou shalt not subject defenseless others to cell phone conversations.** Cell phone etiquette, like all forms of etiquette, centers on having respect for others.
2. **Thou shalt not set thy ringer to play *La Cucaracha* every time thy phone rings.** It's a phone, not a public address system.
3. **Thou shalt turn thy cell phone off during public performances.** Set your phone on vibrate when in meetings or in the company of others and, if necessary, take or return calls at a polite distance.
4. **Thou shalt not dial while driving.** If you must engage in cell phone conversations while driving, use a hands-off device.
5. **Thou shalt not speak louder on thy cell phone than thou would on any other phone.** It's called "cell yell" and it's very annoying to others.

SOURCES: Five basic commandments in bold excerpted from D Brody, "The Ten Commandments of Cell Phone Etiquette," *Infoworld,* February 5, 2005, www.infoworld.com. Five interpretations quoted from R Kreitner, *Management,* 11th ed (Boston: Houghton Mifflin Harcourt, 2009), p 318.

Summary of Key Concepts

1. *Describe the perceptual process model of communication.* Communication is a process of consecutively linked elements. Historically, this process was described in terms of a conduit model. Criticisms of this model led to development of a perceptual process model of communication that depicts receivers as information processors who create the meaning of messages in their own mind. Because receivers' interpretations of messages often differ from those intended by senders, miscommunication is a common occurrence.

2. *Describe the barriers to effective communication.* Every element of the perceptual model of communication is a potential process barrier. There are nine personal barriers that commonly influence communication: (1) variable skills in communicating effectively, (2) variations in how information is processed and interpreted, (3) variations in interpersonal trust, (4) stereotypes and prejudices, (5) big egos, (6) poor listening skills, (7) natural tendency to evaluate others' messages, (8) inability to listen with understanding, and (9) nonverbal communication. Physical barriers pertain to distance, physical objects, time, and work and office noise. Semantic barriers show up as encoding and decoding errors because these phases of communication involve transmitting and receiving words and symbols.

3. *Contrast the communication styles of assertiveness, aggressiveness, and nonassertiveness.* An assertive style is expressive and self-enhancing but does not violate others' basic human rights. In contrast, an aggressive style is expressive and self-enhancing but takes unfair advantage of others. A nonassertive style is characterized by timid and self-denying behavior. An assertive communication style is more effective than either an aggressive or nonassertive style.

4. *Discuss the primary sources of nonverbal communication.* There are several identifiable sources of nonverbal communication effectiveness. Body movements and gestures, touch, facial expressions, and eye contact are important nonverbal cues. The interpretation of these nonverbal cues significantly varies across cultures.

5. *Review the five dominant listening styles and 10 keys to effective listening.* The five dominant listening styles are appreciative, empathetic, comprehensive, discerning, and evaluative. Good listeners use the following 10 listening habits: (1) capitalize on thought speed by staying with the speaker and listening between the lines, (2) listen for ideas rather than facts, (3) identify areas of interest between the speaker and listener, (4) judge content and not delivery, (5) do not judge until the speaker has completed his or her message, (6) put energy and effort into listening, (7) resist distractions, (8) listen to both favorable and unfavorable information, (9) read or listen to complex material to exercise the mind, and (10) take notes when necessary and use visual aids to enhance understanding.

6. *Describe the communication differences between men and women, and explain the source of these differences.* Men and women vary in terms of how they ask for information, express certainty, apologize, accept blame, give criticism and praise, say thank you, build consensus, give directions, claim ownership of ideas, and use tone of voice. There are two competing explanations for these differences. The biological perspective attributes gender differences in communication to inherited drives, needs, and conflicts associated with reproductive strategies used by women and men. The second explanation, which is based on social role theory, contends that females and males learn different ways of speaking as children growing up.

7. *Discuss the formal and informal communication channels.* Formal communication channels follow the chain of command and include vertical, horizontal, and external routes. Vertical communication involves the flow of information up and down the organization. Horizontal communication flows within and between employees working in different work units. External communication flows between employees inside the organization and a variety of stakeholders outside the organization. Informal communication channels do not follow the chain of command. The grapevine and management by walking around represent the two most commonly used informal channels.

8. *Explain the contingency approach to media selection.* Selecting media is a key component of communication effectiveness. Media selection is based on the interaction between the information richness of a medium and the complexity of the problem/situation at hand. Information richness ranges from low to high and is a function of four factors: speed of feedback, characteristics of the channel, type of communication, and language source. Problems/situations range from simple to complex. Effective communication occurs when the richness of the medium matches the complexity of the problem/situation. From a contingency perspective, richer media need to be used as problems/situations become more complex.

9. *Describe the Internet Generation, and discuss the pros and cons of teleworking.* The 81 million people in the United States born between January 1977 and the end of 1997 were the first generation to grow up with the Internet. According to Don Tapscott, members of Net Gen are comfortable with advanced telecommunications and digital information technology and can be characterized by eight norms: freedom, customization, scrutiny, integrity, collaboration, entertainment, speed, and innovation. Teleworking involves doing work that

is generally performed at a central office from various locations using advanced information technologies. It is called telecommuting when done from one's home. Employees who telework enjoy a measure of freedom and flexibility while their employers save on facilities. Telecommuting cuts travel expenses and reduces traffic congestion and pollution. On the downside, teleworkers can experience professional isolation, loss of informal interaction with colleagues, and the pressure of never being away from their work.

10. *Specify practical tips for more effective e-mail and cell phone etiquette.* E-mail can be more effectively managed by doing the following: (1) do not assume e-mail is confidential, (2) be professional and courteous, (3) avoid sloppiness, (4) don't use e-mail for volatile or complex issues, (5) keep messages brief and clear, (6) save people time, and (7) be careful with attachments. Basic cell phone etiquette involves having respect for others by avoiding annoying ring tones, loud conversations in public places, and unsafe dialing while driving.

Key Terms

OB in Action Case Study

Go Ahead, Use Facebook[88]

BusinessWeek Wendy Wilkes was giving a presentation about Unilever's information technology to 30 new hires—most of them barely out of school—and they were not happy. They didn't like the company-issued mobile phones and laptops (or lack thereof). The employee Web site was so 1990s it didn't have interactive features, such as Facebook. And they couldn't download iTunes or instant-messaging software to communicate with people outside the company.

Wilkes can certainly identify with their gripes. The 27-year-old manager also joined the maker of such consumer staples as Lipton, Slim-Fast, and Vaseline right out of college. In school, she was accustomed to using her Hotmail account from any computer. But from her desktop at work she had access to corporate e-mail only. Not to mention that instant messaging—the foundation of her social life in college—was forbidden with anyone outside the company. "It was the amount of lockdown that surprised me the most," she says.

For anyone born after 1985, entering the workforce is a technological shock. Raised on MySpace.com and Wikipedia, these workers can't comprehend why they should have to wait 18 months for a company to build corporate software when they can download what they need instantly. "Technology is an important thing in my personal and work life, and I think the two of them should be connected," says Amy Johannigman, a 22-year-old college senior who worked at a company one summer where the use of social-networking sites was discouraged, camera phones verboten, and the interns were told to limit personal e-mails.

Revolt in the Ranks

Corporate policy isn't stopping Johannigman's contemporaries. Sure, there are official policies against using gear the tech department hasn't sanctioned, but the sheer number of workers who are flouting the rules makes enforcement nearly impossible. Consulting firm Forrester Research even coined a term for workers ignoring corporate policy and taking technology into their own hands: *Technology Populism.*

At Unilever, half of the desktop software and services used by employees comes from outside the company, and a lot of it shouldn't be there—Skype and iTunes, to name just a couple. "We can't stop them," says Chris Turner, Unilever's chief technology officer. "They're not accepting no as an answer."

Neither did Wilkes. She joined Unilever with a degree in information management and soon became a member of the marketing department's support team, where she experienced Unilever's rigid rules firsthand.

So Wilkes put together some ideas about how employees could be more productive using consumer technology and sent her thoughts to Turner.

About six months ago, Turner offered Wilkes a new job, basically, in her words, to "get involved in trying to make a difference." Now Wilkes is one of 13 so-called "consumerization architects" whose job is to spread the use of popular—and in many cases free—technology. For example, Wilkes is looking into letting employees install webcams so they can confer by videoconference and cut down on travel time.

Unilever is still testing how to give employees more digital freedom. It may move users outside the corporate firewall and allow them to connect via their own computers, provided they're using certain security technologies. Anecdotal evidence suggests that the savings could be millions of dollars. "We see this as a real opportunity to start altering the cost model to deliver IT," says Turner.

Turner's ideas are unpopular with some people in his own department. But, as he points out, the social and economic forces are overwhelming.

Questions for Discussion

1. Have you ever been frustrated with out-of-date information technology in the workplace? If so, explain how it hampered your communication.
2. From a strategic standpoint, what are the arguments against uncontrolled information technology in the workplace?
3. As a top-level manager, what information technology policies would you put in place? What would you do to enforce those policies?
4. What is your personal stance on "Technology Populism"? What are the implications of your position for organizations?
5. What evidence of Net Gen norms (see Table 14–6) can you find in this case? Are they potentially positive or disruptive to organizational success? Explain.
6. How can Unilever's Wendy Wilkes give employees more digital freedom without endangering the company? Explain in terms of specific tools such as Skype, Webcam videoconferencing, iPods, Facebook, and Twitter.

Ethical Dilemma

We Know Where You Are[89]

BusinessWeek In this dawn of geo-tracking, many people are more likely to start out swapping data with friends and families. Already 25 million people have installed Facebook on their handsets. And Google is pushing in the same direction. On Feb. 4 [2009] the search engine released Latitude, an app that lets people with high-end mobile phones share location data with friends. Users can check on their buddies stuck in traffic, sneaking out of work early, or catching a ball game. Latitude even provides directions on how to meet up with friends and contacts. . . .

The privacy implications are considerable. Is it OK for a boss to hand an employee a Latitude-loaded BlackBerry and then monitor her whereabouts? Companies that operate fleets of trucks have tracked employees for years. But similar technology in cell phones would potentially let all sorts of companies monitor and measure employee movements. Latitude does offer cloaking options. A user can hide from certain people or ask to be located by city, not by street.

What Are the Ethics of Having Employees Use Geo-tracking Technologies Such as Google's Latitude?

1. When employees are on company time they are fully accountable for their whereabouts. Geo-tracking is acceptable, with or without their knowledge.
2. Geo-tracking your employees is acceptable if they are fully informed about the technology.
3. If employees will be geo-tracked by their employer, then the employees need to fully participate in formulating standards and limits of use. What standards and limits do you recommend?
4. Hello, Big Brother. Geo-tracking employees is an unacceptable infringement of personal privacy rights.
5. Invent other options. Discuss.

Web Resources

For study material and exercises that apply to this chapter, visit our Web site, **www.mhhe.com/kreitner**

Chapter 15

Influence, Empowerment, and Politics

LEARNING OBJECTIVES

When you finish studying the material in this chapter, you should be able to:

LO.1 Explain the concept of mutuality of interest.

LO.2 Name at least three "soft" and two "hard" influence tactics, and summarize the practical lessons from influence research.

LO.3 Identify and briefly describe French and Raven's five bases of power, and discuss the responsible use of power.

LO.4 Define the term *empowerment,* and explain why it is a matter of degree.

LO.5 Explain why delegation is the highest form of empowerment, and discuss the connections among delegation, trust, and personal initiative.

LO.6 Define *organizational politics,* and explain what triggers it.

LO.7 Distinguish between favorable and unfavorable impression management tactics.

LO.8 Explain how to manage organizational politics.

Student Resources for Studying Chapter 15

The Web site for your text includes resources that will help you master the concepts in this chapter. As you read, you'll want to visit the site for these helpful tools:

- Your online Study Guide includes learning objectives, a chapter summary, a glossary of key terms, and discussion questions.
- Take a practice quiz and test your knowledge!
- Scroll through a PowerPoint presentation with key concepts for this chapter.

Your instructor might also direct you to the Web site for these exercises:

- Self-assessments that correspond with the chapter content and a Group Exercise.
- You'll also find Video Cases and Internet Exercises for this chapter online.

www.mhhe.com/kreitner

BusinessWeek The management revolt at Meetup Inc. broke into the open last February. Douglas Atkin, a senior manager, yanked CEO Scott Heiferman into a conference room and showed him a list scrawled on a whiteboard. In bright red letters were all the things Atkin felt were wrong at the New York startup, including "We Aren't a Creative Company" and "I Hate the Org Chart." Atkin pressed his boss to change course. "We need to blow this up and start all over again," he said.

Meetup is a company built on organization. Through its Web site, people can set up local groups for everything from sharing organic gardening tips online to marshaling volunteers for political campaigns. But as the company grew to 52 employees and 5 million members, Meetup's own organization buckled. It was failing at the very thing that was supposed to be its expertise.

What followed Atkin's confrontation was a management experiment that shook the company. Heiferman replaced the old org chart with a highly unusual management strategy in which workers set priorities and pick their own projects. Inspired by the people who use its service, Meetup loosened the reins and dispersed power. For some workers, it felt like chaos, and they fled. Others thrived.

The process is still under way, but the results so far are largely positive. Morale is up, and the company is cranking out products. . . . "We got more done in six weeks than in six months last year," says Heiferman, who expects the projects to boost revenues tenfold, to $100 million, by 2010.

Meetup's approach isn't for everyone. But for managers, especially those responsible for younger workers

with attitudes and expectations so different from those of earlier generations, the experiment holds lessons: Giving up control can lead to better results. Your workers may have better ideas than you. Gary Hamel, who wrote *The Future of Management,* predicts more companies will adopt flexible organizations to

Meetup Inc.'s CEO Scott Heiferman (holding the label) wants everyone to be his or her own boss.

accommodate Internet Age workers and profit from their skills. "With information so broadly shared now, the sources of influence and power are eroding," he says. Companies already using such approaches include Whole Foods Market, and W.L. Gore & Associates, the $2 billion maker of Gore-Tex....

Heiferman isn't throwing out systems entirely. A strategy group tracks how changes affect revenue and customer growth. And the CEO reserves the right to pull what he calls the "red cord" on projects headed in the wrong direction. He hasn't had to use it. At least not yet.[1]

FOR DISCUSSION

How willing and able are you to work in this type of unstructured situation?

LO.1 At the very heart of interpersonal dealings in today's work organizations is a constant struggle between individual and collective interests. For example, Sid wants a raise, but his company doesn't make enough money to both grant raises and buy needed capital equipment. The downside of such misalignment of interests was evident in the results of a recent survey of 150 senior executives who were asked, "What makes good employees quit?" "Unhappiness with management" was the number one response category (35%), followed by "Limited opportunities for advancement" (33%) and "Lack of recognition" (13%).[2] Preoccupation with self-interest is understandable. After all, each of us was born, not as a cooperating organizational member, but as an individual with instincts for self-preservation. It took socialization in family, school, religious, sports, recreation, and employment settings to introduce us to the notion of mutuality of interest. Basically, **mutuality of interest** involves win–win situations in which one's self-interest is served by cooperating actively and creatively with potential adversaries. A pair of organization development consultants offered this managerial perspective of mutuality of interest:

Mutuality of interest

Balancing individual and organizational interests through win–win cooperation.

> Nothing is more important than this sense of mutuality to the effectiveness and quality of an organization's products and services. Management must strive to stimulate a strong sense of shared ownership in every employee, because otherwise an organization cannot do its best in the long run. Employees who identify their own personal self-interest with the quality of their organization's output understand mutuality and strive to maintain it in their jobs and work relations.[3]

Figure 15–1 graphically portrays the constant tug-of-war between employees' self-interest and the organization's need for mutuality of interest. It also shows the linkage between this chapter—influence, empowerment, and politics—and other key topics in this book. Managers need a complete tool kit of techniques to guide diverse individuals, who are often powerfully motivated to put their own self-interests first, to pursue common objectives. At stake in this tug-of-war between

Figure 15–1   *The Constant Tug-of-War between Self-Interest and Mutuality of Interest Requires Managerial Action*

436

PepsiCo's CEO Indra Nooyi Is a Master of Influence

Nooyi came to the United States in 1978 at age 23 to earn her M.B.A. at Yale, where she worked as a dorm receptionist—opting for the graveyard shift because it paid an extra 50 cents per hour. Her parents had told her she was out of her mind and should have stayed in India and gotten married. "I always had this urge, this desire, this passion," she once explained, to "settle in the United States," where she is now the married mother of two daughters.

When Nooyi joined PepsiCo in 1994, it was as the company's chief strategist. From the start, she helped executives make some tough decisions. Seeing less future in fast food, she moved the company to shed KFC, Pizza Hut, and Taco Bell in 1997. Betting instead on beverages and packaged food, she helped engineer a $3 billion acquisition of Tropicana in 1998 and a $14 billion takeover in 2001 of Quaker Oats, maker of Gatorade. The moves proved prescient choices. Company earnings soared, and so, too, did her stature.

By 2006, Nooyi was one of just two finalists to succeed CEO Steven Reinemund as leader of one of the world's best-known brands. After getting the nod, Nooyi flew to visit the other contender. "Tell me whatever I need to do to keep you," she implored. They had worked together for years, both loved music, and Nooyi was persuasive, offering to boost her competitor's compensation to nearly match her own. He agreed to serve as her right-hand man, creating her version of a team of rivals.

What do people need to do (or be) to influence you?

SOURCE: From "New Ideas for This Pepsi Generation," by M Useem, *U.S. News & World Report,* December 1–8, 2008, p 49. Copyright © 2009 U.S. News & World Report, L.P. Reprinted with permission.

Behind the familiar Pepsi name and logo is CEO Indra Nooyi's skillful use of influence and empowerment to attract good people and enact bold new strategies.

---

individual and collective interests is no less than the ultimate survival of organizations such as Meetup, profiled in the opening vignette.

Organizational Influence Tactics

How do you get others to carry out your wishes? Do you simply tell them what to do? Or do you prefer a less direct approach, such as promising to return the favor? Whatever approach you use, the crux of the issue is *social influence.* A large measure of interpersonal interaction involves attempts to influence others, including parents, bosses, coworkers, spouses, children, teachers, friends, and customers. According to noted management author Gary Hamel: "Influence is like water, always flowing somewhere."[4] All of us need to sharpen our influence skills (see the Real World/Real People feature above). A good starting point is familiarity with the following research insights.

> **to the point**
> What practical lessons have researchers taught us about influencing others?

L0.2 Nine Generic Influence Tactics

A particularly fruitful stream of research, initiated by David Kipnis and his colleagues in 1980, reveals how people influence each other in organizations. The

Kipnis methodology involved asking employees how they managed to get either their bosses, coworkers, or subordinates to do what they wanted them to do.[5] Statistical refinements and replications by other researchers over a 13-year period eventually yielded nine influence tactics. The nine tactics, ranked in diminishing order of use in the workplace, are as follows:

1. *Rational persuasion.* Trying to convince someone with reason, logic, or facts.
2. *Inspirational appeals.* Trying to build enthusiasm by appealing to others' emotions, ideals, or values.
3. *Consultation.* Getting others to participate in planning, making decisions, and changes.
4. *Ingratiation.* Getting someone in a good mood prior to making a request; being friendly, helpful, and using praise or flattery.
5. *Personal appeals.* Referring to friendship and loyalty when making a request.
6. *Exchange.* Making express or implied promises and trading favors.
7. *Coalition tactics.* Getting others to support your effort to persuade someone.
8. *Pressure.* Demanding compliance or using intimidation or threats.
9. *Legitimating tactics.* Basing a request on one's authority or right, organizational rules or policies, or express or implied support from superiors.[6]

These approaches can be considered *generic* influence tactics because they characterize social influence in all directions and in a wide variety of settings. Researchers have found this ranking to be fairly consistent regardless of whether the direction of influence is downward, upward, or lateral.[7]

Some call the first five influence tactics—rational persuasion, inspirational appeals, consultation, ingratiation, and personal appeals—*soft* tactics because they are friendlier and not as coercive as the last four tactics. Exchange, coalition, pressure, and legitimating tactics accordingly are called *hard* tactics because they involve more overt pressure. Margaret G McGlynn, president of Merck Vaccines, is a good role model for having made a career out of skillfully using rational persuasion:

> An ability to argue her case in a "relentlessly logical and wonderfully intense way," as ex-boss David Anstice puts it, helped McGlynn rise rapidly. . . .
>
> McGlynn's powers of persuasion have also helped her achieve results on Capitol Hill. Last summer, after Merck won approval to market a vaccine for shingles—a painful disease that strikes the elderly—she started knocking on doors all over Capitol Hill. Turned out that the new Medicare Part D drug plan prevented doctors from getting fully paid to administer vaccines. "I explained to [policymakers] that shingles is a debilitating illness that causes a major impact on quality of life," she says. They seem to have listened: On Dec. 9, [2006], Congress passed a bill that fixes the Medicare payment shortfall, which the President signed.[8]

Three Possible Influence Outcomes

Put yourself in this familiar situation. It's Wednesday and a big project you've been working on for your project team is due Friday. You're behind on the preparation of your computer graphics for your final report and presentation. You catch a friend who is great at computer graphics as he heads out of the office at quitting time. You try this *exchange tactic* to get your friend to help you out: "I'm way behind. I need your help. If you could come back in for two to three hours tonight and help me with these graphics, I'll complete those spreadsheets you've been complaining about." According to researchers, your friend will engage in one of three possible influence outcomes:

1. *Commitment.* Your friend enthusiastically agrees and will demonstrate initiative and persistence while completing the assignment.
2. *Compliance.* Your friend grudgingly complies and will need prodding to satisfy minimum requirements.
3. *Resistance.* Your friend will say no, make excuses, stall, or put up an argument.[9]

The best outcome is commitment because the target person's intrinsic motivation will energize good performance. However, managers often have to settle for compliance in today's hectic workplace. Resistance means a failed influence attempt.

Practical Research Insights

Laboratory and field studies have taught us useful lessons about the relative effectiveness of influence tactics along with other instructive insights:

- Commitment is more likely when people rely on consultation, strong rational persuasion, and inspirational appeals and *do not* rely on pressure and coalition tactics.[10] Interestingly, in one study, managers were not very effective at *downward* influence. They relied most heavily on inspiration (an effective tactic), ingratiation (a moderately effective tactic), and pressure (an ineffective tactic).[11]

- A meta-analysis of 69 studies suggests ingratiation (making the boss feel good) can slightly improve your performance appraisal results and make your boss like you significantly more.[12] Another study, with diversity and ethical implications, found ingratiation to be an effective way for Caucasian men to get a seat on a corporate board of directors in the United States.[13]

- Commitment is more likely when the influence attempt involves something *important* and *enjoyable* and is based on a *friendly* relationship.[14]

- A field study of sales managers in the United States looked at how the quality of the working relationship between a manager and a team member affected willingness to help teammates. When the relationship was *not* good, inspirational appeals and exchange tactics actually *reduced* helping behavior, with lack of credibility being the likely culprit. On the other hand, exchange tactics increased helping behavior when the relationship was good. *Consultation* increased helping behavior, regardless of the quality of the relationship. This is a strong endorsement for participation, whereby managers and leaders solicit input from employees.[15]

- In a survey, 214 employed MBA students (55% female) tended to perceive their superiors' soft influence tactics as fair and hard influence tactics as unfair. *Unfair* influence tactics were associated with greater *resistance* among employees.[16]

- Another study probed male–female differences in influencing work group members. Many studies have found women to be perceived as less competent and less influential in work groups than men. The researchers had male and female work group leaders engage in either task behavior (demonstrating ability and task competence) or dominating behavior (relying on threats). For both women and men, task behavior was associated with perceived competence and effective influence. Dominating behavior was not effective. The following conclusion by the researchers has important practical implications for all current and future managers who desire to successfully influence others: "The display of task cues is an effective means to enhance one's status in groups and . . . the attempt to gain influence in task groups through dominance is an ineffective and poorly received strategy for both men and women."[17]

- Interpersonal influence is culture bound. The foregoing research evidence on influence tactics has a bias in favor of European-North Americans. Much remains to be learned about how to effectively influence others (without unintended insult) in today's diverse labor force and cross-cultural global economy.[18]

Finally, Barbara Moses, consultant and author from Toronto, Canada, offers this advice on influencing your boss:

> If your boss doesn't understand the need for change, this might be partly your fault. You can't make change; you have to sell it. And the key to selling anything is to understand where the other person is coming from—rather than to assume that your boss is a complete jerk. But most of us communicate from an egocentric place. We construct an idea or a project mainly in terms of what makes sense to us. Instead, ask yourself: "What's most important to my boss?" "What are his greatest concerns?" Go forward only after you've answered these questions.[19]

Social Power

to the point
Why do managers need to know about the two types and five bases of power?

The term *power* evokes mixed and often passionate reactions. Citing recent instances of government corruption and corporate misconduct, many observers view power as a sinister force. To these skeptics, Lord Acton's time-honored statement that "power corrupts and absolute power corrupts absolutely" is as true as ever.[20] However, OB specialists remind us that, like it or not, power is a fact of life in modern organizations. According to one management writer,

> [p]ower must be used because managers must influence those they depend on. Power also is crucial in the development of managers' self-confidence and willingness to support subordinates. From this perspective, power should be accepted as a natural part of any organization. Managers should recognize and develop their own power to coordinate and support the work of subordinates; it is powerlessness, not power, that undermines organizational effectiveness.[21]

Social power

Ability to get things done with human, informational, and material resources.

Thus, power is a necessary and generally positive force in organizations. As the term is used here, **social power** is defined as "the ability to marshal the human, informational, and material resources to get something done."[22]

Importantly, the exercise of social power in organizations is not necessarily a downward proposition. Employees can and do exercise power upward and laterally. An example of an upward power play occurred at Alberto-Culver Company, the personal care products firm. Leonard Lavin, founder of the company, was under pressure to revitalize the firm because key employees were departing for more innovative competitors such as Procter & Gamble. Lavin's daughter Carol Bernick, and her husband Howard, both longtime employees, took things into their own hands:

> Even the Bernicks were thinking of jumping ship. Instead, in September 1994, they marched into Lavin's office and presented him with an ultimatum: Either hand over the reins as CEO or run the company without them. It was a huge blow for Lavin, forcing him to face selling his company to outsiders or ceding control to the younger generation. Unwilling to sell, he reluctantly stepped down, though he remains chairman.

How does it feel to push aside your own father and wrest operating control of the company he created? "It isn't an easy thing to do with the founder of any company, whether he's your father or not," says Carol Bernick, 46, now vice chairman and president of Alberto-Culver North America.[23]

Howard Bernick became CEO, the firm's top-down management style was scrapped in favor of a more open culture, and Lavin reportedly was happy with how things have turned out.[24]

L0.3 Dimensions of Power

While power may be an elusive concept to the casual observer, social scientists view power as having reasonably clear dimensions. Two dimensions of power that deserve our attention are (1) socialized versus personalized power and (2) the five bases of power.

Two Types of Power   Behavioral scientists such as David McClelland contend that one of the basic human needs is the need for power (n Pwr), as discussed in Chapter 8. Because this need is learned and not innate, the need for power has been extensively studied. Historically, need for power was said to be high when subjects interpreted TAT pictures in terms of one person attempting to influence, convince, persuade, or control another. More recently, however, researchers have drawn a distinction between **socialized power** and **personalized power.**

> There are two subscales or "faces" in n Pwr. One face is termed "socialized" (s Pwr) and is scored in the Thematic Apperception Test (TAT) as "plans, self-doubts, mixed outcomes and concerns for others, . . ." while the second face is "personalized" power (p Pwr), in which expressions of power for the sake of personal aggrandizement become paramount.[25]

Managers and others who pursue personalized power for their own selfish ends give power a bad name. According to research, personalized power is exhibited when managers

1. Focus more on satisfying their own needs.
2. Focus less on the needs of their underlings.
3. Act like "the rules" others are expected to follow don't apply to them.[26]

For example, Nancy Traversy, cofounder and CEO of the successful children's book publisher Barefoot Books, recently related this story about how she came to be an entrepreneur:

> I was born in Canada to a family of artists. I studied business, which made me the black sheep. After college I worked for the banking division of Pricewaterhouse in London. One day I was wearing a suit. One of the partners said to me, "Women don't wear trousers" and sent me home to change. It was a formative experience.[27]

A series of interviews with 25 American women elected to public office found a strong preference for socialized power.[28] A good case in point is Sheryl Sandberg, Facebook's chief operating officer, who recently wrote:

> My first job was at the World Bank, where I worked on health projects in India—leprosy, AIDS and blindness. During my first trip to India, I was taken on a tour of a village

Socialized power
Directed at helping others.

Personalized power
Directed at helping oneself.

leprosy home, where I saw people in conditions that I would not have thought possible. I promised myself that going forward, I would work only on things that really mattered.

Facebook allows people to be their authentic selves online and therefore use the power of technology to discover each other and share who they really are. The connections they make have a real impact on their lives.[29]

Five Bases of Power

A popular classification scheme for social power traces back 50 years to the work of John French and Bertram Raven. They proposed that power arises from five different bases: reward power, coercive power, legitimate power, expert power, and referent power.[30] Each involves a different approach to influencing others:

Sheryl Sandberg, the chief operating officer at Facebook, dedicated herself to socialized power as a result of working in less-developed parts of the world. What is your experience with personalized versus socialized power?

Reward power
Obtaining compliance with promised or actual rewards.

Coercive power
Obtaining compliance through threatened or actual punishment.

Legitimate power
Obtaining compliance through formal authority.

Expert power
Obtaining compliance through one's knowledge or information.

Referent power
Obtaining compliance through charisma or personal attraction.

- *Reward power.* A manager has **reward power** to the extent that he or she obtains compliance by promising or granting rewards. On-the-job behavior shaping, for example, relies heavily on reward power.

- *Coercive power.* Threats of punishment and actual punishment give an individual **coercive power.** For instance, consider this heavy-handed tactic by Wolfgang Bernhard, a Volkswagen executive: "A ruthless cost-cutter, Bernard, 46, has a favorite technique: He routinely locks staffers in meeting rooms, then refuses to open the doors until they've stripped $1,500 in costs from a future model."[31] Bathroom break, anyone?

- *Legitimate power.* This base of power is anchored to one's formal position or authority. Thus, individuals who obtain compliance primarily because of their formal authority to make decisions have **legitimate power.** Legitimate power may express itself in either a positive or negative manner in managing people. Positive legitimate power focuses constructively on job performance. Negative legitimate power tends to be threatening and demeaning to those being influenced. Its main purpose is to build the power holder's ego. Importantly, there is growing concern today about the limits of managers' legitimate power relative to privacy rights and off-the-job behavior.[32] (For example, see the Real World/Real People feature on page 443.)

- *Expert power.* Valued knowledge or information gives an individual **expert power** over those who need such knowledge or information. The power of supervisors is enhanced because they know about work schedules and assignments before their employees do. Skillful use of expert power played a key role in the effectiveness of team leaders in a study of three physician medical diagnosis teams.[33] Knowledge *is* power in today's high-tech workplaces.

- *Referent power.* Also called charisma, **referent power** comes into play when one's personality becomes the reason for compliance. Role models have referent power over those who identify closely with them.[34]

Regarding charisma, Jack and Suzy Welch recently offered this instructive perspective in their *BusinessWeek* column:

[A]lmost everyone wonders at some point in his or her career how big a role charisma plays in success. So how big is it? In the short term, very. In the long term, very again—but not alone.

Get Healthy. That's an Order!

Getting health insurance from your employer [in the United States] is sometimes seen as an entitlement, but the benefit owes its existence to a quirk of history. During World War II, employers desperate to attract workers began offering health insurance. Providing coverage has been an increasing burden for companies ever since. As a result, businesses have been forcing employees to shoulder more and more of the cost.

Some theorized that higher co-payments and pricier premiums would get people to take better care of themselves. It's not happening. "We have this notion that you can gorge on hot dogs, be in a pie-eating contest, and drink every day, and society will take care of you," says Harvard Business School Professor Michael E Porter, who coauthored *Redefining Health Care.* "We can't afford to let individuals drive up costs because they're not willing to address their health problems."

Hence the wellness fixation at companies as varied as IBM, Microsoft, Harrah's Entertainment, and Scotts. Employees who voluntarily sign up for such programs often receive discounts on health-care premiums, free weight-loss and smoking-cessation programs, gratis gym memberships, counseling for emotional problems, and prizes like vacations or points that can be redeemed for gift cards.

Companies save money. Employees get healthier. What's not to like? But the wellness craze raises important issues. One is that people could start blaming unhealthy colleagues for helping push up premiums. Then there are the privacy and discrimination issues: How far should managers intrude into employees' lives?

What is your position on this issue?

SOURCE: Excerpted from M Conlin, "Get Healthy—or Else," *BusinessWeek,* February 26, 2007, p 60.

Now, we're obviously not talking here about "bad" charisma, exuded without brains, vision, and character. That trait is useless, and even dangerous. In business, wow personalities with less-than-wow minds are called empty suits for good reason. Too many of these individuals manage to ho-ho-ho their way to the top, even to the CEO's office, but most self-destruct after looking great for a couple of years while achieving little. On a larger scale, darkly charismatic leaders have the power to wreck lives and nations. . . .

But good charismatic leaders are everywhere, too, leading with magnetism plus integrity and intelligence. And for them, charisma just makes the job a whole lot easier. Why? Because leaders have always had to energize their people.[35]

go to the Web for the Self-Exercise: What Is Your Self-Perceived Power?

Research Insights about Social Power

In one study, a sample of 94 male and 84 female nonmanagerial and professional employees in Denver, Colorado, completed TAT tests. The researchers found that the male and female employees had similar needs for power (n Pwr) and personalized power (p Pwr). But the women had a significantly higher need for socialized power (s Pwr) than did their male counterparts.[36] This bodes well for today's work organizations where women are playing an ever greater administrative role. Unfortunately, as women gain power in the workplace, greater tension between men and women has been observed. *Training* magazine offered this perspective:

> [O]bservers view the tension between women and men in the workplace as a natural outcome of power inequities between the genders. Their argument is that men still have most of the power and are resisting any change as a way to protect their power base. [Consultant Susan L] Webb asserts that sexual harassment has far more to do with exercising power in an unhealthy way than with sexual attraction. Likewise, the glass ceiling, a metaphor for the barriers women face in climbing the corporate ladder to management and executive positions, is about power and access to power.[37]

Accordingly, "powerful women were described more positively by women than by men" in a study of 140 female and 125 male college students in Sydney, Australia.[38]

A reanalysis of 18 field studies that measured French and Raven's five bases of power uncovered "severe methodological shortcomings."[39] After correcting for these problems, the researchers identified the following relationships between power bases and work outcomes such as job performance, job satisfaction, and turnover:

- Expert and referent power had a generally positive impact.
- Reward and legitimate power had a slightly positive impact.
- Coercive power had a slightly negative impact.

The same researcher, in a follow-up study involving 251 employed business seniors, looked at the relationship between influence styles and bases of power. This was a bottom-up study. In other words, employee perceptions of managerial influence and power were examined. Rational persuasion was found to be a highly acceptable managerial influence tactic. Why? Because employees perceived it to be associated with the three bases of power they viewed positively: legitimate, expert, and referent.[40]

In summary, expert and referent power appear to get the best *combination* of results and favorable reactions from lower-level employees.

Using Power Responsibly and Ethically

As democracy continues to spread around the world, one reality is clear: Leaders who do not use their power responsibly risk losing it. This holds for corporations and nonprofit organizations as well as for government leaders and public figures. A step in the right direction for managers who want to avoid such a turnaround and wield power responsibly is understanding the difference between commitment and mere compliance.

Responsible managers strive for socialized power while avoiding personalized power. Former NATO commander General Wesley Clark put it this way:

> Sometimes threatening works, but it usually brings with it adverse consequences—like resentment and a desire to get even in some way. People don't like to be reminded

that they are inferior in power or status. And so, in business, it is important to motivate through the power of shared goals, shared objectives, and shared standards.[41]

In fact, in a survey, organizational commitment was higher among US federal government executives whose superiors exercised socialized power than among colleagues with "power-hungry" bosses. The researchers used the appropriate terms *uplifting power* versus *dominating power*.[42] How does this relate to the five bases of power? As with influence tactics, managerial power has three possible outcomes: commitment, compliance, or resistance. Reward, coercive, and negative legitimate power tend to produce *compliance* (and sometimes, resistance). On the other hand, positive legitimate power, expert power, and referent power tend to foster *commitment*. Once again, commitment is superior to compliance because it is driven by internal or intrinsic motivation. Employees who merely comply require frequent "jolts" of power from the boss to keep them headed in a productive direction. Committed employees tend to be self-starters who do not require close supervision—a key success factor in today's flatter, team-oriented organizations.

LO.4 Empowerment: From Power Sharing to Power Distribution

to the point
How does empowerment occur and why is effective delegation a difficult challenge?

A promising trend in today's organizations centers on giving employees a greater say in the workplace. This trend wears various labels, including "high-involvement management," "participative management," and "open-book management." Regardless of the label one prefers, it is all about employees taking greater control of their work lives. Those who dismiss the employee empowerment trend as a passing fad need to see it as part of a much, much larger picture. Klaus Schwab, a respected Swiss businessman and philanthropist, recently offered this sweeping perspective:

> [A] general issue will be the changing power equation, which means that everywhere in society and business, the power is moving from the center to the periphery. Vertical command-and-control structures are being eroded and replaced by communities and different platforms. We are moving into the Web 2.0 world, and this has tremendous implications on the national level and on business models.[43]

Empowerment

Sharing varying degrees of power with lower-level employees to tap their full potential.

Management consultant and writer W Alan Randolph offers this definition: "**empowerment** is recognizing and releasing into the organization the power that people already have in their wealth of useful knowledge, experience, and internal motivation."[44] A core component of this process is pushing decision-making authority down to progressively lower levels. Steve Kerr, who has served as the "chief learning officer" at General Electric and Goldman Sachs, adds this important qualification: "We say empowerment

Swiss power broker Klaus Schwab sees an erosion of tra~~d~~itional command-and-control structures in the Web 2.0

is moving decision making down to the lowest level *where a competent decision can be made.*[45] Of course, it is naive and counterproductive to hand power over to unwilling or unprepared employees. Let us explore the dynamics of employee empowerment, while keeping these recent cautionary words from Jack and Suzy Welch in mind: "empowerment, is one of those concepts (like "creative destruction" and "collaborative work teams") that, as books are written and consultants move in, gets surrounded by more hype than honesty."[46]

A Matter of Degree

The concept of empowerment requires some adjustments in traditional thinking (see the Real Word/Real People feature on page 447). First, power is not a zero-sum situation where one person's gain is another's loss. Social power is unlimited. This requires win–win thinking. Frances Hesselbein, the woman credited with modernizing the Girl Scouts of the USA, put it this way: "The more power you give away, the more you have."[47] Authoritarian managers who view employee empowerment as a threat to their personal power are missing the point because of their win–lose thinking.

The second adjustment to traditional thinking involves seeing empowerment as *a matter of degree* not as an either–or proposition.[48] Figure 15–2 illustrates how power can be shifted to the hands of nonmanagers step by step. The overriding goal is to increase productivity and competitiveness in leaner organizations. Each step in this evolution increases the power of organizational contributors who traditionally were told what, when, and how to do things. A good role model for the spirit of empowerment is Motorola executive Greg Brown:

> He boils his philosophy down to three words: listen, learn, lead. It means you need to understand your business down to the nuts and bolts, let your employees know you won't have all the answers, and focus on just a handful of truly crucial things, even though dozens seem as important.[49]

Participative Management

Participative management

Involving employees in various forms of decision making.

Confusion exists about the exact meaning of participative management (PM). Management experts have clarified this situation by defining **participative management** as the process whereby employees play a direct role in (1) setting goals, (2) making decisions, (3) solving problems, and (4) making changes in the organization. Participative management includes, but goes beyond, simply asking employees for their ideas or opinions.

Advocates of PM claim employee participation increases employee satisfaction, commitment, and performance. Consistent with both Maslow's need theory and the job characteristics model of job design (see Chapter 8), participative management is predicted to increase motivation because it helps employees fulfill three basic needs: (1) autonomy, (2) meaningfulness of work, and (3) interpersonal contact. Satisfaction of these needs enhances feelings of acceptance and commitment, security, challenge, and satisfaction. In turn, these positive feelings supposedly lead to increased innovation and performance.[50]

Participative management does not work in all situations. The design of work, the level of trust between management and employees, and the employees'

Power to the People at Cisco Systems

As the old methods fall short, executives need to bring a wider array of skills and backgrounds to the table. Companies are testing fresh methods to develop global leaders while tapping innovative collaboration tools and social networks to speed up productivity and decision-making. Perhaps no company has done more in this vein than Cisco. As part of his move to democratize management, [CEO John] Chambers set up a new hierarchy within the company. "Councils" are teams of executives who make decisions on $10 billion opportunities. "Boards" consist of executives who have authority to make calls on $1 billion bets, and "working groups" are organized to deal with a specific issue for a limited period of time. Chambers—who

typically isn't involved in the decisions—believes his approach is a path others will need to follow. "When you have command and control by the top 10 people, you can only do one or two things at a time," he says. "The future is about collaboration and teamwork and making decisions with a replicable process that offers scale, speed, and flexibility."

What are both the practical and ethical arguments for empowering employees?

SOURCE: Reprinted from J McGregor, "'There is No More Normal,'" March 23, 30, 2009, issue of *BusinessWeek* by special permission. Copyright © 2009 by The McGraw-Hill Companies, Inc.

---

competence and readiness to participate represent three factors that influence the effectiveness of PM. With respect to the design of work, individual participation is counterproductive when employees are highly interdependent on each other, as on an assembly line. The problem with individual participation in this case is that interdependent specialists generally do not have a broad understanding of the entire production process. Participative management also is less likely to succeed when employees do not trust management. Finally, PM is more effective when employees are competent, prepared, and interested in participating. Bonnie

Figure 15–2   *The Evolution of Power: From Domination to Delegation*

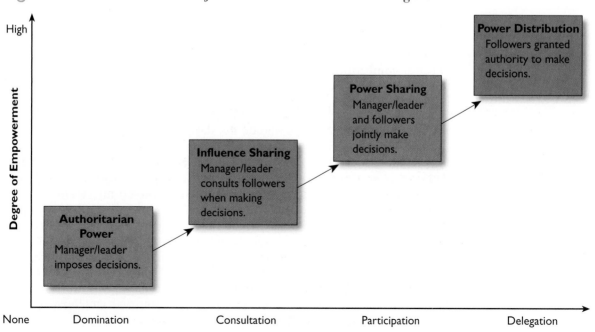

Hammer, president of NBC Universal Cable Entertainment, fosters participation by pushing her staff to the forefront:

> Although she has strong views about projects, she tries to ensure that the team doesn't succumb to groupthink. "I can't tell you how many meetings I open up with, 'My voice is last,'" she says. "I don't want anybody to hear my opinion before I hear everybody else's opinion. I give everyone the license to disagree."[51]

L0.5 Delegation

Delegation

Granting decision-making authority to people at lower levels

The highest degree of empowerment is **delegation,** the process of granting decision-making authority to lower-level employees.[52] This amounts to *power distribution.* Delegation has long been the recommended way to lighten the busy manager's load while at the same time developing employees' abilities.[53] Importantly, delegation gives nonmanagerial employees more than simply a voice in decisions. It empowers them to make their own decisions. A prime example is the Ritz-Carlton Hotel chain:

> At Ritz-Carlton, every worker is authorized to spend up to $2,000 to fix any problem a guest encounters. Employees do not abuse the privilege. "When you treat people responsibly, they act responsibly," said Patrick Mene, the hotel chain's director of quality.[54]

Not surprising, then, that Ritz-Carlton has won national service quality awards.

Barriers to Delegation   Delegation is easy to talk about, but many managers find it hard to actually do. A concerted effort to overcome the following common barriers to delegation needs to be made:

- Belief in the fallacy, "If you want it done right, do it yourself."
- Lack of confidence and trust in lower-level employees.
- Low self-confidence.
- Fear of being called lazy.
- Vague job definition.
- Fear of competition from those below.
- Reluctance to take the risks involved in depending on others.
- Lack of controls that provide early warning of problems with delegated duties.
- Poor example set by bosses who do not delegate.[55]

Delegation Research and Implications for Trust and Personal Initiative   Researchers at the State University of New York at Albany surveyed pairs of managers and employees and did follow-up interviews with the managers concerning their delegation habits. Their results confirmed some important commonsense notions about delegation. Greater delegation was associated with the following factors:

1. Employee was competent.
2. Employee shared manager's task objectives.
3. Manager had a long-standing and positive relationship with employee.
4. The lower-level person also was a supervisor.[56]

Figure 15–3   *Personal Initiative: The Other Side of Delegation*

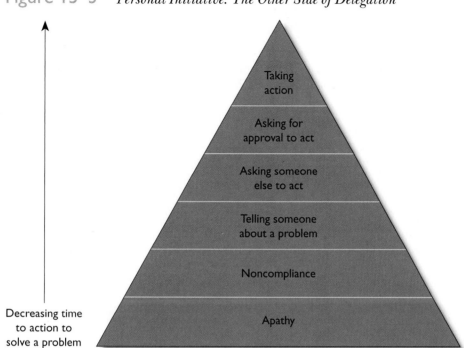

SOURCE: Figure from A L Frohman, "Igniting Organizational Change from Below: The Power of Personal Initiative," *Organizational Dynamics,* Winter 1997, p 46. © 1997, with permission from Elsevier.

This delegation scenario boils down to one pivotal factor, *trust.*[57]

Managers prefer to delegate important tasks and decisions to the people they trust. As discussed in Chapter 11, it takes time and favorable experience to build trust. Of course, trust is fragile; it can be destroyed by a single remark, act, or omission. Ironically, managers cannot learn to trust someone without, initially at least, running the risk of betrayal. This is where the empowerment evolution in Figure 15–2 represents a three-step ladder to trust: consultation, participation, and delegation. In other words, managers need to start small and work up the empowerment ladder. They need to delegate small tasks and decisions and scale up as competence, confidence, and trust grow. Employees need to work on their side of the trust equation as well. One of the best ways to earn a manager's trust is to show *initiative* (see Figure 15–3) and then get results. Researchers in the area offer this instructive definition and characterization:

Personal initiative is a behavior syndrome resulting in an individual's taking an active and self-starting approach to work and going beyond what is formally required in a given job. More specifically, personal initiative is characterized by the following aspects: it (1) is consistent with the organization's mission, (2) has a long-term focus, (3) is goal-directed and action-oriented, (4) is persistent in the face of barriers and setbacks, and (5) is self-starting and proactive.[58]

Personal initiative

Going beyond formal job requirements and being an active self-starter.

Recall our discussion of the *proactive personality* in Chapter 5.

Empowerment: The Research Record and Practical Advice

Like other widely heralded techniques—such as TQM, 360-degree reviews, teams, and learning organizations—empowerment has its fair share of critics and suffers from unrealistic expectations.[59] Research results to date are mixed, with a recent positive uptrend:

- A meta-analysis encompassing 27 studies and 6,732 individuals revealed that employee participation in the performance appraisal process was positively related to an employee's satisfaction with his or her performance review, perceived value of the appraisal, motivation to improve performance after the review, and perceived fairness of the appraisal process.[60]

- Another meta-analysis of 86 studies involving 18,872 people demonstrated that participation had a small statistically significant positive impact on job performance but only a moderate positive effect on job satisfaction.[61]

- Relative to work teams, a field study of 102 hotels in the United States revealed that teams with empowering leadership tended to have more knowledge sharing, a greater sense of team efficacy, and better performance.[62]

- A study of 164 New Zealand companies employing at least 100 people found a positive correlation between high-involvement management practices and employee retention and company productivity.[63]

- A field study with 149 call center employees documented how "high-involvement work processes" more effectively boosted job performance (e.g., customer satisfaction), job satisfaction, and organizational commitment than did self-managed teams.[64]

- A study of 3,000 Canadian companies looked at the relationship between employee empowerment and layoffs. Productivity tended to drop after a layoff in high-involvement workplaces, *except* when the commitment to empowerment was continued during and after the layoff.[65]

We believe empowerment has good promise if managers go about it properly. Empowerment is a sweeping concept with many different definitions. Consequently, researchers use inconsistent measurements, and cause-effect relationships are fuzzy. Managers committed to the idea of employee empowerment need to follow the path of continuous improvement, learning from their successes and failures. Eight years of research with 10 "empowered" companies led Randolph to formulate the three-pronged empowerment plan in Figure 15–4. Notice how open-book management and active information sharing are needed to build the necessary foundation of trust. Beyond that, clear goals and lots of relevant training are needed. Noting that the empowerment process can take several years to unfold, Randolph offered this perspective:

> While the keys to empowerment may be easy to understand, they are hard to implement. It takes tremendous courage to start sharing sensitive information. It takes true strength to build more structure just at the point when people want more freedom of action. It takes real growth to allow teams to take over the management decision-making process. And above all, it takes perseverance to complete the empowerment process.[66]

Figure 15–4   *Randolph's Empowerment Model*

The Empowerment Plan

Share Information
- Share company performance information.
- Help people understand the business.
- Build trust through sharing sensitive information.
- Create self-monitoring possibilities.

**Create Autonomy
through Structure**
- Create a clear vision and clarify the little pictures.
- Create new decision-making rules that support empowerment.
- Clarify goals and roles collaboratively.
- Establish new empowering performance management processes.
- Use heavy doses of training.

**Let Teams Become
the Hierarchy**
- Provide direction and training for new skills.
- Provide encouragement and support for change.
- Gradually have managers let go of control.
- Work through the leadership vacuum stage.
- Acknowledge the fear factor.

**Remember: Empowerment is not magic;
it consists of a few simple steps and a lot of persistence.**

SOURCE: W A Randolph, "Navigating the Journey to Empowerment," *Organizational Dynamics,* Vol. 24, No. 3, p 46, © 1997, with permission from Elsevier.

LO.6 Organizational Politics and Impression Management

> **to the point**
> How can organizational politics and impression management be kept on a positive track?

Most students of OB find the study of organizational politics intriguing. Perhaps this topic owes its appeal to the antics of Hollywood's corporate villains and TV shows like *The Office*.[67] As we will see, however, organizational politics includes, but is certainly not limited to, dirty dealing. Organizational politics is an ever-present and sometimes annoying feature of modern work life. "Executives say that they spend 19% of their time dealing with political infighting with their staffs, according to a survey by OfficeTeam, a staffing services firm."[68] One expert recently observed, "Many 'new economy' companies use the acronym 'WOMBAT'—or waste of money, brains, and time—to describe office politics."[69] On the other hand, organizational politics can be a positive force in modern work organizations. Skillful and well-timed politics can help you get your point across, neutralize resistance to a key project, land a choice job assignment, or simply get the job done.

A recent Accountemps survey asked 572 workers, "How do you deal with office politics?"

Characters Michael Scott (Steve Carell) and Dwight Schrute (Rainn Wilson) of *The Office* frequently engage in office politics that quickly get out of hand. But when real life imitates art, it's not always so funny.

A majority (54%) chose the response "Know what's going on but do not participate," while 16% said "Participate directly" and 29% said they would not participate.[70] It's knowing how "the game" is played that really counts.[71] Actively playing politics at work is a matter of personal preference and ethics. Bill Fox, a manager at a New Jersey firm, offers this practical analogy:

> Just like in judo, where you use your opponent's momentum against them, in bureaucracies if you learn the system you can use it against the bureaucrats. For example, very often bureaucratic requirements are more about form than substance. So as long as you fill out the proper paperwork, dot the i's, and cross the t's, you can get what you want approved; your request complied with the bureaucrats' system and that's their primary concern.[72]

To that end, 32% of 3,447 middle and senior managers responding to an Internet survey said they needed coaching in how to be more politically savvy at work.[73]

We explore this important and interesting area by (1) defining the term *organizational politics,* (2) identifying three levels of political action, (3) discussing eight specific political tactics, (4) considering a related area called *impression management,* and (5) examining relevant research and practical implications.

go to the Web for the Self-Exercise: How Political Are You?

Definition and Domain of Organizational Politics

Organizational politics

Intentional enhancement of self-interest.

"**Organizational politics** involves intentional acts of influence to enhance or protect the self-interest of individuals or groups."[74] An emphasis on *self-interest* distinguishes this form of social influence. Managers are constantly challenged to achieve a workable balance between employees' self-interests and organizational interests, as discussed at the beginning of this chapter. When a proper balance exists, the pursuit of self-interest may serve the organization's interests. Political behavior becomes a negative force when self-interests erode or defeat organizational interests. For example, researchers have documented the political tactic of filtering and distorting information flowing up to the boss. This self-serving practice put the reporting employees in the best possible light.[75]

Uncertainty Triggers Political Behavior   Political maneuvering is triggered primarily by *uncertainty.* Five common sources of uncertainty within organizations are

1. Unclear objectives.
2. Vague performance measures.
3. Ill-defined decision processes.
4. Strong individual or group competition.[76]
5. Any type of change.

Regarding this last source of uncertainty, organization development specialist Anthony Raia noted, "Whatever we attempt to change, the political subsystem becomes active. Vested interests are almost always at stake and the distribution of power is challenged."[77]

Thus, we would expect a field sales representative, striving to achieve an assigned quota, to be less political than a management trainee working on a variety of projects. While some management trainees stake their career success on hard work, competence, and a bit of luck, many do not. These people attempt to gain a competitive edge through some combination of the political tactics discussed below. Meanwhile, the salesperson's performance is measured in actual sales, not in terms of being friends with the boss or taking credit for others' work. Thus, the management trainee would tend to be more political than the field salesperson because of greater uncertainty about management's expectations.

Because employees generally experience greater uncertainty during the earlier stages of their careers, are junior employees more political than more senior ones? The answer is yes, according to a survey of 243 employed adults in upstate New York. In fact, one senior employee nearing retirement told the researcher: "I used to play political games when I was younger. Now I just do my job."[78]

Three Levels of Political Action

Although much political maneuvering occurs at the individual level, it also can involve group or collective action. Figure 15–5 illustrates three different levels of political action: the individual level, the coalition level, and the network level.[79] Each level has its distinguishing characteristics. At the individual level, personal self-interests are pursued by the individual. The political aspects of coalitions and networks are not so obvious, however.

People with a common interest can become a political coalition by fitting the following definition. In an organizational context, a **coalition** is an informal group bound together by the *active* pursuit of a *single* issue. Coalitions may or may not coincide with formal group membership. When the target issue is resolved (a sexual-harassing supervisor is fired, for example), the coalition disbands. Experts note that political coalitions have "fuzzy boundaries," meaning they are fluid in membership, flexible in structure, and temporary in duration.

Coalition
Temporary groupings of people who actively pursue a single issue.

Figure 15–5   *Levels of Political Action in Organizations*

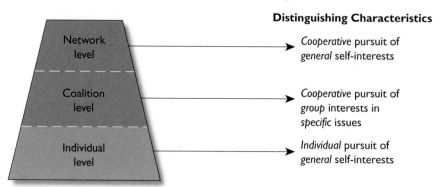

Distinguishing Characteristics

Network level → *Cooperative* pursuit of *general* self-interests

Coalition level → *Cooperative* pursuit of *group* interests in *specific* issues

Individual level → *Individual* pursuit of *general* self-interests

Coalitions are a potent political force in organizations. Consider the situation Charles J Bradshaw faced in a finance committee meeting at Transworld Corporation. Bradshaw, president of the company, opposed the chairman's plan to acquire a $93 million nursing home company:

> [The senior vice president for finance] kicked off the meeting with a battery of facts and figures in support of the deal. "Within two or three minutes, I knew I had lost," Bradshaw concedes. "No one was talking directly to me, but all statements addressed my opposition. I could tell there was a general agreement around the board table." . . .
> Then the vote was taken. Five hands went up. Only Bradshaw voted no.[80]

After the meeting, Bradshaw resigned his $530,000-a-year position, without as much as a handshake or good-bye from the chairman. In Bradshaw's case, the finance committee was a formal group that temporarily became a political coalition aimed at sealing his fate at Transworld. In recent years, coalitions on the corporate boards of Home Depot, Computer Associates, and Hewlett-Packard ousted the heads of those giant companies.

A third level of political action involves networks.[81] Unlike coalitions, which pivot on specific issues, networks are loose associations of individuals seeking social support for their general self-interests. Politically, networks are people oriented, while coalitions are issue oriented. Networks have broader and longer term agendas than do coalitions. For instance, Avon's Hispanic employees have built a network to enhance the members' career opportunities.[82]

Political Tactics

Anyone who has worked in an organization has firsthand knowledge of blatant politicking. Blaming someone else for your mistake is an obvious political ploy. But other political tactics are more subtle. Researchers have identified a range of political behavior.

One landmark study, involving in-depth interviews with 87 managers from 30 electronics companies in southern California, identified eight political tactics. Top-, middle-, and low-level managers were represented about equally in the sample. According to the researchers: "Respondents were asked to describe organizational political tactics and personal characteristics of effective political actors based upon their accumulated experience in *all* organizations in which they had worked."[83] Listed in descending order of occurrence, the eight political tactics that emerged were

1. Attacking or blaming others.
2. Using information as a political tool.
3. Creating a favorable image. (Also known as *impression management.*)
4. Developing a base of support.
5. Praising others (ingratiation).
6. Forming power coalitions with strong allies.
7. Associating with influential people.
8. Creating obligations (reciprocity).

Table 15–1 describes these political tactics and indicates how often each reportedly was used by the interviewed managers.

Table 15–1   *Eight Common Political Tactics in Organizations*

POLITICAL TACTIC	PERCENTAGE OF MANAGERS MENTIONING TACTIC	BRIEF DESCRIPTION OF TACTIC
1. Attacking or blaming others	54%	Used to avoid or minimize association with failure. Reactive when scapegoating is involved. Proactive when goal is to reduce competition for limited resources.
2. Using information as a political tool	54	Involves the purposeful withholding or distortion of information. Obscuring an unfavorable situation by overwhelming superiors with information.
3. Creating a favorable image (impression management)	53	Dressing/grooming for success. Adhering to organizational norms and drawing attention to one's successes and influence. Taking credit for others' accomplishments.
4. Developing a base of support	37	Getting prior support for a decision. Building others' commitment to a decision through participation.
5. Praising others (ingratiation)	25	Making influential people feel good ("apple polishing").
6. Forming power coalitions with strong allies	25	Teaming up with powerful people who can get results.
7. Associating with influential people	24	Building a support network both inside and outside the organization.
8. Creating obligations (reciprocity)	13	Creating social debts ("I did you a favor, so you owe me a favor").

SOURCE: Adapted from R W Allen, D L Madison, L W Porter, P A Renwick, and B T Mayes, "Organizational Politics: Tactics and Characteristics of Its Actors," *California Management Review*, Fall 1979, pp 77–83.

The researchers distinguished between reactive and proactive political tactics. Some of the tactics, such as scapegoating, were *reactive* because the intent was to *defend* one's self-interest. Other tactics, such as developing a base of support, were *proactive* because they sought to *promote* the individual's self-interest.

What is your attitude toward organizational politics? How often do you rely on the various tactics in Table 15–1? You can get a general indication of your political tendencies by comparing your behavior with the characteristics in Table 15–2. Would you characterize yourself as politically *naive,* politically *sensible,* or a political *shark?* How do you think others view your political actions? What are the career, friendship, and ethical implications of your political tendencies?[84]

LO.7 Impression Management

Impression management is defined as "the process by which people attempt to control or manipulate the reactions of others to images of themselves or their ideas."[85]

Impression management

Getting others to see us in a certain manner.

Table 15–2   *Are You Politically Naive, Politically Sensible, or a Political Shark?*

CHARACTERISTICS	NAIVE	SENSIBLE	SHARKS
Underlying attitude	Politics is unpleasant.	Politics is necessary.	Politics is an opportunity.
Intent	Avoid at all costs.	Further departmental goals.	Self-serving and predatory.
Techniques	Tell it like it is.	Network; expand connections; use system to give and receive favors.	Manipulate; use fraud and deceit when necessary.
Favorite tactics	None—the truth will win out.	Negotiate, bargain.	Bully; misuse information; cultivate and use "friends" and other contacts.

SOURCE: From J K Pinto and O P Kharbanda, "Lessons for an Accidental Profession," *Business Horizons,* Vol. 38, No. 2, p 45, © 1995, with permission from Elsevier.

This encompasses how one talks, behaves, and looks. Most impression management attempts are directed at making a *good* impression on relevant others. But, as we will see, some employees strive to make a *bad* impression. For purposes of conceptual clarity, we will focus on *upward* impression management (trying to impress one's immediate supervisor) because it is most relevant for managers. Still, it is good to remember that *anyone* can be the intended target of impression management. Parents, teachers, peers, voters, employees, and customers are all fair game when it comes to managing the impressions of others.

go to the Web for the Group Exercise: You Make Me Feel So Good!

A Conceptual Crossroads   Impression management is an interesting conceptual crossroads involving self-monitoring, attribution theory, and organizational politics.[86] Perhaps this explains why impression management has gotten active research attention in recent years. High self-monitoring employees ("chameleons" who adjust to their surroundings) are likely to be more inclined to engage in impression management than would low self-monitors.[87] Impression management also involves the systematic manipulation of attributions. For example, a bank president will look good if the board of directors is encouraged to attribute organizational successes to her efforts and attribute problems and failures to factors beyond her control. Impression management definitely fits into the realm of organizational politics because of an overriding focus on furthering one's *self-interests.*

Making a Good Impression   If you "dress for success," project an upbeat attitude at all times, and have polished a 15-second elevator speech for top executives, you are engaging in favorable impression management—particularly so if your motive is to improve your lot in life. Is it all worth the effort? In a survey of 2,198 employees, 56% said dressing for success paid off; 44% said no.[88] Too close to call. There are questionable ways to create a good impression, as well. For instance, Stewart Friedman, director of the University of Pennsylvania's Leadership Program, offered this gem:

> Last year, I was doing some work with a large bank. The people there told me a story that astounded me: After 7 PM, people would open the door to their office, drape a spare jacket on the back of their chair, lay a set of glasses down on some reading material on their desk—and then go home for the night. The point of this elaborate gesture was to create the illusion that they were just out grabbing dinner and would be returning to burn the midnight oil.[89]

Impression management can easily stray into unethical territory.

"HATED HIM. LOVED THE CHAIR."

SOURCE: *Harvard Business Review,* November 2008, p 14.

A statistical factor analysis of the influence attempts reported by a sample of 84 bank employees (including 74 women) identified three categories of favorable upward impression management tactics.[90] Favorable upward impression management tactics can be *job-focused* (manipulating information about one's job performance), *supervisor-focused* (praising and doing favors for one's supervisor), and *self-focused* (presenting oneself as a polite and nice person). A moderate amount of upward impression management is a necessity for the average employee today (see the Real World/Real People feature on page 458). Too little, and busy managers are liable to overlook some of your valuable contributions when they make job assignment, pay, and promotion decisions. Too much, and you run the risk of being branded a "schmoozer," a "phony," and other unflattering things by your coworkers. Excessive flattery and ingratiation can backfire by embarrassing the target person and damaging one's credibility. Also, the risk of unintended insult is very high when impression management tactics cross gender, racial, ethnic, and cultural lines. International management experts warn

> [t]he impression management tactic is only as effective as its correlation to accepted norms about behavioral presentation. In other words, slapping a Japanese subordinate on the back with a rousing "Good work, Hiro!" will not create the desired impression in Hiro's mind that the expatriate intended. In fact, the behavior will likely create the opposite impression.[91]

Making a Poor Impression   At first glance, the idea of consciously trying to make a bad impression in the workplace seems absurd. But an interesting new line of impression management research has uncovered both motives and tactics for making oneself look *bad*. In a survey of the work experiences of business students at a large northwestern US university, more than half "reported

"It's Hard to Look Smart with Bad Numbers"

Mark Hurd, CEO, Hewlett-Packard

SOURCE: As quoted in "The Best Advice I Ever Got," *Fortune*, May 12, 2008, p 72.

Nine years after starting at NCR, I moved to a head-office job in Dayton in 1988. An NCR executive was giving a presentation; he had great slides and an even better delivery. The CEO, Chuck Exley, listened to the entire presentation in his typically gracious, courteous manner. At the conclusion, he nodded and said something brief but profound: "Good story, but it's hard to look smart with bad numbers." And as I reflected on it, the presenter, articulate as he was, as good as his slides were, simply had bad numbers.

That comment has always stayed with me. You have to focus on the underlying substance. There's just no way to disguise poor performance. I've tried to follow that advice throughout my career. Deliver good numbers and you earn the right for people to listen to you

How does this approach relate to managing organizational politics and impression management?

When it comes to impression management, Hewlett-Packard's CEO Mark Hurd learned to deliver numbers that really matter.

---

witnessing a case of someone intentionally looking bad at work."[92] Why? Four motives came out of the study:

> (1) *Avoidance:* Employee seeks to avoid additional work, stress, burnout, or an unwanted transfer or promotion. (2) *Obtain concrete rewards:* Employee seeks to obtain a pay raise or a desired transfer, promotion, or demotion. (3) *Exit:* Employee seeks to get laid off, fired, or suspended, and perhaps also to collect unemployment or workers' compensation. (4) *Power:* Employee seeks to control, manipulate, or intimidate others, get revenge, or make someone else look bad.[93]

Within the context of these motives, *unfavorable* upward impression management makes sense.

Five unfavorable upward impression management tactics identified by the researchers are as follows:

- *Decreasing performance*—restricting productivity, making more mistakes than usual, lowering quality, neglecting tasks.
- *Not working to potential*—pretending ignorance, having unused capabilities.
- *Withdrawing*—being tardy, taking excessive breaks, faking illness.
- *Displaying a bad attitude*—complaining, getting upset and angry, acting strangely, not getting along with coworkers.
- *Broadcasting limitations*—letting coworkers know about one's physical problems and mistakes, both verbally and nonverbally.[94]

The Wall Street Journal's Jared Sandberg explains what he calls "strategic incompetence":

> Strategic incompetence isn't about having a strategy that fails, but a failure that succeeds. It almost always works to deflect work one doesn't want to do—without

ever having to admit it. For junior staffers, it's a way of attaining power through powerlessness. For managers, it can juice their status by pretending to be incapable of lowly tasks.[95]

Recommended ways to manage employees who try to make a bad impression can be found throughout this book. They include more challenging work, greater autonomy, better feedback, supportive leadership, clear and reasonable goals, and a less stressful work setting.

Research Evidence on Organizational Politics and Impression Management

Field research involving employees in real organizations rather than students in contrived laboratory settings has yielded these useful insights:

- In a study of 514 nonacademic university employees in the southwestern United States, white men had a greater understanding of organizational politics than did racial and ethnic minorities and white women. The researchers endorsed the practice of using mentors to help women and minorities develop their political skills.[96]

- Another study of 68 women and 84 men employed by five different service and industrial companies in the United States uncovered significant gender-based insights about organizational politics. In what might be termed the battle of the sexes,

  > it was found that political behavior was perceived more favorably when it was performed against a target of the opposite gender. . . . Thus subjects of both sexes tend to relate to gender as a meaningful affiliation group. This finding presents a different picture from the one suggesting that women tend to accept male superiority at work and generally agree with sex stereotypes which are commonly discriminatory in nature.[97]

- In a survey of 172 team members in a large company's research and development unit, perceived higher levels of team politics were associated with lower organizational commitment, lower job satisfaction, poorer job performance, and lower unit effectiveness.[98]

- When 250 British managers were recently polled about organizational politics, political maneuvering was found to be commonplace and back-stabbing behavior reportedly triggered reciprocal back-stabbing. The researchers further concluded:

  > Most managers viewed political behavior as ethical and necessary, and aspects of organizational effectiveness, change, resourcing and reputation were attributed to political tactics, although 80% had no training in this area. Tactics experienced frequently included networking, using "key players" to support initiatives, making friends with power brokers, bending the rules, and self-promotion. Tactics experienced as rare, but not unknown, included misinformation, spreading rumors, and keeping "dirt files" for blackmail.[99]

The results of a cross-cultural laboratory study are noteworthy. A unique study of 38 Japanese Americans and 39 European Americans at the University of Utah showed how impression management can cause problems across cultures. Consistent with Japanese tradition, the Japanese Americans tended to publicly report their job performance in a self-effacing (or modest) way, *despite confiding in private that they had performed as well as the European Americans.* This Japanese cultural tendency toward understatement created a false impression for third-party European American evaluators (who were kept unaware of any cultural distinctions). According to the researchers, "Japanese American participants were seen as less competent and less likeable than their European American counterparts because of their tendency to downplay their performance."[100] The old American expression "It pays to toot your own horn" appears to be as true as ever. Too much tooting, however, can brand one as arrogant, self-centered, and overbearing. This sort of delicate cultural balancing act makes cross-cultural dealings very challenging.

go to the Web for the Self-Exercise: How Much Do You Rely on Upward Impression Management Tactics?

LO.8 Managing Organizational Politics

Organizational politics cannot be eliminated. A manager would be naive to expect such an outcome. But political maneuvering can and should be managed to keep it constructive and within reasonable bounds. Harvard's Abraham Zaleznik put the issue this way: "People can focus their attention on only so many things. The more it lands on politics, the less energy—emotional and intellectual—is available to attend to the problems that fall under the heading of real work."[101] *Measurable objectives are management's first line of defense against counterproductive organizational politics.*

An individual's degree of politicalness is a matter of personal values, ethics, and temperament. People who are either strictly nonpolitical or highly political generally pay a price for their behavior. The former may experience slow promotions and feel left out, while the latter may run the risk of being called self-serving and lose their credibility. People at both ends of the political spectrum may be considered poor team players. A moderate amount of prudent political behavior generally is considered a survival tool in complex organizations. Meanwhile, managers are urged to follow the tips in Table 15–3 and everyone needs to follow

Table 15–3   *How to Keep Organizational Politics within Reasonable Bounds*

- Screen out overly political individuals at hiring time.
- Create an open-book management system.
- Make sure every employee knows how the business works and has a personal line of sight to key results with corresponding measurable objectives for individual accountability.
- Have nonfinancial people interpret periodic financial and accounting statements for all employees.
- Establish formal conflict resolution and grievance processes.
- As an ethics filter, do only what you would feel comfortable doing on national television.
- Publicly recognize and reward people who get real results without political games.

SOURCE: Adapted in part from discussion in L B MacGregor Serven, *The End of Office Politics as Usual* (New York: American Management Association, 2002), pp 184–99.

Irene Rosenfeld's lead. The Brooklyn-born CEO of Kraft says this is the best advice she ever got:

> Be yourself. All too often, particularly in a corporate environment, there's a tendency to want to create a persona that's perceived to be what people are looking for. The opportunity to bring your whole self to work every day is a powerful idea, an inspiring idea, and it's a part of making one feel comfortable at a company.[102]

Summary of Key Concepts

1. *Explain the concept of mutuality of interest.* Managers are constantly challenged to foster mutuality of interest (a win–win situation) between individual and organizational interests. Organization members need to actively cooperate with actual and potential adversaries for the common good.

2. *Name at least three "soft" and two "hard" influence tactics, and summarize the practical lessons from influence research.* Five soft influence tactics are rational persuasion, inspirational appeals, consultation, ingratiation, and personal appeals. They are more friendly and less coercive than the four hard influence tactics: exchange, coalition tactics, pressure, and legitimating tactics. According to research, soft tactics are better for generating commitment and are perceived as more fair than hard tactics. Ingratiation—making the boss feel good through compliments and being helpful—can slightly improve performance appraisal results and make the boss like you a lot more. Influence through domination is a poor strategy for both men and women. Influence is a complicated and situational process that needs to be undertaken with care, especially across cultures.

3. *Identify and briefly describe French and Raven's five bases of power, and discuss the responsible use of power.* French and Raven's five bases of power are reward power (rewarding compliance), coercive power (punishing noncompliance), legitimate power (relying on formal authority), expert power (providing needed information), and referent power (relying on personal attraction). Responsible and ethical managers strive to use socialized power (primary concern is for others) rather than personalized power (primary concern for self). Research found higher organizational commitment among employees with bosses who used uplifting power than among those with power-hungry bosses who relied on dominating power.

4. *Define the term* empowerment, *and explain why it is a matter of degree.* Empowerment involves sharing varying degrees of power and decision-making authority with lower-level employees to tap their full potential. Empowerment is not an either–or, all-or-nothing proposition. It can range from merely consulting with employees, to having them actively participate in making decisions, to granting them decision-making authority through delegation.

5. *Explain why delegation is the highest form of empowerment, and discuss the connections among delegation, trust, and personal initiative.* Delegation gives employees more than a participatory role in decision making. It allows them to make their own work-related decisions. Managers tend to delegate to employees they trust. Employees can get managers to trust them by demonstrating personal initiative (going beyond formal job requirements and being self-starters).

6. *Define organizational politics, and explain what triggers it.* Organizational politics is defined as intentional acts of influence to enhance or protect the self-interests of individuals or groups. Uncertainty triggers most politicking in organizations. Political action occurs at individual, coalition, and network levels. Coalitions are informal, temporary, and single-issue alliances.

7. *Distinguish between favorable and unfavorable impression management tactics.* Favorable upward impression management can be job-focused (manipulating information about one's job performance), supervisor-focused (praising or doing favors for the boss), or self-focused (being polite and nice). Unfavorable upward impression management tactics include decreasing performance, not working to potential, withdrawing, displaying a bad attitude, and broadcasting one's limitations.

8. *Explain how to manage organizational politics.* Since organizational politics cannot be eliminated, managers need to keep it within reasonable bounds. Measurable objectives for personal accountability are key. Participative management also helps, especially in the form of open-book management. Formal conflict resolution and grievance programs are helpful. Overly political people should not be hired, and employees who get results without playing political games should be publicly recognized and rewarded. The "how-would-it-look-on-TV" ethics test can limit political maneuvering.

OB in Action Case Study

Beyond Flextime: Trashing the Workweek[103]

For Linda Skoglund, getting a pedicure on a busy Tuesday afternoon was a career turning point. It ran against her Midwestern work ethic. And certainly, there was plenty of work piled up at J.A. Counter & Associates, the $2.5 million insurance and investment advisory firm she owns in New Richmond, Wisconsin. On the other hand, canceling her visit to the salon that day could have sent a bad message. It risked signaling to her 15 employees that they weren't allowed to do whatever they wanted at any given time during work hours. And that would tank her plans to overhaul the work environment at J.A. Counter.

In recent years, profits had been sluggish, and the company was lagging 15 percent behind industry benchmarks for revenue per employee. Skoglund had started doing more comprehensive performance reviews, increased the company's sales goals, cut expenses, and fired a couple of employees. Those adjustments boosted the bottom line slightly, but at a cost. "There were so many changes, it affected morale," Skoglund says. "A lot of people feared for their jobs." Not only that, she was constantly being forced to put out minor fires, which prevented her from focusing on sales. "I was tired of problems always ending up with management," she says. "I wanted to move away from KinderCare."

Finally, last spring, Skoglund decided to implement a new way of managing—a system known as a results-only work environment, or ROWE. Now, J.A. Counter's employees can leave the office whenever they please. They don't have to tell anyone where they are going or why. If an employee chooses to share the fact that he or she is taking the afternoon off to go to a baseball game, no one's allowed to make muttering comments about his or her work ethic. It's no surprise that this system has boosted morale; perhaps more significant, Skoglund says it has improved productivity as well.

Of course, companies have been touting flexible work arrangements for years. At most businesses, however, freedom has a limit: It's allowed only a couple of days a week or only for certain employees. But Cali Ressler and Jody Thompson, the two women who developed ROWE, say the system doesn't work unless it works for everyone—even the assistants, secretaries, and receptionists who have traditionally been at the mercy of a boss. Ressler and Thompson came up with the idea for ROWE while they were working in the HR department at electronics giant Best Buy, which wound up offering it to 3,000 employees at its corporate headquarters. . . .[In 2008], Ressler and Thompson left Best Buy and ventured out on their own as consultants and authors of the recently published book *Why Work Sucks and How to Fix It.* So far, they have worked with a few small companies, including J.A. Counter, and the results have been surprising. Changing the entire philosophy of work at corporate behemoth Best Buy was hard enough; at smaller companies, the two have found, it can be even harder.

That's because at small companies, employees are more likely to wear many hats—at J.A. Counter, for example, one person is in charge of HR, accounting, and IT. Employees who play so many roles are more hesitant about leaving the office, and their bosses are more reluctant to let them go. Plus, smaller companies often don't have well-defined job descriptions, so it's difficult to judge whether employees are doing their jobs if they are not spending every day in the office. And when an employee in Best Buy's IT department takes the afternoon off, another one can cover for him or her. Not so at a company filled with one-person departments.

Many of Skoglund's employees were skeptical when she announced the move to ROWE. "I'll believe it when I see it," said financial adviser Matt Radintz. Then the kicker: "What about Judy?"

Judy Wentlandt is J.A. Counter's receptionist. The team could readily imagine the salespeople—many of whom already had flexible schedules—moving to ROWE. But a receptionist? Skoglund was adamant—yes, the receptionist. She wasn't sure just how it would work; she told her staff members to figure it out. Two weeks later, they came back with a simple plan. When Wentlandt gave advance notice that she would be at home or off-site, volunteers would be asked to fill the receptionist's role.

New technology allows all employees to view their desktop from any station in the office. The company is considering installing a new phone system that will allow Wentlandt to answer phones from off-site locations, giving her even more flexibility. "I don't have the spontaneity that everyone else has," Wentlandt says. "But if I need coverage, I get it." She has left work to take her grandson to a museum and to attend her father's birthday party. Before, she would have had to take vacation time or skip those events. . . .

But the shift to ROWE has forced J.A. Counter's managers to focus more on outcomes than on hours. Before moving to the new system, each manager met with his or her direct reports and wrote out detailed job descriptions, with expectations and measurements. Now, Mehls says, J.A. Counter's employees are like "mini-entrepreneurs," managing their own schedules and focusing on delivering results instead of just pulling in a paycheck.

Questions for Discussion

1. What influence tactics and power bases are evident in this case? Explain.
2. Where would you plot J.A. Counter's ROWE program on the empowerment grid in Figure 15–2? Explain.
3. Has employee empowerment been taken too far in this case? Explain.
4. What impact do you expect the ROWE program to have on organizational politics at J.A. Counter? Explain.
5. What are your own feelings about the ROWE concept? Would you like to work in such an unstructured situation? Explain why or why not.

Ethical Dilemma

You Say You Never Lie? That's Probably a Lie!

It can be hard to get people to face the truth sometimes. Especially about lying.

You don't want your kids to eat too much, so you say all the cookies are gone.

You don't feel like going out, so you tell your date something important came up.

You're overloaded with errands, so you call in sick.

Lies, all of them, but we don't really like calling them that. In an Associated Press-Ipsos poll, more than half of respondents said lying was never justified. Yet in the same poll, up to two-thirds said it was OK to lie in certain situations, like protecting someone's feelings.

Apparently white lies are an acceptable, even necessary, part of many lives, even though we dislike the idea of lying. . . .

Among the groups more likely to say lying was sometimes OK: people ages 18–29, college graduates and those with higher household incomes.[104]

When, If Ever, Is It Ethical for a Manager to Lie? Explain Your Moral Reasoning.

1. Never. A lie is a lie and it is immoral to deceive others, especially those for whom you are responsible.

2. Harmless "white lies" are okay when used to protect people's feelings. "Say, how do you like my new haircut?" "Do I look like I've gained some weight?"
3. True, it's wrong to lie. But life isn't perfect, so the truth needs to be bent a little bit sometimes. (When, and in what situations, exactly?)
4. Get real. Everyone lies one time or another. The trick is to do it skillfully and not overdo it.
5. A harmless white lie now and then is okay, but care needs to be taken because any sort of lying damages a manager's credibility.
6. Invent other options. Discuss.

Web Resources

For study material and exercises that apply to this chapter, visit our Web site, www.mhhe.com/kreitner

Chapter 16

Leadership

Student Resources for Studying Chapter 16

The Web site for your text includes resources that will help you master the concepts in this chapter. As you read, you'll want to visit the site for these helpful tools:

- Your online Study Guide includes learning objectives, a chapter summary, a glossary of key terms, and discussion questions.
- Take a practice quiz and test your knowledge!
- Scroll through a PowerPoint presentation with key concepts for this chapter.

Your instructor might also direct you to the Web site for these exercises:

- Self-assessments that correspond with the chapter content and a Group Exercise.
- You'll also find Video Cases and Internet Exercises for this chapter online.

www.mhhe.com/kreitner

Despite layoffs and recession-starved budgets, many employers are investing in leadership-development programs, hoping not to be caught short of strong managers when the economy recovers.

Identifying and grooming leaders is important in good times, says Bret Furio, senior vice president of consumer lifestyle for Philips Electronics North America. "In times of crisis when the economy is struggling," he adds, "it's imperative."

Like many companies Philips Electronics NV is trimming its training budget this year. A December survey of 117 large US companies by Watson Wyatt Worldwide Inc. found 23% of respondents had recently cut training programs, and another 18% planned to do so this year.

But Philips will offer its annual Inspire program for 30 high-potential employees, stressing subjects such as business strategy and personal leadership. Participants are assigned to teams to work on a business project. Mr. Furio reasons that investing in leadership development will help Philips through the recession and recovery. . . .

Philips is typical of many companies, according to Bersin & Associates, a research firm that studies corporate training. Bersin estimates that companies cut overall training budgets by 11% last year and projects another decline this year, based on a recent survey of human-resources executives. President Josh Bersin says the deepest cuts are in training for "soft skills' such as communicating with co-workers and conducting meetings. He says leadership development is taking a growing share of training budgets.

Yaarit Silverstone, global managing director for the organizational-effectiveness practice at consulting firm Accenture Ltd., says the emphasis on leadership development is a departure from the past. Ms. Silverstone says companies historically cut leadership-development programs during downturns, but the moves backfired, prompting midlevel managers and top performers to leave when the company recovered. Now, she says, executives believe that without capable managers, "their ability to come through (the recession) in a healthy fashion is diminished."

Consider Estee Lauder Cos. The New York cosmetics maker Thursday reported lower sales and profit for

Philips Electronics may be cutting their training budgets, but they are still selecting the highest potential employees for leadership development.

the period ended Dec. 31, and said it would eliminate 2,000 jobs over the next two years, but Lauder is continuing its leadership-development programs, albeit more cheaply. Lauder typically sends 120 executives to a two-or-three-week summer program at Vassar College. This year, it plans to send 60, for one week. In all its leadership programs, Lauder will emphasize innovation and managing change in volatile business conditions.[1]

FOR DISCUSSION

How can companies justify spending money on leadership development when they are laying off other employees?

The chapter opening vignette highlights that organizations such as Philips Electronics and Estee Lauder understand the value of leadership development during bad economic conditions. This investment has two benefits. First, leadership development enhances a company's leadership capabilities to deal with the current recession. Second, leadership development positions organizations for success once the economy turns around.[2] In support of this conclusion, OB researchers have discovered that leaders can make a difference.

One study, for instance, revealed that leadership was positively associated with net profits from 167 companies over a time span of 20 years.[3] Research also showed that a coach's leadership skills affected the success of his or her team. Specifically, teams in both major league baseball and college basketball won more games when players perceived the coach to be an effective leader. A more recent study further demonstrated that improvements in leadership within bank branches were associated with improvements in customer satisfaction.[4] Oppositely, bad leadership has negative effects on employees and customers. For example, a Swedish study found that employees had higher rates of angina, heart attacks, and death when they perceived that their managers were incompetent.[5] Rest assured, leadership makes a difference.

After formally defining the term *leadership,* this chapter focuses on the following areas: (1) trait and behavioral approaches to leadership, (2) alternative situational theories of leadership, (3) the full-range theory of leadership, and (4) additional perspectives on leadership. Because there are many different leadership theories within each of these areas, it is impossible to discuss them all. This chapter reviews those theories with the most research support.

to the point

What is the difference between leading and managing?

LO.1 What Does Leadership Involve?

Because the topic of leadership has fascinated people for centuries, definitions abound. This section presents a definition of leadership, reviews the different approaches or perspectives used to study leadership, and highlights the similarities and differences between leading and managing.

Leadership Defined

Disagreement about the definition of leadership stems from the fact that it involves a complex interaction among the leader, the followers, and the situation. For example, some researchers define leadership in terms of personality and physical traits, while others believe leadership is represented by a set of prescribed behaviors. In contrast, other researchers define leadership in terms of the power relationship between leaders and followers. According to this perspective, leaders use their power to influence followers' behavior. Leadership also can be seen as an instrument of goal achievement. In other words, leaders are individuals who help others accomplish their goals. Still others view leadership from a skills perspective.

There are four commonalities among the many definitions of **leadership:** (1) leadership is a process between a leader and followers, (2) leadership involves social influence, (3) leadership occurs at multiple levels in an organization (at the individual level, for example, leadership involves mentoring, coaching, inspiring, and motivating; leaders also build teams, generate cohesion, and resolve conflicts at the group level; finally, leaders build culture and generate change at the organizational level), and (4) leadership focuses on goal accomplishment.[6] Based on these commonalities, leadership is defined as "a process whereby an individual influences a group of individuals to achieve a common goal."[7]

There are two components of leadership missing from the above definition: the moral and follower perspectives. Leadership is not a moral concept. History is filled with examples of effective leaders who were killers, corrupt, and morally bankrupt. Barbara Kellerman, a leadership expert, commented on this notion by concluding, "Leaders are like the rest of us: trustworthy and deceitful, cowardly and brave, greedy and generous. To assume that all good leaders are good people is to be willfully blind to the reality of the human condition, and it more severely limits our scope for becoming more effective at leadership."[8] The point is that good leaders develop a keen sense of their strengths and weaknesses and build on their positive attributes.

Moreover, research on leadership has only recently begun to recognize that the expectations, attitudes, and behavior of followers also affect how well the presumed leader can lead. "Followership" is discussed in the last section of this chapter.

Leadership

Process whereby an individual influences others to achieve a common goal.

Approaches to Leadership

Leadership is one of the most frequently investigated topics within the field of OB due to its importance to all organizations. As such, there are several different approaches or perspectives that have guided leadership research. While the popularity of these approaches has changed over time, knowledge of each one provides you with a better understanding of how the leadership process unfolds.

This chapter examines the different leadership approaches outlined in Table 16–1. OB researchers began their study of leadership in the early part of the 20th century by focusing on the traits associated with leadership effectiveness. This perspective was followed by attempts in the 1950s and 1960s to examine the behaviors or styles exhibited by effective leaders. This research led to the realization that there is not one best style of leadership, which in turn spawned various contingency approaches to leadership in the 1960s and 70s. Contingency approaches focused on identifying the types of leadership behaviors that are most effective in different settings. The transformational approach is the most popular perspective for studying leadership today. Research based on this approach began in the early 1980s and adheres to the idea that leaders transform employees to pursue organizational goals through a variety of leader behaviors. Finally, there are several emerging perspectives that examine leadership from new or novel points of view.

You would not believe how many different theories exist for each of these perspectives. There are literally a dozen or two. Moreover, the number of leadership theories exponentially increases if we count those proposed by managerial

Table 16–1   *Approaches to Studying Leadership*

1. Trait Approaches
- Stogdill and Mann's five traits—intelligence, dominance, self-confidence, level of energy, and task-relevant knowledge.
- Leadership prototypes—intelligence, masculinity, and dominance.
- Kouzes and Posner's four traits—honesty, forward-looking, inspiring, and competent.
- Goleman—emotional intelligence.
- Judge and colleagues—two meta-analyses: importance of extraversion, conscientiousness, and openness; importance of personality over intelligence.
- Kellerman's bad traits—incompetent, rigid, intemperate, callous, corrupt, insular, and evil.

2. Behavioral Approaches
- Ohio State studies—two dimensions: initiating structure behavior and consideration behavior.
- University of Michigan studies—two leadership styles: job centered and employee centered.

3. Contingency Approaches
- Fiedler's contingency model—task-oriented style and relationship-oriented style; and three dimensions of situational control: leader–member relations, task structure, and position power.
- House's path–goal revised theory—eight leadership behaviors clarify paths for followers' goals; and employee characteristics and environmental factors are contingency factors that influence the effectiveness of leadership behaviors.

4. Transformational Approach
- Bass and Avolio's four transformational leadership behaviors—inspirational motivation, idealized influence, indivualized consideration, and intellectual stimulation.
- Full-range theory of leadership—leadership varies along a continuum from laissez-faire leadership to transactional leadership to transformational leadership.

5. Emerging Approaches
- Leader–member exchange (LMX) model—dyadic relationships between leaders and followers is critical.
- Shared leadership—mutual influence process in which people share responsibility for leading.
- Greenleaf's servant leadership—providing service to others, not oneself.
- Role of followers in leadership process—followers manage the leader–follower relationship.

SOURCE: From A Kinicki and B Williams, *Management: A Practical Introduction,* 4/e, p 440, McGraw-Hill, 2009. Copyright © 2009 The McGraw-Hill Companies. Reprinted with permission.

consultants. Rather than overwhelm you with all these theories of leadership, we focus on the historical ones that have received the most research support. We also discuss emerging perspectives that appear to have academic and practical application in the future. That said, we created a special learning module that contains descriptions of several leadership theories that are not covered in this chapter (see Learning Module C on the Web site for this book).

Leading versus Managing

It is important to appreciate the difference between leadership and management to fully understand what leadership is all about. Bernard Bass, a leadership expert, concluded that "leaders manage and managers lead, but the two activities are not synonymous."[9] Bass tells us that although leadership and management overlap, each entails a unique set of activities or functions. Broadly speaking, managers typically perform functions associated with planning, investigating, organizing, and control, and leaders deal with the interpersonal aspects of a manager's job. Leaders inspire others, provide emotional support, and try to get employees to rally around a common goal. Leaders also play a key role in creating a vision and strategic plan for an organization. Managers, in turn, are charged with implementing the vision and strategic plan. Table 16–2 summarizes the key characteristics associated with being a leader and a manager.[10]

Table 16–2   *Characteristics of Being a Leader and a Manager*

BEING A LEADER MEANS	BEING A MANAGER MEANS
Motivating, influencing, and changing behavior.	Practicing stewardship, directing and being held accountable for resources.
Inspiring, setting the tone, and articulating a vision.	Executing plans, implementing, and delivering the goods and services.
Managing people.	Managing resources.
Being charismatic.	Being conscientious.
Being visionary.	Planning, organizing, directing, and controlling.
Understanding and using power and influence.	Understanding and using authority and responsibility.
Acting decisively.	Acting responsibly.
Putting people first; the leader knows, responds to, and acts for his or her followers.	Putting customers first; the manager knows, responds to, and acts for his or her customers.
Leaders can make mistakes when 1. They choose the wrong goal, direction or inspiration, due to incompetence or bad intentions; or 2. They overload; or 3. They are unable to deliver on, implement the vision due to incompetence or a lack of follow through commitment.	Managers can make mistakes when 1. They fail to grasp the importance of people as the key resource; or 2. They underlead; they treat people like other resources, numbers; or 3. They are eager to direct and to control but are unwilling to accept accountability.

SOURCE: Reprinted from P Lorenzi, "Managing for the Common Good: Prosocial Leadership," *Organizational Dynamics,* vol. 33, no. 3, p 286. © 2004, with permission from Elsevier.

There are several conclusions to be drawn from the information presented in Table 16–2. First, good leaders are not necessarily good managers, and good managers are not necessarily good leaders. Second, effective leadership requires effective managerial skills at some level. For example, JetBlue ex-CEO David Neeleman was let go because the company needed him to be more managerial and less entrepreneurial.[11] Good managerial skills turn a leader's vision into actionable tasks and successful implementation. Both Carol Bartz, CEO of Yahoo, and Akio Toyoda, CEO of Toyota, endorsed this conclusion by noting that effective execution is a key driver of organizational success.[12] Sergio Marchionne, CEO of Fiat Group, is a good example. He not only let go of people who would not adopt a more participative approach to leading, but he established very challenging performance targets throughout the organization. Here is what he said about his approach toward execution in an interview for the *Harvard Business Review:*

> "As I give people more responsibility, I also hold them more accountable. A leader who fails to meet an objective should suffer some consequences, but I don't believe that failing to meet an objective is the end of the world. Markets and economies aren't perfectly predictable, and in an organization this size, you can always offset a failure here with a success there. But if you want to grow leaders, you can't let explanations and excuses become a way of life.... If you set what people think is an unrealistic target, you have to help them reach it.... Helping them doesn't mean doing the job for them.... A lot of what I do is challenge assumptions—which often look like you're asking stupid questions. That's how we cut out time to market for the Cinquecento down from four years to just 18 months."[13]

All told then, organizational success requires a combination of effective leadership and management. This in turn leads to the realization that today's leaders need to be effective at both leading and managing. While this may seem like a daunting task, the good news is that a recent meta-analysis of leadership interventions shows that people can be taught to be more effective leaders and managers (see the Real World/Real People feature on page 471).[14]

go to the Web for the Self-Exercise: How Ready Are You to Assume the Leadership Role?

to the point

What are the key trait and behavioral approaches to leadership and what are their major takeaways?

LO.2 Trait and Behavioral Theories of Leadership

This section examines the two earliest approaches used to explain leadership. Trait theories focused on identifying the personal traits that differentiated leaders from followers. Behavioral theorists examined leadership from a different perspective. They tried to uncover the different kinds of leader behaviors that resulted in higher work group performance. Both approaches to leadership can teach current and future managers valuable lessons about leading.

AlliedBarton Security Services's Leadership Development Produces Positive Results

AlliedBarton Leadership Boot Camp signaled a shift in how the company views and leads employees. It includes three stages. The first, "On-Ramp Preparation," is a six-week process that includes a 360-degree leadership analysis, personal coaching, and a virtual reality leadership video in which participants practice principles and skills. Another two assessments are delivered to understand the employee's level of engagement. The multi-rater feedback establishes a baseline for performance. The second stage, "Residential," includes three-and-a-half days in which participants engage with peers to build execution plans. The final phase, "On-the-Job Application," occurs over a 16-week period, and includes on-the-job implementation of execution plans. Participants meet with direct reports, deliver a plan to engage employees, and complete the multi-rater survey.

Following Boot Camp, account manager turnover was reduced from 32 percent to 21 percent. Financial impact as of July 31, 2007, was more than $2 million in turnover reduction savings.

Why is this program so successful?

SOURCE: Excerpted from "Best Practices & Outstanding Initiatives," *Training Magazine*, February 2008, p 118.

Trait Theory

Trait theory is the successor to what was called the "great man" theory of leadership. This approach was based on the assumption that leaders such as Abraham Lincoln, Martin Luther King, or Jack Welch were born with some inborn ability to lead. In contrast, trait theorists believed that leadership traits were not innate but could be developed through experience and learning. A **leader trait** is a physical or personality characteristic that can be used to differentiate leaders from followers.

Before World War II, hundreds of studies were conducted to pinpoint the traits of successful leaders. Dozens of leadership traits were identified. During the postwar period, however, enthusiasm was replaced by widespread criticism. This section reviews a series of studies that provide a foundation for understanding leadership traits. We conclude by integrating results across the various studies and summarizing the practical recommendations of trait theory.

Leader trait
Personal characteristic that differentiates leaders from followers.

Stogdill's and Mann's Findings   Ralph Stogdill in 1948 and Richard Mann in 1959 sought to summarize the impact of traits on leadership. Based on his review, Stogdill concluded that five traits tended to differentiate leaders from average followers: (1) intelligence, (2) dominance, (3) self-confidence, (4) level of energy and activity, and (5) task-relevant knowledge. Among the seven categories of personality traits examined by Mann, intelligence was the best predictor of leadership.[15] Vikram Pandit, CEO of Citigroup, is a good example of an intelligent person who has risen through the corporate ranks. He has a PhD from Columbia University and is known for his analytical skills. "People who work with him appear universally to admire his thought processes, calling him 'very smart' to 'brilliant.' Sam Palmisano, CEO of IBM, says he's often leaned on Pandit for strategic advice. 'Vikram sees the big picture,' Palmisano says."[16] Unfortunately, the overall pattern of research findings revealed that both Stogdill's and Mann's key traits did not accurately predict which individuals became leaders in organizations. People with these traits often remained followers.

**Implicit
leadership theory**
Perceptual theory
in which prototypes
determine traits of
effective leaders.

**Leadership
prototype**
Mental
representation
of the traits and
behaviors possessed
by leaders.

Implicit Leadership Theory (ILT)

Implicit leadership theory is based on the idea that people have beliefs about how leaders should behave and what they should do for their followers. These beliefs are summarized in what is called a *leadership prototype.*[17] A **leadership prototype** is a mental representation of the traits and behaviors that people believe are possessed by leaders. It is important to understand the content of leadership prototypes because we tend to perceive that someone is a leader when he or she exhibits traits or behaviors that are consistent with our prototypes (recall our discussion of encoding and simplification in Chapter 7). We also tend to identify with leaders and evaluate them as more effective when they behave in prototypical ways. Robert Lord and his colleagues attempted to identify employees' leadership prototypes by conducting a meta-analysis of past studies. Results demonstrated that people are perceived as leaders when they exhibit traits and behaviors associated with intelligence, masculinity, and dominance.[18] Other studies showed that leadership prototypes tend to be shared throughout an organization and are culturally based.[19] In other words, leadership prototypes are influenced by national cultural values. Researchers have not yet identified a set of global leadership prototypes.

Kouzes and Posner's Research: Is Honesty the Most Critical Leadership Trait?

James Kouzes and Barry Posner attempted to identify key leadership traits by asking the following open-ended question to more than 20,000 people around the world: "What values (personal traits or characteristics) do you look for and admire in your superiors?" The top four traits included honesty, forward-looking, inspiring, and competent.[20] The researchers concluded that these four traits constitute a leader's credibility. This research suggests that people want their leaders to be credible and to have a sense of direction. That said, our discussion in Chapter 3 revealed that an organization's culture significantly influences the extent to which leaders encourage and reinforce integrity at work. Credibility is enhanced by honestly communicating with others and by taking responsibility for one's mistakes or problems. Lego CEO Jørgen Vig Knudstorp believes that this is even more important during a turnaround or crisis.[21] US President Barack Obama followed this advice when he encountered problems with his nomination of Tom Daschle as secretary of Health and Human Services; Daschle failed to pay over $100,000 in taxes on time.

Mr. Obama admitted to mistakes in handling the Daschle matter. "I'm here on television saying I screwed up and that's part of the era of responsibility," he told NBC News. "Ultimately it's important for this administration to send a message that there aren't two sets of rules. You know, one for prominent people and one for ordinary folks who have to pay their taxes."[22]

Tom Daschle, standing behind President Obama, undercut his nomination for being on the president's cabinet by failing to pay his taxes on time. The president admitted on television that he handled the Daschle case poorly.

Goleman's Research on Emotional Intelligence

We discussed Daniel Goleman's research on emotional intelligence in Chapter 5. Recall that *emotional intelligence* is the ability to manage oneself and one's relationships in mature and constructive ways: The six components of emotional intelligence are shown in Table 5–5. Given that leadership is an influence process between leaders and followers, it should come as no surprise that emotional intelligence is predicted to be associated with leadership effectiveness. While Goleman contends he has evidence to support this conclusion, he has not published it in any academic journals or professional magazine. We agree with others who contend that there presently is not enough research published in OB journals to substantiate the conclusion that emotional intelligence is significantly associated with leadership effectiveness.[23]

Judge's Research: Is Personality More Important Than Intelligence?

Tim Judge and his colleagues completed two meta-analyses that bear on the subject of traits and leadership. The first examined the relationship among the Big Five personality traits (see Table 5–2 for a review of these traits) and leadership emergence and effectiveness in 94 studies. Results revealed that extraversion was most consistently and positively related to both leadership emergence and effectiveness. Conscientiousness and openness to experience also were positively correlated with leadership effectiveness.[24] Judge's second meta-analysis involved 151 samples and demonstrated that intelligence was modestly related to leadership effectiveness. Judge concluded that personality is more important than intelligence when selecting leaders.[25]

Kellerman's Research: What Traits Are Possessed by Bad Leaders?

Thus far we have been discussing traits associated with "good leadership." Barbara Kellerman believes this approach is limiting because it fails to recognize that "bad leadership" is related to "good leadership." It also ignores the valuable insights that are gained by examining ineffective leaders. Kellerman thus set out to study hundreds of contemporary cases involving bad leadership and bad followers in search of the traits possessed by bad leaders. Her qualitative analysis uncovered seven key traits:[26]

- *Incompetent.* The leader and at least some followers lack the will or skill (or both) to sustain effective action. With regard to at least one important leadership challenge, they do not create positive change. For example, James Cayne, former CEO of Bear Stearns, was reportedly off playing golf and bridge as the company collapsed.

- *Rigid.* The leader and at least some followers are stiff and unyielding. Although they may be competent, they are unable or unwilling to adapt to new ideas, new information, or changing times. Richard Fuld, former CEO of Lehman Brothers, held firm to his belief that Lehman was too big to fail.

- *Intemperate.* The leader lacks self-control and is aided and abetted by followers who are unwilling or unable effectively to intervene.

- *Callous.* The leader and at least some followers are uncaring and unkind. Ignored or discounted are the needs, wants, and desires of most members of the group or organization, especially subordinates. Steve Jobs is known for parking his car in handicapped spaces and for being so callous that he brings employees to tears.

- *Corrupt.* The leader and at least some followers lie, cheat, or steal. To a degree that exceeds the norm, they put self-interest ahead of the public interest.

- *Insular.* The leader and at least some followers minimize or disregard the health and welfare of "the other," that is, those outside the group or organization for which they are directly responsible. Philip Schoonover, former CEO of Circuit City, fired 3,400 of the most experienced employees because he felt they made too much money.

- *Evil.* The leader and at least some followers commit atrocities. They use pain as an instrument of power. The harm done to men, women, and children is severe rather than slight. The harm can be physical, psychological, or both.[27]

Do you know leaders who possess any of these traits? Unfortunately, there are many examples.

Gender and Leadership   The increase of women in the workforce has generated much interest in understanding the similarities and differences in female and male leaders. Three separate meta-analyses and a series of studies conducted by consultants across the country uncovered the following differences: (1) Men and women were seen as displaying more task and social leadership, respectively;[28] (2) women used a more democratic or participative style than men, and men used a more autocratic and directive style than women;[29] (3) men and women were equally assertive;[30] and (4) women executives, when rated by their peers, managers, and direct reports, scored higher than their male counterparts on a variety of effectiveness criteria.[31]

What Are the Takeaways from Trait Theory?   We can no longer afford to ignore the implications of leadership traits. Traits play a central role in how we perceive leaders, and they ultimately impact leadership effectiveness. What can be learned from the previous research on traits? Integrating across past studies leads to the extended list of positive traits shown in Table 16–3. This list, along with the negative traits identified by Kellerman, provides guidance regarding the leadership traits you should attempt to cultivate if you want to assume a leadership role. Personality tests, which were discussed in Chapter 5, and other trait assessments can be used to evaluate your strengths and weaknesses vis-à-vis these traits. Results can then be used to prepare a personal development plan.[32] We encourage you to use an executive coach in this process.

There are two organizational applications of trait theory. First, organizations may want to include personality and trait assessments into their selection and

Table 16–3   *Key Positive Leadership Traits*

Task competence (intelligence, knowledge, problem-solving skills).
Interpersonal competence (ability to communicate, demonstrate caring and empathy).
Intuition.
Traits of character (conscientiousness, discipline, moral reasoning, integrity, and honesty).
Biophysical traits (physical fitness, hardiness, and energy level).
Personal traits (self-confidence, sociability, self-monitoring, extraversion, self-regulating, and self-efficacy).

SOURCE: These traits were identified in B M Bass and R Bass, *The Bass Handbook of Leadership* (New York: Free Press, 2008), p 135.

promotion processes. It is important to remember that this should only be done with valid measures of leadership traits. Second, management development programs can be used to enhance employees' leadership traits. For example, both small and large companies such as EMC, Loews Hotels, and PricewaterhouseCoopers send targeted groups of managers to developmental programs that include management classes, coaching sessions, trait assessments, and stretch assignments.[33] Many companies also are using information technology to offer developmental classes online.[34]

LO.3 Behavioral Styles Theory

This phase of leadership research began during World War II as part of an effort to develop better military leaders. It was an outgrowth of two events: the seeming inability of trait theory to explain leadership effectiveness and the human relations movement, an outgrowth of the Hawthorne studies. The thrust of early behavioral leadership theory was to focus on leader behavior, instead of on personality traits. It was believed that leader behavior directly affected work group effectiveness. This led researchers to identify patterns of behavior (called *leadership styles*) that enabled leaders to effectively influence others.

The Ohio State Studies   Researchers at Ohio State University began by generating a list of behaviors exhibited by leaders. At one point, the list contained 1,800 statements that described nine categories of leader behavior. Ultimately, the Ohio State researchers concluded there were only two independent dimensions of leader behavior: consideration and initiating structure. **Consideration** involves leader behavior associated with creating mutual respect or trust and focuses on a concern for group members' needs and desires. **Initiating structure** is leader behavior that organizes and defines what group members should be doing to maximize output. These two dimensions of leader behavior were oriented at right angles to yield four behavioral styles of leadership (see Figure 16–1).

Consideration
Creating mutual respect and trust with followers.

Initiating structure
Organizing and defining what group members should be doing.

Figure 16–1   *Four Leadership Styles Derived from the Ohio State Studies*

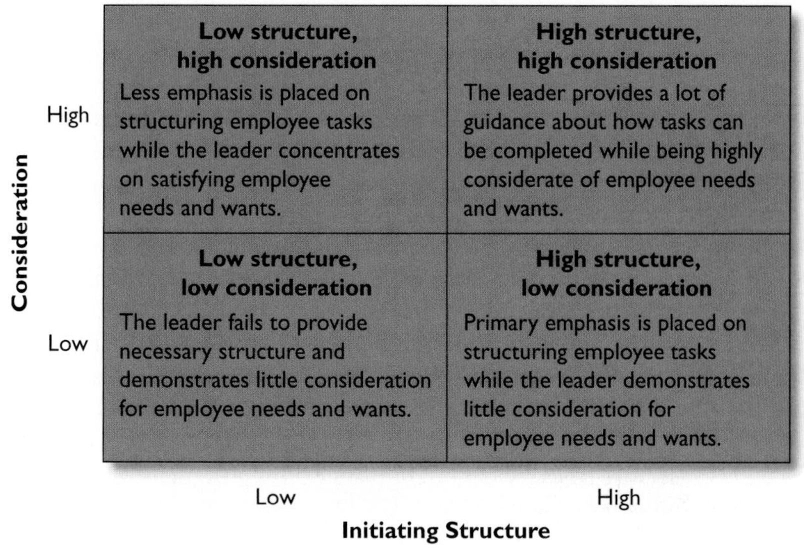

	Low structure, high consideration Less emphasis is placed on structuring employee tasks while the leader concentrates on satisfying employee needs and wants.	**High structure, high consideration** The leader provides a lot of guidance about how tasks can be completed while being highly considerate of employee needs and wants.
	Low structure, low consideration The leader fails to provide necessary structure and demonstrates little consideration for employee needs and wants.	**High structure, low consideration** Primary emphasis is placed on structuring employee tasks while the leader demonstrates little consideration for employee needs and wants.

Consideration: High / Low

Initiating Structure: Low / High

It initially was hypothesized that a high-structure, high-consideration style would be the one best style of leadership. Through the years, the effectiveness of the high-high style has been tested many times.[35] Overall, results have been mixed and there has been very little research about these leader behaviors until just recently. Findings from a 2004 meta-analysis of 130 studies and more than 20,000 individuals demonstrated that consideration and initiating structure had a moderately strong, significant relationship with leadership outcomes. Results revealed that followers performed more effectively for structuring leaders even though they preferred considerate leaders.[36] All told, results do not support the idea that there is one best style of leadership, but they do confirm the importance of considerate and structuring leader behaviors. Follower satisfaction, motivation, and performance are significantly associated with these two leader behaviors. Future research is needed to incorporate them into more contemporary leadership theories.

University of Michigan Studies   As in the Ohio State studies, this research sought to identify behavioral differences between effective and ineffective leaders. Researchers identified two different styles of leadership: one was employee centered; the other was job centered. These behavioral styles parallel the consideration and initiating-structure styles identified by the Ohio State group. In summarizing the results from these studies, one management expert concluded that effective leaders (1) tend to have supportive or employee-centered relationships with employees, (2) use group rather than individual methods of supervision, and (3) set high performance goals.[37]

What Are the Takeaways from Behavioral Styles Theory?   By emphasizing leader behavior, something that is learned, the behavioral style approach makes it clear that leaders are made, not born. This is the opposite of the trait theorists' traditional assumption. Given what we know about behavior shaping and model-based training, leader behaviors can be systematically improved and developed.[38]

Behavioral styles research also revealed that there is no one best style of leadership. The effectiveness of a particular leadership style depends on the situation at hand. For instance, employees prefer structure over consideration when faced with role ambiguity. Finally, research also reveals that it is important to consider the difference between how frequently and how effectively managers exhibit various leader behaviors. For example, a manager might ineffectively display a lot of considerate leader behaviors. Such a style is likely to frustrate employees and possibly result in lowered job satisfaction and performance. Because the frequency of exhibiting leadership behaviors is secondary in importance to effectiveness, managers are encouraged to concentrate on improving the effective execution of their leader behaviors.

Finally, Peter Drucker, an internationally renowned management expert and consultant, recommended a set of nine behaviors (see Table 16–4) managers can focus on to improve their leadership effectiveness. The first two practices provide the knowledge leaders need. The next four help leaders convert knowledge into effective action, and the last two ensure that the whole organization feels responsible and accountable. Drucker refers to the last recommendation as a managerial rule.

Table 16–4   *Peter Drucker's Tips for Improving Leadership Effectiveness*

1. Determine what needs to be done.

2. Determine the right thing to do for the welfare of the entire enterprise or organization.

3. Develop action plans that specify desired results, probable restraints, future revisions, check-in points, and implications for how one should spend his or her time.

4. Take responsibility for decisions.

5. Take responsibility for communicating action plans and give people the information they need to get the job done.

6. Focus on opportunities rather than problems. Do not sweep problems under the rug, and treat change as an opportunity rather than a threat.

7. Run productive meetings. Different types of meetings require different forms of preparation and different results. Prepare accordingly.

8. Think and say "we" rather than "I." Consider the needs and opportunities of the organization before thinking of your own opportunities and needs.

9. Listen first, speak last.

SOURCE: Reprinted by permission of *Harvard Business Review*. Recommendations were derived from "What Makes an Effective Executive," by P F Drucker, June 2004, pp 58–63. Copyright 2004 by the Harvard Business School Publishing Corporation; all rights reserved.

Situational theories

Propose that leader styles should match the situation at hand.

Situational Theories

Situational leadership theories grew out of an attempt to explain the inconsistent findings about traits and styles. **Situational theories** propose that the effectiveness of a particular style of leader behavior depends on the situation. As situations change, different styles become appropriate. This directly challenges the idea of one best style of leadership.[39] Let us closely examine two alternative situational theories of leadership that reject the notion of one best leadership style. We conclude this section by discussing an approach you can use to implement situational theories.

to the point

What are the similarities and differences between Fiedler's contingency model and House's revised path-goal theory and how can managers apply these situational theories?

LO.4 Fiedler's Contingency Model

Fred Fiedler, an OB scholar, developed a situational model of leadership. It is the oldest and one of the most widely known models of situational leadership. He labeled the model *contingency theory* because it is based on the premise that a leader's effectiveness is contingent on the extent to which a leader's style fits or matches characteristics of the situation at hand. To understand how this matching process works, we need to consider the key leadership styles identified by Fiedler and the situational variables that constitute what Fiedler labels *situational control*. We then review relevant research and managerial implications.[40]

Leadership Styles Fiedler believes that leaders have one dominant or natural leadership style that is resistant to change. A leader's style is described as either task-motivated or relationship-motivated. Task-motivated leaders focus on accomplishing goals, whereas relationship-motivated leaders are more interested in developing positive relationships with followers. These basic styles are similar to initiating structure/concern for production and consideration/concern for people that were previously discussed. To determine an individual's leadership style, Fiedler developed the least preferred coworker (LPC) scale. High scores on the survey (high LPC) indicate that an individual is relationship-motivated, and low scores (low LPC) suggest a task-motivated style.

Situational Control   Situational control refers to the amount of control and influence the leader has in her or his immediate work environment. Situational control ranges from high to low. High control implies that the leader's decisions will produce predictable results because the leader has the ability to influence work outcomes. Low control implies that the leader's decisions may not influence work outcomes because the leader has very little influence. There are three dimensions of situational control: leader–member relations, task structure, and position power. These dimensions vary independently, forming eight combinations of situational control (see Figure 16–2).

The three dimensions of situational control are defined as follows:

Leader–member relations

Extent that leader has the support, loyalty, and trust of the work group.

- **Leader–member relations** reflect the extent to which the leader has the support, loyalty, and trust of the work group. This dimension is the most important component of situational control. Good leader–member relations suggest that the leader can depend on the group, thus ensuring that the work group will try to meet the leader's goals and objectives.

Figure 16–2   *Representation of Fiedler's Contingency Model*

Situational Control	High-Control Situations			Moderate-Control Situations				Low-Control Situations
Leader-member relations	Good	Good	Good	Good	Poor	Poor	Poor	Poor
Task structure	High	High	Low	Low	High	High	Low	Low
Position power	Strong	Weak	Strong	Weak	Strong	Weak	Strong	Weak
Situation	I	II	III	IV	V	VI	VII	VIII

Optimal Leadership Style	**Task-Motivated Leadership**	**Relationship-Motivated Leadership**	**Task-Motivated Leadership**

SOURCE: Adapted from F E Fiedler, "Situational Control and a Dynamic Theory of Leadership," in *Managerial Control and Organizational Democracy*, ed B King, S Streufert, and F E Fiedler (New York: John Wiley & Sons, 1978), p 114.

Carol Bartz Uses Task-Motivated Leadership to Turn around Yahoo

Not yet six weeks into the job, Yahoo Inc. Chief Executive Carol Bartz is preparing a company-wide reorganization that underscores the new CEO's belief in a more top-down managerial approach.

The plan aims to speed up decision making and give Yahoo products a more consistent appearance by consolidating certain functions that have previously been spread out across the company. . . .

A straight-talker, Ms. Bartz has become known for stubbornly starting meetings on time, say employees. She doesn't bring her BlackBerry into meetings, according to workers who have begun leaving behind theirs as well.

She's requested briefings with staff at several levels of the organization, seeking updates on major projects and testing employees by asking, "What would you do if you were me?" say people familiar with her process.

And she hasn't shied from changing course on major projects.

Do you think that Ms. Bartz should be more relationship-oriented given that she has only been on the job for six weeks? Explain.

SOURCE: Excerpted from J E Vascellaro, "Yahoo CEO Set to Install Top-Down Management," *The Wall Street Journal*, February 23, 2009, p B1.

- **Task structure** is concerned with the amount of structure contained within tasks performed by the work group. For example, a managerial job contains less structure than that of a bank teller. Because structured tasks have guidelines for how the job should be completed, the leader has more control and influence over employees performing such tasks. This dimension is the second most important component of situational control.

- **Position power** refers to the degree to which the leader has formal power to reward, punish, or otherwise obtain compliance from employees.

Task structure

Amount of structure contained within work tasks.

Position power

Degree to which leader has formal power.

Linking Leadership Motivation and Situational Control   Fiedler suggests that leaders must learn to manipulate or influence the leadership situation in order to create a match between their leadership style and the amount of control within the situation at hand. These contingency relationships are depicted in Figure 16–2. The last row under the Situational Control column shows that there are eight different leadership situations. Each situation represents a unique combination of leader–member relations, task structure, and position power. Situations I, II, and III represent high-control situations. Figure 16–2 shows that task-motivated leaders are hypothesized to be most effective in situations of high control. The Real World/Real People feature above illustrates how Carol Bartz, Yahoo's new CEO, is using task-motivated leadership to turn around the company. We suspect that she is operating within situation III. Under conditions of moderate control (situations IV, V, VI, and VII), relationship-motivated leaders are expected to be more effective. Finally, the results orientation of task-motivated leaders is predicted to be more effective under the condition of very low control (situation VIII).

Research and Takeaways from Fiedler's Model   On the positive side, two meta-analyses provided partial support for this model.[41] At the same time, this theory has generated much criticism and controversy. There are problems with the LPC scale and research does not clearly support all predictions derived from this model.[42] That said, there are three key takeaways from Fiedler's model.

First, this model emphasizes the point that leadership effectiveness goes beyond traits and behaviors. It is a function of the fit between a leader's style and the situational demands at hand. As a case in point, a team of researchers examined the effectiveness of 20 senior-level managers from GE who left the company for other positions. The researchers concluded that

> not all managers are equally suited to all business situations. The strategic skills required to control costs in the face of fierce competition are not the same as those required to improve the top line in a rapidly growing business or balance investment against cash flow to survive in a highly cyclical business....We weren't surprised to find that relevant industry experience had a positive impact on performance in a new job, but that these skills didn't transfer to a new industry.[43]

This study leads to the conclusion that organizations should attempt to hire or promote people whose leadership styles *fit* or *match* situational demands.[44]

Second, this model explains why some people are successful in some situations and not in others. Leaders are unlikely to be successful in all situations. If a manager is failing in a certain context, management should consider moving the individual to another situation. Don't give up on a high-potential person simply because he or she was a poor leader in one context. Finally, leaders need to modify their style to fit a situation. Leadership styles are not universally effective.

LO.5 Path–Goal Theory

Path–goal theory was originally proposed by Robert House in the 1970s.[45] It was based on the expectancy theory of motivation discussed in Chapter 8. Recall that expectancy theory is based on the idea that motivation to exert effort increases as one's effort→performance→outcome expectations improve. Leader behaviors thus are expected to be acceptable when employees view them as a source of satisfaction or as paving the way to future satisfaction. In addition, leader behavior is predicted to be motivational to the extent it (1) reduces roadblocks that interfere with goal accomplishment, (2) provides the guidance and support needed by employees, and (3) ties meaningful rewards to goal accomplishment.

Contingency factors

Variables that influence the appropriateness of a leadership style.

House proposed a model that describes how leadership effectiveness is influenced by the interaction between four leadership styles (directive, supportive, participative, and achievement-oriented) and a variety of contingency factors. **Contingency factors** are situational variables that cause one style of leadership to be more effective than another. Path–goal theory has two groups of contingency variables. They are employee characteristics and environmental factors. Five important employee characteristics are locus of control, task ability, need for achievement, experience, and need for clarity. Two relevant environmental factors are task structure (independent versus interdependent tasks) and work group dynamics. In order to gain a better understanding of how these contingency factors influence leadership effectiveness, we illustratively consider locus of control (see Chapter 5), task ability and experience, and task structure.

Employees with an internal locus of control are more likely to prefer participative or achievement-oriented leadership because they believe they have control over the work environment. Such individuals are unlikely to be satisfied with directive leader behaviors that exert additional control over their activities. In contrast, employees with an external locus tend to view the environment as uncontrollable, thereby preferring the structure provided by supportive or directive leadership. An employee with high task ability and experience is less apt to need additional direction and thus would respond negatively to directive leadership. This person is more likely to be motivated and satisfied by participative and achievement-oriented leadership. Oppositely, an inexperienced employee would find achievement-oriented leadership overwhelming as he or she confronts challenges associated with learning a new job. Supportive and directive leadership would be helpful in this situation. Finally, directive and supportive leadership should help employees experiencing role ambiguity. However, directive leadership is likely to frustrate employees working on routine and simple tasks. Supportive leadership is most useful in this context.

There have been about 50 studies testing various predictions derived from House's original model. Results have been mixed, with some studies supporting the theory and others not.[46] House thus proposed a new version of path–goal theory in 1996 based on these results and the accumulation of new knowledge about OB.

A Reformulated Theory   The revised theory is presented in Figure 16–3.[47] There are three key changes in the new theory. First, House now believes that leadership is more complex and involves a greater variety of leader behavior. He thus identified eight categories of leadership styles or behavior (see Table 16–5). The need for an expanded list of leader behaviors is supported by current research and descriptions of business leaders.

The second key change involves the role of intrinsic motivation (discussed in Chapter 9) and empowerment (discussed in Chapter 15) in influencing leadership effectiveness. House places much more emphasis on the need for leaders to foster intrinsic motivation through empowerment. Shared leadership represents the final change in the revised theory. That is, path–goal theory is based on the premise that an employee does not have to be a supervisor or manager to engage in leader behavior.

Figure 16–3 *A General Representation of House's Revised Path–Goal Theory*

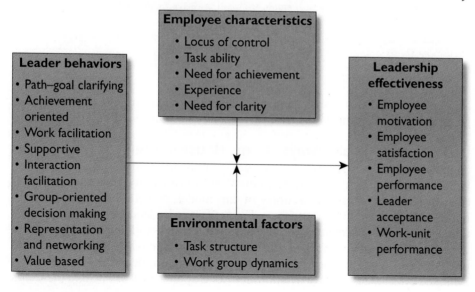

Table 16–5   *Categories of Leader Behavior within the Revised Path–Goal Theory*

CATEGORY OF LEADER BEHAVIOR	DESCRIPTION OF LEADER BEHAVIORS
Path–goal clarifying behaviors	Clarifying employees' performance goals; providing guidance on how employees can complete tasks; clarifying performance standards and expectations; use of positive and negative rewards contingent on performance
Achievement-oriented behaviors	Setting challenging goals; emphasizing excellence; demonstrating confidence in employees' abilities
Work-facilitation behaviors	Planning, scheduling, organizing, and coordinating work; providing mentoring, coaching, counseling, and feedback to assist employees in developing their skills; eliminating roadblocks; providing resources; empowering employees to take actions and make decisions
Supportive behaviors	Showing concern for the well-being and needs of employees; being friendly and approachable; treating employees as equals
Interaction-facilitation behaviors	Resolving disputes; facilitating communication; encouraging the sharing of minority opinions; emphasizing collaboration and teamwork; encouraging close relationships among employees
Group-oriented decision-making behaviors	Posing problems rather than solutions to the work group; encouraging group members to participate in decision making; providing necessary information to the group for analysis; involving knowledgeable employees in decision making
Representation and networking behaviors	Presenting the work group in a positive light to others; maintaining positive relationships with influential others; participating in organizationwide social functions and ceremonies; doing unconditional favors for others
Value-based behaviors	Establishing a vision, displaying passion for it, and supporting its accomplishment; demonstrating self-confidence; communicating high performance expectations and confidence in others' abilities to meet their goals; giving frequent positive feedback

SOURCE: Descriptions were adapted from R J House, "Path–Goal Theory of Leadership: Lessons, Legacy, and a Reformulated Theory," *Leadership Quarterly,* 1996, pp 323–52.

Rather, House believes that leadership is shared among all employees within an organization. More is said about shared leadership in the final section of this chapter.

Research and Takeaways from House's Theory
There are not enough direct tests of House's revised path–goal theory using appropriate research methods and statistical procedures to draw overall conclusions. Future research is clearly needed to assess the accuracy of this model. Nonetheless, there are three important takeaways from this theory. First, effective leaders possess and use more than one style of leadership. Managers are encouraged to familiarize themselves with the different categories of leader behavior outlined in path–goal theory and to try new behaviors when the situation calls for them. Consider the leader behaviors exhibited by Bob Iger, CEO of Walt Disney Co. He prefers to work behind the scenes

and does not host any Disney TV productions. He is known to say hello to everyone he encounters on the Disney campus and participates in a Disney team that competes in the Malibu, California, triathalon to raise money for charity. He loves to study operational statistics and is very interested in studying and using consumers' attitudes to make decisions. Since taking over the healm at Disney, Iger patched up the rocky relationship between Pixar and Disney and ultimately purchased Pixar for $7 billion. He also resolved several contentious issues with former director Roy Disney and Comcast. Iger empowers his employees and allows them plenty of freedom to make decisions. At that same time, he holds people accountable for their work.[48] This example illustrates that Iger uses path–goal clarifying behaviors, achievement-oriented behaviors, work-facilitation behaviors, supportive behaviors, interaction-facilitation behaviors, and represenation and networking behaviors.

Second, the theory offers specific suggestions for how leaders can help employees. Leaders are encouraged to clarify the paths to goal accomplishment and to remove any obstacles that may impair an employee's ability to achieve his or her goals. In so doing, managers need to guide and coach employees during the pursuit of their goals. Third, a small set of employee characteristics (i.e., ability, experience, and need for independence) and environmental factors (task characteristics of autonomy, variety, and significance) are relevant contingency factors.[49] Managers are advised to modify their leadership style to fit these various employee and task characteristics.

Applying Situational Theories

Although researchers and practitioners support the logic of situational leadership, the practical application of such theories has not been clearly developed. A team of researchers thus attempted to resolve this problem by proposing a general strategy that managers can use across a variety of situations. The general strategy contains five steps.[50] We explain how to implement the steps by using the examples of a head coach of a sports team and a sales manager.

1. *Identify important outcomes.* This step entails a determination of the goals the leader is trying to achieve. For example, the head coach may have goals "to win" or "avoid injury to key players" whereas a sales manager's goals might be to "increase sales by 10%" or "decrease customers' complaints." It is important to identify the key goals that exist at a specific point in time.

2. *Identify relevant leadership types/behaviors.* This step requires the manager to identify the specific types of behaviors that may be appropriate for the situation at hand. The list of behaviors shown in Table 16–5 is a good starting point. A head coach in a championship game, for instance, might focus on achievement-oriented and work-facilitation behaviors. In contrast, a sales manager might find path–goal clarifying, work-facilitation, and supportive behaviors more relevant for the sales team. Don't try to use all available leadership behaviors. Rather, select the one or two that appear most helpful.

3. *Identify situational conditions.* Fiedler's contingency theory and House's path–goal theory both identify a set of potential contingency factors to consider. That said, there may be other practical considerations. For example, a star quarterback on a football team may be injured, which might require the team to adopt a different strategy toward winning the game. Similarly, managing a virtual sales team from around the world will affect the types of leadership that are most effective in this context.

4. *Match leadership to the conditions at hand.* This is the step in which research cannot provide conclusive recommendations because there simply are too many possible situational conditions. This means that you should use your knowledge about organizational behavior to determine the best match between leadership styles/behaviors and the situation at hand. The coach whose star quarterback is injured might use supportive and values-based behaviors to instill confidence that the team can win with a different quarterback. Our virtual sales manager also might find it useful to use the empowering leadership associated with work-facilitation behaviors (see Table 16–5) and to avoid directive leadership.

5. *Determine how to make the match.* It's now time to implement the leadership style or behaviors you determined were most appropriate in step 4. There are two basic approaches you can use according to contingency theory and House's path–goal theory. You can either change the person in the leadership role or the leader can change his or her style/behavior. Returning to our examples, it is not possible to change the head coach in a championship game. This means that the head coach needs to change his or her style/behavior. In contrast, the organization employing the sales manager might move him or her to another position because the individual is too directive and does not like to empower others. Alternatively, the sales manager could change his/her behavior.

to the point

What is the difference between transactional and transformational leadership, and how does transformational leadership transform followers and work groups?

LO.6 The Full-Range Model of Leadership: From Laissez-Faire to Transformational Leadership

One of the most recent approaches to leadership is referred to as a *full-range model of leadership.*[51] The authors of this model, Bernard Bass and Bruce Avolio, proposed that leadership behavior varied along a continuum from laissez-faire leadership (i.e., a general failure to take responsibility for leading) to transactional leadership to transformational leadership. Examples of laissez-faire leadership include avoiding conflict, surfing the Internet during work, failing to assist employees in setting performance goals, failing to give performance feedback, or being so hands-off that employees have little idea about what they should be doing.[52] Of course, laissez-faire leadership is a terrible way for any manager to behave and should be avoided. What gender do you think engages in more laissez-faire leadership? A meta-analysis revealed that men displayed more of this type of leadership than women.[53] It is important for organizations to identify managers who lead with this style and to train and develop them to use behaviors associated with transactional and transformational leadership. Both transactional and transformational are positively related to a variety of employee attitudes and behaviors and represent different aspects of being a good leader. Let us consider these two important dimensions of leadership.

Transactional leadership

Focuses on clarifying employees' roles and providing rewards contingent on performance.

Transactional leadership focuses on clarifying employees' role and task requirements and providing followers with positive and negative rewards contingent on performance. Further, transactional leadership encompasses the fundamental managerial activities of setting goals, monitoring progress toward goal achievement, and rewarding and punishing people for their level of goal accomplishment.[54] You can see from this description that transactional leadership is based on using extrinsic motivation (recall our discussion in Chapter 9) to increase employee productivity. Consider how Bijan Khosrowshahi, chief executive of Fuji Fire and Marine Insurance, used transactional leadership to pick up the pace of growth at what had been a slow-moving company.

> He changed reporting lines so more managers talked directly to him. Then he forbade participants from reading prepared reports word-for-word in meetings, as had been customary. . . .
>
> To assess talent, he grilled about 40 senior managers on the details of their jobs, discussing issues from reinsurance schemes to the chances of getting business from Toyota Motor Corp. . . .
>
> Mr. Khosrowshahi is prodding managers to identify solutions as well as problems, and urging employees to take more initiative. Early on, he solicited volunteers to develop new-product ideas. . . .
>
> [Yasunobu] Aoki's team was asked to create a new auto-insurance policy. . . . When Mr. Aoki presented the plan to a Fuji committee including Mr. Khosrowshahi, he was taken aback by their tough questions.
>
> "That's when I realized this wasn't a game," says Mr. Aoki.[55]

Bijan Khosrowshahi, CEO of Fuji Fire and Marine Insurance, uses both transactional and transformational leadership to influence his followers. His leadership is credited with increased financial performance for the firm. Would you like to work for Mr. Khosrowshahi? Why?

In contrast, **transformational leaders** "engender trust, seek to develop leadership in others, exhibit self-sacrifice and serve as moral agents, focusing themselves and followers on objectives that transcend the more immediate needs of the work group."[56] Transformational leaders can produce significant organizational change and results because this form of leadership fosters higher levels of intrinsic motivation, trust, commitment, and loyalty from followers than does transactional leadership. That said, however, it is important to note that transactional leadership is an essential prerequisite to effective leadership and that the best leaders learn to display both transactional and transformational leadership to various degrees. In support of this proposition, research reveals that transformational leadership leads to superior performance when it augments or adds to transactional leadership.[57] Let us return to the example of Fuji's Bijan Khosrowshahi to see how he augmented transactional leadership with transformational leadership so that employees would be inspired to work in new ways.

Transformational leadership

Transforms employees to pursue organizational goals over self-interests.

> Mr. Khosrowshahi also worked on boosting morale, scheduling lunches with employees and launching a training program with Tokyo's Hitotsubashi University. To commemorate Fuji's improved earnings last year, he gave each of its employees 10,000 yen, or around $95, accompanied by thank-you notes in envelopes decorated with his caricature.
>
> Hiroko Ikeno, an office worker who was a member of Mr. Aoki's team, says Mr. Khosrowshahi is so popular that some colleagues have taped his photo to their PCs.[58]

Khosrowshahi's leadership has helped Fuji's net premiums written (equivalent to revenues) rise for the first time in several years. We now turn our attention to examining the process by which transformational leadership influences followers.

LO.7 How Does Transformational Leadership Transform Followers?

Transformational leaders transform followers by creating changes in their goals, values, needs, beliefs, and aspirations. They accomplish this transformation by appealing to followers' self-concepts—namely their values and personal identity. Figure 16–4 presents a model of how leaders accomplish this transformation process.

Figure 16–4 shows that transformational leader behavior is first influenced by various individual and organizational characteristics. For example, research reveals that transformational leaders tend to have personalities that are more extraverted, agreeable, and proactive and less neurotic than nontransformational leaders.[59] Female leaders also were found to use transformational leadership more than male leaders.[60] It is important to note, however, that the relationship between personality traits and transformational leadership is relatively weak. This suggests that transformational leadership is less traitlike and more susceptible to managerial influence. This conclusion reinforces the notion that an individual's life experiences play a role in developing transformational leadership and that transformational leadership can be learned.[61] Finally, Figure 16–4 shows that organizational culture influences the extent to which leaders are transformational. Cultures that are adaptive and flexible rather than rigid and bureaucratic are more likely to create environments that foster the opportunity for transformational leadership to be exhibited.

Figure 16–4   *A Transformational Model of Leadership*

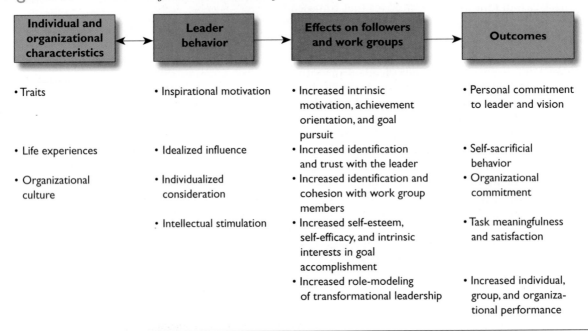

SOURCE: Based in part on D A Waldman and F J Yammarino, "CEO Charismatic Leadership: Levels-of-Management and Levels-of-Analysis Effects," *Academy of Management Review*, April 1999, pp 266–85; and B Shamir, R J House, and M B Arthur, "The Motivational Effects of Charismatic Leadership: A Self-Concept Based Theory," *Organization Science*, November 1993, pp 577–94.

Transformational leaders engage in four key sets of leader behavior (see Figure 16–4).[62] The first set, referred to as *inspirational motivation,* involves establishing an attractive vision of the future, the use of emotional arguments, and exhibition of optimism and enthusiasm. A vision is "a realistic, credible, attractive future for your organization."[63] According to Burt Nanus, a leadership expert, the "right" vision unleashes human potential because it serves as a beacon of hope and common purpose. It does this by attracting commitment, energizing workers, creating meaning in employees' lives, establishing a standard of excellence, promoting high ideals, and bridging the gap between an organization's present problems and its future goals and aspirations. Carl-Henric Svanberg, Ericsson's CEO, understands the importance of establishing an organization's vision. He noted that "[i]n a company this big, you can't just tell everyone, 'Turn left and work fast,' You have to share with them the vision you want to accomplish and get everybody on board and enthusiastic about it. When you get them to march in the same direction, you can really move mountains together."[64]

Idealized influence, the second set of leader behaviors, includes behaviors such as sacrificing for the good of the group, being a role model, and displaying high ethical standards. Home Depot's CEO Frank Blake exhibited idealized influence when he "accepted an annual pay package worth one-quarter of his predecessor's, and he is also finding creative ways to motivate employees, including giving merit awards for great customer service and assigning store workers more decision-making power."[65] Through their actions, transformational leaders like Frank Blake model the desired values, traits, beliefs, and behaviors needed to realize the vision.

The third set, *individualized consideration,* entails behaviors associated with providing support, encouragement, empowerment, and coaching to employees. These behaviors necessitate that leaders pay special attention to the needs of their followers and search for ways to help people develop and grow. You can do this by spending time talking with people about their interests and by identifying new learning opportunities for them. You also may want to serve as a mentor. Showing interest in people by remembering their names and previous conversations are other simple ways in which you can demonstrate consideration. Finally, treating people with respect and telling them the truth with compassion also represent examples of individualized consideration. The Real World/Real People feature on page 488 illustrates how Steve Harrison tries to implement this component of transformational leadership.

Intellectual stimulation, the fourth set of leadership behaviors, involves behaviors that encourage employees to question the status quo and to seek innovative and creative solutions to organizational problems. As you can see, this dimension of transformational leadership pertains to encouraging employee creativity, innovation, and problem solving. The group problem-solving techniques discussed in Chapter 12 can help to stimulate employees. Further, fostering an adhocracy culture—recall our discussion in Chapter 3—will assist in creating a work environment that promotes intellectual stimulation. You can use any of the cultural embedding techniques we discussed in Chapter 3 in this pursuit.

Research and Managerial Implications

Components of the transformational model of leadership have been the most widely researched leadership topic over the last decade. Overall, the relationships outlined in Figure 16–4 generally were supported by previous research. For example, transformational leader behaviors were positively associated with the extent to which

Steve Harrison Uses Business Decencies to Exhibit Individualized Consideration

Steve Harrison, chairman of Lee Hecht Harrison, says leaders can improve a company's culture by using business decencies—gestures "offered without expectation of reward" that show respect for and interest in others. The most effective decencies are actionable (that is, behavior, not just a warm feeling), tangible (something that can be observed or that changes the environment in an observable way), pragmatic (making business sense), affordable (immediately and in terms of setting a precedent), replicable (so others can imitate it), and sustainable (generating goodwill for the long haul).

Harrison offers a few examples:

- Rearrange seating at meetings to dissolve barriers and make it easier to connect with attendees.
- Write one thank-you note on paper or via e-mail each day.
- Give praise in public, criticism in private.
- Take time to talk to receptionists, administrative assistants, and maintenance people.
- Acknowledge the family, friends, and outside interests of people who work for you.
- Convey bad news in person.
- Make yourself easily accessible by having regular open office hours.

Would you like to work for Steve?

SOURCE: Based on S Harrison, "Deliberate Acts of Decency," *HR Magazine*, July 2007, pp 97–99 (list quoted from p 99).

Improving company culture can be easy as introducing yourself to the new receptionist.

---

employees identified with both their leaders and immediate work groups.[66] Followers of transformational leaders also were found to set goals that were consistent with those of the leader, to possess values that were aligned with their manager, to have more positive feelings about the work environment, and to be more highly committed to supporting organizational changes.[67] With respect to the direct relationship between transformational leadership and work outcomes, a meta-analysis of 49 studies indicated that transformational leadership was positively associated with measures of leadership effectiveness and employees' job satisfaction.[68] However, recent research suggests that it is important to use all the forms of transformational leadership. Restaurant managers who used transformational leadership obtained more employee ideas for improvement if they communicated they were open to new ideas.[69] You can probably imagine that if your boss conveyed a passion only for his or her own vision, you might actually be less eager to share your ideas; the same thing seems to have happened in the restaurants studied. At the organizational level, a second meta-analysis demonstrated that transformational leadership was positively correlated with organizational measures of effectiveness.[70]

These results underscore four important managerial implications. First, the best leaders are not just transformational; they are both transactional and transformational, and they avoid a laissez-faire or "wait-and-see" style. This conclusion was reinforced by results from a recent meta-analysis. Findings demonstrated that transactional leadership was positively correlated with followers' job satisfaction, satisfaction with the leader, and motivation as well as group and organizational performance and measures of a leader's effectiveness. The opposite pattern was found for laissez-faire leadership.[71]

Second, transformational leadership not only affects individual-level outcomes like job satisfaction, organizational commitment, and performance, but it also influences group dynamics and group-level outcomes. Managers can thus use the four types of transformational leadership shown in Figure 16–4 as a vehicle to improve group dynamics and work-unit outcomes. This is important in today's organizations because most employees do not work in isolation. Rather, people tend to rely on the input and collaboration of others, and many organizations are structured around teams. The key point to remember is that transformational leadership transforms individuals as well as teams and work groups. We encourage you to use this to your advantage.

Third, employees at any level in an organization can be trained to be more transactional and transformational.[72] This reinforces the organizational value of developing and rolling out a combination of transactional and transformational leadership training for all employees. These programs, however, should be based on an overall corporate philosophy that constitutes the foundation of leadership development.

Fourth, transformational leaders can be ethical or unethical. Whereas ethical transformational leaders enable employees to enhance their self-concepts, unethical ones select or produce obedient, dependent, and compliant followers. Top management can create and maintain ethical transformational leadership by

1. Creating and enforcing a clearly stated code of ethics.
2. Recruiting, selecting, and promoting people who display ethical behavior.
3. Developing performance expectations around the treatment of employees—these expectations can then be assessed in the performance appraisal process.
4. Training employees to value diversity.
5. Identifying, rewarding, and publicly praising employees who exemplify high moral conduct.[73]

go to the Web for the Group Exercise: Exhibiting Leadership within the Context of Running a Meeting

Additional Perspectives on Leadership

This section examines four additional perspectives on leadership: leader–member exchange theory, shared leadership, servant-leadership, and a follower perspective.

LO.8 The Leader–Member Exchange (LMX) Model of Leadership

The leader–member exchange model of leadership revolves around the development of dyadic relationships between managers and their direct reports. This model is quite different from those previously discussed in that it focuses on the

to the point

What are the key conclusions regarding the leader–member exchange model of leadership, shared leadership, servant-leadership, and the role of being a follower?

quality of relationships between managers and subordinates as opposed to the behaviors or traits of either leaders or followers. It also is different in that it does not assume that leader behavior is characterized by a stable or average leadership style as do the previously discussed models. In other words, most models of leadership assume a leader treats all employees in about the same way. In contrast, the LMX model is based on the assumption that leaders develop unique one-to-one relationships with each of the people reporting to them. Behavioral scientists call this sort of relationship a *vertical dyad.* The forming of vertical dyads is said to be a naturally occurring process, resulting from the leader's attempt to delegate and assign work roles. As a result of this process, two distinct types of leader–member exchange relationships are expected to evolve.[74]

In-group exchange

A partnership characterized by mutual trust, respect, and liking.

One type of leader–member exchange is called the **in-group exchange.** In this relationship, leaders and followers develop a partnership characterized by reciprocal influence, mutual trust, respect and liking, and a sense of common fates. In the second type of exchange, referred to as an **out-group exchange,** leaders are characterized as overseers who fail to create a sense of mutual trust, respect, or common fate.[75]

Out-group exchange

A partnership characterized by a lack of mutual trust, respect, and liking.

Research Findings
If the leader–member exchange model is correct, there should be a significant relationship between the type of leader–member exchange and job-related outcomes. Research supports this prediction. For example, a positive leader–member exchange was positively associated with job satisfaction, job performance, commitment to organizational change, trust between managers and employees, work climate, willingness to help coworkers, and satisfaction with leadership.[76] Results from a recent meta-analysis of 50 studies involving 9,324 people also revealed a moderately strong, positive relationship between LMX and organizational citizenship behaviors—recall our discussion in Chapter 6.[77] As you might imagine, positive LMXs were found to predict not only turnover but also career outcomes, such as promotability, salary level, and receipt of bonuses, over a seven-year period.[78] Finally, studies also have identified a variety of variables that influence the quality of an LMX. For example, LMX was related to personality similarity and demographic similarity.[79]

Managerial Implications
There are three important implications associated with the LMX model of leadership. First, leaders are encouraged to establish high-performance expectations for all of their direct reports because setting high-performance standards fosters high-quality LMXs. Second, because personality and demographic similarity between leaders and followers is associated with higher LMXs, managers need to be careful that they don't create a homogeneous work environment in the spirit of having positive relationships with their direct reports. Our discussion of diversity in Chapter 2 clearly documented that there are many positive benefits of having a diverse workforce. The third implication pertains to those of us who find ourselves in a poor LMX. A management consultant offers the following tips for improving the quality of leader–member exchanges.[80]

1. Stay focused on your department's goals and remain positive about your ability to accomplish your goals. An unsupportive boss is just another obstacle to be overcome.

2. Do not fall prey to feeling powerless, and empower yourself to get things done.

3. Exercise the power you have by focusing on circumstances you can control and avoid dwelling on circumstances you cannot control.

4. Work on improving your relationship with your manager. Begin by examining the level of trust between the two of you and then try to improve it by frequently and effectively communicating. You can also increase trust by following through on your commitments and achieving your goals.

5. Use an authentic, respectful, and assertive approach to resolve differences with your manager. It also is useful to use a problem-solving approach when disagreements arise.

go to the Web for the Self-Exercise: Assessing Your Leader–Member Exchange

LO.9 Shared Leadership

A pair of OB scholars noted that "there is some speculation, and some preliminary evidence, to suggest that concentration of leadership in a single chain of command may be less optimal than shared leadership responsibility among two or more individuals in certain task environments."[81] This perspective is quite different from the previous theories and models discussed in this chapter, which assume that leadership is a vertical, downward-flowing process. In contrast, the notion of shared leadership is based on the idea that people need to share information and collaborate to get things done at work. This in turn underscores the need for employees to adopt a horizontal process of influence or leadership. **Shared leadership** is defined as "a dynamic, interactive influence process among individuals in groups for which the objective is to lead one another to the achievement of group or organizational goals or both. This influence process often involves peer, or lateral, influence and at other times involves upward or downward hierarchical influence."[82] The concept of shared leadership was first discussed in Chapter 11 when we reviewed the characteristics of high-performing teams. You may recall that *shared responsibility* is one of the eight attributes associated with high-performing teams.

Shared leadership is most likely to be needed when people work in teams, when people are involved in complex projects, and when people are doing knowledge work—work that requires voluntary contributions of intellectual capital by skilled professionals. Shared leadership also is beneficial when people are working on tasks or projects that require interdependence and creativity.[83] Despite these recommendations, it is important to remember that people vary in the preference for shared leadership. Some of these differences are culturally based (recall our discussion in Chapter 4). For example, we conducted a consulting project with a manufacturing company in Portugal and realized that many employees preferred a directive rather than collaborative approach toward decision making and leadership.

The concept of shared leadership is taking hold at the highest levels in organizations. We are seeing more and more cases in which a CEO and another executive, such as a chief operating officer or chief financial officer, share the overall responsibilities of running the business. A simple way to make this work is for one leader to focus on internal matters while the other is concerned with external issues. Organizations like Goldman Sachs, Adobe, and PepsiCo are using this form of leadership because they find that two people are more likely to possess the varied abilities that are needed to run an organization. The application of shared leadership in this manner also helps organizations build a leadership pipeline for executive-level positions.

Shared leadership
Simultaneous, ongoing, mutual influence process in which people share responsibility for leading.

Table 16−6   *Key Questions and Answers to Consider When Developing Shared Leadership*

KEY QUESTIONS	ANSWERS
What task characteristics call for shared leadership?	Tasks that are highly *interdependent.* Tasks that require a great deal of *creativity.* Tasks that are highly *complex.*
What is the role of the leader in developing shared leadership?	*Designing the team,* including clarifying purpose, securing resources, articulating vision, selecting members, and defining team processes. *Managing the boundaries* of the team.
How can organizational systems facilitate the development of shared leadership?	*Training and development systems* can be used to prepare both designated leaders and team members to engage in shared leadership. *Reward systems* can be used to promote and reward shared leadership. *Cultural systems* can be used to articulate and to demonstrate the value of shared leadership.
What vertical and shared leadership behaviors are important to team outcomes?	*Directive leadership* can provide task-focused directions. *Transactional leadership* can provide both personal and material rewards based on key performance metrics. *Transformational leadership* can stimulate commitment to a team vision, emotional engagement, and fulfillment of higher-order needs. *Empowering leadership* can reinforce the importance of self-motivation.
What are the ongoing responsibilities of the vertical leader?	The vertical leader needs to be able to step in and *fill voids* in the team. The vertical leader needs to continue to *emphasize the importance of the shared leadership approach,* given the task characteristics facing the team.

SOURCE: From C L Pearce, "The Future of Leadership: Combining Vertical and Shared Leadership to Transform Knowledge Work," *Academy of Management Executive: The Thinking Manager's Source,* February 2004, p 48. Copyright © 2004 by The Academy of Management. Reproduced by permission of The Academy of Management via Copyright Clearance Center.

Researchers are just now beginning to explore the process of shared leadership, and results are promising. For example, shared leadership in teams was positively associated with group cohesion, group citizenship, and group effectiveness.[84] Table 16–6 contains a list of key questions and answers that managers should consider when determining how they can develop shared leadership.

Servant-leadership

Focuses on increased service to others rather than to oneself.

Servant-Leadership

Servant-leadership is more a philosophy of managing than a testable theory. The term *servant-leadership* was coined by Robert Greenleaf in 1970. Greenleaf believes that great leaders act as servants, putting the needs of others, including employees, customers, and community, as their first priority. **Servant-leadership** focuses on increased service to others rather than to oneself.[85] Because the focus of servant-leadership is serving others over self-interest, servant-leaders are less likely to engage in self-serving behaviors that hurt others. Embedding servant-leadership into an organization's culture requires actions as well as words. For example, Jack Windolf, CEO of Bollinger Insurance Solutions in New Jersey, took his bonus of $500,000 and distributed $434,000 of it in $1,000 bonus checks to all of the company's 434 employees.[86]

According to Jim Stuart, cofounder of the leadership circle in Tampa, Florida, "[l]eadership derives naturally from a commitment to service. You know that you're practicing servant-leadership if your followers become wiser, healthier, more autonomous—and more likely to become servant-leaders themselves."[87] Servant-leadership is not a quick-fix approach to leadership. Rather, it is a long-term, transformational approach to life and work.

Servant-leaders have the characteristics listed in Table 16–7. An example of someone with these characteristics is Sam Palmisano, chairman and CEO of IBM. Here is what he had to say about his approach to leadership:

Table 16–7   *Characteristics of the Servant-Leader*

SERVANT-LEADERSHIP CHARACTERISTICS	DESCRIPTION
1. *Listening*	Servant-leaders focus on listening to identify and clarify the needs and desires of a group.
2. *Empathy*	Servant-leaders try to empathize with others' feelings and emotions. An individual's good intentions are assumed even when he or she performs poorly.
3. *Healing*	Servant-leaders strive to make themselves and others whole in the face of failure or suffering.
4. *Awareness*	Servant-leaders are very self-aware of their strengths and limitations.
5. *Persuasion*	Servant-leaders rely more on persuasion than positional authority when making decisions and trying to influence others.
6. *Conceptualization*	Servant leaders take the time and effort to develop broader based conceptual thinking. Servant-leaders seek an appropriate balance between a short-term, day-to-day focus and a long-term, conceptual orientation.
7. *Foresight*	Servant-leaders have the ability to foresee future outcomes associated with a current course of action or situation.
8. *Stewardship*	Servant-leaders assume that they are stewards of the people and resources they manage.
9. *Commitment to the growth of people*	Servant-leaders are committed to people beyond their immediate work role. They commit to fostering an environment that encourages personal, professional, and spiritual growth.
10. *Building community*	Servant-leaders strive to create a sense of community both within and outside the work organization.

SOURCE: These characteristics and descriptions were derived from L C Spears, "Introduction: Servant-Leadership and the Greenleaf Legacy," in *Reflections on Leadership: How Robert K Greenleaf's Theory of Servant-Leadership Influenced Today's Top Management Thinkers,* ed L C Spears (New York: John Wiley & Sons, 1995), pp 1–14.

Over the course of my IBM career I've observed many CEOs, heads of state, and others in positions of great authority. I've noticed that some of the most effective leaders don't make themselves the center of attention. They are respectful. They listen. This is an appealing personal quality, but it's also an effective leadership attribute. Their selflessness makes the people around them comfortable. People open up, speak up, contribute. They give those leaders their very best.[88]

Not only do employees *like* servent-leaders, like Sam Palmisano of IBM, but research suggests they work hard for them too.

Researchers have just begun to develop measures of servant-leadership and to examine relationships between this type of leadership and various outcomes. In support of Greenleaf's ideas, servant-leadership was found to be positively associated with employees' performance, organizational commitment, job satisfaction, creativity, helping behaviors, and perceptions of justice. Servant-leadership also was negatively related to counterproductive work behavior.[89] These results suggest that managers would be well served by using the servant-leadership characteristics shown in Table 16–7.

LO.10 The Role of Followers in the Leadership Process

All of the previous theories discussed in this chapter have been leader-centric. That is, they focused on understanding leadership effectiveness from the leader's point of view. We conclude this chapter by discussing the role of followers in the leadership process. Although very little research has been devoted to this topic, it is an important issue to consider because the success of both leaders and followers is contingent on the dynamic relationship among the people involved.[90]

We begin our discussion by noting that both leaders and followers are closely linked. You cannot lead without having followers, and you cannot follow without having leaders. The point is that each needs the other, and the quality of the relationship determines how we behave as followers. This is why it is important for both leaders and followers to focus on developing a mutually rewarding and beneficial relationship.

Followers vary in terms of the extent to which they commit, comply, and resist a leader's influence attempts. For example, one researcher identified three types of followers: helpers, independents, and rebels. *"Helpers* show deference and comply with the leadership; *independents* distance themselves from the leadership and show less compliance; and *rebels* show divergence from the leader and are at least compliant. Among other types of followers, moderate in compliance, are *diplomats, partisans,* and *counselors."*[91] Leaders obviously want followers who are productive, reliable, honest, cooperative, proactive, and flexible. Leaders do not benefit from followers who hide the truth, withhold information, fail to generate ideas, are unwilling to collaborate, provide inaccurate feedback, or are unwilling to take the lead on projects and initiatives.[92]

In contrast, research shows that followers seek, admire, and respect leaders who foster three emotional responses in others: Followers want organizational leaders

Jack and Suzy Welch Identify What Followers Can Expect from Leaders

First, it's reasonable to expect two candid performance appraisals a year that make it absolutely clear how you're doing relative to your peers and ambitions. . . . But no boss is doing his job properly if he's not letting each of his people know where they stand in constructive detail. . . .

Second, it's reasonable to expect a boss who doesn't play favorites. Little else has the power to enervate an organization like a boss who has an "in-group" and an "out-group," like some kind of middle school "mean girl." Such bosses invariably spawn politicking among colleagues who need to trust each other in order to share information, generate ideas, or simply get anything done. So if your boss is poisoning the workplace with favoritism, you shouldn't chalk it up to business as usual. It's not.

Third, it's reasonable to expect a boss who doesn't abandon you in your hour of need. We have a friend, "Carol," whose boss once asked her to present a proposal at a meeting with the organization's executive team. Carol dutifully complied, but when the executives shook their heads, Carol's boss abandoned her, even throwing up her hands as if she found her own idea annoying. Such I-don't-know-you behavior is the hallmark of a manager who feels vulnerable in his or her own position—or is just a jerk.

Fourth, it's reasonable to expect a boss who delivers outsize rewards for outsize performance. We realize that it may sound crazy to be talking about boosting compensation during recessionary times. But any good boss understands how important—and how motivating—it is to differentiate. And very good bosses refuse to resort to the old line hauled out in every downturn: "You were terrific, but this is all I could get you from upstairs."

Finally and most important, it's reasonable to expect a boss who demonstrates integrity. It's awful to go to work each day wondering if your boss is shading the truth, adding spin to his real beliefs, or violating company values. So hold tight to this expectation.

Do you have any expectations that go beyond this list? What are they?

SOURCE: Excerpted from J Welch and S Welch, "An Employee Bill of Rights," *BusinessWeek*, March 16, 2009, p 72.

---

to create feelings of *significance* (what one does at work is important and meaningful), *community* (a sense of unity encourages people to treat others with respect and dignity and to work together in pursuit of organizational goals), and *excitement* (people are engaged and feel energy at work).[93] The Real World/Real People feature above takes follower desires one step further and recommends five key leadership behaviors that followers should expect to receive from their managers. What then can followers do to enhance the achievement of these mutual expectations?

A pair of OB experts developed a four-step process for followers to use in managing the leader–follower relationship.[94] First, it is critical for followers to understand their boss. Followers should attempt to gain an appreciation for their manager's leadership style, interpersonal style, goals, expectations, pressures, and strengths and weaknesses. One way of doing this is to ask your manager to answer the following seven questions:[95]

1. How would you describe your leadership style? Does your style change when you are under pressure?
2. When would you like me to approach you with questions or information? Are there any situations that are off limits (e.g., a social event)?
3. How do you want me to communicate with you?
4. How do you like to work?
5. Are there behaviors or attitudes that you will not tolerate? What are they?
6. What is your approach toward giving feedback?
7. How can I help you?

Second, followers need to understand their own style, needs, goals, expectations, and strengths and weaknesses.[96] The next step entails conducting a gap analysis between the understanding a follower has about his or her boss and the understanding the follower has about him- or herself. With this information in mind, followers are ready to proceed to the final step of developing and maintaining a relationship that fits both parties' needs and styles.

This final step requires followers to build on mutual strengths and to adjust or accommodate the leader's divergent style, goals, expectations, and weaknesses.[97] For example, a follower might adjust his or her style of communication in response to the boss's preferred method for receiving information. Other adjustments might be made in terms of decision making. If the boss prefers a participative approach, then followers should attempt to involve their manager in all decisions regardless of the follower's decision-making style—recall our discussion of decision-making styles in Chapter 12. Good use of time and resources is another issue for followers to consider. Most managers are pushed for time, energy, and resources and are more likely to appreciate followers who save rather than cost them time and energy. Followers should not use up their manager's time discussing trivial matters.

There are two final issues to consider. First, a follower may not be able to accommodate a leader's style, expectations, or weaknesses and may have to seek a transfer or quit his or her job to reconcile the discrepancy. We recognize that there are personal and ethical trade-offs that one may not be willing to make when managing the leader–follower relationship. Second, we can all enhance our boss's leadership effectiveness and our employer's success by becoming better followers. Remember, it is in an individual's best interest to be a good follower because leaders need and want competent employees.

Summary of Key Concepts

1. *Define the term* leadership, *and explain the difference between leading and managing.* Leadership is defined as a process in which an individual influences a group of individuals to achieve a common goal. Although leadership and management overlap, each entails a unique set of activities or functions. Managers typically perform functions associated with planning, investigating, organizing, and control, and leaders deal with the interpersonal aspects of a manager's job. Table 16–2 summarizes the differences between leading and managing. All told, organizational success requires a combination of effective leadership and management.

2. *Review trait theory research and the takeaways from this theoretical perspective.* Historical leadership research did not support the notion that effective leaders possessed unique traits from followers. More recent research showed that effective leaders possessed the following traits: task competence, interpersonal competence, intuition, traits of character, biophysical traits, and personal traits. In contrast, bad leaders displayed the following characteristics:

incompetence, rigid, intemperate, callous, corrupt, insular, and evil. Research also demonstrated that men and women exhibited different styles of leadership. The takeaways from trait theory are that (*a*) we can no longer ignore the implications of leadership traits; traits influence leadership effectiveness; (*b*) organizations may want to include personality and trait assessments into their selection and promotion processes; and (*c*) management development programs can be used to enhance employees' leadership traits.

3. *Explain behavioral styles theory and its takeaways.* The thrust of behavioral styles theory is to identify the leader behaviors that directly affect work-group effectiveness. Researchers at Ohio State uncovered two key leadership behaviors: consideration and initiating structure. These behaviors are similar to the employee-centered and job-centered behaviors uncovered by researchers at the University of Michigan. The takeaways from this theoretical perspective are as follows: (*a*) leaders are made, not born; (*b*) there is no one best style of leadership; (*c*) the effectiveness of a particular style depends on the situation at hand;

and (*d*) managers are encouraged to concentrate on improving the effective execution of their leader behaviors.

4. *Explain, according to Fiedler's contingency model, how leadership style interacts with situational control, and discuss the takeaways from this model.* Fiedler believes leader effectiveness depends on an appropriate match between leadership style and situational control. Leaders are either task motivated or relationship motivated. Situation control is composed of leader–member relations, task structure, and position power. Task-motivated leaders are effective under situations of both high and low control. Relationship-motivated leaders are more effective when they have moderate situational control. The three takeaways are (*a*) leadership effectiveness goes beyond traits and behaviors, (*b*) leaders are unlikely to be successful in all situations, and (*c*) leaders need to modify their style to fit a situation.

5. *Discuss House's revised path–goal theory and its practical takeaways.* There are three key changes in the revised path–goal theory. Leaders now are viewed as exhibiting eight categories of leader behavior (see Table 16–5) instead of four. In turn, the effectiveness of these styles depends on various employee characteristics and environmental factors. Second, leaders are expected to spend more effort fostering intrinsic motivation through empowerment. Third, leadership is not limited to people in managerial roles. Rather, leadership is shared among all employees within an organization. There are three takeaways: (*a*) effective leaders possess and use more than one style of leadership, (*b*) the theory offers specific suggestions for how leaders can help employees, and (*c*) managers are advised to modify their leadership style to fit relevant contingency factors.

6. *Describe the difference between laissez-fair, transactional, and transformational leadership.* Laissez-faire leadership is the absence of leadership. It represents a general failure to take responsibility for leading. Transactional leadership focuses on clarifying employees' role and task requirements and providing followers with positive and negative rewards contingent on performance. Transformational leaders motivate employees to pursue organizational goals above their own self-interests. Transactional and transformational leadership are both important for organizational success.

7. *Discuss how transformational leadership transforms followers and work groups.* Individual characteristics and organizational culture are key precursors of transformational leadership, which is comprised of four sets of leader behavior. These leader behaviors in turn positively affect followers' and work-group goals, values, beliefs, aspirations, and motivation. These positive effects are then associated with a host of preferred outcomes.

8. *Explain the leader–member exchange model of leadership.* The LMX model revolves around the development of dyadic relationships between managers and their direct reports. These leader–member exchanges qualify as either in-group or out-group relationships. Research supports this model of leadership.

9. *Review the concept of shared leadership and the principles of servant-leadership.* Shared leadership involves a simultaneous, ongoing, mutual influence process in which individuals share responsibility for leading regardless of formal roles and titles. This type of leadership is most likely to be needed when people work in teams, when people are involved in complex projects, and when people are doing knowledge work. Shared leadership also is beneficial when people are working on tasks or projects that require interdependence and creativity. Servant-leadership is more a philosophy than a testable theory. It is based on the premise that great leaders act as servants, putting the needs of others, including employees, customers, and community, as their first priority.

10. *Describe the follower's role in the leadership process.* Followers can use a four-step process for managing the leader–follower relationship. Followers need to understand their boss and themselves. They then conduct a gap analysis between the understanding they have about their boss and themselves. The final step requires followers to build on mutual strengths and to adjust or accommodate the leader's divergent style, goals, expectations, and weaknesses.

Key Terms

Indra Nooyi Uses the Full Range of Leadership[98]

Indra Nooyi is an entirely different kind of CEO, a product of her native India as well as of PepsiCo's family-values approach to grooming CEOs. She is not hung up on pay. She's not shy about asking for help when she needs it. She's 52 years old and does not plan for this job to be her last. Her friend Henry Kissinger predicts that it's only a matter of time before she is plucked for a big Washington post, possibly a cabinet job, and Nooyi acknowledges that at some point, she'd like that. She's cosmopolitan, rigorously educated, and a strategic thinker—her background is Boston Consulting Group—much more interested in the burgeoning markets in Russia and China than in the noisy U.S. cola wars.

Since becoming CEO, she has reorganized PepsiCo to make it less fixated on the U.S. and broadened the power structure by doubling her executive team to 29. . . . She has created a motto—"Performance With Purpose"—that puts a positive spin on how she wants PepsiCo to do business both at home and abroad.

It essentially boils down to balancing the profit motive with making healthier snacks, striving for a net-zero impact on the environment, and taking care of your workforce. "If all you want is to screw this company down tight and get double-digit earnings growth and nothing else, then I'm the wrong person," she says. "Companies today are bigger than many economies. We are little republics. We are engines of efficiency. If companies don't do [responsible] things, who is going to? Why not start making change now?" . . .

Indra Krishnamurthy Nooyi has one of those incredible, impeccable track records. She grew up in Chennai (formerly Madras), on the southeast coast of India, the daughter of an accountant and a stay-at-home mother who "encouraged us but held us back, told us we could rule the country as long as we kept the home fires burning," she says. Her grandfather, a retired judge, scrutinized report cards, presided over homework, and in his later years prepared her in advance for all the theorems in her geometry book to be sure she'd be able to excel if he were to die before the school year ended. Every night at dinner her mother would present a world problem to Nooyi and her sister and have them compete to solve it as if they were a President or Prime Minister. Though her family is Hindu, Nooyi attended a Catholic school, was an avid debater, played cricket, badgered her parents (and the nuns) until she was allowed to play the guitar, and then formed an all-girl rock band—the first ever at the Holy Angels Convent. . . .

One of Nooyi's most stunning talents is the art of suasion. She can rouse an audience and rally them around something as mind-numbing as a new companywide software installation. Her new motto, "Performance With Purpose," is both a means of "herding the organization" and of presenting PepsiCo globally. Because these days, she knows, you can't take even an emerging market for granted. . . .

Nooyi sells her ideas with a famous intensity. Her colleagues say she "brings her whole self" to the office. She insists that everybody's birthday is celebrated with a cake . . . and everyone is forever 35. Her karaoke machine is the ubiquitous party game at every PepsiCo gathering. She talks about being a mother. In December one executive recalls how Nooyi described to her whole team what it felt like to be a soccer mom whose week it was to bring the treats. You get a very specific list. You can't have nuts. You can't have wheat. The situation confounds the CEO mom, she confesses, urging them to "make it easy for me so I don't have to think. We can do this. We already have the products."

Just as she was held to very high standards in her youth, she expects everyone around her to measure up. She has red, green, and purple pens and uses them liberally to mark up everything that crosses her desk. "My scribbles are legendary—legendary," she says with a twinkle. Like "I have never seen such gross incompetence." Or " 'This is unacceptable,' and I underline 'unacceptable' three times," she says. She's joking, but she gets her point across. One of her so-called love letters once scared some secretaries so badly that she had to go assure them that their bosses were not about to lose their jobs.

"She challenges you," says Tim Minges, president of the Asia Pacific region. When his team couldn't find an inexpensive alternative to palm oil for its products in Thailand last year, she kept pushing and pushing, saying, "I hear you, I hear you, so what's the right solution?" until they came up with one: rice bran oil. "But don't try to delegate up, because she will bounce it right back in your face," he says. . . .

With her team, there's nothing remote about Nooyi. She is part schoolmarm, part mother hen. She once told Hugh Johnston, who worked for her in corporate strategy, that he was dressed like a bum. At the time he was helping roll out the company's IT program, and he replied, "Indra, these are IT people; this is what we do. We don't go out of the building." When he moved to headquarters, she told him where to shop, and he has acquired a whole new wardrobe. She knows she is demanding, and she worries about it. She throws dinners for members of her team and their spouses, including Q&A sessions in which she insists on getting questions from the spouses and won't sit down until she does.

She appreciates the support from families, she says, because her career has been tough on her own family.

Questions for Discussion

1. Use Table 16–2 to evaluate the extent to which Indra Nooyi displayed the characteristics associated with being a good leader and good manager.

2. Which different positive and negative leadership traits and styles were displayed by Ms. Nooyi? Cite examples.

3. To what extent does Indra display situational approaches toward leadership. Explain.

4. Which of the four types of transformational leadership behavior were displayed by Ms. Nooyi?

5. Would you like to work for Indra Nooyi? Explain why or why not.

6. What did you learn about leadership from this case?

Ethical Dilemma

Should You Cover for a Laid-Off Friend?[99]

You manage a group of software developers for a large organization and several days ago had the difficult task of notifying a friend who works for the company that he is being laid off. Even though he has performed wonderfully in the past and you hate to see him go, your company lost a contract with a major client and thus his position has become obsolete.

The employee wants to build a house, and you're aware that he is 10 days away from closing on a loan for it. He has sold his previous home and now is living with his in-laws. He asks you for a favor: could you extend his employment just 10 more days so that he can qualify for his new home loan? Unfortunately, you don't have the authority to do so, and you tell him you can't help him.

He then tells you that the mortgage company will be calling sometime soon to get a verbal confirmation of his employment. The confirmation is an essential prerequisite if your friend is to obtain the loan for his new home. Would you, he asks, tell the mortgage company that he is still employed?

What Would You Do?

1. Tell the mortgage company your friend is still employed by the company. Your friend needs a break, and you are confident that he'll find a job in the near future.

2. Refuse to lie. It is unethical to falsify information regarding employment.

3. Simply avoid the mortgage company's phone call.

4. Invent other options. Discuss.

Web Resources

For study material and exercises that apply to this chapter, visit our Web site, **www.mhhe.com/kreitner**

Chapter 17

Organizational Design, Effectiveness, and Innovation

When you finish studying the material in this chapter, you should be able to:

LO.1 Describe the four characteristics common to all organizations, and explain the difference between closed and open systems.

LO.2 Define the term *learning organization*.

LO.3 Describe seven basic ways organizations are structured.

LO.4 Discuss Burns and Stalker's findings regarding mechanistic and organic organizations.

LO.5 Identify when each of the seven organization structures is the right fit.

LO.6 Describe the four generic organizational effectiveness criteria.

LO.7 Explain how managers can prevent organizational decline.

LO.8 Discuss the difference between innovation, invention, creativity, and integration.

LO.9 Review the myths about innovation.

LO.10 Explain the model of innovation.

Student Resources for Studying Chapter 17

The Web site for your text includes resources that will help you master the concepts in this chapter. As you read, you'll want to visit the site for these helpful tools:

- Your online Study Guide includes learning objectives, a chapter summary, a glossary of key terms, and discussion questions.
- Take a practice quiz and test your knowledge!
- Scroll through a PowerPoint presentation with key concepts for this chapter.

Your instructor might also direct you to the Web site for these exercises:

- Self-assessments that correspond with the chapter content and a Group Exercise.
- You'll also find Video Cases and Internet Exercises for this chapter online.

www.mhhe.com/kreitner

BusinessWeek Companies have long formed alliances and joint ventures. Recently, they've come together to swap employees, a practice Google and Procter & Gamble have experimented with to share expertise.

The next wave could be "federations." In such arrangements, companies can exchange much more than their knowledge, profits, or workers. They share access to parts of their info tech systems. Today the practice is common between such business partners as employers and their 401(k) providers.

But some tech experts believe federations could have a far broader impact when it comes to cross-company collaboration.

Frank Modruson, chief information officer at Accenture, says his company recently gave Microsoft employees access to its collaboration software. That means staff can find, chat with, instant message, or videoconference with any employee at the other company. Modruson says he has received eight requests from clients in the past month to set up a similar structure with Accenture, up from none in January.

Federating the same software between two companies is fairly simple. But opening up systems that involve multiple applications and dozens, if not hundreds, of companies is much more complex. That's not happening yet, but it should, says John Hagel, co-chairman of Deloitte's Center for Edge Innovation. Companies increasingly design products and run supply chains with large groups of specialized partners. "For the companies that can figure this out," says Hagel, "it's a massive opportunity."

And federated IT systems could be the building blocks for ad hoc ventures that pop up for specific projects. Accenture's chief scientist, Kishore Swaminathan, sees federation as a way to handle sudden spikes in demand or share data between agencies in criminal investigations. Ideally, he says, "it could be turned on and off instantly."[1]

FOR DISCUSSION

Why is the existence of federations growing?

Virtually every aspect of life is affected at least indirectly by some type of organization. We look to organizations to feed, clothe, house, educate, and employ us. Organizations attend to our needs for entertainment, police and fire protection, insurance, recreation, national security, transportation, news and information, legal assistance, and health care. Many of these organizations seek a profit; others do not. Some are extremely large; others are tiny mom-and-pop operations. Despite this mind-boggling diversity, modern organizations have one basic thing in common: they are the primary context for organizational behavior. As mentioned in Chapter 1, organizations are the chessboard upon which the game of organizational behavior is played. Therefore, present and future organizational members need a working knowledge of modern organizations to improve their chances of making the right moves.

The chapter opening vignette highlights some of the changes taking place in today's organizations. Federations of diverse organizations collaborating with each other to achieve an objective was unheard of five years ago. These types of changes are being fueled by a combination of globalization and information technology, which was discussed in Chapter 14.[2] As you will learn in this chapter, these driving forces have caused some organizations to dramatically change their operations and structure. Boeing is a good example.

> Since it was made available for sale in 2003, Boeing has sold 892 Dreamliners to 57 customers around the world. At a list price of $162 million, that's worth about $145 billion. Yet not a single Dreamliner has flown, and the 787 is more than a year behind schedule. One reason is that Boeing has been innovative to a fault. When it decided to engineer a new aircraft, the company also decided to engineer a new manufacturing process. That process includes dozens of partners around the globe that build and preassemble big pieces of the plane. Boeing's job is to manage this far-flung supply chain and to make sure that parts fit together flawlessly on the factory floor in Everett, Wash. That, too, is the future, but only if Boeing can figure out how to do it right.[3]

Time will tell whether or not Boeing's new manufacturing process and structure will define the future construction of commercial aviation.

The overall goal of this chapter is to provide you with a solid foundation for understanding how organizational design influences organizational effectiveness and innovation. We begin by defining the term *organization,* discussing important dimensions of organization charts, and contrasting views of organizations as closed or open systems. Our attention then turns to the various ways organizations are designed, from traditional divisions of work to more recent, popular ideas about lowering barriers between departments and companies. Next, we discuss the contingency approach to designing organizations. We then explore various criteria for assessing an organization's effectiveness, and conclude by discussing the topic of organizational innovation.

Organization

System of consciously coordinated activities of two or more people.

to the point

What are the four characteristics of organizational structure, and what are the key conclusions regarding closed and open systems and a learning organization?

LO.1 Organizations: Definition and Perspectives

As a necessary springboard for this chapter, we need to formally define the term *organization,* clarify the meaning of organization charts, and explore two open-system perspectives of organizations.

What Is an Organization?

According to Chester I Barnard's classic definition cited in Chapter 1, an **organization** is "a system of consciously coordinated activities or forces of two or more persons."[4] Embodied in the *conscious coordination* aspect of this definition are four common denominators of all organizations: coordination of effort, a common goal, division of labor, and a hierarchy of authority.[5] Organization theorists refer to these factors as the organization's *structure.*

Coordination of effort is achieved through formulation and enforcement of policies, rules, and regulations. Division of labor occurs when the common goal is pursued by individuals performing separate but related tasks. The hierarchy of authority, also called the chain of command, is a control mechanism dedicated to making sure the right people do the right things at the right time. Historically, managers have maintained the integrity of the hierarchy of authority by adhering to the unity of command principle. The **unity of command principle** specifies that each employee should report to only one manager. Otherwise, the argument goes, inefficiency would prevail because of conflicting orders and lack of personal accountability. (Indeed, these are problems in today's more fluid and flexible organizations based on innovations such as cross-functional, self-managed, and virtual teams.) Managers in the hierarchy of authority also administer rewards and punishments. When operating in concert, the four definitional factors—coordination of effort, a common goal, division of labor, and a hierarchy of authority—enable an organization to come to life and function.

Unity of command principle
Each employee should report to a single manager.

Organization Charts

An **organization chart** is a graphic representation of formal authority and division of labor relationships. To the casual observer, the term *organization chart* means the family tree–like pattern of boxes and lines posted on workplace walls. Within each box one usually finds the names and titles of current position holders. To organization theorists, however, organization charts reveal much more. The partial organization chart in Figure 17–1 reveals four basic dimensions of organizational structure: (1) hierarchy of authority (who reports to whom), (2) division of labor, (3) spans of control, and (4) line and staff positions.

Organization chart
Boxes-and-lines illustration showing chain of formal authority and division of labor.

Hierarchy of Authority   As Figure 17–1 illustrates, there is an unmistakable hierarchy of authority. Working from bottom to top, the 10 directors report to the two executive directors who report to the president who reports to the chief executive officer. Ultimately, the chief executive officer answers to the hospital's board of directors. The chart in Figure 17–1 shows strict unity of command up and down the line. A formal hierarchy of authority also delineates the official communication network and speaks volumes about compensation. Research shows that there is an increasing wage gap between layers over time. That is, the difference in pay between successive layers tends to increase over time.[6]

Division of Labor   In addition to showing the chain of command, the sample organization chart indicates extensive division of labor. Immediately below the hospital's president, one executive director is responsible for general administration while another is responsible for medical affairs. Each of these two specialities is further subdivided as indicated by the next layer of positions. At each successively lower level in the organization, jobs become more specialized.

Spans of Control   The **span of control** refers to the number of people reporting directly to a given manager.[7] Spans of control can range from narrow to wide. For example, the president in Figure 17–1 has a narrow span of control of two. (Staff assistants usually are not included in a manager's span of control.) The executive administrative director in Figure 17–1 has a wider span of control of five. Historically, spans of seven to ten people were considered best. More recently, however, corporate restructuring and improved communication technologies have

Span of control
The number of people reporting directly to a given manager.

Figure 17–1   *Sample Organization Chart for a Hospital (executive and director levels only)*

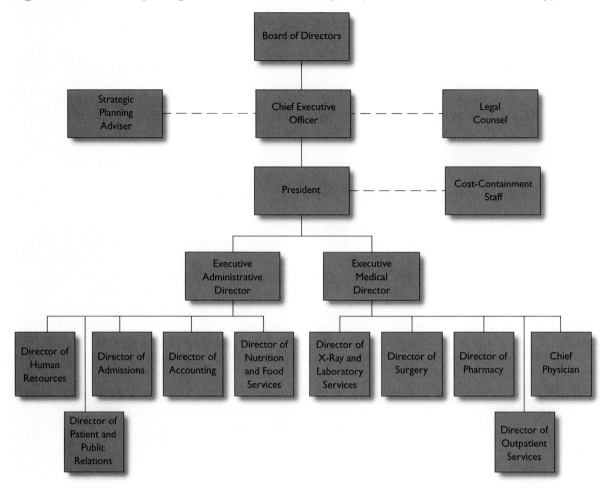

increased the typical span of control.[8] Despite years of debate, organization theorists and senior executives have not arrived at a consensus regarding the ideal span of control (see the Real World/Real People feature on page 505).

Generally, the narrower the span of control, the closer the supervision and the higher the administrative costs as a result of a higher manager-to-worker ratio. Recent emphasis on empowering employees and administrative efficiency dictates spans of control as wide as possible but guarding against inadequate supervision and lack of coordination. Wider spans also complement the trend toward greater worker autonomy and participation.

Staff personnel

Provide research, advice, and recommendations to line managers.

Line managers

Have authority to make organizational decisions.

Line and Staff Positions   The organization chart in Figure 17–1 also distinguishes between line and staff positions. Line managers such as the president, the two executive directors, and the various directors occupy formal decision-making positions within the chain of command. Line positions generally are connected by solid lines on organization charts. Dotted lines indicate staff relationships. **Staff personnel** do background research and provide technical advice and recommendations to their **line managers,** who have the authority to make decisions. For example, the cost-containment specialists in the sample organization chart merely advise the

Companies Have Different Views about the Optimum Span of Control

Consider Pepsico Inc.'s Gemesa cookie business in Mexico as a case in point. There, workers have been briefed on company goals and processes so that they do more themselves to keep production running smoothly. New pay systems reward productivity, quality, service and teamwork while penalizing underperformance. That promotes efficiency, Pepsico says, while letting managers function more as coaches of self-motivating teams.

Gemesa last year ran its factories with 56 employees per boss, Pepsico says, instead of the 12:1 ratio that prevailed in the mid-1990's. The changes have helped Gemesa improve its business results, the company adds. . . .

Not all companies are eager to give bosses more subordinates. Sun Microsystems Inc. prefers work teams of 10 people or fewer, says Ann Bamesberger, vice president, Open Work Services group, at the Santa Clara, Calif., computer company.

Sun lately has put more energy into redesigning work environments, so that teams can expand and contract more easily as projects evolve, says Ms. Bamesberger. Among those initiatives: better support for engineers who sometimes work from home and flexible seating so that growing teams can fit in new members without losing proximity.

One boss with more than two dozen people reporting to her is Cindy Zollinger, president of Cornerstone Research, a litigation-consulting firm.

"I don't really manage them in a typical way," Ms. Zollinger says. "They largely run themselves. I help them in dealing with obstacles they face, or in making the most of opportunities that they find."

Do you think an individual can effectively manage 24 employees? Explain.

SOURCE: Excerpted from G Anders, "Overseeing More Employees—with Fewer Managers," *The Wall Street Journal*, March 24, 2008, p B6.

---

president on relevant matters. Apart from supervising the work of their own staff assistants, they have no line authority over other organizational members. Modern trends such as cross-functional teams and matrix structures, which are discussed later in this chapter, are blurring the distinction between line and staff.

An Open-System Perspective of Organizations

To better understand how organizational models have evolved over the years, we need to know the difference between closed and open systems.[9] A **closed system** is said to be a self-sufficient entity. It is "closed" to the surrounding environment. In contrast, an **open system** depends on constant interaction with the environment for survival. The distinction between closed and open systems is a matter of degree.[10] Because every worldly system is partly closed and partly open, the key question is: How great a role does the environment play in the functioning of the system? For instance, a battery-powered clock is a relatively closed system. Once the battery is inserted, the clock performs its time-keeping function hour after hour until the battery goes dead. The human body, on the other hand, is a highly open system because it requires a constant supply of life-sustaining oxygen from the environment. Nutrients also are imported from the environment. Open systems are capable of self-correction, adaptation, and growth, thanks to characteristics such as homeostasis and feedback control.

Historically, management theorists downplayed the environment as they used closed-system thinking to characterize organizations as either well-oiled machines or highly disciplined military units. They believed rigorous planning and control would eliminate environmental uncertainty. But that proved unrealistic. Drawing upon the field of general systems theory that emerged during

Closed system
A relatively self-sufficient entity.

Open system
Organism that must constantly interact with its environment to survive.

Figure 17–2   *The Organization as an Open System*

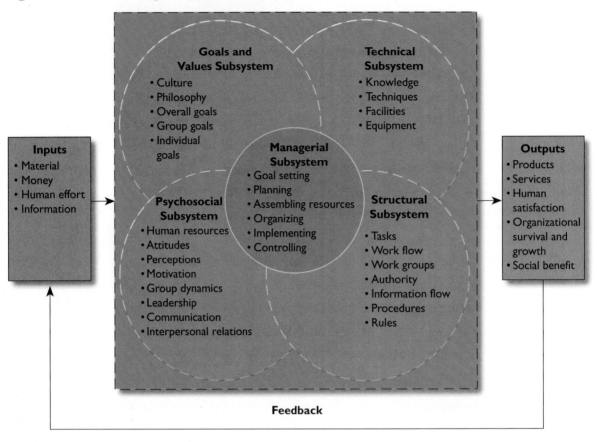

SOURCE: This model is a combination of Figures 5–2 and 5–3 in F E Kast and J E Rosenzweig, *Organization and Management: A Systems and Contingency Approach,* 4th ed (New York: McGraw-Hill, 1986), pp 112, 114. Copyright © 1986. Reprinted with permission of the McGraw-Hill Companies, Inc.

the 1950s, organization theorists suggested a more dynamic model for organizations.[11] The resulting open-system model likened organizations to the human body. Accordingly, the model in Figure 17–2 reveals the organization to be a living organism that transforms inputs into various outputs. The outer boundary of the organization is permeable. People, information, capital, and goods and services move back and forth across this boundary. Moreover, each of the five organizational subsystems—goals and values, technical, psychosocial, structural, and managerial—is dependent on the others. Feedback about such things as sales and customer satisfaction or dissatisfaction enables the organization to self-adjust and survive despite uncertainty and change. In effect, the organization is alive.

LO.2 Learning Organizations

In recent years, organization theorists have extended the open-system model by adding a "brain" to the "living body." Organizations are said to have human-like cognitive functions, such as the abilities to perceive and interpret, solve problems, and learn from experience. Today, managers read and hear a good deal about learning organizations and knowledge management (as discussed in Chapter 12).[12] Peter Senge, a professor at the Massachusetts Institute of Technology, popularized the term *learning organization* in his best-selling book *The Fifth Discipline.* He described a learning organization as "a group of people working together to collectively enhance their capacities to create results that they truly care about."[13] A practical interpretation of these ideas results in the following definition. A **learning organization** is one that proactively creates, acquires, and transfers knowledge and that changes its behavior on the basis of new knowledge and insights.[14]

Learning organization

Proactively creates, acquires, and transfers knowledge throughout the organization.

Learning organizations actively try to infuse their organizations with new ideas and information. They do this by constantly scanning their external environments, hiring new talent and expertise when needed, and devoting significant resources to train and develop their employees. Next, new knowledge must be transferred throughout the organization. Learning organizations strive to reduce structural, process, and interpersonal barriers to the sharing of information, ideas, and knowledge among organizational members. In support of this recommendation, recent research shows that organizational learning was significantly associated with leadership, organizational structure, and organizational culture.[15] Finally, behavior must change as a result of new knowledge. Learning organizations are results oriented. They foster an environment in which employees are encouraged to use new behaviors and operational processes to achieve corporate goals.

An expert recently proposed the following four-step process for developing a learning infrastructure:

> First, organizations that focus on execution-as-learning use the best knowledge obtainable (which is understood to be a moving target) to inform the design of specific process guidelines. Second, they enable their employees to collaborate by making information available when and where it's needed. Third, they routinely capture process data to discover how work is really being done. Finally, they study these data in an effort to find ways to improve.[16]

Employees at learning organizations collaborate with one another to come up with the best results.

Following this four-step process should encourage employees to view learning as a daily activity, thereby increasing overall levels of organizational learning.

L0.3 Organization Design in a Changing World

to the point
What are the similarities and differences between the seven basic ways organizations are structured?

Until a few decades ago, most management theorists thought about organizations' structures mainly in terms of how each organization arranged its hierarchy from top to bottom. More recently, many organizations have emphasized horizontal relationships to carry out entire processes or to operate with teams. In addition, some companies' managers have seen alternatives to working within the boundaries that have traditionally defined organizations. In this section, we look at seven types of structures that have resulted from each of these three points of view.[17]

Traditional Designs

Organizations defined by the traditional approach tended to have functional, divisional, and/or matrix structures. Each of these structures relied on the vertical hierarchy and attempted to define clear departmental boundaries and reporting relationships. Let us consider each type of structure.

Functional Structure   A functional structure groups people according to the business functions they perform, for example, manufacturing, marketing, and finance. A manager is responsible for the performance of each of these functions, and employees tend to identify strongly with their particular function, such as sales or engineering. The organization chart in Figure 17–1 illustrates a functional structure. Responsibility at this hospital is first divided into administrative and medical functions, and within each category, directors are responsible for each of the functions. This arrangement puts together people who are experts in the same or similar activities. Thus, as a small company grows and hires more production workers, salespeople, and accounting staff, it typically groups them together with a supervisor who understands their function.

Divisional Structure   In a divisional structure, the organization groups together activities related to outputs, such as type of product or type (or location) of customer. For example, General Electric has six businesses (major product divisions): GE Commercial Finance, GE Healthcare, GE Industrial, GE Infrastructure, GE Money, and NBC Universal. These major business areas are subdivided into either product or geographic divisions. GE Healthcare is divided into product divisions such as Clinical Systems and Diagnostic Imaging; and GE Money is divided into three geographic divisions: Americas; Asia Pacific; and Europe, Middle East, and Africa.[18] The people in a division can become experts at making a particular type of product or serving the particular needs of their customer group or geographic area. Typically, each division has a functional structure. Some organizations have concluded that using a functional or divisional structure divides people too much, ultimately creating silos within the organization. This in turn detracts from the extent to which employees collaborate and share best practices across functions. One way to address this problem while still focusing on hierarchy is to create a matrix structure.

Matrix Structure   Organizations use matrix structures when they need stronger horizontal alignment or cooperation in order to meet their goals. For example, Hachette Filipacchi Media, the world's largest magazine publisher, is restructuring its U.S. operations into a matrix structure. CEO Alain Lemarchand is doing this because he wants to create greater integration and collaboration between three chief brands of women's titles and the functions of editorial, ad sales, business development, and event marketing.[19] A matrix structure combines a vertical structure with an equally strong horizontal overlay. This generally combines functional and divisional chains of command to form a grid with two command structures, one shown vertically by function, and the other shown horizontally, by product line, brand, customer group, or geographic region. In the example shown in Figure 17–3, Ford might set up vice presidents for each functional group and project managers for each make of car. Employees would report to two managers: one in charge of the function they perform and the other in charge of the project they are working on.

Matrix organizations historically received a bad rap for being too complex and confusing. The reality is that it takes much more collaboration and integration to effectively implement this structure. Jay Galbraith, an expert on matrix structures, noted that matrix structures frequently fail because management fails to create complimentary and reinforcing changes to the organization's IT systems, human resource procedures (e.g., performance appraisals, rewards, selection criteria), planning and

Figure 17–3   *Matrix Structure*

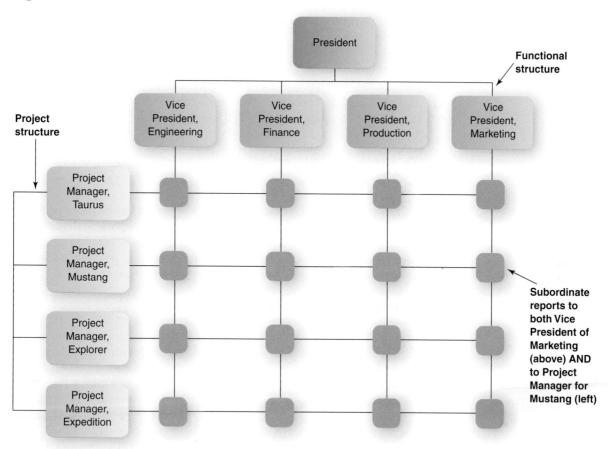

budgeting processes, organizational culture, internal processes, and so on.[20] He concluded that "organization structures do not fail; managements fail at implementation."[21] This type of structure increasingly is being used by companies that are expanding into internal markets.

Focus on Collaboration: Horizontal Design

The traditional approach of dividing up work according to functions, products, and customers is dissatisfying to managers who want to focus on bringing people together, without internal boundaries keeping them apart. If you want people to share knowledge and continually improve the way things are done, you need to create an environment in which collaboration feels easy and natural. Many organizations with this viewpoint have emphasized horizontal relationships among people who are working on shared tasks more than vertical relationships in a traditional organizational design.

This horizontal approach to organizational design tends to focus on work processes. A process consists of every task and responsibility needed to meet a customer need, such as developing a new product or filling a customer order. Completing a process requires input from people in different functions, typically organized into a cross-functional team (described in Chapter 11). Thus, teamwork is a feature of organizations designed horizontally. Two experts in organization design have identified five principles for designing a horizontal organization:

1. Organize around complete workflow processes rather than tasks.
2. Flatten hierarchy and use teams to manage everything.
3. Appoint process team leaders to manage internal team processes.
4. Let supplier and customer contact drive performance.
5. Provide required expertise from outside the team as required.[22]

Designs That Open Boundaries between Organizations

While the horizontal organization aims to break down barriers within organizations, some structures are based on the idea that not even barriers between organizations are always ideal. Sometimes organizations can perform better by creating structures in which they can pool their resources to work toward a shared goal. This strategic approach results in structures that are called hollow, modular, or virtual.

Hollow Structure   A hollow organization results from strategic application of the trend toward outsourcing. The organization's managers identify core competencies—functions the organization can do better and more profitably than other organizations. It then outsources noncore processes to vendors who can do them cheaper or faster. An athletic shoe company, for example, might decide that it can excel at developing new designs, owing to its design talent and knowledge of the market. Then it might find outsourcing partners to handle other activities such as manufacturing, order taking, shipping, and managing employee benefits. The more processes that are outsourced, the more the resulting organization is "hollow"—and focused on what it does best. Furniture company Herman Miller goes outside the organization for design expertise. CEO Brian Walker explains the advantages:

> This external network ensures that we are always taking a fresh look at problems faced by our customers without subjecting it to our own filters. If you have only an internal design staff, even an enormously talented one, you are inherently limited by their existing world view and experiences. Our ability to tap into a broader outside network lets us . . . get a fresh perspective on existing or emerging problems.[23]

Herman Miller also uses other organizations for manufacturing; Walker says the company is "more . . . an integrator than a manufacturer," which makes it less resistant to new product ideas because it doesn't have to change manufacturing processes itself.

A hollow structure is useful when an organization is faced with strong price competition and there are enough companies to perform the required outsourced processes.

Modular Structure   A modular organization, like a hollow organization, uses outsourcing. But instead of outsourcing processes, it outsources parts of a product, such as components of a jet or subroutines of a software program. The modular organization is responsible for ensuring that the parts meet quality requirements, that the parts arrive in a timely fashion, and that the organization is capable of efficiently combining the parts into the final whole. This design is useful when a company can identify product modules and create design interfaces that allow it to assemble parts into a working order. A well-known example is Boeing, in its production of the 787 Dreamliner. As previously mentioned, the delay of the Dreamliner is due to Boeing's difficulties in managing its far-flung supply chain and to making sure the parts fit together flawlessly on the factory floor in Everett, Wash.[24] Modular structures are used in other industries such as automobile manufacturing, bicycle production, home appliances, consumer electronics, and software development.

Virtual Structure   Finally, an organization may identify partners to create a virtual organization, "a company outside a company created specifically to respond to an exceptional market opportunity that is often temporary."[25] Just as "virtual memory" in a computer causes it to seem as if it has more memory, so a virtual organization does more than what its founding organization could do with the resources within the organization's boundaries. The organization identifies partners with the needed talents and negotiates an agreement in which the participants typically work in separate facilities. Instead of relying heavily on face-to-face meetings, however, members of virtual organizations send e-mail and voicemail messages, exchange project information over the Internet, and convene videoconferences among dispersed participants. Information technology clearly enables virtual organizations to work toward common goals, such as developing a new product or entering a new market. For instance, virtual organizations can help in developing cell phones for the US market.

AT&T and Verizon dominate the market for wireless service to such a degree that phone producers must work with them to create compatible products and to develop a pipeline for selling them. Nokia, which had trouble gaining market share in the United States, recently shifted its strategy "to develop phones in partnership with US carriers, in part by assigning 300 product developers each to AT&T and Verizon."[26] Salespeople and R&D personnel also are assigned to work with particular wireless carriers. In general, a virtual organization demands flexibility, and managers must be able to lead and motivate people in separate locations. This structure is valuable for organizations that want to grow through partnerships with other companies.[27]

The company uses a virtual organization design.

Contingency approach to organization design

Creating an effective organization–environment fit.

go to the Web for the Group Exercise: Stakeholder Audit Team

The Contingency Approach to Designing Organizations

to the point
What are the key learning points regarding mechanistic and organic organizations, and when should managers use each of the seven basic organizational structures?

According to the **contingency approach to organization design,** organizations tend to be more effective when they are structured to fit the demands of the situation.[28] For example, the Real World/Real People feature on page 512 illustrates how Toyota is changing the organizational structure of its US operations in response to poor financial performance in 2008 and 2009. The purpose of this section is to introduce you to the contingency approach to organization design by reviewing a landmark study, drawing a distinction between centralized and decentralized

Toyota Changes Its Organizational Structure in Response to a Plunge in Sales

Toyota Motor Corp. is expected to announce as early as Friday a major overhaul of its U.S. operations, bringing engineering, manufacturing and sales under a single executive to revamp the ailing business. . . .

Toyota's U.S. operations for years generated some of the company's biggest profits but now are suffering from plunging sales. . . . As part of the reorganization, Toyota is expected to bring together engineering, manufacturing, and sales under one umbrella run by Mr. Inaba. Currently, U.S. sales reports to one executive and manufacturing and engineering to another. . . .

"The problem is every silo reported back to someone different, but now they need someone in charge of the whole choir," said a former Toyota executive. He said Mr. Inaba is a big-picture thinker and is "much better at 60,000 feet," which means he needs a strong staff that can make his ideas work at ground level. . . .

The U.S. revamping is intended to concentrate more power in a small number of executives and promote more coordination among different units that in the past reported directly to their respective bosses at Toyota's headquarters.

What type of organizational design is Toyota planning to use?

SOURCE: Excerpted from N Shirouzu, "Toyota Plans a Major Overhaul in U.S.," *The Wall Street Journal,* April 10, 2009, p B3.

Toyota is hoping President Yoshimi Inaba can rescue its US operations during the slumping economy.

decision making, and discussing when each of the organization designs is best suited to the context.

LO.4 Mechanistic versus Organic Organizations

A landmark contingency design study was reported by a pair of British behavioral scientists, Tom Burns and G M Stalker. In the course of their research, they drew a very instructive distinction between what they called mechanistic and organic organizations. **Mechanistic organizations** are rigid bureaucracies with strict rules, narrowly defined tasks, and top-down communication. A mechanistic organization generally would have one of the traditional organization designs described earlier in this chapter. Ironically, it is at the cutting edge of technology that this seemingly out-of-date approach has found a home. In the highly competitive business of Web hosting—running clients' Web sites in high-security facilities humming with Internet servers—speed and reliability are everything. Enter military-style managers who require strict discipline, faithful adherence to thick rule books, and flawless execution. But, as *BusinessWeek* observed, "The regimented atmosphere and military themes . . . may be tough to stomach for skilled workers used to a more free-spirited atmosphere."[29]

Oppositely, **organic organizations** are flexible networks of multitalented individuals who perform a variety of tasks. An example is Eileen Fisher, Inc., which designs and manufactures women's clothing. The company's leadership includes Susan Schor, who—in the words of founder Eileen Fisher—"came in and created

Mechanistic organizations

Rigid, command-and-control bureaucracies.

Organic organizations

Fluid and flexible networks of multitalented people.

her own place:" heading all aspects of "people and culture," including employee development, social consciousness, human resources, and internal communications. Schor's accomplishments include crafting an organizational structure in which all employees work in teams run by facilitators and "no one reports to anyone. Instead, we 'connect into' someone else."[30] These qualities of an organic organization are easiest to maintain with the lowered boundaries of horizontal and virtual organizations. Internet technology has made such arrangements more practical by enabling individuals to develop networks of people with whom they can readily share information as needed—a kind of "ecosystem" of people and knowledge.[31] The organization's job then becomes a matter of helping people create and use an optimal network for learning and collaborating.

A Matter of Degree   Importantly, as illustrated in Table 17–1, each of the mechanistic-organic characteristics is a matter of degree. Organizations tend to be relatively mechanistic or relatively organic. Pure types are rare because divisions, departments, or units in the same organization may be more or less mechanistic or organic. From an employee's standpoint, which organization structure would you prefer?

Different Approaches to Decision Making   Decision making tends to be centralized in mechanistic organizations and decentralized in organic organizations. **Centralized decision making** occurs when key decisions are made by top management. Carol Bartz, Yahoo's CEO, for example, has decided to implement a more top-down style of management because she wants to make the company more efficient.[32] **Decentralized decision making** occurs when important decisions are made by middle- and lower-level managers. Generally, centralized organizations are more tightly controlled while decentralized organizations are more adaptive to changing situations.[33] Semco, a Brazilian manufacturer, turned to a more decentralized structure when it needed to spark dramatic change. Ricardo Semler became CEO when Semco was headed for bankruptcy; he eliminated most

Centralized decision making

Top managers make all key decisions.

Decentralized decision making

Lower-level managers are empowered to make important decisions.

Table 17–1 *Characteristics of Mechanistic and Organic Organizations*

CHARACTERISTIC	MECHANISTIC ORGANIZATION		ORGANIC ORGANIZATION
1. Task definition and knowledge required	Narrow; technical	→	Broad; general
2. Linkage between individual's contribution and organization's purpose	Vague or indirect	→	Clear or direct
3. Task flexibility	Rigid; routine	→	Flexible; varied
4. Specification of techniques, obligations, and rights	Specific	→	General
5. Degree of hierarchical control	High	→	Low (self-control emphasized)
6. Primary communication pattern	Top-down	→	Lateral (between peers)
7. Primary decision-making style	Authoritarian	→	Democratic; participative
8. Emphasis on obedience and loyalty	High	→	Low

SOURCE: Adapted from discussion in T Burns and G M Stalker, *The Management of Innovation* (London: Tavistock, 1961), pp 119–25.

senior-management jobs and pushed decision making down to lower levels of self-managed teams. The outcomes have been promising.

> The move initially caused inefficiencies and higher costs but eventually allowed low-level innovation to flourish.... Inventory backlogs have eased, product lines have expanded, and sales have jumped.... After the company's reorganization, revenues climbed from $4 million to $212 million.[34]

Experts on the subject warn against extremes of centralization or decentralization. The challenge is to achieve a workable balance between the two extremes. A management consultant put it this way:

> The modern organization in transition will recognize the pull of two polarities: a need for greater centralization to create low-cost shared resources; and a need to improve market responsiveness with greater decentralization. Today's winning organizations are the ones that can handle the paradox and tensions of both pulls. These are the firms that analyze the optimum organizational solution in each particular circumstance, without prejudice for one type of organization over another. The result is, almost invariably, a messy mixture of decentralized units sharing cost-effective centralized resources.[35]

Centralization and decentralization are not an either–or proposition; they are an and–also balancing act.

Practical Research Insights
When they classified a sample of actual companies as either mechanistic or organic, Burns and Stalker discovered one type was not superior to the other. Each type had its appropriate place, depending on the environment. When the environment was relatively stable and certain, the successful organizations tended to be mechanistic. Organic organizations tended to be the successful ones when the environment was unstable and uncertain.[36]

In a more recent study of 103 department managers from eight manufacturing firms and two aerospace organizations, managerial skill was found to have a greater impact on a global measure of department effectiveness in organic departments than in mechanistic departments. This led the researchers to recommend the following contingencies for management staffing and training:

> If we have two units, one organic and one mechanistic, and two potential applicants differing in overall managerial ability, we might want to assign the more competent to the organic unit since in that situation there are few structural aids available to the manager in performing required responsibilities. It is also possible that managerial training is especially needed by managers being groomed to take over units that are more organic in structure.[37]

Another interesting finding comes from a study of 42 voluntary church organizations. As the organizations became more mechanistic (more bureaucratic) the intrinsic motivation of their members decreased. Mechanistic organizations apparently undermined the volunteers' sense of freedom and self-determination. Additionally, the researchers believe their findings help explain why bureaucracy tends to feed on itself: "A mechanistic organizational structure may breed the need for a more extremely mechanistic system because of the reduction in intrinsically motivated behavior."[38] Thus, bureaucracy begets greater bureaucracy.

Most recently, field research in two factories, one mechanistic and the other organic, found expected communication patterns. Command-and-control (downward) communication characterized the mechanistic factory. Consultative or participative (two-way) communication prevailed in the organic factory.[39]

Both Mechanistic and Organic Structures Have Their Places

Although achievement-oriented students of OB typically express a distaste for mechanistic organizations, not all organizations or subunits can or should be organic. For example, McDonald's could not achieve its admired quality and service standards without extremely mechanistic restaurant operations. Imagine the food and service you would get if McDonald's employees used their own favorite ways of doing things and worked at their own pace! On the other hand, mechanistic structure alienates some employees because it erodes their sense of self-control.

LO.5 Getting the Right Fit

All of the organization structures described in this chapter are used today because each structure has advantages and disadvantages that make it appropriate in some cases. For example, the clear roles and strict hierarchy of an extremely mechanistic organization are beneficial when careful routines and a set of checks and balances are important, as at a nuclear power facility. In a fast-changing environment with a great deal of uncertainty, an organization would benefit from a more organic structure that lowers boundaries between functions and organizations. Let us consider each of the seven basic organization designs.

A functional structure can save money by grouping together people who need similar materials and equipment. Quality standards can be maintained because supervisors understand what department members do and because people in the same function develop pride in their specialty. Workers can devote more of their time to what they do best. These benefits are easiest to realize in a stable environment, where the organization doesn't depend on employees to coordinate their efforts to solve varied problems. Today, fewer organizations see their environment as stable, so more are moving away from strictly functional structures.

Divisional structures increase employees' focus on customers and products. Managers have the flexibility to make decisions that affect several functions in order to serve customer needs. This enables the organization to move faster if a new customer need arises or if a competitor introduces an important product. However, duplicating functions in each division can add to costs, so this structure may be too expensive for some organizations. Also, divisions sometimes focus on their own customer groups or products to the exclusion of the company's overall mission. Ford Motor Company has struggled to unify its geographic and brand divisions to save money by sharing design, engineering, and manufacturing. Managers of geographic divisions have introduced new car models on different time lines and insisted that their customers want different features.[40] In contrast, geographic divisions have helped McDonald's grow by freeing managers to introduce menu items and décor that locals appreciate.[41]

A matrix structure tries to combine the advantages of functional and divisional structures. This advantage is also the structure's main drawback: it violates the unity of command principle, described previously in the chapter. Employees have to balance the demands of a functional manager and a product or project manager. When they struggle with this balance, decision making can slow to a crawl, and political behavior can overpower progress. Employees' role clarity also may be reduced. The success of a matrix organization, therefore, requires superior managers who communicate extensively, foster commitment and collaboration, manage conflict, and negotiate effectively to establish goals and priorities consistent with the organization's strategy.[42] This conclusion underscores the importance of considering the organization's culture prior to adopting a matrix structure. As discussed in Chapter 3, clan and adhocracy cultures, which endorse values related to flexibility and discretion, are more consistent with the requirements of a matrix structure. One organization that has made matrix structures work for decades is Procter & Gamble. To manage 138,000 employees in more than 80 countries, the company has a matrix structure in which global business units are responsible for a brand's development and production, while market development organizations focus on the customer needs for particular regions and the way the brands can meet those needs. Employees have to meet objectives both for the brand and for the market, with different managers responsible for each.[43]

Horizontal designs generally improve coordination and communication in organizations.[44] Cross-functional teams can arrive at creative solutions to problems that arise in a fast-changing environment. Teams can develop new products faster and more efficiently than can functions working independently in a traditional structure. Horizontal designs also encourage knowledge sharing. However, because lines of authority are less clear, managers must be able to share responsibility for the organization's overall performance, build commitment to a shared vision, and influence others even when they lack direct authority.[45] This type of structure is a good fit when specialization is less important than the ability to respond to varied or changing customer needs. It requires employees who can rise to the challenges of empowerment. A horizontal design is a good fit for Research in Motion (RIM) because it builds on employees' deep product and customer knowledge. All employees use the company's BlackBerry pocket computers, so they know what works and what doesn't. RIM's chief executive maintains that because employees know the details of what makes the BlackBerry work, they are well positioned to continue improving it: "We didn't just buy an operating system from one company and a radio technology from another, and then have them assembled somewhere in Asia. We actually built the whole thing. . . . I don't mind investing in it because I know there's a return."[46] RIM applies that knowledge by creating teams to brainstorm new ideas in every aspect of the company's operations.

Finally, organizations that open their boundaries to become hollow, modular, or virtual can generate superior returns by focusing on what they do best.[47] Like functional organizations, they tap people in particular specialties, who may be more expert than the generalists of a divisional or horizontal organization. The downside of these structures is that organizations give up expertise and control in the functions or operations that are outsourced. Still, like divisional and horizontal organizations, they can focus on customers or products, leaving their partners to focus on their own specialty area. In India, when Tata Motors wanted to develop a $2,500 compact car, it decided its own engineers needed assistance, so Tata adopted a modular structure. Each of its suppliers tackled designing particular components to be as inexpensive as possible while still meeting quality standards, and Tata focused on coordinating their work.[48] An example of a successful hollow organization is one global manufacturer that shifted its focus to developing products and contracted with outsourcing firms to make the products in the manufacturer's own facilities, handling the process from ordering materials to shipping the finished product. The arrangement maintained quality while cutting labor costs by 40% by avoiding inefficiency and duplication of work.[49]

The success of organizations that work across boundaries depends on managers' ability to get results from people over whom they do not have direct formal authority by virtue of their position in the organization. As previously mentioned, for example, Boeing has been embarrassed by its setbacks in manufacturing the Dreamliner from components provided by a network of suppliers, which did not always meet their commitments to Boeing.[50] Also, individuals in these organizations may not have the same degree of commitment as do employees of a traditional organization, so motivation and leadership may be more difficult. Therefore, these designs are the best fit when organizations have suitable partners they trust; when efficiency is very important; when the organization can identify functions, processes, or product components to outsource profitably; and in the case of a virtual organization, when the need to be met is temporary. In a study of managers in 20 organizations that extensively collaborate with other companies, these efforts most often succeeded in companies that select and train for teamwork skills, invest in processes that promote collaboration, set up tools and systems for sharing information, and treat collaboration as one of the company's ongoing programs requiring leadership.[51] Another recent study of 177 international strategic alliances further showed that open structures work best when there is a high level of trust between partnering organizations.[52]

Organizational Effectiveness (and the Threat of Decline)

to the point

What are the similarities and differences between the four generic effectiveness criteria, and how can managers prevent organizational decline?

How effective are you? If someone asked you this apparently simple question, you would likely ask for clarification before answering. For instance, you might want to know if they were referring to your grade point average, annual income, actual accomplishments, ability to get along with others, public service, or perhaps something else entirely. So it is with modern organizations. Effectiveness criteria abound.[53]

Assessing organizational effectiveness is an important topic for an array of people, including managers, job hunters, stockholders, government agencies, and OB specialists. The purpose of this section is to introduce a widely applicable and useful model of organizational effectiveness; we also will deal with the related problem of organizational decline.

LO.6 Generic Organizational-Effectiveness Criteria

A good way to better understand this complex subject is to consider four generic approaches to assessing an organization's effectiveness (see Figure 17–4). These effectiveness criteria apply equally well to large or small and profit or not-for-profit organizations. Moreover, as denoted by the overlapping circles in Figure 17–4, the four effectiveness criteria can be used in various combinations. The key thing to remember is "no single approach to the evaluation of effectiveness is appropriate in all circumstances or for all organization types."[54] What do Coca-Cola and France Télécom, for example, have in common, other than being large profit-seeking corporations? Because a multidimensional approach is required, we need to look more closely at each of the four generic effectiveness criteria.

Figure 17–4   *Four Ways to Assess Organizational Effectiveness*

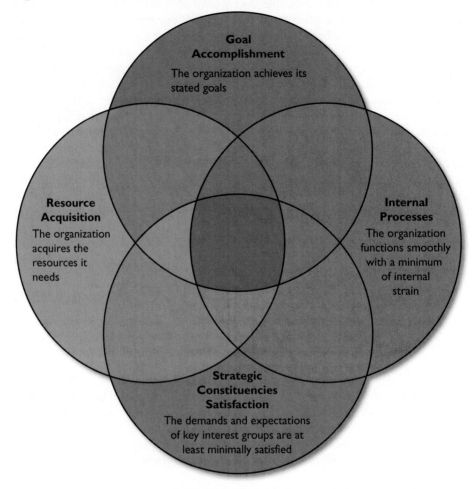

SOURCES: Adapted from discussion in K Cameron, "Critical Questions in Assessing Organizational Effectiveness," *Organizational Dynamics,* Autumn 1980, pp 66–80; and K S Cameron, "Effectiveness as Paradox: Consensus and Conflict in Conceptions of Organizational Effectiveness," *Management Science,* May 1986, pp 539–53.

Goal Accomplishment   Goal accomplishment is the most widely used effectiveness criterion for organizations. Key organizational results or outputs are compared with previously stated goals or objectives. Deviations, either plus or minus, require corrective action. This is simply an organizational variation of the personal goal-setting process discussed in Chapter 9. Effectiveness, relative to the criterion of goal accomplishment, is gauged by how well the organization meets or exceeds its goals.

Productivity improvement, involving the relationship between inputs and outputs, is a common organization-level goal. Goals also may be set for organizational efforts such as minority recruiting, sustainability, customer satisfaction, employee satisfaction, quality improvement, and fair reward systems.[55] Given today's competitive pressures and e-business revolution, *innovation* and *speed* are very important organizational goals worthy of measurement and monitoring.[56] A few years ago, Toyota gave us a powerful indicator of where things are going in this regard. The Japanese automaker announced it could custom-build a car in just five days! A customer's new Toyota would roll off the Ontario, Canada, assembly line just five days after the order was placed. A 30-day lag was the industry standard at the time.[57]

Resource Acquisition

This second criterion relates to inputs rather than outputs. An organization is deemed effective in this regard if it acquires necessary factors of production such as raw materials, labor, capital, and managerial and technical expertise. Charitable organizations such as the Salvation Army judge their effectiveness in terms of how much money they raise from private and corporate donations.[58]

Internal Processes

This dimension of effectiveness focuses on "what the organization must excel at" to effectively meet its financial objectives and customers' expectations. A team of researchers have identified four critical high-level internal processes that managers are encouraged to measure and manage. These processes influence productivity, efficiency, quality, safety, and a host of other internal metrics. The processes include organizational activities associated with (1) innovation, (2) customer service and satisfaction, (3) operational excellence, and (4) being a good corporate citizen.[59] Companies tend to adopt continuous improvement programs, recall our discussion of TQM in Chapter 1, in pursuit of improving their internal processes. Consider how Aclan Packaging Food Americas, a multinational manufacturer of flexible packaging, used continuous improvement (CI).

> Alcan Packaging's CI commitment has grown. We have hundreds of CI projects every year, in support functions as well as manufacturing—leading to millions of dollars in savings and value. They include:
> - A companywide knife-safety project that reduced employee lacerations.
> - A Toronto project that reduced the plant's water consumption by 80 percent.
> - A waste-reduction process at the Neenah, Wis., plant that eliminates 21 truckloads of waste annually. . . .
>
> In the HR department, we continue to deploy CI. It is effective for addressing social networking, college brand awareness, training, work/life balance and trust building.[60]

Strategic Constituencies Satisfaction

Organizations both depend on people and affect the lives of people. Consequently, many consider the satisfaction of key interested parties to be an important criterion of organizational effectiveness.

A **strategic constituency** is any group of individuals who have some stake in the organization—for example, resource providers, users of the organization's products or services, producers of the organization's output, groups whose cooperation is essential for the organization's survival, or those whose lives are significantly affected by the organization.[61]

Strategic constituencies (or *stakeholders*) generally have competing or conflicting interests.[62] For instance, customers at gas pumps were not cheering when ExxonMobil's first quarter 2009 earnings topped $10 billion.[63] Strategic constituents or stakeholders can be identified systematically through a stakeholder audit.[64] A **stakeholder audit** enables management to identify all parties significantly impacted by the organization's performance (see Figure 17–5). Conflicting interests and relative satisfaction among the listed stakeholders can then be dealt with.

Strategic constituency
Any group of people with a stake in the organization's operation or success.

Stakeholder audit
Systematic identification of all parties likely to be affected by the organization.

Figure 17–5   *A Sample Stakeholder Audit Identifying Strategic Constituencies*

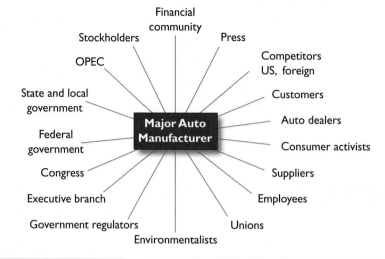

SOURCE: From N C Roberts et al., "The Stakeholder Audit Goes Public," *Organizational Dynamics,* Winter 1989. © 1989. Reprinted with permission from Elsevier.

A never-ending challenge for management is to strike a workable balance among strategic constituencies so as to achieve at least minimal satisfaction on all fronts.

Multiple Effectiveness Criteria: Some Practical Guidelines

Experts on the subject recommend a multidimensional approach to assessing the effectiveness of modern organizations. This means no single criterion is appropriate for all stages of the organization's life cycle. Nor will a single criterion satisfy competing stakeholders. Well-managed organizations mix and match effectiveness criteria to fit the unique requirements of the situation.[65] For example, Irdeto Holdings, which provides content protection for pay TV and video recordings, decided on a structural change after determining that sales were growing fastest in Asia, which already accounted for almost 40% of the company's revenues. To meet business goals for serving this important geographic market, Irdeto's executives decided to convert the company's Beijing office into a second headquarters (the first headquarters is located near Amsterdam). This change serves an important constituency—Asian customers—but raised concerns with Amsterdam employees. Responding to that second constituency, Irdeto's CEO, Graham Kill, announced plans to build a new Amsterdam office building and explained that employees can enjoy an exciting career path if they are willing to rotate between the two headquarters cities. Management also has had to address internal processes, especially in developing Chinese managers to take initiative in decision making and to think about issues affecting the entire corporation, not just Asian markets.[66]

Managers need to identify and seek input from strategic constituencies. This information, when merged with the organization's stated mission and philosophy, enables management to derive an appropriate *combination* of effectiveness criteria. The following guidelines are helpful in this regard:

- *The goal accomplishment approach* is appropriate when "goals are clear, consensual, time-bounded, measurable."[67]

- *The resource acquisition approach* is appropriate when inputs have a traceable effect on results or output. For example, the amount of money the World Wildlife Fund receives through donations dictates the level of services provided.

- *The internal processes approach* is appropriate when organizational performance is strongly influenced by specific processes (e.g., cross-functional teamwork).

- *The strategic constituencies approach* is appropriate when powerful stakeholders can significantly benefit or harm the organization.[68]

Keeping these basic concepts of organizational effectiveness in mind, we turn our attention to preventing organizational decline.

go to the Web for the Self-Exercise: Organization Design Field Study

L0.7 The Ever-Present Threat of Organizational Decline

Sadly, 2008 and 2009 are filled with many examples of organizational decline. Previously successful firms such as AIG, Lehman Brothers, Morgan Stanley, Chrysler, General Motors, and Prologis experienced major decline during this period. These companies tripped up for a number of reasons including strategic blunders, risky investments, lack of responsiveness to customers, bad luck, and managerial resistance to change.[69] Although the problems at these companies varied, some of them turned the corner from success to decline rather suddenly and dramatically. Donald N Sull, a strategy professor at the London Business School, added this perspective:

> One of the most common business phenomena is also one of the most perplexing: when successful companies face big changes in their environment, they often fail to respond effectively. Unable to defend themselves against competitors armed with new products, technologies, or strategies, they watch their sales and profits erode, their best people leave, and their stock valuations tumble. Some ultimately manage to recover—usually after painful rounds of downsizing and restructuring—but many don't.[70]

Researchers call this downward spiral **organizational decline** and define it as "a decrease in an organization's resource base."[71] The term *resource* is used very broadly in this context, encompassing money, talent, customers, and innovative ideas and products. Managers seeking to maintain organizational effectiveness need to be alert to the problem because experts tell us "decline is almost unavoidable unless deliberate steps are taken to prevent it."[72] The first key step is to recognize the early warning signs of organizational decline.

Organizational decline

Decrease in organization's resource base (money, customers, talent, innovations).

Early Warning Signs of Decline

Short of illegal conduct, there are 14 early warning signs of organizational decline:

1. Excess personnel.
2. Tolerance of incompetence.
3. Cumbersome administrative procedures.
4. Disproportionate staff power (e.g., technical staff specialists politically overpower line managers, whom they view as unsophisticated and too conventional).
5. Replacement of substance with form (e.g., the planning process becomes more important than the results achieved).
6. Scarcity of clear goals and decision benchmarks.
7. Fear of embarrassment and conflict (e.g., formerly successful executives may resist new ideas for fear of revealing past mistakes).
8. Loss of effective communication.
9. Outdated organizational structure.[73]
10. Increased scapegoating by leaders.
11. Resistance to change.
12. Low morale.
13. Special interest groups are more vocal.
14. Decreased innovation.[74]

Managers who monitor these early warning signs of organizational decline are better able to reorganize in a timely and effective manner. However, research has uncovered a troublesome perception tendency among entrenched top management teams. In companies where there had been little if any turnover among top executives, there was a tendency to attribute organizational problems to *external* causes (e.g., competition, the government, technology shifts). Oppositely, *internal* attributions tended to be made by top management teams with *many* new members. Thus, proverbial "new blood" at the top appears to be a good insurance policy against misperceiving the early-warning signs of organizational decline.[75]

Preventing Organizational Decline

The time to start doing something about organizational decline is when everything is going *right.* For it is during periods of high success that the seeds of decline are sown.[76] *Complacency* is the number one threat because it breeds overconfidence and inattentiveness. As one management writer recently explained,

> [i]n organizations, complacency is a side effect of success. Growth brings bloat, and bloat slows the organization's response to competitive threats. It is after sustained periods of success that organizations run the highest risk of getting hurt. At the moment of a company's greatest triumph, senior management's most important duty is to make sure that the butterflies are still fluttering in everybody's belly.[77]

Organizational narcissim

Organizational tendency to deny facts, use self-aggrandizement, and feel entitled.

Complacency also leads to **organizational narcissism.** Organizational narcissism occurs when a company "loses sight of the 'reality' of its position in the marketplace and employs denial, self-aggrandizement, and a sense of entitlement to prop up its damaged sense of identity."[78] Narcissism leads companies to deny facts about itself and to use rationalizations and justifications to defend its actions. Organizations can stave off the tendency to become narcissistic by trying to remain fact-based and by realistically considering both supportive and negative evidence about the company's status.[79]

LO.8 Organizational Innovation

Innovation "is the creation of something new that makes money; it finds a pathway to the consumer."[80] This definition highlights two key aspects of innovation. First, innovation is different from *invention,* which entails the creation of something new, and *creativity,* which was was defined in Chapter 12 as a process of developing something new or unique. The CEO of Procter & Gamble A G Lafley discussed this distinction in an interview with *Business Week.* "You need creativity and invention, but until you can connect that creativity to the customer in the form of a product or service that meaningfully changes their lives, I would argue you don't have innovation." He uses the example of diapers to make his case. "We invented a material back in the 60s that would absorb a lot of water. Until we converted it into a Pampers disposable baby diaper, it was just a new kind of material. We created this entirely new product category, and that created an industry."[81] Second, innovation also is different from *integration,* which involves actions associated with getting multiple people, units, departments, functions, or sites to work together in pursuit of a goal, idea, or project.[82] As you will learn in this section, successful innovation relies on invention, creativity, and integration.

We are discussing the topic of innovation in this chapter because it is an organizational issue. That is, innovation requires us to integrate concepts pertaining to individual behavior, groups and social processes, and organizational processes (recall the topical model of OB shown in Figure 1–5). It is important to have a good understanding about innovation because it serves as the gasoline that fuels the economic engine of companies and countries alike. Interestingly, the United States' standing as an innovative nation has been falling over the last decade. A recent study by the Boston Consulting Group and the National Association of Manufacturers revealed that the United States is the eighth most innovative country in the world, behind (1) Singapore, (2) South Korea, (3) Switzerland, (4) Iceland, (5) Ireland, (6) Hong Kong, and (7) Finland. Another recent study further showed that US companies were planning to decrease their spending on innovation in 2009 and to reduce its importance as a strategic priority.[83] Time will tell whether or not this was a good decision.

To guide our investigation into how organizations can be more innovative, this section discusses myths about innovation and presents a model of innovation.

to the point

How can managers increase innovation?

Innovation

Creation of something new that is used by consumers.

LO.9 Myths about Innovation

We would like to dispel two myths about innovation. The first focuses on the notion that innovation involves an epiphany or eureka moment. In other words, some people think that innovation is a spur-of-the-moment thing in which an idea is hatched, such as Isaac Newton discovering gravity after being hit on the head by an apple while sitting under a tree. This is a nice story, but it does not represent reality. Others conceive innovation as something that occurs when a person is in the right place at the right time. Nothing could be further from the truth. Innovation does not occur like a thunderbolt. Rather, it is a time-consuming

Zara Spends Decades to Innovate Its Supply Chain

Inditex's secret? Besides selling relatively cheap clothes, which fit the times, the company maintains an iron grip on every link in its supply chain. That enables it to move designs from sketch pad to store rack in as little as two weeks. This "fast fashion" way of doing things has become a model for other apparel chains, such as Los Angeles-based Forever 21, Spain's Mango, and Britain's Topshop, which is set to open in New York next year.

Inditex has spent more than three decades perfecting its strategy. Along the way it has broken almost every rule in retailing. At most clothing companies supply chain starts with designers, who plan collections as much as a year in advance. At Inditex, Zara store managers monitor what's selling daily—and with up to 70% of their salaries coming from commission, there's a lot of incentive to get it right. They track everything from current sales trends to merchandise customers want but can't find in stores, then shoot orders to Inditex's 300 designers, who fashion what's needed instantly....

Wages are higher at Inditex—its factory workers in Spain make an average of $1,650 a month, vs. $206 in China's Guandong Province. But the company saves time and money on shipping. Also, Inditex's plants use just-in-time systems developed in cooperation with logistics experts from Toyota Motor, which gives the company a level of control that would be impossible if it were entirely dependent on outsiders.

In addition, Inditex supplies every market from warehouses in Spain. Even so, it manages to get new merchandise to European stores within 24 hours, and by flying goods via commercial airliners, to stores in the Americas and Asia in 48 hours or less.

Can other retailers copy Zara's strategy? Explain.

SOURCE: Excerpted from K Capell, "Zara Thrives By Breaking All the Rules," *BusinessWeek*, October 20, 2008, p 66.

At Zara, store managers tell designers what customers want based on what happens in the store. Who knows, maybe that perfect pair of pants was made just for you!

Apple's iPhone is one of the most innovative products of the 21st century. What do you foresee being the next innovative product released by Apple?

activity that takes hard work and dedication. Jack and Suzy Welch note that "it emerges incrementally, in bits and chugs, forged by a mixed bag of coworkers from up, down, and across an organization, sitting and wrangling it out in the trenches."[84] Innovation is hard work and requires an investment in time and resources. For example, Spanish apparel firm Inditex and its Zara chain invested more than three decades in trying to determine how to innovate its supply chain (see the Real World/Real People feature above). Its efforts contributed to the company's fourfold increase in sales since 2000.[85]

Apple's CEO Steve Jobs once was asked "how do you systematize innovation?" He answered, "you don't."[86] The second myth is that innovation can be systematized. If it could, everyone would do it. There simply are too many challenges associated with innovation that make its success unpredictable. These challenges are discussed when we review a model of innovation in the next section.

LO.10 A Model of Innovation

Innovation is not a static event. Rather, it is a dyamic process that ebbs and flows over time and can lead to many potential benefits, including revenue growth, new products and services, lower costs, improved products and services, and improved processes. These benefits can manifest in both the short and long term. Honda Motor, for example, is investing millions in robotics research that is not expected to pay off for quite some time. They invented a robot that can follow four mental commands. "Honda says it foresees consumer applications—thinking a car trunk open, for instance. But R&D director Yasuhisa Arai concedes that 'practical uses are still way in the future.'"[87]

The process of growing a tree is a useful metaphor for understanding how organizations can become more innovative. Seeds are the starting point for growing trees. Over time, seeds evolve into strong trunks with the proper water, oxygen, nutrients, and sunlight. A healthy trunk enables a tree to survive and produce a canopy for all to enjoy its beauty, shade, or pollination. Innovation follows a similar process. You will learn that experts have uncovered six seeds of innovation that organizations can use to begin the process of becoming more innovative. These seeds will not produce innovation, however, unless an organization effectively manages a set of key challenges. Managing the seeds and challenges of innovation produces the trunk of innovation. Finally, innovation also needs special nutrients to help it grow, prosper, and deliver intended benefits. These nutrients include the proper organizational culture, leadership, people, and execution. Figure 17–6 shows that there are three components that influence the benefits of innovation: seeds of innovation,

Figure 17–6   *A Model of Innovation*

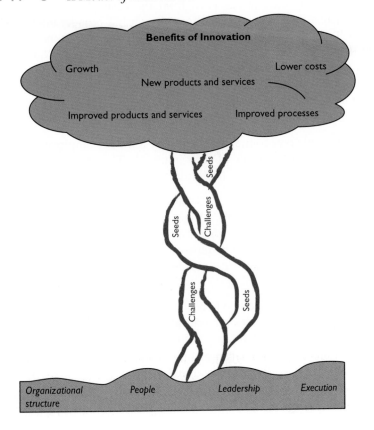

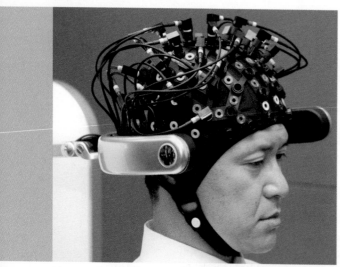

Honda's robotics research is looking to literally tap into our brains for new products.

Seeds of innovation

Starting point of organizational innovation.

challenges of innovation, and nutrients of innovation. Let us consider each component.

Seeds of Innovation   Seeds of innovation represent the starting point of organizational innovation. After studying hundreds of innovations, an expert identified six seeds of innovation.[88] They are

1. *Hard work in a specific direction.* Most innovations come from dedicated people diligently working to solve a well-defined problem. This hard work can span many years.

2. *Hard work with direction change.* Innovations frequently occur when people change their approach toward solving a problem. In other words, hard work closes some doors and opens others.

3. *Curiosity.* Innovations can begin when people are curious about something of interest. Curiosity spawns the experimentation and inventiveness inherent in innovation.

4. *Wealth and money.* Innovations frequently occur because an organization or an individual simply wants to make money. Fiat's being near bankruptcy, for instance, drove the company to look for innovative ways to cut costs and grow market share in the United States. This is the reason Fiat took a stake in Chrysler in return for releasing small-car technology.[89]

5. *Necessity.* Many innovations grow from the desire to achieve something or to complete a task that is needed to accomplish a broader goal. For example, "Xerox hired two researchers the company calls 'innovation managers' who will hunt for inventions and products from Indian startups that Xerox might adapt for North America. And Hewlett-Packard is using its research lab in India to see how it can migrate Web-interface applications for mobile phones in Asia and Africa to developed markets."[90]

6. *Combination of seeds.* Many innovations occur as a result of multiple factors.

For example, Google tries to fuel innovation by allowing employees to spend 20% of their time on projects outside of their main job. This strategy allows employee curiosity to meld with hard work to produce new products.[91]

Challenges of Innovation   Figure 17–6 illustrates that the challenges of innovation and the seeds of innovation are interwoven in a dynamic relationship that unfolds over time. The benefits of innovation are less likely to occur if these two components of innovation are not effectively integrated.[92] The challenges include

1. *Find an idea.* An idea is needed to create something new, and people can get ideas from many different sources: concentrated thinking, past experience, daydreaming, reading, talking with others, or intuition.

2. *Develop a solution.* This challenge entails coming up with a model or prototype of a product or a workable solution to a problem.

3. *Sponsorship and funding.* Innovations require resources and someone to champion whatever organizational changes are needed to develop a new product or

service. Tata Motors, for example, has committed $1.5 billion to research and development. The company also gives out awards for the best annual innovations and the most entrepreneurial employees.[93]

4. *Reproduction.* The company must figure out how to profitably make the new product or deliver a new service.

5. *Reach your potential customer.* Many innovations fail because the company cannot figure out how to get the new product or service in the hands of consumers. Some experts recommend the use of job mapping. Job mapping "breaks down the task the customer wants done into a series of discrete process steps. By deconstructing a job from beginning to end, a company gains a complete view of all the points at which a customer might desire more help from a product or service—namely, at each step in the job."[94] Job mapping helps companies determine how customers might best use new products and services.

6. *Beat your competitors.* Remember that other companies may be pursuing the same breakthroughs. It is better to focus on a smaller number of innovations.

7. *Timing.* Customers must be ready for the new product or service and employees must be prepared to make whatever changes are necessary to turn the innovation into reality. The timing of the innovation needs to be considered.

8. *Keep the lights on.* Organizations must still make money while they are pursuing innovation. It is important to stay focused on keeping current customers happy while engaging in innovative activities.

Nutrients of Innovation

Organizations are more likely to experience the benefits of innovation when the dynamic interplay between the seeds and challenges of innovation are supported and reinforced by the nutrients of innovation: an organization's culture, leadership, people, and ability to execute. For example, a recent meta-analysis revealed that innovation was positively associated with market, adhocracy, and clan cultures—recall our discussion in Chapter 3.[95] GE already has put this research finding into use in a training program called "Leadership, Innovation, and Growth." Teams attending the training complete an internal assessment regarding the extent to which the culture is supportive of creativity. Participants then use the results to discuss how they might make the work environment more innovation friendly.[96] Research also showed that transformational leadership was helpful in creating innovative alliances between companies and in encouraging employees' creativity.[97]

Moreover, research identified several employee characteristics that can help organizations innovate. For example, innovation was positively associated with the individual characteristics associated with creativity (see Chapter 12), the level of skills and abilities possessed by people, and employees' self-efficacy for innovation; employee abilities and self-efficacy were reviewed in Chapter 5.[98] Finally, the ability to execute ultimately makes or breaks an organization's attempts at bringing new products and services to market. Why?

Consider the definition of **execution.**

Execution is a systematic process of rigorously discussing hows and whats, questioning, tenaciously following through, and ensuring accountability. It includes making assumptions about the business environment, assessing the organization's capabilities, linking strategy to operations and the people who are going to implement the strategy, synchronizing those people and their various disciplines, and linking rewards to outcomes. It also includes mechanisms for changing assumptions as the environment changes and upgrading

Execution
Process of discussing hows and whats, questioning, following through, and ensuring accountability.

the company's capabilities to meet the challenges of an ambitious strategy. In its most fundamental sense, execution is a systematic way of exposing reality and acting on it.[99]

This definition highlights that execution requires organizations to effectively manage people, groups, and organizational processes and systems in the pursuit of innovation. In the end, the innovation process must be managed. This is precisely what has been learned by studying innovative companies such as Apple, Google, Toyota, Microsoft, Nintendo, IBM, Hewlett-Packard, Research in Motion, Nokia, and Wal-Mart. These companies were rated by *Business Week* as the 10 most innovative companies in the world in 2009.[100]

Summary of Key Concepts

1. *Describe the four characteristics common to all organizations, and explain the difference between closed and open systems.* They are coordination of effort (achieved through policies and rules), a common goal (a collective purpose), division of labor (people performing separate but related tasks), and a hierarchy of authority (the chain of command). Closed systems, such as a battery-powered clock, are relatively self-sufficient. Open systems, such as the human body, are highly dependent on the environment for survival. Organizations are said to be open systems.

2. *Define the term* learning organization. A learning organization is one that proactively creates, acquires, and transfers knowledge and changes its behavior on the basis of new knowledge and insights.

3. *Describe seven basic ways organizations are structured.* Traditional designs include (1) functional structures, in which work is divided according to function; (2) divisional structures, in which work is divided according to product or customer type or location; and (3) matrix structures, with dual-reporting structures based on product and function. Organizations also may be designed (4) horizontally, with cross-functional teams responsible for entire processes. Organization design also may reduce barriers between organizations, becoming (5) hollow organizations, which outsource functions; (6) modular organizations, which outsource the production of a product's components; or (7) virtual organizations, which temporarily combine the efforts of members of different companies in order to complete a project.

4. *Discuss Burns and Stalker's findings regarding mechanistic and organic organizations.* British researchers Burns and Stalker found that mechanistic (bureaucratic, centralized) organizations tended to be effective in stable situations. In unstable situations, organic (flexible, decentralized) organizations were more effective. These findings underscored the need for a contingency approach to organization design.

5. *Identify when each of the seven organization structures is the right fit.* Mechanistic organizations and functional structures may be necessary when tight control is important and the environment is stable. Organic organizations allow for innovation in a rapidly changing environment. Divisional structures are a good fit when the organization needs deep knowledge of varied customer groups and the ability to respond to customer demands quickly. A matrix organization can deliver the advantages of functional and divisional structures if the company has superior managers who communicate extensively, foster commitment and collaboration, and negotiate effectively to establish goals and priorities consistent with the organization's strategy. A horizontal design is a good fit when specialization is less important than the ability to respond to varied or changing customer needs. Hollow, modular, and virtual designs are best when organizations have suitable partners they trust; efficiency is very important; the organization can identify functions, processes, or product components to outsource; and in the case of a virtual organization, when the need to be met is temporary.

6. *Describe the four generic organizational effectiveness criteria.* They are goal accomplishment (satisfying stated objectives), resource acquisition (gathering the necessary productive inputs), internal processes (building and maintaining healthy organizational systems), and strategic constituencies satisfaction (achieving at least minimal satisfaction for all key stakeholders).

7. *Explain how managers can prevent organizational decline.* Because complacency and organizational

narcissim are the the leading causes of organizational decline, managers need to create a culture of continuous improvement. Decline automatically follows periods of great success if preventive steps are not taken to avoid the erosion of organizational resources (money, customers, talent, and innovative ideas).

8. *Discuss the difference between innovation, invention, creativity, and integration.* Innovation is creating something new that is commercialized. In contrast, invention is simply the creation of something new and creativity is the process of developing something new or unique. Integration involves actions associated with getting multiple people, units, departments, functions, or sites to work together in pursuit of a goal, idea, or project. Innovation relies on invention, creativity, and integration.

9. *Review the myths of innovation.* There are two key myths about innovation. The first is the myth that innovation involves an epiphany or eureka moment. The second is that innovation can be systematized.

10. *Explain the model of innovation.* Innovation is a dynamic process that involves the simultaneous effects of seeds of innovation and challenges of innovation. That said, the benefits of innovation only occur when the interaction between seeds and challenges is nurtured by the nutrients of innovation, which include organizational culture, leadership, people, and execution.

Key Terms

Organization, 502
Unity of command principle, 503
Organization chart, 503
Span of control, 503
Staff personnel, 504
Line managers, 504
Closed system, 505
Open system, 505
Learning organization, 507
Contingency approach to organization design, 511

Mechanistic organizations, 512
Organic organizations, 512
Centralized decision making, 513
Decentralized decision making, 513
Strategic constituency, 519
Stakeholder audit, 519
Organizational decline, 521
Organizational narcissism, 522
Innovation, 523
Seeds of innovation, 526
Execution, 527

OB in Action Case Study

Irdeto Holdings BV Changes Its Organizational Structure[101]

In late 2006. Irdeto Holdings BV Chief Executive Graham Kill concluded his company could no longer be run from an Amsterdam suburb.

Sales at Irdeto, a unit of South American media group Naspers Ltd. that sells content-protection for pay TV and video, were growing faster in Asia, which accounted for about 39% of the company's $170 million annual revenue. In five years, Mr. Kill expected that share to rise to half. To succeed in Asia, he thought, the company should be managed from there.

So last August, Mr. Kill moved with his family to Beijing, site of Irdeto's principal Asian office. He declared Beijing a second headquarters and said other executives would serve multiyear stints there as well. . . .

Irdeto is one of a growing number of companies testing new corporate structures as their businesses get too complex and global to be run from one place. Some have shifted management or product-development responsibilities closer to hot markets or pools of talented workers. SAP AG, for instance, has big development centers in seven locations in addition to its original headquarters in Walldorf, Germany, including the U.S. and India. Other companies have created multiple headquarters or dispensed with headquarters altogether.

Splitting headquarters is challenging, Mr. Kill says. Top executives on different continents need to know what to expect of each other. Employees of the original headquarters need to be assured they're still valuable. Companies also need to compensate for the decline in face-to-face communication, he says; at Irdeto, that has meant frequent phone calls and bolstering technology such as videoconferencing. . . .

Last May, Mr. Kill took his top six executives on a weeklong retreat in the United Kingdom to discuss how they would manage differently. They decided to discontinue weekly face-to-face briefings on operations; instead, they would put the updates in writing and confer once every two weeks on strategy, says Patricia van der Velden, Irdeto's vice president for human relations. To make it easier to communicate remotely, the company created more videoconferencing rooms and gave managers Webcams and videophone software for their laptops.

The executives also suggested Mr. Kill be less involved in operations because he would be harder to reach; top lieutenants would make more decisions on their own, says Ms. Van der Velden.

Mr. Kill and his team announced the changes to all employees a few weeks later. To reassure Amsterdam-based staffers that they remained important, Mr. Kill said Irdeto would build a new office building in the Dutch city.

"When you're communicating a possible threat to people, you have to give them something in return," says Ms. Van der Velden.

Still, Amsterdam-based employees worried about layoffs and career advancement, Ms. Van der Velden says. They also asked whether work hours would shift earlier to better accommodate Beijing, which is seven hours ahead of Amsterdam. She told them that Irdeto didn't plan layoffs but that career opportunities might depend on willingness to relocate to China.

Official working hours didn't change, because that would involve re-writing contracts. But Amsterdam-based workers are making more of an effort to schedule conference calls earlier in their day, during office hours in Beijing.

In Beijing, Mr. Kill is trying to get employees to make decisions as well as follow them—a new idea to many Chinese managers, says Thierry Raymaekers, who was hired in China and has headed Irdeto's marketing there for eight years.

Questions for Discussion

1. Which of the seven organizational designs is Irdeto using? Explain your rationale.

2. Is Irdeto moving to a more mechanistic or organic structure? How can you tell?

3. Based on the contingency approach to designing organizations, which of the seven designs do you think is most appropriate for Irdeto? Discuss your rationale.

4. Why are employees in Amsterdam resisting the organizational redesign?

5. How important is the role of information technology to the success of Irdeto's organizational redesign? Explain.

6. What is your most important takeaway from this case?

Ethical Dilemma

Has Electronic Monitoring Gone Too Far?

Results from an American Management Association national survey: The Electronic Monitoring & Surveillance Survey revealed that 25% of employers have fired employees who misused e-mail (e.g., offensive language or excessive personal use), while roughly 33% discharged people for using the Internet inappropriately (e.g., surfing for pornography).[102] "Computer monitoring takes many forms, with 45% of employers tracking content, keystrokes, and time spent at the keyboard. Another 43% store and review computer files. In addition, 12% monitor the blogosphere to see what is being written about the company, and another 10% monitor social networking sites."[103] Consider how electronic monitoring impacted Kary Nagel.

Kary Nagel, 24, was regarded as a good employee until she criticized the owners of a credit-repair agency on her personal e-mail. She was immediately fired after the owners read her e-mail. "I never signed anything saying it was OK to monitor my e-mail or Internet activity," Nagel said. "So I assumed it wasn't, which was a horrible assumption."[104]

Companies believe that electronic monitoring will reduce the estimated 30 to 40% decrease in productivity associated with Internet surfing during work hours. Interestingly, companies such as WakeMed Health & Hospitals and Butterball do not even inform employees that they are being monitored at work. Some people believe that the failure to tell employees about monitoring activities is just plain wrong.[105]

How Much Electronic Surveillance in the Workplace Is Too Much?

1. Electronic surveillance signals a distrust in employees, erodes morale, and ultimately hampers productivity. Explain your rationale.

2. Employers sign the paychecks and own the equipment, so they have the right to make sure they are getting their money's worth and their equipment is being used properly. Explain.

3. This sort of "snoopervision" creates a cat-and-mouse game in which "beating the system" becomes more important than productivity. Explain.

4. Electronic surveillance is unnecessary if properly trained and equipped employees are held accountable for meeting challenging but fair performance goals. Explain your rationale.

5. No amount of electronic performance monitoring can make up for poor hiring decisions, inadequate training, a weak performance-reward system, and inept supervision. Explain.

6. Invent other interpretations or options. Discuss.

Web Resources

For study material and exercises that apply to this chapter, visit our Web site, www.mhhe.com/kreitner

Chapter 18

Managing Change and Stress

Student Resources for Studying Chapter 18

The Web site for your text includes resources that will help you master the concepts in this chapter. As you read, you'll want to visit the site for these helpful tools:

- Your online Study Guide includes learning objectives, a chapter summary, a glossary of key terms, and discussion questions.
- Take a practice quiz and test your knowledge!
- Scroll through a PowerPoint presentation with key concepts for this chapter.

Your instructor might also direct you to the Web site for these exercises:

- Self-assessments that correspond with the chapter content and a Group Exercise.
- You'll also find Video Cases and Internet Exercises for this chapter online.

www.mhhe.com/kreitner

The nation's business leaders are confronting a confusing and stark reality. Few have ever faced such calamitous circumstances. A daunting task lies before them: making sure their corporations survive and positioning their businesses for the opportunities that lie ahead after this storm subsides. Every action and decision matters. Urgency, speed and flexibility become imperatives. . . .

This is a time for leaders to lead. They must face immense and ambiguous problems head-on and demonstrate to others a way forward, despite the fog. They must get down to serious work. Forget about wishful thinking and cheerleading. They have to dig into the details of their businesses and the external environment. They must seek contributions from other people, but they cannot pass the buck when it comes to making hard decisions. Leaders must own these decisions, being sensitive and compassionate toward the human beings affected by them. The best decisions will reflect the need to survive in the short term while coming out better in the long term. Times of upheaval provide tremendous opportunities for companies with smart leaders to act faster and better and to gain ground against their competition.

What exactly is this "new new reality?" Only a few months ago, leaders were managing their businesses for revenue growth and fatter profits. Then, the global financial system spun out of control and credit dried up. Virtually no corporation, no matter how strong, has been left untouched. All have been hugely affected by the lack of liquidity or flow of cash as the credit spigot got shut off. Even a AAA-rated company such as AIG had to be taken over by the U.S. Government. . . .

In early fall 2008, when DuPont Chairman and Chief Executive Officer Charles O. Holliday Jr. saw that an economic downturn was coming, he immediately put that reality on the table. He pulled together his top team of people to pool their thinking about how serious and long the downturn might be—and how it would affect DuPont's business. Unmistakable signs suggested that a severe downturn was indeed setting in. For example, bookings at the hotel DuPont owns in Wilmington, Del., serving mostly business customers, had fallen sharply.

DuPont was fundamentally strong, but Holliday wanted to ensure that the company stayed ahead of the situation. Cash had to be protected, and the company would have to reduce its costs quickly, ahead of a sharp revenue decline. No one likes to close production facilities, but Holliday did not sidestep the issues of shifting production

DuPont CEO Charles Holliday threw himself into action as the recession quickly became a reality and influenced others around him while doing so.

and perhaps shuttering some facilities. Those sensitive issues had to be explored.

Meanwhile, the CEO tirelessly drove the message about the need to reduce costs and conserve cash throughout the company. Some actions were taken immediately. The company released many of its outside contractors, in some cases shifting work to employees whose work was slowing.

Even as leaders planned their courses of action, Holliday questioned the pace. Conscientious leaders were promising to make changes two or three months out. Holliday realized that many of those actions had to take place right then and pushed execution into high gear.

Holliday rose to the challenge before him, as did many leaders throughout DuPont. He didn't stay in his office or wash his hands of the challenge by delegating. He faced it head-on and drove execution throughout the company. His own confidence in grappling with the uncertain and difficult circumstances became contagious.[1]

FOR DISCUSSION

What are the strengths of DuPont's approach to managing change?

The worldwide recession has created tremendous pressure on organizations to change. The chapter opening vignette, for example, illustrated how DuPont's CEO took a proactive approach toward dealing with this crisis. Other well-known companies such as GE, Intel, Toyota, and Pepsi have similarly implemented corporate-wide change initiatives to help weather the current financial storm.[2] In addition to these forces for change, increased global competition, startling breakthroughs in information technology, and calls for greater corporate ethics are forcing companies to change the way they do business. Employees want satisfactory work environments, customers are demanding greater value, and investors want more integrity in financial disclosures. The rate of organizational and societal change is clearly accelerating.

Furthermore, any type of change, whether it be product driven, personal, or organizational, is likely to encounter resistance even when it represents an appropriate course of action. Even when employees don't actively resist a change, the goal of the change might not be realized if employees feel so negative about it that absenteeism and turnover rise.[3] Peter Senge, a well-known expert on the topic of organizational change, made the following comment about organizational change during an interview with *Fast Company* magazine:

> When I look at efforts to create change in big companies over the past 10 years, I have to say that there's enough evidence of success to say that change is possible—and enough evidence of failure to say that it isn't likely.[4]

If Senge is correct, then it is all the more important for current and future managers to learn how they can successfully implement organizational change.

This final chapter was written to help managers navigate the journey of change. Specifically, we discuss the forces that create the need for organization change, models of planned change, resistance to change, and how managers can better manage the stress associated with organizational change.

to the point

What are the external and internal forces for organizational change?

LO.I Forces of Change

How do organizations know when they should change? What cues should an organization look for? Although there are no clear-cut answers to these questions, cues signaling the need for change are found by monitoring the forces for change.

Organizations encounter many different forces for change. These forces come from external sources outside the organization and from internal sources. This section examines the forces that create the need for change. Awareness of these forces can

Figure 18–1   *The External and Internal Forces for Change*

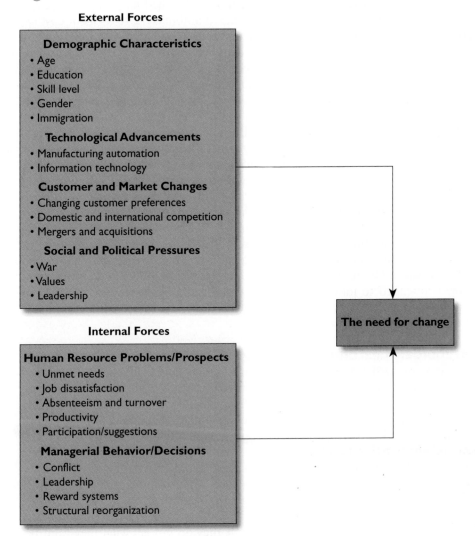

help managers determine when they should consider implementing an organizational change. The external and internal forces for change are presented in Figure 18–1.

External Forces

External forces for change originate outside the organization. Because these forces have global effects, they may cause an organization to question the essence of what business it is in and the process by which products and services are produced. Let us now consider the five key external forces for change: demographic characteristics, technological advancements, market changes, social and political pressures, and a crisis.

External forces for change
Originate outside the organization.

Demographic Characteristics   Chapter 2 provided a detailed discussion of demographic changes occurring in the US workforce. We concluded that organizations need to effectively manage diversity if they are to receive maximum contribution and commitment from employees. An aging US workforce has become an important force for change at Toyota. For years, the company has had an edge in efficiency; its workers were paid less than those at US–based automakers, so its labor cost for producing each car was less. But as the US employees have been with the company nearly two decades, their wages have climbed, even as Toyota's US competitors have laid off many of their older workers and negotiated contracts that pay newer workers lower rates. Now Toyota has to work harder than ever to improve efficiency, cut the cost of health care benefits, and find other ways to keep its competitive edge.[5]

Technological Advancements
Both manufacturing and service organizations are increasingly using technology as a means to improve productivity, competitiveness, and customer service while also cutting costs. For example, information technology is enabling more and more forms of self-service, from Internet stores and banks for customers to online help for employees who want to learn about their benefits packages. Visitors to Adour Alain Ducasse restaurant in New York City can choose their wines by looking up information on a touch screen in the bar. The restaurant's management sees the technology not as a substitute for an educated sommelier but as a way for customers to enjoy learning about and trying new wines.[6] In other applications, including use of robots in factories, technology is intended to improve efficiency without adding employees. There is no question that the development and use of technological advancements is probably one of the biggest forces for change.

Shareholder, Customer, and Market Changes
Shareholders have become more involved with pressing for organizational change in response to ethical lapses from senior management and anger over executives' compensation packages. Companies such as Amgen Inc., Schering-Plough, and Prudential Financial Inc., for example, have gone as far as using Web surveys to obtain shareholder feedback about pay practices (see the Real World/Real People feature on page 537). Aflac has taken this trend one step further by becoming the first US company to allow shareholders to have a say on pay. Say on pay means that shareholders actually provide the deciding vote on executives' compensation practices.[7] Increasing customer sophistication is requiring organizations to deliver higher value in their products and services. Customers are simply demanding more now than they did in the past. Moreover, customers are more likely to shop elsewhere if they do not get what they want because of lower customer switching costs. This has led more and more companies to seek customer feedback about a wide range of issues in order to retain and attract customers. For example, McDonald's actively collects information about consumer preferences and tastes and uses it to revise the menu. This led McDonald's to create more chicken offerings. The company now sells almost as much chicken as beef and its chicken sales are twice those of its leading competitors combined. ConAgra Foods also revamped its Banquet frozen dinners based on customer feedback, and Amazon. com has modified its internal process to overcome customer complaints.[8]

With respect to market changes, companies are experiencing increased pressure to obtain more productivity because global competition is fierce. Swings in the economic cycle also spur a need to change in response to surging or falling demand for products, requiring companies to produce more or survive on less.

Social and Political Pressures
These forces are created by social and political events. For example, widespread concern about the impact of climate change and rising energy costs have been important forces for change in almost

Companies Are Asking Shareholders for Input about Executive Compensation

As outrage grows over executive-pay practices, biotechnology firm Amgen Inc. is taking the unusual step of asking shareholders what they think of its compensation plan.

In its March 26 proxy, Amgen, Thousand Oaks, Calif., directed shareholders to a 10-question online survey. Queries include whether the plan is based on performance and whether the performance goals are clearly disclosed and understandable. Amgen says it will post a summary of the responses on its Web site after its May 6 shareholder meeting.

Amgen's survey, one of the first of its kind, comes as executives and directors seek new ways to reach out to restless shareholders. Drug maker Schering-Plough Corp. had planned a similar survey before it agreed last month to be acquired by Merck & Co.; the company declines to comment on whether it will still conduct the survey. Prudential Financial Inc. this year created a link on its Web site so investors could comment on its compensation plan.

Do you think it makes sense to get shareholder input on executive compensation? Explain.

SOURCE: Excerpted from P Dvorak, "Companies Seek Shareholder Input on Pay Practices," *The Wall Street Journal*, April 6, 2009, p B4.

every industry around the world. Companies have gone "green," looking for ways to use less energy themselves and to sell products that consume less energy. Employees of Microsoft are eagerly claiming spots on the company's free shuttle buses, leaving their cars at home, and employees at 3M have submitted thousands of ideas to the company's 3P (Pollution Prevention Pays) program, saving the company more than $1 billion in the first year alone.[9]

In general, social and political pressure are exerted through legislative bodies that represent the American populace. For example, 27 states have imposed so-called obesity taxes on vending machine snacks in an attempt to reduce obesity in the United States. Such taxes, which also have been considered for nondiet soft drinks, will surely hurt sales for the snack and soft drink industries.[10] Political events also can create substantial change. For example, the war in Iraq created tremendous opportunities for defense contractors and organizations like Halliburton that are involved in rebuilding the country. Although it is difficult for organizations to predict changes in political forces, many organizations hire lobbyists and consultants to help them detect and respond to social and political changes. In the case of climate change, experts predict that some degree of regulation is likely. Harvard business professor Forest Reinhardt advises that companies take bold action, rather than waiting for government constraints:

Microsoft employees getting off the complimentary shuttle bus.

Business leaders must be courageous in betting on the long-term future that will benefit their companies the most. . . . By betting on the future they want, corporations will make that future all the more likely. Prudent businesspeople may balk at the idea that they should stick their necks out and, in some cases, act unilaterally on climate change. But their necks are already exposed.[11]

Internal Forces

Internal forces for change

Originate inside the organization.

Internal forces for change come from inside the organization. These forces may be subtle, such as low job satisfaction, or can manifest in outward signs, such as low productivity and conflict. Internal forces for change come from both human resource problems and managerial behavior/decisions.

Human Resource Problems/Prospects

These problems stem from employee perceptions about how they are treated at work and the match between individual and organization needs and desires. Chapter 6 highlighted the relationship between an employee's unmet needs and job dissatisfaction. Dissatisfaction is a symptom of an underlying employee problem that should be addressed. For example, employees from 3M Co., Sony Corp, and Caterpillar Inc. factories in France took senior managers hostage in response to dissatisfaction with the benefits being received by laid-off workers. A related incident occurred at Republic Windows and Doors when the company closed its plant in Chicago. Employees staged a sit-in until they were paid for 60 days of severance and accrued vacation.[12] Unusual or high levels of absenteeism and turnover also represent forces for change. Organizations might respond to these problems by using the various approaches to job design discussed in Chapter 8; by reducing employees' role conflict, overload, and ambiguity (recall our discussion in Chapter 10); and by removing the different stressors discussed in the final section of this chapter. Prospects for positive change stem from employee participation and suggestions.

Managerial Behavior/Decisions

Excessive interpersonal conflict between managers and their subordinates is a sign that change is needed. Both the manager and the employee may need interpersonal skills training, or the two individuals may simply need to be separated. For example, one of the parties might be transferred to a new department. Inappropriate leader behaviors such as inadequate direction or support may result in human resource problems requiring change. As discussed in Chapter 16, leadership training is one potential solution for this problem. Inequitable reward systems—recall our discussion in Chapters 8 and 9—and the type of structural reorganizations discussed in Chapter 17 are additional forces for change. Finally, managerial decisions are a powerful force for change. Consider the implications of the growing trend for organizations to drop their health care coverage: A recent national survey revealed that 19 percent of US companies are planning to eliminate health care benefits.[13] As discussed in detail in Chapter 8, employees' perceived organizational justice of such a decision may crush employee motivation, satisfaction, and performance.

to the point

How do Lewin's model of change, a systems model of change, and Kotter's model explain the change process, and how does the process of organizational development unfold?

Models and Dynamics of Planned Change

American managers are criticized for emphasizing short-term, quick-fix solutions to organizational problems. When applied to organizational change, this approach is doomed from the start. Quick-fix solutions do not really solve underlying problems, and they have little staying power. This leads to the conclusion that organizational change should be viewed as a natural, normal, and constant characteristic of organizational life. This is what Amy Lessack, Wachovia senior vice president, enterprise learning, had to say about organizational change:

Figure 18–2   *A Generic Typology of Organizational Change*

Change management is not an event for us, it's something we do every day. It is embedded in the work we do, so every time we do learning design or talk to clients or to the business, we talk about change—how it's impacting employees and leaders, how to lead that change, and how can we partner with the business to help employees work through the changes.[14]

Researchers and managers alike have tried to identify effective ways to manage the change process given its importance for organizational survival. This section sheds light on their insights. After discussing different types of organizational changes, we review Lewin's change model, a systems model of change, Kotter's eight steps for leading organizational change, and organizational development.

Types of Change

A useful three-way typology of change is displayed in Figure 18–2.[15] This typology is generic because it relates to all sorts of change, including both administrative and technological changes. Adaptive change is lowest in complexity, cost, and uncertainty. It involves reimplementation of a change in the same organizational unit at a later time or imitation of a similar change by a different unit. For example, an adaptive change for a department store would be to rely on 12-hour days during the annual inventory week. The store's accounting department could imitate the same change in work hours during tax preparation time. Adaptive changes are not particularly threatening to employees because they are familiar.

Innovative changes fall midway on the continuum of complexity, cost, and uncertainty. An experiment with flexible work schedules by a farm supply warehouse company qualifies as an innovative change if it entails modifying the way other firms in the industry already use it. Unfamiliarity, and hence greater uncertainty, make fear of change a problem with innovative changes.

At the high end of the continuum of complexity, cost, and uncertainty are radically innovative changes. Changes of this sort are the most difficult to implement and tend to be the most threatening to managerial confidence and employee job security. At the same time, however, radically innovative changes potentially realize the greatest benefits. Importantly, radical changes must be supported by an organization's culture. Organizational change is more likely to fail if it is inconsistent with any of the three levels of organizational culture: observable artifacts, espoused values, and basic assumptions (see the discussion in Chapter 3).

L0.2 Lewin's Change Model

Most theories of organizational change originated from the landmark work of social psychologist Kurt Lewin. Lewin developed a three-stage model of planned change that explained how to initiate, manage, and stabilize the change process.[16] The three stages are unfreezing, changing, and refreezing. Before reviewing each stage, it is important to highlight the assumptions underlying this model:[17]

1. The change process involves learning something new, as well as discontinuing current attitudes, behaviors, or organizational practices.

2. Change will not occur unless there is motivation to change. This is often the most difficult part of the change process.

3. People are the hub of all organizational changes. Any change, whether in terms of structure, group process, reward systems, or job design, requires individuals to change.

4. Resistance to change is found even when the goals of change are highly desirable.

5. Effective change requires reinforcing new behaviors, attitudes, and organizational practices.

Let us now consider the three stages of change.

Unfreezing   The focus of this stage is to create the motivation to change. In doing so, individuals are encouraged to replace old behaviors and attitudes with those desired by management. Managers can begin the unfreezing process by disconfirming the usefulness or appropriateness of employees' present behaviors or attitudes. In other words, employees need to become dissatisfied with the old way of doing things. Managers frequently create the motivation for change by presenting data regarding levels of effectiveness, efficiency, or customer satisfaction. This helps employees understand the need for change. For example, declines in the stock price and same-store sales of Starbucks, along with the reappointment of Howard Schultz as CEO of the company he once built into an internationally known brand, signaled a need for change in how Starbucks operated. Schultz communicated that in a memo complaining that the company was losing its vision and growing dull in terms of product innovation. He has attempted to create a sense of urgency and motivate a commitment to change through his intense leadership style and frequent trips to meet directly with employees and urge them "not to be 'bystanders' who tolerate mediocrity."[18]

Benchmarking

Process by which a company compares its performance with that of high-performing organizations.

Benchmarking is a technique that can be used to help unfreeze an organization. **Benchmarking** "describes the overall process by which a company compares its performance with that of other companies, then learns how the strongest-performing companies achieve their results."[19] For example, one company for which we consulted discovered through benchmarking that their costs to develop software were twice as high as the best companies in the industry, and the time it took to get a new product to market was four times longer than the benchmarked organizations. These data were ultimately used to unfreeze employees' attitudes and motivate people to change the organization's internal processes in order to remain competitive. Managers also need to devise ways to reduce the barriers to change during this stage.

Changing   This is the stage in which organizational change takes place. This change, whether large or small, is undertaken to improve some process, procedure, product, service, or outcome of interest to management. Because change involves learning and doing things differently, this stage entails providing employees with new information, new behavioral models, new processes or procedures, new equipment, new technology, or new ways of getting the job done. How does management know what to change?

There is no simple answer to this question. Organizational change can be aimed at improvement or growth, or it can focus on solving a problem such as poor customer service or low productivity. Change also can be targeted at different levels in an organization. For example, sending managers to leadership training programs can be a solution to improving individuals' job satisfaction and productivity. In contrast, installing new information technology may be the change required to increase work group productivity and overall corporate profits. The point to keep in mind is that change should be targeted at some type of desired end-result. The systems model of change, which is the next model to be discussed, provides managers with a framework to diagnose the target of change.

Refreezing   The goal of this stage is to support and reinforce the change. Change is supported by helping employees integrate the changed behavior or attitude into their normal way of doing things. This is accomplished by first giving employees the chance to exhibit the new behaviors or attitudes. Once exhibited, positive reinforcement is used to encourage the desired change. Additional coaching and modeling also are used at this point to reinforce the stability of the change. Extrinsic rewards, particularly monetary incentives (recall our discussion in Chapter 9), are frequently used for this purpose.[20]

A Systems Model of Change

A systems approach takes a "big picture" perspective of organizational change. It is based on the notion that any change, no matter how large or small, has a cascading effect throughout an organization.[21] For example, promoting an individual to a new work group affects the group dynamics in both the old and new groups. Similarly, creating project or work teams may necessitate the need to revamp compensation practices. These examples illustrate that change creates additional change. Today's solutions are tomorrow's problems.

A systems model of change offers managers a framework or model to use for diagnosing *what* to change and for determining *how* to evaluate the success of a change effort. To further your understanding about this model, we first describe its components and then discuss a brief application. The four main components of a systems model of change are inputs, strategic plans, target elements of change, and outputs (see Figure 18–3).

Inputs   All organizational changes should be consistent with an organization's mission, vision, and resulting strategic plan. A **mission statement** represents the "reason" an organization exists, and an organization's *vision* is a long-term goal that describes "what" an organization wants to become. Consider how the difference between mission and vision affects organizational change. Your university probably has a mission to educate people. This mission does not necessarily imply anything about change. It simply defines the university's overall purpose.[22] In

Mission statement
Summarizes "why" an organization exists.

Figure 18–3   *A Systems Model of Change*

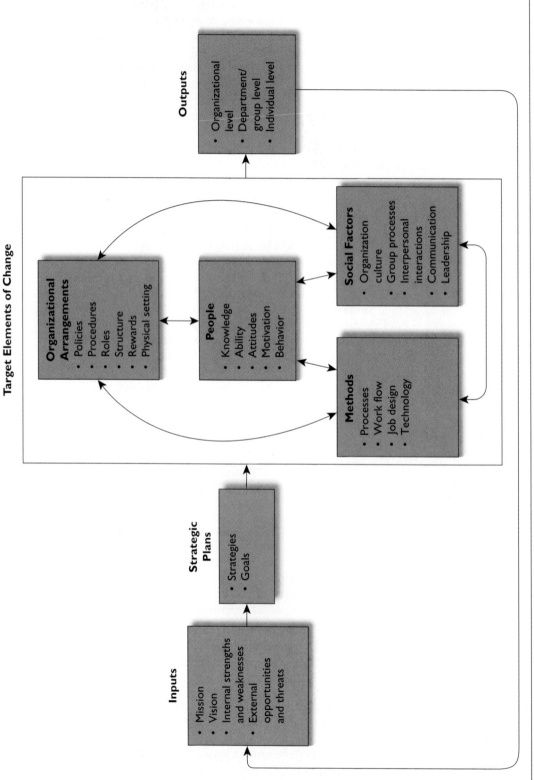

Inputs

- Mission
- Vision
- Internal strengths and weaknesses
- External opportunities and threats

Strategic Plans

- Strategies
- Goals

Target Elements of Change

Organizational Arrangements

- Policies
- Procedures
- Roles
- Structure
- Rewards
- Physical setting

People

- Knowledge
- Ability
- Attitudes
- Motivation
- Behavior

Social Factors

- Organization culture
- Group processes
- Interpersonal interactions
- Communication
- Leadership

Methods

- Processes
- Work flow
- Job design
- Technology

Outputs

- Organizational level
- Department/group level
- Individual level

SOURCES: Adapted from D R Fuqua and D J Kurpius, "Conceptual Models in Organizational Consultation," *Journal of Counseling and Development*, July–August 1993. pp 602–18; and D A Nadler and M L Tushman, "Organizational Frame Bending: Principles for Managing Reorientation," *Academy of Management Executive*, August 1989, pp 194–203.

contrast, the university may have a vision to be recognized as the "best" university in the country. This vision requires the organization to benchmark itself against other world-class universities and to create plans for achieving the vision. For example, the vision of the W P Carey School of Business at Arizona State University is to be among the top 25 business schools in the world. An assessment of an organization's internal strengths and weaknesses against its environmental opportunities and threats (SWOT) is another key input within the systems model. This SWOT analysis is a key component of the strategic planning process.

Strategic Plans   A strategic plan outlines an organization's long-term direction and the actions necessary to achieve planned results. Among other things, strategic plans are based on results from a SWOT analysis. This analysis aids in developing an organizational strategy to attain desired goals such as profits, customer satisfaction, quality, adequate return on investment, and acceptable levels of turnover and employee satisfaction and commitment.

Target Elements of Change   **Target elements of change** are the components of an organization that may be changed. They essentially represent change levers that managers can push and pull to influence various aspects of an organization. The choice of which lever to pull, however, is based on a diagnosis of a problem, or problems, or the actions needed to accomplish a goal: A problem exists when managers are not obtaining the results they desire. The target elements of change are used to diagnose problems and to identify change-related solutions.

As shown in Figure 18–3, there are four targeted elements of change: organizational arrangements, social factors, methods, and people.[23] Each target element of change contains a subset of more detailed organizational features. For instance, the "social factors" component includes consideration of an organization's culture, group processes, interpersonal interactions, communication, and leadership. There are two final issues to keep in mind about the target elements of change shown in Figure 18–3. First, the double-headed arrows connecting each target element of change convey the message that change ripples across an organization. For example, changing a reward system to reinforce team rather than individual performance (an organizational arrangement) is likely to impact organizational culture (a social factor). Second, the "people" component is placed in the center of the target elements of change box because all organizational change ultimately impacts employees. Organizational change is more likely to succeed when managers proactively consider the impact of change on its employees.

Outputs   Outputs represent the desired end-results of a change. Once again, these end-results should be consistent with an organization's strategic plan. Figure 18–3 indicates that change may be directed at the organizational level, department/group level, or individual level. Change efforts are more complicated and difficult to manage when they are targeted at the organizational level. This occurs because organizational-level changes are more likely to affect multiple target elements of change shown in the model.

Applying the Systems Model of Change   There are two different ways to apply the systems model of change. The first is as an aid during the strategic planning process. Once a group of managers have determined their vision and strategic goals, the target elements of change can be considered when developing

Target elements of change

Components of an organization that may be changed.

action plans to support the accomplishment of goals. For example, following the merger of Adolph Coors Company and Molson, the management team of Molson Coors Brewing established goals of cutting costs by $180 million, making Coors Light a global brand, and developing new high-end brands of beer. Target elements of change have included strengthening shared values of the predecessor companies (social factors), keeping production and distribution employees focused on their existing functions (motivation, a people factor), creating a general-management development program (another people factor), and establishing a subsidiary to specialize in new products (organizational arrangements).[24]

The second application involves using the model as a diagnostic framework to determine the causes of an organizational problem and to propose solutions. We highlight this application by considering a consulting project in which we used the model. We were contacted by the CEO of a software company and asked to figure out why the presidents of three divisions were not collaborating with each other—the problem. It turned out that two of the presidents submitted a proposal for the same $4 million project from a potential customer. Our client did not get the work because the customer was appalled at having received two proposals from the same company; hence the CEO's call to us. We decided to interview employees by using a structured set of questions that pertained to each of the target elements of change. For instance, we asked employees to comment on the extent to which the reward system, organizational culture, work flow, and physical setting contributed to collaboration across divisions. The interviews taught us that the lack of collaboration among the division presidents was due to the reward system (an organizational arrangement), a competitive culture and poor communications (social factors), and poor work flow (a methods factor). Our recommendation was to change the reward systems, restructure the organization, and redesign the work flow.

go to the Web for the Self-Exercise: Applying the Systems Model of Change

L0.3 Kotter's Eight Steps for Leading Organizational Change

John Kotter, an expert in leadership and change management, believes that organizational change typically fails because senior management makes a host of implementation errors. Kotter proposed an eight-step process for leading change (see Table 18–1) based on these errors.[25] Unlike the systems model of change, this model is not diagnostic in orientation. Its application will not help managers to diagnose what needs to be changed. Rather, this model is more like Lewin's model of change in that it prescribes how managers should sequence or lead the change process.

Kotter's eight steps, shown in Table 18–1, subsume Lewin's model of change. The first four steps represent Lewin's "unfreezing" stage. Steps 5, 6, and 7 represent "changing," and step 8 corresponds to "refreezing." The value of Kotter's steps is that it provides specific recommendations about behaviors that managers need to exhibit to successfully lead organizational change. It is important to remember that Kotter's research reveals that it is ineffective to skip steps and that managers most often make mistakes at the beginning.[26] For instance, Yahoo cofounder and

Table 18–1   *Steps to Leading Organizational Change*

STEP	DESCRIPTION
1. Establish a sense of urgency	Unfreeze the organization by creating a compelling reason for why change is needed.
2. Create the guiding coalition	Create a cross-functional, cross-level group of people with enough power to lead the change.
3. Develop a vision and strategy	Create a vision and strategic plan to guide the change process.
4. Communicate the change vision	Create and implement a communication strategy that consistently communicates the new vision and strategic plan.
5. Empower broad-based action	Eliminate barriers to change, and use target elements of change to transform the organization. Encourage risk taking and creative problem solving.
6. Generate short-term wins	Plan for and create short-term "wins" or improvements. Recognize and reward people who contribute to the wins.
7. Consolidate gains and produce more change	The guiding coalition uses credibility from short-term wins to create more change. Additional people are brought into the change process as change cascades throughout the organization. Attempts are made to reinvigorate the change process.
8. Anchor new approaches in the culture	Reinforce the changes by highlighting connections between new behaviors and processes and organizational success. Develop methods to ensure leadership development and succession.

SOURCE: The steps were developed by J P Kotter, *Leading Change* (Boston: Harvard Business School Press, 1996).

former CEO Jerry Yang was partially unsuccessful in creating change at Yahoo because "he was slow to consolidate redundant businesses (two photo sharing properties, multiple social-media sites) and failed to explain the strategy behind his Get Google objective."[27] These errors pertain to steps one and three. The Real World/ Real People feature on page 546 provides an example of how MasterCard's Global Talent Management and Development (GTM&D) group used Kotter's model.

L0.4 Creating Change through Organization Development

Organization development (OD) is different from the previously discussed models of change. OD does not entail a structured sequence as proposed by Lewin and Kotter, but it does possess the same diagnostic focus associated with the systems model of change. That said, OD is much broader in orientation than any of the previously discussed models. Specifically, a pair of experts in this field of study and practice defined **organization development** as follows:

OD consists of planned efforts to help persons work and live together more effectively, over time, in their organizations. These goals are achieved by applying behavioral science principles, methods, and theories adapted from the fields of psychology, sociology, education, and management.[28]

Organization development

A set of techniques or tools used to implement planned organizational change.

MasterCard Implements Kotter's Model

To increase the urgency for change (step1), in November 2007, a getAbstract Chat hosted by Chief Marketing Officer Larry Flanagan involved close to a thousand MasterCard employees via a global teleconference of the key themes of Dr. Kotter's work and their application to the company. . . .

The Guiding Team (step 2) consists of CMO Flanagan and his communication team; Valerie Gelb, chief sales development officer and an early adapter; and the GTM&D team, supported by the ISB trainers. "While we focus on creating a culture of change, we allow each business unit to assemble the correct guiding team for each individual change initiative," says Ann Schulte, VP, Learning and Development, who leads GTM&D's MasterCard University. . . .

MasterCard's vision (step 3), reveals Matthew Breitfelder, VP, Management & Leadership Development, is "To be ready, willing, and able to change as the need arises." The company's broad communication efforts (step 4)—including Intranet coverage of the change initiatives—have been enhanced through its strategic partnership with Worldwide Communications (its internal marketing and advertising team). "We have empowered action (step 5) by providing all MasterCard employees access to these concepts through a variety of means. . . ."

As for producing short-term wins (step 6), Schulte says, "While we are early in our process, we already can see improvements in the ways in which teams think about and plan for change. We are beginning to build a common 'language' around change."

Adds Breitfelder, "We know we have to keep the momentum going (step 7), so we spend time with teams helping them see the end goal but also making sure they remember the reason why this work is so important."

Making these changes sustainable (step 8) does not occur by coincidence. "Following each LBC session, the participants have a detailed action plan that prepares them to not only launch their initiative, but to sustain early gains," Ray says. "The GTM&D team follows up with business unit teams, providing guidance, monitoring progress against action plans, and serving as 'group mentors,' all aimed at making the changes a permanent part of our culture."

To what extent was MasterCard deficient in following Kotter's steps? Explain.

SOURCE: Excerpted from "MasterCard Worldwide: Taking Charge of Change," *Training Magazine,* June 2008, pp 30–36.

As you can see from this definition, OD constitutes a set of techniques or interventions that are used to implement "planned" organizational change aimed at increasing "an organization's ability to improve itself as a humane and effective system." OD techniques or interventions apply to each of the change models discussed in this section. For example OD is used during Lewin's "changing" stage. It also is used to identify and implement targeted elements of change within the systems model of change. Finally, OD might be used during Kotter's steps 1, 3, 5, 6, and 7. Finally, OD is put into practice by change agents. A **change agent** is someone who is a catalyst in helping organizations to deal with old problems in new ways. Change agents can be external consultants or internal employees.[29] In this section, we briefly review how OD works and its research and practical implications.

Change agent

Individual who is a catalyst in helping organizations to implement change.

How OD Works   OD change agents follow a medical-like model. They approach the organization as if it were a "sick" patient, "diagnose" its ills, prescribe and implement an "intervention," and "evaluate" progress. If the evaluation reveals that positive change has not occurred, this information provides feedback that is used to refine the diagnosis and/or consider the extent to which the intervention was effectively implemented (see Figure 18–4). Let us consider the components of the OD process shown in Figure 18–4.

1. *Diagnosis: What is the problem and its causes?* Change agents use a combination of interviews, surveys, meetings, written materials, and direct observation to

Figure 18–4   *The OD Process*

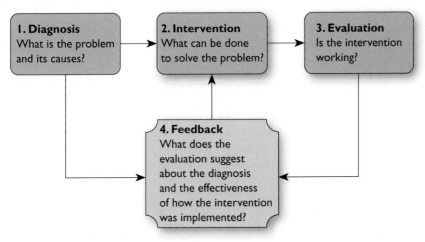

SOURCE: Adapted from W L French and C H Bell Jr, *Organization Development: Behavioral Interventions for Organizational Improvement* (Englewood Cliffs, NJ: Prentice Hall, 1978).

determine the problem and its associated causes. We recommend using the target elements of change in the systems model of change as a vehicle to develop diagnostic questions aimed at indentifying causes. For example, you might ask, "to what extent does the structure or reward system contribute to the problem?"

2. *Intervention: What can be done to solve the problem?* The treatment or intervention represents the changes being made to solve the problem. Treatments are selected based on the causes of the problem. For example, if the cause of low quality is poor teamwork, then team building (see Chapter 11) might be used as the intervention. In contrast, managers might be sent to some type of leadership training if bad leadership is the cause of low quality (see Chapter 16). The key thing to remember is that there is not one "set" of intervention techniques that apply to all situations. Rather, you can use any number of interventions based on theories and models you studied in this book. A contingency approach allows you to select the intervention that seems best suited for the problem and causes at hand.[30]

3. *Evaluation: Is the intervention working?* Evaluation requires the organization to develop measures of effectiveness—recall our discussion of organizational effectiveness in Chapter 17. The proper measure depends on the problem. For example, measures of voluntary turnover and productivity would be appropriate if the problem involved employee turnover and productivity, respectively. If possible, the final evaluation should be based on comparing measures of effectiveness obtained before and after the intervention.

4. *Feedback: What does the evaluation suggest about the diagnosis and the effectiveness of how the intervention was implemented?* If the evaluation reveals that the intervention worked, then the OD process is complete and the change agent can consider how best to "refreeze" the changes. Oppositely, a negative evaluation means one of two things: (1) either the initial diagnosis was wrong or (2) the intervention was not effectively implemented. Negative evaluations generally require the change agent to collect more information about steps 1 and 2 in the OD process shown in Figure 18–4.[31]

OD Research and Practical Implications   Before discussing OD research, note that OD-related interventions produced the following insights:

- A meta-analysis of 18 studies indicated that employee satisfaction with change was higher when top management was highly committed to the change effort.[32]

- A meta-analysis of 52 studies provided support for the systems model of organizational change. Specifically, varying one target element of change created changes in other target elements. Also, there was a positive relationship between individual behavior change and organizational-level change.[33]

- A meta-analysis of 126 studies demonstrated that multifaceted interventions using more than one OD technique were more effective in changing job attitudes and work attitudes than interventions that relied on only one human-process or technostructural approach.[34]

- A survey of 1,700 firms from China, Japan, the United States, and Europe revealed that (1) US and European firms used OD interventions more frequently than firms from China and Japan and (2) some OD interventions are culture free and some are not.[35]

There are four practical implications derived from this research. First, planned organizational change works. However, management and change agents are advised to rely on multifaceted interventions. As indicated elsewhere in this book, goal setting, feedback, recognition and rewards, training, participation, and challenging job design have good track records relative to improving performance and satisfaction. Second, change programs are more successful when they are geared toward meeting both short-term and long-term results. Managers should not engage in organizational change for the sake of change. Change efforts should produce positive results. Third, organizational change is more likely to succeed when top management is truly committed to the change process and the desired goals of the change program. This is particularly true when organizations pursue large-scale transformation. Finally, the effectiveness of OD interventions is affected by cross-cultural considerations. Managers and OD consultants should not blindly apply an OD intervention that worked in one country to a similar situation in another country.[36]

to the point

What are the key causes of resistance to change and how can managers reduce it?

Understanding and Managing Resistance to Change

No matter how technically or administratively perfect a proposed change may be, people make or break it because organizational change represents a form of influence. That is, organizational change is management's attempt to have employees behave, think, or perform differently. Viewing change from this perspective underscores what we discussed about influence techniques and outcomes in Chapter 15. You may recall that resistance is one of the three possible influence outcomes; the other two are commitment and compliance. This perspective has led many people to conclude that resistance to change represents a failed influence attempt by a change agent. Interestingly, recent research indicates a need to rethink this interpretation.

Past research on resistance has been based on the assumption that "change agents are doing the right and proper things while change recipients throw up unreasonable obstacles or barriers intent on 'doing in' or 'screwing up' the change. . . Accordingly, change agents are portrayed as undeserving victims of the irrational and dysfunctional repsonse of change recipients."[37] This is why resistance is viewed as a negative outcome that is caused by irrational and self-serving recipients. While this can be true, it is equally likely that resistance is caused by two other key factors: the change agent's characteristics, actions, inactions, and perceptions and the quality of the relationship between change agents and change recipients. This section is based on the premise that resistance is a natural form of employee feedback and that it can serve a useful purpose. Managers are encouraged to understand the causes of resistance if they are to effectively manage change.[38] Accordingly, this section presents a model that outlines the causes of resistance and practical ways of overcoming resistance to change.

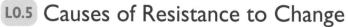

go to the Web for the Self-Exercise: Does Your Commitment to a Change Initiative Predict Your Behavioral Support for the Change?

LO.5 Causes of Resistance to Change

Resistance to change is an emotional/behavioral response to real or imagined threats to an established work routine. Resistance can be as subtle as passive resignation and as overt as deliberate sabotage. Figure 18–5 presents a model of resistance that illustrates the relationship among the three key causes of resistance. The model conceives resistance as a dynamic interaction between these three sources as opposed to being caused solely by irrational and stubborn recipients of change. For example, recipient resistance is partly based on their perceptions of change, which are very much influenced by the attitudes and behaviors exhibited by change agents and the level of trust between change agents and recipients. Similarly, change agents' actions and perceptions are affected by the recipients' actions and inactions and the quality of relationships with recipients. Let us consider each source of resistance.

Resistance to change

Emotional/behavioral response to real or imagined work changes.

Figure 18–5   *A Dynamic Model of Resistance to Change*

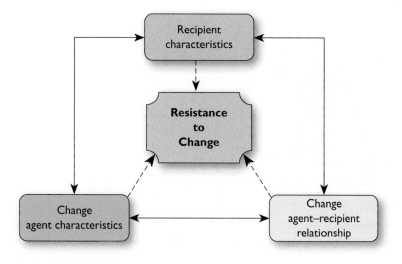

LO.6 **Recipient Characteristics**   Recipient characteristics include a variety of individual differences (see Chapter 5) possessed by recipients. They also represent the actions (e.g., engaging in new behaviors) or inactions (e.g., failing to engage in new behaviors) displayed by recipients. Finally, recipient perceptions of change (e.g., "this change is unfair because I am being asked to do more with no increase in pay") also contribute to resistance. Six of the key recipient characteristics are discussed below:[39]

1. *An individual's predisposition toward change.* This predisposition is highly personal and deeply ingrained. It is an outgrowth of how one learns to handle change and ambiguity as a child. While some people are distrustful and suspicious of change, others see change as a situation requiring flexibility, patience, and understanding.[40] For example, **resilience to change,** which represents a composite characteristic reflecting high self-esteem, optimism, and an internal locus of control, was positively associated with recipients' willingness to accommodate or accept a specific organizational change.[41] Another study of 514 employees from six organizations headquartered on four different continents (North America, Europe, Asia, and Australia) demonstrated that personal dispositions pertaining to having a "positive self-concept" and "tolerance for risk" were positively related to coping with change. That is, people with a positive self-concept and a tolerance for risk handled organizational change better than those without these dispositions.[42]

2. *Surprise and fear of the unknown.* When innovative or radically different changes are introduced without warning, affected employees become fearful of the implications. Rumors fill the void created by a lack of official announcements. This is exactly what happened when General Motors announced its negotiated plan to reduce its workforce through a carefully designed attrition program. The reduction in workforce was needed to help GM lower its operating costs.

> Almost as soon as yesterday's buyout offer from General Motors Corp was announced, news—and rumors—began sweeping through the company's truck assembly plant in Pontiac, Mich. "It spread like wildfire," said 52-year-old Larry Walker, a 33-year veteran of the plant, which employs 2,500 hourly workers and makes the GMC Sierra Truck and Chevrolet Silverado. "I talked about it with my buddies all day long. We're all trying to figure out what we should do."[43]

Resilience to change

Composite personal characteristic reflecting high self-esteem, optimism, and an internal locus of control.

General Motors assembly plant workers read a union bulletin during a meeting called by the Canadian Auto Workers at the Oshawa assembly plant.

3. *Fear of failure.* Intimidating changes on the job can cause employees to doubt their capabilities. Self-doubt erodes self-confidence and cripples personal growth and development. Recall our discussion about self-efficacy in Chapter 5.

4. *Loss of status and/or job security.* Administrative and technological changes that threaten to alter power bases or eliminate jobs generally trigger strong resistance. For example, most corporate restructuring involves the elimination of managerial jobs. One should not be surprised when middle managers resist restructuring and participative management programs that reduce their authority and status.

5. *Peer pressure.* Someone who is not directly affected by a change may actively resist it to protect the interests of his or her friends and coworkers.

6. *Past success.* Success can breed complacency. It also can foster a stubbornness to change because people come to believe that what worked in the past will work in the future. Decades ago the Green Revolution alleviated hunger in Asia and Latin America by equipping farmers with more productive strains of wheat and rice. But in the words of Usha Tuteja, who heads the Agricultural Economics Research Center at Delhi University, "People got complacent." Governments, believing that the problem of feeding a growing population had been solved, stopped funding agricultural research. Unfortunately, today new challenges have again made food supply a major problem, and the solutions will require years of investment in further research.[44]

Change Agent Characteristics
As true for recipients, this cause includes a variey of individual differences (e.g., the big five personality dimensions discussed in Chapter 5) possessed by change agents. For example, one of us recently served as a change agent for a Scandanavian company and encountered resistance from some employees because they had negative views and stereotypes of Americans. Change agent characteristics also represent the actions or inactions displayed by change agents. For example, a change agent who fails to communicate with employees or is perceived as instituting unfair policies is likely to create resistance from recipients.[45] Finally, resistance is a function of the change agent's perceptions of why employees are behaving the way they are in the face of organizational change. A change agent, for instance, might interpret employees' questions as a form of resistance when in fact the questions represent honest attempts at clarifying the change process. Five of the key recipient characteristics are discussed below:

1. *Decisions that disrupt cultural traditions or group relationships.* Whenever individuals are transferred, promoted, or reassigned, cultural and group dynamics are thrown into disequilibrium. For example, Nobuyuki Idei, former CEO of Sony Corp., was worried about employees' resistance to change when he named Sir Howard Stringer as the next chairman and CEO of Sony and asked six corporate officers to resign. Nobuyki's concern, rightfully so, stemmed from the fact that Stringer's appointment is inconsistent with Sony's tradition of promoting an insider with technical background and resignations would create a majority board of foreigners.[46]

2. *Personality conflicts.* Just as a friend can get away with telling us something we would resent hearing from an adversary, the personalities of change agents can breed resistance. Change agents that display any of the traits of bad leadership discussed in Chapter 16 are likely to engender resistance from recipients.

3. *Lack of tact or poor timing.* Undue resistance can occur because change agents introduce change in an insensitive manner or at an awkward time. Proposed organizational changes are more likely to be accepted by others when change agents effectively explain or "sell" the value of their proposed changes. This can be done by explaining how a proposed change is strategically important to an organization's success.

4. *Leadership style.* Research shows that people are less likely to resist change when the change agent uses transformational leadership (see Chapter 16).[47]

5. *Failing to legitimize change.* Change must be internalized by recipients before it will be truly accepted. Active, honest communication and reinforcing reward systems are needed to make this happen. This recommendation underscores the need for change agents to communicate with recipients in a way that considers employees' point-of-view and perspective. It also is important for change agents

to explain how change will lead to positive personal and organizational benefits. This requires that change agents have a clear understanding about how recipients' jobs will change and how they will be rewarded.[48] For example, an employee is unlikely to support a change effort that is perceived as requiring him or her to work longer with more pressure without a commensurate increase in pay.

Change Agent–Recipient Relationship In general, resistance is reduced when change agents and recipients have a postive, trusting relationshp. Trust, as discussed in Chapter 11, involves reciprocal faith in others' intentions and behavior. Mutual mistrust can doom to failure an otherwise well-conceived change. Mistrust encourages secrecy, which begets deeper mistrust. Managers who trust their employees make the change process an open, honest, and participative affair. Employees who, in turn, trust management are more willing to expend extra effort and take chances with something different. In support of this conclusion, a recent study of employees from the oil and banking industries showed that a high-quality relationship between managers and direct reports was associated with less resistance to change.[49]

go to the Web for the Self-Exercise: Assessing Your Organization's Readiness for Change

L0.7 Alternative Strategies for Overcoming Resistance to Change

We previously noted that resistance is a form of feedback and managers need to understand why it is occurring before trying to overcome it. This can be done by considering the extent to which the three sources of resistance shown in Figure 18–5 are contributing to the problem. Consider employee characterisitcs as an example. Employees are more likely to resist when they perceive that the personal costs of change overshadow the benefits. If this is the case, then managers are advised to (1) provide as much information as possible to employees about the change, (2) inform employees about the reasons/rationale for the change, (3) conduct meetings to address employees' questions regarding the change, and (4) provide employees the opportunity to discuss how the proposed change might affect them.[50] Using these recommendations also will improve the agent–recipient relationship because they enhance the level of trust between the parties.

Moreover, Figure 18–5 cautions managers not to assume that people are consciously resisting change. Resistance has a cause and, according to John Kotter's research of more than 100 companies, the cause generally involves some obstacle in the work environment. He noted that obstacles in the organization's structure or in a "performance appraisal system [that] makes people choose between the new vision and their own self-interests" impeded change more than an individual's direct resistance.[51] This perspective implies that it is important for management to obtain employee feedback about any obstacles that may be affecting their ability or willingness to accept change. In the end, change agents should not be afraid to modify the targeted elements of change or their approach toward change based on employee resistance. If people are resisting for valid reasons, then a new change initiative is needed.

In addition to these suggestions, employee participation in the change process is another generic approach for reducing resistance. That said, however, organizational change experts have criticized the tendency to treat participation as a cure-all for resistance to change. They prefer a contingency approach because resistance can take many forms and, furthermore, because situational factors vary (see Table 18–2). As shown in Table 18–2, Participation + Involvement does have its place, but it takes time that is not always available. Also as indicated in Table 18–2, each of the other five methods has its situational niche, advantages,

Table 18–2   *Six Strategies for Overcoming Resistance to Change*

APPROACH	COMMONLY USED IN SITUATIONS	ADVANTAGES	DRAWBACKS
Education + communication	Where there is a lack of information or inaccurate information and analysis.	Once persuaded, people will often help with the implementation of the change.	Can be very time-consuming if lots of people are involved.
Participation + involvement	Where the initiators do not have all the information they need to design the change and where others have considerable power to resist.	People who participate will be committed to implementing change, and any relevant information they have will be integrated into the change plan.	Can be very time-consuming if participators design an inappropriate change.
Facilitation + support	Where people are resisting because of adjustment problems.	No other approach works as well with adjustment problems.	Can be time-consuming, expensive, and still fail.
Negotiation + agreement	Where someone or some group will clearly lose out in a change and where that group has considerable power to resist.	Sometimes it is a relatively easy way to avoid major resistance.	Can be too expensive in many cases if it alerts others to negotiate for compliance.
Manipulation + co-optation	Where other tactics will not work or are too expensive.	It can be a relatively quick and inexpensive solution to resistance problems.	Can lead to future problems if people feel manipulated.
Explicit + implicit coercion	Where speed is essential and where the change initiators possess considerable power.	It is speedy and can overcome any kind of resistance.	Can be risky if it leaves people mad at the initiators.

SOURCE: Reprinted by permission of *Harvard Business Review.* Exhibit from "Choosing Strategies for Change," by J P Kotter and L A Schlesinger, March/April 1979. Copyright 1979 by the Harvard Business School Publishing Corporation; all rights reserved.

and drawbacks. For example, Manipulation + Co-optation may appear to be a negative approach, but it works in the right context. We once used co-optation, which involves giving a resistor a desirable role in the change process, in order to motivate the individual to endorse the change process. This approach ultimately led to a modification in the change process and the resistor's final endorsement. In short, there is no universal strategy for overcoming resistance to change. Managers need a complete repertoire of change strategies.[52]

go to the Web for the Group Exercise: Creating Change at Best Buy

to the point

What are the key conclusions regarding the model of occupational stress, stress moderators, and stress reduction techniques?

LO.8 Dynamics of Stress

We all experience stress on a daily basis. Although stress is caused by many factors, researchers conclude that stress triggers one of two basic reactions: active fighting or passive flight (running away or acceptance), the so-called **fight-or-flight response.**[53] Physiologically, this stress response is a biochemical "passing gear" involving hormonal changes that mobilize the body for extraordinary demands. Imagine how our prehistoric ancestors responded to the stress associated with a charging saber-toothed tiger. To avoid being eaten, they could stand their ground and fight the beast or run away. In either case, their bodies would have been energized by an identical hormonal change, involving the release of adrenaline into the bloodstream.

In today's hectic urbanized and industrialized society, charging beasts have been replaced by problems such as deadlines, role conflict and ambiguity, financial responsibilities, information overload, technology, traffic congestion, noise and air pollution, family problems, and work overload. As with our ancestors, our response to stress may or may not trigger negative side effects, including headaches, ulcers, insomnia, heart disease, high blood pressure, strokes, insomnia, allergies, skin disorders, and mental illness.[54] The same stress response that helped our prehistoric ancestors survive has too often become a factor that seriously impairs our daily lives.

Fight-or-flight response

To either confront stressors or try to avoid them.

Because stress and its consequences are manageable, it is important for managers to learn as much as they can about occupational stress. After defining stress, this section provides an overview of the dynamics associated with stress by presenting a model of occupational stress, discussing moderators of occupational stress, and reviewing the effectiveness of several stress-reduction techniques.

This lion has clearly created a flight response from its targeted prey. Have you ever run away from danger?

Defining Stress

To an orchestra violinist, stress may stem from giving a solo performance before a big audience. While heat, smoke, and flames may represent stress to a firefighter, delivering a speech or presenting a lecture may be stressful for those who are shy. In short, stress means different things to different people. Managers need a working definition.

Formally defined, **stress** is "an adaptive response, mediated by individual characteristics and/or psychological processes, that is a consequence of any external action, situation, or event that places special physical and/or psychological demands upon a person."[55] This definition is not as difficult as it seems when we reduce it to three interrelated dimensions of stress: (1) environmental demands, referred to as stressors, that produce (2) an adaptive response that is influenced by (3) individual differences. Unfortunately, the worldwide recession has been driving up stress levels across the world, which in turn has prompted an increase in the number of people seeking psychological assistance.[56]

Hans Selye, considered the father of the modern concept of stress, pioneered the distinction between stressors and the stress response. Moreover, Selye emphasized that both positive and negative events can trigger an identical stress response that can be beneficial or harmful. He referred to stress that is positive or produces a positive outcome as **eustress.** Receiving an award in front of a large crowd or successfully completing a difficult work assignment both are examples of stressors that produce eustress. He also noted that

- Stress is not merely nervous tension.
- Stress can have positive consequences.
- Stress is not something to be avoided.
- The complete absence of stress is death.[57]

These points make it clear that stress is inevitable. Efforts need to be directed at managing stress, not at somehow escaping it altogether.

Stress
Behavioral, physical, or psychological response to stressors.

Eustress
Stress that is good or produces a positive outcome.

A Model of Occupational Stress

Figure 18–6 presents an instructive model of occupational stress. The model shows that an individual initially appraises four types of stressors. This appraisal then motivates an individual to choose a coping strategy aimed at managing stressors, which, in turn, produces a variety of outcomes. The model also specifies several individual differences that moderate the stress process. A moderator is a variable that causes the relationship between two variables—such as stressors and cognitive appraisal—to be stronger for some people and weaker for others. Three key moderators are discussed in the next section. Let us now consider the remaining components of this model in detail.

Stressors   Stressors are environmental factors that produce stress. Stated differently, stressors are a prerequisite to experiencing the stress response. Figure 18–6 shows the four major types of stressors: individual, group, organizational, and extraorganizational. Individual-level stressors are those directly associated with a person's job duties. The most common examples of individual stressors are job demands, work overload, role conflict, role ambiguity, everyday hassles, perceived control over events occurring in the work environment, and job characteristics.[58]

Stressors
Environmental factors that produce stress.

Figure 18–6   *A Model of Occupational Stress*

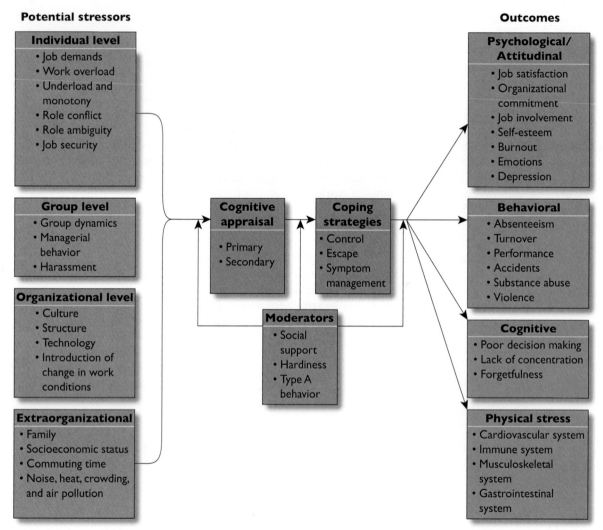

Losing one's job is another important individual-level stressor. Job loss is a very stressful event that is associated with decreased psychological and physical well-being.[59] Finally, sleep-related issues are important stressors. Research shows that most people need about seven hours of sleep per night and that alertness, energy, performance, creativity, and thinking are related to how refreshed an employee feels when starting his/her workday.[60]

Group-level stressors are caused by group dynamics (recall our discussion in Chapter 10) and managerial behavior. Managers create stress for employees by (1) exhibiting inconsistent behaviors, (2) failing to provide support, (3) showing lack of concern, (4) providing inadequate direction, (5) creating a high-productivity environment, and (6) focusing on negatives while ignoring good performance. Sexual harassment experiences represent another group-level stressor. A recent meta-analysis of 90 studies involving over 19,000 people demonstrated that harassing experiences were negatively associated with self-esteem, life and job satisfaction, and organizational commitment, and positively with intentions to quit, absenteeism, anxiety, depression, and physical symptoms of stress.[61] Another review of 110 studies showed that bullying and incivility at work represent group-level stressors that are correlated with higher stress, anger, anxiety, and lower organizational commitment.[62]

Organizational stressors affect large numbers of employees. Organizational culture, which was discussed in Chapter 3, is a prime example. For instance, a high-pressure environment that fuels employee fear about performing up to standard can increase the stress response. The increased use of information technology is another source of organizational stress, as is the air quality and ventilation found throughout the organization. The World Health Organization, for instance, reports that roughly 30% of all new and remodeled buildings have problems related to air quality, and air quality is associated with a variety of conditions such as headaches, dizziness, and the ability to concentrate.[63]

Extraorganizational stressors are those caused by factors outside the organization. For instance, in Chapter 6 we discussed how conflicts associated with balancing one's career and family life are stressful.[64] Socioeconomic status is another extraorganizational stressor. Stress is higher for people with lower socioeconomic status, which represents a combination of (1) economic status, as measured by income; (2) social status, assessed by education level; and (3) work status, as indexed by occupation. These stressors are likely to become more important in the future. In support of this conclusion, two recent national surveys revealed that the majority of Americans cited money and the economy as their biggest stressors.[65]

Cognitive Appraisal of Stressors
Cognitive appraisal reflects an individual's overall perception or evaluation of a situation or stressor. It is an important component within the stress process because people interpret the same stressors differently. For example, some individuals perceive unemployment as a positive liberating experience, whereas others perceive it as a negative debilitating one.

Figure 18–6 shows that people make two types of appraisals when evaluating the potential impact of stressors on their lives: primary and secondary appraisals.[66] A **primary appraisal** results in categorizing a situation or stressor as irrelevant, positive, or stressful. Stress appraisals are obviously the most important in terms of our current discussion because they imply that a situation or stressor is perceived as harmful, threatening, or challenging.[67]

A **secondary appraisal** only occurs in response to a stressful primary appraisal and entails an assessment of what might and can be done to reduce the level of perceived stress. During this evaluation a person considers which coping strategies are available and which ones are most likely to help resolve the situation at hand. Ultimately, the combination of an individual's primary and secondary appraisal influences the choice of coping strategies used to reduce stress.

Coping Strategies
Coping strategies are characterized by the specific behaviors and cognitions used to cope with a situation. People use a combination of three approaches to cope with stressors and stress (see Figure 18–6). The first, called a **control strategy,** consists of using behaviors and cognitions to directly anticipate or solve problems. A control strategy has a take-charge tone. Examples include talking to your boss about workload if you feel overwhelmed with your responsibilities, and confronting someone who is spreading negative rumors. Results from a meta-analysis of 34 studies and more than 4,000 people indicated

Primary appraisal
Determining whether a stressor is irrelevant, positive, or stressful.

Secondary appraisal
Assessing what might and can be done to reduce stress.

Control strategy
Coping strategy that directly confronts or solves problems.

that control coping was positively related to overall health outcomes.[68] Research further shows that people are more apt to use control coping when they possess high self-esteem, self-efficacy, and problem-solving skills.[69]

In contrast to tackling the problem head-on, an **escape strategy** amounts to avoiding the problem. Behaviors and cognitions are used to avoid or escape situations. Individuals use this strategy when they passively accept stressful situations or avoid them by failing to confront the cause of stress (an obnoxious coworker, for instance). Finally, a **symptom management strategy** consists of using methods such as relaxation, meditation, medication, or exercise to manage the symptoms of occupational stress.[70] A vacation, for example, can be a good way to reduce the symptoms of stress.

Escape strategy

Coping strategy that avoids or ignores stressors and problems.

Symptom management strategy

Coping strategy that focuses on reducing the symptoms of stress.

Stress Outcomes   Theorists contend stress has psychological/attitudinal, behavioral, cognitive, and physical health consequences or outcomes. A large body of research supports the negative effects of perceived stress on many aspects of our lives. Workplace stress is negatively related to job satisfaction, organizational commitment, organizational citizenship behavior, positive emotions, and performance, and positively with emotional exhaustion, absenteeism, and turnover.[71] Research also shows that stress is associated with negative behaviors such as yelling and verbal abuse and violence toward others. It also is associated with the frequency of drinking and taking illicit drugs.[72] These stress outcomes are very costly. The American Institute of Stress estimates that one million people miss work daily as a result of stress. All told, "the annual tab for all these lost hours due to absenteeism; reduced productivity; turnover; and medical, legal, and insurance costs comes to $300 billion or $7,500 per worker."[73] Finally, ample evidence supports the conclusion that stress negatively affects our physical and psychological health. Stress contributes to the following physical and mental health problems: lessened ability to ward off illness and infection, high blood pressure, coronary artery disease, tension headaches, back pain, diarrhea, constipation, and psychological well-being.[74] In fact, it's stressful to even think about all these problems!

L0.9   Moderators of Occupational Stress

Moderators, once again, are variables that cause the relationships between stressors, perceived stress, and outcomes to be weaker for some people and stronger for others. Managers with a working knowledge of important stress moderators can confront employee stress in the following ways:

1. Awareness of moderators helps identify those most likely to experience stress and its negative outcomes. Stress-reduction programs then can be formulated for high-risk employees.

2. Moderators, in and of themselves, suggest possible solutions for reducing negative outcomes of occupational stress.

Keeping these objectives in mind, we will examine three important moderators: social support, hardiness, and Type A behavior.

Social Support   Talking with a friend or taking part in a bull session can be comforting during times of fear, stress, or loneliness. For a variety of reasons, meaningful social relationships help people do a better job of handling stress.

Social support is the amount of perceived helpfulness derived from social relationships. Importantly, social support is determined by both the quantity and quality of an individual's social relationships. We receive four types of social support from others:

- *Esteem support.* Providing information that a person is accepted and respected despite any problems or inadequacies.
- *Informational support.* Providing help in defining, understanding, and coping with problems.
- *Social companionship.* Spending time with others in leisure and recreational activities.
- *Instrumental support.* Providing financial aid, material resources, or needed services.[75]

Research shows that social support is negatively related to physiological processes and mortality. In other words, people with low social support tend to have poorer cardiovascular and immune system functioning and tend to die earlier than those with strong social support networks. Further, social support protects against the perception of stress, depression, psychological problems, pregnancy complications, anxiety, loneliness, high blood pressure, and a variety of other ailments. In contrast, negative social support, which amounts to someone undermining another person, negatively affects one's mental health.[76] We are well advised to avoid people who try to undermine us.

Social support research highlights two practical recommendations. First, managers are advised to keep employees informed about external and internal social support systems. Internally, managers can use all four forms of social support when employees experience a personal crisis. Coping with a divorce is a good example. Second, participative management programs and company-sponsored activities that make employees feel they are an important part of an extended family can be rich sources of social support. Employees need time and energy to adequately maintain their social relationships. If organizational demands are excessive, employees' social relationships and support networks will suffer, resulting in stress-related illness and decreased performance.[77]

Social support
Amount of helpfulness derived from social relationships.

Social support helps us deal with the ups and downs of life. A simple touch can be very comforting to someone in need.

Hardiness   Suzanne Kobasa, a behavioral scientist, identified a collection of personality characteristics that neutralize occupational stress. This collection of characteristics, referred to as **hardiness,** involves the ability to perceptually or behaviorally transform negative stressors into positive challenges. Hardiness embraces the personality dimensions of commitment, locus of control, and challenge.[78]

Commitment reflects the extent to which an individual is involved in whatever he or she is doing. Committed people have a sense of purpose and do not give up under pressure because they tend to invest themselves in the situation. As discussed in Chapter 5, individuals with an *internal locus of control* believe they can influence the events that affect their lives. People possessing this trait are more likely to foresee stressful events, thereby reducing their exposure to anxiety-producing

Hardiness
Personality characteristic that neutralizes stress.

situations. Moreover, their perception of being in control leads "internals" to use proactive coping strategies. *Challenge* is represented by the belief that change is a normal part of life. Hence, change is seen as an opportunity for growth and development rather than a threat to security.

Research supports the moderating influence of hardiness on the stress process. For example, a five-year study of 259 managers from a public utility revealed that hardiness—commitment, locus of control, and challenge—reduced the probability of illness following exposure to stress.[79] The three components of hardiness also were found to directly influence how 276 members of the Israeli Defense Forces appraised stressors and ultimately coped with them. Hardy individuals interpreted stressors less negatively and were more likely to use control coping strategies than unhardy people.[80] Furthermore, additional research demonstrated that hardy individuals displayed lower stress and burnout and higher job satisfaction than their less hardy counterparts.[81]

One practical offshoot of this research is organizational training and development programs that strengthen the characteristics of commitment, personal control, and challenge. For example, a team of researchers developed a hardiness training program based on this recommendation and tested it on a group of students and working adults. Results revealed that students' grade point average, retention, and health improved after the training. Training also resulted in increased performance, job satisfaction, and health for the working adults.[82] The hardiness concept also meshes nicely with job design. Enriched jobs are likely to fuel the hardiness components of commitment and challenge. A final application of the hardiness concept is as a diagnostic tool. Employees scoring low on hardiness would be good candidates for stress-reduction programs.

Type A Behavior Pattern

According to Meyer Friedman and Ray Rosenman (the cardiologists who isolated the Type A syndrome in the 1950s):

Type A behavior pattern

Aggressively involved in a chronic, determined struggle to accomplish more in less time.

Type A behavior pattern is an action-emotion complex that can be observed in any person who is aggressively involved in a chronic, incessant struggle to achieve more and more in less and less time, and if required to do so, against the opposing efforts of other things or persons. It is not psychosis or a complex of worries or fears or phobias or obsessions, but a socially acceptable—indeed often praised—form of conflict. Persons possessing this pattern also are quite prone to exhibit a free-floating but, extraordinarily well-rationalized hostility. As might be expected, there are degrees in the intensity of this behavior pattern.[83]

While labeling Type A behavior as "hurry sickness," Friedman and Rosenman noted that Type A individuals frequently tend to exhibit most of the behaviors listed in Table 18–3.

Because Type A behavior is a matter of degree, it is measured on a continuum. This continuum has the hurried, competitive Type A behavior pattern at one end and the more relaxed Type B behavior pattern at the other. Let us now consider the pros and cons of being Type A. OB research has demonstrated that Type A employees tend to be more productive than their Type B coworkers. For instance, Type A behavior yielded a significant and positive correlation with 766 students' grade point averages, the quantity and quality of 278 university professors' performance, and sales performance of 222 life insurance brokers.[84] On the other hand, Type A behavior is associated with some negative consequences. A recent meta-analysis of 729 studies revealed that Type A individuals had higher cardiovascular hyperactivity (e.g., heart rates, diastolic blood pressure, and systolic blood

Table 18–3   *Type A Characteristics*

1. Hurried speech; explosive accentuation of key words.

2. Tendency to walk, move, and eat rapidly.

3. Constant impatience with the rate at which most events take place (e.g., irritation with slow-moving traffic and slow-talking and slow-to-act people).

4. Strong preference for thinking of or doing two or more things at once (e.g., reading this text and doing something else at the same time).

5. Tendency to turn conversations around to personally meaningful subjects or themes.

6. Tendency to interrupt while others are speaking to make your point or to complete their train of thought in your own words.

7. Guilt feelings during periods of relaxation or leisure time.

8. Tendency to be oblivious to surroundings during daily activities.

9. Greater concern for things worth *having* than with things worth being.

10. Tendency to schedule more and more in less and less time; a chronic sense of time urgency.

11. Feelings of competition rather than compassion when faced with another Type A person.

12. Development of nervous tics or characteristic gestures.

13. A firm belief that success is due to the ability to get things done faster than the other guy.

14. A tendency to view and evaluate personal activities and the activities of other people in terms of "numbers" (e.g., number of meetings attended, telephone calls made, visitors received).

SOURCE: Adapted from M Friedman and R H Rosenman, *Type A Behavior and Your Heart* (Greenwich, CT: Fawcett Publications, 1974), pp 100–2.

pressure) than Type B people. In turn, this hyperactivity was associated with heart disease and cardiac mortality.[85] Type A people also showed greater cardiovascular activity when they encountered the following situations:

1. Receipt of positive or negative feedback.

2. Receipt of verbal harassment or criticism.

3. Tasks requiring mental as opposed to physical work.[86]

Unfortunately for Type A individuals, these situations are frequently experienced at work. A second meta-analysis of 83 studies further demonstrated that the hard-driving and competitive aspects of Type A are related to coronary heart disease, but the speed and impatience and job involvement aspects are not. This meta-analysis also showed that feelings of anger, hostility, and aggression were more strongly related to heart disease than was Type A behavior.[87] Do these results signal the need for Type A individuals to quit working so hard? Not necessarily. First off, the research indicated that feelings of anger, hostility, and aggression were more detrimental to our health than being Type A. We should all attempt to reduce these negative emotions. Second, researchers have developed stress-reduction techniques to help Type A people pace themselves more realistically and achieve better balance in their lives; they are discussed in the next section. Management can help Type A people, however, by not overloading them with work despite their apparent eagerness to take an ever-increasing workload. Managers need to actively help rather than unthinkingly exploit Type A individuals.

go to the Web for the Self-Exercise: Where Are You on the Type A–B Behavior Continuum?

LO.10 Stress-Reduction Techniques

Stress is very costly to organizations. The American Institute of Stress estimates that work stress costs US industries about $300 billion a year. It thus is not surprising that organizations are increasingly implementing a variety of stress-reduction programs to help employees cope with modern-day stress.[88]

There are many different stress-reduction techniques available. The four most frequently used approaches are muscle relaxation, biofeedback, meditation, and cognitive restructuring. Each method involves somewhat different ways of coping with stress (see Table 18–4). Although research supports the positive benefits of all these techniques, a recent meta-analysis of 55 stress management interventions demonstrated that cognitive restructuring was most effective.[89] Despite these positive results, however, some researchers advise organizations not to implement stress-reduction programs despite their positive outcomes. They rationalize that

Table 18–4   *Stress-Reduction Techniques*

TECHNIQUE	DESCRIPTION	ASSESSMENT
Muscle relaxation	Uses slow, deep breathing and systematic muscle tension reduction.	Inexpensive and easy to use; may require a trained professional to implement.
Biofeedback	A machine is used to train people to detect muscular tension; muscle relaxation is then used to alleviate this symptom of stress.	Expensive due to costs of equipment; however, equipment can be used to evaluate effectiveness of other stress-reduction programs.
Meditation	The relaxation response is activated by redirecting one's thoughts away from oneself; a four-step procedure is used to attain passive stress-free state of mind.	Least expensive, simple to implement, and can be practiced almost anywhere.
Cognitive restructuring	Irrational or maladaptive thoughts are identified and replaced with those that are rational or logical.	Expensive because it requires a trained psychologist or counselor.
Holistic wellness	A broad, interdisciplinary approach that goes beyond stress reduction by advocating that people strive for personal wellness in all aspects of their lives.	Involves inexpensive but often behaviorally difficult lifestyle changes.

The Recession Results in Increased Demand for Employee Assistance Programs (EAPs)

Many of the employees calling EAPs are seeking help with their finances, and some who have lost their homes to foreclosures are asking for housing assistance. But the vast majority call to get help managing the stress associated with today's dire economic conditions, EAP vendors say.

"I've been in the business for 20 years and I've never seen anything like it," said Mike Garfield, senior VP of global business development at ComPsych Corp. in Chicago.

"Call volume for EAPs' financial counselors was up more than 30% in October [2008]," he said. . . .

"People are swimming in debt, struggling to pay the mortgage, uncertain about their future and turning to their EAP because it's free, confidential and personalized help," said Ann Clark, chief executive officer and founder of the San Diego-based EAP vendor.

Do you think it makes sense for companies to pay for EAP assistance for employees that have been laid off? Explain.

SOURCE: Excerpted from J Wojcik, "EAP Vendors Report Surge in Number of Help Line Calls," *Business Insurance*, November 3, 2008, p 28.

---

these techniques relieve *symptoms* of stress rather than eliminate stressors themselves.[90] Thus, they conclude that organizations are using a Band-Aid approach to stress reduction.

This recommendation has led to the creation of much broader approaches toward stress reduction. Two of the broadest approaches entail the use of employee assistance programs and for individuals to use a holistic wellness approach. Let us consider each of these approaches toward stress reduction.

Employee Assistance Programs (EAPs)

Employee assistance programs consist of a broad array of programs aimed at helping employees to deal with personal problems such as substance abuse, health-related problems, family and marital issues, and other problems that negatively affect their job performance. For example, the current recession has led to a surge in requests from employers asking EAP providers to offer financial assistance and coping with stress programs (see the Real World/Real People feature above).[91] EAPs are typically provided by employers or in combination with unions. Employees use these services as part of their benefit package. Alternatively, referral-only EAPs simply provide managers with telephone numbers that they can distribute to employees in need of help. Employees then pay for these services themselves.

> **Employee assistance programs**
>
> Help employees to resolve personal problems that affect their productivity.

Holistic Wellness Approach

A **holistic wellness approach** encompasses and goes beyond stress reduction by advocating that individuals strive for "a harmonious and productive balance of physical, mental, and social well-being brought about by the acceptance of one's personal responsibility for developing and adhering to a health promotion program."[92] Organizations are encouraged to consider the benefits of wellness programs in light of a recent meta-analysis of 17 studies. Results revealed that employee participation in wellness programs was positively associated with job satisfaction and negatively with absenteeism.[93] Five

> **Holistic wellness approach**
>
> Advocates personal responsibility for healthy living.

Farcus

by David Waisglass
Gordon Coulthart

© 1991 Farcus Cartoons   WAISGLASS/COULTHART

www.farcus.com

When stress management works too well.

dimensions of a holistic wellness approach are as follows:

1. *Self-responsibility.* Take personal responsibility for your wellness (e.g., quit smoking, moderate your intake of alcohol, wear your seat belt, and eat less food). As a case in point, experts estimate that 50 to 70% of all diseases are caused by lifestyle choices under our control.[94]

2. *Nutritional awareness.* Because we are what we eat, try to increase your consumption of foods high in fiber, vitamins, and nutrients—such as fresh fruits and vegetables, poultry, and fish—while decreasing those high in sugar and fat.

3. *Stress reduction and relaxation.* Use techniques to relax and reduce the symptoms of stress.

4. *Physical fitness.* Exercise regularly to maintain strength, flexibility, endurance, and a healthy body weight. A review of employee fitness programs indicated that they were a cost-effective way to reduce medical costs, absenteeism, turnover, and occupational injuries. Because many people do not like to exercise, more companies have begun to use incentives as vehicles to motivate employees to exercise. For example, over 1,000 employees from Home Depot increased their exercise sessions over six weeks after being promised a reward for meeting exericse-related goals.[95] Fitness programs also were positively linked with job performance and job satisfaction.

5. *Environmental sensitivity.* Be aware of your environment and try to identify the stressors that are causing your stress. A control coping strategy might be useful to eliminate stressors.

Summary of Key Concepts

1. *Discuss the external and internal forces that create the need for organizational change.* Organizations encounter both external and internal forces for change. There are five key external forces for change: demographic characteristics, technological advancements, customer and market changes, social and political pressures, and organizational crises. Internal forces for change come from both human resource problems and managerial behavior/decisions.

2. *Describe Lewin's change model and the systems model of change.* Lewin developed a three-stage model of planned change that explained how to initiate, manage, and stabilize the change process. The three stages were unfreezing, which entails creating the motivation to change; changing; and stabilizing change through refreezing. A systems model of change takes a big picture perspective of change. It focuses on the interaction among the key components of change. The three main components of change are inputs, target elements of change, and outputs. The target elements of change represent the components of an organization that may be changed. They include organizational arrangements, social factors, methods, and people.

3. *Discuss Kotter's eight steps for leading organizational change.* John Kotter believes that organizational

change fails for one or more of eight common errors. He proposed eight steps that organizations should follow to overcome these errors. The eight steps are (1) establish a sense of urgency, (2) create the guiding coalition, (3) develop a vision and strategy, (4) communicate the change vision, (5) empower broad-based action, (6) generate short-term wins, (7) consolidate gains and produce more change, and (8) anchor new approaches in the culture.

4. *Define organization development (OD), and explain the OD process.* Organization development is a set of tools or techniques that are used to implement planned organizational change. OD is broader in focus and has a diagnostic focus. OD is guided by a four-step process. The steps are (1) diagnosis, (2) intervention, (3) evaluation, and (4) feedback.

5. *Explain the dynamic model of resistance to change.* The model contradicts the traditional assumption that resistance to change is caused by irrational and self-serving recipients. Rather, resistance is viewed as being caused by the dynamic interactions among three key sources of resistance. They are recipient characteristics, change agent characteristics, and the quality of the change agent–recipient relationships. Managers need to consider all three sources of resistance when trying to manage resistance to change.

6. *Discuss the key recipient and change agent characteristics that cause resistance to change.* There are six key recipient characteristics. They are (1) an individual's predisposition toward change, (2) surprise and fear of the unknown, (3) fear of failure, (4) loss of status and/or job security, (5) peer pressure, and (6) past success. The five key change agent characteristics include the following: (1) decisions that disrupt cultural traditions or group relationships, (2) personality conflicts, (3) lack of tact or poor timing, (4) leadership style, and (5) failing to legitimize change.

7. *Identify alternative strategies for overcoming resistance to change.* The first step is to use the dynamic model of resistance to diagnose the causes of employee resistance. The second is to consider characteristics in the work environment that may represent obstacles to change. These obstacles then need to be eliminated. Finally, managers can adopt one or more of the generic strategies for overcoming resistance to change. They are education + communication, participation +

involvement, facilitation + support, negotiation + agreement, manipulation + co-optation, and explicit + implicit coercion. Each has its situational appropriateness and advantages and drawbacks.

8. *Define the term* stress *and describe the model of occupational stress.* Stress is an adaptive reaction to environmental demands or stressors that triggers a fight-or-flight response. This response creates hormonal changes that mobilize the body for extraordinary demands. According to the occupational model of stress, the stress process begins when an individual cognitively appraises stressors. This appraisal then motivates an individual to choose a coping strategy aimed at reducing stressors, which, in turn, results in a variety of stress outcomes.

9. *Discuss the stress moderators of social support, hardiness, and Type A behavior.* People use each of these moderators to help reduce the impact of stressors that are appraised as harmful, threatening, or challenging. Social support represents the amount of perceived helpfulness derived from social relationships. People use four types of support (esteem, informational, social, and instrumental) to reduce the impact of stress. Hardiness is a collection of personality characteristics that neutralize stress. It includes the characteristics of commitment, locus of control, and challenge. The Type A behavior pattern is characterized by someone who is aggressively involved in a chronic, determined struggle to accomplish more and more in less and less time. Management can help Type A individuals by not overloading them with work despite their apparent eagerness to take on an ever-increasing workload.

10. *Discuss employee assistance programs (EAPs) and a holistic approach toward stress reduction.* Employee assistance programs help employees to resolve personal problems that affect their productivity. EAPs are typically funded by organizations or in combination with unions. A holistic approach toward wellness goes beyond stress-reduction techniques by advocating that people strive for a harmonious balance among physical, mental, and social well-being. This approach to stress management has five key components: self-responsibility, nutritional awareness, stress reduction and relaxation, physical fitness, and environmental sensitivity.

Key Terms

External forces for change, 535
Internal forces for change, 538
Benchmarking, 540
Mission statement, 541

Target elements of change, 543
Organization development, 545
Change agent, 546
Resistance to change, 549

OB in Action Case Study

Wyeth Implements Major Organizational Change[96]

When Denise Peppard was studying for her master's degree in business administration at the University of Michigan more than 20 years ago, she decided to pursue a career in human resources management. . . .

Peppard realized that potential when she became senior vice president of HR for Wyeth last January. . . .

Corporate and cultural change at Wyeth has served as Peppard's focal point. She began her present job in the midst of a large-scale corporate restructuring program called Project Impact. Peppard began implementing the project while serving as the head of HR for Wyeth Pharmaceuticals—the largest division, employing approximately 92 percent of Wyeth's 50,000 employees worldwide.

"The change we're experiencing is throughout the pharma industry right now. You can look at it as an opportunity," Peppard says, "because it's good change. It's the kind of change that we should be doing and will ultimately make Wyeth a better company."

Project Impact goals include:

- Streamlining Wyeth's operations.
- Exploring opportunities for alliances for research and development.
- Reducing production costs.

One of the first steps in implementing the restructuring plan was a series of job cuts. Just as Peppard began her new job, Wyeth officials announced the company would reduce its workforce by 10 percent during the next five years. In March, the company laid off 1,200 sales representatives in a cost-cutting move. The job cuts came after Wyeth's patent expired on its popular Protonix acid-relief medication and the company began facing stiffer competition from manufacturers of generic drugs.

Yet Project Impact appears to meet the intended short-term result: Compared with 2007, Wyeth's revenue and earnings have grown approximately 6 percent in 2008. The company reported revenue of $11.65 billion for the first six months of 2008.

"If there's one thing to regret in this change process, [it's] that we began with a short-term cost reduction associated with Protonix production and the sales force," says Peppard. "I don't think everyone in the company has quite grasped that this effort is not just about job reductions and that it is actually about changing the way we work."

For examples, Peppard points to ideas such as using fewer manufacturing facilities and possibly using more third-party suppliers. Research and development partnerships with other pharmaceutical companies represent other avenues for Wyeth leaders to ponder.

"We really have to restructure the way people are working, and that's a massive, massive change," Peppard says during an interview at Wyeth's headquarters. . . .

Peppard sees the changes within Wyeth and the pharmaceutical industry as the natural response to its shifts in the global market. In the past year and for the first time ever, Wyeth's international sales surpassed the company's U.S. sales. Nearly half of Wyeth's employees now work outside the United States.

Still, the workforce reductions ultimately impact individuals, and Peppard admits that making decisions that affect the livelihoods of people proves to be the toughest part of her job.

"These are not decisions that are taken lightly," Peppard says. Wyeth leaders "take great care with decisions to cut jobs and make sure that each affected individual is treated with care and dignity. Even though it's a business decision, ultimately it comes down to a personal level, and that's the really tough part."

Questions for Discussion

1. What were the external and internal forces for change at Wyeth?
2. To what extent did Denise Peppard follow the change models proposed by Lewin and Kotter? Explain.

3. Which of the target elements of change within the systems model of change were affected by the changes at Wyeth?

4. Would you expect Ms. Peppard to encounter resistance to change? Why? What might be done to reduce this resistance? Explain.

5. What did this case teach you about organizational change? Discuss.

Is There an Ethical Way to Implement Downsizing without Hurting Your Best Employees?[97]

Intel has restructured and eliminated about 10,500 jobs during the past 20 months. The company decided to make these cuts owing to declining revenue and market share. Intel used a quantitative approach in making the cuts. That is, the company studied workforce demographics and determined what areas were most in need of cuts and then reassigned people based on where they might best contribute to the company's future plans. The managerial ranks were reduced the most. Corporate executives are pleased with the process because the company is now more profitable and competitive.

In contrast, some employees believe that the company "botched the restructuring in ways that have harmed morale, employee development and long-term leadership quality." Interviews with employees uncovered complaints that "Intel disregarded employees' passions in reorganizing, squandered the talents of HR specialists and unwisely shifted leadership training efforts from lower-level managers to upper-level executives." Disgruntled employees believe that Intel did not consider employees interests during the restructuring. An internal memo obtained by Workforce Management indicated that senior management knew they would be losing quality employees. The memo states: "We know we are losing good people in this move. But we have too many managers, and this manager reduction is necessary to improve our decision making and communication and to resize the company. In addition, since we need to become a leaner company and are limiting job openings, redeploying their skills, as individual contributors or as managers, is not a reasonable option."

Solving the Dilemma: How Would You Have Handled the Layoffs at Intel?

1. Intel's approach sounds logical to me. Revenues are up, and the company just unveiled a new processing chip that *Time* called the best invention of the year. You can't make everyone happy when you let go more than 10,000 people.

2. Downsizing solely by the numbers is bad. Management should have accommodated employees' passions and interests when restructuring, even if it resulted in less cuts than desired. In the long run, this will lead to higher employee satisfaction and performance.

3. It sounds like the criticisms are being leveled by people who don't like their new assignments. They should quit complaining and be happy that they are still employed.

4. I am not sure that there is an optimum approach. It is impossible to balance the short-term goal of reducing costs while maintaining a positive work environment in which people are doing the type of work they are passionate about.

5. Invent other interpretations or options. Discuss.

For study material and exercises that apply to this chapter, visit our Web site, **www.mhhe.com/kreitner**

Photo Credits

CHAPTER 10

Page 279 AP Photo/Misha Japaridze

Page 281 © Lori Adamski Peek/Getty Images

Page 286 © Digital Vision

Page 291 © Getty Images

Page 292 © The McGraw-Hill Companies, Inc./Lars A. Niki, photographer

Page 300 © Thomas Barwick/Getty Images

CHAPTER 11

Page 305 AP Photo/Bebeto Matthews

Page 309 © Royalty-Free/Corbis

Page 313 © Lance Cpl. Jeremy T. Ross/United States Marine Corp

Page 317 Courtesy of Ledalite.

Page 320 AP Photo/Gautam Singh

Page 322 Photo provided by author.

Page 328 (top) © Richard Foreman

Page 328 (bottom) © Getty Images

CHAPTER 12

Page 335 Courtesy of Landscape Forms

Page 338 © Somos/Veer/Getty Images

Page 343 © Ryan McVay/Getty Images

Page 356 © Tom Merton/Getty Images

CHAPTER 13

Page 371 © Big Cheese Photo/Jupiter Images

Page 376 © Digital Vision/Getty Images

Page 378 © Prakash Singh/AFP/Getty Images

Page 380 © Getty Images

Page 381 © AFP/Getty Images

Page 387 © Comstock/Getty Images

Page 392 © John Hasyn/Getty Images

CHAPTER 14

Page 404 © Paul Harris/Getty Images

Page 410 © AFP/Getty Images

Page 414 © Jon Feingersh/Getty Images

Page 419 © Flying Colours Ltd/Getty Images

Page 424 © Allison Michael Orenstein/Getty Images

Page 427 © Annie Marie Musselman/Getty Images

CHAPTER 15

Page 435 Chris Mueller/Redux

Page 437 AP Photo/Al Behrman

Page 442 Courtesy of Facebook.

Page 443 © Peter DaSilva

Page 445 © Reuters/ARC-Dominic Favre

Page 451 NBC-TV/THE KOBAL COLLECTION/HASTON, CHRIS

Page 458 AP Photo/Paul Sakuma

CHAPTER 16

Page 465 © AFP/Getty Images

Page 472 © Getty Images

Page 485 Courtesy of Fuji Fire and Marine Insurance Co., Ltd.

Page 488 © Ryan McVay/Getty Images

Page 494 AP Photo/Gautam Singh

CHAPTER 17

Page 507 © Sam Roberts/Getty Images

Page 511 Courtesy of Nokia.

Page 512 © AFP/Getty Images

Page 524 (top) © Aly Song/Reuters/Landov

Page 524 (bottom) PRNewsFoto/Apple

Page 526 AP Photo/Koji Sasahara

CHAPTER 18

Page 533 AP Photo/Wade Payne

Page 537 © Rick Dahms

Page 550 AP Photo/The Canadian Press, J.P. Moczulski

Page 554 © Digital Vision/Getty Images

Page 559 © Getty Images

Endnotes

CHAPTER 1

1 Reprinted by permission of *Harvard Business Review*. Excerpt from "The Best Advice I Ever Got," by D W Dowling, October 2008. Copyright 2008 by the Harvard Business School Publishing Corporation; all rights reserved.

2 Based on J Pfeffer, *The Human Equation: Building Profits by Putting People First* (Boston: Harvard Business School Press, 1998); and J Pfeffer and J F Veiga, "Putting People First for Organizational Success," *Academy of Management Executive,* May 1999, pp 37–48.

3 Data from Pfeffer and Veiga, "Putting People First for Organizational Success," p 47. Also see C A O'Reilly and J Pfeffer, *Hidden Value: How Great Companies Achieve Extraordinary Results with Ordinary People* (Boston: Harvard Business School Press, 2000); and J Combs, Y Liu, A Hall, and D Ketchen, "How Much Do High-Performance Work Practices Matter? A Meta-Analysis of Their Effects on Organizational Performance," *Personnel Psychology,* Autumn 2006, pp 501–28.

4 See H Maurer and C Lindblad, "All Arrows Are Pointing Down" *BusinessWeek,* January 26–February 2, 2009, p 6; J Reingold, J Caplin, and B Kowitt, "The New Jobless," *Fortune,* February 16, 2009, pp 60–69; and B Hagenbaugh and S Kirchhoff, "Unemployment 'Truly Gruesome,'" *USA Today,* January 8, 2009, p 1B.

5 As quoted in J Shambora, A Lashinsky, B Gimbel, and J Schlosser, "A View from the Top," *Fortune,* March 16, 2009, p 107. Other people-centered organizations are profiled in B Morris, "What Makes Apple Golden," *Fortune,* March 17, 2008, pp 68–74; and J Chu and K Rockwood, "Thinking Outside the Big Box," *Fast Company,* November 2008, pp 128–32.

6 "Layoffs Pack Punch to 'Surviving' Employees," *HR Magazine,* February 2009, p 18. Also see E Thornton, "The Hidden Perils of Layoffs," *BusinessWeek,* March 2, 2009, pp 52–53; M Kimes, "Does Your Team Have PLSD?" *Fortune,* March 2, 2009, p 24; R Zeidner, "Cutting Hours without Raising Hackles," *HR Magazine,* April 2009, pp 44–48; and T Francis and B Levisohn, "Cushioning Workweek Cuts," *BusinessWeek,* April 20, 2009, p 11.

7 Excerpted from M Boyle, "Cutting Costs without Cutting Jobs," *BusinessWeek,* March 9, 2009, p 55. Also see M Weinstein, "Kind Cuts?" *Training,* January 2009, p 8; O Kharif, "Chopping Hours, Not Heads," *BusinessWeek,* January 5, 2009, p 85; and L O'Neil, "Bucking the Layoff Trend with Creative HR," *HR Magazine,* March 2009, p 8.

8 See K A Powell, "More Than the Math: CFOs Should Be 'People People' Too," *HR Magazine,* February 2008, pp 87–91; E E Lawler III, "HBR Case Study: Why Are We Losing All Our Good People?" *Harvard Business Review,* June 2008, pp 41–45; and "Benchmark with the Best," *HR Magazine,* July 2008, p 49.

9 C I Barnard, *The Functions of the Executive* (Cambridge, MA: Harvard University Press, 1938), p 73.

10 F Zakaria, "The Education of Paul Wolfowitz," *Newsweek,* March 28, 2005, p 37.

11 Data from J B Miner, "The Rated Importance, Scientific Validity, and Practical Usefulness of Organizational Behavior Theories: A Quantitative Review," *Academy of Management Learning and Education,* September 2003, pp 250–68. Also see G Symon and C Cassell, "Neglected Perspectives in Work and Organizational Psychology," *Journal of Occupational and Organizational Psychology,* September 2006, pp 307–14; and W F Cascio and H Aguinis, "Research in Industrial and Organizational Psychology from 1963 to 2007: Changes, Choices, and Trends," *Journal of Applied Psychology,* September 2008, pp 1062–81.

12 E E Lawler III, *Treat People Right! How Organizations and Individuals Can Propel Each Other into a Virtuous Spiral of Success* (San Francisco: Jossey-Bass, 2003), p 19.

13 See M Weinstein, "You Softie," *Training,* June 2007, p 18.

14 Excerpted from J Welch and S Welch, "Growing Up but Staying Young," *BusinessWeek,* December 11, 2006, p 112.

15 B S Lawrence, "Historical Perspective: Using the Past to Study the Present," *Academy of Management Review,* April 1984, p 307.

16 See L T Benjamin Jr, "Hugo Munsterberg's Attack on the Application of Scientific Psychology," *Journal of Applied Psychology,* March 2006, pp 414–25.

17 Evidence indicating that the original conclusions of the famous Hawthorne studies were unjustified may be found in R G Greenwood, A A Bolton, and R A Greenwood, "Hawthorne a Half Century Later: Relay Assembly Participants Remember," *Journal of Management,* Fall–Winter 1983, pp 217–31; and R H Franke and J D Kaul, "The Hawthorne Experiments: First Statistical Interpretation," *American Sociological Review,* October 1978, pp 623–43. For a positive interpretation of the Hawthorne studies, see J A Sonnenfeld, "Shedding Light on the Hawthorne Studies," *Journal of Occupational Behaviour,* April 1985, pp 111–30.

18 See M Parker Follett, *Freedom and Coordination* (London: Management Publications Trust, 1949).

19 See D McGregor, *The Human Side of Enterprise* (New York: McGraw-Hill, 1960).

20 A manager's Theory X and Y management challenges are illustrated in A Fisher, "Changing Course," *Fortune,* November 27, 2006, p 278.

21 S Bates, "Getting Engaged," *HR Magazine,* February 2004, pp 44, 46.

22 See D W Organ, "Elusive Phenomena," *Business Horizons,* March–April 2002, pp 1–2.

23 See, for example, R Zemke, "TQM: Fatally Flawed or Simply Unfocused?" *Training,* October 1992, p 8.

24 R O Crockett, "Six Sigma Pays Off at Motorola," *BusinessWeek,* December 4, 2006, p 50. Also see B Hindo, "Six Sigma: So Yesterday?" *BusinessWeek,* June 2007, p 11; S E Ante, "Rubbing Customers the Right Way," *BusinessWeek,* October 8, 2007, pp 88–89; and B Hindo, "Rewiring Westinghouse," *BusinessWeek,* May 19, 2008, pp 48–49.

25 J McGregor, "The Performance Paradox," *Fast Company,* April 2005, pp 29–30. Also see A Levin, "Fewer Crashes Caused by Pilots," *USA Today,* March 2, 2004, p 1A.

26 M Sashkin and K J Kiser, *Putting Total Quality Management to Work* (San Francisco: Berrett-Koehler, 1993), p 39.

27 R J Schonberger, "Total Quality Management Cuts a Broad Swath—Through Manufacturing and Beyond," *Organizational Dynamics,* Spring 1992, p 18. Also see A G Lafley and R Charan, "The Consumer Is Boss," *Fortune,* March 17, 2008, pp 120–26; and "Katsuaki Watanabe," *Newsweek,* January 5, 2009, p 64.

28 Based on C Hui, S S K Lam, and J Schaubroeck, "Can Good Citizens Lead the Way in Providing Quality Service? A Field Quasi Experiment," *Academy of Management Journal,* October 2001, pp 988–95. Also see H Liao and M Subramony, "Employee Customer Orientation in Manufacturing Organizations: Joint Influences of Customer Proximity and the Senior Leadership Team," *Journal of Applied Psychology,* March 2008, pp 317–28.

29 Deming's landmark work is W E Deming, *Out of the Crisis* (Cambridge, MA: MIT, 1986). Also see B Kenney, "Whatever Happened to Quality?" *Industry Week,* April 2008, pp 42–47. Another quality pioneer, Joseph M Juran, is profiled in S Miller, "Pioneer of Quality Control Kept Searching for 'A Better Way' to Make and Manage," *The Wall Street Journal,* March 8, 2008, p A7.

30 See M Trumbull, "What Is Total Quality Management?" *The Christian Science Monitor,* May 3, 1993, p 12; J Hillkirk, "World-Famous Quality Expert Dead at 93," *USA Today,* December 21, 1993, pp 1B–2B; and O Port, "The Kings of Quality," *BusinessWeek,* August 30, 2004, p 20.

31 Based on discussion in M Walton, *Deming Management at Work* (New York: Putnam/Perigee, 1990).

32 Ibid., p 20.

33 Adapted from D E Bowen and E E Lawler III, "Total Quality-Oriented Human Resources Management," *Organizational Dynamics,* Spring 1992, pp 29–41. Also see J Jarvis, "The Buzz from Starbucks Customers," *BusinessWeek,* April 28, 2008, pp 106–7; D Frisch, "Human Resources: Part of the Team—Continuous Improvement Tools Move Out of the Plant," *HR Magazine,* July 2008, pp 66–67; and R Clark, "Success on a Shoestring," *BusinessWeek,* August 25–September 1, 2008, pp 43–44.

34 For details, see T J Douglas and W Q Judge Jr, "Total Quality Management Implementation and Competitive Advantage: The Role of Structural Control and Exploration," *Academy of Management Journal,* February 2001, pp 158–69; and K B Hendricks and V R Singhal, "The Long-Run Stock Price Performance of Firms with Effective TQM Programs," *Management Science,* March 2001, pp 359–68.

35 Data from J Gillum, "A Third of Adults without Internet Don't Want It," *USA Today,* February 3, 2009, p 7D; and R D Hof, "Google," *BusinessWeek,* December 22, 2008, p 53.

36 See G T Lumpkin and G G Dess, "E-Business Strategies and Internet Business Models: How the Internet Adds Value," *Organizational Dynamics,* no. 2, 2004, pp 161–73.

37 M J Mandel and R D Hof, "Rethinking the Internet," *BusinessWeek,* March 26, 2001, p 118. For the future of the Internet, see M Fitzgerald, "Technology: When the Forecast Calls for Clouds," *Inc.,* January–February 2009, pp 100–102; T Ilube, "What You Need to Know about the Semantic Web," *Harvard Business Review,* February 2009, p 36; and S Baker, "The Next Web," *BusinessWeek,* March 9, 2009, pp 42–46.

38 D Tapscott, *Grown Up Digital: How the Net Generation Is Changing Your World* (New York: McGraw-Hill, 2009), p 96. Also see J Graham, "Social Nets More Popular Than E-mail," *USA Today,* March 10, 2009, p 10B; and H Green and R D Hof, "Six Million Users: Nothing to Twitter At," *BusinessWeek,* March 16, 2009, pp 51–52.

39 See J Welch and S Welch, "The Connected Leader," *BusinessWeek,* June 23, 2008, p 86; "E-Training: The Source for Innovative Online Learning Strategies," supplement to *Training,* September 2008; and E Hutchinson, "'People People' Work at Home, Too," *HR Magazine,* September 2008, pp 60–62.

40 See S Boehle, "Hidden Potential," *Training,* July–August 2008, pp 42–44; M B Arthur, R J DeFillippi, and V J Lindsay, "On Being a Knowledge Worker," *Organizational Dynamics,* October–December 2008, pp 365–77; and E E Lawler III, "Make Human Capital a Source of Competitive Advantage," *Organizational Dynamics,* January–March 2009, pp 1–7.

41 For details on these trends, see K Dychtwald, T J Erickson, and R Morison, *Workforce Crisis: How to Beat the Coming Shortage of Skills and Talent* (Boston: Harvard Business School Press, 2006); P Cappelli, "Talent Management for the Twenty-First Century," *Harvard Business Review,* March 2008, pp 74–81; and M Hilton, "Skills for Work in the 21st Century: What Does the Research Tell Us?" *Academy of Management Perspectives,* November 2008, pp 63–78.

42 B E Becker, M A Huselid, and D Ulrich, *The HR Scorecard: Linking People, Strategy, and Performance* (Boston: Harvard Business School Press, 2001), p 4. Also see S Baker, "How Much Is That Worker Worth?" *BusinessWeek,* March 23–30, 2009, pp 46, 48.

43 See www.intel.com/education/index.htm?iid=intel_edu+body_ initiative.

44 See "North Carolina Girl Wins Intel Prize," *USA Today,* March 3, 2008, p 7; and D J Der Bedrosian, "Intel Science Talent Search Crowns 10 Promising Young Scientists," *USA Today,* March 12, 2009, p 7D.

45 Inspired by P S Adler and S Kwon, "Social Capital: Prospects for a New Concept," *Academy of Management Review,* January 2002, pp 17–40. Also see M Weinstein, "Charity Begins @ Work," *Training,* May 2008, pp 56–58; M Lazarova and S Taylor, "Boundaryless Careers, Social Capital, and Knowledge Management: Implications for Organizational Behavior," *Journal of Organizational Behavior,* January 2009, pp 119–30; J Alter, "Don't Muffle the Call to Serve," *Newsweek,* January 12, 2009, p 48; and S Hamm, "The Globe is IBM's Classroom," *BusinessWeek,* March 23–30, 2009, pp 56–57.

46 L Prusak and D Cohen, "How to Invest in Social Capital," *Harvard Business Review,* June 2001, p 93. Also see D Somaya, I O Williamson, and N Lorinkova, "Gone But Not Lost: The Different Performance Impacts of Employee Mobility between Cooperators versus Competitors," *Academy of Management Journal,* October 2008, pp 936–53; and B L Fredrickson, M A Cohn, K A Coffey, J Pek, and S M Finkel, "Open Hearts Build Lives: Positive Emotions, Induced through Loving-Kindness Meditation, Build Consequential Personal Resources," *Journal of Personality and Social Psychology,* November 2008, pp 1045–62.

47 Data from "What Makes a Job OK," *USA Today,* May 15, 2000, p 1B. Also see S Baker, "You're Fired—But Stay in Touch," *BusinessWeek,* May 4, 2009, pp 54–55.

48 Based on E D Heaphy and J E Dutton, "Positive Social Interactions and the Human Body at Work: Linking Organizations and Physiology," *Academy of Management Review,* January 2008, pp 137–62.

49 Adapted from R Kreitner, *Management,* 11th ed (Boston: Houghton Mifflin Harcourt, 2009), pp 5–6.

50 See J Welch and S Welch, "An Employee Bill of Rights," *BusinessWeek,* March 16, 2009, p 72.

51 J Covert and T Sattersten, "Learning from Heroes," *Harvard Business Review,* March 2009, p 24.

52 C Edwards, "How HP Got the Wow! Back," *BusinessWeek,* December 22, 2008, pp 60–61.

53 See, for example, H Mintzberg, "Managerial Work: Analysis from Observation," *Management Science,* October 1971, pp B97–B110. Also see N Fondas, "A Behavioral Job Description for Managers," *Organizational Dynamics,* Summer 1992, pp 47–58.

54 See L B Kurke and H E Aldrich, "Mintzberg Was Right!: A Replication and Extension of *The Nature of Managerial Work,*" *Management Science,* August 1983, pp 975–84.

55 Validation studies can be found in E Van Velsor and J B Leslie, *Feedback to Managers, Volume II: A Review and Comparison of Sixteen Multi-Rater Feedback Instruments* (Greensboro, NC: Center for Creative Leadership, 1991); F Shipper, "A Study of the Psychometric Properties of the Managerial Skill Scales of the Survey of Management Practices," *Educational and Psychological Measurement,* June 1995, pp 468–79; and C L Wilson, *How and Why Effective Managers Balance Their Skills: Technical, Teambuilding, Drive* (Columbia, MD: Rockatech Multimedia Publishing, 2003).

56 See F Shipper, "Mastery and Frequency of Managerial Behaviors Relative to Sub-Unit Effectiveness," *Human Relations,* April 1991, pp 371–88.

57 Ibid.

58 Data from F Shipper, "A Study of Managerial Skills of Women and Men and Their Impact on Employees' Attitudes and Career Success in a Nontraditional Organization," paper presented at the Academy of Management Meeting, August 1994, Dallas, Texas. The same outcome for on-the-job studies is reported in A H Eagly and B T Johnson, "Gender and Leadership Style: A Meta-Analysis," *Psychological Bulletin,* September 1990, pp 233–56.

59 For instance, see J B Rosener, "Ways Women Lead," *Harvard Business Review,* November–December 1990, pp 119–25; and C Lee, "The Feminization of Management," *Training,* November 1994, pp 25–31.

60 A similar finding is reported in J Kornik, "Bosses Say They're Great: Employees Not So Sure," *Training,* October 2006, p 20.

61 Based on F Shipper and J E Dillard Jr, "A Study of Impending Derailment and Recovery of Middle Managers across Career Stages," *Human Resource Management,* Winter 2000, pp 331–45. Also see K Sulkowicz, "When You're the Abusive Boss's Pet," *BusinessWeek,* January 15, 2007, p 14; B Grow, "Out at Home Depot," *BusinessWeek,* January 15, 2007, pp 56–62; and L Buchanan, "The Bully Rulebook: How to Deal with Jerks," *Inc.,* February 2007, pp 43–44.

62 See E Thornton, "Managing through a Crisis: The New Rules," *BusinessWeek,* January 19, 2009, pp 30–34.

63 See G M Parker, *Team Players and Teamwork: New Strategies for Developing Successful Collaboration,* 2nd ed (San Francisco: Jossey-Bass, 2008).

64 G Hamel, "Moon Shots for Management," *Harvard Business Review,* February 2009, p 92. Also see G Hamel with B Breen, *The Future of Management* (Boston: Harvard Business School Press, 2007); and R Khurana and N Nohria, "It's Time to Make Management a True Profession," *Harvard Business Review,* October 2008, pp 70–77.

65 As quoted in P LaBarre, "The Industrial Revolution," *Fast Company,* November 2003, pp 116, 118. The contingency approach was used in G E R Tummers, G G van Merode, and J A Landeweerd, "Organizational Characteristics as Predictors of Nurses' Psychological Work Reactions," *Organization Studies,* April 2006, pp 559–84.

66 See G Johns, "The Essential Impact of Context on Organizational Behavior," *Academy of Management Review,* April 2006, pp 386–408.

67 See N Varchaver, "Long Island Confidential," *Fortune,* November 27, 2006, pp 172–86; and J Feeley and T Weidlich, "Skilling Gets New Sentence Hearing," *USA Today,* January 7, 2009, p 3B.

68 See D Henry, "Not Everyone Hates SarbOx," *BusinessWeek,* January 29, 2007, p 37; A Pomeroy, "Sox Compliance Costs Still High," *HR Magazine,* September 2007, p 12; and D R Dalton and C M Dalton, "Corporate Governance in the Post Sarbanes-Oxley Period: Compensation Disclosure and Analysis (CD&A)," *Business Horizons,* March–April 2008, pp 85–92.

69 See T Demos, "Will Madoff's Enablers Get Hard Time?" *Fortune,* January 19, 2009, p 24; D Kansas, "Madoff Does Minneapolis," *Fortune,* February 2, 2009, pp 80–86; K McCoy, "Trading His Penthouse for Prison: Madoff Leaves Court Cuffed," *USA Today,* March 13, 2009, pp 1B–2B; R Parloff, "The Impostor," *Fortune,* April 13, 2009, pp 58–66; and J Bandler, N Varchaver, and D Burke, "How Bernie Did It," *Fortune,* May 11, 2009, pp 51–71.

70 See R Parloff, "Wall Street: It's Payback Time," *Fortune,* January 19, 2009, pp 56–69.

71 T M Jones, "Corporate Social Responsibility Revisited, Redefined," *California Management Review,* Spring 1980, pp 59–60. Also see P Neron and W Norman, "Citizenship, Inc.: Do We Really Want Businesses to Be Good Corporate Citizens?" *Business Ethics Quarterly,* January 2008, pp 1–26; D Matten and J Moon, "'Implicit' and 'Explicit' CSR: A Conceptual Framework for a Comparative Understanding of Corporate Social Responsibility," *Academy of Management Review,* April 2008, pp 404–24; and P A Heslin and J D Ochoa, "Understanding and Developing Strategic Corporate Social Responsibility," *Organizational Dynamics,* April–June 2008, pp 125–44.

72 See K Basu and G Palazzo, "Corporate Social Responsibility: A Process Model of Sensemaking," *Academy of Management Review,* January 2008, pp 122–36; and S Waddock, "Building a New Institutional Infrastructure for Corporate Responsibility," *Academy of Management Perspectives,* August 2008, pp 87–108.

73 See, for example, J Welch and S Welch, "The Real Verdict on Business," *BusinessWeek,* June 12, 2006, p 100.

74 A B Carroll, "Managing Ethically with Global Stakeholders: A Present and Future Challenge," *Academy of Management Executive,* May 2004, p 118.

75 Ibid., pp 117–18.

76 E Levenson, "Citizen Nike," *Fortune,* November 24, 2008, p 166.

77 D Callahan, *The Cheating Culture: Why More Americans Are Doing Wrong to Get Ahead* (Orlando: Harcourt, 2004), pp 19–20. Also see M Baucus, W I Norton Jr, B Davis-Sramek, and W Meek, "Cheating and NASCAR: Who's at the Wheel?" *Business Horizons,* September–October 2008, pp 379–89; and S Block, "Americans May Be More Inclined to Cheat on Their Taxes," *USA Today,* February 5, 2009, p 3B.

78 Based on T Jackson, "Cultural Values and Management Ethics: A 10-Nation Study," *Human Relations,* October 2001, pp 1267–1302. Also see M Kaptein, "Developing and Testing a Measure for the Ethical Culture of Organizations: The Corporate Ethical Virtues Model," *Journal of Organizational Behavior,* October 2008, pp 923–47.

[79] Results can be found in "HR Poll Results," http://hr2.blr.com/index.cfm/Nav/11.0.0.0/Action/Poll_Question /qid/170, accessed April 8, 2005.

[80] Based on L K Trevino, G R Weaver, and M E Brown, "It's Lovely at the Top: Hierarchical Levels, Identities, and Perceptions of Organizational Ethics," *Business Ethics Quarterly,* April 2008, pp 233–52.

[81] Results can be found in Matthew Boyle, "By the Numbers: Liar Liar!" *Fortune,* May 26, 2003, p 44.

[82] P Babcock, "Spotting Lies," *HR Magazine,* October 2003, p 47. Also see D Macsai, ". . . And I Invented Velcro," *BusinessWeek,* August 4, 2008, p 15.

[83] Data from N Byrnes, "Profiles in Pilfering," *BusinessWeek,* October 13, 2008, p 16. Also see C Dugas, "More Consumers, Workers Shoplift as Economy Slows," *USA Today,* June 19, 2008, pp 1B–2B.

[84] M Conlin, "To Catch a Corporate Thief," *BusinessWeek,* February 16, 2009, p 52.

[85] "Say No: International Anti-Corruption Day," *Fast Company,* January 2009, p 44.

[86] Supporting research can be found in J B Cullen, K P Parboteeah, and M Hoegl, "Cross-National Differences in Managers' Willingness to Justify Ethically Suspect Behaviors: A Test of Institutional Anomie Theory," *Academy of Management Journal,* June 2004, pp 411–21. Also see the debate in L D Ordonez, M E Schweitzer, A D Galinsky, and M H Bazerman, "Goals Gone Wild: The Systematic Side Effects of Overprescribing Goal Setting," *Academy of Management Perspectives,* February 2009, pp 6–16; and E A Locke and G P Latham, "Has Goal Setting Gone Wild, or Have Its Attackers Abandoned Good Scholarship?" *Academy of Management Perspectives,* February 2009, pp 17–23.

[87] S Jayson, "Teens Face Up to Ethics Choices—If You Can Believe Them," *USA Today,* December 6, 2006, p 6D.

[88] Ibid. Also see D O Neubaum, M Pagell, J A Drexler Jr, F M McKee-Ryan, and E Larson, "Business Education and Its Relationship to Student Personal Moral Philosophies and Attitudes toward Profits: An Empirical Response to Critics," *Academy of Management Learning and Education,* March 2009, pp 9–24.

[89] Data and quotation from http://charactercounts.org/programs/reportcard/index.html, accessed March 14, 2009. Also see C L Grossman, "Almost All Denominations Losing Ground, Survey Finds," *USA Today,* March 9, 2009, pp 1A–2A.

[90] See Chapter 6 in K Hodgson, *A Rock and a Hard Place: How to Make Ethical Business Decisions When the Choices Are Tough* (New York: AMACOM, 1992), pp 66–77.

[91] See R M Fulmer, "The Challenge of Ethical Leadership," *Organizational Dynamics,* August 2004, pp 307–17; and S Ambec and P Lanoie, "Does It Pay to Be Green? A Systematic Overview," *Academy of Management Perspectives,* November 2008, pp 45–62.

[92] Results can be found in "Tarnished Employment Brands Affect Recruiting," *HR Magazine,* November 2004, pp 16, 20.

[93] Adapted in part from W E Stead, D L Worrell, and J Garner Stead, "An Integrative Model for Understanding and Managing Ethical Behavior in Business Organizations," *Journal of Business Ethics,* March 1990, pp 233–42. Also see D Lange, "A Multidimensional Conceptualization of Organizational Corruption Control," *Academy of Management Review,* July 2008, pp 710–29; and J DesJardins, *An Introduction to Business Ethics,* 3rd ed (New York: McGraw-Hill, 2009).

[94] L W Fry and J W Slocum Jr, "Maximizing the Triple Bottom Line through Spiritual Leadership," *Organizational Dynamics,* January–March 2008, pp 86–96.

[95] For an excellent review of integrity testing, see D S Ones and C Viswesvaran, "Integrity Testing in Organizations," in *Dysfunctional Behavior in Organizations: Violent and Deviant Behavior,* ed R W Griffin et al. (Stamford, CT: JAI Press, 1998), pp 243–76. Also see J McGregor, "Background Checks That Never End," *BusinessWeek,* March 20, 2006, p 40.

[96] Guidelines for conducting ethics training are discussed by K Tyler, "Do the Right Thing," *HR Magazine,* February 2005, pp 99–101. Also see J Porter, "Using Ex-Cons to Scare MBAs Straight," *BusinessWeek,* May 5, 2008, p 58.

[97] See B Levisohn, "Getting More Workers to Whistle," *BusinessWeek,* January 28, 2008, p 18; M Der Hovanesian, "Sex, Lies, and Mortgage Deals," *BusinessWeek,* November 24, 2008, pp 71–74; and M Isikoff, "The Fed Who Blew the Whistle," *Newsweek,* December 22, 2008, pp 40–48.

[98] See C Hirschman, "Giving Voice to Employee Concerns," *HR Magazine,* August 2008, pp 50–53; and M Kimes, "Fluor's Corporate Crime Fighter," *Fortune,* February 16, 2009, p 26.

[99] Based on S J Reynolds, "Moral Attentiveness: Who Pays Attention to Moral Aspects of Life?" *Journal of Applied Psychology,* September 2008, pp 1027–41.

[100] As quoted in D Jones, "Military a Model for Execs," *USA Today,* June 9, 2004, p 4B. Also see B George with P Sims, *True North: Discover Your Authentic Leadership* (San Francisco: Jossey-Bass, 2007).

[101] Complete discussion of this technique can be found in J E Hunter, F L Schmidt, and G B Jackson, *Meta-Analysis: Cumulating Research Findings across Studies* (Beverly Hills, CA: Sage Publications, 1982); J E Hunter and F L Schmidt, *Methods of Meta-Analysis: Correcting Error and Bias in Research Findings* (Newbury Park, CA: Sage Publications, 1990); H Le, I Oh, J Shaffer, F Schmidt, "Implications of Methodological Advances for the Practice of Personnel Selection: How Practitioners Benefit from Meta-Analysis," *Academy of Management Perspectives,* August 2007, pp 6–15; and I Oh, F L Schmidt, J A Shaffer, and H Le, "The Graduate Management Admission Test (GMAT) Is Even More Valid Than We Thought: A New Development in Meta-Analysis and Its Implications for the Validity of the GMAT," *Academy of Management Learning and Education,* December 2008, pp 563–70.

[102] Limitations of meta-analysis technique are discussed in P Bobko and E F Stone-Romero, "Meta-Analysis May Be Another Useful Tool, but It Is Not a Panacea, in *Research in Personnel and Human Resources Management,* vol. 16, ed G R Ferris (Stamford, CT: JAI Press, 1998), pp 359–97; and J Carey, "When Medical Studies Collide," *BusinessWeek,* August 6, 2007, p 38.

[103] Excerpted from S Hamm, "A Passion for the Planet," August 21–28, 2006, issue of *BusinessWeek* by special permission. Copyright © 2006 by The McGraw-Hill Companies, Inc.

[104] As quoted in S Sanghi, "Leader Must See Big Picture in Layoff Debate," *The Arizona Republic,* March 8, 2009, p D5.

CHAPTER 2

1. Excerpted from A M Chaker, "High Schools Add Classes Scripted by Corporations," *The Wall Street Journal,* March 16, 2008, pp. A1, A3.

2. K Maher, "Lockheed Settles Racial-Discrimination Suit," *The Wall Street Journal,* January 2, 2008, p A4.

3. M Schoeff Jr. "Clamping Down on Race Bias," *Workforce Management,* January 14, 2008, pp 1, 3, www.workforce.com.

4. L Wasmer Andrews, "Hard-Core Offenders," *HR Magazine,* December 2004, p 44.

5. Excerpted from "Jury Awards $1.7M to Woman Spanked on Job," *USA Today,* May 16, 2006, www.usatoday.com/news/nation/2006-04-28-spanking-trial_x.htm.

6. H Collingwood, "Who Handles a Diverse Work Force Best?" *Working Women,* February 1996, p 25.

7. See K Gurchiek, "EEOC Addresses Religious Discrimination," *HR Magazine,* September 2008, p 21; and D Levine, "Religious Beliefs, Job Abandonment, Reductions in Force," *HR Magazine,* July 2008, p 29.

8. See "Best Practices & Outstanding Initiatives," *Training,* February 2008, pp 114–20; and "Training Top 125 2008," *Training,* February 2008, pp 76–81.

9. For information on equal employment opportunity legislation, see J Bravin, "Justices Reject Anew Retaliation at Work," *The Wall Street Journal,* January 27, 2009, p A2; K M Puburn Jr, R E Ployhart, and D A Kravitz, "The Diversity-Validity Dilemma: Overview and Legal Context," *Personnel Psychology,* Spring 2008, pp 143–51; and R E Ployhart and B C Holtz, "The Diversity-Validity Dilemma: Strategies for Reducing Racioethnic and Sex Subgroup Differences and Adverse Impact in Selection," *Personnel Psychology,* Spring 2008, pp 153–72.

10. Results can be found in D A Harrison, D A Kravitz, D M Mayer, L M Leslie, and D Lev-Arey, "Understanding Attitudes toward Affirmative Action Programs in Employment: Summary and Meta-Analysis of 35 Years of Research," *Journal of Applied Psychology,* September 2006, pp 1013–36. Also see A Levi and Y Fried, "Differences between African Americans and Whites in Reactions to Affirmative Action Programs in Hiring, Promotion, Training, and Layoffs," *Journal of Applied Psychology,* September 2008, pp 1118–29; and D A Kravitz, T M Bludau, and S L Klineberg, "The Impact of Anticipated Consequences, Respondent Group, and Strength of Affirmative Action Plan on Affirmative Action Attitudes," *Group and Organization Management,* August 2008, pp 361–91.

11. For a thorough review of relevant research, see M E Heilman, "Affirmative Action: Some Unintended Consequences for Working Women," in *Research in Organizational Behavior,* vol. 16, ed B M Staw and L L Cummings (Greenwich, CT: JAI Press, 1994), pp 125–69.

12. Results from this study can be found in M E Heilman, W S Battle, C E Keller, and R A Lee, "Type of Affirmative Action Policy: A Determinant of Reactions to Sex-Based Preferential Selection?" *Journal of Applied Psychology,* April 1998, pp 190–205.

13. A M Morrison, *The New Leaders: Guidelines on Leadership Diversity in America* (San Francisco, CA: Jossey-Bass, 1992), p 78.

14. Results can be found in E Kearney and D Gebert, "Managing Diversity and Enhancing Team Outcomes: The Promise of Transformational Leadership," *Journal of Applied Psychology,* January 2009, pp 77–89.

15. See R Levering and M Moskowitz, "100 Best Companies to Work for: And the Winners Are . . .," *Fortune,* February 2, 2009, pp 67–78; and S Meisinger, "Diversity: More Than Just Representation," *HR Magazine,* January 2008, p 8.

16. Results can be found in A A Cannella Jr, J-H Park, and H-U Lee, "Top Management Team Functional Background Diversity and Firm Performance: Examining the Roles of Team Member Colocation and Environmental Uncertainty," *Academy of Management Journal,* August 2008, pp 768–84.

17. See S Schechner and V Kumar, "Retirement Living TV Gets Boost," *The Wall Street Journal,* January 16, 2009, p B9; and K Helliker, "The Solution to Hunting's Woes? Setting Sights on Women," *The Wall Street Journal,* October 1, 2008, pp A1, A20.

18. These trends are discussed in G Toppo, "Study: 1 in 7 U.S. Adults Lacks Basic Literary Skills," *The Arizona Republic,* January 9, 2009, p A6; "Immigration Counters.com—Live Counters, News, Resources, Facts," http://immigrationcounters.com, last modified February 4, 2009; "High School Graduation Rates Plummet Below 50 Percent in Some U.S. Cities," www.foxnews.com/story/0,2933,344190,00.html, April 1, 2008; D Goldman, "America 2050: Minorities in Majority," *CNNMoney.com,* http://cnnmoney.printthis.clickability.com/pt/cpt?action=cpt&title=Minorities+will+become+the+majority, August 13, 2008; and "Immigation Policy Issues," www.newsbatch.com/immigration.htm, updated July 2007.

19. See "AAUW's Position on Pay Equity," www.aauw.org/advocacy/issue_advocacy/actionpages/payequity.cfm?RenderForPrint=1, January 29, 2009; R R Hastings, "Male, Female Executives' Bonuses Uneven," *HR Magazine,* October 2008, p 28; and K S Lyness and D E Thompson, "Above the Glass Ceiling: A Comparison of Matched Samples of Female and Male Executives," *Journal of Applied Psychology,* June 1997, pp 359–75.

20. These conclusions were based on A H Eagly and L L Carli, *Through the Labyrinth* (Boston: Harvard Business School Press, 2007); M Heilman and T G Okimoto, "Motherhood: A Potential Source of Bias in Employment Decisions," *Journal of Applied Psychology,* January 2008, pp 189–98; and T A Judge and B A Livingston, "Is the Gap More Than Gender? A Longitudinal Analysis of Gender, Gender Role Orientation, and Earnings," *Journal of Applied Psychology,* September 2008, pp 994–1012.

21. See ibid.

22. These statistics were taken from ibid., and D R Dalton and C M Dalton, "Women Gain (Hidden) Ground in the Boardroom," *Harvard Business Review,* January 2009, p 23.

23. Ibid., pp 26–27.

24. *The American Heritage Dictionary* (New York: Bantam Dell, 2004), p 475.

25. For details regarding these statistics, see Goldman, "America 2050: Minorities in Majority."

26. See Bureau of Labor Statistics, "Employed Persons by Occupation, Sex, Race, and Hispanic or Latino Ethnicity, 2007 Annual Averages," www.bls.gov, accessed February 5, 2009.

27. See Equal Employment Opportunity Commission, "Race-Based Charges FY 1997–FY 2007," www.eeoc.gov, last updated February 26, 2008; and B Leonard, "Web, Call Center Fuel Rise in EEOC Claims," *HR Magazine,* June 2008, p 30.

28. Bureau of Labor Statistics, "Weekly and Hourly Earnings Data from the Current Population Survey," http://data.bls.gov,

accessed March 14, 2008. But see R R Hastings, "The Forgotten Minority," *HR Magazine,* July 2007, pp 62–67.

29 See T DeAngelis, "Unmasking 'Racial Micro Aggressions,'" *Harvard Business Review,* February 2009, pp 42–46; D R Avery, P F McKay, and D C Wilson, "What Are the Odds? How Demographic Similarity Affects the Prevalence of Perceived Employment Discrimination," *Journal of Applied Psychology,* March 2008, pp 235–49; and J W Kunstman and E A Plant, "Racing to Help: Racial Bias in High Emergency Helping Situations," *Journal of Applied Psychology,* December 2008, pp 1499–1510.

30 See Census Bureau, *Statistical Abstract of the United States,* 2008, Table 27, "Educational Attainment by Race and Hispanic Origin," www.census.gov.

31 See S Miller, "Skills Critical for a Changing Workforce," *HR Magazine,* August 2008, p 24; and C Boles, "Last Call? Gates Pushes Globalism in Remarks," *The Wall Street Journal,* March 13, 2009, p B3.

32 "Facts on Literacy," *National Literacy Facts,* August 27, 1998, www.svs.net/wpci/Litfacts.htm.

33 Literacy statistics can be found in R R Britt, "Culture: 14 Percent of U.S. Adults Can't Read," *LiveScience,* www.livescience.com/culture/090110-illerate-adults.html, January 10, 2009; and "US: Measuring Up 2008," *University World News,* www.universityworldnews.com, December 7, 2008.

34 The New Commission on the Skills of the American Workforce, *Tough Choices or Tough Times* (San Francisco, CA: Jossey-Bass, 2007), pp xvi, xvii.

35 See the related discussion in S Miller, "Retiring Boomers Spark Phased Retirement Interest," *HR Magazine,* September 2008, p 32; and D A Ready, L A Hill, and J A Conger, "Winning the Race for Talent in Emerging Markets," *Harvard Business Review,* November 2008, pp 63–70.

36 See R Strack, J Baier, and A Fahlander, "Managing Demographic Risk," *Harvard Business Review,* February 2008, pp 119–28.

37 These examples are discussed in E White, "Managers Take Advantage of Generation Gap," *The Arizona Republic,* September 3, 2008, p CL1.

38 See T Erickson, "Gen Y in the Workplace," *Harvard Business Review,* February 2009, pp 43–46; K Auby, "A Boomer's Guide to Communicating with Gen X and Gen Y," *BusinessWeek,* September 1, 2008, p 63; and P Bathurst, "Millennials at Work," *The Arizona Republic,* May 4, 2008, p EC1.

39 For details, see T W H Ng and D C Feldman, "The Relationship of Age to Ten Dimensions of Job Performance," *Journal of Applied Psychology,* March 2008, pp 392–423.

40 Ibid., p 403.

41 S J Wells, "Say Hola! to the Majority Minority," *HR Magazine,* September 2008, p 38.

42 Examples are provided in E Hutchinson, "'People People' Work at Home, Too," *HR Magazine,* September 2008, pp 60–62; R Zeidner, "Bending with the Times," *HR Magazine,* July 2008, p 10; and P Babcock, "Elder Care at Work," *HR Magazine,* September 2008, pp 111–18.

43 See D M Owens, "Success Factors," *HR Magazine,* August 2008, pp 87–89.

44 C Hymowitz, "Women Tell Women: Life in the Top Jobs Is Worth the Effort," *The Wall Street Journal,* November 20, 2006, p B1.

45 See Eagly and Carli, *Through the Labyrinth;* and T DeAngelis, "Mentoring for Mid-Career Women," *Monitor on Psychology,* November 2008, p 65.

46 L Lowen, "Breaking the Grass Ceiling: Women Playing Golf," *About.com,* http://womenissues.about.com, February 28, 2008.

47 For details, see S Boehle, "Voices of Opportunity," *Training,* January 2009, pp 38–39.

48 D A Thomas, "The Truth about Mentoring Minorities: Race Matters," *Harvard Business Review,* April 2001, p 107.

49 See B Mirza, "Build Employee Skills, Help Nonprofits," *HR Magazine,* October 2008, p 30.

50 See J Weber, "This Time, Old Hands Keep Their Jobs," *BusinessWeek,* February 9, 2009, p 50; R J Grossman, "Keep Pace with Older Workers," *HR Magazine,* May 2008, pp 39–46; and D Wessel, "Older Staffers Get Uneasy Embrace," *The Wall Street Journal,* May 15, 2008, p A2.

51 E White, "The New Recruits: Older Workers," *The Wall Street Journal,* January 14, 2008, p B3.

52 These recommendations were taken from G M McEvoy and M J Blahana, "Engagement or Disengagement? Older Workers and the Looming Labor Shortage," *Business Horizons,* September–October 2001, p 50.

53 R R Hastings, "Do Younger Employees Sabotage Boomers?" *HR Magazine,* October 2008, p 33.

54 T J Erickson, "Task, Not Time: Profile of a Gen Y Job," *Harvard Business Review,* February 2008, p 19.

55 P O'Connell, "What's Eating Gen X," *BusinessWeek,* September 1, 2008, p 62.

56 Examples are discussed in L Gerdes, "The Best Places to Launch a Career," *BusinessWeek,* September 15, 2008, pp 37–46; R King, "Go Ahead, Use Facebook," *BusinessWeek,* September 1, 2008, p 65; and S Banjo, "A Perfect Match?" *The Wall Street Journal,* October 13, 2008, p R1.

57 D van Knippenberg, C K W De Dreu, and A C Homan, "Work Group Diversity and Group Performance: An Integrative Model and Research Agenda," *Journal of Applied Psychology,* December 2004, p 1009.

58 See ibid., pp 1008–22; and S E Jackson and A Joshi, "Diversity in Social Context: A Multi-Attribute, Multilevel Analysis of Team Diversity and Sales Performance," *Journal of Organizational Behavior,* September 2004, pp 675–702.

59 See D Sandy and L Zhao, "The Effects of Cultural Diversity in Virtual Teams versus Face-to-Face Teams," *Group Decision and Negotiation,* July 2006, p 389; and J L Berdahl and C Moore, "Workplace Harassment: Double Jeopardy for Minority Women," *Journal of Applied Psychology,* March 2006, pp 426–36.

60 See Jackson and Joshi, "Diversity in Social Context."

61 Results can be found in J M Sacco and N Schmitt, "A Dynamic Multilevel Model of Demographic Diversity and Misfit Effects," *Journal of Applied Psychology,* March 2005, pp 203–31; and H Liao and A Joshi, "Sticking Out Like a Sore Thumb: Employee Dissimilarity and Deviance at Work," *Personnel Psychology,* Winter 2004, pp 969–1000.

62 van Knippenberg, De Dreu, and Homan, "Work Group Diversity and Group Performance," p 1009.

63 These conclusions were derived from Jackson and Joshi, "Diversity in Social Context."

[64] See J Wegge, C Roth, B Neubach, K-H Schmidt, and R Kanfer, "Age and Gender Diversity as Determinants of Performance and Health in a Public Organization: The Role of Task Complexity and Group Size," *Journal of Applied Psychology,* November 2008, 1301–13; and Jackson and Joshi, "Diversity in Social Context."

[65] See S Schulz-Hardt, F C Brodbeck, A Mojzisch, R Kerschreiter, and D Frey, "Group Decision Making in Hidden Profile Situations: Dissent as a Facilitator for Decision Quality," *Journal of Personality and Social Psychology,* December 2006, pp 1080–93.

[66] See R Moss-Kanter, *The Change Masters* (New York: Simon and Schuster, 1983).

[67] See K Y Williams, "Demography and Diversity in Organizations: A Review of 100 Years of Research," in *Research in Organizational Behavior,* vol. 20, ed B M Staw and L L Cummings (Greenwich, CT: JAI Press, 1998), pp 77–140.

[68] See M J Pearsall, A P J Ellis, and J M Evans, "Unlocking the Effects of Gender Faultlines on Team Creativity: Is Activation the Key?" *Journal of Applied Psychology,* January 2008, pp 225–34.

[69] D C Lau and J K Murnighan, "Demographic Diversity and Faultlines: The Compositional Dynamics of Organizational Groups," *Academy of Management Review,* April 1998, p 328.

[70] Supportive results can be found in A C Homan, J R Hollenbeck, S E Humphrey, D V Knippenberg, D R Ilgen, and G A V Kleff, "Facing Differences with an Open Mind: Openness to Experience, Salience of Intragroup Differences, and Performance of Diverse Work Groups," *Academy of Management Journal,* December 2008, pp 1204–22.

[71] See ibid; and A H Van De Ven, R W Rogers, J P Bechara, and K Sun, "Organizational Diversity, Integration and Performance," *Journal of Organizational Behavior,* April 2008, pp 335–54.

[72] Support groups are discussed by J T Arnold, "Employee Networks," *HR Magazine,* June 2006, pp 145–52; and C McGlothlen, "Inclusive, Exclusive or Outlawed?" *HR Magazine,* July 2006, pp 107–12.

[73] These barriers were taken from discussions in M Loden, *Implementing Diversity* (Burr Ridge, IL: Irwin, 1996); E E Spragins, "Benchmark: The Diverse Work Force," *Inc.,* January 1993, p 33; and Morrison, *The New Leaders.*

[74] C Ostroff, A J Kinicki, and M M Tamkins, "Organizational Culture and Climate," in *Handbook of Psychology*, vol. 12, ed W C Borman, D R Ilgen, and R J Klimoski (Hoboken, NJ: John Wiley & Sons, 2003), p 571.

[75] J A Gonzalez and A DeNisi, "Cross-Level Effects of Demography and Diversity Climate on Organizational Attachment and Firm Effectiveness," *Journal of Organizational Behavior,* January 2009, p 24.

[76] See ibid., pp 21–40; P F McKay, D R Avery, and M A Morris, "Mean Racial-Ethnic Differences in Employee Sales Performance: The Moderating Role of Diversity Climate," *Personnel Psychology,* Summer 2008, pp 349–74; and L-E Petersen and J Dietz, "Employment Discrimination: Authority Figures' Demographic Preferences and Followers' Affective Organizational Commitment," *Journal of Applied Psychology,* November 2008, pp 1287–1300.

[77] MG Danaher, "Prompt Response Avoids Liability for Hostile Work Environment," *HR Magazine,* June 2004, p 181.

[78] See the related results in L Torres and D Rollock, "Acculturation and Depression among Hispanics: The Moderating Effect of Intercultural Competence," *Cultural Diversity and Ethnic Minority Psychology,* January 2007, pp 10–17.

[79] This example was taken from G Colvin, "Lafley and Immelt: In Search of Billions," *Fortune,* December 11, 2006, pp 70–72.

[80] This discussion is based on R R Thomas Jr, *Redefining Diversity* (New York: AMACOM, 1996). Also see J Brett, K Behfar, and M C Kern, "Managing Multicultural Teams," *Harvard Business Review,* November 2006, pp 84–91.

[81] D J Gaiter, "Eating Crow: How Shoney's, Belted by a Lawsuit, Found the Path to Diversity," *The Wall Street Journal,* April 16, 1996, pp A, A11.

[82] P Dass and B Parker, "Strategies for Managing Human Resource Diversity: From Resistance to Learning," *Academy of Management Executive,* May 1999, p 69.

[83] Gaiter, "Eating Crow."

[84] E White, "Fostering Diversity to Aid Business," *The Wall Street Journal,* May 20, 2006, p B3.

[85] Excerpted from C Tuna, "Initiative Moves Women Up Corporate Ladder," *The Wall Street Journal,* October 20, 2008, p B4. Copyright © 2008 by Dow Jones & Company, Inc. Reproduced with permission of Dow Jones & Company, Inc. via Copyright Clearance Center.

[86] Excerpted from D Roberts and P Engardio, "Secrets, Lies, and Sweatshops," January 22, 2007, issue of *BusinessWeek* by special permission. Copyright © 2007 by The McGraw-Hill Companies, Inc.

CHAPTER 3

[1] C Barrett, "Talking Southwest Culture," *Spirit,* May 2008, p 12.

[2] These companies are discussed in R Levering and M Moskowitz, "The 100 Best Companies to Work For," *Fortune,* February 2, 2009, pp 67–78.

[3] D Seidman, *Training,* February 2009, p 8.

[4] E H Schein, "Culture: The Missing Concept in Organization Studies," *Administrative Science Quarterly,* June 1996, p 236.

[5] Excerpted from J McGregor, "The 2008 Winners," *BusinessWeek,* March 3, 2008, p 49.

[6] See P Glader, "GE's Chief Declines $12 Million Bonus Amid Crisis," *The Wall Street Journal,* February 19, 2009, p B4.

[7] S H Schwartz, "Universals in the Content and Structure of Values: Theoretical Advances and Empirical Tests in 20 Countries," in *Advances in Experimental Social Psychology,* ed M P Zanna (New York: Academic Press, 1992), p 4.

[8] See Y Berson, S Oreg, and T Dvir, "CEO Values, Organizational Culture and Firm Outcomes," *Journal of Organizational Behavior,* July 2009, pp 615–33; and Y Ling, Z Simsek, M H Lubatkin, and J F Veiga, "The Impact of Transformational CEOs on the Performance of Small-to-Medium-Sized Firms: Does Organizational Context Matter?" *Journal of Applied Psychology,* July 2008, pp 923–34.

[9] A Fox, "Get in the Business of Being Green," *HR Magazine,* June 2008, pp 45–46.

[10] See T L Friedman, "Yes, They Could. So They Did." *New York Times.com,* February 14, 2009, www.nytimes. com/2009/02/15/opinion/15friedman.html.

[11] See the related discussion in D Seidman, "Outgreening Delivers Sustainable Competitive Advantage," *Business Week Online,* December 5, 2008, www/businessweek.com/managing/content/dec2008/ca2008125_029230.htm; M Conlin, "Suddenly, It's Cool to Take the Bus," *Business Week,* May 5, 2008, p 24; and "The World's Most Influential Companies," *Business Week,* December 22, 2008, pp 43–53.

[12] P Babcock, "Is Your Company Two-Faced?" *HR Magazine,* January 2004, p 43.

[13] M Herbst, "Starbucks' Karma Problem," *Business Week,* January 12, 2009, p 26.

[14] B Leonard, "Stay True to Your Values," *HR Magazine,* July 2008, pp 45–46.

[15] Results are discussed in "Executing Ethics," *Training,* March 2007, p 8. Ethical cultures are also discussed by M Kaptein, "Developing and Testing a Measure for the Ethical Culture of Organizations: The Corporate Ethical Virtues Model," *Journal of Organizational Behavior,* March 2008, pp 923–47.

[16] See "Employees Trust Managers More Than Top Brass," *HR Magazine,* October 2008, p 10; and R J Grossman, "Hiring to Fit the Culture," *HR Magazine,* February 2009, p 41.

[17] Related discussion is provided by R J Grossman, "What Is Culture?" *HR Magazine,* February 2009, pp 42–44; and R J Grossman, "How to Screen for Cultural Fit," *HR Magazine,* February 2009, pp 46–50.

[18] M Bolch, "Closing the Sale," *HR Magazine,* October 2008, p 88.

[19] Statistics and data contained in the Southwest Airlines example can be found in the "Southwest Airlines Fact Sheet," updated December 15, 2008, www.southwest.com.

[20] "Southwest Airlines Careers," accessed February 2009, www.southwest.com.

[21] Southwest's mission statement can be found in "The Mission of Southwest Airlines," December 2008, www.southwest.com.

[22] See C Ostroff, A Kinicki, and M Tamkins, "Organizational Culture and Climate," in *Handbook of Psychology,* vol. 12, ed W C Borman, D R Ilgen, and R J Klimoski (New York: Wiley and Sons, 2003), pp 565–93.

[23] See the related discussion in S Ten Have, W Ten Have, A F Stevens, M Vander Elst, and F Pol-Coyne, *Key Management Models: The Management Tools and Practices That Will Improve Your Business* (San Francisco, CA: Jossey-Bass, 2003).

[24] A thorough description of the CVF is provided in K S Cameron, R E Quinn, J Degraff, and A V Thakor, *Competing Values Leadership* (Northampton, MA: Edward Elgar, 2006).

[25] Excerpted from K R Spors, "Top Small Workplaces 2008," *The Wall Street Journal,* October 13, 2008, p R4.

[26] See R Levering and M Moskowitz, "100 Best Companies to Work For," p 67.

[27] Zappos is discussed in J M O'Brien, "Zappos Knows How to Kick It," *Fortune,* February 2, 2009, pp 55–60.

[28] Excerpted from J McGregor, "How Failure Breeds Success," *Business Week,* July 10, 2006, pp 45–46. Also see N T Sheehan and G Vaidyanathan, "The Path to Growth," *The Wall Street Journal,* March 3–4, 2007, p R8.

[29] These examples were taken from D Welch, D Kiley, and M Ihlwan, "My Way or the Highway at Hyundai," *Business Week,* March 17, 2008, pp 48–51; and E Frauenheim, "Culture Crash," *Workforce Management,* January 14, 2008, pp 12–17.

[30] See J Welch and S Welch, "The Loyalty Factor," *Business Week,* January 19, 2009, p 68.

[31] For details on Home Depot and Exelon, see J Reingold, "Home Depot's Total Rehab," *Fortune,* September 29, 2008, pp 159–66; and "Exelon Announces Fourth Quarter and Full Year 2008 Results: Reaffirms 2009 Earnings Guidance," *Exelon Newsroom,* January 22, 2009, www.exeloncorp.com.

[32] See H Takeuchi, E Osono, and N Shimizu, "The Contradictions That Drive Toyota's Success," *Harvard Business Review,* June 2008, pp 96–104.

[33] The Ritz-Carlton's culture is discussed in J Gordon, "Redefining Elegance," *Training,* March 2007, pp 14–18.

[34] Results can be found in C Hartnell, Y Ou, and A Kinicki, "Assessing the Organizational Culture-Organizational Effectiveness Link: A Meta-Analytic Review," manuscript under review, September 2009. Also see Y Berson, S Oreg, and T Dvir, "CEO Values, Organizational Culture, and Firm Outcomes," *Journal of Organizational Behavior,* July 2008, pp 615–33.

[35] Mergers are discussed by J Silver-Greenberg, "Dealmakers Test the Waters," *Business Week,* March 2, 2009, pp 18–20; in C Palmeri, "What FedEx Isn't Delivering," *Business Week,* December 29, 2008, pp 78–79; and in M J Epstein, "The Drivers of Success in Post-Merger Integration," *Organizational Dynamics,* May 2004, pp 174–89.

[36] See the related discussion in V Sathe and E J Davidson, "Toward a New Conceptualization of Culture Change," in *Handbook of Organizational Culture & Climate,* ed N M Ashkanasay, C P M Wilderom, and M F Peterson (Thousand Oaks, CA: Sage Publications, 2000), pp 279–96.

[37] W Disney, quoted in B Nanus, *Visionary Leadership: Creating a Compelling Sense of Direction for Your Organization* (San Francisco, CA: Jossey-Bass, 1992), p 28; reprinted from B Thomas, *Walt Disney: An American Tradition* (New York: Simon & Schuster, 1976), p 247.

[38] D-A Durbin, "Ford Cuts Part of Culture Shift," *The Arizona Republic,* January 24, 2006, p D3.

[39] The mechanisms were based on material contained in E H Schein, "The Role of the Founder in Creating Organizational Culture," *Organizational Dynamics,* Summer 1983, pp 13–28.

[40] J Collins, "The Secret of Enduring Greatness," *Fortune,* May 5, 2008, pp 73–76.

[41] D Clark, "Why Silicon Valley Is Rethinking the Cubicle Office," *The Wall Street Journal,* October 15, 2007, http://online.wsj.com.

[42] See M Kimes, "Fluor's Corporate Crime Fighter," *Fortune,* February 16, 2009, p 26.

[43] D Moss, "Triage: Methodically Developing Its Employees," *HR Magazine,* July 2007, p 45.

[44] C Jarnagin and J W Slocum Jr, "Creating Corporate Cultures through Mythopoetic Leadership," *Organizational Dynamics,* 2007, pp 288–302.

45 See S Denning, "Stories in the Workplace," *HR Magazine,* September 2008, pp 129–32.

46 C Hymowitz, "New CEOs May Spur Resistance if They Try to Alter Firm's Culture," *The Wall Street Journal,* August 13, 2007, p B1.

47 See N M Davis, "Scaling Mountains, Literally and Figuratively," *HR Magazine,* July 2008, pp 47–48.

48 See N Shirouzu, "Toyota, Needing Change, Taps a Scion to Lead," *The Wall Street Journal,* January 12, 2009, pp B1, B2.

49 These examples are explored in B Roberts, "Social Networking at the Office," *HR Magazine,* March 2008, pp 81–83.

50 L Grensing-Pophal, "Building Service with a Smile," *HR Magazine,* November 2006, p 87.

51 J Van Maanen, "Breaking In: Socialization to Work," in *Handbook of Work, Organization, and Society,* ed R Dubin (Chicago: Rand-McNally, 1976), p 67.

52 See R Alsop, *The Trophy Kids Grow Up* (San Francisco, CA: Jossey-Bass, 2008).

53 Supportive evidence is provided by R W Griffeth and P W Hom, *Retaining Valued Employees* (Thousand Oaks, CA: Sage Publications, 2001), pp 46–65.

54 See B Roberts, "Manage Candidates Right from the Start," *HR Magazine,* October 2008, pp 73–76.

55 See J M Phillips, "Effects of Realistic Job Previews on Multiple Organizational Outcomes: A Meta-Analysis," *Academy of Management Journal,* December 1998, pp 673–90.

56 Onboarding programs are discussed by M Weinstein, "SCC's Keys to Success," *Training,* February 2009, pp 36–40; P Post, "Perspective Matters," *Training,* February 2009, p 112; and S Fall, "The Executive Entrance," *Training,* August 2008, pp 46–48.

57 Excerpted from S Reed, "The Stealth Oil Giant," *BusinessWeek,* January 14, 2008, p 45.

58 These results are presented in M M Smith, "Recognition ROI . . . Now More Than Ever," *HR Magazine: Special Advertisement Supplement—The Power of Incentives, HR Magazine,* 2008, pp 87–94; and "Outsider Longer," *Training,* March 2007, p 6. Also see M Weinstein, "In on Onboarding," *Training,* July/August 2008, p 8.

59 See J P Slattery, T T Selvarajan, and J E Anderson, "Influences of New Employee Development Practices on Temporary Employee Work-Related Attitudes," *Human Resource Development Quarterly,* 2006, pp 279–303.

60 See E H Offstein and R L Dufresne, "Building Strong Ethics and Promoting Positive Character Development: The Influence of HRM at the United States Military Academy at West Point," *Human Resource Management,* Spring 2007, pp 95–114.

61 J Fan and J P Wanous, "Organizational and Cultural Entry: A New Type of Orientation Program for Multiple Boundary Crossings," *Journal of Applied Psychology,* November 2008, pp 1390–1400.

62 R Levering and M Moskowitz, "The 100 Best Companies to Work For: And the Winners Are . . .," *Fortune,* January 23, 2006, p 94.

63 A review of stage model research can be found in B E Ashforth, *Role Transitions in Organizational Life: An Identity-Based Perspective* (Mahwah, NJ: Lawrence Erlbaum Associates, 2001).

64 See A M Saks and B E Ashforth, "Proactive Socialization and Behavioral Self-Management," Journal of Vocational Behavior, June 1996, pp 301–23.

65 For a thorough review of research on the socialization of diverse employees with disabilities, see A Colella, "Organizational Socialization of Newcomers with Disabilities: A Framework for Future Research," in *Research in Personnel and Human Resources Management,* ed G R Ferris (Greenwich, CT: JAI Press, 1996), pp 351–417.

66 This definition is based on the network perspective of mentoring proposed by M Higgins and K Kram, "Reconceptualizing Mentoring at Work: A Developmental Network Perspective," *Academy of Management Review,* April 2001, pp 264–88.

67 Results can be found in T D Allen, L T Eby, M L Poteet, and E Lentz, "Career Benefits Associated with Mentoring for Protégés: A Meta-Analysis," *Journal of Applied Psychology,* February 2004, pp 127–36; H-G Wolff and K Moser, "Effects of Networking on Career Success: A Longitudinal Study," *Journal of Applied Psychology,* January 2009, pp 196–206; and S M Carraher, S E Sullivan, and M M Crocitto, "Mentoring across Global Boundaries: An Empirical Examination of Home-and-Host-Country Mentors on Expatriate Career Outcomes," *Journal of International Business Studies,* December 2008, pp 1310–26.

68 Career functions are discussed in detail in K Kram, *Mentoring of Work: Developmental Relationships in Organizational Life* (Glenview, IL: Scott, Foresman, 1985).

69 T J DeLong, J J Gabarro, and R J Lees, "Why Mentoring Matters in a Hypercompetitive World," *Harvard Business Review,* January 2008, pp 115–21.

70 This discussion is based on Higgins and Kram, "Reconceptualizing Mentoring at Work."

71 See W C Byham, "Start Networking Right Away (Even If You Hate It)," *Harvard Business Review,* January 2009, p 22; K E Kram and M C Higgins, "A New Approach to Mentoring," *The Wall Street Journal,* September 22, 2008, p R10; and N Wingfield and P-W Tam, "Out of the Office: Job Loss in the Age of Blogs and Twitter," *The Wall Street Journal,* February 3, 2009, p A11.

72 See Higgins and Kram, "Reconceptualizing Mentoring at Work."

73 See L T Eby, J R Durley, S C Evans, and B R Ragins, "Mentors' Perceptions of Negative Mentoring Experiences: Sale Development and Nomological Validation," *Journal of Applied Psychology,* March 2008, pp 358–73.

74 See A Pentland, "How Social Networks Network Best," *Harvard Business Review,* February 2009, p 37; J S Lublin, "Networking? Here's How to Stand Out," *The Wall Street Journal,* November 4, 2008, p D4; and R Zeidner, "Employee Networking," *HR Magazine,* November 2008, pp 58–60.

75 See T Gutner, "Finding Anchors in the Storm: Mentors," *The Wall Street Journal,* January 27, 2009, p D4; and H Lollis, "Be a Steppingstone," *HR Magazine,* November 2008, pp 112–14.

76 See P Parker, D T Hall, and K E Kram, "Peer Coaching: A Relational Process for Accelerating Career Learning," *Academy of Management Learning & Education,* December 2008, pp 487–503.

[77] A Pomeroy, "Internal Mentors and Coaches Are Popular," *HR Magazine,* September 2007, p 12.

[78] M Kimes, "Cisco Systems Layers It On," *Fortune,* December 8, 2008, p 24.

[79] Excerpted from J Silver-Greenberg, "The Credit-Card Blowup Ahead," *Business Week,* October 20, 2008, pp 24–25.

CHAPTER 4

[1] From S Gupta, "Mine the Potential of Multicultural Teams," *HR Magazine,* October 2008, pp. 79–80. Copyright 2008 by Society for Human Resource Management (SHRM). Reproduced with permission of Society for Human Resource Management via Copyright Clearance Center.

[2] See M Mandel, "Multinationals: Are They Good for America?" *Business Week,* March 10, 2008, pp. 41–46; P Engardio, G Smith, and J Sasseen, "Refighting NAFTA," *Business Week,* March 31, 2008, pp 56–59; S E Ante, "Mobsters without Borders," *Business Week,* May 5, 2008, p 76; and D Rocks, "Sweat and Striving on China's Factory Floor," *Business Week,* October 20, 2008, p 94.

[3] R Zeidner, "Uncovering Offshoring's Invisible Costs," *HR Magazine,* January 2009, p 26. Also see M Boyle, "Mapping the iPod Economy," *Business Week,* November 3, 2008, p 30.

[4] See M Srivastava, "Bangalore Backlash," *Business Week,* November 17, 2008, pp 53–54.

[5] D J Lynch, "Developing Nations Poised to Challenge USA as King of the Hill," *USA Today,* February 8, 2007, p 2B. Also see M V Copeland, "Boeing's Big Dream," *Fortune,* May 5, 2008, pp 180–91; S LeVine, "5,000 Years of Raucous Trade," *Business Week,* June 16, 2008, pp 97–98; and M Goldsmith, "We're All Entrepreneurs," *Business Week,* August 25–September 1, 2008, p 46.

[6] K Hall, "Japan: Google's Real-Life Lab," *Business Week,* February 25, 2008, p 56.

[7] Data from M A Carpenter, W G Sanders, and H B Gregersen, "Bundling Human Capital with Organizational Context: The Impact of International Assignment Experience on Multinational Firm Performance and CEO Pay," *Academy of Management Journal,* June 2001, pp 493–511. Also see "Kent Is It at Coke," *Business Week,* July 14–21, 2008, pp 7–8; P Engardio, "Mom-and-Pop Multinationals," *Business Week,* July 14–21, 2008, pp 77–78; K Capell, "Unilever," *Business Week,* December 22, 2008, p 47; and H Dolezalek, "Global Yet Local," *Training,* January 2009, pp 34–36.

[8] See E McGirt, "¡Hola Surfers!" *Fast Company,* March 2008, pp 57–58; P A Parham and H J Muller, "Review of Workforce Diversity Content in Organizational Behavior Texts," *Academy of Management Learning and Education,* September 2008, pp 424–28; and A Campo-Flores and S Kliff, "Campfire Questions," *Newsweek,* January 26, 2009, pp 66–67.

[9] G Dutton, "Building a Global Brain," *Management Review,* May 1999, p 35.

[10] M Mabry, "Pin a Label on a Manager—and Watch What Happens," *Newsweek,* May 14, 1990, p 43.

[11] Ibid. Also see G K Stahl and A Voigt, "Do Cultural Differences Matter in Mergers and Acquisitions? A Tentaive Model and Examination," *Organization Science,* January–February 2008, pp 160–76; M W Morris, J Podolny, and B N Sullivan, "Culture and Coworker Relations: Interpersonal Patterns in American, Chinese, German, and Spanish Divisions of a Global Retail Giant," *Organization Science,* July–August 2008, pp 517–32; and M A Lyles, "Appreciating Cultural Differences in China: An Interview with Robert A. Eckert, Chairperson of the Board and CEO of Mattel, Inc." *Business Horizons,* November–December 2008, pp 463–68.

[12] M Javidan and R J House, "Cultural Acumen for the Global Manager: Lessons from Project GLOBE," *Organizational Dynamics,* Spring 2001, p 292 (emphasis added).

[13] For instructive discussion, see J S Black, H B Gregersen, and M E Mendenhall, *Global Assignments: Successfully Expatriating and Repatriating International Managers* (San Francisco: Jossey-Bass, 1992), ch 2.

[14] F Trompenaars and C Hampden-Turner, *Riding the Waves of Culture: Understanding Cultural Diversity in Global Business,* 2nd ed (New York: McGraw-Hill, 1998), pp 6–7. The concept of "cultural mosaic" is discussed in G T Chao and H Moon, "The Cultural Mosaic: A Metatheory for Understanding the Complexity of Culture," *Journal of Applied Psychology,* November 2005, pp 1128–40. Also see C Wan, C Chiu, S Peng, and K Tam, "Measuring Cultures through Intersubjective Cultural Norms," *Journal of Cross-Cultural Psychology,* March 2007, pp 213–26.

[15] As quoted in *Business Week,* August 25–September 1, 2008, p 44.

[16] As quoted in "How Cultures Collide," *Psychology Today,* July 1976, p 69.

[17] J Main, "How to Go Global—and Why," *Fortune,* August 28, 1989, p. 73.

[18] W D Marbach, "Quality: What Motivates American Workers?" *Business Week,* April 12, 1993, p 93. Service quality is discussed in F X Frei, "The Four Things a Service Business Must Get Right," *Harvard Busness Review,* April 2008, pp 70–80.

[19] See G A Sumner, *Folkways* (New York: Ginn, 1906).

[20] As quoted in C Levinson, "In Kirkuk, Ethnic Tension Simmers," *USA Today,* August 14, 2008, p 2A.

[21] D A Heenan and H V Perlmutter, *Multinational Organization Development* (Reading, MA: Addison-Wesley, 1979), p 17. Also see S S Kahn and J H Liu, "Intergroup Attributions and Ethnocentrism in the Indian Subcontinent," *Journal of Cross-Cultural Psychology,* January 2008, pp 16–36.

[22] Data from R Kopp, "International Human Resource Policies and Practices in Japanese, European, and United States Multinationals," *Human Resource Management,* Winter 1994, pp 581–99. Also see D DeLuca and H Hu, "Evaluate Workforces in Emerging Economies," *HR Magazine,* September 2008, pp 64–70.

[23] Fareed Zakaria, *The Post-American World* (New York: W W Norton, 2008), p 46.

[24] Data from M B Marklein, "High Mark for Foreign Students Here," *USA Today,* November 17, 2008, p 4D; and M B Marklein, "An 'Interdependent' World Welcomes More U.S. Students," *USA Today,* November 17, 2008, p 4D.

[25] See R R McCrae, A Terracciano, A Realo, and J Allik, "Interpreting GLOBE Societal Practices Scales," *Journal of Cross-Cultural Psychology,* November 2008, pp 805–10.

[26] J S Osland and A Bird, "Beyond Sophisticated Stereotyping: Cultural Sensemaking in Context," *Academy of Management Executive,* February 2000, p 67.

[27] "Fujio Mitarai: Canon," *Business Week,* January 14, 2002, p 55.

28 P C Earley and E Mosakowski, "Cultural Intelligence," *Harvard Business Review,* October 2004, p 140. Also see P C Earley and E Mosakowski, "Toward Culture Intelligence: Turning Cultural Differences into a Workplace Advantage," *Academy of Management Executive,* August 2004, pp 151–57; H C Triandis, "Cultural Intelligence in Organizations," *Group and Organization Management,* February 2006, pp 20–26; and D S Elenkov and I M Manev, "Senior Expatriate Leadership's Effects on Innovation and the Role of Cultural Intelligence," *Journal of World Business,* in press, 2009.

29 See J M Shapiro, J L Ozanne, and B Saatcioglu, "An Interpretive Examination of the Development of Cultural Sensitivity in International Business," *Journal of International Business Studies,* January–February 2008, pp 71–87; L Nardon and R M Steers, "The New Global Manager: Learning Cultures on the Fly," *Organizational Dynamics,* January–March 2008, pp 47–59; and K A Crowne, "What Leads to Cultural Intelligence?" *Business Horizons,* September–October 2008, pp 391–99.

30 J Porter, "How to Stand Out in the Global Crowd," *BusinessWeek,* November 24, 2008, pp 52, 54.

31 See "How Cultures Collide," pp 66–74, 97; and M Munter, "Cross-Cultural Communication for Managers," *Business Horizons,* May–June 1993, pp 69–78.

32 S Reed, "Meet the Master of Mideast Buyouts," *BusinessWeek,* March 10, 2008, p 70.

33 The German management style is discussed in R Stewart, "German Management: A Challenge to Anglo-American Managerial Assumptions," *Business Horizons,* May–June 1996, pp 52–54.

34 I Adler, "Between the Lines," *Business Mexico,* October 2000, p 24.

35 The tips were excerpted from R Drew, "Working with Foreigners," *Management Review,* September 1999, p 6.

36 For background, see Javidan and House, "Cultural Acumen for the Global Manager," pp 289–305; the entire Spring 2002 issue of *Journal of World Business;* R J House, P J Hanges, M Javidan, P W Dorfman, and V Gupta, eds, *Culture, Leadership, and Organizations: The GLOBE Study of 62 Societies* (Thousand Oaks, CA: Sage, 2004); and www.thunderbird.edu/wwwfiles/ms/globe/.

37 R House, M Javidan, P Hanges, and P Dorfman, "Understanding Cultures and Implicit Leadership Theories across the Globe: An Introduction to Project GLOBE," *Journal of World Business,* Spring 2002, p 4.

38 Adapted from the list in ibid., pp 5–6. Also see M Javidan, G K Stahl, F Brodbeck, and C P M Wilderom, "Cross-Border Transfer of Knowledge: Cultural Lessons from Project GLOBE," *Academy of Management Executive,* May 2005, pp 59–76; and D A Waldman, M Sully de Luque, N Washburn, R J House, et al., "Cultural and Leadership Predictors of Corporate Social Responsibility Values of Top Management: A GLOBE Study of 15 Countries," *Journal of International Business Studies,* November 2006, pp 823–37.

39 See M Javidan, "Forward-Thinking Cultures," *Harvard Business Review,* July–August 2007, p 20.

40 As quoted in J Reingold, "Secrets of Their Success," *Fortune,* November 24, 2008, p 162. For more detail, see Malcolm Gladwell, *Outliers: The Story of Success* (New York: Little, Brown, 2008), ch 7.

41 See D Oyserman, H M Coon, and M Kemmelmeier, "Rethinking Individualism and Collectivism: Evaluation of

Theoretical Assumptions and Meta-Analyses," *Psychological Bulletin,* January 2002, pp 3–72; and B Erdogan and R C Liden, "Collectivism as a Moderator of Responses to Organizational Justice: Implications for Leader-Member Exchange and Ingratiation," *Journal of Organizational Behavior,* February 2006, pp 1–17.

42 M Edwards, "As Good as It Gets," *AARP: The Magazine,* November–December 2004, p 48.

43 See table in ibid., p 49.

44 Data from Trompenaars and Hampden-Turner, *Riding the Waves of Culture,* ch 5. For related research, see E G T Green and J Deschamps, "Variation of Individualism and Collectivism within and between 20 Countries," *Journal of Cross-Cultural Psychology,* May 2005, pp 321–39; and S Begley, "You Can Blame the Bugs," *Newsweek,* April 14, 2008, p 41.

45 As quoted in E E Schultz, "Scudder Brings Lessons to Navajo, Gets Some of Its Own," *The Wall Street Journal,* April 29, 1999, p C12.

46 Trompenaars and Hampden-Turner, *Riding the Waves of Culture,* p 56.

47 For interesting reading, see P Zimbardo and J Boyd, *The Time Paradox: The New Psychology of Time That Will Change Your Life* (New York: Free Press, 2008); and J Hodgins, "You Can't Make More Time," *BusinessWeek,* August 25–September 1, 2008, p 71.

48 As quoted in D W Dowling, "The Best Advice I Ever Got," *Harvard Business Review,* May 2008, p 21.

49 S Smith, "A Pirate's Life," *Newsweek,* June 26, 2006, p 45.

50 R W Moore, "Time, Culture, and Comparative Management: A Review and Future Direction," in *Advances in International Comparative Management,* vol. 5, ed S B Prasad (Greenwich, CT: JAI Press, 1990), pp 7–8.

51 J Deschenaux, "Less Time for Lunch," *HR Magazine,* June 2008, p 125.

52 See E T Hall, *The Hidden Dimension* (Garden City, NY: Doubleday, 1966).

53 "How Cultures Collide," p 72.

54 See S Prothero, "The Islam You Don't Hear About," *USA Today,* June 23, 2008, p 13A; B Einhorn and C Tschang, "Praying for Success in Shanghai," *BusinessWeek,* July 14–21, 2008, pp 87–89; and R J Grossman, "Religion at Work," *HR Magazine,* December 2008, pp 26–33.

55 Results adapted from and value definitions quoted from S R Safranski and I-W Kwon, "Religious Groups and Management Value Systems," in *Advances in International Comparative Management,* vol. 3, ed R N Farner and E G McGoun (Greenwich, CT: JAI Press, 1988), pp 171–83.

56 Ibid., p 180.

57 N J Adler with A Gundersen, *International Dimensions of Organizational Behavior,* 5th ed (Mason, OH: Thomson South-Western, 2008), p 13 (emphasis added).

58 Drawn from F F Chen, "What Happens if We Compare Chopsticks with Forks? The Impact of Making Inappropriate Comparisons in Cross-Cultural Research," *Journal of Personality and Social Psychology,* November 2008, pp 1005–18. Also see G T M Hult et al., "Data Equivalence in Cross-Cultural International Business Research: Assessment and Guidelines," *Journal of International Business Studies,*

September 2008, pp 1027–44; and G A Jack, M B Calas, S M Nkomo, and T Peltonen, "Critique and International Management: An Uneasy Relationship," *Academy of Management Review,* October 2008, pp 870–84.

[59] M Javidan and R J House, "Leadership and Cultures around the World: Findings from GLOBE—An Introduction to the Special Issue," *Journal of World Business,* Spring 2002, p 1.

[60] For complete details, see G Hofstede, *Culture's Consequences: International Differences in Work-Related Values,* abridged ed (Newbury Park, CA: Sage, 1984); G Hofstede, "The Interaction between National and Organizational Value Systems," *Journal of Management Studies,* July 1985, pp 347–57; and G Hofstede, "Management Scientists Are Human," *Management Science,* January 1994, pp 4–13. Also see M H Hoppe, "Introduction: Geert Hofstede's *Culture's Consequences: International Differences in Work-Related Values,*" *Academy of Management Executive,* February 2004, pp 73–74; M H Hoppe, "An Interview with Geert Hofstede," *Academy of Management Executive,* February 2004, pp 75–79; J W Bing, "Hofstede's Consequences: The Impact of His Work on Consulting and Business Practices," *Academy of Management Executive,* February 2004, pp 80–87; B L Kirkman, K B Lowe, and C B Gibson, "A Quarter Century of *Culture's Consequences:* A Review of Empirical Research Incorporating Hofstede's Cultural Values Framework," *Journal of International Business Studies,* May 2006, pp 285–320; L Tang and P E Koveos, "A Framework to Update Hofstede's Cultural Value Indices: Economic Dynamics and Institutional Stability," *Journal of International Business Studies,* September 2008, pp 1045–63; and G Ailon, "Mirror, Mirror on the Wall: *Culture's Consequences* in a Value Test of Its Own Design," *Academy of Management Review,* October 2008, pp 885–904.

[61] A similar conclusion is presented in the following replication of Hofstede's work: A Merritt, "Culture in the Cockpit: Do Hofstede's Dimensions Replicate?" *Journal of Cross-Cultural Psychology,* May 2000, pp 283–301. Also see K Gilbert and S Cartwright, "Cross-Cultural Consultancy Initiatives to Develop Russian Managers: An Analysis of Five Western Aid-Funded Programs," *Academy of Management Learning and Education,* December 2008, pp 504–18.

[62] For related reading, see E Van de Vliert, "Autocratic Leadership around the World," *Journal of Cross-Cultural Psychology,* January 2006, pp 42–59; M Javidan, P W Dorfman, M Sully de Luque, and R J House, "In the Eye of the Beholder: Cross Cultural Lessons in Leadership from Project GLOBE," *Academy of Management Perspectives,* February 2006, pp 67–90; G B Graen, "In the Eye of the Beholder: Cross-Cultural Lesson in Leadership from Project GLOBE: A Response Viewed from the Third Culture Bonding (TCB) Model of Cross-Cultural Leadership," *Academy of Management Perspectives,* November 2006, pp 95–101; R J House, M Javidan, P W Dorfman, and M Sully de Luque, "A Failure of Scholarship: Response to George Graen's Critique of GLOBE," *Academy of Management Perspectives,* November 2006, pp 102–14; and P Caligiuri and I Tarique, "Predicting Effectiveness in Global Leadership Activities," *Journal of World Business,* in press, 2009.

[63] J Guyon, "David Whitwam," *Fortune,* July 26, 2004, p 174.

[64] M Vande Berg, "Siemens: Betting That Big Is Once Again Beautiful," *Milken Institute Review,* Second Quarter 2002, p 47.

[65] See Del Jones, "At Johnson Controls, Growth Is Good: Expansion Abroad Is Key, New CEO Says," *USA Today,* February 18, 2008, p 6B.

[66] J Welch and S Welch, "Red Flags for the Decade Ahead," *BusinessWeek,* May 19, 2008, p 82. Also see "Work Abroad? No Thanks," *BusinessWeek,* June 16, 2008, pp 8, 10.

[67] Data from J Clark, "New Travel Rules Set Off Confusion, Rush for Passports," *USA Today,* January 19, 2007, p 3D; and *NBC Nightly News,* January 27, 2007.

[68] J S Black and H B Gregersen, "The Right Way to Manage Expats," *Harvard Business Review,* March–April 1999, p 53. A more optimistic picture is presented in R L Tung, "American Expatriates Abroad: From Neophytes to Cosmopolitans," *Journal of World Business,* Summer 1998, pp 125–44. Also see D M Brock, O Shenkar, A Shoham, and I C Siscovick, "National Culture and Expatriate Deployment," *Journal of International Business Studies,* December 2008, pp 1293–1309.

[69] Data from G S Insch and J D Daniels, "Causes and Consequences of Declining Early Departures from Foreign Assignments," *Business Horizons,* November–December 2002, pp 39–48.

[70] S Dallas, "Rule No. 1: Don't Diss the Locals," *BusinessWeek,* May 15, 1995, p 8. Also see S M Toh and A S DeNisi, "A Local Perspective to Expatriate Success," *Academy of Management Executive,* February 2005, pp 132–46; and M A Shaffer, D A Harrison, H Gregersen, J S Black, and L A Ferzandi, "You Can Take It with You: Individual Differences and Expatriate Effectiveness," *Journal of Applied Psychology,* January 2006, pp 109–25.

[71] P Capell, "Employers Seek to Trim Pay for US Expatriates," April 16, 2005, www.careerjournal.com. Also see E Krell, "Evaluating Returns on Expatriates," *HR Magazine,* March 2005, pp 60–65.

[72] These insights come from Tung, "American Expatriates Abroad"; R L Tung, "Female Expatriates: The Model Global Manager?" *Organizational Dynamics,* no. 3, 2004, pp 243–53; A Varma, S M Toh, and P Budhwar, "A New Perspective on the Female Expatriate Experience: The Role of Host Country National Categorization," *Journal of World Business,* June 2006, pp 112–20; M Janssens, T Cappellen, and P Zanoni, "Successful Female Expatriates as Agents: Positioning Oneself through Gender, Hierarchy, and Culture," *Journal of World Business,* June 2006, pp 133–48; and A Pomeroy, "Outdated Policies Hinder Female Expats," *HR Magazine,* December 2006, p 16.

[73] A good resource book is D C Thomas, *Cross-Cultural Management: Essential Concepts,* 2nd ed (Thousand Oaks, CA: Sage, 2008).

[74] E Levenson, "Leaders of the Pack," *Fortune,* October 16, 2006, p 189.

[75] "The Best Managers: Irene Rosenfeld," *BusinessWeek,* January 19, 2009, p 41.

[76] See L Grensing-Pophal, "Expat Lifestyles Take a Hit," *HR Magazine,* March 2008, pp 50–54; K A Manion, "Venturing Abroad," *HR Magazine,* June 2008, pp 86–90.

[77] Data from "E-Pulse," *Training,* January 2002, p 60. Also see M Weinstein, "Mismanaged Mobility," *Training,* June 2008, p 11.

[78] J S Lublin, "Younger Managers Learn Global Skills," *The Wall Street Journal,* March 31, 1992, p B1. For more, see M Weinstein, "Foreign but Familiar," *Training,* January 2009, pp 20–23; M Weinstein, "Taking the (Global) Initiative," *Training,* January 2009, pp 28–32; and P Burrows, "Cisco: Tuning a Workforce to Local Markets," *BusinessWeek,* March 23–30, 2009, p 55.

79 See P C Earley, "Intercultural Training for Managers: A Comparison of Documentary and Interpersonal Methods," *Academy of Management Journal,* December 1987, pp 685–98.

80 E Iwata, "Time to Cut Back, Hunker Down," *USA Today,* February 20, 2008, p 6B. Also see M Fitzgerald, "What Are You Trying to Say? Translators for Your Business," *Inc.,* April 2008, pp 56–57; M Weinstein, "Speaking My Language," *Training,* May 2008, p 14; and A Madhani, "ROTC Recruits Paid to Command New Languages," *USA Today,* December 23, 2008, p 1A.

81 Data from "USA Today Snapshots: Learning the Lingo," *USA Today,* January 26, 2006, p 1A.

82 Data from "Diverse Landscape of Newest Americans," *USA Today,* December 4, 2006, p 8A. For interesting reading, see H Hitchings, *The Secret Life of Words: How English Became English* (New York: Farrar, Straus and Giroux, 2008).

83 See E Marx, *Breaking through Culture Shock: What You Need to Succeed in International Business* (London: Nicholas Brealey Publishing, 2001). Also see R Takeuchi, J P Shay, and J Li, "When Does Decision Autonomy Increase Expatriate Managers' Adjustment? An Empirical Test," *Academy of Management Journal,* February 2008, pp 45–60.

84 See S Overman, "Mentors without Borders," *HR Magazine,* March 2004, pp 83–85; and J T Arnold, "Tracking Business Travelers," *HR Magazine,* November 2008, pp 107–10.

85 K L Miller, "How a Team of Buckeyes Helped Honda Save a Bundle," *BusinessWeek,* September 13, 1993, p 68.

86 B Newman, "For Ira Caplan, Re-Entry Has Been Strange," *The Wall Street Journal,* December 12, 1995, p A12.

87 See Black, Gregersen, and Mendenhall, *Global Assignments,* p 227.

88 Ibid., pp 226–27.

89 See A B Bossard and R B Peterson, "The Repatriate Experience as Seen by American Expatriates," *Journal of World Business,* February 2005, pp 9–28; K Tyler, "Retaining Repatriates," *HR Magazine,* March 2006, pp 97–102; and L Albright, "How Can My Company Best Retain Repatriated Employees?" *HR Magazine,* March 2008, p 35.

90 Excerpted from T Lowry and F Balfour, "It's All About the Face-to-Face," January 28, 2008, issue of *BusinessWeek* by special permission. Copyright © 2008 by the McGraw-Hill Companies, Inc.

91 Excerpted from M V Gratchev, "Making the Most of Cultural Differences," *Harvard Business Review,* October 2001, pp 28, 30. For relevant background information, see C J Robertson, K M Gilley, and M D Street, "The Relationship between Ethics and Firm Practices in Russia and the United States," *Journal of World Business,* November 2003, pp 375–84.

CHAPTER 5

1 Excerpted from B Basler, "Brain Cancer: Could Adult Stem Cells Be the Cause—and the Cure?" *AARP Bulletin,* November 2008, pp 22–24. Copyright © 2008 AARP. All rights reserved.

2 Data from www.census.gov/main/www/popclock.html.

3 Data from B Horovitz, "Ice Cream Shops Thaw Sales with Scoops of Fun," *USA Today,* June 9, 2006, pp 1B–2B.

4 D Seligman, "The Trouble with Buyouts," *Fortune,* November 30, 1992, p 125.

5 See H Dolezalek, "The Path to Inclusion," *Training,* May 2008, pp 52–54; R R Hastings, "Obama Election a Boost for Diversity," *HR Magazine,* December 2008, p 23; and J Schramm, "Human Resources Gets Religion," *HR Magazine,* January 2009, p 96.

6 See R S Kaplan, "What to Ask the Person in the Mirror," *Harvard Business Review,* January 2007, pp 86–95; S Begley, "Our Imaginary, Hotter Selves," *Newsweek*, February 25, 2008, p 49; and C J Wakslak, S Nussbaum, N Liberman, and Y Trope, "Representations of the Self in the Near and Distant Future," *Journal of Personality and Social Psychology,* October 2008, pp 757–73.

7 Drawn from E Porter, "Mirror, Mirror on the Wall," *Best Friends Magazine,* January–February 2007, pp 8–9.

8 Data from "If We Could Do It Over Again," *USA Today,* February 19, 2001, p 4D.

9 As quoted in G Colvin, "Star Power," *Fortune,* February 6, 2006, p 56.

10 V Gecas, "The Self-Concept," in *Annual Review of Sociology,* ed R H Turner and J F Short Jr (Palo Alto, CA: Annual Reviews Inc., 1982), vol. 8, p 3. Also see R E Johnson, C C Rosen, and P E Levy, "Getting to the Core of Core Self-Evaluation: A Review and Recommendations," *Journal of Organizational Behavior,* April 2008, pp 391–413.

11 L Festinger, *A Theory of Cognitive Dissonance* (Stanford, CA: Stanford University Press, 1957), p 3. Self-awareness cognitions in a practical context are discussed in K Sulkowicz, "Analyze This," *BusinessWeek,* April 21, 2008, p 17.

12 Based in part on a definition found in Gecas, "The Self-Concept." Also see W B Swann Jr, C Chang-Schneider, and K L McClarty, "Do People's Self-Views Matter? Self-Concept and Self-Esteem in Everyday Life," *American Psychologist*, February–March 2007, pp 84–94.

13 H W Marsh, "Positive and Negative Global Self-Esteem: A Substantively Meaningful Distinction or Artifacts?" *Journal of Personality and Social Psychology,* April 1996, p 819.

14 Ibid.

15 Based on D A Stinson et al., "The Cost of Lower Self-Esteem: Testing a Self- and Social-Bonds Model of Health," *Journal of Personality and Social Psychology,* March 2008, pp 412–28; S M McCrea, "Self-Handicapping, Excuse Making, and Counterfactual Thinking: Consequences for Self-Esteem and Future Motivation," *Journal of Personality and Social Psychology,* August 2008, pp 274–92; and U Orth, R W Robins, and B W Roberts, "Low Self-Esteem Prospectively Predicts Depression in Adolescence and Young Adulthood," *Journal of Personality and Social Psychology,* September 2008, pp 695–708.

16 See D G Gardner, L Van Dyne, and J L Pierce, "The Effects of Pay Level on Organization-Based Self-Esteem and Performance: A Field Study," *Journal of Occupational and Organizational Psychology,* September 2004, pp 307–22. Relationship-based self-esteem is discussed in C R Knee, A Canevello, A L Bush, and A Cook, "Relationship-Contingent Self-Esteem and the Ups and Downs of Romantic Relationships," *Journal of Personality and Social Psychology,* September 2008, pp 608–27.

17 A J Fiacco, "Over 50? Keep Foot in Door," *The Arizona Republic,* June 20, 2004, p D4. Similar situations are addressed in K Sulkowicz, "Analyze This," *BusinessWeek,* May 19, 2008, p 15; and N Byrnes, "A City That Must Evolve—Again," *BusinessWeek,* December 22, 2008, p 28.

[18] Ibid.

[19] E Diener and M Diener, "Cross-Cultural Correlates of Life Satisfaction and Self-Esteem," *Journal of Personality and Social Psychology,* April 1995, p 662. Also see J J A Denissen, L Penke, D P Schmitt, and M A G van Aken, "Self-Esteem Reactions to Social Interactions: Evidence for Sociometer Mechanisms across Days, People, and Nations," *Journal of Personality and Social Psychology,* July 2008, pp 181–96; H C Boucher, K Peng, J Shi, and L Wang, "Culture and Implicit Self-Esteem," *Journal of Cross-Cultural Psychology,* January 2009, pp 24–45; and J D Brown, H Cai, M A Oakes, and C Deng, "Cultural Similarities in Self-Esteem Functioning," *Journal of Cross-Cultural Psychology,* January 2009, pp 140–57.

[20] Based on data in F L Smoll, R E Smith, N P Barnett, and J J Everett, "Enhancement of Children's Self-Esteem through Social Support Training for Youth Sports Coaches," *Journal of Applied Psychology,* August 1993, pp 602–10.

[21] W J McGuire and C V McGuire, "Enhancing Self-Esteem by Directed-Thinking Tasks: Cognitive and Affective Positivity Asymmetries," *Journal of Personality and Social Psychology,* June 1996, p 1124.

[22] Drawn from J M Twenge and W K Campbell, "Increases in Positive Self-Views among High School Students: Birth-Cohort Changes in Anticipated Performance, Self-Satisfaction, Self-Liking, and Self-Competence," *Psychological Science,* November 2008, pp 1082–86.

[23] See M Elias, "Study: Today's Youth Think Quite Highly of Themselves," *USA Today,* November 19, 2008, p 7D.

[24] Data from P Coy, "The Competition Issue: The Poll," *BusinessWeek,* August 21–28, 2006, p 46.

[25] See G Chen, S M Gully, and D Eden, "General Self-Efficacy and Self-Esteem: Toward Theoretical and Empirical Distinction between Correlated Self-Evaluations," *Journal of Organizational Behavior,* May 2004, pp 375–95.

[26] M E Gist, "Self-Efficacy: Implications for Organizational Behavior and Human Resource Management," *Academy of Management Review,* July 1987, p 472. Also see A Bandura, "Self-Efficacy: Toward a Unifying Theory of Behavioral Change," *Psychological Review,* March 1977, pp 191–215; J B Vancouver, K M More, and R J Yoder, "Self-Efficacy and Resource Allocation: Support for a Nonmonotonic, Discontinuous Model," *Journal of Applied Psychology,* January 2008, pp 35–47; A P Tolli and A M Schmidt, "The Role of Feedback, Causal Attributions, and Self-Efficacy in Goal Revision," *Journal of Applied Psychology,* May 2008, pp 692–701; and K Ng, S Ang, and K Chan, "Personality and Leader Effectiveness: A Moderated Mediation Model of Leadership Self-Efficacy, Job Demands, and Job Autonomy," *Journal of Applied Psychology,* July 2008, pp 733–43.

[27] Based on D H Lindsley, D A Brass, and J B Thomas, "Efficacy-Performance Spirals: A Multilevel Perspective," *Academy of Management Review,* July 1995, pp 645–78. Also see J B Vancouver and L N Kendall, "When Self-Efficacy Negatively Relates to Motivation and Performance in a Learning Context," *Journal of Applied Psychology,* September 2006, pp 1146–153.

[28] See, for example, V Gecas, "The Social Psychology of Self-Efficacy," in *Annual Review of Sociology,* ed W R Scott and J Blake (Palo Alto, CA: Annual Reviews, Inc., 1989), vol. 15, pp 291–316; C K Stevens, A G Bavetta, and M E Gist, "Gender Differences in the Acquisition of Salary Negotiation Skills: The Role of Goals, Self-Efficacy, and Perceived Control,"

Journal of Applied Psychology, October 1993, pp 723–35; D Eden and Y Zuk, "Seasickness as a Self-Fulfilling Prophecy: Raising Self-Efficacy to Boost Performance at Sea," *Journal of Applied Psychology,* October 1995, pp 628–35; S M Jex, P D Bliese, S Buzzell, and J Primeau, "The Impact of Self-Efficacy on Stressor-Strain Relations: Coping Style as an Explanatory Mechanism," *Journal of Applied Psychology,* June 2001, pp 401–409; and C A Shields, L B Brawley, and T I Lindover, "Self-Efficacy as a Mediator of the Relationship between Causal Attributions and Exercise Behavior," *Journal of Applied Social Psychology,* November 2006, pp 2785–802.

[29] G Toppo, "A Solution to How to Teach Math: Subtract," *USA Today,* March 13, 2008, p 6D.

[30] Data from A D Stajkovic and F Luthans, "Self-Efficacy and Work-Related Performance: A Meta-Analysis," *Psychological Bulletin,* September 1998, pp 240–61.

[31] As quoted in G Colvin, "How One CEO Learned to Fly," *Fortune,* October 30, 2006, p 100.

[32] M Snyder and S Gangestad, "On the Nature of Self-Monitoring: Matters of Assessment, Matters of Validity," *Journal of Personality and Social Psychology,* July 1986, p 125.

[33] As quoted in K Sulkowicz, "Me, Me, Me, Me, Me," *BusinessWeek,* April 23, 2007, p 14.

[34] Data from D V Day, D J Schleicher, A L Unckless, and N J Hiller, "Self-Monitoring Personality at Work: A Meta-Analytic Investigation of Construct Validity," *Journal of Applied Psychology,* April 2002, pp 390–401.

[35] Data from M Kilduff and D V Day, "Do Chameleons Get Ahead? The Effects of Self-Monitoring on Managerial Careers," *Academy of Management Journal,* August 1994, pp 1047–60.

[36] Data from D B Turban and T W Dougherty, "Role of Protege Personality in Receipt of Mentoring and Career Success," *Academy of Management Journal,* June 1994, pp 688–702.

[37] See F Luthans, "Successful vs. Effective Managers," *Academy of Management Executive,* May 1988, pp 127–32.

[38] M G Pratt, "To Be or Not to Be? Central Questions in Organizational Identification," in *Identity in Organizations,* ed D A Whetten and P C Godfrey (Thousand Oaks, CA: Sage Publications, 1998), p 172. Also see D van Knippenberg and E Sleebos, "Organizational Identification versus Organizational Commitment: Self-Definition, Social Exchange, and Job Attitudes," *Journal of Organizational Behavior,* August 2006, pp 571–84.

[39] R Levering and M Moskowitz, "Fortune 100 Best Companies to Work For," *Fortune,* January 22, 2007, p 108.

[40] For more, see B Filipczak, "The Soul of the Hog," *Training,* February 1996, pp 38–42. Also see B Kowitt, "True Obsessions," *Fortune,* May 11, 2009, pp 84–91.

[41] C Fishman, "What if You'd Worked at Enron?" *Fast Company,* May 2002, pp 104, 106.

[42] For related discussion, see G E Kreiner, E C Hollensbe, and M L Sheep, "Where Is the 'Me' among the 'We'? Identity Work and the Search for Optimal Balance," *Academy of Management Journal,* October 2006, pp 1031–57.

[43] For a good overview, see L R James and M D Mazerolle, *Personality in Work Organizations* (Thousand Oaks, CA: Sage Publications, 2002). Also see D P McAdams and J L Pals, "A New Big Five: Fundamental Principles for an Integrative

Science of Personality," *American Psychologist,* April 2006, pp 204–17.

44 See N Nicolaou, S Shane, L Cherkas, J Hunkin, and T D Spector, "Is the Tendency to Engage in Entrepreurship Genetic?" *Management Science,* January 2008, pp 167–79; L Szabo, "Premature Babies Grow Up to Be Less Social," *USA Today,* July 17, 2008, p 6D; and R L Hotz, "The Biology of Ideology," *The Wall Street Journal,* September 5, 2008, p A10.

45 Data from M C Ashton, K Lee, and L R Goldberg, "A Historical Analysis of 1,710 English Personality-Descriptive Adjectives," *Journal of Personality and Social Psychology,* November 2004, pp 707–21.

46 The landmark report is J M Digman, "Personality Structure: Emergence of the Five-Factor Model," *Annual Review of Psychology,* vol. 41, 1990, pp 417–40. Also see M R Barrick and M K Mount, "Autonomy as a Moderator of the Relationships between the Big Five Personality Dimensions and Job Performance," *Journal of Applied Psychology,* February 1993, pp 111–18; and S Jayson, "Can Your Personality Help You Weather Tough Economic Times?" *USA Today,* December 4, 2008, p 10D.

47 Based on S E Hampson and L R Goldberg, "A First Large Cohort Study of Personality Trait Stability over the 40 Years between Elementary School and Midlife," *Journal of Personality and Social Psychology,* October 2006, pp 763–79. Also see B W Roberts, K E Walton, and W Viechtbauer, "Patterns of Mean-Level Change in Personality Traits across the Life Course: A Meta-Analysis of Longitudinal Studies," *Psychological Bulletin,* January 2006, pp 1–25; C J Soto, O P John, S D Gosling, and J Potter, "The Developmental Psychometrics of Big Five Self-Reports: Acquiescence, Factor Structure, Coherence, and Differentiation from Ages 10 to 20," *Journal of Personality and Social Psychology,* April 2008, pp 718–37; and J M Ganiban, K J Saudino, J Ulbricht, J M Neiderhiser, and D Reiss, "Stability and Change in Temperament during Adolescence," *Journal of Personality and Social Psychology,* July 2008, pp 222–36.

48 Data from S V Paunonen et al., "The Structure of Personality in Six Cultures," *Journal of Cross-Cultural Psychology,* May 1996, pp 339–53; and K Yoon, F Schmidt, and R Ilies, "Cross-Cultural Construct Validity of the Five-Factor Model of Personality among Korean Employees," *Journal of Cross-Cultural Psychology,* May 2002, pp 217–35.

49 J Allik and R R McCrae, "Escapable Conclusions: Toomela (2003) and the Universality of Trait Structure," *Journal of Personality and Social Psychology,* August 2004, p 261. Also see D P Schmitt, J Allik, R R McCrae, and V Benet-Martinez, "The Geographic Distribution of Big Five Personality Traits," *Journal of Cross-Cultural Psychology,* March 2007, pp 173–212; and D P Schmitt, A Realo, M Voracek, and J Allik, "Why Can't a Man Be More Like a Woman? Sex Differences in Big Five Personality Traits across 55 Cultures," *Journal of Personality and Social Psychology,* January 2008, pp 168–82.

50 Based on B De Raad and D P H Barelds, "A New Taxonomy of Dutch Personality Traits Based on a Comprehensive and Unrestricted List of Descriptors," *Journal of Personality and Social Psychology,* February 2008, pp 347–64.

51 See M R Barrick and M K Mount, "The Big Five Personality Dimensions and Job Performance: A Meta-Analysis," *Personnel Psychology,* Spring 1991, pp 1–26. Also see R P Tett, D N Jackson, and M Rothstein,

"Personality Measures as Predictors of Job Performance: A Meta-Analytic Review," *Personnel Psychology,* Winter 1991, pp 703–42.

52 Barrick and Mount, "The Big Five Personality Dimensions and Job Performance," p 18. For more research on conscientiousness, see G Yeo and A Neal, "Subjective Cognitive Effort: A Model of States, Traits, and Time," *Journal of Applied Psychology,* May 2008, pp 617–31; R D Zimmerman, "Understanding the Impact of Personality Traits on Individuals' Turnover Decisions: A Meta-Analytic Path Model," *Personnel Psychology,* Summer 2008, pp 309–48; and K A Orvis, N M Dudley, and J M Cortina, "Conscientiousness and Reactions to Psychological Contract Breach: A Longitudinal Field Study," *Journal of Applied Psychology,* September 2008, pp 1183–93.

53 See H Zhao and S E Seibert, "The Big Five Personality Dimensions and Entrepreneurial Status: A Meta-Analytical Review," *Journal of Applied Psychology,* March 2006, pp. 259–71.

54 Based on S E Seibert and M L Kraimer, "The Five-Factor Model of Personality and Career Success," *Journal of Vocational Behavior,* February 2001, pp 1–21. For more insights on extraversion, see D S DeRue, J R Hollenbeck, M D Johnson, D R Ilgen, and D K Jundt, "How Different Team Downsizing Approaches Influence Team-Level Adaptation and Performance," *Academy of Management Journal,* February 2008, pp 182–96; and J Welch and S Welch, "Release Your Inner Extrovert," *BusinessWeek,* December 8, 2008, p 92.

55 J M Crant, "Proactive Behavior in Organizations," *Journal of Management,* 2000, p 439. Also see S K Parker, H M Williams, and N Turner, "Modeling the Antecedents of Proactive Behavior at Work," *Journal of Applied Psychology,* May 2006, pp 636–52; and D A Major, J E Turner, and T D Fletcher, "Linking Proactive Personality and the Big Five to Motivation to Learn and Development Activity," *Journal of Applied Psychology,* July 2006, pp 927–35.

56 For an excellent overview, see J B Rotter, "Internal versus External Control of Reinforcement: A Case History of a Variable," *American Psychologist,* April 1990, pp 489–93.

57 Crant, "Proactive Behavior in Organizations," pp 439–41. Also see J B Fuller, L E Marler, and K Hester, "Promoting Felt Responsibility for Constructive Change and Proactive Behavior: Exploring Aspects of an Elaborated Model of Work Design," *Journal of Organizational Behavior,* December 2006, pp 1089–120.

58 For inspiring examples, see D Fenn, "Cool, Determined & Under 30," *Inc.,* October 2008, pp 97–105; T Banks, "What Matters Most in My Work and My Life," *Newsweek,* October 13, 2008, p 54; and L Buchanan, "Legacy: Ed Justice Sr., 1921–2008," *Inc.,* November 2008, p 144.

59 As quoted in C Salter, "Matt Glotzbach," *Fast Company,* March 2008, p 78.

60 R Kurtz, "Testing, Testing," *Inc.,* June 2004, p 36. Also see "Personality Assessment Soars at Southwest," *Training,* January 2008, p 14.

61 See A Murphy Paul, *The Cult of Personality: How Personality Tests Are Leading Us to Miseducate Our Children, Mismanage Our Companies, and Misunderstand Ourselves* (New York: Free Press, 2004).

62 As quoted in H Dolezalek, "Tests on Trial," *Training,* April 2005, p 34. Also see M Bolch, "Nice Work," *HR Magazine,* February 2008, pp 78–81; and M Weinstein, "Personalities & Performance," *Training,* July–August 2008, pp 36–40.

63 For details, see S Komar, D J Brown, C Robie, and J A Komar, "Faking and the Validity of Conscientiousness: A Monte Carlo Investigation," *Journal of Applied Psychology,* January 2008, pp 140–54.

64 As quoted in V O'Connell, "Test for Dwindling Retail Jobs Spawns a Culture of Cheating," *The Wall Street Journal,* January 7, 2009, pp A1, A10.

65 As quoted in A Smith, "Experts: Tests, Job Steering Raise Flags," *HR Magazine,* June 2008, p 36.

66 For details, see H J Foldes, E E Duehr, and D S Ones, "Group Differences in Personality: Meta-Analyses Comparing Five U.S. Racial Groups," *Personnel Psychology,* Autumn 2008, pp 579–616.

67 J Kullman, "'Wii' Bit of Technology Aids Medical Education," *ASU Insight,* February 22, 2008, pp 1, 6.

68 See M J Frase, "Smart Selections," *HR Magazine,* December 2007, pp 63–67; "Study Suggests New SAT Is Nothing to Write Home About," *USA Today,* June 18, 2008, p 6D; and "Too Soon to Drop SAT," *USA Today,* October 7, 2008, p 10A.

69 Data from "People Rate How They Sleep," *USA Today,* April 12, 2005, p 1A. Also see S Armour, "Lack of Sleep Catches Up with Today's Workforce," *USA Today,* March 3, 2008, p 1B.

70 See M Healy, "Sleep Matters for a Healthy Heart," *USA Today,* December 24, 2008, p 6D; C M Barnes and J R Hollenbeck, "Sleep Deprivation and Decision-Making Teams: Burning the Midnight Oil or Playing with Fire?" *Academy of Management Review,* January 2009, pp 56–66; C Binnewies, S Sonnentag, and E J Mojza, "Daily Performance at Work: Feeling Recovered in the Morning as a Predictor of Day-Level Job Performance," *Journal of Organizational Behavior,* January 2009, pp 67–93; and M Healy, "Plenty of Sleep May Help Prevent Colds," *USA Today,* January 13, 2009, p 4D.

71 A Pomeroy, "Sleep Deprivation and Medical Errors," *HR Magazine,* February 2002, p 42.

72 See K Fackelmann, "Americans Skip Sleep to Make Time for Leisure Activities," *USA Today,* August 30, 2007, p 7D.

73 As quoted in A Weintraub, "Napping Your Way to the Top," *BusinessWeek,* November 27, 2006, pp 98–99.

74 T Peng, "Take a Three-Martini Nap," *Newsweek,* June 30, 2008, p 56. Also see A Fox, "The Brain at Work," *HR Magazine,* March 2008, pp 37–42.

75 For interesting reading on intelligence, see D Lubinski, R M Webb, M J Morelock, and C P Benbow, "Top 1 in 10,000: A 10-Year Follow-Up of the Profoundly Gifted," *Journal of Applied Psychology,* August 2001, pp 718–29; T A Judge, A E Colbert, and R Ilies, "Intelligence and Leadership: A Quantitative Review and Test of Theoretical Propositions," *Journal of Applied Psychology,* June 2004, pp 542–52; and L T Benjamin Jr, "The Birth of American Intelligence Testing," *Monitor on Psychology,* January 2009, pp 20–21.

76 For an excellent overview of intelligence, including definitional distinctions and a historical perspective of the IQ controversy, see R A Weinberg, "Intelligence and IQ," *American Psychologist,* February 1989, pp 98–104. Also see R Plomin and F M Spinath, "Intelligence: Genetics, Genes, and Genomics," *Journal of Personality and Social Psychology,* January 2004, pp 112–29; G Toppo, "Poverty Dramatically Affects Children's Brains," *USA Today,* December 8, 2008, p 4D; and S Begley, "Sex, Race and IQ: Off Limits?" *Newsweek,* April 20, 2009, p 53.

77 See Weinberg, "Intelligence and IQ"; and W A Walker and C Humphries, "Starting the Good Life in the Womb," *Newsweek,* September 17, 2007, pp 56, 58.

78 B Azar, "People Are Becoming Smarter—Why?" *APA Monitor,* June 1996, p 20. Also see S Begley and J Interlandi, "The Dumbest Generation? Don't Be Dumb," *Newsweek,* June 2, 2008, pp 42–44.

79 See D Lubinski, "Introduction to the Special Section on Cognitive Abilities: 100 Years after Spearman's (1904) 'General Intelligence, Objectively Determined and Measured,'" *Journal of Personality and Social Psychology,* January 2004, pp 96–111; and R Gilkey and C Kilts, "Cognitive Fitness," *Harvard Business Review,* November 2007, pp 53–66.

80 See F L Schmidt and J E Hunter, "Employment Testing: Old Theories and New Research Findings," *American Psychologist,* October 1981, p 1128; and H D Nguyen and A M Ryan, "Does Stereotype Threat Affect Test Performance of Minorities and Women? A Meta-Analysis of Experimental Evidence," *Journal of Applied Psychology,* November 2008, pp 1314–34.

81 See H Gardner, *Frames of Mind: The Theory of Multiple Intelligences,* 10th anniversary ed (New York: Basic Books, 1993); H Gardner, *Intelligence Reframed: Multiple Intelligences for the 21st Century* (New York: Basic Books, 2000); and H Gardner, *Five Minds for the Future* (Boston: Harvard Business School Press, 2009).

82 For a good overview of Gardner's life and work, see M K Smith, "Howard Gardner and Multiple Intelligences," *Encyclopedia of Informal Education,* 2002, www.infed.org/thinkers/gardner.htm. Also see B Fryer, "The Ethical Mind: A Conversation with Psychologist Howard Gardner," *Harvard Business Review,* March 2007, pp 51–56.

83 See S A Snook, "Love and Fear and the Modern Boss," *Harvard Business Review,* January 2008, pp 16–17; S C Douglas, C Kiewitz, M J Martinko, P Harvey, Y Kim, and J U Chun, "Cognitions, Emotions, and Evaluations: An Elaboration Likelihood Model for Workplace Aggression," *Academy of Management Review,* April 2008, pp 425–51; J Welch and S Welch, "Emotional Mismanagement," *BusinessWeek,* July 28, 2008, p 84; and M A Hazen, "Grief and the Workplace," *Academy of Management Perspectives,* August 2008, pp 78–86.

84 D Kirkpatrick, "Microsoft after Gates," *Fortune,* July 7, 2008, p 118.

85 G Anders, "John Chambers after the Deluge," *Fast Company,* July 2001, p 108.

86 R S Lazarus, *Emotion and Adaptation* (New York: Oxford University Press, 1991), p 6. Also see S G Barsade and D E Gibson, "Why Does Affect Matter in Organizations?" *Academy of Management Perspectives,* February 2007, pp 36–59; and P Kuppens, A Realo, and E Diener, "The Role of Positive and Negative Emotions in Life Satisfaction Judgment across Nations," *Journal of Personality and Social Psychology,* July 2008, pp 66–75.

87 Based on discussion in R D Arvey, G L Renz, and T W Watson, "Emotionality and Job Performance: Implications for Personnel Selection," in *Research in Personnel and Human Resources Management,* vol. 16, ed G R Ferris (Stamford, CT: JAI Press, 1998), pp 103–47. Also see T Masuda et al., "Placing the Face in Context: Cultural Differences in the Perception of Facial Emotion," *Journal of Personality and Social Psychology,* March 2008, pp 365–81; K Byron, "Carrying Too Heavy a Load? The Communication and Miscommunication of Emotion by Email," *Academy of Management Review,* April 2008, pp 309–27; and E Bould and N Morris, "Role of Motion Signals in Recognizing Subtle Facial Expressions of Emotion," *British Journal of Psychology,* May 2008, pp 167–89.

88 J A Byrne and H Timmons, "Tough Times," *BusinessWeek,* October 29, 2001, p 66. Also see K Sulkowicz, "Analyze This," *BusinessWeek,* January 12, 2009, p 16; and J Welch and S Welch, "Put Your Rage on the Back Burner," *BusinessWeek,* April 6, 2009, p 98.

89 J McGregor, "#1 Taryn Rose," *Fast Company,* May 2005, p 69.

90 D Goleman, *Emotional Intelligence* (New York: Bantam Books, 1995), p 34. For more, see S Cote and C T H Miners, "Emotional Intelligence, Cognitive Intelligence, and Job Performance," *Administrative Science Quarterly,* March 2006, pp 1–28; J D Mayer, P Salovey, and D R Caruso, "Emotional Intelligence: New Ability or Eclectic Traits?" *American Psychologist,* September 2008, pp 503–17; and J Antonakis, N M Ashkanasy, and M T Dasborough, "Does Leadership Need Emotional Intelligence?" *The Leadership Quarterly*, April 2009, pp 247–61.

91 Data from S D Pugh, "Service with a Smile: Emotional Contagion in the Service Encounter," *Academy of Management Journal,* October 2001, pp 1018–27; and P Totterdell, S Kellett, K Teuchmann, and R B Briner, "Evidence of Mood Linkage in Work Groups," *Journal of Personality and Social Psychology,* June 1998, pp 1504–15. Also see Z Song, M Foo, and M A Uy, "Mood Spillover and Crossover among Dual-Earner Couples: A Cell Phone Event Sampling Study," *Journal of Applied Psychology,* March 2008, pp 443–52; M S Cole, F Walter, and H Bruch, "Affective Mechanisms Linking Dysfunctional Behavior to Performance in Work Teams: A Moderated Mediation Study," *Journal of Applied Psychology,* September 2008, pp 945–58; and M Weisbuch and N Ambady, "Affective Divergence: Automatic Responses to Others' Emotions Depend on Group Membership," *Journal of Personality and Social Psychology,* November 2008, pp 1063–79.

92 N M Ashkanasy and C S Daus, "Emotion in the Workplace: The New Challenge for Managers," *Academy of Management Executive,* February 2002, p 79. Also see J P Trougakos, D J Beal, S G Green, and H M Weiss, "Making the Break Count: An Episodic Examination of Recovery Activities, Emotional Experiences, and Positive Affective Displays," *Academy of Management Journal,* February 2008, pp 131–46; J D Margolis and A Molinsky, "Navigating the Bind of Necessary Evils: Psychological Engagement and the Production of Interpersonally Sensitive Behavior," *Academy of Management Journal,* October 2008, pp 847–72; and D P Skarlicki, D D van Jaarsveld, and D D Walker, "Getting Even for Customer Mistreatment: The Role of Moral Identity in the Relationship between Customer Interpersonal Injustice and Employee Sabotage," *Journal of Applied Psychology,* November 2008, pp 1335–47.

93 Data from A M Kring and A H Gordon, "Sex Differences in Emotions: Expressions, Experience, and Physiology," *Journal of Personality and Social Psychology,* March 1998, pp 686–703.

94 As quoted in B Schlender, "The Bill & Warren Show," *Fortune,* July 20, 1998, p 52. Also see T A Judge and C Hurst, "How the Rich (and Happy) Get Richer (and Happier): Relationship of Core Self-Evaluations to Trajectories in Attaining Work Success," *Journal of Applied Psychology,* July 2008, pp 849–63; D Jones, "Knowledge of Failure Helps Lead to Success," *USA Today,* January 19, 2009, p 3B; and G Mannes, "Be Prepared for the Long Haul," *Money,* February 2009, pp 86–89.

95 As quoted in H Mackay, "Always Follow the Advice of Dr. Lou," *The Arizona Republic,* January 18, 2009, p D2. Also see Coach John Wooden's "pyramid of success" in J Wooden and

S Jamison, *Wooden on Leadership* (New York: McGraw-Hill, 2005), p 2; and M Goldsmith with M Reiter, *What Got You Here Won't Get You There: How Successful People Become Even More Successful* (New York: Hyperion, 2007).

96 F Luthans, C M Youssef, and B J Avolio, *Psychological Capital: Developing the Human Competitive Edge* (Oxford, UK: Oxford University Press, 2007), p 3 (emphasis added). Also see F Luthans, J B Avey, and J L Patera, "Experimental Analysis of a Web-Based Training Intervention to Develop Positive Psychological Capital," *Academy of Management Learning and Education,* June 2008, pp 209–21. For background reading on positive psychology, see M E P Seligman and M Csikszentmihalyi, "Positive Psychology: An Introduction," *American Psychologist,* January 2000, pp 5–14; and S Begley, "Happiness: Enough Already," *Newsweek,* February 11, 2008, pp 50–52.

97 As quoted in "Melody Gardot," *Spirit,* September 2008, p 71. Also see A Siebert, "Develop Resiliency Skills," *Training and Development,* September 2006, pp 88–89; J A Sonnenfeld and A J Ward, "Firing Back: How Great Leaders Rebound after Career Disasters," *Harvard Business Review, Special Issue: The Tests of a Leader,* January 2007, pp 76–84; and G E Mangurian, "Realizing What You're Made Of," *Harvard Business Review,* March 2007, pp 125–30.

98 M Gladwell, *Outliers: The Story of Success* (New York: Little, Brown, 2008), pp 38–41.

99 G Colvin, *Talent Is Overrated: What Really Separates World-Class Performers from Everybody Else* (New York: Penguin, 2008), p 66 (emphasis added). Also see S Berfield, "The Truth about Tech Startups," *BusinessWeek,* May 19, 2008, p 16; and A B H de Bruin, N Smits, R M J P Rikers, and H G Schmidt, "Deliberate Practice Predicts Performance over Time in Adolescent Chess Players and Drop-Outs: A Linear Mixed Models Analysis," *British Journal of Psychology,* November 2008, pp 473–97.

100 S DMeglio, "How No. 1 Keeps Getting Better," *USA Today,* March 21, 2008, p 2A.

101 For more, see R Wiseman, *The Luck Factor: The Four Essential Principles* (New York: Miramax, 2004); D H Pink, "How to Make Your Own Luck," *Fast Company,* July 2003. pp 78–82; K R Olson, Y Dunham, C S Dweck, E S Spelke, and M R Banaji, "Judgments of the Lucky across Development and Culture," *Journal of Personality and Social Psychology,* May 2008, pp 757–76; B Sherwood, "What It Takes to Survive," *Newsweek,* February 2, 2009, pp 50–53; and www.richardwiseman.com.

102 Robert Solomon, as quoted in D Vera and A Rodriguez-Lopez, "Strategic Virtues: Humility as a Source of Competitive Advantage," *Organizational Dynamics,* no. 4, 2004, pp 394–95. Also see W Isaacson, "Benjamin Franklin and The Art of Humility," *Newsweek,* Commemorative Inaugural Edition, 2009, pp 59–60.

103 Robert Solomon, as quoted in Vera and Rodriguez-Lopez, "Strategic Virtues," p 395.

104 Reprinted by permission of *Harvard Business Review.* Excerpt from "The Best Advice I Ever Got," by D W Dowling, June 2008. Copyright 2008 by the Harvard Business School Publishing Corporation; all rights reserved.

105 Excerpted from E Gibson, "Mental Pick-Me-Ups: The Coming Boom," January 5, 2009, issue of *BusinessWeek* by special permission. Copyright © 2009 by The McGraw-Hill Companies, Inc. Also see L Lee, "Boosting Our Gray Matter," *BusinessWeek,* August 20–27, 2007, p 87; and "Surprising Use of 'Cognitive Enhancers,'" *USA Today,* April 10, 2008, p 4D.

CHAPTER 6

[1] Excerpted from J Sandberg, "Cubicle Culture: For Many Employees, a Dream Job Is One That Isn't a Nightmare," *The Wall Street Journal,* April 15, 2008, p B1.

[2] Schwartz's theory is discussed in S H Schwartz, "Universals in the Content and Structure of Values: Theoretical Advances and Empirical Tests in 20 Countries," in *Advances in Experimental Social Psychology,* ed M Zanna (New York: Academic Press, 1992), pp 1–65.

[3] A Bardi and S H Schwartz, "Values and Behavior: Strength and Structure of Relations," *Personality and Social Psychology Bulletin,* October 2003, p 1208.

[4] Ibid., pp 1207–20; and A Bardi, R M Calogero, and B Mullen, "A New Archival Approach to the Study of Values and Value-Behavior Relations: Validation of the Value Lexicon," *Journal of Applied Psychology,* May 2008, pp 483–97.

[5] See E Davidov, P Schmidt, and S H Schwartz, "Bringing Value Back in the Adequacy of the European Social Survey to Measure Values in 20 Countries," *Public Opinion Quarterly,* Fall 2008, pp 420–45.

[6] See Bardi and Schwartz, "Values and Behavior: Strength and Structure of Relations."

[7] K Helliker, "You Might as Well Face It: You're Addicted to Success," *The Wall Street Journal,* February 10, 2009, p D1. Value conflicts are also discussed by B Azar, "American Culture Set Us Up for the Economic Fall, Psychologists Say," *Monitor on Psychology,* January 2009, p 31.

[8] This example was derived from D Lieberman, "L.A. Times' Publisher Forced Out Over Refusal to Cut Staff," *USA Today,* October 6, 2006, p 1B.

[9] For a thorough discussion of person-culture fit, see A L Kristof-Brown, R D Zimmerman, and E C Johnson, "Consequences of Individuals' Fit at Work: A Meta-Analysis of Person-Job, Person-Organization, Person-Group, and Person-Supervisor Fit," *Personnel Psychology,* Summer 2005, pp 281–342.

[10] Supportive results can be found in H A Elfenbein and C A O'Reilly III, "Fitting In: The Effects of Relational Demography and Person-Culture Fit on Group Process and Performance," *Group and Organization Management,* February 2007, pp 109–42.

[11] See G Colvin, "How to Manage Your Business in a Recession," *Fortune,* January 19, 2009, pp 88–93; and J Welch and S Welch, "Finding Your Inner Courage," *BusinessWeek,* February 23, 2009, p 84.

[12] P L Perrewé and W A Hochwarter, "Can We Really Have It All? The Attainment of Work and Family Values," *Current Directions in Psychological Science,* February 2001, p 31.

[13] See B A Livingston and T A Judge, "Emotional Response to Work-Family Conflict: An Examination of Gender Role Orientation among Working Men and Women," *Journal of Applied Psychology,* January 2008, pp 207–16; and Z Song, M-D Foo, and M A Uy, "Mood Spillover and Crossover among Dual-Earner Couples: A Cell-Phone Event Sampling Study," *Journal of Applied Psychology,* March 2008, pp 443–52.

[14] Results can be found in A H Eagly and L L Carli, *Through the Labyrinth* (Boston: Harvard Business School Press, 2007).

[15] Examples can be found in R Levering and M Moskowitz, "100 Best Companies to Work For," *Fortune,* February 2, 2009,

pp 67–78; and T DeAngelis, "Making Time for Family Time," *Monitor on Psychology,* January 2008, pp 38–39.

[16] "Best Practices & Outstanding Initiatives," *Training,* February 2009, p 96.

[17] The need for flexibility is discussed by S Shellenbarger, "Reasons to Hold Out Hope for Balancing Work and Home," *The Wall Street Journal,* January 11, 2007, p D1; and S Shellenbarger, "Time on Your Side: Rating Your Boss's Flexible Scheduling," *The Wall Street Journal,* January 25, 2007, p D1.

[18] See "Fast Fact," *Training,* July/August 2008, p 9.

[19] See D A Major, T D Fletcher, D D Davis, and L M Germano, "The Influence of Work-Family Culture and Workplace Relationships on Work Interference with Family: A Multilevel Model," *Journal of Organizational Behavior,* October 2008, pp 881–97; and A B Bakker, E Demerouti, and M F Dollard, "How Job Demands Affect Partners' Experience of Exhaustion: Integrating Work-Family Conflict and Crossover Theory," *Journal of Applied Psychology,* July 2008, pp 901–11.

[20] Results can be found in M T Ford, B A Heinen, and K L Langkamer, "Work and Family Satisfaction and Conflict: A Meta-Analysis of Cross-Domain Relations," *Journal of Applied Psychology,* January 2007, pp 57–80; and W J Casper, L T Eby, C Cordeaux, A Lockwood, and D Lambert, "A Review of Research Methods in IO/OB Work-Family Research," *Journal of Applied Psychology,* January 2007, pp 28–43. Also see R Ilies, K S Wilson, and D T Wagner, "The Spillover of Daily Job Satisfaction onto Employees' Family Lives: The Facilitating Role of Work-Family Integration," *Academy of Management Journal,* February 2009, pp 87–102.

[21] See K S Lyness and M K Judiesch, "Can a Manager Have a Life and Career? International and Multisource Perspectives on Work-Life Balance and Career Advancement Potential," *Journal of Applied Psychology,* July 2008, pp 789–805.

[22] These results are discussed in L Winerman, "A Healthy Mind, a Longer Life," *Monitor on Psychology,* November 2006, pp 42–44.

[23] See D A Harrison, D A Newman, and P L Roth, "How Important Are Job Attitudes? Meta-Analytic Comparisons of Integrative Behavioral Outcomes and Time Sequences," *Academy of Management Journal,* April 2006, pp 305–25; M Riketta, "The Causal Relation between Job Attitudes and Performance: A Meta-Analysis of Panel Studies." *Journal of Applied Psychology,* March 2008, pp 472–81; and M Subramony, N Krause, J Norton, and G N Burns, "The Relationship between Human Resource Investments and Organizational Performance: A Firm-Level Examination of Equilibrium Theory," *Journal of Applied Psychology,* July 2008, pp 778–88.

[24] M Fishbein and I Ajzen, *Belief, Attitude, Intention and Behavior: An Introduction to Theory and Research* (Reading, MA: Addison-Wesley Publishing, 1975), p 6.

[25] The components or structure of attitudes is thoroughly discussed by A P Brief, *Attitudes in and around Organizations* (Thousand Oaks, CA: Sage, 1998), pp 49–84.

[26] Research on the components of attitudes was conducted by M S Cole, F Walter, and H Bruch, "Affective Mechanism Linking Dysfunctional Behavior to Performance in Work Teams: A Moderated Mediation Study," *Journal of Applied Psychology,* September 2008, pp 945–58; and Y H M See, R E Petty, and L R Fabrigar, "Affective and Cognitive Meta-Bases of Attitudes: Unique Effects on Information Interest and Persuasion," *Journal of Personality and Social Psychology,* June 2008, pp 938–55.

27 For details about this theory, see L Festinger, *A Theory of Cognitive Dissonance* (Stanford, CA: Stanford University Press, 1957). Also see A Bawa and P Kansal, "Cognitive Dissonance and the Marketing of Services: Some Issues," *Journal of Services Research,* October 2008–March 2009, pp 31–51; and M M Cheng, A K-D Schulz, and P Booth, "Knowledge Transfer in Project Reviews: The Effect of Self-Justification Bias and Moral Hazard," *Accounting and Finance,* March 2009, pp 75–94.

28 See B M Staw and J Ross, "Stability in the Midst of Change: A Dispositional Approach to Job Attitudes," *Journal of Applied Psychology,* August 1985, pp 469–80. Also see J Schaubroeck, D C Ganster, and B Kemmerer, "Does Trait Affect Promote Job Attitude Stability?" *Journal of Organizational Behavior,* March 1996, pp 191–96.

29 Data from P S Visser and J A Krosnick, "Development of Attitude Strength over the Life Cycle: Surge and Decline," *Journal of Personality and Social Psychology,* December 1998, pp 389–410.

30 This example is discussed in J L Lunsford, "Outsourcing at Crux of Boeing Strike," *The Wall Street Journal,* September 8, 2008, pp B1, B4.

31 I Ajzen, "The Theory of Planned Behavior," *Organizational Behavior and Human Decision Processes,* vol. 50 (1991), p 188.

32 See R P Steel and N K Ovalle II, "A Review and Meta-Analysis of Research on the Relationship between Behavioral Intentions and Employee Turnover," *Journal of Applied Psychology,* November 1984, pp 673–86.

33 Results can be found in M R Barrick and R D Zimmerman, "Reducing Voluntary Turnover through Selection," *Journal of Applied Psychology,* January 2005, pp 159–66.

34 Drawn from I Ajzen and M Fishbein, *Understanding Attitudes and Predicting Social Behavior* (Englewood Cliffs, NJ: Prentice Hall, 1980); J Zikic, "Job Search and Social Cognitive Theory: The Role of Career-Related Activities," *Journal of Vocational Behavior,* February 2009, pp 117–27; W S Chow and L S Chan, "Social Network, Social Trust, and Shared Goals in Organizational Knowledge Sharing," *Information & Management,* November 2008, pp 458–92; F A White, M A Charles, and J K Nelson, "The Role of Persuasive Arguments in Changing Affirmative Action Attitudes and Expressed Behavior in Higher Education," *Journal of Applied Psychology,* November 2008, pp 1271–86; G J Golan and S A Banning, "Exploring a Link between the Third-Person Effect and the Theory of Reasoned Action: Beneficial Ads and Social Expectations," *The American Behavioral Scientist,* October 2008, pp 208–24; and P W Hom and C L Hulin, "A Competitive Test of the Prediction of Reenlistment by Several Models," *Journal of Applied Psychology,* February 1981, pp 23–39.

35 Supportive research is presented in T L Webb and P Sheeran, "Does Changing Behavioral Intentions Engender Behavior Change: A Meta-Analysis of the Experimental Evidence," *Psychological Bulletin,* March 2006, pp 249–68.

36 "Top Small Workplaces 2008," *The Wall Street Journal,* October 13, 2008, p 5.

37 L Yerkes, *Fun Works: Creating Places Where People Love to Work* (San Francisco, CA: Berrett-Koehler, 2001), p 73.

38 The concept of commitment and its relationship to motivated behavior is thoroughly discussed by O N Solinger, W V Olffen, and R A Roe, "Beyond the Three-Component Model of Organizational Commitment," *Journal of Applied Psychology,* January 2008, pp 70–83; and J P Meyer, T E Becker, and

C Vandenberghe, "Employee Commitment and Motivation: A Conceptual Analysis and Integrative Model," *Journal of Applied Psychology,* December 2004, pp 991–1007.

39 J P Meyer and L Herscovitch, "Commitment in the Workplace: Toward a General Model," *Human Resource Management Review,* Autumn 2001, p 301.

40 J P Meyer and N J Allen, "A Three-Component Conceptualization of Organizational Commitment," *Human Resource Management Review,* Spring 1991, p 67.

41 See T H Shore, W H Bommer, and L M Shore, "An Integrative Model of Managerial Perceptions of Employee Commitment: Antecedents and Influences on Employee Treatment," *Journal of Organizational Behavior,* July 2008, pp 635–55; and Y Gong, K S Law, S Chang, and K R Xin, "Human Resource Management and Firm Performance: The Differential Role of Managerial Affective and Continuance Commitment," *Journal of Applied Psychology,* January 2009, pp 263–75.

42 "Top Small Workplaces 2008," p R9.

43 This definition was provided by D M Rousseau, "Psychological and Implied Contracts in Organizations," *Employee Responsibilities and Rights Journal,* June 1989, pp 121–39.

44 See T Dulac, J A-M Coyle-Shariro, D J Henderson, and S J Wayne, "Not All Responses to Breach Are the Same: The Interconnection of Social Exchange and Psychological Contract Processes in Organizations," *Academy of Management Journal,* December 2008, pp 1079–98; K A Orvis, N M Dudley, and J M Cortina, "Conscientiousness and Reactions to Psychology Contract Breach: A Longitudinal Field Study," *Journal of Applied Psychology,* September 2008, pp 1183–93; and Z X Chen, A S Tsui, and L Zhong, "Reactions to Psychological Contract Breach: A Dual Perspective," *Journal of Organizational Behavior,* July 2008, pp 527–48.

45 Results can be found in N P Podsakoff, J A LePine, and M A LePine, "Differential Challenge Stressor–Hindrance Stressor Relationships with Job Attitudes, Turnover Intentions, Turnover, and Withdrawal Behavior: A Meta-Analysis," *Journal of Applied Psychology,* March 2007, pp 438–54.

46 Results can be found in M Riketta, "Attitudinal Organizational Commitment and Job Performance: A Meta-Analysis," *Journal of Organizational Behavior,* March 2002, pp 257–66.

47 Results can be found in R W Griffeth, P W Hom, and S Gaertner, "A Meta-Analysis of Antecedents and Correlates of Employee Turnover: Update, Moderator Tests, and Research Implications for the Next Millennium," *Journal of Management,* 2000, pp 463–88.

48 These examples were discussed by R Levering and M Moskowitz, "100 Best Companies to Work For," *Fortune,* February 2, 2009, pp 67–78.

49 Supportive research is provided by L H Nishi, D P Lepak, and B Schneider, "Employee Attributions of the 'Why' of HR Practices: Their Effects on Employee Attitudes and Behaviors, and Customer Satisfaction," *Personnel Psychology,* Autumn 2008, pp 503–45.

50 R Levering and M Moskowitz, "The 100 Best Companies to Work For," *Fortune,* January 24, 2005, p 84.

51 Levering and Moskowitz, "The 100 Best Companies to Work For" (2009), p 75.

[52] I M Paullay, G M Alliger, and E F Stone-Romero, "Construct Validation of Two Instruments Designed to Measure Job Involvement and Work Centrality," *Journal of Applied Psychology,* April 1994, p 224.

[53] Yerkes, *Fun Works,* p 126.

[54] Results can be found in S P Brown, "A Meta-Analysis and Review of Organizational Research on Job Involvement," *Psychological Bulletin,* September 1996, pp 235–55.

[55] Results can be found in J M Diefendorff, D J Brown, A M Kamin, and R G Lord, "Examining the Roles of Job Involvement and Work Centrality in Predicting Organizational Citizenship Behaviors and Job Performance," *Journal of Organizational Behavior,* February 2002, pp 93–108.

[56] See J K Harter, F L Schmidt, and T L Hayes, "Business-Unit-Level Relationship between Employee Satisfaction, Employee Engagement, and Business Outcomes: A Meta-Analysis," *Journal of Applied Psychology,* April 2002, pp 268–79.

[57] See W H Macey and B Schneider, "The Nature of Employee Engagement," *Industrial and Organizational Psychology: Perspectives on Science and Practice,* 2008, pp 3–30; and A J Wefald and R G Downey, "Job Engagement in Organizations: Fad, Fashion, or Folderol?" *Journal of Organizational Behavior,* January 2009, pp 141–45.

[58] Results can be found in Harter, Schmidt, and Hayes, "Business-Unit-Level Relationship between Employee Satisfaction, Employee Engagement, and Business Outcomes: A Meta-Analysis."

[59] See J Robison, "Building Engagement in This Economic Crisis," *Gallup Management Journal,* February 19, 2009, http://gmj.gallup.com/content/115213/Building-Engagement-Economic-Crisis.aspx.

[60] See M Day, "Engagement Requires a Rethink," *Human Resources,* February 2009, p 19; S Stern, "How to Engage a Workforce That Is Fearing the Worst," *Financial Times,* February 10, 2009, p 14; and B Kelleher, "Employee Engagement Carries ENSR through Organizational Challenges and Economic Turmoil," *Global Business and Organizational Effectiveness,* March/April 2009, pp 6–19.

[61] See J Robison, "How the Ritz-Carlton Manages the Mystique," *Gallup Management Journal,* December 11, 2008, http://gmj.gallup.com/content/112906.

[62] Results can be found in R R Hastings, "Silent Generation Speaks Up about Work, *HR Magazine,* September 2008, p 30.

[63] For a review of the development of the JDI, see P C Smith, L M Kendall, and C L Hulin, *The Measurement of Satisfaction in Work and Retirement* (Skokie, IL: Rand-McNally, 1969).

[64] For a review of these models, see Brief, *Attitudes in and around Organizations.*

[65] S Miller, "HR, Employees Vary on Job Satisfaction," *HR Magazine,* August 2007, p 32.

[66] For a review of need satisfaction models, see E F Stone, "A Critical Analysis of Social Information Processing Models of Job Perceptions and Job Attitudes," in *Job Satisfaction: How People Feel about Their Jobs and How It Affects Their Performance,* ed C J Cranny, P Cain Smith, and E F Stone (New York: Lexington Books, 1992), pp 21–52.

[67] See J P Wanous, T D Poland, S L Premack, and K S Davis, "The Effects of Met Expectations on Newcomer Attitudes and Behaviors: A Review and Meta-Analysis," *Journal of Applied Psychology,* June 1992, pp 288–97. Also see J Schaubroeck, J D Shaw, M K Duffy, and A Mitra, "An Under-Met and Over-Met Expectations Model of Employee Reactions to Merit Raises," *Journal of Applied Psychology,* March 2008, pp 424–34.

[68] A complete description of this model is provided by E A Locke, "Job Satisfaction," in *Social Psychology and Organizational Behavior,* ed M Gruneberg and T Wall (New York: John Wiley & Sons, 1984).

[69] "Top Small Workplaces 2008," p 8.

[70] Results can be found in J Cohen-Charash and P E Spector, "The Role of Justice in Organizations: A Meta-Analysis," *Organizational Behavior and Human Decision Processes,* November 2001, pp 278–321.

[71] A thorough discussion of this model is provided by C L Hulin, and T A Judge, "Job Attitudes," in *Handbook of Psychology,* vol. 12, ed W C Borman, D R Ilgen, and R J Klimoski (Hoboken, NJ: John Wiley & Sons, Inc., 2003), pp 255–76.

[72] A summary and interpretation of this research is provided by B M Staw and Y Choen-Charash, "The Dispositional Approach to Job Satisfaction: More Than a Mirage, but Not Yet an Oasis," *Journal of Organizational Behavior,* February 2005, pp 59–78.

[73] See R D Arvey, T J Bouchard Jr, N L Segal, and L M Abraham, "Job Satisfaction: Environmental and Genetic Components," *Journal of Applied Psychology,* April 1989, pp 187–92. Also see S E Hammpson, L R Goldberg, T M Vogt, and J P Dubanoski, "Mechanisms by Which Childhood Personality Traits Influence Adult Health Status: Educational Attainment and Healthy Behaviors," *Health Psychology,* January 2007, pp 121–25.

[74] See C Dormann and D Zapf, "Job Satisfaction: A Meta-Analysis of Stabilities," *Journal of Organizational Behavior,* August 2001, pp 483–504.

[75] P Wakeman, "The Good Life and How to Get It," *Inc.,* February 2001, p 50.

[76] See A J Kinicki, F M McKee-Ryan, C A Schriesheim, and K P Carson, "Assessing the Construct Validity of the Job Descriptive Index: A Review and Meta-Analysis," *Journal of Applied Psychology,* February 2002, pp 14–32.

[77] See Brown, "A Meta-Analysis and Review of Organizational Research on Job Involvement."

[78] D W Organ, "The Motivational Basis of Organizational Citizenship Behavior," in *Research in Organizational Behavior,* ed B M Staw and L L Cummings (Greenwich, CT: JAI Press, 1990), p 46.

[79] Results can be found in B J Hoffman, C A Blair, J P Meriac, and D J Woehr, "Expanding the Criterion Domain? A Quantitative Review of the OCB Literature," *Journal of Applied Psychology,* March 2007, pp 555–66.

[80] See N P Podsakoff, S W Whiting, P M Podsakoff, and B D Blume, "Individual- and Organizational-Level Consequences of Organizational Citizenship Behaviors: A Meta-Analysis," *Journal of Applied Psychology,* January 2009, pp 122–41.

[81] This issue is discussed by K M Dudley and J M Cortina, "Knowledge and Skills That Facilitate the Personal Support Dimension of Citizenship," *Journal of Applied Psychology,* November 2008, pp 1249–70; and D S Chiaburu and D A Harrison, "Do Peers Make the Place? Conceptual Synthesis and Meta-Analysis of Coworker Effects on Perceptions, Attitudes,

OCBs and Performance," *Journal of Applied Psychology,* September 2008, pp 1082–103.

82 See N E Fassina, D A Jones, and K L Uggerslev, "Meta-Analytic Tests of Relationships between Organizational Justice and Citizenship Behavior: Testing Agent-System and Shared-Variance Models," *Journal of Organizational Behavior,* August 2008, pp 805–28; and H Moon, D Kamdar, D H Mayer, and R Takeuchi, "Me or We? The Role of Personality and Justice as Other-Centered Antecedents to Innovate Citizenship Behaviors within Organizations," *Journal of Applied Psychology,* January 2008, pp 84–94.

83 These results can be found in K Gurchiek, " 'I Can't Make It to Work Today, Boss . . . Gotta Round Up My Ostriches,' " *HR Magazine,* March 2005, p 30.

84 These cost estimates are provided in "How Much Does Absenteeism Cost Your Business," *Perfect Labor Storm 2.0,* December 10, 2008, http://hrblog.typepad.com/perfect-labor-storm/2018.

85 See R D Hackett, "Work Attitudes and Employee Absenteeism: A Synthesis of the Literature," *Journal of Occupational Psychology,* 1989, pp 235–48.

86 Results can be found in P W Hom and A J Kinicki, "Toward a Greater Understanding of How Dissatisfaction Drives Employee Turnover," *Academy of Management Journal,* October 2001, pp 975–87. Also see Y Fried, A Shirom, S Gilboa, and C L Cooper, "The Mediating Effects of Job Satisfaction and Propensity to Leave on Role Stress–Job Performance Relationship: Combining Meta-Analysis and Structural Equation Modeling," *International Journal of Stress Management,* November 2008, pp 305–28.

87 See "How Important Is Retention?" *Training,* June 2008, p 11.

88 See A Coombes, "Wedded to the Job," *The Arizona Republic,* February 22, 2009, p EC1.

89 Y Lermusiaux, "Calculating the High Cost of Employee Turnover," www.ilogos.com/en/expertviews/articles/strategic/200331007_YL.html, accessed April 15, 2005, p 1.

90 See ibid. An automated program for calculating the cost of turnover can be found at "Calculate Your Turnover Costs," www.keepemployees.com/turnovercalc.htm, accessed February 28, 2009.

91 Results can be found in Griffeth, Hom, and Gaertner, "A Meta-Analysis of Antecedents and Correlates of Employee Turnover."

92 Results can be found in Podsakoff, LePine, and LePine, "Differential Challenge Stressor–Hindrance Stressor Relationships with Job Attitudes, Turnover Intentions, Turnover, and Withdrawal Behavior: A Meta-Analysis."

93 The various models are discussed in T A Judge, C J Thoresen, J E Bono, and G K Patton, "The Job Satisfaction–Job Performance Relationship: A Qualitative and Quantitative Review," *Psychological Bulletin,* May 2001, pp 376–407.

94 Results can be found in ibid.

95 One example is provided by D J Schleicher, J D Watt, and G J Greguras, "Reexamining the Job Satisfaction–Performance Relationship: The Complexity of Attitudes," *Journal of Applied Psychology,* February 2004, pp 165–77.

96 Results can be found in Harter, Schmidt, and Hayes, "Business-Unit-Level Relationship between Employee Satisfaction, Employee Engagement, and Business Outcomes: A Meta-Analysis."

97 D S Ones, "Introduction to the Special Issue on Counterproductive Behaviors at Work," *International Journal of Selection and Assessment,* 10/1–2 (2002), pp 1–4 (quoting p 1).

98 M Conlin, "To Catch a Corporate Thief," *BusinessWeek,* February 16, 2009, p 52.

99 B Leonard, "Study: Bully Bosses Prevalent in U.S.," *HR Magazine,* May 2007, pp 22, 28.

100 See B J Tepper, C A Henle, L S Lambert, R A Giacalone, and M K Duffy, "Abusive Supervision and Subordinates' Organization Deviance," *Journal of Applied Psychology,* July 2008, pp 721–32; and P Bordia, S L D Restubog, and R L Tang, "When Employees Strike Back: Investigating Mediating Mechanisms between Psychological Contract Breach and Workplace Deviance," *Journal of Applied Psychology,* September 2008, pp 1104–17.

101 J B Olson-Buchanan and W R Boswell, "An Integrative Model of Experiencing and Responding to Mistreatment at Work," *Academy of Management Review,* January 2008, pp 76–96.

102 C Hymowitz, "Bosses Have to Learn How to Confront Troubled Employees," *The Wall Street Journal,* April 23, 2007, p B1.

103 Ibid. Also see R A Clay, "Keeping Employees Safe at Home," *Monitor on Psychology,* January 2009, pp 54–55.

104 B W Roberts, P D Harms, A Caspi, and T E Moffitt, "Predicting the Counterproductive Employee in a Child-to-Adult Prospective Study," *Journal of Applied Psychology,* September 2007, pp 1427–36.

105 S Dilchert, D S Ones, R D Davis, and C D Rostow, "Cognitive Ability Predicts Objectively Measured Counterproductive Work Behaviors," *Journal of Applied Psychology,* May 2007, pp 616–27. Also see M Inness, M M LeBlanc, and J Barling, "Psychosocial Predictors of Supervisor-, Peer-, Subordinate-, and Service-Provider-Targeted Aggression," *Journal of Applied Psychology,* November 2008, pp 1401–11.

106 J R Detert, L K Treviño, E R Burris, and M Andiappan, "Managerial Modes of Influence and Counterproductivity in Organizations: A Longitudinal Business-Unit-Level Investigation," *Journal of Applied Psychology,* July 2007, pp 993–1005.

107 J McGregor, "Keeping Talent in the Fold," *BusinessWeek,* November 3, 2008, pp 51–52.

108 Excerpted from J W Miller, "Belgians Take Lots of Sick Leave, and Why Not, They're Depressed," *The Wall Street Journal,* January 9, 2009, pp A1, A6.

CHAPTER 7

1 Excerpted from C Binkley, "Want to Be CEO? You Have to Dress the Part," *The Wall Street Journal,* January 10, 2008, pp D1, D2.

2 D Steiner, "Bernie, I Hardly Knew Ya," *ReportOnBusiness.com,* February 26, 2009, http://business.theglobeandmail.com/servlet/story/RTGAM.20090224.rmmadoff0224/BNST; and J Epstein, " 'Uncle Bernie' and the Jews," *Newsweek,* January 19, 2009, pp 36–37.

3 Examples can be found in S Berfield, "Getting the Most Out of Every Shopper," *BusinessWeek,* February 9, 2009, pp 45–46; and G F Seib, "Issues Recede in '08 Contest as Voters Focus on Candidates' Character," *The Wall Street Journal,* February 5, 2009, pp A1, A14.

[4] See L Winerman, "Screening Surveyed," *Monitor on Psychology,* January 2006, pp 28–29.

[5] S T Fiske and S E Taylor, *Social Cognition,* 2nd ed (Reading, MA: Addison-Wesley Publishing, 1991), pp 1–2.

[6] The negative bias was examined by C Unkelbach, K Fiedler, M Bayer, M Stegmüller, and D Danner, "Why Positive Information Is Processed Faster: The Density Hypothesis," *Journal of Personality and Social Psychology,* July 2008, pp 36–49.

[7] E Rosch, C B Mervis, W D Gray, D M Johnson, and P BoyesBraem, "Basic Objects in Natural Categories," *Cognitive Psychology,* July 1976, p 383.

[8] Results can be found in M Rotundo, D-H Nguyen, and P R Sackett, "A Meta-Analytic Review of Gender Differences in Perceptions of Sexual Harassment," *Journal of Applied Psychology,* October 2001, pp 914–22. Also see J L Berdahl, "The Sexual Harassment of Uppity Women," *Journal of Applied Psychology,* March 2007, pp 425–37.

[9] See J Halberstadt, "Featural Shift in Explanation-Biased Memory for Emotional Faces," *Journal of Personality and Social Psychology,* January 2005, pp 38–49.

[10] See T Mussweiler and L Damisch, "Going Back to Donald: How Comparisons Shape Judgmental Priming Effects," *Journal of Personality and Social Psychology,* December 2008, pp 1295–1315.

[11] For a thorough discussion about the structure and organization of memory, see L R Squire, B Knowlton, and G Musen, "The Structure and Organization of Memory," in *Annual Review of Psychology,* ed L W Porter and M R Rosenzweig (Palo Alto, CA: Annual Reviews Inc., 1993), vol. 44, pp 453–95.

[12] Implicit cognition is discussed by B Azar, "IAT: Fad or Fabulous," *Monitor on Psychology,* July/August 2008, pp 44–45; and L S Son Hing, G A Chung-Yan, L K Hamilton, and M P Zanna, "A Two-Dimensional Model That Employs Explicit and Implicit Attitudes to Characterize Prejudice," *Journal of Personality and Social Psychology,* June 2008, pp 971–87.

[13] See M Orey, "White Men Can't Help It," *BusinessWeek,* May 15, 2006, pp 54, 57. Also see G L Stewart, S L Dustin, M R Barrick, and T C Carnold, "Exploring the Handshake in Employment Interviews," *Journal of Applied Psychology,* September 2008, pp 1139–46.

[14] Details of this study can be found in C K Stevens, "Antecedents of Interview Interactions, Interviewers' Ratings, and Applicants' Reactions," *Personnel Psychology,* Spring 1998, pp 55–85.

[15] See R C Mayer and J H Davis, "The Effect of the Performance Appraisal System on Trust for Management: A Field Quasi-Experiment," *Journal of Applied Psychology,* February 1999, pp 123–36.

[16] Results can be found in W H Bommer, J L Johnson, G A Rich, P M Podsakoff, and S B Mackenzie, "On the Interchangeability of Objective and Subjective Measures of Employee Performance: A Meta-Analysis," *Personnel Psychology,* Autumn 1995, pp 587–605.

[17] See J I Sanchez and P D L Torre, "A Second Look at the Relationship between Rating and Behavioral Accuracy in Performance Appraisal," *Journal of Applied Psychology,* February 1996, pp 3–10.

[18] The effectiveness of rater training was supported by D V Day and L M Sulsky, "Effects of Frame-of-Reference Training and Information Configuration on Memory Organization and Rating Accuracy," *Journal of Applied Psychology,* February 1995, pp 158–67.

[19] Results can be found in J S Phillips and R G Lord, "Schematic Information Processing and Perceptions of Leadership in Problem-Solving Groups," *Journal of Applied Psychology,* August 1982, pp 486–92. Also see M Van Vugt and B R Spisak, "Gender Biases in Leadership Selection during Competitions within and between Groups," *Psychology.com,* October 30, 2008, www.physorg.com/news144587356.html.

[20] See K Tyler, "Generation Gaps," *HR Magazine,* January 2008, pp 69–72; Binkley, "Want to Be CEO? You Have to Dress the Part"; and P Bathurst, "Success: Share, Play Nice," *The Arizona Republic,* December 23, 2007, p EC1.

[21] See B J Tepper, C A Henle, L S Lambert, R A Giacalone, and M K Duffy, "Abusive Supervision and Subordinates' Organizational Deviance," *Journal of Applied Psychology,* July 2008, pp 721–32; and P Bordia, S L D Restubog, and R L Tang, "When Employees Strike Back: Investigating Mediating Mechanisms between Psychological Contract Breach and Workplace Deviance," *Journal of Applied Psychology,* September 2008, pp 1104–17.

[22] See H K Knudsen, L J Ducharme, and P M Roman, "Turnover Intention and Emotional Exhaustion 'at the Top': Adapting the Job Demands-Resources Model to Leaders of Addiction Treatment Organizations," *Journal of Occupational Health Psychology,* January 2009, pp 84–95; and W Darr and G Johns, "Work Strain, Health, and Absenteeism: A Meta-Analysis," *Journal of Occupational Health Psychology,* October 2008, pp 293–318.

[23] See E C Baig, "Survey Offers a 'Sneak Peek' into Net Surfers' Brains," *USA Today,* March 27, 2006, p 4B; and L Winerman, "Screening Surveyed," *Monitor on Psychology,* January 2006, pp 28–29.

[24] These recommendations were excerpted from Baig, "Survey Offers a 'Sneak Peek' into Net Surfers' Brains," p 4B.

[25] S Power, "Mickey Mouse, Nike Give Advice on Air Security," *The Wall Street Journal,* January 24, 2002, p B4.

[26] C M Judd and B Park, "Definition and Assessment of Accuracy in Social Stereotypes," *Psychological Review,* January 1993, p 110.

[27] For a discussion of stereotype accuracy, see T R Cain, J T Crawford, K Harber, and F Cohen, "The Unbearable Accuracy of Stereotypes," in *Handbook of Prejudice, Stereotyping, and Discrimination,* ed T D Nelson (New York: Psychology Press, 2009), pp 199–225; and N O Rule, N Ambady, R B Adams Jr, and C N Macrae, "Accuracy and Awareness in the Perception and Categorization of Male Sexual Orientation," *Journal of Personality and Social Psychology,* November 2008, 1019–28.

[28] Stereotype formation and maintenance is discussed by J V Petrocelli, Z L Tormala, and D D Rucker, "Unpacking Attitude Certainty: Attitude Clarity and Attitude Correctness," *Journal of Personality and Social Psychology,* January 2006, pp 30–41.

[29] See S Madon, M Guyll, S J Hilbert, E Kyriakatos, and D L Vogel, "Stereotyping the Stereotypic: When Individuals Match Social Stereotypes," *Journal of Applied Social Psychology,* January 2006, pp 178–205.

[30] Results are presented in E Tahmincioglu, "Men Rule—At Least in Workplace Attitudes," *MSNBC,* www.msnbc.msn.com/id/17345308/, accessed March 6, 2007.

[31] See V K Gupta, D B Turban, and N M Bhawe, "The Effect of Gender Stereotype Activation on Entrepreneurial Intentions," *Journal of Applied Psychology,* September 2008, pp 1053–61.

[32] See J D Olian, D P Schwab, and Y Haberfeld, "The Impact of Applicant Gender Compared to Qualifications on Hiring Recommendations: A Meta-Analysis of Experimental Studies," *Organizational Behavior and Human Decision Processes,* April 1988, pp 180–95.

[33] Results from the meta-analyses are discussed in K P Carson, C L Sutton, and P D Corner, "Gender Bias in Performance Appraisals: A Meta-Analysis," paper presented at the 49th Annual Academy of Management Meeting, Washington, DC: 1989. Results from the field study can be found in T J Maurer and M A Taylor, "Is Sex by Itself Enough? An Exploration of Gender Bias Issues in Performance Appraisal," *Organizational Behavior and Human Decision Processes,* November 1994, pp 231–51.

[34] See J Landau, "The Relationship of Race and Gender to Managers' Ratings of Promotion Potential," *Journal of Organizational Behavior,* July 1995, pp 391–400.

[35] Results can be found in K S Lyness and M E Heilman, "When Fit Is Fundamental: Performance Evaluations and Promotions of Upper-Level Female and Male Managers," *Journal of Applied Psychology,* July 2006, pp 777–85.

[36] For a complete review, see S R Rhodes, "Age-Related Differences in Work Attitudes and Behavior: A Review and Conceptual Analysis," *Psychological Bulletin,* March 1983, pp 328–67. Also see J C Santora and W J Seaton, "Age Discrimination: Alive and Well in the Workplace?" *Academy of Management Perspectives,* May 2008, pp 103–105.

[37] See T W H Ng and D C Feldman, "The Relationship of Age to Ten Dimensions of Job Performance," *Journal of Applied Psychology,* March 2008, pp 392–423.

[38] For details, see B J Avolio, D A Waldman, and M A McDaniel, "Age and Work Performance in Nonmanagerial Jobs: The Effects of Experience and Occupational Type," *Academy of Management Journal,* June 1990, pp 407–22.

[39] D H Powell, "Aging Baby Boomers: Stretching Your Workforce Options," *HR Magazine,* July 1998, p 83.

[40] Results can be found in R W Griffeth, P W Hom, and S Gaertner, "A Meta-Analysis of Antecedents and Correlates of Employee Turnover: Update, Moderator Tests, and Research Implications for the Next Millennium," *Journal of Management,* 2000, pp 463–88.

[41] See J J Martocchio, "Age-Related Differences in Employee Absenteeism: A Meta-Analysis," *Psychology and Aging,* December 1989, pp 409–14.

[42] T DeAngelis, "Unmasking 'Racial MicroAggressions,'" *Monitor on Psychology,* February 2009, p 44. Also see J W Kunstman and E A Plant, "Racing to Help: Racial Bias in High Emergency Situations," *Journal of Personality and Social Psychology,* December 2008, pp 1499–1510; and A R McConnell, R J Rydell, L M Strain, and D M Mackie, "Forming Implicit and Explicit Attitudes toward Individuals: Social Group Association Cues," *Journal of Personality and Social Psychology,* May 2008, pp 792–807.

[43] Ibid., p 43.

[44] See J K Robbennolt and M Taksin, "Jury Selection, Peremptory Challenges, and Discrimination," *Monitor on Psychology,* January 2009, pp 16–17.

[45] This information was obtained from the official Web site of Tiger Woods, www.tigerwoods.com, accessed March 3, 2009; and www.wikipedia.org, accessed March 3, 2009.

[46] Results from these studies can be found in A I Huffcutt and P L Roth, "Racial Group Differences in Employment Interview Evaluations," *Journal of Applied Psychology,* April 1998, pp 179–89; and T-R Lin, G H Dobbins, and J-L Farh, "A Field Study of Race and Age Similarity Effects on Interview Ratings in Conventional and Situational Interviews," *Journal of Applied Psychology,* June 1992, pp 363–71.

[47] See D A Waldman and B J Avolio, "Race Effects in Performance Evaluations: Controlling for Ability, Education, and Experience," *Journal of Applied Psychology,* December 1991, pp 897–901; and E D Pulakos, L A White, S H Oppler, and W C Borman, "Examination of Race and Sex Effects on Performance Ratings," *Journal of Applied Psychology,* October 1989, pp 770–80.

[48] H-H D Nguyen and A M Ryan, "Does Stereotype Threat Affect Test Performance of Minorities and Women? A Meta-Analysis of Experimental Evidence," *Journal of Applied Psychology,* November 2008, p 1314.

[49] See ibid., pp 1314–34; and D Buyens, H Van Dijk, T Dewilde, and A De Vos, "The Aging Workforce: Perceptions of Career Ending," *Journal of Managerial Psychology,* 2009, pp 102–17.

[50] See S J Wells, "Counting on Workers with Disabilities," *HR Magazine,* April 2008, pp 45–49.

[51] See "New Monthly Data Series on the Employment Status of People with a Disability," U.S. Bureau of Labor Statistics. Last modified February 6, 2009, http://data.bls.gov/cgi-bin/print.pl/ cps/cpsdisability.htm.

[52] These statistics were reported in C Komp, "Unemployment, Poverty Higher for People with Disabilities," *The New Standard,* October 4, 2006, http://newstandardnews.net/content/index.cfm/ items/3727.

[53] The ADA and its associated accommodation requirements are discussed by A Smith, "Out with the Old ADA, in with the New ADAAA," *HR Magazine,* November 2008, p 22.

[54] R A Posthuma and M A Campion, "Age Stereotypes in the Workplace: Common Stereotypes, Moderators, and Future Research Directions," *Journal of Management,* February 2009, pp 158–88.

[55] See Day and Sulsky, "Effects of Frame-of-Reference Training and Information Configuration on Memory Organization and Rating Accuracy."

[56] The background and results for this study are presented in R Rosenthal and L Jacobson, *Pygmalion in the Classroom: Teacher Expectation and Pupils' Intellectual Development* (New York: Holt, Rinehart & Winston, 1968).

[57] D B McNatt, "Ancient Pygmalion Joins Contemporary Management: A Meta-Analysis of the Result," *Journal of Applied Psychology,* April 2000, pp 314–22. Also see B J Avolio, R J Reichard, S T Hannah, F O Walumbwa, and A Chan, "A Meta-Analytic Review of Leadership Impact Research: Experimental and Quasi-Experimental Studies," *The Leadership Quarterly,* in press, 2009.

[58] See G Natanovich and D Eden, "Pygmalion Effects among Outreach Supervisors and Tutors: Extending Sex Generalizability," *Journal of Applied Psychology,* November 2008, pp 1382–89.

[59] See ibid.

[60] The Golem effect is defined and investigated by O B Davidson and D Eden, "Remedial Self-Fulfilling Prophecy: Two Field Experiments to Prevent Golem Effects among Disadvantaged Women," *Journal of Applied Psychology,* June 2000, pp 386–98.

[61] The role of positive expectations at Google is discussed by A Lashinsky, "Search and Joy," *Fortune,* January 22, 2007, pp 70–82.

[62] See S M Heathfield, "The Two Most Important Management Secrets: The Pygmalion and Galatea Effects," *About.com Human Resources,* accessed March 2009, http://humanresources.about.com; D Eden, D Geller, A Gewirtz, R Gordon-Terner, I Inbar, M Liberman, Y Pass, I Salomon-Segev, and M Shalit, "Implanting Pygmalion Leadership Style through Workshop Training: Seven Field Experiments," *The Leadership Quarterly,* Summer 2000, pp 171–210.

[63] Kelley's model is discussed in detail in H H Kelley, "The Processes of Causal Attribution," *American Psychologist,* February 1973, pp 107–28.

[64] See A M Grant, S Parker, and C Collins, "Getting Credit for Proactive Behavior: Supervisor Reactions Depend on What You Value and How You Feel," *Personnel Psychology,* Spring 2009, pp 31–55; and K White, D R Lehman, K J Hemphill, D R Mandel, and A M Lehman, "Causal Attributions, Perceived Control, and Psychological Adjustment: A Study of Chronic Fatigue Syndrome," *Journal of Applied Social Psychology,* January 2006, pp 75–99.

[65] Examples can be found in C Meyer and A Schwager, "Understanding Customer Experience," *Harvard Business Review,* February 2007, pp 117–26; and C Lakshman, "Attributional Theory of Leadership: A Model of Functional Attributions and Behaviors," *Leadership & Organization Development,* 2008, pp 317–39.

[66] Results from these studies can be found in D A Hofmann and A Stetzer, "The Role of Safety, Climate, and Communication in Accident Interpretation: Implications for Learning from Negative Events," *Academy of Management Journal,* December 1998, pp 644–57; and I Choi, R E Nisbett, and A Norenzayan, "Causal Attribution across Cultures: Variation and Universality," *Psychological Bulletin,* January 1999, pp 47–63.

[67] Results can be found in G Kolev, "The Stock Market Bubble, Shareholders' Attribution Bias and Excessive Top CEO Pay," *The Journal of Behavioral Finance,* April 2008, pp 62–71.

[68] These cases are discussed in J A Segal, "Woman in the Moon," *HR Magazine,* August 2007, pp 107–14.

[69] See M T Billett and Y Qian, "Are Overconfident CEOs Born or Made? Evidence of Self-Attribution Bias from Frequent Acquirers," *Management Science,* June 2008, pp 1037–51; and R Madrigal and J Chen, "Moderating and Mediating Effects of Team Identification in Regard to Causal Attributions and Summary Judgments Following a Game Outcome," *Journal of Sport Management,* November 2008, pp 717–33.

[70] Results can be found in E W K Tsang, "Self-Serving Attributions in Corporate Annual Reports: A Replicated Study," *Journal of Management Studies,* January 2002, pp 51–65.

[71] This research is summarized by T S Duval and P J Silvia, "Self-Awareness, Probability of Improvement, and the Self-Serving Bias," *Journal of Personality and Social Psychology,* January 2002, pp 49–61.

[72] Ibid., p 58.

[73] Details may be found in S E Moss and M J Martinko, "The Effects of Performance Attributions and Outcome Dependence on Leader Feedback Behavior following Poor Subordinate Performance," *Journal of Organizational Behavior,* May 1998, pp 259–74; and E C Pence, W C Pendleton, G H Dobbins, and J A Sgro, "Effects of Causal Explanations and Sex Variables on Recommendations for Corrective Actions Following Employee Failure," *Organizational Behavior and Human Performance,* April 1982, pp 227–40.

[74] See M O'Neill, "Luck, or Hard Work?" *Forbes,* February 26, 2007, p 38.

[75] See D Konst, R Vonk, and R V D Vlist, "Inferences about Causes and Consequences of Behavior of Leaders and Subordinates," *Journal of Organizational Behavior,* March 1999, pp 261–71.

[76] See M Miserandino, "Attributional Retraining as a Method of Improving Athletic Performance," *Journal of Sport Behavior,* August 1998, pp 286–97.

[77] Excerpted from J. Lublin, "A Question to Make a Monkey of You," *The Wall Street Journal,* February 3, 2009, p D4.

[78] Excerpted from A McConnon, "Mad Ave: If I Only Had a Brain Scan," *BusinessWeek,* January 22, 2007, p 19.

CHAPTER 8

[1] Excerpted from G Colvin, "Rewarding Failure," *Fortune,* April 28, 2008, p 22.

[2] E E Lawler III, "Make Human Capital a Source of Competitive Advantage," *Organizational Dynamics,* January–March 2009, p 3.

[3] M Kimes, "How I Got Started: The Accidental CEO," *Fortune,* March 2, 2009, p 26.

[4] T R Mitchell, "Motivation: New Direction for Theory, Research, and Practice," *Academy of Management Review,* January 1982, p 81.

[5] A review of content and process theories of motivation is provided by R M Steers, R T Mowday, and D L Shapiro, "The Future of Work Motivation Theory," *Academy of Management Review,* July 2004, pp 379–87.

[6] For a complete description of Maslow's theory, see A H Maslow, "A Theory of Human Motivation," *Psychological Review,* July 1943, pp 370–96.

[7] See W B Swann Jr, C Chang-Schneider, and K L McClarty, "Do People's Self-Views Matter?" *American Psychologist,* February–March 2007, pp 84–94.

[8] Applications of Maslow's theory are found in M Hofman, "The Idea That Saved My Company," *Inc.,* October 2007, www.inc.com; and C Conley, *How Great Companies Get Their Mojo from Maslow* (San Francisco, CA: Jossey-Bass, 2007).

[9] The use of surveys is discussed by J Welch and S Welch, "Employee Polls: A Vote in Favor," *BusinessWeek,* January 28, 2008, p 90.

[10] For a complete review of ERG theory, see C P Alderfer, *Existence, Relatedness, and Growth: Human Needs in Organizational Settings* (New York: Free Press, 1972).

[11] L Buchanan, "Managing One-to-One," *Inc.,* October 2001, p 87.

[12] H A Murray, *Explorations in Personality* (New York: John Wiley & Sons, 1938), p 164.

[13] See K G Shaver, "The Entrepreneurial Personality Myth," *Business and Economic Review,* April/June 1995, pp 20–23.

[14] See S W Spreier, M H Fontaine, and R L Malloy, "Leadership Run Amok," *Harvard Business Review,* June 2006, pp 72–82.

[15] See H Heckhausen and S Krug, "Motive Modification," in *Motivation and Society,* ed A J Stewart (San Francisco, CA: Jossey-Bass, 1982).

[16] Results can be found in D B Turban and T L Keon, "Organizational Attractiveness: An Interactionist Perspective," *Journal of Applied Psychology,* April 1993, pp 184–93.

[17] Quoted in Spreier, Fontaine, and Malloy, "Leadership Run Amok," p 2. Also see H Moon, D Kamdar, D M Mayer, and R Takeuchi, "Me or We? The Role of Personality and Justice as Other-Centered Antecedents to Innovative Citizenship Behaviors within Organizations," *Journal of Applied Psychology,* January 2008, pp 84–94.

[18] See G Anand, "Friends Try to Reconcile 2 Sides of Indian Executive," *The Wall Street Journal,* January 8, 2009, p A9; and "Ramalinga Raju," *Wikipedia,* last updated February 27, 2009, http:wikipedia.org.

[19] See F Herzberg, B Mausner, and B B Snyderman, *The Motivation to Work* (New York: John Wiley & Sons, 1959).

[20] See R Hastings, "Silent Generation Speaks Up about Work," *HR Magazine,* September 2008, p 30; and Y Fried, A Shirom, S Gilboa, and C L Cooper, "The Mediating Effects of Job Satisfaction and Propensity to Leave on Role-Stress-Job Performance Relationships: Combining Meta-Analysis and Structural Equation," *International Journal of Stress Management,* November 2008, pp 305–28.

[21] F Herzberg, "One More Time: How Do You Motivate Employees?" *Harvard Business Review,* January–February 1968, p 56.

[22] For a thorough review of research on Herzberg's theory, see C C Pinder, *Work Motivation: Theory, Issues, and Applications* (Glenview, IL: Scott, Foresman, 1984).

[23] "Top Small Workplaces 2008," *The Wall Street Journal,* October 13, 2008, p R8.

[24] Recognition suggestions are offered by H Dolezalek, "Good Job!" *Training,* July/August 2008, pp 32–34; and L Anderson, "Turn Best Practices into Common Practices with On-the-Spot Recognition," *HR Magazine: Special Advertisement Supplement—The Power of Incentives,* 2008, pp 97–102.

[25] See S Gorman, "Virus Was Set to Destroy Fannie Mae Data," *The Wall Street Journal,* February 1, 2009, p A2.

[26] The comparison process was studied by E C Hollensbe, S Khazanchi, and S S Masterson, "How Do I Assess If My Supervisor and Organization Are Fair? Identifying the Rules Underlying Entity-Based Justice Perceptions," *Academy of Management Journal,* December 2008, pp 1099–1116; and M H Harris, F Anseel, and F Lievens, "Keeping Up with the Joneses: A Field Study of the Relationships among Upward, Lateral, and Downward Comparisons and Pay Level Satisfaction," *Journal of Applied Psychology,* May 2008, pp 665–73.

[27] See M C Bolino and W H Turnley, "Old Faces, New Places: Equity Theory in Cross-Cultural Contexts," *Journal of Organizational Behavior,* January 2008, pp 29–50; and "Selected Cross-Cultural Factors in Human Resource Management," *Society for Human Resource Management Research Quarterly,* Third Quarter 2008, pp 1–9.

[28] These statistics were obtained from C Graham, "Top Execs Earn Far More Than Proposed $500,000 Cap," *The Arizona Republic,* February 5, 2009, p D1; and K Hall, "CEO Pay: Don't Look to Japan For Answers," *BusinessWeek,* February 23, 2009, p 60.

[29] S J Wells, "Layoff Aftermath," *HR Magazine,* November 2008, p 37.

[30] M N Bing and S M Burroughs, "The Predictive and Interactive Effects of Equity Sensitivity in Teamwork-Oriented Organizations," *Journal of Organizational Behavior,* May 2001, p 271.

[31] Types of equity sensitivity are discussed by ibid. Also see O H Akan, R S Allen, and C S White, "Equity Sensitivity and Organizational Citizenship Behavior in a Team Environment," *Small Group Research,* February 2009, pp 94–112.

[32] For a thorough review of organizational justice theory and research, see R Cropanzano, D E Rupp, C J Mohler, and M Schminke, "Three Roads to Organizational Justice," in *Research in Personnel and Human Resources Management,* vol. 20, ed G R Ferris (New York: JAI Press, 2001), pp 269–329.

[33] J A Colquitt, D E Conlon, M J Wesson, C O L H Porter, and K Y Ng, "Justice at the Millennium: A Meta-Analytic Review of 25 Years of Organizational Justice Research," *Journal of Applied Psychology,* June 2001, p 426.

[34] Results from these studies can be found in N E Fassina, D A Jones, and K L Uggerslev, "Meta-Analytic Tests of Relationships between Organizational Justice and Citizenship Behavior: Testing Agent-System and Shared-Variance Models," *Journal of Organizational Behavior,* August 2008, pp 805–28; Y Cohen-Charash and P E Spector, "The Role of Justice in Organizations: A Meta-Analysis," *Organizational Behavior and Human Decision Processes,* November 2001, pp 278–321; Colquitt, Conlon, Wesson, Porter, and Ng, "Justice at the Millennium;" and M S Hershcovis, N Turner, J Barling, K A Arnold, K E Dupré, M Inness, M M LeBlanc, and N Sivanathan, "Predicting Workplace Aggression: A Meta-Analysis," *Journal of Applied Psychology,* January 2007, pp 228–38.

[35] For recent studies of justice, see J Schaubroeck, J D Shaw, M K Duffy, and A Mitra, "An Under-Met and Over-Met Expectations Model of Employee Reactions to Merit Raises," *Journal of Applied Psychology,* March 2008, pp 424–34; and D M Mayer, R L Greenbaum, M Kuenzi, and G Shteynberg, "When Do Fair Procedures Not Matter: A Test of the Identity Violation Effect," *Journal of Applied Psychology,* January 2009, pp 142–61.

[36] Results from this study were reported in K Gurchiek, "Show Workers Their Value, Study Says," *HR Magazine,* October 2006, p 40.

[37] Voice was examined by E R Burris, J R Detert, and D S Chiaburu, "Quitting Before Leaving: The Mediating Effects of Psychological Attachment and Detachment on Voice," *Journal of Applied Psychology,* July 2008, pp 912–22; and J Ullrich, O Christ, and R van Dick, "Substitutes for Procedural Fairness: Prototypical Leaders Are Endorsed Whether They Are Fair or Not," *Journal of Applied Psychology,* January 2009, pp 235–44.

[38] E Thornton, "Managing through a Crisis: The New Rules," *BusinessWeek,* January 19, 2009, pp 30–34.

[39] The impact of groups on justice perceptions was investigated by D A Jones and D P Skarlicki, "The Effects of Overhearing Peers to Discuss an Authority's Fairness Reputation on Reactions to Subsequent Treatment," *Journal of Applied Psychology,* March 2005, pp 363–72.

40 See B J Tepper, M K Duffy, C A Henle, and L S Lambert, "Procedural Injustice, Victim Precipitation, and Abusive Supervision," *Personnel Psychology,* Spring 2006, pp 101–23.

41 G Colvin, "The World's Most Admired Companies 2009," *Fortune,* March 16, 2009, p 78.

42 Climate for justice was studied by S Tangirala and R Ramanujam, "Employee Silence on Critical Work Issues: The Cross Level Effects of Procedural Justice Climate," *Personnel Psychology,* Spring 2008, pp 37–68.

43 See M Subramony, N Krause, J Norton, and G N Burns, "The Relationship between Human Resource Investments and Organizational Performance: A Firm-Level Examination of Equilibrium Theory," *Journal of Applied Psychology,* July 2008, pp 778–88; and D P Skarlicki, D D van Jaarsveld, and D D Walker, "Getting Even for Customer Mistreatment: The Role of Moral Identity in the Relationship between Customer Interpersonal Injustice and Employee Sabotage," *Journal of Applied Psychology,* November 2008, pp 1335–47.

44 See V H Vroom, *Work and Motivation* (New York: John Wiley & Sons, 1964).

45 E E Lawler III, *Motivation in Work Organizations* (Belmont, CA: Wadsworth, 1973), p 45.

46 See C C Pinder, *Work Motivation* (Glenview, IL: Scott, Foresman, 1984), ch 7.

47 "Federal Express's Fred Smith," *Inc.,* October 1986, p 38.

48 Results can be found in W van Eerde and H Thierry, "Vroom's Expectancy Models and Work-Related Criteria: A Meta-Analysis," *Journal of Applied Psychology,* October 1996, pp 575–86. Also see R D Pritchard, M M Harrell, D DiazGranados, and M J Guzman, "The Productivity Measurement and Enhancement System: A Meta-Analysis," *Journal of Applied Psychology,* May 2008, pp 540–67.

49 See J P Wanous, T L Keon, and J C Latack, "Expectancy Theory and Occupational/Organizational Choices: A Review and Test," *Organizational Behavior and Human Performance,* August 1983, pp 66–86.

50 See J Cameron and W D Pierce, *Rewards and Intrinsic Motivation: Resolving the Controversy* (Alberta, Canada: Cameron and Pierce, 2002); K L Scott, J D Shaw, and M K Duffy, "Merit Pay Raises and Organization-Based Self-Esteem," *Journal of Organizational Behavior,* October 2008, pp 967–80; and P Berrone and L R Gomez-Mejia, "Environmental Performance and Executive Compensation: An Integrated Agency-Institutional Perspective," *Academy of Management Journal,* February 2009, pp 103–26.

51 See the discussion in T R Mitchell and D Daniels, "Motivation," in *Handbook of Psychology,* vol. 12, eds W C Borman, D R Ilgen, and R J Klimoski (Hoboken, NJ: John Wiley & Sons, Inc., 2003), pp 225–54.

52 "Top Small Workplaces," *The Wall Street Journal,* October 13, 2008, p R5.

53 L Scott, "Grocery Bagger Set Course to Be President of Bashas'," *The Arizona Republic,* February 11, 2007, p D2.

54 E A Locke, K N Shaw, L M Saari, and G P Latham, "Goal Setting and Task Performance: 1969–1980," *Psychological Bulletin,* July 1981, p 126.

55 Sustainability goals are discussed in N H Woodward, "New Breed of Human Resource Leader," *HR Magazine,* June 2008, pp 52–56; and E Levenson, "Citizen Nike," *Fortune,* November 24, 2008, pp 165–70.

56 Examples are discussed in J Adamy, "Starbucks CEO, Top Officials Didn't Get Bonuses for 2008," *The Wall Street Journal,* January 23, 2009, p B3; and C Tuna, "Shareholders to Focus on Executive Compensation," *The Wall Street Journal,* January 12, 2009, p B4.

57 S Miller, "Many Don't Disclose Executive Pay Goals," *HR Magazine,* March 2008, p 33.

58 R Millward, "Harrington Hungry for More," *The Arizona Republic,* July 24, 2007, p C6. Also see S Banjo, "Shared Goals," *The Wall Street Journal,* April 14, 2008, p R3.

59 M Frese, S I Krauss, N Keith, S Escher, R Grabarkiewicz, S T Luneng, C Heers, J Unger, and C Friedrich, "Business Owners' Action Planning and Its Relationship to Business Success in Three African Countries," *Journal of Applied Psychology,* November 2007, pp 1481–98.

60 See G P Latham and E A Locke, "Enhancing the Benefits and Overcoming the Pitfalls of Goal Setting," *Organizational Dynamics,* November 2006, pp 332–40.

61 See A P Tolli and A M Schmidt, "The Role of Feedback, Causal Attributions, and Self-Efficacy in Goal Revision," *Journal of Applied Psychology,* May 2008, pp 692–701.

62 See E A Locke and G P Latham, *A Theory of Goal Setting and Task Performance* (Englewood Cliffs, NJ: Prentice Hall, 1990).

63 See M J Ferguson, "On Becoming Ready to Pursue a Goal You Don't Know You Have: Effects of Nonconscious Goals on Evaluative Readiness," *Journal of Personality and Social Psychology,* December 2008, pp 1268–94. Action planning in a sales context is discussed by P Keegan, "Sales Slip-Ups," *Fortune,* September 29, 2008, p 108.

64 Supportive results can be found in S E Humphrey, J D Nahrgang, and F P Morgeson, "Integrating Motivational, Social, and Contextual Work Design Features: A Meta-Analytic Summary and Theoretical Extension of the Work Design Literature," *Journal of Applied Psychology,* September 2007, pp 1332–56.

65 See J J Donovan and D J Radosevich, "The Moderating Role of Goal Commitment on the Goal Difficulty-Performance Relationship: A Meta-Analytic Review and Critical Reanalysis," *Journal of Applied Psychology,* April 1998, pp 308–15. Also see M Koo and A Fishbach, "Dynamics of Self-Regulation: How (Un)accomplished Goal Actions Affect Motivation," *Journal of Personality and Social Psychology,* February 2008, pp 183–95.

66 See Latham and Locke, "Enhancing the Benefits and Overcoming the Pitfalls of Goal Setting."

67 J L Bowditch and A F Buono, *A Primer on Organizational Behavior* (New York: John Wiley & Sons, 1985), p 210.

68 This framework was proposed by M A Campion and P W Thayer, "Development and Field Evaluation of an Interdisciplinary Measure of Job Design," *Journal of Applied Psychology,* February 1985, pp 29–43.

69 G D Babcock, *The Taylor System in Franklin Management,* 2nd ed (New York: Engineering Magazine Company, 1917), p 31.

70 For a thorough discussion, see F B Copley, *Frederick W Taylor: The Principles of Scientific Management* (New York: Harper & Brothers, 1911).

71 See the related discussion in S Wagner-Tsukamoto, "An Institutional Economic Reconstruction of Scientific

Management: On the Lost Theoretical Logic of Taylorism," *Academy of Management Review,* January 2007, pp 105–17.

[72] This type of program was developed and tested by M A Campion and C L McClelland, "Follow-Up and Extension of the Interdisciplinary Costs and Benefits of Enlarged Jobs," *Journal of Applied Psychology,* June 1993, pp 339–51.

[73] See M Weinstein, "Foreign but Familiar," *Training,* January 2009, pp 20–23.

[74] Benefits of job rotation are discussed by J T Arnold, "Kicking Up Cross-Training," *HR Magazine,* August 2008, pp 96–100; and M Fisher, "Job Rotation, Total Rewards, Measuring Value," *HR Magazine,* August 2008, p 33.

[75] J R Hackman, G R Oldham, R Janson, and K Purdy, "A New Strategy for Job Enrichment," *California Management Review,* Summer 1975, p 58.

[76] Definitions of the job characteristics were adapted from J R Hackman and G R Oldham, "Motivation through the Design of Work: Test of a Theory," *Organizational Behavior and Human Performance,* August 1976, pp 250–79.

[77] See Humphrey, Nahrgang, and Morgeson, "Integrating Motivational, Social, and Contextual Work Design Features: A Meta-Analytic Summary and Theoretical Extension of the Work Design Literature."

[78] These examples were taken from R Levering and M Moskowitz, "The 100 Best Companies to Work for 2007," *Fortune,* January 22, 2007, p 94; and R Levering and M Moskowitz, "The 100 Best Companies to Work For," *Fortune,* January 24, 2005, p 76.

[79] Supportive results were found by S K Parker, H M Williams, and N Turner, "Modeling the Antecedents of Proactive Behavior at Work," *Journal of Applied Psychology,* May 2006, pp 636–52.

[80] See Humphrey, Nahrgang, and Morgeson, "Integrating Motivational, Social, and Contextual Work Design Features: A Meta-Analytic Summary and Theoretical Extension of the Work Design Literature."

[81] Results can be found in M R Kelley, "New Process Technology, Job Design, and Work Organization: A Contingency Model," *American Sociological Review,* April 1990, pp 191–208.

[82] Productivity studies are reviewed in R E Kopelman, *Managing Productivity in Organizations* (New York: McGraw-Hill, 1986).

[83] C Vander Doelen, "Virtual Assembly Weeds Out 'Bad' Jobs," *Windsor (ON) Star,* December 15, 2007, www.canada.com.

[84] This description was taken from J R Edwards, J A Scully, and M D Brtek, "The Nature and Outcome of Work: A Replication and Extension of Interdisciplinary Work-Design Research," *Journal of Applied Psychology,* December 2000, pp 860–68.

[85] M Maynard, "At Toyota, a Global Giant Reaches for Agility," *New York Times,* February 22, 2008, www.nytimes.com. Also see N Woodward, "Easing Back Pain," *HR Magazine,* April 2008, pp 57–60.

[86] National Institute of Neurological Disorders and Stroke, "NINDS Repetitive Motion Disorders Information Page," www.ninds.nih.gov, last updated February 14, 2007.

[87] Bureau of Labor Statistics, "Nonfatal Occupational Injuries and Illnesses Requiring Days Away from Work, 2006," news release, November 8, 2007, www.bls.gov.

[88] J Welch and S Welch, "An Employee Bill of Rights," *BusinessWeek,* March 16, 2009, p 72.

[89] See C Elton, "Carrots in a Crisis," *Training,* January 2009, p 12; and S Baker, "Will Work for Praise," *BusinessWeek,* February 16, 2009, pp 46–49.

[90] "HMO Clerks Who Pare Doctor Visits Rewarded," *The Arizona Republic,* May 18, 2002, p A10.

[91] Compensation plans are discussed by N Byrnes, "A Better Way to Reward Executives," *BusinessWeek,* February 16, 2009, p 29; and P Dvorak and J S Lublin, "Firms Rethink Compensation Plans," *The Wall Street Journal,* January 20, 2009, pp B1, B2.

[92] Excerpted from S Simon, "Denver Teachers Object to Changes in Pay-for-Performance Plan," *The Wall Street Journal,* August 18, 2008, p A3.

[93] Excerpted from M Kimes, "Nomenclature: Your Swiss Bank May Be Getting Kickbacks," *Fortune,* February 16, 2009, p 19.

CHAPTER 9

[1] From R Zeidner, "Uncommon Benefits," *HR Magazine,* July 2008, pp 44–45. Copyright 2008 by Society for Human Resource Management (SHRM). Reproduced with permission of Society for Human Resource Management via Copyright Clearance Center.

[2] B Tulgan, "The Under-Management Epidemic," *HR Magazine,* October 2004, p 119.

[3] S Meisinger, "Management Holds Key to Employee Engagement," *HR Magazine,* February 2008, p 8.

[4] See E E Lawler III, *Treat People Right! How Organizations and Individuals Can Propel Each Other into a Virtuous Spiral of Success* (San Francisco, CA: Jossey-Bass, 2003); T R Clark, "Engaging the Disengaged," *HR Magazine,* April 2008, pp 109–12; H Lollis, "Be a Steppingstone," *HR Magazine,* November 2008, pp 112–14; and L Petersen, "Can Our Company's Vision and Values Be Reflected in Our Performance Management System?" *HR Magazine,* January 2009, p 30.

[5] This distinction is drawn from G P Latham, J Almost, S Mann, and C Moore, "New Developments in Performance Management," *Organizational Dynamics,* no. 1, 2005, pp 77–87.

[6] See K Sulkowicz, "Analyze This," *BusinessWeek,* March 10, 2008, p 19; S A Culbert, "Get Rid of the Performance Review!" *The Wall Street Journal,* October 20, 2008, p R4; and A Fox, "Curing What Ails Performance Reviews," *HR Magazine,* January 2009, pp 52–56.

[7] As quoted in P B Brown, "What I Know Now," *Fast Company,* April 2005, p 104. Also see J Welch and S Welch, "Hiring Is Hard Work," *BusinessWeek,* July 7, 2008, p 80; and A Fox, "Prune Employees Carefully," *HR Magazine,* April 2008, pp 66–70.

[8] See M Weinstein, "A Better Blend," *Training,* September 2008, pp 30–39; S J Armstrong and E Sadler-Smith, "Learning on Demand, at Your Own Pace, in Rapid Bite-Sized Chunks: The Future Shape of Management Development?" *Academy of Management Learning and Education,* December 2008, pp 571–86; and K Tyler, "Training on a Shoestring," *HR Magazine,* January 2009, pp 66–69.

[9] Adapted and quoted from "ThermoSTAT," *Training,* July–August 2003, p 16. Also see M Weinstein, "They're Not Getting It," *Training,* September 2008, p 8.

10 Based on W R Boswell, J B Bingham, and A J S Colvin, "Aligning Employees through 'Line of Sight,'" *Business Horizons,* November–December 2006, pp 499–509.

11 C J Loomis, "The Bloomberg," *Fortune,* April 16, 2007, p 68.

12 G H Seijts and G P Latham, "Learning versus Performance Goals: When Should Each Be Used?" *Academy of Management Executive,* February 2005, pp 126–27. Also see L D Ordonez, M E Schweitzer, A D Galinsky, and M H Bazerman, "Goals Gone Wild: The Systematic Side Effects of Overprescribing Goal Setting," *Academy of Management Perspectives,* February 2009, pp 6–16; E A Locke and G P Latham, "Has Goal Setting Gone Wild, or Have Its Attackers Abandoned Good Scholarship?" *Academy of Management Perspectives*, February 2009, pp 17–23; and G Hirst, D Van Knippenberg, and J Zhou, "A Cross-Level Perspective on Employee Creativity: Goal Orientation, Team Learning Behavior, and Individual Creativity," *Academy of Management Journal,* April 2009, pp 280–93.

13 Thorough discussions of MBO are provided by P F Drucker, *The Practice of Management* (New York: Harper, 1954); and P F Drucker, "What Results Should You Expect? A User's Guide to MBO," *Public Administration Review,* January–February 1976, pp 12–19.

14 As quoted in M Kimes, "How Do I Groom and Keep Talented Employees?" *Fortune,* November 10, 2008, p 26.

15 Results from both studies can be found in R Rodgers and J E Hunter, "Impact of Management by Objectives on Organizational Productivity," *Journal of Applied Psychology,* April 1991, pp 322–36; and R Rodgers, J E Hunter, and D L Rogers, "Influence of Top Management Commitment on Management Program Success," *Journal of Applied Psychology,* February 1993, pp 151–55.

16 D Foust, "Why Did IndyMac Implode?" *Business Week,* August 4, 2008, p. 24.

17 For a good update, see G P Latham and E A Locke, "Enhancing the Benefits and Overcoming the Pitfalls of Goal Setting," *Organizational Dynamics,* no. 4, 2006, pp 332–40.

18 See J A Colquitt and M J Simmering, "Conscientiousness, Goal Orientation, and Motivation to Learn during the Learning Process: A Longitudinal Study," *Journal of Applied Psychology,* August 1998, pp 654–65. Also see S D Bond, K A Carlson, and R L Keeney, "Generating Objectives: Can Decision Makers Articulate What They Want?" *Management Science,* January 2008, pp 56–70.

19 D VandeWalle, S P Brown, W L Cron, and J W Slocum Jr, "The Influence of Goal Orientation and Self-Regulated Tactics on Sales Performance: A Longitudinal Field Test," *Journal of Applied Psychology,* April 1999, p 250. Also see G H Seijts, G P Latham, K Tasa, and B W Latham, "Goal Setting and Goal Orientation: An Integration of Two Different Yet Related Literatures," *Academy of Management Journal,* April 2004, pp 227–39; and C L Porath and T S Bateman, "Self-Regulation: From Goal Orientation to Job Performance," *Journal of Applied Psychology,* January 2006, pp 185–86.

20 For more, see Y Gong and J Fan, "Longitudinal Examination of the Role of Goal Orientation in Cross-Cultural Adjustment,*"* *Journal of Applied Psychology,* January 2006, pp 176–84; S C Payne, S S Youngcourt, and J M Beaubien, "A Meta-Analytic Examination of the Goal Orientation Nomological Net," *Journal of Applied Psychology,* January 2007, pp 128–50; and M Koo and A Fishbach, "Dynamics of Self-Regulation: How (Un)Accomplished Goal Actions Affect Motivation," *Journal of Personality and Social Psychology,* February 2008, pp 183–95.

21 As quoted in "The Best Managers," *Business Week,* January 19, 2009, p 41.

22 See G Jones, "How the Best of the Best Get Better and Better," *Harvard Business Review,* June 2008, pp 123–27; and R S Kaplan, "Reaching Your Potential," *Harvard Business Review,* July–August 2008, pp 45–49.

23 See E A Locke, "Linking Goals to Monetary Incentives," *Academy of Management Executive,* November 2004, pp 130–33.

24 E A Locke and G P Latham, *Goal Setting: A Motivational Technique That Works!* (Englewood Cliffs, NJ: Prentice Hall, 1984), p 79. Also see D C Kayes, "The Destructive Pursuit of Idealized Goals," *Organizational Dynamics,* no. 4, 2005, pp 391–401.

25 K Tyler, "One Bad Apple," *HR Magazine,* December 2004, p 85. Also see J Welch and S Welch, "Emotional Mismanagement," *BusinessWeek,* July 28, 2008, p 84.

26 Data from "500 Largest U.S. Corporations," *Fortune,* May 5, 2008, pp 114, 122.

27 As quoted in C Fishman, "Fred Smith," *Fast Company,* June 2001, p F-54.

28 C D Lee, "Feedback, Not Appraisal," *HR Magazine,* November 2006, p 111. Also see S P Kaufman, "Evaluating the CEO," *Harvard Business Review,* October 2008, pp 53–57; and A Bruzzese, "No Worker Should Tolerate Personal Criticism," *The Arizona Republic,* January 11, 2009, p EC1.

29 Both the definition of feedback and the functions of feedback are based on discussion in D R Ilgen, C D Fisher, and M S Taylor, "Consequences of Individual Feedback on Behavior in Organizations," *Journal of Applied Psychology,* August 1979, pp 349–71; and R E Kopelman, *Managing Productivity in Organizations: A Practical People-Oriented Perspective* (New York: McGraw-Hill, 1986), p 175.

30 See P C Earley, G B Northcraft, C Lee, and T R Lituchy, "Impact of Process and Outcome Feedback on the Relation of Goal Setting to Task Performance," *Academy of Management Journal,* March 1990, pp 87–105.

31 Data from A N Kluger and A DeNisi, "The Effects of Feedback Interventions on Performance: A Historical Review, a Meta-Analysis, and a Preliminary Feedback Intervention Theory," *Psychological Bulletin,* March 1996, pp 254–84. Also see G Morse, "Feedback Backlash," *Harvard Business Review,* October 2004, p 28.

32 Data from K D Harber, "Feedback to Minorities: Evidence of a Positive Bias," *Journal of Personality and Social Psychology,* March 1998, pp 622–28.

33 See D M Herold and D B Fedor. "Individuals' Interaction with Their Feedback Environment: The Role of Domain-Specific Individual Differences," in *Research in Personnel and Human Resources Management,* vol. 16, ed G R Ferris (Stamford, CT: JAI Press, 1998), pp 215–54.

34 See T Matsui, A Okkada, and T Kakuyama, "Influence of Achievement Need on Goal Setting, Performance, and Feedback Effectiveness," *Journal of Applied Psychology,* October 1982, pp 645–48.

35 S J Ashford, "Feedback-Seeking in Individual Adaptation: A Resource Perspective," *Academy of Management Journal,* September 1986, pp 465–87. Also see D B Fedor, R B Rensvold, and S M Adams, "An Investigation of Factors Expected to Affect Feedback Seeking: A Longitudinal Field Study," *Personnel Psychology,* Winter 1992, pp 779–805; M F Sully De Luque and S M Sommer, "The Impact of Culture on Feedback-Seeking Behavior: An Integrated Model and Propositions," *Academy of Management Review,* October 2000,

pp 829–49; and K J Sulkowicz, "Analyze This," *Business Week,* May 4, 2009, p 16.

36 See D B Turban and T W Dougherty, "Role of Protege Personality in Receipt of Mentoring and Career Success," *Academy of Management Journal,* June 1994, pp 688–702.

37 See B D Bannister, "Performance Outcome Feedback and Attributional Feedback: Interactive Effects on Recipient Responses," *Journal of Applied Psychology,* May 1986, pp 203–10; J B Vancouver and E C Tischner, "The Effect of Feedback Sign on Task Performance Depends on Self-Concept Discrepancies," *Journal of Applied Psychology,* December 2004, pp 1092–98; and C Unkelbach, K Fielder, M Bayer, M Stegmuller, and D Danner, "Why Positive Information Is Processed Faster: The Density Hypothesis," *Journal of Personality and Social Psychology,* July 2008, pp 36–49.

38 For complete details, see P M Podsakoff and J L Farh, "Effects of Feedback Sign and Credibility on Goal Setting and Task Performance," *Organizational Behavior and Human Decision Processes,* August 1989, pp 45–67.

39 W S Silver, T R Mitchell, and M E Gist, "Responses to Successful and Unsuccessful Performance: The Moderating Effect of Self-Efficacy on the Relationship between Performance and Attributions," *Organizational Behavior and Human Decision Processes,* June 1995, p 297. Also see A P Tolli and A M Schmidt, "The Role of Feedback, Causal Attributions, and Self-Efficacy in Goal Revision," *Journal of Applied Psychology,* May 2008, pp 692–701.

40 J M Kouzes and B Z Posner, *Credibility: How Leaders Gain and Lose It, Why People Demand It* (San Francisco, CA: Jossey-Bass, 1993), p 25. For research support, see A J Kinicki, G E Prussia, B Wu, and F M McKee-Ryan, "A Covariance Structure Analysis of Employees' Response to Performance Feedback," *Journal of Applied Psychology,* December 2004, pp 1057–69. Also see J Pfeffer, *What Were They Thinking? Unconventional Wisdom about Management* (Boston: Harvard Business School Press, 2007), pp 104–6.

41 See K Leung, S Su, and M W Morris, "When Is Criticism *Not* Constructive? The Roles of Fairness Perceptions and Dispositional Attributions in Employee Acceptance of Critical Supervisory Feedback," *Human Relations,* September 2001, pp 1123–54; and D Heath and C Heath, "I Love You, Now What?" *Fast Company,* October 2008, pp 95–96.

42 Based on discussion in Ilgen, Fisher, and Taylor, "Consequences of Individual Feedback on Behavior in Organizations," pp 367–68. Also see A M O'Leary-Kelly, "The Influence of Group Feedback on Individual Group Member Response," in *Research in Personnel and Human Resources Management,* vol. 16, ed G R Ferris (Stamford, CT: JAI Press, 1998), pp 255–94.

43 See P C Earley, "Computer-Generated Performance Feedback in the Magazine-Subscription Industry," *Organizational Behavior and Human Decision Processes,* February 1988, pp 50–64.

44 See M De Gregorio and C D Fisher, "Providing Performance Feedback: Reactions to Alternate Methods," *Journal of Management,* December 1988, pp 605–16.

45 For details, see R A Baron, "Countering the Effects of Destructive Criticism: The Relative Efficacy of Four Interventions," *Journal of Applied Psychology,* June 1990, pp 235–45. Also see A Maingault, "Q: I'm Trying to Help a Manager Who Inadvertently Destroys Morale When Providing Criticism," *HR Magazine,* May 2008, p 36.

46 C O Longenecker and D A Gioia, "The Executive Appraisal Paradox," *Academy of Management Executive,* May 1992, p 18.

47 See M Carson, "Saying It Like It Isn't: The Pros and Cons of 360-Degree Feedback," *Business Horizons,* September–October 2006, pp 395–402; T van Rensburg and G Prideaux, "Turning Professionals into Managers Using Multisource Feedback," *Journal of Management Development,* no. 6, 2006, pp 561–71; and J T Polzer, "Making Diverse Teams Click," *Harvard Business Review,* July–August 2008, pp 20–21.

48 J W Smither, M London, and R R Reilly, "Does Performance Improve Following Multisource Feedback? A Theoretical Model, Meta-Analysis, and Review of Empirical Findings," *Personnel Psychology,* Spring 2005, p 33. Also see F Shipper, R C Hoffman, and D M Rotondo, "Does the 360 Feedback Process Create Actionable Knowledge Equally across Cultures?" *Academy of Management Learning and Education,* March 2007, pp 33–50.

49 D Jones, "It's Lonely—and Thin-Skinned—at the Top," *USA Today,* January 16, 2007, p 1B.

50 D E Coates, "Don't Tie 360 Feedback to Pay," *Training,* September 1998, pp 68–78. Also see the second Q&A in J Welch and S Welch, "The Importance of Being There," *Business Week,* April 16, 2007, p 92.

51 For more on coaching, see P Parker, D T Hall, and K E Kram, "Peer Coaching: A Relational Process for Accelerating Career Learning," *Academy of Management Learning and Education,* December 2008, pp 487–503; and D Coutu and C Kauffman, "What Can Coaches Do for You?" *Harvard Business Review,* January 2009, pp 91–97.

52 See S N Kaplan, "Are U.S. CEOs Overpaid?" *Academy of Management Perspectives,* May 2008, pp 5–20; J C Bogle, "Reflections on CEO Compensation," *Academy of Management Perspectives,* May 2008, pp 21–25; J Welch and S Welch, "CEO Pay: No Easy Answer," *Business Week,* July 14–21, 2008, p 106; and S Miller, "U.S. Top Executives' Total Pay Down," *HR Magazine,* October 2008, p 26.

53 "The Stat," *Business Week,* October 4, 2004, p 16.

54 See, for example, S Kerr with G Rifkin, *Reward Systems: Does Yours Measure Up?* (Boston: Harvard Business Press, 2009).

55 See L Kerschner, "A Farmer's Labor of Love," *Newsweek,* April 28, 2008, p 17; G Gloeckler, "Here Come the Millennials," *Business Week,* November 24, 2008, pp 46–50; and R Eisenberger and J Aselage, "Incremental Effects of Reward on Experienced Performance Pressure: Positive Outcomes for Intrinsic Interest and Creativity," *Journal of Organizational Behavior,* January 2009, pp 95–117.

56 List adapted from J L Pearce and R H Peters, "A Contradictory Norms View of Employer–Employee Exchange," *Journal of Management,* Spring 1985, pp 19–30.

57 B Hindo, "Rewiring Westinghouse," *Business Week,* May 19, 2008, p 49. Also see "Delta, Northwest Pilots Can't Agree," *USA Today,* March 18, 2008, p 2B; M Orey, "Will Cravath Swaine Turn Off the Meter?" *Business Week,* December 8, 2008, p 20; and R R Hastings, "Length-of-Service Awards Becoming More Personal," *HR Magazine,* December 2008, pp 43–47.

58 R Levering and M Moskowitz, "100 Best Companies to Work For: And the Winners Are . . .," *Fortune,* February 2, 2009, pp 67–78.

59 See K W Thomas, *Intrinsic Motivation at Work: Building Energy and Commitment* (San Francisco, CA: Berrett-Koehler

Publishers, 2000). Also see A M Grant, "Does Intrinsic Motivation Fuel the Prosocial Fire? Motivational Synergy in Predicting Persistence, Performance, and Productivity," *Journal of Applied Psychology,* January 2008, pp 48–58.

[60] See E L Deci and R M Ryan, "The 'What' and 'Why' of Goal Pursuits: Human Needs and Self-Determination of Behavior," *Psychological Inquiry,* December 2000, pp 227–68.

[61] This study is summarized by S Ellingwood, "On a Mission," *Gallup Management Journal,* Winter 2001, pp 6–7.

[62] R Randazzo, "Nuclear Watchdog," *The Arizona Republic,* November 2, 2008, p D1.

[63] M Littman, "Best Bosses Tell All," *Working Woman,* October 2000, p 55.

[64] A Carter, "Lighting a Fire under Campbell," *BusinessWeek,* December 4, 2006, p 96.

[65] D R Spitzer, "Power Rewards: Rewards That Really Motivate," *Management Review,* May 1996, p 47. Also see S Kerr, "An Academy Classic: On the Folly of Rewarding A, while Hoping for B," *Academy of Management Executive,* February 1995, pp 7–14.

[66] List adapted from discussion in Spitzer, "Power Rewards," pp 45–50. Also see W F Cascio, "The High Cost of Low Wages," *Harvard Business Review,* December 2006, p 23; and S Miller, "Satisfaction with Pay, Benefits Falling," *HR Magazine,* January 2007, pp 38–39.

[67] See J Stinson, "How Much Do You Make? It'd Be No Secret in Scandinavia," *USA Today,* June 19, 2008, p 8A; A Collis, "Q: What Are Total Rewards Strategies?" *HR Magazine,* August 2008, p 34; and L Grensing-Pophal, "And Now, a Word about Salary Increases," *HR Magazine,* November 2008, pp 93–98.

[68] "Performance-Based Pay Plans," *HR Magazine,* June 2004, p 22. Also see J O'Donnell, "Slow Times Mean Pay Cuts for Many," *USA Today,* June 2, 2008, pp 1B–2B; R Zeidner, "Bright Future for Performance Pay," *HR Magazine,* December 2008, p 12; and R Zeidner, "Falling Stock Values Erode Bonus Pool," *HR Magazine,* January 2009, p 27.

[69] For arguments against incentive compensation, see B W Heineman Jr, "The Fatal Flaw in Pay for Performance," *Harvard Business Review,* June 2008, pp 31, 34; W F Cascio and P Cappelli, "Lessons from the Financial Services Crisis," *HR Magazine,* January 2009, pp 46–50; and D Heath and C Heath, "The Curse of Incentives," *Fast Company,* February 2009, pp 48–49.

[70] Data from D Kiley, "Crafty Basket Makers Cut Downtime, Waste," *USA Today,* May 10, 2001, p 3B.

[71] N J Perry, "Here Come Richer, Riskier Pay Plans," *Fortune,* December 19, 1988, p 51. Also see J McGregor, "Merit Pay? Not Exactly," *BusinessWeek,* September 22, 2008, p 17; J Spolsky, "Employees Will Always Game Incentive Plans," *Inc.,* October 2008, pp 85–86; and K Wehrum, "The Gift That Stops Giving—Dealing with an Empty Bonus Pool," *Inc.,* November 2008, pp 52, 54.

[72] Data from M Bloom and G T Milkovich, "Relationships among Risk, Incentive Pay, and Organizational Performance," *Academy of Management Journal,* June 1998, pp 283–97.

[73] For details, see G D Jenkins Jr, N Gupta, A Mitra, and J D Shaw, "Are Financial Incentives Related to Performance? A Meta-Analytic Review of Empirical Research," *Journal of Applied Psychology,* October 1998, pp 777–87. Also see S J Peterson and F Luthans, "The Impact of Financial and Nonfinancial Incentives on Business-Unit Outcomes over Time," *Journal of Applied Psychology,* January 2006, pp 156–65.

[74] See M J Mandel, "Those Fat Bonuses Don't Seem to Boost Performance," *BusinessWeek,* January 8, 1990, p 26; S F O'Byrne and S D Young, "Why Executive Pay Is Failing," *Harvard Business Review,* June 2006, p 28; and A Pomeroy, "Pay for Performance Is Working, Says a New Study," *HR Magazine,* January 2007, pp 14, 16.

[75] Based on discussion in R Ricklefs, "Whither the Payoff on Sales Commissions?" *The Wall Street Journal,* June 6, 1990, p B1. Also see S Greco, "Fighting the Sales Force Blues," *Inc.,* September 2008, pp 47–49.

[76] "Performance-Based Pay Plans," p 22.

[77] See "Inc. Guidebook: Performance Pay," *Inc.,* December 2008, p 2; N Byrnes, "A Steely Resolve," *BusinessWeek,* April 6, 2009, p 54; and S Lackey, "Fill Those Unpopular Shifts," *HR Magazine,* April 2009, pp 63–66.

[78] See B E Litzky, K A Eddleston, and D L Kidder, "The Good, the Bad, and the Misguided: How Managers Inadvertently Encourage Deviant Behaviors," *Academy of Management Perspectives,* February 2006, pp 91–103; and M Conlin, "The Case for Unequal Perks," *BusinessWeek,* March 23–30, 2009, pp 54–55.

[79] See E L Thorndike, *Educational Psychology: The Psychology of Learning, Vol. II* (New York: Columbia University Teachers College, 1913).

[80] Discussion of an early behaviorist who influenced Skinner's work can be found in P J Kreshel, "John B Watson at J Walter Thompson: The Legitimation of 'Science' in Advertising," *Journal of Advertising,* no. 2, 1990, pp 49–59. Recent discussions involving behaviorism include M R Ruiz, "B F Skinner's Radical Behaviorism: Historical Misconstructions and Grounds for Feminist Reconstructions," *Psychology of Women Quarterly,* June 1995, pp 161–79; J A Nevin, "Behavioral Economics and Behavioral Momentum," *Journal of the Experimental Analysis of Behavior,* November 1995, pp 385–95; and H Rachlin, "Can We Leave Cognition to Cognitive Psychologists? Comments on an Article by George Loewenstein," *Organizational Behavior and Human Decision Processes,* March 1996, pp 296–99.

[81] For discussion, see J W Donahoe, "The Unconventional Wisdom of B F Skinner: The Analysis-Interpretation Distinction," *Journal of the Experimental Analysis of Behavior,* September 1993, pp 453–56.

[82] See B F Skinner, *The Behavior of Organisms* (New York: Appleton-Century-Crofts, 1938).

[83] For modern approaches to respondent behavior, see B Azar, "Classical Conditioning Could Link Disorders and Brain Dysfunction, Researchers Suggest," *APA Monitor,* March 1999, p 17.

[84] For interesting discussions of Skinner and one of his students, see M B Gilbert and T F Gilbert. "What Skinner Gave Us," *Training,* September 1991, pp 42–48; and "HRD Pioneer Gilbert Leaves a Pervasive Legacy," *Training,* January 1996, p 14. Also see F Luthans and R Kreitner, *Organizational Behavior Modification and Beyond: An Operant and Social Learning Approach* (Glenview, IL: Scott, Foresman, 1985).

[85] Praise and recognition are explored in K Painter, "Stepping Up the Gratitude," *USA Today*, April 24, 2008, p 6D; H Dolezalek, "Good Job!" *Training,* July–August 2008, pp 32–34; and C Elton, "Carrots in a Crisis," *Training,* January 2009, p 12.

86 R Levering and M Moskowitz, "100 Best Companies to Work For: And the Winners Are . . .," *Fortune,* February 2, 2009, pp 67–78.

87 Research on punishment is reported in L E Atwater, D A Waldman, J A Carey, and P Cartier, "Recipient and Observer Reactions to Discipline: Are Managers Experiencing Wishful Thinking?" *Journal of Organizational Behavior,* May 2001, pp 249–70; and T K Peng and M F Peterson, "Nation, Demographic, and Attitudinal Boundary Conditions on Leader Social Rewards and Punishments in Local Governments," *Journal of Organizational Behavior,* January 2008, pp 95–117.

88 See C B Ferster and B F Skinner, *Schedules of Reinforcement* (New York: Appleton-Century-Crofts, 1957).

89 See L M Saari and G P Latham, "Employee Reactions to Continuous and Variable Ratio Reinforcement Schedules Involving a Monetary Incentive," *Journal of Applied Psychology,* August 1982, pp 506–8.

90 P Brinkley-Rogers and R Collier, "Along the Colorado, the Money's Flowing," *The Arizona Republic,* March 4, 1990, p A12.

91 J M O'Brien, "Zappos Knows How to Kick It," "*Fortune,* February 2, 2009, p 58.

92 K Gurchiek, "'New Collar' Workers Choose Hourly Careers," *HR Magazine,* September 2008, p 24.

93 See D Jones, "Training Workers the SeaWorld Way," *USA Today,* August 21, 2006, p 3B; J Yabroff, "How to Train a Husband," *Newsweek,* February 18, 2008, pp 58–59; and D Heath and C Heath, "Your Boss Is a Monkey," *Fast Company,* April 2008, pp 75–76.

94 Data from K L Alexander, "Continental Airlines Soars to New Heights," *USA Today,* January 23, 1996, p 4B; and M Knez and D Simester, "Making Across-the-Board Incentives Work," *Harvard Business Review,* February 2002, pp 16–17.

95 K Rockwood, "The Employee Whisperer," *Fast Company,* November 2008, pp 72, 74.

96 Reprinted by permission of *Harvard Business Review.* Excerpt from "Working in the Gray Zone," by M Anteby, May 2008. Copyright 2008 by the Harvard Business School Publishing Corporation; all rights reserved. Also see D J Ketchen Jr, C W Craighead, and M R Buckley, "Time Bandits: How They Are Created, Why They Are Tolerated, and What Can Be Done about Them," *Business Horizons,* March–April 2008, pp 141–49.

CHAPTER 10

1 From R Zeidner, "Employee Networking," *HR Magazine,* November 2008, pp 58–60. Reprinted with permission of Society for Human Resource Management.

2 Drawn from C O Longenecker, M J Neubert, and L S Fink, "Causes and Consequences of Managerial Failure in Rapidly Changing Organizations," *Business Horizons,* March–April 2007, pp 145–55.

3 See P S Adler and S Kwon, "Social Capital: Prospects for a New Concept," *Academy of Management Review,* January 2002, pp 17–40; and J Savage and S Kanazawa, "Social Capital and the Human Psyche: Why Is Social Life 'Capital'?" *Sociological Theory,* September 2004, pp 504–24.

4 D Goleman, *Social Intelligence: The New Science of Human Relationships* (New York: Bantam, 2006); and D Goleman and R Boyatzis, "Social Intelligence and the Biology of Leadership," *Harvard Business Review,* September 2008, pp 74–81.

5 See D Zohar and O Tenne-Gazit, "Transformational Leadership and Group Interaction as Climate Antecedents: A Social Network Analysis," *Journal of Applied Psychology,* July 2008, pp 744–57; and A M Grant, J E Dutton, and B D Rosso, "Giving Commitment: Employee Support Programs and the Prosocial Sensemaking Process," *Academy of Management Journal,* October 2008, pp 898–918.

6 This definition is based in part on one found in D Horton Smith, "A Parsimonious Definition of 'Group': Toward Conceptual Clarity and Scientific Utility," *Sociological Inquiry,* Spring 1967, pp 141–67.

7 E H Schein, *Organizational Psychology,* 3rd ed (Englewood Cliffs, NJ: Prentice Hall, 1980), p 145.

8 For related research, see H H M Tse and M T Dasborough, "A Study of Exchange and Emotions in Team Member Relationships," *Group and Organization Management,* April 2008, pp 194–215.

9 M R della Cava, "Jobless? Join the Club," *USA Today,* December 7, 2008, pp 1D–2D.

10 J Castro, "Mazda U.," *Time,* October 20, 1986, p 65.

11 See M Bartiromo, "Chris DeWolf on MySpace's Widening Web of Users," *BusinessWeek,* June 2, 2008, pp 25–26; and S Kapner, "Facebook Tries to Sell Its Friends Again," *Fortune,* February 16, 2009, p 24.

12 www.pcmag.com/encyclopedia_term/0,2542,t=social+networking&i=55316,00.asp, accessed February 7, 2009.

13 Data from S Jayson, "A Few Wrinkles Are Etching Facebook, Other Social Sites," *USA Today,* January 15, 2009, p 9D.

14 See M Chafkin, "Anything Could Happen," *Inc.,* March 2008, pp 116–23.

15 See B Roberts, "Social Networking at the Office," *HR Magazine,* March 2008, pp 81–83; D Kirkpatrick, "Web 2.0 Gets Over Its Goofing-Off Phase," *Fortune,* March 31, 2008, pp 32, 34; A M Kleinbaum and M L Tushman, "Managing Corporate Social Networks," *Harvard Business Review,* July–August 2008, pp 26–27; and J Swartz, "Social Networks Go to Work," *USA Today,* October 8, 2008, p 5B.

16 Reprinted from J Welch and S Welch, "From the Old, Something New," November 20, 2006, issue of *BusinessWeek* by special permission. Copyright © 2006 by The McGraw-Hill Companies, Inc.

17 For an instructive overview of five different theories of group development, see J P Wanous, A E Reichers, and S D Malik, "Organizational Socialization and Group Development: Toward an Integrative Perspective," *Academy of Management Review,* October 1984, pp 670–83.

18 See B W Tuckman, "Developmental Sequence in Small Groups," *Psychological Bulletin,* June 1965, pp 384–99; and B W Tuckman and M A C Jensen, "Stages of Small-Group Development Revisited," *Group & Organization Studies,* December 1977, pp 419–27.

19 See G A Ballinger and F D Schoorman, "Individual Reactions to Leadership Succession in Workgroups," *Academy of Management Review,* January 2007, pp 118–36.

20 For related research, see J C Biesanz, S G West, and A Millevoi, "What Do You Learn about Someone over Time? The Relationship between Length of Acquaintance and

Consensus and Self-Other Agreement in Judgments of Personality," *Journal of Personality and Social Psychology,* January 2007, pp 119–35; and R I Swaab, K W Phillips, D Diermeier, and V H Medvec, "The Pros and Cons of Dyadic Side Conversations in Small Groups," *Small Group Research,* June 2008, pp 372–90.

21 Based on B L Riddle, C M Anderson, and M M Martin, "Small Group Socialization Scale: Development and Validity," *Small Group Research,* October 2000, pp 554–72; and M Van Vugt and C M Hart, "Social Identity as Social Glue: The Origins of Group Loyalty," *Journal of Personality and Social Psychology,* April 2004, pp 585–98.

22 L N Jewell and H J Reitz, *Group Effectiveness in Organizations* (Glenview, IL: Scott, Foresman, 1981), p 19.

23 Based on J F McGrew, J G Bilotta, and J M Deeney, "Software Team Formation and Decay: Extending the Standard Model for Small Groups," *Small Group Research,* April 1999, pp 209–34.

24 Ibid., p 232.

25 Ibid., p 231.

26 D Davies and B C Kuypers, "Group Development and Interpersonal Feedback," *Group & Organization Studies,* June 1985, p 194.

27 Ibid., pp 184–208.

28 C J G Gersick, "Marking Time: Predictable Transitions in Task Groups," *Academy of Management Journal,* June 1989, pp 274–309.

29 D K Carew, E Parisi-Carew, and K H Blanchard, "Group Development and Situational Leadership: A Model for Managing Groups," *Training and Development Journal,* June 1986, pp 48–49. For evidence linking leadership and group effectiveness, see G R Bushe and A L Johnson, "Contextual and Internal Variables Affecting Task Group Outcomes in Organizations," *Group & Organization Studies,* December 1989, pp 462–82.

30 See D McCullough, "Timeless Leadership: The Great Leadership Lessons Don't Change," *Harvard Business Review,* March 2008, pp 45–49; L Freifeld, "Leading the Way," *Training,* May 2008, p 6; and J Spolsky, "My Style of Servant Leadership," *Inc.,* December 2008, pp 77–78.

31 See A T Church, et al., "Culture, Cross-Role Consistency, and Adjustment: Testing Trait and Cultural Psychology Perspectives," *Journal of Personality and Social Psychology,* September 2008, pp 739–55.

32 G Graen, "Role-Making Processes within Complex Organizations," in *Handbook of Industrial and Organizational Psychology,* ed M D Dunnette (Chicago: Rand-McNally, 1976), p 1201.

33 Data from D S Chiaburu and D A Harrison, "Do Peers Make the Place? Conceptual Synthesis and Meta-Analysis of Coworker Effects on Perceptions, Attitudes, OCBs, and Performance," *Journal of Applied Psychology,* September 2008, pp 1082–1103.

34 G L Miles, "Doug Danforth's Plan to Put Westinghouse in the 'Winner's Circle,'" *BusinessWeek,* July 28, 1986, p 75.

35 Schein, *Organizational Psychology,* p 198.

36 Ibid. The relationship between interrole conflict and turnover is explored in P W Hom and A J Kinicki, "Toward a Greater Understanding of How Dissatisfaction Drives Employee Turnover," *Academy of Management Journal,* October 2001, pp 975–87. Also see B E Ashforth, C T Kulik, and M A Tomiuk,

"How Service Agents Manage the Person-Role Interface," *Group and Organization Management,* February 2008, pp 5–45.

37 Data from M Healy and K Simmons, "Kitchen Duties," *USA Today,* November 13, 2008, p 1D. Also see C Arnst, "Are There Too Many Women Doctors?" *BusinessWeek,* April 28, 2008, p 104; and S Jayson, "Gender Roles See a 'Conflict' Shift," *USA Today,* March 26, 2009, p 1A.

38 See J Porter, "Using Ex-Cons to Scare MBAs Straight," *BusinessWeek,* May 5, 2008, p 58; S J Reynolds, "Moral Attentiveness: Who Pays Attention to the Moral Aspects of Life?" *Journal of Applied Psychology,* September 2008, pp 1027–41; and J DesJardins, *An Introduction to Business Ethics,* 3rd ed (New York: McGraw-Hill, 2009).

39 Schein, *Organizational Psychology,* p 198. Four types of role ambiguity are discussed in M A Eys and A V Carron, "Role Ambiguity, Task Cohesion, and Task Self-Efficacy," *Small Group Research,* June 2001, pp 356–73.

40 Drawn from M Peterson et al., "Role Conflict, Ambiguity, and Overload: A 21-Nation Study," *Academy of Management Journal,* April 1995, pp 429–52.

41 Based on Y Fried, H A Ben-David, R B Tiegs, N Avital, and U Yeverechyahu, "The Interactive Effect of Role Conflict and Role Ambiguity on Job Performance," *Journal of Occupational and Organizational Psychology,* March 1998, pp 19–27.

42 R R Blake and J Srygley Mouton, "Don't Let Group Norms Stifle Creativity," *Personnel,* August 1985, p 28.

43 See R Youngreen and C D Moore, "The Effects of Status Violations on Hierarchy and Influence in Groups," *Small Group Research,* October 2008, pp 569–87.

44 A Dunkin, "Pepsi's Marketing Magic: Why Nobody Does It Better," *BusinessWeek,* February 10, 1986, p 52.

45 For related reading, see R L Paetzold, R L Dipboye, and K D Elsbach, "A New Look at Stigmatization in and of Organizations," *Academy of Management Review,* January 2008, pp 186–93; and D L Ferris, D J Brown, J W Berry, and H Lian, "The Development and Validation of the Workplace Ostracism Scale," *Journal of Applied Psychology,* November 2008, pp 1348–66.

46 D C Feldman, "The Development and Enforcement of Group Norms," *Academy of Management Review,* January 1984, pp 50–52. Also see S Maitlis and T B Lawrence, "Triggers and Enablers of Sensegiving in Organizations," *Academy of Management Journal,* February 2007, pp 57–84.

47 Feldman, "The Development and Enforcement of Group Norms." Also see D Abrams, G R de Moura, J M Marques, and P Hutchison, "Innovation Credit: When Can Leaders Oppose Their Group's Norms?" *Journal of Personality and Social Psychology,* September 2008, pp 662–78.

48 See R G Netemeyer, M W Johnston, and S Burton, "Analysis of Role Conflict and Role Ambiguity in a Structural Equations Framework," *Journal of Applied Psychology,* April 1990, pp 148–57; and G W McGee, C E Ferguson Jr, and A Seers, "Role Conflict and Role Ambiguity: Do the Scales Measure These Two Constructs?" *Journal of Applied Psychology,* October 1989, pp 815–18.

49 See S E Jackson and R S Schuler, "A Meta-Analysis and Conceptual Critique of Research on Role Ambiguity and Role Conflict in Work Settings," *Organizational Behavior and Human Decision Processes,* August 1985, pp 16–78.

50 Based on C S Crandall, A Eshleman, and L O'Brien, "Social Norms and the Expression and Suppression of

Prejudice: The Struggle for Internalization," *Journal of Personality and Social Psychology,* March 2002, pp 359–78. Also see L Ashburn-Nardo, K A Morris, and S A Goodwin, "The Confronting Prejudiced Responses (CPR) Model: Applying CPR in Organizations," *Academy of Management Learning and Education,* September 2008, pp 332–42.

[51] See B Weber and G Hertel, "Motivation Gains of Inferior Group Members: A Meta-Analytic Review," *Journal of Personality and Social Psychology,* December 2007, pp 973–93.

[52] See K D Benne and P Sheats, "Functional Roles of Group Members," *Journal of Social Issues,* Spring 1948, pp 41–49. For an alternative typology, see T V Mumford, C H Van Iddekinge, F P Morgeson, and M A Campion, "The Team Role Test: Development and Validation of a Team Role Knowledge Situational Judgment Test," *Journal of Applied Psychology,* March 2008, pp 250–67.

[53] See G P Latham and E A Locke, "Enhancing the Benefits and Overcoming the Pitfalls of Goal Setting," *Organizational Dynamics,* no. 4, 2006, pp 332–40.

[54] A Zander, "The Value of Belonging to a Group in Japan," *Small Group Behavior,* February 1983, pp 7–8. Also see N J Adler with A Gundersen, *International Dimensions of Organizational Behavior,* 5th ed (Mason, OH: Thomson South-Western, 2008), ch 5.

[55] Data from M Vella, "InData," *BusinessWeek,* April 28, 2008, p 58. Also see P R Laughlin, E C Hatch, J S Silver, and L Boh, "Groups Perform Better Than the Best Individuals on Letters-to-Numbers Problems: Effects of Group Size," *Journal of Personality and Social Psychology,* April 2006, pp 644–51; and J L Yang, "The Power of Number 4.6," *Fortune,* June 12, 2006, p 122.

[56] For example, see B Grofman, S L Feld, and G Owen, "Group Size and the Performance of a Composite Group Majority: Statistical Truths and Empirical Results," *Organizational Behavior and Human Performance,* June 1984, pp 350–59.

[57] See P Yetton and P Bottger, "The Relationships among Group Size, Member Ability, Social Decision Schemes, and Performance," *Organizational Behavior and Human Performance,* October 1983, pp 145–59.

[58] This copyrighted exercise may be found in J Hall, "Decisions, Decisions, Decisions," *Psychology Today,* November 1971, pp 51–54, 86, 88.

[59] Yetton and Bottger, "The Relationships among Group Size, Member Ability, Social Decision Schemes, and Performance," p 158.

[60] Based on R B Gallupe, A R Dennis, W H Cooper, J S Valacich, L M Bastianutti, and J F Nunamaker Jr, "Electronic Brainstorming and Group Size," *Academy of Management Journal,* June 1992, pp 350–69. Also see J Barauh and P B Paulus, "Effects of Training on Idea Generation in Groups," *Small Group Research,* October 2008, pp 523–41.

[61] Data from E Salas, D Rozell, B Mullen, and J E Driskell, "The Effect of Team Building on Performance: An Integration," *Small Group Research,* June 1999, pp 309–29.

[62] Drawn from B Mullen, C Symons, L-T Hu, and E Salas, "Group Size, Leadership Behavior, and Subordinate Satisfaction," *Journal of General Psychology,* April 1989, pp 155–69.

[63] D S Carlson, K M Kacmar, and D Whitten, "What Men Think They Know about Executive Women," *Harvard Business Review,* September 2006, p 28. Also see T A Judge and B A Livingston, "Is the Gap More Than Gender? A Longitudinal Analysis of Gender, Gender Role Orientation, and Earnings," *Journal of Applied Psychology,* September 2008, pp 994–1012.

[64] See K Tyler, "Sign in the Name of Love," *HR Magazine,* February 2008, pp 40–43; K Deveny, "We're Bossy—And Proud of It," *Newsweek,* June 30, 2008, p 58; G Garcia, "Men: The New Misfits," *Fortune,* October 13, 2008, pp 185–86; and J Wegge, C Roth, B Neubach, K Schmidt, and R Kanfer, "Age and Gender Diversity as Determinants of Performance and Health in a Public Organization: The Role of Task Complexity and Group Size," *Journal of Applied Psychology,* November 2008, pp 1301–13.

[65] G L Stewart, S L Dustin, M R Barrick, and T C Darnold, "Exploring the Handshake in Employment Interviews," *Journal of Applied Psychology,* September 2008, p 1145.

[66] See L Smith-Lovin and C Brody, "Interruptions in Group Discussions: The Effects of Gender and Group Composition," *American Sociological Review,* June 1989, pp 424–35.

[67] L Karakowsky, K McBey, and D L Miller, "Gender, Perceived Competence, and Power Displays: Examining Verbal Interruptions in a Group Context," *Small Group Research,* August 2004, p 407.

[68] E M Ott, "Effects of the Male–Female Ratio at Work," *Psychology of Women Quarterly,* March 1989, p 53.

[69] "Daily Downer," *Training,* April 2005, p 12.

[70] M Elias, "15% of Female Veterans Tell of Sexual Trauma," *USA Today,* October 28, 2008, p 6D.

[71] J L Berdahl and C Moore, "Workplace Harassment: Double Jeopardy for Minority Women," *Journal of Applied Psychology,* March 2006, p 426.

[72] See S Jayson, "Abusive Teen Dating Behavior Goes High-Tech," *USA Today,* February 8, 2007, p 1D; S Jayson, "Guys Try to Read Society's Road Map for Behavior," *USA Today,* August 26, 2008, p 9D; and J Kornblum, "Bullying Devastates Lives," *USA Today,* November 19, 2008, p 7D.

[73] Data from B A Gutek, A Groff Cohen, and A M Konrad, "Predicting Social-Sexual Behavior at Work: A Contact Hypothesis," *Academy of Management Journal,* September 1990, pp 560–77. Also see S Jayson, "Infidelity Today Has a New Face," *USA Today,* July 1, 2008, pp 1D–2D.

[74] Data from M Rotundo, D Nguyen, and P R Sackett, "A Meta-Analytic Review of Gender Differences in Perceptions of Sexual Harassment," *Journal of Applied Psychology,* October 2001, pp 914–22. Also see N A Bowling and T A Beehr, "Workplace Harassment from the Victim's Perspective: A Theoretical Model and Meta-Analysis," *Journal of Applied Psychology,* September 2006, pp 998–1012; and J A Segal, "I Did It, But. . .," *HR Magazine,* March 2008, pp 91–95.

[75] S J South, C M Bonjean, W T Markham, and J Corder, "Female Labor Force Participation and the Organizational Experiences of Male Workers," *Sociological Quarterly,* Summer 1983, p 378.

[76] R R Hirschfeld, M H Jordan, H S Field, W F Giles, and A A Armenakis, "Teams' Female Representation and Perceived Potency as Inputs to Team Outcomes in a Predominantly Male Field Setting," *Personnel Psychology,* Winter 2005, p 893. Also see M J Pearsall, A P J Ellis, and J M Evans, "Unlocking the

Effects of Gender Faultlines on Team Creativity: Is Activation the Key?" *Journal of Applied Psychology,* January 2008, pp 225–34; and A M Konrad, V Kramer, and S Erkut, "The Impact of Three or More Women on Corporate Boards," *Organizational Dynamics,* April–June 2008, pp 145–64.

[77] B T Thornton, "Sexual Harassment, 1: Discouraging It in the Work Place," *Personnel,* April 1986, p 18. Also see R K Robinson, G M Franklin, and W J Davis, "Sexual Harassment Redux," *Business Horizons,* July–August 2004, pp 3–5; J W Janove, "Conclude and Communicate," *HR Magazine,* August 2004, pp 131–34; T O McCarthy, "Sexual Conduct: Equal Abuse Unequal Harm," *HR Magazine,* January 2005, pp 93–94; and J A Segal, "Deconstructing Documentation," *HR Magazine,* June 2006, pp 175–86.

[78] Data from T Galvin, "2001 Industry Report," *Training,* October 2001, pp 41, 54. Also see J Deschenaux, "EEOC: Train Managers on Harassment," *HR Magazine,* May 2008, p 26.

[79] See M Elias, "Do We All Have a Dark Side?" *USA Today,* March 14, 2007, p 7D; and G D Reeder, A E Monroe, and J B Pryor, "Impressions of Milgram's Obedient Teachers: Situational Cues Inform Inferences about Motives and Traits," *Journal of Personality and Social Psychology,* July 2008, pp 1–17.

[80] For additional information, see S E Asch, *Social Psychology* (Englewood Cliffs, NJ: Prentice Hall, 1952), ch 16.

[81] See T P Williams and S Sogon, "Group Composition and Conforming Behavior in Japanese Students," *Japanese Psychological Research,* no. 4, 1984, pp 231–34; T Amir, "The Asch Conformity Effect: A Study in Kuwait," *Social Behavior and Personality,* no. 2, 1984, pp 187–90; and Y Takano and S Sogon, "Are Japanese More Collectivistic Than Americans," *Journal of Cross-Cultural Psychology,* May 2008, pp 237–50.

[82] Data from R Bond and P B Smith, "Culture and Conformity: A Meta-Analysis of Studies Using Asch's (1952b, 1956) Line Judgment Task," *Psychological Bulletin,* January 1996, pp 111–37.

[83] J L Roberts and E Thomas, "Enron's Dirty Laundry," *Newsweek,* March 11, 2002, p 26. Also see G Farrell, "Pride at Root of Skilling's Downfall," *USA Today,* October 24, 2006, p 3B.

[84] See K R Morrison and D T Miller, "Distinguishing between Silent and Vocal Minorities: Not All Deviants Feel Marginal," *Journal of Personality and Social Psychology,* May 2008, pp 871–82; and P Bordia, S L D Restubog, and R L Tang, "When Employees Strike Back: Investigating Mediating Mechanisms between Psychological Contract Breach and Workplace Deviance," *Journal of Applied Psychology,* September 2008, pp 1104–17.

[85] For a comprehensive update on groupthink, see the entire February–March 1998 issue of *Organizational Behavior and Human Decision Processes* (12 articles). Also see W Schiano and J W Weiss, "Y2K All Over Again: How Groupthink Permeates IS and Compromises Security," *Business Horizons,* March–April 2006, pp 115–25; D H Freedman, "Leadership Lessons," *Inc.,* March 2008, p 26; and J Carey, "The Unwisdom of Crowds," *BusinessWeek,* May 11, 2009, pp 69–70.

[86] I L Janis, *Groupthink,* 2nd ed (Boston: Houghton Mifflin, 1982), p 9. Alternative models are discussed in K Granstrom and D Stiwne, "A Bipolar Model of Groupthink: An Expansion of Janis's Concept," *Small Group Research,* February 1998, pp 32–56; and A R Flippen, "Understanding Groupthink from a Self-Regulatory Perspective," *Small Group Research,* April 1999, pp 139–65.

[87] Ibid. For an alternative model, see R J Aldag and S Riggs Fuller, "Beyond Fiasco: A Reappraisal of the Groupthink Phenomenon and a New Model of Group Decision Processes," *Psychological Bulletin,* May 1993, pp 533–52. Also see A A Mohamed and F A Wiebe, "Toward a Process Theory of Groupthink," *Small Group Research,* August 1996, pp 416–30.

[88] N Byrnes and J Sasseen, "Board of Hard Knocks," *BusinessWeek,* January 22, 2007, pp 37–38. Also see J W Lorsch and R C Clark, "Leading from the Boardroom," *Harvard Business Review,* April 2008, pp 105–11; and K Pick, "Can You Hear Me Now?" *Harvard Business Review,* July–August 2008, pp 23–24.

[89] Details of this study may be found in M R Callaway and J K Esser, "Groupthink: Effects of Cohesiveness and Problem-Solving Procedures on Group Decision Making," *Social Behavior and Personality,* no. 2, 1984, pp 157–64. Also see C R Leana, "A Partial Test of Janis's Groupthink Model: Effects of Group Cohesiveness and Leader-Behavior on Defective Decision Making," *Journal of Management,* Spring 1985, pp 5–17; and G Moorhead and J R Montanari, "An Empirical Investigation of the Groupthink Phenomenon," *Human Relations,* May 1986, pp 399–410. A more modest indirect effect is reported in J N Choi and M U Kim, "The Organizational Application of Groupthink and Its Limitations in Organizations," *Journal of Applied Psychology,* April 1999, pp 297–306.

[90] Adapted from discussion in Janis, *Groupthink,* ch 11.

[91] D Jones, "P&G CEO Wields High Expectations but No Whip," *USA Today,* February 19, 2007, p 3B. Also see G S Day and P J H Schoemaker, "Are You a 'Vigilant Leader'?" *MIT Sloan Management Review,* Spring 2008, pp 43–51.

[92] Based on discussion in B Latane, K Williams, and S Harkins, "Many Hands Make Light the Work: The Causes and Consequences of Social Loafing," *Journal of Personality and Social Psychology,* June 1979, pp 822–32; and D A Kravitz and B Martin, "Ringelmann Rediscovered: The Original Article," *Journal of Personality and Social Psychology,* May 1986, pp 936–41. Also see A Jassawalla, H Sashittal, and A Malshe, "Students' Perceptions of Social Loafing: Its Antecedents and Consequences in Undergraduate Business Classroom Teams," *Academy of Management Learning and Education,* March 2009, pp 42–54.

[93] See J A Shepperd, "Productivity Loss in Performance Groups: A Motivation Analysis," *Psychological Bulletin,* no. 1, 1993, pp 67–81; R E Kidwell Jr and N Bennett, "Employee Propensity to Withhold Effort: A Conceptual Model to Intersect Three Avenues of Research," *Academy of Management Review,* July 1993, pp 429–56; and S J Karau and K D Williams, "Social Loafing: Meta-Analytic Review and Theoretical Integration," *Journal of Personality and Social Psychology,* October 1993, pp 681–706.

[94] See S J Zaccaro, "Social Loafing: The Role of Task Attractiveness," *Personality and Social Psychology Bulletin,* March 1984, pp 99–106; J M Jackson and K D Williams, "Social Loafing on Difficult Tasks: Working Collectively Can Improve Performance," *Journal of Personality and Social Psychology,* October 1985, pp 937–42; and J M George, "Extrinsic and Intrinsic Origins of Perceived Social Loafing in Organizations," *Academy of Management Journal,* March 1992, pp 191–202.

[95] For complete details, see K Williams, S Harkins, and B Latane, "Identifiability as a Deterrent to Social Loafing: Two Cheering Experiments," *Journal of Personality and Social Psychology,* February 1981, pp 303–11.

[96] See J M Jackson and S G Harkins, "Equity in Effort: An Explanation of the Social Loafing Effect," *Journal of Personality and Social Psychology,* November 1985, pp 1199–206.

[97] Both studies are reported in S G Harkins and K Szymanski, "Social Loafing and Group Evaluation," *Journal of Personality and Social Psychology,* June 1989, pp 934–41. Also see R Hoigaard, R Safvenbom, and F E Tonnessen, "The Relationship between Group Cohesion, Group Norms, and Perceived Social Loafing in Soccer Teams," *Small Group Research,* June 2006, pp 217–32.

[98] Data from J A Wagner III, "Studies of Individualism-Collectivism: Effects on Cooperation in Groups," *Academy of Management Journal,* February 1995, pp 152–72. Also see R C Liden, S J Wayne, R A Jaworski, and N Bennett, "Social Loafing: A Field Investigation," *Journal of Management,* no. 2, 2004, pp 285–304.

[99] S G Rogelberg, J L Barnes-Farrell, and C A Lowe, "The Stepladder Technique: An Alternative Group Structure Facilitating Effective Group Decision Making," *Journal of Applied Psychology,* October 1992, p 730.

[100] Reprinted by permission of *Harvard Business Review,* "Unmasking Manly Men," by R J Ely and D Meyerson, August 2008. Copyright 2008 by the Harvard Business School Publishing Corporation; all rights reserved.

[101] Excerpted from J Sandberg, "My Boss Wants to Be My Online Friend," *The Arizona Republic,* July 14, 2007, p D3.

[102] Data from J Yang and S Parker, "Characterizing Relationship with Boss," *USA Today,* October 16, 2008, p 1B.

CHAPTER 11

[1] Excerpted from D Foust, "U.S. Airways: After the 'Miracle on the Hudson,'" March 2, 2009, issue of *BusinessWeek* by special permission. Copyright © 2009 by The McGraw-Hill Companies, Inc.

[2] See M Wilson, "Flight 1549 Pilot Tells of Terror and Intense Focus," *New York Times,* February 9, 2009, www.nytimes.com/2009/02/09/nyregion/09interview.html?_r=1.

[3] J Welch and S Welch, "Company Man or Free Agent," *BusinessWeek,* February 12, 2007, p 106. Also see M de Rond, "Lessons from the Oxford and Cambridge Boat Race," *Harvard Business Review,* September 2008, p 28; and E Catmull, "How Pixar Fosters Collective Creativity," *Harvard Business Review,* September 2008, pp 64–72.

[4] Data from "Workforce Readiness and the New Essential Skills," SHRM *Workplace Visions,* no. 2, 2008, Table 3, p 5.

[5] As quoted in A Fisher, "How to Get Hired by a 'Best' Company," *Fortune,* February 4, 2008, p 96.

[6] J R Katzenbach, and D K Smith, *The Wisdom of Teams: Creating the High-Performance Organization* (New York: HarperBusiness, 1999), p 45.

[7] See J Welch and S Welch, "Team Building: Wrong and Right," *BusinessWeek,* November 24, 2008, p 130.

[8] J R Katzenbach and D K Smith, "The Discipline of Teams," *Harvard Business Review,* March–April 1993, p 112 (emphasis added).

[9] A Gardiner, "Perfect Fit: Holtz Leads East Carolina Revival," *USA Today,* September 12, 2008, p 8C.

[10] "A Team's-Eye View of Teams," *Training,* November 1995, p 16.

[11] See E Sundstrom, K P DeMeuse, and D Futrell, "Work Teams," *American Psychologist,* February 1990, pp 120–33.

[12] For an alternative typology of teams, see S G Scott and Walter O Einstein, "Strategic Performance Appraisal in Team-Based Organizations: One Size Does Not Fit All," *Academy of Management Executive,* May 2001, pp 107–16. Also see R Rico, M Sanchez-Manzanares, F Gil, and C Gibson, "Team Implicit Coordination Processes: A Team Knowledge-Based Approach," *Academy of Management Review,* January 2008, pp 163–84; "Innovative Work Teams in a Challenging Business Environment," SHRM *Workplace Visions,* no 1, 2009, pp 1–6; and D M Wallace and V B Hinsz, "Group Members as Actors and Observers in Attributions of Responsibility for Group Performance," *Small Group Research,* February 2009, pp 52–71.

[13] S Hamm and K Hall, "Perfect: The Quest to Design the Ultimate Portable PC," *BusinessWeek,* February 25, 2008, p 45. Also see J McGregor and M Kripalani, "GE: Reinventing Tech for the Emerging World," *BusinessWeek,* April 28, 2008, p 68.

[14] For example, see J Goldstein, "As Doctors Get a Life, Strains Show," *The Wall Street Journal,* April 29, 2008, pp A1, A14; and A Zimmerman, "Wal-Mart's Emergency-Relief Team Girds for Hurricane Gustav," *The Wall Street Journal,* August 30, 2008, p A3.

[15] P King, "What Makes Teamwork Work?" *Psychology Today,* December 1989, p 16.

[16] See J A LePine, R F Piccolo, C L Jackson, J E Mathieu, and J R Saul, "A Meta-Analysis of Teamwork Processes: Tests of a Multidimensional Model and Relationship with Team Effectiveness Criteria," *Personnel Psychology,* Summer 2008, pp 273–307; J E Mathieu and T L Rapp, "Laying the Foundation for Successful Team Performance Trajectories: The Roles of Team Charters and Performance Strategies," *Journal of Applied Psychology,* January 2009, pp 90–103; and F A Kennedy, M L Loughry, T P Klammer, and M M Beyerlein, "Effects of Organizational Support on Potency in Work Teams," *Small Group Research,* February 2009, pp 72–93.

[17] "Collaboration Provides Edge," *The Arizona Republic,* April 10, 2005, p 2. Also see L L Berry, "The Collaborative Organization: Leadership Lessons from Mayo Clinic," *Organizational Dynamics,* no. 3, 2004, pp 228–42.

[18] See M Bolch, "Rewarding the Team," *HR Magazine,* February 2007, pp 91–93.

[19] P Burrows, "Cisco's Comeback," *BusinessWeek,* November 24, 2003, p 124. For updates, see M Kimes, "Cisco Systems Layers It On," *Fortune,* December 8, 2008, p 24; and J Fortt, "Cisco Aims to Serve," *Fortune,* March 16, 2009, pp 33–34.

[20] See T V Mumford, C H Van Iddekinge, F P Morgeson, and M A Campion, "The Team Role Test: Development and Validation of a Team Role Knowledge Situational Judgment Test," *Journal of Applied Psychology,* March 2008, pp 250–67; A W Woolley, M E Gerbasi, C F Chabris, S M Kosslyn, and J R Hackman, "Bringing in the Experts: How Team Composition and Collaborative Planning Jointly Shape Analytic Effectiveness," *Small Group Research,* June 2008, pp 352–71; and S E Humphrey, F P Morgeson, and M J Mannor, "Developing a Theory of the Strategic Core of Teams: A Role Composition Model of Team Performance," *Journal of Applied Psychology,* January 2009, pp 48–61.

[21] As quoted in P B Brown, "What I Know Now," *Fast Company,* January 2005, p 96. Also see G Hirst, D Van Knippenberg, and J Zhou, "A Cross-Level Perspective on Employee Creativity: Goal Orientation, Team Learning Behavior, and Individual Creativity," *Academy of Management Journal,* April 2009, pp 280–93.

22 J Vesterman, "From Wharton to War," *Fortune,* June 12, 2006, p 108.

23 For more on team effectiveness, see D S DeRue, J R Hollenbeck, M D Johnson, D R Ilgen, and D K Jundt, "How Different Team Downsizing Approaches Influence Team-Level Adaptation and Performance," *Academy of Management Journal,* February 2008, pp 182–96; R R Hirschfeld and J B Bernerth, "Mental Efficacy and Physical Efficacy at the Team Level: Inputs and Outcomes among Newly Formed Action Teams," *Journal of Applied Psychology,* November 2008, pp 1429–37; and S Sonnentag and J Volmer, "Individual-Level Predictors of Task-Related Teamwork Processes: The Role of Expertise and Self-Efficacy in Team Meetings," *Group and Organization Management,* February 2009, pp 37–66.

24 For more, see P Falcone, "On the Brink of Failure," *HR Magazine,* February 2008, pp 82–84; the first Q&A in J Welch and S Welch, "When a Star Slacks Off," *BusinessWeek,* March 17, 2008, p 88; and C M Barnes, J R Hollenbeck, D T Wagner, D S DeRue, J D Nahrgang, and K M Schwind, "Harmful Help: The Costs of Backing-Up Behavior in Teams," *Journal of Applied Psychology,* May 2008, pp 529–39.

25 P Raeburn, "Whoops! Wrong Patient," *BusinessWeek,* June 17, 2002, p 85.

26 See C M Christensen, M Marx, and H H Stevenson, "The Tools of Cooperation and Change," *Harvard Business Review,* October 2006, pp 73–80.

27 J Gordon, "Redefining Elegance," *Training,* March 2007, p 20.

28 See A Kohn, "How to Succeed without Even Vying," *Psychology Today,* September 1986, pp 27–28. Sports psychologists discuss "cooperative competition" in S Sleek, "Competition: Who's the Real Opponent?" *APA Monitor,* July 1996, p 8.

29 As quoted in M C Meaney, "Seeing Beyond the Woman: An Interview with a Pioneering Academic and Board Member," *The McKinsey Quarterly,* September 2008, pp 7–8.

30 D W Johnson, G Maruyama, R Johnson, D Nelson, and L Skon, "Effects of Cooperative, Competitive, and Individualistic Goal Structures on Achievement: A Meta-Analysis," *Psychological Bulletin,* January 1981, pp 56–57. An alternative interpretation of the foregoing study that emphasizes the influence of situational factors can be found in J L Cotton and M S Cook, "Meta-Analysis and the Effects of Various Reward Systems: Some Different Conclusions from Johnson et al.," *Psychological Bulletin,* July 1982, pp 176–83.

31 R Zemke, "Office Spaces," *Training,* May 2002, p 24.

32 S W Cook and M Pelfrey, "Reactions to Being Helped in Cooperating Interracial Groups: A Context Effect," *Journal of Personality and Social Psychology,* November 1985, p 1243. Also see R R Hastings, "Poll Finds Mistrust among Racial Groups," *HR Magazine,* February 2008, p 26.

33 See A J Stahelski and R A Tsukuda, "Predictors of Cooperation in Health Care Teams," *Small Group Research,* May 1990, pp 220–33.

34 See, for example, E Nordwall, "Former AIG Exec Gets Prison Term," *USA Today,* January 28, 2009, p 1B; R Parloff, "Wall Street: It's Payback Time," *Fortune,* January 19, 2009, pp 56–69; and D Kansas, "Madoff Does Minneapolis," *Fortune,* February 2, 2009, pp 80–86.

35 Data from D Jones, "Leadership Crisis Blamed for Some of Nation's Problems," *USA Today,* November 5, 2008, p 6B.

36 Data and quote from R Zeidner, "Employees Trust Managers More Than Top Brass," *HR Magazine,* October 2008, p 10. Also see A R Carey and V Salazar, "Trust in Business World Sliding," *USA Today,* September 10, 2008, p 1A; and R J Grossman, "Executive Pay: Perception and Reality," *HR Magazine,* April 2009, pp 26–32.

37 J Barbian, "Short Shelf Life," *Training,* June 2002, p 52.

38 See F D Schoorman, R C Mayer, and J H Davis, "An Integrative Model of Organizational Trust: Past, Present, and Future," *Academy of Management Review,* April 2007, pp 344–54; R Y J Chua, P Ingram, and M W Morris, "From the Head and the Heart: Locating Cognition- and Affect-Based Trust in Managers' Professional Networks," *Academy of Management Journal,* June 2008, pp 436–52; and D C Lau and R C Liden, "Antecedents of Coworker Trust: Leaders' Blessings," *Journal of Applied Psychology,* September 2008, pp 1130–38.

39 J D Lewis and A Weigert, "Trust as a Social Reality," *Social Forces,* June 1985, p 971.

40 H Mackay, "Truth or Consequences," www.harveymackay.com/columns/column_this_week.cfm, accessed March 6, 2009.

41 See E C Tomlinson and R C Mayer, "The Role of Causal Attribution Dimensions in Trust Repair," *Academy of Management Review,* January 2009, pp 85–104; and N Gillespie and G Dietz, "Trust Repair after an Organization-Level Failure," *Academy of Management Review,* January 2009, pp 127–45.

42 R C Mayer, J H Davis, and F D Schoorman, "An Integrative Model of Organizational Trust," *Academy of Management Review,* July 1995, p 715.

43 Lewis and Weigert, "Trust as a Social Reality," p 970. Also see R F Hurley, "The Decision to Trust," *Harvard Business Review,* September 2006, pp 55–62.

44 M Powell, "Betrayal," *Inc.,* April 1996, p 24.

45 Adapted from F Bartolomé, "Nobody Trusts the Boss Completely—Now What?" *Harvard Business Review,* March–April 1989, pp 135–42. Also see M Williams, "Building Genuine Trust through Interpersonal Emotion Management: A Threat Regulation Model of Trust and Collaboration across Boundaries," *Academy of Management Review,* April 2007, pp 595–621; C J Roussin, "Increasing Trust, Psychological Safety, and Team Performance through Dyadic Leadership Discovery," *Small Group Research,* April 2008, pp 224–48; and S S Webber, "Development of Cognitive and Affective Trust in Teams," *Small Group Research,* December 2008, pp 746–69.

46 S M R Covey with R R Merrill, *The Speed of Trust: The One Thing That Changes Everything* (New York: Free Press, 2006), p 45 (emphasis added).

47 W Foster Owen, "Metaphor Analysis of Cohesiveness in Small Discussion Groups," *Small Group Behavior,* August 1985, p 416.

48 This distinction is based on discussion in A Tziner, "Differential Effects of Group Cohesiveness Types: A Clarifying Overview," *Social Behavior and Personality,* no. 2, 1982, pp 227–39.

49 B Mullen and C Copper, "The Relation between Group Cohesiveness and Performance: An Integration," *Psychological Bulletin,* March 1994, p 224.

50 Ibid. Additional research evidence is reported in M I Norton, J H Frost, and D Ariely, "Less Is More: The Lure of

Ambiguity, or Why Familiarity Breeds Contempt," *Journal of Personality and Social Psychology,* January 2007, pp 97–105.

51 Based on B Mullen, T Anthony, E Salas, and J E Driskell, "Group Cohesiveness and Quality of Decision Making: An Integration of Tests of the Groupthink Hypothesis," *Small Group Research,* May 1994, pp 189–204. Also see M C Andrews, K M Kacmar, G L Blakely, and N S Bucklew, "Group Cohesion as an Enhancement to the Justice-Affective Commitment Relationship," *Group and Organization Management,* December 2008, pp 736–55.

52 G L Miles, "The Plant of Tomorrow Is in Texas Today," *BusinessWeek,* July 28, 1986, p 76.

53 See, for example, P Jin, "Work Motivation and Productivity in Voluntarily Formed Work Teams: A Field Study in China," *Organizational Behavior and Human Decision Processes,* 1993, pp 133–55. Also see S Reysen, "Construction of a New Scale: The Reysen Likability Scale," *Social Behavior and Personality,* no. 2, 2005, pp 201–8.

54 Based on discussion in E E Lawler III and S A Mohrman, "Quality Circles: After the Honeymoon," *Organizational Dynamics,* Spring 1987, pp 42–54.

55 See D L Duarte and N Tennant Snyder, *Mastering Virtual Teams: Strategies, Tools, and Techniques,* 3rd ed (San Francisco, CA: Jossey-Bass, 2006).

56 "Internet Use Grows in Importance, Time," *USA Today,* November 29, 2006, p 6D.

57 J Yang and K Gelles, "Working Remotely vs. In the Office," *USA Today,* June 10, 2008, p 1B.

58 See A Malhotra , A Majchrzak, and B Rosen, "Leading Virtual Teams," *Academy of Management Perspectives,* February 2007, pp 60–70; B Rosen, S Furst, and R Blackburn, "Overcoming Barriers to Knowledge Sharing in Virtual Teams," *Organizational Dynamics,* no. 3, 2007, pp 259–73; and J Thilmany, "Live but Not in Person," *Training,* September 2008, pp 40–42.

59 Based on P Bordia, N DiFonzo, and A Chang, "Rumor as Group Problem Solving: Development Patterns in Informal Computer-Mediated Groups," *Small Group Research,* February 1999, pp 8–28.

60 See K A Graetz, E S Boyle, C E Kimble, P Thompson, and J L Garloch, "Information Sharing in Face-to-Face, Teleconferencing, and Electronic Chat Groups," *Small Group Research,* December 1998, pp 714–43.

61 Based on F Niederman and R J Volkema, "The Effects of Facilitator Characteristics on Meeting Preparation, Set Up, and Implementation," *Small Group Research,* June 1999, pp 330–60; and B Whitworth, B Gallupe, and R McQueen, "Generating Agreement in Computer-Mediated Groups," *Small Group Research,* October 2001, pp 625–65.

62 Based on J J Sosik, B J Avolio, and S S Kahai, "Inspiring Group Creativity: Comparing Anonymous and Identified Electronic Brainstorming," *Small Group Research,* February 1998, pp 3–31. Also see S S Kahai, J J Sosik, and B J Avolio, "Effects of Participative and Directive Leadership in Electronic Groups," *Group and Organization Management,* February 2004, pp 67–105.

63 Based on M M Montoya-Weiss, A P Massey, and M Song, "Getting It Together: Temporal Coordination and Conflict Management in Global Virtual Teams," *Academy of Management Journal,* December 2001, pp 1251–62.

64 J Hyatt, "A Surprising Truth about Geographically Dispersed Teams," *MIT Sloan Management Review,* Summer 2008, pp 5–6.

65 B Dumaine, "Who Needs a Boss?" *Fortune,* May 7, 1990, p 52.

66 Adapted from Table 1 in V U Druskat and J V Wheeler, "Managing from the Boundary: The Effective Leadership of Self-Managing Work Teams," *Academy of Management Journal,* August 2003, pp 435–57.

67 See L Fleming, "Perfecting Cross-Pollination," *Harvard Business Review,* September 2004, pp 22–24; J I Cash Jr, M J Earl, and R Morison, "Teaming Up to Crack Innovation Enterprise Integration," *Harvard Business Review,* November 2008, pp 90–100; and "Ask Stephen Covey," *Inc.,* December 2008, p 68.

68 L Tischler, "Twenty People, Four Notes: How Microsoft Created the Sound of Vista," *Fast Company,* February 2007, p 24.

69 Excerpted from "Fast Talk," *Fast Company,* February 2004, p 50.

70 See "1996 Industry Report: What Self-Managing Teams Manage," *Training,* October 1996, p 69.

71 See L L Thompson, *Making the Team: A Guide for Managers* (Upper Saddle River, NJ: Prentice Hall, 2000).

72 See P S Goodman, R Devadas, and T L Griffith Hughson, "Groups and Productivity: Analyzing the Effectiveness of Self-Managing Teams," in *Productivity in Organizations,* ed J P Campbell, R J Campbell, and Associates (San Francisco, CA: Jossey-Bass, 1998), pp 295–327. Also see S Kauffeld, "Self-Directed Work Groups and Team Competence," *Journal of Occupational and Organizational Psychology,* March 2006, pp 1–21; and K A Smith-Jentsch, J A Cannon-Bowers, S L Tannenbaum, and E Salas, "Guided Team Self-Correction: Impacts on Team Mental Models, Processes, and Effectiveness," *Small Group Research,* June 2008, pp 303–27.

73 See C Douglas and W L Gardner, "Transition to Self-Directed Work Teams: Implications of Transition Time and Self-Monitoring for Managers' Use of Influence Tactics," *Journal of Organizational Behavior,* February 2004, pp 47–65.

74 J M O'Brien, "Team Building in Paradise," *Fortune,* May 26, 2008, p 113.

75 As quoted in C Tkaczyk, "Keeping Creatives Happy," *Fortune,* March 16, 2009, p 40.

76 See A McConnon, "My Mentor, Flicka," *BusinessWeek,* January 14, 2008, p 56; L Thomas, "Japan's Teamwork-Building Employee Dorms Make a Comeback," *The Wall Street Journal,* August 15, 2008, p A9; and S Prokesch, "How GE Teaches Teams to Lead Change," *Harvard Business Review,* January 2009, pp 99–106.

77 See J Brett, K Behfar, and M C Kern, "Managing Multicultural Teams," *Harvard Business Review,* November 2006, pp 83–91.

78 S Bucholz and T Roth, *Creating the High-Performance Team* (New York: John Wiley & Sons, 1987), p xi. Also see S E Kohn and V D O'Connell, *6 Habits of Highly Effective Teams* (Franklin Lakes, NJ: Career Press, 2007); and S A Miles and N Bennett, "6 Steps to (Re)Building a Top Management Team," *MIT Sloan Management Review,* Fall 2008, pp 60–64.

79 Bucholz and Roth, *Creating the High-Performance Team,* p 14.

80 P King, "What Makes Teamwork Work?" *Psychology Today,* December 1989, p 17.

81 For more, see D L Kirkpatrick and J D Kirkpatrick, *Evaluating Training Programs: The Four Levels,* 3rd ed (San Francisco, CA: Berrett-Koehler, 2006).

82 J M O'Brien, "Zappos Knows How to Kick It," *Fortune,* February 2, 2009, p 58.

83 For related research, see C B Gibson, C D Cooper, and J A Conger, "Do You See What We See? The Complex Effects of Perceptual Distance between Leaders and Teams," *Journal of Applied Psychology,* January 2009, pp 62–76; S W J Kozlowski, D Watola, J M Jensen, B Kim, and I Botero, "Developing Adaptive Teams: A Theory of Dynamic Leadership," in *Team Effectiveness in Complex Organizations,* ed E Sales, G F Goodwin, and C S Burke (New York: Routledge Academic, 2009); and J B Wu, A S Tsui, and A J Kinicki, "Leading Individuals or Leading Teams? Implications of Dual-Level Leadership Process for Team Effectiveness," *Academy of Management Journal,* 2009, in press.

84 L A Hill, "Becoming the Boss," *Harvard Business Review,* January 2007, p 54. Also see the second Q&A in J Welch and S Welch, "It's Business-Bashing Time," *BusinessWeek,* March 10, 2008, p 92; and D Coutu, "Why Teams Don't Work," *Harvard Business Review,* May 2009, pp 99–105.

85 See B Frisch, "When Teams Can't Decide," *Harvard Business Review,* November 2008, pp 121–26; and S A Eisenbeiss, D van Knippenberg, and S Boerner, "Transformational Leadership and Team Innovation: Integrating Team Climate Principles," *Journal of Applied Psychology,* November 2008, pp 1438–46.

86 Excerpted from N Heintz, "In Spanish It's *Un Equipo.* In English, It's a Team. Either Way, It's Tough to Build," *Inc.: The Magazine for Growing Companies,* April 2008. Copyright © 2008 by Mansueto Ventures LLC. Reproduced with permission of Mansueto Ventures LLC via Copyright Clearance Center.

87 Excerpted from B Levisohn, "Bailing Out of the Bailout," *BusinessWeek,* March 16, 2009, p 45.

CHAPTER 12

1 "Top Small Workplaces 2008," *The Wall Street Journal,* October 13, 2008, p R6.

2 See D Welch, "GM Live Green or Die," *BusinessWeek,* May 26, 2008, pp 36–41; and J S Lublin, "CEO Firing on the Rise as Downturn Gains Steam," *The Wall Street Journal Online,* January 13, 2009, http://online.wsj.com.

3 See S Tully, "Divorce Bank of America Style," *Fortune,* February 16, 2009, p 72; S Craig, "Merrill's $10 Million Men," *The Wall Street Journal Online,* March 4, 2009, http://online.wsj.com; and S Craig, "Heat Turns Up on Merrill Bonuses' Timing," *The Wall Street Journal,* March 12, 2009, p C1.

4 Strengths and weaknesses of the rational model are discussed by M H Bazerman, *Judgment in Managerial Decision Making* (Hoboken, NJ: John Wiley & Sons, Inc., 2006).

5 J L Yang, "Mattel's CEO Recalls a Rough Summer," *Fortune,* January 22, 2008, http://cnn.money.com (interview with Bob Eckert).

6 See J MG Boaventura and A A Fischmann, "Is Your Vision Consistent? A Method for Checking, Based on the Scenario Concepts," *Futures,* September 2008, pp 597–612; and J O Schwarz, "Assessing the Future of Future Studies in Management," *Futures,* April 2008, pp 237–46.

7 This study was conducted by P C Nutt, "Expanding the Search for Alternatives during Strategic Decision-Making," *Academy of Management Executive,* November 2004, pp 13–28.

8 Results can be found in J P Byrnes, D C Miller, and W D Schafer, "Gender Differences in Risk Taking: A Meta-Analysis," *Psychological Bulletin,* May 1999, pp 367–83.

9 Yang, "Mattel's CEO Recalls a Rough Summer."

10 H A Simon, "Rational Decision Making in Business Organizations," *American Economic Review,* September 1979, p 510. Also see M Price, "Mind over Money," *Monitor on Psychology,* January 2009, pp 28–29.

11 These conclusions were proposed by R Brown, *Rational Choice and Judgment* (Hoboken, NJ: John Wiley & Sons, Inc., 2005), p 9.

12 Bounded rationality is discussed by M Bazerman and D Chugh, "Decisions without Blinders," *Harvard Business Review,* January 2006, pp 88–97; and H A Simon, *Administrative Behavior,* 2nd ed (New York: Free Press, 1957).

13 These conclusions were excerpted from "Poor Decisions Hurt Company Performance," *HR Magazine,* February 2007, p 16.

14 The model is discussed in detail in M D Cohen, J G March, and J P Olsen, "A Garbage Can Model of Organizational Choice," *Administrative Science Quarterly,* March 1981, pp 1–25.

15 Ibid., p 2.

16 This discussion is based on material presented in J G March and R Weissinger-Baylon, *Ambiguity and Command* (Marshfield, MA: Pitman Publishing, 1986), pp 11–35.

17 See A Carter, "Lighting a Fire under Campbell," *BusinessWeek,* December 4, 2006, pp 96, 99.

18 Garbage can processes are also discussed by L Backer and T S Clark, "Eco-Effective Greening Decisions and Rationalizations," *Organization & Environment,* September 2008, pp 227–44; and D A Samuelson, "Understanding Organizational Anarchy," *OR-MS Today,* August 2008, pp 34–39.

19 See D J Snowden and M E Boone, "A Leader's Framework for Decision Making," *Harvard Business Review,* November 2007, pp 69–76.

20 Ibid., p 76.

21 Biases associated with using shortcuts in decision making are discussed by A Tversky and D Kahneman, "Judgment under Uncertainty: Heuristics and Biases," *Science,* September 1974, pp 1124–31.

22 See J Groopman, "A Doctor's Rx for CEO Decision Makers," *Harvard Business Review,* February 2008, pp 19–20; R L Hotz, "The Brain, Your Honor, Will Take the Witness Stand," *The Wall Street Journal,* January 16, 2009, p A7; and A Campbell, J Whitehead, and S Finkelstein, "Why Good Leaders Make Bad Decisions," *Harvard Business Review,* February 2009, pp 60–66.

23 See K Sengupta, T L Abdel-Hamid, and L N Van Wassenhove, "The Experience Trap," *Harvard Business Review,* February 2008, pp 94–101.

24 Results can be found in R A Lowe and A A Ziedonis, "Overoptimism and the Performance of Entrepreneurial Firms," *Management Science,* February 2006, pp 173–86.

25 G Flaccus, "Risky Decisions Are Faulted in Death of California Firefighters," *The Arizona Republic,* May 23, 2007, p A13. Another example is provided by E Hoffman, "Fooled by Nice Duds and a Fancy Degree," *BusinessWeek,* February 11, 2008, p 72.

26 This scenario was taken from Bazerman, *Judgment in Managerial Decision Making,* p 41.

27 See S T Certo, B L Connelly, and L Tihany, "Managers and Their Not-So Rational Decisions," *Business Horizons,* 2008, pp 113–19.

28 See J D Stoll and S Terlep, "GM to Offer Two Choices: Bankruptcy or More Aid," *The Wall Street Journal,* February 14, 2009, pp A1, A6; C A Denison, "Real Options and Escalation of Commitment: A Behavioral Analysis of Capital Investment Decisions," *The Accounting Review,* January 2009, pp 133–55; and J E Berg, J W Dickhaut, and C Kanodia, "The Role of Information Asymmetry in Escalation Phenomena: Empirical Evidence," *Journal of Economic Behavior & Organization,* February 2009, pp 135–47.

29 See J Ross and B M Staw, "Organizational Escalation and Exit: Lessons from the Shoreham Nuclear Power Plant," *Academy of Management Journal,* August 1993, pp 701–32.

30 D W De Long and P Seemann, "Confronting Conceptual Confusion and Conflict in Knowledge Management," *Organizational Dynamics,* Summer 2000, p 33.

31 See T H Davenport, L Prusak, and B Strong, "Putting Ideas to Work," *The Wall Street Journal,* March 10, 2008, p R11; T Davenport, "How to Design Smart Business Experiments," *Harvard Business Review,* February 2009, pp 68–76.

32 R Lubit, "Tacit Knowledge and Knowledge Management: The Keys to Sustainable Competitive Advantage," *Organizational Dynamics,* 2001, p 166. Also see S J Armstrong and A Mahmud, "Experiential Learning and the Acquisition of Managerial Knowledge," *Academy of Management Learning & Education,* June 2008, pp 189–208.

33 See T J Friel and R S Duboff, "The Last Act of a Great CEO," *Harvard Business Review,* January 2009, pp 82–89; and "Best Practices & Outstanding Initiatives," *Training,* February 2009, pp 96–100.

34 Excerpted from "Top Small Workplaces 2008," *The Wall Street Journal,* October 13, 2009, p R6.

35 See A C Edmondson, "The Competitive Imperative of Learning," *Harvard Business Review,* July–August 2008, pp 60–67; J Welch and S Welch, "The Importance of Being Sticky," *BusinessWeek,* September 22, 2008, p 112.

36 This definition was derived from A J Rowe and R O Mason, *Managing with Style: A Guide to Understanding, Assessing and Improving Decision Making* (San Francisco, CA: Jossey-Bass, 1987).

37 The discussion of styles was based on material contained in ibid.

38 Excerpted from B Gimbel, "Keeping Planes Apart," *Fortune,* June 27, 2005, p 112.

39 B Bremner and D Roberts, "A Billion Tough Sells," *BusinessWeek,* March 20, 2006, p 44.

40 Y I Kane and P Dvorak, "Howard Stringer, Japanese CEO," *The Wall Street Journal,* March 3–4, 2007, p A1, A6.

41 See K H Hanzaee, "Iranian Generation Y Female & Male Decision-Making Styles: Are They Different," *Journal of American Academy of Business,* March 2009, pp 57–64; and Rowe and Mason, *Managing with Style.*

42 D S Goldsmith, "Creating Master Decision Makers," *Leadership in Action,* November/December 2008, pp 22–23.

43 J Lehrer, *How We Decide* (Boston: Houghton Mifflin, 2009).

44 E Sadler-Smith and E Shefy, "The Intuitive Executive: Understanding and Applying 'Gut Feel' in Decision-Making," *Academy of Management Executive,* November 2004, p 77.

45 Excerpted from C C Miller and R D Ireland, "Intuition in Strategic Decision Making: Friend or Foe in the Fast-Paced 21st Century," *Academy of Management Executive,* February 2005, p 20.

46 Ibid., pp 19–30.

47 See E Dane and M G Pratt, "Exploring Intuition and Its Role in Managerial Decision Making," *Academy of Management Review,* January 2007, pp 33–54.

48 N M Tichy and W G Bennis, "Making Judgment Calls: The Ultimate Act of Leadership," *Harvard Business Review,* October 2007, p 99.

49 See D Begley, "You Might Help a Teen Avoid Dumb Behavior by Nurturing Intuition," *The Wall Street Journal,* November 3, 2006, p B1.

50 See T J Chermack and K Nimon, "The Effects of Scenario Planning on Participant Decision-Making Style," *Human Resource Development Quarterly,* Winter 2008, pp 351–72.

51 See M J Mauboussin, "What Good Are Experts?" *Harvard Business Review,* February 2008, pp 43–44.

52 Results were reported in "The Ethical Mind," *Harvard Business Review,* March 2007, pp 51–56.

53 The decision tree and resulting discussion are based on C E Bagley, "The Ethical Leader's Decision Tree," *Harvard Business Review,* February 2003, pp 18–19.

54 Details of this example can be found in E E Schultz and T Francis, "Financial Surgery: How Cuts in Retiree Benefits Fatten Companies' Bottom Lines," *The Wall Street Journal,* March 1, 2004, p A1.

55 See R Müller, K Spang, and S Ozcan, "Cultural Differences in Decision Making in Project Teams," *International Journal of Managing Projects in Business,* 2009, pp 70–93.

56 Excerpted from "Top Small Workplaces 2008," *The Wall Street Journal,* October 13, 2008, p R4.

57 Results can be found in C K W De Dreu and M A West, "Minority Dissent and Team Innovation: The Importance of Participation in Decision Making," *Journal of Applied Psychology,* December 2001, pp 1191–201.

58 These recommendations were derived from L Lorber, "Running the Show: An Open Book," *The Wall Street Journal,* February 23, 2009, p R8; B Frisch, "When Teams Can't Decide," *Harvard Business Review,* November 2008, pp 121–26; and F W Kellermanns, S W Floyd, A W Pearson, and B Spencer, "The Contingent Effect of Constructive Confrontation on the Relationship between Shared Mental Models and Decision Quality," *Journal of Organizational Behavior,* January 2008, pp 119–37.

59 These guidelines were derived from G P Huber, *Managerial Decision Making* (Glenview, IL: Scott, Foresman, 1980), p 149.

60 G W Hill, "Group versus Individual Performance: Are N +1 Heads Better Than One?" *Psychological Bulletin,* May 1982, p 535.

61 J H Davis, "Some Compelling Intuitions about Group Consensus Decisions, Theoretical and Empirical Research, and Interpersonal Aggregation Phenomena: Selected Examples, 1950–1990," *Organizational Behavior and Human Decision Processes,* June 1992, pp 3–38.

62 Supporting results can be found in J Hedlund, D R Ilgen, and J R Hollenbeck, "Decision Accuracy in Computer-Mediated versus Face-to-Face Decision-Making Teams," *Organizational Behavior and Human Decision Processes,* October 1998, pp 30–47.

63 See J R Winquist and J R Larson Jr, "Information Pooling: When It Impacts Group Decision Making," *Journal of Personality and Social Psychology,* February 1998, pp 371–77.

64 G M Parker, *Team Players and Teamwork: The New Competitive Business Strategy* (San Francisco, CA: Jossey-Bass, 1990).

65 These recommendations were obtained from ibid.

66 See A F Osborn, *Applied Imagination: Principles and Procedures of Creative Thinking,* 3rd ed (New York: Scribners, 1979).

67 See P A Heslin, "Better Than Brainstorming? Potential Contextual Boundary Conditions to Brainwriting for Idea Generation in Organizations," *Journal of Occupational and Organizational Psychology,* March 2009, pp 129–45.

68 A summary of brainstorming research is provided by R C Litchfield, "Brainstorming Reconsidered: A Goal-Based View," *Academy of Management Review,* July 2008, pp 649–68.

69 These recommendations and descriptions were derived from B Nussbaum, "The Power of Design," *BusinessWeek,* May 17, 2004, pp 86–94.

70 See J Baruah and P B Paulus, "Effects of Training on Idea Generation in Groups," *Small Group Research,* October 2008, pp 523–41.

71 Applications of the NGT can be found in M Utley, S Gallivan, M Mills, and M Mason, "A Consensus Process for Identifying a Prioritized List of Study Questions," *Health Care Management,* February 2007, pp 105–10.

72 For details see T H Davenport, "How to Design Smart Business Experiments," *Harvard Business Review,* February 2009, pp 69–76.

73 See L Thompson, "Improving the Creativity of Organizational Work Groups," *Academy of Management Executive,* February 2003, pp 96–109.

74 See N C Dalkey, D L Rourke, R Lewis, and D Snyder, *Studies in the Quality of Life: Delphi and Decision Making* (Lexington, MA: Lexington Books: D C Heath and Co., 1972).

75 An application of the Delphi technique can be found in T Grisham, "The Delphi Technique: A Method for Testing Complex and Multifaceted Topics," *International Journal of Managing Projects in Business,* 2009, pp 112–30.

76 See P Dvorak, "Best Buy Taps 'Prediction Market'; Imaginary Stocks Let Workers Forecast Whether Retailer's Plans Will Meet Goals," *The Wall Street Journal,* September 16, 2008, p B1.

77 See K Maher, "Wal-Mart Seeks New Flexibility in Worker Shifts," *The Wall Street Journal,* January 3, 2007, pp A1, A11.

78 See Z Guo, J D'Ambra, T Turner, and H Zhang, "Improving the Effectiveness of Virtual Teams: A Comparison of Video-Conferencing and Face-to-Face Communication in China," *IEEE Transactions on Professional Communication,* March 2009, pp 1–16; and K McNamara, A R Dennis, and T A Carte, "It's the Thought That Counts: The Mediating Effects of Information Processing in Virtual Team Decision Making," *Information Systems Management,* Winter 2008, pp 20–32.

79 M Weinstein, "So Happy Together," *Training,* May 2006, p 38.

80 Supportive results can be found in S S Lam and J Schaubroeck, "Improving Group Decisions by Better Polling Information: A Comparative Advantage of Group Decision Support Systems," *Journal of Applied Psychology,* August 2000, pp 565–73.

81 See D Tapscott, *Grown Up Digital* (New York: McGraw-Hill, 2009).

82 See S Berkun, *The Myths of Innovation* (Sebastopol, CA: O'Reilly Media, Inc., 2007).

83 This definition was adapted from one provided by R K Scott, "Creative Employees: A Challenge to Managers," *Journal of Creative Behavior,* First Quarter 1995, pp 64–71.

84 See C Palmeri and S Reed, "New Frugality in the Oil Patch," *BusinessWeek,* March 16, 2009, p 48; and A Weintraub, "The Inside Track in Medical Cameras," *BusinessWeek,* December 15, 2008, p 70.

85 R Eisenberger and J Aselage, "Incremental Effects of Reward on Experienced Performance Pressure: Positive Outcomes for Intrinsic Interest and Creativity," *Journal of Organizational Behavior,* January 2009, pp 95–117.

86 T A Matherly and R E Goldsmith, "The Two Faces of Creativity," *Business Horizons,* September–October 1985, p 9.

87 This discussion is based on research reviewed in M A Collins and T M Amabile, "Motivation and Creativity," in *Handbook of Creativity,* ed R J Sternberg (Cambridge, UK: Cambridge University Press, 1999), pp 297–311.

88 Personality and creativity were investigated by M Baer and G R Oldham, "The Curvilinear Relations between Experienced Creative Time Pressure and Creativity: Moderating Effects of Openness to Experience and Support for Creativity," *Journal of Applied Psychology,* July 2006, pp 963–70.

89 J M Higgins, "Innovate or Evaporate: Seven Secrets of Innovative Corporations," *The Futurist,* September–October 1995, p 46.

90 J Y Kim, "A Lifelong Battle against Disease," *U.S. News & World Report,* November 19, 2007, pp 62, 64.

91 Quoted on pp 48–49 of D Coutu, "Creativity Step by Step," *Harvard Business Review,* April 2008, pp 47–51 (interview with Twyla Tharp).

92 F Balfour, "Catching the Eye of China's Elite," *BusinessWeek*, February 11, 2008, pp 55–56.

93 Results can be found in E Tahmincioglu, "Gifts That Gall," *Workforce Management,* April 2004, p 45.

94 Details of this study can be found in M Basadur, "Managing Creativity: A Japanese Model," *Academy of Management Executive,* May 1992, pp 29–42.

95 See "You Are Getting Creative . . . Very Creative," *BusinessWeek,* May 12, 2008, p 18.

96 See L Gumusluoglu and A Ilsev, "Transformational Leadership, Creativity, and Organizational Innovation," *Journal of Business Research,* April 2009, pp 461–73; and M Jackson, "Quelling Distraction," *HR Magazine,* August 2008, pp 43–46.

97 These recommendations were derived from E Catmull, "How Pixar Fosters Collective Creativity," *Harvard Business Review,* September 2008, pp 65–72; "Keeping Creatives Happy," *Fortune,* March 16, 2009, p 40 (interview with Jeffrey Katzenberg); and L Tischler, "A Designer Takes on His Biggest Challenge Ever," *Fast Company,* February 2009, pp 78–83.

98 See A Oke, N Munshi, and F O Walumbwa, "The Influence of Leadership on Innovation Processes and Activities," *Organizational Dynamics,* January–March 2009, pp 64–72.

99 K K Spors, "Productive Brainstorms Take the Right Mix of Elements," *The Wall Street Journal,* July 24, 2008, p B5.

100 Excerpted from D Kiley, "Ford's Savior?" *BusinessWeek,* March 16, 2009, pp 31–34.

101 Excerpted from R Berner and C Terhune, "Linking Credit Scores to Hospital Care," *BusinessWeek,* December 1, 2008, pp 80–81.

CHAPTER 13

1 Excerpted from J Sandberg, "Avoiding Conflicts: The Too-Nice Boss Makes Matters Worse," *The Wall Street Journal,* February 26, 2008. Copyright © 2008 by Dow Jones & Company, Inc. Reproduced with permission of Dow Jones & Company, Inc. via Copyright Clearance Center.

2 D Tjosvold, *Learning to Manage Conflict: Getting People to Work Together Productively* (New York: Lexington Books, 1993), p xi.

3 Ibid., pp xi–xii. Also see A O'Leary-Kelly, E Lean, C Reeves, and J Randel, "Coming into the Light: Intimate Partner Violence and Its Effects at Work," *Academy of Management Perspectives,* May 2008, pp 57–72; and B Morris, "You Have Victims Working for You. You Have Batterers Working for You, Too," *Fortune,* November 24, 2008, pp 122–33.

4 J A Wall Jr and R Robert Callister, "Conflict and Its Management," *Journal of Management,* no. 3 (1995), p 517. Also see M Sheehan, "Understanding Opposition," *Harvard Business Review,* February 2008, p 21.

5 Wall and Callister, "Conflict and Its Management," p 544.

6 D Stead, "The Big Picture," *BusinessWeek,* January 8, 2007, p 11.

7 See J B Olson-Buchanan and W R Boswell, "An Integrative Model of Experiencing and Responding to Mistreatment at Work," *Academy of Management Review,* January 2008, pp 76–96.

8 K Cloke and J Goldsmith, *Resolving Conflicts at Work: A Complete Guide for Everyone on the Job* (San Francisco, CA: Jossey-Bass, 2000), pp 25, 27, 29. Also see R Lipsyte, "'Jock Culture' Permeates Life," *USA Today,* April 10, 2008, p 11A.

9 D Brady, "It's All Donald, All the Time," *BusinessWeek,* January 22, 2007, p 51.

10 C Day, "Learn to Love the Spotlight," *Fortune,* November 10, 2008, p 36.

11 Cloke and Goldsmith, *Resolving Conflicts at Work,* pp 31–32. Also see K Fackelmann, "Arguing Hurts the Heart in More Ways Than One," *USA Today,* March 6, 2006, p 10D; D Meyer, "The Saltshaker Theory," *Inc.,* October 2006, pp 69–70; J Welch and S Welch, "The Blame Game—Forget It," *BusinessWeek,* March 5, 2007, p 92; and J Welch and S Welch, "The Right Way to Say Goodbye," *BusinessWeek,* March 26, 2006, p 144.

12 See J Deschenaux, "Bills Prohibit Employer Bans on Firearms," *HR Magazine,* February 2007, pp 34, 39; S C Douglas, C Kiewitz, M J Martinko, P Harvey, Y Kim, and J U Chun, "Cognitions, Emotions, and Evaluations: An Elaboration Likelihood Model for Workplace Aggression," *Academy of Management Review,* April 2008, pp 425–51; and M Inness, M M LeBlanc, and J Barling, "Psychosocial Predictors of Supervisor-, Peer-, Subordinate-, and Service-Provider-Targeted Aggression," *Journal of Applied Psychology,* November 2008, pp 1401–11.

13 See T Simons and R S Peterson, "When to Let Them Duke It Out," *Harvard Business Review,* June 2006, pp 23–24; and E Agnvall, "Case Closed. Now What?" *HR Magazine,* February 2008, pp 69–72.

14 S P Robbins, "'Conflict Management' and 'Conflict Resolution' Are Not Synonymous Terms," *California Management Review,* Winter 1978, p 70. Also see P S Hempel, Z Zhang, and D Tjosvold, "Conflict Management between and within Teams for Trusting Relationships and Performance in China," *Journal of Organizational Behavior,* January 2009, pp 41–65.

15 Excerpted from K Sulkowicz, "Analyze This," *BusinessWeek,* September 29, 2008, p 19.

16 Excerpted from T Ursiny, *The Coward's Guide to Conflict: Empowering Solutions for Those Who Would Rather Run Than Fight* (Naperville, IL: Sourcebooks, 2003), p 27.

17 See D Jones, "Could Insecurity Be the Secret to CEOs' Success?" *USA Today,* February 1, 2007, pp 1B–2B.

18 Adapted in part from discussion in A C Filley, *Interpersonal Conflict Resolution* (Glenview, IL: Scott, Foresman, 1975), pp 9–12; and B Fortado, "The Accumulation of Grievance Conflict," *Journal of Management Inquiry,* December 1992, pp 288–303. For a situation with many of these antecedents of conflict, see M Adams, "Pilots Have Much to Lose during Mergers," *USA Today,* March 10, 2008, p 3B.

19 Adapted from discussion in Tjosvold, *Learning to Manage Conflict,* pp 12–13.

20 L Gardenswartz and A Rowe, *Diverse Teams at Work: Capitalizing on the Power of Diversity* (New York: McGraw-Hill, 1994), p 32.

21 Reprinted from F Keenan, "EMC: Turmoil at the Top?" March 11, 2002, issue of *BusinessWeek* by special permission. Copyright © 2002 by The McGraw-Hill Companies, Inc.

22 For more, see S Hamm, "The Fine Art of Tech Mergers," *BusinessWeek,* July 10, 2006, pp 70, 72; and www.emc.com/about/index.htm, accessed March 18, 2009.

23 C M Pearson and C L Porath, "On the Nature, Consequences, and Remedies of Workplace Incivility: No Time for 'Nice'? Think Again," *Academy of Management Executive,* February 2005, p 7. Also see L M Cortina, "Unseen Injustice: Incivility as Modern Discrimination in Organizations," *Academy of Management Review,* January 2008, pp 55–75; and S Lim, L M Cortina, and V J Magley, "Personal and Workgroup Incivility: Impact on Work and Health Outcomes," *Journal of Applied Psychology,* January 2008, pp 95–107.

24 S Keeler, "Study Calls Out Workplace Bullies," *ASU Insight,* December 8, 2006, p U1. Also see R Zeidner, "Taking Bullies to the Woodshed," *HR Magazine,* May 2008, p 12; and the third Q&A in A Maingault, "Economic Trends, Buddy Systems, Receiving Criticism," *HR Magazine,* March 2009, p 27.

25 C Farrell, "Is the Workplace Getting Raunchier?" *BusinessWeek,* March 17, 2008, p 19.

26 Data and quote from J Yang and S Ward, "USA Today Snapshots," *USA Today,* September 15, 2008, p 1B.

27 P Falcone, "Days of Contemplation," *HR Magazine,* February 2007, p 107.

28 Data from D Stamps, "Yes, Your Boss Is Crazy," *Training,* July 1998, pp 35–39. Also see "Grim Report on Youth Mental Disorders," *USA Today,* December 2, 2008, p 10D; and B D Gelb and P W Corrigan, "How Managers Can Lower Mental Illness Costs by Reducing Stigma," *Business Horizons,* July–August 2008, pp 293–300.

29 See L P Postol, "ADAAA Will Result in Renewed Emphasis on Reasonable Accommodations," SHRM *Legal Report,* January 2009, pp 1–6; and M B Marcus, "Web Initiative Urges People to Think before They Drink," *USA Today,* March 9, 2009, p 5D.

30 Drawn from J C McCune, "The Change Makers," *Management Review,* May 1999, pp 16–22.

31 Based on discussion in C W Leach et al., "Group-Level Self-Definition and Self-Investment: A Hierarchical (Multicomponent) Model of In-Group Identification," *Journal of Personality and Social Psychology,* July 2008, pp 144–65; J Gillispie and J H Chrispeels, "Us and Them," *Small Group Research,* August 2008, pp 397–437; and A C Homan, J R Hollenbeck, S E Humphrey, D Van Knippenberg, D R Ilgen, and G A Van Kleef, "Facing Differences with an Open Mind: Openness to Experience, Salience of Intragroup Differences, and Performance of Diverse Work Groups," *Academy of Management Journal,* December 2008, pp 1204–22.

32 See T F Pettigrew and L R Tropp, "A Meta-Analytic Test of Intergroup Contact Theory," *Journal of Personality and Social Psychology,* May 2006, pp 751–83.

33 G Labianca, D J Brass, and B Gray, "Social Networks and Perceptions of Intergroup Conflict: The Role of Negative Relationships and Third Parties," *Academy of Management Journal,* February 1998, p 63 (emphasis added).

34 For example, see S C Wright, A Aron, T McLaughlin-Volpe, and S A Ropp, "The Extended Contact Effect: Knowledge of Cross-Group Friendships and Prejudice," *Journal of Personality and Social Psychology,* July 1997, pp 73–90; and E Page-Gould, R Mendoza-Denton, and L R Tropp, "With a Little Help from My Cross-Group Friend: Reducing Anxiety in Intergroup Contexts through Cross-Group Friendship," *Journal of Personality and Social Psychology,* November 2008, pp 1080–94.

35 See A Karacanta and J Fitness, "Majority Support for Minority Out-Groups: The Roles of Compassion and Guilt," *Journal of Applied Social Psychology,* November 2006, pp 2730–49; D A Butz and E A Plant, "Perceiving Outgroup Members as Unresponsive: Implications for Approach-Related Emotions, Intentions, and Behavior," *Journal of Personality and Social Psychology,* December 2006, pp 1066–79; and C M Fiol, M G Pratt, and E J O'Connor, "Managing Intractable Identity Conflicts," *Academy of Management Review,* January 2009, pp 32–55.

36 For a good overview, see N J Adler and A Gundersen, *International Dimensions of Organizational Behavior,* 5th ed (Mason, OH: South-Western, 2007). Also see M B Teagarden and D H Cai, "Learning from Dragons Who Are Learning from Us: Developmental Lessons from China's Global Companies," *Organizational Dynamics,* January–March 2009, pp 73–81; and D Roberts, "A Bartending Banker Rocks China Finance," *BusinessWeek,* March 2, 2009, pp 50–51.

37 See M Alexander and H Korine, "When You Shouldn't Go Global," *Harvard Business Review,* December 2008, pp 70–77; and C M Dalton, "Strategic Alliances: There Are Battles and There Is War," *Business Horizons,* March–April 2009, pp 105–108.

38 "Negotiating South of the Border," *Harvard Management Communication Letter,* August 1999, p 12.

39 Excerpted from A Rosenbaum, "Testing Cultural Waters," *Management Review,* July–August 1999, p 43. Copyright © 1999 by American Management Association. Reproduced with permission of American Management Association via Copyright Clearance Center.

40 See R L Tung, "American Expatriates Abroad: From Neophytes to Cosmopolitans," *Journal of World Business,* Summer 1998, pp 125–44.

41 See K A Crowne, "What Leads to Cultural Intelligence?" *Business Horizons,* September–October 2008, pp 391–99.

42 See J Weiss and J Hughes, "What Collaboration? Accept—and Actively Manage—Conflict," *Harvard Business Review,* March 2005, pp 92–101; G Colvin, "The Wisdom of Dumb Questions," *Fortune,* June 27, 2005, p 157; and B Frisch, "When Teams Can't Decide," *Harvard Business Review,* November 2008, pp 121–26.

43 R A Cosier and C R Schwenk, "Agreement and Thinking Alike: Ingredients for Poor Decisions," *Academy of Management Executive,* February 1990, p 71. Also see J P Kotter, "Combating Complacency," *BusinessWeek,* September 15, 2008, pp 54–55.

44 For example, see "Facilitators as Devil's Advocates," *Training,* September 1993, p 10.

45 Good background reading on devil's advocacy can be found in C R Schwenk, "Devil's Advocacy in Managerial Decision Making," *Journal of Management Studies,* April 1984, pp 153–68.

46 See G Katzenstein, "The Debate on Structured Debate: Toward a Unified Theory," *Organizational Behavior and Human Decision Processes,* June 1996, pp 316–32; J Baruah and P B Paulus, "Effects of Training on Idea Generation in Groups," *Small Group Research,* October 2008, pp 523–41; and L Buchanan, "Armed with Data: How the Military Can Help You Learn from Your Mistakes," *Inc.,* March 2009, pp 98, 100.

47 See D M Schweiger, W R Sandberg, and P L Rechner, "Experiential Effects of Dialectical Inquiry, Devil's Advocacy, and Consensus Approaches to Strategic Decision Making," *Academy of Management Journal,* December 1989, pp 745–72.

48 See J S Valacich and C Schwenk, "Devil's Advocacy and Dialectical Inquiry Effects on Face-to-Face and Computer-Mediated Group Decision Making," *Organizational Behavior and Human Decision Processes,* August 1995, pp 158–73.

49 As quoted in D Jones, "CEOs Need X-Ray Vision in Transition," *USA Today,* April 23, 2001, p 4B.

50 Based on C K W De Dreu and M A West, "Minority Dissent and Team Innovation: The Importance of Participation in Decision Making," *Journal of Applied Psychology,* December 2001, pp 119–201. Also see P Shachaf, "Cultural Diversity and Information and Communication Technology Impacts on Global Virtual Teams: An Exploratory Study," *Information and Management,* March 2008, pp 131–42; and H P Sims Jr, S Faraj, and S Yun, "When Should a Leader Be Directive or Empowering? How to Develop Your Own Situational Theory of Leadership," *Business Horizons,* March–April 2009, pp 149–58.

[51] A statistical validation for this model can be found in M A Rahim and N R Magner, "Confirmatory Factor Analysis of the Styles of Handling Interpersonal Conflict: First-Order Factor Model and Its Invariance across Groups," *Journal of Applied Psychology,* February 1995, pp 122–32. Also see M A Rahim, *Managing Conflict in Organizations* (Westport, CT: Greenwood Publishing Group, 2001); W G Stephan, "Psychological and Communication Processes Associated with Intergroup Conflict Resolution," *Small Group Research,* February 2008, pp 28–41; and D Bargal, "Group Processes to Reduce Intergroup Conflict," *Small Group Research,* February 2008, pp 42–59.

[52] M A Rahim, "A Strategy for Managing Conflict in Complex Organizations," *Human Relations,* January 1985, p 84.

[53] For an alternative approach, see H Ren and B Gray, "Repairing Relationship Conflict: How Violation Types and Culture Influence the Effectiveness of Restoration Rituals," *Academy of Management Review,* January 2009, pp 105–26.

[54] "Female Officers Draw Fewer Brutality Suits," *USA Today,* May 2, 2002, p 3A. Also see L W Andrews, "When It's Time for Anger Management," *HR Magazine,* June 2005, pp 131–36.

[55] P Ruzich, "Triangles: Tools for Untangling Interpersonal Messes," *HR Magazine,* July 1999, p 129. Also see P Falcone, "Avoid Pre-emptive Strikes," *HR Magazine,* May 2007, pp 101–104.

[56] M Orey, "Fear of Firing," *BusinessWeek,* April 23, 2007, p 54.

[57] For background, see P S Nugent, "Managing Conflict: Third-Party Interventions for Managers," *Academy of Management Executive,* February 2002, pp 139–54; F P Phillips, "Ten Ways to Sabotage Dispute Management," *HR Magazine,* September 2004, pp 163–68; and R Zeidner, "What's Important about Dispute Resolution?" *HR Magazine,* September 2008, p 10.

[58] See M Bordwin, "Do-It-Yourself Justice," *Management Review,* January 1999, pp 56–58; and E Jensen, D Wagner, and D FitzGerald, "Mediators Help Take Bite Out of Dog Disputes," *USA Today,* March 16, 2009, p 3A.

[59] B Morrow and L M Bernardi. "Resolving Workplace Disputes," *Canadian Manager,* Spring 1999, p 17. For related research, see J M Brett, M Olekalns, R Friedman, N Goates, C Anderson, and C Cherry Lisco, "Sticks and Stones: Language, Face, and Online Dispute Resolution," *Academy of Management Journal,* February 2007, pp 85–99.

[60] Adapted from discussion in K O Wilburn, "Employment Disputes: Solving Them Out of Court," *Management Review,* March 1998, pp 17–21; and Morrow and Bernardi, "Resolving Workplace Disputes," pp 17–19, 27. Also see W H Ross and D E Conlon, "Hybrid Forms of Third-Party Dispute Resolution: Theoretical Implications of Combining Mediation and Arbitration," *Academy of Management Review,* April 2000, pp 416–27.

[61] Wilburn, "Employment Disputes," p 19. Also see B P Sunoo, "Hot Disputes Cool Down in Online Mediation," *Workforce,* January 2001, pp 48–52.

[62] For background on this contentious issue, see S Armour, "Arbitration's Rise Raises Fairness Issue," *USA Today,* June 12, 2001, pp 1B–2B; T J Heinsz, "The Revised Uniform Arbitration Act: An Overview," *Dispute Resolution Journal,* May–July 2001, pp 28–39; and J B Thelen, "Manager Who Refused to Sign Agreement Must Arbitrate," *HR Magazine,* January 2007, p 111.

[63] For example, see M G Danaher, "Employee's Arbitration Victory Had Limits," *HR Magazine,* March 2007, p 116.

[64] See R E Jones and B H Melcher, "Personality and the Preference for Modes of Conflict Resolution," *Human Relations,* August 1982, pp 649–58.

[65] See R A Baron, "Reducing Organizational Conflict: An Incompatible Response Approach," *Journal of Applied Psychology,* May 1984, pp 272–79.

[66] See G A Youngs Jr, "Patterns of Threat and Punishment Reciprocity in a Conflict Setting," *Journal of Personality and Social Psychology,* September 1986, pp 541–46.

[67] For more details, see V D Wall Jr and L L Nolan, "Small Group Conflict: A Look at Equity, Satisfaction, and Styles of Conflict Management," *Small Group Behavior,* May 1987, pp 188–211. Also see S M Farmer and J Roth, "Conflict-Handling Behavior in Work Groups: Effects of Group Structure, Decision Processes, and Time," *Small Group Research,* December 1998, pp 669–713.

[68] K J Behfar, R S Peterson, E A Mannix, and W M K Trochim, "The Critical Role of Conflict Resolution in Teams: A Close Look at the Links between Conflict Type, Conflict Management Strategies, and Team Outcomes," *Journal of Applied Psychology,* January 2008, p 185. The first student to read this and e-mail r.kreitner@cox.net before December 31, 2010, will receive a $100 grant for being a serious scholar.

[69] Based on B Richey, H J Bernardin, C L Tyler, and N McKinney, "The Effects of Arbitration Program Characteristics on Applicants' Intentions toward Potential Employers," *Journal of Applied Psychology,* October 2001, pp 1006–13.

[70] See M E Schnake and D S Cochran, "Effect of Two Goal-Setting Dimensions on Perceived Intraorganizational Conflict," *Group & Organization Studies,* June 1985, pp 168–83. Also see O Janssen, E Van De Vliert, and C Veenstra, "How Task and Person Conflict Shape the Role of Positive Interdependence in Management Teams," *Journal of Management,* no. 2, 1999, pp 117–42.

[71] Drawn from L H Chusmir and J Mills, "Gender Differences in Conflict Resolution Styles of Managers: At Work and at Home," *Sex Roles,* February 1989, pp 149–63.

[72] See K K Smith, "The Movement of Conflict in Organizations: The Joint Dynamics of Splitting and Triangulation," *Administrative Science Quarterly,* March 1989, pp 1–20.

[73] Based on C Tinsley, "Models of Conflict Resolution in Japanese, German, and American Cultures," *Journal of Applied Psychology,* April 1998, pp 316–23; and S M Adams, "Settling Cross-Cultural Disagreements Begins with 'Where' Not 'How,'" *Academy of Management Executive,* February 1999, pp 109–10.

[74] Based on a definition in M A Neale and M H Bazerman, "Negotiating Rationally: The Power and Impact of the Negotiator's Frame," *Academy of Management Executive,* August 1992, pp 42–51. Also see D Malhotra, "When Contracts Destroy Trust," *Harvard Business Review,* May 2009, p 25.

75 For example, see J L Lunsford, "Boeing Strikers Dig In Heels Even as Economy Turns South," *The Wall Street Journal,* October 23, 2008, pp A1, A9; and J McGregor, "Costco's Artful Discounts," *BusinessWeek,* October 20, 2008, pp 58–60.

76 Data and quote from J Yang and K Carter, "USA Today Snapshots," *USA Today,* March 9, 2009, p 1B.

77 M H Bazerman and M A Neale, *Negotiating Rationally* (New York: Free Press, 1992), p 16. Also see M Kaplan, "How to Negotiate Anything," *Money,* May 2005, pp 117–19; D Malhotra, G Ku, and J K Murnighan, "When Winning Is Everything," *Harvard Business Review,* May 2008, pp 78–86; and E T Amanatullah, M W Morris, and J R Curhan, "Negotiators Who Give Too Much: Unmitigated Communion, Relational Anxieties, and Economic Costs in Distributive and Integrative Bargaining," *Journal of Personality and Social Psychology,* September 2008, pp 723–38.

78 Good win–win negotiation strategies can be found in R R Reck and B G Long, *The Win–Win Negotiator: How to Negotiate Favorable Agreements That Last* (New York: Pocket Books, 1987); R Fisher and W Ury, *Getting to YES: Negotiating Agreement without Giving In* (Boston: Houghton Mifflin, 1981); and R Fisher and D Ertel, *Getting Ready to Negotiate: The Getting to YES Workbook* (New York: Penguin Books, 1995). Also see B Spector, "An Interview with Roger Fisher and William Ury," *Academy of Management Executive,* August 2004, pp 101–108; B Booth and M McCredie, "Taking Steps toward 'Getting to Yes' at Blue Cross and Blue Shield of Florida," *Academy of Management Executive,* August 2004, pp 109–12; and N Brodsky, "The Paranoia Moment. Are They Stalling? Is This Deal about to Fall Apart?" *Inc.,* April 2007, pp 67–68.

79 See L R Weingart, E B Hyder, and M J Prietula, "Knowledge Matters: The Effect of Tactical Descriptions on Negotiation Behavior and Outcome." *Journal of Personality and Social Psychology,* June 1996, pp 1205–17.

80 For more, see A Valenzuela, J Srivastava, and S Lee, "The Role of Cultural Orientation in Bargaining under Incomplete Information: Differences in Causal Attributions," *Organizational Behavior and Human Decision Processes,* January 2005, pp 72–88; K Lee, G Yang, and J L Graham, "Tension and Trust in International Business Negotiations: American Executives Negotiating with Chinese Executives," *Journal of International Business Studies,* September 2006, pp 623–41; and L E Metcalf, A Bird, M Shankarmahesh, Z Aycan, J Larimo, and D D Valdelamar, "Cultural Tendencies in Negotiation: A Comparison of Finland, India, Mexico, Turkey, and the United States," *Journal of World Business,* December 2006, pp 382–94.

81 For supporting evidence, see J K Butler Jr, "Trust Expectations, Information Sharing, Climate of Trust, and Negotiation Effectiveness and Efficiency," *Group and Organization Management,* June 1999, pp 217–38.

82 See H J Reitz, J A Wall Jr, and M S Love, "Ethics in Negotiation: Oil and Water or Good Lubrication?" *Business Horizons,* May–June 1998, pp 5–14; M E Schweitzer and Jeffrey L Kerr, "Bargaining under the Influence: The Role of Alcohol in Negotiations," *Academy of Management Executive,* May 2000, pp 47–57; and A M Burr, "Ethics in Negotiation: Does Getting to Yes Require Candor?" *Dispute Resolution Journal,* May–July 2001, pp 8–15.

83 For related research, see E van Dijk, G A van Kleef, W Steinel, and I van Beest, "A Social Functional Approach to Emotions in Bargaining: When Communicating Anger Pays and When It Backfires," *Journal of Personality and Social Psychology,* April 2008, pp 600–14; and D R Dalton and C M Dalton, "On the *Many* Limitations of Threat in Negotiation, as Well as Other Contexts," *Business Horizons,* March–April 2009, pp 109–15.

84 Based on R L Pinkley, T L Griffith, and G B Northcraft, "'Fixed Pie' a la Mode: Information Availability, Information Processing, and the Negotiation of Suboptimal Agreements," *Organizational Behavior and Human Decision Processes,* April 1995, pp 101–12.

85 Based on A E Walters, A F Stuhlmacher, and L L Meyer, "Gender and Negotiator Competitiveness: A Meta-Analysis," *Organizational Behavior and Human Decision Processes,* October 1998, pp 1–29.

86 Based on B Barry and R A Friedman, "Bargainer Characteristics in Distributive and Integrative Negotiation," *Journal of Personality and Social Psychology,* February 1998, pp 345–59. Also see K J Sulkowicz, "The Psychology of the Deal," *BusinessWeek,* April 9, 2007, p 14.

87 For more, see J P Forgas, "On Feeling Good and Getting Your Way: Mood Effects on Negotiator Cognition and Bargaining Strategies," *Journal of Personality and Social Psychology,* March 1998, pp 565–77.

88 Data from B Campbell and M M Marx, "Toward More Effective Stakeholder Dialogue: Applying Theories of Negotiation to Policy and Program Evaluation," *Journal of Applied Social Psychology,* December 2006, pp 2834–63.

89 Drawn from J M Brett and T Okumura, "Inter- and Intracultural Negotiation: US and Japanese Negotiators," *Academy of Management Journal,* October 1998, pp 495–510.

90 Excerpted from L Buchanan, "The Ultimate Business Makeover," *Inc.: The Magazine for Growing Companies,* March 2009. Copyright © 2009 by Mansueto Ventures LLC. Reproduced with permission of Mansueto Ventures LLC via Copyright Clearance Center.

91 Excerpted from K Sulkowicz, "Sparring Execs Need a Time Out," *BusinessWeek,* December 18, 2006, p 18.

CHAPTER 14

1 Excerpted from J McGregor, "Job Review in 140 Keystrokes," *BusinessWeek,* March 23–30, 2009, p 58.

2 See D G Kolb, P D Collins, and E A Lind, "Requisite Connectivity: Finding Flow in a Not-So-Flat World," *Organizational Dynamics,* April–June 2008, pp 181–89; and N R Lockwood, "Effective Organizational Communication: A Competitive Advantage," SHRM Research Quarterly, *HR Magazine,* December 2008, pp 1–9.

3 Data from G Naik, "A Hospital Races to Learn Lessons of Ferrari Pit Stop," *The Wall Street Journal,* November 14, 2006, pp A1, A10.

4 Based on "Why Am I Here," *Training,* April 2006, p 13. For a similar interpretation, see D Robb, "From the Top," *HR Magazine,* February 2009, pp 61–63.

5 J L Bowditch and A F Buono, *A Primer on Organizational Behavior,* 4th ed (New York: John Wiley & Sons, 1997), p 120.

6 Data from H Hitchings, *The Secret Life of Words: How English Became English* (New York: Farrar, Straus and Giroux, 2008), p 7.

[7] G A Fowler, "In China's Offices, Foreign Colleagues Might Get an Earful," *The Wall Street Journal,* February 13, 2007, p B1.

[8] See S Boehle, "Voices of Opportunity," *Training,* January 2009, pp 37–39; and A Campo-Flores and S Kliff, "Campfire Questions," *Newsweek,* January 26, 2009, pp 66–67.

[9] See A Damast, "For Communication Skills, the Play's the Thing," *BusinessWeek,* April 7, 2008, p 92; and M Weinstein, "Mane Event," *Training,* March–April 2009, pp 20–24.

[10] See R Y J Chua, P Ingram, and M W Morris, "From the Head and the Heart: Locating Cognition- and Affect-Based Trust in Managers' Professional Networks," *Academy of Management Journal,* June 2008, pp 436–52.

[11] See R R Hastings, "Poll Finds Mistrust among Racial Groups," *HR Magazine,* February 2008, p 26.

[12] For a thorough discussion of these barriers, see C R Rogers and F J Roethlisberger, "Barriers and Gateways to Communication," *Harvard Business Review,* July–August 1952, pp 46–52.

[13] Ibid., p 47.

[14] Physical barriers are discussed in E Woyke, "Wanted: A Clutter Cutter," *BusinessWeek,* April 9, 2007, p 12.

[15] Excerpted from J Sandberg, "'It Says Press Any Key. Where's the Any Key?'" *The Wall Street Journal,* February 20, 2007, p B1.

[16] See B Levisohn, "Techie Charm School," *BusinessWeek,* August 25–September 1, 2008, p 13.

[17] Results can be found in J D Johnson, W A Donohue, C K Atkin, and S Johnson, "Communication, Involvement, and Perceived Innovativeness," *Group and Organization Management,* March 2001, pp 24–52; and B Davenport Sypher and T E Zorn Jr, "Communication-Related Abilities and Upward Mobility: A Longitudinal Investigation," *Human Communication Research,* Spring 1986, pp 420–31. Also see M Weinstein, "Leadership Tails," *Training,* March–April 2009, p 24.

[18] J Swartz, "Yahoo's New CEO Finds Plenty on Her Plate," *USA Today,* January 15, 2009, p 3B. For more, see J Swartz, "Yahoo to Lay Off Up to 700 Staffers after Profit Drops," *USA Today,* April 22, 2009, p 3B.

[19] These recommendations were adapted from J Yadegaran, "Just Say 'No,'" *The Arizona Republic,* September 14, 2006, p E3.

[20] W D St. John, "You Are What You Communicate," *Personnel Journal,* October 1985, p 40. Also see M E Mangelsdorf, "The Power of Nonverbal Communication," *The Wall Street Journal,* October 20, 2008, p R2; and S Baker, "Reading the Body Language of Leadership," *BusinessWeek,* March 23–30, 2009, p 48.

[21] This statistic was reported in R O Crockett, "The 21st Century Meeting," *BusinessWeek,* February 26, 2007, pp 72–79.

[22] A study of decoding nonverbal cues was conducted by E L Cooley, "Attachment Style and Decoding of Nonverbal Cues," *North American Journal of Psychology,* 2005, pp 25–33.

[23] Based on J A Hall, "Male and Female Nonverbal Behavior," in *Multichannel Integrations of Nonverbal Behavior,* ed A W Siegman and S Feldstein (Hillsdale, NJ: Lawrence Erlbaum, 1985), pp 195–226.

[24] See B Kachka, "Etiquette 101," *Condé Nast Traveler,* April 2008, pp 112–18; and S Pika, E Nicoladis, and P Marentette, "How to Order a Beer: Cultural Differences in the Use of Conventional Gestures for Numbers," *Journal of Cross-Cultural Psychology,* no. 1, 2009, pp 70–80.

[25] Results can be found in Hall, "Male and Female Nonverbal Behavior."

[26] See J A Russell, "Facial Expressions of Emotion: What Lies beyond Minimal Universality?" *Psychological Bulletin,* November 1995, pp 379–91. Also see B Azar, "A Case for Angry Men and Happy Women," *Monitor on Psychology,* April 2007, pp 18–19.

[27] Norms for cross-cultural eye contact are discussed by C Engholm, *When Business East Meets Business West: The Guide to Practice and Protocol in the Pacific Rim* (New York: John Wiley & Sons, 1991).

[28] These recommendations were adapted from those in P Preston, "Nonverbal Communication: Do You Really Say What You Mean?" *Journal of Healthcare Management,* March–April 2005, pp 83–86.

[29] See R D Ramsey, "Ten Things That Never Change for Supervisors," *SuperVision,* April 2007, pp 16–18; "CEOs Emphasize Listening to Employees," *HR Magazine,* January 2007, p 14; and M Marchetti, "Listen to Me!" *Sales and Marketing Management,* April 2007, p 12.

[30] The discussion of listening styles is based on "5 Listening Styles," www.crossroadsinstitute.org/listyle.html, accessed May 5, 2005; and J Condrill, "What Is Your Listening Style?" *Authors Den.Com,* July 7, 2005, www.authorsden.com/visit/viewarticle. asp?id=18707.

[31] As quoted in J Weber, "Against the Grain," *BusinessWeek,* January 12, 2009, p 37. Also see D W Dowling, "Maureen Chiquet: The Best Advice I Ever Got," *Harvard Business Review,* November 2008, p 30.

[32] These recommendations were excerpted from J Jay, "On Communicating Well," *HR Magazine,* January 2005, pp 87–88.

[33] D Tannen, "The Power of Talk: Who Gets Heard and Why," *Harvard Business Review,* September–October 1995, p 139.

[34] For a thorough review of the evolutionary explanation of sex differences in communication, see A H Eagly and W Wood, "The Origins of Sex Differences in Human Behavior," *American Psychologist,* June 1999, pp 408–23. A critique of evolutionary psychology was also provided by S Begley, "Evolutionary Psych May Not Help Explain Our Behavior after All," *The Wall Street Journal,* April 29, 2005, p B1.

[35] See Tannen, "The Power of Talk," pp 160–73; and D Tannen, *You Just Don't Understand: Women and Men in Conversation* (New York: Ballantine Books, 1990).

[36] See M Dainton and E D Zelley, *Applying Communication Theory for Professional Life: A Practical Introduction* (Thousand Oaks, CA: Sage, 2005); and "The Differences between Boys and Girls…At the Office," *Training,* November 2006, p 8.

[37] This definition was taken from J C Tingley, *Genderflex: Men and Women Speaking Each Other's Language at Work* (New York: American Management Association, 1994), p 16.

[38] Tannen, "The Power of Talk," pp 147–48.

[39] See C Hirschman, "Giving Voice to Employee Concerns," *HR Magazine,* August 2008, pp 50–53; L Grensing-Pophal, "To Ask or Not to Ask," *HR Magazine,* February 2009, pp 53–55; and M Kimes, "How Can I Get Candid Feedback from My Employees?" *Fortune,* April 13, 2009, p 24.

[40] For practical advice and examples, see M Marquardt, *Leading with Questions: How Leaders Find the Right Solutions by Knowing What to Ask* (San Francisco, CA: Jossey-Bass, 2005); and S Freeman, "Ask the 'Dumb' Questions," *USA Today,* January 13, 2009, p 11A.

[41] J Yang and S Ward, "USA Today Snapshots," *USA Today,* February 26, 2008, p 1B.

[42] J Yang and V Salazar, "USA Today Snapshots," *USA Today,* November 20, 2008, p 1B. Also see the first Q&A in "Ask Inc.: Tough Questions, Smart Answers," *Inc.,* January–February 2009, pp 104–105.

[43] These recommendations were taken from N H Woodward, "Doing Town Hall Meetings Better," *HR Magazine,* December 2006, p 70. Also see J L Yang, "What's the Secret to Running Great Meetings?" *Fortune,* October 27, 2008, p 26; N Morgan, "How to Become an Authentic Speaker," *Harvard Business Review,* November 2008, pp 115–19; and S B Fink, "Address the Human Side of M&As," *Training,* March–April 2009, p 16.

[44] For more, see L Sussman, "Disclosure, Leaks, and Slips: Issues and Strategies for Prohibiting Employee Communication," *Business Horizons,* July–August 2008, pp 331–39.

[45] H B Vickery III, "Tapping into the Employee Grapevine," *Association Management,* January 1984, pp 59–60.

[46] Drawn from S M Crampton, J W Hodge, and J M Mishra, "The Informal Communication Network: Factors Influencing Grapevine Activity," *Public Personnel Management,* Winter 1998, pp 569–84; "Pruning the Company Grapevine," *Supervision,* September 1986, p 11; and J Yang and V Salazar, "What Is the Most Taboo Topic to Discuss at Work?" *USA Today,* June 17, 2008, p 1B.

[47] J Yang and S Parker, "Top Managers Don't Appreciate Office Gossip," *USA Today,* December 24, 2008, p 1B.

[48] J McGregor, "Mining the Office Chatter," *BusinessWeek,* May 19, 2008, p 54. Also see D McGinn, "Managing Along the Cutting Edge," *Newsweek,* February 9, 2009, pp 46–47.

[49] Management by walking around is discussed by T Peters and N Austin, *A Passion for Excellence: The Leadership Difference* (New York: Random House, 1985).

[50] L Dulye, "Get Out of Your Office," *HR Magazine,* July 2006, p 99.

[51] These recommendations were adapted from ibid., pp 100–101.

[52] Data from J M O'Brien, "Zappos Knows How to Kick It," *Fortune,* February 2, 2009, pp 54–60.

[53] R Levering and M Moskowitz, "And the Winners Are. . .," *Fortune,* February 2, 2009, pp 67–78.

[54] R L Daft and R H Lengel, "Information Richness: A New Approach to Managerial Behavior and Organizational Design," in *Research in Organizational Behavior,* ed B M Staw and L L Cummings (Greenwich, CT: JAI Press, 1984), p 196.

[55] Details of this example are provided in L Grensing-Pophal, "Spread the Word—Correctly," *HR Magazine,* March 2005, pp 83–88. Also see N Byrnes, "A Steely Resolve," *BusinessWeek,* April 6, 2009, p 54.

[56] See E Binney, "Is E-Mail the New Pink Slip?" *HR Magazine,* November 2006, pp 32, 38; and D M Cable and K Y T Yu, "Managing Job Seekers' Organizational Image Beliefs: The Role of Media Richness and Media Credibility," *Journal of Applied Psychology,* July 2006, pp 828–40.

[57] See B Barry and I S Fulmer, "The Medium and the Message: The Adaptive Use of Communication Media in Dyadic Influence," *Academy of Management Review,* April 2004, pp 272–92; and A F Simon, "Computer-Mediated Communication: Task Performance and Satisfaction," *The Journal of Social Psychology,* June 2006, pp 349–79.

[58] See R E Rice and D E Shook, "Relationships of Job Categories and Organizational Levels to Use of Communication Channels, Including Electronic Mail: A Meta-Analysis and Extension," *Journal of Management Studies,* March 1990, pp 195–229.

[59] For more, see A Lashinsky, "The True Meaning of Twitter," *Fortune,* August 18, 2008, pp 39–42; D Kadlec, "How Not to Act Your Age at Work," *Money,* December 2008, pp 44, 46; S H Wildstrom, "What to Entrust to the Cloud," *BusinessWeek,* April 6, 2009, pp 89–90; and C Edwards, "Soon TVs and PCs May Work Like the Wii," *BusinessWeek,* April 13, 2009, p 52.

[60] A Fisher, "E-Mail Is for Liars," *Fortune,* November 24, 2008, p 57.

[61] A Pentland, "How Social Networks Network Best," *Harvard Business Review,* February 2009, p 37. Also see G Morse, "Conversation: Wikipedia Founder Jimmy Wales on Making the Most of Company Wikis," *Harvard Business Review,* April 2008, p 26; E M Lira, P Ripoll, J M Peiro, and A M Zornoza, "The Role of Information and Communication Technologies in the Relationship between Group Effectiveness and Group Potency," *Small Group Research,* December 2008, pp 728–45; and G Dutton, "Tech Check," *Training,* January 2009, pp 24–26.

[62] Data from www.ic3.gov/media/2009/090331.aspx, accessed April 7, 2009.

[63] R Zeidner, "Out of the Breach," *HR Magazine,* August 2008, p 39. Also see "Help! Somebody Save Our Files! How to Handle and Prevent the Most Common Data Disasters," *Inc.,* August 2008, pp 33–37; R Zeidner, "Customers Threatened with Extortion after Data Breach," *HR Magazine,* January 2009, p 22; and "Cybercrooks' Website Spotlights Extent of Identity Theft," *USA Today,* March 16, 2009, p 7B.

[64] See M V Copeland, "On the Internet, Everybody Knows Your Dog's Name," *Fortune,* September 29, 2008, p 58; and K Wehrum, "When IT Workers Attack: How to Prevent Tech Sabotage," *Inc.,* April 2009, pp 132, 134.

[65] D Tapscott, *Grown Up Digital: How the Net Generation Is Changing Your World* (New York: McGraw-Hill, 2009), p 36. Also see the table "How Does Your Generation Communicate?" in "Generation Gap," *Executive Travel,* November–December 2008, pp 60–61.

[66] J L Yang, "How to Get a Job," *Fortune,* April 13, 2009, p 51. Also see J Graham, "Cake Decorator Finds Twitter a Tweet Recipe for Success," *USA Today,* April 1, 2009, p 5B; and S Jayson, "For Teens, a Friend Online Usually a Friend Offline, Too," *USA Today,* April 2, 2009, p 7D.

[67] See E Agnvall, "Meetings Go Virtual," *HR Magazine,* January 2009, pp 74–77; J Mullich, "How to Pick Your Mobile Lifestyle," *The Wall Street Journal,* April 1, 2009, pp A11–A12; and L Cauley, "FCC Pursues Goal of Nationwide Affordable, Fast Internet," *USA Today,* April 8, 2009, p 5B.

[68] Data from E Reed, "Telecommuting by the Numbers," *HR Magazine,* September 2008, p 61. Also see "Benchmark with the Best," *HR Magazine,* July 2008, p 49.

[69] Reprinted from M Conlin, "Home Offices: The New Math," March 9, 2009, issue of *BusinessWeek* by special permission.

Copyright © 2009 by The McGraw-Hill Companies, Inc. Also see J Schramm, "Work Turns Flexible," *HR Magazine,* March 2009, p 88.

70 J A Pearce II, "Successful Corporate Telecommuting with Technology Considerations for Late Adopters," *Organizational Dynamics,* January–March 2009, p 17.

71 Data from "The Virtual Workforce," *BusinessWeek,* March 5, 2007, p 6; and T D Golden, J F Veiga, and Z Simsek, "Telecommuting's Differential Impact of Work-Family Conflict: Is There No Place Like Home?" *Journal of Applied Psychology,* November 2006, pp 1240–50.

72 M Conlin, "Telecommuting: Out of Sight, Yes. Out of Mind, No," *BusinessWeek,* February 18, 2008, p 60.

73 Results are reported in K Gurchiek, "Telecommuting Could Hold Back Careers," *HR Magazine,* March 2007, p 34.

74 T D Golden, J F Veiga, and R N Dino, "The Impact of Professional Isolation on Teleworker Job Performance and Turnover Intentions: Does Time Spent Teleworking, Interacting Face-to-Face, or Having Access to Communication-Enhancing Technology Matter?" *Journal of Applied Psychology,* November 2008, p 1412.

75 C R Stoner, P Stephens, and M K McGowan, "Connectivity and Work Dominance: Panacea or Pariah?" *Business Horizons,* January–February 2009, p 67. Also see D G Kolb, P D Collins, and E A Lind, "Requisite Connectivity: Finding Flow in a Not-So-Flat World," *Organizational Dynamics,* April–June 2008, pp 181–89.

76 See T W Briggs, "Book's Not Closed on Texting," *USA Today,* September 4, 2007, p 9D; B Levisohn, "Write On, Dood," *BusinessWeek,* August 4, 2008, p 16; and M B Marklein, "Community Colleges Must Expect More," *USA Today,* November 17, 2008, p 4D.

77 L Stone, "Living with Continuous Partial Attention," *Harvard Business Review,* February 2007, p 28. Also see L McCreary, "My BlackBerry Ate My Accountability," *Harvard Business Review,* February 2008, p 38; N L Reinsch Jr, J W Turner, and C H Tinsley, "Multicommunicating: A Practice Whose Time Has Come?" *Academy of Management Review,* April 2008, pp 391–403; and N Croal, "The Peril of Digital Fidgeting," *Newsweek,* July 21, 2008, p 64.

78 R Scoble, "Reengineering Your Inbox," *Fast Company,* February 2009, p 50.

79 Based on K Byron, "Carrying Too Heavy a Load? The Communication and Miscommunication of Emotion by Email," *Academy of Management Review,* April 2008, pp 309–27.

80 B Roberts, "Stay Ahead of the Technology Use Curve," *HR Magazine,* October 2008, p 58.

81 M Kessler, "Fridays Turning E-mail Free," *The Arizona Republic,* October 7, 2007, p D3. Also see J McGregor, "E-mail: Can't It Wait Till Monday?" *BusinessWeek,* May 19, 2008, p 54.

82 Data from "Americans More Dependent on Cellphones Than Landlines," *The Arizona Republic,* March 8, 2008, p D3; J Kornblum, "Text Messaging Taps Out a Family-Friendly Result," *USA Today,* October 20, 2008, p 7D; and A R Carey and J Snider, "Replacing Land-Line Phones with Cellphones," *USA Today,* April 7, 2009, p 1A.

83 See W Koch, "More Teens Caught Up in 'Sexting,'" *USA Today,* March 12, 2009, p 1A; and J Michaels, "Cellphones Put to 'Unnerving' Use in Gaza," *USA Today,* January 14, 2009, p 4A.

84 K Freking and D Nguyen, "Engineer of Doomed Train Had Invited Teen to Run It," *USA Today,* March 4, 2009, p 5A. Also see D Searcey, "Generation Text: Emailing on the Go Sends Some Users into Harm's Way," *The Wall Street Journal,* July 25, 2008, pp A1, A11.

85 See J O'Donnell, "Efforts to Limit Cellphone Use While Driving Grow," *USA Today,* March 30, 2009, p 1B.

86 A Novotney, "Dangerous Distraction," *Monitor on Psychology,* February 2009, p 34.

87 See the 10 tips in www.microsoft.com/smallbusiness/resources/technology/communications/cell-phone-etiquette-10-dos-and-donts.aspx#Cellphoneetiquettedosanddonts, accessed April 10, 2009.

88 Reprprinted from R King, "Go Ahead, Use Facebook," August 25–September 1, 2008, issue of *BusinessWeek* by special permission. Copyright © 2009 by The McGraw-Hill Companies, Inc. Seven Twitter tools are discussed in R Scoble, "Brand New Day," *Fast Company,* May 2009, p 52.

89 Reprinted from S Baker, "The Next Net," March 9, 2009, issue of *BusinessWeek* by special permission. Copyright © 2009 by The McGraw-Hill Companies, Inc. Also see K Boehret, "Tracking Friends the Google Way," *The Wall Street Journal,* February 4, 2009, p D2; and L Cauley, "Feel Like Someone's Watching You?" *USA Today,* February 9, 2009, pp 1B–2B.

CHAPTER 15

1 Reprinted from H Green, "How Meetup Tore Up the Rule Book," June 16, 2008, issue of *BusinessWeek* by special permission. Copyright © 2008 by The McGraw-Hill Companies, Inc.

2 Quotes and data from J Yang and V Salazar, "USA Today Snapshots," *USA Today,* February 10, 2009, p 1B. Also see A L Kalleberg, "The Mismatched Worker: When People Don't Fit Their Jobs," *Academy of Management Perspectives,* February 2008, pp 24–40; and L Petrecca, "Many Satisfied with Job Despite Tough Times," *USA Today,* March 13, 2009, p 3B.

3 H Malcolm and C Sokoloff, "Values, Human Relations, and Organization Development," in *The Emerging Practice of Organizational Development,* ed W Sikes, A Drexler, and J Gant (San Diego, CA: University Associates, 1989), p 64.

4 As quoted in "The World's Most Influential Companies," *BusinessWeek,* December 22, 2008, p 44. For more of Hamel's ideas, see G Hamel, "Moon Shots for Management," *Harvard Business Review,* February 2009, pp 91–98.

5 See D Kipnis, S M Schmidt, and I Wilkinson, "Intraorganizational Influence Tactics: Explorations in Getting One's Way," *Journal of Applied Psychology,* August 1980, pp 440–52. Also see C A Schriesheim and T R Hinkin, "Influence Tactics Used by Subordinates: A Theoretical and Empirical Analysis and Refinement of the Kipnis, Schmidt, and Wilkinson Subscales," *Journal of Applied Psychology,* June 1990, pp 246–57; G Yukl and C M Falbe, "Influence Tactics and Objectives in Upward, Downward, and Lateral Influence Attempts," *Journal of Applied Psychology,* April 1990, pp 132–40; and G Yukl and B Tracey, "Consequences of Influence Tactics Used with Subordinates, Peers, and the Boss," in *Organizational Influence Processes,* 2nd ed, ed L W Porter, H L Angle, and R W Allen (Armonk, NY: M E Sharpe, 2003), pp 96–116.

6 Based on Table 1 in G Yukl, C M Falbe, and J Y Youn, "Patterns of Influence Behavior for Managers," *Group*

and Organization Management, March 1993, pp 5–28. An additional influence tactic is presented in B P Davis and E S Knowles, "A Disrupt-Then-Reframe Technique of Social Influence," *Journal of Personality and Social Psychology,* February 1999, pp 192–99. For more on ingratiation, see D B Yoffie and M Kwak, "With Friends Like These: The Art of Managing Complementors," *Harvard Business Review,* September 2006, pp 88–98.

[7] For comprehensive coverage, see L W Porter, H L Angle, and R W Allen, eds, *Organizational Influence Processes,* 2nd ed (Armonk, NY: M E Sharpe, 2003); and The Society for Human Resource Management and Harvard Business School Press, *The Essentials of Power, Influence, and Persuasion* (Boston: Harvard Business School Press, 2006).

[8] Excerpted from A Weintraub, "Making Her Mark at Merck," *BusinessWeek,* January 8, 2007, p 65. Also see J Grenny, D Maxfield, and A Shimberg, "How to Have Influence," *MIT Sloan Management Review,* Fall 2008, pp 47–52; J Reingold, "Meet Your New Leader," *Fortune,* November 24, 2008, pp 145–46; and M Kimes, "The Accidental CEO," *Fortune,* March 2, 2009, p 26.

[9] Based on discussion in G Yukl, H Kim, and C M Falbe, "Antecedents of Influence Outcomes," *Journal of Applied Psychology,* June 1996, pp 309–17.

[10] Data from ibid.

[11] Data from G Yukl and J B Tracey, "Consequences of Influence Tactics Used with Subordinates, Peers, and the Boss," *Journal of Applied Psychology,* August 1992, pp 525–35. Also see C M Falbe and G Yukl, "Consequences for Managers of Using Single Influence Tactics and Combinations of Tactics," *Academy of Management Journal,* August 1992, pp 638–52.

[12] Data from R A Gordon, "Impact of Ingratiation on Judgments and Evaluations: A Meta-Analytic Investigation," *Journal of Personality and Social Psychology,* July 1996, pp 54–70.

[13] Based on J D Westphal and I Stern, "Flattery Will Get You Everywhere (Especially if You Are a Male Caucasian): How Ingratiation, Boardroom Behavior, and Demographic Minority Status Affect Additional Board Appointments at U.S. Companies," *Academy of Management Journal,* April 2007, pp 267–88; and N Byrnes, "Profiles in Sycophancy," *BusinessWeek,* August 13, 2007, p 12.

[14] Data from Yukl, Kim, and Falbe, "Antecedents of Influence Outcomes."

[15] Based on R T Sparrowe, B W Soetjipto, and M L Kraimer, "Do Leaders' Influence Tactics Relate to Members' Helping Behavior? It Depends on the Quality of the Relationship," *Academy of Management Journal,* December 2006, pp 1194–208. Also see F A White, M A Charles, and J K Nelson, "The Role of Persuasive Arguments in Changing Affirmative Action Attitudes and Expressed Behavior in Higher Education," *Journal of Applied Psychology,* November 2008, pp 1271–86.

[16] Data from B J Tepper, R J Eisenbach, S L Kirby, and P W Potter, "Test of a Justice-Based Model of Subordinates' Resistance to Downward Influence Attempts," *Group and Organization Management,* June 1998, pp 144–60.

[17] J E Driskell, B Olmstead, and E Salas, "Task Cues, Dominance Cues, and Influence in Task Groups," *Journal of Applied Psychology,* February 1993, p 51. No gender bias was found in H Aguinis and S K R Adams, "Social-Role versus Structural Models of Gender and Influence Use in Organizations: A Strong Inference Approach," *Group and Organization Management,* December 1998, pp 414–46.

[18] See P P Fu et al., "The Impact of Societal Cultural Values and Individual Social Beliefs on the Perceived Effectiveness of Managerial Influence Strategies: A Meso Approach," *Journal of International Business Studies,* July 2004, pp 284–305. Also see C Anderson, S E Spataro, and F J Flynn, "Personality and Organizational Culture as Determinants of Influence," *Journal of Applied Psychology,* May 2008, pp 702–10.

[19] B Moses, "You Can't Make Change; You Have to Sell It," *Fast Company,* April 1999, p 101. Also see S R Covey, "Rising Stars," *Training,* March–April 2008, p 64; H Green, "Google: Harnessing the Power of Cliques," *BusinessWeek,* October 6, 2008, p 50; and N J Goldstein, "Harnessing Social Pressure," *Harvard Business Review,* February 2009, p 25.

[20] See D H Gruenfeld, M E Inesi, J C Magee, and A D Galinsky, "Power and the Objectification of Social Targets," *Journal of Personality and Social Psychology,* July 2008, pp 111–27; D Coutu, "Smart Power," *Harvard Business Review,* November 2008, pp 55–59; and J Meacham, "The Story of Power," *Newsweek,* January 5, 2009, pp 32–35.

[21] D Tjosvold, "The Dynamics of Positive Power," *Training and Development Journal,* June 1984, p 72. Also see D Tjosvold and B Wisse, eds, *Power and Interdependence in Organizations* (Cambridge, UK: Cambridge University Press, 2009).

[22] M W McCall Jr, *Power, Influence, and Authority: The Hazards of Carrying a Sword,* Technical Report No. 10 (Greensboro, NC: Center for Creative Leadership, 1978), p 5. For an excellent discussion, see J O Hagberg, *Real Power: Stages of Personal Power in Organizations,* 3rd ed (Salem, WI: Sheffield Publishing, 2003).

[23] D Weimer, "Daughter Knows Best," *BusinessWeek,* April 19, 1999, pp 132, 134. Also see "How to Stage a Coup," *Inc.,* March 2005, p 52.

[24] For an update, see C L Bernick, "When Your Culture Needs a Makeover," *Harvard Business Review,* June 2001, pp 53–61.

[25] L H Chusmir, "Personalized versus Socialized Power Needs among Working Women and Men," *Human Relations,* February 1986, p 149.

[26] R I Sutton, "Are You Being a Jerk Again?" *BusinessWeek,* August 25–September 1, 2008, p 52.

[27] As quoted in L Buchanan, "That's Quite a Story: How I Did It," *Inc.,* November 2006, p 113.

[28] Based on D W Cantor and T Bernay, *Women in Power: The Secrets of Leadership* (Boston: Houghton Mifflin, 1992). Also see S Jayson, "At Home, Women Hold the Power," *USA Today,* September 25, 2008, p 8D; and J Shambora and B Kowitt, "50 Most Powerful Women," *Fortune,* October 13, 2008, pp 165–78.

[29] S Sandberg, "Changing the World, One Job at a Time," *Newsweek,* October 13, 2008, p 68.

[30] See J R P French and B Raven, "The Bases of Social Power," in *Studies in Social Power,* ed D Cartwright (Ann Arbor: University of Michigan Press, 1959), pp 150–67. Also see S M Farmer and H Aguinis, "Accounting for Subordinate Perceptions of Supervisor Power: An Identity-Dependence Model," *Journal of Applied Psychology,* November 2005, pp 1069–83.

[31] G Edmondson, "Power Play at VW," *BusinessWeek,* December 4, 2006, p 45.

[32] See, for example, M Weinstein, "Off-Duty But on Your Mind," *Training,* March–April 2008, p 11; M Conlin, "Hide the Doritos! Here Comes HR," *BusinessWeek,* April 28, 2008, pp 94, 96; S Boehle, "They're Watching You. . .," *Training,* September 2008, pp 22–29; and R Jana, "A Shot in the Arm for E-Health," *BusinessWeek,* December 8, 2008, pp 58–59.

[33] Data from J R Larson Jr, C Christensen, A S Abbott, and T M Franz, "Diagnosing Groups: Charting the Flow of Information in Medical Decision-Making Teams," *Journal of Personality and Social Psychology,* August 1996, pp 315–30.

[34] See D J Ketchen Jr, G L Adams, and C L Shook, "Understanding and Managing CEO Celebrity," *Business Horizons,* November–December 2008, pp 529–34; and F Zakaria, "Barack Obama," *Newsweek,* January 5, 2009, p 37.

[35] Excerpted from the first Q&A with J Welch and S Welch, "It's Not about Empty Suits," October 16, 2006, issue of *BusinessWeek* by special permission. Copyright © 2006 by The McGraw-Hill Companies, Inc.

[36] Details may be found in Chusmir, "Personalized versus Socialized Power Needs among Working Women and Men," pp 149–59. For a review of research on individual differences in the need for power, see R J House, "Power and Personality in Complex Organizations," in *Research in Organizational Behavior,* ed B M Staw and L L Cummings (Greenwich, CT: JAI Press, 1988), pp 305–57.

[37] B Filipczak, "Is It Getting Chilly in Here?" *Training,* February 1994, p 27.

[38] Data from J Onyx, R Leonard, and K Vivekananda, "Social Perception of Power: A Gender Analysis," *Perceptual and Motor Skills,* February 1995, pp 291–96.

[39] P M Podsakoff and C A Schriesheim, "Field Studies of French and Raven's Bases of Power: Critique, Reanalysis, and Suggestions for Future Research," *Psychological Bulletin,* May 1985, p 388. Also see C A Schriesheim, T R Hinkin, and P M Podsakoff, "Can Ipsative and Single-Item Measures Produce Erroneous Results in Field Studies of French and Raven's (1950) Five Bases of Power? An Empirical Investigation," *Journal of Applied Psychology,* February 1991, pp 106–14.

[40] See T R Hinkin and C A Schriesheim, "Relationships between Subordinate Perceptions and Supervisor Influence Tactics and Attributed Bases of Supervisory Power," *Human Relations,* March 1990, pp 221–37.

[41] W Clark, "The Potency of Persuasion," *Fortune,* November 12, 2007, p 48.

[42] Based on P A Wilson, "The Effects of Politics and Power on the Organizational Commitment of Federal Executives," *Journal of Management,* Spring 1995, pp 101–18. For related research, see J B Arthur, "Effects of Human Resource Systems on Manufacturing Performance and Turnover," *Academy of Management Journal,* June 1994, pp 670–87.

[43] As quoted in M Bartiromo, "What to Expect at Davos," *BusinessWeek,* January 29, 2007, p 100. Also see the empowerment-related case studies in L Buchanan, "When Absence Makes the Team Grow Stronger: A CEO Rethinks His Role after a Tour in Iraq," *Inc.,* June 2008, pp 40–43; H C Steiman, "A Socialist CEO Grows Up. His Company Tries to, Too," *Inc.,* July 2008, pp 45–46; and J Spolsky, "I Hoped to Create a Utopian Workplace. Instead, I Caused an Employee Revolt," *Inc.,* September 2008, pp 65–67.

[44] As quoted in W A Randolph and M Sashkin, "Can Organizational Empowerment Work in Multinational Settings?" *Academy of Management Executive,* February 2002, p 104 (emphasis added). Also see B Frisch, "When Teams Can't Decide," *Harvard Business Review,* November 2008, pp 121–26; E McGirt, "Revolution in San Jose," *Fast Company,* January 2009, pp 88–94; and H P Sims Jr, S Faraj, and S Yun, "When Should a Leader Be Directive or Empowering? How to Develop Your Own Situational Theory of Leadership," *Business Horizons,* March–April 2009, pp 149–58.

[45] R M Hodgetts, "A Conversation with Steve Kerr," *Organizational Dynamics,* Spring 1996, p 71. Also see M T Hansen, "When Internal Collaboration Is Bad for Your Company," *Harvard Business Review,* April 2009, pp 82–88.

[46] J Welch and S Welch, "Why Your Office Isn't Like Google's," *BusinessWeek,* August 25–September 1, 2008, p 100.

[47] L Shaper Walters, "A Leader Redefines Management," *Christian Science Monitor,* September 22, 1992, p 14. Also see B George, P Sims, A N McLean, and D Mayer, "Discovering Your Authentic Leadership," *Harvard Business Review,* February 2007, pp 129–38.

[48] For a 15-item empowerment scale, see Table 1 on p 103 of B P Niehoff, R H Moorman, G Blakely, and J Fuller, "The Influence of Empowerment and Job Enrichment on Employee Loyalty in a Downsizing Environment," *Group and Organization Management,* March 2001, pp 93–113.

[49] F Vogelstein, "Star Power: Greg Brown, Motorola," *Fortune,* February 6, 2006, p 57.

[50] For an extended discussion of this model, see M Sashkin, "Participative Management Is an Ethical Imperative," *Organizational Dynamics,* Spring 1984, pp 4–22.

[51] D Lieberman, "Hammer Determined to Extend Cable Reach," *USA Today,* March 23, 2009, p 6B. Also see R Jana, "Let's All Rearrange the Office," *BusinessWeek,* September 22, 2008, p 45.

[52] For more on delegation, see L Bossidy, "The Job No CEO Should Delegate," *Harvard Business Review,* March 2001, pp 46–49.

[53] See S Gazda, "The Art of Delegating," *HR Magazine,* January 2002, pp 75–78.

[54] M Memmott, "Managing Government Inc.," *USA Today,* June 28, 1993, p 2B. Also see R C Ford and C P Heaton, "Lessons from Hospitality That Can Serve Anyone," *Organizational Dynamics,* Summer 2001, pp 30–47.

[55] R Kreitner, *Management,* 11th ed (Boston: Houghton Mifflin Harcourt, 2009), p 254.

[56] Drawn from G Yukl and P P Fu, "Determinants of Delegation and Consultation by Managers," *Journal of Organizational Behavior,* March 1999, pp 219–32. Also see Z X Chen and S Aryee, "Delegation and Employee Work Outcomes: An Examination of the Cultural Context of Mediating Processes in China," *Academy of Management Journal,* February 2007, pp 226–38.

[57] See B W Heineman Jr, "Avoiding Integrity Land Mines," *Harvard Business Review,* April 2007, pp 100–108; R Y J Chua, P Ingram, and M W Morris, "From the Head to the Heart: Locating Cognition- and Affect-Based Trust in Managers' Professional Networks," *Academy of Management Journal,* June 2008, pp 436–52; and D Moyer, "Broken Trust," *Harvard Business Review,* April 2009, p 120.

[58] M Frese, W Kring, A Soose, and J Zempel, "Personal Initiative at Work: Differences between East and

West Germany," *Academy of Management Journal,* February 1996, p 38 (emphasis added). Also see D N Den Hartog and F D Belschak, "Personal Initiative, Commitment and Affect at Work," *Journal of Occupational and Organizational Psychology,* December 2007, pp 601–22.

59 See W A Randolph, "Re-thinking Empowerment: Why Is It So Hard to Achieve?" *Organizational Dynamics,* Fall 2000, pp 94–107.

60 Results can be found in B D Cawley, L M Keeping, and P E Levy, "Participation in the Performance Appraisal Process and Employee Reactions: A Meta-Analytic Review of Field Investigations," *Journal of Applied Psychology,* August 1998, pp 615–33.

61 Results are contained in J A Wagner III, C R Leana, E A Locke, and D M Schweiger, "Cognitive and Motivational Frameworks in US Research on Participation: A Meta-Analysis of Primary Effects," *Journal of Organizational Behavior,* 1997, pp 49–65.

62 Based on A Srivastava, K M Bartol, and E A Locke, "Empowering Leadership in Management Teams: Effects on Knowledge Sharing, Efficacy, and Performance," *Academy of Management Journal,* December 2006, pp 1239–251.

63 Based on J P Guthrie, "High-Involvement Work Practices, Turnover, and Productivity: Evidence from New Zealand," *Academy of Management Journal,* February 2001, pp 180–90.

64 Based on M Workman and W Bommer, "Redesigning Computer Call Center Work: A Longitudinal Field Experiment," *Journal of Organizational Behavior,* May 2004, pp 317–37.

65 Based on C D Zatzick and R D Iverson, "High-Involvement Management and Workforce Reduction: Competitive Advantage or Disadvantage?" *Academy of Management Journal,* October 2006, pp 999–1015.

66 W A Randolph, "Navigating the Journey to Empowerment," *Organizational Dynamics,* Spring 1995, p 31. For more on empowerment, see B Burlingham, "How Has It Come to This?" *Inc.,* February 2008, pp 102–109; S Mantere and E Vaara, "On the Problem of Participation in Strategy: A Critical Discursive Perspective," *Organization Science,* March–April 2008, pp 341–58; and F Kiel, "Flaws in the Selfish-Worker Theory," *BusinessWeek,* October 6, 2008, p 78.

67 See www.nbc.com/The_Office, accessed March 24, 2009.

68 D J Burrough, "Office Politics Mirror Popular TV Program," *The Arizona Republic,* February 4, 2001, p EC1.

69 L B MacGregor Serven, *The End of Office Politics as Usual* (New York: American Management Association, 2002), p 5. Also see K J McGregor, "Sweet Revenge: The Power of Retribution, Spite, and Loathing in the World of Business," *BusinessWeek,* January 22, 2007, pp 64–70.

70 Quotes and data from J Yang and K Simmons, "USA Today Snapshots," *USA Today,* November 17, 2008, p 1B.

71 For a wide range of perspectives, see www.businessweek.com/magazine/content/08_34/b4097030713566.htm?chan=magazine+channel_special+report, accessed March 24, 2009. For practical tips, see C Hawley, *100+ Tactics for Office Politics,* 2nd ed (Hauppauge, NY: Barron's Educational Series, 2008).

72 As quoted in M Keohan, "Breaking Out of the Box," *BusinessWeek,* August 25–September 1, 2008, p 55. Also see S B Bacharach, "Politically Proactive," *Fast Company,* May 2005, p 93; and R M Kramer, "The Great Intimidators," *Harvard Business Review,* February 2006, pp 88–96.

73 Data from M Weinstein, "Training Today: Q&A," *Training,* January–February 2007, p 7. Also see B Kowitt, "5 Tips for Keeping Your Job," *Fortune,* December 8, 2008, p 14; J Welch and S Welch, "Resisting the Pull of Office Politics," *BusinessWeek,* December 22, 2008, p 84; and S Johnson, "With Frenemies Like These," *Fast Company,* January 2009, p 148.

74 R W Allen, D L Madison, L W Porter, P A Renwick, and B T Mayes, "Organizational Politics: Tactics and Characteristics of Its Actors," *California Management Review,* Fall 1979, p 77. A comprehensive overview can be found in M G McIntyre, *Secrets to Winning at Office Politics: How to Achieve Your Goals and Increase Your Influence at Work* (New York: St. Martin's, 2005).

75 See P M Fandt and G R Ferris, "The Management of Information and Impressions: When Employees Behave Opportunistically," *Organizational Behavior and Human Decision Processes,* February 1990, pp 140–58.

76 First four based on discussion in D R Beeman and T W Sharkey, "The Use and Abuse of Corporate Politics," *Business Horizons,* March–April 1987, pp 26–30. For supportive evidence, see C C Rosen, P E Levy, and R J Hall, "Placing Perceptions of Politics in the Context of the Feedback Environment, Employee Attitudes, and Job Performance," *Journal of Applied Psychology,* January 2006, pp 211–20.

77 A Raia, "Power, Politics, and the Human Resource Professional," *Human Resource Planning,* no. 4, 1985, p 203.

78 As quoted in A J DuBrin, "Career Maturity, Organizational Rank, and Political Behavioral Tendencies: A Correlational Analysis of Organizational Politics and Career Experience," *Psychological Reports,* October 1988, p 535. Also see T Lowry, "Extreme Experience," *BusinessWeek,* September 8, 2008, pp 46–51.

79 This three-level distinction comes from A T Cobb, "Political Diagnosis: Applications in Organizational Development," *Academy of Management Review,* July 1986, pp 482–96. Also see M A Valenti and T Rockett, "The Effects of Demographic Differences on Forming Intragroup Relationships," *Small Group Research,* April 2008, pp 179–202; and P Sellers, "The New Valley Girls," *Fortune,* October 13, 2008, pp 152–62.

80 L Baum, "The Day Charlie Bradshaw Kissed off Transworld," *BusinessWeek,* September 29, 1986, p 68. Also see C J Loomis, "How the HP Board KO'd Carly," *Fortune,* March 7, 2005, pp 99–102.

81 See H Ibarra and M Hunter, "How Leaders Create and Use Networks," *Harvard Business Review,* January 2007, pp 40–47; N Anand and J A Conger, "Capabilities of the Consummate Networker," *Organizational Dynamics,* no. 1, 2007, pp 13–27; and R Cross and R J Thomas, "How Top Talent Uses Networks and Where Rising Stars Get Trapped," *Organizational Dynamics,* April–June 2008, pp 165–80.

82 Drawn from J T Arnold, "Employee Networks," *HR Magazine,* June 2006, pp 145–52.

83 Allen et al., "Organizational Politics," p 77. Also see D C Treadway, W A Hochwarter, C J Kacmar, and G R Ferris, "Political Will, Political Skill, and Political Behavior," *Journal of Organizational Behavior,* May 2005, pp 229–45.

84 See B Fryer, "When Your Colleague Is a Saboteur," *Harvard Business Review,* November 2008, pp 41–45; M Conlin, "How

to Shine in Dark Times," *BusinessWeek,* November 3, 2008, pp 52–53; and J Welch and S Welch, "The Loyalty Fallacy," *BusinessWeek,* January 19, 2009, p 68.

[85] A Rao, S M Schmidt, and L H Murray, "Upward Impression Management: Goals, Influence Strategies, and Consequences," *Human Relations,* February 1995, p 147.

[86] See W H Turnley and M C Bolino, "Achieving Desired Images While Avoiding Undesired Images: Exploring the Role of Self-Monitoring in Impression Management," *Journal of Applied Psychology,* April 2001, pp 351–60.

[87] See L Ryan, "The Reengineered Resume," *BusinessWeek,* December 3, 2007, p SC12; L Ali, "Google Yourself—And Enjoy It," *Newsweek,* February 18, 2008, p 49; and M Conlin, "Are People in Your Office Acting Oddly?" *BusinessWeek,* April 13, 2009, p 54.

[88] Data from "Dressing for Success," *USA Today,* October 24, 2006, p 1B. Also see S Grobart, "Allow Me to Introduce Myself (Properly)," *Money,* January 2007, pp 40–41.

[89] S Friedman, "What Do You Really Care About? What Are You Most Interested In?" *Fast Company,* March 1999, p 90.

[90] See S J Wayne and G R Ferris, "Influence Tactics, Affect, and Exchange Quality in Supervisor-Subordinate Interactions: A Laboratory Experiment and Field Study," *Journal of Applied Psychology,* October 1990, pp 487–99. For another version, see Table 1 (p 246) in S J Wayne and R C Liden, "Effects of Impression Management on Performance Ratings: A Longitudinal Study," *Academy of Management Journal,* February 1995, pp 232–60. Also see M C Bolino, J A Varela, B Bande, and W H Turnley, "The Impact of Impression-Management Tactics on Supervisor Ratings of Organizational Citizenship Behavior," *Journal of Organizational Behavior,* May 2006, pp 281–97.

[91] M E Mendenhall and C Wiley, "Strangers in a Strange Land: The Relationship between Expatriate Adjustment and Impression Management," *American Behavioral Scientist,* March 1994, pp 605–20.

[92] T E Becker and S L Martin, "Trying to Look Bad at Work: Methods and Motives for Managing Poor Impressions in Organizations," *Academy of Management Journal,* February 1995, p 191.

[93] Ibid., p 181. Also see M K Duffy, D C Ganster, and M Pagon, "Social Undermining in the Workplace," *Academy of Management Journal,* April 2002, pp 331–51; and M K Duffy, J D Shaw, B J Tepper, and K L Scott, "The Moderating Roles of Self-Esteem and Neuroticism in the Relationship between Group and Individual Undermining Behavior," *Journal of Applied Psychology,* September 2006, pp 1066–77.

[94] Adapted from Becker and Martin, "Trying to Look Bad at Work," pp 180–81.

[95] J Sandberg, "The Art of Showing Pure Incompetence at an Unwanted Task," *The Wall Street Journal,* April 17, 2008, p B1.

[96] Data from G R Ferris, D D Frink, D P S Bhawuk, J Zhou, and D C Gilmore, "Reactions of Diverse Groups to Politics in the Workplace," *Journal of Management,* no. 1, 1996, pp 23–44. For other findings from the same database, see G R Ferris, D D Frink, M C Galang, J Zhou, K M Kacmar, and J L Howard, "Perceptions of Organizational Politics: Prediction, Stress-Related Implications, and Outcomes," *Human Relations,* February 1996, pp 233–66.

[97] A Drory and D Beaty, "Gender Differences in the Perception of Organizational Influence Tactics," *Journal of Organizational*

Behavior, May 1991, pp 256–57. Also see B A Pontari and B R Schlenker, "Helping Friends Manage Impressions: We Like Helpful Liars but Respect Nonhelpful Truth Tellers," *Basic and Applied Social Psychology,* June 2006, pp 177–83.

[98] Based on L A Witt, T F Hilton, and W A Hochwarter, "Addressing Politics in Matrix Teams," *Group and Organization Management,* June 2001, pp 230–47. Also see D S Conner, "Human-Resource Professionals' Perceptions of Organizational Politics as a Function of Experience, Organizational Size, and Perceived Independence," *The Journal of Social Psychology,* December 2006, pp 717–32.

[99] D A Buchanan, "You Stab My Back, I'll Stab Yours: Management Experience and Perceptions of Organizational Political Behaviour," *British Journal of Management,* March 2008, p 49. Also see C Porath and C Pearson, "How Toxic Colleagues Corrode Performance," *Harvard Business Review,* April 2009, p 24.

[100] S A Akimoto and D M Sanbonmatsu, "Differences in Self-Effacing Behavior between European and Japanese Americans," *Journal of Cross-Cultural Psychology,* March 1999, pp 172–73.

[101] A Zaleznik, "Real Work," *Harvard Business Review,* January–February 1989, p 60. Also see J Welch and S Welch, "Stop the B.S. Budgets," *BusinessWeek,* June 26, 2006, p 114; and S Sanghi, "How to Handle Boss Who Plays Politics," *The Arizona Republic,* January 14, 2007, p D2.

[102] As quoted in D Lieberman, "Kraft Sees Benefits as Consumers Stay Home," *USA Today,* December 11, 2008, p 4B.

[103] Excerpted from S Westcott, "Beyond Flextime: Trashing the Workweek," *Inc.: The Magazine for Growing Companies,* August 2008. Copyright © 2008 by Mansueto Ventures LLC. Reproduced with permission of Mansueto Ventures LLC via Copyright Clearance Center. For more on ROWE, see C Ressler and J Thompson, "Make Results Matter," *HR Magazine,* April 2009, pp 77–79.

[104] Excerpted from J Noveck, "Poll: Lying Always Bad, but White Lies Are Frequent," *The Arizona Republic,* July 16, 2006, p A22.

CHAPTER 16

[1] Excerpted from D Mattioli, "Despite Cutbacks, Firms Invest in Developing Leaders," *The Wall Street Journal,* February 9, 2009, p B4.

[2] Leadership development is discussed by M Weinstein, "Rx for Excellence," *Training,* February 2009, pp 48–52; and "Still Haven't Closed the Gap," *Training,* March/April 2009, p 9.

[3] See S Lieberson and J F O'Connor, "Leadership and Organizational Performance: A Study of Large Corporations," *American Sociological Review,* April 1972, pp 117–30. The importance of leadership is also discussed by B M Bass and R Bass, *The Bass Handbook of Leadership* (New York: Free Press, 2008), pp 3–26.

[4] Results can be found in K T Dirks, "Trust in Leadership and Team Performance: Evidence from NCAA Basketball," *Journal of Applied Psychology,* December 2000, pp 1004–12; D Jacobs and L Singell, "Leadership and Organizational Performance: Isolating Links between Managers and Collective Success," *Social Science Research,* June 1993, pp 165–89; and A G Walker, J W Smither, and D A Waldman, "A Longitudinal Examination of Concomitant Changes in Team Leadership and Customer Satisfaction," *Personnel Psychology,* Autumn 2008, pp 547–77.

5 See "Bad-Boss Peril," *The Arizona Republic,* November 30, 2008, p A29.

6 The four commonalities were identified by P G Northouse, *Leadership: Theory and Practice,* 4th ed (Thousand Oaks, CA: Sage Publications, 2007), p 3.

7 Ibid.

8 B Kellerman, "Leadership—Warts and All," *Harvard Business Review,* January 2004, p 45.

9 B M Bass, *Bass & Stogdill's Handbook of Leadership: Theory, Research, and Managerial Applications,* 3rd ed (New York: Free Press, 1990), p 383.

10 For a discussion about the differences between leading and managing, see Bass and Bass, *The Bass Handbook of Leadership*, pp 651–81.

11 See S Carey, "Budget Airline Makes Its Debut in Brazil," *The Wall Street Journal,* December 14, 2008, p B3.

12 See J E Vascellaro and J S Lublin, "Yahoo Names Bartz as CEO; Decker Resigns," *The Wall Street Journal,* January 14, 2009, pp B1, B4; and J Murphy and N Shirouzu, "Toyota Management Heads toward a Shakeup," *The Wall Street Journal,* January 21, 2009, p B3.

13 S Marchionne, "Fiat's Extreme Makeover," *Harvard Business Review,* December 2008, p 46.

14 See B J Avolio, R J Reichard, S T Hannah, F O Walumbwa, and A Chan, "A Meta-Analytic Review of Leadership Impact Research: Experimental and Quasi-Experimental Studies," *The Leadership Quarterly,* in press.

15 For a summary, see Bass and Bass, *The Bass Handbook of Leadership*, pp 103–35.

16 C J Loomis, "Can Anyone Run Citigroup?" *Fortune,* May 5, 2008, p 86; and D Enrich, "Pandit's Puzzle: How to Fix Citigroup," *The Wall Street Journal,* January 16, 2009, p C3.

17 Implicit leadership theory is discussed by Bass and Bass, *The Bass Handbook of Leadership*, pp 46–78; J Ullrich, O Christ, and R van Dick, "Substitutes for Procedural Fairness: Prototypical Leaders Are Endorsed Whether They Are Fair or Not," *Journal of Applied Psychology,* January 2009, pp 235–44; A S Rosette, G J Leonardelli, and K W Phillips, "The White Standard: Racial Bias in Leader Categorization," *Journal of Applied Psychology,* July 2008, pp 758–77; and C Anderson and G J Kilduff, "Why Do Dominant Personalities Attain Influence in Face-to-Face Groups? The Competence-Signaling Effects of Trait Dominance," *Journal of Personality and Social Psychology,* February 2009, pp 491–503.

18 Results can be found in R G Lord, C L De Vader, and G M Alliger, "A Meta-Analysis of the Relation between Personality Traits and Leadership Perceptions: An Application of Validity Generalization Procedures," *Journal of Applied Psychology,* August 1986, pp 402–10.

19 See M W Dickson, C J Resick, and P J Hanges, "Systematic Variation in Organizationally-Shared Cognitive Prototypes of Effective Leadership Based on Organizational Form," *The Leadership Quarterly,* October 2006, pp 487–505; and F C Brodbeck et al., "Cultural Variation of Leadership Prototypes across 22 European Countries," *Journal of Occupational and Organizational Psychology,* March 2000, pp 1–29.

20 Results can be found in J M Kouzes and B Z Posner, *The Leadership Challenge* (San Francisco, CA: Jossey-Bass, 1995). Also see R Birchfield, "Leaders Must Restore Trust," *New Zealand Management,* March 2009, pp 32–33.

21 See A O'Connell, "Conversation: Lego CEO Jørgen Vig Kundstorp on Leading through Survival and Growth," *Harvard Business Review,* January 2009, p 25.

22 J Weisman, L Meckler, and N Ben-David, "Obama on Defense as Daschle Withdraws," *The Wall Street Journal,* February 4, 2009, pp A1, A2.

23 See J Antonakis, N M Ashkanasy, and M T Dasborough, "Does Leadership Need Emotional Intelligence?" *The Leadership Quarterly,* April 2009, pp 247–61; and M P McEnrue, K S Groves, and W Shen, "Emotional Intelligence Development: Leveraging Individual Characteristics," *Journal of Management Development,* 2009, pp 150–74.

24 Results can be found in T A Judge, J E Hono, R Ilies, and M W Gerhardt, "Personality and Leadership: A Qualitative and Quantitative Review," *Journal of Applied Psychology,* August 2002, pp 765–80.

25 See T A Judge, A E Colbert, and R Ilies, "Intelligence and Leadership: A Quantitative Review and Test of Theoretical Propositions," *Journal of Applied Psychology,* June 2004, pp 542–52.

26 Kellerman's research can be found in B Kellerman, *Bad Leadership* (Boston: Harvard Business School Press, 2004).

27 The trait definitions were quoted from ibid., pp 40–46. The personal examples were taken from "The Worst Managers," *BusinessWeek,* January 19, 2009, p 42; and P Elkind, "The Trouble with Steve," *Fortune,* March 17, 2008, p 88.

28 Gender and the emergence of leaders was examined by A H Eagly and S J Karau, "Gender and the Emergence of Leaders: A Meta-Analysis," *Journal of Personality and Social Psychology,* May 1991, pp 685–710; and J L Prime, N M Carter, and T M Welbourne, "Women 'Take Care,' Men 'Take Charge': Managers' Stereotypic Perceptions of Women and Men Leaders," *The Psychologist-Manager Journal,* January 2009, pp 25–49.

29 See A H Eagly, S J Karau, and B T Johnson, "Gender and Leadership Style among School Principals: A Meta-Analysis," *Educational Administration Quarterly,* February 1992, pp 76–102.

30 Supportive findings are contained in J M Twenge, "Changes in Women's Assertiveness in Response to Status and Roles: A Cross-Temporal Meta-Analysis, 1931–1993," *Journal of Personality and Social Psychology,* July 2001, pp 133–45.

31 For a summary of this research, see H Ibarra and O Obodaru, "Women and Vision Thing," *Harvard Business Review,* January 2009, pp 62–70.

32 See B Conchie, "Strengths-Based Leaders," *Leadership Excellence,* February 2009, p 10.

33 Examples can be found in S Boehle, "True Vision," *Training,* February 2008, pp 32–39; H Dolezalek, "We Train to Please," *Training,* March/April 2008, pp 34–36; and M Weinstein, "Leadership Leader," *Training,* February 2008, pp 41-46.

34 See B Reeves, T W Malone, and T O'Driscoll, "Leadership's Online Labs," *Harvard Business Review,* May 2008, pp 59–66.

35 This research is summarized and critiqued by Bass and Bass, *The Bass Handbook of Leadership*, pp 497–538.

36 Results can be found in T A Judge, R F Piccolo, and R Ilies, "The Forgotten Ones? The Validity of Consideration and Initiating Structure in Leadership Research," *Journal of Applied Psychology,* February 2004, pp 36–51.

[37] See V H Vroom, "Leadership," in *Handbook of Industrial and Organizational Psychology,* ed M D Dunnette (Chicago: Rand-McNally, 1976).

[38] Supportive results can be found in F Shipper, R C Hoffman, and D M Rotondo, "Does the 360 Feedback Process Create Actionable Knowledge Equally across Cultures?" *Academy of Management Learning & Education,* March 2007, pp 33–50.

[39] Situational theories are discussed by Bass and Bass, *The Bass Handbook of Leadership,* pp 497–538; and M D Watkins, "Picking the Right Transition Strategy," *Harvard Business Review,* January 2009, pp 47–53.

[40] For more on this theory, see F E Fiedler, "A Contingency Model of Leadership Effectiveness," in *Advances in Experimental Social Psychology,* vol. 1, ed L Berkowitz (New York: Academic Press, 1964); and F E Fiedler, *A Theory of Leadership Effectiveness* (New York: McGraw-Hill, 1967).

[41] See L H Peters, D D Hartke, and J T Pohlmann, "Fiedler's Contingency Theory of Leadership: An Application of the Meta-Analyses Procedures of Schmidt and Hunter," *Psychological Bulletin,* March 1985, pp 274–85. The meta-analysis was conducted by C A Schriesheim, B J Tepper, and L A Tetrault, "Least Preferred Co-worker Score, Situational Control, and Leadership Effectiveness: A Meta-Analysis of Contingency Model Performance Predictions," *Journal of Applied Psychology,* August 1994, pp 561–73.

[42] See the related discussion in J R Hackman and R Wageman, "Asking the Right Questions about Leadership," *American Psychologist,* January 2007, pp 43–47; and V H Vroom and A G Jago, "The Role of the Situation in Leadership," *American Psychologist,* January 2007, pp 17–24.

[43] B Groysberg, A N McLean, and N Nohria, "Are Leaders Portable?" *Harvard Business Review,* May 2006, pp 95, 97.

[44] See B J Avolio, "Promoting More Integrative Strategies for Leadership Theory-Building," *American Psychologist,* January 2007, pp 25–33.

[45] For more detail on this theory, see R J House, "A Path–Goal Theory of Leader Effectiveness," *Administrative Science Quarterly,* September 1971, pp 321–38.

[46] This research is summarized by R J House, "Path–Goal Theory of Leadership: Lessons, Legacy, and a Reformulated Theory," *The Leadership Quarterly,* Autumn 1996, pp 323–52. Also see S Sarin, "First among Equals: The Effect of Team Leader Characteristics on the Internal Dynamics of Cross-Functional Product Development Teams," *Journal of Product Innovation Management,* March 2009, pp 188–205; and R P Vecchio, J E Justin, and C L Pearce, "The Utility of Transactional and Transformational Leadership for Predicting Performance and Satisfaction within a Path–Goal Theory Framework," *Journal of Occupational and Organizational Psychology,* March 2008, pp 71–82.

[47] See House, "Path–Goal Theory of Leadership: Lessons, Legacy, and a Reformulated Theory."

[48] See R Siklos, "Bob Iger Rocks Disney," *Fortune,* January 19, 2009, pp 80–86.

[49] Results can be found in P M Podsakoff, S B MacKenzie, M Ahearne, and W H Bommer, "Searching for a Needle in a Haystack: Trying to Identify the Illusive Moderators of Leadership Behaviors," *Journal of Management,* 1995, pp 422–70.

[50] The steps were developed by H P Sims Jr, S Faraj, and S Yun, "When Should a Leader Be Directive or Empowering? How to Develop Your Own Situational Theory of Leadership," *Business Horizons,* March–April 2009, pp 149–58.

[51] For a complete description of this theory, see B J Avolio and B M Bass, *A Manual for Full-Range Leadership Development* (Binghamton, NY: Center for Leadership Studies, 1991). The manual is now published by www.mindgarden.com.

[52] Examples can be found in J Sandberg, "Too-Nice Boss?" *The Arizona Republic,* March 2, 2008, p EC1; and K Kelly, "Cayne to Step Down as Bear Stearns CEO," *The Wall Street Journal,* January 8, 2008, pp A1, A18.

[53] Results can be found in A H Eagly, M C Johannesen-Schmidt, and M L van Engen, "Transformational, Transactional, and Laissez-Faire Leadership Styles: A Meta-Analysis Comparing Women and Men," *Psychological Bulletin,* June 2003, pp 569–91.

[54] A definition and description of transactional leadership is provided by Bass and Bass, *The Bass Handbook of Leadership,* pp 618–48.

[55] Excerpted from P Dvorak, "Outsider CEO Translates A New Message in Japan," *The Wall Street Journal,* March 10, 2008, p B4.

[56] U R Dumdum, K B Lowe, and B J Avolio, "A Meta-Analysis of Transformational and Transactional Leadership Correlates of Effectiveness and Satisfaction: An Update and Extension," in *Transformational and Charismatic Leadership: The Road Ahead,* ed B J Avolio and F J Yammarino (New York: JAI Press, 2002), p 38.

[57] Supportive research is summarized by Bass and Bass, *The Bass Handbook of Leadership,* pp 618–48.

[58] Dvorak, "Outsider CEO Translates a New Message in Japan."

[59] Supportive results can be found in T M Hautala, "The Relationship between Personality and Transformational Leadership," *Journal of Management Development,* 2006, pp 777–94; and J E Bono and T A Judge, "Personality and Transformational and Transactional Leadership: A Meta-Analysis," *Journal of Applied Psychology,* October 2004, pp 901–10.

[60] See Eagly, Johannesen-Schmidt, and van Engen, "Transformational, Transactional, and Laissez-Faire Leadership Styles."

[61] See Avolio, Reichard, Hannah, Walumbwa, and Chan, "A Meta-Analytic Review of Leadership Impact Research: Experimental and Quasi-Experimental Studies."

[62] These definitions are derived from R Kark, B Shamir, and C Chen, "The Two Faces of Transformational Leadership: Empowerment and Dependency," *Journal of Applied Psychology,* April 2003, pp 246–55.

[63] B Nanus, *Visionary Leadership* (San Francisco, CA: Jossey-Bass, 1992), p 8.

[64] T Bisoux, "Making Connections," *BizEd,* January/February 2009, p 22.

[65] J Reingold, "Meet Your New Leader," *Fortune,* November 24, 2008, p 146.

[66] Supportive research can be found in J B Wu, A S Tsui, and A J Kinicki, "Leading Groups: Consequences of Differentiated Leadership in Groups," *Academy of Management Journal,* in press; and F O Walumbwa, B J Avolio, and W Zhu, "How Transformational Leadership Weaves Its Influence on Individual

Job Performance: The Role of Identification and Efficacy Beliefs," *Personnel Psychology,* Winter 2008, pp 793–825.

67 See M E Brown, "Leader-Follower Values Congruence: Are Socialized Charismatic Leaders Better Able to Achieve It?" *Journal of Applied Psychology,* March 2009, pp 478–90; A E Colbert, A L Kristoff-Brown, B H Bradley, and M R Barrick, "CEO Transformational Leadership: The Role of Goal Importance Congruence in Top Management Teams," *Academy of Management Journal,* February 2008, pp 81–96; A Erez, V F Misangyi, D E Johnson, M A LePine, and K C Halverson, "Stirring the Hearts of Followers: Charismatic Leadership as the Transferal of Affect," *Journal of Applied Psychology,* May 2008, pp 602–15; and D M Herold, D B Fedor, S Caldwell, and Y Liu, "The Effects of Transformational and Change Leadership on Employees' Commitment to Change: A Multilevel Study," *Journal of Applied Psychology,* March 2008, pp 346–57.

68 Results can be found in U R Dumdum, K B Lowe, and B J Avolio, "A Meta-Analysis of Transformational and Transactional Leadership Correlates of Effectiveness and Satisfaction: An Update and Extension," in *Transactional and Charismatic Leadership: The Road Ahead,* ed B J Avolio and F J Yammarino (New York: JAI, 2002), pp 35–66.

69 See J R Detert and E R Bussi, "Leadership Behavior and Employee Voice: Is the Door Really Open?" *Academy of Management Journal,* August 2007, pp 869–84.

70 See K B Lowe, K G Kroeck and N Sivasubramaniam, "Effectiveness Correlates of Transformational and Transactional Leadership: A Meta-Analytic Review of the MLQ Literature," *The Leadership Quarterly,* 1996, pp 385–425. Also see L Gumusluoglu and A Ilsev, "Transformational Leadership, Creativity, and Organizational Innovation," *Journal of Business Research,* April 2009, pp 461–73.

71 Results can be found in T A Judge and R F Piccolo, "Transformational and Transactional Leadership: A Meta-Analytic Test of Their Relative Validity," *Journal of Applied Psychology,* October 2004, pp 755–68. Also see T R Hinkin and C A Schriesheim, "An Examination of 'Nonleadership': From Laissez-Faire Leadership to Leader Reward Omission and Punishment Omission," *Journal of Applied Psychology,* November 2008, pp 1234–48.

72 See A J Towler, "Effects of Charismatic Influence Training on Attitudes, Behavior, and Performance," *Personnel Psychology,* Summer 2003, pp 363–81; and M Frese and S Beimel, "Action Training for Charismatic Leadership: Two Evaluations of Studies of a Commercial Training Module on Inspirational Communication of a Vision," *Personnel Psychology,* Autumn 2003, pp 671–97.

73 These recommendations were derived from J M Howell and B J Avolio, "The Ethics of Charismatic Leadership: Submission or Liberation?" *Academy of Management Executive,* May 1992, pp 43–54.

74 See F Dansereau Jr, G Graen, and W Haga, "A Vertical Dyad Linkage Approach to Leadership within Formal Organizations," *Organizational Behavior and Human Performance,* February 1975, pp 46–78.

75 These descriptions were taken from D Duchon, S G Green, and T D Taber, "Vertical Dyad Linkage: A Longitudinal Assessment of Antecedents, Measures, and Consequences," *Journal of Applied Psychology,* February 1986, pp 56–60.

76 Supportive results can be found in S A Furst, "Employee Resistance to Organizational Change: Managerial Influence

Tactics and Leader–Member Exchange," *Journal of Applied Psychology,* March 2008, pp 453–62; L Van Dyne, D Kamdar, and J Joireman, "In-Role Perceptions Buffer the Negative Impact of Low LMX on Helping and Enhance the Positive Impact of High LMX on Voice," *Journal of Applied Psychology,* November 2008, pp 1195–1207; D J Henderson, S J Wayne, L M Shore, W H Bommer, and L E Tetrick, "Leader–Member Exchange, Differentiation, and Psychological Contract Fulfillment: A Multilevel Examination," *Journal of Applied Psychology,* November 2008, pp 1208–19; and M Ozer, "Personal and Task-Related Moderators of Leader–Member Exchange among Software Developers," *Journal of Applied Psychology,* September 2008, pp 1174–82.

77 Results can be found in R Ilies, J D Nahrgang, and F P Morgeson, "Leader–Member Exchange and Citizenship Behaviors: A Meta-Analysis," *Journal of Applied Psychology,* January 2007, pp 269–77.

78 A turnover study was conducted by G B Graen, R C Liden, and W Hoel, "Role of Leadership in the Employee Withdrawal Process," *Journal of Applied Psychology,* December 1982, pp 868–72. The career progress study was conducted by M Wakabayashi and G B Graen, "The Japanese Career Progress Study: A 7-Year Follow-Up," *Journal of Applied Psychology,* November 1984, pp 603–14.

79 See J B Bernerth, A A Armenakis, H S Field, W F Giles, and H J Walker, "The Influence of Personality Differences between Subordinates and Supervisors on Perceptions of LMX," *Group and Organization Management,* April 2008, pp 216–40.

80 These recommendations were derived from G C Mage, "Leading Despite Your Boss," *HR Magazine,* September 2003, pp 139–44.

81 R J House and R N Aditya, "The Social Scientific Study of Leadership Quo Vadis?" *Journal of Management,* 1997, p 457.

82 C L Pearce and J A Conger, "All Those Years Ago: The Historical Underpinnings of Shared Leadership," in *Shared Leadership: Reframing the Hows and Whys of Leadership,* ed C L Pearce and J A Conger (Thousand Oaks, CA: Sage), p 1.

83 A thorough discussion of shared leadership is provided by C L Pearce, "The Future of Leadership: Combining Vertical and Shared Leadership Transform Knowledge Work," *Academy of Management Executive,* February 2004, pp 47–59; and C L Pearce, J A Conger, and E A Locke, "Shared Leadership Theory," *The Leadership Quarterly,* October 2008, pp 622–28.

84 This research is summarized in B J Avolio, J J Sosik, D I Jung, and Y Berson, "Leadership Models, Methods, and Applications," in *Handbook of Psychology: Industrial and Organizational Psychology,* vol. 12, ed W C Borman, D R Ilgen, and R J Klimoski (Hoboken, NJ: John Wiley & Sons, 2003), pp 277–307. Also see S J Zaccaro, A L Rittman, and M A Marks, "Team Leadership," *The Leadership Quarterly,* 2001, pp 451–83.

85 An overall summary of servant-leadership is provided by L C Spears, *Reflections on Leadership: How Robert K Greenleaf's Theory of Servant-Leadership Influenced Today's Top Management Thinkers* (New York: John Wiley & Sons, 1995).

86 "America Needs More CEOs Like Windolf," www .courierpostonline.com, April 3, 2009.

87 J Stuart, *Fast Company,* September 1999, p 114.

88 "The Best Advice I Ever Got," *Fortune,* May 12, 2008, p 74.

89 See R C Liden, S J Wayne, H Zhao, and D Henderson, "Servant Leadership: Development of a Multidimensional

Measure and Multi-Level Assessment," *The Leadership Quarterly,* April 2008, pp 161–77; M J Neubert, K M Kacmar, D S Carlson, L B Chonko, and J A Roberts, "Regulatory Focus as a Mediator of the Influence of Initiating Structure and Servant Leadership on Employee Behavior," *Journal of Applied Psychology,* November 2008, pp 1220–33; and D M Mayer, M Bardes, and R F Piccolo, "Do Servant-Leaders Help Satisfy Follower Needs? An Organizational Justice Perspective," *European Journal of Work and Organizational Psychology,* June 2008, pp 180–97.

[90] The role of followers is discussed by Bass and Bass, *The Bass Handbook of Leadership,* pp 400–36; and A C Bluedorn and K S Jaussi, "Leaders, Followers, and Time," *The Leadership Quarterly,* December 2008, pp 654–68.

[91] Bass and Bass, *The Bass Handbook of Leadership,* p 408.

[92] See L Bossidy, "What Your Leader Expects of You and What You Should Expect in Return," *Harvard Business Review,* April 2007, pp 58–65.

[93] See R Goffee and G Jones, "Followership: It's Personal, Too," *Harvard Business Review,* December 2001, p 148.

[94] This checklist was proposed by J J Gabarro and J P Kotter, "Managing Your Boss," *Harvard Business Review,* January 2005, pp 92–99.

[95] These ideas were partially based on B Dattner, "Forewarned Is Forearmed," *BusinessWeek,* September 1, 2008, p 50; and P Drucker, "Managing Oneself," *Harvard Business Review,* January 2005, pp 2–11.

[96] See the related discussion in B George, P Sims, A N McLean, and D Mayer, "Discovering Your Authentic Leadership," *Harvard Business Review,* February 2007, pp 129–38.

[97] The following suggestions were discussed by Gabarro and Kotter, "Managing Your Boss." Also see J Banks and D Coutu, "How to Protect Your Job in a Recession," *Harvard Business Review,* September 2008, pp 113–16.

[98] Excerpted from B. Morris, "The Pepsi Challenge: Can This Snack and Soda Giant Go Healthy?" *Fortune,* March 3, 2008, pp 55–66.

[99] A Kinicki and B Williams, *Management: A Practical Introduction* (New York: McGraw-Hill, 2009), p 467.

CHAPTER 17

[1] J McGregor, "Can Companies Have One Nervous System?" *BusinessWeek,* March 23 and 30, 2009, pp 40–41.

[2] See G Hamel, "Moon Shots for Management," *Harvard Business Review,* February 2009, pp 91–98; D Tapscott, *Grown Up Digital* (New York: McGraw-Hill, 2009); and T O'Driscoll, "Join the Webvolution," *Training,* February 2008, p 24.

[3] M V Copeland, "Boeing's Big Dream," *Fortune,* May 5, 2008, p 182.

[4] C I Barnard, *The Functions of the Executive* (Cambridge, MA: Harvard University Press, 1938), p 73.

[5] Drawn from E H Schein, *Organizational Psychology,* 3rd ed (Englewood Cliffs, NJ: Prentice Hall, 1980), pp 12–15.

[6] See V Smeets and F Warzynski, "Too Many Theories, Too Few Facts: What the Data Tell Us about the Link between Span of Control, Compensation, and Career Dynamics," *Labour Economics,* August 2008, pp 688–704.

[7] For an excellent overview of the span of control concept, see D D Van Fleet and A G Bedeian, "A History of the Span of Management," *Academy of Management Review,* July 1977, pp 356–72. Also see Smeets and Warzynski, "Too Many Theories, Too Few Facts: What the Data Tell Us about the Link between Span of Control, Compensation, and Career Dynamics."

[8] See G Anders, "Overseeing More Employees—With Fewer Managers," *The Wall Street Journal,* March 24, 2008, p B6.

[9] For a discussion about organizational metaphors, see C Oswick and P Jones, "Beyond Correspondence? Metaphor in Organization Theory," *Academy of Management Review,* April 2006, pp 483–85.

[10] For open-system perspectives, see G Sewell and J R Barker, "Coercion versus Care: Using Irony to Make Sense of Organizational Surveillance," *Academy of Management Review,* October 2006, pp 934–61.

[11] A management-oriented discussion of general systems theory may be found in K E Boulding, "General Systems Theory— The Skeleton of Science," *Management Science,* April 1956, pp 197–208. For more recent systems-related ideas, see A J Kinicki, K J L Jacobson, B M Galvin, and G E Prussia, "A Multi-Systems Model of Leadership," manuscript under review.

[12] See T G Weldy, "Learning Organization and Transfer: Strategies for Improving Performance," *The Learning Organization,* 2009, pp 58–68; F M Nafukho, C M Graham, and M H Muyia, "Determining the Relationship among Organizational Learning Dimensions of a Small-Size Business Enterprise," *Journal of European Industrial Training,* 2009, pp 32–51; and Jim Grieves, "Why We Should Abandon the Idea of the Learning Organization," *The Learning Organization,* 2008, pp 463–73.

[13] R M Fulmer and J B Keys, "A Conversation with Peter Senge: New Development in Organizational Learning," *Organizational Dynamics,* Autumn 1998, p 35.

[14] This definition was based on D A Garvin, "Building a Learning Organization," *Harvard Business Review,* July–August 1993, pp 78–91.

[15] See S T Hannah and P B Lester, "A Multilevel Approach to Building and Leading Learning Organizations," *The Leadership Quarterly,* February 2009, pp 34–48; A Willem and M Buelens, "Knowledge Sharing in Inter-Unit Cooperative Episodes: The Impact of Organizational Structure Dimensions," *International Journal of Information Management,* April 2009, pp 151–60; and H D Fard, A A A Rostamy, and H Taghiloo, "How Types of Organisational Cultures Contribute in Shaping Learning Organisations," *Singapore Management Review,* 2009, pp 49–64.

[16] A C Edmondson, "The Competitive Imperative of Learning," *Harvard Business Review,* July–August 2008, p 62.

[17] The three categories of thinking about organizational design are based on N Anand and R L Daft, "What Is the Right Organization Design?" *Organizational Dynamics,* 2007, pp 329–44.

[18] General Electric Company, "Fact Sheet," Our Company: Our Businesses, GE Web site, www.ge.com, accessed April 8, 2009. Also see M Vella, "Why GE Is Getting Out of the Kitchen," *BusinessWeek,* May 16, 2008, www.businessweek.com.

[19] See R Adams, "Hachette to Break through 'Silos' as It Restructures Women's Magazines," *The Wall Street Journal,* March 2, 2009, p B1.

[20] See J R Galbraith, *Designing Matrix Organizations That Actually Work* (San Francisco, CA: Jossey-Bass, 2009). The role

of HR integration is discussed by S H Appelbaum, D Nadeau, and M Cyr, "Performance Evaluation in a Matrix Organization: A Case Study (Part One)," *Industrial and Commercial Training,* 2008, pp 236–41; S H Appelbaum, D Nadeau, and M Cyr, "Performance Evaluation in a Matrix Organization: A Case Study (Part Two)," *Industrial and Commercial Training,* 2008, pp 295–99; and S H Appelbaum, D Nadeau, and M Cyr, "Performance Evaluation in a Matrix Organization: A Case Study (Part Three)," *Industrial and Commercial Training,* 2009, pp 9–14.

21 Galbraith, *Designing Matrix Organizations That Actually Work,* p ix.

22 Ibid., p 332.

23 P Lawrence, "Herman Miller's Creative Network," *BusinessWeek,* February 15, 2008, www.businessweek.com (interview with Brian Walker).

24 See Copeland, "Boeing's Big Dream," pp 180–82. Also see L Lunsford, "Boeing to Cut Production of 777 Jets," *The Wall Street Journal,* April 10, 2009, p B3.

25 Anand and Daft, "What Is the Right Organization Design?" p 338.

26 D Kiley, "Nokia Starts Listening," *BusinessWeek,* May 5, 2008, p 30.

27 See Y Zuo and B Panda, "Two-Level Trust-Based Decision Model for Information Assurance in a Virtual Organization," *Decision Support Systems,* May 2008, pp 291–309; and A Gunasekaran, K-H Lai, and T C Edwin, "Responsive Supply Chain: A Competitive Strategy in a Networked Economy," *Omega,* August 2008, pp 549–64.

28 See S Raisch, "Balanced Structures: Designing Organizations for Profitable Growth," *Long Range Planning,* October 2008, pp 483–508; and H G Barkema and M Schijven, "Toward Unlocking the Full Potential of Acquisitions: The Role of Organizational Restructuring," *Academy of Management Journal,* August 2008, pp 696–722. Practical examples are provided by N Shirouzu, "Toyota Plans a Major Overhaul in U.S.," *The Wall Street Journal,* April 10, 2009, p B3; and G Colvin, "The World's Most Admired Companies," *Fortune,* March 16, 2009, pp 75–78.

29 B Elgin, "Running the Tightest Ships on the Net," *BusinessWeek,* January 29, 2001, p 126.

30 A Pomeroy, "Passion, Obsession Drive the 'Eileen Fisher Way,'" *HR Magazine,* July 2007, p 55.

31 T O'Driscoll, "Join the Webvolution," *Training,* February 2008, p 24.

32 See J E Vascellaro, "Bartz Remakes Yahoo's Top Ranks," *The Wall Street Journal,* February 27, 2009, p B3; and J E Vascellaro, "Yahoo CEO Set to Install Top-Down Management," *The Wall Street Journal,* February 23, 2009, p B1.

33 See G P Huber, C C Miller, and W H Glick, "Developing More Encompassing Theories about Organizations: The Centralization-Effectiveness Relationship as an Example," *Organization Science,* no. 1, 1990, pp 11–40.

34 J Ewers, "No Ideas? You're Not Alone," *U.S. News & World Report,* June 18, 2007, pp 50–52, quoting from p 51.

35 P Kaestle, "A New Rationale for Organizational Structure," *Planning Review,* July/August 1990, p 22.

36 Details of this study can be found in T Burns and G M Stalker, *The Management of Innovation* (London: Tavistock, 1961).

37 D J Gillen and S J Carroll, "Relationship of Managerial Ability to Unit Effectiveness in More Organic versus More Mechanistic Departments," *Journal of Management Studies,* November 1985, pp 674–75.

38 J D Sherman and H L Smith, "The Influence of Organizational Structure on Intrinsic versus Extrinsic Motivation," *Academy of Management Journal,* December 1984, p 883.

39 See J A Courtright, G T Fairhurst, and L E Rogers, "Interaction Patterns in Organic and Mechanistic Systems," *Academy of Management Journal,* December 1989, pp 773–802.

40 A Taylor III, "Can This Car Save Ford?" *Fortune,* April 22, 2008, http://money.cnn.com.

41 P Gumbel, "Big Mac's Local Flavor," *Fortune,* May 2, 2008, http://money.cnn.com.

42 See Galbraith, *Designing Matrix Organizations That Actually Work.*

43 Procter & Gamble, "Corporate Info: Structure," Careers page of P&G Web site, www.pg.com, accessed May 22, 2008; and Procter & Gamble, "Facts about P&G," 2007, www.pg.com.

44 Anand and Daft, "What Is the Right Organization Design?" pp 331–33.

45 Y L Doz and M Kosonen, "The New Deal at the Top," *Harvard Business Review,* June 2007, pp 98–104; and E White, "Art of Persuasion Becomes Key," *The Wall Street Journal,* May 19, 2008, http://online.wsj.com.

46 A Hesseldahl, "BlackBerry: Innovation behind the Icon," *BusinessWeek,* April 4, 2008, www.businessweek.com.

47 Anand and Daft, "What Is the Right Organization Design?" pp 333–40.

48 M Kripalani, "Inside the Tata Nano Factory," *BusinessWeek,* May 9, 2008, www.businessweek.com.

49 J Holland, "Innovative Outsourcing Model Saves Company Millions," *Industry Week,* April 25, 2007, www.industryweek.com.

50 Copeland, "Boeing's Big Dream."

51 A MacCormack and T Forbath, "Learning the Fine Art of Global Collaboration," *Harvard Business Review,* January 2008, pp 24, 26.

52 See M J Robson, C S Katsikeas, and D C Bello, "Drivers and Performance Outcomes of Trust in International Strategic Alliances: The Role of Organizational Complexity," *Organization Science,* July–August 2008, pp 647–65.

53 See T Kelly, "Measuring Informal Learning: Encourage a Learning Culture and Track It!" *TrainingIndustry.com,* April 2, 2009, www.trainingindustry.com/articles/measuring-informal-learning.aspx; K R Thompson and M J Mathys, "The Aligned Balanced Scorecard: An Improved Tool for Building High Performance Organizations," *Organizational Dynamics,* October–December 2008, pp 378–93; and R J Grossman, "Measuring Up," *HR Magazine,* January 2008, pp 29–35.

54 K Cameron, "Critical Questions in Assessing Organizational Effectiveness," *Organizational Dynamics,* Autumn 1980, p 70.

55 For examples, see R Masson, "That's Not Fair," *Journal of Compensation and Benefits,* March/April 2009, pp 29–35; J Schramm, "Rich, Green Perspective," *HR Magazine,* July

2008, p 112; and N Madjar and R Ortiz-Walters, "Customers as Contributors and Reliable Evaluators of Creativity in the Service Industry," *Journal of Organizational Behavior,* October 2008, pp 949–66.

56 See R Agarwal and C E Helfat, "Strategic Renewal of Organizations," *Organization Science,* March–April 2009, pp 281–93; and S Yu-Shan, E W K Tsang, and M W Peng, "How Do Internal Capabilities and External Partnerships Affect Innovativeness?" *Asia Pacific Journal of Management,* June 2009, pp 309–32.

57 Data from M Maynard, "Toyota Promises Custom Order in 5 Days," *USA Today,* August 6, 1999, p 1B.

58 See E Bazar, "Red Cross Announces Restructuring to Restore Image," *USA Today,* October 31, 2006, p 3A.

59 See R S Kaplan and D P Norton, "Having Trouble with Your Strategy? Then Map It," *Harvard Business Review,* September–October 2000, pp 167–76.

60 D Frisch, "Human Resources: Part of the Team," *HR Magazine,* July 2008, p 67.

61 Cameron, "Critical Questions in Assessing Organizational Effectiveness," p 67.

62 See R J Martinez and P M Norman, "Whither Reputation? The Effects of Different Stakeholders," *Business Horizons,* September–October 2004, pp 25–32.

63 See E Iwata, "Exxon's $10.9B in Profit Disappoints Street," *USA Today,* May 2, 2008, p 3B.

64 See N C Roberts and P J King, "The Stakeholder Audit Goes Public," *Organizational Dynamics,* Winter 1989, pp 63–79.

65 See C Ostroff and N Schmitt, "Configurations of Organizational Effectiveness and Efficiency," *Academy of Management Journal,* December 1993, pp 1345–61.

66 P Dvorak, "How Irdeto Split Headquarters," *The Wall Street Journal,* January 7, 2008, p B3.

67 K S Cameron, "Effectiveness as Paradox: Consensus and Conflict in Conceptions of Organizational Effectiveness," *Management Science,* May 1986, p 542.

68 Alternative effectiveness criteria are discussed in ibid.

69 See D Welch, "Should GM Split Itself in Two?" *BusinessWeek,* April 6, 2009, p 72; A Lucchetti, "Morgan Stanley to Post a Loss from Volatile, Complex Bonds," *The Wall Street Journal,* April 19, 2009, p C1; J McCracken and K Linebaugh, "Chrysler, Banks Far Apart in Talks," *The Wall Street Journal,* April 10, 2009, pp B1, B2; and A Troianovski, "Prologis Gets Some Relief in Stock Sale," *The Wall Street Journal,* April 9, 2009, p B3.

70 D N Sull, "Why Good Companies Go Bad," *Harvard Business Review,* July–August 1999, pp 42–52.

71 M A Mone, W McKinley, and V L Barker III, "Organizational Decline and Innovation: A Contingency Framework," *Academy of Management Review,* January 1998, p 117.

72 P Lorange and R T Nelson, "How to Recognize—and Avoid—Organizational Decline," *Sloan Management Review,* Spring 1987, p 47.

73 Excerpted from ibid., pp 43–45.

74 For details, see K S Cameron, M U Kim, and D A Whetten, "Organizational Effects of Decline and Turbulence," *Administrative Science Quarterly,* June 1987, pp 222–40. Also see

S F Latham and M Braun, "Managerial Risk, Innovation, and Organizational Decline," *Journal of Management,* April 2009, pp 258–81.

75 Data from V L Barker III and P W Patterson Jr, "Top Management Team Tenure and Top Manager Causal Attributions at Declining Firms Attempting Turnarounds," *Group and Organization Management,* September 1996, pp 304–36.

76 See H Ma and R Karri, "Leaders Beware: Some Sure Ways to Lose Your Competitive Advantage," *Organizational Dynamics,* no. 1, 2005, pp 63–76; and J Pfeffer, "The Agony of Victory," *Business 2.0,* January–February 2007, p 62.

77 B Treasurer, "How Risk-Taking Really Works," *Training,* January 2000, p 43.

78 D Duchon and M Burns, "Organizational Narcissism," *Organizational Dynamics,* October–December 2008, p 355.

79 See ibid., pp 354–64.

80 A Fisher, "America's Most Admired Companies," *Fortune,* March 17, 2008, p 66.

81 "How P&G Plans to Clean Up," *BusinessWeek,* April 13, 2009, p 44.

82 J I Cash Jr, M J Earl, and R Morison, "Teaming Up to Crack Innovation Enterprise Integration," *Harvard Business Review,* November 2008, pp 90–100.

83 See "Innovation Nations," *BusinessWeek,* April 6, 2009, p 10; and R Jana, "Spending on Innovation: A Casualty of the Recession," *BusinessWeek,* April 20, 2009, p 58.

84 J Welch and S Welch, "Finding Innovation Where It Lives," *BusinessWeek,* April 21, 2008, p 84.

85 See K Capell, "Zara Thrives by Breaking All the Rules," *BusinessWeek,* October 20, 2008, p 66. Also see E Svoboda, "Grand Experiment," *Fast Company,* February 2009, pp 36-40.

86 Source quoted in S Berkum, *The Myths of Innovation* (Sebastopol, CA: O'Reilly Media, Inc., 2007), p 44.

87 I Rowley, "Drive, He Thought," *BusinessWeek,* April 20, 2009, p 12.

88 This discussion is based on Berkum, *The Myths of Innovation.*

89 See D Kiley and C Matlack, "Fiat: On the Road Back to America," *BusinessWeek,* April 20, 2009, p 28.

90 R Jana, "Inspiration from Emerging Economies," *BusinessWeek,* March 23 and 30, 2009, p 41.

91 See "How Google Fuels Its Idea Factory," *BusinessWeek,* May 12, 2008, pp 54–55.

92 This discussion is based on Berkum, *The Myths of Innovation.*

93 See M Kripalani, "Tata Taps a Vast R&D Shop—Its Own," *BusinessWeek,* April 20, 2009, p 50.

94 L A Bettencourt, "The Customer-Centered Innovation Map," *Harvard Business Review,* May 2008, p 109. Also see M W Johnson, C M Christensen, and H Kagermann, "Reinventing Your Business Model," *Harvard Business Review,* December 2008, pp 51–59.

95 See C Hartnell, Y Ou, and A Kinicki, "Assessing the Organizational Culture-Organizational Effectiveness Link: A Meta-Analytic Review," paper presented at the National Academy of Management Meeting, 2009.

[96] See S Prokesch, "How GE Teaches Teams to Lead Change," *Harvard Business Review,* January 2009, pp 99–106.

[97] See L Gumusluoglu and A Ilsev, "Transformational Leadership and Organizational Innovation: The Roles of Internal and External Support for Innovation," *Journal of Product Innovation Management,* May 2009, pp 264–75; L Gumusluoglu and A Ilsev, "Transformational Leadership, Creativity, and Organizational Innovation," *Journal of Business Research,* April 2009, pp 461–73; R N Osborn and R Marion, "Contextual Leadership, Transformational Leadership and the Performance of International Innovation Seeking Alliances," *The Leadership Quarterly,* April 2009, pp 191–206; and A Oke, M Munshi, and F O Walumbwa, "The Influence of Leadership on Innovation Processes and Activities," *Organizational Dynamics,* January–March 2009, pp 64–72.

[98] See J N Choi and J Y Chang, "Innovation Implementation in the Public Sector: An Integration of Institutional and Collective Dynamics," *Journal of Applied Psychology,* January 2009, pp 245–53; and B Verworn and C Hipp, "Does the Ageing Workforce Hamper the Innovativeness of Firms? (No) Evidence from Germany," *International Journal of Human Resources Development and Management,* 2009, pp 180–97.

[99] L Bossidy and R Charan, *Execution: The Discipline of Getting Things Done* (New York: Crown Business, 2002), p 22.

[100] See R Jana, "Do Ideas Cost Too Much?" *BusinessWeek,* April 20, 2009, pp 46–47.

[101] Excerpted from P Dvorak, "How Irdeto Split Headquarters," *The Wall Street Journal,* January 7, 2008, p B3.

[102] See "Electronic Monitoring & Surveillance Survey: Employers Get Serious about Fighting E-Mail & Internet Abuse," *Wireless News,* March 4, 2008, NA. General Reference Center.

[103] Ibid.

[104] F Norton, "Every E-Mail You Send, Every Time You Click . . .: . . .The Boss Might Be Watching You: Count on It," *News & Observer,* March 28, 2008, http://find.galegroup.com.ezproxy.crystallakelibrary.org/itx/p.

[105] Ibid.

CHAPTER 18

[1] Excerpted from R. Charan, "Confront Reality," *HR Magazine,* February 2009, pp 34–36.

[2] See J McGregor, "From Great to Good," *BusinessWeek,* April 13, 2009, pp 32–35; I Rowley and H Tashiro, "There's Even Trouble in Toyota City," *BusinessWeek,* April 27, 2009, pp 50–51; and B Helm, "Blowing Up Pepsi," *BusinessWeek,* April 27, 2009, pp 32–36.

[3] See, for example, M Fugate, A J Kinicki, and G E Prussia, "Employee Coping with Organizational Change: An Examination of Alternative Theoretical Perspectives and Models," *Personnel Psychology,* Spring 2008, pp 1–36.

[4] A M Webber, "Learning for a Change," *Fast Company,* May 1999, p 180.

[5] See N Shirouzu and J Murphy, "A Scion Drives Toyota Back to Basics," *The Wall Street Journal,* February 24, 2009, pp A1, A11; and D Welch, "What Could Dull Toyota's Edge," *BusinessWeek,* April 28, 2008, p 38.

[6] S E Ante, "The Sommelier Will Take Your Order," *BusinessWeek,* February 25, 2008, p 72.

[7] See P Dvorak, "Companies Seek Shareholder Input on Pay Practices," *The Wall Street Journal,* April 6, 2009, p B4; S E Needleman, "Severance Plans Face Squeeze Amid Scramble to Preserve Cash," *The Wall Street Journal,* March 19, 2009, p B2; and F Hansen, "A Nation under TARP?" *Workforce Management,* April 20, 2009, pp 15–19.

[8] See J Shambora, A Lashinsky, B Gimbel, and J Schlosser, "A View from the Top," *Fortune,* March 16, 2009, p 110; J Weber, "Over a Buck for Dinner? Outrageous," *BusinessWeek,* March 9, 2009, p 57; and H Green, "How Amazon Aims to Keep You Clicking," *BusinessWeek,* March 2, 2009, pp 34–39.

[9] M Conlin, "Suddenly, It's Cool to Take the Bus," *BusinessWeek,* May 5, 2008, p 24.

[10] See C Arnst, "Taxing the Rich—Foods, That Is," *BusinessWeek,* February 23, 2009, p 62.

[11] Quoted from p 44 of F L Reinhardt, "Place Your Bets on the Future You Want," *Harvard Business Review,* October 2007, pp 42, 44.

[12] See J Marquez, "Hostage-Taking in France Has U.S. Observers on Their Guard," *Workforce Management,* April 20, 2009, p 10.

[13] See F Hansen, "Health Care Collapse," *Workforce Management,* April 20, 2009, p 12.

[14] L Wheeler, "Change Every Day," *Training,* October 2008, p 51.

[15] This three-way typology of change was adapted from discussion in P C Nutt, "Tactics of Implementation," *Academy of Management Journal,* June 1986, pp 230–61.

[16] For a thorough discussion of the model, see K Lewin, *Field Theory in Social Science* (New York: Harper & Row, 1951); and J Helms, K Dye, and A J Mills, *Understanding Organizational Change* (New York: Routledge, 2009) pp 39–55.

[17] These assumptions are discussed in E H Schein, *Organizational Psychology,* 3rd ed (Englewood Cliffs, NJ: Prentice Hall, 1980).

[18] J Adamy, "Schultz's Second Act Jolts Starbucks," *The Wall Street Journal,* May 19, 2008, http://online.wsj.com.

[19] C Goldwasser, "Benchmarking: People Make the Process," *Management Review,* June 1995, p 40.

[20] An application of this model can be found in B C Medle and O H Akan, "Creating Positive Change in Community Organizations: A Case for Rediscovering Lewin," *Nonprofit Management & Leadership,* Summer 2008, pp 485–96.

[21] See N Beck, J Brüderl, and M Woywode, "Momentum or Deceleration? Theoretical and Methodological Reflections on the Analysis of Organizational Change," *Academy of Management Journal,* June 2008, pp 413–35.

[22] Mission statements for academic institutions are discussed by T B Palmer and J C Short, "Mission Statements in U.S. College of Business: An Empirical Examination of Their Content with Linkages to Configurations and Performance," *Academy of Management Learning & Education,* December 2008, pp 454–70.

[23] A thorough discussion of the target elements of change can be found in M Beer and B Spector, "Organizational Diagnosis: Its Role in Organizational Learning," *Journal of Counseling and Development,* July–August 1993, pp 642–50.

[24] Details of this example can be found in D Kesmodel, "How 'Chief Beer Taster' Blended Molson, Coors," *The Wall Street Journal,* October 1, 2007, pp B1, B5.

25 These errors are discussed in J P Kotter, "Leading Change: When Transformation Efforts Fail," *Harvard Business Review,* January 2007, pp 96–103.

26 See L Freifeld, "Changes with Penguins," *Training,* June 2008, pp 24–28; and J P Kotter, "Transformation," *Leadership Excellence,* December 2008, p 20.

27 J Fortt, "Yahoo's Taskmaster," *Fortune,* April 27, 2009, p 83.

28 P G Hanson and B Lubin, "Answers to Questions Frequently Asked about Organization Development," in *The Emerging Practice of Organization Development,* ed W Sikes, A Drexler, and J Grant (Alexandria, VA: NTL Institute, 1989), p 16.

29 Characteristics of change agents are discussed by J Welch and S Welch, "What Change Agents Are Made Of," *BusinessWeek,* October 20, 2008, p 96; and F Bryant, "The Proper Consultant's Stance in Diversity and Inclusion: 'Be All You Can Be' Typified by the Four 'Be Attitudes,'" *Diversity Factor (online),* Winter 2009, pp 1–6.

30 Over 60 different intervention techniques are discussed by P Holman, T Devane, and S Cady, *The Change Handbook,* 2nd ed (San Francisco, CA: Berrett-Kohler, 2007).

31 Sample interventions can be found in F Blackler and S Regan, "Intentionality, Agency, Change: Practice Theory and Management," *Management Learning,* April 2009, pp 161–76; and C C Cataldo, J O Raelin, and M Lambert, "Reinvigorating the Struggling Organization: The Unification of Schein's Oeuvre into a Diagnostic Model," *The Journal of Applied Behavioral Science,* March 2009, pp 122–40.

32 See R Rodgers, J E Hunter, and D L Rogers, "Influence of Top Management Commitment on Management Program Success," *Journal of Applied Psychology,* February 1993, pp 151–55.

33 Results can be found in P J Robertson, D R Roberts, and J I Porras, "Dynamics of Planned Organizational Change: Assessing Empirical Support for a Theoretical Model," *Academy of Management Journal,* June 1993, pp 619–34.

34 Results from the meta-analysis can be found in G A Neuman, J E Edwards, and N S Raju, "Organizational Development Interventions: A Meta-Analysis of Their Effects on Satisfaction and Other Attitudes," *Personnel Psychology,* Autumn 1989, pp 461–90.

35 Results can be found in C-M Lau and H-Y Ngo, "Organization Development and Firm Performance: A Comparison of Multinational and Local Firms," *Journal of International Business Studies,* First Quarter 2001, pp 95–114.

36 See N Orkin, "Focus on Japan," *Training,* February 2008, p 30.

37 J D Ford, L W Ford, and A D'Amelio, "Resistance to Change: The Rest of the Story," *Academy of Management Review,* April 2008, p 362.

38 See J D Ford and L W Ford, "Decoding Resistance to Change," *Harvard Business Review,* April 2009, pp 99–103; and B Gullickson, "Working with Resistance," *Strategic Finance,* February 2009, pp 8, 10.

39 Adapted from R J Marshak, *Covert Processes at Work* (San Francisco, CA: Berrett-Koehler Publishers, 2006); and A S Judson, *Changing Behavior in Organizations: Minimizing Resistance to Change* (Cambridge, MA: Blackwell, Inc., 1991).

40 An individual's predisposition to change was investigated by S Oreg, M Bayazit, M Vakola, L Arciniega, and A Armenakis,

et al., "Dispositional Resistance to Change: Measurement Equivalence and the Link to Personal Values across 17 Nations," *Journal of Applied Psychology,* July 2008, pp 935–44.

41 Research regarding resilience is discussed by K Kersting, "Resilience: The Mental Muscle Everyone Has," *Monitor on Psychology,* April 2005, pp 32–33; and K Sulkowicz, "Analyze This," *BusinessWeek,* January 12, 2009, p 16.

42 See C R Wanberg and J T Banas, "Predictors and Outcomes of Openness to Changes in a Reorganizing Workplace," Journal of Applied Psychology, February 2000, pp 132–42. Also see R Evenson, "Prepare Yourself: Like It or Not, Change Is Coming!" *Supervision,* February 2009, pp 8–11.

43 G Chon, K Maher, and C Dade, "On Plant Assembly Lines and at Kitchen Tables, Worry about the Future," *The Wall Street Journal,* March 23, 2006, p A1.

44 L Goering, "Land of Plenty No Longer," *Chicago Tribune,* May 20, 2008, sec 1, p 8.

45 See I H Gleibs, A Mummendey, and P Noack, "Predictors of Change in Postmerger Identification during a Merger Process: A Longitudinal Study," *Journal of Personality and Social Psychology,* November 2008, pp 1095–1112.

46 Details of this example are provided by B Schlender, "Inside the Shakeup at Sony," *Fortune,* April 4, 2005, pp 94–104.

47 See D A Waldman and M Javidan, "Alternative Forms of Charismatic Leadership in the Integration of Mergers and Acquisitions," *The Leadership Quarterly,* April 2009, pp 130–42; and D M Harold, D B Fedor, S Caldwell, and Y Liu, "The Effects of Transformational and Change Leadership on Employees' Commitment to Change: A Multilevel Study," *Journal of Applied Psychology,* March 2008, pp 346–57.

48 See J D Ford and L W Ford, "Decoding Resistance to Change;" and J D Ford, L W Ford, and A D'Amelio, "Resistance to Change: The Rest of the Story."

49 See S A Furst and D M Cable, "Employee Resistance to Organizational Change: Managerial Influence Tactics and Leader-Member Exchange," *Journal of Applied Psychology,* March 2008, pp 453–62.

50 See R Charan, "Home Depot's Blueprint for Culture Change," *Harvard Business Review,* April 2006, pp 61–70.

51 J P Kotter, "Leading Change: Why Transformation Efforts Fail," *Harvard Business Review,* 1995, p 64.

52 J P Kotter and L A Schlesinger, "Choosing Strategies for Change," *Harvard Business Review,* July–August 2008, pp 130–39.

53 The stress response is thoroughly discussed by H Selye, *Stress without Distress* (New York: J B Lippincott, 1974).

54 See M Beck, "Stress So Bad It Hurts—Really," *The Wall Street Journal,* March 17, 2009, pp D1, D6; and D L Blustein, "The Role of Work in Psychological Health and Well-Being," *American Psychologist,* May–June 2008, pp 228–40.

55 J M Ivancevich and M T Matteson, *Stress and Work: A Managerial Perspective* (Glenview, IL: Scott, Foresman, 1980), pp 8–9.

56 M Elias, "Economy Prompts More Calls to Suicide Hotlines," *USA Today,* January 12, 2009, p 6D.

57 See Selye, *Stress without Distress.*

[58] See S Gilboa, A Shirom, Y Fried, and C Cooper, "A Meta-Analysis of Work Demand Stressors and Job Performance: Examining Main and Moderating Effects," *Personnel Psychology,* Summer 2008, pp 227–71; and J L Xie, J Schaubroeck, and S S K Lam, "Theories of Job Stress and the Role of Traditional Values: A Longitudinal Study in China," *Journal of Applied Psychology,* July 2008, pp 831–48.

[59] Supportive results can be found in F M McKee-Ryan, Z Song, C R Wanberg, and A J Kinicki, "Psychological and Physical Well-Being during Unemployment: A Meta-Analytic Study," *Journal of Applied Psychology,* January 2005, pp 53–76; and F M McKee-Ryan, M Virick, G E Prussia, J Harvey, and J D Lilly, "Life after the Layoff: Getting a Job Worth Keeping," *Journal of Organizational Behavior,* May 2009, pp 561–80.

[60] See C Binnewies, S Sonnentag, and E J Mojza, "Daily Performance at Work: Feeling Recovered in the Morning as a Predictor of Day-Level Job Performance," *Journal of Organizational Behavior,* January 2009, pp 67–93; and A Fox, "The Brain at Work," *HR Magazine,* March 2008, pp 37–42.

[61] Results are reported in N A Bowling and T A Beehr, "Workplace Harassment from the Victim's Perspective: A Theoretical Model and Meta-Analysis," *Journal of Applied Psychology,* September 2006, pp 998–1012.

[62] See J Chamberlin, A Novotney, E Packard, and M Price, "Enhancing Worker Well-Being," *Monitor on Psychology,* May 2008, pp 26–29.

[63] The issue of environmental conditions is discussed by A Bruzzese, "Is the Building Making You 'Sick' of Work?" *The Arizona Republic,* January 29, 2005, p D3.

[64] See H H Wierda-Boer, J R M Gerris, and A A Vermulst, "Managing Multiple Roles: Personality, Stress, and Work-Family Interference in Dual-Earner Couples," *Journal of Individual Differences,* 2009, pp 6–19.

[65] See L Young and C Palmeri, "Coping with Portfolio Panic," *BusinessWeek,* March 16, 2009, pp 60–61; and "USA Today Snapshots: Money Weighs Us Down," *USA Today,* January 12, 2009, p 1A.

[66] The discussion of appraisal is based on R S Lazarus and S Folkman, *Stress, Appraisal, and Coping* (New York: Springer Publishing, 1984).

[67] M Fugate, A J Kinicki, and G E Prussia, "Employee Coping with Organizational Change: An Examination of Alternative Theoretical Perspectives and Models," *Personnel Psychology,* Spring 2008, pp 1–36.

[68] Results are presented in J A Penley, J Tomaka, and J S Wiebe, "The Association of Coping to Physical and Psychological Health Outcomes: A Meta-Analytic Review," *Journal of Behavioral Medicine,* December 2002, pp 551–609.

[69] See J D Kammeyer-Mueller, T A Judge, and B A Scott, "The Role of Core Self-Evaluations in the Coping Process," *Journal of Applied Psychology,* January 2009, pp 177–95; and J C Hellmuth and J K McNulty, "Neuroticism, Marital Violence, and the Moderating Role of Stress and Behavioral Skills," *Journal of Personality and Social Psychology,* July 2008, pp 166–80.

[70] See S Sonnentag and J Stefanie, "Job Stressors and the Pursuit of Sports Activities: A Day-Level Perspective," *Journal of Occupational Health Psychology,* April 2009, pp 165–81.

[71] Supportive results can be found in J K Ito and C M Brotheridge, "Predictors and Consequences of Promotion Stress: A Bad Situation Made Worse by Employment Dependence," *International Journal of Stress Management,* February 2009, pp 65–85; H K Knudsen, L J Ducharme, and P M Roman, "Turnover Intention and Emotional Exhaustion 'at the Top': Adapting the Job Demands-Resources Model to Leaders of Addiction Treatment Organizations," *Journal of Occupational Health Psychology,* January 2009, pp 84–95; W Darr and G Johns, "Work Strain, Health, and Absenteeism: A Meta-Analysis," *Journal of Occupational Health Psychology,* October 2008, pp 293–318; and Y Fried, A Shirom, S Gilboa, and C L Cooper, "The Mediating Effects of Job Satisfaction and Propensity to Leave on Role Stress-Job Performance Relationships: Combining Meta-Analysis and Structural Equation Modeling," *International Journal of Stress Management,* November 2008, pp 305–28.

[72] See M R Frone, "Are Work Stressors Related to Employee Substance Use? The Importance of Temporal Context in Assessments of Alcohol and Illicit Drug Use," *Journal of Applied Psychology,* January 2008, pp 199–206.

[73] S Caminiti, "A New Health Care Prescription," *Fortune,* January 24, 2005, special advertising section, p S3. Also see L Cole, "I Can't Cope Any More," *ICIS Chemical Business,* February 2009, p 28.

[74] Supportive results can be found in T A Wright, R Cropanzano, D G Bonett, and W J Diamond, "The Role of Employee Psychological Well-Being in Cardiovascular Health: When the Twain Shall Meet," *Journal of Organizational Behavior,* February 2009, pp 193–208; P Steel, J Schmidt, and J Shultz, "Refining the Relationship between Personality and Subjective Well-Being," *Psychological Bulletin,* January 2008, pp 138–61; and G E Miller, E Chen, and E S Zhou, "If It Goes Up, Must It Come Down? Chronic Stress and the Hypothalamic-Pituitary-Adrenocortical Axis in Humans," *Psychological Bulletin,* January 2007, pp 25–45.

[75] Types of support are discussed by S Cohen and T A Wills, "Stress, Social Support, and the Buffering Hypothesis," *Psychological Bulletin,* September 1985, pp 310–57.

[76] See H S Kim, D K Sherman, and S E Taylor, "Culture and Social Support," *American Psychologist,* September 2008, pp 518–26; R A Clay, "One Heart—Many Threats," *Monitor on Psychology,* January 2007, pp 46–54.

[77] See J C Wallace, B D Edwards, T Arnold, M L Frazier, and D M Finch, "Work Stressors, Role-Based Performance, and the Moderating Influence of Organizational Support," *Journal of Applied Psychology,* January 2009, pp 254–63; and C Maslach and M P Leiter, "Early Predictors of Job Burnout and Engagement," *Journal of Applied Psychology,* May 2008, pp 498–512.

[78] This pioneering research is presented in S C Kobasa, "Stressful Life Events, Personality, and Health: An Inquiry into Hardiness," *Journal of Personality and Social Psychology,* January 1979, pp 1–11.

[79] See S C Kobasa, S R Maddi, and S Kahn, "Hardiness and Health: A Prospective Study," *Journal of Personality and Social Psychology,* January 1982, pp 168–77.

[80] Results can be found in V Florian, M Mikulincer, and O Taubman, "Does Hardiness Contribute to Mental Health during a Stressful Real Life Situation? The Roles of Appraisal and Coping," *Journal of Personality and Social Psychology,* April 1995, pp 687–95.

[81] See D Spurlick Jr, "Work Stress, Hardiness, and Burnout among Nursing Faculty," *Dissertation Abstracts International,* 2008.

82 Results from this study are discussed in S R Maddi, "On Hardiness and Other Pathways to Resilience," *American Psychologist,* April 2005, pp 261–62.

83 M Friedman and R H Rosenman, *Type A Behavior and Your Heart* (Greenwich, CT: Fawcett Publications, 1974), p 84. (Boldface added.)

84 See C Lee, L F Jamieson, and P C Earley, "Beliefs and Fears and Type A Behavior: Implications for Academic Performance and Psychiatric Health Disorder Symptoms," *Journal of Organizational Behavior,* March 1996, pp 151–77; S D Bluen, J Barling, and W Burns, "Predicting Sales Performance, Job Satisfaction, and Depression by Using the Achievement Strivings and Impatience–Irritability Dimensions of Type A Behavior," *Journal of Applied Psychology,* April 1990, pp 212–16; and M S Taylor, E A Locke, C Lee, and M E Gist, "Type A Behavior and Faculty Research Productivity: What Are the Mechanisms?" *Organizational Behavior and Human Performance,* December 1984, pp 402–18.

85 Results are contained in Y Chida and M Hamer, "Chronic Psychological Factors and Acute Physiological Responses to Laboratory-Induced Stress in Healthy Populations: A Quantitative Review of 30 Years of Investigations," *Psychological Bulletin,* November 2008, pp 829–85.

86 See S A Lyness, "Predictors of Differences between Type A and B Individuals in Heart Rate and Blood Pressure Reactivity," *Psychological Bulletin,* September 1993, pp 266–95.

87 See T Q Miller, T W Smith, C W Turner, M L Guijarro, and A J Hallet, "A Meta-Analytic Review of Research on Hostility and Physical Health," *Psychological Bulletin,* March 1996, pp 322–48; and D I Pickering, "The Role of Perceived Social Support and Stress in the Type A Cognition-Symptom Relationship," *Journal of Rational-Emotive and Cognitive-Behavior Therapy,* March 2009, pp 1–22.

88 See S J Wells, "Finding Wellness's Return on Investment," *HR Magazine,* June 2008, pp 75–84; and A Cynkar, "Whole Workplace Health," *Monitor on Psychology,* March 2007, pp 28–32.

89 Results are presented in K M Richardson and H R Rothstein, "Effects of Occupational Stress Management Intervention Programs: A Meta-Analysis," *Journal of Occupational Health Psychology,* January 2008, pp 69–93.

90 See D C Ganster, B T Mayes, W E Sime, and G D Tharp, "Managing Organizational Stress: A Field Experiment," *Journal of Applied Psychology,* October 1982, pp 533–42.

91 See N Whitfield, "Layoffs Spark Surge in Assistance Program Usage," *Business Insurance,* January 19, 2009, pp 16–17; and T Craig, "How to . . . Get Value from Your EAP," *Personnel Today,* January 27, 2009, p 25.

92 R Kreitner, "Personal Wellness: It's Just Good Business," *Business Horizons,* May–June 1982, p 28.

93 See K M Parks and L A Steelman, "Organizational Wellness Programs: A Meta-Analysis," *Journal of Occupational Health Psychology,* January 2008, pp 58–68.

94 This statistic was reported in "Meeting the Challenge of Motivating Employees to Embrace Wellness," *HR Magazine,* May 2005, pp 15–17.

95 See "Workout Incentives for Employees Work," *USA Today,* January 7, 2009, p 6D; and E B Solomont, "Companies Find Inexpensive Ways to Promote Wellness," *Workforce Management Online,* March 2009, www.workforce.com.

96 Excerpted from B Leonard, "Insightful Career Choice," *HR Magazine,* October 2008, pp 50–51.

97 This case is based on material contained in E Frauenheim, "Culture Crash: Lost in the Shuffle," *Workforce Management,* January 14, 2008, pp 1, 12–17.

Glossary

ability Stable characteristic responsible for a person's maximum physical or mental performance.

action plan Outlines the activities or tasks that need to be accomplished in order to obtain a goal.

adhocracy culture A culture that has an external focus and values flexibility.

affective component The feelings or emotions one has about an object or situation.

affirmative action Focuses on achieving equality of opportunity in an organization.

alternative dispute resolution Avoiding costly lawsuits by resolving conflicts informally or through mediation or arbitration.

Americans with Disabilities Act Prohibits discrimination against the disabled.

anticipatory socialization phase Occurs before an individual joins an organization, and involves the information people learn about different careers, occupations, professions, and organizations.

Asch effect Giving in to a unanimous but wrong opposition.

attention Being consciously aware of something or someone.

attitude Learned predisposition toward a given object.

behavioral component How one intends or expects to act toward someone or something.

benchmarking Process by which a company compares its performance with that of high-performing organizations.

bounded rationality Constraints that restrict rational decision making.

brainstorming Process to generate a quantity of ideas.

care perspective Involves compassion and an ideal of attention and response to need.

case study In-depth study of a single person, group, or organization.

causal attributions Suspected or inferred causes of behavior.

centralized decision making Top managers make all key decisions.

change agent Individual who is a catalyst in helping organizations to implement change.

change and acquisition phase Requires employees to master tasks and roles and to adjust to work group values and norms.

clan culture A culture that has an internal focus and values flexibility rather than stability and control.

closed system A relatively self-sufficient entity.

coalition Temporary groupings of people who actively pursue a single issue.

coercive power Obtaining compliance through threatened or actual punishment.

cognitions A person's knowledge, opinions, or beliefs.

cognitive categories Mental depositories for storing information.

cognitive component Beliefs or ideas one has about an object or situation.

cognitive dissonance Psychological discomfort experienced when attitudes and behavior are inconsistent.

cohesiveness A sense of "we-ness" helps group stick together.

collectivist culture Personal goals less important than community goals and interests.

communication Interpersonal exchange of information and understanding.

communication competence Ability to communicate effectively in specific situations.

competing values framework A framework for categorizing organizational culture.

conflict One party perceives its interests are being opposed or set back by another party.

conflict triangle Conflicting parties involve a third person rather than dealing directly with each other.

consensus Presenting opinions and gaining agreement to support a decision.

consideration Creating mutual respect and trust with followers.

content theories of motivation Identify internal factors influencing motivation.

contingency approach Using management tools and techniques in a situationally appropriate manner; avoiding the one-best-way mentality.

contingency approach to organization design Creating an effective organization–environment fit.

contingency factors Variables that influence the appropriateness of a leadership style.

continuous reinforcement Reinforcing every instance of a behavior.

control strategy Coping strategy that directly confronts or solves problems.

core job dimensions Job characteristics found to various degrees in all jobs.

corporate social responsibility The idea that corporations are expected to go above and beyond following the law and making a profit.

counterproductive work behaviors (CWBs) Types of behavior that harm employees and the organization as a whole.

creativity   Process of developing something new or unique.

credibility   Being believable through integrity, intent, capabilities, and results.

cross-cultural management Understanding and teaching behavioral patterns in different cultures.

cross-cultural training   Structured experiences to help people adjust to a new culture/country.

cross-functionalism   Team made up of technical specialists from different areas.

cultural intelligence   The ability to interpret ambiguous cross-cultural situations accurately.

culture   Beliefs and values about how a community of people should and do act.

culture shock   Anxiety and doubt caused by an overload of new expectations and cues.

day of contemplation   A one-time-only day off with pay to allow a problem employee to recommit to the organization's values and mission.

decentralized decision making Lower-level managers are empowered to make important decisions.

decision making   Identifying and choosing solutions that lead to a desired end result.

decision-making style   A combination of how individuals perceive and respond to information.

decision tree   Graphical representation of the process underlying decision making.

delegation   Granting decision-making authority to people at lower levels.

deliberate practice   A demanding, repetitive, and assisted program to improve one's performance.

Delphi technique   Process to generate ideas from physically dispersed experts.

demographic faultline   A hypothetical dividing line that splits groups into demographically based subgroups.

developmental relationship strength   The quality of relationships among people in a network.

devil's advocacy   Assigning someone the role of critic.

dialectic method   Fostering a debate of opposing viewpoints to better understand an issue.

differentiation   Division of labor and specialization that causes people to think and act differently.

discrimination   Occurs when employment decisions are based on factors that are not job related.

distributive justice   The perceived fairness of how resources and rewards are distributed.

diversity   The host of individual differences that make people different from and similar to each other.

diversity climate   Employees' aggregate perceptions about an organization's policies, practices, and procedures pertaining to diversity.

diversity of developmental relationships   The variety of people in a network used for developmental assistance.

dysfunctional conflict   Threatens organization's interests.

e-business   Running the *entire* business via the Internet.

emotional intelligence   Ability to manage oneself and interact with others in mature and constructive ways.

emotions   Complex human reactions to personal achievements and setbacks that may be felt and displayed.

employee assistance programs Help employees to resolve personal problems that affect their productivity.

employee engagement   An individual's involvement, satisfaction, and enthusiasm for work.

empowerment   Sharing varying degrees of power with lower-level employees to tap their full potential.

enacted values   The values and norms that are exhibited by employees.

encounter phase   Employees learn what the organization is really like and reconcile unmet expectations.

equity sensitivity   An individual's tolerance for negative and positive equity.

equity theory   Holds that motivation is a function of fairness in social exchanges.

ERG theory   Three basic needs—existence, relatedness, and growth—influence behavior.

escape strategy   Coping strategy that avoids or ignores stressors and problems.

espoused values   The stated values and norms that are preferred by an organization.

ethics   Study of moral issues and choices.

ethnocentrism   Belief that one's native country, culture, language, and behavior are superior.

eustress   Stress that is good or produces a positive outcome.

execution   A systematic process of discussing hows and whats, questioning, tenaciously following through, and ensuring accountability.

expatriate   Anyone living or working in a foreign country.

expectancy   Belief that effort leads to a specific level of performance.

expectancy theory   Holds that people are motivated to behave in ways that produce valued outcomes.

expert power   Obtaining compliance through one's knowledge or information.

explicit knowledge   Information that can be easily put into words and shared with others.

external factors   Environmental characteristics that cause behavior.

external forces for change Originate outside the organization.

external locus of control Attributing outcomes to circumstances beyond one's control.

extinction Making behavior occur less often by ignoring or not reinforcing it.

extrinsic rewards Financial, material, or social rewards from the environment.

feedback Objective information about performance.

field study Examination of variables in real-life settings.

fight-or-flight response To either confront stressors or try to avoid them.

formal communication channels Follow the chain of command or organizational structure.

formal group Formed by the organization.

functional conflict Serves organization's interests.

fundamental attribution bias Ignoring environmental factors that affect behavior.

Galatea effect An individual's high self-expectations lead to high performance.

garbage can model Holds that decision making is sloppy and haphazard.

genderflex Temporarily using communication behaviors typical of the other gender.

glass ceiling Invisible barrier blocking women and minorities from top management positions.

goal What an individual is trying to accomplish.

goal commitment Amount of commitment to achieving a goal.

goal specificity Quantifiability of a goal.

Golem effect Loss in performance due to low leader expectations.

grapevine Unofficial communication system of the informal organization.

group Two or more freely interacting people with shared norms and goals and a common identity.

group cohesiveness A "we feeling" binding group members together.

groupthink Janis's term for a cohesive in-group's unwillingness to realistically view alternatives.

hardiness Personality characteristic that neutralizes stress.

hierarchy culture A culture that has an internal focus and values stability and control over flexibility.

high-context cultures Primary meaning derived from nonverbal situational cues.

holistic wellness approach Advocates personal responsibility for healthy living.

human capital The productive potential of one's knowledge and actions.

humility Considering the contributions of others and good fortune when gauging one's success.

hygiene factors Job characteristics associated with job dissatisfaction.

implicit cognition Any thought or belief that is automatically activated without conscious awareness.

implicit leadership theory Perceptual theory in which prototypes determine traits of effective leaders.

impression management Getting others to see us in a certain manner.

individualistic culture Primary emphasis on personal freedom and choice.

informal communication channels Do not follow the chain of command or organizational structure.

informal group Formed by friends or those with common interests.

information/decision-making theory Diversity leads to better

task-relevant processes and decision making.

in-group exchange A partnership characterized by mutual trust, respect, and liking.

initiating structure Organizing and defining what group members should be doing.

innovation Creation of something new that is used by consumers.

instrumental cohesiveness Sense of togetherness based on mutual dependency needed to get the job done.

instrumentality A performance → outcome perception.

integration Cooperation among specialists to achieve a common goal.

intelligence Capacity for constructive thinking, reasoning, problem solving.

interactional justice Extent to which people feel fairly treated when procedures are implemented.

intermittent reinforcement Reinforcing some but not all instances of behavior.

internal factors Personal characteristics that cause behavior.

internal forces for change Originate inside the organization.

internal locus of control Attributing outcomes to one's own actions.

intrinsic motivation Motivation caused by positive internal feelings.

intrinsic rewards Self-granted, psychic rewards.

intuition Making a choice without the use of conscious thought or logical inference.

jargon Language or terminology that is specific to a particular profession, group, or company.

job design Changing the content or process of a specific job to increase job satisfaction and performance.

job enlargement Putting more variety into a job.

job enrichment   Building achievement, recognition, stimulating work, responsibility, and advancement into a job.

job involvement   Extent to which an individual is immersed in his or her present job.

job rotation   Moving employees from one specialized job to another.

job satisfaction   An affective or emotional response to one's job.

judgmental heuristics   Rules of thumb or shortcuts that people use to reduce information-processing demands.

justice perspective   Based on the ideal of reciprocal rights and driven by rules and regulations.

knowledge management   Implementing systems and practices that increase the sharing of knowledge and information throughout an organization.

laboratory study   Manipulation and measurement of variables in contrived situations.

law of effect   Behavior with favorable consequences is repeated; behavior with unfavorable consequences disappears.

leader–member relations   Extent that leader has the support, loyalty, and trust of the work group.

leader trait   Personal characteristic that differentiates leaders from followers.

leadership   Process whereby an individual influences others to achieve a common goal.

leadership prototype   Mental representation of the traits and behaviors possessed by leaders.

learning goal   Encourages learning, creativity, and skill development.

learning organization   Proactively creates, acquires, and transfers knowledge throughout the organization.

legitimate power   Obtaining compliance through formal authority.

liaison individuals   Those who consistently pass along grapevine information to others.

line managers   Have authority to make organizational decisions.

line of sight   Employees know the company's strategic goals and how they need to contribute.

linguistic style   A person's typical speaking pattern.

listening   Actively decoding and interpreting verbal messages.

low-context cultures   Primary meaning derived from written and spoken words.

maintenance roles   Relationship-building group behavior.

management   Process of working with and through others to achieve organizational objectives, efficiently and ethically, amid constant change.

management by objectives   Management system incorporating participation into decision making, goal setting, and feedback.

management by walking around   Managers walk around and informally talk to people from all areas and levels.

managing diversity   Creating organizational changes that enable all people to perform up to their maximum potential.

market culture   A culture that has a strong external focus and values stability and control.

mechanistic organizations   Rigid, command-and-control bureaucracies.

media richness   Capacity of a given communication medium to convey information and promote understanding.

mentoring   Process of forming and maintaining developmental relationships between a mentor and a junior person.

met expectations   The extent to which one receives what he or she expects from a job.

meta-analysis   Pools the results of many studies through statistical procedure.

micro aggressions   Biased thoughts, attitudes, and feelings that exist at an unconscious level.

mission statement   Summarizes "why" an organization exists.

monochronic time   Preference for doing one thing at a time because time is limited, precisely segmented, and schedule driven.

morally attentive   Faithfully considering the ethical implications of one's actions.

motivation   Psychological processes that arouse and direct goal-directed behavior.

motivators   Job characteristics associated with job satisfaction.

mutuality of interest   Balancing individual and organizational interests through win–win cooperation.

need for achievement   Desire to accomplish something difficult.

need for affiliation   Desire to spend time in social relationships and activities.

need for power   Desire to influence, coach, teach, or encourage others to achieve.

need hierarchy theory   Five basic needs—physiological, safety, love, esteem, and self-actualization—influence behavior.

needs   Physiological or psychological deficiencies that arouse behavior.

negative inequity   Comparison in which another person receives greater outcomes for similar inputs.

negative reinforcement   Making behavior occur more often by contingently withdrawing something negative.

negotiation   Give-and-take process between conflicting interdependent parties.

noise   Interference with the transmission and understanding of a message.

nominal group technique   Process to generate ideas and evaluate solutions.

nonrational models Explain how decisions actually are made.

nonverbal communication Messages sent outside of the written or spoken word.

norm Shared attitudes, opinions, feelings, or actions that guide social behavior.

onboarding Programs aimed at helping employees integrate, assimilate, and transition to new jobs.

open system Organism that must constantly interact with its environment to survive.

operant behavior Skinner's term for learned, consequence-shaped behavior.

optimizing Choosing the best possible solution.

organic organizations Fluid and flexible networks of multitalented people.

organization System of consciously coordinated activities of two or more people.

organization chart Boxes-and-lines illustration showing chain of formal authority and division of labor.

organization development A set of techniques or tools used to implement organizational change.

organizational behavior Interdisciplinary field dedicated to better understanding and managing people at work.

organizational citizenship behaviors (OCBs) Employee behaviors that exceed work-role requirements.

organizational commitment Extent to which an individual identifies with an organization and its goals.

organizational culture Shared values and beliefs that underlie a company's identity.

organizational decline Decrease in organization's resource base (money, customers, talent, innovations).

organizational identification Organizational values or beliefs become part of one's self-identity.

organizational moles Those who use the grapevine to enhance their power and status.

organizational narcissism Organizational tendency to deny facts, use self-aggrandizement, and feel entitled.

organizational politics Intentional enhancement of self-interest.

organizational socialization Process by which employees learn an organization's values, norms, and required behaviors.

ostracism Rejection by other group members.

out-group exchange A partnership characterized by a lack of mutual trust, respect, and liking.

participative management Involving employees in various forms of decision making.

pay for performance Monetary incentives tied to one's results or accomplishments.

perception Process of interpreting one's environment.

perceptual model of communication Process in which receivers create their own meaning.

performance management Continuous cycle of improving job performance with goal setting, feedback and coaching, and rewards and positive reinforcement.

performance outcome goal Targets a specific end-result.

personal barriers Any individual attribute that hinders communication.

personal initiative Going beyond formal job requirements and being an active self-starter.

personality Stable physical and mental characteristics responsible for a person's identity.

personality conflict Interpersonal opposition driven by personal dislike or disagreement.

personalized power Directed at helping oneself.

polychronic time Preference for doing more than one thing at a time because time is flexible, multidimensional, and based on relationships and situations.

position power Degree to which leader has formal power.

positive inequity Comparison in which another person receives lesser outcomes for similar inputs.

positive reinforcement Making behavior occur more often by contingently presenting something positive.

primary appraisal Determining whether a stressor is irrelevant, positive, or stressful.

proactive personality Action-oriented person who shows initiative and perseveres to change things.

problem Gap between an actual and a desired situation.

procedural justice The perceived fairness of the process and procedures used to make allocation decisions.

process theories of motivation Identify the process by which internal factors and cognitions influence motivation.

programmed conflict Encourages different opinions without protecting management's personal feelings.

propensity to trust A personality trait involving one's general willingness to trust others.

proxemics Hall's term for the study of cultural expectations about interpersonal space.

psychological capital Striving for success by developing one's self-efficacy, optimism, hope, and resiliency.

psychological contract An individual's perception about the terms and conditions of a reciprocal exchange with another party.

punishment Making behavior occur less often by contingently presenting something negative or withdrawing something positive.

rational model Logical four-step approach to decision making.

realistic job preview Presents both positive and negative aspects of a job.

referent power Obtaining compliance through charisma or personal attraction.

repetitive motion disorders (RMDs) Muscular disorders caused by repeating motions.

resilience to change Composite personal characteristic reflecting high self-esteem, optimism, and an internal locus of control.

resiliency The ability to handle pressure and quickly bounce back from personal and career setbacks.

resistance to change Emotional/behavioral response to real or imagined work changes.

respondent behavior Skinner's term for unlearned stimulus–response reflexes.

reward power Obtaining compliance with promised or actual rewards.

role ambiguity Others' expectations are unknown.

role conflict Others have conflicting or inconsistent expectations.

role overload Others' expectations exceed one's ability.

roles Expected behaviors for a given position.

sample survey Questionnaire responses from a sample of people.

satisficing Choosing a solution that meets a minimum standard of acceptance.

scenario technique Speculative forecasting method.

schema Mental picture of an event or object.

scientific management Using research and experimentation to find the most efficient way to perform a job.

script A mental picture of an event.

secondary appraisal Assessing what might and can be done to reduce stress.

seeds of innovation Starting point of organizational innovation.

self-concept Person's self-perception as a physical, social, spiritual being.

self-efficacy Belief in one's ability to do a task.

self-esteem One's overall self-evaluation.

self-fulfilling prophecy Someone's high expectations for another person result in high performance.

self-managed teams Groups of employees granted administrative oversight for their work.

self-serving bias Taking more personal responsibility for success than failure.

semantics The study of words.

servant-leadership Focuses on increased service to others rather than to oneself.

sex-role stereotype Beliefs about appropriate roles for men and women.

shaping Reinforcing closer and closer approximations to a target behavior.

shared leadership Simultaneous, ongoing, mutual influence process in which people share responsibility for leading.

situational theories Propose that leader styles should match the situation at hand.

skill Specific capacity to manipulate objects.

social capital The productive potential of strong, trusting, and cooperative relationships.

social categorization theory Similarity leads to liking and attraction.

social loafing Decrease in individual effort as group size increases.

social networking site (SNS) A Web-enabled community of people who share all types of information.

social power Ability to get things done with human, informational, and material resources.

social support Amount of helpfulness derived from social relationships.

socialized power Directed at helping others.

socio-emotional cohesiveness Sense of togetherness based on emotional satisfaction.

span of control The number of people reporting directly to a given manager.

staff personnel Provide research, advice, and recommendations to line managers.

stakeholder audit Systematic identification of all parties likely to be affected by the organization.

stereotype Beliefs about the characteristics of a group.

stereotype threat The predicament in which members of a social group must deal with the possibility of being judged or treated stereotypically, or of doing something that would confirm the stereotype.

strategic constituency Any group of people with a stake in the organization's operation or success.

strategic plan A long-term plan outlining actions needed to achieve desired results.

stress Behavioral, physical, or psychological response to stressors.

stressors Environmental factors that produce stress.

sustainability Meeting humanity's needs without harming future generations.

symptom management strategy Coping strategy that focuses on reducing the symptoms of stress.

tacit knowledge Information gained through experience that is difficult to express and formalize.

target elements of change Components of an organization that may be changed.

task roles   Task-oriented group behavior.

task structure   Amount of structure contained within work tasks.

team   Small group with complementary skills who hold themselves mutually accountable for common purpose, goals, and approach.

team building   Experiential learning aimed at better internal functioning of groups.

team viability   Team members satisfied and willing to contribute.

telecommuting/teleworking Doing work generally performed in the office at home or in other convenient locations using advanced communication technologies.

Theory Y   McGregor's modern and positive assumptions about employees being responsible and creative.

360-degree feedback   Comparison of anonymous feedback from one's superior, subordinates, and peers with self-perceptions.

total quality management   An organizational culture dedicated to training, continuous improvement, and customer satisfaction.

transactional leadership   Focuses on clarifying employees' roles and providing rewards contingent on performance.

transformational leadership Transforms employees to pursue organizational goals over self-interests.

trust   Reciprocal faith in others' intentions and behavior.

Type A behavior pattern Aggressively involved in a chronic, determined struggle to accomplish more in less time.

unity of command principle   Each employee should report to a single manager.

valence   The value of a reward or outcome.

value attainment   The extent to which a job allows fulfillment of one's work values.

value system   The organization of one's beliefs about preferred ways of behaving and desired end-states.

value congruence or person–culture fit   The similarity between personal values and organizational values.

values   Enduring belief in a mode of conduct or end-state.

virtual team   Information technology allows group members in different locations to conduct business.

vision   Long-term goal describing "what" an organization wants to become.

whistle-blowing   Reporting unethical/illegal acts to outside third parties.

withdrawal cognitions   Overall thoughts and feelings about quitting a job.

workforce demographics Statistical profiles of adult workers.

Name/Company Index

X

Y

Z

Subject Index